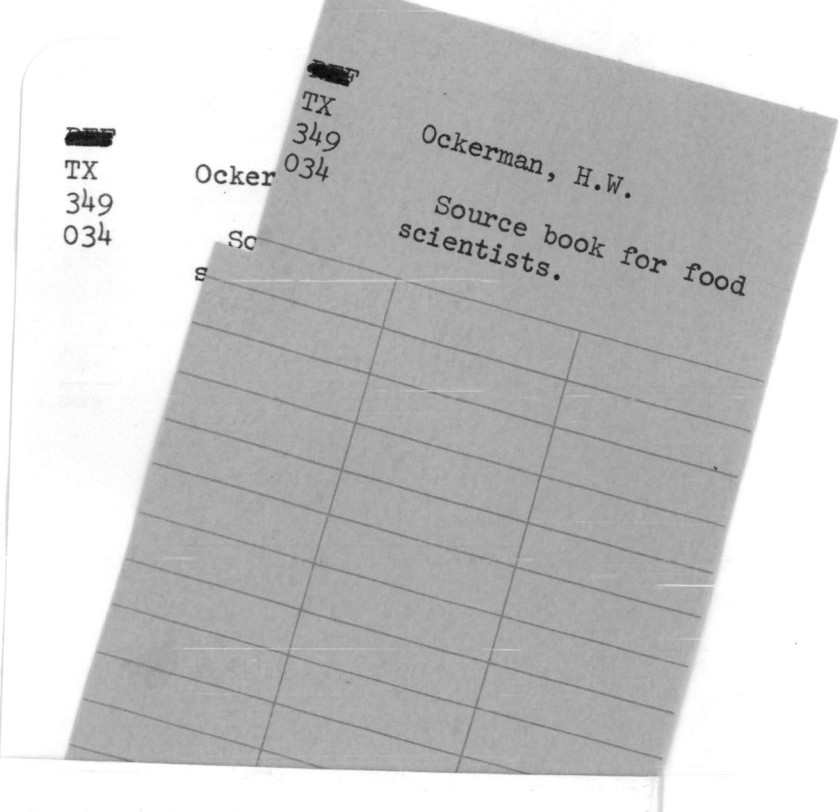

Source Book for Food Scientists

HERBERT W. OCKERMAN, Ph.D.
Professor of Animal Science,
The Ohio State University,
and
The Ohio Agricultural Research
and Development Center,
Columbus, Ohio

THE AVI PUBLISHING COMPANY, INC.,
Westport, Connecticut

Library of Congress Cataloging in Publication Data

Ockerman, Herbert W
Source book for food scientists.

1. Food—Dictionaries. 2. Food—Composition—Tables. I. Title.
TX349.034 664′.003 77-17406
ISBN 0-87055-228-7

Printed in the United States of America

Preface

The *Source Book for Food Scientists* materialized as the result of accumulating current data and relevant facts in the field of food science and technology. Since reference sources are often scattered, there has been a need for a one-volume data book of this type. A number of my colleagues have urged me to make my data bank available to others, hence this volume.

Such a book could be organized as follows: a dictionary interpretation of terms used in food science and technology; tabular material giving detailed information on food composition and properties; chemical formulas and structures; uses of food-stuffs; harvesting; slaughtering and related information concerning the meat industry . . . . in fact, almost any and every type of subject one might encounter dealing with food.

I have organized the material in two parts. Part 1 covers what I call my "personal dictionary" of pertinent information. Part 2 contains the tabular and general information which broadens the base of Part 1 with factual data.

I have found it invaluable. My earnest desire, now that the material is to be published, is that it will equally serve other food scientists and technologists working in various capacities in industry, government and the academic community.

I wish to acknowledge the encouragement given me by Dr. Donald K. Tressler, President, AVI Publishing Company, and to express my appreciation for his belief and support in this project.

It is also a special pleasure for me to acknowledge the editorial assistance provided by Mrs. Lucy Long, Senior Editor at AVI, and to Mr. Gessner Hawley, Editor of the *Condensed Chemical Dictionary* and Co-editor of the *Encyclopedia of Chemistry*. It was their collaboration and assistance that transformed a very rough draft into a publishable manuscript. However, errors of omission or commission are mine alone to bear.

I would also like to thank the scores of publishers and authors who have granted me permission to reprint their copyrighted materials. Thanks are also extended to the many authors and contributors to government publications for information obtained from those sources. Specific acknowledgment is noted for each source as it appears in this book.

I also wish to extend grateful thanks to my wife, Frances, for her assistance in typing and proofreading. Her patience and help contributed much to the completion of this book.

This is the First Edition of the *Source Book* and I would greatly appreciate communications from readers for suggestions or recommendations on how to improve it and also to call to my attention errors which may be corrected in the next printing.

HERBERT W. OCKERMAN
Columbus, Ohio

Jan 1, 1978

Dedicated to Frances

How to Use the Source Book

For ease of retrieval, the information in this book is organized in two parts.

Part 1 consists of dictionary terms and descriptions wherein the definitions usually contain internal detailed information on the subject and, where feasible, some data concerning its use or properties.

With the majority of these *Source Book* terms and descriptions in Part 1, there is reference to Part 2 giving a list of subjects for further information. (See breakdown of artichoke entry below.)

Part 2 is comprised of alphabetical sections containing food composition, properties and general data designed as the basis for the initiation of a broader search for further information relevant to the dictionary term given in Part 1. Part 2 is, in truth, a "data book" of Tables, Figures, charts, formulas, etc. Part 1 will lead the reader to a pertinent, appropriate section in Part 2; or, one can refer to Part 2 independently of the Part 1 dictionary descriptions, since it is all organized alphabetically.

Term — Generic name — Description

artichoke (*Cynara scolymus*) A deep-rooted perennial, thistle-like plant, belonging to the daisy family; grows well in cold, moist climate; — **Growth preferences**
the flower-heads or chokes have scales with
Portion eaten — fleshy bases. The fleshy base of scales are eaten raw, baked, fried, stuffed, served with sauces, — **Preparation methods**
or preserved in oil; the base of the flower head and the center leaf stalk are also eaten. *See also* — **For more information**
This is a reference subject found in Part 1 Section J — Jerusalem artichoke.
Store at 31°-32°F, 90-95% relative humidity; — **Storage information**
use in 1 to 2 weeks.
Composition: 86% H_2O, 3% protein, 11% fiber, 0.8% ash, pH 5.6.
For more information — *See* Part 2: Iron; Minerals, Food; Niacin; Phosphorus; Potassium; Potassium-rich Foods; Vegetables, Canning Dates; Vegetable Composition; Vegetable Plants — **These are reference subjects found in Part 2 under Sections I, M, N, P and V**

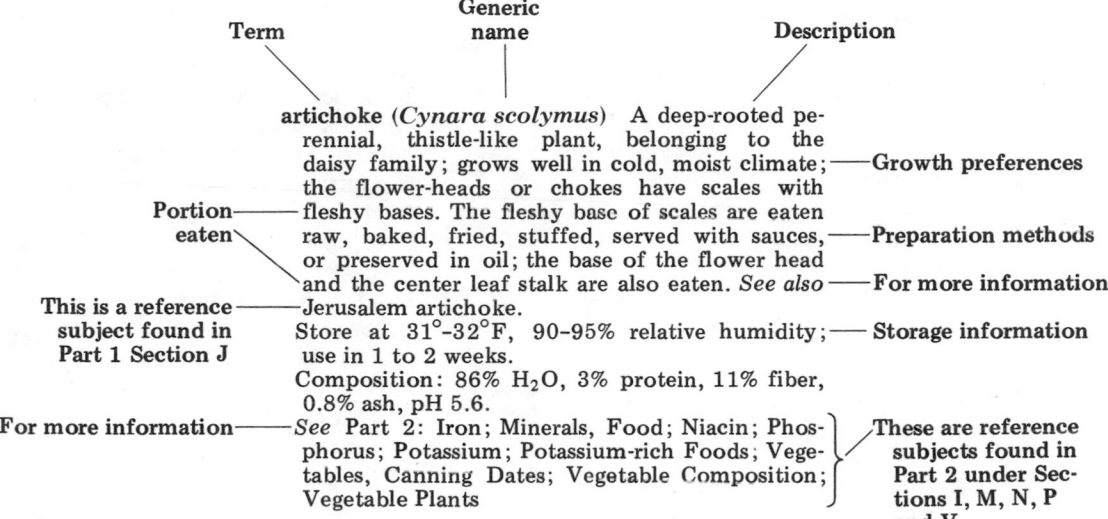

Other ready-reference material is to be found in the book:

Inside the front cover is a Table for temperature conversion from Fahrenheit to Celsius or vice versa.

Inside the back cover will be found conversion factors for units of weight, units of liquid measure, oven temperatures and units of volume.

And following is a list of the most-often-used abbreviations for quick reference.

Common Abbreviations

NOTE: Where the abbreviation denotes either the singular or plural, the spelled-out version of the abbreviation carries an asterisk (*).

AAAS	American Association for the Advancement of Science
amp	ampere*
AOAC	Association of Official Analytical Chemists
apoth	apothecary
approx	approximately
atm	atmosphere
at. no.	atomic number
at. wt.	atomic weight
avg	average
av	avoirdupois
bp	boiling point
Brit	British
Btu	British thermal units
bu	bushel*
c	calorie*
C	Centigrade or Celsius
ca	circa or about
cc	cubic centimeter*
CAMP	computer assisted menu planning
CFN	Council on Food and Nutrition of the American Medical Association
cg	centigram*
chem	chemical or chemistry
cl	centiliter*
cm	centimeter*
cp	chemically pure
cps	cycles per second
cu	cubic
cwt	hundredweight
d	density
DC	direct current
deg	degree*
df	degrees of freedom
dg	decigram*
diam	diameter
dkg	dekagram*
dkl	dekaliter*
dl	deciliter*
dm	decimeter*
doz	dozen*
dr	dram*
dwt	pennyweight
e.g.	for example
EMF	electromotive force
equiv wt	equivalent weight
F	Fahrenheit
FAO	Food and Agricultural Organization, United Nations
FDA	Federal Drug Administration
ffa	free fatty acid*
fl	fluid
FNS	Food and Nutrition Service, U.S. Department of Agriculture
FNB	Food and Nutrition Board of the National Academy of Science—National Research Council
fp	freezing point
fpm	feet per minute
fps	feet per second
ft	foot*
g	gram*
gal.	gallon*
gpm	gallon* per minute
gr	grain*
h	hectare*
hg	hectogram*
Hg	mercury
hhd	hogshead*
hp	horse power
hr	hour*
i.d.	inside dimension
i.e.	that is
imp	imperial
in.	inch*
I.U.	International Units

j	joule*
l	liter* (more often spelled out to avoid misinterpretation with numeral one)
lat	latitude
lb	pound*
K	Kelvin
kcal	kilocalorie*
Keq	equilibrium constant
kg	kilogram*
km	kilometer*
kw	kilowatt*
m	meter*
M	Molal
max	maximum
MDR	minimum daily requirement (no longer used; see RDA)
med	medium
mg	milligram*
MHz	megahertz
mi	mile*
MID	Meat Inspection Division, U.S. Department of Agriculture
min	minimum
ml	milliliter*
mm	millimeter*
mo	month*
mol wt	molecular weight
mp	melting point
mps	meters per second
mv	millivolt*
No.	number (when followed by numeral)
NFE	nitrogen free extract
NIH	National Institutes of Health
NMR	nuclear magnetic resonance
NPU	net protein utilization
NPV	net protein value
NRC	National Research Council
NSF	National Science Foundation
o.d.	outside dimension
opt	optimum, optional
oz	ounce*
PER	protein efficiency ratio
pk	peck*
ppm	parts per million
ppt	precipitate; parts per trillion
prob	probable
psf	per square foot*
psi	per square inch*
psia	per square inch atmosphere*
pt	pint*
qt	quart*
r	correlation
R	Reaumur
rd	rod*
RDA	recommended daily allowance
RH	relative humidity
rpm	revolutions per minute
sec	second*
sig	significant
sp	specific
sp. gr.	specific gravity
sq	square
tbsp	tablespoon*
temp	temperature
tsp	teaspoon*
USDA	United States Department of Agriculture
U.S.P.	U.S. Pharmocopeia
vit	vitamin (rarely used)
vol	volume
wt	weight
yd	yard*
yr	year*

Contents

PART 1

SOURCE BOOK TERMS AND DESCRIPTIONS

A

A (1) Abbreviation for absolute temperature. (2) Abbreviation for acre.

Å Abbreviation for angstrom.

a_w *See* **water activity**

abalone (*Haliotis*) Mollusk or shellfish.
Composition: 76% water, 19% protein, 0.5% fat, 3.5% carbohydrate, 1.6% ash.
See Part 2: Minerals (Trace), Food

A-band Dark bands (anisotropic) in muscle fiber; they contain all the myosin and the ends of the actin filaments.

abattoir Slaughterhouse.

abductor A muscle which draws a limb, wing, or other body appendage away from a medial position.

Aberdeen-Angus Solid black breed of beef cattle which has no horns; origin, Northeastern Scotland; imported into America by G. Grant of Victoria, Kansas.
See Part 2: Beef and Dual-Purpose Cattle; Gestation Periods

Aberdeen-Angus-Hereford cross Offspring will be polled and have a white face and black body; if 2 of the above offspring are crossed, the following ratio of offspring will result:
27 polled, white face, black body
9 horned, white face, black body
9 polled, entirely black
9 polled, white face, red body
3 horned, entirely black
3 horned, white face, red body
3 polled, colored face, red body
1 horned, colored face, red body

abomasum 4th section of the ruminant stomach, which is located on the right side; often called the "true stomach"; it functions very much like the entire monogastric stomach; a bovine abomasum may contain from 2 to 5 gallons.

Abruzzi A variety of rye.

abscissa (*x*-axis) Horizontal axis on rectangular coordinates.

abscission Detachment or separation of a fruit from a tree or shrub. Treatment with chemicals before harvesting aids this separation.

absolute alcohol Contains about 99.8% alcohol; can be made as follows: (1) heat crystalline copper sulfate until it is a white powder; (2) add to commercial alcohol (96%) until it no longer turns blue; (3) filter into a clean, dry, tight-capped bottle.

absolute temperature (A)
°K (Kelvin) = °C + 273.16
°R (Rankine) = °F + 459.69
See Part 2: Temperature (Conversion Table)

absolute value |n| A number without a + or − sign.

absolute zero −459.69°F; −273.16°C.

absorption Penetration of a liquid into the fine structure of a solid, the liquid being retained within the solid. Cellulosic materials (absorbent cotton, paper) readily absorb liquids, and absorption of nutrients by the intestinal walls is an important factor in metabolism. The word also means the tendency of a material to accept energy in the form of certain wavelengths of light (absorption band). *See also* **spectrophotometric analysis.**

aburage *See* **tofu**

ABY agar *See* Part 2: Microorganism, Media

Ac Symbol for the element actinium.

AC *See* **alternating current**

acacia gum *See* **gum arabic**

acerola cherry (West Indian cherry, Barbados cherry) A tropical berry (*Malpighia punicifolia, M. glabra*) high in vitamin C (1700 mg ascorbic acid/100 g pitted fruit); it resembles a cherry but is an entirely different fruit.

Composition	Pulp & Skin (%)	Juice (%)
Water	92	94
Protein	0.4	0.4
Fat	0.3	0.3
Carbohydrate	7	5
pH		3–3.5

See Part 2: Fruit Storage I

acetabulum Hip joint cavity.

acetate differential agar *See* Part 2: Microorganism, Media

acetic acid 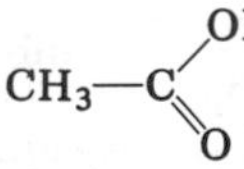 A saturated carboxylic acid occurring as a free fatty acid in natural fat; found in vinegar (4 to 12%); formed by the bacterial fermentation (*Acetobacter aceti*) of alcohol:

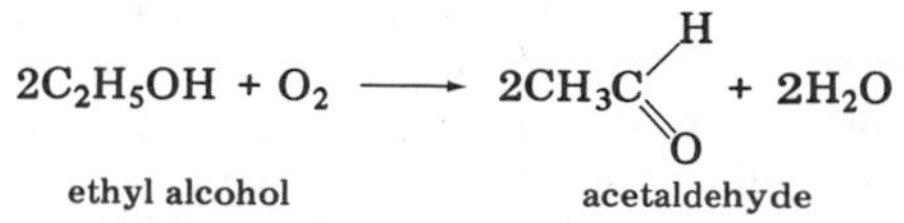

ethyl alcohol acetaldehyde

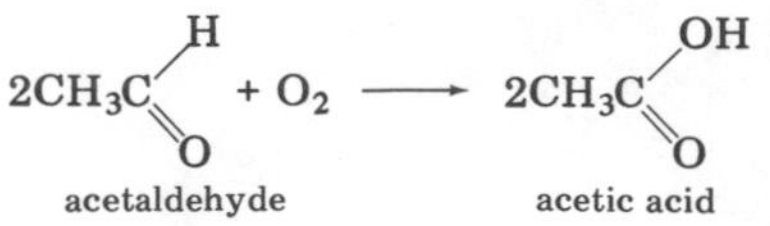

Mol. wt. 60.03; Eq. wt. 60.03

Commercial grades	Moles/ liter	g/ liter	% by wt	Specific gravity	*N*
acetic acid, glacial	17.4	1045	99.5	1.050	17.4
acetic acid	6.27	376	36	1.045	6.27

Can be obtained also by destructive distillation of wood and by reaction of carbon monoxide with methanol. Used in preserving food.

ml of 99.5% CH_3COOH to dilute to 10 liter	approx. normality
580	1.00

See Part 2: Concentration of Commercial Strengths of Acids and Bases; Normal Solutions; pH, Standard Solutions; Reagents, Normal Solutions

Acetobacter A rod-shaped (2-μm long) microorganism that occurs in pairs of long or short chains; they are important in the carbon cycle, the production of vinegar, the oxidation of ethanol to acetic acid and acetate or lactate to carbon dioxide and water.
See Part 2: Spoilage, Carbohydrate Foods

Acetomonas A rod-shaped (3-μm long) obligate aerobic microorganism that oxidizes ethanol to acetic acid; they are found on fruits and in fermented beverages.
See Part 2: Spoilage, Carbohydrate Foods

acetone bodies Compounds such as β-hydroxybutyric acid, acetoacetic acid, and acetone; these are *sometimes* end products of metabolism and are excreted as such; they are acidic and moderately toxic.

acetonemia Metabolic cattle disease usually occurring early in lactation; loss of flesh and milk production, and an unsteady gait are symptoms; prevented by a balanced ration.

acetylated monoglycerides Esters of glycerin with a mixture of acetic acid and edible fatty acids. Made by interesterification of edible fats with triacetin and glycerol; the CH_3CO- group is attached to the glycerol. Used as emulsifiers.

acetylene *See* **alkyne**

achar Cucumbers, shallots and chilies marinated in vinegar, sugar and salt.

achene A small, dry, 1-seeded fruit that remains closed at maturity, e.g., strawberry seed.

Achilles tendon A tendon which attaches the gastrocnemius muscle to the os calcis.
See Part 2: Connective Tissue, Composition

***Achromobacter* (*Alcaligenes*)** Small, Gram-negative, strictly aerobic, nonpathogenic, usually motile, microorganisms found in the intestinal tract; in dairy products, rotting eggs, and other foods; in soil, and fresh and salt water; responsible for spoilage of meat and fish.
See Part 2: Spoilage, Protein Foods

acid A compound that may be either organic or inorganic and is characterized by the following properties: gives up (donates) protons (hydrogen ions, H^+) to other substances; contains hydrogen atoms that are replaceable by positive components; reacts with a base to form a salt and water (neutralization); has a pH less than 7.0. Inorganic acids ionize strongly in water, e.g., sulfuric, hydrochloric. Organic acids ionize slightly or not at all in water; they may be saturated or unsaturated. They all contain one or more carboxyl groups (—COOH), and have the generalized formula 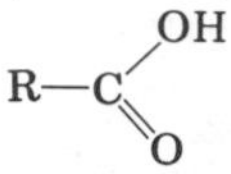 . *See also* **fatty acid.**

Acids have a sour, sharp taste; many inorganic acids are severely corrosive to the skin and must be handled with care. In mixing, always add acid to water—*never* the reverse.
See Part 2: Concentration of Commercial Strengths of Acids and Bases; Indicators, pH, and Acid Base; Organic Acids in Fruits and Vegetables

acid alcohol A mixture of 50 ml of 35% alcohol and 3 drops of pure hydrochloric acid.

acid-forming foods Foods that leave an acid residue in the body after the food has been utilized (e.g., meat, eggs, fish and cereal).

acid halides 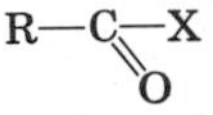 Named after the acid by dropping the -ic and adding -yl, followed by the name of the halide.

acidity The pH of a solution between 7.1 and 1.0.
See Part 2: Bananas, Composition; Lemon Juice Composition; Lime Juice Composition; Milk, Physical Properties; pH, Buffer Solutions; pH, Standard Solutions; pH, Universal Indicators; pH Values of Biological Materials

acid-modified starch Acid modification lowers the paste viscosity of a starch solution.

acid nitriles Organic compounds having the generalized formula R—CN.

acid number *See* **acid value**

acidophilus milk A cultured milk produced by adding acidophilus bacteria (*Lactobacillus acidophilus*).
See Part 2: Fluid and Fermented milks, Composition

acidulant An organic acid added to food to aid in preservation, chelate metals (which also aids in retarding oxidation), and modify taste (both acid and sweetness); it may be used with buffers

to adjust pH, which in turn modifies physical properties.
See Part 2: Acidulants

acid value (acid number) Mg of caustic potash (potassium hydroxide) needed to neutralize the free fatty acid in 1 g of fat; a measure of processing care and storage deterioration. *See also* **free fatty acid.**

AC medium An infusion-free, general culture medium for the propagation of anaerobes, microaerophiles, and aerobes; it is recommended for controlling sterility of products.
See Part 2: Microorganism, Media

acorn A winter variety of squash, from its resemblance to the seed of an oak tree.

acre (A) A measure of surface area.
1A = 6,272,640 sq in.
= 43,560 sq ft
= 4,840 sq yd
= 4,046.87 sq m (m^2)
= 0.40469 hectare (ha)
= 0.004047 sq kilometer (km^2)
= 0.001563 sq mile statute
See Part 2: Acre, Plants; Acre, Trees

acre-inch A measure of volume; 3630 cu ft.

A.C.S. grade Designation of a grade of chemical purity that meets the specifications of the American Chemical Society.

actin *See* **actomyosin**

actinin A myofibrillar protein which is a portion of the thin filament in muscle tissue; it is divided into α-actinin which promotes the lateral association of F-actin and β-actinin which inhibits the polymerization of F-actin.
See Part 2: Myofibrillar Proteins of Muscle

actinium (Ac) An element; at. no. 89; mass number of most stable isotope 227; electron configuration 2-8-18-32-18-9-2
orbit K L M N O P Q
oxidation state + 3; parent member of the actinide series of radioactive elements; Group III B of Periodic Table.

Actinomyces A microorganism in the soil, from which certain antibiotics are derived.
See Part 2: Microorganism, Media

actinomycete isolation agar *See* Part 2: Microorganism, Media

actinomycetin Antibiotic agent effective against certain Gram-positive and Gram-negative organisms.

activator An ion whose presence promotes enzyme activity.

active oxygen method A method of measuring fat stability by bubbling oxygen through heated fat and following peroxide formation.

actomyosin The globulin complex responsible for muscle contraction; consists of actin and myosin proteins.
See Part 2: Myofibrillar Proteins of Muscle

acyl group 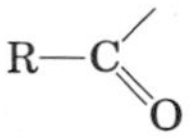 An organic group formed by attachment of a carbonyl group (C=O) to an alkyl or aryl group.

additive Any substance, the intended use of which results or may reasonably be expected to result directly or indirectly in its becoming a component or otherwise affecting the characteristics of any food (FDA). Intentional additives in extremely low percentages perform specific functions in foods, e.g., antioxidants, anticaking agents, colorants, flavor agents, acidulants, etc. Unintentional additives are unwanted substances such as insecticide residues and other contaminants that may find their way into food products.

addled egg *See* **mixed rot**

adductor (muscle) Large inside thigh muscle that is cranial to the semimembranosus and caudal, and medial to the femur.

adenine A purine that occurs in ribonucleic acid and certain coenzymes.

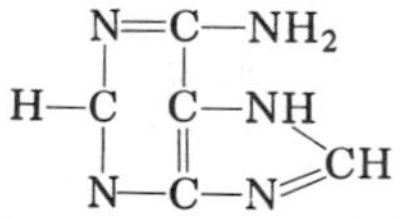

adenine-riboflavin dinucleotide A dinucleotide containing riboflavin phosphate and adenylic acid.

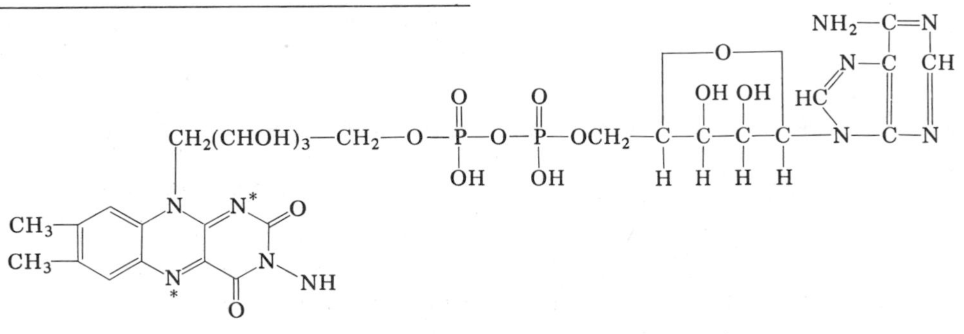

(*take on H here)

adenosine A nucleoside composed of adenine and ribose.

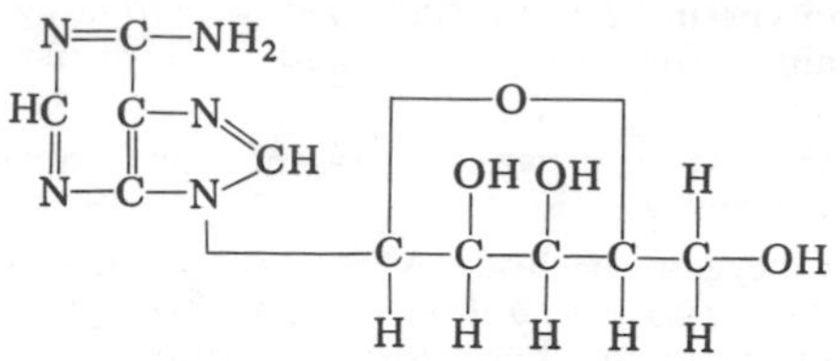

adenylic acid A mononucleotide of adenine.

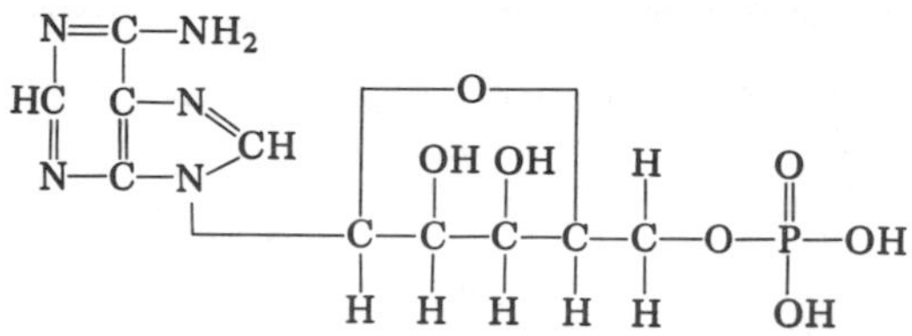

adipic acid An acidulant.

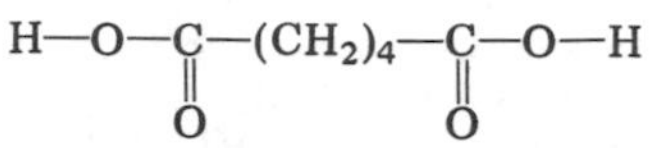

It is 110–115% as tart as anhydrous citric acid.
See Part 2: Acidulants

adipose tissue Tissue that contains fat; its average composition is: 11–17% water, 3–7% protein, 75–85% fat, 3–8 calories/g.
See Part 2: Hide, Layers; Hides, Salt Absorption

ad lib Without restraint or limit.

adobo Meat cut into cubes, with vinegar, salt, garlic and pepper added, cooked in water, fried in lard and stored in lard.

adrenal cortex extract A drug extracted from the outer portion (cortex) of the adrenal glands of cattle, hogs and sheep and used to treat Addison's disease and shock.

adrenal glands Two small reddish brown glands located near the kidneys; inner section of the gland is known as the medulla; outer portion is the cortex. This gland is stimulated by the adrenocorticotropic hormone produced by the pituitary gland: I. Inner portion produces a secretion which makes the blood vessels smaller and speeds up the heart rate; II. Outer portion produces a secretion the lack of which causes Addison's disease.

adrenosterone $C_{19}H_{24}O_3$; an androgenic steroid isolated from the adrenal cortex.
See Part 2: Steroids

adsorption Adherence of molecules of a gas, liquid, or solid to the surface of a solid. It is important in deodorizing (activated carbon) and decolorizing (clays). It also plays a part in catalysis.

Aerobacter A Gram-negative rod type of microorganism that will ferment glucose and lactose to produce acid and gas; found in dairy products, grain, sewage, water, and the alimentary tract.
See Part 2: Microorganism Reactions on Differential Tube Media

aerobe Microorganism that can grow in the presence of free oxygen.
See Part 2: Microbiological Media

aerobic Descriptive of bacteria which require air or oxygen to survive. *See also* **facultative anaerobe; obligate aerobes.**

Aeromonas A small rod-shaped (3-μm long), facultative aerobic microorganism that is found in water and may be pathogenic to aquatic animals; breaks down carbohydrate to yield acid and gas.
See Part 2: Spoilage, Protein Foods

aerosol A suspension in air of a liquid or solid in finely divided form, as discharged through a small orifice by a propellant gas or other pressure source, e.g., spray drying of milk.

AFDOUS code Association of Food and Drug Officials of the U.S.; a frozen food handling code.

aflatoxin A metabolic toxin produced by *Aspergillus flavus* and other fungi. It is carcinogenic.

African rue (*Peganum harmala*) An African plant from which are isolated harmine and harmaline both of which are stimulants to the central nervous system.
See Part 2: Poisonous Plants

after-taste Taste that follows the removal of the initial stimulus; it may be continuous with or follow the initial stimulus after a period of time.

Ag Symbol for the element silver (Latin *argentum*).

agar-agar (agar, Japanese gelatin, vegetable gelatin) A dried hydrophilic, polygalactoside gelling agent made from sea grass (*Gelidium cartilagineum, Gracilaria confervoides* and other red algae); used as a bacterial media and in foods (soups, jellies, ice cream) as a stabilizer, emulsifier and thickener. 1.5% concentration congeals at 32–40°C, and liquefies at 85–95°C. Gel strength is proportional to concentration (0.5 to 2.0%); it is increased with sugar and locust bean gum content. MW-5,000 to 30,000; store in well closed container.
See Part 2: Gums and Gelling Agents; Gums and Gelling Agents, Characteristics; Gum Characteristics; Gum Physicochemical Properties; Stabilizers-thickeners

agaric Any mushroom, particularly the species, *Agaricus*; fungus.

age The passage of time (or other units) from the beginning of an event.
See Part 2: Bone Age; Teeth Eruption

aged cheese *See* **cured (cheese)**

aged meat Meat held at refrigeration temperatures to improve flavor and tenderness; *Thamnidium* mold contributes to flavor of aged meat.

aggregate fruit Fruit formed from a flower containing many pistils (e.g., blackberry).
See Part 2: Fruit Classification

aging Holding a food product under specific conditions of temperature, humidity, etc. for an extended period of time to improve its texture, flavor, and other properties, or to determine its shelf life. *See also* **aged meat.**
See Part 2: Cheese Characteristics; Tenderness of Poultry

agricultural limestone Liming material composed of 58% $CaCO_3$ and 42% $MgCO_3$; each pound has the neutralizing equivalent of 0.95 to 1.08 lb of $CaCO_3$ (or approx. this quantity of dolomitic limestone).

agronomy The science of soil structure, fertility, and management and application of its principles to agricultural crop production.

aïoli A garlic-flavored mayonnaise.

air The atmosphere enveloping the earth, composed chiefly of oxygen (21%), nitrogen (78%), argon (0.93%) and carbon dioxide (0.03%).
See Part 2: Ingestion and Inhalation; Insulation.

air cell An air-containing vacuole within an egg.
See Part 2: Egg Structure

air-slaked lime Liming material composed of 80–95% $Ca(OH)_2$; each pound has the neutralizing equivalent of 0.85 to 1 lb of $CaCO_3$ (or approx. this quantity of dolomitic limestone).

aitch bone *See* **ischium**
See Part 2: Beef Round, Bone Structure; Beef Wholesale Cuts; Lamb Wholesale Cuts; Pork Wholesale Cuts; Veal Wholesale Cuts; Bone; Bone Age

akee A medium-size tree that bears a 3-inch red fruit; when ripe the fruit opens and a cream-colored aril is exposed; the aril is consumed raw, fried, or boiled.

akene Dry carpel having a single seed.

AK medium (Arret & Kirshbaum) Microbiological medium designed for the production of spores of *B. subtillis*, which, in turn, are used for the detection of antibiotics in milk.
See Part 2: Microbiological Examination of Dairy Products

Al Symbol for the element aluminum.

-al Ending for an aldehyde compound.

à la Newburg A seafood (especially lobster, shrimp, etc.) served with a thick sauce made from cream, eggs and butter, usually flavored with wine. The name is said to be taken from that of the chef who invented it (Wenburg), in which the first and third letters were inverted.

alanine Monoamino-monocarboxylic non-essential amino acid;

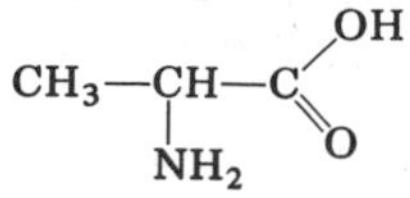

See Part 2: Amino Acids; Amino Acid, Solubilities; Corn, Amino Acids; Egg Products Nutritive Value; Grain Analysis; Manure Analysis; Wheat, Amino Acids; Wheat Products, Amino Acid Compositions

à la provençal With olive oil, lemon juice, parsley and garlic.

albacore An alternate name for tuna.

albedo Whiteness; light reflected by a surface.
See Part 2: Orange Structure

albumin A simple protein which is soluble in water and dilute salt solutions and coagulable by heat.
See Part 2: Milk and Milk Products, Vitamin Content; Milk, Species; Wheat Products, Amino Acid Compositions

albuminoid A simple protein that is insoluble in water, dilute salt solutions, dilute acids or alkalies, absolute or 70–80% alcohol (e.g., keratin, elastin, collagen, and fibroin).

Alcaligenes A Gram-negative, aerobic to facultatively anaerobic rod (8-µm long) type of microorganism found in dairy products, soil, water, and the intestinal tract; no gas is produced by carbohydrates.
See Part 2: Intestinal Microorganisms in Triple-sugar Iron Agar; Microorganism Reactions on Differential Tube Media

alcohol A class of organic compounds in which one or more alkyl or aryl groups and one or more hydroxyl groups are present. The suffix -ol is approved by IUPAC, e.g., methanol, ethanol, etc. Both straight-chain and ring structures of various types occur. Aliphatic alcohols are subclassified as monohydric, dihydric, trihydric and polyhydric (polyol), the names indicating the number of OH groups present. *See also* **absolute alcohol; industrial alcohol; acid alcohol; ethyl alcohol; methyl alcohol; glycerol; glycol; cholesterol.**

alcoholic beverage A drink in which ethyl alcohol is present; the content varies widely with the nature of the drink.
See Part 2: Alcoholic Solutions; Minerals (Trace), Limits

alcoholometer A hydrometer calibrated in % alcohol.

aldehyde A class of organic compounds characterized by the presence of the unsaturated carbonyl group (C=O). A hydrogen atom is also attached to the carbon atom, so that the generalized formula is represented by

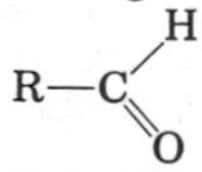

. The characteristic suffix is -al in IUPAC nomenclature. e.g., methanal (formaldehyde). Aldehydes may be aliphatic or aromatic.

aldehydo *See* Part 2: Sugar, D-aldehydo

aldosterone $C_{21}H_{28}O_5$; a hormone; a mineralocorticoid which causes the retention of sodium

and the loss of potassium; it is isolated from adrenals.
See Part 2: Steroids

aldrin A toxic insecticide which may be carcinogenic. Its use on food crops has been prohibited.

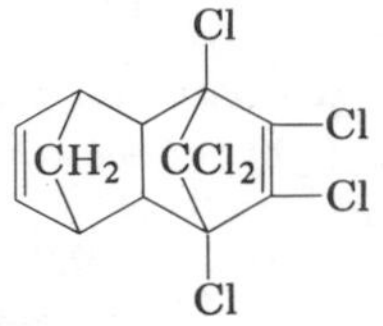

ale An alcoholic beverage made from barley malt and hops by a top fermenting yeast; it used to differ (little difference today) from beer in that less hops were used, was lighter in color and sweeter; English beer with 3.1 to 6.6% alcohol by volume.

aleuronat Flour made from the aleurone portion of grain.

aleurone layer The 2nd layer or layer beneath the pericarp in grain; contains protein grain or granules.
See Part 2: Corn Kernel; Rice Kernel; Wheat Kernel; Wheat Kernel Parts; Wheat, Parts of Grain; Wheat, Parts of Grain, Vitamins

alewife A shad-like fish.

alfalfa A perennial plant used for hay and pasture; cut when 1/10 flowers open; pH, 6.5–6.8; inoculation is essential. Varieties: Certified Atlantic, Certified Buffalo, Certified Williamsburg, DuPuits, Narragansett, and Oklahoma Common; Approx. nutrients used by 3 tons of hay—170 lb N, 48 lb P_2O_5, 150 lb K_2O; plant 10 to 12 lb per acre. 1 bu alfalfa seed = 50 lb.
See Part 2: Nutrients in Crops; pH Values of Biological Materials; Seed, Germination

alfalfa meal 0.6 lb/qt; 19 lb/bu.

alfol Crumpled aluminum foil used as insulation.
See Part 2: Insulation, Conductivity Values

al fresco In the open air, usually in reference to dining.

algae Chlorophyll-bearing plants that are primarily aquatic; subclassified as green, blue-green, red and brown. They include many types of seaweed, e.g., kelp, and are the chief source of carrageenan used as a texturing aid in ice cream, etc. *See also* **algin; carrageenan; agar-agar.**
See Part 2: Microorganism, Media

algin A hydrophilic gum extracted from sea-growing brown algae (*Macrocystis pyrifera*) composed of D-mannuronic and L-galacturonic acid residues; MW—35,000 to 200,000. *See also* **alginic acid; alginate.**

alginate A derivative of alginic acid. *See also* **alginic acid.**
See Part 2: Gums and Gelling Agents; Gum Characteristics; Stabilizers-thickeners; Minerals, Trace, Limits

alginic acid $(C_6H_8O_6)_n$ A hydrophilic carbohydrate extracted from seaweed; used as a stabilizer. *See also* **algin.**
Types used in food industry are as follows:

sodium alginate	$(C_6H_7O_6Na)_n$	sodium salt of alginic acid
ammonium alginate	$(C_6H_7O_6NH_4)_n$	ammonium salt of alginic acid
potassium alginate	$(C_6H_7O_6K)_n$	potassium salt of alginic acid
propylene glycol alginate	$(C_9H_{14}O_7)_n$	propylene glycol ester of alginic acid

See Part 2: Minerals (Trace), Limits

alicyclic A class of organic compounds in which the carbon atoms form closed rings of various geometrical shapes. They may be saturated or unsaturated and have properties resembling those of aliphatic compounds. They may be hydrocarbons (cyclohexane) or alcohols (cholesterol).

aliphatic A class of organic compounds in which the carbon atoms are arranged in a straight (open) or branched chain. They may be either saturated or unsaturated. They include hydrocarbons, organic acids, ketones, amines, aldehydes, and the more common alcohols, e.g., methanol, ethanol, butanol, etc. *See also* **alkane, alkene, alkadiene, alkyne.**

aliquot Exactly measured volume; a definite part of a whole.

alkadiene (C_nH_{2n-2}) An unsaturated aliphatic hydrocarbon that contains 2 double bonds. Also called diolefin.

alkalescens A species of *Shigella* microorganism; renders milk alkaline with changing appearance, taste, or odor; occasionally causes diarrhea.
See Part 2: Intestinal Microorganisms; Intestinal Microorganisms in Triple-Sugar Iron Agar

alkali A substance with mild to caustic properties; pH in excess of 7; turns litmus paper blue and neutralizes acids. *See also* **base; caustic soda.**

alkali metal The strongly electropositive metals occurring in Group IA of the Periodic Table. They have a valence of 1.

alkaline-earth metal The metals occurring in Group IIA of the Periodic Table, with the exception of beryllium. They are electropositive, and have a valence of 2.

alkaloid A product of plant metabolism, many of which are poisonous. They belong to the class of nitrogenous heterocyclic compounds. Well-known examples are nicotine, caffeine, morphine and strychnine.

alkane (C_nH_{2n+2}) A class of saturated aliphatic hydrocarbons containing only single bonds. Also called paraffins.

alkanesulfonic *See* **sulfonic acid**

alkanet A vegetable color (brown-red) from the alkanet root.

alkanethiol (R—SH) An alcohol-type organic compound in which the oxygen atom of the OH group is replaced by sulfur, forming a sulfhydryl group. Such compounds were formerly called mercaptans.

alkene (C_nH_{2n}) A class of unsaturated aliphatic hydrocarbon containing one double bond. Also called paraffins.

alkyl cyanide *See* **nitrile**

alkyl group (C_nH_{2n+1}) An aliphatic saturated hydrocarbon group having one valence (CH_3, C_2H_5, etc.), often represented by R.

alkyl halide ($C_nH_{2n+1}X$) Any alkane in which one hydrogen atom has been replaced by an atom of either fluorine, chlorine, bromine, or iodine (X).

alkyl metallic sulfate $R—O—SO_2—O^{-+}M$, where M stands for a metal.

alkyl sulfate $R'—O—SO_2—O—R$

alkyl sulfide *See* **alkylthioalkane**

alkylthioalkane (R'—S—R) An ether-type organic compound in which the oxygen atom is replaced by sulfur.

alkyne (C_nH_{2n-2}) A class of unsaturated aliphatic hydrocarbons containing one triple bond; also called acetylene compounds.

Allemande A smooth, yellow sauce made from the strained stock of veal, fish or chicken and mixed with egg yolks, cream, lemon juice and spices.

allies Small stalked fungi.

alligator pear *See* **avocado**

allose $C_6H_{12}O_6$; A synthetic aldohexose sugar. *See* Part 2: Sugar, D-aldehydo

allspice (pimento, not pimiento) (*Pimenta officinalis* Lindl) Dried nearly ripe fruit of pimento tree (tropical) used as a spice; contains: not less than 8% quercitannic acid; not more than 0.4% ash insoluble in HCl; not more than 25% crude fiber; and not more than 6% total ash; has an aroma similar to a mixture of nutmeg, cinnamon, and cloves. For labeling purposes the word "allspice" indicates Jamaican origin only.
See Part 2: Essential Oils; Spices, Microbial Content

allumette Potatoes or other vegetables that are cut like matches.

almond (*Prunus dulcis*) A small tree grown for nut and oil production; a hard shell ellipsoidal nut.

Variety	Common name	Use
amara	bitter	almond oil for flavoring and emollient
dulcis	sweet	edible nuts

natural almond: shelled nut with brown skin left on
blanched almond: brown skin removed, skin loosened by bringing to boil in water (1/3 cup = 1 oz)
roasting in butter or oil; 300°F oven for 15-20 min
toasted 300°F oven for 15-20 min
Storage: shelled nuts should be stored in tightly closed containers in refrigerator or freezer
1 lb almond nutmeats = 3-4 cups nutmeats
1 cup shelled nutmeats = 150 g (5.4 oz)
1 lb shelled nutmeats = 3½ lb imported unshelled
1 lb shelled nutmeats = 2 lb Calif. unshelled

Composition	% H_2O	% Protein	% Fat	% Carbohydrate	% Ash
Dried	5	19	54	20	3
Roasted and salted	1	19	57	20	3.5

See Part 2: Beans, Peas and Nuts; Flavor Ingredients, Taste and Flavor Type; Fruit and Nut Rootstock; Minerals, Food; Nut, Grades; Protein Factors; Tocopherols

almond black Black pigment produced by charring almond shells.

almond oil An oil obtained from bitter almonds, after removal of hydrocyanic acid. 0.914-0.920 specific gravity; 1.472-1.475 refractive index (15.5°C); 188-195 saponification number; 93-100 iodine number; 2.85 acid number.

almond paste Made by water cooking blanched and ground sweet and bitter almonds with sugar or dextrose; max. 14% water; max. 40% total sugar expressed as invert sugar.

alpha (A, α) Greek letter, the English equivalent of "A."

alpha amino acid *See* **amino acid**

alpha particle A form of radiation given off by radium and other radioactive elements; it is actually a helium nucleus and has low penetrating power.

alpha-tocopherol ($C_{29}H_{50}O_2$) A chemical with vitamin E activity found in some food stuffs. It occurs in alfalfa.

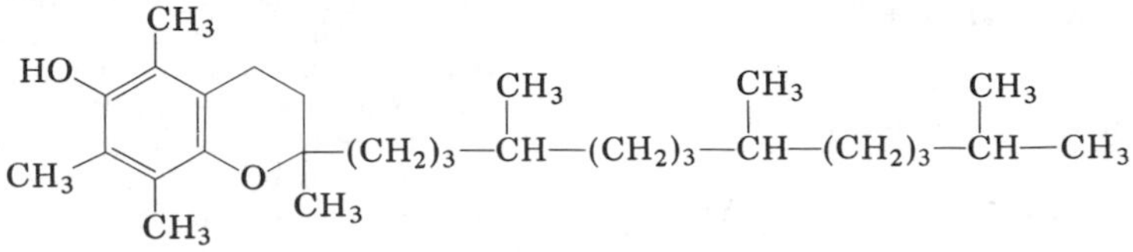

Alsatian wine A dry white wine with a clean flavor produced in the Alsace area of eastern France.

alsike clover A perennial hay; seed 2 to 4 lb/acre, (60 lb/bu); pH 6-6.8; inoculation is necessary; cut in full bloom.

Alta A variety of fescue.

Alternaria A genus of *Fungi Imperfect*; one of the plant diseases caused by this fungus is carrot blight which appears as irregular necrotic areas on older leaves.
See Part 2: Mold, Food; Molds, Mycotoxins; Rot Spoilage

alternating current (AC) An electric current that reverses its direction of flow at constant intervals.

altitude Distance above sea level.
Cooking time table alterations:

Boiling water bath:
add 1 min/1000 ft if cooking time is less than 20 min
add 2 min/1000 ft if cooking time is more than 20 min

Pressure cook:
add 1 lb/2000 ft; time remains the same

Cake recipes alteration/cake:

Altitude	Shortening	Sugar	Baking Powder	Temp.
3000-5000 ft	1 tablespoon less	1½ tablespoons less	—	—
5000-7000 ft	2 tablespoons less	3 tablespoons less	reduce ¼	—
over 8000 ft	3 tablespoons less	4 tablespoons less	reduce ½	increase 25°F

See Part 2: Altitude Adjustments for Baking; Temperatures Corresponding to Gauge Pressure at Various Altitudes

altrose $C_6H_{12}O_6$; An artificially obtained sugar; isomeric with glucose.
See Part 2: Sugar, D-aldehydo

alum An inclusive term for several aluminum-type compounds. *See also* **aluminum potassium sulfate; aluminum sulfate.**

alum-cochineal Potassic alum, 6 g; powdered cochineal, 6g; distilled water, 90 ml; boil 30 min on steam bath; allow to settle and pour off the liquid; add water to bring up to 180 cc, boil down to 90 cc, cool, filter, add a small amount of thymol or salicylic acid.

aluminum (Al) A metallic element; at. no. 13; at. wt. 26.98; oxidation state + 3; electron configuration 2-8-3
orbit K L M
Nontoxic; used in food machinery and cooking utensils.

aluminum potassium sulfate (potassium aluminum sulfate) $K_2SO_4 \cdot Al_2(SO_4)_3 \cdot 24H_2O$. A double salt of aluminum used in water purification, as a food additive, and as an astringent.

aluminum sulfate $[Al_2(SO_4)_3]$ A variety of alum used to clarify fats and oils, and in water purification.
See Part 2: Reagents, Normal Solutions

Am Symbol for the element americium.

amanori *See* **nori**

amaranth (FD&C Red No. 2) The red azo dye extensively used for many years as a food colorant, but prohibited in 1976 because of suspected carcinogenicity. It has been replaced for many applications by Red No. 40.

amebiasis Infected with amebae.
See Part 2: Infectious Diseases, Food-Borne

ameliorate To improve. *See also* modified wine.

American cheddar A semi-hard, aged cheese.

American cheese A mild, semi-soft process cheese with a cheddar-like flavor; pH 4.9.

American leg of lamb A leg from which the tibia is removed and the meat that surrounded it is tucked under the fell.

American mackerel *See* **mackerel**

American system A system for grading wool based on Merino wool, which is fine. Grades: Fine, half blood, ⅜ blood, ¼ blood, low ¼ blood, common, braid.

americium (Am) A radioactive element of the actinide series; Group IIIB of the Periodic Table; at. No. 95; mass No. of most stable isotope 243; oxidation state +3, +4, +5, +6; electron configuration 2-8-18-32-24-9-2
orbit K L M N O P Q.

amide A class of compounds derived from ammonia, some of which are inorganic (sodamide, $NaNH_2$) and some organic. Organic amides contain an acyl group; $R\text{—}\overset{\overset{\displaystyle O}{\|}}{C}\text{—}NH_2$. They are related to organic acids, in which the OH group is replaced by NH_2. *See also* **acyl group.**

AMIF-72 An antioxidant containing butylated hydroxyanisole.

amine A class of organic compounds that may be derived from ammonia (NH_3) by substituting an alkyl or aryl group (CH_3 or C_6H_5) for one or more of the hydrogen atoms. *See also* **amino acid.**

aminoacetic acid *See* **glycine**

amino acid A basic unit of protein containing at least one amino group (NH_2) and at least one carboxyl group or a derivative of this basic structure; they are of L-configuration, except glycine which has no asymmetric carbon. 22 amino acids are constituents of proteins, and many others exist independently. 8 of the 22 are called "essential" as they must be obtained from outside the human body, that is, in the diet.

See Part 2: Amino Acids; Amino Acid, Solubilities; Coconut, Amino Acids; Corn, Amino Acids; Egg Products Nutritive Value; Manure Analysis; Milk, Amino Acids; Protein and Amino Acid, Color Reactions; Wheat, Amino Acids; Wheat Products, Amino Acid Compositions; Wheat Products Composition

***p*-aminobenzoic acid (PABA)** $NH_2C_6H_4COOH$ A vitamin-like compound essential for growth of some organisms; also antagonizes sulfanilamide.
See **antagonism** and Part 2: Wheat, Vitamins

α-aminocaproic acid *See* **norleucine**

aminodimethylaniline oxalate A reagent for certain bacteria.
See Part 2: Microorganism, Media

α-aminoglutaric acid *See* **glutamic acid**

α-aminoisocaproic acid *See* **leucine**

α-aminoisovaleric acid *See* **valine**

α-aminopropionic acid *See* **alanine**

α-aminosuccinic acid *See* **aspartic acid**

ammeter An instrument connected in series with the circuit which measures electric current.

ammonia, anhydrous (NH_3) A liquid fertilizer material which becomes gaseous at atmospheric pressure. Fertilizer notation 82-0-0. Acidic in nature; requires 1.47 lb of dolomitic limestone to neutralize each pound applied. B.p. -33.35°C; f.p. -77.7°C; heat of vaporization 327 cal/g; specific heat 1.07 cal/gram-degree. An end product of animal metabolism. Made from natural gas or synthesis gas. Low electrical conductivity. Pungent, suffocating smell. Very soluble in water, giving an alkaline solution of ammonium hydroxide. Also used as a refrigerant.

ammonia, aqua A solution of ammonia in water, forming ammonium hydroxide (NH_4OH). Solutions vary in strength from 10 to 29%. Pressure 40 psi at 25°F; 197 psi at 100°F. *See also* **ammonium hydroxide.**
See Part 2: Ammonia Solutions; Concentration of Commercial Strengths of Acids and Bases; Fertilizer; Fertilizer Materials; Normal Solutions; pH, Standard Solutions; Refrigerant; Sanitizing Chemicals; Sanitizers; Wheat Products, Amino Acid Compositions

ammonia water *See* **ammonia, aqua**

ammonification The production of ammonia by bacteria from protein.

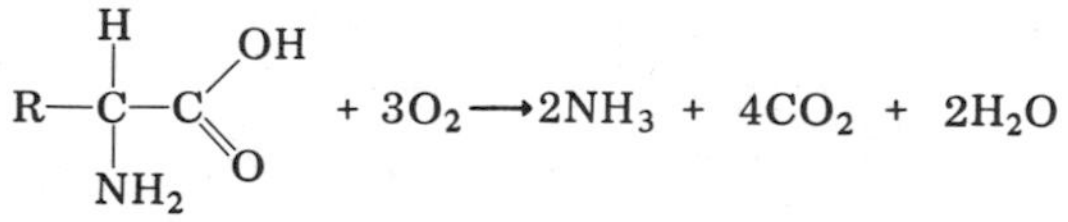

ammonium alginate *See* **algin**

ammonium carbamate ($H_2N \cdot C(=O) \cdot O—NH_4$)

A white water-soluble powder which gives off ammonia on decomposition at 60°C. Used in fertilizers.

ammonium carbonate A mixture of ammonium carbamate and ammonium acid carbonate. Used to aid fermentation in wine mfg. and general-purpose food additive.

ammonium chloride NH_4Cl. Water-soluble crystals. Used in fertilizers and in bakery products.
See Part 2: Normal Solutions

ammonium hydroxide (NH_4OH) (NH_3 in water); mol. wt. 35.05; eq. wt. 35.05.

Commercial strength	Mole/ liter	g/ liter	% by wt	Specific gravity	Normality
—	14.8	251	28	0.898	14.8

ml of 27% ammonium hydroxide to dilute to 10 liter	approximate normality
710	1.00

See also **ammonia (aqua).**
See Part 2: Reagents, Normal Solutions

ammonium nitrate A fertilizer material; fertilizer notation-33.5-0-0; NH_4NO_3; 33.5% nitrogen (50% of this is ammonia and 50% is nitrate); acid in nature and would require 0.58 lb of dolomitic limestone to neutralize each pound applied. *See also* **ANL; calnitro.**
See Part 2: Fertilizer; Fertilizer Materials

ammonium nitrate and lime *See* **ANL**

ammonium phosphate A fertilizer material; fertilizer notation 11-48-0.

ammonium sulfate A fertilizer material; fertilizer notation 20.5-0-0; $(NH_4)_2SO_4$; acid in nature and would require 1.1 lb of dolomitic limestone to neutralize each pound applied.
See Part 2: Fertilizer Materials; Normal Solutions

ammonium thiocyanate *See* Part 2: Normal Solutions

amontillado A sherry with more body and color than fino from which it is often made by aging in the cask.

amorphous Lacking a crystalline structure, a characteristic of the liquid state of matter; some materials that are apparently solid, such as glass, are not crystalline and are considered to be liquids of extremely high viscosity.

amp *See* **ampere**

ampalaya Balsam apple; an East Indian yellow, bitter gourd used in pickles and curries.
See Part 2: Vegetable Storage

ampere (a) (amp) The rate of current flow (I or i). 1 amp = 6.24 × 10^{18} electrons per second.

$$\text{ampere} = \frac{\text{volt}}{\text{ohm}}$$

amphoteric Elements which are in the center of the activity or electromotive force series, and may either gain or lose electrons (act as a base or an acid) depending upon what elements they are associated with (e.g., sulfur).

amphoteric hydroxides Hydroxides which have the properties of both acids and bases.

amylase An enzyme that hydrolyzes α $(1 \rightarrow 4)$ glucosidic linkages in polysaccharides such as starch and glycogen; e.g.,

$$\text{starch} \xrightarrow{\alpha\text{-amylase}} \text{dextrin + maltose}$$

$$\xrightarrow{\beta\text{-amylase}} \text{maltose}$$

$$\xrightarrow{\gamma\text{-amylase}} \text{glucose}$$

amylase, β An enzyme that splits off maltose units from non-reducing end of starch molecules.

amyloglucosidase An enzyme. *See also* **glucoamylase.**

amylolytic Denotes enzymes which act on carbohydrates.

amylopectin A starch constructed in a bush-shaped arrangement; most of the α-D-glucopyranosyl sections are linked $1 \rightarrow 4$, but branches are attached $1 \rightarrow 6$ approximately every 26 monosaccharide units.
See Part 2: Amylopectin; Amylose and Amylopectin; Starch

amylopsin (amylase) Enzyme capable of hydrolysis of starch, glycogen, or their breakdown products.
See Part 2: pH Values of Biological Materials

amylose A starch constructed of a linear chain of α-D-glucopyranosyl units joined by $1 \rightarrow 4$ linkages.
See Part 2: Amylose; Amylose and Amylopectin; Starch

amyris oil West Indian sandalwood oil.

anabolism Digestion or reduction of food, synthesis of complex products and storage of energy which takes place in a living organism.

anadas Collection of wine of any one year.

anaerobic Descriptive of bacteria that can live without air or oxygen. *See also* **facultative anaerobe; obligate anaerobes.**
See Part 2: Microbiological Media

anaerogenic Forming little or no gas.
See Part 2: Intestinal Microorganisms in Triple-sugar Iron Agar

analysis of variance (for measurement data of 2 or more trials)

n indiv. observations per treatment		*a* Treatments 1	2 · · ·	*i* · · ·	*a*	
	1	X_{11}	X_{21}	X_{i1}	X_{a1}	
	2 · ·	X_{12}	X_{22}	X_{i2}	X_{a2}	
	j · ·	X_{1j}	X_{2j}	X_{ij}	X_{aj}	
	n	X_{1n}	X_{2n}	X_{in}	X_{an}	Total
Treat. ΣX		$X_{1.}$	$X_{2.}$	$X_{i.}$	$X_{a.}$	Total Sum $X_{..}$
Treat. Mean $\Sigma X/n = \bar{x}$		$\bar{x}_{1.}$	$\bar{x}_{2.}$	$\bar{x}_{i.}$	$\bar{x}_{a.}$	Total Mean $\bar{x}_{..}$
ΣX^2		$\Sigma X^2_{1.}$	$\Sigma X^2_{2.}$	$\Sigma X^2_{i.}$	$\Sigma X^2_{a.}$	Total Sum Squares $\Sigma X^2_{..}$
$C = (\Sigma X)^2/n$		$C_{1.}$	$C_{2.}$	$C_{i.}$	$C_{a.}$	$C_{..} = (\Sigma X_{..})^2/\text{total } n$
$\Sigma x^2 = \Sigma X^2 - C$		$\Sigma x^2_{1.}$	$\Sigma x^2_{2.}$	$\Sigma x^2_{i.}$	$\Sigma x^2_{a.}$	$\Sigma x^2_{..} = \Sigma X^2_{..} - C_{..}$

Source of Variation	d.f.	Sum of Squares	Mean Squares
Total	$(an) - 1$	$\text{total } \Sigma X^2_{..} - \dfrac{(\text{total } \Sigma X_{..})^2}{an}$	
Treatment Mean (a)	$a - 1$	$\dfrac{\Sigma(\text{Treat } \Sigma X_{i.})^2}{n} - \dfrac{(\text{total } \Sigma X_{..})^2}{an}$	$SS/df = \sigma^2 + nK^2$
Indiv. or Error (n)	Sub or $(n-1)a$	Subtract or Σ treat $\Sigma x^2_{i.}$	$SS/df = \sigma^2$

$$\text{Ho}: u_1 = u_2 = u_i = \cdots u_a \qquad F = \frac{\text{MS of Treatment}}{\text{MS of Individual}} \qquad df\ f1 = a - 1 \quad df\ f2 = a(n-1)$$

If F is Sig. then see Mean Test to see which means are Sig.

analysis of variance (sub treatments)

Treatment (a) $i = 1 \cdots a$

Sub treat b, $j = 1 \cdots b$		1		$\cdots$	$\cdots$	i	$\cdots$	$\cdots$	a	
		1	j	b	1	j	b	1	j	b
n obs per sub treat $k = 1 \cdots n$	1	X_{111}	X_{1j1}	X_{1b1}	X_{i11}	X_{ij1}	X_{ib1}	X_{a11}	X_{aj1}	X_{ab1}
	$\cdot$ $\cdot$ k	X_{11k}	X_{1jk}	X_{1bk}	X_{i1k}	X_{ijk}	X_{ibk}	X_{a1k}	X_{ajk}	X_{abk}
	$\cdot$ $\cdot$ n	X_{11n}	X_{1jn}	X_{1bn}	X_{i1n}	X_{ijn}	X_{ibn}	X_{a1n}	X_{ajn}	X_{abn}
Σ		$X_{11.}$	$X_{1j.}$	$X_{1b.}$	$X_{i1.}$	$X_{ij.}$	$X_{ib.}$	$X_{a1.}$	$X_{aj.}$	$X_{ab.}$
Σ		$X_{1..}$			$X_{i..}$			$X_{a..}$		
Σ					$X_{...}$					

	df
(1) $C = (X_{...})^2/abn$	
(2) Total $SS = \Sigma X_{ijk} - C = (X_{111})^2 + \cdots (X_{abn})^2 - C$	$abn - 1$
(3) Total SS for sub treat $= \Sigma X_{ij.}^2/n = (X_{11.}) + \cdots (X_{ab.})^2/n$	$ab - 1$
(4) SS for error or Individual = total $SS(2)$ − total SS sub treat(3)	$(abn - 1) - (ab - 1)$
(5) Total SS for treatment $= (\Sigma X_{i..})^2/bn - C$ $= (X_{1..})^2 + \cdots (X_{a..})/bn - C$	$a - 1$
(6) SS sub treat of same treat = total sub treat(3) − SS treat(5)	$(b - 1)a$

Sources of variation	df	SS	MS	
Total	$abn - 1$	(2)		
Total for treatment	$a - 1$	(5)	SS/df	$\sigma^2 + n\sigma B^2 + b\sigma A^2$
SS Sub treat of Same treat	$(b - 1)a$	(6)	SS/df	$\sigma^2 + n\sigma B^2$
Individuals	$(abn - 1) - (ab - 1)$	(4)	SS/df	σ^2

$$F \text{ for treatment} = \frac{\text{MS}(5)}{\text{MS}(6)} \qquad \begin{matrix} df - (5) \\ df - (6) \end{matrix}$$

$$F \text{ for sub treat} = \frac{\text{MS}(6)}{\text{MS}(4)} \qquad \begin{matrix} df - (6) \\ df - (4) \end{matrix}$$

analysis of variance (two-way classification)

groups	a treatment 1	2 $\cdots$	i $\cdots$	a	Σ groups ΣX
1	X_{11}	X_{21}	X_{i1}	X_{a1}	$X_{.1}$
2	X_{12}	X_{22}	X_{i2}	X_{a2}	$X_{.2}$
$\cdot$					
$\cdot$					
j	X_{1j}	X_{2j}	X_{ij}	X_{aj}	$X_{.j}$
$\cdot$					
$\cdot$					
n	X_{1n}	X_{2n}	X_{in}	X_{an}	$X_{.n}$
Total ΣX	$X_{1.}$	$X_{2.}$	$X_{i.}$	$X_{a.}$	$X_{..}$

Correction term $= (X_{..})^2/an = C$

(Continued)

$$\text{Total } SS = (X_{11})^2 + \cdots (X_{an})^2 - C$$

$$\text{Group } SS = \frac{(X_{.1})^2 + \cdots (X_{.n})^2}{a} - C$$

$$\text{Treatment } SS = \frac{(X_{1.})^2 + \cdots (X_{a.})^2}{n} - C$$

$$\text{Error } SS = \text{Total } SS - \text{group } SS - \text{treatment } SS$$

Sources of Variation	*df*	*SS*	MS
Group	$n - 1$	Group *SS*	$SS/n - 1$
Treatment	$a - 1$	Treat *SS*	$SS/a - 1$
Error	$(n - 1)(a - 1)$	Error *SS*	$SS/(n - 1)(a - 1)$
Total	$an - 1$	Total *SS*	

$$\text{Group } F = \frac{\text{MS of Group}}{\text{MS of Error}} \qquad \begin{matrix} df - \text{group} \\ df - \text{error} \end{matrix}$$

$$\text{Treat } F = \frac{\text{MS of treat}}{\text{MS of Error}} \qquad \begin{matrix} df - \text{treat} \\ df - \text{error} \end{matrix}$$

---

anchovy A pungent, salted and pickled herring-like fish (*Engraulidae*) usually packed in oil and canned or made into a sauce.

Composition	Pickled
% H_2O	59
% protein	19
% fat	10
% carbohydrate	0.3
% ash	11.5

anchovy pear Fruit eaten as a pickle from the *Grias cauliflora* tree.

ancona A mediterranean class of chickens that lays a white-shelled egg; greenish black with some white tip feathers; varieties, single-comb and rose-comb.

andouille A large pork sausage; a kind of sausage made of tripe.

androstenedione A steroid hormone.
See Part 2: Steroids

-ane I.U.P.A.C. ending for alkane (paraffin) series of hydrocarbons.

aneurin *See* **thiamin**

angelica (*Angelica archangelica*) A many blossomed large biennial herb of which the leaf stalks and midribs are used as food garnishes and confections; grown in cold climates.

young stems and leaves	crystallized with sugar	confectionery flavoring
	essential oil	decorating
root	essential oil	gin
seed	essential oil	vermouth, chartreuse

See Part 2: Essential Oils

angico gum (Brazilian gum) A brown gum from a South American tree used in tanning and varnishes.
See Part 2: Gum Distribution

ang-khak An oriental food made from fungus growth on rice.
See Part 2: Fungi Food Products

angostura bitters An extract from the bark of *Galipea officinalis*, used to flavor drinks.
See Part 2: Essential Oils

angstrom (Å) (A.U.) A measure of length.

1 angstrom = 0.1 millimicron (mμ) = 1 nanometer (nm)
= 10^{-4} (0.0001) micron (μ)
= 3.937×10^{-7} in.
= 10^{-7} mm
= 10^{-8} cm
= 10^{-10} m

Angus *See* **Aberdeen-Angus**
See Part 2: Beef and Dual-Purpose Cattle

anhydride A compound obtained by removing a molecule of water from an acid, e.g., CO_2 is the anhydride of carbonic acid (H_2CO_3). Amino acids may be considered the anhydrides of proteins by hydrolysis.

anhydrous Of a solid, containing no water of crystallization, or water closely bound to the molecule as in a hydrate; of a gas, not dissolved in water.

anhydrous ammonia *See* **ammonia, anhydrous**

aniline A colorless coal-tar or indigo derivative which is the basis for many brilliant biological stains. It is quite toxic.

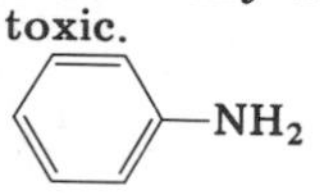

Animal and Plant Health Inspection Service (APHIS) A Federal agency responsible for meat inspection.

animal fat A product obtained from the tissues of mammals and poultry; contains not less than 90% total fatty acids; not more than 2.5% unsaponifiable matter; and not more than 1% insoluble matter.
See Part 2: Saturated Fatty Acids

animal foods Human foods obtained from animal sources.
See Part 2: Animal Foods, Composition

animal protein factor (APF) *See* **vitamin B_{12}**

animal starch *See* **glycogen**
See Part 2: Sweetening Compounds

animation An abundance of life; opposite of sleepiness or dullness.

anion A negative ion, e.g., the chloride ion (Cl^-) formed when sodium chloride (NaCl) ionizes in water.
See Part 2: Sanitizers

anise (*Pimpinella anisum L.*) An annual herb which bears small, hard, grayish-brown, ribbed, aromatic fruit that is used for flavoring beverages, soups and sweets; seed from a Mediterranean plant used as spice; not more than 9% total ash; not more than 1.5% HCl insoluble ash.
See Part 2: Flavoring Agents, Natural; Flavor Ingredients, Taste and Flavor Type

aniseed *See* **anise**
See Part 2: Essential Oils

anisole Methylphenyl ether ($C_6H_5OCH_3$).

anisotropic Yielding different characteristics in different directions; predetermined axis.

ANL (ammonium nitrate and lime) A neutral fertilizer material made from ammonium nitrate (NH_4NO_3) and lime; 9% CaO, 7% MgO.

annatto (annotto, arnatto) A vegetable of brown-red color from the fruit (seed) of the *Bixa orellana L.*; used in coloring oils and food.

annatto extract *See* **bixin**

anode The positive electrode in an electrolytic cell.

anonaceous fruit (custard apples) A small tree that bears a multiple fruit with a scaly surface. Varieties are:
- Bullock's Heart: buff or red-brown heart-shaped fruit that is firm, granular and sweet
- Cherimoya: green fruit with a pineapple-like flavor
- Ilama: similar to Cherimoya but grown in lowlands
- Soncoya: large fruit
- Sour Sop: fruit has soft spine on green rind; flesh is white and acid
- Sweet Sop: sweet custard-like flesh
- Raw composition 71-82% H_2O; 1-2% protein; 0.3-0.6% fat; 16-25% carbohydrate; 1% ash

antagonism The competitive or inhibiting effect of one substance upon another of similar molecular structure, e.g., between paraaminobenzoic acid and sulfanilimide. Substances having this effect are called antimetabolites. The antigen-antibody relationship is based on this behavior.
See also **antibody**.

ante mortem Before death.

anterior *See* **ventral** (belly); in comparative anatomy, *see* **cranial** (front or head).

anterior pituitary *See* **pituitary**

anther Pollen-bearing end of stamen.
See Part 2: Flower, Perfect

anthocyanin A red plant pigment; also found in blue and purple plants.

anthracene $C_6H_4(CH)_2C_6H_4$ A fused ring aromatic hydrocarbon obtained by distillation of coal tar

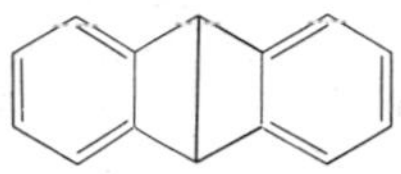

antiberiberi *See* **thiamin**

antibiotic A substance which occurs in nature and is usually of mold origin; inhibits the growth of bacteria.
See Part 2: Antibiotic Standards; Wastes, Agricultural and Industrial

antibiotic medium (seed agar) A microbiological medium used for preparation of test cultures prepared for antibiotic assays of ointments, tablets, milk, and for assaying antibiotics.
See Part 2: Microbiological Examination of Dairy Products; Microorganism, Culture Media, Dairy and Food Products

antiblack tongue factor *See* **niacin**

antibody A protective substance formed in the blood when antigens (bacteria or viruses) are present. Both antigen and antibody are proteins. The antibody is able to inhibit or destroy the invading organism, partly as a result of the antagonism between the molecules of antigen and antibody.

anticaking agent An additive used to prevent caking of dry material; in salt, cures or seasonings (up to 2% in combination in meat-curing ingredients). Substances used are as follows:
- tricalcium phosphate
- tetrasodium pyrophosphate
- calcium carbonate
- magnesium carbonate
- calcium stearate
- silica gel
- calcium aluminum silicate*
- calcium silicate*
- magnesium silicate*
- sodium alumino-silicate
- sodium calcium alumino-silicate
- sorbitol
- glycerol (glycerin)
- propylene glycol

*In table salt
In salt (13 ppm in meat-curing ingredients)

yellow prussiate of soda (sodium ferrocyanide decahydrate)

anticoagulant A substance used to prevent the coagulation of liquids containing colloids; i.e., heparin, dicoumarin, oxalate, citrate, hirudin.

antiegg white injury factor *See* **biotin**

antifoaming agent An additive used in low percentages to retard foaming of liquids, i.e., silicones (fats, methyl polysilicone), octanol, sulfonated oils.

antigen *See* **antibody**
See Part 2: Microorganism, Media

antihemorrhagic *See* **vitamin K**

antimetabolite *See* **antagonism; metabolite**

antimony (Sb, from Latin stibium) A metallic element; Group VA of the Periodic Table; at. no. 51; at. wt. 121.76; oxidation states +3, +5, −3; electron configuration 2-8-18-18-5
orbit K L M N O

antineuritic *See* **thiamin**

antioxidant A substance that retards oxidation of organic substances, including fat rancidity, e.g., propyl gallate, ascorbic acid, butylated hydroxyanisole (BHA), butylated hydroxytoluene (BHT). Not more that 3/1000 of 1% BHA or 1/1000 of 1% citric acid may be used in unsmoked dry sausage during preparation for trichinae treatment.
See Part 2: Antioxidants, Formula; Antioxidant Mixtures; Antioxidant Structure; Antioxidant Activity

antipasto First course of relishes, or smoked or pickled meat or fish; hors d'oeuvres or appetizers usually eaten with a fork.

antipernicious anemia factor *See* **vitamin B_{12}**

antirachitic vitamin *See* **vitamin D**

antiscorbutic vitamin *See* **ascorbic acid**

antiseptic A bactericidal material, especially for use in contact with the body of man or animals, e.g., hexachlorophene, hydrogen peroxide, iodine, silver compounds, thiomersal. They are not identical with disinfectants. *See also* **disinfectant.**

antiserum A serum that contains antibodies; it is obtained from animals that have been subjected to antigen.
See Part 2: Microorganism, Media

antisterility factor *See* **vitamin E**

antixerophthalmia *See* **vitamin A**

AOM *See* **active oxygen method**

A.P. As purchased.

aperitif A short drink of an alcoholic beverage offered before dinner to increase the appetite; from Latin aperire, to open.

apex The tip of a cone or cone-shaped structure.

APF (animal protein factor) *See* **vitamin B_{12}**

aphid A small insect (less than 1/8 in.) that has the following characteristics: soft, oblong, 6 legs, winged or wingless, green, yellow or black; they suck sap from cotton leaves and produce honeydew which causes the leaves to curl downward.
See Part 2: Insect Control

APHIS *See* **Animal and Plant Health Inspection Service**

aphthous fever *See* **foot and mouth disease**

apothecary wrap *See* **drug store wrap**

appetizer A food used to introduce a meal; it includes hors d'oeuvres, cocktails and canapés.
See Part 2: Salad Dressing and Mayonnaise Variations

apple A fleshy round fruit (pome) of the tree of the genus *Malus*; there are more than 3,000 apple classifications.

Size

1 pound fresh	= 3 med. size apples
	= 2-3/4-3 cups pared and sliced
1 cup pared and sliced	= 120 g (4.3 oz)
1 pound dried	= 8 lbs fresh
	= 4 1/2 cups dried
1 cup dried	= 105 g (3.7 oz)
1 qt canned	= 2 to 3 lbs fresh
	= 7-8 med. size apples
1 case (24) No. 2 1/2 can	= 1.4 bu. fresh
1 bu. fresh	= 40-50 lbs
	= 16-22 qts canned
1 barrel	= 3 bu. = 150 lbs
1 Northwest box (10.5 × 11.5 × 18 in.)	= 44 lbs
1 Eastern box (11 × 13 × 17 in.)	= 54 lbs

Comparison (pared) 70-80% edible

	fresh	dried
water	85%	24%
protein	0.2%	1%
fat	0.3%	1.6%
carbohydrate	12-14%	72%
ash	0.3%	2%
pH	2.9-3.3	—

Storage

cool place or refrigerate (30-31°F)
relative humidity 85-90%
freezing point 28°F
use ripe apples within 1 week

Varieties

1. Fresh 39% of total

Grimes Golden	Red Delicious
Jonathan	Winesap

2. Dual-purpose 47% of total

Cortland	Rome
Golden Delicious	Stayman
McIntosh	Yellow Newtown
Newton	Wealthy

3. Processing 14% of total

Baldwin	Rhode Island Greening
Gravenstein	Winesap
Northern Spy	York Imperial

Size (in.)	Yield of slices (%)
3	78
2.75	73
2.5	66
2.25	53

See Part 2: Ascorbic Acid; Calories, Daily Recommendations; Canned Spoilage Related to pH; Canned Yield; Flavor Ingredients, Taste and Flavor Type; Food, Composition; Frozen Food Storage; Fruit and Nut Rootstock; Fruit and Vegetable Diseases; Fruit, Availability; Fruit Harvest Dates; Fruit Classification; Fruit Composition; Fruit, Cooking; Fruit Dried Simmering; Fruit Frozen Yield; Fruit, Growing Season, Storage Life; Fruit Sauces; Fruit Servings per Pound; Fruit Simmering; Fruit Storage; Iron; Microwave Cooking, Fruit; Minerals, Food; Minerals, Trace, Limits; Nicotinic Acid, Food; Nutrients in Crop; Organic Acids in Fruits and Vegetables; Pectin Content; pH Values of Biological Materials; Plant Food, Composition; Potassium; Riboflavin; Riboflavine, Food; Rot Spoilage; Standards, Processed Fruit and Vegetable Products; Storage; Storage, Dry; Storage Times; Sugar, Fruit; Thiamin; Transit Temperature; Vitamin C; Wastes, Agricultural and Industrial

apple brandy *See* **cider**

apple butter *See* **butter (fruit)**

Composition	
% H_2O	52%
% protein	0.4%
% fat	0.8%
% carbohydrate	47%
% ash	0.4%

apple (cider) vinegar A condiment made from apple juice.

Min.: 4% acetic acid
1.6% apple solids (max. 50% reducing sugars)
0.25% apple ash (min. water-soluble ash 0.01% of phosphoric acid, P_2O_5)

apple grades

USDA	Western states
Extra fancy	Extra fancy
Fancy	Fancy
No. 1	C

applejack *See* **cider**

apple juice *See* **cider**

apple pie spice Includes: cinnamon, cloves, nutmeg or mace, allspice, and ginger.

apple sauce A sauce made from apples and sugar.

1 case (24) No. 2½ cans	= 1.2 bu fresh
1 lb apple sauce	= 1.75 cups
1 cup apple sauce	= 260 g (9.1 oz)

Composition	Unsweetened	Sweetened
% H_2O	88	76
% protein	0.2	0.2
% fat	0.2	0.2
% carbohydrate	11	24
% ash	0.3	0.2
pH	3.3	3.3

See Part 2: Microwave Cooking, Fruit

apricot (*Prunus armeniaca*) A medium-size tree that bears fruit from pale yellow to deep orange, which is eaten fresh, canned, dried and frozen or made into jam; intermediate between peach and plum.

Three species of plum are known as apricots:

Prunus armeniaca	common
Prunus mume	Japanese
Prunus dasycarpa	black

Size

1 lb	= 8–12 med. raw apricots (small 20/lb.; large 10/lb.)
	= 2½ cups fresh sliced (155 g or 5.5 oz/cup)
	= 56 med. dried apricots
	= 3 cups dried apricots (150 g or 5.3 oz/cup)
	= 8–12 whole canned
	= 12–20 halfs canned
1 lb dried	= 5–6 cups cooked apricots
	= 6–8 lbs fresh
1 bu fresh	= 40–50 lbs raw apricots
	= 20–24 qts canned

1 lug (4.6 × 12.5 × 16.1 in.) = 24 lb
1 crate (4.5 × 16 × 16.1 in.) = 24 lb

To ripen store in open air at room temperature and keep out of sun

Storage, when ripe store uncovered in refrigerator (31–32°F) and 85–90% relative humidity; use in 3 to 14 days; frozen (0°F) storage life, 1 year

Composition	Fresh	Dried
% H_2O	85	25
% protein	1	5
% fat	0.2	0.5
% carbohydrate	13	66
% ash	0.7	3
pH	3.3–4.0	3.4–4.0

See Part 2: Flavor Ingredients, Taste and Flavor Type; Frozen Food Storage; Fruit and Nut Rootstock; Fruit and Vegetables Composition; Fruit, Availability; Fruit Harvest Dates; Fruit Classification; Fruit Composition; Fruit, Cooking; Fruit Dried Simmering; Fruit Frozen Yield; Fruit, Growing Season, Storage Life; Fruit Servings per Pound; Fruit Simmering; Fruit Storage; Microwave Cooking, Fruit; Minerals, Food; Organic Acids in Fruits and Vegetables; Plant Foods, Composition; Potassium-Rich Foods; Standards, Processed Fruit and Vegetable Products; Storage; Sugar, Fruit; Vitamin A; Vitamin A, Food

APT agar Microbiological agar for growth of lactic acid bacteria; often used for heterofermentative lactobacilli that cause greening in meat.
See Part 2: Microbiological Media

aqua fortis Nitric acid (HNO_3).

aqua regia Mixture of 3 parts hydrochloric and 1 part nitric acid ($3HCl + HNO_3$).

Ar Symbol for the element argon.

arabic gum *See* **gum arabic**
See Part 2: Gums and Gelling Agents; Gums and Gelling Agents, Characteristics; Gum Distribution; Pentosans; Stabilizers-Thickeners

arabinogalactan *See* **larch gum**

arabinose A 5-carbon monosaccharide (pentose) sugar found in fruit juices and gum.
See Part 2: Sugar, D-aldehydo

arachidic acid (arachic acid) $CH_3(CH_2)_{18}C\begin{smallmatrix}OH\\O\end{smallmatrix}$ 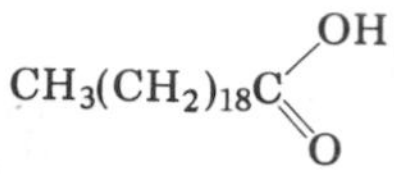

A 20-carbon saturated acid found in peanut oil.
See Part 2: Fats and Oils, Fatty Acid Composition; Fatty Acids; Fatty Acids, Fats and Oils; Fatty Acids and Their Properties; Milk, Fatty Acids, Seasonal; Saturated Fatty Acids; Wheat, Fatty Acids

arachidonic acid

$$CH_3(CH_2)_4CH=CHCH_2CH=CHCH_2CH=CHCH_2CH=CH(CH_2)_3C\begin{smallmatrix}OH\\O\end{smallmatrix}$$

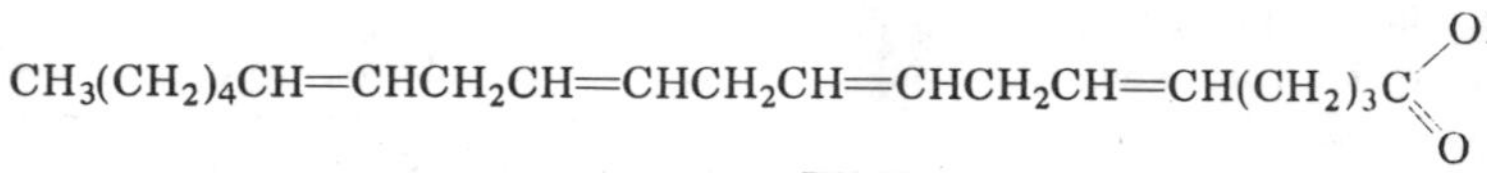

A 20-carbon unsaturated acid found in animals.
See Part 2: Fats and Oils, Composition; Fatty Acids; Fatty Acids, Fats and Oils; Fatty Acids and Their Properties; Unsaturated Fatty Acids

arachis oil *See* **Peanut oil**

arak An alcoholic drink made from dates and flavored with mastik; an alcoholic drink made from grapes and flavored with anise seed.

arbutus (strawberry tree) A shrub-like tree that produces a red, warty berry that is used to make liqueurs and confectionery.

archil A coloring material derived from a vegetable and used in food; produces violet red, blue or purple colors.

are A measure of area; 1 are = 119.6 sq yards
= 100 sq m
= 0.025 acre

area (A) A measure of surface.
area of triangle = ½(base × height);
area of circle = πR^2 or = 0.7854 $(D)^2$; (π = 3.1416);
square and circle of equal area: side of square = (D) 0.8862
area of sphere = $(D)^2 \times 3.1416$

areolar connective tissue Connective tissue in the form of a loose network with a great deal of space between fibers.

arginine A nonessential amino acid

$$NH_2-\underset{\underset{NH}{\|}}{C}-NH-(CH_2)_3-\underset{\underset{NH_2}{|}}{CH}-C\begin{smallmatrix}OH\\O\end{smallmatrix}$$

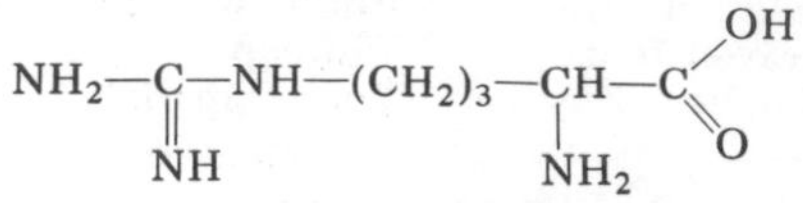

See Part 2: Amino Acids; Corn, Amino Acids; Egg Products Nutritive Value; Grain Analysis; Manure Analysis; Seed, Chemical Composition; Wheat, Amino Acids; Wheat Products, Amino Acid Compositions

argon (Ar) An element; noble gas group of Periodic Table; at. no. 18; at. wt. 39.944; oxidation state 0; electron configuration 2-8-8;
orbit K L M
0.94% present in air.

aril The external fleshy covering of a seed; an extra seed covering.

Arlington A variety of lespedeza (*Sericea*).

arm The upper limb of a human or the forelimb of a vertebrate.
See Part 2: Beef Chuck; Beef Cuts; Beef Retail Yield; Bone; Meat Identification; Pork Cookery; Veal Chart; Veal Cuts; Veal Wholesale Cuts

Armagnac A dry French brandy containing 40-50% alcohol.

arm bone Humerus.
See Part 2: Beef Wholesale Cuts; Lamb Wholesale Cuts; Pork Wholesale Cuts

arm roast Beef roast made by cutting across the fore arm bone.

arm steak Steak made from the same area as an arm roast.

armyworm A worm whose larva feeds on small grain and strips it of its leaves. *See also* **fall armyworm**.
See Part 2: Insect Control

aroma Fragrance or odor.

aromatic An unsaturated organic compound in which the carbon atoms are joined in a closed hexagonal ring and whose structure is based on that of benzene. Such rings are called carbocyclic when composed only of carbon atoms, and heterocyclic if atoms of other elements are constituents of the ring. *See also* **benzene**.

aromatic acid An acid in which one or more of the hydrogen atoms of the aromatic nucleus has been replaced by a carboxyl group.

aromatic alcohol An alcohol derived from benzene in which one or more of the hydrogen atoms of the benzene ring is replaced by a hydroxyl or hydroxyl-containing group, e.g., phenol (C_6H_5OH) and benzyl alcohol ($C_6H_5CH_2OH$).

arracacha (*Arracacia xanthorrhiza*) A Mexican plant used for starch production.
See Part 2: Starches and Starchy Roots, Composition

arrack An alcoholic liquid fermented from sugar obtained from the palm tree.

arrowgrass (*Triglochin*) Popular name for several grass-like plants such as marsh arrowgrass and sea-side arrowgrass.
See Part 2: Poisonous Plants

arrowroot (*Maranta arundinacea*) A perennial that produces starchy rhizomes; a very digestible starch is made from these tubers; refined starch from the tubers of this plant is also referred to as arrowroot.
Composition: 0.4% protein, 0.1% fat, 94% carbohydrate.

arrowroot flour Flour produced from the rhizome of a tropical perennial herb. *See also* **arrowroot.**

arrowroot powder A powder produced from the rhizome of a tropical perennial herb. *See also* **arrowroot.**

arrowroot starch A starch obtained from roots of a West Indian tropical plant and used as a thickening agent in cooking. *See also* **arrowroot**.

arsenic (As) A nonmetallic element; at. no. 33; at. wt. 74.92; Group VA of Periodic Table; oxidation states +3, +5, -3; electron configuration 2-8-18-5
orbit K L M N
Toxic and possibly carcinogenic.
See Part 2: Minerals, Trace, Limits; Water Drinking Standards

arsine (AsH_3) A highly toxic gas derived from arsenic.

artefact *See* **artifact**

artery cure Pumping the curing pickle into a ham through the femoral and allowing the blood vessels to distribute the cure to the ham.

artichoke (*Cynara scolymus*) A deep-rooted perennial, thistle-like plant, belonging to the daisy family; grows well in cold, moist climate; the flower-heads or chokes have scales with fleshy bases. The fleshy base of scales are eaten raw, baked, fried, stuffed, served with sauces, or preserved in oil; the base of the flower head and the center leaf stalk are also eaten. *See also* **Jerusalem artichoke.**
Store at 31°-32°F, 90-95% relative humidity; use in 1 to 2 weeks.
Composition: 86% H_2O, 3% protein, 11% fiber, 0.8% ash, pH 5.6.
See Part 2: Iron; Minerals, Food; Niacin; Phosphorus; Potassium; Potassium-rich Foods; Vegetable Composition; Vegetable Plants; Vegetables, Canning Dates

artichoke noodle A noodle made from the flour from the tuber of the Jerusalem artichoke (which is not an artichoke).

artifact A tissue structure which has been changed by artificial means.

artificial insemination The introduction of spermatozoa into the vagina or uterus by instrumental rather than natural means.

aryl group An aromatic group such as C_6H_5, C_6H_4, etc. representing a benzene nucleus minus one, two or more hydrogen atoms which are replaced by various groups or side chains. Often represented in formulas by R.

As Symbol for the element arsenic.

asafetida (*asafoetida*) A semi-solid plant gum obtained from the root of the genus *Ferula*; it has a bitter taste and a distinctive odor.
See Part 2: Essential Oils

asbestos Magnesium silicate ($Mg_3Si_2O_7 \cdot 2H_2O$). There are two major types, serpentine (chrysotile) and amphibole. Both are extremely fibrous and are completely noncombustible. Asbestos fiber is a carcinogen when inhaled.
See Part 2: Insulation

Ascaris suis Round intestinal worms that are parasites in hogs.

asclepian A protease enzyme found in the juice of the milkweed.

ascorbic acid (vitamin C) ($C_6H_8O_6$) A water-soluble vitamin whose deficiency causes a disease known as scurvy; body does not store. Deficiency symptoms: bleeding gums, sore joints; source—citrus fruits, tomatoes, cabbage, lettuce, carrots, apples, potatos, liver. It is used as a preservative, antioxidant and nutrient and is added to frozen food to prevent darkening.
It can be used in cured meat to speed up color reaction.

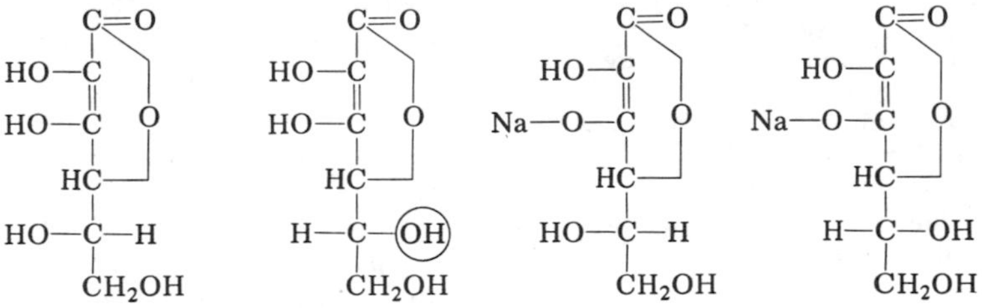

ascorbic acid | isoascorbic (erythorbic) acid | sodium ascorbate | sodium isoascorbate

¾ oz ascorbic or isoascorbic acid per 100 lb. meat; 0.875 oz sodium ascorbate or sodium isoascorbate per 100 lb. meat; 75 oz ascorbic or isoascorbic acid per 100 gal pickle (10% pump); 87.5 oz sodium ascorbate or sodium isoascorbate per 100 gal pickle (10% pump); 10% spray solution may be applied to outer surface.

See Part 2: Ascorbic Acid; Ascorbic Acid, Food; Ascorbic Acid, Fruit Juices; Beans, Peas and Nuts; Cereal Fortification; Cereals, Vitamin and Mineral Content; Composition of Food; Dairy Products, Composition; Egg Composition; Fats and Oils Composition; Fish and Shellfish Composition; Fruit and Vegetables Composition; Fruit Composition; Grain Products Composition; Lemon Juice Composition; Lime Juice Composition; Meat Composition; Meat Pigment; Milk and Milk Products, Vitamin Content; Milk Composition; Plant Foods, Composition; Poultry Composition; Recommended Daily Dietary Allowance; Sausage Composition; Soups Composition; Sugars and Sweets Composition; Tomato and Tomato Products, Composition; Variety Meat Percentage of Daily Recommended Allowances; Vegetable Composition; Vitamins; Vitamin Sources, Functions, and Stability

-ase Suffix used in naming certain enzymes, e.g., zymase, diastase.

ash The solids remaining after the complete combustion of a material.

See Part 2: Concentrated and Dried Milk Products; Connective Tissue, Composition; Creams, Butter and Frozen Desserts; Cultured Dairy Products, Composition; Egg Products Nutritive Value; Bananas Composition; Cherry Composition; Corn Kernal Composition; Egg Composition, Fluid and Fermented Milks, Composition; Fruit Composition; Grain Analysis; Honey Composition; Lime Juice Composition; Manure Analysis; Maple Syrup Composition; Milk and Cheese Composition; Milk, Breeds, Composition Milk Composition; Milk, Concentrated Products; Milk, Dry Products; Milk, Mammals, Composition; Milk, Species; Oil Meals Composition; Oils and Fats Composition; Packing-house Byproducts Composition; Plant Foods, Composition; Pulses, Nuts and Seeds Composition; Seed, Chemical Composition; Seed Composition; Soybean Composition; Starches and Starchy Roots Composition; Sugars and Syrups Composition; Sweetening Agents; Tomato and Tomato Products, Composition; Turkey Composition; Wastes, Agricultural and Industrial; Wheat and Flour Composition; Wheat, Carbohydrate Composition; Wheat, Parts of Grain; Wheat Products Composition

ash analysis A value determined by incinerating a sample material at high temp. (525°C) for 16 to 18 hr.

ash gourd *See* **gourd**

asiago A mild, light yellow, cylindrical and smokey after-dinner cheese (2 to 6 mo. ripening); longer ripening (min. 12 mo.) produces a hard, sharp cheese used for grating.

asparagine A derivative of aspartic acid. *See also* **aspartic acid**.

See Part 2: Amino Acids

asparagus (***Asparagus officinalis***) This cool-weather plant is a member of the lily family; young white shoot or "spear" (green or purple-tipped); it is cooked in water and served with butter or sauce; can be frozen and canned;

1 lb	= 16–20 spears
	= 2 cups cooked
1 cup cooked	= 180 g (6.4 oz)
2½–6 lbs fresh	= 1 qt canned
2–2½ lbs fresh	= 1 qt frozen
1 bu	= 40–50 lb
1 bu. fresh	= 9–14 qt canned
1 crate	= 30 lb

Storage: 32°F; 90–95% relative humidity; use in 3–4 weeks.

Composition (fresh): 92% H_2O; 3% protein; 0.2% fat; 5% carbohydrate; 0.6% ash; pH 5.4–6.1.

Size:	
pencil	- less than ⅜ in. diam.
medium	- ⅜ to ⅝ in.
jumbo	- ⅝ to ⅞ in.
colossal	- ⅞ & up.

See Part 2: Ascorbic Acid; Asparagus Terms; Calories, Daily Recommendations; Frozen Food Storage; Fruit and Vegetables Composition; Iron; Canned Spoilage Related to pH; Microwave Cooking, Fresh Vegetables; Microwave Cooking Frozen Vegetables; Microwave Processing Time; Minerals, Food; Niacin; Nicotinic Acid, Food; Phosphorus; Plant Foods, Composition; Portion Size; Riboflavin; Riboflavin, Daily Recommendations; Riboflavin, Food; Soups Composition; Storage; Sugar, Vegetables; Thiamin; Tocopherols; Transit Temperature; Vegetable Boiling; Vegetable Composition; Vegetable Cooking, Frozen; Vegetable Frozen Yield; Vegetable Plants; Vegetables, Boiling Time, Frozen; Vegetables, Canning Dates; Vegetables Classification; Vegetables, Cooking Frozen; Vegetable Servings; Vegetable Storage; Vegetable Yield; Vegetable Yield Canned and Frozen; Vegetable Yield Frozen, Canned and Fresh; Vitamin A; Vitamin A, Daily Recommendations; Vitamin C; Wastes, Agricultural and Industrial

asparagus pea (***Lotus tetragonolobus***) Young pea pods used as human food.

aspartic acid A nonessential monoamino-dicarboxylic amino acid.

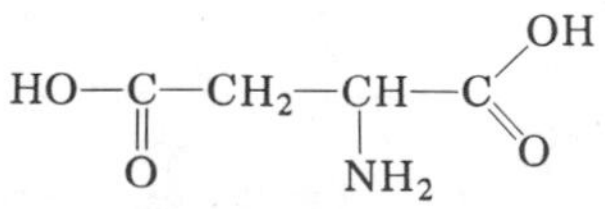

See Part 2: Amino Acids; Amino Acid, Solubilities; Corn, Amino Acids; Egg Products Nutritive Value; Grain Analysis; Manure Analysis; Wheat, Amino Acids; Wheat Products, Amino Acid Compositions

Aspergillus A common mold.
See Part 2: Mold, Food; Moulds, Mycotoxins; Rot Spoilage; Spoilage, Fat in Foods

Aspergillus flavusoryzae group A group of proteolytic enzymes used to soften beef tissue.

Aspergillus oryzae A proteolytic enzyme used to soften beef tissue.

asphalt A complex mixture of bitumins obtained from mid-continent and western petroleum; occurs naturally in Trinidad.
See Part 2: Insulation

aspic Jellied (gelatin) broth used for molding.

aspirin (acetylsalicylic acid)

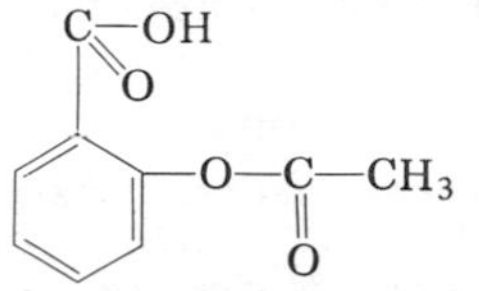

A common anodyne which often causes bleeding, especially from the gums.

as purchased As ordinarily obtained from a typical retail store.
See Part 2: Fruit Composition

assam *See* **black tea**

astatine (At) A halogen element; Group VII A of Periodic Table; at. no. 85; mass number of most stable isotope 210; electron configuration 2-8-18-32-18-7
orbit K L M N O P

asternal rib *See* **false rib; rib**

astrakhan fur The fur of fat-tailed sheep.

asymmetric carbon atom A carbon atom to which are attached 4 different atoms or groups of atoms; a compound containing one such atom displays optical rotation.

At Symbol for the element astatine.

-ate Suffix indicating a salt whose metal is in the highest oxidation state.

Atlantic herring *See* **sea herring**

atlas First cervical vertebra (neck bone) which attaches to the head.
See Part 2: Beef Chuck; Beef Wholesale Cuts; Bone; Lamb Wholesale Cuts; Pork Wholesale Cuts; Veal Wholesale Cuts

atmosphere (standard, 760 mm) A measure of pressure; 1 standard atmosphere
= 1,013,250 dynes/cm^2
= 2,116.35 lb per sq ft (psf)
= 760 mm (column of mercury (Hg) 13.59593 sp. gr. at 0°C and under standard acceleration of gravity)
= 33.9006 ft (column of water, max. density at 4°C, 39°F)
= 29.9212 in. (column of mercury) (Hg) 13.59593 sp. gr.)
= 14.6969 lb per sq in. (psi)
= 10.3329 m (column of water, max. density at 4°C, 39°F)
= 1.03329 kg per sq cm (kg/cm^2)
At atmospheric pressure, there are 2.7×10^{19} molecules per cubic centimeter.

atom The smallest particle of an element that exhibits the properties of that element.

atomic number The number of protons in an atomic nucleus, ranging from 1 for hydrogen to 106 for the most recently discovered element. This number indicates the position of an element in the periodic table and determines its chemical properties and behavior.

atomic weight The mass (weight) of an atom of an element, obtained by averaging the mass of all its isotopes, in relation to the mass of carbon-12 isotope (exactly 12.00), which is now the official standard.

atrio-ventricular node Area of the heart which receives the impulse after the auricles have contracted and passes it on by the "bundle of His" to the ventricles.

atrium *See* **auricle**

ATS medium (American Trudeau Society) Microbiological medium for the determination of tubercle bacilli.
See Part 2: Microorganism, Media

atto (one quintillionth) = 0.000 000 000 000 000 001. Prefix for quantities smaller than the base unit.

Au Symbol for the element gold (from Latin *aurum*).

A.U. Abbreviation for angstrom.

aubergine *See* **eggplant**

au fait Brick ice cream with layers of frozen fruit.

au gratin Covered with cheese and cooked.

au jus With natural juice.

Aureomycin An antibiotic. *See also* **chlortetracycline**

aureomycin rose Microbiological media used for the detection of yeast and mold.
See Part 2: Microbiological Examination of Dairy Products

aureus A specie of *Staphylococcus* microorganism found in dairy products and water.
See Part 2: Water Activity, Organisms and Food

auricle The upper chambers of the heart, called right and left auricle.

auslese Made from grape bunches that are late-gathered and specially selected for ripeness.

Australian lettuce Curly head lettuce that resembles chicory.

Australorp An English class of chickens with black plumage, white skin and lays a brown shelled egg.
See Part 2: Poultry Breeds and Varieties

autoclave A container for sterilizing by steam under pressure.

Pressure	Boiling Point of Water
atmospheric	100°C (212°F)
atmospheric + 10 lb	115°C (239°F)
atmospheric + 15 lb	121°C (250°F)
atmospheric + 20 lb	126°C (259°F)

average error A method of expressing error for a single observation and an average of a series of measurements. Average error for a *single* determination (a):

$$a = \frac{\pm \Sigma V}{n}$$

ΣV = sum of deviation from the average regardless of sign
n = number of observations

Average error for an *averaged* value for n observations (A):

$$A = \pm \frac{\Sigma V}{n\sqrt{n}}$$

average error 0.8453 = probable error
average error 1.2532 = mean square error

avidin A toxic principle occurring in egg white, which is inactivated by heat; it is a protein which combines with biotin, thus inactivating it; however it loses this ability on heating; also, it inactivates biotin and makes it unavailable to animals.

avocado (Alligator pear) (*Persea americana*) A medium-size tree that produces a fruit about the size and shape of a pear which may be green or yellow when ripe; the flesh, which may be eaten raw, used as a vegetable or fruit, or spread like butter, surrounds a single stone;

Varieties	Size (in.)	Peeled & Pitted wt (oz)	% H_2O	% Protein	%* Fat	% Carbohydrate	% Ash
California	3½ X 4¼	10	74	2.2	17	6	1
Florida	3 X 4	12	78	1.3	11	9	1

*some varieties up to 30%

High in protein, vitamin B, vitamin A
1 lb = 2½ cups sliced
1 cup = 140 g (5 oz)
1 lug (4.5 X 12.5 X 16.1 in.) = 12–15 lb

To ripen: open air
room temperature
out of sun

Storage: Fruit is easily bruised; when ripe, store in refrigerator (45–55°F) at 85–90% relative humidity; use in 3 to 10 days. Storage in paper bag in the dark at room temperature accelerates ripening.

See Part 2: Calories, Daily Recommendations; Fruit, Availability; Fruit Classification; Fruit Composition; Fruit Storage; Minerals, Food; Plant Foods, Composition; Potassium-rich Foods; Storage; Transit Temperature

avocado oil A semi-drying oil separated from the pulp of the avocado; 70–95 iodine number.

Avogadro's number (N) The number of material units (molecules, atoms, ions, electrons, etc.) present in one mole of substance, namely, 6.023×10^{23}. *See also* **mole.**

See Part 2: Constants, Fundamental

awn A small pointed projection (i.e., beard on grain).

axial The axis of a structure.

axillary The angle between stem and leaf-stalk; the armpit.

See Part 2: Lymph Nodes, Ox

Ayrshire A breed of dairy cattle which originated in Scotland; they are white with patches of red to brown.

See Part 2: Dairy Cattle Breeds; Gestation Periods; Milk Breeds, Composition; Milk Composition

azarole (*Crataegus azarolus*) A hawthorn fruit used for jams and flavoring (apple-like).

azeotrope A mixture of 2 or more liquids that distills at a constant temperature and has a constant composition.

See Part 2: Refrigerant

azide blood agar Microbiological selective medium used for the isolation of streptococci; sodium azide inhibits gram-negative organisms.

See Part 2: Microbiological Media

azide dextrose broth Microbiological broth used for quantitative determination of streptococci; other organisms that will also grow in this broth include gram-positive bacilli, coliforms, and enterococci.

See Part 2: Microbiological Media; Microorganisms, Culture Media, Water and Sewage, Standard Methods

B

B *See* **boron**

Ba Symbol for the element barium.

baba A yeast cake flavored with rum or fruit.

babassu A nut from the babassu palm native to Brazil, from which oil is obtained by pressing.
See Part 2: Fats and Oils, Fatty Acid Composition; Fats or Oils, Physical and Chemical Properties; Fatty Acids, Fats and Oils; Fats and Oils, Characteristics; Iodine and Saponification Values; Melting Points, Fats and Oils; Oil or Fat, Characteristics; Saturated Fatty Acids; Specific Gravities, Fats and Oils; Titer, Fats and Oils; Unsaponifiable Matter

Babcock test A fat test for milk, developed in 1890 by S. M. Babcock.

baby beef Young cattle (15 months or less) that have been well fed.

baccharis A plant with a fragrant root; a genus of American plants of the thistle family.
See Part 2: Poisonous Plants

Bacillaceae A family of small rod or coccoid shaped, aerobic or obligate anaerobic, usually Gram-positive microorganisms found in soil and animals; a few produce disease.
See Part 2: Water Activity, Organisms and Food

bacilli (plural of bacillus) A subdivision of bacteria whose shape resembles a rod (Latin, stick).
See Part 2: Canned Spoilage Manifestations; Canned Spoilage Related to pH; Rot Spoilage; Spoilage, Carbohydrate Foods; Spoilage, Protein Foods; Thermophiles

Bacillus botulinus Anaerobic bacteria that produce a toxin which causes food poisoning known as botulism.

Bacillus cereus Faculative bacteria found in soil and water that may utilize bound oxygen to cause spoilage in canned foods.
See Part 2: Food Poisoning, Bacteria

back The upper part of an animal from the neck to the pelvis area.
See Part 2: Meat Identification

backbone (spinal column) *See* **thoracic vertebrae; lumbar vertebrae; sacral vertebrae**
See Part 2: Beef Wholesale Cuts; Bone; Bone in Retail Cuts; Lamb Wholesale Cuts; Pork, Cooking; Pork Loin Cooking; Pork Wholesale Cuts; Veal Wholesale Cuts

back-packed Cured meat product packed in a weak pickle (25°F) and stored at −15°F to await a more favorable market.

backsettler *See* **black tea**

back strap A wide elastin yellow band located along the top of the shoulder of an animal and used to support the head; it should be removed from a roast since it will remain tough; also called *ligamentum nuchae.*
See Part 2: Beef Rib Nomenclature

bacon A belly or side of a hog that has been cured or smoked; about 12% of a hog carcass (head and leaf fat on).

Cured pork belly, thin-sliced = 35 slices/lb
regular-sliced = 22 slices/lb
thick-sliced = 18 slices/lb

Bacon, Canadian style is made from boned pork loin.
Bacon squares are made from jowl.
Salt pork (white bacon) is salted back fat.

Storage: keep in original wrappers; refrigerate at 36–42°F; should be used within 1 week after opening.

Composition	Raw bacon (%)	Cooked and drained bacon (%)	Canadian, unheated (%)	Canadian, cooked and drained (%)
Water	19	8	62	50
Protein	8	30	20	28
Fat	69	52	14	17
Carbohydrate	1	3.2	0.3	0.3
Ash	2	6.3	3.6	4.7

See Part 2: Bacon Dressing; Broiling Griddle, Meat; Broiling Meat; Broiling Time and Temperature; Calories, Daily Recommendations; Food, Composition; Meat and Meat Products Composition; Meat Composition; Meat, Frozen Storage; Meat Identification; Meat Storage; Minerals, Food; Pork Chart; Pork Cookery; Pork, Cooking; Pork Cooking Methods; Pork Cuts; Pork Cuts and Uses; Pork Storage; Pork Yield; Portion Size; Spoilage, Protein Foods; Storage Times; Thiamin, Food

bacon fat Fat obtained from cooking bacon; smoke point 290–300°F.

bacon type A classification of hogs that usually includes the following breeds: Landrace, Tamworth, and Yorkshire.

bacteria Microorganisms usually consisting of a single cell composed of proteinaceous substances. They may be of several shapes, e.g., rod-like

(bacilli), or spherical (cocci), filamentous, etc. Many types are infectious, but others are beneficial. They play a part in the oxidation and spoilage of foodstuffs.
See Part 2: Bacteria, Molds, and Yeasts; Bacteria on Chickens at Various Holding Temperatures; Culture Media; Egg Specifications; Food Poisoning, Bacteria; Illness from Food; Intestinal Microorganisms; Intestinal Microorganisms in Triple-Sugar Agar; Most Probable Number; Most Probable Number, Bacterial; Spices, Microbial Content

bacterial starter culture A preparation used in manufacturing some sausage; not to exceed 0.5%; e.g., (1) thuringer (2) Lebanon bologna (3) salami (4) pork roll (5) cervelat.

bactericidal Causing death of bacteria.

bacteriophage An organism (often a virus) that inhibits the growth of bacteria by surrounding and gradually disintegrating the bacterial cell ("phage" = "eat").
See Part 2: Sanitizing Chemicals

bacteriostat An agent that inhibits or stops the growth of bacteria.

bactofugation Centrifugal force and heat applied to food to reduce bacterial count.

bacto-tryptone A peptone used in microbiological differential test media based on the elaboration of indole by bacteria; used in examination of water and sewage, dairy products and in canned goods for "flat sour" and "sulfide spoilage".
See Part 2: Microorganism, Culture Media, Dairy and Food Products; Microorganism, Selective and Differential Broths and Media, Water Filtration Plant

badiane The fruit of a Chinese anise tree; its aromatic volatile oil is used as a condiment and for flavoring; an alcoholic beverage flavored with bitter almonds.
See Part 2: Essential Oils

bagasse Cellulosic waste remaining after the processing of sugar cane. Used as insulation board, and locally as a boiler fuel.
See Part 2: Fuel, Heating Value

bagel A small roll or biscuit made from high-gluten flour, given a short fermentation period, boiled in syrup and baked in a hot oven.
See Part 2: Fermented Ingredients

BAGG broth *See* Part 2: Microorganism, Media

baguilumbang nut (soft lumbag) (*Aleurites trisperma*) Tree native to the Philippines that is very similar to the tung oil tree and from the seed a drying oil is extracted.
See Part 2: Unsaturated Fatty Acids

Bahia grass (*Helminthosporium sativum*) A tropical America, perennial pasture grass.
See Part 2: Seed, Germination

Baird Parker agar *See* **agar-agar** and Part 2: Microorganism, Media

bake To cook covered or uncovered in an oven usually by dry heat; to cook by covering with coals, heated stones or heated metal.
See Part 2: Poultry Class; Lamb Cuts; Pork Cuts; Pork Loin Cooking; Veal Chart; Altitude Adjustments for Baking

baked Alaska A frozen dessert consisting of a block of ice cream over which is spread a coating of meringue made of beaten egg whites, sugar and flavoring. The combination is baked in a hot oven for 3 to 5 min, till meringue is delicately browned.

baked beans Dried beans that are soaked, boiled and retorted with pork and tomato products, often baked before serving; 6% protein, 17% carbohydrate. *See also* Haricot Bean.
See Part 2: Portion Size

baked goods Foods that have been cooked by baking.
See Part 2: Calories, Daily Recommendations; Frozen Food Storage

baked oyster shells A liming material composed of 85% $CaCO_3$; each pound has the neutralizing equivalent of 0.8 to 0.9 lb of $CaCO_3$ (or approx. this quantity of dolomitic limestone).

baking powder A mixture of dry acid or acid salt and baking soda and starch or flour (stabilizer); contents:

baking soda: sodium bicarbonate ($NaHCO_3$)
acid salt: cream of tartar, or tartaric acid, calcium acid phosphate, or sodium aluminum sulfate
starch: cornstarch

Must liberate at least 12% CO_2; may be single- or double-acting. In the presence of moisture as well as heat, carbon dioxide is evolved as a result of the chemical reaction of the acid on the carbonate.

Double-acting
sodium aluminum sulfate: reacts with baking soda on heating; calcium acid phosphate: reacts with baking soda when mixture is cold; most commonly used; yields gas when combined with liquid and when heated (4 teaspoons = ½ oz) 1 tsp = 3.6 g; 1 teaspoon double-acting = 1½ teaspoons single-acting.

sodium aluminum sulfate

$$\underset{}{2NaAl(SO_4)_2} + \underset{\text{sodium bicarbonate}}{6NaHCO_3} \xrightarrow{H_2O+\Delta} \underset{\text{sodium sulfate}}{4Na_2SO_4} + \underset{\text{aluminum hydroxide}}{2Al(OH)_3} + \underset{\text{carbon dioxide}}{6CO_2}\uparrow$$

monocalcium phosphate

$$CaH_4(PO_4)_2 + \underset{\text{sodium bicarbonate}}{2NaHCO_3} \xrightarrow{H_2O} \underset{\text{dicalcium phosphate}}{CaHPO_4} + \underset{\text{disodium phosphate}}{Na_2HPO_4} + \underset{\text{carbon dioxide}}{2CO_2}\uparrow + \underset{\text{water}}{2H_2O}$$

calcium acid phosphate and/or sodium acid pyrophosphate; may be double-acting; intermediate between other two as to when CO_2 is released.
Single-acting
potassium acid tartrate (cream of tartar) and tartaric acid; yields gas when combined with liquid and gas expands when heated.

$$\underset{\text{cream of tartar}}{KHC_4H_4O_6} + \underset{\text{sodium bicarbonate}}{NaHCO_3} \xrightarrow{H_2O} \underset{\text{potassium sodium tartrate}}{KNaC_4H_4O_6} + CO_2\uparrow + H_2O$$

or

$$\underset{\text{tartaric acid}}{H_2C_4H_4O_6} + \underset{\text{sodium bicarbonate}}{2NaHCO_3} \xrightarrow{H_2O} \underset{\text{sodium tartrate}}{Na_2C_4H_4O_6} + 2CO_2\uparrow + 2H_2O$$

1 tsp = 3.8 g.
1 tsp baking powder = ¼ tsp baking soda + ½ tsp cream of tartar
= ¼ tsp baking soda + ½ cup of fully soured milk or buttermilk
= ¼ tsp baking soda + ½ tablespoon vinegar or lemon juice + ½ cup sweet milk
= ¼ tsp baking soda + ¼ to ½ cup molasses

2½ cups baking powder = 1 lb
2½ tbsp baking powder = 1 oz

Altitude adjustment for cake baking.

Elevation Ft	Decrease baking powder/cake Tsp
2,000	¼
3,500	⅓
5,000	½
6,500	⅔
8,000	¾

See also **altitude.**
See Part 2: Altitude Adjustments for Baking; Minerals, Trace, Limits

baking soda (sodium bicarbonate) An ingredient of baking powders. (Potassium bicarbonate can be used in low-sodium diets.) When heated, it evolves carbon dioxide which acts as a leavening agent in cooking.

$$2NaHCO_3 \xrightarrow{\Delta} Na_2CO_3 + H_2O + CO_2$$

1 tsp = 4.1g
Altitude adjustment for cake:

Elevation Ft	Decrease baking soda/cake Tsp
2,000	¼
3,500	⅓
5,000	½
6,500	⅔
8,000	¾

balachan A fermented shrimp paste.

balamuth medium *See* Part 2: Microorganism, Media

balance of payment Difference between total payment made to foreign nations for goods purchased and the receipts from them for goods sold.

balance of trade Difference between money value of merchandise imported and exported.

Baldwin A variety of apple which is in season from Nov. to March; good sauce and cooking apple and fair eating apple.

ball and socket *See* **ground glass joint**

ball mill A porcelain container filled about ½ full with flintlike balls and rotated in the horizontal position; used to mix and grind chemicals.

balsa wood A light strong wood from tropical America.

balsam One of several varieties of resinous tree products characterized by a distinctive pleasant aroma and a sticky consistency. Used in certain types of medications such as cough syrups, e.g., Tolu balsam, Canada balsam, and Peru balsam.
See Part 2: Organic Acids in Fruits and Vegetables; Essential Oils

balsam pear (bitter gourd) (*Momordica charantia*) A tropical climbing plant that produces a rough ribbed elongated (up to 8 in.) fruit that is orange-yellow or white; uses: fruit—cooked and eaten; tender shoots and leaves can be cooked like greens.

balsam wool A heat insulating and sound reducing material made from shredded wood fibers.
See Part 2: Insulation

bamboo shoots Thick (3 in. in diameter) pointed (6 to 12 in. long) shoots that grow from the ground under a bamboo plant; if not harvested, they would grow into new stems. They are boiled, salted, or pickled.
Composition: 91% H_2O, 3% protein, 0.3% fat, 5% carbohydrate, 1% ash.

banana (*Musa*) A giant herb that produces bunches of fruit; each bunch contains 9 to 12 half-spirals (hands) of fruit, each containing 12 to 16 fruits (fingers); one bunch may contain 120 to 200 bananas and weigh 50 to 80 lb; the skin of the fruit is green and turns yellow when ripe; 60% edible;

Types:
dessert: eaten raw; 17–19% sugar
lady fingers: short fruit
red-skinned: red skin and orange tint to flesh
cooking: high starch, low sugar, picked green

Forms: most are eaten fresh, some cooked, some dried and some made into flour, some fermented into beer

1 lb = 3 to 4 bananas
= 2 cups sliced (1 cup = 140 g or 5 oz)
= 1¼ cups mashed (1 cup = 230 g or 8.2 oz)
1 box (13 × 12 × 32 in.) = 40 lb

Storage Conditions: unwrapped; keep out of sun; temperature 55° to 60°F (refrigeration impairs flavor and stops ripening); relative humidity 90%; freezing point 26°–30°F

Composition: 76% H_2O, 1% protein, 0.2% fat, 22% carbohydrate, 0.8% ash, pH 4.5–4.7.

See Part 2: Ascorbic Acid; Banana, Areas of Production; Bananas Composition; Calories, Daily Recommendations; Canned Spoilage Related to pH; Flavor Ingredients, Taste and Flavor Type; Food, Composition; Fruit and Vegetable Diseases; Fruit Availability; Fruit Classification; Fruit Composition; Fruit Servings Per Pound; Fruit Storage; Iron; Microwave Cooking, Fruit; Minerals, Food; Niacin; Niacin, Daily Recommendations; Organic Acids in Fruits and Vegetables; Phosphorus; pH Values of Biological Materials; Plant Foods, Composition; Potassium; Potassium-Rich Foods; Riboflavin; Storage; Thiamin; Transit Temperature; Vitamin A, Daily Recommendations; Vitamin C

Banda mace Dried arillodes of nutmeg from Banda (Nile area of Africa) which contain 13% essential oil.
See Part 2: Spices, Microbial Content

Bang's disease A cattle disease causing abortion, weak calves, sterility and retaining afterbirth; usually spread by infected animals; infected animals should be slaughtered; called undulant fever in man. *See also* **brucellosis.**
See Part 2: Illness from Food

bar A measure of atmospheric pressure equal to one million dynes/sq cm
1 bar = 33.46 ft of water at 4°C
= 29.53 in. of mercury at 0°C
= 14.504 lb/sq in.
= 1.020 kg/sq cm
= 0.987 standard atmosphere

Barbados An island in the West Indies; often indicating products produced there. *See also* **molasses.**

barbecue A meat with sauce roasted over coals or in an oven; to roast or broil, basting with a highly seasoned sauce (to cook in or served with barbecue sauce).
See Part 2: Poultry Class; Sauce, Barbecue

barbecue pit An earth (sometimes masonry) pit in which food is steam-cooked; heat is supplied by coals, hot rocks or hot metal; moisture is supplied by the food or other vegetable matter added to the pit; it is a slow cooking process.

barding Thin strips of bacon fat secured to meat.

Bardolino A light red wine with a touch of sharpness produced in the Veneto region of northeastern Italy.

barium (Ba) An alkali metal element; at. no. 56; at. wt. 137.36; oxidation state +2; electron configuration 2-8-18-18-8-2
orbit K L M N O P
Group IIA of Periodic Table. Barium and all its soluble compounds are toxic; insoluble barium sulfate is not.
See Part 2: Grain Analysis; Normal Solutions; Water Drinking Standards

barium carbonate *See* Part 2: Normal Solutions

barium chloride *See* Part 2: Normal Solutions

barium fluosilicate ($BaSiF_6$) An inorganic insecticide.

barium hydroxide *See* Part 2: Normal Solutions

barium nitrate *See* Part 2: Reagents, Normal Solutions

barium oxide *See* Part 2: Normal Solutions

bark Outer covering of a tree or fat covering of an animal.
See Part 2: Beef Rib Nomenclature; Wastes, Agricultural and Industrial

barley (***Hordeum vulgare***) An annual grain used for malt, meal and livestock feed; matures in 265–280 days.

Type	Genus	Description	Use
2-row	*Hordeum distichon*	Only middle spikelet of each three produces seed	Malting, pearl barley-soup and stew, patent barley meal, livestock feed
6-row	*Hordeum vulgare*	3 spikelets develop per node; more hardy than 2-row	Same uses

47–48 lb per bu; 1.5 lb/qt
plant 80–100 lb (2 bu.) per acre
2 cups pearl barley = 1 lb
1 qt ground barley = 1.1 lb
pH 6.0; variety-Davie.

Composition (pearled) 11% H_2O, 9% protein, 1% fat, 78% carbohydrate, 1% ash; moisture content for storage should be less than 13%.

See Part 2: Cereal Composition; Cereal Fortification; Cereal Nutrient Content; Cereals, Vitamin and Mineral Content; Grain Products Composition; Minerals, Food; Nutrients in Crop; Pentosans; Plant Foods, Composition; Protein Factors; Seed, Chemical Composition; Seed Composition; Seed, Germination; Soups Composition; Spoilage, Fat in Foods; Tocopherols; Vitamin A, Food

barley sugar Sucrose which has been heated until it melts and allowed to recrystallize in large granules.

baron of beef 2 unseparated sirloins.

barracuda A small shark.
See Part 2: Vitamin D, Fish

barrel (oil) 42 U.S. gal. of petroleum.

barrel (U.S.) (liquid) A measure of volume.
1 barrel = 1.1924×10^5 ml
= 32256 drams (U.S. fl)
= 7276.5 cu in.
= 4196.7 oz (Br. fl)
= 4032 oz (U.S. fl)
= 119.2369 liters
= 31.5 gal. (U.S.)
= 26.23 gal. (Br)
= 4.2109 cu ft
= 0.11924 cu m
See Part 2: Barrel Size

barrow A male hog that has been castrated before advanced sexual development.
See Part 2: Swine Market Classes and Grades

Barsac A full, sweet wine of high sugar content produced by allowing the grapes to stay on the vine until they are attacked by mold, dehydrated (concentrating the sugar) and pressed (of the small quantity of juice remaining) to produce a very expensive wine. *See also* **sauterne**.

Bartlett A variety of pears of small size, rusty color.

basal Near the base; the leaves of plants that are often used to flavor soups, ragoûts, sauces, sausages and salads. Physiologically, the metabolism of a human or animal organism under rest conditions.

basa wood *See* Part 2: Insulation

base Any substance which accepts or acquires protons (H^+), has a pH higher then 7.0 and reacts with acids to form salts. *See also* **alkali**.
See Part 2: Concentration of Commercial Strengths of Acids and Bases; Indicators: pH and Acid Base

base-forming foods Foods that leave an alkaline residue in the body after the food has been utilized (e.g., milk, nuts, most fruits, potatoes, and legumes).

base line In gas chromatography, a straight line drawn when no sample is going through the detector.

basic slag A fertilizer material which is a byproduct of the steel industry; fertilizer notation 0-9-0; basic in nature and equal to 0.5-0.7 lb of dolomitic limestone for each lb of material; 8-10% P_2O_5, 46% CaO, 6% MgO.

basil (sweet basil) (herbe royale) (*Ocimum basilicum* L.) A spicy annual herb of the mint family; green 1½-in. leaves used as seasoning.
See Part 2: Essential Oils; Flavoring Agents, Natural; Spices, Microbial Content

bass A species of fish found in both fresh and salt water.
See Part 2: Frozen Food Storage; Minerals, Food; Vitamin A, Fish; Vitamin D, Fish

bassora gum *See* **gum tragacanth**

baste To moisten food during cooking by spooning or conveying by other means the pan liquor, butter, fat or other liquid over the food at frequent intervals to prevent drying and/or to add flavor.

basterma A salted dried meat.

bate A digesting process used on hides prior to tanning to make them soft or pliable; agents used: (1) manures (2) desiccated pancreas enzyme (3) a wood enzyme. *See also* **puering**.

batter (1) A mixture of flour and liquid.

Name	Parts Flour	Parts Liquid
Pour	1	1
Soft drop	1⅓ to 2	1
Medium	3	1
Stiff drop	4	1

(2) A mixture of tissue for a sausage product

Baumé A scale used to measure density of a liquid; the specific gravity at 60°F corresponds (not same value) to degree Baumé.
See Part 2: Brine, Meat Curing; Salt Brine; Salt, Brine Table; Sugar Solutions

bay An inlet of water; a section of a barn; the bark of a dog; light red color in horses; an evergreen tree of the laurel family whose leaf has a very aromatic flavor; it is used with meat, fish, poultry, soups, stuffing and pickling solutions.
See Part 2: Essential Oils; Spices, Microbial Content

bay leaves (laurel) (*Laurus nobilis* L.) Dried leaves from an evergreen tree used as an herb; dark green, wavy-edged leaves (2-4 in. long); they are very aromatic when crushed.

bay oil *See* **myrcia**

bay smelt *See* **smelt**

B.C. Beef casing.

BCP-D agar *See* **agar-agar**
See Part 2: Microorganism, Media

BDG broth *See* Part 2: Microorganism, Media

Be Symbol for the element beryllium.

bean A vegetable food, the dried seeds of which are also used as food; several are contained in a pod. Storage temp., 32° to 45°F (refrigerator crisper or plastic bags); relative humidity, 90%; freezing temp, 30°F; pH, 5.0-6.0; use within 3 to 5 days.
See Part 2: Beans Dry, Cooking; Beans, Peas and Nuts; Calories, Daily Recommendations; Canned Spoilage Related to pH; Canned Yield; Food, Composition; Frozen Food Storage; Fruit and Vegetables Composition; Iron; Iron, Daily Recommendations; Microwave Cooking,

Fresh Vegetables; Microwave Cooking, Frozen Vegetables; Microwave Processing Time; Minerals, Food; Niacin; Niacin, Daily Recommendations; Nicotinic Acid, Food; Nitrate, Vegetables; Nutrients in Crop; Organic Acids in Fruits and Vegetables; Pentosans; Phosphorus; pH Values of Biological Materials; Plant Foods, Composition; Portion Size; Protein Factors; Pulses, Nuts and Seeds Composition; Riboflavin; Riboflavin, Food; Seed, Chemical Composition; Seed, Germination; Soups Composition; Standards, Processed Fruit and Vegetable Products; Storage; Storage, Dry; Storage Times; Sugar Legumes; Thiamin; Thiamin, Daily Recommendations; Transit Temperature; Vegetable Boiling; Vegetable Composition; Vegetable Cooking, Frozen; Vegetable Frozen Yield; Vegetable Plants; Vegetables, Boiling Time, Frozen; Vegetables, Canning Dates; Vegetables Classification; Vegetables, Cooking Frozen; Vegetable Servings; Vegetables Panned; Vegetable Storage; Vegetable Yield; Vegetable Yield Canned and Frozen; Vegetable Yield Frozen, Canned and Fresh; Vitamin A, Food

bean beetle *See* Part 2: Insect Control

bean, dry The mature seed, dried to below 4% moisture.
Types: pea (navy), pinto, great northern, kidney, lima.
Colors: white, red, pinto (mottled), black, brown.
100 lb fresh = 11-13 lb dry beans; 60 lb/bu.
Composition: 8-13% H_2O, 22% protein, 1.5% fat, 61% carbohydrate, 4% ash; spacing 4-8 in.; harvest when pod is full.

bean grades (edible) U.S. Grades 1, 2, 3; handpicked grades: U.S. No. 1 choice handpicked; U.S. No. 1 handpicked; U.S. No. 2 handpicked; U.S. No. 3 handpicked.

bean, green (string) A moderately mature but not dried bean, usually eaten with pod.
1 lb fresh = 3 cups
1 cup fresh = 115 g (4 oz)
1 lb fresh = 2½ cups cooked
1 cup cooked = 125 g (4.4 oz)
1½-2 lb fresh = 1 qt canned
1 bu fresh = 24-40 lb
= 12-22 qt canned
Storage: 45°F, 85-90% relative humidity, 8 days storage life
Composition: 90% H_2O, 2.2% protein, 0.2% fat, 7% carbohydrate, 0.7% ash; pH 4.6

Size	Thickness
1	less than 29/128 in.
2	29/128 in. but not including 36/128 in.
3	36/128 in. but not including 21/64
4	21/64 in. but not including 24/64
5	24/64 in. but not including 27/64
6	27/64 in. or more

bean, kidney (*Phaseolus vulgaris; P. coccineus*) A common kidney-shaped bean that is often dried.
1 lb = 2½ cups
1 cup = 185 g (6.5 oz)
1 lb dried = 5½ cups cooked
1 cup cooked = 185 g (6.5 oz)

bean, lima (*Phaseolus lunatus*) A common bean that has a flat seed which is used for food; 2 lb unshelled = 1 lb shelled.
Shelled
1 lb fresh = 2 cups
1 cup fresh = 155 g (5.5 oz)
1 bu fresh = 28-30 lb
= 6-10 qt canned
1 lb dried = 2½ cups
1 cup dried = 180 g (6.3 oz)
1 bu dried = 56 lbs
1 lb dried = 5½ cups cooked
1 cup cooked = 186 g (6.6 oz)
1 qt canned = 2-5 lb fresh
In pod
1 bu fresh = 28-35 lb
= 6-10 qt canned
1 qt canned = 3-4 qt fresh
= 3-5 lb fresh
1 qt frozen = 4-4.5 lb fresh
Seed
50-75 lb/acre
Storage: Leave in pods; refrigerate 32-40°F; 85-90% relative humidity; use within 1 to 15 days; frozen (0°F) storage life 12 mo.

Composition	Raw Immature Seed	Dried Mature Seed
H_2O (%)	67	10
Protein (%)	8	20
Fat (%)	0.5	1.5
Carbohydrate (%)	22	64
Ash (%)	2	3.6
pH	6.5	—

bean, Navy White seed variety of kidney bean.
1 lb dried = 2⅓ cups dried
1 cup dried = 190 g (6.7 oz)
1 lb dried = 5½ cups cooked
1 cup cooked = 190 oz (6.7 oz)

bean pork Fresh jowls.

bean, snap or wax (*Phaseolus vulgaris*)
1½-2 lb fresh = 1 qt frozen
1 bu = 30 lb
1½-2½ lb fresh = 1 qt canned
1 ton fresh = 100 cases (24) No. 2½ cans
Storage: 45°F; 85-90% relative humidity; 8-10 days storage life; frozen (0°F) storage life 8 mo; seed 50 lb/acre; spacing 3 in. in rows 3 feet apart.

beard Hair on the face of men; or projections on animals in the same general location; projections on grain.
See Part 2: Rice Kernel

bear grass Southern and western North American pasture grass of several species that have similar grass-like foliage.
See Part 2: Poisonous Plants

bearish A downward price trend in the market.

Bearnaise A thick meat or fish hot sauce made of eggs, butter, vinegar, tarragon and seasonings.

Beaujolais Any of several light, fresh, fruity and brilliant purple-colored wine produced in the Beaujolais region of France.

beechnut Edible nut from the beech (*Fagus*) tree.
Composition: 7% H_2O, 19% protein, 50% fat, 20% carbohydrate, 4% ash

beef Flesh from bovine animal at least 10 months old; 1 barrel = 200 lb.
See Part 2: Animal Foods, Composition; Beef and Dual-Purpose Cattle; Beef, Boneless Cuts; Beef Chart; Beef Chuck; Beef Cuts; Beef Cuts and Uses; Beef Degrees of Doneness; Beef Percentages of Daily Recommended Allowances; Beef Retail Yield; Beef Rib Carving; Beef Rib Nomenclature; Beef Roasting; Beef Round, Bone Structure; Beef Round Cuts; Beef Rounds; Beef Yields; Bone Age; Braising Time; Broiling Time and Temperature; Calories, Daily Recommendations; Cattle; Cooking in Liquid, Time; Food, Composition; Frozen Food Storage; Frozen Meat Storage Time; Gland Weights; Glutamate; Glutamate Addition; Grades, Meat; Iron, Daily Recommendations; Lamb Chart; Liver; Meat and Meat Products Composition; Meat Composition; Meat, Frozen Storage; Meat Identification; Meat Label; Meat Nutritive Value; Meat, Servings per Pound; Meat Storage; Minerals, Food; Niacin, Daily Recommendations; Nicotinic Acid, Food; Portion Size; Potassium-Rich Foods; Riboflavin, Daily Recommendations; Riboflavin, Food; Roasting Meat; Roasting, Time and Temperature; Sauce, Beef Steak; Simmering Meat; Soups Composition; Specific Heat, Meat; Tallow, Beef, Triglyceride Mole Percent Composition; Thiamin, Daily Recommendations; Thiamin, Food; Vitamin A, Food; Yield Grade Meat

beefalo A type of cattle (buffalo-bison hybrids).

beef briskets A cut of beef located between the fore shanks which is usually cooked by simmering or made into corned beef; maximum gain in weight on curing, 20% over fresh uncured weight.

beef carcass *See* Part 2: Beef Carcass, Cutting Yield; Beef Carcass, Yield Grade; Beef Chart; Beef Yields

beef cooking *See* Part 2: Beef, Cooking

beef cutting *See* Part 2: Beef, New York-style Cutting; Beef, Chicago-Style Cutting; Beef Chart; Beef Yields

beef extract A product obtained by boiling lean beef under vacuum, straining the broth, evaporating it to 50% water, and adding salt.

beef fat *See* Part 2: Fat and Oil Composition; Fat and Oil, Fatty Acid Composition; Fatty Acids, Fats and Oils; Tallow, Beef, Triglyceride Mole Percent Composition; Unsaturated Fatty Acids

beef grades Prime
Choice
Good
Commercial
Utility
Cutter
Canner

beef hams *See* **dried beef**

beef lactose agar *See* Part 2: Microorganism, Culture Media, Dairy and Food Products

Beefmaster A cross of Brahman on both the Hereford and Shorthorn in a 3-way cross.
See Part 2: Beef and Dual-Purpose Cattle

beef stroganoff Beef cooked with onions, mushrooms, sour cream, tomato puree, Worcestershire sauce and sometimes wine and often served over noodles.

beef tea An extract made by simmering beef in water.

beef tongues *See* **cured beef tongues**

beef tree An instrument attached to the rear legs of a beef carcass during slaughter which is attached to a hoist for raising the carcass.

beef with barbecue sauce A sauce containing at least 50% meat (wt of cooked and trimmed meat) or 72% uncooked meat.

beef yield *See* Part 2: Beef Yields

beer An alcoholic drink produced from wort fermentation by yeast (*Saccharomyces cerevisiae*); pH 4.0–5.0; storage 32°–40°F.

Beeren-Auslese A wine made from specially selected single grapes from the best bunches.

beeswax A wax from the honeycomb of the bee; used to glaze candy.
See Part 2: Saturated Fatty Acids; Wax

beet (***Beta vulgaris***) A cool-weather annual or biennial member of the goosefoot family, closely related to sugar beets; the red beetroot may be used as a salad root, boiled, fried, packed in vinegar, stuffed, canned, made into soup or wine; the root may be spherical to oblong or ovoid.
1 lb fresh topped = 2 cups
1 cup topped fresh = 145 g (5.1 oz)
2–3½ lb fresh topped = 1 qt canned
2½–3 lb fresh topped = 1 qt frozen
1 bu topped = 50–60 lb
1 bu topped = 16–24 qt canned
1 crate (8 × 12 × 22 in.) bunched = 40 lb
100 lb fresh beets = 14–17 lb dry beets
Storage: Remove tops and store covered in a refrigerator (32°F); 90–95% relative humidity; use within 1 week to 3 mo.
Composition: 87% H_2O, 1.5% protein, 0.1% fat, 10% carbohydrate, 1% ash; pH 4.9–5.5.
See Part 2: Canned Yield; Canned Spoilage Related to pH; Food, Composition; Glutamate; Minerals, Food; Nitrate, Vegetables; Pentosans;

Plant Foods, Composition; Portion Size; Seed, Germination; Standards, Processed Fruit and Vegetable Products; Storage; Sugar, Vegetables; Vegetable Boiling; Vegetable Composition; Vegetable Cooking; Vegetable Plants; Vegetables, Canning Dates; Vegetables Classification; Vegetables, Cooking Frozen; Vegetable Servings; Vegetable Storage; Vegetable Yield; Vegetable Yield Canned and Frozen; Vegetable Yield Frozen, Canned and Fresh; Wastes, Agricultural and Industrial

beet greens Beet tops used as greens; 15 lb per bushel.
Storage: Wash and drain; store in refrigerator crisper or plastic bag; use within 1 to 2 days.

beet pulp Dried, 0.6 lb/qt.

beet sugar *See* **sucrose**

behenic acid A saturated fatty acid found in peanut oil.
See Part 2: Fats and Oils, Fatty Acid Composition; Fatty Acids; Fatty Acids and Their Properties; Fatty Acids, Fats and Oils; Saturated Fatty Acids

behen oil (oil of ben) A nondrying oil from ben nut (*Moringa*) used in food, for extraction and lubrication.
See Part 2: Saturated Fatty Acids

beignet A paste fritter.

belachan A fermented paste of prawns or shrimp.

Belgian endive *See* **French endive**

belling A method of testing eggs: gently tap eggs together; checked eggs give a dead sound, those without checks give clear, bell-like sound.

bell scraper A metal dome-shaped scraper with a wooden handle used to remove hair or dirt from a hog carcass.

belly The area of a hog carcass from which bacon is made and spare ribs removed; trimmed hog belly is 14% of hog carcass.
See Part 2: Pork Cuts

bel paese A mild, mellow, light yellow interior, gray surface, semi-soft Italian dessert cheese made from whole (cows) milk; ripened 6–8 weeks.
See Part 2: Cheese Characteristics; Cheese Vitamin Content; Milk and Milk Products, Vitamin Content

Belted Galloway Black Scottish beef cattle with white belt circling body between shoulders and hooks.
See Part 2: Beef and Dual-Purpose Cattle

Beltsville No. 1 A breed of hogs originated by U.S.D.A.; consists of a cross between Danish Landrace (75%) and Poland China (25%); it is black with white spots and has drooping ears.
See Part 2: Swine Breeds

Beltsville No. 2 A breed of hogs originated by U.S.D.A. by crossing Yorkshire (58%) and Duroc (32%) and also adding 5% Hampshire and 5% Landrace blood; it is red in color and has a white underline and occasional black spots.

Beltsville Small White *See* Part 2: Turkey Varieties

Benedict A test for reducing sugar.

bene seed (benne seed, benni seed) *See* **sesame seed**

bengal agar *See* **agar-agar**
See Part 2: Microbiological Examination of Dairy Products

bengal gram *See* **chick pea**

bent grass (*Agrostis*) A reedy stiff wiry grass used for pasture or turf; neglected pasture.
See Part 2: Seed, Germination

benzene C_6H_6 A liquid hydrocarbon made from petroleum or coal tar; it is an unsaturated aromatic substance which is the chemical basis for hundreds of derivatives, e.g., dyes, pharmaceuticals, insecticides, plastics, detergents, etc. Many of its derivatives are made by substituting various groups or side chains for one or more of the hydrogen atoms. *See also* **aromatic.**

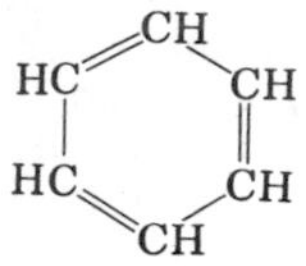

benzene hexachloride C_6Cl_6 A poisonous chlorinated hydrocarbon used as an insecticide. It is a mixture of several isomers, and contains 12-14% of the toxic gamma isomer. *See also* **lindane.**

benzoic acid $C_6H_5C\begin{matrix} OH \\ O \end{matrix}$ An aromatic acid used as an antimicrobial agent (preservative) in foods, but only up to 0.1%. Occurs naturally in cinnamon, cranberries, greengage plums, prunes, ripe olives and benzoin resin.
See Part 2: Organic Acids in Fruits and Vegetables.

bergamot An essential oil used in flavoring.
See Part 2: Essential Oils; Flavoring Agents, Natural

beriberi A nutritional deficiency disease caused by lack of thiamin (vitamin B_1) in the diet.

berkelium (Bk) A synthethic radioactive element of the actinide series; Group IIIB of the Periodic Table; at. no. 97; mass number of most stable isotope 249; oxidation states +3, +4; electron configuration 2–8–18–32–26–9–2
orbit K L M N O P Q

Berkshire A meat type breed of hogs that originated in South Central England from Chinese, Siamese and Italian strains; it is black, preferably with 6 white points, has an erect ear, and a turned-up snout.
See Part 2: Swine Breeds

Berkshire Knot Large, horned, dark-face breed of sheep.

berliner (New England) A coarse cut pork (small quantity of beef) stuffed into large casings; it is held 3 days before stuffing to allow curing.
See Part 2: Sausage Identification

Bermuda grass (*Cynodon dactylon*), **(wire grass)** A perennial plant used for pasture and lawns; hard to eradicate; pH 5.0-5.5; approx. nutrients used in growing 3 tons for grazing: 85 lb N, 18 lb P_2O_5, 60 lb K_2O; varieties: Coastal, Common. 1 bu Bermuda grass seed = 35 lb.
See Part 2: Seed, Germination

berry (true) A subdivision of simple fruit; it has a fleshy ovary wall enclosing one or more seeds and attached to a fleshy placenta; (e.g., gooseberry, currant, cranberry, grape, banana, tomato, eggplant); fruit usually referred to as berries fall under the aggregate fruit classification.
Storage: keep whole, unstemmed, uncovered, unwashed; temperature 31°F; relative humidity 85-90%; freezing point 29-30°F; use in 1 to 2 days.
Berries (except strawberries) -
2 cups fresh = 1 lb
1 qt fresh = 1½ lb fresh
1¼-3 lb (fresh) = 1 qt canned
5 cups (fresh) = 1 qt canned
1 crate (fresh) = 36-40 lb
= 16-20 qt canned
50-gal barrel = 380 lb
Composition: 85% water; 1% protein; 1% fat; 13% carbohydrate; 0.5% ash.
See Part 2: Calories, Daily Recommendations; Fruit, Availability; Fruit Harvest Dates; Fruit Classification; Fruit Composition; Fruit Frozen Yield; Fruit Storage; Standards, Processed Fruit and Vegetable Products; Storage Times; Vegetables Classification

beryllium (Be) A metallic element; at. no. 4; at. wt. 9.013; Group IIA of the Periodic Table; oxidation state +2; electron configuration 2-2
orbit K L
Beryllium and its compounds are poisonous.

beta (B, β) Greek letter with an English equivalent of b.

beta-carotene ($C_{40}H_{56}$) A carotenoid which is transformed to vitamin A in the liver.

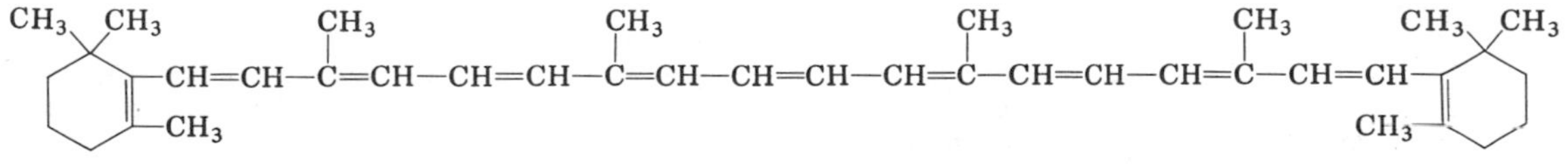

betaine ($C_5H_{11}O_2N$)
See Part 2: Grain Analysis; Wheat Products Composition

beta ray A stream of high-speed, negatively charged particles coming from the nucleus of radioactive elements; physically similar to electrons, with moderate penetrating power.

betel Leaf of a creeper pepper, *Piper betel*, which is chewed for its stimulating effect; dried seed of *Areca catechu*, pinnate-leaved palm also chewed for its stimulatory effect.
See Part 2: Vegetable Storage

Betula A genus of birch trees; the black birch (*B. lenta*) bark is extracted for methyl salicylate.
See Part 2: Flavoring Agents, Natural

beurre noir (Black butter) (French) Butter melted over low heat until it is dark brown. Used as a sauce for fish or meat.

beverage Inclusive name for any liquid drink, usually agreeable, consumed by humans.
See Part 2: Beverage Carbonated, Ingredients; Microbiological Media; Minerals, Trace, Limits

BG sulfa agar *See* **agar-agar**
See Part 2: Microorganism, Media

BHA *See* **butylated hydroxyanisole**
See Part 2: Antioxidant Activity; Antioxidant Mixtures; Antioxidants, Formula; Antioxidant Structure

BHC Abbreviation for benzene hexachloride. *See also* **lindane.**

BHT *See* **butylated hydroxytoluene**
See Part 2: Antioxidant Activity; Antioxidant Mixtures; Antioxidants, Formula; Antioxidant Structure

bi- Prefix meaning two; di- is more frequent.

Bi Symbol for the element bismuth.

bibb lettuce (limestone) Similar to Boston lettuce, deep green and crisp leaves. *See also* **lettuce.**

biceps brachii A muscle of the chuck that lies in front of the humerus; attaches to the head of the radius.

biceps femoris A thigh muscle running from the ischium (ox) or from the ilium over the ischium (other animals) to the back of the tibia; it is the large lateral muscle of the round; part of the bottom round.
See Part 2: Edible Meat and Chilled Carcass

biddy Slang or colloquial term for a hen.

big Boston *See* **Boston lettuce**

Biggy agar *See* **agar-agar**
See Part 2: Microorganism, Media

big packer hides Hides removed from the carcass by relatively skilled labor.

Big Stem Jersey A dry mealy variety of sweet potato.

bilberry (blaeberry, whortleberry) (*Vaccinium myrtillus*) A low shrub bearing a juicy, bluish-black, globose fruit; the fruit is acid when raw but is used in tarts and jam.

bile broth Microbiological broth used in the detection of coliform organisms; bile is inhibitory for most other bacteria.
See Part 2: Microbiological Examination of Dairy Products

bile salts Salts formed from bile acids; their function is emulsification of fats, which can then be hydrolyzed more rapidly.

billbug An insect that makes holes in corn stalks near the ground or across the corn leaves; often kills buds of young plant. Control: early planting, rotation; avoid infested area for few years; treat plowed area.

billion A numerical term; in France and U.S. it is 1,000,000,000; in England and Germany 1,000,000,000,000.

biltong Meat cut into strips, rubbed with a curing mixture, and dried.

binder (sausage) A term used in sausage manufacture to indicate a material that will absorb and hold moisture at elevated temperatures; may not contain over 3½% collectively or individually: (1) cereal (2) vegetable starch (3) starchy vegetable flour (4) soya flour (5) non-fat dry milk (dried skim milk) (6) dried milk (7) max. 2% isolated soy protein.

binders Cross fibers that bind sheep fleece together.

binomial distribution A population which can be divided into 2 classes; (e.g., yes and no); the variable is a discrete value in contrast to a continuous variable.

bioassay A measure of the physiological effects of a substance on a living organism, including higher animals.

biogas Methane admixed with other hydrocarbon gases obtained by destructive distillation of animal manures and other agricultural wastes; used as a fuel.

biological value (protein) The percentage of true digestible protein used by the body.

biosate agar *See* **agar-agar**
See Part 2: Microbiological Media

biotin ($C_{10}H_{16}O_3N_2S$) A water-soluble member of the vitamin B complex necessary for growth and health. It occurs in yeast, liver, and milk. Persons who consume large amounts of raw egg white may develop a nutritional deficiency because the avidin in the egg-white combines with biotin in such a way as to make it unavailable. Withdrawal of egg-white from the diet will correct this deficiency. *See also* **avidin**.

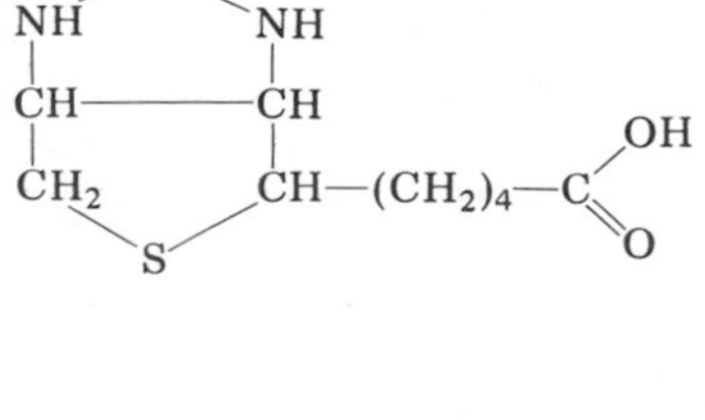

See Part 2: Biotin Content; Egg Products Nutritive Value; Cheese Vitamin Content; Milk and Milk Products, Vitamin Content; Milk Composition; Vitamin Sources, Functions, and Stability; Wheat, Vitamins

birch An artificial flavoring used in soft drinks, e.g., birch beer.
See Part 2: Flavors, Beverage

bird A member of the Aves classification of animals.
See Part 2: Egg Incubation Periods; Meat and Meat Products Composition

bird cherry *See* **cherry**

birdsfoot trefoil (Lotus) A plant with clawlike pods; a perennial legume. 60 lb per bushel; plant 4 to 6 lb per acre. Varieties: Cascase, Granger, Parker, Viking.

bird's nest A Chinese soup made from the gelatinous material (derived from sea weed) which lines the nest of some swallows; also a fungus.

bis- A prefix used in chemical terminology to indicate that a group occurs twice in a molecule, as the phenol group in bisphenol A $(CH_3)_2C(C_6H_5OH)_2$.

biscuit (literally, twice-cooked, from French *cuivre*) A small bread-like cake made from flour, milk, shortening and baking powder, baked at about 400°F and served hot.
See Part 2: Calories, Daily Recommendations; Grain Products Composition; Spoilage, Fat in Foods; Thiamin, Food

bisk *See* **bisque**

bismuth (Bi) A metallic element; at. no. 83; at. wt. 208.99; Group VA of Periodic Table; oxidation states +3, +5; electron configuration 2-8-18-32-18-5
orbit K L M N O P

bismuth sulfite agar *See* **agar-agar**
See Part 2: Microorganism, Media; Microorganism, Selective and Differential Broths and Media, Water Filtration Plant

bismuth sulfite broth *See* Part 2: Microorganism, Selective and Differential Broths and Media, Water Filtration Plant

bison A species of buffalo.
See Part 2: Gestation Periods

bisque A thick fish or game soup that has been strained; high-fat ice cream that contains bread or confection products.

bisulfate group $—O—SO_2—OH$

bisulfate ion $(HSO_4)^-$

bitter A basic taste response.
See Part 2: Bitter Flavors; Bitter, Herbs; Flavor Ingredients, Taste and Flavor Type

bitter almond *See* **almond**
See Part 2: Essential Oils

bitter chocolate *See* **chocolate**

bitter gourd *See* **balsam pear**

bitter orange *See* **sour orange**

bittersweet A flavor of bitter and sweet; the root and bark of a climbing plant (*Celastrus scandens*) which when consumed can increase perspiration; poisonous nightshade (*Solanum dulcamara*).
See Part 2: Flavor Ingredients, Taste and Flavor Types

bitterweed A grass which will cause off-flavors in milk when eaten by cows.
See Part 2: Poisonous Plants

Biuret Test A general test for protein; a pink to purple color is formed when protein is heated with alkali and copper sulfate; the color is due to the presence of two 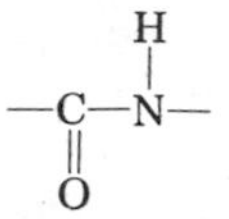 groups. Tripeptides and all native proteins give a positive test.
See Part 2: Protein and Amino Acid, Color Reactions

bixin (annatto extract) A yellow to peach coloring material obtained by extracting the seed of *Bixa orellana* tree.

Bk Symbol for the element berkelium.

black and gray fleece Wool containing some dark fibers; cannot be used for making light-colored fabric.

black and white bass *See* **sea bass**

blackback *See* **flounder**

blackberry (***Rubus alleghaniensis***) A prickly (there are thornless sports) climbing plant that produces a fruit composed of a large number of one-seeded drupelets which are closely set together on a core; the fruit is borne in clusters at the end of older shoots; the berries are consumed fresh, canned and made into jam; 100 lb fresh berries = 16–20 lb dried berries; pH 3.2–4.5 (3.5 av.).
See Part 2: Fruit Harvest Dates; Fruit Classification; Fruit Composition; Fruit Frozen Yield; Minerals, Food; Plant Foods, Composition; Storage; Sugar, Fruit

black bread *See* **rye**

Blackface Hampshire, Oxford and Shropshire sheep or lambs sired by a ram of one of these breeds.

Black-faced Highland A long-fleece breed of sheep originating in Scotland.
See Part 2: Sheep Breeds

blackfish *See* **sea bass**

black gram (urd, woolly pyrol) (*Phaseolus mungo*) A hairy plant (pulse) which has a pod that contains up to 10 black seeds with a white hilum; harvested in 4 months.

Parts of Plant	Use
Total plant	Green manure
Dry seed	Human food (pulse)
Young pods	Boiled and eaten

black grouper *See* **grouper**

Black Leaf 40 An insecticide that is a 40% solution of nicotine sulfate.

black pepper *See* **pepper**

black rice *See* **wild rice**

black rot Egg yolk which becomes black, hard and solid, evolving hydrogen sulfide; albumin becomes liquefied, granular and dark in color.

black salsify *See* **scorzonera**

black sea bass *See* **sea bass**

blackstrap molasses A molasses from which most of the sugar has been removed; it is dark in color, strong in flavor, high in ash content, and used for fermentation purposes. It contains 30% sucrose, 20% reducing sugars, 20% nonsugars, 20% water; ash 10%. *See also* **molasses**.
See Part 2: Sugars and Sweets Composition

black tea Tea made from leaves that have been fermented (oxidized) to darken the leaves and soften the flavor before being steamed, rolled and dried. Types are:
assam: a strong, pungent, brisk flavor and mellow body
backsettler: a hearty, brisk flavor
darjeeling: reddish color and fragrant aroma
keemun: smooth flavor and light body
lapsang souchong: slate gray color, smokey flavor, medium body
orange pekoe: flowery light body, mild clear taste
pamir tura: coppery color, flavorful, mild taste;
See also **tea**.

black teeth Long tusks of young pigs.

black tongue A deficiency disease in dogs due to improper diet. *See also* **pellagra**.

black walnut (***Juglans nigra***) A tall North American tree grown for lumber and nuts; the nuts are larger but shells are thicker than European walnuts; the nut flavor is strong and is used in confectionery and ice cream.
1 lb shelled walnuts = 4 cups nutmeats
1 lb in shell = 1⅔ cups nutmeats
8½ lb in shell = 1 lb shelled
1 bu in shell = 50 lb
See also **walnut**.

bladder (1) A hollow sac within the body which serves one or more functional purposes, e.g., gall bladder, urinary bladder. (2) Any similar structure in plants.
See Part 2: Casings, Animal; Casing, Terms; Organ Weights

bladder pod *See* Part 2: Poisonous Plants

blade A cut of meat.
See Part 2: Beef Chuck; Beef Cuts; Beef Retail Yield; Beef Rib Nomenclature; Bone; Bone in Retail Cuts; Meat Identification; Meat Label; Pork Cooking Methods; Pork Loin Nomenclature; Pork Shoulder; Pork Yield; Veal Chart; Veal Cuts; Veal Wholesale Cuts

bladebone *See* **scapula**
See Part 2: Beef Wholesale Cuts; Lamb Wholesale Cuts; Pork Wholesale Cuts

bladebone steak meat *See* **clear cut shoulder**

blade rib roast *See* **chuck rib roast**

blaeberry *See* **bilberry**

blanch To place in boiling water to loosen skin, set color or remove color.

blanc mange A thickened, molded milk dessert. From French "white food" (manger-eat).
See Part 2: Cornstarch Pudding Variations

blarney A semi-hard Irish cheese with small "eyes" and a red coating.

bleach To remove color from an oil; agents used are activated carbon; activated clay; diatomaceous earth; fuller's earth.
See Part 2: Margarine Production

bleaching powder Calcium oxychloride ($CaOCl_2$).

blemish A mark, injury, or deformity of the skin or adjacent tissue that would mar the appearance but not impair the usefulness of an animal.

blend To combine well; to mix thoroughly.

blended whiskey Mixture of 2 or more straight whiskeys (100 proof) or of straight whiskey with silent spirit or water; caramel is usually added.

bleu cheese *See* **blue cheese**

bleu de bresse A blue-veined cheese made from cow's milk; it has a thin rind and a soft mottled texture.

bleu des causses A rich, creamy textured, blue-veined cheese made from cow's milk and matured in caves; it is gold-foil wrapped and weighs about 5 lb.

blewits (*Lepista*) An edible fungus that has a mushroom shape with a gray or brown cap.

blind end Closed at one end.
See Part 2: Casings, Hogs and Beef; Casings, Terms

bloat A condition caused by failure to eliminate normal gases from the rumen; usually occurs after placing on lush pasture; swelling high above the left flank, unsteady gait, causing the animal to fall.

bloater A herring (fish) that has received a medium salt cure and has been smoked overnight.

block Edam cheese Same as Edam except that it is made in the shape of a rectangle or cube.

blocky Deep, compact, wide and low set.

blood Red fluid tissue circulated by the heart; buffering system compounds HCO_3^-, H_2CO_3, HPO_4^{2-}, $H_2PO_4^-$;

$$\text{hemoglobin} + \text{acid } H^+ + HCO_3^- \longrightarrow H_2CO_3$$
$$+ \text{base } OH^- + H_2CO_3 \longrightarrow H_2O + HCO_3^-$$

The volume obtained on slaughtering is as follows:

Species	Avg Volume (Approx 50-75% of Total Volume) Lb
Cattle	30
Sheep	4-5
Pigs	5-8

Normal pH range 7.3 to 7.5.
See Part 2: Blood; Gland Weights; Minerals, Plant or Animal Tissue; Moisture in Biological Materials; Organ Weights; pH Values of Biological Materials

blood agar *See* **agar-agar**
See Part 2: Microorganism, Media

blood albumin Blood serum that has been clarified and dried. *See also* **albumin.**

blood flour Dried blood in fine powder form.

blood meal Dried ground blood; approximately 85% protein.

blood orange A sweet orange in which the flesh has blood-red streaks.

blood system *See* **American system**

bloom Bright red color of meat when it is fresh. *See also* **fat bloom.**

blue (bleu) A semi-hard, Danish or French white cheese which contains veins of blue mold, has a zesty flavor and is made from whole (cow's) milk.
Ripening time: 2 mo. minimum; 3-4 mo. usually; 9 mo. pronounced flavor. *See also* **blue cheese.**
See Part 2: Cheese Characteristics; Cheese Vitamin Content; Milk and Milk Products, Vitamin Content; Vitamin A, Milk and Milk Products

Blue Andalusian A mediterranean class of chickens that lays a white-shelled egg.

blueback A Maine trout; a Columbia salmon; a river herring.
See Part 2: Salmon and Trout

blueberry (*Vaccinium*) A shrub that bears a bluish-black fruit that is used in pies, stewed with sugar or in puddings. Types are high-bush and low bush, the latter usually being smaller and of lighter color. 1 lb = 2 cups; 1 cup = 145 g (5.2 oz); ph 3.7.
See Part 2: Fruit, Availability; Fruit Harvest Dates; Fruit Classification; Fruit Composition; Fruit Frozen Yield; Fruit Servings per Pound; Minerals, Food; Organic Acids in Fruits and Vegetables; Plant Foods, Composition; Standards, Processed Fruit and Vegetable Products; Sugar, Fruit

bluebonnet (*Lupinus*) A silky annual leguminous herb which grows in the southwestern U.S.
See Part 2: Poisonous Plants

blue channel *See* **catfish**

blue cheese A white, semi-soft, blue-veined cheese made from whole (cow's) milk. It is an attempt to duplicate the French roquefort made from the milk of sheep; it is usually in a wheel shape

and has a piquant spicy flavor; ripened by internal mold (*Penicillium roquefortü*). 1 cup crumbled = 4 oz; Composition 40-42% H_2O, 21-22% protein, 30-31% fat, 2% carbohydrate, 6% ash, 4% salt.
Other blue-veined cheeses are danablu, gorgonzola, roquefort, and stilton.

blue cheese dressing *See* Part 2: Fats and Oils, Composition

blue fin *See* **tuna**

bluefish (skipjack, skip-mackerel) Many types of dark or bluish fishes such as *Pomatomus saltatrix* (Atlantic coast of U.S.), *Labridoe* (Florida and West Indies), pollack, cunner and seabass.
See Part 2: Fish and Shellfish Composition; Minerals, Food

bluegrass (Kentucky, common, *Poa pratensis*) A perennial grass used for pasture and lawns; 15-22 lb per bushel; plant 2 to 10 lb per acre; pH 6.0-6.8.
See Part 2: Nutrients in Crops; Seed, Germination

Blue Lake A green bean variety grown in the northwestern U.S.

blue mackerel *See* **mackerel**

blue stem cattle Cattle from (1) Osage of Oklahoma or (2) Flint hills of Kansas.

bluestone $CuSO_4 \cdot 5H_2O$; cupric sulfate.

blutwurst Blood sausage.
See Part 2: Sausage Identification

boar An uncastrated male pig or hog.
See Part 2: Meat and Meat Products Composition; Swine Market Classes and Grades

board foot A measure of lumber.

$$\text{board feet} = \frac{\text{width (inches)} \times \text{thickness (inches)} \times \text{length (feet)}}{12}$$

1 board foot = 144 cu in.
= 0.0024 cu m

bob veal Carcass of immature veal.

bockwurst An imitation sausage made from veal and pork and a substantial proportion of milk; sold in fresh state.
See Part 2: Sausage Identification; Sausage, Types

body *See* Part 2: Bone and Body Weight

body weight *See* Part 2: Fat and Body Weight

boil To cook in water at boiling temperature (100°C; 212°F).
See Part 2: Beans Dry, Cooking; Vegetable Boiling; Vegetables, Boiling Time, Frozen.

boiled ham A cured, unsmoked ham which is boned, cooked, compressed and shaped. *See also* **ham, boiled.**

boiled soap A hard soap made from tallow or grease, using a soda base and removing the glycerin formed.

boiling point (b.p.) The temperature at which a liquid vaporizes; normal boiling point is the temperature at which the vapor pressure of a liquid reaches 760 mm of mercury.
See Part 2: Boiling Point, Altitude; Boiling Points, Sodium Chloride, Calcium Chloride; Temperature of Vaporization, Latent Heat of Vaporization, Boiling Point

bolar roast A beef roast made from the lower half of a clear-cut shoulder (shoulder clod).

boletes A species of fleshy central stalk fungi (mushrooms) several of which are edible.

boll weevil Insect that lays its eggs in cotton buds and bolls; the larvae destroy the fruit; adults are gray brown with long snout, about ¼ in. long; larva are white with brown head.

bollworm A moth which lays its eggs on squares, blooms and bolls of cotton and the larva destroys the fruit; adults are a gray brown moth with green areas, wing spread approximately 1½ in.; larva (young) are white and brown; (old) green to orange with brown stripes.

bologna A comminuted, cooked, smoked, large casing sausage; normally contains 60% beef and 40% pork; however, the following percentages are found in formulations:

20-60%	bull or beef trimmings
30-60%	regular pork trimmings (50-50)
0-10%	hearts
0-32%	pork cheek meat
0-25%	veal
0-35%	beef brisket & cheek meat
0-10%	cooked beef tripe
0-25%	back fat
10-40%	ice
2-3%	salt
0-8%	binder: non fat dry milk, dry skim milk, soya flour

*¼ oz/100 lb sodium nitrite
*0-2 oz/100 lb sodium nitrate
*7-16 oz/100 lb sugar
*0-⅞ oz/100 lb (add late in chopping) sodium ascorbate
*4-6 oz/100 lb white pepper
or
4-6 oz/100 lb black pepper
*0-2½ oz/100 lb ground cardamon
*2-2½ oz/100 lb coriander
*0-1¾ oz/100 lb allspice
*0-1 oz/100 lb mace
*0-2 oz/100 lb sage
0-1½ lb/100 lb fresh onions
0-2 oz/100 lb nutmeg
0-¾ oz/100 lb fresh garlic
0-2 oz/100 lb ginger
*combination often used

Processing:
1. Grind through 3/8 in. plate
2. Chop beef
3. Add seasoning and cure (not ascorbate)
4. Add binder and ice as needed
5. Add pork, ice and ascorbate
6. Do not exceed 65°F
7. Stuff
8. Smokehouse temperature:

Time Hr	Temp °F	Conditions
1/2	130	dry
1	155	smoke
1 1/2	160	smoke
1 1/2	185	cook (until internal temperature of 150 to 155°F is reached)

shower for 20-30 min; room temperature, 1 hr; store in cooler.
Home storage: Keep in original wrapper; refrigerate.
See Part 2: Sausage Composition; Sausage Identification; Sausage Nutritive Value; Sausage, Types

bologna bull An aged lean bull.

bolus Food that a ruminant regurgitates for remastication before reswallowing.

bombe A ball-shaped dessert or confection.

bonavist *See* **lablab**

bone The fundamental structural system of the body. Composed of connective tissue and $[Ca_3(PO_4)_2]_n$ $CaCO_3$; retail meat store bones will yield 60% meat scraps; 30% moisture; 10% tallow.
See Part 2: Beef Chuck; Beef Round, Bone Structure; Beef Wholesale Cuts; Beef Yields; Bone; Bone Age; Bone and Body Weight; Bone and Retail Cuts; Bones, Composition; Gland Weights; Moisture in Biological Materials; Organ Weights; Poultry Yield

bone grease Fat obtained from rendered bones; oil obtained by dry distillation; tallow obtained by boiling.
See Part 2: Iodine and Saponification Values

boneless sirloin Boned muscle of the loin end wholesale cut.

bone meal A meal made from pulverized animal bones, either steamed or unsteamed. The former is used for animal feeds and the latter, called "raw," for fertilizer. Feed grade must have 65-75% tricalcium phosphate and 2% max. ammonia. Fertilizer grade has 40-55% tricalcium phosphate 20-25% phosphoric acid and 4-5% ammonia.
See Part 2: Fertilizer Materials; Packinghouse By-Products Composition.

boning yield The percent of boneless meat in a carcass.

bonito Common name for the food fishes, *Sardi chilensis* and *Sardi velox*.
See Part 2: Vitamin A, Fish; Vitamin D, Fish

borassus palm *See* **palmyra**

borax Hydrated sodium salt of boric acid, $Na_2B_4O_7 \cdot 10H_2O$ (sodium tetraborate). There is also an anhydrous grade used as an herbicide.
See Part 2: Fertilizer Materials

Bordeaux A region in southwestern France in which red (claret) and white wine of the same name is produced. *See also* **cabernet.**

Bordeaux mixture A mixture of slaked lime and copper sulfate solution; used as an insecticide, especially for potato bugs.

bordelaise A sauce made of red wine, shallots, thyme and pepper.

Bordetella A genus of microorganisms that are Gram-negative coccobacilli; they cause respiratory-tract infections.
See Part 2: Microorganism, Media

bordet gengou agar *See* **agar-agar**
See Part 2: Microorganism, Media

boric acid broth *See* Part 2: Microorganism, Culture Media, Water and Sewage, Standard Methods

borneo (green butter, tangkawang) A fat used in chocolate industry as a substitute for cocoa butter; obtained from the fruit of *Dipterocarpus* or *Shorea stenoptera*.
See Part 2: Iodine and Saponification Values; Melting Points, Fats and Oils; Refractive Indices, Fats and Oils; Titer, Fats and Oils

boron (B) A nonmetallic element; at. no. 5; at. wt. 10.82; Group III A of Periodic Table; oxidation state +3; electron configuration 2-3
orbit K L
A trace element in plant nutrition.
See Part 2: Grain Analysis; Nutrients in Crops; pH and Availability of Plant Nutrients

borsch (borsht) A fermented or fresh vegetable stock soup colored with red beet juice and of Russian origin.

bos A zoological genus which includes all cattle (and buffalo).

Boston baked beans Baked beans slowly cooked and flavored with molasses. *See also* **haricot bean.**

Boston bluefish *See* **pollock**

Boston butt Upper portion of a pork shoulder.
See Part 2: Meat, Servings per Pound; Pork Carcass, Retail Yield; Pork Chart; Pork Cookery; Pork, Cooking; Pork Cooking Yield; Pork Cuts; Pork Cuts and Uses; Pork Shoulder; Pork Wholesale Cuts; Pork Yield

Boston cut (English cut) A rectangular cut of meat from the thin end of the 4th and 5th ribs of the beef chuck.
See Part 2: Beef Cuts; Beef Retail Yield

Boston lettuce (big Boston, butterhead) A type of lettuce having velvety spreading leaves, which separate easily. *See* **lettuce**

Botrytis A genus of fungi causing rotting in plants and diseases in insects.
See Part 2: Mold, Food; Rot Spoilage

bottled in bond A straight whiskey, produced and bottled in accordance with the Bottling-In-Bond Act, a Federal law dating back to 1897; e.g., bonded bourbon must conform to all the requirements and standards of any straight whiskey and in addition the whiskey must be at least 4 years old (most are older), must be bottled at 100 proof (suggestions have been made to reduce this level), produced in a single distillery, by the same distiller and is the product of a single season and year.

bottle gourd *See* **gourd**

bottom chuck Inside portion of a beef chuck when this area is divided along the blade bone.

bottom round Outside muscle of the round; it is tougher than top round. *See also* **outside round.**
See Part 2: Beef, Boneless Cuts; Beef Round Cuts; Meat Identification

botulinum *See* ***Clostridium botulinum***

botulism A type of food poisoning caused by consuming toxin produced by the anaerobic bacteria *Clostridium botulinum*; most potent poison known to man; neurotoxin formed during growth of *Clostridium botulinum* (spore-forming bacteria that requires no oxygen). Six antigenic types of toxin (different species): Man (A, B, E, F) Animals (C, D). *See also Clostridium botulinum.*
See Part 2: Diseases, Food-Borne; Food Poisoning, Bacteria; Illness from Food; Infectious Diseases, Food-Borne; Microbial Toxins

bouillabaisse A chowder made from at least two kinds of fish (several types of fish are used); a stew made from fish, shellfish, onions, tomatoes and spices.

bouilli To boil or stew food (French).

bouillir To boil (French).

bouillon A clarified liquid prepared by simmering meat.
See Part 2: Soups Composition

bouillon cube (or powder) A dehydrated cube containing salt, hydrolyzed vegetable protein and fat, dextrin, sugar, meat extract and coloring.
Composition: 4% H_2O, 20% protein, 3% fat, 5% carbohydrate, 68% ash.

Bouin's picro-formol Picric acid, saturated:

aqueous solution (1g/75 ml H_2O)	75 parts
formalin	25 parts
glacial acetic acid	5 parts

Not for use with kidney or cells containing mucin
1. Fix for 4 to 16 hr
2. Wash with several changes of 50% alcohol
3. Wash with several changes of 70% alcohol
4. Store in 70 or 80% alcohol

boula boula A soup made of turtle, sherry wine and whipped cream.

bound water Water that has been adsorbed by the colloids (proteins) of a living cell.

bouquet The smell or scent that characterizes an alcoholic beverage, especially a fine wine.

bouquet garni A bunch of mixed herbs, (often bay leaf, onion, parsley and thyme) used in soup.

bouquetière, à la With several vegetables.

bourbon whiskey An alcoholic beverage made from a mash which contains at least 51% corn in its grain content (usually 65 to 75% corn); aged in charred new oak containers.

bourg Red and some white wines produced on the right bank of the Gironde in France.

bovine Pertaining to cattle (Latin *bos*).
See Part 2: Molds, Mycotoxins

bovine TB medium *See* Part 2: Microorganism, Media

box curing (pressure) Curing bacon in a box and applying pressure to it during cure. Use ¾-oz cure/lb bacon; time of cure is not too important, since bacon will not over-cure.

boysenberry A seedless, dark, juice berry developed by crossing raspberry, blackberry and loganberry; very similar to loganberry.
See Part 2: Fruit Frozen Yield

Br Symbol for the element bromine.

Brabham A variety of cowpeas.

brachio-cephalicus A muscle that runs from the shoulder to the head along the ventral side of the neck.

bracken fern A poisonous plant.
See Part 2: Poisonous Plants

bract A modified leaf below a flower or flowering part.

bracteole A small or secondary modified leaf below a flower or flowering part.

Bradford system *See* **English system**

Braford A cross of Brahman and Hereford beef cattle.

Brahma An Asiatic class of chickens that have feathered shanks, pea comb, yellow skin, and lay a brown-shelled egg.

Varieties	Plumage color
*Light	Generally white, neck feathers black with white edging, tail feathers dark
*Dark	(Female) neck and back—greenish black with edging of white, front of neck black; rest of body—mostly black
	(Male) head and upper neck—gray; rest of body gray with black penciling; tail—black
*Buff	Similar to Light except the white areas are replaced by buff

*bantam varieties
See Part 2: Poultry Breeds and Varieties

Brahman (Zebu) (Indian cattle) A breed of beef cattle derived from several breeds of native India cattle; they have a prominent hump above the shoulders and excess skin below the neck and brisket; have flat horns and drooping ears; their color ranges from gray to red. Guzerat strain most popular in U.S.; can withstand extreme heat and repel both flies and ticks.
See Part 2: Beef and Dual-Purpose Cattle

Brahorn A cross of Brahman and Shorthorn beef cattle.

brain Nerve tissue in the skull of animals; some types are used as food, e.g., calves.
Store in coldest part of refrigerator; use within 1 to 2 days.
Composition: 79% H_2O, 10% protein, 9% fat, 1% carbohydrate, 1.4% ash.
See Part 2: Beef Cuts and Uses; Gland Weights; Lamb Cuts and Uses; Moisture in Biological Materials; Organ Weights; Pork Cuts and Uses; Unsaturated Fatty Acids; Variety Meat, Cooking; Variety Meat Percentage of Daily Recommended allowances; Variety Meat Preparation; Veal Cuts and Uses

brain heart infusion agar *See* Part 2: Microorganism, Media

brain veal agar *See* Part 2: Microorganism, Media

braise To cook slowly in a covered utensil with a small amount of liquid; a moist heat method of cooking; moisture is added and the product placed in a closed container and cooked either in an oven or on top of a stove.
See Part 2: Beef, Cooking; Beef Cuts; Braising Meat; Braising Time; Lamb Braising; Lamb Cuts; Lamb Cuts and Uses; Meat Composition; Pork, Cooking; Pork Cuts; Pork Cuts and Uses; Pork Loin Cooking; Variety Meat, Cooking; Variety Meat Preparation; Veal Chart; Veal Cuts; Veal Cuts and Uses; Vitamin Retention, Meat

bran The outer protective layer (pericarp) and the layer just under it (aleurone layer) in cereal grains; 20 lb/bu.
See Part 2: Wheat and Flour Composition; Wheat, Carbohydrate Composition; Wheat, Fatty Acids; Wheat Kernel Parts; Wheat Products Composition

branched chain A linear series or chain of carbon atoms occurring in hydrocarbons and alcohols in which one or more substituent groups is present. Compounds containing branched chains are notably more reactive than normal or straight-chain compounds, especially in catalytic cracking processes; for example, normal heptane has an octane number of zero, while isooctane rates 100. The more extended the branching, the more reactive the compound in organic synthesis. Branched chain compounds are isomeric with the corresponding straight-chain compounds and are indicated by the prefix iso-. An example is butane:

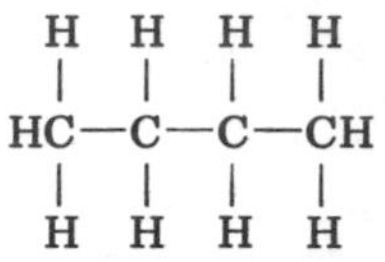

or $CH_3CH_2CH_2CH_3$

normal butane
(straight-chain)

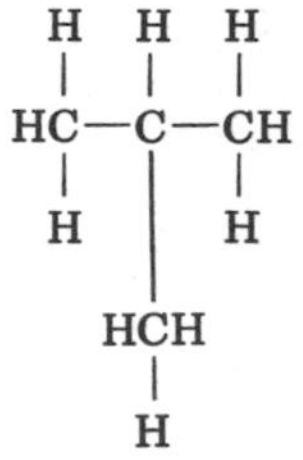

or $CH_3CHCH_3CH_3$

isobutane
(branched-chain)

brandy An alcoholic beverage made by the distilling of wine or wine residues; the distillate or mixture of distillates from fermented juice, mash, or wine of fruit distilled at less than 190° proof; usual range 37–43% alcohol by volume.
See Part 2: Minerals (Trace), Limits

bran flakes A breakfast cereal made from 40% of the outer coarse coat of grain.
See Part 2: Grain Products Composition

Brangus A cross of Brahman and Angus beef cattle.
See Part 2: Beef and Dual-Purpose Cattle

bratwurst A sausage product made from lean pork trimmings. Ingredients:
pork trimmings (70% lean)
2% salt
6 oz white pepper/100 lb
½ oz celery seed/100 lb
½ oz mace/100 lb
1 oz sage/100 lb
Grind ⅛-in plate; mix; stuff; cook in water to internal temp. of 148°F
See Part 2: Sausage Identification; Sausage, Types

braunschweiger A sausage normally made of 50% pork liver and 50% pork jowl; however, the following percentages are found in formulations:

40–50% pork liver
20–50% pork jowl
0–12% bacon ends or cured meat
0–15% veal
20–40% pork trimmings
0–20% beef trimmings
0–7½% ice
0–5% binder
*1.6–2.5% salt
*6–16 oz sugar/100 lb
*⅛–2 oz $NaNO_3$/100 lb
*⅛–¼ oz $NaNO_2$/100 lb
*2–6 oz pepper/100 lb
0–5 lb onion/100 lb

0-4 oz onion powder/100 lb
*0-1 oz sweet marjoram/100 lb
*0-1 oz cardamon/100 lb
*0-1 oz mace/100 lb
0-1 oz caraway seed/100 lb
0-3 oz mustard/100 lb
0-½ oz clove/100 lb
0-2 oz coriander/100 lb
0-½ oz sage/100 lb

Processing:
1. Slash liver and place in ice water to bleach, drain
2. Chop liver, ice and seasoning
3. Add meat and chop
4. Stuff
5. Cook in 160°F water until internal temp. of 145°F
6. Chill in ice water (internal temp. 90-100°F)

*This combination is used in some formulations.
See Part 2: Sausage Identification; Sausage Nutritive Value

Braunvieh German brown cattle.

Brazilian santos A Brazilian coffee; it is sharp, refreshing, strong, and light-colored in cup.

Brazil nut (cream nut) (*Bertholletia excelsa*) A hardshelled nut used for food and oil; a wild South American tree that produces woody fruit (2-4 lb) that contains 12-24 nuts; the nuts have to be cracked to obtain the kernel, which is eaten raw.
Kernel composition: 5% H_2O, 14% protein, 67% fat, 11% carbohydrate, 3% ash. 1 lb shelled kernels = 2 lb unshelled.
See Part 2: Beans, Peas and Nuts; Minerals, Food; Nut, Grades; Plant Foods, Composition; Protein Factors

bread (1) A leavened mixture made from flour or meal and baked in an oven. (2) To coat with bread crumbs, as breaded cutlets; coating should not exceed 30% of weight of finished product.
Composition of bread based on flour (%):

Ingredients	White (%)	Whole Wheat (%)
Flour	100	100
Water	60-65	66
Yeast	2-3	2
Salt	2	2.25
Sugar	4-8	4
Mold inhibitor	0.125	
NFDM* solids	3-4	
Shortening	2-4	5
Emulsifier	0.25	0.2-0.4

*Nonfat dry milk.

2½ pullman loaves bread = 50 servings; Yeast (*Saccharomyces cerevisiae*) produces CO_2 in bread.
Frozen storage: 0°F quick storage life 2-4 mo.; yeast storage life 6-12 mo.; rolls 2-4 mo.

Composition	H_2O (%)	Protein (%)	Fat (%)	Carbohydrate (%)	Ash (%)	pH
White	36	9	3	51	2	5.0-6.0
Rye	36	9	1	52	2	
Whole wheat	36	10	3	48	2	

contains: 62% total solids
1.1-1.8 mg thiamin/lb
.7-1.6 mg riboflavin/lb
10-15 mg niacin or niacinamide/lb
8-12.5 mg Fe/lb
optional: 150-750 U.S. Pharmacopeia units of vitamin D/lb.
See Part 2: Bread and Flour Enrichment; Calcium Daily Requirements; Calories, Daily Recommendations; Cereal Enrichment; Food, Composition; Frozen Food Storage; Grain Products Composition; Iron, Daily Recommendations; Minerals, Food; Niacin, Daily Recommendations; Nicotinic Acid, Food; Pantothenic Acid Content; Portion Size; Riboflavin, Daily Recommendations; Spoilage, Carbohydrate Foods; Thiamin, Daily Recommendations; Thiamin, Food; Vitamin A, Food; Wheat, Minerals; Wheat, Vitamins

bread crumbs Small particles of bread, 1/16 to 1/8 in. diameter.
1 lb soft = 10 cups
1 cup soft = 45 g (1.6 oz)
1 lb dry = 4.4 cups
1 cup dry = 115 g (3.6 oz)
See Part 2: Water Activity, Organisms and Food

bread flour *See* **hard-wheat flour**

breadfruit (*Artocarpus communis*) A tall tropical tree that produces fruit up to 8 in. in diameter with a thick warty skin; the fruit is high in starch and is eaten after roasting; can also be preserved by fermentation; Jak (Jack fruit) is a related species with larger and more odoriferous fruit that is eaten raw or cooked.
Composition: 71-72% H_2O, 1-2% protein, 0.3% fat, 25-26% carbohydrate, 1% ash.
See Part 2: Fruit Composition

bread wheat *See* **wheat**

breakfast sausage May be made from fresh or cured beef, pork, veal, lamb or mutton and may be fresh or cured; max. 50% fat.

break joint A temporary cartilage located ½ in. above the ankle of a sheep. If this breaks clean, the carcass is considered a lamb.
See Part 2: Bone Age; Lamb, Wholesale Cuts

bream *See* **demersal fish**

breast The sternum.
See Part 2: Bone; Bone in Retail Cuts; Braising Meat; Braising Time; Lamb Chart; Lamb Cuts; Lamb Cuts and Uses; Lamb Wholesale Cuts; Lamb Yield; Meat Identification; Meat, Servings

per Pound; Turkey Composition; Veal Chart; Veal Cuts; Veal Cuts and Uses

breastbone Sternum sternebrae.
See Part 2: Lamb Wholesale Cuts; Pork Wholesale Cuts; Veal Wholesale Cuts

breech wool The coarsest wool of the fleece, which grows on the outer thighs and crotch area.

breed A race of animals having well-defined distinguishing characteristics and the ability to reproduce these characteristics in their offspring.

breed character A combination of masculinity or femininity with breed type features, and head type being very important.

breeding age First breeding:

Jersey	16 mo.	Beef cattle	18 mo.
Guernsey	18 mo.	Swine	8 mo.
Ayrshire	19 mo.	Sheep	12 mo.
Holstein	20 mo.		

breed type A characteristic form of a breed, along with typical color, marking and head.

brewer anaerobic agar *See* Part 2: Microorganism, Media

brewers' grain *See* Part 2: Cereal By-Products Composition

brewers' yeast *See* **yeast**

brick *See* Part 2: Insulation; Insulation, Conductivity Values

brick cheese An American, moist, semi-soft, white to cream-colored (some light yellow to orange) cheese made from whole milk; contains many small holes; it may be either natural or processed; it is brick-shaped and has mild to sharp flavor; ripened by bacteria surface growth; often used in sandwiches.
Composition: 41-42% H_2O, 21-22% protein, 30-31% fat, 2% carbohydrate, 2% salt; 3-4% ash.
See Part 2: Cheese Characteristics; Cheese Vitamin Content; Vitamin A, Milk and Milk Products

brie A dessert cheese that is disk-shaped, light-colored, soft and savoury textured; has a flowery rind, sharp flavor and is very soft when ripe; made from cows' milk; medium and small wheels ripened 4-8 weeks by external molds.
Storage: refrigerate, tightly covered, use within 2 weeks.
Composition: 45-51% H_2O, 20-22% protein, 26-30% fat, 3-4% ash, 2% salt.
See Part 2: Cheese Characteristics; Cheese Vitamin Content; Milk and Milk Products, Vitamin Content; Vitamin A, Milk and Milk Products

Briggsian logarithms *See* **logarithm base 10**

brightness A term applied to the color of wool.

bright wool Wool of a clean nature and uniform shrinkage; produced east of the "semi-bright" area.

brilliant-green agar *See* Part 2: Intestinal Microorganisms; Microbiological Media; Microorganism, Selective and Differential Broths and Media, Water Filtration Plant

brilliant green bile *See* Part 2: Microorganism, Culture Media, Water and Sewage, Standard Methods; Microorganism, Selective and Differential Broths and Media, Water Filtration Plant

brilliant green bile broth *See* Part 2: Microbiological Media; Microorganism, Culture Media, Dairy and Food Products

brilliant green lactose *See* Part 2: Microbiological Examination of Dairy Products

brine Sodium chloride dissolved in water; natural brines contain from 2.6% (sea water) to 20% or more, plus other salts.
See Part 2: Brine, Meat Curing; Meat Curing Ingredients; Salt Brine; Salt, Brine Table; Salt Penetration Rate; Salt Solution, Freezing

bringall (*brinjal*) *See* **eggplant**
See Part 2: Vegetable Storage

brinza (brinzen, brinsen) A Hungarian (Carpathian mountains) cheese, also known as Liptau, made from ewes' milk or the mixed milk of sheep and goats and rennet.
See Part 2: Vitamin A, Milk and Milk Products

brioche A soft, sweet, yeast breakfast roll.

brisket The front of the breast of quadruped animals.
See Part 2: Beef, Boneless Cuts; Beef Chart; Beef Cuts; Beef Cuts and Uses; Beef Retail Yield; Beef Wholesale Cuts; Bone in Retail Cuts; Meat Identification; Riboflavin, Food

britch Fleece that comes from the rear legs of sheep. *See also* **breech wool.**

British pharmaceutical codex *See* Part 2: Minerals (Trace), Limits

British pharmacopoeia *See* Part 2: Minerals (Trace), Limits

British Proof Spirit An alcoholic beverage that contains 57.07% alcohol by volume (49.24% by weight) at 15.6°C.

British thermal unit (Btu) (B) A measure of heat, energy, and work.
1 Btu = heat required to raise the temperature of 1 lb of water 1°F
= 1,054.90 joules (10^7 ergs)
= 777.98 foot pounds (ft-lb)
= 107.577 kilogram meters (kg-m)
= 0.252 kg-cal (thermal units)
= 0.0003984 metric horsepower-hours (75 kg-m-hr)
= 0.0003930 U.S. horsepower-hours (hp-hr)
= 0.0002930 kilowatt hours (kw-hr)

British thermal units per second (Btu/sec) A measure of power, rate of energy, and heat.
1 Btu/sec = 1,054.90 watts (10^7 ergs/sec)
= 778.104 foot-pounds per second (ft-lb/sec)
= 107.577 kilogram meters per second (kg-m/sec)

= 1.43436 metric horsepower (75 kg-m/sec)
= 1.41474 U.S. horsepower (550 ft-lb/sec)
= 1.05490 kilowatt (kw)
= 0.25200 kg-cal/sec (thermal units per sec)

British wines Wines containing 16% alcohol by volume.

brix A hydrometer used for testing the sugar content of syrups.
See Part 2: Brix Table; Brix, Temperature Correction; Cherry Brix; Sugar Solutions

broad bean (*Vicia faba*) A large podded bean; young pods are cooked whole or sliced, or the bean may be harvested when fully grown, shelled and cooked.

Composition	H_2O (%)	Protein (%)	Fat (%)	Carbohydrate (%)	Ash (%)
Immature seed	72	8	0.5	18	1
Dry mature seed	12	25	2	58	3

broadbill *See* **swordfish**

broad leaf endive *See* **escarole**

broccoli (*Brassica oleracea*) A vegetable whose flower is used as food; winter cauliflower.
Types: Sprouting (*Brassica oleracea* var. *botrytis*); produces a number of loose terminal heads; white or purple (turns green on cooking) heads. Green sprouting broccoli, Calabrese; loose terminal head of green flower buds; may be boiled, used in soups and purée; often quick-frozen or canned. 2 lb fresh = 1 qt frozen; 1 lb fresh = 2 cups cooked; 1 cup cooked = 165 g (5.8 oz).
Storage: refrigerator crisper (32°F) or plastic bag; 90-95% relative humidity; use in 1 to 7 days; frozen (0°F) storage 1 year.
Raw spears composition: 89% H_2O, 4% protein, 0.3% fat, 6% carbohydrate, 1% ash, pH 6.5.
See Part 2: Ascorbic Acid; Calcium Daily Requirements; Calories, Daily Recommendations; Food, Composition; Frozen Food Storage; Iron; Microwave Cooking, Frozen Vegetables; Microwave Processing Time; Minerals, Food; Niacin; Nitrate, Vegetables; Phosphorus; Plant Foods, Composition; Potassium; Riboflavin; Storage; Sugar, Vegetables; Thiamin; Vegetable Boiling; Vegetable Composition; Vegetable Cooking; Vegetable Frozen Yield; Vegetable Plants; Vegetables, Boiling Time, Frozen; Vegetables, Cooking Frozen; Vegetable Servings; Vegetable Storage; Vegetable Yield; Vegetable Yield Canned and Frozen; Vegetable Yield Frozen, Canned and Fresh; Vitamin A; Vitamin A, Daily Recommendations; Vitamin C

brochette, en Cooked on a skewer or spit.

broil *See* **broiling**

broiler A young chicken from 1 to 3¼ lb.
See Part 2: Bone Age; Poultry Dressing Percentage; Poultry Roasting; Poultry Yield

broiler-fryer (1) chicken of either sex from 9 to 12 weeks old, (2) duck of either sex about 8 weeks old.

broiling A dry-heat method of cooking used for the more tender cuts; the meat is exposed directly to the heat.
See Part 2: Beef, Cooking; Beef Cuts; Broiling Griddle, Meat; Broiling Meat; Broiling Time and Temperature; Lamb Broiling; Lamb Cuts; Lamb Cuts and Uses; Pork Cookery; Pork, Cooking; Pork Cuts; Pork Cuts and Uses; Pork Loin Cooking; Poultry Class; Variety Meat, Cooking; Variety Meat Preparation; Veal Cuts and Uses; Vitamin Retention, Meat

broken mouth A sheep having some missing teeth.

bromcresol green An indicator showing yellow to blue color change over pH range 3.8 to 5.4; 0.1 g in 100 ml alcohol.

bromcresol purple An indicator which is yellow at pH 5.2 and purple at pH 6.8; 0.1 g in 9.25 ml $N/50$ NaOH; dilute to 250 ml.

bromegrass (*Bromus*) A type of oat; some species are considered weeds; 14 lb per bushel; plant 6 lb per acre.

bromelin (bromelain) An enzyme found in pineapple and used to tenderize meat.

brominated vegetable oil (BVO) An oil made by addition of bromine to unsaturated fatty acids; used in citrus-flavored soft drinks.

Iodine No.	Made from	Specific Gravity
80-90	olive	1.24
105-115	sesame	1.33
	corn	
	cottonseed	

bromine (Br) A liquid halogen element; at. no. 35; at. wt. 79.916; Group VIIA of Periodic Table; electron configuration 2-8-18-7; oxidation states
orbit K L M N
+1, +5, +3, -1.
See Part 2: Normal Solutions; Sanitizers

bromthymol blue An indicator that is yellow below pH 6.0, green between 6 and 7; and blue above 7; 0.1 g in 100 ml of 50% alcohol.

bronze *See* Part 2: Turkey Varieties

bronze beauty lettuce Leaf lettuce with reddish tinted leaves. *See* **lettuce**

brood sow A sow kept for the production of pigs.

broomcorn *See* **millet**. Seed 44-50 lb/bu.
See Part 2: Poisonous Plants; Seed, Germination

broomweed Several species of plants have this common name;

Genus	Region of Growth
Gutierrezia texana	Southwest U.S.
Scoparia dulcis	tropical and sub-tropical
Corchorus siliquosus	tropical
Sida or Triumfetta	tropical

See Part 2: Poisonous Plants

broth An extract from meat, vegetables, or grain, cooked in water.
See Part 2: Microorganism, Selective and Differential Broths and Media, Water Filtration Plant

Brownian movement Continuous zigzag motion of small particles in a suspension caused by bombardment by molecules of the dispersion medium.

browning Darkening of cut surface of some fruits and vegetables;

$$\text{mono-orthodiphenolic} \xrightarrow[\text{enzymic oxidation}]{\text{phenolase}} \text{quinone} \longrightarrow \text{unstable hydroxyquinone} \xrightarrow[\text{oxidation}]{\text{nonenzymatic}} \text{dark brown polymer}$$

browning reaction (Maillard reaction) A reaction involving amino acids and reducing sugars that determines the color of many processed foods. It causes discoloration of freshly peeled fruits and vegetables and occurs in some canned fish products; may be inhibited by ascorbic or citric acid.

brown rice Hulled, unpolished grain; contains more minerals and vitamins than polished white rice. *See also* **rice; unpolished rice.**

brown sherry A sherry made by blending olorosos with sweetening and coloring wines.

brown sugar Sugar made from sugar cane or beets that has not been as highly refined as white sugar.

Brown Swiss A dairy type breed of cattle that originated in Switzerland; solid color from light to dark brown.
See Part 2: Dairy Cattle Breeds; Gestation Periods; Milk Breeds, Composition; Milk Composition

Brucella A genus of non-motile short rod-shaped to coccoid, gram-negative encapsulated microorganisms; causes brucellosis, contagious abortion (Bang's disease) and undulant fever (Malta fever).
See Part 2: Microbiological Media; Microorganism, Culture Media, Dairy and Food Products; Microorganism, Media

brucellosis (Bang's disease) A cattle disease which causes a loss of a large percentage of calves; calfhood vaccination is available.
See Part 2: Diseases, Food-Borne; Illness from Food; Infectious Diseases, Food-Borne; Microbiological Media

brunoise Finely dried vegetables.

brush Hair at tip of wheat kernel, gynoecium of hop.
See Part 2: Wheat Kernel

Brussels sprouts (*Brassica oleracea* var. *gemmifera*) Auxillary buds of this plant resemble miniature cabbages and are used as a green vegetable; a vegetable whole leaf is used as food.

2 lb fresh	= 1 qt frozen
1 lb fresh	= 4 cups
1 cup fresh	= 100 g (3.6 oz)
1 lb fresh	= 2½ cups cooked
1 cup cooked	= 180 g (6.4 oz)

Storage: May be quick-frozen. If fresh, place in refrigerator crisper (32°F) or plastic bag (90-95% relative humidity); use within 1 to 21 days.
Raw composition: 85% H_2O, 5% protein, 0.4% fat, 8% carbohydrate, 1% ash, pH 6.3.
Size:

1	¾ to 1 in.	3	1.25 to 1.50 in.
2	1 to 1.25 in.	4	1.50 in. or more

See Part 2: Ascorbic Acid; Frozen Food Storage; Iron; Microwave Cooking, Frozen Vegetables; Minerals, Food; Niacin; Phosphorus; Plant Foods, Composition; Potassium; Potassium-Rich Foods; Riboflavin; Storage; Sugar, Vegetables; Thiamin; Vegetable Boiling; Vegetable Composition; Vegetable Cooking; Vegetable Frozen Yield; Vegetable Plants; Vegetables, Boiling Time, Frozen; Vegetables, Canning Dates; Vegetables Classification; Vegetables, Cooking Frozen; Vegetable Servings; Vegetable Storage; Vegetable Yield Frozen, Canned and Fresh; Vitamin C

Brut champagne A very dry, unsweetened, light wine with a piquant yet delicate flavor made in France.

Btu *See* **British thermal unit**

buck A male sheep.

buckeye (*Aesculus*) A poisonous plant.
See Part 2: Poisonous Plants

Buckeye (chicken) An American class of chickens that lays a brown-shelled egg. Color: mahogany, undercolor red; tail feathers, black.

buck-kneed Knees bent slightly forward.

buckling A salted and smoked herring.
See Part 2: Fish, Smoke-Cured

buck shad *See* **shad**

buckwheat (*Fagopyrum esculentum, F. tartaricum,* or *F. emarginatum*) A hardy grasslike herb that produces a 3-cornered seed (kasha or buckwheat groats); 1.6 lb/qt; 48-52 lb/bu.
Whole grain composition: 10% H_2O, 11% protein, 2.5% fat, 75% carbohydrate, 2% ash.
See Part 2: Cereal Composition; Grain Products Composition; Minerals, Food; Pantothenic Acid Content; Seed, Germination

buckwheat bran Covering of buckwheat; 1 lb/qt; 29 lb/bu.

buckwheat flour Gray flour speckled with black made from buckwheat; obtained by sifting buckwheat meal; 100 lb buckwheat flour = 3.5 bu buckwheat.
Composition: 12% H_2O, 6-15% protein, 1-3% fat, 68-80% carbohydrate, 1-2% ash.

buckwheat grits Coarsely ground buckwheat.

buckwheat groats Whole kernel buckwheat cracked without grinding.

buck wool Wool from rams; coarser and with higher shrink than wether or ewe wool.

bud An undeveloped shoot, stem, flower or leaf.
See Part 2: Vegetable Classification

budu Fermented, salted, dried whitebait or anchovies.

budworm Any of several worms that eat plant buds.
See Part 2: Insect Control

buffalo A type of cattle native to western U.S. *See also* **bison.**
See Part 2: Meat and Meat Products Composition; Milk and Cheese Composition; Milk, Mammals, Composition

buffer A mixture of compounds which, when added to a solution, protects it from any substantial change in pH. Such mixtures are usually in solution form, and contain either a weak acid and its related salt or a mixture of two acid salts. Buffering compounds often used are carbonates, phosphates and ammonium salts. The acid-base balance of the blood is controlled by the presence of carbonic (a weak acid) and bicarbonate (its related salt).
See Part 2: Buffer Solutions; pH, Buffer Solutions

buffet A meal in which the dishes are placed on a sideboard, the diners serving themselves and eating either standing up or seated informally.

builders lime A liming material composed of 85% CaO; each lb has the neutralizing equivalent of 1.5 to 1.75 lb of $CaCO_3$ (or approximately this quantity of dolomitic limestone).

bulb The resting state of a plant with a subterraneal bud composed of scale-like overlapping leaves that contains food for regrowth.
See Part 2: Vegetable Classification; Vegetable Composition

bulgur Cracked wheat that retains the bran and germ of the grain; sometimes called parboiled wheat; it is cooked, dried, partly debranned and cracked; in nutrition it resembles whole wheat.

bulk comb honey *See* **chunk honey**

bull Uncastrated male cattle.

bullhead *See* **catfish**

bull hide A hide of a mature male uncastrated cattle weighing from 60 to over 100 lb.

bullish An upward price trend on the market.

bull meat Boneless beef tissue from bull carcasses; boneless beef.

bullock A mature steer, ox or stag.

bullocks heart *See* **anonaceous fruit**

bundle of His (Wilhelm His, Jr., German physician) Connecting length in the heart between the atrioventricular nodes.

bung A natural casing used in the meat trade; in beef it comes from the caecum and in hogs it comes from the terminal end of the large intestine.
See Part 2: **Casings, Animal; Casings, Hog and Beef; Casings, Hog Bungs; Casings, Terms**

Burgundy wine A red or white table wine with a robust fruity flavor produced in the valleys of Saône and Yonne in France; 14% alcohol by volume. *See also* **Chardonnay; Pineau Noir; Sparkling Burgundy.**

burned oyster shells A liming material composed of 55% CaO and 5% MgO; each pound has the neutralizing equivalent of 0.9 to 1.1 lb of $CaCO_3$ (or approx. this quantity of dolomitic limestone).

Burong babi Pork fermented with Ang-kak (red mold grown on rice).

burro Specie of ass that is small in size.

bushel, dry (Imp.) (Br.) A dry measure of volume.
1 bu = 2218.192 cu in.
= 36.368 liter
= 4 Br. pecks (Br.)
= 1.2843 cu ft
= 1.032 bu (U.S.)

bushel (Winchester bushel) (U.S.) (bu) A dry measure of volume and capacity.
1 bu = 2,150.42 cu in.
= 64 pints (U.S.)
= 37.2368 U.S. liquid quarts
= 35.2393 cubic decimeters (dm^3)
= 35.238 liter
= 32 U.S. dry quarts (d. qt.)
= 9.30920 U.S. liquid gallons
= 8 U.S. dry gallons (d. gal)
= 4 pecks (U.S.)
= 1.24446 cu ft
= 0.04609 cu yd;
See Part 2: Canned Yield

bust A ruptured hog.

butane (C_4H_{10}) A gaseous aliphatic hydrocarbon derived from petroleum and used as a fuel and refrigerant.
See Part 2: Refrigerant

butanoic *See* Part 2: Saturated Fatty Acids

butcher cattle Cattle having good flesh.

butcher's pepper Coarsely ground black pepper.

butcher's round Round of beef without the rump.

butcher's wrap A hand-wrapping or packaging procedure in which the object is laid diagonally on paper close to one corner; this corner is placed over the object and the object is rolled to the diagonal corner, bringing the ends of the paper over the object while rolling it.

butt A measure of volume; 1 butt = 2 hogsheads.

butt end sirloin First sirloin taken from the rump end of the wholesale cut loin end.

butter A colorless, semisolid consisting of the glycerides of the fatty acids of cows' milk. It contains a high percentage of butyric acid, from which the word "butter" is derived. It is made by mechanical agitation of milk or cream, which disrupts the protective layer of protein on the fat particles, allowing them to coalesce. After churning, the product is washed and usually salted. Permissible colorants are also added. *See also* **churning.**

21–23 lb milk yield 1 lb butter
1 qt cream yields 1 lb butter
1 oz = 2 tablespoons of butter
1 stick = ½ cup = ¼ lb butter
1 lb = 2 cups
1 cup = 225 g (7.9 oz)
1 lb = 3 cups (whipped)
1 cup whipped = 150 g (5.4 oz)
1 cup butter = 1 cup margarine
= ⅞ cup hydrogenated fat or lard + ½ teaspoon of salt

Storage: Tightly wrap and protect from light

Temperature	Relative humidity	Storage life
32–36°F	80–85	2 mo.
−10 to −20°F	80–85	1 yr

Composition: 9.5–16% H_2O, 0.4–0.6% protein, 81%–88% fat (min. 80% milk fat), 0.4% carbohydrate, 0.5–5.0% ash (2.5% ash-salted butter), 0.5–1.50% curd; pH 6.1–6.4, m.p. 97°F. *See also* **butter (fruit).**

See Part 2: Animal Foods, Composition; Butter and Butter Products, Composition; Calories, Daily Recommendations; Cream, Butter and Frozen Desserts; Dairy Products, Composition; Fats and Oils Composition; Flavor Ingredients, Taste and Flavor Type; Food, Composition; Melting Points, Fats and Oils; Microbiological Standards, Dairy; Milk and Milk Products, Vitamin Content; Minerals, Food; Oils and Fats Composition; Spoilage, Fat in Foods; Storage Times; Unsaturated Fatty Acids; Vitamin A, Daily Recommendations; Vitamin A, Food; Vitamin A, Milk and Milk Products; Vitamin D, Food

butter bean (lima) (Madagascar bean) (***Phaseolus lunatus***) A tropical bean with a large white seed; harvesting begins about 100 days after planting.

buttercup A Mediterranean class of chickens that lays a white-shelled egg.

butterfat The natural fat in cows' milk (glycerides of fatty acids listed below).

28–35°C melting point
0.930–0.940 specific gravity
0.911 specific gravity 40/15°C
1.445–1.449 refractive index (60°C)
26–38 iodine value
221–233 saponification value

Composition (acid)

Acid	%	Acid	%
Butyric	4	Stearic	9
Caproic	2	Arachidic	2
Capric	2	Palmitoleic	5
Lauric	2	Oleic	27
Myristic	11	Linoleic	4
Palmitic	29		

See Part 2: Butter and Butter Products, Composition; Fats and Oils Composition; Fat and Oils, Fatty Acid Composition; Fats and Oils, Physical and Chemical Properties; Fatty Acids, Fats and Oils; Iodine and Saponification Values; Oil or Fat, Characteristics; Refractive Indices, Fats and Oils; Saturated Fatty Acids; Titer, Fats and Oils; Unsaturated Fatty Acids

butterfly chop A thick boneless pork chop, which is folded open to double the original surface area.
See Part 2: Pork Cuts; Pork Loin Cooking

butterfly fillet A double fillet.

butter (fruit) Usually made of large fruits cooked until soft and the pulp passed through a sieve (0 to ½ lb sugar/lb fruit), e.g., apple butter.

butter grade

USDA grades:	Made from:
AA	top quality sweet cream
A	lesser-quality sweet cream
B	sour sweet cream

butter head A variety of head lettuce. *See also* **Boston lettuce; lettuce.**

buttermilk The liquid that remains after milk or cream (sweet or sour) is churned.

1 cup = 245 g (8.5 oz);
1 cup buttermilk = 1 cup sour milk
= 1 cup sweet milk + 1 tablespoon lemon juice (let stand for 5 min)
= 1 cup sweet milk + 1 tablespoon vinegar (let stand for 5 min)
= 1 cup sweet milk + 1¾ teaspoon cream of tartar.

See also **buttermilk, cultured.**

Composition of buttermilk made from skim milk: 90% H_2O, 3.6% protein, 0.1% fat, 5% carbohydrate, 0.7% ash, pH 4.5; Min. 8.25% milk solids other than fat.

Storage: 40°F, use in 4–6 days.

See Part 2: Animal Foods, Composition; Cultured Dairy Products, Composition; Dairy Products, Composition; Dairy Terms; Fluid and Fermented Milks, Composition; Glutamate; Milk and Cheese Composition; Milk and Milk Products, Vitamin

Content; Milk, Concentrated Products; Milk, Dry Products; Minerals, Food; Vitamin A, Milk and Milk Products

buttermilk, cultured Made by treating pasteurized skimmed or part skimmed milk with a lactic acid starter culture; min. 8.25% non-fat milk solids. *See also* **lactic acid.**

butternut (white walnut, *Juglans cinerea*) A tall North American tree that produces an edible nut; the shell is hard and the kernel has a rich, pleasant flavor.

Kernel composition: 4% H_2O, 24% protein, 61% fat, 8% carbohydrate, 3% ash.

See Part 2: Minerals, Food; Protein Factors

buttons White cartilagenous area on the ends of the feather bones of young animals.

See Part 2: Beef Rib Nomenclature; Beef Wholesale Cuts; Bone; Lamb Wholesale Cuts; Pork Wholesale Cuts; Veal Wholesale Cuts

butt tenderloin Ilio-psoas (iliacus and psoas major) muscle; lies ventral to the shaft of the ilium in cross section of sirloin; is the psoas major and psoas minor in pin bone area and lies ventral to the lateral process of lumbar vertebra.

butylated hydroxyanisole (BHA) An antioxidant which needs a synergist to be very effective; it will carry through to the baked product; 0.01% in fat (total antioxidant, 0.02% in combination); 0.003% in smoked dry sausage.

See Part 2: Antioxidant Activity; Antioxidant Mixtures; Antioxidants, Formula; Antioxidant Structure

butylated hydroxytoluene (BHT) An antioxidant; 0.01% in fat (total antioxidant, 0.02% in combination).

See Part 2: Antioxidant Activity; Antioxidant Mixtures; Antioxidants, Formula; Antioxidant Structure

butyric acid $CH_3(CH_2)_2C\begin{smallmatrix}\diagup OH\\ \diagdown\!\!\diagdown O\end{smallmatrix}$ An aliphatic fatty acid occurring in milk fat.

See Part 2: Fatty Acids and Their Properties; Fatty Acids; Fatty Acids, Fats and Oils; Milk, Fatty Acids, Seasonal; Saturated Fatty Acids

by-product *See* Part 2: Packing-House By-Products Composition

Byssochlamys fulva A heat-resistant (30 min at 85°C) mold that causes spoilage and swells in canned fruit.

See Part 2: Rot Spoilage; Spoilage, Carbohydrate Foods

C

C Symbol for the element carbon. Symbol used also for capacitor.

Ca Symbol for the element calcium.

Cabbage (*Brassica oleracea capitata*) A vegetable whose leaf is used as food; a plant whole enlarged terminal bud is used as a green vegetable or salad greens.

Types:

early or new varieties: conical or painted heads

spring cabbage: young cabbage at any time of year

Danish: tight, white, compact heads

savoy: round shape, yellowish wrinkled leaves; mild flavor and makes good cole slaw

red: tight head, deep purple hue (anthocyanin pigments); used for pickling and in salads

Seed 4-8 oz/acre (150 to 300 ft bed space), spacing 12 in. in rows 3 ft apart.

Size:

1 lb fresh = 3½-4½ cups shredded

1 cup shredded = 80 g (2.8 oz)

1 lb fresh = 2 cups cooked

1 cup cooked = 145 g (5.2 oz)

wire-bound crate = 50 lb

western crate (13 × 18 × 21.6 in.) = 80 lb

100 lb fresh cabbage = 8-10 lb dry cabbage

Storage: Separate and discard injured tissue; store in refrigerator (32°F) crisper or plastic bag (90-95% relative humidity); freezing point 31°F; use within 1 week to 2 mo.

Composition	Water (%)	Protein (%)	Fat (%)	Carbohydrate (%)	Ash (%)	pH
Raw	92	1	0.2	5	0.7	5.2-5.4
Dried	4	14	2	72	7	

See also **Chinese cabbage.**

See Part 2: Ascorbic Acid; Calcium Daily Requirements; Calories, Daily Recommendations; Food, Composition; Fruit and Vegetable, Diseases; Microwave Processing Time; Minerals, Food; Minerals, Plant or Animal Tissue; Nicotinic Acid, Food; Nitrate, Vegetables; Nutrients in Crops; Pentosans; Phosphorus; Plant Foods, Composition; Portion Size; Rot Spoilage; Storage; Sugar, Vegetables; Vegetable Boiling; Vegetable Composition; Vegetable Plants; Vegetables, Canning Dates; Vegetables Classification; Vegetable Servings; Vegetables Panned; Vegetable Storage; Vegetable Yield Frozen, Canned and Fresh; Vitamin A, Food; Vitamin C

cabbage worm A cabbage infestation.

See Part 2: Insect Control

cabernet A variety of bluish-black grapes that is fermented to yield the red wines of Bordeaux (clarets).

cacao *See* **cocoa**

See Part 2: Fatty Acids, Fats and Oils; Iodine and Saponification Values; Melting Points, Fats and Oils; Refractive Indices, Fats and Oils; Titer, Fats and Oils; Unsaponifiable Matter

caciocavallo cheese A cheese with a salty-smoky, robust flavor; a dinner or grating cheese in tenpin shape and bound by cord; tan surface, light interior; made from goat or cows' milk; ripening time 3 mo. min., 12 mo. or more for grating.

See Part 2: Cheese Characteristics; Milk and Cheese Composition

cadmium (Cd) A metallic element; at. no. 48; at. wt. 112.41; Group IIB of Periodic Table; oxidation state +2; electron configuration 2-8-18-18-2

orbit K L M N O

Cadmium and its compounds are poisonous.

See Part 2: Water Drinking Standards

caecum *See* **cecum**

Caesar salad A salad made of romaine, grated cheese, olive oil and croutons, over which a raw egg is broken before final mixing.

café au lait Equal parts of hot coffee and scalded milk (French).

café noir Black coffee (French).

caffeine A plant alkaloid which acts as a stimulant; it occurs in coffee, cola, tea, etc. It increases pulse rate, accelerates heart action and sometimes causes high blood pressure.

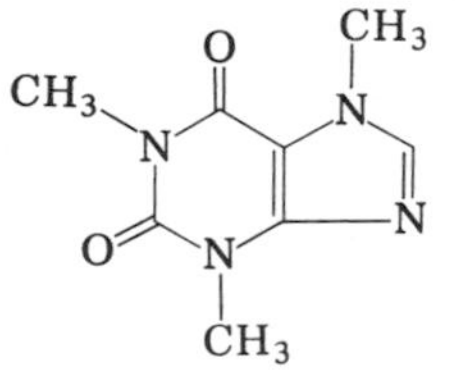

	Mg caffeine per fl oz	% in plant
Coffee	16-18	1
Chocolate milk	14	
Tea	13	2
Instant coffee	11	
Cola beverage	4-6	1.5
Cocoa	0.3	

cainito (*Chrysophyllum cainito*) Star apple from the word, cayomito; a tropical 500 to

1000 g berry; a West Indies small tree grown for its apple-shaped, greenish-purple edible fruit.
See Part 2: Fruit Classification; Fruit Storage

cake A mixture of flour, milk, egg, sugar, flavoring, and leavening agent, packed into a mass and baked; one 3-layer cake (10″ diam.) = 50 servings; frozen (0°F) storage life 4-6 mo.
See Part 2: Calories, Daily Recommendations; Frozen Food Storage; Grain Products Composition; Portion Size; Stabilizers, Thickeners; Thiamin, Food

cake flour *See* **soft-wheat flour**

cake mix A commercially prepared mixture containing most cake ingredients; only water and sometimes eggs need be added. *See also* **cake.**

cala Cured and smoked picnic (lower portion of pork shoulder).

calabrese *See* **broccoli**

calamondin A small, loose skin, acid orange.
See Part 2: Fruit Storage

calcareous A soil that is high in calcium carbonate ($CaCO_3$) or its derivative, lime (CaO).

calciferol $C_{28}H_{43}OH$ Vitamin D_2, which can be produced by ultraviolet irradiation of ergosterol.

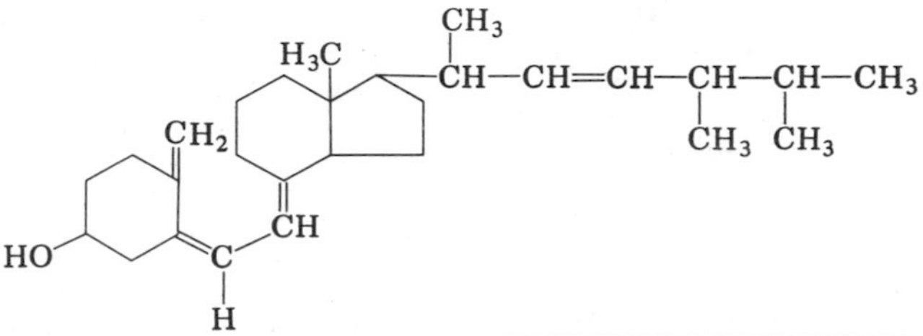

calcium (Ca) An alkaline-earth element; at. no. 20; at. wt. 40.08; Group IIA of the Periodic Table; oxidation state +2; electron configuration 2-8-8-2
orbit K L M N
daily requirements 0.8 to 2 g
body functions: bone and tooth formation, contraction of muscles, clotting of blood, irritability of nerves
occurrence in foods:

High	Low
milk & milk products	seed
vegetables	lean meat
egg yolk	

See Part 2: Beans, Peas and Nuts; Calcium; Calcium, Daily Requirements; Cereal Fortification; Cereal Nutrient Content; Cereals, Vitamin and Mineral Content; Cheese Composition; Composition of Food; Concentrated and Dried Milk Products; Creams, Butter and Frozen Desserts; Dairy Products, Composition; Egg Composition; Egg Products, Nutritive Value; Fats and Oils, Composition; Fish and Shellfish Composition; Fluid and Fermented Milks, Composition; Food, Composition; Fruit Composition; Grain Analysis; Grain Products Composition; Lemon Juice Composition; Lime Juice Composition; Macaroni and Noodles Composition; Manure Analysis; Maple Syrup Composition; Meat Composition; Meat, Nutritive Value; Milk Composition; Minerals, Food; Minerals, Plant or Animal Tissue; Normal Solutions; Nutrients in Crop; pH and Availability of Plant Nutrients; Plant Foods, Composition; Poultry Composition; Recommended Daily Dietary Allowance; Sausage Composition; Soups Composition; Sugars and Sweets Composition; Tomato and Tomato Products, Composition; Variety Meat Percentage of Daily Recommended Allowances; Vegetable Composition; Water Drinking Standards; Wheat, Minerals

calcium acetate $(CH_3COO)_2Ca \cdot H_2O$ Used as a source of acetic acid and as a sequestrant and mold-control agent in baked goods.

calcium acid phosphate $Ca(H_2PO_4)_2$ Used in baking powder, self-rising flour; same as superphosphate.

calcium arsenate $Ca_3(AsO_4)_2$ A poisonous insecticide.

calcium carbonate $CaCO_3$ The calcium salt of carbonic acid (H_2CO_3). Rocks of the sedimentary class are chiefly composed of $CaCO_3$; it is thus one of the most abundant inorganic materials on earth. It is the primary source of lime.
See Part 2: Fertilizer Materials; Liming Materials; Normal Solutions

calcium carbonate equivalent A value used in calculating soil sweetening efficiency: = % $CaCO_3$ + 1.19 (% $MgCO_3$).

calcium caseinate A complex molecule that may be considered the calcium salt of the protein casein, present in cows' milk in about 3% concentration. Used in cheese making.

calcium chloride $CaCl_2$ Approved as a sequestrant and general-purpose food additive; used in evaporated milk up to 0.1% by weight.
See Part 2: Boiling Points, Sodium Chloride, Calcium Chloride; Normal Solutions

calcium cyanamide $CaCN_2$ A nitrogenous compound used as a fertilizer ingredient.
See Part 2: Fertilizer Materials

calcium cyclamate *See* **cyclamate**

calcium hydrate *See* **calcium hydroxide**

calcium hydroxide $Ca(OH)_2$ Hydrated lime, made by adding water to calcium oxide; used as a fertilizer ingredient.

See Part 2: Liming Materials; Normal Solution; Reagents, Normal Solution

calcium hypochlorite $Ca(OCl)_2$ An inorganic chemical used for chlorination of water, bleaching, and disinfectant; chloride of lime, chlorinated lime, and HTH have a high content of this compound.
See Part 2: Chlorine Availability; Chlorine Compounds; Sanitizers

calcium metaphosphate $Ca(PO_3)_2$ A fertilizer material: 0-63-0.

calcium nitrate $Ca(NO_3)_2 \cdot 4H_2O$ A fertilizer ingredient.
See Part 2: Fertilizer Materials

calcium oxide CaO Synonymous with lime. Obtained by heating limestone (calcium carbonate) in a furnace. Used as a fertilizer ingredient and in poultry feeds.
See Part 2: Liming Materials; Normal Solutions

calcium pectinate A complex salt of the polysaccharide pectin, derived from citrus or apple sources; can be used as an edible gel coating for meat products. *See also* **pectin.**

calcium phosphate A hydrated compound existing in several modifications.
(1) calcium phosphate, dibasic; dicalcium phosphate; $CaHPO_4 \cdot 2H_2O$. Animal feeds; fertilizer ingredient; dough conditioner.
(2) calcium phosphate, monobasic; monocalcium phosphate; calcium biphosphate; acid calcium phosphate $CaH_4(PO_4)_2 \cdot H_2O$. Ingredient of baking powders, fertilizers; pH control.
(3) calcium phosphate, tribasic; tricalcium phosphate; precipitated calcium phosphate; $Ca_3(PO_4)_2 \cdot H_2O$. Anticaking agent; pH control; fertilizer ingredient; tenderizer.

calcium silicate slag A liming material that is equal to 0.8 lb of dolomitic limestone per each pound used.

calf Young bovine species (cattle), either sex, usually under 12 months old. Dressing percentage 55.5%.
See Part 2: Cattle

calf carcass The body of a bovine animal 3 to 8 months old at slaughter.

calf knees Knees bent too far to the rear.

Calgon Proprietary name for sodium hexametaphosphate. Used for water softening and corrosion and scale prevention. *See also* **hexametaphosphate.**

californium (Cf) A synthetic radioactive element of the actinide series; Group IIIB of Periodic Table; at. no. 98; mass number of most stable isotope 249; oxidation state +3; electron configuration 2-8-18-32-28-8-2
orbit K L M N O P Q

calnitro A neutral fertilizer material made from ⅔ ammonium nitrate (NH_4NO_3) and ⅓ dolomitic limestone; 20.5-0-0.

Calorie *See* **kilocalorie**

calorie (gram calorie) (small calorie) (standard calorie) The heat required to raise the temperature of 1 gram of water from 15 to 16°C.
1000 gram calories = 1 kilocalorie (kcal)
1 calorie = 0.001 kilocalorie
= 4.186×10^7 ergs
= 4.186 joules
= 3.968×10^{-3} Btu
= 3.0874 ft-lb
See Part 2: Beans, Peas and Nuts; Beef Percentages of Daily Recommended Allowances; Calories, Basal, Per 24 Hours; Calories, Daily Recommendations; Cereal Nutrient Content; Cherry Composition; Composition of Food; Dairy Products, Composition; Egg Composition; Egg Products Nutritive Value; Fats and Oils, Composition; Fish and Shellfish Composition; Flour, Extraction Rates; Food, Composition; Fruit Composition; Grain Analysis; Grain Products Composition; Lamb Percentages of Daily Recommended Allowances; Lime Juice Composition; Macaroni and Noodles Composition; Meat and Meat Products Composition; Meat Composition; Meat, Nutritive Value; Milk and Cheese Composition; Oils and Fats Composition; Plant Foods, Composition; Pork, Percentages of Daily Recommended Allowances; Poultry Composition; Pulses, Nuts and Seeds Composition; Recommended Daily Dietary Allowance; Sausage Composition; Sausage Nutritive Value; Soups Composition; Starches and Starchy Roots Composition; Sugars and Sweets Composition; Sugars and Syrups Composition; Tomato and Tomato Products, Composition; Turkey Composition; Variety Meat Percentage of Daily Recommended Allowances; Vegetable Composition; Wheat, Parts of Grain

caltrop *See* **water chestnut**

calvados *See* **cider**

calyx The outer portion of flowering parts of plants.

calza *See* Part 2: Iodine and Saponification Values

camel A large ruminant quadruped with a characteristic hump (Arabian or dromedary) or two humps (Central Asiatic) used for work and food (meat and milk).
See Part 2: Gestation Periods; Milk and Cheese Composition; Milk, Mammals, Composition

camembert A very soft dessert cheese having a creamy yellow interior, edible thin whitish crust, and pungent aroma; made from (whole) cows' milk; wheel shape, smaller in size than coulommiers; mild to pungent in flavor; ripened 4-5 weeks by external molds.
Storage: Refrigerate, tightly covered; use within 2 weeks.
Composition: 50-52% H_2O, 17-20% protein, 25-26% fat, 2% carbohydrate, 4% ash, 2.5% salt, pH 7.4.
See Part 2: Cheese Characteristics; Cheese Composition; Cheese, Vitamin Content; Glutamate; Milk and Cheese Composition; Milk and Milk

Products, Vitamin Content; Vitamin A, Milk and Milk Products

camphor $C_{10}H_{16}O$ A product derived by distillation of a wood native to Taiwan; has a strong, sharp odor; it is also synthesized from pinene; used as a moth-proofing agent.
See Part 2: Essential Oils

can A metal container of various sizes used for preserving heat-processed foods; made of steel coated with an extremely thin electroplated layer of tin and a further coating of a lacquer or enamel composed of a polymerized natural or synthetic resin; the body is lap-jointed and soldered; *see also* **canning** and entries under **canned.**

Size	Measure (cups)	Weight (lb)	(oz)
No. 10	13	6	10
No. 5	7	3	8
No. 3 cyl	5 & 3/4	3	3
No. 3	4		33
No. 2½	3½		28
No. 2	2½		20
No. 303	2		16
No. 1 tall	2		16
No. 300	1 & 3/4		15
12 oz	1½		12
No. 1	1 & 1/3		11
Picnic	1¼		10½
8 oz	1		8
No. ½ (8 oz)	1		8

See Part 2: Cans, Sizes; Cans, Conversion Table; Cans, Equivalent Sizes; Canned Spoilage Manifestations; Canned, Spoilage Related to pH; Canned Yield; Cans, Construction; Cherries, Canned Weights; Frozen Food Containers; Fruit and Vegetables, Cost Per Serving

Canadian bacon Pork sirloin muscle that has been cured, placed in an artificial casing and smoked.
See Part 2: Broiling Time and Temperature; Pork Cookery; Pork, Cooking; Pork, Cooking Methods; Pork Cuts; Pork Cuts and Uses; Pork Loin Cooking; Roasting, Time and Temperature

cananga An essential oil obtained by distilling flowers of the *Cananga odorata* plant native to Java. Used as a flavoring agent.
See Part 2: Essential Oils

canapé A small, shaped, white, rye or brown toasted bread or cracker covered with a well-seasoned spread; it is usually garnished with brightly colored food and served as an appetizer.

canary grass (*Phalaris canaiensis* or *Lepidium* or *peppergrass*) Any of a number of grass seeds used to feed birds.
See Part 2: Seed, Germination

cancellated bone tissue A tissue found inside most bones; it has the appearance of a sponge.

candelilla A light brown wax obtained from the under side of the leaves of certain plants in Latin America and Texas. Used for waterproofing, paper coating, etc.
See Part 2: Wax

Candida albicans A yeast-like fungus that may cause human infection.
See Part 2: Microorganism, Media

candida BCG agar *See* Part 2: Microorganism, Media

candied fruit Fruit impregnated with syrup until sugar concentration is high enough to inhibit bacterial growth; the fruit is then washed and dried.

candle power Illumination power of a standard sperm oil candle; 1 candle power (spherical) = 12.566 lumens. *See also* **foot candle; lux.**

candy To cook in sugar or syrup; a sugar-flavored confection. *See also* **confection; caramel.**

Description	Temperature of Syrup (F°)	(C°)	Product
Syrup	220-230	104-110	
Thread (spins thread when dropped from fork)	230-234	110-112	Syrup
Soft ball (ball in cold water flattens when removed)	234-238	112-114	Fondant, fudge, panocha
Medium ball	238-244	114-118	
Firm (stiff) ball (firm in cold water, does not flatten in fingers)	244-248	118-120	Caramels
Hard ball (pliable but holds shape)	248-254	120-123	Divinity, Marshmallows, Popcorn balls
Very hard ball	254-265	123-124	Divinity, Marshmallows, Popcorn balls
Light (soft) crack (threads are hard but not brittle in cold water)	265-285	124-141	Butterscotch, Taffy
Hard crack (threads are hard and brittle in cold water)	290-300	143-149	Brittle, Glacé
Caramel stage	320-360	160-182	

See Part 2: Candy Storage; Storage Times; Sugars and Sweets Composition

cane sugar *See* **sucrose**

cane syrup *See* **top syrup**

canned fruit A fruit such as peaches, pears, grapefruit, etc. that has been packed in cans and heat-treated. *See also* **canning.** There are three grades: A (Fancy); B (Choice); C (Standard).
See Part 2: Fruit Servings Per Pound; Storage, Dry

canned goods Any food product that has been preserved by canning. *See also* **canning.**
See Part 2: Storage Times; Thermophiles; Vegetables, Canned Grades; Vegetables, Canning Dates

canned ham A ham that has been preserved by canning.
See Part 2: Pork Storage

canned meat A meat or meat product that has been preserved by canning.
See Part 2: Meat and Meat Products Composition; Meat Composition

canned pork A pork product that has been preserved by canning. Maximum increase in weight is 8% over fresh uncured weight. *See also* **canning.**

canned vegetables Vegetables (beans, peas, corn, beets, etc.) that have been preserved by canning.
See Part 2: Storage, Dry; Vegetables, Canned Grades; Vegetables, Canning Dates; Vegetable Yield, Canned and Frozen; Vegetable Yield, Frozen, Canned and Fresh

canner Thin, aged cattle used for boneless beef and canning.
See Part 2: Grades, Meat

cannery A factory devoted to canning food products, often with a high degree of automation.
See Part 2: Wastes, Agricultural and Industrial

canning Preservation of a foodstuff by enclosing it in a sealed air-tight container and heating under high-pressure steam for specified periods of time at temperatures from 190°F for acidic foods to 250°F for other types. The heat treatment is essential to destroy bacterial spores (sterilization). *See also* **can.**

cannon Live animal area on front legs below knee and above fetlock; on rear legs below hock and above fetlock; carcass. *See also* **shank bone.**

can size *See* **can**

cantal A semi-hard cheese fairly strong in flavor; matures after 2½ mo.
See Part 2: Cheese, Vitamin Content; Milk and Milk Products, Vitamin Content; Vitamin A, Milk and Milk Products

cantaloupe A species of muskmelon; 50 lb/bu; seed 2-3 lb/acre; space in hills 2 ft apart in 5-foot rows; thin to 2 plants/hill. 5 in. diameter = 1⅔ lb; Jumbo crate (13 × 13 × 22.1 in.) = 83 lb; pH 6.1-7.1.
See Part 2: Calcium, Daily Requirements; Food, Composition; Fruit and Vegetable, Diseases; Fruit, Availability; Fruit Composition; Fruit Frozen Yield; Minerals, Food; Plant Foods, Composition; Potassium-Rich Foods; Protein Factors; Storage; Transit Temperature; Vegetable Storage; Vitamin A; Vitamin A, Daily Recommendations; Vitamin C

Cantino PYG agar *See* Part 2: Microorganism, Media

cap A natural casing used in the meat trade, made of pork caecum.
See Part 2: Casings, Animal; Casings, Hog and Beef; Casings, Terms

capacitance The ability to store an electrical charge.

capacitor (C) 2 conductors separated by an insulator –| |–

q = quantity of electricity necessary to charge the capacitor in coulomb ($q = Ce_c$).
C = capacitance of capacitor in farad, ratio of charge to voltage
e_c = potential across capacitor

The larger the conductors and the thinner the insulator, the higher the capacitance value.

capacola (capicola, capicolla, cappicola) A meat product made from boneless cala butts and seasoned with red pepper pods. *See also* **capocollo.**
See Part 2: Sausage Identification; Sausage, Types.

cape gooseberry *See* **gooseberry**

caper (*Capparis spinosa*) An unopened bud of the Mediterranean shrub (caperbush); used as flavoring in cooking, and as a sauce.

capicola *See* **capacola**

capicolla *See* **capacola**

capillary A small vein, 0.0007 in. in diameter.

capocollo (coppa) Trimmed center portion of a pork shoulder that is dry-cured for several weeks; it is rolled in paprika and red pepper, heat-processed (may be smoked) and air-dried; may or may not be cooked. *See also* **capacola.**

capon A desexed young male chicken less than 8 mo. old that was castrated when 6 weeks old or implanted with a female sex hormone.
See Part 2: Poultry Dressing Percentage; Poultry Roasting; Poultry Yield

cappicola *See* **capacola**

capric acid (decanoic acid) $CH_3(CH_2)_8C(=O)OH$ A 10-carbon saturated fatty acid (glyceride) found in butter, coconut and palm oil.
See Part 2: Fat and Oils, Fatty Acid Composition; Fatty Acids; Fatty Acids, Fats and Oils; Fatty Acids and Their Properties; Milk, Fatty Acids, Seasonal; Saturated Fatty Acids

caproic acid (hexanoic acid) $CH_3(CH_2)_4C(=O)OH$ A 6-carbon saturated fatty acid found in butter, coconut and palm oil.
See Part 2: Fatty Acids; Fatty Acids, Fats and Oils; Fatty Acids and Their Properties; Milk, Fatty Acids, Seasonal; Saturated Fatty Acids

caproleic acid An unsaturated fatty acid found in vegetable oils.
See Part 2: Unsaturated Fatty Acids

caprylic acid $CH_3(CH_2)_6C(=O)OH$ An 8-carbon saturated acid found in butter, coconut and palm oil.

See Part 2: Fat and Oil, Fatty Acid Composition; Fatty Acids; Fatty Acids, Fats and Oils; Fatty Acid Properties; Milk, Fatty Acids, Seasonal; Saturated Fatty Acids

capsicum (*Capsicum*) A classification which in-includes many essential spices: cayenne pepper, chili pepper, chili powder, hot red pepper, paprika, pimiento, tabasco.

capsule ink India ink used to stain bacteria and the unstained capsule is delineated by the ink; material used in the differentiation and serological identification of *Klebsiella* microorganisms.
See Part 2: Microorganism, Media

carabao Water buffalo.
See Part 2: Meat and Meat Products Composition; Milk and Cheese Composition; Milk, Mammals, Composition

carambola A small tree that bears 3 to 5 in. long, ribbed, yellow fruit; the juice and flavor vary from sweet to acid; it is consumed fresh, as tarts, in preserves and as a drink; the acid-sweet fruit is star-shaped in cross section.
Raw composition: 90% H_2O, 0.7% protein, 0.5% fat, 8% carbohydrate, 0.4% ash.

caramel (burnt sugar) (1) An amorphous brown material obtained upon heating carbohydrates; often used as a coloring for soft drinks, food, candy and bakery products. (2) A confection cooked to a stiff paste.
See Part 2: Colors Permanently Listed; Minerals (Trace), Limits; Sugars and Sweets Composition

caramelization Sucrose (sugar) heated past the melting point so that it decomposes, gives off water and turns slightly brown.

carapace One-piece shell covering the head and thorax (body and tail) of a lobster or turtle.

caraway (*Carum carvi* L.) A dried fruit (seed) of the parsley family; it has a distinctive flavor and is used as a spice. Seed is hard, with 5 ridges, gray-brown in color; ⅛-³⁄₁₆ in. in length; curved and tapered at the ends; used in pastries, soups, breads, cheese and kummel liqueur; immature leaves used in soup; not more than 8% total ash; not more than 1.5% HCl-insoluble ash.
See Part 2: Essential Oils; Flavoring Agents, Natural

carbamide *See* **urea**

carbocyclic A ring structure containing only carbon atoms in the ring.

carbohydrate $C_x(H_2O)_y$ 75% of dry weight of a plant is composed of this class of substances; it is composed of C, H and O and contains the saccharose group

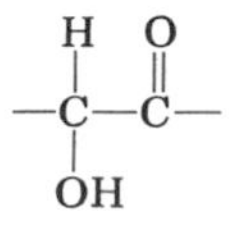

The hydrogen and oxygen occur in the same ratio as in water. Carbohydrates include all sugars and polysaccharides; starches; and all forms of cellulose.
See Part 2: Bananas Composition; Beans, Peas and Nuts; Cereal Nutrient Content; Cherry Composition; Composition of Food; Concentrated and Dried Milk Products; Corn Kernel Composition; Cultured Dairy Products, Composition; Dairy Products, Composition; Egg Composition; Egg Products, Nutritive Value; Egg Specifications; Fats and Oils, Composition; Fish and Shellfish Composition; Flour, Extraction Rates; Food, Composition; Fruit Composition; Grain Products Composition; Macaroni and Noodles Composition; Meat and Meat Products Composition; Meat Composition; Meat, Nutritive Value; Milk and Cheese Composition; Milk Composition; Oils and Fats Composition; Plant Foods, Composition; Poultry Composition; Pulses, Nuts and Seeds Composition; Sausage Composition; Seed, Chemical Composition; Soups, Composition; Spoilage, Carbohydrate Foods; Starches and Starchy Roots Composition; Sugars and Sweets Composition; Sugars and Syrups Composition; Tomato and Tomato Products, Composition; Vegetable Composition; Wheat, Carbohydrate Composition; Wheat, Parts of Grain

carbohydrate equivalent A value that measures the fattening power of a ration; = % protein (1.9) + % fat (2.5) + % carbohydrate.

carbolic acid *See* **phenol**

carbon (C) A non-metallic element; at no. 6; at. wt. 12.011; Group IV A of Periodic Table; electron configuration 2-4;
orbit K L
oxidation states +2, +4, −4. Carbon is present in all organic matter; it has the unique ability to form four covalent bonds, thus readily combining with itself and other nonmetallic elements to form hydrocarbons, carbohydrates, alcohols, amino acids, and many other types of organic molecules. *See also* **photosynthesis.**
See Part 2: Manure Analysis

carbon, activated A pure form of carbon which has been made porous by destructive distillation of carbonaceous materials followed by treatment with steam or CO_2—a process called activation. Cellulose residues, coal, coconut shells, coke, lignite, peat or sawdust are used. It is used to decolorize or deodorize food; the tremendous surface area of the microporous carbon serves to adsorb molecules of odors and colors in colloidal suspension.

carbonate A salt or ester of carbonic acid (H_2CO_3) characterized by the divalent CO_3 group.

carbonated beverage A supersaturated solution of CO_2 and H_2O under pressure; a beverage made by absorbing carbon dioxide (15 to 75 lb of gas pressure/sq in., which is 1 to 5 volumes of gas) in potable water; other ingredients in-

clude sweetening agents (dry or liquid sugars, invert sugar, dextrose, fructose, corn syrup, glucose, sorbitol or non-nutrient sweeteners), acids (acetic, adipic, citric, fumaric, gluconic, lactic, malic, tartaric and phosphoric), flavors (derived from fruit, vegetables, bark, roots and leaves or artificial flavor), color (food or artificial color), preservatives and numerous optional ingredients.
See Part 2: Beverage Carbonated, Ingredients; Microbiological Media

carbon dioxide CO_2 An inorganic compound; a colorless, odorless gas at room temperature, 1.5 times as dense as air; a volatile colorless liquid at -37°C; a white, snow-like solid at -78°C, which volatilizes directly into gas at room temperature (sublimes). It is nontoxic and noncombustible, and is the end product of combustion and respiration. It is present in air in concentrations of from 0.02 to 0.04%. It is essential in the photosynthetic reaction. Its uses and properties are:
(1) Food preservation (refrigeration storage of fresh fruits and meats)
(2) Carbonation of beverages
(3) Leavening agent in baked goods, resulting from acid-carbonate reaction in baking powders
Critical temperature 87.9°F (31.0°C); pressure 1071 psia; b.p. (sublimes) -109.3°F (-78.5°C); heat absorbed during sublimation 247 Btu per lb; solid density 97.5 lb/cu ft; f.p. -69.9°F (-50.6°C).
1 lb solid = 8.7 cu ft gas at 70°C at 1 atm pressure. *See also* **Dry Ice** and **carbonated beverage.**
See Part 2: Carbon Dioxide Dissolved in Water; Carbon Dioxide, Weight and Volume; Refrigerant

carbon disulfide (CS_2) Highly flammable inorganic liquid. Has lowest autoignition point of any liquid (212°F). Used as solvent and fumigant.
See Part 2: Fumigants

carbonic acid H_2CO_3 A weak acid formed by the combination of CO_2 and H_2O; the CO_2 may be removed from H_2O by boiling.

$$H_2CO_3 \rightleftharpoons H^+ + HCO_3^- \qquad K_1 = 4.2 \times 10^{-7}$$
$$HCO_3^- \rightleftharpoons H^+ + CO_3^{--} \qquad K_2 = 4.8 \times 10^{-11}$$
$$H_2CO_3 \rightleftharpoons 2H^+ + CO_3^{--} \qquad K_T = 2 \times 10^{-17}$$

carbon monoxide CO A highly toxic inorganic gas resulting from incomplete combustion, as in automobile exhausts; it combines with hemoglobin in the blood 200 times as readily as oxygen.

carbon tetrachloride CCl_4 A liquid chlorinated hydrocarbon which may be used as a fumigant. Its toxicity has caused it to be prohibited from household use, as a cleaning agent or as a fire extinguisher.
See Part 2: Fumigants

carbonyl group $-\underset{\underset{O}{\Vert}}{C}-$ Occurs in aldehydes, ketones and organic acids. Also forms coordination compounds with metals; nickel carbonyl is extremely poisonous as it gives off carbon monoxide.

carboxyl group $-\underset{\underset{O}{\Vert}}{C}-OH$ Occurs in carboxylic and fatty acids. Usually written COOH.

carboxymethylcellulose (CMC; **sodium carboxymethylcellulose**) A synthetic water-soluble gum (polymer) used as a stabilizing and thickening agent in such foods as ice cream, dairy substitutes, puddings, fruit concentrates, sauces, and baked and frozen products. Since the reaction occurs in an alkaline medium (Na) it is also called sodium carboxymethylcellulose.
See Part 2: Stabilizers, Thickeners

carcass (carcase) The dressed body of a slaughtered animal, offal having been removed. MID definition: all parts, including viscera, of a slaughtered animal which are capable of being used as human food.
See Part 2: Edible Meat and Chilled Carcass; Pork Carcass, Retail Yield; Pork Chart

carcinogen A substance that causes cancer in experimental animals or in man, for example, benzopyrene, benzidine and phenanthrene. The list of known or suspected carcinogens includes several hundred compounds (some of which are insecticides), and is constantly increasing.

cardamom (cardamon) (*Elettaria cardamomum Maton*) Tiny black seeds of a plant of the ginger family used for spices; buff-colored pods have been bleached but the dark ones have not. Seeds containing the spicy essence are enclosed in a capsule; they are harvested and carefully dried to prevent splitting of this protective covering. Dried seeds have not more than 8% total ash; not more than 3% acid-insoluble ash.
See Part 2: Flavoring Agents, Natural

cardoon (*Cynara cardunculus*) A plant similar to the artichoke that is grown for its leaf-stalks that are blanched and eaten as celery, in salads, and in soups.
See Part 2: Vegetable Plants

carmine A brilliant red or purplish coloring substance obtained from cochineal (insect) and used to color food and stain biological specimens; can be decolorized with 0.1 to 1% HCl; aluminum lake of carminic acid.

carminic acid $C_{22}H_{20}O_{13}$ The compound responsible for the color of cochineal.

carnauba The hardest wax known, obtained from a Brazilian palm.
See Part 2: Wax

carob bean gum *See* **locust bean gum**

carob gum A vegetable gum containing polysaccharides.

See Part 2: Gums and Gelling Agents; Gum Distribution

carob pod (Saint John's bread) The flat leathery seed pods of the carob tree, used as a chocolate substitute.

carob powder A flour-like powder made from ground carob pod; it resembles cocoa and is used as a chocolate substitute; 3 teaspoons carob powder plus 2 tablespoons of water or milk = 1 square of unsweetened chocolate.
Composition: 11% H_2O, 4% protein, 1% fat, 81% carbohydrate, 2% ash.

carob seed gum *See* **locust bean gum**

carotene $C_{40}H_{56}$ A yellow organic pigment found in green plants and carrots; can be converted by the animal body to vitamin A. Used as a coloring agent. *See also* **beta-carotene.**
See Part 2: Colors Permanently Listed; Histochemical Test; Lime Juice Composition; Vitamin Sources, Functions, and Stability

carotenoid A class of pigments, e.g., carotene (carrots); xanthophyll (yellow corn); lycopene (tomatoes), apricots, lobster, oranges. There are many kinds of carotenoids and some have Vitamin A activity.

carpal bone Fore-foot bones located above the metacarpal bones.
See Part 2: Bone

carpel A one-celled ovary or fruit.

carpet grass A perennial plant used for lawns.
See Part 2: Seed, Germination

carpet wool A rough coarse wool; classification of breeds that produce this type of wool, e.g., Blackfaced Highland Breed.
See Part 2: Sheep Breeds

carrageen (carragheen) (Irish moss) (*Chondrus crispus*) (*Gigartina stellata*) A red algae seaweed which grows in the North Atlantic from which carrageenan is produced; the gum extracted is used as an emulsifier in many foods; it may form both aqueous and milk gels.
See Part 2: Gum Characteristics; Gums, Physicochemical Properties; Gums and Gelling Agents; Minerals, Trace, Limits; Stabilizers, Thickeners

carrageenan (carrageenin) A phycocolloid extracted from carrageen and used in foods as an emulsifier. *See also* **carrageen; phycocolloid.**

carré de l'est A soft, mild-tasting, square-shaped, floury rind cheese which is made from pasteurized cows' milk; packed in square wooden chip boxes.

carré demi-sel A creamy-textured, mild-flavored, slightly salted cheese made from pasteurized cows' milk and cream.

carrot (*Daucus carota*) A biennial herb that has an orange cylindrical to spherical root; the root is high in vitamin A (carotene) and sugar content and is used for human food and livestock feed.
Storage: Remove tops (increases storage life) and store covered (90–95% relative humidity) in refrigerator (32°F); use within 1 week to 4 mo.; frozen (0°F) storage 1 year.

one 5½ × 1 in. carrot = 50 g
1 lb without top = 3 cups = 2½ cups shredded
2–3 lb fresh without tops = 1 qt canned
2½–3 lb fresh without tops = 1 qt frozen
1 bu fresh without tops = 50 to 60 lb = 17 – 22 qt canned
1 western crate (13 × 13 × 22.5 in.) bunched = 75 lb
100 lb fresh carrots = 10–12 lb dry carrots

	H_2O (%)	Protein (%)	Fat (%)	Carbohydrate (%)	Ash (%)	pH
Raw	88	1–2	0.2	10	0.8	4.9–5.3
Dried	4	4	1.4	85	6	
Canned juice						5.2–5.8

See Part 2: Calories, Daily Recommendations; Canned Yield; Essential Oils; Food, Composition; Frozen Food Storage; Fruit and Vegetable, Diseases; Glutamate; Microwave Cooking, Frozen Vegetables; Minerals, Food; Niacin; Nicotinic Acid, Food; Nitrate, Vegetables; Organic Acids in Fruits and Vegetables; Pectin Content; pH Values of Biological Materials; Plant Foods, Composition; Portion Size; Potassium; Rot Spoilage; Standards, Processed Fruit and Vegetable Products; Storage; Sugar, Vegetables; Tocopherols; Vegetable Boiling; Vegetable Composition; Vegetable Cooking; Vegetable Frozen Yield; Vegetable Plants; Vegetables, Boiling Time, Frozen; Vegetables, Canning Dates; Vegetables, Classification; Vegetables, Cooking Frozen; Vegetable Servings; Vegetables Panned; Vegetable Storage; Vegetable Yield; Vegetable Yield, Canned and Frozen; Vegetable Yield, Frozen, Canned and Fresh; Vitamin A; Vitamin A, Daily Recommendations; Vitamin A, Food

cartilage Strong, elastic connective tissue associated with the bony system of the body.
See Part 2: Bone Age

carving Cutting a cooked roast or fowl into portions for serving.
See Part 2: Beef Rib Carving; Ham Carving; Lamb Crown Roast Carving; Lamb Leg Carving; Pork Loin Carving

caryopsis A grain in which the seed coat is attached to the ovary wall, the fruit and seed forming a single grain (i.e., wheat, barley).

cascade A variety of birdsfoot trefoil.

cascarilla oil Sweetwood bark oil; an essential oil.

case An enclosure, usually of standard size to hold a given quantity of units.
See Part 2: Cans, Equivalent Sizes

case hardening A crusty outside layer formed on a food product by heat and chemical action.

casei factor *See* **folic acid**

casein A phosphoprotein in milk; major protein fraction of milk; 3% of milk; purest dairy form is low-fat cottage cheese; 2.5 lb from 100 lb skim milk; pH 4.6 (isoelectric point). It is clearly associated with calcium. *See also* calcium caseinate.

Composition: 8-12% moisture, 83-84% protein, 1.5% fat, ash 2.1%.

See Part 2: Dairy Products, Composition; Glutamate; Milk, Amino Acids; Milk and Milk Products, Vitamin Content; Milk Composition; Milk, Species

caseinate Casein solubilized with an alkaline substance, e.g., sodium caseinate and calcium caseinate. Caseinates improve smoothness and texture of foods.

casein soy peptone agar *See* Part 2: Microbiological Examination of Dairy Products

Caserta pepperoni A meat product consisting of 75% pork and 25% beef; it originated in Italy.

cashew nut (*Anacardium occidentale*) A hard-shell nut used for food and oil; a medium-size tree that will grow in dryer areas and produces a large fleshy "apple" below which hangs a single nut; the nut kernel must be roasted and shelled. Kaju is a fermented liquor made from the cashew "apples". Cashew shells contain an oil that is used in varnishes, resins, etc.

Composition: 5% H_2O, 17% protein, 46% fat, 29% carbohydrate, 3% ash. 1 lb shelled cashew nuts = 4.6 lb unshelled.

See Part 2: Beans, Peas and Nuts; Fruit Classification; Fruit Storage; Iodine and Saponification Values

casing A membranous case used to encase sausages and various processed meats. Colors used in casings are FDA-approved colors.

hog bung casing:

Grade	Width (in.)	No. pieces/ tierce
Export	over 2⅛	400
Large prime	1 15/16-2⅛	500
Medium prime	1 12/16-1 15/16	550
Special prime	1 9/16-1 12/16	580
Small prime	1 7/16-1 9/16	600
Skips	1 4/16-1 7/16	700
No. 1 broken shorts export & large primes	over 1 15/16	800
No. 2 broken shorts medium, special & small primes	1 15/16-1 7/16	1050

natural casing (small hog casing):

Grade	Width (mm)
Extra narrow	under 28
Narrow medium	28-32
Selected medium	32-35
English medium	35-38
Wide	38-42
Extra wide	over 42

sheep casing:

Grade	Width (mm)	Length of Hank (yd)
Narrow	16-18	100
Narrow mediums	18-20	100
Special mediums	20-22	100
Wide	22-24	100
Extra wide	24-26	100

See Part 2: Casings, Animal; Casings, Hog; Casings, Hog and Beef; Casings, Hog Bungs; Casings, Sheep; Casings, Terms

casitone starch agar *See* Part 2: Microorganism, Media

Casman medium base A noninfusion media developed for use as a single blood medium instead of fresh blood agar plus chocolated blood plate; used for growth of fastidious pathogens.

See Part 2: Microorganism, Media

cassaba A large melon, light yellow to white in color, with light green interior.

See Part 2: Storage

cassareep Concentrated juice of the cassava tuber.

cassava (tapioca; manioc) (*Manihot utilissima*) A woody South American tropical plant from the roots of which starch is extracted. A shrub that produces swollen tuberous roots; the tubers are high in starch and low in protein, and must be cooked before eating; the tuber may be made into meal; the starch is extracted and dried, and fermented into liquor. 1 lb = 3 cups; 1 cup = 150 g (5.4 oz).

Dry composition: 13% H_2O; 0.4-0.6% protein, 0.1-0.2% fat, 86-95% carbohydrate, 0.2% ash. *See also* **tapioca flour.**

See Part 2: Starches and Starchy Roots Composition

casserole A dish prepared as a mixture of meats, fish, vegetables, flavoring, etc. and baked in a glass or ceramic container, usually with a cover.

See Part 2: Microwave Processing Time; Portion Size

cassia (*Cinnamomum cassia* **Blume**) A dried bark, ground or stick, of the cassia tree, used as a spice; essential oil is oil of cinnamon or cassia containing not more than 5% total ash nor more than 2% acid-insoluble ash.

See Part 2: Essential Oils; Flavoring Agents, Natural

cassoulet Large dark red kidney-shaped bean. *See also* **haricot bean.**

castor bean The fruit or seed pod of the castor plant *Ricinus communis*.

See Part 2: Poisonous Plants; Protein Factors; Oil, Seed and Fruit

castor oil The nondrying oil expressed from castor beans; used as a laxative, and other pharmaceuticals.

Specific gravity	0.960-0.967
Refractive index (15.5°C)	1.479-1.481
Saponification number	175-185

Iodine number 82-90
Flash point 230°C

See Part 2: Fats or Oils, Physical and Chemical Properties; Fatty Acids, Fats and Oils; Oil or Fat, Characteristics; Refractive Indices, Fats and Oils; Specific Gravities, Fats and Oils; Unsaponifiable Matter

castor sugar Granulated sugar refined to a finer grain; 2 cups = 1 lb.

castration Removal of the testicles from a male or sex glands from a female.
Desired age: calves, 2 weeks to 2 months; pigs, 3 to 4 weeks; lambs, 1 to 2 weeks.
Methods: knife (use a fly-repellent, e.g., pine tar, and disinfectant around wound); elastrator (rubber rings); emasculatome (clamp).

catabolism Release of energy and the burning of materials, a biochemical process of degradation which takes place in the body.

catalana A Mediterranean class of chickens that lays a white-shelled egg.

catalase An enzyme that breaks down hydrogen peroxide to water and oxygen.

catalyst A substance which speeds up a reaction without undergoing permanent chemical change. Enzymes are organic catalysts. Most catalysts used in industry are inorganic, e.g., metals or their oxides. Nickel is a catalyst for hydrogenation of vegetable oils to solid fats used in cooking, e.g., Crisco.

catchup (catsup; ketchup) A tomato sauce with vinegar, sugar and spices. 1 cup = 275 g (9.6 oz).
Storage: After opening, cover and refrigerate.
Composition: 69% H_2O, 2% protein, 0.4% fat, 25% carbohydrate, 4% ash.
See Part 2: Standards, Processed Fruit and Vegetable Products; Tomato and Tomato Products, Composition; Vegetable Composition

catfish (Bullhead; Blue Channel; Ocean catfish; Wolf fish) A lean fish caught in rivers and used for food; it is scaleless and has cat-like teeth.
See Part 2: Minerals, Food

catgut Dried colons of sheep and oxen split into threads.

cation A positive ion, e.g., Na^+, Ca^{++}.

catsup *See* **catchup**

Cattalo A buffalo-bison hybrid.

cattle Bovine animals raised for milk, beef and work; *Bos taurus*, European; *Bos indicus*, India and Africa; dressing percentage 54.9.
See Part 2: Cattle; Muscle and Body Weight; Reproductive Cycle; Teeth Eruption

caudal Associated with or relating to the tail of an animal.
See Part 2: Bone

caudal vertebrae Tail bone located to the rear of the sacral vertebrae; number varies with species and individual animals in the same breed. *See also* **vertebrae.**

caul fat A loop of fat that supports the stomach. *See also* **web fat.**

cauliflower (*Brassica oleracea*) A vegetable whose flower is used for food. A single-stem plant with a compact white head (curd) composed of flower buds and surrounded by green leaves; may be eaten raw but is usually cooked or pickled.
1 lb fresh = 1½ cups
1 cup = 105 g (3.7 oz)
2⅔ lb = 1 qt frozen
1.5 bu crate = 37 lb
100 lb fresh = 12-14 lb dry
Storage: In refrigerator (32°F); crisper or plastic bags (85-90% relative humidity); use within 3-14 days; frozen (0°F) storage 1 year.
Raw composition: 91% H_2O, 3% protein, 0.2% fat, 5.2% carbohydrate, 1% ash, pH 5.6.
See Part 2: Calories, Daily Recommendations; Frozen Food Storage; Fruit and Vegetables Composition; Fruit and Vegetable, Diseases; Frying Time; Iron; Microwave Cooking, Frozen Vegetables; Microwave Processing Time; Minerals, Food; Niacin; Nitrate, Vegetables; Organic Acids in Fruits and Vegetables; Phosphorus; Plant Foods, Composition; Portion Size; Riboflavin; Storage; Sugar, Vegetables; Thiamin: Vegetable Boiling; Vegetable Composition; vegetable Cooking; Vegetable Frozen Yield; Vegetable Plants; Vegetables, Boiling Time, Frozen; Vegetables Classification; Vegetables, Cooking Frozen; Vegetable Servings; Vegetable Storage; Vegetable Yield; Vegetable Yield Canned and Frozen; Vegetable Yield, Frozen, Canned and Fresh; Vitamin C

caustic lime A liming material composed of 85% CaO; each lb has the neutralizing equivalent of 1.5 to 1.75 lb of $CaCO_3$ (or approximately this quantity of dolomitic limestone).

caustic potash Potassium hydroxide (KOH).

caustic soda (sodium hydroxide) NaOH A strongly alkaline cleaner with high germicidal and dissolving action but with poor deflocculating and emulsifying power; it is very corrosive and will burn skin; usually in solutions of various concentrations.
See Part 2: Concentration of Commercial Strengths of Acids and Bases; Detergent Properties; Normal Solutions; pH, Standard Solutions; Reagents, Normal Solutions; Sodium Hydroxide Solution

caviar (caviare) Roe eggs of sturgeon or other fish prepared by a special process (maturation and salting); should be labeled to indicate type of fish; red caviar is roe of salmon; pH 5.4.

	H_2O (%)	Protein (%)	Fat (%)	Carbohydrate (%)	Ash (%)
granular	46-57	27	15	0-3	9
pressed	36	34	17	5	8

cayenne (*Capsicum frutescens* L.) Pods of the red pepper plant used as seasoning. Extremely "hot", burning taste. *See also* **tobasco sauce.**

Cd Symbol for the element cadmium.

Ce Symbol for the element cerium.

cecum Blind end section of the digestive tract between the small and large intestine; larger size in non-ruminants that utilize forage.

cedar An essential oil obtained from the cedar tree.
See Part 2: Essential Oils

celeriac (turnip-rooted celery) (*Apium graveolens* var. *rapaceum*) A plant similar to celery; the swollen base of the stem is the part eaten as a cooked vegetable.
Storage: 32°F, 90-95% relative humidity, use in 3 mo.
Raw root composition: 88% H_2O, 2% protein, 0.3% fat, 8% carbohydrate, 1% ash.
See Part 2: Storage; Vegetable Plants

celery (*Apium graveolens*) A shallow-rooted biennial vegetable whose leaf stem is used as food.
Leaf-stalk: consumed raw in salads and hors d'oeuvres; cooked as vegetables and soup.
Seed: flavoring
1 crate = 60 lb; 1 lb = 2 bunches; 7 bunches = 50 servings; 100 lb fresh = 8-9 lb dry.

Storage: In refrigerator (31-32°F), crisper or plastic bag (90-95% relative humidity). Use within 3 days to 2 mo.
Raw composition: 94% H_2O, 0.9% protein, 0.1% fat, 4% carbohydrate, 1% ash, pH 5.7-6.0.
See Part 2: Essential Oils; Flavoring Agents, Natural; Fruit and Vegetable, Diseases; Minerals, Food; Nitrate, Vegetables; Plant Foods, Composition; Potassium; Rot Spoilage; Soups Composition; Storage; Sugar, Vegetables; Transit Temperature; Vegetable Boiling; Vegetable Composition; Vegetable Plants; Vegetables Classification; Vegetable Servings; Vegetable Storage

celery cabbage *See* **Chinese cabbage**

celery flake Flaked leaves and stalks of celery that have been dehydrated.

celery salt A mixture of ground celery seed and salt.

celery seed (*Apium graveolens*) Tiny brown dried fruit (seed) used as a spice; should not contain more than 10% total ash and 2% acid-insoluble ash.
See Part 2: Spices, Microbial Content

cellophane A transparent film made of regenerated cellulose and coated or treated with lacquers or polymers; relatively permeable to air and moisture when wet, less permeable when dry.
See Part 2: Frozen Food Containers; Film Gauge.

cellular glass A porous glass used as an insulating material.
See Part 2: Insulating Value

cellulose $(C_6H_{10}O_5)_n$ A carbohydrate polymer made up of glucose units joined in the form of long chains; the links are 1 and 4 as in starch, but the linkage to carbon 1 is beta in cellulose and alpha in starch. It occurs in plants (⅓ of all vegetable matter) and is not digestible by man. Cellulose content: wood 40-50%, annual plants 35-40%, cotton fiber 98%.
See Part 2: Cellulose Formula; Histochemical Test; Wheat, Parts of Grain

cellulose acetate A cellulose ester used as a packaging material.
See Part 2: Plastic Permeability

cellulose gum *See* **carboxymethylcellulose**

Celotex A proprietary product made from sugarcane waste (bagasse) and used as insulating board.
See Part 2: Insulation

Celsius Temperature scale also known as the centigrade scale in which one degree is equivalent to 1/100 the difference between the temperature of melting ice and boiling water at standard atmospheric pressure.

cement A mixture of alumins, silica and lime (often with sand) that will harden when water is added. Such mixtures are called hydraulic cements, the water entering into a chemical reaction to form a hydrate. Portland cement is of this type. 1 barrel = 4 bags = 376 lb.
See Part 2: Insulation, Conductivity Values

centare A measure of area equivalent to 1 sq meter.

center Middle point or place.
See Part 2: Pork Loin Nomenclature; Pork Yield

centi- (one-hundredth) (0.01); prefix for quantities 100 times as small as the base unit.

centigrade (C) A temperature scale in standard scientific use invented by Celsius, and now generally called by his name.

$C = \frac{5}{9}(F - 32)$	F = Fahrenheit
$C = R\,(\frac{5}{4})$	R = Réaumur
$K = C + 273.15$	K = Kelvin
$F = (C \times \frac{9}{5}) + 32$	Boiling point of water = 100°C
$R = C \times \frac{4}{5}$	Freezing point of water = 0°C

See Part 2: Temperature

centigram (cg) A unit of metric weight.
1 centigram = 10 milligrams (mg)

centiliter (cl) A unit of metric volume.
1 centiliter = 10 milliliters

centimeter (cm) A unit of metric length.
1 centimeter = 1×10^8 angstrom units
= 10,000 microns
= 10 millimeters (mm)
= 0.3937 in. (US)
= 0.032808 feet (US)
= 10^{-2} meter
= 6.2137×10^{-6} statute U.S. miles
2.54 cm = 1 inch
30.48 cm = 1 foot

centimeter of mercury A measure of pressure.
1 cm of mercury at 0°C = 27.845 lb/sq ft
= 13.595 g/sq cm
= 0.446 feet of water at 4°C
= 0.019337 lb/sq in.
= 0.013158 atmosphere
= 0.013 kilogram/sq cm

centimeter per second (cm per sec) A measure of velocity.
1 cm per sec = 1.9685 ft per min
= 0.6000 meter/min
= 0.03600 kilometer/hr
= 0.0328083 ft per sec
= 0.02237 miles per hr
= 3.728×10^{-4} mile/min

centimeter per second per second A measure of acceleration.
1 cm/sec/sec = 0.03281 foot/sec/sec
= 0.02237 mile/hr/sec

centrifugal force A force exerted outward from the center of gravity.
centrifugal force = 0.00001118 (radius in cm) $(\text{rpm})^2$ (no. of times greater than gravity)

$$\text{centrifugal force (gravity)} = \frac{\text{velocity in ft/sec}^2}{32.16 \times \text{radius of circle in ft}}$$

centrifugal force (grams) = 1.118 (wt in grams) (radius in cm) $(\text{rpm})^2\ 10^{-5}$

$$\text{centrifugal force (pounds)} = \frac{\text{wt of body in lb} \times (\text{velocity in ft/sec})^2}{32.16 \times \text{radius of circle in feet}}$$

centriole A division center of a cell.

century plant A Mexican *Agava* plant that flowers once and dies.
See Part 2: Poisonous Plants

cep (*Boletus edulis*) An edible fungus with a smooth brown cap, white tinged with pink flesh, and a stout stalk.

cephalin A phospholipid associated with lecithins in egg yolk, and some animal tissues; a compound of fatty acids and phosphones.

cereal Dry fruit of certain grasses.
See Part 2: Calcium Daily Requirements; Calories, Daily Recommendations; Cereal By-Products Composition; Cereal Composition; Cereal Enrichment; Cereal Fortification; Cereals, Vitamin and Mineral Content; Cereal Nutrient Content; Iron, Daily Recommendations; Niacin, Daily Recommendations; Nicotinic Acid, Food; Portion Size; Protein Factors; Riboflavin, Daily Recommendations; Riboflavin, Food; Spoilage, Carbohydrate Foods; Storage, Dry; Storage, Times; Thiamin, Daily Recommendations; Thiamin, Food; Vitamin A, Food

cerebellum Rear portion of the brain which directs coordination of movements.

cerebrum The front area of the brain that consists of 2 hemispheres and is responsible for consciousness.

ceriman A climbing vine that has a cone-like fruit.

cerium (Ce) A rare earth element of the lanthanide series; at. no. 58; at. wt. 104.13; Group IIIB of Periodic Table; oxidation states +3, +4; electron configuration 2-8-18-19-9-2
orbit K L M N O P

cero *See* **mackerel**

cérons A full, sweet white wine.

cerotic acid $CH_3(CH_2)_{24}COOH$ A saturated fatty acid obtained from various waxes.
See Part 2: Saturated Fatty Acids

Certified Atlantic A variety of alfalfa.

Certified Buffalo A variety of alfalfa.

Certified Williamsburg A variety of alfalfa.

cervalat (cervelet) A finely chopped, semi-dry sausage made chiefly from beef (or all beef) with a little pork; it is given a heavy smoke and allowed to dry.
Varieties: farmer (smaller casings), holsteiner. *See also* **summer sausage.**
See Part 2: Sausage Identification; Sausage, Types

cervical vertebrae Neck bone in all mammals, numbered from front to back.
See Part 2: Bone

cesium (Cs) An alkali metal element; at. no. 55; at. wt. 132.91; Group IA of Periodic Table; oxidation state +1; electron configuration 2-8-18-18-8-1
orbit K L M N O P

cetoleic An unsaturated fatty acid occurring in vegetable oils.
See Part 2: Unsaturated Fatty Acids

cetrimide agar *See* Part 2: Microorganism, Media

cevitamic acid *See* **ascorbic acid**

Cf Symbol for the element californium.

Chaetomium *See* Part 2: Molds, Mycotoxins

chaff The inedible portion of wheat or other grain which remains after threshing.
See Part 2: Wastes, Agricultural and Industrial

chain (surveyors' or Gunter's) A measure of length.
1 chain = 100 links (Gunter's)
= 66 feet
= 22 yards
= 20.117 meters
= 4 rods
= 0.0125 mile
10 sq chain = 1 acre

chain, carbon A series of carbon atoms in an organic molecule connected by single, double or triple bonds. *See also* **aliphatic, aromatic, branched chain.**

chalaza Strands of coagulated albumin which hold the yolk of an egg in position by attachment to the shell.
See Part 2: Egg Structure

chaldron A dry measure; 36 bushels (US) or 32 bu (Br.) = 1 chaldron.

chamois (chammy) A soft leather made from the inner layer of sheep skin; formerly from chamois (antelope).

chamomile An Egyptian herb used as tea.
See Part 2: Essential Oils; Flavoring Agents, Natural

champagne A blend of wines (10-13% alcohol) from various black and white grapes; a second fermentation in the bottle produces the natural sparkle. Types are burt, driest; extra dry, less dry; sec, sweet; demi-sec, sweeter; doux, sweetest; pink, (grape skins removed later in fermentation process). *See also* **brut champagne; chardonnay; dry champagne; pink champagne; wine.**

Chantecler An American breed of chicken that lays a brown-shelled egg. Varieties; white, partridge.

chantelle cheese A dessert cheese with a rich, light-orange, tangy flavor.
See Part 2: Cheese Vitamin Content; Vitamin A, Milk and Milk Products

chanterelle (*Cantharellus cibarius*) A yellow, funnel shaped, edible fungus.

Chapman Stone medium Selective medium for the isolation of staphylococci which uses sodium chloride as the selective agent.
See Part 2: Microorganism, Media

characteristic *See* **logarithm**

Charbray A cross of French Charolais and Brahman beef cattle.
See Part 2: Beef and Dual-Purpose Cattle

charcoal A dark, porous fuel (carbon) made by destructive distillation of wood; 6 lb hardwood yields 1 lb charcoal. Various types are lump (odd size just as it comes from retorts) and briquettes (lump charcoal that is ground, mixed with a starch binder and pressed into uniform size blocks). 2 lb charcoal for average size grill; 20 min burning required before ready to cook.
See Part 2: Insulation, Conductivity Values

charcoal agar *See* Part 2: Microorganism, Media

chard A beet whose leaf and stalk is used as food; also blanched artichoke leaves. *See also* **seakale beet.**
See Part 2: Minerals, Food; Sugar, Vegetables; Vegetable Composition; Vegetable Cooking; Vegetable Frozen Yield; Vegetable Plants; Vegetables, Cooking Frozen

Chardonnay (pineau blanc) A variety of yellowish-green grape that is fermented to yield white burgundy or champagne. *See also* **wine.**

Charolais (Charollais) A French breed of beef cattle.
See Part 2: Beef and Dual-Purpose Cattle; Gestation Periods

charqui *See* **jerked beef**

chasseur (hunter style) A tomato-wine sauce with mushrooms, peppers, olives and garlic.

chateaubriand Thick beef.
See Part 2: Portion Size

chats The tailing or rejects in a mining operation.
See Part 2: Fertilizer Materials

chaulmoogra oil A vegetable oil used for treatment of leprosy; composed of glycerides of chaulmoogric and hydnocarpic acids.
See Part 2: Fatty Acids and Their Properties

chayote (*Sechium edule*) An herbaceous, perennial vine whose fruit may differ in shape (often pear-shaped or round), size (3 to 8 in. long), and color (white to dark green). The fruit quality is similar to a squash and contains a single seed often 2 in. long.
Part of plant:
Fruit: cooked, in sauces, puddings, tarts and salads
Young shoots and leaves: vegetables
Flesh roots (up to 20 lb): used like a yam
Raw composition: 92% H_2O, 0.6% protein, 0.1% fat, 7% carbohydrate, 0.4% ash.
See Part 2: Vegetables classification; Vegetable Storage

checharron Brown lard that is highly flavored.

cheddar cheese (American, American cheddar) A cheese made by cooking the curd at 98-106°F and pressing for 15-20 hr; cured at 35 to 55°F; sharp flavor 9-12 mo.; color, white to orange; flavor more definite upon aging (mild to sharp); made from whole milk (10 lb milk/1 lb cheese); shape, brick to large round circular cakes; texture, hard; ripening, 2-12 mo. by bacteria; use, sandwich, cook or dessert; 4 cups grated = 1 lb.
Composition: 39% moisture maximum (37% av.); solids contain not less than 50% milk fat; 0.02% calcium chloride maximum; 22-25% protein; 32-33% fat (min. 50% in solids or min. 30.5% in cheese); 2% carbohydrate; 4% ash; 1.5-2% salt; pH 5.9; grades U.S. AA, A, B, C.
Other cheddar types:
Stirred or granular curd (more open texture)
Colby (softer body, open texture, milder flavor)
Washed curd (higher moisture, bland flavor)
Monterry Jack (white, higher moisture, soft, open texture)
See Part 2: Cheese Characteristics; Cheese Composition; Cheese Vitamin Content; Food, Composition; Milk and Cheese Composition; Milk and Milk Products, Vitamin Content; Vitamin A, Food; Vitamin A, Milk and Milk Products

cheese A food made from milk. Essential processing steps are:
1. Adjust temperature to 86-96°F.
2. Add starter culture (lactic acid and flavor-producing varieties).

3. Color may be added or removed.
4. Add rennet when proper acidity is reached.
5. Culturing or Ripening, usually 15-90 min.
6. Curd is cut.
7. Stir.
8. Heat.
9. Remove curd from whey.

10 lb milk required to make 1 lb cheese.
4-4½ cups grated cheese/lb.
1 cup grated = 110 g (4 oz).
pH = 4.8-6.4.
In surface-ripened cheese, microorganisms are added to exterior of cheese.

Storage: After opening, cover (65-70% relative humidity) and refrigerate (35°F); will keep for several weeks; longer holding will result in additional curing and a sharper flavor; natural cheese can be frozen for 6 weeks to 2 mo. *See also* **club cheese; coldpack cheese; coldpack cheese food; comminuted cheese; cured (cheese); natural cheese; pasteurized process cheese; pasteurized process cheese food.**

See Part 2: Animal Foods, Composition; Calcium Daily Requirements; Calories, Daily Recommendations; Cheese Characteristics; Cheese Composition; Cheese Grade Stamps; Cheese Label; Cheese Vitamin Content; Dairy Products, Composition; Glutamate; Microbiological Standards, Dairy; Milk and Cheese Composition; Milk and Milk Products, Vitamin Content; Minerals, Food; Portion Size; Riboflavin, Daily Recommendations; Riboflavin, Food; Spoilage, Protein Foods; Stabilizers, Thickeners; Storage Times; Thiamin, Food; Vitamin A, Daily Recommendations; Vitamin A, Food; Vitamin A, Milk and Milk Products; Vitamin D, Food

cheese, American *See* **cheddar cheese**

cheese, cheddar *See* **cheddar cheese**

cheese cracker *See* Part 2: Fermented Ingredients

cheese, cream *See* **cream cheese; cheese**

cheese mite A pest that feeds on hams and cheese.

cheese skipper *See* **ham skipper**

chela The claw of a crustacean, e.g., crab or lobster.

chemically pure (C.P.) A grade of chemical purity that is suitable for routine use; C.P. indicates absence of any detectable impurity.

chemical poisoning Poisoning due to presence of a toxic substance in the body resulting from ingestion, inhalation or skin absorption.
See Part 2: Chemical Poisoning

chemise, en Unpeeled boiled potatoes.

chemurgy Utilization of agricultural and farm wastes for fuel or industrial use. Conversion of manure to methane is under experimentation; bagasse and corn cobs are used locally for boiler fuels. There is growing interest in this field for energy sources.

chenchalok Spicy pickle made from onions, salt and pepper and added to shrimp.

chendol A drink made of rose-colored syrup and containing cooked rice, flour, peas colored green with a pandanus leaf, passion fruit seeds and condensed milk; poured over shaved ice.

Chenopodiaceae Goosefoot family of plants having utricular fruit.
See Part 2: Vegetables Classification

cherimoya (*Anona cherimolia*) (Vegetable ice cream) A highland tropical small tree fruit with a pineapple flavor, juicy white pulp, custard-like center and a scaly surface. *See also* **anonaceous fruit.**
See Part 2: Fruit Composition

cherry (*Prunus*) A tree that produces a thin-skinned, shiny fruit with juicy flesh; it contains one stone (one-seeded drupe); the cherries are in clusters on relatively long stalks.

Type	Name	Use
Sour (*P. cerasus*) (acid; tart) (lighter red & softer than sweet)	morello, Flemish, kentish red, amarelles, griottes	liqueurs, cooking, baking
Sweet (*P. avium*)	mazzard, gean	fruit
Bird	—	flavoring rum

Varieties:
Sour: montmorency, early Richmond, English morello;
Sweet:
bing, black tartarian, black republican, lambert, schmidt, windsor, napoleon (Royal Ann).

Not pitted:
1 lb = 120 med. cherries
1½ qt (fresh) = 1 qt canned
1 crate (fresh) = 24 qt = 45-55 lb = 18-22 qt canned
1 case (24) No. 2½ cans = 0.023 tons fresh cherries
1 lug (4.1 × 11.5 × 14 in.) = 16 lb
1 (25-lb) lug = 22 pt canned
100 lb fresh = 17-21 lb sour cherries = 22-26 lb sweet cherries

Pitted:
1 lb fresh = 2⅓ cups (1 cup = 155 g or 5.4 oz)
1½-2½ lb (fresh) = 1 qt canned
1½-2 qt (fresh) = 1 qt canned
1 bu (fresh) = 56 lb = 25 qt canned.

Storage: Keep whole, unstemmed; uncovered (85-90% relative humidity); unwashed; refrigerate (31-32°F); use in 1 to 10 days; freezing point 24-28°F

	H_2O (%)	Protein (%)	Fat (%)	Carbohydrate (%)	Ash (%)	pH
sour	84	1	0.3	14	0.5	3.1-4
sweet	80	1	0.3	17	0.5	3.5-4.4

See Part 2: Calories, Daily Recommendations; Canned Yield; Cherries, Canned Weights; Cherry

Brix; Cherry Composition; Flavor Ingredients, Taste and Flavor Type; Flavors, Beverage; Frozen Food Storage; Fruit and Nut Rootstock; Fruit and Vegetables Composition; Fruit, Availability; Fruit Harvest Dates; Fruit Classification; Fruit Composition; Fruit, Cooking; Fruit Frozen Yield; Fruit, Growing Season, Storage Life; Fruit Sauces; Fruit Servings per Pound; Fruit Storage; Minerals, Food; Organic Acids in Fruits and Vegetables; Plant Foods, Composition; Standards, Processed Fruit and Vegetable Products; Storage; Sugar, Fruit; Transit Temperature; Vitamin A

cherry, acerola *See* **acerola cherry**

cherry gum A gum similar to arabic exudated from *Prunus* species.
See Part 2: Pentosans

cherry laurel A toxic plant of the cherry family. *See also* **bay leaves.**
See Part 2: Poisonous Plants

cherrystone A small hard-shelled clam. *See also* **clam.**

cherry tomato *See* **tomato**

chervil (*Anthriscus cerefolium* L. Hoffm) A smallish annual herb of the parsley family with delicate white flowers; its leaves are used whole or ground; curled leaves used fresh for salads and soups and garnishing.
Composition: 81% H_2O, 3% protein, 1% fat, 12% carbohydrate, 3.5% ash.

Cheshire cheese A hard cheese made in England; it resembles cheddar and when aged it has a sharp flavor.
See Part 2: Cheese Vitamin Content; Milk and Milk Products, Vitamin Content; Vitamin A, Milk and Milk Products

Chester White A meat-type breed of hog originating in Southeastern Pennsylvania from a number of local strains; solid white with a drooping ear.
See Part 2: Swine Breeds

chestnut (a) A hard-shell nut requiring cooking before eating (*Castanea sativa*); (b) a horny growth on the inside of a horse's leg; (c) sorrel (reddish brown) color of horses. *See also* **sweet chestnut.**
See Part 2: Minerals, Food; Pulses, Nuts and Seeds Composition

Cheviot A medium-wool mutton-type breed of sheep originating in Scotland; its face, ears, and legs are white and have no wool.
See Part 2: Sheep Breeds

chevon The flesh of goats.

chevres A cheese made from goat's milk, covered with mold; curd is close and white, and flavor is mild. *See also* **cheese.**

chewing gum A sweetened, flavored gum that is chewed to obtain flavor.
Composition: 17-30% chicle gum (latex of sapodilla); 46-59% glucose; 18-23% water; glycerol; flavor ingredients; colorants. *See also* **sapodilla.**

chewy Characteristic of a food (usually candy) that resists breaking up by the teeth, but slowly dissolves in the mouth. *See also* **confection.**

chi (χ, x) A Greek letter with an English equivalent of x.

Chianina An extremely large, white breed of cattle originating in Italy; used for work and beef production; claimed to be the world's largest cattle and a very old breed.

chianti A fruity red wine. *See also* **wine.**

chiaretto A rosé wine. *See also* **wine.**

chia seed Black seeds from the wild sage that can be used as food.

Chicago round A cut of beef.
See Part 2: Beef Rounds

Chicago style A method of cutting beef; the fore quarter is divided into chuck, rib, shank, brisket, and short plate; the hind quarter is divided into round, rump, loin end, short loin, and flank; the sirloin tip (obtained in the National style of cutting) is left on the loin end in the Chicago style.

chicha Fermented corn or other plants.

chick antidermatitis factor A vitamin-related complex. *See also* **pantothenic acid**

chicken A domesticated fowl (poultry) that is raised for eggs and meat production. Young chicken meat has 71% H_2O, 20% protein, 7% fat, 1% ash; dressing percentage 72%; 3 lb dressed chicken = 4½ cups chopped cooked meat = 1½ lb chopped cooked meat; 8-18% fat absorption during frying.
Storage: Coldest part of refrigerator; use within 1 to 2 days.
See Part 2: Bacteria on Chickens at Various Holding Temperatures; Bone; Calories, Daily Recommendations; Egg Incubation Periods; Food, Composition; Frozen Food Storage; Frying Time; Glutamate; Glutamate Addition; Iron, Daily Recommendations; Liver; Meat and Meat Products Composition; Microwave Processing Time; Minerals, Food; Portion Size; Poultry Breeds and Varieties; Poultry Class; Poultry Composition; Poultry Cooking, Frozen; Poultry Dressing Percentage; Poultry Roasting; Poultry Yield; Soups Composition; Spoilage, Protein Foods; Turkey Composition

chicken cacciatore A skillet dish prepared with chicken, onion, garlic, tomatoes, wine, noodles and olive oil.

chicken fat Fat removed from the carcass of chickens; smoke point 400-430°F.
See Part 2: Iodine and Saponification Values

chicken grade *See* **poultry grades**

chicken salad A salad made from cooked chicken meat tossed with other ingredients such as mayonnaise, chopped celery, etc.

5 chickens for salad = 50 servings.

chick pea (Bengal gram) (*Cicer arietinum*) A tropical pulse with a small round pod containing 1 to 2 seeds; harvested in 4 to 6 mo.; used to make "dhal."
See Part 2: Seed Germination

chick's first breath An air space in large end of egg between two membranes.

chicle gum *See* **chewing gum; sapodilla**

chico Sapodilla tropical fruit with rough brownish skin and sweet pulp; marmalade, tropical, egg-shaped single seeded fruit.
See Part 2: Fruit Classification

chicory (*Cichorium intybus*) A perennial herb used as a substitute for or mixed with coffee; and adds a bitter flavor. The root is chopped, roasted, ground and the water extract used as a beverage. The leaves and shoots are usually blanched to reduce bitter taste and are used as salads or vegetables. The hearts are blanched and used as a cooked vegetable.
Types: French endive (large-rooted); summer chicory or escarole; curly endive (greens with a somewhat bitter taste).
Composition: 95% H_2O, 1% protein, 0.1% fat, 3% carbohydrate, 0.6% ash.
See Part 2: Minerals, Trace, Limits; Vegetable Composition; Vegetable Plants

chiffonade Shredded vegetables or meat.
See Part 2: French Dressing Variations

Chile saltpeter $NaNO_3$; sodium nitrate derived from guano on islands off coast of Chile.

chili Strongest fruit (pepper) of herbaceous plant belonging to *Capsicum* family which has a hot and pungent flavor; used in chili con carne, chili sauce, cayenne pepper, chili vinegar and pickles.
See Part 2: Wastes, Agricultural and Industrial

chili con carne A dish made of 40% (min.) meat (computed on fresh meat wt); 25% (max.) of meat as hearts, cheek meat, head meat or weasand meat; 8% (max.) cereal or soya flour.
See Part 2: Meat Composition; Microwave Processing Time; Portion Size

chili pepper A spice of the capsicums group ground coarser than paprika.

chili powder A preparation for seasoning that contains chili pepper, cumin, oregano, garlic, salt, and sometimes other spices.

chili sauce A hot spiced tomato sauce.
Storage: After opening, cover and refrigerate.
See Part 2: Standards, Processed Fruit and Vegetable Products; Tomato and Tomato Products, Composition

chill room A refrigeration area for meats and vegetables; regulation temp. 38 ± 2°F; tolerance of 10°F for reasonable time after the entry of fresh food; ideal temp. 30 ± 2°F.

chinaberry A berry containing a toxic principle.
See Part 2: Poisonous Plants

China wood oil *See* **tung oil**

chinch bug An insect that sucks the sap from corn and other small grains after they have been harvested. Control: segregate corn and small grains.

chine bone Body of cervical, thoracic, lumbar, and sacral vertebrae.
See Part 2: Beef Rib Nomenclature; Beef Wholesale Cuts; Bone; Lamb Wholesale Cuts; Meat Identification; Pork Wholesale Cuts; Veal Wholesale Cuts

Chinese cabbage (celery cabbage, ***Brassica pekinensis*** **and** ***B. chinensis*****)** A salad green with a long, oval, firm head; cabbage taste; outer leaves green; inside and center of leaves white. *See also* **pak-choi.**

Chinese vegetable tallow *See* Part 2: Iodine and Saponification Values

Chinese water chestnut (pi-tsi) (***Eleocharis tuberosa***) A water plant; a tuber which is sliced and used as food; it has a very crisp texture.
Raw composition: 96% H_2O, 0.4% protein, 0.2% fat, 3% carbohydrate, 0.2% ash.

chinook A grade of Alaskan salmon. *See also* **salmon.**
See Part 2: Salmon and Trout

chipped beef Beef sliced in thin fragments.
See Part 2: Meat Composition; Meat, Servings per Pound.

chi-square (χ^2) A measure of deviation from a hypothesis;
$\chi^2 = \Sigma(f - F)^2/F$
f = no. found in sample
F = no. expected by hypothesis
df = total possible classes -1
e.g., $df = 1$ if 2 categories (e.g., yes and no)
χ^2 of 6.635 or larger there is a 1% possibility of this taking place if the hypothesis is true: χ^2 of 3.841 (5%). Percentage values *cannot* be used without returning to a known sample size.

chitin A water-insoluble polysaccharide containing amine groupings; tends to form horny layers such as occur in protective coatings of shellfish. Its chemical structure is not unlike that of cellulose except for the presence of nitrogen.
See Part 2: Histochemical Tests

chitterling (chittlin') Intestine of swine; considered a food delicacy by some people.

chive (*Allium schoenoprasum*) An onion-like plant that grows in tufts and whose leaves, fresh or freeze-dried, are used as a mild flavoring in cream cheese, potato salad, etc.
Composition: 91% H_2O, 2% protein; 0.3% fat; 6% carbohydrate; 0.8% ash.

chlamydospore agar *See* Part 2: Microorganism, Media

chloramine T A topical antiseptic and sanitizer.
See Part 2: Chlorine Availability; Chlorine Compounds; Sanitizers

chlordan(e) A toxic chlorinated hydrocarbon insecticide; its use on food crops has been prohibited.

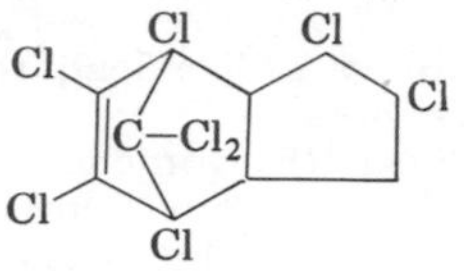

chlorella agar *See* Part 2: Microorganism, Media

chloride A salt of hydrochloric acid. *See also* **chlorine.**
See Part 2: Chloride Salt, Injury; Chlorine Availability

chlorinated hydrocarbon A hydrocarbon in which some or all of the hydrogen atoms have been replaced by chlorine; carbon tetrachloride is an example; as a group, they are quite toxic; many that have been used as insecticides (DDT, chlordane) are no longer permitted on food crops, though a number of others are still in approved use.

chlorine (Cl) A halogen element; a toxic gas at room temperature. at. no. 17; at. wt. 35.457; Group VIIA of Periodic Table; oxidation states +1, +5, +7, −1; electron configuration 2-8-7
orbit K L M
As hydrochloric acid, it imparts intensely acid pH to gastric juice (about pH 2.0). *See also* **hydrochloric acid.**
See Part 2: Chloride Salt, Injury; Chlorine Availability; Chlorine Compounds; Chlorine, Water Treatment; Egg Products Nutritive Value; Lemon Juice Composition; Minerals, Food; Normal Solutions; Sanitizers; Sanitizing Chemicals; Water Drinking Standards

chloroform ($CHCl_3$) A chlorinated hydrocarbon that has anesthetic properties and is a solvent for fat. Its use in cough medicines etc. has been prohibited because of its suspected carcinogenicity.

chlorophyll A green pigment present in all green plants; it is essential for the formation of carbohydrates by the plant since it acts as an energy converter.

R in chlorophyll a —CH_3
R in chlorophyll b —C(=O)—H

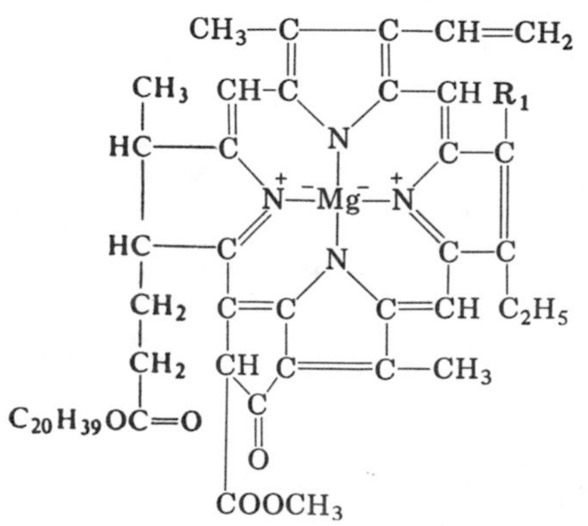

See also **photosynthesis.**

chloropicrin CCl_3NO_2 A very poisonous liquid used as a fumigant. Inhalation of fumes may be serious.
See Part 2: Fumigants

chlortetracycline $C_{22}H_{23}ClN_2O_8$ A broad-spectrum antibiotic.

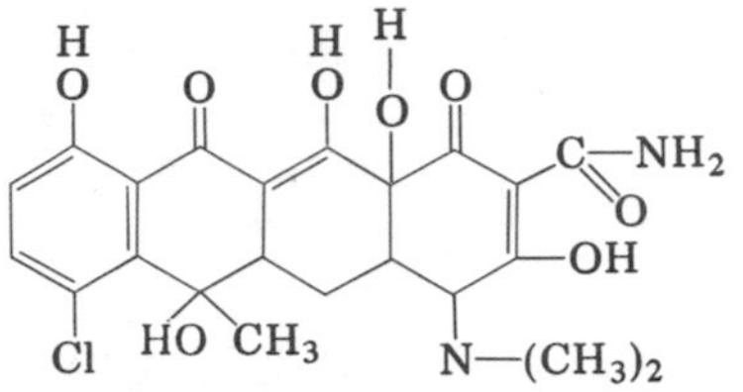

See Part 2: Antibiotic Standards

chocolate A solid or semiplastic food made from chocolate liquor derived from cocoa nibs which are obtained from the cocoa bean, a seed of the *Theobroma cacao* tree. The beans are dried, removed from the pod, fermented, pulp is removed, washed, dried and roasted (146-300°C). The kernels are broken, removed from the shell, heated and ground. This product is called bitter chocolate; it contains not less than 50% cacao fat; max. 8% ash on fat-free moisture-free basis; max. 0.4% ash insoluble in HCl on fat-free moisture-free basis; max. 7% crude fiber on fat-free moisture-free basis.

Types	Chocolate Liquor (%)	Milk Solids (%)	Sweetened	Fat (%)
Bitter or baking	100			50+
Semi-sweet or bitter-sweet	Min. 35	Max. 12	yes	
Sweet	Min. 15	Max. 12	yes	
Milk	Min. 10	⩾3.66 milk fat & ⩾12 solids	yes	
Dark		0		

1 oz chocolate can be substituted by 3 tbsp of cocoa + 1 tbsp of fat; 1 lb = 2 cups; 1 cup = 225 g (7.9 oz); 1 square = 1 oz.
Cooking chocolate composition: 2-3% H_2O, 10-11% protein, 53% fat, 28-29% carbohydrate, 3-4% ash.
Storage: 38-42°F. *See also* **cocoa; semi-sweet chocolate, semi-sweet chocolate pieces, sweet cooking chocolate; unsweetened chocolate.**
See Part 2: Calories, Daily Recommendations; Coatings; Dairy Terms; Flavor Ingredients, Taste and Flavor Type; Nicotinic Acid, Food; Spoilage, Carbohydrate Foods; Sugars and Sweets Composition

chocolate agar *See* Part 2: Microorganism, Media

chocolate drink Milk with less than 3.25% fat to which sugar and chocolate have been added.

chocolate-flavored drink Milk with less than 3.25% fat to which sugar and cocoa have been added.

chocolate-flavored milk Whole milk to which sugar and cocoa have been added; min. fat 3.25%.

chocolate milk Whole milk to which sugar and chocolate have been added; min. fat 3.25%.

choice A marketing grade of meat, fruit or vegetable.
See Part 2: Grades, Meat; Meat Grade Stamps

choke (1) A condition in cattle in which a foreign object is lodged in the throat. (2) The flower head of an artichoke. *See also* **artichoke.**

chokecherries A toxic berry.
See Part 2: Poisonous Plants

cholecalciferol A form of vitamin D designated as D_3; activated 7-dehydrocholesterol.
See Part 2: Vitamins

cholera, hog An infectious and fatal swine disease caused by *Vibrio cholerae*; may be prevented by vaccination.
See Part 2: Illness from Food

cholesterol A sterol found in all animal tissues, especially in the brain, egg yolk, cod liver oil; the unsaponifiable fraction of animal fats and gall stones.

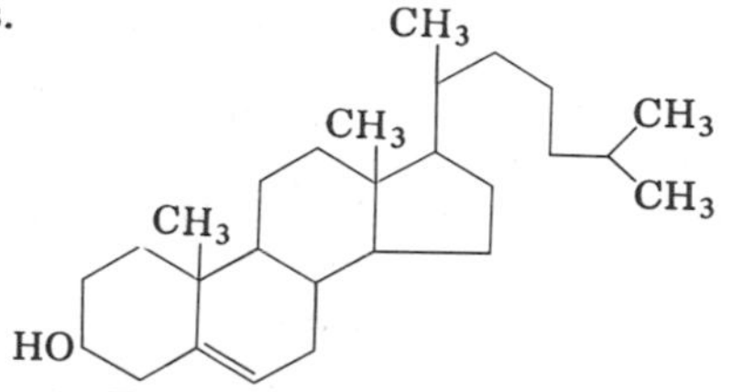

See Part 2: Egg Products Nutritive Value; Histochemical Test; Steroids

choline A water-soluble member of the vitamin B complex, whose deficiency causes "fatty livers" in rats, damage to kidneys in rats, damage to leg tendons in the chick and reduced egg production in hens; it is widely distributed in biological material and made synthetically.

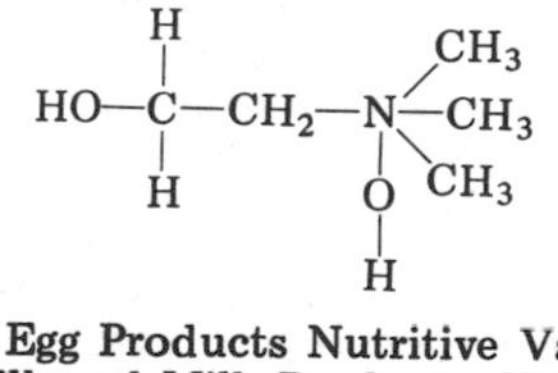

See Part 2: Egg Products Nutritive Value; Grain Analysis; Milk and Milk Products, Vitamin Content; Wheat Products Composition; Wheat, Vitamins

cholinesterase An enzyme that neutralizes the toxic effect of the acetylcholine formed by the nervous system.

cholinesterase inhibitor An ester of phosphoric acid that has the effect of preventing the enzyme cholinesterase from functioning, thus causing serious illness and often death from acetylcholine poisoning; a number of insecticides of the parathion type act in this way, and though they are not persistent they are dangerous to handle.

chop A slice of pork, veal or lamb, including the bone.
Storage: Coldest part of refrigerator; original wrapper, 1 to 2 days storage; unwrapped and covered loosely, 3 to 5 days storage.
See Part 2: Braising Time; Broiling Griddle, Meat; Broiling Meat; Broiling Time and Temperature; Lamb Cuts; Lamb Cuts and Uses; Meat Composition; Meat, Frozen Storage; Meat Identification; Meat, Servings Per Pound; Pork Chart; Pork Cookery; Pork Cooking; Pork Cooking Methods; Pork Cooking Yield; Pork Cuts; Pork Loin Cooking; Pork Storage; Portion Size; Roasting Meat; Veal Chart

chopped beef Ground beef containing 20% fat.

chopped steak Ground steak containing 20% fat.

chopper Medium-finished, aged ewes.

chop suey A dish made with pork, veal and/or chicken, vegetables, soy sauce, rice or noodles.
See Part 2: Microwave Processing Time; Pork Loin Cooking

chorizos A coarsely ground, highly spiced (pimento and red pepper) Spanish sausage in which pork predominates (sometime a little beef is used); it is dried and lightly smoked.
See Part 2: Sausage Identification

chow-chow A fine-ground pickle mixture, with mustard, used as a relish.
See Part 2: Vegetable Storage

chowder (1) A large size of hard, soft or surf clams. (2) A soup made with clams or fish boiled in milk.

Christensen agar *See* Part 2: Microorganism, Media

chrome tanning Making leather from hides using sodium dichromate ($Na_2Cr_2O_7$) as the tanning solution; it is converted to chromic sulfate, which combines with the protein of the hide.

chromium (Cr) A metallic element; at. no. 24; at. wt. 52.01; Group VIB of Periodic Table; oxidation states +2, +3, +6; electron configuration 2-8-13-1
orbit K L M N
The 6-valent form is poisonous.

chromoprotein A protein attached to a color group, e.g., hemoglobin.

chuck Part of fore quarter of beef consisting of the thick area of the first 5 ribs; about 26% of a choice steer carcass.
See Part 2: Beef, Boneless Cuts; Beef Chart; Beef Chuck; Beef Cuts; Beef Cuts and Uses; Beef Retail Yield; Beef Roasting; Beef Wholesale Cuts; Beef Yields; Lamb Chart; Potassium-Rich Foods

chuck rib roast A beef roast made from the chuck area (first 5 ribs).

chuck tender *See* **Scotch tender**
See Part 2: Beef, Boneless Cuts

chuffy Very compact and blocky.

chum *See* **salmon**
See Part 2: Salmon and Trout

chunk *See* Part 2: Fish Forms

chunk honey Pieces of honeycomb covered with extracted honey.

churning Mechanical agitation of whole milk or cream so that the fat globules stick together to form butter and are separated from the buttermilk. *See also* **butter**.

chute Inclined ramp used for loading and unloading.

chutney (chutnee) A spicy India relish composed of sweets, acids and fruits.

chyme The food material that leaves the stomach and enters the small intestine.

chymosin *See* **rennin**

chymotrypsin A proteolytic enzyme which attacks native proteins and is found in *pancreatic* juices in the small intestine; it is secreted in the inactive form called chymotrypsinogen.

chymotrypsinogen Inactive form of chymotrypsin and the form in which it is secreted; it is activated by trypsin.

CI *See* **color index**

ciboule *See* **onion**

cider Juice from apples; bitterness or astringency from tannins in the juice is desirable; the juice will ferment due to yeast in 24 hr unless this action is stopped by pasteurization. Hard cider = fermented apple juice; soft cider = unfermented apple juice; champagne cider = sparkling cider; distilled liquors from cider are apple brandy, calvados, and applejack.

Cider apple classification:
- Sweet (low acid content)
- Sharp (high acid content)
- Bittersweet (sweet with high tannin content)
- Bittersharp (sharp with high tannin content)

In making cider usually 2 or more varieties are mixed. In U.S. cider means unfermented apple juice; internationally it means fermented apple juice or light apple wine (4.3% alcohol by volume).

Composition (apple juice): 88% H_2O, 0.1% protein, 0% fat, 12% carbohydrate, 0.2% ash, pH 2.9-4.0.

Storage: 32-36°F.

See Part 2: Minerals (Trace), Limits

cider vinegar *See* **apple (cider) vinegar**

cinnamon (*Cinnamomum cassia Blume* or *Cinnamomum zeylanicum Nees*) A spice made from the dried bark of an evergreen tree of the cinnamomum family; may be in ground or stick form; bark is peeled and slowly dried into quills, which are folded together for packing. Used in curry powders and confectionery. *See also* **cassia**.

See Part 2: Essential Oils; Flavoring Agents, Natural; Flavor Ingredients, Taste and Flavor Type; Spices, Microbial Content

cinnamon leaf oil An essential oil distilled from the cinnamon leaf.

cinnamon oil An essential oil distilled from broken cinnamon bark.

C.I.P. Cleaned in place.

circumference (C) The perimeter of a circle, 360° or 2π radians.

C = D (3.1416)	D = diameter
C = 2R (3.1416)	R = radius

***cis-trans* isomers** So-called geometric isomers, in which the location of substituent groups in relation to double-bonded carbons is indicated by either cis- (Latin for "on this side") or trans- (Latin for "on the other side"). In structures below the *cis* form has both R groups on one side of the double bond, while in the *trans* form they are diagonally opposite each other:

cis *trans*

citrange Hybrid between citron and orange.
See Part 2: Fruit and Nut Rootstock

citrangequat Hybrid between citrange and kumquat.

citrate A salt of citric acid. Sodium citrate ($C_6H_5Na_3O_7 \cdot 2H_2O$) combines with calcium to prevent blood from clotting; 600 mg of Na citrate/100 ml blood.

citrate azide agar *See* Part 2: Microbiological Examination of Dairy Products

citrate mannitol agar *See* Part 2: Microorganism, Media

citrate medium *See* Part 2: Microorganism, Media

citrate monoglyceride *See* Part 2: Antioxidant Mixtures

citric acid

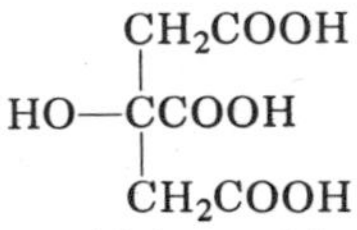

A tricarboxylic acid formed in the cells of plants and animals in a sequence of reactions known as the Krebs cycle; it acts as a catalyst of tissue oxidation. Obtained by fermentation of molasses and used in foods as an antioxidant and acidulant. 0.2% in fresh blood prevents clotting (sodium citrate is also used). *See also* **Krebs cycle**.

See Part 2: Acidulants; Antioxidants, Formulas; Antioxidant Mixtures; Maple Syrup Composition; Normal Solutions; Organic Acids in Fruits and Vegetables; Reagents, Normal Solutions

citron (*Citrus medica*) A small citrus tree that produces an elongated fruit (up to 8 in.) with a rough greenish-yellow to golden yellow rind, under which is a thick white inner skin enclosing a sour pulp.

See Part 2: Minerals, Food; Vegetable Plants

citronella An essential oil distilled by steam from a southeast Asian grass; contains geraniol, camphene and dipentene. Has strong odor and is used as an insect repellent (especially mosquitoes).
See Part 2: Essential Oils

citrus fruit (*Citrous*) Any of the *Rutaceae* family of plants. Tropical or subtropical small trees that contain a winged leafstalk, e.g., citrangequat, citrange, citron, clementine, grapefruit, kumquat (not a true citrus), lemon, lime, limequat, orange, orangequat, ortanique, papeda, pomelo (pummelo), shaddock, tangelos, tangerine, tangor, ugli.

Juice	80–90% sugar and acid; high in vitamin C
Skin	essential oil source
Flowers and leaves	essential oil source
Fruit	citric acid; pectin source

Storage: Unwrap; keep at lowest possible room temperature; use within 1 week; short-term refrigeration not harmful.
See Part 2: Flavor Ingredients, Taste and Flavor Type; Fruit and Nut Rootstock; Fruit and Vegetable Diseases; Fruit Composition; Fruit Storage; Microbiological Media; Pectin Content; Rot Spoilage; Storage Times

city chicken Alternate layers of veal and pork placed on a skewer.
See Part 2: Veal Chart; Veal Cuts

civil defense agar *See* Part 2: Microorganism, Media

Cl Symbol for the element chlorine.

clabber Milk soured to a point where a firm curd is formed but not to the point of whey separation.

Cladosporium *See* Part 2: Mold, Food; Spoilage, Fat in Food

clam A lean, bivalve mollusk; a shellfish.

Types	Occurrence
Butter (*Saxidomus nuttalli*)	Pacific coast
Hard, quahog, hard shell, cherrystones (*Mercenaria mescenaria*)	New England, middle and south Atlantic
Little neck (*Protothaca steminea*)	Pacific coast
Razor (*Siliqua patula*)	Pacific coast
Soft, soft shell (*Mya arenaria*)	North & Middle Atlantic coast
Surf, skimmer (*Spisula solidissima*)	Middle Atlantic

Form	Amount needed for one serving
In shell as appetizer	6
In shell as entree	15–20
Shucked	½–¾ cup

Equivalents:
1 pt shucked = 18 in the shell = 15 oz in the can, minced
1 cup canned = 160 g (5.6 oz)

As purchased	yield (%)	Quantity/serving (oz)	Quantity/serving (No.)
Breaded	85	3.75	
In shell-hard	15	22	½ doz
In shell-soft	30	10	1 doz
Shucked	48	6.5	
Canned	—	3.0	

Clam meat composition: 80–82% H_2O, 11–14% protein, 1–2% fat, 1–6% carbohydrate, 2% ash, pH 5.9–7.1 (av. 6.5).

Clams may contain a toxic substance *Gonyaulax catenella* derived from a plankton organism, and should be periodically tested.
See Part 2: Fish and Shellfish Composition; Fish, Storage; Frozen Food Storage; Frying Time; Minerals, Food; Portion Size; Soups Composition

claret A dry red table wine; red wine of Bordeaux; 10% alcohol by volume. *See also* **cabernet; wine.**

clarification Purification of a liquid such as drinking water, sugar solution, or vegetable oils by adsorbing the suspended solid particles on activated clays or carbon, or by use of aluminum sulfate; impurities causing undesirable color, odor, and taste in the liquid are thus removed. *See also* **colloid.**

clary oil (clary sage oil) (oil of muscatel) A yellowish essential oil used as a flavoring.

classification Separating small solid units into groups of uniform size, by passing them over a selective device such as a wide-mesh screen. Such fruits as peas, olives, etc., are graded in this way.

class mark The center value for a class interval (e.g., class interval 12.5 to 17.5—class mark 15).

clavicle *See* Part 2: Bone

clay (aluminum silicate), $(Al_2O_3SiO_2 \cdot H_2O)$ (1) A firm fine soil that is coherent when wet and hard when dry. *See also* **kaolin.** (2) A variety of cowpeas.
See Part 2: Soil Classes

clean cut A method of describing a live animal.
head and neck: finely sculptured appearance, no coarseness
bone: no puffy or meaty joints
cannon or shank: free from coarseness or meatiness

cleaning solution A solution made by adding 500 ml concentrated sulfuric acid to 25 ml saturated sodium dichromate; allow to cool before use; this red solution will turn green when oxidizing power has been exhausted.

clear cut shoulder (shoulder clod) A beef roast made from muscle on the fore shank, to the rear of the forearm bone.

clear flour A grade of white flour which may be made from the poorer 5 to 60% of all the white flour milled; it is further subdivided into the following grades:

fancy clear	or	first clear
first clear		second clear

clearing agents *See* Part 2: Minerals, Trace, Limits

clear plate *See* Part 2: Pork Shoulder

cled agar *See* Part 2: Microorganism, Media

clementine A citrus fruit between an orange and a tangerine in size, color and ease of peeling.

Climax A variety of lespedeza.

cloak fern A plant having a toxic principle.
See Part 2: Poisonous Plants

cloche, sous Under a bell.

clod Deltoideus and infraspinatus muscles of the chuck; they lie lateral to the scapula and ventral to its spine; the large muscle from a beef chuck.
See Part 2: Beef, Boneless Cuts

clod bone The humerus.

Clorox Proprietary name for sodium hypochlorite ($NaClO \cdot 5H_2O$); % available chlorine 2–6% home use, 10–18% industrial use.

closed side (beef) The right side.

Clostridium botulinum The bacteria (at least 5 types) that produce the toxin responsible for the food poisoning known as botulism; anaerobic bacteria which produce very heat resistant spores; this is the most serious but rarest type of food poisoning, with from 30 to 65% of the cases ending in death; it is a gram-positive rod; the bacteria should be heated to 250°F for at least 24 mins to kill them. *See also* ***Bacillus botulinus*** **; botulism.**
See Part 2: Microbial Toxins; Microbiological Media; Microorganism, Media; Spoilage, Carbohydrate Foods; Spoilage, Protein Foods; Thermophiles

Clostridium perfringens An anaerobic microbe that causes food poisoning; some spores have extreme heat resistance; it is universally prevalent, the greatest problem being heat-resistant spores that have survived the cooking process and germinate and multiply when the food is left at an intermediate temperature. The key to safety is temperature control (danger range 65–122°F) after cooking.
See Part 2: Food Poisoning, Bacteria; Illness from Food; Infectious Diseases, Food-borne; Microbiological Media

clostrisel agar *See* Part 2: Microbiological Media

clothing wool Wool that is too short to reach the combing grade.

cloudberry (*Rubus chamaemorus*) A berry that is often used like the blackberry; it grows in very cold climates and is of a golden color.

clouding agent *See* Part 2: Clouding Agents

clove (*Caryophyllus aromaticus* or *Eugenia caryophyllata Thunb.*) The unopened flower bud of the clove tree (evergreen) is used for spices; buds are picked by hand and sun-dried.

They have a round head and are spike-like in shape, and may be obtained ground or whole; should contain the following: not more than 5% clove stems; not less than 15% volatile ether extract; not less than 12% quercitannic acid; not more than 10% crude fiber; not more than 7% total ash; not more than 0.5% acid-insoluble ash.
See Part 2: Essential Oils; Flavoring Agents, Natural; Flavor Ingredients, Taste and Flavor Type; Spices, Microbial Content

clove oil An essential oil distilled from bud, stalks and leaves of the clove plant; used for making vanillin.

clover (*Trifolium*) Many members of the pea family with trifoliolate leaves and flowers with a dense head; used as forage; 60 lb of seed per bushel.
See Part 2: Seed Germination

club *See* Part 2: Beef Cuts; Beef Cuts and Uses; Beef Retail Yield; Broiling Meat

club cheese *See* **coldpack cheese**

club sandwich A sandwich containing bacon, turkey or chicken, lettuce, mayonnaise, and sometimes tomato between slices of toast. May be either two or three "decks," and served open or closed.

club steak Steak cut from the rib end of the short loin, located in front of the T-bone steak.

clupanodonic A fatty acid.
See Part 2: Fatty Acids, Fats and Oils; Fatty Acids and Their Properties; Unsaturated Fatty Acids

Cm Symbol for the element curium.

cm *See* **centimeter**

CMC *See* **carboxymethylcellulose**

Co Symbol for the element cobalt.

CO_2 *See* **carbon dioxide; Dry Ice**

coagulase An enzyme that induces coagulation.
See Part 2: Microbiological Media

coagulation Aggregation of protein macromolecules into clusters or clumps of semisolid material, which may be initiated by heat (egg white), by a change in pH (milk), or by enzymatic activation (blood). The change is usually irreversible.

coal A mineral comprised of about 90% carbon, used as fuel and source of coke and coal tar.

anthracite: 1 cubic foot = approx. 53 lb
bituminous: 1 cubic foot = approx. 48 lb

See Part 2: Fuel, Heating Value

coarse hominy *See* **hominy**

Coastal Bermuda A variety of Bermuda grass used for pastures.

coatepec *See* **Mexican altura**

coating (1) A natural hard cellulosic layer on a seed or fruit. (2) A thin layer of material applied to a product either mechanically or by dipping, as chocolate on candy or casein solution on paper.
See Part 2: Coatings

cob (1) The fibrous inner portion of the ear of corn (maize) from which the kernels have been removed; used for smoking meats and as fuel in some agricultural areas. (2) A short-legged horse. *See also* **hazel.**

cobalamine Vitamin B_{12}, which cures pernicious anemia; it contains trivalent cobalt.

cobalt (Co) A metallic element; at. no. 27; at. wt. 58.94; Group VIII of Periodic Table; oxidation states +2, +3; electron configuration 2–8–15–2
orbit K L M N
It is necessary for hemoglobin formation.
See Part 2: Grain Analysis; Normal Solutions; Wheat, Minerals

cobnut *See* **hazel**

cocarboxylase A coenzyme ($C_{12}H_{19}ClN_4O_7P_2S \cdot H_2O$). *See also* **thiamin pyrophosphate.**

cocci A subdivision of bacteria whose shape resembles that of a sphere (Greek, berry).
See Part 2: Bacteria, Molds and Yeasts

coccygeal vertebrae *See* **caudal vertebrae**
See Part 2: Bone

Cochin An Asiatic class of chickens that has feathered shanks, yellow skin, long feathering and lay a brown egg; varieties: buff*, partridge*, white*, black* (* indicates there are also bantam varieties).
See Part 2: Poultry Breeds and Varieties

cochineal A purplish red coloring matter made from dried bodies of the insect, *Coccus cacti.*
See Part 2: Unsaturated Fatty Acids

cock (old rooster) Mature male chicken over 10 months of age; hardened breast bone. *See also* rooster.

cockerel A male fowl. *See also* **toms.**

cockle (1) A shellfish; 20% edible (10–12% protein). (2) A weed.

cocklebur A plant having a toxic principle.
See Part 2: Poisonous Plants

cocktail sauce A sauce made with peppers, tomato, etc., usually served with seafood cocktails.
See Part 2: French Dressing Variations

cocoa (***Theobroma cacao***) A small tree that produces yellow or red pods, which contain beans encased in white mucilage. The beans and mucilage are fermented; the dull red beans are then dried, shelled, roasted and ground. Cocoa is made in much the same manner as chocolate except some of the fat is removed and the final product is ground; it contains less than 8% fat. The bean contains 50–57% cocoa butter (fat).
Terms
Cocoa (drinking): cocoa butter removed;
Chocolate: extra cocoa butter, sugar and milk added;
Nib: cotyledon
Manufacturing terms
Winnowing: separation of shells from nibs;
Nib grinding: by grinding, nibs are converted into chocolate liquor;
Dutching (alkalizing): color becomes darker and flavor milder;
Pressing: cocoa butter is separated from powder.
2–3½ tablespoons cocoa + ½ tablespoon butter = 1 oz or one square of chocolate
4 tablespoons = 1 oz; 4 cups = 1 lb; ¼ cup = 1 oz (28 g).
Cocoa composition without milk (%): H_2O 1, protein 4, fat 2, carbohydrate 89, ash 2, pH 6.3.
See also **cacao.**
See Part 2: Cocoa, Composition; Cocoa Cultivation; Food, Composition; Minerals, Food; Minerals, Trace, Limits; Wastes, Agricultural and Industrial

cocoa butter (theobroma oil) Fat expressed from cacao bean

specific gravity	0.950 –0.975
refractive index (60°C)	1.449 –1.451
melting point	28°–33°C
saponification no.	188 –202
iodine no.	32 –40
pH	6.6

Acid composition (%): myristic 0.5, palmitic 25, stearic 35, oleic 37, linoleic 3, linolenic 0.5.
Used for confectionery, soaps and pharmaceutical products (suppositories).
See Part 2: Fats and Oils, Composition; Fats and Oils, Fatty Acid Composition; Fats and Oils, Physical and Chemical Properties; Fatty Acids, Fats and Oils

cocoa nibs Broken kernels of the cacao bean.

coconut (cocoanut) (***Cocos nucifera***) The hard shelled nut of a palm that grows in tropical lowlands; begins fruiting in 6–9 years; 50 nuts/yr/tree; 23 lb copra/yr/tree.
Part of plant
Palm trunk: building timber;
Leaves: house thatching;
Husk (coir): ropes and coconut matting;
Meat (copra), residue after oil extraction (oil cake): livestock feed;
1000 lb coconuts = 500 lb copra = 25 gal. oil = 170 lb desiccated or shredded coconut;
1 lb = 5⅓ to 8 cups shredded coconut;
1 cup shredded coconut = 2⅘ to 3 oz (80 g).
The milk is more abundant in green nuts; it contains sugar and oil.
See Part 2: Beans, Peas and Nuts; Coconut, Amino Acids; Flavor Ingredients, Taste and Flavor Type; Fruit Classification; Minerals, Food; Oils and Fats Composition; Oil, Seed and Fruit; Plant Foods, Composition; Protein Factors; Pulses, Nuts and Seeds Composition; Storage; Unsaponifiable Matter

coconut, desiccated Coconut with reduced moisture content; will keep for 1 month without refrigeration.

coconut meat Endosperm of coconut.

Composition	H_2O (%)	Protein (%)	Fat (%)	Carbohydrate (%)	Ash (%)
Fresh	51	3	35	9	1
Dried, unsweetened	3	7	65	23	1.5

coconut oil (copra oil) A non-drying, highly saturated, very stable oil.

Saturated fatty acid carbons	unhydrogenated	hydrogenated
6	0.2	trace
8	5-8	8
10	7	7
12	45-48	48
14	17-18	18
16	9-10	10
18	2-7	10
Monounsaturated		
18	6	trace
Polyunsaturated	2	trace
Iodine value	7-10	23
Saponification value	250-260	250-260
Melting point	37°-39°C	25°C
Acid number	0.01	
Specific gravity 20°/4°C	0.9226	
Unsaponifable (%)	<0.5	
Saponification no.	246-260	
Titer	20°-24°C	

See Part 2: Fats and Oils, Composition; Fats and Oils, Fatty Acid Composition; Fats and Oils, Physical and Chemical Properties; Fatty Acids, Fats and Oils; Fats and Oils, Characteristics; Iodine and Saponification Values; Melting Points, Fats and Oils; Oil or Fat, Characteristics; Refractive Indices, Fats and Oils; Saturated Fatty Acids; Specific Gravities, Fats and Oils; Spoilage, Fat in Food; Titer, Fats and Oils; Tocopherols

coconut oil cake (copra meal) Ground cake after oil extraction of copra; used for livestock feed.
Composition (%): H_2O 5, protein 23, fat 8, fiber 9.

coconut water Liquid from the interior of the coconut.
Composition (%): H_2O 5-12, protein 22-23, fat 7-8, fiber 9-13, nitrogen-free extract 40.

cod (1) The scrotum after removal of testicles on a steer; it usually contains fat. (2) A saltwater fish. *See also* **cod fish; demersal fish.**

coddle To cook slowly and gently; to cook below the boiling point, as of eggs.

codeine $C_{18}H_{21}NO_3$ A narcotic alkaloid derived from morphine (poppy) and used for relief of coughs. Allergic reactions may occur.

Codex Alimentarius A group formed to set up food standards to be used in international trade; works cooperately with FAO and WHO.

cod fat A large piece of fat on the flank of both steers and heifers.

cod fish (cod; scrod (baby)) A soft-finned lean fish caught on Middle Atlantic and Pacific coasts.
Atlantic cod = *Gadus morhua*
Pacific cod = *Gadus macrocephalus*
market classes: snapper, up to 1½ lb; scrod, 1½ to 2½ lb; market, 2½ to 10 lb; large, 10 to 25 lb; whale, over 25 lb; yield, 43%.
Muscle composition (%): H_2O 81, protein 16-18, fat 0.3, ash 1.
See Part 2: Fish and Shellfish Composition; Fish, Smoke-cured; Fish, Storage; Frozen Food Storage; Glutamate; Minerals, Food; Riboflavin, Food; Thiamin, Food; Unsaponifiable Matter; Vitamin A, Fish; Vitamin D, Fish; Vitamin D, Food; Water Activity, Organisms and Food

cod liver oil Oil expressed from livers of *Gadidae* species of fish;

specific gravity	0.922-0.930
refractive index (15.5°C)	1.479-1.485
saponification no.	180-190
iodine no.	135-180
I.U. vitamin A/g	400-4,000
I.U. vitamin D/g	40-400

See Part 2: Fats and Oils, Physical and Chemical Properties; Iodine and Saponification Values; Titer, Fats and Oils; Unsaturated Fatty Acids; Vitamin A, Food

coefficient of variation (C) A measure of variation of observations that has been adjusted for sample magnitude so that variation between samples with different magnitude can be compared.

$$C = \frac{s}{\bar{x}}$$

s = estimate of standard deviation (σ)
$\bar{x}$ = sample mean

Sometimes expressed as a percentage $\frac{\sigma}{\bar{x}} \cdot 100 = \%$

coenzyme A complex organic compound (nucleotide) which combines with and activates an enzyme system; an essential factor in such biochemical transformations as cellular oxidation, Krebs cycle and vitamin activation. *See also* **prosthetic group.**

coenzyme I (CoI) *See* **diphosphopyridine nucleotide**

coenzyme II (CoII) *See* **triphosphopyridine nucleotide**

coenzyme R *See* **biotin**

coffee A berry or bean of the coffee tree (*Coffea arabica*) which must be roasted (230–250°C) before using as a drink; a tropical plant whose beans are roasted, ground and brewed in hot water to yield a stimulating non-alcoholic drink; 1½ lb green dried beans per tree.

Species

Coffea arabica: a small tree that bears a green berry that turns red when ripe; each berry contains 2 beans.

mild coffee: berry is opened by a machine, beans are fermented in water and sun-dried; bean retains parchment skin.

hard coffee: sun-drying whole berry and removing pump by machine; parchment skin removed.

Coffea canephora: yields a smaller bean and is known as robusta.

Coffea liberica: very robust

origin	name
Colombia	medellins, armenias, mamizales, (MAM's)
Brazil	santos, paranas, minas
Mexico	coatepecs, oaxacas, tapachulas
Guatemala	antiguas
Honduras	copans
Ethiopia	djimmas, harrars
Congo	oicru
Angola	ambriz
Hawaii	kona

Roasting: 400°F internal temperature to develop aroma and taste; 10–12% moisture removed; caramelization of sucrose; pyrolysis of carbohydrate and protein; 16% weight loss.

Grinding: to facilitate water extraction. Size: regular, 1 mm; drip, 0.75 mm; fine, 0.38 mm.

Regular:
4⅓ to 5½ cups = 1 lb
1 cup = 85 g (3.0 oz)
70 to 80 tbsp = 1 lb

Instant:
10 to 12 cups = 1 lb
1 cup = 40 grams (1.4 oz)
1 lb yields 480 cups

Yield:
For 50 people (2 cups each): 6 oz instant coffee to 4 gal. water; steep for 5 min; 40 to 50 servings = 1 lb of regular coffee and 1 qt cream.

Storage limits:

	Bean	Ground
Room temperature	3–4 weeks	7–10 days
Refrigerator	do not store	3 weeks
Freezer	3 months	—

Composition (%)

	Mocha	
	Green	Roasted
Caffeine	1.3	1.3
Water extract	31	30
Fat	14	14
Protein	9	10
Fiber	22	15
Ash	4	4
Moisture	9	3

Beverage coffee has no nutritional value; stimulating value 1.1 to 1.2% caffeine. *See also* **caffeine.**

See Part 2: Coffee Berry; Coffee Composition; Coffee Granule Designation; Coffee Particle Size; Coffee Yield; Minerals, Food; Minerals, Trace, Limits; Portion Size; Wastes, Agricultural and Industrial

coffee bean The seed or bean of the coffee tree (*Coffea arabica*).
See Part 2: Poisonous Plants

coffee creamer Container to hold cream; (coffee cream is 16–30% fat); coffee creamer (coffee whitener, a more modern term) is usually made from corn syrup solids, casein, vegetable fat, sodium caseinate, emulsifiers and gums; can also be a nondairy whitener.
See Part 2: Cultured Dairy-Products, Composition

coffee substitutes Roasted grains, figs, beans, dandelion roots, chicory roots.

coffee whitener Imitation, nondairy, fabricated cream and half-and-half substitutes; they are generally made from vegetable oil, carbohydrate, and a low level of protein; term can also include cream.
See Part 2: Coffee Whitener, Composition

cognac A brandy from the cognac region of France; letters on bottles mean: E, especial; F, fine; O, old; S, superior; P, pale; X, extra; C, cognac.
See Part 2: Flavor Ingredients, Taste and Flavor Type

cognac oil, green Wine yeast oil obtained by steam distillation of wine lees; has odor of cognac.

coho A type of salmon. *See also* **salmon.**
See Part 2: Salmon and Trout

cohune A nut obtained from a Central American palm; the oil contains 45% lauric, 17% myristic and 10% oleic acids; it is edible and nondrying.
See Part 2: Iodine and Saponification Values

coir Coconut husk fiber used for padding and fiber type products; approx 23% of the nut.

coke The residue of thermal decomposition (destructive distillation) of coal or petroleum; it is 90% carbon; one ton of coal yields about 0.7 ton coke.

cola (kola) The kola nut or an extract prepared from it; used in beverages; nut contains 1.5% caffeine. *See also* **kola nut.**

See Part 2: Beverage Carbonated, Ingredients; Calories, Daily Recommendations; Flavor Ingredients, Taste and Flavor Type; Flavors, Beverage

colada An alcoholic beverage prepared as follows: Place in a shaker, ½ cup crushed ice, 1 jigger (1½ oz) bourbon, 1 oz cream of coconut, 2 oz unsweetened pineapple juice; shake and pour into tall glass filled with ice cubes; add cherry.

Colbeck EY agar *See* Part 2: Microorganism, Media

colby cheese A hard (softer than cheddar), light yellow to orange cheese made from whole milk; cylindrical in shape, with mild to mellow flavor; ripens in 1-3 mo. by bacteria.
Composition (%): H_2O 39%, protein 21%, fat 31%, salt 1.7%, ash 4%.
See Part 2: Cheese Characteristics; Cheese Vitamin Content

cold cuts Comminuted cooked meat products that are often served without further cooking; sliced cold meat with or without cheese.
Storage: original wrapper, refrigerate; use within 3 to 5 days of opening.
See Part 2: Storage Times

coldpack cheese A blend of fresh and aged natural cheese; the flavor is that of natural cheese but the texture is softer.

coldpack cheese food Similar to coldpack cheese but also includes other dairy products and sweetening agents and has a higher moisture content.

cold soap (semi-boiled soap) A soft soap made from tallow and grease using a potash base; glycerin fraction remains in the soap; it is less harsh than boiled soap.

cold test A test for evaluation of winterization of an oil. The oil is held in ice water and the time required for first cloudiness to appear is noted. *See also* **winterization.**

cole *See* **rape**

coleoptile The first leaf (seed leaf or primary leaf) in seeding of monocotyledon which forms a protective sheath.
See Part 2: Wheat Kernel; Wheat Kernel Parts

coleorhiza The sheath surrounding the radicle (primary root) that the roots grow through.
See Part 2: Wheat Kernel; Wheat Kernel Parts

coleseed *See* **rape**

cole slaw A mixture of shredded cabbage and salad dressing or mayonnaise and many different varieties of seasoning.
See Part 2: Portion Size

coli A type of bacteria.
See Part 2: Microorganism Reactions on Differential Tube Media

coliform Sieve-like; resembling the *Escherichia coli*; coliform group—all aerobic and facultative anaerobic, gram-negative, nonspore-forming bacilli which ferment lactose and produce gas.
See Part 2: Egg Specifications; Intestinal Microorganisms; Intestinal Microorganisms in Triple-Sugar Agar; Microbiological Media; Microbiological Standards, Dairy; Microorganism, Culture Media, Dairy and Food Products; Microorganism, Culture Media, Water and Sewage, Standard Methods; Microorganism, Media

collagen Proteinaceous connective tissue of meat made up of parallel fibers which can be converted to gelatin by boiling in water.
See Part 2: Connective Tissue, Composition; Connective Tissue Proteins

collard (*Brassica oleracea* var. *viridis*) A kale whose leaf is used as food.
Storage: wash and drain; store in refrigerator crisper or plastic bag; use within 1 to 2 days.
Raw composition (%):
H_2O 87%, protein 4%, fat 0.7%, carbohydrate 7%, ash 1.6%.
See Part 2: Minerals, Food; Plant Foods, Composition; Vegetable Boiling; Vegetable Composition; Vegetable Frozen Yield; Vegetable Plants

collective fruits *See* **multiple fruit**

Colletotricum A type of mold.
See Part 2: Mold, Food

colloid A particle whose size range lies between the lower limit of resolution of an optical microscope (1 micron) and the size of an average molecule (1 millimicron). Such particles are too large to pass through a parchment membrane, but they remain suspended in dispersions because they are too small to settle out by gravity. Colloidal systems may be of several types; solid in liquid (casein in milk), solid in gas (smoke) gas in solid or liquid (foam); liquid in gas (fog); liquid in liquid (emulsion), etc. Many protein molecules are of colloidal dimensions; when they form a coating on a fat particle, as in milk, they are called protective colloids. *See also* **dispersed phase; continuous phase.**

colloidal phosphate $Ca_3(PO_4)_2$ calcium phosphate A fertilizer material; 20% total P_2O_5.

Colocasia Tuberous-rooted aroids; e.g., the taro whose rootstock is an edible starchy staple in the tropics and which can be fermented into poi.
See Part 2: Vegetable Storage

cologne spirit *See* **silent spirit**

color *See* **colorant**

Colorados hide A hide branded on rump or side.

colorant Any substance that imparts color; they are broadly classified as either pigments or dyes, although the distinction is not precise, e.g., chlorophyll is an organic pigment and lakes are organic pigments precipitated on an inorganic base. Most food colorants (FD&C colors) are synthetic coal-tar dyes and lakes. They require approval by the FDA before use.

Many natural colorants are vegetable-derived, e.g., alkanet, annatto, carotene, chlorophyll, saffron, tumeric.

See Part 2: Color Additives; Color, Meat; Colors Permanently Listed; Minerals (Trace), Limits.

colorimetric analysis An optical method of analysis in which concentration is determined by comparing light transmitted (a specific wave length) through known concentrations of the compound with light transmitted through the sample.

color index (C.I.) Colorants are given a color index number by the British Society of Dyers and Colorists which identifies an individual dye.

color wheel A device in which papers of various colors arranged in spectral sequence are placed as sectors on a disc; by spinning the disc, the colors appear to fuse and form a single color; used as a comparison for food color.

colostrum Milk produced for several days after parturition; it is quite different in composition from normal milk.

colt A young male horse 4 years or under.

Columbia (1) A medium-wool breed of sheep developed in Wyoming and Idaho by crossing Lincoln rams on Rambouillet ewes; they are white-faced sheep with no horns and their fleece grades approximately 3/8. (2) A variety of trefoil.

See Part 2: Sheep Breeds

Columbia CNA agar *See* Part 2: Microorganism, Media

Columbia river smelt *See* **smelt**

Columbian Excelso A Columbian coffee that has strong body, mellow aroma, and is smooth and rich-tasting.

Columbian 5-Year Aged A very smooth aged coffee.

columbium *See* **niobium**

colza *See* **rapeseed oil**

comb honey Honey as it comes from the hive in wooden frames.

combinations The number of groupings that can be formed from objects without regard to order (e.g., n objects taken r at a time:

$$C_r^n = \frac{n!}{r!\,(n-r)!}$$

combination of w, x, y, z taken 3 at a time:

$$C_r^n = \frac{1 \times 2 \times 3 \times 4}{(1 \times 2 \times 3)\,(1)} = 4 \quad wxy \quad xyz \quad wyz \quad wxz$$

sum of all combinations from 1 to n in a group:

$$S_c = 2^n - 1 = 2^4 - 1 = 15$$

w	wxy
x	wxz
y	wyz
z	xyz
wx	$wxyz$
wy	
wz	
xy	
xz	
yz	

See also **permutations.**

combing wool Wool that is both long-stapled and strong-fibered.

combustion A chemical reaction, usually caused by heat, between oxygen and another substance. Oxides result from inorganic combustion (water is the product of combustion of hydrogen). Combustion of organic materials always yields carbon dioxide and water as end products, with evolution of heat. It can be considered the opposite of photosynthesis.

commercial grade *See* **technical or commercial**

See Part 2: Grades, Meat; Meat Grade Stamps

comminute To reduce to a very small particle size.

comminuted cheese *See* **coldpack cheese**

common A variety of lespedeza (sericea).

common bass *See* **sea bass**

Common Bermuda A variety of Bermuda grass used for lawns.

compact bone The outer, hard, brittle, white shell of bones.

comparisons *See* Part 2: Paired Comparisons

complete protein A protein when used alone in the diet that is adequate for normal growth.

complexus Triangular muscle in the neck area between the ligamentum nuchae and the cervical vertebrae.

See Part 2: Beef Rib Nomenclature

Compositae A large order of plants including the aster.

See Part 2: Vegetables Classification

composition The substances included in a given mixture, by name and percentage.

See Part 2: Composition of Food

compote A dessert or appetizer consisting of fruit sliced and served in natural juice, or cooked in syrup.

compound A substance, either organic or inorganic, that is composed of two or more elements; compounds are homogeneous and can be separated only by a chemical reaction. *See also* **mixture.**

compressed yeast A moist mixture of yeast and cornstarch.

shelf life, refrigerated (31°F) 2 weeks;
frozen 2 months;
activation temperature 105°F

comrcl *See* **commercial**

concentrate A product from which water has been removed and which will be reconstituted prior to use; milk, ⅔ water removed.
See Part 2: Dairy Terms; Milk, Concentrated Products

concentrated milk *See* **plain condensed milk; plain condensed skimmed milk**
See Part 2: Concentrated and Dried Milk Products

concentrated skimmed milk *See* **plain condensed skimmed milk**

concentration The percentage of solute dissolved in a given amount of solvent.

Concord A variety of grape, dark blue in color.

concrete Portland cement (hydraulic cement) containing various percentages of aggregate (gravel, cinders, fly ash, etc.). *See also* **cement.**
See Part 2: Insulation; Insulation, Conductivity Values

condemned An animal carcass or parts of carcass that an Inspector has found unfit for human consumption.

condensed Reduced to denser consistency by removal of moisture.

condensed milk Milk preserved by evaporation and the addition of sugar; 2.3 lb milk = 1 lb condensed milk (whole); specific gravity 1.16. *See also* **plain condensed milk; sweetened condensed milk.**
See Part 2: Condensed Milk Dressing; Dairy Terms; Milk and Cheese Composition; Milk and Milk Products, Vitamin Content; Milk Composition; Milk, Concentrated Products; Vitamin A, Milk and Milk Products

condiment A flavoring agent having a sharp spicy taste, e.g., mustard, pepper.
See Part 2: Stabilizers, Thickeners

condition (of meat animals or draft horses) Degree of Fatness; (of race horses) Fitness to race.

condol Tropical vegetable.
See Part 2: Vegetable Storage

conductance (G) The reciprocal of resistance in an electrolytic solution.

$$G = \frac{1}{R} \qquad \begin{array}{l} R = \text{resistance in ohms} \\ G = \text{in reciprocal ohms} \end{array}$$

conductivity The ability of a material to conduct electricity. The opposite of resistivity.
See Part 2: Insulation, Conductivity Values

cone wheat *See* **wheat**

confection A cooked mixture of sugar, flavoring, fruits, and the like having a predominantly sweet taste; candy.
Hard candies (high-boiled sweets): highly saturated, super-cooled sugar solutions.
Chewy confections: (grained) supersaturated sugar solutions such as fudges, cream centers, pulled grained mints, rigid grained marshmallows, hard and soft panned centers; (nongrained) unsaturated sugar solutions, e.g., marshmallows, taffies, nougats, caramels, jellies, gums, kisses.
Aerated or whipped confections: agitation with incorporation of air.
See Part 2: Minerals, Trace, Limits

confectioners coatings *See* Part 2: Coatings

confectioner's sugar (icing sugar) (1) A highly refined sugar made into a very fine powder, suited to confectioner's use; 3½ cups = 1 lb; powdered sugar; fine (XXXX). (2) Sugar which is extra coarse in size (sometimes called manufacturers' sugar).

congealing point (C.P.) The temperature at which a liquid oil becomes solid; used to follow hydrogenation. *See also* **freezing point.**

congeners Flavorful substances generated with alcohol during fermentation.

connective tissue A tough proteinaceous material associated with muscles.
See Part 2: Connective Tissue, Composition; Connective Tissue Proteins

conserve A combination of several fruits and nuts cooked until thick and clear; a blend of 2 or more fruits and nut meats in a thick syrup or jelly (½ to ¾ lb of sugar/lb fruit).

consistency A measure of firmness or viscosity; a penetrometer is used to measure the consistency of fats; for oils and other thick liquids a viscometer is used.

consommé A clarified, highly seasoned thin soup made by simmering meat and vegetables.

constitutional formula *See* **structural formula**

contignac *See* **quince**

continental roast *See* **French roast**

continuous phase (external phase) The dispersion medium in a colloidal or other heterogeneous system. For example, air is the continuous phase in a water-in-air suspension (fog, aerosol); water is the continuous phase in a solid-in-liquid suspension (milk). *See also* **dispersed phase.**

controlled atmosphere (CA) storage A storage environment in which not only the temperature but the concentration of oxygen, nitrogen and carbon dioxide are adjusted to an optimum level and maintained constant for a desired period. This practice was adopted in 1940 for fruit and vegetable storage. *See also* **storage.**

convenience food Preprepared or semiprepared foods that require a minimum of preparation prior to consumption.

converted rice A patented process for transferring some of the B vitamins from the outer layer of the rice grains into the interior before milling.

Convolvulaceae The large morning-glory family of plants.
See Part 2: Vegetable Classification

cooked (fully cooked) (thoroughly cooked) (ready-to-eat) (ready-to-serve) (meat label) A meat product which must have a cooked appearance, which usually requires an internal temperature of at least 148°F. *See also* **smoked meat.**

cooked dressing *See* Part 2: Cooked Dressing

cooked meat *See* Part 2: Meat Storage

cooked meat medium *See* Part 2: Microorganism, Media

cooked salad dressing A thickened sauce containing:
liquid (water or milk)
acid (vinegar or acid fruit juice)
seasoning (sugar, salt, etc.)
fat (butter, lard)
thickening agent (flour, starch or eggs)

cooked salami *See* **salami cotto**

Cooke Rose Bengal agar *See* Part 2: Microorganism, Media

cookie A dry, sweet, flat cake; frozen (0°F) storage 4-6 mo.
See Part 2: Calories, Daily Recommendations; Grain Products Composition

cooking Preparation of food by exposure to heat (baking, frying, roasting, boiling).
See Part 2: Beef, Cooking; Beef Degrees of Doneness; Braising Meat; Cooking in Liquid, Time; Fruit, Cooking; Frying Time; Lamb Braising; Lamb Broiling; Lamb Roasting; Lamb Simmering; Microwave Cooking, Fresh Vegetables; Microwave Cooking, Frozen Vegetables; Micro-Cooking, Fruit; pH, Post Mortem; Pork Cookery; Pork Loin Cooking; Poultry Cooking, Frozen; Variety Meat, Cooking; Variety Meat Preparation; Vegetables, Cooking Frozen; Vitamin Retention, Meat

cooking oil A vegetable oil that has been refined, bleached and deodorized but not winterized.
Storage: short-term, room temperature; long-term, refrigerate; if it becomes cloudy or solid, this is not harmful and the oil will clear when heated.

cooking temperatures (roast meat)

Meat	Cut (Lb)	Oven Temp. (°F)	Meat Temp. (°F)	Total Time (Hr)	Min per Lb
Beef					
well-done	Standing rib	325	170	2¾-3¼	27-30
	5-7				
medium	5-7	325	160	2¼-2¾	22-25
rare	5-7	325	140	2-2¼	18-20
well-done	Rolled rib	325	170	4½-5½	48-52
	5-7				
medium	5-7	325	160	3½-4	33-38
rare	5-7	325	140	3-3½	30-32
Lamb					
shoulder, rolled	4-6	325	175	3-4	40-45
shoulder	5-7	325	175	3-3½	30-35
leg	6-7	325	175	3¼-4	30-35
Pork					
shoulder, rolled	4-5	300-350	170	1¾-3⅓	35-40
shoulder	5-8	300-350	170	2½-4¾	30-35
½-loin	5-7	300-350	170	3-4¾	35-40
½-fresh ham (bone in)	5-8	300-350	170	3-6	30-35
Pork, cured*					
½-ham*	6-8	325	130	1¼-1¾	14
ham*	Boned	325	130	Varies with size	12-15
ham*	Canned 8-13	325	130	2-2¼	10-15
Veal					
rump	4	325	175	2¾-3	40
leg	Whole 6-8	325	175	3¼-4	30-35
½-leg	3	325	175	2	40
Chicken	2-3	350	185	1¼-1½	30-40

(Continued)

Meat	Cut (Lb)	Oven Temp. (°F)	Meat Temp. (°F)	Total Time (Hr)	Min per Lb
Turkey	6–8	325	185	3½–4	30–35
	8–12	325	185	4–4½	22–30

*"Cook before eating" hams and picnics should be cooked to meat temp. of 160°F; this will take approx. ⅓ more cooking time.

coomys *See* **koumiss**

coon cheese A subdivision of cheddar cheese.

cooperative group A wholesale grocery operation owned by the retailers.

coorg Mandarin type citrus orange.
See Part 2: Fruit Storage

copaiba A type of balsamic resin from Brazil and Venezuela, used as a flavoring and oderant.
See Part 2: Flavoring Agents, Natural

coppa *See* **capocollo**

coppa picante Square molded cala butts that have been cured and covered with black pepper.

copper (Cu) A metallic element; at. no. 29; at. wt. 63.54; Group IB of Periodic Table; oxidation states +1, +2; electron configuration 2-8-18-1 orbit K L M N
body function: necessary for utilization of Fe in hemoglobin synthesis.

Food:	high	low
	Meat, liver, fish, cereals	Milk

See Part 2: Egg Products Nutritive Value; Grain Analysis; Minerals, Food; Minerals, Plant or Animal Tissue; Minerals (Trace), Limits; Normal Solutions; Nutrients in Crops; pH and Availability of Plant Nutrients; Water Drinking Standards; Wheat, Minerals

copperas Ferrous sulfate ($FeSO_4 \cdot 7H_2O$).
See Part 2: Fertilizer Materials

copper oxide CuO or Cu_2O.
See Part 2: Fertilizer Materials; Normal Solutions

copper sulfate $CuSO_4$.
See Part 2: Fertilizer Materials; Normal Solutions

copperweed A plant having a toxic principle.
See Part 2: Poisonous Plants

copra Dried coconut meat used for food in tropical countries.

coquille, en Served in a shell.

coracoid A cartilage or bone extending from the scapula toward the sternum.
See Part 2: Bone

cord A measure of volume of cut wood equivalent to a stack 8 × 4 × 4 ft. *See also* **wood**.

cordial (American term), liqueur (European term) An alcoholic beverage produced by mixing or redistilling neutral spirits, brandy, gin or other distilled spirits with or over fruits, flowers, plants, juices or other natural flavoring materials; min, 2½% sugar; less than 10% dry.
See Part 2: Minerals (Trace), Limits

core The central seed-bearing portion of certain fruits.
See Part 2: Orange Structure

coriander (***Coriandrum sativum*** **L.**) A small plant of the parsley family; seed, whole (⅛-in. in diameter, prominently ridged) or ground. Used as a condiment, in curries, in liquor; color range from white to yellowish brown; not more than 7% total ash; not more than 1.5% acid-insoluble ash; approx. 0.5% volatile oil; approx. 13% fatty matter.
See Part 2: Essential Oils; Flavoring Agents, Natural; Unsaturated Fatty Acids; Vegetable Storage

corium (1) The second layer of skin containing tissue and lying beneath the epidermis. (2) A genus of viruses.
See Part 2: Hide, Layers; Hides, Salt Absorption

cork The bark of an oak tree (*Quercus suber*) native to Spain and cultivated in California. Used for insulation, bottle stoppers, life belts, etc.

Size No.	Approx Diam of Large End of Cork (mm)	Size No.	Approx Diam of Large End of Cork (mm)
000	7	12	28
00	8	13	30
0	10	14	31
1	11	15	33
2	12	16	35
3	14	17	36
4	15	18	38
5	17	19	39
6	19	20	41
7	20	22	44
8	22	24	47
9	24	26	50
10	25		
11	27		

See Part 2: Insulation; Insulation, Conductivity Values

corkboard An insulating layer or panel made of cork.
See Part 2: Insulation

corm A short bulb-like underground stem, where reserve materials are stored.

corn (*Zea mays*) (maize, Indian corn, mealies) A grain crop of American origin grown in tropical, sub-tropical and temperate regions; an annual vegetable whose seed is used as food. The term varies in meaning depending on country: in England it means wheat, in Scotland oats and in U.S. maize or Indian corn. It requires 3-5 months to mature. The characteristic protein of corn is zein.

Type	Characteristics
Dent	Depression at tip of seed
Flint	Grains are harder and somewhat translucent
Flour	Soft grains
Pop	Hard grains that burst on heating
Sweet	Higher in sugar content
Hybrid	Higher yield

Color: Controlled by male tassel; white, yellow (contains carotene), red, purple and black.

Use: Human food, animal feed, silage, meal, flour, hominy, starch, sugar, oil, alcohol.

Food Value: Good source of starch; protein lower in nutritional value than other grains; lysine is first limiting amino acid and tryptophan is the second.

1 bu fresh = 50-72 lb = 8-12½ qt canned;
6-20 (12 avg) ears cut = 1 qt canned;
3-6 lb fresh in husk = 1 qt canned;
4-4½ lb fresh in husk = 1 qt frozen;
2 cups canned = 1 lb;
1 case (24) no. 2 cans = 0.038 ton fresh.
1 bu husked ear corn = 2¼ to 2½ cu. ft;
52-56 lb/bu (dent whole corn) or 1.7 lb/qt;
Ground whole corn 1.5 lb/qt; 70-80 lb/bu in shuck;
1 bu ear corn with husk = 3½ cu ft;
100 lb fresh = 26-33 lb dry corn.

	Lb/qt	Lb/bu
Husked ear	—	70
Cracked	1.6	50
Shelled	1.8	56
Meal	1.6	50
Corn & cob meal	1.4	45

Storage (sweet corn): unhusked and uncovered (85-90% relative humidity); refrigerate (31-32°F); use within 1 to 8 days; frozen (0°F) storage cut corn, 1 yr.

Components of kernel (%): germ, 12 (contains 80% of the oil); endosperm, 82; pericarp (bran coat), 5; tip cap 1.

	H_2O (%)	Protein (%)	Fat (%)	Carbohydrate (%)	Ash (%)	pH
Sweet raw	73	3.5	1	22	1	6.0-6.5
Dry field corn	13	9-11	4-5	64-80	1-1.5	

Dry Corn Milling Products	Wet Corn Milling Products
grits	cornstarch
coarse meal	corn oil
flour	corn gluten feed
germ	
hominy feeds	

Approx nutrient used for growth (lb):

	100 bu grain	3 ton stover
N	90	70
P_2O_5	35	25
K_2O	25	95

See Part 2: Calories, Daily Recommendations; Canned Spoilage Related to pH; Canned Yield; Cereal Composition; Cereal Nutrient Content; Cereal Enrichment; Cereal Fortification; Cereals, Vitamin and Mineral Content; Corn; Corn; Amino Acids; Corn Kernel; Corn Kernel Composition; Food, Composition; Frozen Food Storage; Fruit and Vegetables Composition; Frying Time; Glutamate; Glutamate Addition; Grain Analysis; Grain Products Composition; Iron; Microwave Cooking, Frozen Vegetables; Microwave Processing Time; Minerals, Food; Niacin; Niacin, Daily Recommendations; Nicotinic Acid, Food; Nitrate, Vegetables; Nutrients in Crops; Pentosans; Phosphorus; Plant Foods, Composition; Portion Size; Potassium; Protein Factors; Riboflavin; Seed, Chemical Composition; Seed Composition; Seed, Germination; Standards, Processed Fruit and Vegetable Products; Starch Microappearance; Starch Modified; Starch; Storage; Sugars and Syrups Composition; Sugar, Vegetables; Sweetness of Sweeteners; Sweetening Agents; Thiamin; Tocopherols; Unsaponifiable Matter; Vegetable Boiling; Vegetable Composition; Vegetable Cooking; Vegetable Frozen Yield; Vegetable Plants; Vegetables, Boiling Time, Frozen; Vegetables, Canning Dates; Vegetables, Cooking Frozen; Vegetables Panned; Vegetable Storage; Vegetable Yield; Vegetable Yield Canned and Frozen; Vegetable Yield Frozen, Canned and Fresh; Vitamin A; Vitamin A, Food; Vitamin C

corn (pop) (*Zea mays everta*) An annual plant used for food; 60 lb/bu; 13.5% moisture for electric popping; variety Purdue.

corn and cob meal A mixture of fine ground corn and corn cobs; 1.4 lb per qt.

corn belt Midwest U.S. where large quantities of corn are grown.

corn cockle A plant having a toxic principle.
See Part 2: Poisonous Plants

corn, ear The fruit (seed) unit of the plant *Zea mays* covered with cellulosic husk lined with silk-like fibers. 1 doz ears = 2½ cups cooked; 1 cup cooked = 165 g (5.8 oz); 70 lb shucked corn per bu; 74 lb corn in ear with husk/bu; a bushel = cubic feet of volume × 0.4.

corn earworm A striped yellow-headed worm that destroys the leaves of young corn plants and feeds in the top of ears of older plants; also eats pods or beans of soybeans; Control: resistant varieties with tight husk.

corned In reference to meat, salted; from the word "korn" which means grain (grain salt).

corned beef Beef that has been dry- or brine-cured with salt and some of the following: sugar, baking soda, saltpeter, or cream of tartar; a typical corned beef cure is:

use 1 oz/lb of meat:
- 8 lb salt
- 3 lb sugar
- 3 oz saltpeter (or 4 oz cream of tartar)
- 4 oz baking soda

Apply 1/3 of the above on each of the 1st, 4th and 10th days; cure 2 to 3 weeks; for brine cure, add 4½ gal. water. Meat to use: brisket, plate or rump; is not smoked; also see **dried beef**; max. gain in weight on curing is 10% over fresh uncured weight.

See Part 2: Beef Cuts and Uses; Cooking in Liquid, Time; Meat and Meat Products Composition; Meat Composition; Meat Storage; Portion Size; Sausage, Types; Simmering Meat

corned beef hash A mixture of ground corned beef and potato.
See Part 2: Meat Composition

corn fed Cattle that have been fattened on corn.

corn, flaked Crushed whole corn kernels.
See Part 2: Food, Composition; Grain Products Composition

corn flakes A breakfast cereal made from toasted flakes of corn; produced from corn grain by precooking, flaking and toasting; 1 cup = 1 oz.
Composition (%): H_2O 4, protein 7-8, fat 0.4, carbohydrate 85-89, ash 3.

corn flour Finely ground kernels of white, yellow or blue corn; finely ground maize (corn) meal; used as pancake flour.
Composition (%): H_2O 12, protein 8, fat 3, carbohydrate 77, ash 1.

corn gluten feed *See* Part 2: Cereal By-Products Composition

corn grits (grits; hominy grits) Ground white or yellow corn from which germ and bran have been removed; coarser ground than corn meal; ground hominy.
See Part 2: Grain Products Composition

corn ground Comminuted corn whose volume is 25 lb per cubic foot.

corn-hog ratio The number of bushels of corn that is equal in value to 100 lb of live hog.

$$\text{corn-hog ratio} = \frac{\text{price per cwt of hogs}}{\text{price per bu of corn}}$$

below 11.4 = high corn prices, low hog prices, loss to feeder
11.4 = normal, break-even point
above 11.4 = low corn prices, high hog prices, profit to feeder

cornhusker A type of cheese.
See Part 2: Cheese Vitamin Content

cornification Hardening of tissue due to keratin formation. *See also* **keratinization.**

corning Preservation of beef by salting.

cornish A class of English chickens which has a yellow skin, pea comb, and lays a brown egg. Varieties: Dark*, White*, White laced red*, Buff; (* indicates there is also a bantam variety).
See Part 2: Poultry Breeds and Varieties; Poultry Cooking, Frozen

corn meal A meal made from white corn or yellow corn; a variety of coarseness of grind is available (bolted is finer grind). The old process used the entire grain; the new process uses corn from which the bran and most of the germ has been removed.

100 lb degermed corn meal = 3.16 bu corn
100 lb non-degermed corn meal = 2 bu corn
1 bu = 50 lb corn meal
2-3¼ cups = 1 lb.

Whole grain, unbolted composition (%): H_2O 12 (max 15% H_2O), protein 9, fat 5 (original corn fat content (± 0.3% is permissible range), carbohydrate 74, not less than 1.2% crude fiber (not more than original corn).
Whole grain, bolted composition (%): protein 9, fat 3, carbohydrate 75, ash 1.
See Part 2: Food, Composition; Grain Products Composition; Minerals, Food; Storage, Dry

corn meal agar *See* Part 2: Microorganism, Media

corn muffin A small cake made of cornmeal, milk, egg, and leavening agent.
See Part 2: Grain Products Composition

corn oil An oil obtained by extraction of the germ of corn.

specific gravity	0.916-0.927
refractive index (15.5°C)	1.475-1.477
% unsaponifiable	1-2.2
iodine no.	103-130
melting point	−20° to−10°C
titer	16°-20°C

The oil comprises 5% of whole moisture-free grain and contains the following fatty acids: myristic 1 ± 0.9%, palmitic 10 ± 3%, stearic 3.5 ± 1%, hexadecenoic 1 ± 0.8%, oleic 34 ± 15%, linoleic 48 ± 15%. 1 qt = 4 cups; 1 cup = 210 g (7.4 oz).

	Smoke Point		Flash Point		Fire Point	
	(°F)	(°C)	(°F)	(°C)	(°F)	(°C)
crude	352	178	562	294	655	346
refined	440	227	618	326	678	359

See Part 2: Fats and Oils Composition; Fat and Oils, Fatty Acid Composition; Fats and Oils, Physical and Chemical Properties; Fatty Acids, Fats and Oils; Fats and Oils, Characteristics; Fats and Oils, Composition; Free Fatty Acid, Smoke, Flash, Fire Points; Iodine and Saponification Values; Oil, Seed and Fruit; Oil, Triglyceride Mole Percent Composition; Refractive Indices, Fats and Oils; Specific Gravities, Fats and Oils; Spoilage, Fat in Foods; Titer, Fats and Oils; Tocopherols

corn, puffed Breakfast cereal made by heating grain (corn) under pressure and rapidly releasing pressure causing the superheated steam and the kernel to expand.
See Part 2: Grain Products Composition

corn salad *See* **field salad**
See Part 2: Vegetable Plants

corn, shelled 56 lb per bu; plant 10 to 15 lb per acre.

cornstarch A starch made from the endosperm of corn and used as a thickening agent in gravies, puddings, etc. and as a filler in baking powders.

Types	Process	Use
Waxy	waxy corn (amylopectin)	frozen sauces and pie fillings
Flavored	sugar and flavoring added	puddings and pie fillings
Instant	dehydrated gelatinized starch, sugar and flavoring	pudding and pie filling

3 tbsp = 1 oz; 3 cups = 1 lb; 1 cup (stirred) = 130 g.
For thickening: 1 tbsp cornstarch = 2 tbsp flour
Composition (%): H_2O 12, protein 0.3, carbohydrate 88, ash 0.1, pH 4-7. *See also* **corn flour.**
See Part 2: Cornstarch Pudding Variations

corn sugar The glucose obtained by complete hydrolysis of cornstarch; occurs naturally in honey, some fruits, and vegetables.

corn syrup A syrup made by partial hydrolysis of cornstarch; contains dextrose, maltose and dextrins. Light and dark forms available: the light form has had clarifying and decolorizing treatment; the dark is a mixture of corn syrup and refiner's syrup (pH = 5.0). 1 cup = 328 g (11.6 oz) = 1 cup of sugar plus ¼ cup liquid. It can be used in meat curing: (a) corn syrup solids, (b) corn syrup, (c) glucose syrup. Total cannot exceed 2% (dry basis) of all ingredients in meat product.
See Part 2: Sweetening Compounds

coronet A horse's leg at the top of the hoof.

corrected wine *See* **modified wine**

correlation (r)

$$r = \frac{\Sigma xy}{[(\Sigma x^2)(\Sigma y^2)]^{1/2}}$$

$$= \frac{\Sigma XY - \dfrac{(\Sigma X)(\Sigma Y)}{n}}{\left\{\left[\Sigma X^2 - \dfrac{(\Sigma X)^2}{n}\right]\left[\Sigma Y^2 - \dfrac{(\Sigma Y)^2}{n}\right]\right\}^{1/2}}$$

$$= \frac{n\Sigma XY - \Sigma X\,\Sigma Y}{\{[n\Sigma X^2 - (\Sigma X)^2]\,[n\Sigma Y^2 - (\Sigma Y)^2]\}^{1/2}}$$

r ranges from -1 to 0 to $+1$
-1 and $+1$ are perfect correlations
0 is no correlation

t test Ho: $r = 0$ Prob. of greater $|r|$ value if r were drawn from a normal population in which $r = 0$

$$t = r\left(\frac{n-2}{1-r^2}\right)^{1/2}$$

n = no. of X's or Y's
$df = n - 2$

Check Levels of Sig. Tables $df = n - 2$
Confidence Limits (CL) can be set only by transformation to a quantity which is distributed normally.
See Part 2: Correlation Significance

Corriedale A medium-wool breed of sheep that originated in New Zealand primarily from the crossing of Merino ewes with Lincoln rams; white face with dark nostrils and hooves and has no horns; the wool fleece grade is usually ⅜.
See Part 2: Sheep Breeds

cortex (1) The outer portion or bark of a tree. (2) The protective covering of the cerebrum or of the adrenal glands.

corticosterone A hormone obtained from the adrenal cortex.
See Part 2: Steroids

cortisol A steroid hormone obtained from the adrenal cortex or made synthetically.
See Part 2: Steroids

cortisone A steroid hormone obtained from the adrenal cortex or made synthetically.
See Part 2: Steroids

cortland A variety of apples that are in season in September to December; make excellent sauce and are good eating and cooking apples.

Corynebacterium A genus of slightly curved rods, usually aerobic microorganisms; it includes both nonpathogenic and organisms that cause animal or plant diseases; e.g., diphtheria type organisms.
See Part 2: Microorganism, Media

cos A variety of head lettuce. *See also* **lettuce; romaine lettuce.**

cosecant A trigonometric function:

$$\text{cosecant} = \frac{\text{hypotenuse}}{\text{ordinate}}$$

cosine A trigonometric function:

$$\text{cosine} = \frac{\text{abscissa}}{\text{hypotenuse}}$$

cossettes Sugar beet slices.

costae Ribs (Latin).

costal Pertaining to the ribs.
See Part 2: Bone

costal cartilage Rib cartilage on lower ends (opposite ends that are attached to backbones) of ribs.

costs per serving *See* Part 2: Fruit and Vegetables, Cost per Serving

cotangent A trigonometric function:

$$\text{cotangent} = \frac{\text{abscissa}}{\text{ordinate}}$$

Cotswold A long-wool breed of sheep originating in England.
See Part 2: Sheep Breeds

cottage cheese A soft, moist, delicate, nonripened, perishable, creamy and white cheese made from pasteurized skim milk by lactic acid fermentation (*Streptococcus lactis*) and adding cream dressing; it is mild and slightly acid. *See also* **curd**.
Forms:
large curd or small curd
dry form or creamed form
1 gal. milk yields 1 qt cottage cheese
6.25 lb skim milk = 1 lb cottage cheese
1 lb cottage cheese = 2 cups
1 cup = 240 g (8.3 oz)
Manufacturing steps:
1. Let milk stand until it thickens.
2. Gently heat until the whey (clear liquid) rises to the top.
3. Strain.
4. Chop.
5. Add butter, cream, salt.

Storage: Refrigerate, tightly covered; use within 3 to 5 days.

Composition:	H_2O (%)	Protein (%)	Fat (%)	Carbohydrate (%)	Ash (%)	Salt (%)	pH
Creamed	78-90	13-14	4-5	3	1-2	1	
Uncreamed	79-80	15-17	0.3-0.4	3	1-2	1	5.0
Partially creamed or low fat			max 2				

See Part 2: Calcium Daily Requirements; Calories, Daily Recommendations; Cheese Characteristics; Cheese Composition; Cheese Vitamin Content; Food Composition; Microbiological Standards, Dairy; Milk and Cheese Composition; Milk and Milk Products, Vitamin Content; Minerals, Food; Riboflavin, Daily Recommendations; Stabilizers, Thickeners; Vitamin A, Milk and Milk Products

cottage roll Boneless cylinder-shaped piece of pork cut from the top of the Boston butt; may be fresh, cured, or cured and smoked.

cotted fleeces Wool that is tangled and will require special processing; characteristic of certain breeds and illness in some breeds.

cotton ***Gossypium*** An annual plant whose vegetable fiber is composed primarily of cellulose and is used for cloth; seed 30 lb/bu; pH 6-6.5; 1 bale = 480 lb.
3.25 lb seed cotton including trash equals 1 lb ginned cotton.
32 lb cotton seed = 1 bu; seed yields edible oil.

Approx nutrients used:

Lb	500 Lb Lint	1000 Lb Seed	1500 Lb Plant
N	1.4	36	38
P_2O_5	0.5	15	15
K_2O	3	15	27

See Part 2: Insulation; Nutrients in Crops; Seed, Chemical Composition; Seed Germination

cotton candy Spinning sugar that has been boiled at a high temperature.

cottonseed Seed of cotton plant; cotton plant (100 lb fiber) = 170 lb cottonseed; cottonseed yield, 850 lb/acre.
Components (%): linters 10; hull 35; kernels 55. Kernels contain: 7% moisture; 30% protein; 30% oil; 24% nitrogen-free extract; 5% crude fiber; 4-5% ash.
See Part 2: Oil, Seed and Fruit; Oils and Fats Composition; Pentosans; Protein Factors; Refractive Indices, Fats and Oils; Seed Composition; Unsaponifiable Matter

cottonseed flour Flour made from ground cottonseed specially processed to minimize the toxic properties of gossypol.
Composition: 6% H_2O, 48-50% protein, 7% fat, 33% carbohydrate, 6% ash.

cottonseed hulls Waste remaining after processing the seed. 0.3 lb/qt.
See Part 2: Fertilizer Materials; Insulation

cottonseed meal The product remaining after expression of the oil. Used for both animal feeds and as fertilizer. 2.10 lb cottonseed = 1 lb cottonseed meal; 1.5 lb/qt; 41-50% protein; used as a protein supplement in livestock feed. Can be used as an agricultural fertilizer material 5.7-2.5-1.5 or 6.6-2.5-1.5; acid in nature and would require 0.1 lb of dolomitic limestone to neutralize each pound applied.
See Part 2: Fertilizer Materials; Oil Meals Composition

cottonseed oil A semidrying vegetable oil containing glycerides of oleic, palmitic and linoleic acids. 5.88 lb cottonseed = 1 lb cottonseed oil.

Saturated Carbon Atoms	%
14	1
16	23
18	2
Mono-unsaturated	
18	24
Polyunsaturated	
18-2	50

Iodine no. 97-115; specific gravity 0.9187 (20°/4°C); saponification no. 189-200; unsaponifiable 0.5-1.5%; cloud point 40°-50°F; melting point -2° to +2°C; smoke point 410°-430°F; acid number 14.24; titer 31-37°C; refractive index (15.5°C) 1.473-1.476; 1 qt = 4 cups; 1 cup = 210 g (7.4 oz).

Good source of linoleic acid; used for shortening and margarine; may be hydrogenated.
See Part 2: Fats and Oils Composition; Fat and Oils, Fatty Acid Composition; Fats and Oils, Physical and Chemical Properties; Fatty Acids, Fats and Oils; Fats and Oils, Characteristics; Fats and Oils Composition; Free Fatty Acids; Smoke, Flash, Fire Points; Iodine and Saponification Values; Oil or Fat, Characteristics; Oil, Triglyceride Mole Percent Composition; Specific Gravities, Fats and Oils; Spoilage, Fat in Foods; Titer, Fats and Oils; Tocopherols

cottonseed stearin A fat obtained from cottonseed.

specific gravity	0.918-0.923
melting point	26-40°C
saponification no.	194-195
iodine no.	89-103

cotyledon The rudimentary form the leaf of seed plants; some types have one (monocots); others have two (dicots).
See Part 2: Wheat Kernel Parts

coulomb A charge of approximately 6.24×10^{18} electrons passing a point in one second when the current is one amp; electrical measurement; x ampere times y seconds = xy coulomb.

coulommiers A round, flat, light-colored flowery rind cheese made from cow's milk; it weighs about 1 pound is packed in a wood chip box; it is larger than a camembert and smaller than a brie.

counterfeit Poorly bred cattle that give an impression of good breeding.

country-cure *See* **dry cure**

country hides Hides removed by an unconventional pattern, containing cuts, and handled under various storage conditions.

country-style pork sausage Coarsely ground pork sausage that contains 10 to 20% beef. *See also* **pork sausage.**

coupling Area on back of quadruped between dorsal vertebrae and pelvis.

courgette *See* **marrow**

cover pickle The pickle in which meat is placed to cure.

cow Female of bovine species (cattle) after she has dropped her first calf; gestation period 283 days (range 240-311); duration of heat period, 12-24 hr; normal recurrence of heat 18-24 days.
See Part 2: Milk, Mammals, Composition; Milk, Species; Muscle and Body Weight

cowberry (mountain cranberry) An evergreen shrub with fruit similar to the cranberry.

cow-hocked Hocks closer together than ankles and rear toes pointed out; hocks bent in on rear view.

cowpea (***Vigna sinensis***) An annual legume; southern peas; annual plant used for hay; pH - 5.5; cut when first pods have matured. Varieties: black, brabham, clay, iron, whipporwill.

Country	Use
U.S.A.	mature seeds are dried and eaten; green manure and forage
China	young tender pods are eaten
Sudan	starchy root used for food

	H_2O (%)	Protein (%)	Fat (%)	Carbohydrate (%)	Ash (%)
Immature seed raw	67	9	0.8	22	2
Young pod with seed raw	86	3	0.3	9	1
Dry mature seed	10	23	1.5	62	3.5

Dried: 1.9 lb/qt; 60 lb/bu.
See Part 2: Minerals, Food; Nutrients in Crops; Seed, Chemical Composition; Seed, Germination; Sugar, Legumes; Vegetables Classification; Vegetable Composition; Vegetable Plants

cowpox A contagious cattle disease in which the udder and teats redden and eruption appears; this area is surrounded by purplish skin; when given to man, protects against smallpox.

cozymase *See* **diphosphopyridine nucleotide**

C.P. *See* **chemically pure**

CPF *See* Part 2: Swine Breeds

cps Cycles per second.

Cr Symbol for the element chromium.

crab A lean crustacean; shellfish; 50% edible (average 20% protein);

Types	Where caught	Weight Lb
Blue (*Callinectes sapidus*)	Middle, south Atlantic Gulf	½-2
Dungeness (*Cancer magister*)	Northern Pacific coast	1¼-2½
King (*Paralithodes camtschatica*)	Alaska	6-20
Stone (*Menippe merenaria*)	Florida, Texas	
Tanner; Snow (*Chionoectes tanneri*)	Alaska, Canada	

Cook by boiling in salt water for 20 to 25 minutes.

	Amount for for one serving Oz
Crab meat	4
Whole blue crab	2 to 4
Whole dungeness crab	½ to 1

1 cup crab meat = 165 g (5.7 oz)
Equivalents: 8-10 oz King crab leg in shell = 6 oz

frozen crab meat = 7½ oz canned crab meat = 1 cup cooked and flaked.

As purchased in shell	Oz to purchase per serving	% Yield
Blue	22	12–16
Dungeness (½ crab meat is body & ½ is leg meat)	12	25
King	—	20–26
King crab legs	6	52
Soft shell	4.5	65

Blue crab Grade	Name	From	% of Meat
Premium	lump	large muscle controlling swimming legs	25
Second	regular or flake	remainder of body muscle	50
Lowest	claw meat	claw	25

King crab	% of Meat
Leg meat	70
Shoulder	15
Body	15

See also **crabmeat.**
See Part 2: Fish and Shellfish Composition; Frozen Food Storage; Minerals, Food

crabapple (*Malus pumila*) Parent species for most cultivated apples; many varieties; planted for decorative value and used to make excellent jam and jellies; 1 lb fresh = 1 qt canned.
Raw composition (%):
H_2O 81, protein 0.4, fat 0.3, carbohydrate 18, ash 0.4.

crabmeat Edible meat obtained various crabs; pH 7.0. *See also* **crab.**

Common Name	Scientific Name
King crabmeat	*Paralithodes camtschatica* *Paralithodes platypus*
King crabmeat or hanasaki crabmeat	*Paralithodes brevipes*
Korean variety crabmeat or kegani crabmeat	*Erimacrus isenbeckii*
Snow crabmeat	*Chionoecetes oplio* *Chionoecetes tanneri* *Chionoecetes bairdii* *Chionoecetes angulatus*

cracked Particle size reduced by breaking, crushing, or grinding.

cracker A flat, thin biscuit.
Composition (based on flour as 100%):

Ingredient	%
Flour	100
Water	56
Yeast	1.5
Salt	1.75
Sugar	1
Shortening	5
Emulsifier	0.1–0.3

Graham:
1 lb = 66 crackers = 4.3 cups crumbs.
1 cup crumbs = 85 g (3 oz).
Soda:
1 lb = 82 crackers = 7 cups crumbs = 6.8 cups fine crumbs.
1 cup fine crumbs = 70 g (2.5 oz).
Saltines:
1 lb = 130–160 crackers (2-in. square).

	H_2O (%)	Protein (%)	Fat (%)	Carbohydrate (%)	Ash (%)	pH
Graham	6	8	9	73	3	
Sandwich type	3	15	24	56	3	7 8.5

See Part 2: Calories, Daily Recommendations; Fermented Ingredients; Grain Products Composition

cracklings The residue left from rendered pork fat that has had the lard extracted.

cradle roast *See* Part 2: Pork Loin Cooking

cramp bone *See* **patella**

crampy Raising rear foot with a jerk.

cranberry (*Vaccinium macrocarpum*) An evergreen with wiry stems that produces a bright red round fruit; these tart, acid fruits are used for making cranberry sauce and cranberry juice.
1 barrel = 100 lb; 1 bu. = 55 lb; 1 pk = 8 lb = 12 pt canned.
1 lb = 4–5 cups fresh (1 cup = 115 g or 4 oz) = 3–3½ cups sauce (1 cup = 215 g or 7.6 oz) = 1–⅔ cups canned sauce (1 cup = 280 g or 9.8 oz);
1½ qt fresh = 1½ qt canned;
1 qt juice = 4 cups (1 cup = 250 g or 8.8 oz).
Storage: 36° to 40°F, 85 to 90% relative humidity, 1 to 3 mo. storage life, 27° F freezing point.

	H_2O (%)	Protein (%)	Fat (%)	Carbohydrate (%)	Ash (%)	pH
Raw	88	0.4	0.7	11	0.2	
Juice (33% juice)	83	0.1	0.1	16	0.1	2.3–2.7
Sauce (sweetened, strained)	62	0.1	0.2	37	0.1	2.3–2.4

See Part 2: Fruit, Availability; Fruit, Canning Dates; Fruit Classification; Fruit Composition; Fruit Cooking; Fruit Frozen Yield; Fruit Sauces; Microwave Cooking, Fruit; Minerals, Food; Organic Acids in Fruits and Vegetables; Plant Foods, Composition; Salad Dressing and Mayonnaise Variations; Standards, Processed Fruit and Vegetable Products; Storage; Transit Temperature

cranial Of or pertaining to the head.

cream (1) The fat of milk (butterfat) obtained by gravity separation on long standing. (2) A syrupy liqueur. *See also* **cordial.**

	Milk Fat (%)	Milk Fat (range) (%)	Remarks
Light cream, coffee, table	20	18–30	
Light whipping cream		30–36	Will whip but not freeze
Half and half		10–12	
Heavy cream		36–40	
Sour cream, salad cream, cream dressing		18–20	
Half and half sour cream		10–12	

1 pt = 2 cups = 4 cups whipped;
1 cup coffee cream (20%) = 3 tbsp butter + ⅞ cup milk;
1 cup heavy cream (40%) = ⅓ cup butter + ¾ cup milk.
Storage: Temperature 40°F; keep out of direct sunlight; use within 3 to 5 days.

	H_2O (%)	Protein (%)	Fat (%)	Carbohydrate (%)	Ash (%)	pH	Min Milk Fat (%)
Half & half	80	3	12	5	0.6		10.5
Coffee, table, light	71	3	21	4	0.6		18
Light whipping	62	2.5	31	4	0.5	6.5	30
Heavy whipping	57	2	38	3	0.4		36

	Specific Gravity	Wt of Cup
20% Cream	—	240 g (8.5 oz)
40% Cream	0.99	236 g (8.3 oz)
100% Cream	0.54	—
Sour	—	240 g (8.5 oz)
Half and half	—	242 g (8.5 oz)

Dry cream: 1 lb = 19 lb milk.
See Part 2: Animal Foods, Composition; Calories, Daily Recommendations; Creams, Butter and Frozen Desserts; Dairy Products, Composition; Dairy Terms; Fluid and Fermented Milks, Composition; Milk and Cheese Composition; Milk and Milk Products, Vitamin Content; Milk, Dry Products; Minerals, Food; Sour Cream Dressing; Spoilage, Fat in Foods; Stabilizers, Thickeners; Vitamin A, Milk and Milk Products

cream cheese A non-ripened, perishable, pure white, soft cheese made from cream and whole (cow's) milk; the milk and cream are pasteurized and coagulated by a lactic acid starter; it is foil-wrapped in rectangular portions; its flavor is mild and slightly acid; texture is buttery.
3-oz package = 6⅔ tbsp; 8 oz = 1 cup; 1 cup = 230 g (8.1 oz). 33% min fat content (38% avg); neufchâtel has min fat content of 20%.
Composition (%): H_2O 51–54, fat 35, protein 8–9, carbohydrate 2, ash 1–2, salt 1; pH 4.9.
Storage: Refrigerate tightly covered, use within 2 weeks.
See Part 2: Cheese Characteristics; Cheese Vitamin Content; Salad Dressing and Mayonnaise Variations; Stabilizers, Thickeners; Vitamin A, Milk and Milk Products

cream (liquor) A full-bodied, sweet alcoholic beverage or cordial, e.g., cream sherry, creme de menthe, etc.

creaming properties Properties obtained by using a shortening that will incorporate large quantities of air and produce light baked goods.

cream nut *See* **Brazil nut**

cream of tartar Acid salt of tartaric acid; $KHC_4H_4O_6$ (potassium acid (hydrogen) tartrate); potassium bitartrate; 1 teaspoon = 3.1 g. *See also* **baking powder.**

Cream of Wheat Proprietary name of a breakfast cereal made of wheat flour with added vitamins and minerals.
See Part 2: Portion Size

cream puff A pastry shell filled with whipped cream or custard.
See Part 2: Storage Times

cream (créme) sherry Wine of special richness; e.g., sweetness.

cream soda A flavor of carbonated beverage; soft drink flavored with sugar and vanilla.

cream, whipping *See* **whipping cream; cream**

creamy dressing Cream added to French dressing, salad dressing, or mayonnaise and used on greens and vegetables.
See Part 2: French Dressing Variations; Salad Dressing and Mayonnaise Variations

crème de cacao A liqueur made from the cacao plant. *See also* **cacao; liqueur.**

créme de gruyére A processed cheese in which various types of cheeses are melted together and to which butter, milk or cream are added.

créme de menthe A liqueur made from mint. *See also* **liqueur.**

creosote, coal-tar A distillate made from bituminous coal; used to treat wood for protection against rot and worms. *See also* **fence post treatment**; wood creosote, not coal-tar creosote, is usually used for medical purposes.

crêpe A thin pancake made with fruit and flaming liqueur sauce.

crêpes suzettes Thin pancakes, rolled with or without creamed meat filling and seasoned with brandy sauce.

crescenza A soft, creamy, uncooked fast ripening, milky sweet yellowish cheese made from cow's milk and rennet; similar to Bel-Paese.
See Part 2: Cheese, Vitamin Content

cress Several species of vegetables (family *cruciferae*) whose leaf is used as food.
See Part 2: Vegetable Plants

crest Top of the neck of a male animal; the comb on the head of a bird.

cribber An animal that clamps teeth on something and "sucks wind."

crimp Waves in wool fiber.

crimson clover (Italian) (*Trifolium incarnatum*) An annual plant used for hay and pasture; seed 60 lb/bu; seed 20-25 lb/acre; pH 6.0; approx nutrients used for one ton of hay: N 65 lb, P_2O_5 14 lb, K_2O 60 lb.

croaker (hardhead) A lean fish that makes a croaking sound; caught on the Atlantic and Gulf Coasts.
Composition: 79% H_2O, 18-19% protein, 1-3% fat, 1.3% ash.

croissant A breakfast roll that is crescent-shaped.

crop (1) In a beef animal, from topline to half-way down the side and just behind upper half of shoulder. (2) First stomach of a bird. (3) A riding whip. (4) To cut or trim.

croquette A meat, fish or vegetable that is chopped, shaped, rolled in crumbs, and deep-fried.

cross-bred An animal whose sire and dam come from different breeds.
See Part 2: Sheep Breeds

cross cells Layer of kernel beneath the mesocarp.
See Part 2: Corn Kernel; Rice Kernel; Wheat Kernel Parts

cross firing Hitting a front foot with an opposite hind foot.

cross rib roast *See* **arm roast**

crotalaria Several species of an annual green manure crop; seed 60 lb/bu; use 20 lb/acre; pH 6; crotalaria seed may injure livestock.
See Part 2: Poisonous Plants; Seed, Germination

croup On horse, between hips and tailhead; called rump on other species of farm livestock.

crouton A cube of dry-toasted or sautéed bread.

crow hops A mild bucking motion.

crown roast A roast made from an unsplit rib rack; the backbone is removed, opposite end ribs tied together and the tip of the rips are frenched.
See Part 2: Lamb Crown Roast Carving; Lamb Cuts and Uses; Lamb Roasting; Pork, Cooking; Pork Cookery; Pork Cuts; Pork Loin Cooking; Veal Chart; Veal Cuts

crucible A small platinum or porcelain container that can stand high heat and used in chemical analysis.

Cruciferae Mustard, watercress, cabbage, and radish family.
See Part 2: Vegetables Classification

crude fat *See* **fat analysis**

crude fiber The unprocessed cellulosic component of a plant. Analysis is an attempt to measure the non-digestible carbohydrate material; the sample is freed of fat, boiled in weak acid and then in weak alkali; the residue thus contains crude fiber and ash and thus the loss in weight by ashing is reported as crude fiber.
See Part 2: Sodium Hydroxide Solution; Sulfuric Acid Solution

crude oil Unrefined petroleum, used as an insecticide for hogs.

crude protein determination *See* **Kjeldahl determination**

crustacean A class of shellfish that have a segmented, crust-like shell and jointed appendages; i.e., crab, crayfish, lobster, shrimp.
See Part 2: Fish and Shellfish Composition

cryolite Na_3AlF_6; an inorganic insecticide.

Cryovac Trademark of organic chemicals division of W. R. Grace & Co.; a vinylidene chloride—vinyl chloride film which can be heat-shrunk.

cryptorchidism Retention of one or both of the testes within the abdomen.

crystal That structure of matter which is characteristic of the solid state; the constituent atoms are arranged in a geometric pattern called a lattice, which may be of many different shapes (cubic, rhomboid, etc.). Identification can be obtained by X-rays, which are diffracted by the lattice at various angles. *See also* **amorphous.**

crystalline Systematic arrangement of atoms in space; resembling a crystal; transparent.

crystallized honey Honey that has naturally hardened or been made to harden (crystal formed).

crystal violet broth *See* Part 2: Microorganism, Selective and Differential Broths and Media, Water Filtration Plant

crystal violet stain *See* Part 2: Gram Stain

Cs Symbol for the element cesium.

CT Cellar trimmed.

Cu Symbol for the element copper.

cubeb An essential oil used in flavorings.
See Part 2: Essential Oils

cube steak A thin slice of beef that has been passed through a machine to reduce toughness, by partially disintegrating the fibers.

cubic centimeter (cc) (cm^3) (cu cm) A measure of volume.

1 cc = 0.999972 milliliter (ml)
= 0.27051 dram (U.S. liquid)
= 0.0610234 cubic inch (U.S.)
= 0.0338 ounce (U.S. fluid)
= 0.0021 pint (U.S. liquid)
= 0.0011 quart (U.S. liquid)
= 2.6417×10^{-4} gallon (U.S)
= 2.1997×10^{-4} gallon (Imperial)
= 3.5314×10^{-5} cubic foot (U.S.)
= 2.83776×10^{-5} bushel (U.S.)
= 1.3079×10^{-6} cubic yard (U.S.)

A cubic centimeter of water weighs approx 1 gram.

cubic decimeter (dm^3) A measure of volume.
1 dm^3 = 1000.0 cubic centimeters (cc)
= 61.0234 cubic inches (cu. in.)
= 1.05668 liquid quarts (liquid qt)
= 0.99997 liter (l)
= 0.90808 U.S. dry quart (dry qt)
= 0.264178 U.S. liquid gallon (liquid gal.)
= 0.22702 U.S. dry gallon (dry gal.)
= 0.035314 cubic foot (cu. ft)
= 0.02838 U.S. bushel (bu.)
= 0.001308 cubic yard (cu. yd)

cubic foot (cu ft) (ft^3) A measure of volume.
1 cu ft (Br.) = 2.831677×10^4 cubic centimeters (cu cm)
1 cu ft (U.S.) = 28317.016 cubic centimeters (cm^3)
= 2.8316×10^4 milliliters (ml)
= 7660.60 drams (U.S. fl.)
= 1,728 cubic inches (cu in.)
= 997.37 ounces (Br. fl.)
= 957.568 ounces (U.S. fl.)
= 62.427 pounds of H_2O at 4°C
= 59.844 pints (U.S. liquid)
= 29.9221 liquid quarts (liquid qt) (U.S.)
= 28.3170 cubic decimeters (dm^3)
= 28.31625 liters (l)
= 25.7140 dry quarts (dry qt) (U.S.)
= 7.48055 liquid gallons (liquid gal) (U.S.)
= 6.42851 dry gallons (dry gal) (U.S.)
= 6.229 gallons (Br.)
= 0.80357 bushel (bu) (U.S.) (approx 4/5 bu)
= 0.23743 barrel (U.S.)
= 0.118739 hogshead (U.S.)
= 0.03704 cubic yard (cu yd)
= 0.02831701 cubic meter (m^3)
27 cu ft (U.S.) = 1 cubic yard (cu yd)
1 cu ft water = 62.4 lb

cubic feet per minute (cfm) A measure of flow.
1 cfm = 472.0 cubic centimeters per second (cc/sec)
= 0.1247 gallon per second (gal/sec)

cubic inch (cu in.) ($in.^3$) A measure of volume.
1 cu in. (Br.) = 16.3870253 cubic centimeters (cu cm)
= 0.003606 gallon (Br.)
1 cu in. (U.S.) = 276.842 minims (Br.)
= 256.976 minims (U.S.)
= 16.387162 cubic centimeters (cm^3)
= 16.3868 milliliters (ml)
= 4.4329 drams (U.S. fl.)
= 0.57651 ounce (Br. fl.)
= 0.5541 ounce (U.S. fl.)
= 0.01732 liquid quart (liquid qt) (U.S.)
= 0.01639 cubic decimeter (dm^3)
= 0.0163868 liter (l)
= 0.014881 dry quart (dry qt) (U.S.)
= 0.004329 liquid gallon (liquid gal) (U.S.)
= 0.003720 dry gallon (dry gal) (U.S.)
= 3.606×10^{-3} gallon (Br.)
= 0.000578704 cubic foot (cu ft)
= 0.0004650 bushel (bu) (U.S.)
= 1.37429×10^{-4} barrel
= 0.00002143347 cubic yard (cu yd)
= 1.639×10^{-5} cubic meter (m^3)
231 cu in. (U.S.) = 1 liquid gallon (liquid gal) (U.S.)
1728 cu in. (U.S.) = 1 cubic foot (cu ft)
2150.40 cu in (U.S.) = 1 bushel (bu)

cubic meter (cu m) (m^3) A measure of volume.
1 cubic meter = 61023.38 cubic inches (U.S.)
= 999.973 liters (l)
= 264.173 gallons (U.S. liquid)
= 219.9 gallons (Br.)
= 35.31477 cubic feet (Br.)
= 35.3144 cubic feet (U.S.)
= 28.3776 bushels (U.S.)
= 1.307954 cubic yards (Br.)
= 1.3079428 cubic yards (U.S.)

cubic millimeter (mm^3) A measure of volume.
1 cubic millimeter = 0.000061023 cubic inch (cu in.)
= 1×10^{-9} cubic meter (cu m)

cubic yard (cu yd) (yd^3) (U.S.) A measure of volume.
1 cu yd = 7.646×10^5 cubic centimeters (cu cm)
= 46,656 cubic inches (cu in.)
= 807.896 U.S. liquid quarts (liquid qt) (U.S.)
= 764.559 cubic decimeters (dm^3)
= 764.54 liters (l)
= 694.279 U.S. dry quarts (dry qt)
= 201.974 U.S. liquid gallons (liquid gal) (U.S.)
= 173.570 U.S. dry gallons (dry gal)
= 168.17 gallons (Br.)
= 27 cubic feet (cu ft)
= 21.6962 U.S. bushels (bu)
= 0.764559 cubic meter (cu m)

cucumber (*Cucumis sativus*) A vegetable whose fruit is used as food; a climbing plant; different varieties produce different shapes, sizes and rind textures of fruit; the rind color is usually green to yellow and some reach 15 in. in length; they may be eaten raw, pickled, in soup, fried or boiled; 48 lb per bushel; seed 2–3 lb/acre; spacing, one plant per 12 in. in 6-foot rows. *See also* **gherkin.**
Pared Composition: 96% H_2O, 0.6% protein, 0.1% fat, 3.2% carbohydrate, 0.4% ash, pH 5.1.
Storage: 45–50°F; 90–95% relative humidity; 10–14 days.

See Part 2: Fruit and Vegetable, Diseases; Fruit Classification; Minerals, Food; Minerals, Plant or Animal Tissue; Nitrate, Vegetables; pH Values of Biological Materials; Plant Foods, Composition; Spoilage, Carbohydrate Foods; Standards, Processed Fruit and Vegetable Products; Storage; Sugar, Vegetables; Tocopherols; Transit Temperature; Vegetables, Canning Dates; Vegetables Classification; Vegetable Composition; Vegetable Plants; Vegetable Storage

cucumber beetle A pest that infests cucumber vines and fruit.
See Part 2: Insect Control

Cucurbitaceae A family of herbaceous tendril-bearing vines; e.g., cucumber, gourd, pumpkin, and squash.

cucurbits Inclusive name for cucumbers, muskmelons, watermelons, squash, pumpkins, gourds and chayote.

cud *See* **bolus**

cuissot de chevreuil rôti Roast venison that has been marinated in wine.

cull Stock (usually inferior) that is separated from group and sold separately.
See Part 2: Grades, Meat

cultured dairy products *See* Part 2: Cultured Dairy Products, Composition; Dairy Terms

cultured pearl A pearl made by inserting foreign material in an oyster and allowing it to deposit on it a coating called nacre.

culture media Nutritive substances such as agar which promote the growth of bacteria.
See Part 2: Culture Media

cumberland (1) A cold meat sauce of orange and lemon juice and peel, port wine and red currant jelly. (2) A variety of red clover.

cumin seed (cummin) (comino seed) (*Cuminum cyminum* L.) A small (⅛-¼-inch) dried, oblong seed from a Mediterranean plant used as a culinary spice; both whole or ground form; used in making curry powder and flavoring cordials; not more than 9.5% total ash; not more than 1.5% HCl-insoluble ash; and not more than 5% harmless foreign matter.

cu-nic A treatment for internal parasites; mix 1 oz copper sulfate (bluestone) in 3 qt water, add ¾ oz of a 40% solution nicotine sulfate (Black leaf 40); dose per sheep: 1 to 4 fluid oz depending on size.

cup A container used as a measuring vessel. *See also* **measuring cup.**
See Part 2: Ladle Size; Volume

curb (1) Unsoundness. (2) A chain on a bit used to restrain a horse.

curd A gel or precipitate (casein) of sour milk caused by the action of lactic acid on calcium caseinate forming free casein; solid or casein portion of milk separated from the liquid (whey) by action of rennet or lactic acid; used in cottage cheese.
See Part 2: Vegetables Classification

cured beef tongues Max. gain in wt on curing is 10% over fresh uncured wt; smoked beef tongues —should not exceed green wt.

cured cheese Cheese that has been ripened by long aging. The flavor and texture characteristics of cheese are determined by: (1) enzymes that develop; (2) microorganisms that develop; (3) length of storage time (ripening). Mild cheese is cured 2-3 mo.; it has slight flavor and a slightly rubbery body. Medium-aged cheese is cured up to 6 mo.; it has a mellow body and smooth texture. Sharp (or aged) cheese is cured over 6 mo and has a richer flavor.

curie The amount of radioactivity produced by 1 g of radium. Defined as 3.7×10^{10} atomic disintegrations per second.
See Part 2: Constants, Fundamental

curing A process involving various physicochemical changes in such food products as meats, fish, and cheese. Meat may be cured by addition of certain chemicals such as sodium nitrite, salt and sugar; some types are also subjected to the action of smoke.
See Part 2: Ham, Curing; Hide Curing; Meat and Meat Products Composition; Meat Composition; Meat Curing Ingredients; Meat, Servings Per Pound

curium (Cm) A radioactive element of the actinide series; Group IIIB of Periodic Table. at. no. 96; mass number of most stable isotope 247; oxidation state +3; electron configuration 2-8-18-32-25-9-2
orbit K L M N O P Q

curly endive A salad green with a large head composed of ragged, bitter-flavored leaves.

currant (*Ribes*) A shrub that produces a round berry, with a thin skin, a juicy flesh and a number of seeds; fruit colors may be black, red, or white.
Composition (raw): 84-86% H_2O, 1-1.7% protein, 0.1% fat, 12-13% carbohydrate, 0.6% ash, red-pH 2.9-3.1. Also, a raisin made from a small black grape.
Composition (dried fruit): 2% protein, 63% carbohydrate; used for making jams, jellies and juice. 1 lb (dried) = 3.25 cups; 1 cup dried = 140 g (4.9 oz).
Storage: 32°F; 80-85% relative humidity; 10-14 days.
See Part 2: Flavor Ingredients, Taste and Flavor Type; Fruit Classification; Fruit Composition; Fruit Frozen Yield; Minerals, Food; Organic Acids in Fruits and Vegetables; Plant Foods, Composition; Riboflavin, Food; Sugar, Fruit

current (I, i) Rate of movement of electronic charge from one point to another; measured in amperes (a).

curry A stew made of meat, rice, etc. seasoned with curry powder.
See Part 2: Minerals (Trace), Limits

curry powder A blend of many spices (black pepper, cinnamon, cloves, cumin, ferugreek, ginger, red pepper, etc.) used in seasoning; contains tumeric which gives it color. *See also* **pepper (capsicum).**

custard A dessert consisting of a thick mixture of eggs, milk, sugar and flavoring; a thickening agent may be added. The liquid type is cooked at low heat in an open pan, but the solid type is oven-baked.
See Part 2: Calories, Daily Recommendations; Stabilizers, Thickeners; Storage Times

custard apple *See* **anonaceous fruit**
See Part 2: Fruit Composition; Fruit Storage

custard marrow *See* **marrows**

cut Of shellac, the number of pounds of shellac gum dissolved in each gallon of pure alcohol.

cutability *See* Part 2: Grades, Meat

cutlet A small slice of veal or other meat cuts from the ribs or leg; often coated with bread crumbs.
See Part 2: Braising Time; Meat Composition; Meat, Frozen Storage; Meat Identification; Pork Loin Cooking; Portion Size; Veal Chart; Veal Cuts and Uses

cut-out An animal separated from the group.

cutter One grade better than canner.
See Part 2: Grades, Meat

cutting yield *See* Part 2: Beef Carcass, Cutting Yield

cwt Hundredweight (100 lb).

cyanamid (cyanamide) $CaCN_2$ A fertilizer material; 21-0-0; nitrogen goes through several states such as urea, ammonium and nitrate; it is basic in nature and each pound is equivalent to 0.63 lb of dolomitic limestone.

cyanide A compound containing the CN group, such as HCN (hydrogen cyanide).
See Part 2: Water Drinking Standards

cyanocobalamin $C_{63}H_{88}CoN_{14}O_{14}P$ An active form of vitamin B_{12}.
See Part 2: Vitamins

cyanogen C_2N_2 A toxic gas used as a fumigant.
See Part 2: Normal Solutions

cyclamate Any of a group of non-nutritive sweeteners derived from cyclamic acid, $C_6H_{11}NHSO_4H$. Because of their tendency to form a toxic and possibly carcinogenic compound hexylamine, their use was prohibited in soft drinks and other food products by the FDA some years ago. Efforts to have the ban removed have so far been unsuccessful.

cyclic Moving in cycles or a chemical closed ring formation.

cyclic compound An organic compound in which the carbon atoms are arranged in a closed ring. *See also* **alicyclic, aromatic, heterocyclic.**

cycloalkane $(CH_2)_n$ A saturated cyclic series of compounds. *See also* **alicyclic.**

cycloalkene An unsaturated cyclic series of compounds. *See also* **alicyclic.**

cymling A summer variety of squash.

cysteine A non-essential sulfur-containing amino acid; 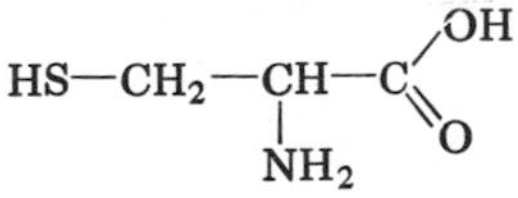 can be oxidized to cystine.
See Part 2: Amino Acids

cystine A nonessential sulfur-containing amino acid

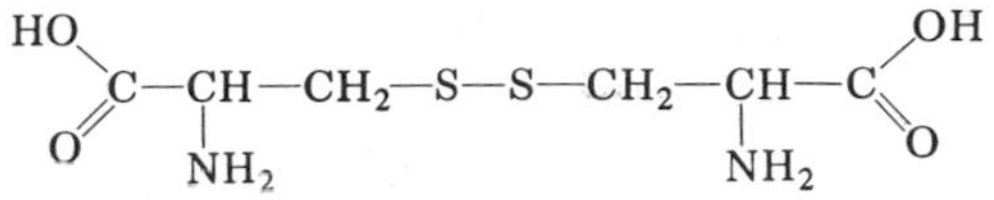

See Part 2: Amino Acids; Amino Acid, Solubilities; Corn, Amino Acids; Egg Products Nutritive Value; Grain Analysis; Manure Analysis; Milk, Amino Acids; Wheat, Amino Acids; Wheat Products, Amino Acid Compositions

cystine heart agar *See* Part 2: Microorganism, Media

cystine tryptic agar *See* Part 2: Microbiological Media

-cyte A suffix meaning "cell," e.g., erythrocyte (red cell).

cyto- A prefix meaning tube or cover, e.g., cytoplasm.

cytochrome There are many separate cytochromes in the cells and they can be oxidized and reduced and play a major role in transporting hydrogen from substrate to atmospheric oxygen.

cytology A microscopic study of cells.

cytoplasm A specific type of protoplasm which includes all of the cell's protoplasm except that of the nucleus.

cytosine A base found in nucleic acids (both in DNA and RNA).

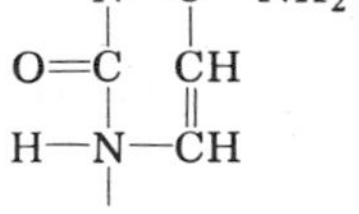

D

D Designates the right-handed (dextro) enantiomer (optical isomer) of a compound containing an asymmetric carbon atom. While such compounds (e.g., glyceraldehyde) are optically active, the D indicates only the structure of the compound, *not* the direction of optical rotation, which is shown by either *d* or a plus sign (+). *See also* **dextrorotatory; enantiomer; optical isomers; asymmetric carbon atom.**

2,4-D An organic herbicide (diclorophenoxyacetic acid). It is moderately toxic.

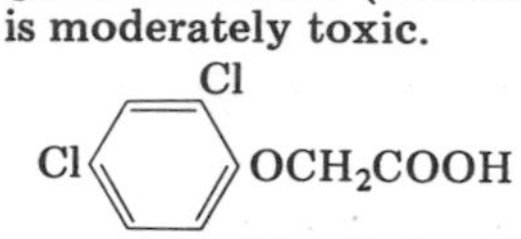

daikon A Japanese radish; it is often preserved by drying and fermentation.

dairy An establishment in which milk and its products are processed.
See Part 2: Microbiological Standards, Dairy

dairy cattle Collective term for commercial milk-producing animals.
See Part 2: Dairy Cattle Breeds

Dairy Herd Improvement Association (DHIA) An association that will assist dairymen in testing the production of a herd.

dairy products Milk, cream, cheese, and products made directly from them (ice cream).
See Part 2: Animal Foods, Composition; Calories, Daily Recommendations; Dairy Products, Composition; Dairy Terms; Glutamate; Microbiological Examination of Dairy Products; Microbiological Media; Microorganism, Culture Media, Dairy and Food Products; Mold, Food; Riboflavin, Food; Storage Times; Thiamin, Food; Vitamin A, Food; Vitamin D, Food

daisy cheese A type of cheddar cheese. *See also* **cheddar cheese.**

Dallis grass (*Paspalum dilatatum*) A perennial bunch-type grass used for pasture; seed 15 lb/bu; 12–15 lb/acre; soil pH 5–5.6.
See Part 2: Seed, Germination

dam A female parent (of animals).

damson *See* **plum**

dandelion (*Leontodon taraxacum*) A vegetable whose leaf is used as food; a perennial herb whose ground root is used for dandelion coffee; leaves are used in salads or boiled; flower heads are fermented to yield dandelion wine.
Composition (of raw greens): 86% H_2O, 3% protein, 0.7% fat, 9% carbohydrate, 2% ash.

Danish agar *See* **furcellaran**

Danish bread *See* Part 2: Fermented Ingredients

Danish Landrace *See* **Landrace**

darjeeling *See* **black tea**

dark cutter A dark condition in the muscle of a fresh beef carcass caused by high pH resulting from low muscle glycogen at the time of slaughter; no flavor or health hazard seems to be associated with this condition.
See Part 2: pH, Post Mortem

dash Less than ⅛ tsp of dry material, or 4 to 6 drops of liquid.

dasheen (*Colocasia esculenta*) *See* **taro**

date palm (*Phoenix dactylifera*) A tall palm that produces fruit (86% edible) in bunches that contain about 40 strands, each strand containing 25 to 35 dates; trees average 100 lb fruit per year.
Types of fruit:
soft dates: sold in pressed masses; eaten raw or in confectionery (60% sugar);
semi-dry dates: sold in boxes still attached to strand;
dry dates: hard; can be ground into flour (70% sugar);
date sap: fermented to palm wine or toddy; used for sugar production.
1 lb pitted dates = 2½–2⅔ cups pitted (1 cup = 180 g or 6.3 oz);
1 lb dried whole dates = 60 dates.
Dry date composition: 22% H_2O, 2% protein, 0.5% fat, 64–80% carbohydrate, 2% ash, pH 6.2–6.4.
See Part 2: Fruit Availability; Fruit Classification; Fruit Composition; Fruit Storage; Minerals, Food; Plant Foods, Composition; Potassium-rich Foods; Storage; Transit Temperature

date plum *See* **persimmon**

datum (sing.) A bit or item of information ("The datum is - - - -");
data (plural) More than one item of information ("The data are - - - -").

Davie A variety of barley.

d-c Direct current.

DDD *See* **TDE**

DDT (dichlorodiphenyltrichloroethane) A chlorinated hydrocarbon insecticide which is toxic to fish and some birds; content in foods is limited to 5 ppm. Largely because of its ecologically damaging effects it has been prohibited from use on food crops; it is highly persistent and not biodegradable. It is widely used in some foreign countries (India).

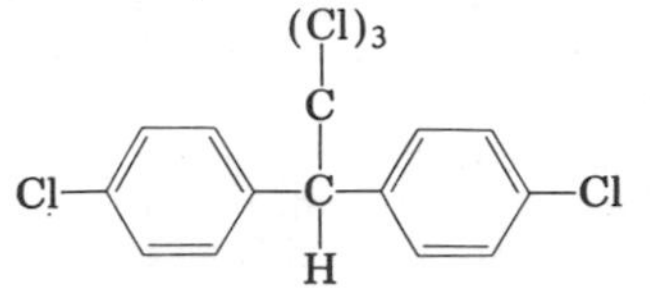

deacon A young calf sometimes considered too young for food.

deacon skin Skin from bob veal.

dead wool Wool taken from sheep shortly after death.

deamination Removal of an amino ($—NH_2$) group from a compound.

death camas A plant having a toxic principle.
See Part 2: Poisonous Plants

Debouillet A breed of sheep.
See Part 2: Sheep Breeds

decalcifying solution A solution used to dissolve calcareous matter; 1 part nitric acid and 9 parts 70% alcohol.

decanoic acid (capric acid) $CH_3(CH_2)_8COOH$ A saturated fatty acid found in coconut oil.
See Part 2: Saturated Fatty Acids

decarboxylase An enzyme that removes CO_2 from carboxylic acids.
See Part 2: Microorganism, Media; Microorganism, Selective and Differential Broths and Media, Water Filtration Plant

decenoic acid An unsaturated fatty acid.
See Part 2: Milk, Fatty Acids, Seasonal; Unsaturated Fatty Acids

deci- (one-tenth) (0.1) A prefix for quantities one-tenth the size of the base unit.

decigram (dg) A unit of metric weight.
1 decigram = 100 milligrams (mg)
= 10 centigrams (cg)
= 1.54324 grams
= 0.1 gram

deciliter (dl) A unit of metric volume.
1 deciliter = 100.003 cc
= 100 milliliters
= 10 centiliters
= 3.3815 ounces (U.S. fluid)
= 0.1 liter

decimal reduction time (D) (sometimes Z) The time required in minutes to kill 90% of the bacterial cells of a population at a given temperature.

decimeter (dm) A linear measure.
1 decimeter = 100 millimeters
= 10 centimeters
= 3.937 inches (U.S.)
= 0.1 meter

deckle Inner layer of meat and fat from a brisket.
See Part 2: Beef, Boneless Cuts

deep-fat fry To cook in fat deep enough to cover the product.

deep-sea fillet *See* **hake** and **pollock**

deer *See* Part 2: Gestation Periods; Meat and Meat Products Composition

defatted soy flour The primary flour made from soybean; chemical extraction of the fat has reduced it to less than 1%; protein 52–55%; crude fiber 2.5%; ash 6%.

defectives Items of substandard quality or appearance.
See Part 2: Defectives in Lot

defrost To remove frost from a refrigeration unit; to allow frozen food to thaw.
See Part 2: Defrosting Time

degree (deg) (°) (1) A measurement used for angles
1 degree = 3600 seconds
= 60 minutes
= 0.0175 radian
circle = 360 degrees
(2) A unit of temperature measurement. *See also* **absolute temperature; absolute zero; Celsius; Fahrenheit; centigrade.**

degrees of freedom Number of unrestricted variables.

degrees per second (angular)
1 degree per second = 0.167 revolution/min
= 0.0175 radian/sec
= 2.778×10^{-3} revolution/sec

degum To remove unwanted oxidation products.
See Part 2: Margarine Production

dehair To remove hair from hides by use of a solution of 8 lb dehydrated lime in 4 gal water; the enzyme trypsin is also used.

dehorn To remove horns from animals. Age (preferable) 1 week to 2 months. Methods: (1) chemical: 1 to 3 weeks old; clip hair and rough skin until irritated; apply ring of Vaseline around the budding horn; apply caustic (stick, paste, or liquid). Caution: caustic will burn—keep off of body; (2) electric: age 2 weeks to 3 months; (3) mechanical: use fly repellent (e.g., pine tar).

dehydrated food A food dried in artificially heated and mechanically circulated air to less than 5% moisture content.
See Part 2: Meat and Meat Products Composition

dehydration Removal of 95% or more of free water from a material by thermal means.

dehydrofrozen A product held in frozen form during dehydration.

dehydrogenase An enzyme which can oxidize a substrate by removal of hydrogen.

dehydrogenation Removal of hydrogen from a compound (a type of oxidation).

deka- (ten) (10) Prefix for quantities ten times larger than the base unit.

dekagram (dkg) A unit of metric weight.
1 dekagram = 10 grams

dekaliter (dkl) A unit of metric volume.
1 dekaliter = 10 liters

Delaine Merino A breed of sheep. *See also* **Merino-C type**

Delaware (1) A variety of grape. (2) An American class of single-comb chicken that lays a dark-shelled egg; color, white to white and black bars.

Delicious *See* **Red Delicious** and **Golden Delicious**

deliquescent Descriptive of a substance (usually water-soluble salts) that pick up water vapor from the air and gradually liquefy, e.g., sodium hydroxide.

Delmonico A cut of beef.
See Part 2: Beef Cuts; Roasting, Time and Temperature

delta (Δ, δ) Greek letter with English equivalent of "d."

deltoideus A muscle of the chuck filling the angle between the scapula and the humerus; it lies lateral to the triceps; attaches to the upper part of the humerus.

demersal fish (white fish) Fish that live on the sea bottom; 40% edible portion; average analysis of the edible portion, 16% protein; most are less than 1% fat (halibut 4%), 80% water, 80 calories/100 g. Example of types: bream, cod, dogfish, flounder, haddock, halibut, sole, whiting.

demeton A poisonous insecticide; a cholinesterase inhibitor which is a mixture of

$$(CH_3{-}CH_2{-}O)_2{-}\overset{S}{\overset{\nearrow}{P}}{-}O{-}(CH_2)_2{-}S{-}CH_2{-}CH_3$$

and

$$(CH_3{-}CH_2{-}O)_2{-}\overset{O}{\overset{\nearrow}{P}}{-}S{-}(CH_2)_2{-}S{-}CH_2{-}CH_3$$

demisel A soft light French cream cheese.
See Part 2: Cheese Vitamin Content

denaturation A change in the molecular structure of a protein due to exposure to heat, pH modification or contact with certain detergents; this results in reduction of its enzymatic activity and its solubility properties.

denatured alcohol Industrial alcohol to which has been added a low percentage of methyl alcohol or a number of other substances to make it unfit to drink (for taxation purposes).

densimetric analysis Determination of concentration by determination of density.

density The weight (in vacuum) per unit volume at a specific temperature.

$$\text{density} = \frac{\text{weight}}{\text{volume}}$$

See also **specific gravity**.

dent corn *See* **corn**

deodorant A compound such as aluminum chlorohydrate that neutralizes the acids in perspiration; also a highly porous solid such as activated carbon that adsorbs molecules of odorous gases.

deodorization Removal of odor, e.g., by steam distillation of a fat under reduced pressure; reduces odor, free fatty acids and color.
See Part 2: Margarine Production

deoxyribonucleic acid (desoxyribonucleic acid; DNA) A nucleoprotein (nucleic acid + protein) whose extremely complex double helix structure has only recently been determined. It controls the sequence of amino acids in the genes and thus programs the genetic code which determines heredity.
See Part 2: Histochemical Test

DEPC *See* **diethyl pyrocarbonate**

desalination Removal of salts from sea water or brine to make irrigation water and potable water. Some form of distillation (flash distillation) and reverse osmosis are in general use.

desiccator A laboratory device for maintaining a dry (or constant humidity) atmosphere for experimental samples. It is a sealed container in which has been placed an adsorptive material such as silica gel or calcium chloride.

desoxycholate agar *See* Part 2: Microorganism, Culture Media, Dairy and Food Products; Microorganism, Media

desoxycholate citrate agar *See* Part 2: Microorganism, Selective and Differential Broths and Media, Water Filtration Plant; Microorganism, Media

desoxycholate lactose agar *See* Part 2: Microbiological Media; Microorganism, Culture Media, Dairy and Food Products; Microorganism, Media; Microorganism, Selective and Differential Broths and Media, Water Filtration Plant

desoxycorticosterone A steroid hormone.
See Part 2: Steroids

destructive distillation (pyrolysis) Heating of a solid material out of contact with air; destructive distillation of coal yields coal tar and coke, and of wood, turpentine.

detergent A surface-active organic compound that aids emulsification by lowering the surface tension of water. Common soap is an effective detergent; alcohol and linear alkyl sulfonates also have this effect.
See Part 2: Detergent Properties; Detergents

deuterium (H^2) (D) Heavy hydrogen, at. wt. 2.0147.

de-veined shrimp Shrimp from which shell and black sand veins have been removed.

deviations (x_1, $x_2 \cdots x_n$) Individual variations from the sample mean; e.g.: $x_1 = X_1 - \bar{x}$

X_1 = observation no. 1
$\bar{x}$ = sample mean
$\Sigma x = 0$

Devon A dual-purpose type of cattle; red in color.
See Part 2: Beef and Dual-purpose Cattle

dewberry (*Rubus alleghaniensis*) A berry similar to blackberry except fruit is smaller and less compact, and ripens before the blackberry.
Composition: 85% H_2O, 1% protein, 1% fat, 13% carbohydrate, 0.5% ash.
See Part 2: Fruit Classification; Fruit Frozen Yield; Storage

dewclaw In cattle, sheep and swine, horny growth at the rear of the pastern.
See Part 2: Bone

dewlap Loose skin in brisket and neck of cattle.

Dexter *See* Part 2: Beef and Dual-purpose cattle

dextrin(e) $(C_6H_{10}O_5)_x$ Intermediate product in the hydrolysis of starch to maltose, made up of glucose units.
See Part 2: Stabilizers, Thickeners; Sweetening Agents

dextro- Right; right-handed. *See also* **enantiomer; optical rotation.**

dextrorotatory (*d*) (+) Rotation of polarized light to the right. *See also* **optical rotation.**

dextrose *See* **corn sugar; glucose**
See Part 2: Microorganism, Media; Minerals, Trace, Limits; Sweetening Agents; Sweetening Compounds

dextrose proteose agar *See* Part 2: Microorganism, Media

dextrose salt agar *See* Part 2: Microbiological Media

dextrose tryptone agar *See* Part 2: Microbiological Media; Microorganism, Culture Media, Dairy and Food Products

DHIA *See* **Dairy Herd Improvement Association**

di- Prefix meaning two.

diacetate (sodium and calcium) $CH_3COONa \cdot CH_3COOH$ Inhibits mold.

diacetyl $CH_3CO \cdot COCH_3$ Flavoring agent in butter.

dialysis Separation of molecules by difference in rate of diffusion through a membrane.

α, ε-diaminocaproic acid *See* **lysine**

diammonium phosphate $(NH_4)_2HPO_4$
See Part 2: Fertilizer

diamond round A cut of beef.
See Part 2: Beef Rounds

diaphragm A muscle and connective tissue sheet that separates the thoracic from the abdomen section of the body.
See Part 2: Beef Rib Nomenclature

Diaporthe A genus of sac fungi responsible for rot or blight in potatoes and beans.
See Part 2: Mold, Food

diarrhea An intestinal disorder causing loose and watery stools.
See Part 2: Infectious Diseases, Food-borne

diastase An enzyme that hydrolyzes starch to malt sugar.
See Part 2: Honey Composition

diastole Muscle expansion.

diatomaceous earth (kieselguhr) A siliceous earth of low specific gravity used as a clarifying and refining agent.

diazinon A poisonous insecticide of the cholinesterase-inhibiting type.

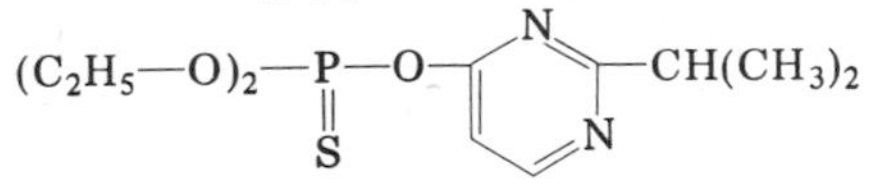

See Part 2: Insect Control

dibasic acid An acid with 2 replaceable hydrogens, e.g.,

$$H_2SO_4 \longrightarrow H^+ + HSO_4^-$$

$$HSO_4^- \rightleftharpoons H^+ + SO_4^{--}$$

dicalcium phosphate $CaHPO_4 \cdot 2H_2O$ A neutral fertilizer material; 0–40–0; also a good source of calcium and phosphorus; low in fluorine (toxic).

dice Cut into small pieces, as potatoes, carrots, etc.

dichlorobenzene A chlorinated hydrocarbon insecticide, especially for moth control.

ortho para

dichlorodifluoromethane CCl_2F_2 A chlorofluorocarbon refrigerant; formerly used as an aerosol propellant. Nonflammable gas.
See Part 2: Refrigerant

dichlorodimethyl hydantoin *See* Part 2: Chlorine Availability; Chlorine Compounds

dichloroethylene ClCHCHCl An unsaturated flammable liquid used as a solvent.
See Part 2: Refrigerant

dichloroisocyanuric acid OCNClCONClCONH Sanitizer used in dishwashing compounds, bleaches, etc. Has 70% available chlorine.
See Part 2: Chlorine Availability; Sanitizers

dichloromethane (methylene chloride) CH_2Cl_2 Used as solvent, fumigant and refrigerant.
See Part 2: Refrigerant

dichloromonofluoromethane $CHCl_2F$ Nonflammable gas used as a refrigerant.
See Part 2: Refrigerant

dichlorotetrafluoroethane $CCl_2F_2CClF_2$ Nonflammable gas used as a refrigerant.
See Part 2: Refrigerant

dicoumarol (dicumarol) $C_{19}H_{12}O_6$ A substance found in spoiled sweetclover that increases the clotting time of blood; an anticoagulant.

dicysteine *See* **cystine**

dieldrin A poisonous chlorinated hydrocarbon insecticide. Use on food crops prohibited.

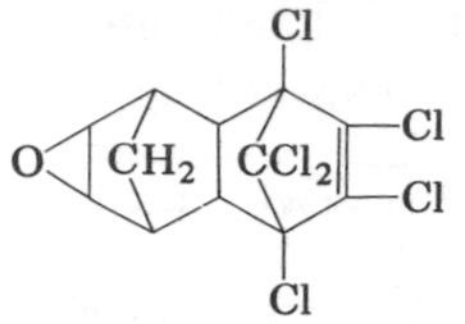

dielectric constant

$$\text{dielectric constant (of a substance)} = \frac{\left[\begin{array}{l}\text{Electrical capacity of a condenser when the substance is}\\ \text{between the plates}\end{array}\right]}{\left[\begin{array}{l}\text{Electrical capacity of a condenser when there is a vac-}\\ \text{uum between the plates}\end{array}\right]}$$

The dielectric constant measures the distance between charges in a molecule and is decreased with increasing temperature. *See also* **polar; non-polar.**

dielectric heating Heating by establishing a high-frequency alternating electric field within a material (electrical nonconductor).

diet A restricted food intake to reduce fat or counteract a functional disorder.
See Part 2: Sodium-restricted Diet

diethyl pyrocarbonate (DEPC)
$C_2H_5O-\underset{\underset{O}{\|}}{C}-O-\underset{\underset{O}{\|}}{C}-O-C_2H_5$ A chemical used to retard mold growth in food; it hydrolyzes in aqueous solutions to ethanol and CO_2.

diethylstilbestrol (DES) *See* **stilbestrol**

difference test An organoleptic test to determine differences in taste perception. *See also* **organoleptic.**
See Part 2: Taste Panel, Difference Tests

differential media Media designed for separation or isolation or differentiation of related organisms.
See Part 2: Microorganism, Selective and Differential Broths and Media, Water Filtration Plant; Microorganism Reactions on Differential Tube Media

differentiation disk *See* Part 2: Microorganism, Media

digester A pressure cooker.

digester tankage *See* **meat meal tankage**

digestibility Percent of food absorbed into bloodstream.

diglyceride Glycerol esterified with two molecules of an acid; has good emulsifying properties. *See also* **fatty acid.**

dihydric alcohol An alcohol whose molecule contains two hydroxyl groups; collectively, these are called glycols; an example is ethylene glycol CH_2OHCH_2OH.

dihydrogenphosphate group
$-O-P(\rightarrow O)-(OH)_2$

dihydroxystearic acid $C_{17}H_{33}(OH)_2COOH$ A hard fatty acid.
See Part 2: Fatty Acids, Fats and Oils; Fatty Acids and Their Properties

diiodotyrosine An iodine-containing amino acid

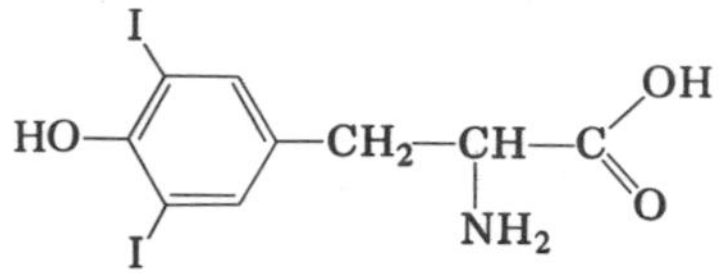

dilan A chlorinated organic insecticide

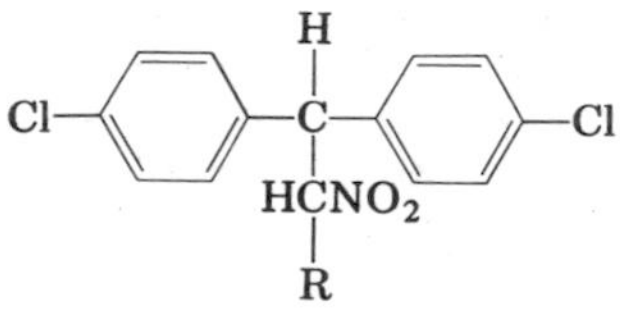

$R=C_2H_5$ (3parts)

$R=CH_3$ (1 part)

dilatometry A method of determining the solid-liquid ratio in a fat; it is based on the specific volume of the liquid and solid phases.

dilauryl thiodipropionate $(C_{12}H_{25}OOCCH_2CH_2)_2S$ An antioxidant used in fats and oils and in packaging materials.
See Part 2: Antioxidant Structure

dill (*Anethum graveolens L.*) A small oval-shaped tan seed; leaves and stems of a shrub used in seasoning. The seed and leaves are used in pickling cucumbers, pastries, soups and sauces. The seed is ridged, flattened, brown with yellow ridges.
See Part 2: Essential Oils; Flavoring Agents, Natural

dill pickles Pickles cured in a solution containing dill.
Composition: 93% H_2O, 0.8% protein, 0.2% fat, 2.2% carbohydrate, 4% ash, pH 3.2–3.5.

dill weed Leaves of dill plant.

diode An electrical component that has a much higher resistance to current passage in one direction than in the other.

diolefin *See* **alkadiene**

diphenyl (biphenyl) $C_6H_5C_6H_5$ A poisonous compound used for treatment of mold in fruit.

diphosphopyridine nucleotide (DPN) (coenzyme I) A coenzyme which functions in several dehydrogenation reactions; it has the ability to take up and give off H, as shown in its formula:

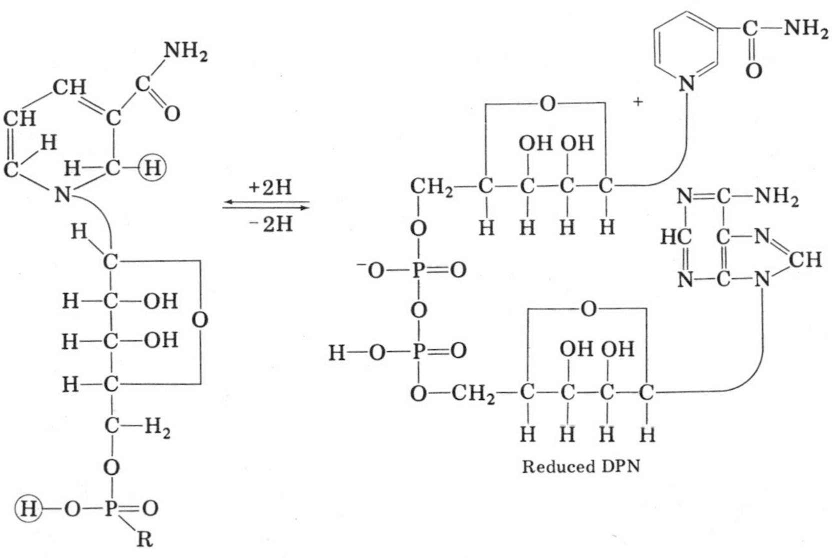

Oxidized DPN

Reduced DPN

Dichloroacetic acid	5×10^{-2}
Chloroacetic	1.5×10^{-3}
Formic	2.1×10^{-4}
Acetic	1.8×10^{-5}
Carbonic (first H)	1×10^{-7}
(second H)	5×10^{-11}
Water	1×10^{-16}

diphosphothiamin *See* **thiamin pyrophosphate**

diphtheria An infectious disease characterized by blocked air passages in the throat, especially in children.
See Part 2: Illness from Food; Infectious Diseases, Food-Borne

directs Stock purchased directly by packers.

disease A malfunctioning of an organism usually accompanied by fever, and caused by bacteria or viruses.
See Part 2: Diseases, Food-Borne; Fruit and Vegetable, Diseases

disinfectant A substance used on inanimate objects (e.g., food processing equipment) to kill or inhibit bacteria. *See also* **antiseptic.**
See Part 2: Microbiological Media

disodium phosphate Na_2HPO_4
See Part 2: Phosphate

dispersed phase (internal phase) The finely divided particles of a colloidal system which remain in continued suspension. *See also* **continuous phase.**

dispersion medium *See* **continuous phase**

dissection Precise and systematic separation or cutting apart of a living or recently living organism, as practiced by biologists and surgeons.

dissociation (ionization) Separation of an electrolyte into positive and negative ions when in aqueous solution, e.g., sodium chloride, sulfuric acid. *See also* **ionization.**

dissociation constant (k_1) A value resulting from the reaction $HAc \rightleftharpoons H^+ + Ac^-$

$$k_1 = \frac{(H^+)(Ac^-)}{(HAc)} \text{ in moles per liter}$$

dissolve To separate a crystalline solid into its component molecules or ions (dissociation) by immersion in water or other solvent.

distal Farther away or remote from the point of attachment, as of a bone or muscle.

distillate Condensed vapor of distillation.

distillation An operation utilized for separating the components of a solution or of a mixture of liquids by heating the liquid to its boiling point and condensing the resulting vapor. Thus, e.g., salt can be removed from a saline solution, and mixtures composed of liquids of different boiling points can be separated (fractional distillation of petroleum). *See also* **destructive distillation.**

distilled vinegar Vinegar made by fermentation of dilute distilled alcohol; min.: 4% acetic acid.

distilled water Water purified by condensation from the vapor phase, e.g., rain.

distiller's corn grain *See* Part 2: Cereal By-Products Composition

distiller's corn soluble *See* Part 2: Cereal By-Products Composition

distillers grain Grain from which alcohol or alcoholic beverages have been removed after fermentation; 19 lb/bu; 0.6 lb/qt.

distillers' soluble Dried liquor that is left from whiskey after distilling the spirit.

ditali lisci *See* **macaroni**

ditali rigati *See* **macaroni**

DNA *See* **deoxyribonucleic acid**

DNase *See* Part 2: Microorganism, Media

do *See* **mean lethal dose**

do'a A condiment containing salt, pepper mixed with marjoram, mint or cumin and either coriander, cinnamon or sesame.

dock Part of tail left on an animal after clipping or cutting; sometimes the region near tail or base of the tail.

dockage Weight deducted from stags and pregnant sows.

docking Removing the tail of an animal; methods include: elastrator, knife or hot iron; best age for sheep, 1 to 2 weeks old, 1 inch from body.

docosanoic acid (behenic acid) $CH_3(CH_2)_{20}COOH$ A saturated fatty acid found in peanut oil.
See Part 2: Saturated Fatty Acids

docosapentaenoic acid *See* Part 2: Unsaturated Fatty Acids

docosenoic acid (erucic acid) A 22-carbon unsaturated fatty acid found in rapeseed oil.
See Part 2: Unsaturated Fatty Acids

Doddies Early Scotch black-polled cattle.

dodecanoic acid (lauric acid) $CH_3(CH_2)_{10}COOH$ A saturated fatty acid found in coconut oil.
See Part 2: Fats and Oils, Fatty Acid Composition; Fatty Acids and Their Properties; Fatty Acids; Fatty Acids, Fats and Oils; Milk, Fatty Acids, Seasonal; Oil, Seed and Fruit; Saturated Fatty Acids

dodecenoic acid A 12-carbon unsaturated fatty acid.
See Part 2: Milk, Fatty Acids, Seasonal; Unsaturated Fatty Acids

dodol A jelly-like sweetmeat made from rice flour, coconut milk and manisan.

dog (grayfish, *Squalus acanthias*) A 20-lb shark used for food, oil, and fertilizer; any of various small sharks.
See Part 2: Salmon and Trout

dogey A small common bred cattle.

dogfish (rock salmon) *See* **demersal fish**

dog rose (*Rosa rugosa*) An urn-shaped fruit (rose-hip) used to make rose hip syrup, jellies, preserves and sauces.

dolomite A type of limestone containing magnesium carbonate in which 40% or more of the neutralizing power is magnesium carbonate. *See also* **dolomitic limestone; limestone.**
See Part 2: Fertilizer Materials; Liming Materials

dolomitic hydrate *See* Part 2: Liming Materials

dolomitic limestone (ground) A liming material composed of 52% $CaCO_3$ and 42% $MgCO_3$ (must be 10–39.9% neutralizing value for dolomitic). Each pound has the neutralizing equivalent of 0.95 to 1.08 pounds of $CaCO_3$; also see **limestone and agricultural limestone.**

domestic sausage Sausages that originated in or are now made in large quantities in the U.S.

domiati A soft salty cheese, ripened by bacteria. Composition: 55% H_2O, 20% protein, 25% fat, 5% salt.

Dominique An American class of chicken with a rose comb that lays a brown-shelled egg; color, bluish slate with light and dark bars; undercolor is slate.

Dorking An English class of chickens with white skin, 5 toes that lays a white-shelled egg; Varieties: white, silver-grey, colored.

Dorman A variety of soybean.

dorsal Located on the back, as a dorsal fin.

Dorset A medium-wool, mutton type, breed of sheep originating in southern England; a white face breed of sheep with both sexes having horns; this breed can lamb at almost any season of the year.
See Part 2: Sheep Breeds

dotriacontanoic A saturated fatty acid.
See Part 2: Saturated Fatty Acids

double bond A type of linkage that occurs in unsaturated compounds, in which not all the available valences of an atom are satisfied. Such linkages occur most frequently between carbon atoms; unsaturated compounds tend to be more reactive than saturated compounds, as one valence is free to attach itself to another atom.
See Part 2: Oil, Triglyceride Mole Percent Composition; Rapeseed Oil, Triglyceride Mole Percent Composition

double bone sirloin (flat bone) A sirloin steak found in the loin end wholesale cut; it is located between the round bone sirloin and the pin bone sirloin; in retail cuts, one of the bones is usually removed.

double gloucester A hard, mellow English cheese.

Double Standard Polled Hereford Hornless Hereford cattle that originated from registered Hereford stock.

Double Standard Polled Shorthord Polled Shorthorn originating from registered Shorthorn stock.

double superphosphate $Ca(H_2PO_4)_2$ A neutral fertilizer material; 0-46-0; it is superphosphate from which the gypsum has been removed.

doughnut A deep-fried circular cake, usually with a hole in the center, made of water, flour, sugar, shortening and some form of leavening.

Types	Frying Temp. (°F)	Sugar (%)	Shortening (%)	Frying Fat (%)
Yeast-raised	375–390	3	5	15–25
Cake type (chemical leavening)	375–390	15	2	18

See Part 2: Calories, Daily Recommendations; Frozen Food Storage; Frying Time; Grain Products Composition

Dover sole *See* **sole**

Down breeds Breeds of sheep such as Hampshire; Oxford; Shropshire; Southdown.

DPN *See* **diphosphopyridine nucleotide**

drachm (Br.) *See* **dram (troy)** for weight; for volume: 1 drachm = 60 minims
= 3.55 ml

dragées de Verdun Almonds coated with sugar.

dram (dr.) (1) Apothecary's or troy weight. A measure of weight used for gold, silver, and jewels.
1 dram = 3.888×10^3 milligrams
= 60 grains
= 3.8879351 grams
= 3 scruples (apoth.)
= 2.5 pennyweights
= 2.194286 drams (avoirdupois)
= 0.1371429 ounce (av.)
= 0.1250 ounce (troy) (apoth.)
= 1.0416667×10^{-2} pound (troy) (apoth.)
= 3.888×10^{-3} kilogram
= 8.571429×10^{-3} pound (av.)
= 4.284×10^{-6} ton (short)
= 3.826×10^{-6} ton (long)
(2) Avoirdupois. A measure of weight
1 dram = 1.77184×10^3 milligrams
= 27.34375 grains
= 1.7718454 grams
= 1.3671875 scruples (apoth.)
= 1.139323 pennyweights
= 0.4557292 dram (apothecary's or troy)
= 0.0625 ounce (av.)
= 0.056966146 ounce (troy) (apoth.)
= 4.7471788×10^{-3} pound (troy) (apoth.)
= 0.00390625 pound (av.)
= 1.772×10^{-3} kilogram
= 1.953×10^{-6} ton (short)
= 1.744×10^{-6} ton (long)
(3) (U.S. fluid) (Apoth.) A liquid measure.
1 dram = 62.451 minims (Br.)
= 60 minims (U.S.)
= 3.6967 cubic centimeters
= 3.6966 ml
= 0.22559 cu. in.
= 0.13011 ounce (Br. fl.)
= 0.125 ounce (fluid)
= 0.0078125 pint (liquid, U.S.)
= 3.6966×10^{-3} liter
= 9.7656×10^{-4} gallon (U.S.)
= 8.13165×10^{-4} gallon (Br.)
= 1.3054×10^{-4} cu. ft
= 3.1×10^{-5} barrel (U.S.)

draw To remove the viscera of a fowl in preparation for cooking.

drawn (1) Of animal and fish carcasses, eviscerated. (2) Of butter or other fat, melted.
See Part 2: Fish Drawn; Fish Yields

drawn butter Melted butter, often with added flavoring, served with lobster or other sea food.

drawn poultry Dressed poultry from which the entrails, head and feet have been removed.

dredge To coat meat with flour or a mixture of flour, butter and salt, prior to baking or roasting.

dressed Prepared for cooking.
See Part 2: Fish Dressed; Fish Forms; Fish Yields

dressing (1) Stuffing for roast fowl, pork, etc. made with bread, oysters, chestnuts, etc. and seasoned with herbs. (2) A sauce for salads made with vegetable oils, vinegar and various herbs and spices.
See Part 2: Bacon Dressing; Calories, Daily Recommendations; Condensed Milk Dressing; Cooked Dressing; Fats and Oils Composition; French Dressing; French Dressing Variations; Fruit Dressing; Fruit Salad Dressing; Mayonnaise; Mayonnaise and Salad Dressing; Salad Dressing and Mayonnaise Variations; Sour Cream Dressing; Stabilizers, Thickeners

dressing percentage Percent of live weight that is represented by chilled carcass weight.

$$\text{dressing percentage} = \frac{\text{chilled carcass wt}}{\text{live wt}} \times 100$$

carcass wt = live wt × dressing percentage

$$\text{live wt} = \frac{\text{carcass wt}}{\text{dressing percentage}}$$

carcass value per hundred wt (cwt) =

$$\frac{\text{price per hundred wt (live)}}{\text{dressing percentage}}$$

live value (cwt) = carcass value (cwt) × dressing percentage

	Cattle (%)	Hogs (%)	Sheep	(%)
Prime	60–67	(head &	ewes	40–60
Choice	58–62	leaf fat		
Good	52–59	on)	fat	48–52
Commercial	45–56	74–84	lambs	
Utility	47–53			
Cutter & Canner	38–47			

See Part 2: Poultry Dressing Percentage

dried A food product from which most of the water has been removed. See following entries.
See also **sun-dried food; dehydrated food.**
See Part 2: Milk, Amino Acids; Milk and Milk Products, Vitamin Content; Milk Composition; Milk, Dry Products; Minerals, Food; Nicotinic Acid, Food; Storage, Dry; Storage Times; Vitamin A, Milk and Milk Products

dried beef (beef hams) Beef that has been dry or sweet-pickle cured with salt, sugar and sodium nitrate and/or sodium nitrite and then smoked and allowed to dry; meat generally used is inside, outside, and knuckles of round; cure:

79.8% by wt water
14 % salt
6% sugar
0.2% sodium nitrate
} pump to 5% of wt

See also **corned beef.**
See Part 2: Meat Composition; Meat, Servings Per Pound

dried fruit Fruit preserved by partial removal of water; most contain approx. 24% water.
Storage: 32°F; 50–60% relative humidity; 9–12 mo. storage life.
See Part 2: Calcium Daily Requirements; Calories, Daily Recommendations; Fruit, Dried, Simmering; Fruit Servings Per Pound; Iron, Daily Recommendations; Niacin, Daily Recommendations; Storage; Storage, Dry; Storage Times

dried milk *See* **binder**
See Part 2: Concentrated and Dried Milk Products

dried skim milk Contains not more than 1½% milk fat and not more than 5% water.

dried whole milk Contains 26% milk fat and not more than 5% water.

drier (dryer) (1) A soap of a heavy metal, e.g., cobalt naphthenate, used in some paints, printing inks, etc., to accelerate polymerization of drying oils; (2) equipment used for drying (dehydrating) foods.
See Part 2: Dryer Types

Drierite ($CaSO_4$) Proprietary name for a desiccant used to keep the atmosphere dry.

drift Weight loss of cattle off feed prior to slaughter.

drip grind Particle size of coffee made by the drip method; finer than regular grind.
See Part 2: Coffee Particle Size

dripping *See* Part 2: Vitamin Retention, Meat

drug store wrap A single thickness of paper is placed under an object; the ends of the paper that go around the sides of the object are brought together on top; they are then folded in ½-inch folds till the paper is down to the object; the ends are then folded into a triangle; the tip of the triangle is then folded under; next, the entire end is folded under smooth and fastened.

drupe A one-celled fruit with one or two seeds; pericarp divided into a thin epicarp (outer layer or peel), a fleshy sarcocarp (mesocarp), and a hard endocarp (inner layer, surrounding seed or stone); e.g., almond, apricot, cherry, peach, plum.

dry bulb *See* Part 2: Relative Humidity

dry champagne *See* **dry wine**

dry cure A curing procedure in which the curing ingredients are dry powders that are rubbed on the meat; many variations in curing ingredients are used; (most widely used formula is 8 lb salt, 3 lb sugar, 3 oz saltpeter); ham, 1 oz cure/lb meat, 3 rubbings, 2 days/lb in cure; bacon, 1 oz cure/lb meat, 2 rubbings, 7 days/inch in cure.

dry heat cooking A method of cooking tender meat by surrounding it with dry air; it includes broiling, panbroiling and roasting.

Dry Ice Compressed solid carbon dioxide (CO_2); −110°F (−79°C).

drying Evaporation of water or organic solvent. *See also* **dehydration.**
See Part 2: Moisture, Drying

drying oil A vegetable oil that hardens to a film due to polymerization of its molecules when exposed to air. Such oils were once widely used in the paint industry, but have been largely replaced by synthetic resins. Examples are linseed oil and tung oil.

drymary A plant having a toxic principle.
See Part 2: Poisonous Plants

dry milk 1 lb dry milk, whole = 7.6 lb milk. *See also* **whole dry milk.**
See Part 2: Dairy Terms

dry pack Sugar-free processed fruit.

dry-processed lard Lard rendered in a steam jacket tank under vacuum.

dry salt cure A cure in which only salt is rubbed on meat and fat products; 7 to 10 lb salt/100 lb meat.

dry sugar cure *See* **dry cure**

dry whole milk *See* **whole dry milk; dry milk**

dry wine A wine in which all the sugar that can be perceived by taste has been fermented. In 100 cc (20°C):
less than 1 g sugar;
not less than 0.16 g ash in red dry wine;
not less than 0.13 g ash in white dry wine;
not less than 1.6 g sugar-free grape solids in red dry wine;
not less than 1.4 g sugar-free grape solids in white dry wine

dry yeast A dry, granular mixture of yeast and a filler mixture (i.e., starch, cornmeal).
1 tbsp active dry yeast = 1 package of active dry yeast = 1 cake compressed yeast.
Storage: Keep in cool dry place for several months; activation temperature, 115°F.

dry-zero *See* Part 2: Insulation

DTM agar *See* Part 2: Microorganism, Media

dual-purpose cattle Cattle developed for the production of both milk and meat; triple purpose: developed for milk, meat, and draft.
See Part 2: Beef and Dual-Purpose Cattle

dual standard Method of difference testing; two known samples are presented, two unknown samples are presented and the observer is asked to identify.
See Part 2: Taste Panel, Difference Tests

Dubos oleic agar *See* Part 2: Microorganism, Media

Duchesse potatoes Potatoes with eggs and butter placed in a pastry tube.

duck An amphibious game bird used for food. *See* Part 2: Animal Foods, Composition; Frozen Food Storage; Glutamate; Meat and Meat Products Composition; Minerals, Food; Portion Size; Poultry Class; Poultry Dressing Percentage; Poultry Roasting; Poultry Yield

duhat *See* Part 2: Fruit Classification

dulcin $H_2NOCNHC_6H_4OC_2H_5$ A synthetic sweetener. Restricted by FDA.
See Part 2: Sweetness of Sweeteners

dulse (*Rhodymenia palmata*) A red algae seaweed used for food and for making an alcoholic drink.

Duncan A variety of early Florida grapefruit.

dungeness *See* **crab**

dunnage Platforms on which cartons are stacked.

duo-trio *See* Part 2: Taste Panel, Difference Tests

dupe *See* Part 2: Fruit Classification

Du puits A variety of alfalfa.

Durham Name once used for the Shorthorn breed of cattle.

durian A large tree that produces a 6 to 8-lb dull-yellow fruit covered with spines; a taste has to be acquired for the pulp which is eaten fresh and made into drinks.
See Part 2: Fruit Classification; Fruit Storage

Duroc A meat-type breed of hogs that originated in New England from several strains of red hogs (primarily the Jersey Reds of New Jersey and Durocs of New York); it is cherry red in color and has drooping ears.
See Part 2: Swine Breeds

Duroc-Jersey Early name of the hog association now known as Duroc.

durra A plant having a toxic principle.
See Part 2: Poisonous Plants

durum flour Flour made from durum wheat with a particle size of 140 μ or less; used to make noodles and to a lesser extent, macaroni.

durum granular A milled product from durum wheat that may contain 20% flour; used in macaroni products.

durum wheat (*Tricilum durum*) A hard wheat with high gluten content used in making macaroni products. *See also* **wheat.**

Dutch Belted A dairy-type breed of cattle.

Dutchess A variety of apples that are in season in July to Sept. that make good pies and sauce but only fair eating.

Dutch loaf *See* Part 2: Sausage Nutritive Value

D-value *See* **decimal reduction time**

dwarf cape gooseberry *See* **gooseberry**

dwarfism Small, midget type animals usually associated with cattle; (y-gene for dwarf and x-normal gene):

(1) dwarf carrier (xy) X non-dwarf carrier (xx) $\longrightarrow$ ½ offsprings carrier (xy) and ½ offsprings non-carrier (xx)

(2) dwarf carrier (xy) X dwarf carrier (xy) $\longrightarrow$ ¼ offsprings dwarf calf (yy), ½ offsprings carrier calf (xy), and ¼ offsprings non-dwarf carrier (xx)

dwt *See* **grain (troy)**

Dy Symbol for the element dysprosium.

dye A soluble organic substance that absorbs certain wavelengths of radiant energy in the visible spectrum. *See also* **colorant.**

dyne-centimeter A measure of heat, energy, and work.
1 dyne-centimeter = 1 erg
= 0.00101979 gram-centimeter
= 0.0000000737612 foot-pound

dyne per cubic centimeter A measure of density.
1 dyne (per cubic centimeter = 0.00118528 poundal/in.^{3}
= 0.00101979 gram/cm^3

dyne per square centimeter A measure of pressure.
1 dyne (per sq centimeter) = 0.0010197 gram/cm^2
= 0.000466646 poundal/in.^{2}

dysentery An infectious disease of the intestines characterized by loss of water.
See Part 2: Infectious Agents; Diseases, Food-Borne

dysprosium (Dy) A rare earth element of the lanthanide series; at. no. 66; at. wt. 162.51; Group IIIB of Periodic Table, oxidation state +3; electron configuration 2-8-18-28-8-2
orbit K L M N O P

E

E *See* **volt**

ear *See* **corn**
See Part 2: Corn; Pork Cuts and Uses

early maturity Of a plant, quick attainment of full development.

early Ohio An all-purpose variety of potato.

earthnut *See* **peanut**

earthstars A type of fungus.

earth tongues A type of fungus.

earworm A pest that infests corn.
See Part 2: Insect Control

Eastern style A method of cutting beef.

ebonite Hard rubber.
See Part 2: Insulation, Conductivity Values

ecdysis Molting.

éclair (from French meaning "lightning") A finger-shaped pastry filled with custard or whipped creme.

E C medium A selective broth for the growth of coliform bacteria at 37°C and for *Escherichia coli* at 45.5°C.
See Part 2: Microorganism, Culture Media, Water and Sewage, Standard Methods; Microorganism, Selective and Differential Broths and Media, Water Filtration Plant

E. coli An infective microorganism.
See Part 2: Microorganism, Media

ecology Study of relationships between animals and plants.

Edam A mild semi-solid cheese from Holland; a mellow cheese, softer than cheddar, with cheddar-type flavor (mild, nut-like); made from partly skimmed milk; its shape is a round ball with a red wax covering; it has a creamy yellow interior; ripened 2 mo.; a dessert or cooking cheese.
Composition: 39% H_2O, 28-31% protein, 24-25% fat, 5% ash, 2% salt, pH 5.4.
See Part 2: Cheese Characteristics; Cheese Composition; Cheese Vitamin Content; Milk and Cheese Composition; Milk and Milk Products, Vitamin Content; Vitamin A, Milk and Milk Products

eddo *See* **taro**

edelweiss (1) A soft ripened cheese from Germany. (2) A perennial herb growing in high mountain areas (Alps).

edible meat *See* Part 2: Edible Meat and Chilled Carcass

edible oil A vegetable oil used as food, e.g., coconut oil, corn oil, etc.

edible-podded pea *See* **sugar pea**

EE broth An enrichment broth for the detection of enteric bacilli in foods; it is a brilliant green bile broth modified by incorporation of dextrose.
See Part 2: Microbiological Media

eel (*Apodes*) Any of the elongated, snake-like fishes with a smooth skin; some are strictly marine and others live in fresh water but descend to the ocean as they approach sexual maturity; many are important as a food source; up to 30% fat. *See also* **fresh-water fish.**
See Part 2: Minerals, Food

eel brass mats A medium density material sometimes used for its heat insulation value in refrigeration systems.
See Part 2: Insulation

EFA Essential fatty acids. *See also* **essential (2).**

egg Reproductive cell of the female. Following data refer to hen's eggs:

1 egg = 1½-2 oz (50 g)
8 to 10 eggs = 1 lb
1 case or crate (eggs in shell) = 30 dozen = 47 to 60 lb
1 case eggs, in shell = 39.5 lb liquid whole eggs = 10.8 lb dried whole eggs
1 carload = 500 cases (30 dozen each) = 15,000 dozen

Equivalents	Frozen Eggs (lb)	No. of Eggs in Shell	Dry Egg Solids (lb)
Whole	1	9 eggs	0.25 + 0.75 water
Yolk	1	23 yolks	0.45 + 0.55 water
White	1	15 whites	0.12 + 0.88 water

1 cup of whole or white or yolk = 240 g
1 whole egg = 2 egg yolks = 3 tbsp + 1 tsp frozen egg = 2 tbsp + 2 tsp dry whole egg powder + equal amounts of water.
1 egg yolk = 3½ tsp thawed frozen egg yolk = 2 tbsp dry egg yolk + 2 tsp water.
12 to 14 egg yolks = 1 cup.
1 egg white = 2 tbsp thawed frozen egg white = 2 tsp dry egg whites + 2 tbsp water.
7 to 10 egg whites = 1 cup.
small egg
  3 small eggs = ⅓ cup
  3 small eggs = 2 medium eggs
medium
  2 medium eggs = ⅓ cup
  3 medium eggs = ½ cup

5 medium eggs = 1 cup
2 medium eggs = 3 small eggs
3 medium eggs = 2 large eggs

large egg
2 large eggs = ½ cup
2 large eggs = 3 medium eggs

Storage:
in shell: refrigerate (28-31°F); use within 1 week.
yolks: Cover with cold water and refrigerate; use within 1 to 2 days.
white: Cover and refrigerate; use within 1 to 2 days.
frozen (−10°F): 1 Year.
dried: Refrigerate (35°F), low as possible relative humidity; use in 6 months to 1 year.

Cooking:

	Boiled Water Temp. (°F)	Boiled Time (min)	Coddled Water Temp. (°F)	Coddled Time (min)	Baked Oven Temp. (°F)	Baked Time (min)
Soft	212	2-4	180-200	6-10	250-350	6-10
Hard	212	20-30	180-200	30-45	250-360	25-40

Composition

Chicken Egg	% of Egg	H_2O (%)	Protein (%)	Fat (%)	Carbohydrate (%)	Ash (%)	pH
Whole	88-89	73-74	13	11-11½	1	1	
Yolk (40% of edible)	30-32	49-51	16	31.2	0.6-1	2	6-6.8
White (60% of edible)	57-58	87-88	11	0	0.8-1	1	7-9
Shell	11-12						

See Part 2: Animal Foods, Composition; Calcium Daily Recommendations; Calories, Daily Recommendations; Egg Composition; Egg Dried, Equivalents; Egg Equivalents; Egg Incubation Periods; Egg Products Nutritive Value; Egg Quality; Egg Quality, Broken; Egg Specifications; Egg Structure; Egg Volume; Food, Composition; Glutamate; Iron, Daily Recommendations; Minerals, Food; Minerals, Plant or Animal Tissue; Nicotinic Acid, Food; Pantothenic Acid Content; Protein Factors; Riboflavin, Daily Recommendations; Riboflavin, Food; Spoilage, Protein Foods; Storage Times; Thiamin, Daily Recommendations; Thiamin, Food; Unsaturated Fatty Acids; Vitamin A, Daily Recommendations; Vitamin A, Food; Vitamin D, Food

egg albumin Egg white.

egg foo yong Entrée containing eggs, beef, onions, tomatoes, water chestnuts, bean sprouts, mushrooms, soy sauce and monosodium glutamate.

egg grade Measure of firmness and height of yolk and thickness of white. USDA Grades: AA or fresh fancy quality; A; B; C.

Quality	Air Cell	White	Yolk
AA	not more than ⅛ in. in depth, regular	clear, firm	slightly defined, no defects
A	not more than 3/16 in. in depth, regular	clear, reasonably firm	fairly well defined, practically free of defects
B	not more than ⅜ in. depth, unlimited movement, free or bubbly	clear, slightly weak	well defined, no serious defects
C	over ⅜ in. in depth, free and bubbly	weak	plainly visible, serious but edible defects

Dirty: adhering foreign material; stains covering ¼ of surface.
Check: broken shell but membrane intact.
Leaker: contents leaking; cannot be used for human consumption.
Loss: contents lost.

egg incubation time Time required for an egg to incubate; days required are:

Duck	28	Hen	21
Geese	30-35	Pigeon	17
Guinea	28	Turkey	28

egg meat medium Liquid medium containing meat, egg white, and calcium carbonate; it is used for determination of microorganisms' proteolytic activity and for carrying stock cultures of anaerobes.
See Part 2: Microorganism, Media

eggnog An egg beaten with sugar, milk, and sometimes liquor.

egg noodle A flat pasta made of wheat flour and eggs; contains min. 5½% egg solids by weight of finished product.

eggplant (aubergine, brinjal, bringall); (*Solanum melongena*) A deep-rooted plant producing a glossy deep purple (sometimes white), firm-fleshed berry containing a lot of seed; the large berry is oblong, egg-shaped or sausage-shaped and from 4 to 12 inches long; the vegetable is sliced and cooked; 1 lb = 2½ cups diced.
Storage: Cool room temp. (45-50°F); 85-90% relative humidity; will keep several months below 60°F; will keep one week above 60°F.
Raw Composition: 92% H_2O, 1% protein, 0.2% fat, 6% carbohydrate, 1% ash, pH 4.5.
See Part 2: Fruit Classification; Frying Time; Minerals, Food; Plant Foods, Composition; Storage; Sugar, Vegetables; Vegetable Composi-

tion; Vegetable Plants; Vegetables Classification; Vegetable Storage

egg shell 94% calcium carbonate; fertilizer notation 1.2–0.6–0.3.

egg size

USDA	Min. Weight (oz/doz)
Jumbo	30
Extra large	27
Large	24
Medium	21
Small (pullet)	18
Peewee	15

medium size, good buy if 1/8 less than large
small size, good buy if 1/4 less than large

egg spaghetti A pasta containing min. 5½% egg solids by weight of finished product.

egg white Min. 11.5% egg solids; max. 0.03% fat. *See also* **egg**.

egg white factor *See* **biotin**

egg, whole Min. 25.5% egg solids.

egusi melon *See* **gourd**

Ehrlich Color reaction of the indole nucleus in such compounds as tryptophan.
See Part 2: Protein and Amino Acid, Color Reactions

eicosanoic acid (arachidic acid) $CH_3(CH_2)_{18}COOH$ A saturated fatty acid found in peanut oil.
See Part 2: Saturated Fatty Acids

eicosatetraenoic acid (arachidonic acid) A C_{20} unsaturated fatty acid found in lecithin.
See Part 2: Unsaturated Fatty Acids

eicosenoic acid An unsaturated fatty acid.
See Part 2: Unsaturated Fatty Acids

Eijkman lactose medium Broth used for the differentiation of fecal strains of *Escherichia coli* from other coliform organisms.
See Part 2: Microorganism, Selective and Differential Broths and Media, Water Filtration Plant

einsteinium (Es) A radioactive element of the actinide series; at. no. 99; Group III B of the Periodic Table; mass number of most stable isotope 254; electron
configuration 2-8-18-32-29-8-2
orbit K L M N O P Q

elastic The property of recovering original shape after being stressed or otherwise deformed. Glass is 100% elastic, but most organic materials are less than 95% elastic after rupture.

elastin Connective tissue protein of meat made up of branched fibers; cooking does not appreciably alter the properties of elastin fibers.
See Part 2: Connective Tissue, Composition; Connective Tissue Proteins

elastrator A tight rubber ring placed on an animal for the purpose of docking or castration; this cuts off the blood circulation and results in sloughing off of the tail or scrotum.

Elberta A variety of freestone peaches.

elder (***Sambucus nigra***) A small tree that produces berries that are made into tea, wine and jelly.
Raw berry composition: 80% H_2O, 3% protein, 0.5% fat, 16% carbohydrate, 1% ash.
See Part 2: Fruit Frozen Yield

elderberry tea Tea made from the berries (sometimes the bark, roots, leaves and flowers) of the elder tree. *See also* **elder**

elderberry wine *See* **elder**

electrolyte A compound which ionizes in aqueous solution and thus increases the electrical conductivity of the solution, e.g., sodium chloride.

electrolytic capacitor A metal foil with a dielectric metal oxide film in an electrolytic solution.

electromotive force series (emf) (activity series) Elements arranged according to decreasing tendency to lose electrons and become positive ions: sodium, magnesium, zinc, cadmium, iron, cobalt, nickel, tin, lead, hydrogen, copper, mercury, silver, platinum, gold.

electron A small negatively charged particle that orbits the nucleus of an atom; negative charge on electron(e) = 1.59×10^{-19} coulomb = 4.802×10^{-10} esu (electrostatic unit); mass (at rest) = 9.11×10^{-28} g; radius = 2.8×10^{-13} cm.
See Part 2: Constants, Fundamental

electronegative Descriptive of an element which has a tendency to acquire electrons and become a negative ion and is, therefore, low in the electromotive force series; e.g., chlorine.

electrophoresis The movement of electrically charged particles in a d-c current field.

electropositive Descriptive of an element that has a strong tendency to lose electrons and is, therefore, high in the electromotive force series, e.g., sodium.

element One of the distinct, basic types of matter that has characteristic chemical properties; 106 elements are known, 92 of which occur in nature.
See Part 2: Elements; Equivalent Weights

elemi A natural resin from a Philippine tree.
See Part 2: Essential Oils

eleostearic acid An unsaturated fatty acid found in vegetable oils.
See Part 2: Fatty Acids, Fats and Oils; Fatty Acids and Their Properties; Oil, Seed and Fruit; Unsaturated Fatty Acids

elk *See* Part 2: Gestation Periods

elliker broth Media for the isolation and propagation of lactobacilli.
See Part 2: Microorganism, Media

EMB agar *See* Part 2: Intestinal Microorganisms; Microorganism, Media

embryo (1) Of a seed, located at one end of the endosperm. (2) of an animal, a fetus.
See Part 2: Wheat Grain; Wheat Kernel Parts; Wheat, Parts of Grain; Wheat Parts of Grain, Vitamins

embryology Study of development of the embryo.

Emerson YpSs agar *See* Part 2: Microorganism, Media

emf *See* **volt; electromotive force series**

emincé Thin-sliced beef.

emjeo (kieserite) $MgSO_4$; magnesium sulfate.
See Part 2: Fertilizer Materials

emmentaler cheese A light yellow, semi-hard, cheese similar to Swiss in texture (large holes), color and taste. *See also* **Swiss cheese.**
See Part 2: Cheese Characteristics; Cheese Composition

emmer-wheat *See* **wheat**

empire wine A wine containing 15-22% alcohol by volume. *See also* **wine.**

empirical formula A chemical formula which expresses the atoms in simplest ratio; it shows only composition, not structure. Empirical formula of both benzene and acetylene is CH.

emulsifying agent (1) A surface-active compound whose molecule is composed of a long chain hydrocarbon terminating in a water-soluble group (OH or COOH), e.g., certain alcohols and fatty acids. When placed in a mixture of oil and water, the molecule orients itself with the water-soluble end in the water and the oil-soluble end in the oil; it thus reduces the interfacial tension between the two liquids and enables them to form a stable colloidal dispersion. Egg yolk, which contains lecithin, is used in making mayonnaise; other commonly-used food emulsifying agents are albumin, agar, casein, gums, etc. (2) A substance which emulsifies by coating fat particles suspended in water, thus preventing them from cohering, e.g., albumin in milk, algin in ice cream. *See also* **protective colloid.**

emulsion A dispersion of oil or fat particles in water (or water in oil) obtained by use of either a surface-active agent (detergent) or a protective colloid. The particles may be of colloidal dimensions, as in mayonnaise, or much larger (fat particles in milk or hydrocarbon particles in rubber latex).
See Part 2: Margarine Production

enantiomer (enantiomorph) Either of the two forms (dextro- and levo-) of an optical isomer. *See also* **optical isomer.**

en brochette Broiled on a skewer.

Endamoeba histolytica Parasitic amoebae found in the intestine and liver of higher animals causing amoebic dysentery and liver abscesses.
See Part 2: Microorganism, Media

endive (chicory) A vegetable (*Cichorium endivia*) whose leaf is used as food or salad green; a curled leaf salad plant that is usually bitter until blanched.
Storage: 32°F; 90-95% relative humidity; 2-3 weeks.
Raw Composition: 93% H_2O, 2% protein, 0.1% fat, 4% carbohydrate, 1% ash. *See also* **chicory; escarole.**
See Part 2: Minerals, Food; Storage; Sugar, Vegetables; Vegetable Composition; Vegetable Plants

endo- A prefix meaning within, as in endosperm, endocrine, etc.

endo agar *See* Part 2: Microbiological Examination of Dairy Products; Microorganism, Culture Media, Dairy and Food Products; Microorganism, Culture Media, Water and Sewage, Standard Methods; Microorganism, Media

endo broth Broth for the detection of coliform and other enteric organisms; Gram-positive organisms are inhibited by sodium sulfite and basic fuchsin.
See Part 2: Microorganism, Culture Media, Water and Sewage, Standard Methods; Microorganism, Media

endocrine gland A ductless organ that secretes hormones into the blood stream.

endocrinology Study of the function and structure of endocrine glands and of function of the hormones they secrete.

endo-enzyme An enzyme which acts in the cell that produced it.

endomysium Connective tissue separating the muscle fibers.

endosperm The large center starchy portion of cereal grain; 83% of wheat. The part of a seed that contains the plant's nutritive tissue.
See Part 2: Corn Kernel; Corn Kernel Composition; Rice Kernel; Wheat, Fatty Acids; Wheat Grain; Wheat Kernel; Wheat Kernel Parts; Wheat, Parts of Grain; Wheat, Parts of Grain, Vitamins

endrin A poisonous chlorinated hydrocarbon insecticide that is an isomer of dieldrin. Use may be prohibited on food crops.

energy value of food The heat given off by burning a stated weight of food. *See also* **calorie.**
See Part 2: Recommended Daily Dietary Allowance

English chop *See* Part 2: Lamb Cuts and Uses

English cut A beef cut made from the thin ends of 4th and 5th ribs.
See Part 2: Beef Cuts

English dairy cheese An aged, sharp-flavored type of cheddar.

English medium hog casing A hog casing 35 to 38 mm in width.

English sole *See* **sole**

English style side of pork *See* **Wiltshire side**

English system A method of grading wool based on the number of hanks of yarn that can be produced from a pound of scoured wool.

English wheat *See* **wheat**

enhancer To make greater, intensify or heighten; a substance added to a food to increase its flavor without contributing any taste of its own, e.g., monosodium glutamate.

enriched rice Rice that is enriched with iron, thiamin, riboflavin, and niacin.
See Part 2: Cereal Enrichment

enrichment Bringing a food up to a specified nutritional standard by adding nutrients during manufacture. For example, rice is enriched with iron, thiamin, riboflavin and niacin. *See also* **fortification.**
See Part 2: Cereal Enrichment

enrobe To dip a candy center into liquid chocolate or other coating mixture by means of a machine designed for this purpose.

ensilage Green fodder stored in a silo or trench.

enteric bacilli Rod-shaped microorganisms that infect the intestines.
See Part 2: Microbiological Media

enterococci Spherical microorganisms that infect the intestines.
See Part 2: Microbiological Media

Enterococcus agar *See* Part 2: Microorganism, Culture Media, Water and Sewage, Standard Methods

Enterprise Seedless A variety of midsummer Florida orange.

entire wheat flour *See* **graham flour**

ento- *See* **endo-**

entrecôte Bercy Sirloin steak and sauce.

entre deux mers Light medium-sweet (some are dryer) white wine.

entrée A dish that can be served before the main course, between courses, or may be the main course; appetizer; meat, fish or poultry not classed as a roast; food other than a roast served as the main course.

entropion Either or both eyelids roll inward soon after birth, resulting in eventual blindness.

enzyme An organic thermolabile catalyst for metabolic reactions produced by living cells; they can often be separated from the cell that produces them and still retain their activity.
See Part 2: Enzymes, Food Industry; pH Values of Biological Materials

eosin methylene-blue agar *See* Part 2: Intestinal Microorganisms; Microbiological Examination of Dairy Products

E.P. Edible portion.

epi- Prefix meaning upon or exterior, e.g., epidermis.

epiblast (ectoderm) Outer layer of gastrula or blastoderm.
See Part 2: Wheat Kernel; Wheat Kernel Parts

epicarp (exocarp) Outer layer of the pericarp.
See Part 2: Orange Structure; Rice Kernel; Wheat Kernel Parts

epicure A connoisseur of find foods, wines and liquors; a discriminating diner.

epidermis The thin, outer pigmented layer of the skin.
See Part 2: Corn Kernel; Hide, Layers; Hide, Salt Absorption; Wheat Kernel Parts

epimysium The connective tissue surrounding an entire muscle.

epinephrine A drug that is extracted from the inner portion (medulla) of the adrenal glands of cattle, hogs and sheep and can be used for shrinking of mucous membranes, as a heart stimulant, and a muscle relaxant.

epithelium Cellular tissue covering a surface or lining a cavity. *See also* **epidermis.**
See Part 2: Wheat Kernel Parts

epoxy group An organic group in which an oxygen atom lies outside the carbon chain:

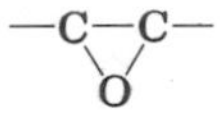

epsilon (E, ϵ) Greek letter with an English equivalent of ĕ.

epsom salts Magnesium sulfate ($MgSO_4 \cdot 7H_2O$). Named from Epsom, England.
See Part 2: Fertilizer Materials

equilibrium A state of balance between reactants and products in a chemical reaction:

$$A + B \underset{r_2}{\overset{r_1}{\rightleftarrows}} C + D$$

At equilibrium $r_1 = r_2$ (rate of reaction)
Amounts of A, B, C, and D remain constant

equilibrium constant (Keq) For the reaction

$$wA + xB \rightleftarrows yC + zD$$

$$\text{Keq} = \frac{(C)^y \times (D)^z}{(A)^w \times (B)^x}$$

Capital letters in moles per liter.

equivalent Equal; corresponding; same.
See Part 2: Fruit and Vegetables, Cost Per Serving

equivalent weight The weight of an element that will combine with one-half the atomic weight of oxygen (7.9997 g). Also called combining weight.
See Part 2: Equivalent Weights

Er Symbol for the element erbium.

erbium (Er) A rare-earth element of the lanthanide series; at. no. 68; at. wt. 167.27; Group IIIB of Periodic Table; oxidation state +3; electron configuration 2-8-18-30-8-2
orbit K L M N O P

erepsin An enzyme (mixture of peptidases) secreted into the small intestine which converts polypeptides into amino acids.
See Part 2: pH Values of Biological Materials

erg A measure of work and energy
1 erg = 1×10^{-7} joule
= 7.3756×10^{-8} foot lb
= 2.3889×10^{-8} g calories (mean)
= 9.4805×10^{-11} Btu (mean)
= 2.3889×10^{-11} kg calories (mean)

erg per second A measure of power, rate of energy and heat.
1 erg per sec = 1 dyne-cm/sec
= 4.4254×10^{-6} ft-lb/min
= 1×10^{-7} watt
= 0.0000000737612 ft-lb/sec
= 5.688×10^{-9} Btu/min
= 1.34×10^{-10} horsepower
= 1×10^{-10} kilowatt

ergosterol $C_{28}H_{43}OH$ A steroid alcohol which on irradiation with ultraviolet light yields calciferol (vitamin D_2).

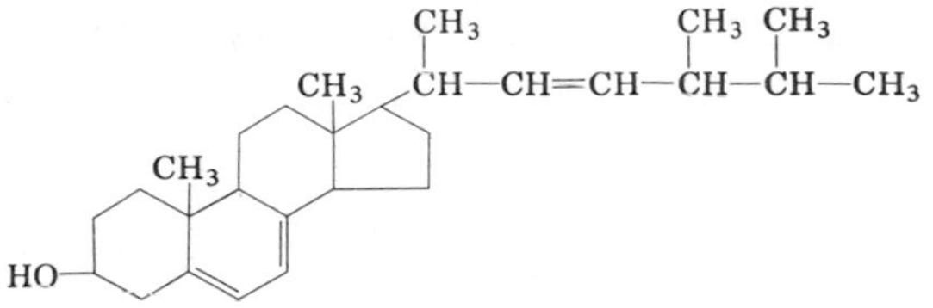

See Part 2: Vitamins

ergot (1) In horses, a horny growth behind the fetlock joint. (2) A fungus that grows on grasses. *See also* **rye.**

Erlenmeyer flask A flat-bottom glass container that gradually tapers to a narrow mouth; used in chemical laboratories.

erucic acid *See* **docosenoic acid**

Erwinia A genus of vegetable pathogens related to coliform.
See Part 2: Rot Spoilage; Spoilage, Carbohydrate Foods

erythorbic acid *See* **ascorbic acid**

erythrocyte A red blood cell, which contains hemoglobin. *See also* **red blood cell.**

erythromycin An antibiotic.
See Part 2: Antibiotic Standards

erythroplastid *See* **erythrocyte**

erythrose *See* Part 2: Sugar, D-aldehydo

Es Symbol for the element einsteinium

escalopes Thin pieces of meat.

escarole (broad-leafed endive) A salad green, with large, ruffled, bitter leaves which are dark green, edging into yellow; it resembles chicory but the leaves are broader and less curly. *See also* **chicory.**
See Part 2: Minerals, Food; Sugar, Vegetables

Escherichia A genus of Gram-negative, rod-shaped, usually nonpathogenic, bacteria found in the intestine of animals and man.
See Part 2: Microorganism Reactions on Differential Tube Media; Spoilage, Carbohydrate Foods

esparto A coarse grass of northern Africa from which a wax is obtained; it is also used for specialty papers. *See* Part 2: Wax

Espresso roast (Italian roast) A procedure for roasting coffee that produces a black-brown bean that shines with coffee oil; the coffee has a penetrating, robust flavor.

essang seed oil An unsaturated fatty acid found in essang seeds.
See Part 2: Unsaturated Fatty Acids

essential (1) A distilled flower product in which the "essence" of the flower is evidenced by the fragrant odor. *See also* **essential oil.** (2) A dietary factor that must be obtained from external sources, as it is not synthesized by bodily metabolism. *See also* **essential amino acid; essential fatty acid.**

essential amino acid An amino acid that is not synthesized within the body, namely, leucine, isoleucine, lysine, methionine, phenylalanine, threonine, trytophan, valine.

essential fatty acid A fatty acid required for good nutrition that must be present in the diet, as it is not produced within the body, e.g., linoleic and linolenic acids.

essential oil A fragrant volatile oily liquid derived from the flowers, stems or leaves of plants by steam distillation, dry distillation, vacuum distillation, or expressed or extracted with solvents; insoluble in water; used as basis of perfumes and flavors.
See Part 2: Essential Oils

ester $R'-C(=O)-O-R$ An organic compound formed by reacting an alcohol with an acid; a molecule of water being removed in the reaction:

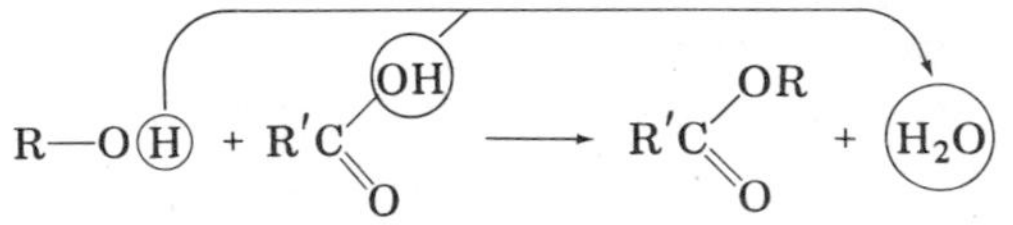

esterase An enzyme that attacks simple esters.

estragon *See* **tarragon**

estrogen A female sex hormone isolated from bovine ovaries which is used in treatment of menopausal syndromes.

eta (H, η) Greek letter with an English equivalent of ē.

etaerio (eterio) An aggregate fruit composed of archenes, berries, druples, follicles, or samaras as in the mulberry.
See Part 2: Fruit Classification

ethane C_2H_6 A flammable odorless gas derived from petroleum.
See Part 2: Refrigerant

ethanol *See* **ethyl alcohol**

ether ($R'-O-R$) A class of organic compounds in which 2 alkyl groups are attached to an oxygen atom. *See also* **ethyl ether.**

ether extract *See* **fat analysis**

ethion A poisonous pesticide; a cholinesterase inhibitor; a phosphorus ester.

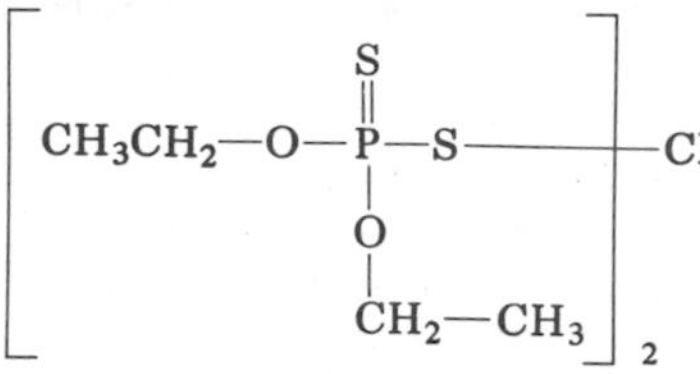

ethoxyquin (6-ethoxy-1,2,dihydro-2,2,4-trimothylquinoline); an effective antioxidant; used as a herbicide.
See Part 2: Antioxidant Structure

ethyl alcohol (CH_3-CH_2) with OH attached to the CH_2; A flammable liquid used as a solvent and beverage. A noncumulative poison. Commercial grade is 95% (92.3% by wt; 94.9% by vol.); often called ethanol or simply alcohol.

sp. gr. = 0.798 at 60°F
b.p. = 78.5°C
heat value = 7 Cal. per gram

0.08 to 0.15% concentration in blood is considered "under influence."
See Part 2: Alcoholic Solutions; Antioxidant Mixtures; Fluid and Fermented Milks, Composition

ethyl chloride C_2H_5Cl A flammable gas (liquid when compressed).
See Part 2: Refrigerant

ethylene $CH_2=CH_2$ A flammable gas used in ripening some fruit; the gas destroys the chlorophyll so that the other pigments may become visible. Also as a refrigerant.
See Part 2: Refrigerant

ethylene dichloride $(CH_2)_2Cl_2$ A toxic flammable liquid used as a fumigant.
See Part 2: Fumigants

ethylene oxide $(CH_2)_2O$ A toxic flammable gas used for the sterilization of food, particularly spices; max. residual 50 ppm.
See Part 2: Fumigants

ethyl ether $CH_3CH_2-O-CH_2CH_3$ A flammable liquid sometimes used as a general anesthetic and extraction solvent. Dangerous!

$$d_4^{25} = 0.708; \quad b = 34.6°C$$

Test for peroxide in ether:
1. Shake for 1 hour 10 ml of ether with 1 ml of aqueous potassium iodine (1 to 10)
2. Protect from light
3. When viewed transversely against a white background no color should be seen in either layer

ethyl formate ($HCOOC_2H_5$) A flammable liquid used as a fumigant and flavoring agent.
See Part 2: Fumigants

ethylidene chloride CH_3CHCl_2 A flammable liquid used as a fumigant and refrigerant.
See Part 2: Refrigerant

ethyl violet azide broth *See* Part 2: Microbiological Media; Microorganism, Culture Media, Water and Sewage, Standard Methods

Eu Symbol for the element europium.

eucalyptus oil An essential oil obtained from the eucalyptus tree (Australia).
See Part 2: Essential oils

euda A ripened cheese made from low fat or skimmed milk.
Composition: 56–57% H_2O, 30% protein, 6–7% fat, 1–2% carbohydrate, 2.6% salt.

euglena agar *See* Part 2: Microorganism, Media

Eugon agar *See* Part 2: Microbiological Media; Microorganism, Media

eulachon smelt *See* **smelt**

European corn-borer An insect that bores through the stalk of corn at any spot. Control: destroy and plow under stalks.

europium (Eu) A rare-earth element of the lanthanide series; at. no. 63; at. wt. 152.0; oxidation states +2, +3; Group IIIB of Periodic Table; electron configuration 2-8-18-25-8-2
orbit K L M N O P

eutectic plate (cold plate) A portable plate that contains a solution; they are frozen and used to maintain temporary refrigeration temperatures in containers.

EVA (Ethyl Violet Azide) broth Broth used for detection, enumeration and confirmation of enterococci which is an index of pollution; other organisms are inhibited by sodium azide and ethyl violet.
See Part 2: Microorganism, Media

evaporated food Food dried by artificial heat.

evaporated milk Produced from whole milk by reducing the volume 40 to 50% by evaporating the water; concentrated milk that has 2.25 times the solids content as whole milk. Raw whole milk is clarified, concentrated (60% water removed), fortified with vitamin D, homogenized, placed in can, and sterilized (245°F for 15 minutes).

Total milk solids not less than 25.5%.
Min. 7.9% milk fat
25.9% total milk solids
Max. 0.1% {disodium phosphate, sodium citrate, calcium chloride}
Min. 25 U.S.P. units of vitamin D/fluid ounce.

Usually diluted with an equal volume of water for use as milk; ½ cup evaporated milk + ½ cup water = 1 cup milk; 2.1–2.4 lb milk = 1 lb evaporated milk (whole); 1 cup = 250 g (8.9 oz); sp. gr. 1.066; pH = 5.9–6.3.

Types:

whole: min. 7.9% milk fat and 25.9% total milk solids;

skim: 0.2 to 0.3% milk fat and min. 15% total milk solids.

Sold in 13½-oz "tall" can, 6-oz "baby" can.

See also **sweetened condensed milk.**

evaporation Conversion of a liquid to a vapor; this occurs at room temperature or lower, but is usually done by heating. The vapor becomes steam at 100°C.

See Part 2: Dairy Terms; Milk and Cheese Composition; Milk and Milk Products, Vitamin Content; Milk Composition; Milk, Concentrated Products; Minerals, Food; Stabilizers, Thickeners; Storage Times; Vitamin A, Milk and Milk Products

ewe A female ovine animal (sheep) of any age; average gestation period 147 days (range 142–157); duration of heat 1–3 days; normal recurrence of heat 15 to 21 days.

See Part 2: Milk, Mammals, Composition; Milk, Species; Sheep Market Classes and Grades; Teeth Eruption

ewe neck A depression at the top of the neck forward of the withers.

ex-light steer hide A steer hide weighing less than 48 lb.

exo-enzyme An enzyme which acts outside of the cell which produced it.

expiration date The date after which a product cannot be sold and should not be used.

exports Commodities conveyed (traded) from one area to another.

See Part 2: Casings, Hog Bungs

expressed oil A vegetable oil obtained by pressing in a hydraulic press or expeller.

extensor A muscle that extends (straightens) a joint.

external abdominal oblique An outside sheet of muscles of the flank whose fibers point down and backward.

extra narrow hog casing A hog casing 29 or less millimeters in diameter.

extra wide hog casing A hog casing 43 or more millimeters in diameter.

extract (flavoring) An alcohol or alcohol-water solution containing a flavoring ingredient, e.g., vanilla.

extracted honey Honey separated from comb by centrifugal force.

extraction Removal of soluble components from a substance or mixture by use of a solvent, e.g., water (coffee), alcohol, ether, acetone, etc.

eye of round (*semitendinosus*) A small triangular muscle of the round. *See also* **semitendinosus.**

See Part 2: Beef, Boneless Cuts; Beef Round Cuts; Meat Identification

F

F Symbol for the element fluorine.

F_1 Offspring of parental generation (P_1).

F_2 Offspring of crossing F_1.

F.A.C. Fat Analysis Committee.

FAC albicans *See* Part 2: Microorganism, Media

face To remove a slice from a piece of meat which has become dark.

factor (1) One of two (or more) numbers which yield a given product when multiplied together, e.g., 2 and 4 are factors of 8; 3 and 4 and 6 and 2 are factors of 12. (2) In biochemistry, an active nutrient substance. *See also* **filtrate factor; folic acid.**

factor, prime Numbers that are divisible only by themselves and 1, and which yield a given quantity when multiplied together; e.g., the prime factors of 45 are 5 × 3 × 3.

factorial $1n$, $n!$ A number multiplied by each number lower than itself until 1 is reached, e.g.: 7 factorial

$$7! = 7 \times 6 \times 5 \times 4 \times 3 \times 2 \times 1 = 5040$$

It can be estimated by Stirling's approximation formula:

$$1n = n^{n} \cdot e^{-n} \cdot \sqrt{2\pi n} \cdot \left(1 + \frac{1}{12n} + \frac{1}{288n^2} + \cdots\right)$$

The value in parentheses is practically unity for large values of n.

facultative anaerobe Bacteria that can grow with or without oxygen.

F.A.D. Flavine adenine dinucleotide.

fagot (faggot) Pork that is cooked and then mixed with ground livers, hearts, and onions; this is made into a ball and covered with caul fat and baked with bundle of thyme, marjoram and bay leaf.

Fahrenheit (F) A measure of temperature.
Freezing of water 32°F
Boiling of water 212°F at 760 mm
Absolute zero −459.6°F
Normal body temp. 98.6°F
Conversion formulas:
F = 9/5 C + 32
C = (F − 32) 5/9
F = (R 9/4) + 32
Rankine = F + 459.67
R = (F − 32) 4/9
C = Celsius or Centigrade
R = Reaumur
See Part 2: Temperature

fairy-ring champignon (*Marasmius oreades*) A small brown to pink edible fungus that creates the "fairy-rings" in short grass.

fall armyworm A worm that feeds on young leaves and ears of corn plant. *See also* **armyworm.**

fall salmon *See* **salmon**
See Part 2: Salmon and Trout

false hellebore A plant having a poisonous principle.
See Part 2: Poisonous Plants

false morels An irregular to saddle-shaped, wrinkled-capped, central stalk fungus.

false rib (asternal) A rib whose cartilage is attached to the cartilage of the rib in front of it. *See also* **rib.**

fancy sausage Usually uncooked, dry or semi-dry sausage.

FAO *See* **Food and Agricultural Organization**

farad A unit of capacitance (1 coulomb charging a capacitor to 1 volt).

faraday (F) An electrical measurement.
1 faraday = 96,500 coulombs (the amount of electricity required to deposit 1 g equivalent weight in electrolysis).
See Part 2: Constants, Fundamental

farci Stuffed.

farfals A mixture of wheat flour and water (sometimes also milk and eggs) that has been dried and then ground.

farina Wheat (durum not used) in granular form from which the bran and most of the germ have been removed. *See also* **potato starch.**
See Part 2: Cereal Composition; Cereal Enrichment; Food, Composition; Grain Products Composition

farinha Meal made from cassava tubers.

farmer sausage A 65% beef, 35% pork product that is ground fine, seasoned and smoked heavily.

farmers cheese (pressed, pot) A soft, white, dry cottage cheese pressed into packages; it is made from partly skimmed milk and has a mild flavor.

farmer style hog carcass A hog carcass split on both sides of the backbone.

farrow To give birth to pigs.

FAS broth A medium used in the enrichment serology method for detecting *Salmonella* in foods and feeds.
See Part 2: Microorganism, Media

fascia A covering of connective tissue which supports and protects internal organs of the body.

fast food service As the name indicates this is a restaurant that serves food quickly; in the past, it has centered around a short order counter (drug store soda fountain, luncheonette or snack bar) where the customer sat on a stool or remained standing or self-service service such as a cafeteria or buffet; currently, the concept applies to feeding establishments that fall into the following categories: utilization of time-saving equipment, utilization of labor-saving equipment or utilization of self-service devices or methods.

fat An ester of glycerol and a fatty acid.

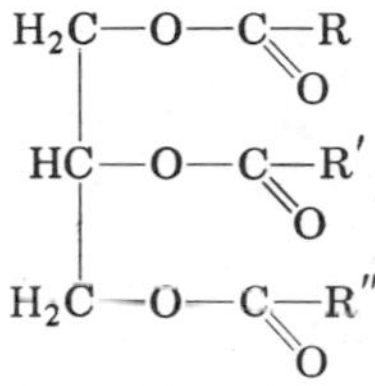
triglyceride

Natural fat is a mixture of various glycerides; physiological value 9 calories/gram.

Fats are lighter than water and are poor conductors of heat. They are solid at room temperature (18–25°C), and are called oils if they are liquid at this temperature.

2 cups = 1 lb; 2 tbsp = 1 oz

Storage: Refrigerate, tightly covered; protect from light; use within 2 weeks.

See Part 2: Bananas Composition; Beans, Peas and Nuts; Cereal Nutrient Content; Cheese Composition; Cherry Composition; Composition of Food; Concentrated and Dried Milk Products; Connective Tissue, Composition; Corn Kernel Composition; Creams, Butter and Frozen Desserts; Cultured Dairy Products, Composition; Dairy Products, Composition; Egg Composition; Egg Products, Nutritive Value; Fat and Body Weight; Fats and Oils, Composition; Fats and Oils, Fatty Acid Composition; Fats and Oils, Physical and Chemical Properties; Fats and Oils, Characteristics; Fish and Shellfish Composition; Flour, Extraction Rates; Fluid and Fermented Milks, Composition; Food, Composition; Fruit Composition; Grain Analysis; Grain Products Composition; Lemon Juice Composition; Lime Juice Composition; Macaroni and Noodles Composition; Manure Analysis; Meat and Meat Products Composition; Meat Composition; Meat, Nutritive Value; Melting Points, Fats and Oils; Milk and Cheese Composition; Milk Breeds, Composition; Milk Composition; Milk, Concentrated Products; Milk, Dry Products; Milk, Mammals, Composition; Milk, Species; Minerals (Trace), Limits; Oil Meals Composition; Oil or Fat, Characteristics; Oils and Fats Composition; Oil, Seed and Fruit; Organ Weights; Packinghouse By-Products Composition; Plant Foods, Composition; Pork Carcass, Retail Yield; Poultry Composition; Pulses, Nuts and Seeds Composition; Refractive Indices, Fats and Oils; Sausage Composition; Seed, Chemical Composition; Seed Composition; Soups Composition; Soybean Composition; Specific Gravities, Fats and Oils; Spoilage, Fat in Food; Starches and Starchy Roots Composition; Sugars and Sweets Composition; Sugars and Syrups Composition; Titer, Fats and Oils; Tomato and Tomato Products, Composition; Turkey Composition; Vegetable Composition; Wheat and Flour Composition; Wheat, Fatty Acids; Wheat, Parts of Grain; Wheat Products Composition

fat analysis (crude fat) Determination of fat content by extracting the dried sample with anhydrous ethyl ether or petroleum ether; the loss in sample wt or residue after solvent evaporation is reported as fat.

fat bloom A white crystalline coating resulting from separation of the fat in chocolate, which rises to the surface.

fat end The fat animals in a group.

fat-end middle Natural casings used in the meat trade; it comes from the last part of the large intestine of beef.

fathom A measurement of length or depth: 1 fathom = 2 yards = 1.829 meters = 6 feet.

fatigue A condition which results in loss of ability to respond to a stimulus.

fat-liquoring Adding a fat or oil (e.g., neats-foot oil) to damp leather to keep it from becoming hard and dry.

fat-soluble A substance which is easily soluble in fat.

fat-soluble vitamins Vitamins A, D, E, and K.

fat stability The hours required for a fat to reach a specific peroxide value under a given set of conditions, which include aeration of the sample at an elevated temperature.

fatty acid $R-\underset{\underset{O}{\|}}{C}-OH$ An aliphatic acid occurring in both plants and animals; it may be saturated or unsaturated, the molecule being comprised of a chain of alkyl groups of varying lengths ending in a carboxyl group. Many are derived from glycerides by hydrolysis. *See also* **glyceride**.

See Part 2: Beans, Peas and Nuts; Fatty Acids; Milk, Fatty Acids, Seasonal; Poultry Composition; Sausage Composition; Soups Composition; Sugars and Sweets Composition; Unsaturated Fatty Acids; Vegetable Composition; Wheat, Fatty Acids

fauna The animal life of an area.

FC broth base *See* Part 2: Microorganism, Culture Media, Water and Sewage, Standard Methods; Microorganism, Media

FDA *See* **Food and Drug Administration**

FD&C color *See* **colorant**

See Part 2: Colors Permanently Listed

F-distribution (z-distribution) Frequency distribution of the ratio of two variance estimates; $F = \frac{s_1^2}{s_2^2}$; the F-distribution has two numbers for degrees of freedom which are the degrees of freedom of the respective variance estimates, the first refers to the numerator (s_1^2) and the second to the denominator (s_2^2).
See Part 2: F-distribution

Fe Symbol for the element iron.

feather (1) A proteinaceous process elaborated by birds; the units grow out from skin follicles analogous to mammalian hair. The chief protein component is keratin. (2) Long hair at the rear of the cannons and ankles of a horse (horse feathers).

feather bone A superior spinous process or flat process on the vertebrae in the thoracic region.
See Part 2: Beef Chuck; Beef Rib Nomenclature; Beef Wholesale Cuts; Bone; Lamb Wholesale Cuts; Meat Identification; Pork Wholesale Cuts; Veal Wholesale Cuts

feces Indigestible residue evacuated from digestive tract.

fedelini *See* **spaghetti**

feed cattle grades Fancy, choice, good, medium, cull.

feeders Cattle that are of the proper size to be put on a fattening ration before slaughter; animals with sufficient size to go into a feedlot.

feeding limestone A good source of dietary calcium which contains almost no magnesium.

feeding tankage *See* **meat meal tankage**

feet-column of water A measure of pressure.
1 = 62.426 pounds per sq foot (psf)
= 22.4185 millimeters (columns of mercury, Hg 13.59593 sp. gr.)
= 0.88262 inch (columns of mercury, Hg 13.59593 sp. gr.)
= 0.43353 pound per sq inch (psi)
= 0.30480 meter (columns of water, max. density at 4°C, 39°F)
= 0.03048 kilogram per sq centimeter (kg/cm^2)
= 0.0299 bar
= 0.02950 atmosphere, standard (760 mm)

feet fallen from rest Feet fallen from rest = (seconds)^2 × 16.08.

feet per minute (fpm) A measure of velocity.
1 fpm = 0.508 centimeter/second
= 0.305 meter/min
= 0.018288 kilometer/hr
= 0.017 ft/second
= 0.011364 mile/hour

feet per second (fps) A measure of velocity.
1 fps = 1.09728 kilometer per hour
= 0.68182 mile per hour (mph)
= 0.59209 knot U.S.
= 0.30480 meter per second (mps)

feet per sec/sec (fps^2) A measure of acceleration.
1 fps^2 = 0.68182 mile per hour/sec (mph-s)
= 0.30480 meter per sec/sec (mps^2)

Fehling's solution A test reagent consisting of two solutions; one contains 173 g sodium potassium tartrate and 50 g sodium hydroxide diluted to 500 ml with water; the other solution contains 34.6 g copper sulfate diluted to 500 ml with water; mix prior to use ($NaKCuC_4H_2O_6$); on reacting with a reducing sugar, it yields cuprous oxide (Cu_2O) (dark red).

feldspar Anhydrous silicates of alumina; used as component of fertilizers and poultry feed.

fell A membrane between muscle and the skin of an animal.

felt A fabric made from short wool (also hair or fur); it is pounded together while the wool is hot and moist; has less strength than woolen fabric. Used for insulation.

female Sex that produces the ovum. *See also* **sex**.

femoral artery An artery located in the rear legs and used to distribute the curing pickle when artery-curing hams.

femorotibial *See* Part 2: Bone

femto- Prefix meaning one quadrillionth (0.000 000 000 000 001).

femur Rear leg (thigh) bone.
See Part 2: Bone

fence post treatment Chemical solutions to use:
1. Coal-tar creosote (100% or can be mixed with 50% kerosene or fuel oil).
2. 5% solution of pentachlorophenol (very toxic).
3. 5% solution of copper naphthenate.

Methods in order of preference:
1. Pressure
2. Hot and cold bath
3. Cold soaking

fender rail A rail placed around the wall of a farrowing pen to keep the sow from mashing her pigs.

fennel (Marathon) (*Foeniculum vulgare Mill*) A plant having a flattened, oblong-ovoid, green to brown seed with yellow ridges, ⅙ in. long; sweet fennel or bitter fennel is used in seasoning; leaves used in sauce, soups, and salad dressing; oil from seed in confectionery, condiments, pickles, liquor. *See also* **Florence fennel.**
See Part 2: Essential Oils; Flavoring Agents, Natural

fenugreek seed (*Trigonella foenum-graecum L.*) A small reddish-brown seed that grows in a pod of a plant of the pea family; fresh plant is eaten as a vegetable; seeds are used as one of the constituents of artificial maple flavoring; used in curry powder.

fermentation Decomposition of sugar to CO_2 and alcohol, catalyzed by bacteria or enzymes:

$C_6H_{12}O_6 \rightarrow 2C_2H_5OH + 2CO_2$.
See Part 2: pH, Post-Mortem; Fermented Ingredients

fermented vinegar Vinegar made by fermentation without distillation; min.: 2% solids; 0.25% ash.

fermière, à la With discs of carrots, potatoes, celery, onions, cabbage, and turnips.

fermium (Fm) A synthetic radioactive element of the actinide series; Group VIIB of Periodic Table; at. no. 100; mass number of most stable isotope 255; electron configuration 2-8-18-32-30-8-2
orbit K L M N O P Q

ferric Iron in highest valence state: Fe^{+++}.

ferro-therm Proprietary name for an insulating material.
See Part 2: Insulation

ferrous Iron in a lower valence state: Fe^{++}.

fertilizer Any of a number of agricultural chemicals applied to the soil to increase its fertility and productivity. Among the more widely used are superphosphates, ammonium nitrate, potassium compounds, and lime. Processed municipal wastes are also used. Animal manures are natural fertilizers.
See Part 2: Fertilizer; Fertilizer Materials; Sugar Beet Yield

fertilizer analysis $x - y - z$
x = total nitrogen; y = available P_2O_5; z = available K_2O.

fescue (Festuca) A perennial grass used for pasture; seed 24 lb/bu; 8 to 10 lb/acre in mixtures; 15-20 lb/acre alone. Varieties: Kentucky 31, alta; nutrient used for 3 tons of grazing, 135 lb N; 60 lb P_2O_5; 210 lb K_2O.
See Part 2: Seed, Germination

feta cheese A pure white, semi-soft, salted, table, salad or cooking cheese; a dry salty cheese made from goat's milk.
Composition: 51-57% H_2O, 18-20% protein, 24% fat, 3% carbohydrate, 4-5% salt.
See Part 2: Milk and Cheese Composition

fetlock Area on legs below cannon and above pastern (ankle).

fetticus *See* **field salad**

fettuccelle *See* **spaghetti**

F.F.A. or (ffa) *See* **Free Fatty Acid Analysis; Fresh Freezer Accumulation**

fiber A long, thin and generally crystalline form of matter whose dimensions may be from 1 micron to 0.05 in. in diameter and up to a foot or more long (for some cellulosic fibers). Many proteins are fibrous, e.g., keratin in hair and wool. Asbestos also has a fibrous structure.
See Part 2: Cherry Composition; Egg Composition; Flour, Extraction Rates; Fruit Composition; Grain Analysis; Macaroni and Noodles Composition; Manure Analysis; Meat and Meat Products Composition; Milk and Cheese Composition; Oil Meals Composition; Packinghouse By-Products Composition; Plant Foods; Composition; Pulses, Nuts and Seeds Composition; Seed Composition; Soybean Composition; Starches and Starchy Roots Composition; Sugars and Syrups Composition; Tomato and Tomato Products, Composition; Vegetable Composition; Wheat, Carbohydrate Composition; Wheat Products Composition

fibroin The principal protein of silk, made up of the amino acids glycine, alanine, tyrosine, and arginine.

fibrous connective tissue Connective tissue in which the fibers are closely woven with little space between them.

fibula The small hind shank bone running parallel to the tibia and often fused to it.
See Part 2: Bone

ficin A proteolytic enzyme from the sap of the fig tree.

fidelini *See* **spaghetti**

field salad Spoon-shaped leaves used for salad greens.
Raw Composition: 93% H_2O, 2% protein, 0.4% fat, 4% carbohydrate, 1% ash.

fifth (of a gallon) A measure of liquid volume used chiefly for liquor; 1 fifth = 25.6 oz.

fig (*Ficus carica L.*) A shrub that produces a pear-shaped fruit that may be green, brown (yellow) or purple (black); the fruit has a thin skin and does not keep well; it may be eaten fresh, dried or canned; it has mild laxative properties.
1 lb = 12 raw medium fresh figs = 2½ cups dried whole figs (44 medium figs) = 2-⅔ cups fine-cut dried figs (1 cup = 170 g or 5.9 oz)
1 lb dried figs = 3 lb fresh California figs = 4 lb fresh figs from other places.
Composition:

	H_2O (%)	Protein (%)	Fat (%)	Carbohydrate (%)	Ash (%)	pH	Storage Temp. (°F)	Storage R.H. (%)	Storage Life
Raw	77	1	0.3	20	1	4.6	28-32	80-85	7 days
Dried	23-24	3.6-4.0	1	53-69	2		32-40	50-60	9-12 mo

See Part 2: Calcium Daily Recommendations; Fruit and Nut Rootstock; Fruit, Availability; Fruit, Canning Dates; Fruit Classification; Fruit Composition; Fruit Storage; Minerals, Food; Plant Foods, Composition; Standards, Processed Fruit and Vegetable Products; Storage

fig bars *See* Part 2: Grain Products Composition

filament (1) An extremely long fiber. (2) Portion of the stamen supporting the anther.
See Part 2: Flower Perfect

filbert (*Corylus maxima*) A hazel-type plant that grows on a large tree; the nut is covered by a more extensive husk. *See also* **hazel.**
1 lb shelled = 2.5 lb unshelled
1 lb whole shelled = 3.5 cups
1 cup whole shelled = 135 g (4.7 oz)
Composition: 6% H_2O, 13% protein, 62% fat, 17% carbohydrate, 2.5% ash.
See Part 2: Fruit and Nut Rootstock; Minerals, Food; Nut, Grades

filé Leaves and leaf buds of sassafras that have been dried and powdered; used as seasoning and for thickening.

filet *See* **fillet**

filet mignon Filet of beef tenderloin garnished with bacon.
See Part 2: Broiling Time and Temperature; Portion Size

fill Animal weight due to recently consumed feed and water.

filled milk Milk in which the butter fat has been replaced by vegetable fat.
See Part 2: Cultured Dairy Products, Composition

fillet A strip of lean meat or meaty sides of fish without bone. *See also* **psoas major; tenderloin.**
See Part 2: Fish Fillets; Fish Forms; Fish, Smoke-Cured; Fish Yields

filly A young female horse that has not produced a foal.

film gauge Film thickness.
See Part 2: Film Gauge

filter To remove suspended matter from a gas or liquid by passing it through a porous article (e.g., paper, fine mesh) or mass (e.g., sand).

filtrate Liquid which has passed through a filter.

filtrate factor *See* **pantothenic acid**

fin Bony but flexible structure attached to the bodies of fish at various locations to serve in locomotion and act as stabilizers.
See Part 2: Fish Nomenclature

fin bone *See* **feather bones**

fine grind Smallest particle size (of coffee beans).
See Part 2: Coffee Granule Designation; Coffee Particle Size

fine-wool sheep Classification of sheep which includes the following breeds: American Merino, Delaine Merino, and Rambouillet.
See Part 2: Sheep Breeds

finger Transverse processes on vertebra.
See Part 2: Beef Wholesale Cuts; Bone; Lamb Wholesale Cuts; Pork Wholesale Cuts; Veal Wholesale Cuts

finings The material for clarifying used in connection with the processing of metal, glass, liquid, beer, etc.
See Part 2: Minerals, Trace, Limits

finish The amount and distribution of fat on an animal; fatness, smoothness.

finnan haddie Smoked haddock, usually baked and served in a cream sauce.
See Part 2: Fish, Smoke-Cured

finnochio dolce *See* **Florence fennel**

fino A pale, dry, light-bodied sherry.

fired The heating step in processing tea to stop fermentation; used to control the amount of fermentation that takes place.

fire point Temperature at which oil when heated under specific conditions will ignite and burn for at least 5 seconds. *See also* **flash point.**
See Part 2: Free Fatty Acid, Smoke, Flash, Fire Points

fir needle oil An essential oil obtained by steam distillation of needles from Canadian or Siberian pine or balsam.

fish Aquatic, cold-blooded vertebrates, equipped with fins and usually scales; they also have gills by which they extract dissolved oxygen from the water.

Form	Quantity for one serving (oz)	Yield (%)
Dressed	8	38
Fillets	5	60
Pan dressed	8	38
Portions	5	90
Steaks	5	60
Sticks	4	90
Whole	12	27

Storage:

	Temp. (°F)	Relative Humidity (%)	Storage Life
Fresh	28–30	90–95	1–5 days
Frozen	−10	90–95	8 mo.
Salted	40–50	90–95	10 mo.
Smoked	40–50	50–60	6 mo.

11–15% fat absorption during frying.

		Minimum flesh content (%)
Fish	1½–8 oz	75
Portions breaded	1½–8 oz fried	65
Fish sticks	¾–1½ oz	72
Fish steaks breaded	¾–1½ oz fried	60

See Part 2: Animal Foods, Composition; Calcium Daily Requirements; Calories, Daily Recommendations; Fish and Shellfish Composition; Fish Cross Section; Fish Drawn; Fish Dressed; Fish Fillets; Fish Forms; Fish Nomenclature; Fish, Smoke-Cured; Fish Steaks; Fish, Storage; Fish Yields; Food, Composition; Frozen Food Storage; Frying Time; Glutamate; Iron, Daily Recommendations; Meat, Servings Per Pound; Minerals, Food; Minerals, Trace, Limits; Moisture in Biological Materials; Niacin, Daily Recommendations; Nicotinic Acid, Food; Portion Size; Riboflavin, Daily Recommendations; Riboflavin, Food; Spoilage, Protein Foods; Storage Times; Thiamin, Daily Recommendations; Thiamin, Food; Vitamin A, Fish; Vitamin A, Food; Vitamin D, Fish; Vitamin D, Food

fish flour Produced by treating whole, comminuted fish with a solvent that removes water and fat, after which the solvent is removed.
Whole fish flour composition: 2% H_2O, 78% protein, 0.3% fat, 20% ash.

fish meal A 70% protein animal food made from fish house waste; 1 lb/qt; 35 lb/bu.
See Part 2: Packinghouse By-Products Composition; Water Activity, Organisms and Food

fish oil An oil obtained from the bodies of fish, especially the livers, which are rich in vitamins.
See Part 2: Fats and Oils, Characteristic; Oil or Fat, Characteristics; Saturated Fatty Acids; Vitamin D, Food

fish scrap Waste fish products used as an agricultural fertilizer; 9.5-6-0; it is slightly acid in nature and would require 0.05 lb of dolomitic limestone to neutralize each pound applied.

fish stick *See* Part 2: Fish and Shellfish Composition; Fish, Storage

fistula An abscess in the area of the withers; an opening into an internal organ.

five-gaited horse A horse that has 3 natural gaits (walk, trot, canter) and 2 man-made gaits (slow gait, rack).

fixative A substance used to reduce over-all volatility of flavoring agents.

fixing agent A substance used to preserve protoplasm with the least amount of alteration; solutions used are alcohol, formalin, mercuric bichloride, potassium bichromate, acetic acid, formic acid, osmic acid, picric acid; mixtures used are Zenker's fluid, Bouin's fluid, and Mueller's fluid.

flake (1) Dehydrated vegetables used as flavoring materials. (2) To break into small flat pieces.

flake tapioca Dough made from tapioca flour, rolled in thin sheets, baked; if ground, it is called granular tapioca.

flame A variety of grape.

flank About 4% of a choice cattle carcass.
See Part 2: Beef Chart; Beef Cuts; Beef Cuts and Uses; Beef Retail Yield; Beef Wholesale Cuts; Lamb Chart; Lamb Yield; Meat Identification; Veal Cuts and Uses

flank steak (***Rectus abdominus***) A tear-shaped steak removed from the flank area; a membrane is removed from it and it is usually cut across the fibers; only two of these steaks may be obtained from an animal.
See Part 2: Beef, Boneless Cuts; Beef Chart; Braising Meat

Flash 18 (Swift & Co.) A canning system in a pressurized (18 lb) can-filling room; this raises the boiling point of a liquid (250°–255°F is normally used).

flash point That temperature at which an ignitable concentration of vapor develops above the surface of an organic liquid. Liquids that evolve such concentrations at or below 80°F are considered flammable, e.g., ethyl alcohol.

	smoke point	flash point	fire point
Fats (range)	320–500°F (160–260°C)	554–626°F (290–330°C)	644–689°F (340–365°C)
Cottonseed oil	450°F (232°C)	625°F (330°C)	685°F (363°C)

See Part 2: Free Fatty Acid, Smoke, Flash, Fire Points

flat bone *See* Part 2: Bone and Retail Cuts

flat bone sirloin *See* **double bone sirloin**

flat sour A type of spoiled can.
See Part 2: Canned Spoilage Manifestations; Canned Spoilage Related to pH

flavanone Any of a group of plant pigments producing yellow and orange colors.
See Part 2: Lemon Juice Composition

flavedo Yellowness.
See Part 2: Orange Structure

Flavobacterium *See* Part 2: Spoilage, Protein Foods

flavoprotein A complex of a flavin nucleotide and an enzyme. *See also* **adenine-riboflavin dinucleotide; riboflavin phosphate.**

flavor The ability of food to stimulate the senses located in the alimentary and respiratory tracts. Closely associated with odor, color and texture. *See also* **taste.**

flavored milk drink *See* Part 2: Cultured Dairy Products, Composition

flavored triple creme A soft, thin-rind cheese; 75% fat gives a buttery texture; may be eaten in its natural state or mixed with spices.

flavoring A substance added to a food to give it a specific taste; e.g., vanilla, chocolate. Many of them are made synthetically. *See also* taste; flavor.
See Part 2: Flavoring Agents, Natural; Flavor Ingredients, Taste and Flavor Type; Flavors, Beverage; Minerals (Trace), Limits

flax A vegetable fiber composed primarily of cellulose.
See Part 2: Wax

flax seed (linseed) A seed from which a drying oil is produced.
1 bu flaxseed = 2.5 gal. oil
= 56 lb
See Part 2: Oil, Seed and Fruit; Protein Factors; Seed, Chemical Composition; Seed Composition; Seed, Germination

flay To remove the skin from an animal in a uniform pattern.

fleabeetle *See* Part 2: Insect Control

Fleckvieh German Simmental cattle.

fleece The wool of a sheep.

fleischig Of meat origin, including fowl.

flesh Muscular tissue of animals.

Fletcher medium base Used for the isolation, cultivation, and maintenance of *Leptospira*.
See Part 2: Microorganism, Media

flexor A muscle that flexes (bends) a joint.

flint corn *See* **corn**

floating rib A rib with no cartilage.

flor A white yeast that floats on the surface of wine.

flora The plant life of an area.

Florence fennel (finnochio dolce) (*Foeniculum vulgare dulce*) A plant resembling celery with a swollen leaf base, which is eaten raw, in salads or cooked.

florentine, à la With spinach.

Florida and Walters A variety of mid-season Florida grapefruit.

flounder (sole, fluke, blackback, yellowtail) A lean flat fish caught in the middle and north Atlantic and on the east and west coasts. *See also* **demersal fish**.
See Part 2: Fish, Storage; Frozen Food Storage, Minerals, Food; Vitamin D, Fish

flour (white flour, wheat flour, plain flour) A fine-ground powder made by milling and sifting wheat from inner portion of wheat grain; consists essentially of endosperm; may be bleached or unbleached.
100 lb flour = 2.3 bu wheat
3–4 tbsp flour = 1 oz
2½ to 3¾ cups flour = 1 lb
4 cups all-purpose flour = 1 lb
1 cup sifted enriched flour = 110 g
4 cups sifted enriched flour = 1 lb
1 qt sifted flour = 1 lb
4–5 cups sifted cake flour = 1 lb
3¾ cups stirred graham flour = 1 lb
1 barrel = 196 lb
Adjustment for altitude:

elevation (ft)	increase flour/cake (tbsp)
4,000	1
5,500	2
7,000	3
8,000	4

Thickening:
2 tbsp flour = 1 tbsp cornstarch, potato starch, rice starch, arrowroot starch, or 2 tbsp quick-cooking tapioca.
1 cup flour = ⅞ cup all-purpose flour + ⅛ cup corn starch.
pH 6.0 to 6.5

specific gravity: flour loose 0.40–0.50
flour pressed 0.70–0.80
Straight hard wheat composition: 12% H_2O, 12% protein, 1.2% fat, 75% carbohydrate, 0.5% ash.
Straight soft wheat composition: 12% H_2O, 10% protein, 1% fat, 77% carbohydrate, 0.4% ash.
13–16.5 mg Fe/lb; 16–20 mg niacin or niacinamide/lb; 1.2–1.5 mg riboflavin/lb; 2–2.5 mg thiamin /lb.
See Part 2: Bread and Flour Enrichment; Cereal Composition; Cereal Enrichment; Cereal Fortification; Cereals, Vitamin and Mineral Content; Flour, Extraction Rates; Food, Composition; Grain Products Composition: Minerals, Food; Minerals, Trace, Limits; Riboflavin, Food; Soybean Composition; Storage, Dry; Storage Times; Thiamin, Food; Vitamin A, Food; Wastes, Agricultural and Industrial; Water Activity, Organisms and Food; Wheat and Flour Composition; Wheat, Carbohydrate Composition; Wheat, Minerals; Wheat Products, Amino Acid Compositions; Wheat, Vitamins

flour, all-purpose (general purpose) Flour made from blends of wheat that are satisfactory for most household cooking.
1 cup (sifted) = 110 g = 1 cup unsifted minus 2 tbsp.
Composition: 12% H_2O, 10% protein, 1% fat, 76% carbohydrate, 0.4% ash.

flour, bread Flour made for bakers and manufactured from hard wheat; high in protein (gluten); granular; bleached or unbleached.

flour, cake Flour made from soft wheat, most highly refined flour, low protein, very fine.
1 cup, sifted = 100 g = ⅞ cup sifted all-purpose flour = 1 cup sifted minus 2 tbsp sifted all-purpose flour.
It contains more starch and less gluten (gluten is less elastic) than bread flour.
Composition: 12% H_2O, 7% protein, 1% fat, 79% carbohydrate, 0.3% ash, pH 5.0–5.2.

flour, enriched Flour with added vitamins and minerals.

Ingredient	Per Pound Min (mg)	Max (mg)
Iron	13	16.5
Niacin	16	20
Riboflavin	1.2	1.5
Thiamin	20	20
May contain:		
Calcium	500	625
Vitamin D	250 U.S.P. units	1000 U.S.P. units

flour, entire wheat *See* **flour, whole wheat**

flour, graham Flour made from entire wheat grain; less finely granulated than whole wheat flour; 3½–4½ cups = 1 lb.

flour, instant (instantized, instant blending, quick-mixing) A general all-purpose flour that blends rapidly with liquids.

flour, pancake A prepared flour that contains leavening and salt and sometimes other ingredients.

flour, pastry A flour made mostly from soft but sometimes from hard wheat; low in protein; finely milled (not as fine as cake flour); used by bakers and biscuit cooks.

flour, ready-mixed *See* **flour, pancake**

flour, self-rising Flour to which leavening ingredients (soda, monocalcium phosphate) and salt are added; 1 cup = 110 g; 500–1500 mg calcium/lb.

flour, whole wheat (entire wheat) A flour made from entire wheat grain (durum or red durum not used); more finely granulated than graham flour; 1 cup (stirred) = 120 g; 3⅓ cups = 1 lb.
Composition: 12% H_2O, 9-13% protein, 2-5% fat, 71–75% carbohydrate, 1-2% ash.

flower The pigmented blossom of a plant which contains the reproductive organs (anther, ovary, pistils, etc.).
See Part 2: Flower, Imperfect; Flower Perfect

fluffy dressing *See* Part 2: Salad Dressing and Mayonnaise Variations

fluke *See* **flounder**

fluorescence The ability of a compound (anthracene, fluorescein) to absorb light of one wavelength and radiate light at another wavelength.

fluorine (F) The most active halogen element; at. no. 9; at. wt. 19.00; Group VIIA of the Periodic Table; oxidation state −1; electron configuration 2–7
orbit K L
1 ppm is often added to drinking water.
See Part 2: Egg Products Nutritive Value; Minerals, Trace, Limits; Water Drinking Standards

fly (horn) A small black fly; a large number will concentrate on a small area of an animal.

fly (horse) A large black fly.

fly (house) A parasite.

flyer Silent cutter.

flying Chopping.

fly-poison A plant having a toxic principle.
See Part 2: Poisonous Plants

Fm Symbol for the element fermium.

F35M hajna *See* Part 2: Microorganism, Media

foal A colt or filly less than one year old.

foam A gas dispersed in a liquid or solid; such dispersions are often of colloidal dimensions. Soapsuds and ordinary sea foam are examples of gas (air)/liquid dispersions; bread and cake are examples of gas (CO_2)/solid dispersions.

foamglas *See* Part 2: Insulation

fog A colloidal system in which a liquid is dispersed in a gas (air).

folacin *See* Part 2: Recommended Daily Dietary Allowance

folded rib roast A standing rib roast with a portion of the ribs removed and the roast folded.

folic acid (PGA) A factor necessary for the production of red and white blood cells; found in the liver in the form of pteroyl-glutamic acid. Sources: liver, kidney, dried beans, beef, yeast, green leafy vegetables, wheat, mushrooms.
See Part 2: Cereal Fortification; Cereals, Vitamin and Mineral Content; Cheese, Vitamin Content; Egg Products, Nutritive Value; Grain Analysis; Lemon Juice Composition; Milk and Milk Products, Vitamin Content; Vitamins; Vitamin Sources, Functions, and Stability; Wheat Products Composition; Wheat, Vitamins

fondant An aqueous solution of invert sugar and corn syrup used by confectioners.
See Part 2: Water Activity, Organisms and Food

fondue A hot cheese dip served with crisp bread or small pieces of toast.

fontina A sweet, mellow, hard Italian cheese; there are also French and Swiss versions.
See Part 2: Cheese Vitamin Content

food Any substance or mixture (except oxygen and water) that nourishes an organism, builds tissue and supplies heat.
See Part 2: Food, Water Intake

Food and Agricultural Organization (FAO) Specialized agency of the United Nations concerned with the development of world agriculture, fisheries and forestry. It is headquartered in Rome.

Food and Drug Administration Federal agency responsible for enforcement of Federal Food, Drug and Cosmetic Act which prohibits the movement in interstate commerce of adulterated or misbranded food; this law covers all food except meat and poultry as well as drugs, devices, and cosmetics.

food color *See* **colorant**

food energy *See* **Calorie**

food poisoning *See* ***Clostridium botulinum; Staphylococcus aureus; salmonellosis***
See Part 2: Food Poisoning, Bacteria; Infectious Diseases, Food-Borne

food starch, modified Native starches treated with chemical agents to modify their physical properties.

foot (ft) A measure of length.
1 foot = 30.48006096 centimeters (cm)
= 12 inches (in.)
= 3.048006 decimeters
= 3 hands (U.S.)
= 0.33333 yard (yd)
= 0.3048006 meter (m)
= 0.06061 rod (rd)
= 0.0151515 chain (Gunter's)
= 0.0003048 kilometer (km)

1 foot = 0.0001894 statute mile
= 0.00016447 U.S. nautical mile
3 feet = 1 yard
3.28 ft = 1 meter

foot and mouth disease A virus-caused disease that affects all cloven-footed animals; it is highly infectious.

foot-candle Unit of illumination.
1 foot-candle = 10.764 lux
= 1.0764 milliphots
= 1 lumen/sq foot

foot-pound (ft-lb) A measure of heat, energy, and work.
1 foot-pound = 13,557,300 ergs or centimeter dynes
= 13,825.5 gram-centimeters
= 32.174 foot poundals
= 1.35573 joules (10^7 ergs) (j)
= 0.32389 g calory (mean)
= 0.13826 kilogram meter (kg-m)
= 0.001285 British thermal unit (mean)
= 0.0003239 kg-cal thermal unit (mean)
= 0.0000005121 metric horsepower-hour (75 kg-m-hr)
= 0.0000005051 U.S. horsepower-hour (hp-hr)
= 0.00000037662 kilowatt hour (kw-hr)

foot-pound per second (ft-lb/sec) A measure of power, rate of energy and heat.
1 ft-lb/sec = 13,557,300 ergs/sec
= 13,825.5 gram-cm/sec
= 60 ft lbs/min
= 1.35573 watts (10^7 ergs/sec)
= 0.13826 kilogram meter per second (kg-m/sec)
= 0.077124 Btu/min (mean)
= 0.001843 metric horsepower (75 kg-m/sec)
= 0.001818 U.S. horsepower (550 ft-lb/sec)
= 0.001356 kilowatt (kw)
= 0.001285 Btu/sec (thermal unit per sec)
= 0.0003237 kg-cal/sec (thermal unit per sec)

foot rot (foul foot) An infection of the foot of cattle and sheep causing swelling around top of foot and inflammation between digits; soak in 5% copper sulfate.

foots Soapstock, alkali soap. *See also* **soapstock**.

foramen An opening in a bone.

forati *See* **spaghetti**

foratini *See* **spaghetti**

forcemeat Meat which has been chopped fine, spiced and highly seasoned; used as a stuffing for fowl, etc.

fore end Shoulders from Wiltshire sides.

forefoot *See* Part 2: Bone; Pork Wholesale Cuts

foreleg *See* Part 2: Bone Age

fore quarter The front portion of a beef carcass that has usually been divided between the 12th and 13th rib (approx. 52% of carcass); it is usually divided into wholesale cuts called chuck, rib, brisket, shank, plate and short ribs.

fore saddle A wholesale cut of veal or lamb consisting of all in front of the 12th rib; the 2 quarters are not split.
See Part 2: Veal Wholesale Cuts

fore shank Made up of the ulna and radius of a carcass.
See Part 2: Beef Cuts; Bone; Lamb Chart; Lamb Yield

forestière With mushrooms.

forget fredette agar *See* Part 2: Microorganism, Media

forging Overreaching or striking heel of forefoot with hindfoot on the same side.

formaldehyde (methanal) HCHO A poisonous water-soluble gas; produced in smoke used for smoking food; used as a fumigant and for smut control.

formalin (formol, formolose) Commercial formalin is 40% formaldehyde in water; approx. 37%, formaldehyde, 10–15% methanol in water (same as 40% formalin); disinfectant in a 1:2000 to 1:200 solution; fixing fluid; preservative.

Formate Ricinoleate broth Medium used for detection of coliform by formation of gas.
See Part 2: Microorganism, Culture Media, Dairy and Food Products; Microorganism, Culture Media, Water and Sewage, Standard Methods; Microorganism, Selective and Differential Broths and Media, Water Filtration Plant

formic acid 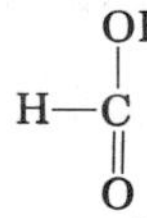 A poisonous liquid found in the venom of ants and bees; m.p. 8.4°C; b.p. 100.5°C; commercial acid has sp. gr. 1.20 (90% by wt) and 1.06 (25% by wt).
See Part 2: Concentration of commercial strengths of Acids and Bases

Formosa oolong *See* **oolong tea**

formyl group (aldehyde group) 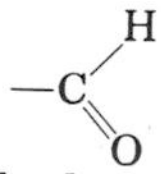 A chemical group characteristic of aldehydes.

fortification The addition of selected nutrients to food to provide higher levels than are naturally present.
See Part 2: Cereal Fortification; Dairy Terms

fortified dry wine A dry wine to which brandy has been added.

fortified sweet wine A sweet wine to which wine spirits have been added.

fortified wine A wine to which grape spirits have been added during or after fermentation; this increases the strength of the wine; if added during fermentation it will stop fermentation and produce a sweeter wine, since not all the sugar has been converted to alcohol. Common types are marsala, madeira, port, sherry.

fossa A depression in a bone.

Foster A variety of late Florida grapefruit.

foul foot *See* **foot rot**

founder Of an animal, to overeat.

fovantini *See* **macaroni**

fowl A mature hen (chicken) usually more than 10 months old; used for stewing. *See also* **hen.**

foxtail A variety of millet.

Fr Symbol for the element francium.

fraction That component of a mixture which can be separated by distillation (liquids of different boiling points) or by filtration or centrifugation (solids of different weights).

fractional crystallization A separation method in which the temperature is slowly lowered, allowing the higher-melting compounds to crystallize.

fractional distillation Separation of the components of petroleum and other liquid mixtures by boiling off and condensing them in sequence; this is possible because of the wide difference in boiling points of the several components. *See also* **distillation.**

francium (Fr) An alkali metal element; at. no. 87; Group IA of Periodic Table; mass number of most stable isotope 223; oxidation state +1; electron configuration 2-8-18-32-18-8-1
orbit K L M N O P Q

frankfurter (wiener, wienies, frank, red hot, vienna sausage) A comminuted, cooked, smoked, small casing sausage; normally 60% beef, 40% pork.

30-70% beef
25-50% pork
0-40% veal
0-8% pork liver & hearts
0-15% defatted pork solids
0-20% tripe
20-40% ice*
2-3% salt*
7-16 oz sugar/100 lb*
0-7% binder
2 oz $NaNO_3$/100 lb*
¼ oz $NaNO_2$/100 lb*
4-7 oz white pepper/100 lb*
1-3 oz coriander/100 lb*
1-2 oz ginger or mace/100 lb*
0-3 oz onion juice/100 lb
0-1 oz cardamon/100 lb
0-1 oz cinnamon/100 lb
0-1 oz sage/100 lb
0-1 oz garlic 100/lb
0-⅞ oz ascorbate/100 lb
0-1 oz mustard/100 lb
0-2 oz nutmeg/100 lb

*Combination of additives used in some formulations

Procedure:
1. Grind ⅛ in. plate
2. Mix beef, seasoning, ice, binder
3. Chop
4. Add pork, ascorbate
5. Chop; max. temp. 65°F
6. Stuff and link
7. Smoke

Temp. (°F)	Time (hr)	Condition
130	½	No smoke
140	½	Smoke
150	¼	"
160	¼	"
170	¼	"
180	Internal temp. of 152°F	Steam

8. Shower 15 minutes
9. Cool

Home Storage: Keep in original wrappers; refrigerate.

See Part 2: Calories, Daily Recommendations; Food, Composition; Meat, Servings per Pound; Meat Storage; Pork Storage; Sausage Composition; Sausage Identification; Sausage Nutritive Value; Sausage, Types

frankincense A fragrant resin obtained from Arabian and African sources; gives off an aromatic smoke used in religious ceremonies.
See Part 2: Essential Oils

frappé A semi-frozen ice or fruit juice; a soft sherbet.

free fatty acid (ffa) A specification for fats used in cooking; a good frying fat has 0.05% max; and emulsifier, 1% max. It is determined by mixing hot fat with hot neutralized ethyl alcohol and then titrating the mixture with a standard weak base; results usually are expressed as oleic acid. *See also* **acid value.**
See Part 2: Free Fatty Acid, Smoke, Flash, Fire Points

freemartin A sterile female calf born twin with a male calf.

free water Water that is not an integral part of the living cell with which it is associated.

freeze drying A preservation technique in which a food is frozen and placed in a vacuum; the ice is vaporized and trapped, leaving a dried product; used especially for coffee.

freezer burn Dehydration of frozen food; can be eliminated by proper wrapping.

freezing point Temperature at which a liquid becomes a solid.
See Part 2: Defrosting Time; Freezer Sizes; Freezing Rate; Thermal-Arrest Time

French-Alpine *See* Part 2: Goats, Milk Breeds

French artichoke A vegetable whose flower is used as food.

French bean (kidney bean), (*Phaseolus vulgaris*) One of many varieties of edible beans that produce a variety of shapes and colors of pods and beans.

French Canadian A breed of dairy cattle.

French Charollais *See* **Charolais**

French combing wool Wool that is shorter than normal combing wool yet can be combed on the French style of combs.

French dressing A temporary emulsion (shake before use) of oil, and acid (vinegar or lemon juice) and seasoning; paprika gives it a red color; min 35% vegetable oil; emulsifier, egg yolk and designated emulsifiers, max 0.75%; acid, vinegar or lemon juice (citric acid can be used for ¼ acetic acid in vinegar).

Combinations often used: ¾ cup salad oil (corn, cottonseed, olive, peanut, or soybean oil); ¼ cup vinegar (cider, white or wine); 1 tsp salt; 1 tsp sugar; dash pepper; ½ tsp paprika; ¼ tsp mustard. Other spices sometimes used; basil, catsup, celery, cloves, curry, garlic, ginger, nutmeg, oregano, tarragon.

See Part 2: Fats and Oils, Composition; French Dressing; French Dressing Variations

French endive (Witloof chicory) (Monk's beard) A salad green with a long compact head grown by placing chicory roots horizontally in moist soil; pale slender leaves 6-10 in. long are slightly bitter.

frenching Removing the meat (2 inches) from the end of a bone.

French leg of lamb Tibia is left in the leg and frenched.

French Merino *See* **Rambouillet**

French mustard *See* Part 2: Mustard, French

French roast (continental roast) A procedure for roasting coffee that produces a deep brown bean with the oil brought to the surface; it is darker than American roast and has a heartier body and sharper taste.

French style bean Green beans cut at an angle rather than horizontally.

Freon Proprietary name for a series of non-flammable refrigerants based on fluorocarbons.

Freon		m.p. (°C)	b.p. (°C)
11	Trichloromonofluoro-methane	-111	23.7
12	Dichlorodifluoro-methane	-158	-29.8
114	1,2 dichloro -1,1,2,2-tetrafluoroethane	-94	4.1
C318	Octafluorocyclobutane	-41.4	-6.0

frequency Number of cycles/second.

Fresh Freezer Accumulation (F.F.A.) Meat that is fresh, partly frozen or solidly frozen, which has been accumulated in the last 15 days and is in good condition.

freshness date *See* **quality assurance date**

fresh receipts Merchandise that has just arrived.

fresh-water fish (ocean-dwelling caught in fresh water) Fish caught in fresh water; i.e., Pacific salmon, Atlantic salmon, and salmon trout; composition of edible portion 16% avg protein; up to 20% fat in salmon.

Fresian European black and white cattle; a mature bull weighs 2200 lb.

fricase Meat with sauce.

fricassee To cook fowl or rabbit by braising; braised meat.

See Part 2: Braising Meat

fries Testicles of food animals.

Friesian *See* **Holstein-Friesian**

Friewer Shaughnessy medium *See* Part 2: Micro-organism Reactions on Differential Tube Media

fritted glass Ground glass that has been fused to form a sheet of filtering (porous) material.

fritter A deep-fried ball of dough in which apples, bananas, etc. are enclosed.

See Part 2: Frying Time

friulana A cheddar type cheese.

frizzes *See* Part 2: Sausage Identification

frizzie (soppresata) A dried pork and beef sausage that is stuffed in a hog middle and dried without smoking for 60 to 90 days; it has a crinkled shape.

frog A smooth-skinned, amphibious animal which lives around water and is capable of jumping long distances; rear legs of larger frogs are used for food.

See Part 2: Minerals, Food; Portion Size

fromage, au With cheese.

See Part 2: Milk and Cheese Composition

frostfish *See* **whiting**

frosting temperature *See* **candy**

frozen dessert *See* Part 2: Creams, Butter and Frozen Desserts; Dairy Terms

frozen food Food kept at or below zero Fahrenheit (-17.5°C).

See Part 2: Fruit Frozen Yield; Meat, Frozen Storage; Meat Storage; Microbiological Media; Poultry Cooking, Frozen; Vegetable Frozen Yield; Vegetables, Boiling Time, Frozen; Vegetables, Cooking Frozen

frozen fruit *See* Part 2: Fruit Servings per Pound

frozen storage *See* Part 2: Frozen Food Containers; Frozen Food Storage

fructose (levulose, fruit sugar) $C_6H_{12}O_6$ A 6-carbon monosaccharide (hexose) which is widely distributed in nature; 173% as sweet as sucrose; m.p. 103°C; found naturally in honey, fruits.

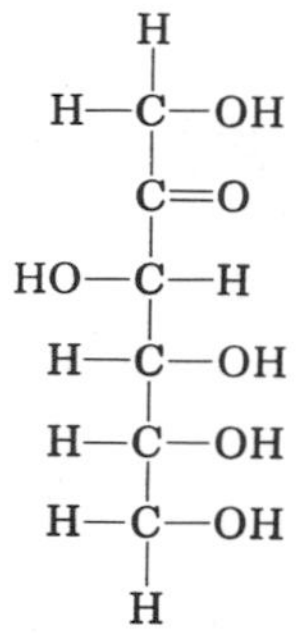

See Part 2: Honey Composition; Sugar, Fruit; Sugar, Legumes; Sugar, Vegetables; Sweeteners, Sweetness; Sweetening Agents; Sweetening Compounds

fruit Edible tissue resulting from the flower of a plant and usually containing the ripened seed; formed from the ovary of the flower. Dried form: 2 cups = 1 lb. *See also* **vegetable.**
See Part 2: Calcium; Calories, Daily Recommendations; Canned Spoilage Related to pH; Food, Composition; Frozen Food Storage; Fruit and Nut Rootstock; Fruit and Vegetable, Diseases; Fruit and Vegetables Composition; Fruit, Availability; Fruit Harvest Dates; Fruit Classification; Fruit Composition; Fruit, Cooking; Fruit Dressing; Fruit Dried Simmering; Fruit Frozen Yield; Fruit Growing Season, Storage Life; Fruit Juice Flavors; Fruit Salad Dressing; Fruit Sauces; Fruit Servings per Pound; Fruit Simmering; Fruit Storage; Microwave Cooking, Fruit; Minerals, Plant or Animal Tissue; Moisture in Biological Materials; Mold, Food; Nicotinic Acid, Food; Nutrients in Crops; Oil, Seed and Fruit; Organic Acids in Fruits and Vegetables; Portion Size; Potassium-Rich Foods; Riboflavin, Food; Rot Spoilage; Salad Dressing and Mayonnaise Variations; Spoilage, Carbohydrate Foods; Standards, Processed Fruit and Vegetable Products; Storage Times; Sugar, Fruit; Thiamin, Food; Vitamin A, Daily Recommendations; Vitamin A, Food

fruitcake A rich cake containing raisins and candied fruit.
See Part 2: Grain Products Composition; Water Activity, Organisms and Food

fruit cocktail Mixed pieces or sections of fresh or canned fruit, served as an appetizer.
See Part 2: Calories, Daily Recommendations; Standards, Processed Fruit and Vegetable Products

fruit grade

(fresh consumer)	U.S. Grades A, B, C
(fresh wholesale)	U.S. Extra Fancy
	U.S. Fancy (in some fruits, this is the top grade)
	U.S. No. 1
	U.S. Utility or U.S. No. 2
	No. 1 cookers
	Combination
(processed)	U.S. Grade A or U.S. Fancy
	U.S. Grade B or U.S. Choice or U.S. Extra Standard
	U.S. Grade C or U.S. Standard

fruit juice *See* Part 2: Fruit Juice Flavors; Minerals, Trace, Limits; Spoilage, Carbohydrate Foods; Stabilizers, Thickeners

fruit sugar *See* **fructose**
See Part 2: Sweetening Compounds

fry To cook in fat.
See Part 2: Frying Time; Lamb Cuts and Uses; Pork Cuts and Uses; Poultry Class; Variety Meat Preparation; Veal Cuts and Uses; Vitamin Retention, Meat

fryer A young chicken from 3¼ to 4¼ lb.
See Part 2: Poultry Roasting

fryer-roaster A turkey of either sex about 16 weeks old.

F-test A test of the hypothesis that two population variances (s_1^2 and s_2^2) are equal; the variance ratio is computed and compared to table *F*-values.
See Part 2: F-Distribution

fuchsin lactose broth Selective medium used in examination of water for *Escherichia coli*; the basic fuchsin dye inhibits Gram-positive organisms.
See Part 2: Microorganism, Selective and Differential Broths and Media, Water Filtration Plant

fudge A confection consisting of a flavored supersaturated sugar solution.
See Part 2: Calories, Daily Recommendations; Sugars and Sweets Composition

fuel A carbonaceous solid, liquid or gas used for heating and cooking.
See Part 2: Fuel, Heating Value

fuller's earth A refining agent for fats and oils, composed of colloidal clay and silicious material.

full fat soy flour A flour made from soy beans that are hulled, ground and processed without fat removal; up to 23% fat, 43% protein.

full pension Hotel room plus 3 meals (breakfast is Continental).

fully cooked *See* **cooked; smoked temperature**

fumaric acid 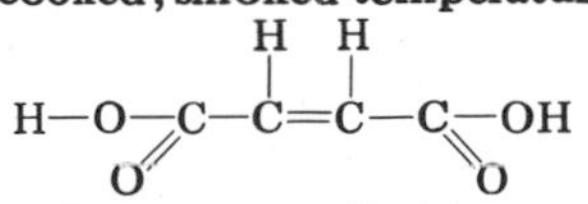 An organic acid used in beverages and baking powder and as an antioxidant; 67-72% as tart as anhydrous citric.
See Part 2: Acidulants; Maple Syrup Composition; Organic Acids in Fruits and Vegetables

fumeol Refined smoke used to make liquid smoke.

fumigation Killing pests by exposure to fumes or gases, e.g., sulfur dioxide, hydrogen cyanide.
See Part 2: Fumigants

fungi A group of plants which contain no chlorophyll.
See Part 2: Fungi Food Products; Microorganism, Media

fungicide A chemical used to destroy or to protect against fungi (and other related growth) on plants, e.g., sulfur, lime, Bordeaux mixture.

F° unit Heat treatment equivalent to minutes at 250°F.

F unit The thermal death time of organisms may be expressed as F values with a subscript indicating the temperature in Fahrenheit (Example: F_{200}).
See Part 2: Thermal-Death-Time Curve

furcellaran (Danish agar) A gum extracted from a sea-growing red algae (*Furcellaria fastigiata*).

furfural *See* **oat**

furlong (fur) A unit of linear measure.
1 furlong = 660 feet
= 220 yards
= 201.168 meters
= 40 rods
= 0.125 mile
8 furlongs = 1 statute mile

fur-sheep *See* Part 2: Sheep Breeds

Fusarium *See* Part 2: Mold, Food; Moulds, Mycotoxins

fused rock phosphate A fertilizer material that contains 30% total P_2O_5.

fusel oil A by-product of alcohol fermentation containing a high percentage of mixed amyl alcohols.

fusion point *See* **melting point**

futira Wheat pastry filled with dates, honey, raisins, sugar, cinnamon and cloves.

F-value *See* **F-unit**

G

G *See* **conductance**

G-4 A Griffith antioxidant containing propyl gallate, lecithin, corn oil, and citric acid.

Ga Symbol for the element gallium.

gado-gado A cooked vegetable (cabbage, carrot, bean, bean sprout) salad with a sauce.

gadoleic acid An unsaturated fatty acid found in certain vegetable oils.
See Part 2: Fats and Oils, Fatty Acid Composition; Fatty Acids and Their Properties; Unsaturated Fatty Acids

gadolinium (Gd) A rare earth element of the lanthanide series; at. no. 64; at. wt. 157.26; Group IIIB of Periodic Table; oxidation state +3; electron configuration 2–8–18–25–9–2
orbit K L M N O P

gaffelbitar Herring preserved in 10–12% salt.

gag *See* **grouper**

gahi A variety of millet.

galactose $C_6H_{12}O_6$ A 6-carbon monosaccharide (hexose) found in combination with other sugars in legumes, agar, pectin and gum; 32% as sweet as sucrose; a constituent of lactose.

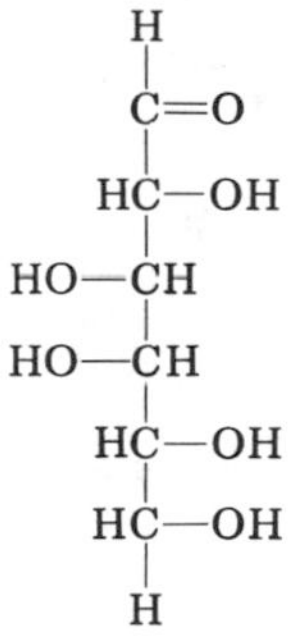

See Part 2: Sugar, D-aldehydo; Sweetening Compounds

gall Bile secreted by the liver.

gallbladder A sac or receptacle located close to the liver whose function is storage of bile.
See Part 2: Liver

gallium (Ga) A metallic element; at. no. 31; at. wt. 69.72; Group IIIA of Periodic Table; oxidation state +3; liquid at 85°F; electron configuration 2–8–18–3
orbit K L M N

gallon (dry) (U.S.) (dry gal.) A measure of volume.
1 d. gal. = 268.803 cubic inches (cu in.)
= 4.65460 U.S. liquid quarts (liquid qt)
= 4.40492 cubic decimeters (dm^3)
= 4 U.S. dry quarts (dry qt)
= 1.16365 U.S. liquid gallons (liquid gal.)
= 0.15556 cubic foot (cu ft)
= 0.125 U.S. bushel (bu)
= 0.005761 cubic yards (cu yd)

gallon (Imperial) (Br.) (Canadian) (Imp.) (gal.) A measure of volume.
1 Imperial gal. = 4545.96 ml
= 277.274 cubic inches (cu in.)
= 160 British fluid oz
= 10.0221 lb (av) of water at 60°F or 10 lb at 16.7°C (62°F)
= 4.546 liters
= 4.54 cubic decimeters (dm^3)
= 4.30128 U.S. liquid quarts (liquid qt)
= 4.1267 U.S. dry quarts (dry qt)
= 4 quarts (Br. fl.)
= 1.20094 U.S. liquid gallons (liquid gal.)
= 1.0317 U.S. dry gallons (dry gal.)
= 0.1605 cubic foot (cu ft)
= 0.12896 U.S. bushel (bu)
= 0.0059429 cubic yard (cu yd)
= 4.546×10^{-3} cu meter

gallon (liquid) (U.S.) (liquid gal.) A measure of volume.
1 l. gal. = 61440 minims
= 3785.434 cubic centimeters (cu cm)
= 3785.33 ml
= 1024 drams (U.S. fl.)
= 231.00 cubic inches (cu in.)
= 133.23 ounces (Br. fl.)
= 128 fluid ounces (U.S.)
= 32 gills
= 8.34545 lb (av), pure H_2O at max. density
= 8.3370 pounds H_2O at 60°F
= 8.330 pounds H_2O at 20°C
= 8 pints (liquid)
= 4 U.S. liquid quarts (liquid qt)
= 3.78533 liters
= 3.43747 U.S. dry quarts (dry qt)
= 0.85937 U.S. dry gallon (dry gal.)
= 0.83268 gallon (British)
= 0.13368 cubic foot (cu ft)
= 0.10742 U.S. bushel (bu)
= 0.004951 cubic yard (cu yd)
= 3.785×10^{-3} cubic meter
= 3.78543 cubic decimeter (dm^3)
= 0.031746 barrel (U.S. liquid)
See Part 2: Volume; Water, Weight and Volume

gallon (U.S. or Br.) per acre Weight per unit of area.
1 gallon (U.S.)/acre = 9.353 liter/ha
1 gallon (Br.)/acre = 11.232 liter/ha

gallon per minute (gpm) A rate of flow.
1 gpm = 2.228×10^{-3} cu ft/sec
= 0.227 cubic meter/hr
= 0.06308 liter/second

Galloway A breed of beef cattle that originated in Southwestern Scotland; they are black, polled, with long curly hair, and smaller than the Angus.
See Part 2: Beef and Dual-purpose Cattle

gallstone A calculus in the gallbladder usually formed from cholesterol or calcium; they may require surgical removal.

gambrel stick A metal or wooden stick placed in the tendons of the rear legs and used to support the carcass when it is hung on the rail.

game Any edible wild animal or bird shot by an individual, either for food or for amusement. Big game usually refers to deer, moose, etc.
See Part 2: Meat and Meat Products Composition

gamma (Γ, γ) Greek letter with an English equivalent of g; 3rd in a series; sometimes used as a metric unit of weight equivalent to a microgram:
1 gamma = 0.001 milligram
= 0.000001 gram

gamma ray High-energy electromagnetic radiation released by disintegration of an atomic nucleus; similar to X-rays but of shorter wavelength.

gammon Ham or strip of bacon that has been salted and smoked or dried; hind legs from Wiltshire sides.

gamy An off-flavor in meat due to incipient decomposition.

garbage Miscellaneous food waste; a possible energy source.
See Part 2: Wastes, Agricultural and Industrial

garbage hogs Hogs that are fed garbage.

garbure A bacon and vegetable soup.

garden cress A green vegetable similar to watercress salad greens but grown in soil.

gardenia *See* Part 2: Essential Oils

garget *See* **mastitis**

garlic (*Allium sativum L.*) Bulb-like root containing several bulbils (cloves) encased in a membrane which are used as spice and seasoning; allicin is responsible for the characteristic odor; it is available in fresh, dried (crushed, ground flakes, powder), oil, and mixed-with-salt forms.
1 oz raw garlic = ½ oz garlic juice
= ¼ oz garlic powder.
When eaten by cattle garlic imparts an off-flavor to milk and meat.
Raw clove composition: 61% H_2O, 6% protein, 0.2% fat, 31% carbohydrate, 1.5% ash.
Storage (dry): 32°F; 70–75% relative humidity; 6 mo. storage life.
See Part 2: Essential Oils; Minerals, Food; Minerals, Plant or Animal Tissue; Spices, Microbial Content; Storage; Vegetables Classification; Vegetable Storage

garlic salt A mixture of garlic powder, salt and starch.

garri Meal made from cassava tubers.

gas (1) The least dense of the three states of matter, in which the molecules move about freely, exerting pressure equally in all directions. At constant temperature the volume of a confined gas is inversely proportional to the applied pressure (Boyle's law). Equal volumes of different gases contain the same number of molecules (Avogadro's law). *See also* **gas law**. (2) *See also* **natural gas.**
See Part 2: Fuel, Heating Value

gas constant (*R*)
8.316 joules per °C
1.9885 calories per °C
0.08207 liter atmosphere per °C

gaskin Stifle to hock of hindfoot of a horse.

gas law $pv = RT$, where

p = pressure
v = volume
R = gas constant
T = absolute temp.

gasoline A mixture of hydrocarbon liquids used for automotive fuel.
See Part 2: Fuel, Heating Value

gastric juice A mixture of hydrochloric acid and pepsin secreted by glands in the stomach to aid digestion; pH about 2.0.
See Part 2: pH Values of Biological Materials

gastrocnemius A large muscle behind the tibia which is attached to Achilles tendon; in cross section of the hind shank it is a large U-shaped muscle to the rear of the tibia.

gastroenteritis A disorder affecting the stomach.
See Part 2: Infectious Diseases, Food-borne

gastrointestinal Relating to the digestive organs (stomach and intestines).
See Part 2: Organ Weights

gastronomy The preparation and appreciation of gourmet food; epicurean taste. *See also* **gourmet**; **epicure.**

gatty gum *See* **gum ghatti**

gaufrettes Wafers with dessert.

gauge Thickness of a metal or other material.
See Part 2: Film Gauge

GC medium *See* Part 2: Microorganism, Media

Gd Symbol for the element gadolinium.

Ge Symbol for the element germanium.

gel A colloidal solution of such hydrophilic materials as gelatin, agar, and pectins dispersed in water; such solutions set to a firm jelly as a

result of interlocking of the long-chain macromolecules; this can be returned to liquid form by heating (reversible gel).
See Part 2: Gums and Gelling Agents; Gums and Gelling Agents, Characteristics

gelatin A hydrophilic protein made from collagen which forms stiff gels when added to water (2–5%). It is widely used in food products for its thickening and water-binding properties. *See also* **collagen.**
granulated: unsweetened and unflavored
4 tbsp granulated = 1 oz
4 cups granulated = 1 lb
1 cup = 150 g (5.3 oz)
powdered: sweetened and flavored
Composition: 13% H_2O, 86% protein, 0.1% fat, 1% ash; has poor nutritive value because of low tryptophan content.
See Part 2: Calories, Daily Recommendations; Gums and Gelling Agents; Gums and Gelling Agents, Characteristics; Minerals (Trace), Limits; Protein Factors; Salad Dressing and Mayonnaise Variations; Stabilizers, Thickeners

Gelbvieh German yellow cattle.

gelding A male horse castrated before advanced sexual development (2 years old).

gelling agent *See* **gel; gelatin; pectin; agar-agar**

generation time The time required for a newly divided cell to grow and divide again.

$$\text{generation time} = \frac{\text{time}}{\text{no. of generations}}$$

$$= \frac{\text{elapsed time}}{3.3 \log \dfrac{\text{no. bacteria at end of period}}{\text{no. bacteria at start or zero time}}}$$

geneva (genierve) Dutch gin.
See Part 2: Minerals, Trace, Limits

geometric isomers *See* ***cis-trans*** **isomers**

Georg fungus medium Microbiological medium used for the isolation of fungi; medium contains penicillin, streptomycin and cycloheximide; all dermatophyte species grow while bacteria and saprophytic fungi are inhibited.
See Part 2: Microorganism, Media

geranium oil *See* Part 2: Essential Oils

germ (1) A common name for bacteria. (2) The embryo (at one end of the kernel) and scutellum in seed, usually separated from the endosperm during milling. The part of the seed kernel necessary for new plant life.
See Part 2: Wheat and Flour Composition; Wheat, Carbohydrate Composition; Wheat, Fatty Acids; Wheat Kernel Parts; Wheat Products Composition

germanium (Ge) A metallic element; at. no. 32; at. wt. 72.60; Group IVA of Periodic Table; oxidation states +2, +4; electron configuration 2–8–18–4
orbit K L M N
A semiconductor.

germicide A substance that destroys microorganisms. *See also* **disinfectant; antiseptic.**

germinate To sprout (of a seed).
See Part 2: Seed, Germination

germ spot (germ cell, disc blastoderm) A small light-colored spot (germinal disc) on the upper surface of an egg yolk (avian) which, in a fertile egg and favorable environmental conditions, develops into the embryo.
See Part 2: Egg Structure

gestation period Length of normal pregnancy (between breeding and birth of offspring).

Animal	Average Age of Puberty (months)	Average Duration of Heat (hr)	Average Heat Interval (days)	Average Gestation Period (days)	Frequency of Twinning
Cattle	12 ± 1	15 ± 10	21 ± 3	283 ± 5	1 in 200
Sheep	5.5 ± 1	28 ± 25	16.5 ± 3	148 ± 4	Depends on breed
Swine	5 ± 1	60 ± 15	21 ± 3	114 ± 12	*
Horses	20 ± 5	156 ± 30	21 ± 4	340 ± 30	

*6.5 pigs per litter

See Part 2: Gestation Periods

ghatti gum *See* **gum ghatti**

ghee A clarified butter from India, made by boiling buffalo milk and cream; can also be made from cow's milk; stores well.
See Part 2: Creams, Butter and Frozen Desserts; Iodine and Saponification Values; Oils and Fats Composition

gherkin (*Cucumis anguria*) A cucumber that produces a small (1 to 3 in.) ovoid, prickly fruit; a small cucumber; the immature fruit is used for pickling; other small cucumbers are often pickled and sold as gherkins (pH 5.8).

giant granadilla A climbing plant that has a large green or greenish-yellow fruit; tastes more insipid than passion fruit; may be boiled in unripe state as vegetable or eaten fresh when ripe.

Gibberella *See* Part 2: Molds, Mycotoxins

gibberellic acid $C_{19}H_{22}O_6$ A plant growth regulator (hormone) occurring in the seeds of some plants which aids in germination.

giblet Primarily the fleshy portion of the diaphragm muscle which is used in sausage; also the heart, liver and gizzard of fowl. *See also* **poultry giblet.**
See Part 2: Poultry Dressing Percentage

gibna beida Dry salty cheese made from goat's milk.

giga Prefix for quantities one billion times larger than the base unit.

gigot Leg of mutton.

gill (gi) A measure of liquid volume.
1 gill = 2 wine glasses = 0.25 pint

gilt A young female hog or pig that has never farrowed and has not reached an evident stage of pregnancy.
See Part 2: Swine Market Classes and Grades

gimmer Yearling ewe.

gin An alcoholic beverage made by original distillation from mash; its flavor is from juniper berries; usual range, 37–43% alcohol by volume.
See Part 2: Minerals, Trace, Limits

ginger (***Zingiber officinale Roscoe***) The underground stem (Rhizome) of a reedlike plant obtained whole, cracked or ground. Good ginger rhizomes are washed and soaked, sometimes boiled, sometimes peeled and dried; rhizome contains starch and can be used for making ginger beer.
Fresh root composition: 87% H_2O, 1% protein, 1% fat, 10% carbohydrate, 1% ash.
Dried:
Not less than 42% starch;
Not less than 12% cold water extract (Jamaica 15%);
Not less than 2% water-soluble ash;
Not more than 8% crude fiber;
Not more than 1% lime;
Not more than 2% acid-insoluble ash.
See Part 2: Essential Oils; Flavors, Beverage; Spices, Microbial Content; Vegetable Storage; Wastes, Agricultural and Industrial

gingerbread A cake sweetened with molasses, and flavored with ginger.
See Part 2: Grain Products Composition

ginger extract 100 cc must contain the alcohol-soluble matter from a minimum of 20 g of ginger.

gingko (***Gingko biloba*****, maidenhair tree**) A deciduous tree with fan-shaped leaves; the female produces a fleshy unpleasant smelling fruit.
See Part 2: Seed, Chemical Composition

ginseng The root (sometimes also leaves and flowers) of a plant used for tea.

gizzard Digestive organ that precedes the stomach in birds.
Chicken raw composition: 75% H_2O, 20% protein, 3% fat, 1% carbohydrate, 1.5% ash.
See Part 2: Poultry Dressing Percentage

gjetost (brown sugar cheese) A goat's milk Norwegian hard cheese with a chocolate brown color and a cubical or rectangular shape; it is unripened and has a sweetish, caramel, buttery flavor.
See Part 2: Cheese Characteristics

glacéd fruit Candied fruit coated with a heavy syrup that is allowed to dry. *See also* **glaze**.

glacial acetic acid *See* **acetic acid**

gland An organ that produces a secretion, thyroid, pituitary, etc.
See Part 2: Gland Weights

glanders An infectious disease of horses characterized by swelling in the jaw area and mucous discharge from the nostrils.

glass container A glass jar or bottle for preservation of fruits or vegetables.
See Part 2: Cans, Conversion Table; Cans, Equivalent Sizes

glass fiber An extruded glass filament of extremely small diameter; woven into mats, it is used for insulation.
See Part 2: Insulation; Insulation, Conductivity Values; Insulating Value

glass wool *See* **glass fiber**

glaze To coat with syrup.
See Part 2: Stabilizers, Thickeners

gliadin A protein found in gluten.
See Part 2: Wheat Products, Amino Acid Compositions

globulin A simple group of proteins that are insoluble in water but soluble in neutral salt solution (5% NaCl) and are coagulable by heat.
See Part 2: Wheat Products, Amino Acid Compositions

Glomerella *See* Part 2: Mold, Food

glucoamylase (amyloglucosidase) An enzyme that hydrolyzes glucose units from the non-reducing end of the starch molecule.

glucoprotein *See* **glycoprotein**

glucose (dextrose), (grape sugar), (blood sugar) $C_6H_{12}O_6$ A 6-carbon monosaccharide (hexose) which has a wide distribution in nature. It is 74% as sweet as sucrose. Glucose-1-phosphate:

OH on no. 1 carbon is replaced by $-O-P(OH)(=O)-OH$.

Glucose-6-phosphate: OH on no. 6 carbon is replaced by the same group. Commercial glucose is a mixture of glucose, dextrin and maltose made by incomplete hydrolysis of starch. *See also* **corn sugar**.

Carbon

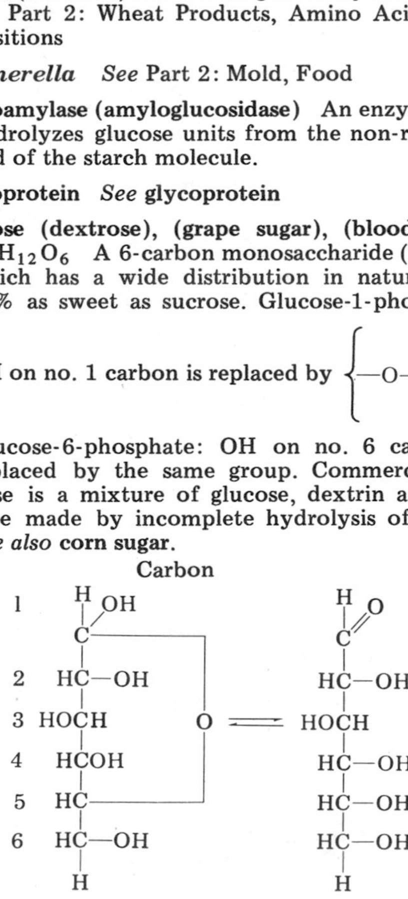

See Part 2: Amylose and Amylopectin; Honey Composition; Minerals (Trace), Limits; Sugar, D-aldehydo; Sugar, Fruit; Sugar, Legumes; Sugar, Vegetables; Sweetness of Sweeteners; Sweetening Agents; Sweetening Compounds

glucose syrup *See* **corn syrup**

glue A colloidal protein mixture made from materials high in collagen; types of animal glue are: (1) hide glue, (2) bone glue, (3) blood albumin glue (water-resistant); (4) fish glue (from skin and bones of fish). *See also* **collagen.**

glumes A chaffy or membranous bract enclosing the spikelet or flowers of grasses and sedges.
See Part 2: Rice Kernel

glutamic acid A monoamino-dicarboxylic amino acid; the sodium salt is used to give meat flavor to foods.

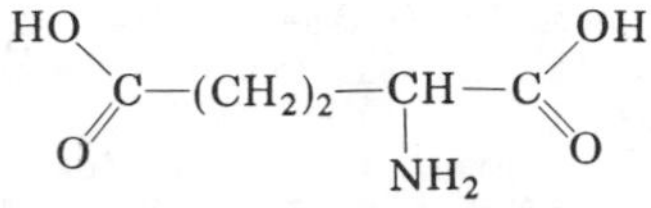

See Part 2: Amino Acids; Amino Acid, Solubilities; Corn, Amino Acids; Egg Products, Nutritive Value; Glutamate; Glutamate Addition; Grain Analysis; Manure Analysis; Wheat, Amino Acids; Wheat Products, Amino Acid Compositions

glutamine A nonessential amino acid.
See Part 2: Amino Acids

glutathione A widely distributed tripeptide of glutamic acid, cysteine and glycine, found in all living cells.

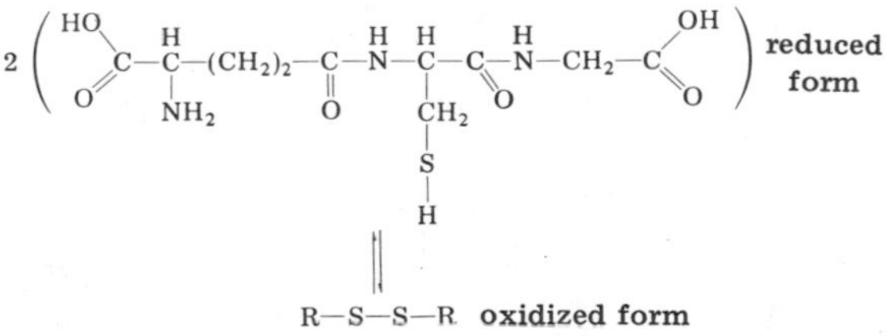

glutelins A group of simple proteins that are insoluble in water or salt solution but are soluble in dilute acids or alkalies.

gluten The tough, viscous nitrogenous substance (protein) remaining when the flour of grain is washed to remove the starch.
See Part 2: Corn Kernel Composition

gluten flour Wheat flour with the starch removed; a mixture of wheat flour and gluten which contains 41% protein.
See Part 2: Gluten-free Diet

glutenin One of the principal proteins of cereal grain that interacts with gliadin to form gluten; a glutelin found in seed; it varies with wheat varieties.
See Part 2: Wheat Products, Amino Acid Compositions

gluteus A muscle of the thigh that runs from the spinous processes of the sacrum, over the ilium to the outside of the femur.

glyceraldehyde $HOCH_2CHOHCHO$ A product of sugar metabolism in the body. Its molecule contains an asymmetric carbon; its conformation is the reference standard for optical isomers of carbohydrates. *See also* **enantiomer; optical isomers.**
See Part 2: Sugar, D-aldehydo

glyceride An ester of glycerol and fatty acids in which one or more hydroxyl groups of the glycerol have been replaced by an acid radical; glycerides are the main constituents of vegetable and animal fats and oils. *See also* **triglyceride.**

glycerin *See* **glycerol**

glycerol (glycerin) $C_3H_5(OH)_3$ A trihydric alcohol; a viscous clear liquid obtained by hydrolysis of natural fats and as a by-product of soap manufacture.

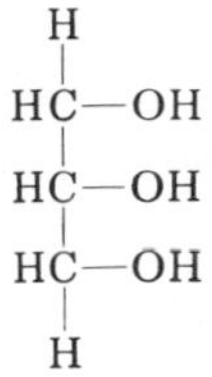

It is used for the manufacture of explosives and as a humectant and solvent; sweet taste; b.p. 290°C.

glycerol-lacto oleate An emulsifying agent.

glycerol-lacto palmitate An emulsifying agent.

glycerol-lacto stearate An emulsifying agent.

glyceryl mono-oleate *See* Part 2: Antioxidant Mixtures

glycine Monoamino-monocarboxylic amino acid (nonessential).

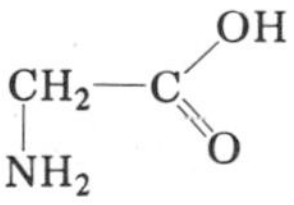

Used to retard rancidity in fat; 0.01% in fat (total antioxidant, 0.02% in combination); 70% as sweet as sucrose.
See Part 2: Amino Acids; Amino Acid, Solubilities; Corn, Amino Acids; Egg Products, Nutritive Value; Grain Analysis; Manure Analysis; Wheat, Amino Acids; Wheat Products, Amino Acid Composition

glycogen (animal starch) $(C_6H_{10}O_5)_x$ The chief form in which carbohydrates are stored in the animal body; made up of glucose units (1 & 4 α linkage); it is stored mainly in the liver and is soluble in cold water.
See Part 2: Histochemical Test; Sweetening Compounds

glycol Ethylene glycol; broadly any aliphatic alcohol containing two hydroxyl groups, i.e., dihydric.

glycolysis Anaerobic enzymatic decomposition of carbohydrates, with release of energy; occurs in yeast fermentation and in some metabolic processes. Lactic acid is one of the products formed.

glycoprotein A combination of a carbohydrate and a protein; N content is 9–13%.

glyoxylic acid HCOCOOH Flavoring intermediate and agricultural chemicals.
See Part 2: Protein and Amino Acid, Color Reactions

GN broth Gram-negative broth is a selective enrichment medium used for the growth of Gram-negative bacilli of the enteric group; desoxycholate and citrate inhibits growth of Gram-positive; mannitol and dextrose inhibits *Proteus* and encourages enteric pathogens.
See Part 2: Microorganism, Selective and Differential Broths and Media, Water Filtration Plant

gnocchi Dumplings of cornmeal or potatoes, eggs and parmesan cheese; entrée made from potatoes, flour and parmesan cheese.

gnotobiote An organism free from contamination or associated with known organisms; mono: without contaminants; di, tri, poly: organism contains one or more known contaminants.

gnotobiotics (Greek: known life) Study of living things by themselves or in association with other known organisms.

goat A hollow-horned ruminant animal; gestation period 150 days (range 142–160).
See Part 2: Gestation Periods; Goats, Milk Breeds; Milk and Cheese Composition; Milk, Mammals, Composition; Milk, Species; Minerals, Food; Reproductive Cycle; Teeth Eruption; Unsaturated Fatty Acids

goat acid A short-chain acid that has an animal odor, e.g., caproic, caprylic, and capric acids (Latin caprus = goat).

goat meat *See* Part 2: Meat and Meat Products Composition

goat's horn *See* **gum tragacanth**

goatweed A plant having a toxic principle.
See Part 2: Poisonous Plants

gobby Lumpy in fleshing.

gold (Au) A metallic element; at. no. 79; at. wt. 197.0; m.p. 1063°C; Group IB of Periodic Table; sp. g. 19.4; oxidation states +1, +3; electron configuration 2–8–18–32–18–1
orbit K L M N O P

golden apple *See* **tomato**

Golden Delicious A variety of apples that is in season from October to March; an excellent eating apple, and a fair to good cooking apple.

gomasio A mixture of sea salt and sesame seeds; reported to give a source of salt without inducing thirst.

Gooch crucible A funnel device with a perforated bottom used in a laboratory with suction to filter precipitates.

goody *See* **spot**

goose A large amphibious bird used for food; its liver is used for paté de foiegras.
See Part 2: Animal Foods, Composition; Frozen Food Storage; Minerals, Food; Meat and Meat Products Composition; Poultry Class; Poultry Roasting

gooseberry (ground cherry, strawberry tomato, dwarf cape gooseberry, cape gooseberry, tomatillo, jamberry) An annual plant that produces a round berry, ½ to ¾-inch in length, with a thin skin, a juicy flesh, a number of seeds, and covered by a light-brown husk; it is eaten raw or is used in stews, sauces and preserves.
Types: Yellowish with hairy skin; reddish skin; dark green skin; pale whitish-green skin; black; red-purple skin.
1 qt fresh = 1 qt canned
Raw composition: 85–89% H_2O, 1–2% protein, 0.2–1% fat, 10–11% carbohydrate, 0.4% ash, pH 2.8–3.1.
See Part 2: Fruit, Canning Dates; Fruit Classification; Fruit Composition; Fruit Frozen Yield; Fruit Storage; Minerals, Food; Organic Acids in Fruits and Vegetables; Riboflavin, Food; Sugar, Fruit

goose grade *See* **poultry grades**

gorgonzola cheese A blue-veined, whole milk cheese very similar to roquefort or blue cheese; soft and creamy yellow interior; light-brown surface; marbled with blue-green mold; cylindrical shape; piquant and spicy flavor; made from goats' and/or cows' milk; ripened 3 mo. by internal mold; a semi-hard cheese from Italy.
Composition: 36% H_2O, 26% protein, 32% fat, 5% ash, 2.4% salt.
See Part 2: Cheese Characteristics, Cheese, Vitamin Content; Milk and Cheese Composition

gorlic *See* Part 2: Fatty Acids and Their Properties

goteborg (hard cervelat) (Swedish sausage) A dry sausage made from coarsely ground beef (60%) and pork (40%) that has a sweet flavor (cardamon); it is given a heavy smoke and dried; a cervelat that has been air-dried for several weeks.

gothaer A summer sausage.

gouda cheese A hard (softer than cheddar), mild to sharp, nut-like, creamy yellow cheese similar to edam but higher in fat; used as a cooking or dessert cheese; the shape is an ellipsoid ball with a red wax covering. It is made from partly skimmed milk; ripened 2–4 mo.
Composition: 36–37% H_2O, 25% protein, 29% fat, 1–2% lactose, 2.7–3.7% ash, 1.7–2% salt.
See Part 2: Cheese Characteristics; Cheese, Vitamin Content; Vitamin A, Milk and Milk Products

goulash A beef and vegetable stew.
See Part 2: Portion Size

gourd A climbing plant whose fruit is often used as food.

bottle gourd: dry hard shell, used as container; young fruit, boiled as a vegetable;
wax or ash gourd: vegetable;
egusi melon: oily seeds are cooked and eaten. *See also* **snake gourd.**
See Part 2: Vegetable Storage; Wastes, Agricultural and Industrial

gourmand One who is given to overeating; a glutton.

gourmandise Luxurious epicurean discrimination in eating and drinking.

gourmet One who is accustomed to the best of foods. *See also* **epicure.**

"government" carcass A term used widely by those employed in the meat packing industry indicating a carcass rejected by USDA Meat Inspectors as being unfit for human consumption.

gracillis The inside thigh muscle just below the skin; only visible in cross-section on approximately last half of cross cut round steaks.

grade (1) Classification according to breeding. Animals that are not pure-bred are often produced by mating a purebred sire with a dam of less than pure breeding; high grade: possessing 87½% or more of pure breeding but not 100%. (2) Classification according to quality (eggs, fruits, vegetables, etc.). (3) Classification according to chemical purity. Chemical specification grades in order of decreasing purity are the following: (1) Primary Standards; (2) Spectro; (3) Reagent; (4) A.C.S.; (5) Chemically Pure; (6) U.S. Pharmacopeia; (7) National Formulary (N.F.); (8) Purified; (9) Technical or Commercial. *See also* **specific entry.**
See Part 2: Cheese Grade Stamps; Egg Quality; Egg Quality, Broken; Grades, Meat; Meat Grade Stamps; Nut, Grades; Poultry Grade Stamp; Poultry Inspection and Grade Stamp; Sheep Market Classes and Grades; Swine Market Classes and Grades; Tomato Grades; Vegetables, Canned Grades; Wheat Grades

graham cracker A soft cracker made from graham flour.
1 cup = 9 coarsely crumbled = 11 finely crumbled
40 crackers = 1 lb
See Part 2: Fermented Ingredients; Grain Products Composition; Minerals, Food

graham flour Flour made from the whole-wheat grain; whole hard wheat flour. It has superior nutritive value and poorer keeping quality. *See also* **flour.**

Graham's salt *See* **sodium phosphate**

grain (troy) (gr) (apoth.) (av.) A measure of weight used for gold, silver, and jewels; grain avoirdupois = grain troy = grain apoth.
1 grain (gr) = 64.798918 milligrams
= 0.3240 carat (metric)
= 0.064798918 gram
= 0.05 scruple (apoth.)
= 0.04166667 pennyweight (troy)
= 0.03657143 dram (av.)
= 0.01666671 dram (apothecary or troy)
= 0.00228571 av. ounce (oz av.)
= 0.00208333 troy or apothecary ounce (oz troy) (oz apoth.)
= 0.0001736111 troy or apothecary pound (lb troy); (lb apoth.)
= 0.0001428571 av. pound (lb av.)
= 0.00006480 kilogram (kg)
= 0.00000007143 net-short ton (2,000 lb)
= 0.00000006378 gross-long ton (2,240 lb)
= 0.00000006480 metric ton (1,000 kg)
24 grains = 1 dwt
20 dwt = 1 ounce
12 ounces = 1 pound

grain (1) Small seeds of grass. (2) In wood and paper, the direction of the fibers.
See Part 2: Food, Composition; Grain Analysis; Grain Products Composition; Nutrients in Crops; Tocopherols; Wheat, Parts of Grain; Wheat, Parts of Grain, Vitamins

grain alcohol *See* **ethyl alcohol**

grain per gallon (Br.) 14.254 parts per million in water (ppm) (by weight).

grain per gallon (U.S.) 142.86 pounds/million gallons = 17.118 parts per million in water (ppm) (by weight).

grain (vinegar) Grain = 10 × % acid.

gram (food) Pulse and/or tropical legumes.

gram (gramme) (g) (gm) A measure of weight.
1 gram = 1,000,000 micrograms (μg)
= 1,000 milligrams (mg)
= 980.665 dynes
= 100 centigrams (cg)
= 15.4323561 grains (troy)
= 10 decigrams (dg)
= 5 carats (metric)
= 1 milliliter of water at its maximum density (4°C) and 1 atm. pressure
= 0.771618 scruple (apoth.)
= 0.64301485 pennyweight (dwt)
= 0.5643833 dram (av.)
= 0.2572059 dram (troy) (apoth.)
= 0.03527396 av. ounce (common) (av.)
= 0.03215074 troy or apothecary ounce
= 2.67923×10^{-3} pound (troy) (apoth.)
= 0.00220462 pound (av.)
= 0.001 kilogram (kg)
= 1.10231×10^{-6} ton (short)
= 9.842×10^{-7} ton (long)
See Part 2: Weight

gram calorie *See* **calorie**

gram-centimeter A measure of heat, energy and/or work.
1 gram-centimeter = 980.5966 ergs = 0.000072330 foot-pound

gram-centimeter per second A measure of power, rate of energy and heat.
1 gram-centimeter per second = 980.5966 ergs/sec = 9.80665×10^{-5} watt = 0.00007238 foot-pound/sec

gram equivalent Atomic weight of an element divided by its valence.

gramicidin An antibiotic polypeptide that is effective against most gram-positive bacteria; obtained by extraction of tyrothricin.

gram molecular weight *See* **mole**

Gram-negative *See* **Gram's stain**

gram per cubic centimeter (g/cm^3) A measure of density or concentration.
1 g/cm^3 = 1,685.56 pounds per cu yard (lb/yd^3)
= 1,000 kilograms per cu meter (kg/m^3)
= 980.5966 $dynes/cm^3$
= 77.6893 pounds per bushel (U.S.)
= 62.4283 pounds per cu foot (lb/ft^3)
= 9.71116 pounds per gallon, dry (U.S.)
= 8.34545 pounds per gallon, liquid (U.S.)
= 1.162283 $poundals/in.^3$
= 0.036127 pound per cu inch ($lb/in.^3$)

gram per liter A measure of density or concentration.
1 g per l = 1,000 parts/million (by wt) in water
= 58.43 grains/gallon
= 8.345 pounds/1,000 gallons
= 0.062427 pound/cu foot

gram per square centimeter A measure of pressure.
1 gram per cm^2 = 980.5966 $dynes/cm^2$
= 0.457592 $poundal/in.^2$
= 0.014223 $pound/in.^2$
= 9.6784×10^{-4} atmosphere

gram per square meter (g/m^2) Weight per unit area.
1 g/m^2 = 0.029 oz/sq yd

Gram-positive *See* **Gram's stain**

Gram's stain A staining method developed by Gram in 1880 which differentiates Gram-positive from Gram-negative bacteria by their ability to retain crystal violet dye.

Negative	Positive
Aerobacter aerogenes	*Clostridium*
E. coli	*Staphyloccus*
Pseudomonas aeruginosa	*Streptococcus*
Salmonella	
Shigella	

See Part 2: Gram Stain; Sanitizing Chemicals; Water Activity, Organisms and Food

Grand Rapids lettuce A leaf lettuce with tightly curled leaves.

Granger A variety of birdsfoot trefoil.

granular tapioca *See* **flake tapioca**

granulated hominy *See* **hominy**

grape (*Vitis vinifera*) A vine which produces fruit used for food and wine; classification is complex and is usually grouped according to the following:
1. wine or dessert
2. outdoor or indoor
3. black or white
4. time of ripening

1 lb seeded = 2 cups (1 cup = 185 g or 6.5 oz)
1 lb seedless = 2½ cups (1 cup = 170 g or 6 oz)
1 qt canned = 2¼ to 3 lb fresh
1 bu = 48 to 50 lb = 16 to 20 qt canned
one 4-qt basket = 6 lb
one 12-qt basket = 18 lb
1 lug (5.75 × 13.5 × 16.5 in.) = 28 lb
1 basket crate (4.75 × 16 × 16.1 in.) = 20 lb

To ripen: Store in open air at room temperature; keep out of sun.
Storage (when ripe): Uncovered (85-90% relative humidity); refrigerate (30-32°F); freezing point 24-27°F; use in 3 to 5 days.
Raw grape composition: 81-82% H_2O, 0.6-1.4% protein, 0.3-1% fat, 15-17% carbohydrate, 0.4% ash, pH 3.4-4.5.
Varieties:
European
- Thompson seedless (green)
- tokay (red)
- cardinal (red)
- emperor (red)

American
- Concord (black)
- Delaware
- catawba

See Part 2: Beverage Carbonated, Ingredients; Flavor Ingredients, Taste and Flavor Type; Flavors, Beverage; Frozen Food Storage; Fruit Availability; Fruit Canning Dates; Fruit Classification; Fruit Composition; Fruit Servings per Pound; Fruit Storage; Minerals, Food; Minerals, Plant or Animal Tissue; Organic Acids in Fruits and Vegetables; Plant Foods, Composition; Rot Spoilage; Standards, Processed Fruit and Vegetable Products; Storage; Sugar, Fruit

grape cheese A mild-flavored, white, buttery-textured cheese; the rind is covered by black grape skin and seeds.

grapefruit (*Citrus paradisi*) A medium-large tree in which the large yellow-rind citrus fruit grows in clusters; the fruit may have a yellow or pinkish pulp with or without seed; consumed fresh, canned in segments, or made into juice and marmalade.
Size:
1 medium-size grapefruit = 4½ in. in diameter = 570 g (1¼ lb)
1 lb fresh (1 medium-size grapefruit) = 1 cup sections (195 g or 6.8 oz)
1 Florida, Texas box (12 × 12 × 24 in.) = 80 lb
1 California box (11.5 × 11.5 × 24 in.) = 64-67 lb
1 case (24) No. 2½ cans = 0.83 box fresh grapefruit
1 serving = ½ grapefruit and sugar

Storage: Unwrapped (80-85% relative humidity); in cool room (32-50°F); use within 1 to 4 weeks; short-term refrigeration is not harmful.

Composition (50% edible):

	H_2O (%)	Protein (%)	Fat (%)	Carbohydrate (%)	Ash (%)	pH
raw pulp	87-89	0.3-0.5	0.1	10-11	0.4	3.0-3.5
juice	89-90	0.5	0.1	9-10	0.2	3.0-3.3

See also **citrus fruit.**
See Part 2: Ascorbic Acid; Calcium, Daily Recommendations; Calories, Daily Recommendations; Flavoring Agents, Natural; Flavors, Beverage; Fruit and Nut Rootstock; Fruit and Vegetables Composition; Food Composition; Fruit, Availability; Fruit Harvest Dates; Fruit Classification; Fruit Composition; Fruit Storage; Fruit Juice Flavors; Microwave Cooking Fruit; Minerals, Food; pH Values of Biological Materials; Plant Foods, Composition; Potassium-Rich Foods; Standards, Processed Fruit and Vegetable Products; Storage; Thiamin; Transit Temperature; Vitamin C

grapefruit oil *See* Part 2: Grapefruit Oil Composition; Grapefruit Oil Properties

grape sugar *See* **glucose**

grape (wine) vinegar A vinegar made from juice of grapes.
Min.: 4% acetic acid; 1% grape solids; 0.13% grape ash.

GRAS Abbreviation of "generally regarded as safe," used by Food and Drug Administration in classifying food additives.

grass Any of a large group of plants of the order *Gramineae*, including cereal grains.

grasser Cattle direct from pasture.

grate To comminute a soft food, especially cheese or nutmeg, by friction against a roughened surface.

gravel Small stones; 1 dry cu ft = 95 lb.
See Part 2: Insulation, Conductivity Values

graves Dry white wine; (also, a red); a wine of fine bouquet and good flavor.

gravimetric analysis An analysis in which results are based upon weight, e.g., specific gravity.

gravitational acceleration The gravity constant $g = 32.1717$ ft/sec/sec.
See Part 2: Constants, Fundamental

gravity A measure of velocities and acceleration.
1 gravity = 980.5966 centimeters per sec per sec
= 32.1717 ft per sec per sec

gravy Cooked meat juice sometimes thickened with flour or cornstarch.
See Part 2: Storage Times

grayfish *See* Part 2: Vitamin A, Fish; Vitamin D, Fish

gray sole *See* **sole**

gray trout *See* **sea trout**

grease Fat with a titer of less than 40°C.

greasewood A plant having a toxic principle.
See Part 2: Poisonous Plants

grease wool Wool that is shorn from sheep and has not been processed.

greater than Symbol used in scientific notations is $>$; greater than or equal to notation is $\geqslant$.

green bug An insect that sucks the sap of small grain.

green clover worm An insect whose larva eats the leaves of soybean.

greengage A variety of plum.

green gram (mung, *Phaseolus aureus*) A tropical pulse that has a pod containing up to 15 seeds that may be green, brown or mottled; used as a pulse or to produce bean sprouts.

greening A variety of apples that is in season from October to January; they are good cooking and sauce apples and fair eating apples.

greenland turbot Common name for food fish, *Reinhardtius hippoglossoides*, a species of *Pleuronectidae*, right-eye flounders.

Green mountain A variety of potato.

greens The leaves of certain vegetables that are cooked and used for food, e.g., beet greens, spinach, etc.
1 lb fresh = 4-6 cups cooked
1 cup cooked = 190 g (6.7 oz)
1½-6 (2 lb avg) lb fresh = 1 qt canned
2-2½ lb fresh = 1 qt frozen
1 bu fresh = 12-18 lb = 3-8 qt canned.
See Part 2: Canned Yield; Minerals, Food; Vegetable Composition; Vegetable Cooking; Vegetable Frozen Yield; Vegetables, Cooking Frozen; Vegetable Storage

green shrimp Raw in-shell shrimp.

green tea Tea made from leaves that have been steamed, rolled and dried without fermentation; fired immediately after picking; lowest in caffeine content.
Types:
gunpowder green: flowery taste, sharp body
panfired Formosa: light in cup, mellow, tart
panfired Japan: sweet, clear and soothing

green white An egg infected with *Pseudomonas*; in the advanced stages the white takes on a greenish cast.

griddle A flat utensil for frying or broiling.
See Part 2: Broiling Griddle, Meat

griddle cake A pancake.
See Part 2: Calories, Daily Recommendations

Griess reagent A mixture of sulfanilic acid and alphanaphthylamine used to develop color in nitrite determinations. *See also* **nitrite.**

grill To broil. *See also* **broil.**

Grimes Golden A variety of apples that are in season from September to December; excellent sauce and eating apples, and fair to good cooking apples.

grind To reduce to small pieces, usually with a machine designed for the purpose.

grits Coarsely ground grain (largely endosperm) from which the bran and germ have been removed. *See also* **corn grits; oat.**

groats Husked oats or wheat.

gross national product (GNP) Total market value of a country's output of final goods and services for a year; can be in either current or constant dollars.

ground beef Comminuted skeletal beef, normally 30% fat; chuck averages 20% fat. *See also* **hamburger.**
See Part 2: Beef Cuts; Beef Retail Yield; Broiling Griddle, Meat; Broiling Meat; Broiling Time and Temperature

ground cherry *See* **gooseberry**

ground glass joint Standard taper all are a 1:10 taper; first number is diameter (in mm) of the large end; second number is length of ground zone (e.g., 24/40 = 24 mm in diameter large end of ground zone and ground zone is 40 mm in length). Ball & socket: first number is ball diameter in mm; second number is inside diameter of tubing.

ground lamb *See* Part 2: Lamb Cuts

ground lean *See* Part 2: Meat Composition

ground limestone A liming material composed of 80-95% $CaCO_3$; each pound has the neutralizing equivalent of 0.85-1.00 lb of $CaCO_3$ (or approximately this quantity of dolomitic limestone).

ground meat Comminuted meat, usually by passing it through a machine equipped with a worm or screw of decreasing flight which forces the meat through a cutting die.
Storage: Coldest part of refrigerator; use within 1 to 2 days.
See Part 2: Meat, Frozen Storage; Meat, Servings per Pound

groundnut *See* **peanut**

groundsel A plant having a toxic principle.
See Part 2: Poisonous Plants

ground substance Aqueous matter containing connective tissue and surrounding the cell.
See Part 2: Connective Tissue Proteins

group (1) One of the major vertical divisions of the Periodic Table of elements. (2) An uncharged combination of two or more elements which acts as a unit in a chemical reaction, e.g., hydroxyl group (OH), sulfate group (SO_4), carbonate group (CO_3), carbonyl group (C=O). When such a group is ionized it acquires an electric charge and is then called a radical. *See also* **alkyl group; aryl group.**

grouper (red, black, yellowfin, speckled hind, gag, scamp) Any of a number of lean fish that resemble the sea bass; caught in the south Atlantic and Gulf.
Raw Composition: 79% H_2O, 19% protein, 0.5% fat, 1.2% ash.

growing season *See* Part 2: Fruit, Growing Season, Storage Life

grub A parasite of cattle which makes holes in the hide in the back area.

grunion smelt *See* **smelt**

gruyère cheese A semi-hard, light-yellow, dessert and cooking cheese from Switzerland; usually sold in small wedges wrapped in foil or flat wheels. It has a nut-like sweet flavor and is made from partly skimmed cow's milk; it is ripened for 3 mo. or more.
See Part 2: Cheese Vitamin Content; Milk and Cheese Composition; Milk and Milk Products, Vitamin Content; Vitamin A, Milk and Milk Products

guaiac (1) An antioxidant used (up to 0.1%) to retard rancidity in fats. (2) A vegetable gum from West Indies.
See Part 2: Antioxidant Structure.

guajillo A plant having a toxic principle.
See Part 2: Poisonous Plants

guanidine A nitrogenous compound found in animal and plant tissue; made by reaction of urea and ammonia.

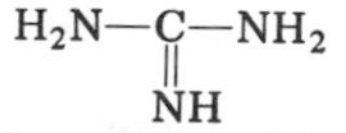

δ-guanidino-α-aminovaleric acid *See* **arginine**

guanine A nitrogenous compound found in animal and vegetable tissue; made by hydrolysis of nucleic acids.

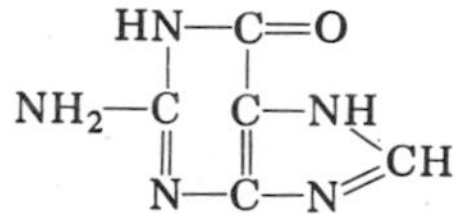

5′-guanosine monophosphate Flavor potentiator; also an important growth factor (nucleotide).

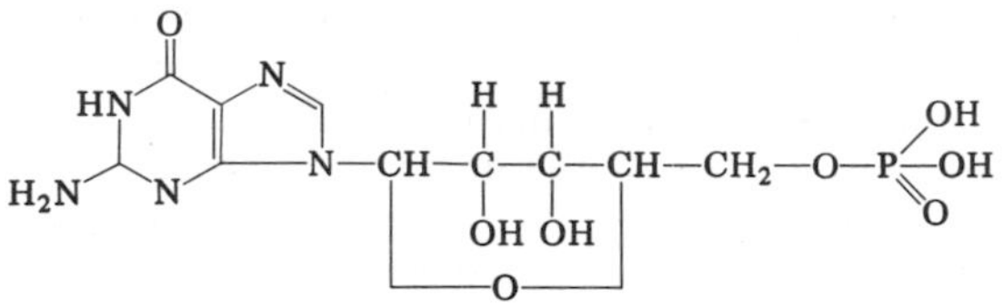

guarana A South American plant used to brew a bitter-tasting drink that has 3 to 5 times as much caffeine as coffee.

guar gum A water-soluble gum obtained from the endosperm of seed of a leguminous plant (*Cyamopsis tetragonolobus*); mol. wt., 200,000-300,000. Used as a suspending agent, thickener, water-binding agent, and texture aid in ice cream; in cakes, pie fillings, cheese, canned food, beverages, icings and dressings; also as livestock feed.
See Part 2: Gums and Gelling Agents; Gum Characteristics; Gums, Physicochemical Properties; Stabilizers, Thickeners

Guatemalan high grown coffee A hard bean coffee that has a light and dry wine-like flavor.

guava (***Psidium guajava***) A small tree that produces a green fruit that becomes yellow when ripe; the pulp (white, yellow, pink or red) is juicy and full of small seeds; can be eaten raw, stewed, made into tarts, jam, jelly, or canned; high in vitamin C content.
Raw Composition: 81-83% H_2O, 1% protein, 0.6% fat, 16% carbohydrate, 0.7% ash.
See Part 2: Fruit Classification; Fruit Composition; Fruit Storage; Plant Foods, Composition

Guernsey A breed of dairy cattle that originated on the island of Guernsey; color is shade of fawn with white markings clearly defined.
See Part 2: Dairy Cattle Breeds; Gestation Periods; Milk Breeds, Composition; Milk Composition

guinea A breed of poultry.
See Part 2: Poultry Class

guinea corn *See* **millet**

guinea grade *See* **poultry grades**

guinea pig A rodent *Cavia cobaya*, much used for experimental work.

gula malacca A brown sugar made from the coconut.

gulose $C_6H_{12}O_6$ A water-soluble syrup that is not fermentable by yeast.
See Part 2: Sugar, D-aldehydo

gum A hydrophilic colloid obtained from tropical trees and shrubs as well as from seaweeds. They are polysaccharides which, when dissolved or dispersed in water, give a viscous solution or dispersion.
See Part 2: Gum Characteristics; Gum Distribution; Gums, Physicochemical Properties; Gums and Gelling Agents; Gums and Gelling Agents, Characteristics; Pentosans; Stabilizers, Thickeners; Water Activity, Organisms and Food

gum acacia *See* **gum arabic**

gum arabic (acacia, gum acacia) A dried gummy exudation from branches of the *Acacia* tree grown in the Sudan area of Africa; a mixture of Ca, Mg and K salts of arabic acid. Used as a stabilizer, thickener and emulsifier.
See Part 2: Gum Characteristics; Gum Distribution; Gums, Physicochemical Properties; Stabilizers, Thickeners

gumbo A soup thickened with filé or okra. *See also* **okra.**

gum dragon *See* **gum tragacanth**

gum gatto *See* **locust bean gum**

gum ghatti (gatty gum; ghatti gum; Indian gum) A polysaccharide exudate from the *Anogeissus latifolia* tree.
See Part 2: Gum Distribution; Gums and Gelling Agents

gum karaya (*Sterculia*, Indian tragacanth, India gum) Dried exudate from the *Sterculia urens* tree grown in India; mol. wt. 9,500,000; used as emulsifier in dairy frozen desserts, cheese, meat sausages, bakery products, and salad dressings.
See Part 2: Gums and Gelling Agents; Gum Characteristics; Gum Distribution; Gums, Physicochemical Properties

gumming Polymerization of fat caused by heating; forms an insoluble syrupy material; occurs more often in unsaturated fatty acids.

gummy An old ewe with incisor teeth broken or missing.

gum rosin Rosin remaining after distillation of gum spirits of turpentine.

gum spirits of turpentine Spirits of turpentine made from the oleoresin from a tree of the pine species.

gum tragacanth (Syrian gum, bassora gum, goat's horn, leaf gum) Exudate from *Astragalus* bush which yields the highest viscosities at the lowest concentration for edible gums; used for emulsions in food industry.

gum tragans Edible gum secretion of a shrub.
See Part 2: Gum Characteristics

gum tragon *See* **locust bean gum**

gunpowder green *See* **green tea**

guns *See* **stitches**

gur *See* **sugar cane**

gut bread The pancreas.

Guthion Proprietary name for a poisonous insecticide of the phosphorus ester type.

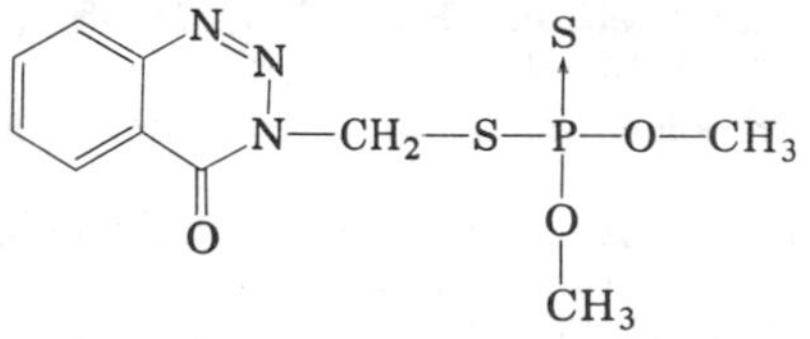

Guzerat A strain of Brahman cattle.

gypsum A fertilizer material used to supply calcium; 85% $CaSO_4$.
See Part 2: Fertilizer Materials

H

H Symbol for the element hydrogen.

ha Abbreviation for hectare.

haché Minced.

hackamore A rope halter.

hackery Ox cart.

Hackney A pony not over 14.2 hands; shown only at 2-trot speeds: park pace, trot on; docked tails; manes braided close to neck; pulls a viceroy (4-wheeled coach).

haddock [scrod (baby)] A lean fish similar to but smaller than the cod; caught in the North Atlantic.
Raw Composition: 80% H_2O, 18% protein, 0.1% fat, 1.4% ash.
See also **demersal fish.**
See Part 2: Fish and Shellfish Composition; Fish, Smoke-Cured; Fish, Storage; Frozen Food Storage; Minerals, Food

hafnium (Hf) A metallic element; at. no. 72; at. wt. 178.50; Group IVB of the Periodic Table; oxidation state +4; electron configuration 2-8-18-32-10-2
orbit K L M N O P

haggerel *See* **hoggett**

hair felt *See* Part 2: Insulation

hairy A variety of vetch.

hake (white, silver, red, squirrel, ling, deep-sea fillet) A lean codlike fish with a fin under the throat; used for food and oil; caught in Gulf of St. Lawrence.
Raw Composition: 82% H_2O, 16.5% protein, 0.4% fat, 1.3% ash.

halal To slaughter food animals under Moslem law.

half-and-half A mixture of approximately 50% whole milk and 50% cream.
See Part 2: Dairy Terms

half-life (half-value) (1) The time required for an unstable substance to lose half of its radioactivity. (2) The time required for half of a particular tissue to be replaced.

halibut A lean large flat fish caught on the Pacific coast and in the North Atlantic. Atlantic halibut is *Hippoglossus hippoglossus*; Pacific halibut is *Hippoglossus stenolepis*.
Raw Composition: 74–78% H_2O, 16–20% protein, 1–8% fat, 1–1.4% ash.
See also **demersal fish.**
See Part 2: Frozen Food Storage; Minerals, Food; Vitamin D, Fish

halibut liver oil (haliver oil) An oil obtained by steaming the livers of halibut or flounder; rich in vitamin A. A dietary supplement.

halite Rock salt.

halogen A group of electronegative elements (Group VIIA of Periodic Table); it includes fluorine, chlorine, bromine and iodine.

halogeton A plant having a toxic principle.
See Part 2: Poisonous Plants

halophilic Descriptive of microorganisms that will grow only if a very high salt concentration is present; salt-loving.
See Part 2: Water Activity, Organisms and Food

ham Hind thigh area of a pork carcass; it may be cut in several lengths depending on desired size of the ham; a short-cut skinned ham is about 18% of the carcass.
Storage: Original wrapper; refrigerate; ½ ham or slices should be used in 3 to 5 days; whole ham should be used in 1 week.
See Part 2: Broiling Griddle, Meat; Broiling Meat; Broiling Time and Temperature; Calories, Daily Recommendations; Cooking in Liquid, Time; Ham Carving; Ham, Curing; Meat and Meat Products Composition; Meat Composition; Meat, Frozen Storage; Meat Identification; Meat, Servings Per Pound; Meat Storage; Microwave Processing Time; Pork Carcass, Retail Yield; Pork Chart; Pork Cookery; Pork, Cooking; Pork, Cooking Methods; Pork Cooking Yield; Pork Cuts; Pork Cuts and Uses; Pork Storage; Pork Wholesale Cuts; Pork Yield; Portion Size; Riboflavin, Food; Roasting Meat; Roasting, Time and Temperature; Simmering Meat; Spoilage, Protein Foods; Storage Times; Water Activity, Organisms and Food

ham beetle (*Corynetes rufipes*) Larva found in cured hams.

ham, boiled A deboned and defatted ham is placed in a press mold; cooked in a water bath of 165°-185°F to internal temp. of 142°-150°F; pressure on ham is increased while ham is cooling.

hamburger (hamburg) Ground skeletal beef; max. 30% fat. *See also* **ground beef.**
Storage: Coldest part of refrigerator; use within 1 to 2 days.
See Part 2: Frozen Food Storage; Meat Composition; Portion Size; Potassium-Rich Foods

ham capocollo Ham used to prepare capocollo.

ham, cured Regular smoked product: finished smoked weight will not exceed fresh uncured weight; water-added product: *water* not in excess of 10% of fresh uncured wt; must be so labeled, other curing ingredients are not included in this 10% so total added substances might be 12–14%.

Hamlin A variety of early Florida oranges.

Hamprace *See* Montana No. 1

Hampshire (hog) A meat-type breed of hog that originated in Southern England, probably from the Norfolk Thin Rind Hog; the hog is black with a 6-inch white belt that encircles the shoulders and includes the 2 front legs.
See Part 2: Swine Breeds

Hampshire (sheep) A medium-wool, mutton-type breed of sheep originating in South-Central England from the Weltshire and Berkshire Knot breeds; has a dark brown to black face, with no horns and a fleece grade of about ¼.
See Part 2: Sheep Breeds

ham roll Ham used to prepare capocollo.

ham skipper An insect that feeds on stored meat and cheese.

hamster A small rodent, *Cricetus cricetus*, used for experimental feeding tests.

hamstringing Cutting of the Achilles tendon.

hand (1) A 4-inch measurement (hand width) used to measure a horse's height at its shoulder. (2) A cluster of bananas on the original stem.

hand cheese Cheese that has a pungent odor and sharp flavor.

hanging tender A pillar of the diaphragm muscle located close to the kidney and is used as a by-product item; on the left or "open" side of a beef carcass; usual weight is 3–4 lbs.
See Part 2: Beef Retail Yield; Beef Wholesale Cuts

hank (1) (Casing). *See also* **sheep casing.** (2) (Cotton) 840 yd. (3) Woollen yarn, 560 yd.

Hanss A variety of clingstone peaches.

Hanus iodine number *See* **iodine value analysis**

hard butter A processed fat with high solid fat index, brittle at room temperature, narrow melting range; used in confections.

hard cider *See* **cider**

hard coal Anthracite.

hard glass Glass with a high melting point, a low coefficient of expansion, that will withstand thermal shock.

hardhead *See* **croaker**

hardness Resistance of a material to penetration by any of several types of needle-like instruments. Hardness of metals is measured with the Rockwell and Brinell testers; softer materials are measured with the Shore Durometer.

hardness (water) A measure (in ppm) of the presence of bicarbonates, sulfates, chlorides, and silicates of calcium, magnesium and iron in the water which form insoluble precipitates with soap; a precipitation of the salts can be obtained by the following:

Heat:

$$Ca(HCO_3)_2 \xrightarrow{\Delta} CaCO_3 + H_2O + CO_2$$

Lime:

$$Ca(HCO_3)_2 + Ca(OH)_2 \longrightarrow 2CaCO_3 + 2H_2O$$

Washing soda:

$$Ca(HCO_3)_2 + Na_2CO_3 \longrightarrow CaCO_3 + 2NaHCO_3$$

$$CaSO_4 + Na_2CO_3 \longrightarrow CaCO_3 + Na_2SO_4$$

Phosphates:

$$3Ca(HCO_3)_2 + 2Na_3PO_4 \longrightarrow Ca_3(PO_4)_2 + 6NaHCO_3$$

$$3CaSO_4 + 2Na_3PO_4 \longrightarrow Ca_3(PO_4)_2 + 3Na_2SO_4$$

Silicate:

$$Ca(HCO_3)_2 + Na_2O \cdot Al_2O_3 \cdot 2SiO_2 \cdot 6H_2O \longrightarrow CaO \cdot Al_2O_3 \cdot 2SiO_2 \cdot 6H_2O + 2NaHCO_3$$

Regeneration of silicate:

$$CaO \cdot Al_2O_3 \cdot 2SiO_2 \cdot 6H_2O + 2NaCl \longrightarrow Na_2O \cdot Al_2O_3 \cdot 2SiO_2 \cdot 6H_2O + CaCl_2$$

See Part 2: Water, Hardness

hard radiation Radiation of extremely short wavelength, including certain x-rays, gamma rays and cosmic rays.

hardtack Flat-shaped, low-moisture, crisp bread made from whole meal grain; air is incorporated by whipping or yeast fermentation.

hard-wheat flour Dough made from this flour has a "rubbery" consistency and thus can hold the carbon dioxide evolved from the leavening agent; it is thus a good bread flour.

hardwood Wood from deciduous trees.
See Part 2: Fuel, Heating Value

hare A large rodent with longer ears and legs than a rabbit.
See Part 2: Gestation Periods

haricot (1) A dish of meat. (2) Seed of string bean.

haricot bean (*Phaseolus vulgaris*) A bean grown for the ripe seed (brown or white) which are usually dried; dried seeds store well and are soaked in water before cooking; used to make Boston baked beans and cassoulet.

haricot, vert Green string beans.

Harris hematoxylin 1 gram of hematoxylin is dissolved in 10 ml absolute alcohol; add this to a warm solution of 20 g ammonia alum in 200 ml H_2O; boil and add 0.5 g mercuric oxide; boil 1 minute and cool rapidly under faucet; just before using, add 4% acetic acid; keeps well.

harrow A toothed (may or may not have springs) framework tool used to break the soil; a disk harrow consists of circular rotating knives attached to a mandrel and pulled by a tractor.

hasen pfeffer A rabbit dish containing vinegar, pepper, sour cream and a number of seasonings.

haver Oats.

Haversian canals Blood vessel carrying canals in compact bone.

Hawaiian *See* Part 2: Salad Dressing and Mayonnaise Variations

hay Mowed and cured grass and clover.
Space requirements: Loose, equal 3.3 to 4.4 lb per cubic foot; baled, 6 to 10 lb per cubic foot; chopped, 5 to 7 lb per cubic foot. Should not be stored while damp.
See Part 2: Nutrients in Crops

hazel (cob), (*Corylus avellana*) A small tree that produces nuts, in clusters (1 to 4), that are ¾ inch long, have a hard brown shell and are enclosed in a husk; similar to a filbert. *See also* **filbert.**
See Part 2: Minerals, Food; Protein Factors

Hb Symbol for hemoglobin.

H-band A light area in the center of the A-band in muscle fiber.

H broth Used for preparation of the "H" agglutination antigen for identification of the *Salmonella* group.
See Part 2: Microorganism, Media

He Symbol for the element helium.

head (1) The close-packed involuted leaves of certain vegetables (lettuce, cabbage, etc.). *See* Part 2: Pork Cuts and Uses; Poultry Dressing Percentage

head cheese Hog head (jaws, eyes, and ears removed); jowl, hearts and tongues are cooked, ground, seasoned and placed in crocks to jell; eaten cold.
See Part 2: Pork Cuts and Uses; Sausage Identification; Sausage Nutritive Value; Sausage, Types

head cheese and sulze (souce) (souse) A sausage product made from meat and/or snouts and/or tongues of hogs, cattle or sheep; contains added gelatin, salt, vinegar, sugar, spices, sodium or potassium nitrate and nitrite; max. 40% gelatin in finished product.

heart The muscular structure that functions as a blood pump in the body. The fibers are branched, multinucleated, small in diameter, and contain intercalated discs.
Blood flow is to:

1. extremities
2. superior and inferior vena cava
3. right auricle
4. right ventricle
5. pulmonary artery
6. lungs
7. pulmonary vein
8. left auricle
9. left ventricle
10. aorta
11. extremities

Animal hearts may be cooked and used for food.
See Part 2: Beef Cuts and Uses; Calories, Daily Recommendations; Gland Weights; Iron, Daily Recommendations; Lamb Cuts and Uses; Meat Composition; Meat, Servings Per Pound; Minerals, Food; Nicotinic Acid, Food; Organ Weights; Pork Cooking Yield; Pork Cuts and Uses; Poultry Dressing Percentage; Thiamin, Food; Variety Meat, Cooking; Variety Meat Percentage of Daily Recommended Allowances; Variety Meat Preparation; Veal Cuts and Uses; Vitamin A, Food

heart beat

	resting rate (per min)
horses	35–40
oxen	40–60
hogs	55–75
sheep	60–80
goats	60–80

heart infusion agar *See* Part 2: Microorganism, Culture Media, Dairy and Food Products; Microorganism, Media

heat A period of sexual excitement in animals that occurs in cycles. Its indications are:

1. nervousness
2. bellowing
3. drop in milk
4. riding or being ridden
5. discharge of mucous
6. vulva red and swollen

See also **gestation period** for time interval for animals.

heat evolution Heat (BTU's) produced during storage of fruit per unit weight per unit time.
See Part 2: Fruit Storage

heating *See* Part 2: Fuel, Heating Value

heat transfer (1) The rate at which heat moves into and through a solid or liquid; it is of primary importance in cooking, baking and canning. (2) The rate at which heat is conducted away from a mechanical system by a coolant.

heavy calfskin A calfskin weighing between 9 and 15 lb.

heavy cowhide A cowhide weighing over 53 lb.

heavy steer hide A steer hide weighing more than 58 lb.

heavy water Deuterium oxide, D_2O.

hectare (ha) A measure of surface area.
1 hectare = 107,638.7 sq feet (sq ft)
= 15,499,969 sq inches (sq in.)
= 11,959.95 sq yards (sq yd)
= 10,000 sq meters (m^2)
= 2.47106 acres (Br.)
= 2.47104 acres (A) (U.S.)
= 0.01 sq. kilometer (km^2)
= 0.003861 sq mile statute

hecto- Prefix for quantities 100 times larger than the base unit.

hectogram (hg) A unit of metric weight.
1 hectogram = 100 grams
= 10 dekagrams (dkg)
= 3.527 ounces (av.)

hectoliter (hl) A unit of metric volume.
1 hectoliter = 100 liters
= 10 dekaliters
= 2.838 bushels (U.S.)

heel flies *See* **ox warbles**

heel of round A boneless roast made from the area to the rear of the stifle joint; the round muscles are considerably smaller in this area and, therefore, it contains a large amount of connective tissue.
See Part 2: Beef, Boneless Cuts

heifer Bovine female that has not produced a calf; desirable age at time of first breeding: Jersey 16 mo., Guernsey 18 mo., Ayrshire 19 mo., Holstein 20 mo.

hektòen enteric agar *See* Part 2: Microorganism, Media

helianthin *See* **methyl orange**

helium (He) A gaseous element; at. no. 2; at. wt. 4.003; oxidation state 0; noble gas group of Periodic Table; electron configuration 2
orbit K

hematoxylin A blue stain ($C_{16}H_{14}O_6 + 3H_2O$) containing logwood dye. *See also* **Harris hematoxylin; iron-hematoxylin solution.**

hemi- Prefix meaning one-half.

hemicellulose A carbohydrate of plants that is intermediate between cellulose and simple sugars.

hemlock A coniferous tree having a toxic principle.
See Part 2: Poisonous Plants

hemmes 7-in medium Media used for the differentiation of *Shigella* and *Salmonella* type organisms.
See Part 2: Microorganism, Media

hemoglobin (Hb) Oxygen-carrying red pigment of blood; a protein-iron complex.
See Part 2: Histochemical Tests; Blood

hemophilus *See* Part 2: Microorganism, Media

hemopoiesis The process by which blood cells are formed.

hemorrhagic septicemia *See* **shipping fever**

hemp A vegetable fiber composed primarily of cellulose; used for cordage.

hempseed oil A drying oil similar to linseed oil.
See Part 2: Iodine and Saponification Values; Protein Factors; Seed, Chemical Composition; Titer, Fats and Oils; Unsaponifiable Matter; Unsaturated Fatty Acids

hen A mature female bird 1 year or older.

henry A measure of inductance; 1 henry will induce a counter emf of 1 volt when current changes at the rate of 1 ampere per second.

heparin A complex carbohydrate acid that is an anticoagulant for blood; it is prepared (isolated) from liver and lungs; 1 International Unit (World Health Organization) = 1 U.S.P. unit.

hepatitis A disease of the liver.
See Part 2: Infectious Diseases, Food-Borne

hepta- Prefix meaning 7.

heptachlor A poisonous chlorinated hydrocarbon insecticide. Use on food crops prohibited.

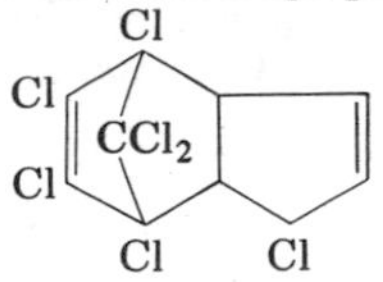

herb A plant whose seed, stems, leaves, flowers or roots are used for seasoning food. It may be annual, biennial or perennial; belongs to one of the following families: Boraginaceae (borage family), Compositae (aster family), Cruciferae (mustard family), Labitae (mint family), Liliaceae (lily family), Umbelliferae (parsley family). Maximum shelf-life of dried herbs, approximately 8 months; ¼ to ⅓ part dried herb = 1 part minced fresh herb.
See Part 2: Herb Vinegars; Minerals (Trace), Limits; Salad Dressing and Mayonnaise Variations

herbe royale *See* **basil**

herbicide Weed killer.

herds grass *See* **redtop**

Hereford (cattle) A breed of beef cattle that is red with a white face and underline; have horns that curve outward and downward; origin, Hereford, England; originally imported to America by Henry Clay, Lexington, Ky.; *See also* **Double Standard Polled Hereford; Polled Hereford; Single Standard Polled Hereford.**
See Part 2: Gestation Periods

Hereford (hogs) A breed of meat-type hogs that is red with white faces and underlines.
See Part 2: Swine Breeds

Hereford-Aberdeen-Angus cross *See* **Aberdeen-Angus-Hereford cross**

Herellea A coccoid bacteria, often occurring as a diplococci, which has the ability to oxidize carbohydrate.
See Part 2: Microorganism, Media

herkimer A type of cheddar cheese.

herring Any of several similar species of pelagic food fish found in the North Atlantic and North Pacific; they include sardines, shads, etc. Some types are salted and pickled; others are canned. The % of fat content varies greatly with the season of the year. *See also* **pelagic fish.**
Raw Composition: 69-79% H_2O, 17% protein, 2-11% fat, 1-2% ash.
See Part 2: Fish Cross Section; Fish, Smoke-Cured; Fish, Storage; Minerals, Food; Nicotinic

Acid, Food; Riboflavin, Food; Thiamin, Food; Vitamin A, Fish; Vitamin A, Food; Vitamin D, Fish; Vitamin D, Food

herring oil A edible fish oil obtained from herring.
See Part 2: Fats and Oils, Physical and Chemical Properties; Fats and Oils, Characteristics; Iodine and Saponification Values; Unsaturated Fatty Acids

hesperidium A subdivision of simple fruit; it has a fleshy ovary wall enclosing one or more seeds, attached to a fleshy placenta, and a leathery rind, e.g., citrus fruit.
See Part 2: Fruit Classification

Hessian fly An insect that damages the central shoot of small grain. Control: sow late in fall.

hetero- A prefix meaning unlike or dissimilar.

heterocyclic A cyclic organic compound having one or more atoms of an element other than carbon in the ring. The other element is usually nitrogen.

heterogeneous A mixture of two or more substances, whether or not they are uniformly dispersed. Milk is a heterogeneous system, even when "homogenized." Heterogeneous systems can be separated by mechanical means. *See also* **homogeneous.**

HETP (hexaethyl tetraphosphate) A poisonous organic phosphorus insecticide containing 10-20% TEPP.

hexa- Prefix meaning 6.

hexacosanoic acid (cerotic acid) $CH_3(CH_2)_{24}COOH$ A saturated fatty acid occurring in beeswax, carnauba wax, etc.
See Part 2: Saturated Fatty Acids

hexadecatrienoic acid *See* Part 2: Unsaturated Fatty Acids

hexadecanoic acid (palmitic acid) $CH_3(CH_2)_{14}COOH$ A saturated fatty acid occurring in natural fats and oils.
See Part 2: Saturated Fatty Acids

hexadecenoic acid (palmitoleic acid) $CH_3(CH_2)_5CH{=}CH(CH_2)_7COOH$ An unsaturated fatty acid found in many fats.
See Part 2: Milk, Fatty Acids, Seasonal; Unsaturated Fatty Acids

hexadienoic acid *See* **sorbic acid**

hexametaphosphate A cleaning agent that has excellent calcium sequestering power; magnesium lowers this sequestering power. It is unstable under high temperatures and high alkaline conditions. *See also* **phosphate; Calgon.**
See Part 2: Phosphate

hexanoic acid (caproic acid) $CH_3(CH_2)_4COOH$ A saturated fatty acid in milk fat (2%).
See Part 2: Saturated Fatty Acids

hexose A 6-carbon sugar.
See Part 2: Maple Syrup Composition

Hf Symbol for the element hafnium.

Hg Symbol for the element mercury (Latin hydrargyrum).

hickory nut (*Carya*) A sweet, edible nut produced by a hardwood tree of the walnut family; 50 lb/bu.
Composition: 3% H_2O, 13% protein, 69% fat, 13% carbohydrate, 2% ash.
See Part 2: Minerals, Food

hide An animal pelt. Cattle hides weigh over 30 lb after curing, skins under 30 lb).
See Part 2: Hide Curing; Hide, Layers; Hides, Salt Absorption

Highland *See* Part 2: Beef and Dual-purpose Cattle

hilus Opening in the capsule of an organ through which the blood vessels and tubes pass.

hind foot *See* Part 2: Bone

hind quarter The rear portion of a beef carcass that is usually separated between the 12th and 13th ribs; it is approximately 48% of the side; it contains the following wholesale cuts: round, rump, loin end, short loin, flank, kidney, and suet.

hind saddle A wholesale cut of veal or lamb consisting of all behind the 12th rib; the two quarters are not split.

hind shank A cut of beef or lamb.
See Part 2: Beef, Boneless Cuts; Beef Cuts; Beef Round, Bone Structure; Bone; Lamb Chart

hind shank bone An animal bone made up of tibia and fibula.

hinny A hybrid animal produced by crossing a stallion with a jennet.

hip (haunch) Region of articulation of femur with pelvis; lateral part of pelvis.
See Part 2: Bone; Lamb, Wholesale Cuts; Meat Identification; Pork Wholesale Cuts; Veal Wholesale Cuts

hip bone *See* **ilium**

hip joint The femero-pelvic joint; there is a strong central ligament attachment.

hip loin *See* **loin end**

hiragonic acid $C_{16}H_{20}O_2$; a liquid, unsaturated (3 double bonds) fatty acid found in sardine oil.
See Part 2: Unsaturated Fatty Acids

histidine A nonessential amino acid;

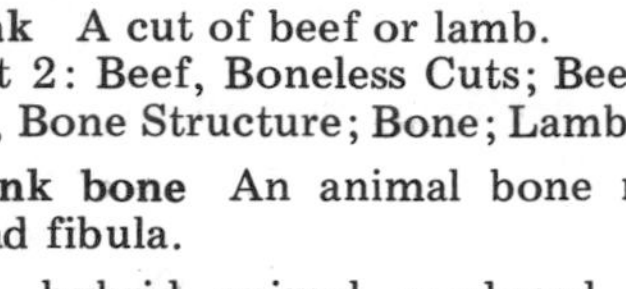

See Part 2: Amino Acids; Amino Acid, Solubilities; Corn, Amino Acids; Egg Products, Nutritive Value; Grain Analysis; Manure Analysis; Seed, Chemical Composition; Wheat, Amino Acids; Wheat Products, Amino Acid Compositions

histochemistry Study of the composition of plant and animal tissues.
See Part 2: Histochemical Test

histogram A graphical presentation of a frequency distribution table.

histology A microscopic study of tissue.

histone A simple protein which is strongly basic, coagulable by heat, soluble in water, dilute acids or alkalis, but insoluble in dilute ammonia.

HMM Heavy meromyosin.

Ho Symbol for the element holmium.

hock (1) A large joint half-way down the hind leg of a horse; the tibia-tarsal joint.
See Part 2: Bone; Pork Carcass, Retail Yield; Pork Chart; Pork Cookery; Pork, Cooking; Pork Cooking Methods; Pork Cuts; Pork Yield; Veal Wholesale Cuts
(2) A wine containing 10% alcohol by volume.

hoechst A mineral wax obtained by oxidizing montan (hydrocarbon extracted from lignites).
See Part 2: Wax

hog Swine of either sex, 120 lb or over in weight; average dressing percentage 70% (68-75%); average 57% excluding lard.
See Part 2: Gland Weights; Swine Breeds; Swine Market Classes and Grades; Teeth Eruption

hog bung *See* **casing (hog bung)**

hog dressed Lamb carcass with the head and pelt left on but with feet and viscera removed. *See also* **hog style.**

hogget (1) A yearling male sheep that has never been shorn. (2) A 1 to 2-year old boar.

hog grades
U.S. #1 proper finish
U.S. #2 excessive finish
U.S. #3 overfinish
U.S. #4 extremely overfinished
Utility underfinished and low quality

hogshead (hhd.) (U.S.) A measure of tobacco; (burley) approx. 950 lb.
1 hogshead = 238.48 liters
= 63 gallons (U.S.); also sometimes from 100 to 140 wine gallons
= 8.42184 cubic feet

hog style A method of dressing veal in which the skin is left on the carcasses.

Holland An American class of chickens that lays a light-colored egg; varieties: White, Barred.

holmium (Ho) A rare earth metallic element; at. no. 67; at. wt. 164.94; Group III B of Periodic Table; oxidation state +3; electron configuration 2-8-18-29-8-2
orbit K L M N O P

Holstein *See* **Holstein-Friesian**

holsteiner A farmer sausage with ends tied together.

Holstein-Friesian A dairy-type breed of cattle that originated in northern part of the Netherlands; commonly called Holstein in North America and Friesian in other countries; color is black and white, areas clearly defined.
See Part 2: Dairy Cattle Breeds; Gestation Periods; Milk Breeds, Composition; Milk Composition

hominy A cereal made from dry corn kernels.
See also **corn; corn grits.**
Types:
pearl: whole grain, hulls removed mechanically;
lye: whole grain, hulls removed by caustic soda solution;
granulated: ground form;
grits: broken grains.
1 cup (raw) = 6 oz; pH 3.9; lye type 6.8 to 8.0.
See Part 2: Cereal Composition; Minerals, Food

homo- Prefix meaning "the same."

homocyclic A ring compound in which all the atoms in the ring are the same element, e.g., benzene.

homogeneous From the Latin words meaning "the same kind," this often misused term refers properly to substances that are of identical constitution throughout and that cannot be mechanically separated, i.e., chemical compounds. It is loosely used to mean mixtures that are uniformly dispersed in each other, but which can be separated by mechanical means. For example, copper sulfate and sucrose are homogeneous, but an alcohol-water solution is heterogeneous. *See also* **compound; mixture.**

homogenized milk Milk in which the fat globules have been mechanically reduced to approximately the same size so that they form a stable emulsion; it is, however, a heterogeneous system. *See also* **heterogeneous.**
See Part 2: Dairy Terms

homologous series A series of organic compounds which differ only by a CH_2 group, e.g., methane, ethane, propane, etc.

honey A plant nectar and saccharine which has been collected and modified by the honey bee (*Apis mellifica* and *A. dorsata*); contains primarily levulose (fructose) and dextrose (glucose).
Composition: not more than 8% sucrose (normally 2%, range ½-8%); not more than 25% water (avg 18%); not more than 0.25% ash; 0-10% dextrin; 65-80% dextrose and levulose.
Flavor and color vary according to nectar collected from the plants.
1 cup = 330 g (11.7 oz); 1 cup honey can be substituted by 1¼ cups sugar and ¼ cup water.
Storage: Unopened, room temperature; opened, refrigerate; if crystals form, dissolve by putting container in hot water.
Strained composition; 17% H_2O (maximum 18.6%), 0.3% protein, 0% fat, 82% carbohydrate, 0.2% ash, pH 3.9.
Properties: Specific gravity 20/20°C 1.4225; viscosity ca.70 poises; weight per gallon 11 lb 13 oz; calories 1380/lb; color, 7 classes but not a factor in grading.

See Part 2: Flavor Ingredients, Taste and Flavor Type; Honey Composition; Minerals, Food; Riboflavin, Food; Storage, Dry; Sugars and Sweets Composition; Sugars and Syrups Composition; Sweetness of Sweeteners; Sweetening Agents; Sweetening Compounds

honeyball *See* Part 2: Fruit and Vegetable Diseases

honeycomb Hexagonal waxy cells built by honeybees. *See also* **reticulum.**

honeydew melon A white muskmelon.
See Part 2: Fruit and Vegetable, Diseases; Fruit, Availability; Storage; Sugar, Vegetables; Transit Temperature; Vegetable Storage

honey loaf A meat loaf that contains a minimum of 5% honey.
See Part 2: Sausage Identification

honeysuckle A flower frequented by honey bees; when eaten by cattle, it gives an off-flavor to milk.

hoof The horny terminal portion of the feet of horses and cattle.

hoof and mouth disease *See* **foot and mouth disease**

hooks Points of the hips.

hop ***Humulus lupulus*** A flower used in beer production. It is a perennial vine of the hemp family that is grown on a framework; resin glands at the base of the bracteoles produce lupulin and its essential oil and soft resins which together flavor beer.
Storage: 28-32°F, 50-60% relative humidity; will keep several months.
See Part 2: Flavoring Agents, Natural; Minerals, Trace, Limits; Wastes, Agricultural and Industrial

hop clover An annual early spring growing grass.

Hopkins-Cole Test A test for the tryptophan radical or the protein containing this radical; a purplish color is developed when this radical is treated with a magnesium glyoxylate reagent.
See Part 2: Protein and Amino Acids, Color Reactions

horehound (hoarhound) A weedy-looking perennial herb.

hormone Any of several organic substances secreted from the endocrine glands; they exercise specific control over the conduct, character and development of the body. Examples are thyroxine, pituitrin, adrenalin.
(sex) hormones:

	Male (androgens)	Female (estrogens)
natural	testosterone androsterone	estradiol estrone progesterone
synthetic		stilbestrol hexoestrol

hors d'oeuvres Colorful and attractive dishes used as appetizers; French term for relish.

horse An animal of the equine family; male is called a stallion or a horse (less common); castrated male is a gelding; female is a mare.
See Part 2: Bone; Gestation Periods; Liver; Milk, Mammals, Composition; Molds, Mycotoxins; Reproductive Cycle; Teeth Eruption

horsebrush A plant having a toxic principle.
See Part 2: Poisonous Plants

horse fat *See* Part 2: Iodine and Saponification Values; Melting Points, Fats and Oils; Specific Gravities, Fats and Oils; Titer, Fats and Oils

horsefly (gadfly) The family *Tabanidae* of flies that sucks the blood of animals.

horsemeat *See* Part 2: Meat and Meat Products Composition

horse mule A male mule.

horse nettle A plant having a toxic principle.
See Part 2: Poisonous Plants

horsepower (boiler) = 33,479 British thermal units per hour = 9.803 kilowatts.

horsepower (metric) (cheval vapeur) (75 kg-m/sec) A measure of power, rate of energy and heat.
metric hp = 735.448 watts (10^7 ergs/sec)
= 542.475 foot-pounds per second (ft-lb/sec)
= 75 kilogram meters per second (kg-m/sec)
= 0.98632 U.S. horsepower (550 ft-lb/sec)
= 0.73545 kilowatt (kw)
= 0.69718 Btu/sec (thermal unit per sec)
= 0.17569 kg-calory/sec (thermal unit per sec)

horsepower (U.S.) (550 ft-lb/sec) (hp) A measure of power, rate of energy and heat.
1 U.S. hp = 33,000 foot-pounds per min
= 2545.08 Btu (mean)/hour
= 745.650 watts (10^7 ergs/sec)
= 550 foot-pounds per second (ft-lb/sec)
= 76.0404 kilogram meters per second (kg-m/sec)
= 42.4176 Btu/min
= 10.688 kg-calory (mean)/minute
= 1.01387 metric horsepower (75 kg-m/sec)
= 0.74565 kilowatt (kw)
= 0.70685 Btu/sec (thermal unit per sec)
= 0.17812 kg-calory/sec (thermal unit per sec)
= 7.457×10^{-9} erg/sec

horsepower-hour (75 kg-m-hr) (metric) A measure of heat, energy, work.
1 metric horsepower-hour = 2,647,610 joules (10^7 ergs) (j)
= 1,952,910 foot pounds (ft-lb)
= 270,000 kilogram meters (kg-m)

= 2,509.83 Btu (thermal units)
= 632.467 kg-calory (thermal units)
= 0.98632 U.S. horsepower-hour (hp-hr)
= 0.73545 kilowatt hour (kw-hr)

horsepower-hour (U.S.) (hp-hr) A measure of heat, energy, work.
1 U.S. hp-hr = 2,684,340 joules (10^7 ergs) (j)
= 1,980,000 foot pounds (ft-lb)
= 273,745 kilogram meters (kg-m)
= 2,544.65 Btu (thermal units)
= 641.240 kg-calory (thermal units)
= 1.01387 metric horsepower-hours (75 kg-m-hr)
= 0.74565 kilowatt hour (kw-hr)

horseradish A condiment made from the root of *Armoracia lapathifolia* or *A. rusticana*. An off-white sauce (pH 5.3) is made from it by crushing or powdering the root with cooking vinegar, milk and seasoning.
See Part 2: Flavoring Agents, Natural; Minerals, Food; Storage

horse-shoe sausage *See* **holsteiner**

hotel rack *See* **rib rack**
See Part 2: Lamb Chart

hothouse lambs 30 to 60-pound lambs (6 to 10 weeks old) dropped between Oct. and Jan. and sold between Christmas and Easter; Grades; Extra Fancy, Fancy, Good, Fair, Plain; usually hog dressed; the pluck and liver are usually left in the carcass.
See Part 2: Sheep Market Classes and Grades

hot salt cure A meat-curing procedure using saltpeter, sugar and hot salt.

H_2S test strip *See* Part 2: Microorganism, Media

Hubbard A winter variety of squash.

huckleberry An insipid berry used in pies and preserves.
See Part 2: Fruit Classification; Fruit Frozen Yield; Minerals, Food

hull The outer protective layer of a seed or berry.
See Part 2: Corn Kernel; Rice Kernel

humane slaughter (1) All animals are rendered insensible to pain by: a single blow, gunshot, electrical, chemical or other means that is rapid and effective before being shackled, hoisted, thrown, cast, or cut. (2) Loss of consciousness by anemia of the brain caused by simultaneous severance of the carotid arteries with a sharp instrument.

humectant A liquid that absorbs moisture from the air and thus maintains constant humidity in a closed container. Glycerol and propylene glycol are examples. *See also* **hygroscopic**.

humerus Upper forearm bone between scapula and ulna.
See Part 2: Bone

humidity Degree of moisture in the air or other gas.
absolute humidity: grains/cu ft
relative humidity: % of moisture in a gas compared to saturated (100%) gas
See Part 2: Humidity, Solutions.

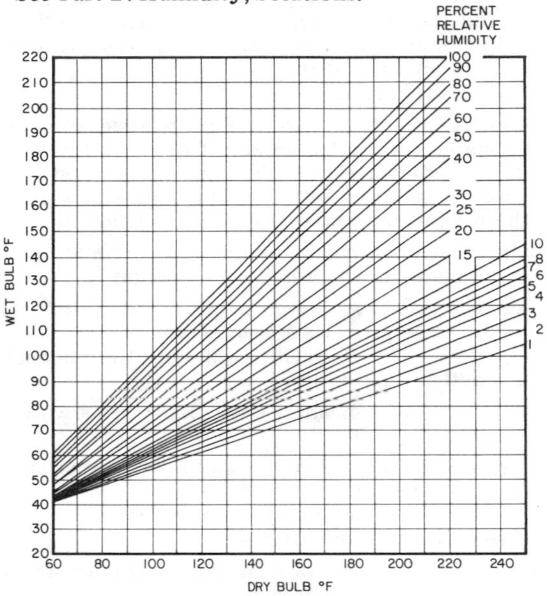

Humlies Early Scotch black-polled cattle.

humpback *See* **salmon**
See Part 2: Salmon and Trout

humus Bacterial-decomposed vegetable matter in the soil.

hundredweight (U.S.) A measure of weight.
1 hundredweight (long) = 112 lb
= 50.8024 kg
= 8 stone
= 4 quarters
= 0.05 long ton
} In units of a long ton

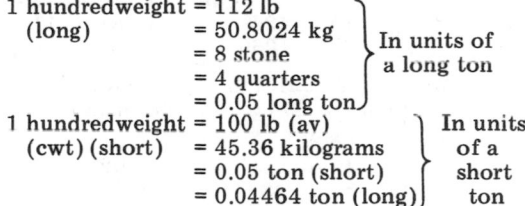

1 hundredweight (cwt) (short) = 100 lb (av)
= 45.36 kilograms
= 0.05 ton (short)
= 0.04464 ton (long)
} In units of a short ton

Hungarian pepper *See* **paprika**

hunter style *See* **chasseur**

husk Leaves enveloping corn, kernels or seed especially when dry and membranous.

hyacinth *See* **lablab**

hyaline Transparent; glassy.
See Part 2: Wheat, Parts of Grain; Wheat, Parts of Grain, Vitamins

hybrid The offspring of a cross between different species, varieties or genera.

hydantoin (glycolylurea) $NHCONHCOCH_2$ A nitrogenous pharmaceutical intermediate.
See Part 2: Sanitizers

hydnocarpic acid *See* **chaulmoogra oil**

hydrate A crystalline product made up of salts and closely associated water molecules, e.g., $CuSO_4 \cdot 5H_2O$; $CrCl_3 \cdot 6H_2O$ (water of crystallization). In some types of hydrates (hydrated lime) the water reacts chemically with a base to form a new compound.

hydrated lime $Ca(OH)_2$ A liming material; each pound has the neutralizing equivalent of 1.2 to 1.35 pounds of $CaCO_3$ (or approx. this quantity of dolomitic limestone).
See Part 2: Fertilizer

hydration number The average relative amount of water carried by an ion of one element or a group compared to the amount carried by another; it varies with concentration—the higher the hydration number, the slower the ion moves.

hydride An inorganic compound of hydrogen and a metal in which hydrogen is negative.

hydriodic acid A water solution of hydrogen iodide (a gas) used as a disinfectant.
See Part 2: Concentration of Commercial Strengths of Acids and Bases

hydro- A prefix meaning water; hydrogen = water-maker.

hydrobromic acid A water solution of hydrogen bromide (a gas).
See Part 2: Concentration of Commercial Strengths of Acids and Bases

hydrocarbon A chemical compound that contains only carbon and hydrogen.

hydrochloric acid (muriatic acid) (spirits of salts) A strong acid; an aqueous solution of hydrogen chloride (a gas). Strong irritant to tissue.

Commercial Strength	Mole/l	g/l	% by wt	Sp gr	Normality
	—	—	38	1.188	12.4
	11.6	424	36	1.18	11.3
	2.9	105	10	1.05	—

Ml of 35-37% HCl to dilute to 10 l	Approx. Normality
8.9	0.01
17.8	0.02
89.0	0.10
445.0	0.50
890.0	1.00

See Part 2: Concentration of Commercial Strengths of Acids and Bases; Hydrochloric Acid, Solution; Normal Solutions; pH, Standard Solutions; Reagents, Normal Solutions

hydrocolloid *See* **hydrophilic colloid; gum; protective colloid**

hydrocyanic acid (hydrogen cyanide) HCN Highly toxic liquid used as a fumigant and insecticide.
See Part 2: Concentration of Commercial Strengths of Acids and Bases; Normal Solutions; Fumigants

hydrofluoric acid An aqueous solution of hydrogen fluoride. Corrosive to tissue.
See Part 2: Concentration of Commercial Strengths of Acids and Bases

hydrofluosilicic acid (fluosilicic acid) H_2F_6Si Fuming liquid, corrosive to tissue.
See Part 2: Concentration of Commercial Strengths of Acids and Bases

hydrogen (H) A gaseous element; at. no. 1; at. wt. 1.0080; Group I A of Periodic Table. Oxidation states +1, −1; electron configuration 1
orbit K
A diatomic gas. The most abundant element in the universe.
See Part 2: Constants, Fundamental

hydrogenated shortening An oil to which hydrogen has been chemically added to convert it to a fat, e.g., Crisco. *See also* **hydrogenation.**
1 cup = 190 g (6.6 oz)
1 lb = 2⅓ cups
Storage: Room temperature.

hydrogenation The saturation or hardening of vegetable oils by adding hydrogen to the double bond with the aid of heat, pressure and a catalyst.
See Part 2: Margarine Production

hydrogen cyanide *See* **hydrocyanic acid**

hydrogen ion (H^+) A positively charged ion with mass of 1; equivalent to a proton.

hydrogen peroxide H_2O_2 A toxic liquid used to remove color in tripe; must be rinsed off; also used as a preservative in milk (0.05% or less) in some areas.

hydrogen sulfide (H_2S) A toxic, flammable gas with offensive odor; a weak dibasic acid.

$$H_2S \rightleftharpoons H^+ + HS^- \quad K_1 = 1 \times 10^{-7}$$
$$HS^- \rightleftharpoons H^+ + S^{--} \quad K_2 = 1.3 \times 10^{-13}$$
$$\text{Total } H_2S \rightleftharpoons 2H^+ + S^{--} \quad K_t = 1.3 \times 10^{-20}$$

hydrolysis A reaction of water with a complex organic compound in which both the water molecule and the organic molecule split, to form two simpler organic compounds; e.g.,

$$R{-}O{-}\underset{\underset{O}{\|}}{C}{-}R + H_2O \longrightarrow ROH + HO{-}\underset{\underset{O}{\|}}{C}{-}R$$

Thus for example proteins are hydrolyzed to amino acids.
See Part 2: Enzyme, Food Industry

hydrolyzed poultry feathers A product obtained from treatment under pressure of feathers from slaughtered poultry; crude protein must be 70% digestible protein. *See also* **feather.**

hydrophilic colloid A macromolecular substance such as a protein or polysaccharide which swells by absorption of water, in some cases forming stiff gels. *See also* **gum; protective colloid; gel.**

hydrometer A floating device used to determine specific gravity of liquids.

hydronium ion (H_3O^+) H^+ ion attached to one water molecule.

hydrophobic Water-repellent; opposite of hydrophilic.

hydroxide ion (hydroxyl ion) $(OH)^-$ A radical formed by dissociation of a hydroxide compound in water solution. *See also* **hydroxyl group.**

β-hydroxyalanine *See* **serine**

β-hydroxy-α-amino-butyric acid *See* **threonine**

hydroxyglutamic acid A monoamino-dicarboxylic amino acid.

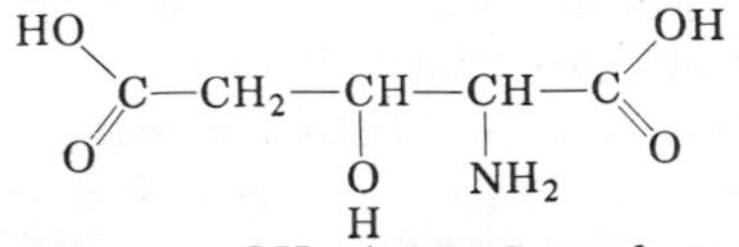

hydroxyl group —OH An uncharged combination of atoms that remains unchanged in chemical reactions. *See also* **hydroxide ion.**

4-hydroxymethyl-2, 6-tert-butylphenone *See* Part 2: Antioxidant Structure

p-hydroxyphenylalanine *See* **tyrosine**

hydroxyproline A heterocylic amino acid.

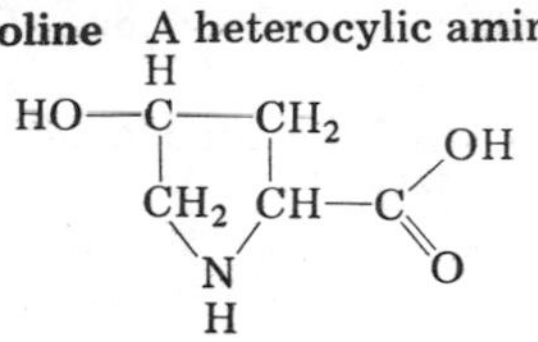

See Part 2: Amino Acids; Amino Acid, Solubilities; Manure Analysis

hygiene The science of public health and prevention of disease.

hygro- Prefix denoting moisture.

hygroscopic Descriptive of a liquid or solid material that picks up atmospheric water vapor, and thus acts as a drying agent, e.g., silica gel. Propylene glycol is a hygroscopic liquid (humectant).

hyper- Prefix meaning above or over; e.g., hypersensitive.

hypo Sodium thiosulfate.

hypo- Prefix meaning under or beneath; e.g., hypodermic.

hypochlorite ion ClO^-

hypoderm *See* Part 2: Orange Structure

hypodermis *See* Part 2: Wheat Kernel Parts

hypoglycemia A low concentration of blood sugar; normal blood sugar level in man is 0.07 to 0.10 percent.

hypophosphorous acid H_3PO_2 *See* Part 2: Concentration of Commercial Strengths of Acids and Bases

hypotenuse The long side of a right triangle; $(\text{hypotenuse})^2 = (\text{side})^2 + (\text{side})^2$

I

I (1) Symbol for the element iodine. (2) *See also* **ampere; current.**

I-band Light band (isotropic) in muscle fibers.

ice (1) Solid state of water, specific gravity 0.92; 1 cu ft = 56 lb; heat absorbed during melting 144 Btu/pound (80 cal./gram).
See Part 2: Ice, Vapor Pressure; Freezing Rate
(2) A frozen dessert that contains no milk fat.
Composition: 67% H_2O, 0.4% protein, trace fat, 32% carbohydrate; trace ash. *See also* **sherbet; ice cream.**

iceberg lettuce A variety of head lettuce; firm compact heads with light green leaves; 1 medium head = 220 g. *See also* **lettuce.**

ice cream A frozen dessert made from milk, cream, sugar, stabilizer, flavoring and often eggs. 4.5 lb/gal.; min. 1.6 lb food solids/gal.; 15 lb milk = 1 gal. ice cream; 1½ gal. brick ice cream = 50 servings; 2½ gal. bulk ice cream = 50 servings; 1 qt = 4 cups; 1 cup = 140 g (5 oz).

Freezer Size (qt)	Lbs Ice for Making & Ripening	Cups Salt for Making Rock	Cups Salt for Making Table	Cups Salt for Ripening Rock	Cups Salt for Ripening Table
2½	15	1½	1	1½	1
4	20	2½	1½	2½	1½
6	25	3½	2⅓	3½	2⅓

Storage: −15°F; storage life is several months.
Composition:

	H_2O (%)	Protein (%)	Fat (%)	Carbohydrate (%)	Ash (%)	Minimum Milk Fat (%)	Minimum Total Milk Solids (%)
Ice cream (10% fat)	63	4.5	10.6	21	1	10	20
Ice cream (12% fat)	62	4	12.5	21	0.8		
Ice cream (16% fat)	63	2.6	16.1	18	0.5		

See Part 2: Calories, Daily Recommendations; Creams, Butter and Frozen Desserts; Dairy Products, Composition; Dairy Terms; Food, Composition; Frozen Food Storage; Milk and Milk Products, Vitamin Content; Minerals (Trace), Limits; Portion Size; Stabilizers, Thickeners

ice milk A frozen dessert made from milk, sugar, stabilizers, flavoring and sometimes eggs; between 2–7% milk fat; min. 11% total milk solids; 1 qt = 4 cups; 1 cup = 185 g (6.6 oz).
Composition: 67% H_2O, 4.8% protein, 5.1% fat, 22% carbohydrate, 1% ash. *See also* **ice cream.**
See Part 2: Calories, Daily Recommendations

icing A coating for cakes made of sugar, milk and flavoring.
See Part 2: Stabilizers, Thickeners

Idaho potato *See* **Russett Burbank**

IDF *See* **International Dairy Federation**

idla A steamed rice cake made from fermented or unfermented dough.

idose A water-soluble aldose syrup not fermented by yeast; isomeric with glucose.
See Part 2: Sugar, D-aldehydo

ikan bilis Salted, dried whitebait or anchovies.

ilama *See* **anonaceous fruit**

iliac *See* Part 2: Lymph Nodes, Ox; Lymph Nodes, Pig

iliacus A muscle of the hind quarter that runs across the inner face of the ilium.

ilium A triangular portion of the pelvic (hip) bone that articulates with the spine and directs a shaft downward and to the rear; called hip bone, pin bone.
See Part 2: Bone

illipe The fat of *Bassia latifolia* or *B. longifolia* used in the chocolate industry.
See Part 2: Iodine and Saponification Values; Refractive Indices, Fats and Oils

imidazole (glyoxalin) A nitrogenous organic compound that inhibits the action of histamine.

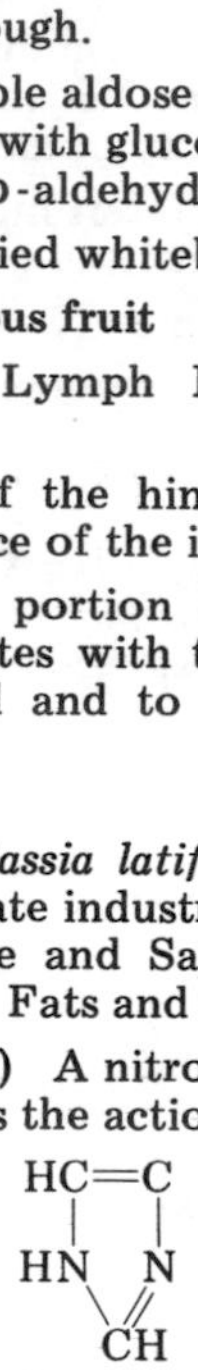

β-imidazole-alanine *See* **histidine**

In Symbol for the element indium.

in-breeding Mating of *very* closely related animals.

incannestrata A sharp wine or dinner cheese; also a grating cheese.

inch A measure of length; 1 in. (British) = 2.539998 cm.
1 in. (U.S.) = 2.5400 × 10^8 angstrom
= 25400.0508 microns
= 1,000 mils
= 72 points (printer's type)
= 25.4000508 millimeters (mm)
= 6 picas (printer's type)
= 2.54000508 centimeters (cm)
= 0.08333 foot (ft)
= 0.02778 yard (yd)
= 0.02540 meter (m)
= 0.005051 rod (rd)
= 0.00002540 kilometer (km)

= 0.0000157828 statute mile
= 0.00001371 U.S. nautical mile
39.37 in. = 1 meter
12 in. = 1 foot
7.92 in. = 1 link

inch-column of mercury (Hg sp gr = 13.59593) A measure of pressure.
1 = 70.7310 pounds per sq foot (psf)
= 25.4001 millimeters (columns of mercury)
= 1.13299 feet (columns of water, max. density at 4°C, 39°F)
= 0.49119 pound per sq inch (psi)
= 0.34534 meter (columns of water, max. density at 4°C, 39°F)
= 0.03453 kilogram per sq centimeter (kg/ cm^2)
= 0.034 bar
= 0.03342 atmosphere, standard (760 mm)

inch-column of water (4°C) A measure of pressure.
1 = 5.2022 pounds/foot
= 2.4583×10^{-3} standard atmospheres
= 0.57802 ounce/sq inch
= 0.074 inch of mercury at 0°C
= 0.03613 pound/sq in.

incisor A front tooth; there are four in each jaw (in man).

incubate To hatch eggs by keeping them warm with body heat or artificial heat.
See Part 2: Egg Incubation Periods

India gum *See* **gum karaya**

Indian cattle *See* **Brahman**

Indian corn (*Zea mays*) *See* **corn**

Indian gum *See* **gum ghatti**

Indian pudding A dessert made with cornmeal and molasses.
See Part 2: Cornstarch Pudding Variations

Indian rice *See* **rice; wild rice**

Indian tragacanth *See* **gum karaya**

indicator A substance which shows a physical change (usually color) when a reaction has taken place, without affecting the reaction; used in acid-base titrations, e.g., litmus, methylene Blue, methyl orange.
See Part 2: Indicators: pH and Acid Base; pH, Buffer Solutions; pH, Universal Indicators

indigo $C_{16}H_{10}N_2O_2$ A blue coloring substance derived from a vegetable and used to color food.

indium (In) A metallic element; at. no. 49; at. wt. 114.82; Group IIIA of Periodic Table; oxidation state +3; electron configuration 2-8-18-18-3
orbit K L M N O

indole An indigo derivative; also made synthetically. A carcinogenic agent.

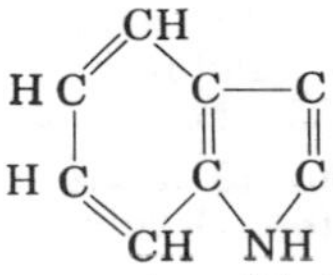

See Part 2: Microorganism, Media

indolealanine *See* **tryptophan**

Indu Brazil *See* Part 2: Beef and Dual-purpose Cattle

inductance The property of matter which resists change in a current passing through it, and is measured in henrys.

inductor An electrical coil used to resist change in current.

industrial alcohol A mixture of 95% ethyl alcohol and 5% water to which are added various chemicals to make the alcohol unfit for drinking. Methyl alcohol is commonly used as a denaturant.

infection Contagion or inflammation caused by bacteria or viruses.
See Part 2: Illness From Food; Infectious Agents; Infectious Diseases, Food-borne

inferior *See* **caudal**; also means beneath, below, or lower.

infra- Prefix meaning beneath, i.e., infrared.

infrared Wavelengths of radiation longer than visible red; i.e., over 7500–8000 angstrom.

infraspinatus A muscle of the chuck that is located laterally to the scapula and below the spine of the scapula.

ingestion Taking any substance into the body by mouth.
See Part 2: Ingestion and Inhalation

inguinal Located in the groin.
See Part 2: Lymph Nodes, Ox; Lymph Nodes, Pig

inhalation Taking air into the lungs by breathing.
See Part 2: Ingestion and Inhalation

injera A fermented bread made from teff (cereal).

ink (meat inspection) Coloring ingredients approved by Food & Drug Administration, and may also include other food grade ingredients.
Purple ink composed of:
1. FD&C blue (Violet No. 1 has been discontinued).
2. water
3. alcohol
4. sugar

Acetone may be added to shorten drying time.

Green ink (used for horse meat) composed of:

	Percent
1. FD&C green	3½
2. dextrose (corn sugar)	3
3. water	16
4. edible shellac	2
5. 95% ethyl alcohol	75

ink blue agar *See* Part 2: Microorganism, Media

inkweed A plant having a toxic principle.
See Part 2: Poisonous Plants

innominate bone *See* **ossa coxarum**

inorganic The branch of chemistry concerned with substances that do not contain carbon (except the carbon oxides and metallic carbonates).

5-inosine monophosphate A flavor enhancer.

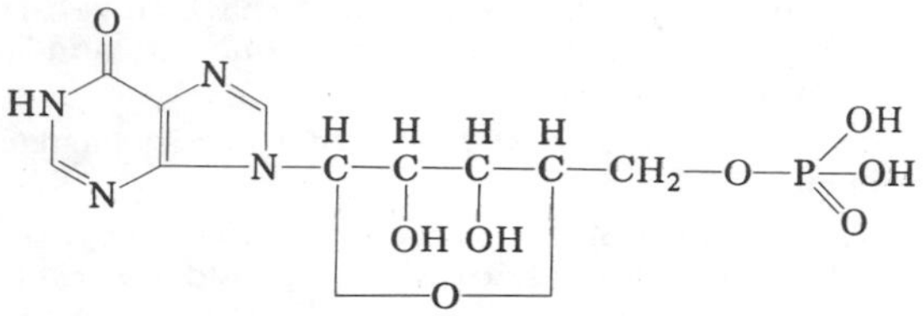

inositol $C_6H_6(OH)_6$ A growth factor.
See Part 2: Egg Products, Nutritive Value; Lemon Juice Composition; Wheat, Vitamins

insect Any species of small flying animals having 6 legs and usually two pairs of wings.
See Part 2: Insect Control; Radiation Preservation

insecticide A chemical used to destroy insects either by contact or by internal poisoning. Some types are toxic to man and ecologically damaging.
See Part 2: Chemical Poisoning

insemination time The effective time for insemination, just prior to ovulation.
mare: last half of heat period;
sow: mid point of heat period;
ewe: last day of heat period;
cow: last half of heat period

insertion Movable (bone that moves) attachment of a muscle.

inside chuck (bottom chuck) A muscle medial to the scapula of which the major ones are teres major, subscapularis, scalenus dorsalis, serratus ventralis, spinalis dorsi, complexus, longissimus dorsi, and longissimus costarum. *See also* **bottom chuck.**
See Part 2: Beef, Boneless Cuts

inside cut *See* Part 2: Beef Round Cuts; Meat Identification

inside round (top round) A beef cut made up of semimembranosus, adductor and gracilis muscles.
See Part 2: Beef, Boneless Cuts

in situ In an undisturbed or normal position.

INSP'D &P's'D "Inspected and passed" (meat inspection).
See Part 2: Meat Inspection Stamp

inspection *See* Part 2: Meat Inspection Stamp; Poultry Inspection and Grade Stamp; Poultry Inspection Stamp

instantizing Physical or chemical treatment (agglomeration) that will improve the water dispersibility of dry powders.

insulation A material that resists penetration by heat or cold, e.g., air, glass wool, felt.
See Part 2: Insulating Value; Insulation; Insulation, Conductivity Values; Insulation, Thickness

insulin A hormone isolated from the pancreas and used to treat diabetes; controls sugar metabolism. It is a protein composed of 16 amino acids.

insulite *See* Part 2: Insulation

integer A whole number.

intercostal Located between the ribs.
See Part 2: Lymph Nodes, Ox

intercostal muscle Two layers of muscle between the ribs.

interesterification A procedure for changing the arrangement of the fatty acids on the glycerin molecule; it gives more plastic range, better consistency, and higher solid content; dry heat, 110° to 200°F.

internal abdominal oblique The inside sheet of muscles of the flank whose fibers point downward and forward.

internal phase *See* **dispersed phase**

International Dairy Federation (IDF) An international group whose purpose was to standardize dairy products; it is now a part of FAO.

International Union of Pure and Applied Chemistry An international group which recommends nomenclature, standards for chemical weights and measures, symbols, etc.

internode The portion of the plant stem between the nodes from which the leaves grow.
See Part 2: Corn

intertransversales A muscle that connects adjacent transverse processes.

intervertebral disc A cartilage disc between vertebrae.

intestinal fat *See* **killing fat**

intestines Digestive tract from the stomach to the rectum. The average length in feet is:

	Small	Large
cattle	120	30
sheep	85	20
swine	55	15

See Part 2: Intestine, Cross Section; Organ Weights

intoxication Literally, poisoning. Usual meaning is presence of alcohol in the brain, causing behavior characteristic of drunkenness. Alcohol is a noncumulative poison.
See Part 2: Illness From Food; Microbial Toxins

intra- Prefix meaning within, e.g., intracellular.

inulin $(C_6H_{10}O_5)_{3,4}$ A form of sugar that can be eaten by diabetics.

in vacuo In a vacuum or a space without air.

invertase (sucrase) An enzyme that hydrolyzes sucrose to glucose and fructose.
See Part 2: pH Values of Biological Materials

invert sugar A 50–50 mixture of glucose (dextrose) and fructose (levulose) used primarily in the confectionery industry. It occurs naturally in honey, and is formed by hydrolysis of sucrose:

$$\underset{\text{(dextrorotatory)}}{\underset{\text{sucrose}}{C_{12}H_{22}O_{11}}} + H_2O \xrightarrow[\text{dilute acid, } 80^\circ C]{\text{hydrolysis}} \underset{\text{(dextrorotatory)}}{\underset{\text{dextrose}}{C_6H_{12}O_6}} + \underset{\text{(levorotatory)}}{\underset{\text{levulose}}{C_6H_{12}O_6}}$$

mix → levorotatory

See Part 2: Sweetening Agents; Sweetening Compounds

in vitro Literally, in glass; a reaction carried out in a test tube as opposed to one carried out in a living organism (*in vivo*).

in vivo In living matter; a reaction carried out in an organism rather than one carried out in a test tube (*in vitro*).

involuntary muscle *See* **smooth muscle**

iodine (I) A halogen element; at. no. 53; at. wt. 126.91; Group VIIA of Periodic Table; oxidation states +1, +5, +7, −1; electron configuration 2–8–18–18–7
orbit K L M N O
Deficiency causes goiter; body function: essential to thyroid gland; in thyroxin; varies in food depending on its origin; in seaweed, seafoods, and in some water supplies; in iodized table salt.
Tincture of iodine: 3% iodine in alcohol solution.
See Part 2: Cereal Fortification; Cereals, Vitamin and Mineral Content; Egg Products, Nutritive Value; Minerals, Food; Minerals, Plant or Animal Tissue; Normal Solutions; Recommended Daily Dietary Allowance; Sanitizers; Sanitizing Chemicals

iodine number A value indicating the degree of unsaturation of a fat or oil; the larger the number, the greater the unsaturation. It is expressed as the percentage of iodine by weight that a fat or oil will absorb; oils range from 80 to 200. *See also* **iodine value analysis.**

Fat	Iodine No.
Butter	22–45
Coconut oil	6–10
Corn oil	103–130
Cottonseed oil	104–114
Lard	46–70
Linseed oil	107–202
Peanut oil	84–100
Poultry fat	66–71
Soybean oil	120–141
Tallow	35–55

See Part 2: Fats and Oils, Composition; Fat and Oil, Fatty Acid Composition; Fats and Oils and Their Physical and Chemical Properties; Fatty Acids and Their Properties; Fats and Oils, Characteristics; Iodine and Saponification Values

iodine solution *See* **iodine**
See Part 2: Gram Stain

iodine value analysis Grams of iodine absorbed by 100 grams of fat; a measure of the unsaturation of a fat. It is determined by adding iodine monobromide to fat; the excess iodine is titrated with standard sodium thiosulfate and calculated as percent by weight of iodine absorbed and reported as iodine number. *See also* **iodine number.**

iodized salt Table salt to which 0.01% sodium or potassium iodide has been added, as well as a small amount of magnesium carbonate for free flowing properties.

iodoform CHI_3 An antiseptic iodine compound.

ion A positive or negative charged atom or group, i.e., H^+, OH^-.

ionization *See* **dissociation**

ionization constant *See* **dissociation constant**

iota (Ι, ι) Greek letter with an English equivalent of i.

I.Q.F. Individually quick-frozen.

Ir Symbol for the element iridium.

iridium (Ir) Metallic element; at. no. 77; at. wt. 192.2; Group VIII of the Periodic Table; oxidation states +3, +4; electron configuration 2–8–18–32–15–2
orbit K L M N O P

Irish cobbler An all-purpose variety of potato.

Irish moss *See* **carrageen; carrageenan**

Irish potato *See* **potato, Irish**

iron (Fe) A metallic element; at. no. 26; at. wt. 55.85; Group VIII of Periodic Table; electron configuration 2–8–14–2;
orbit K L M N
oxidation states +2, +3; body function: in hemoglobin, cytochrome, catalase, peroxidase.

High in iron	Low in iron
peas, beans, leafy green vegetables, meat, fish, egg yolk	white flour, fruits, milk, egg white

See Part 2: Beans, Peas and Nuts; Beef Percentages of Daily Recommended Allowances; Cereal Enrichment; Cereal Fortification; Cereal Nutrient Content; Cereals, Vitamin and Mineral Content; Composition of Food; Dairy Products, Composition; Egg Composition; Egg Products, Nutritive Value; Fats and Oils, Composition; Fish and Shellfish Composition; Flour, Extraction Rates; Food, Composition; Fruit and Vegetables Composition; Fruit Composition; Grain Analysis; Grain Products Composition;

Histochemical Tests; Iron; Iron, Daily Recommendations; Lamb Percentages of Daily Recommended Allowances; Lemon Juice Composition; Lime Juice Composition; Macaroni and Noodles Composition; Manure Analysis; Meat Composition; Meat, Nutritive Value; Minerals, Food; Minerals, Plant or Animal Tissue; Minerals, Trace, Limits; pH and Availability of Plant Nutrients; Plant Foods, Composition; Pork, Percentages of Daily Recommended Allowances; Poultry Composition; Recommended Daily Dietary Allowance; Sausage Composition; Sausage Nutritive Value; Soups, Composition; Sugars and Sweets Composition; Tomato and Tomato Products, Composition; Variety Meat Percentage of Daily Recommended Allowances; Vegetable Composition; Water Drinking Standards; Wheat, Minerals; Wheat Products Composition

iron-hematoxylin Solution

Solution I	
ammonio-ferric sulfate	2.5 g
distilled water	100 ml
Solution II	
hematoxylin	0.5 g
dissolve in 95% alcohol	10 ml
add distilled water	100 ml

iron sulfate (ferric sulfate) $Fe_2(SO_4)_3$ Flocculant in water purification; soil conditioner.
See Part 2: Fertilizer Materials

ischiatic Location near the ischium or haunch.
See Part 2: Lymph Nodes, Ox

ischium Posterior portion of the pelvic bone; joins the ilium at the cavity for the head of the femur; the aitch bone area of the pelvis bone; called pin bone.
See Part 2: Bone; Bone Age

ishinagi A food fish caught in the Pacific.
See Part 2: Vitamin D, Fish

iso- Prefix meaning "the same."

iso-ascorbic acid *See* **ascorbic acid**

isobutane $(CH_3)_2CHCH_3$ Liquefied petroleum gas.
See Part 2: Refrigerant

isocitric acid *See* Part 2: Organic Acids in Fruits and Vegetables

isodrin An isomer of aldrin; a toxic insecticide whose use may be restricted.

isoelectric point pH at which the net charge is zero and there is no migration in an electric field; also the pH of minimum solubility.

isoleucine A monoamino-monocarboxylic amino acid.

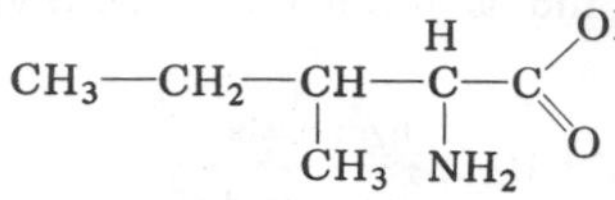

See Part 2: Amino Acids; Amino Acid, Solubilities; Corn, Amino Acids; Egg Products, Nutritive Value; Grain Analysis; Manure Analysis; Milk, Amino Acids; Seed, Chemical Composition; Wheat, Amino Acids; Wheat Products, Amino Acid Compositions

isomerism Compounds which have the same elements in the same proportions by weight but different structure and properties. *See also* **stereoisomer; optical isomers; geometric isomers.**

isotope One of two or more forms of an element whose atomic weights differ by one or more mass units because of the presence of an abnormal number of neutrons in their nuclei. For example, ordinary hydrogen (H^1) contains no neutrons, but isotopic hydrogen (H^2, deuterium) has one neutron. The properties of isotopes are identical except for atomic weight. A number of elements have no isotopes, but most have from 2 to 8 or more.

isotropic A material which has equivalent properties in all directions of test. *See also* **anisotropic.**

isovaleric acid $(CH_3)_2CHCH_2COOH$ A saturated fatty acid occurring in tobacco, hop oil and valerian.
See Part 2: Fatty Acids

Italian cheese A number of different types of cheese; the shape usually determines its name; they are usually smoked, cured and have a tangy, salty flavor.

Italian dressing A salad dressing that usually contains: oil, water, vinegar, sugar, salt, lemon juice, garlic, spices, and pepper.

Italian fennel A plant having anise-flavored green leaves, blanched stalk and a bulbous root.

Italian plum A variety of plum. *See also* **ryegrass.**

Italian roast (coffee) *See* **Espresso roast**

Italian sausage *See* Part 2: Sausage, Types

I.U. International Units (vitamins).

IUPAC *See* **International Union of Pure and Applied Chemistry**

IUTM base *See* Part 2: Microorganism, Media

ivebush *See* Part 2: Poisonous Plants

J

jaboty Fat or tallow from *Erisma calcaratum* and *E. uncinatum* used as a substitute for cocoa butter.
See Part 2: Iodine and Saponification Values

jack A male ass.

jackbean (*Canavalia ensiformis*) A large podded bean used for green manure or fodder or both; whole young pod or mature seed can be cooked and eaten.

jack cheese A light-colored cheddar.

jack fruit *See* **breadfruit**
See Part 2: Fruit Classification; Fruit Composition; Fruit Storage

jack rail A switch and rail for transferring meat-hangers to another rail.

jacksmelt *See* **smelt**

Jackson A variety of soybean.

Jaffa A variety of midsummer Florida orange.

jaggery *See* **sugar cane**

jak *See* **breadfruit**

jam A jel of fruit (often berries) preserve; jel caused by reaction of acid (pH 2.5–3.5) with pectin (½–1%) and sugar (opt. 67%); fruits cooked in sugar until soft and jelly-like; made from crushed fruit, sugar (½ to ¾ part sugar to 1 part fruit), cooked and sealed for storage; pH 3.1–4.0. *See also* **gel.**
Storage: After opening, cover and refrigerate.
See Part 2: Calories, Daily Recommendations; Standards, Processed Fruit and Vegetable Products; Sugars and Sweets Composition; Water Activity, Organisms and Food

jamberry *See* **gooseberry**

jandagum *See* **locust bean gum**

Japanese gelatin *See* **agar-agar**

Japanese medlar *See* **loquat**

Japanese millet *See* **millet**

Japanese rice wine *See* **sake**

Japanese walnut (*Jaglans sieboldiana*) A tree producing edible nuts.

jar *See* Part 2: Glass Jar Tops

jardinière Fresh vegetables.

jasmine *See* Part 2: Essential Oils

Java (1) An American class of chicken that lays a brown-shelled egg.

Varieties	Plumage color	Shank	Beak
Black	Greenish black undercolor black	Black to yellow	Black
Mottled	Black mottled with white, undercolor slate	Blue to yellow	Yellow

(2) A variety of coffee originating in Java.

Java arabicia A coffee bean (tan when unroasted) that produces a coffee that is robust, with a gentle aroma and creamy taste.

jelly A colloidal suspension (usually fruit-flavored) that has gelled; made from pectin, agar, or gelatin by combining 45 parts of clarified fruit juice with 55 parts sugar. The fruit is cooked and strained; sugar (⅔ sugar to 1 part fruit juice) and commercial pectin are added; product is then sealed for storage; pH 3.0–3.5. *See also* **gel.**
Storage: After opening, cover and refrigerate.
See Part 2: Calories, Daily Recommendations; Standards, Processed Fruit and Vegetable Products; Sugars and Sweets Composition

jennet A small horse.

jenny A female ass.

jerked beef Meat cut in strips and hung to dry.

jerky Thin dried strips of meat.

Jersey A breed of dairy cattle that originated on the island of Jersey; color: shades of fawn with or without white markings; gives rich milk.
See Part 2: Dairy Cattle Breeds; Gestation Periods; Milk Breeds, Composition; Milk Composition

Jersey Giant The largest of American class of chickens; it lays a brown-shelled egg;

Varieties	Plumage color	Shank	Beak
Black	Blackish green, undercolor—slate	Black to yellow	Black to yellow
White	White	Green to yellow	Yellow

Jersey Red A breed of red hogs that contributed to the Duroc breed.

Jerusalem artichoke (*Helianthus tuberosus*) A vegetable whose stem tuber is used as food; a member of the daisy family that produces an underground, whitish, yellowish or pinkish, knobby, stem-tuber; the tubers are used as cooked vegetables and contain inulin.

Raw Composition: 80% H_2O, 2% protein, 0.1% fat, 17% carbohydrate, 1% ash.
See Part 2: Storage; Vegetable Composition

Jerusalem cherry A plant having a toxic principle.
See Part 2: Poisonous Plants

jessamine A plant having a toxic principle.
See Part 2: Poisonous Plants

jiffy steak Same as cube steak.

jigger A volume measure of liquor (1.5 oz).

jimmy fern A plant having a poisonous principle.
See Part 2: Poisonous Plants

jimson weed A plant having a poisonous principle.
See Part 2: Poisonous Plants

jinnie *See* **jenny**

Johnson grass A perennial grass that is very difficult to eradicate.
See Part 2: Poisonous Plants; Seed, Germination

jojoba oil A vegetable oil containing unsaturated fatty acids; it has a unique waxy consistency.
See Part 2: Unsaturated Fatty Acids

Jonathan A variety of apples that is in season in Sept. to January; is an excellent eating and cooking apple and a good sauce apple.

joule (j) A measure of heat, energy, work.
1 joule (j) = 1×10^7 ergs
= 0.73761 foot pound (ft-lb.)
= 0.23889 calorie (thermal unit)
= 0.10198 kilogram meter (kg-m)
= 0.0009480 Btu (thermal unit)
= 0.0002389 kg-calory (thermal unit)
= 0.0000003777 metric horsepower-hour (75 kg-m-hr)
= 0.0000003725 U.S. horsepower-hour (h.p.-hr)
= 0.0000002778 kilowatt hour (kw-hr)

A unit of electrical work:
x volt times y coulomb = xy joule;
x watt times y second = xy joule.

jowl Pork carcass area (cheek) parallel with the ribs and located in front of the shoulder and below the ear area; it is cured to make jowl bacon or used fresh in sausage; for sausage use, should be sliced every inch to inspect for abscesses (3–4% of carcass).
See Part 2: Pork Carcass, Retail Yield; Pork Chart; Pork Cuts; Pork Wholesale Cuts; Pork Yield

joy of the mountain *See* **oregano**

Judaism, dietary rules

A. Orthodox
1. Permitted: fruit, vegetables, grain, tea, coffee
2. Permitted if processed by prescribed methods: meat, poultry, fish
3. Not permitted: pork, blood, shellfish, birds of prey, insects except locusts, reptiles, amphibians, cartilaginous fishes
4. Dairy products and meats:
(a) cannot be cooked together;
(b) food mixtures of these not permitted;
(c) some utensils, dishes and cutlery may not be used for both;
(d) milk may not be consumed within 1, 3 or 6 hours after meat.

B. Reformed (used primarily on religious holidays)
1. Avoid dairy and animal products at same meal.
2. Avoid 2 vegetables from same botanical family at same meal.
3. Use chicken fat or vegetable oil instead of lard or tallow.
4. Rework leftovers as a new dish rather than re-serving them.

See also **kosher.**

Judas goat A goat used to lead sheep to slaughter.

jujube A Chinese date.
See Part 2: Fruit Composition

julienne Vegetables cut in long strips.

jumping mullet *See* **mullet**

Juniper (*Juniperus communis*) A dark blue berry from an evergreen tree used in flavoring gin, liqueurs and cordials.

junket Milk which has had a concentrated extract tablet of rennin added; after warming to 98°F, a small amount of rennet is added; the mixture is then allowed to cool and clot.

jus Extract of meat; au jus = with natural meat juice.

jute A vegetable fiber composed of extremely long fibers of cellulose; used for twine.

K

K *See* **kelvin, kilohm, potassium**

K_A *See* **dissociation constant**

kabob Alternating chunks of food cooked on a skewer.
See Part 2: Pork Cookery; Pork, Cooking; Pork Loin Cooking

kaffir corn 50–56 lb/bu; *See also* **millet.**

kafir A plant having a toxic principle.
See Part 2: Poisonous Plants

kainite A neutral fertilizer material; contains potassium chloride (KCl) and magnesium sulfate ($MgSO_4$). 0–0–20

kaju *See* **cashew nut**

kale (*Brassica oleracea* var. *viridis*) A plant whose leaves are used as greens, garnish and livestock feed.
Storage: Wash thoroughly; drain well; store in refrigerator (32°F) crisper or plastic bag (90–95% relative humidity); use within 1 to 12 days.
Raw leaf composition: 83–87% H_2O, 4–6% protein, 0.8% fat, 6–9% carbohydrate, 1.5% ash.
See Part 2: Minerals, Food; Nicotinic Acid, Food; Nitrate, Vegetables; Plant Foods, Composition; Sugar, Vegetables; Vegetable Boiling; Vegetable Composition; Vegetable Cooking; Vegetable Frozen Yield; Vegetable Plants; Vegetables, Boiling Time, Frozen; Vegetables, Cooking Frozen; Vegetable Servings; Vegetable Yield Canned and Frozen; Vegetable Yield Frozen, Canned and Fresh

kanaffa A sweet of shredded grain soaked in sugar solution.

kaolin A purified clay used as an anti-caking agent. Also used in manufacture of china and other ceramic products.

kapok A light vegetable fiber used for insulation and the seeds yield an oil used for soap manufacture.
See Part 2: Fatty Acids; Insulation; Iodine and Saponification Values; Oil or Fat, Characteristics; Refractive Indices, Fats and Oils; Specific Gravities, Fats and Oils; Titer, Fats and Oils; Unsaponifiable Matter

kappa (K, k) Greek letter with an English equivalent of k.

karakul A broadtail breed of sheep whose greatest value is for young lamb pelts that are used for fur.
See Part 2: Sheep Breeds

karaya *See* **gum karaya**

kasha Buckwheat groats or seed.

kasher *See* **kosher**

katsuobushi *See* Part 2: Fungi Food Products

kava (*Piper methysticum*) The root of this plant is mashed and fermented to produce a beverage.

kc Kilocycles/second.

KCN broth base Media containing potassium cyanide used for differentiation; permits differential growth of *Enterobacteriaceae*; *E. coli*, Salmonella and Shigella are inhibited but Klebsiella, *Bethesda-Ballerup* and Proteus grow unrestricted.
See Part 2: Microorganism, Media; Microorganism, Selective and Differential Broths and Media, Water Filtration Plant

keemun *See* **black tea**

kefir (kefyr, kephir) A fermented milk produced by a double lactic acid-alcohol fermentation.
See Part 2: Fluid and Fermented Milks, Composition; Milk and Milk Products, Vitamin Content

kefyr *See* **kefir**

kelp A brown seaweed high in trace minerals (especially iodine); used as food; a type of algae. May grow to lengths up to 100 ft, and is mechanically harvested.

Kelvin (K) *See* **absolute temperature**; K = C + 273.15.
See Part 2: Temperature

kemp Coarse hair or dead fibers or white fibers found in wool, usually from the outer thighs and crotch area; it will not take dye.

kench A container used for salt curing.

Kenland A variety of red clover.

Kentucky 31 A variety of fescue.

Kentucky bluegrass A variety of bluegrass.

kephalin *See* **cephalin**

kephir *See* **kefir**

kerasin A glycolipid which on hydrolysis yields galactose, sphingosine and lignoceric acid.

keratin Principal protein in wool, hair, hooves, horns, nails, and outer layer of epidermis; some of its amino acids are: arginine, aspartic acid, cystine, glutamic acid, lysine, tryptophan and tyrosine.

keratinization Production of a horny layer.

kerosene (kerosine) An oil obtained from distillation of petroleum and from oil shale; 1 gal. = 7 lb.
See Part 2: Fuel, Heating Value

Kerry An Irish breed of small black dairy cattle.

kerupok A prawn or fish puff or cracker.

keta *See* Part 2: Salmon and Trout

ketchup *See* **catchup**

ketjap (shoyu or soy sauce) A liquid produced from fermented soy products.
See Part 2: Fungi Food Products

ketone 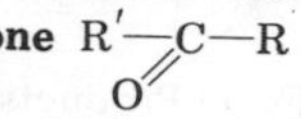 A class of organic compounds in which two alkyl or aryl groups are attached to a carbonyl group. The most common ketones are acetone and methyl ethyl ketone.

ketupat A cake made from eggs, rice flour, sugar, grated coconut and manisan.

KF streptococcus agar *See* Part 2: Microorganism, Culture Media, Water and Sewage, Standard Methods

kidney An organ of the body which excretes liquid waste products of metabolism and is found in a fatty deposit.
Storage: Coldest part of the refrigerator; use within 1 to 2 days.
Raw composition: 76–79% H_2O, 15–17% protein, 3–7% fat, 1% carbohydrate, 1.3% ash.
See Part 2: Beef Retail Yield; Gland Weights; Lamb Cuts and Uses; Meat, Servings Per Pound; Minerals, Food; Nicotinic Acid, Food; Organ Weights; Pantothenic Acid Content; Thiamin, Food; Vitamin A, Food; Variety Meat, Cooking; Variety Meat Percentage of Daily Recommended Allowances; Variety Meat Preparation

kidney bean ***Phaseolus vulgaris*** **bean** *See* **French bean**

kidney chop *See* Part 2: Veal Chart; Veal Cuts; Veal Cuts and Uses

kidney suet A large piece of beef fat which encases the kidney.

kielbasa *See* Part 2: Sausage Identification

kieserite $MgSO_4 \cdot H_2O$ *See* **magnesium sulfate**
See Part 2: Fertilizer Materials

killing fat Fat from the intestinal area, usually used in making soap.

kilo- Prefix for quantities 1000 times larger than the base unit.

kilo-calorie (Calorie, large calorie) A measure of heat, energy, work.
1 kg-cal = 4.186×10^{10} ergs
= 4,186.17 joules (10^7 ergs) (j)
= 3,087.77 foot pounds (ft-lb.)
= 1,000 gram calories or small calories = 3.968 Btu
= 426.900 kilogram meters (kg-m)
= 3.96832 Btu (thermal units)
= 0.001581 metric horsepower-hour (75 kg-m-hr)
= 0.001559 U.S. horsepower-hour (h.p.-hr)
= 0.001163 kilowatt hour (kw-hr)
4 kg-cal = 1 gram of protein
= 1 gram of carbohydrate
9 kg-cal = 1 gram of fat

kilo-calorie per second (kg-calorie/sec) Thermal units per second; a measure of power, rate of energy and heat.
1 kg-cal/sec = 4,186.17 watts (10^7 ergs/sec)
= 3,087.77 foot-pounds per second (ft-lb/sec)
= 426.900 kilogram meters per second (kg-m/sec)
= 5.69200 metric horsepower (75 kg-m/sec)
= 5.61412 U.S. horsepower (550 ft-lb/sec)
= 4.18617 kilowatt (kw)
= 3.96832 Btu/sec (thermal units per sec)

kilogram (kg) (K.G.) (kilo) A measure of weight.
1 kilogram (kg) = 1×10^6 milligrams
= 15,432.35639 grains (gr)
= 1,000 grams (10^3 g)
= 771.6178 scruples (apoth.)
= 643.01485 pennyweight (dwt)
= 564.38332 drams (av.)
= 257.20594 drams (troy) (apoth.)
= 35.27396 avoir ounces (oz av.)
= 32.150742 troy ounces (oz troy) or apothecary
= 10 hectograms (hg)
= 2.6792285 troy pounds (lb troy) or apothecary
= 2.204622341 avoir pounds (lb av.)
= 1 liter or cu decimeter (dm^3) of water at 4°C (at 45° Lat. and sea level)
= 0.001102 net-short ton (2,000 lb)
= 0.001 metric ton (1,000 kg)
= 0.0009842 gross-long ton (2,240 lb)

kilogram-meter (kg-m) A measure of heat, energy, work.
1 kilogram-meter (kg-m) = 9.80597 joules (10^7 ergs) (j)
= 7.23300 foot-pounds (ft-lb)
= 0.009296 Btu (thermal units)
= 0.002342 kg-calory (thermal units)
= 0.000003704 metric horsepower-hours (75 kg-m-hr)
= 0.000003653 U.S. horsepower-hour (h.p.-hr)
= 0.000002724 kilowatt hour (kw-hr)

kilogram meter per second (kg-m/sec) A measure of power, rate of energy and heat.

1 kg-m/sec = 9.80597 watts (10^7 ergs/sec)
= 7.23300 foot-pounds per second (ft-lb/sec)
= 0.01333 metric horsepower (75 kg-m-sec)
= 0.01315 U.S. horsepower (550 ft-lb/sec)
= 0.009806 kilowatt (kw)
= 0.009296 Btu-sec (thermal units per sec)
= 0.002342 kg-calory/sec (thermal units per sec)

kilogram per cubic meter (kg/m^3) A measure of density.
1 kg/m^3 = 1.68556 pound per cubic yard (lb/yd^3)
= 0.07769 pound per bushel (U.S.)
= 0.06243 pound per cubic foot (lb/ft^3)
= 0.009711 pound per gallon, dry (U.S.)
= 0.008345 pound per gallon, liquid (U.S.)
= 0.001 gram per cubic centimeter (g/cm^3)
= 0.00003613 pound per cubic inch (lb/in^3)

kilogram per hectare (kg/ha) Weight per unit area.
1 kg/ha = 0.890 lb/acre

kilogram per square centimeter (kg/cm^2) A measure of pressure.
1 kg/cm^2 = 2,048.17 pounds per sq foot (psf)
= 735.514 millimeters (columns of mercury, Hg)
= 32.8083 feet (columns of water, max. density at 4C, 39F)
= 28.9572 inches (columns of mercury, Hg)
= 14.2234 pounds per sq inch (psi)
= 10 meters (columns of water, max. density at 4C, 39F)
= 0.9807 bar
= 0.96778 atmosphere, standard (760 mm Hg).

kilohm (K) 1000 ohms.

kiloliter (kl) A unit of metric volume.
1 kiloliter = 61,023.0 cu. inch
= 1,000 liters (l)
= 264.18 gallons (U.S. liquid)
= 10 hectoliter (hl)
= 1.308 cu. yards
= 1 cubic meter

kilometer (km) A measurement of length.
1 km = 39,370 inches (in.)
= 3,280.83 feet (ft)
= 1,093.61 yard (yd)
= 1000 meters (m) (10^3 m)
= 198.838 rods (rd)
= 0.62137 statute mile
= 0.53959 U.S. nautical mile
1 mile = 1.6093 kilometers

kilometer per hour A measure of velocity.
1 km/hr = 54.68 feet/minute
= 27.78 centimeters/second
= 16.67 meter/minute
= 0.91134 feet per second (fps)
= 0.62137 mile per hour (mph)
= 0.53959 knot (U.S.)
= 0.27778 meter per second (mps)

kilometer per hour per sec A measure of acceleration.
1 km/hr/sec = 0.91134 foot per sec/sec (fps^2)
= 0.62137 mile per hour/sec (mph-s)
= 0.27778 meter per sec/sec (mps^2)

kilowatt (kw) A measure of power.
1 kw = 1×10^{10} erg/sec
= 4.4254×10^4 ft-lb/minute
= 1,000 watts (10^7 ergs/sec)
= 737.612 foot-pounds per second (ft-lb/sec)
= 101.979 kilogram meters per second (kg-m/sec)
= 56.884 Btu/minute
= 1.35972 metric horsepower (75 kg-m/sec)
= 1.34111 U.S. horsepower (550 ft-lb/sec)
= 0.94796 Btu/sec (thermal units per sec)
= 0.23888 kg-calory/sec (thermal units per sec)

kilowatt hour (kw-hr) A measure of energy, work.
1 kilowatt hour = 3,600,000 joules (10^7 ergs) (j)
= 2,655,403 foot pounds (ft-lb.)
= 367,123 kilogram meters (kg-m)
= 3,412.66 Btu (thermal units)
= 859.975 kg-calory (thermal units)
= 1.35972 metric horsepower-hours (75 kg-m-hr)
= 1.34111 U.S. horsepower-hours (h.p.-hr)

kingfish *See* mackerel

kingklip *See* Part 2: Vitamin D, Fish

king mackerel *See* mackerel

king orange *See* tangerine

king salmon *See* salmon
See Part 2: Salmon and Trout

kipper Herring that are split, lightly salted, and smoked over-night.
See Part 2: Fish, Smoke-Cured; Riboflavin, Food

kip skin Calf skin weighing between 15 and 25 lb.

Kirchner medium A microorganism media used for the propagation of *Mycobacterium tuberculosis*.
See Part 2: Microorganism, Media

kiska An imitation cooked sausage made from pork, oat groats, pork liver, pork spleen, salt, beef blood and spices.

kiskatom Hickory nut.

Kjeldahl (1849–1900) A Danish chemist who developed a method of determination of nitrogen which bears his name.

Kjeldahl determination A determination of total nitrogen by oxidizing the carbon and hydrogen and converting the nitrogen into ammonium sulfate; sulfuric acid is the oxidizing reagent; $H_2SO_4 \longrightarrow H_2 + SO_2 + O_2$. Sodium or potassium sulfate raises the boiling point and thus aids in the oxidation; copper sulfate acts as a catalyst:

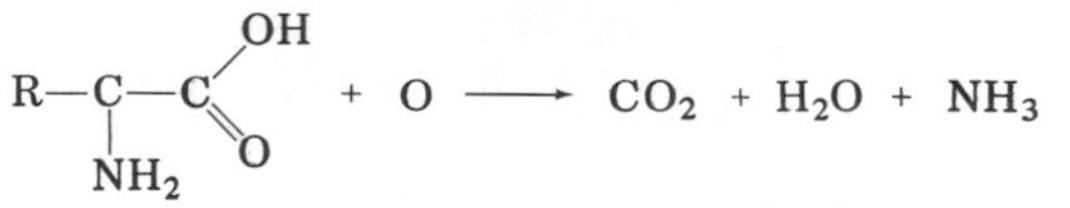

$$NH_3 + H_2SO_4 \longrightarrow NH_4HSO_4$$

Concentrated NaOH is then added and the ammonia is liberated and collected in a standard acid; from the amount of acid neutralized the ammonia nitrogen and crude protein (N × 6.25) can be calculated.

KL Microorganism media used for the serological identification of *Corynebacterium*.
See Part 2: Microorganism, Media

klamath weed A plant having a toxic principle.
See Part 2: Poisonous Plants

Klebsiella A nonmotile genus of plump short rods with rounded ends usually found in the respiratory or intestinal tract and some are pathogenic.
See Part 2: Microorganism, Media; Microorganism Reactions on Differential Tube Media

kligler iron agar *See* Part 2: Microorganism, Media; Microorganism Reactions on Differential Tube Media

knead To work dough or similar semisolid mixture, either by hand or in a machine with revolving agitator blades.
See Part 2: Margarine Production

knee Hinge joint between tibia and femur.
See Part 2: Bone

kneecap Patella.

knockwurst A sausage formulation similar to bologna; no blinders are added and garlic is used in the flavoring; it is stuffed in a large casings and linked every 4 inches.
See Part 2: Sausage Identification

knotted wrack (*Ascophyllum nodosum*) A brown algae seaweed used for livestock feed and the production of alginates used for thickening, emulsification, and food film formation.

knuckle (tip) A meat cut made up primarily of quadriceps muscles cranial to the femur; often made into dried beef. *See also* **sirloin.**
See Part 2: Beef, Boneless Cuts; Beef Round, Bone Structure; Beef Round Cuts; Meat Identification

Kobe A variety of lespedeza.

kohlrabi (*Brassica oleracea* var. *gongylodes*) A cabbage-like plant with a swollen base stem that looks like a turnip; the stem is used as a cooked vegetable or as livestock feed.
Storage: 32°F, 90–95% relative humidity, 1–3 weeks storage life.
Raw stem composition: 90% H_2O, 2% protein, 0.1% fat, 7% carbohydrate, 1% ash.
See Part 2: Minerals, Food; Storage; Sugar, Vegetables; Vegetable Composition; Vegetable Cooking; Vegetable Plants; Vegetables Classification; Vegetables, Cooking Frozen

kola *See* **cola; kola nut**

kolachy A bun filled with prune, apricot or cottage cheese.

kola nut The seed of the *Sterculiaceae* tree.
Varieties: *Cola nitida* (large nuts); *Cola acuminata* (small nuts).
60% alcoholic extract of nuts is used in soft drink industry; beverage contains 120 ppm of extract.

kolbassie (kielbasa) A cooked, smoked, and cured Polish sausage made from pork and beef seasoned with pepper, garlic, salt, sugar and thyme.
See Part 2: Sausage Nutritive Value

Korean A variety of lespedeza.

kori todu *See* **tofu**

koser citrate medium *See* Part 2: Microorganism, Culture Media, Dairy and Food Products; Microorganism, Selective and Differential Broths and Media, Water Filtration Plant

kosher Hebrew term for ritually clean foods. *See also* **Judaism, dietary rules.**

kosher stick Cutting the throat just back of the jaw.

koumiss (koumyss, coomys) Fermented mare's milk; double lactic and alcoholic fermentation; sometimes made with the milk of an ass, camel or cow.

koya dofu *See* **tofu**

KP organic acid base *See* Part 2: Microorganism, Media

Kr Symbol for the element krypton.

kraft paper General-purpose paper manufactured from pine pulp (sulfate pulp). It is strong and relatively cheap; it is the highest tonnage paper produced in U.S.

Kramwiede agar *See* Part 2: Microorganism Reactions on Differential Tube Media

K ration A military ration consisting of a 32-oz, 3-meal concentrated food package (3726 calories). It is easy to carry and of pocket-size. Example of components: pemmican canned cheese, veal loaf, ham spread, malted milk tablets, candy bars, bouillon cubes, and soluble coffee.

kraut Sauerkraut.
See Part 2: Vegetables, Canning Dates

Krebs cycle (citric acid cycle, TCA cycle) A metabolism cycle in which pyruvic acid in the presence of O_2 is broken down into carbon dioxide and water. *See also* **citric acid.**

Kreis Test A test for oxidative rancidity in fats.

krypton (Kr) A gaseous element; at. no. 36; at. wt. 83.80; noble gas group of Periodic Table; oxidation state 0; electron configuration 2-8-18-8
orbit K L M N

kudzu A perennial plant that is used to reclaim gullies and waste land; pH 6.0.
See Part 2: Seed, Germination

kumquat (*Fortunella spp.*) A fruit resembling a small orange though it is not a citrus; the pulp has an acid taste and is used for pickling and conserves.
Raw composition: 81% H_2O, 1% protein, 0.1% fat, 17% carbohydrate, 0.6% ash.
See Part 2: Fruit Classification; Minerals, Food

Kupferberg Media used for the isolation and propagation of *Trichomonas*.
See Part 2: Microorganism, Media

kurrat An onion-like plant closely related to the leek.

kurrol's salt *See* **sodium phosphate**

kutira gum *See* Part 2: Gum Distribution

kwashiorkor A nutritional deficiency of protein.

L

L Designates the left-handed (levo-) enantiomer (optical isomer) of a compound containing an asymmetric carbon atom. It indicates only the structure of the compounds, *not* its optical rotation. *See also* **D; optical isomer; enantiomer.**

La Symbol for the element lanthanum.

label A printed notice stamped on or attached to a food product indicating the following items:

1. True name of product
2. A list of ingredients in descending order of the amount used in formulating the product
3. Name and place of packer or for whom the product is prepared
4. Quantity of product
5. Inspection legend

See Part 2: Cheese Label; Meat Label

labitae The mint family.

lablab (bonavist bean, hyacinth bean, lubia; *Dolichos lablab*) A legume which produces white, reddish, black or mottled seed; young pods are boiled and eaten; ripe seed used for split pulse (cooked); foliage for livestock feed and hay.

laboratory table top dressing A formula that is composed of 600 cc raw linseed oil; 30 cc glacial acetic acid; and 2700 cc spirits of turpentine. Allow 2 weeks for drying.

lacceroic acid *See* Part 2: Saturated Fatty Acids

lachschinken A meat product made by placing two boneless cured pork loins in a casing and smoking; may or may not be cooked.

Lacombe A breed of hogs.
See Part 2: Swine Breeds

lactalbumin A protein found in milk, in which it aids in stabilization of the fat particles.
See Part 2: Milk, Amino Acids

lactase A carbohydrate digestive enzyme which catalyzes hydrolysis of lactose to glucose and galactose.

lactation Secretion of milk from the mammary glands of the female, especially during the period immediately following parturition.
See Part 2: Food, Water Intake; Milk, Mammals, Composition

lactic acid 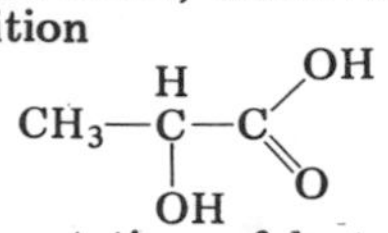 The acid in sour milk (by fermentation of lactose), sauerkraut, silage and muscle after work and after death. A widely distributed asymmetric acid used as a food additive (acidulant and preservative). Can be made by hydrolysis of lactonitrile.
See Part 2: Concentrated and Dried Milk Products; Concentration of Commercial Strengths of Acids and Bases; Cultured Dairy Products, Composition; Fluid and Fermented Milks, Composition; Milk, Dry Products; Normal Solutions; Thermophiles

lacto A frozen dessert made from cultured milk, eggs, sugar and usually flavoring.

Lactobacillus A microorganism causing fermentation spoilage in foods.
See Part 2: Canned Spoilage Manifestations; Canned Spoilage Related to pH; Microbiological Media; Microorganism, Culture Media, Dairy and Food Products; Microorganism, Media; Spoilage, Carbohydrate Foods; Spoilage, Protein Foods; Thermophiles; Water Activity, Organisms and Food

lactometer (galactometer) A floating instrument similar to a hydrometer used to measure specific gravity of milk.

Lactosaprophiticus A microorganism causing food spoilage.
See Part 2: Spoilage, Fat in Food

lactose

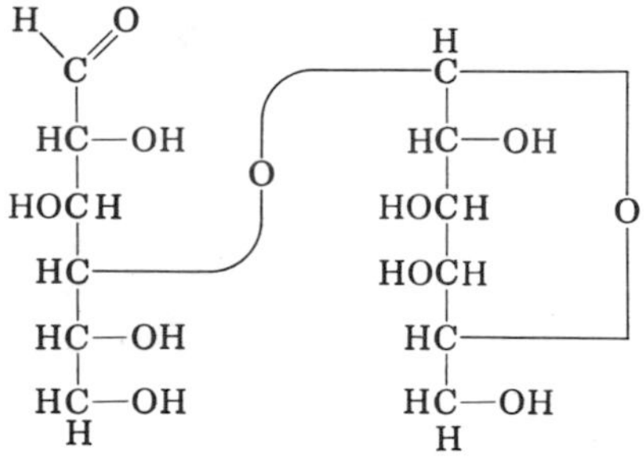

Milk sugar that yields D-glucose and D-galactose on hydrolysis; occurs only in the milk (4-7%) of mammals; the alpha form is 16% as sweet as sucrose. It is obtained from whey during cheese or casein manufacture.
See Part 2: Concentrated and Dried Milk Products; Creams, Butter and Frozen Desserts; Dairy Products, Composition; Fluid and Fermented Milks, Composition; Milk Breeds, Composition; Milk Composition; Milk, Concentrated Products; Milk, Dry Products; Milk, Mammals, Composition; Milk, Species; Sweetening Compounds

lactose broth Medium used in presumptive tests for coliform (*Escherichia*, *Aerobacter*) group by the production of gas.

See Part 2: Microbiological Examination of Dairy Products; Microbiological Media; Microorganism, Culture Media, Dairy and Food Products; Microorganism, Culture Media, Water and Sewage, Standard Methods

ladino clover A perennial legume used for pasture; approx. nutrient used for 3 tons of grazing: 175 lb N; 54 lb P_2O_5; 140 lb K_2O.

ladle A large spoon in the form of a hollow hemisphere, usually with a long curved handle, used for serving soups, stews, and similar dishes.
See Part 2: Ladle Size

lady finger (1) A small finger-shaped sponge cake; (2) A common name for okra.

Lafayette *See* **spot**

L agar *See* Part 2: Microbiological Media

lagbi Sap from the stem of a palm; it is often fermented.

lager In beer manufacturing, the aging, clarification and carbonation process.

lag phase A stage of bacterial growth in which the cell increases in size but not in numbers.

lake A pigment made by precipitating an oil-soluble organic dye on an inorganic substrate, e.g., alumina on aluminum hydroxide. Lakes color food by dispersion. *See also* **colorant.**

lake perch (yellow perch) A lean fish caught in inland fresh waters.

lake trout (togue) A fat fish caught in the lakes of North America.

La Mancha A breed of goat.
See Part 2: Goats, Milk Breeds

lamb (1) Young of ovine species (sheep) of either sex and less than 12 months old; does not have 1st pair of permanent teeth and will produce a clean break at the "break joint"; dressing percentage, avg. 52%.
See Part 2: Animal Foods, Composition; Bone; Bone Age; Braising Time; Broiling Time and Temperature; Calories, Daily Recommendations; Cooking in Liquid, Time; Food, Composition; Frozen Food Storage; Frozen Meat Storage Time; Glutamate; Grades, Meat; Iron, Daily Recommendations; Lamb Braising; Lamb Broiling; Lamb Chart; Lamb Crown Roast Carving; Lamb Cuts; Lamb Cuts and Uses; Lamb Leg Carving; Lamb Percentages of Daily Recommended Allowances; Lamb Roasting; Lamb Simmering; Lamb, Wholesale Cuts; Lamb Yield; Liver; Meat and Meat Products Composition; Meat Composition; Meat, Frozen Storage; Meat Identification; Meat Label; Meat, Nutritive Value; Meat, Servings per Pound; Meat Storage; Minerals, Food; Niacin, Daily Recommendations; Riboflavin, Daily Recommendations; Roasting Meat; Roasting, Time and Temperature; Sheep Market Classes and Grades; Simmering Meat; Thiamin, Daily Recommendations; Vitamin A, Food
(2) The flesh of young (less than 12 to 14 months old) ovine animals of both sexes. Lamb grades are Prime, Choice, Good, Medium (spring lambs only), Plain, Cull. *See also* **hothouse lambs** for their grades.

lamb chuck A wholesale cut of lamb consisting of all in front of the 4th rib.

lambda (Λ, λ) Greek letter with an English equivalent of l; used as a symbol for wavelength of light; also a measure of volume or weight.

1 lambda = 1 microliter
= 1×10^{-3} milliliter
= 1×10^{-6} liter
= 1 microgram
= 1×10^{-3} milligram
= 1×10^{-6} gram

lambert A unit of brightness; 0.3183 candle/sq cm.

lamb hog *See* **hogget**

lambkill A plant having a toxic principle.
See Part 2: Poisonous Plants

lamb leg *See* Part 2: Lamb Chart; Lamb Roasting; Lamb Yield

lamb rack An elevated, trough-like skinning rack used in the slaughter of lambs.

lamb's lettuce *See* **field salad**

Lamona An American class of chicken that lays a light-colored egg; color, white.

land plaster (rock gypsum) A fertilizer material; 70–75% $CaSO_4$; used for calcium supply for peanuts; 0–0–0.

Landrace A bacon-type hog originating in Denmark.
See Part 2: Swine Breeds

langsat *See* Part 2: Fruit Storage

Langshan An Asiatic class of chickens that have feathered shanks and lay a brown-shelled egg. Varieties: Black (white skin); White (yellow skin).

lanolin Refined wool grease; a mixture of cholesterol palmitate, cholesterol oleate, and cholesterol stearate; base for ointments and creams.

lanthanum (La) A metallic element; at. no. 57; at. wt. 138.92; Group IIIB of Periodic Table. Electron configuration 2-8-18-18-9-2;
orbit K L M N O P
oxidation state +3.

lanzones *See* Part 2: Fruit Classification

lapsang souchong *See* **black tea**

larch gum (*Arabinogalactan*) A gum obtained by water extraction from the western larch tree.

lard A natural fat extracted from pork fat.
240°F max. rendering temperature
1 cup = 220 g (7.8 oz)
2 cups = 1 lb
Fatty acid composition: 1% myristic, 27–28% palmitic, 3% palmitoleic, 0.5% margaric, 12–13%

stearic, 44-47% oleic, 6-10% linoleic, 0.5% linolenic.
Storage: Keep covered (90-95% relative humidity); hydrogenated with antioxidants, room temperature; not stabilized, refrigerate (45°F), 4 mo. storage life.
Composition: Fat 100%; ash 0%; protein 0%; carbohydrate 0%.
80-85% yield from rind fat
75-78% yield from nonrind fat (hand press)
Properties:
Acid number 3.4
Smoke point (varies with FFA content) 250-425°F; (continuous process) 420°F; (steam-rendered) 340-372°F.
Saponification value 190-205
Unsaponifiable 0.8%
Specific gravity 0.917-0.938
Refractive index (60°C) 1.441-1.461
Mixed lard melting point 36-45°C; back fat 86-104°F leaf fat 110-118°F
Iodine value 45-75

	Killing fat Depot fat	Cutting fat
Hog fat (%)	35	65
Iodine Value	67-70	57-60

Fat from peanut fed hog has iodine value over 85.
See Part 2: Altitude Adjustments for Baking; Calories, Daily Recommendations; Fats and Oils, Composition; Fat and Oils, Fatty Acid Composition; Fats and Oils, Physical and Chemical Properties; Fatty Acids, Fats and Oils; Fats and Oils, Characteristic; Iodine and Saponification Values; Lard, Triglyceride Mole Percent Composition; Melting Points, Fats and Oils; Minerals, Food; Oils and Fats Composition; Pork Carcass, Retail Yield; Pork Yield; Saturated Fatty Acids; Specific Gravities, Fats and Oils; Spoilage, Fat in Food; Titer, Fats and Oils; Unsaponifiable Matter; Unsaturated Fatty Acids

larder beetle An insect that feeds on stored meat and cheese.

larding A method of securing pieces of bacon fat to meat to keep from drying during cooking. *See also* **lardoon.**

lard oil Liquid (primarily olein, stearin) obtained by pressing prime steam lard.

Specific gravity	0.905-0.916
Refractive index (15.5°C)	1.469-1.472
Saponification number	193-198
Iodine number	56-82

lardoon (lardon) Narrow strips of bacon fat used to keep meat from drying during cooking. *See also* **larding.**

lard type A classification of hogs that has been changed to meat type due to the trend toward leaner hogs.

Laredo A variety of soybean.

Large White A breed of hogs.
See Part 2: Swine Breeds

larkspur A plant having a toxic principle.
See Part 2: Poisonous Plants

lasagne Baked dish made from several cheeses, tomatoes and meat sauce.

Lash Serum *See* Part 2: Microorganism, Media

latent heat Heat absorbed or lost by a substance as it changes state without a change in temperature; e.g., for water the latent heat of fusion (ice to water) is 80 cal per gram; latent heat of condensation (steam to water) is 540 cal per gram.
See Part 2: Temperature of Vaporization, Latent Heat of Vaporization, Boiling Point

latex A white, milky fluid obtained from many varieties of shrubs and trees. Most common is rubber latex (from the tree *Hevea Braziliensis*) which contains about 30% rubber hydrocarbon, which is separated by addition of acetic or formic acid. The hydrocarbon particles are coated with a proteinaceous protective colloid. The latex of the sapodilla plant is called chicle.

latin square columns = rows = treatments

Column

	A	B	C
Row	C	A	B
	B	C	A

Key
$X_{\text{column row treatment}}$

Row	Column 1	2..	i...	a	Row ΣX
1	X_{111}	X_{212}	X_{i1K}	X_{a1R}	$X_{\cdot 1K}$
2	X_{122}	X_{22K}	X_{i2R}	X_{a21}	$X_{\cdot 2K}$
j	X_{1jK}	X_{2jR}	X_{ij1}	X_{aj2}	$X_{\cdot jK}$
n	X_{1nR}	X_{2n1}	X_{in2}	X_{anK}	$X_{\cdot nK}$
Col ΣX	$X_{1\cdot K}$	$X_{2\cdot K}$	$X_{i\cdot K}$	$X_{a\cdot K}$	$X_{\cdots}$

Treatment Summary

	1	2	K	R	
Treat ΣX	$X_{\cdot\cdot 1}$	$X_{\cdot\cdot 2}$	$X_{\cdot\cdot K}$	$X_{\cdot\cdot R}$	$X_{\cdots}$

Correction $= (X_{\cdots})^2/an = C \qquad a = n = R$

Total SS $= (X_{111})^2 + \cdots (X_{anK})^2 - C$

$$\text{Row SS} = \frac{(X_{\cdot 1K})^2 + \cdots (X_{\cdot nK})^2}{a} - C$$

$$\text{Column SS} = \frac{(X_{1\cdot K})^2 + \cdots (X_{a\cdot K})^2}{n} - C$$

$$\text{Treatment SS} = \frac{(X_{\cdot\cdot 1})^2 + \cdots (X_{\cdot\cdot R})^2}{\#\text{ of obs. in Treat. Sum.}} - C$$

Error = Total SS − Row SS − Column SS − Treatment SS

Sources of Variation	df	SS	MS
Total	an − 1	Total SS	
Row	n − 1	Row SS	Row SS/n − 1
Column	a − 1	Column SS	Column SS/a − 1
Treatment	R − 1	Treat. SS	Treat. SS/R − 1
Error	(a − 1) · (a − 2)	Error SS	Error SS/a^2 − 3a + 2

F = MS of Row or Col or Treat/MS Error

df = a − 1, $a^2 - 3a + 2$

latissimus dorsi The broad muscle of the back; it is the lateral muscle in the rib end of a rib steak; runs from spinous processes of the lumbar to the humerus.

laurel *See* **bay leaves**

laurel kernel oil *See* Part 2: Saturated Fatty Acids

lauric acid *See* **dodecanoic acid**

lauroleic acid *See* Part 2: Fatty Acids and Their Properties; Unsaturated Fatty Acids

lauryl sulfate broth *See* Part 2: Microbiological Media

lauryl tryptose broth *See* Part 2: Microorganism, Culture Media, Water and Sewage, Standard Methods

lavandin oil An essential oil steam-distilled from a plant of the lavender species.
See Part 2: Flavoring Agents, Natural

lavender oil An essential oil steam-distilled from flowers of *Landula officinalis*.
See Part 2: Essential Oils

laver (***Porphyra umbilicalis***) A red algae seaweed used for food.

Law of Chemical Equilibrium *See* **equilibrium constant**

Law of Mass Action *See* **equilibrium constant**

L.C.L. Less-than carload lot.

leach To wash out water-soluble components, as from the soil.

lead (Pb) A metallic element; at. no. 82; at. wt. 207.21; Group IVA of Periodic Table; oxidation states +2, +4;
electron configuration 2-8-18-32-18-4
orbit K L M N O P
Lead and its compounds are toxic to man and animals.
See Part 2: Chemical Poisoning; Minerals (Trace), Limits; Water Drinking Standards

lead arsenate $PbHAsO_4$ A poisonous inorganic insecticide.

leaf That portion of a plant in which photosynthesis occurs.
See Part 2: Corn; Vegetables, Classification; Wastes, Agricultural and Industrial

leaf gum *See* **gum tragacanth**

leaf-hopper *See* Part 2: Insect Control

leaf lard The rendered internal abdominal fat of the hog; fat located on the interior of a pork loin; max. iodine number 50; m.p. 110-118°F.

leaf lettuce A crisp, light-green, curly-edged, lettuce used for salad greens. *See also* **lettuce.**

leafminer Any of several insects whose larva burrow into the parenchyma of leaves.
See Part 2: Insect Control

leaf-roller *See* Part 2: Insect Control

league A linear measurement; 1 league = 15,840 feet = 5280 yards = 3 miles.

lean cuts (hog carcass) Boston butt, picnic, loin and ham. Lean pork trimmings contain 20-25% fat.

least significant difference A value that can be used if only 2 means are compared (a = 2) (a = no. of treatments); if 3 or more means are compared, too many will be judged significant; difference in means = $t_{s\bar{x}}\sqrt{2}$.

least squares A principle that states that if deviations are measured from the sample mean and then squared that the sum of these squares will be a minimum value; if the deviations were compared to any value other than the mean, then squared and summed, the resulting sum would be larger than when compared to the mean.

leather The skin or hide of an animal that has been tanned. *See also* **tannic acid.**

leavening agent *See* **baking powder; yeast**

Lebanon An all-beef semi-dry sausage that is given a 6-14 days cold smoke; it has a tangy flavor due to microbial growth.

lebkuchen Cookie containing candied orange peel, cherries, citrons and honey, almonds and seasoning.

lecheguilla A plant having a toxic principle.
See Part 2: Poisonous Plants

lechon Festive pig cooked over live charcoals.

lecithin (trimethyl hydroxyethyl ammonium hydroxide) A phosphatidyl choline. Lecithins are mixtures of fatty acid diglycerides combined with the choline ester of phosphoric acid. Extracted from soybean flake of which it constitutes 0.2 to 0.6%. Lecithins occur in brains, nerves, liver, egg yolk, soybeans, pancreas, heart and blood.

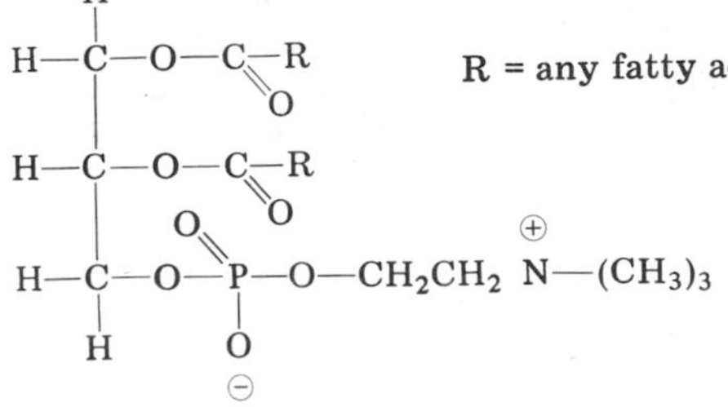

R = any fatty acid

Uses: Emulsifying agents, foam stabilizers, suspending agents, release agents, surface-active agents, wetting agents, nutritive supplements, antispattering, and antioxidant (0.075%).
See Part 2: Minerals (Trace), Limits

lecithinated soy flour Defatted soy flour to which 15% lecithin has been added.

lecithoprotein Protein attached to lecithin or some other phospholipid.

Lee A variety of soybean.

leek (*Allium porrum*) An onion-like plant with an elongated bulb.
Storage: 32°F, 90–95% relative humidity, storage life 1 mo.
Raw bulb composition: 85% H_2O, 2% protein, 0.3% fat, 11% carbohydrate, 1% ash.
See Part 2: Minerals, Food; Storage; Sugar, Vegetables; Vegetables, Classification; Vegetable Composition; Vegetable Plants; Vegetable Storage

leg *See* Part 2: Bone; Bone in Retail Cuts; Lamb Cuts; Lamb Cuts and Uses; Lamb Roasting; Lamb, Wholesale Cuts; Meat Composition; Meat Identification; Meat, Servings Per Pound; Pork Cookery; Pork Cuts and Uses; Pork Wholesale Cuts; Poultry Dressing Percentage; Roasting, Time and Temperature; Turkey Composition; Veal Chart; Veal Cuts; Veal Cuts and Uses; Veal Roasting; Veal Wholesale Cuts

leg bone *See* Part 2: Beef Wholesale Cuts; Lamb, Wholesale Cuts; Pork Wholesale Cuts; Veal Wholesale Cuts

Leghorn A Mediterranean class of chickens that is early-maturing, a good egg producer, and lays a white-shelled egg. Varieties;
*Single-comb white
Rose-comb white
Single-comb light brown
Rose-comb light brown
Single-comb dark brown
Rose-comb dark brown
Single-comb buff
Single-comb black
Single-comb silver
Single-comb red
Single-comb black tailed red
Single-comb Columbian
*Bantam variety also
See Part 2: Poultry Breeds and Varieties

leg of lamb A meat cut that can be prepared in several lengths, but is usually cut in front of the hip bone. *See also* **American leg of lamb**; **French leg of lamb**.

legume *See* **pulse**
See Part 2: Sugar, Legumes; Vegetables Classification

leguminosae *See* Part 2: Vegetables Classification

Leicester A long-wool breed of sheep originating in central England.
See Part 2: Sheep Breeds

lemon (*Citrus limon*) A citrus fruit with a yellow skin and a high concentration of citric acid in the pulp; the juice is used in flavoring, cooking, confectionery and in preparing lemonade; a good source of vitamin C. It is also used as a root stock for other citrus plants. *See also* **citrus fruit**.
1 lb = 3–5 lemons
1 avg. size lemon = 2 to 4 tablespoons juice = 1½ to 3 teaspoons grated rind
3 lb or 1 doz fresh = 2 cups juice (1 cup = 250 g or 8.7 oz)
1 box (9.9 × 13 × 25 in.) = 76 lb
1 carton (10.25 × 10.7 × 16.4 in.) = 70 lb
Storage: 32°F, 85–90% relative humidity, 1 to 2 mo. storage life; f.p. 28°F.

Composition	H_2O (%)	Protein (%)	Fat (%)	Carbohydrate (%)	Ash (%)	pH
Peeled fruit	90	1	0.3	8	0.3	2.2–2.4
Juice	91	0.5	0.2	8	0.3	2.3–2.6
Peel	82	1.5	0.3	16	0.6	

See Part 2: Essential Oils; Flavor Ingredients, Taste and Flavor Type; Flavors, Beverage; Fruit and Nut Rootstock; Fruit, Availability; Fruit Harvest Dates; Fruit Classification; Fruit Composition; Fruit Storage; Fruit Juice Flavors; Lemon Juice Composition; Lemon Oil Composition; Lemon Oil Properties; Minerals, Food; Minerals (Trace), Limits; Organic Acids in Fruits and Vegetables; Plant Foods, Composition; Rot Spoilage; Standards, Processed Fruit and Vegetable Products; Storage

lemonade A drink made from lemon juice, sugar and water.

lemon extract 5% by volume of oil of lemon, which is obtained by pressure from the peel or rind of a lemon.

lemon-lime A carbonated beverage made with lemon juice with small amount of lime juice.
See Part 2: Beverage Carbonated, Ingredients

lemon sole *See* **sole**

lentil (*Lens culinaris*) A leguminous plant whose seeds are dried and used in soups and stews; one to two seeds are contained in the flattened pod and the seeds are green, greenish-brown, reddish or mottled.
1 lb dried = 2¼ cups
1 cup dried = 190 g (6.7 oz)
1 lb dried = 5 cups cooked
1 cup cooked = 200 g (7.1 oz)
Raw dry seed composition: 11% H_2O, 25% protein, 1% fat, 60% carbohydrate, 3% ash.
See Part 2: Beans Dry, Cooking; Minerals, Food; Seed, Chemical Composition; Vegetable Servings

Leptospira Finely coiled aerobic organisms (6–20 μ long) and some are pathogenic to man and animals.
See Part 2: Microorganism, Media

leptospirosis (lepto) A highly contagious disease of cattle, hogs, dogs, rodents and man; there are blood tests and vaccinations available.

lespedeza An annual legume used for hay; seed, 25 to 50 lb per bushel; plant 6 to 40 lb per acre;

pH 6.0; varieties: climax, kobe, Korean, rowan; approx. nutrient used for 2 tons of hay, 77 lb N, 16 lb P_2O_5, 41 lb K_2O.
See Part 2: Seed, Germination

lespedeza, sericea A perennial grass used for forage and erosion control; seed, 60 lb/bu; plant 20–40 lb/acre; pH 6.0; harvest when 12 inches tall, 2 to 3 times/yr; varieties: common, Arlington.

less than Symbol used in scientific notation is $<$, less than or equal to notation is $\leqslant$.

Letheen broth A medium made with trypticase glucose extract, lecithin, and polysorbate 80; used for testing the action of quaternary ammonium compounds in cleaning (phenol coefficient).

lettuce (*Lactuca sativa*) An annual or biennial plant belonging to the daisy family and used as a salad green.
Types
bibb: small cup-shaped head, green exterior and white interior;
Boston: loose oval head, dark green exterior and almost white interior;
iceberg: firm head, medium green exterior and light green interior;
leaf: unheaded, light green, leaves with ruffled edges;
romaine or cos: elongated head, stiff leaves, dark green exterior, light green interior.
1 crate (13 × 18 × 21.6 in.) = 70 lb
3 heads of lettuce for serving salad = 50 servings
Composition: 94–95% H_2O, 1–1.3% protein, 0.1–0.3% fat, 2.5–3.5% carbohydrate, 0.6–1% ash, pH 6.0
Storage: Wash and dry; store in refrigerator (32°F), crisper or plastic bags (90–95% relative humidity); use within 1 to 4 days. *See also* **Australian lettuce; bibb lettuce; Boston lettuce; bronze beauty lettuce; Grand Rapids lettuce; iceberg lettuce; leaf lettuce; New York lettuce; oak leaf lettuce; prize head lettuce; romaine lettuce.**
See Part 2: Ascorbic Acid; Calories, Daily Recommendations; Food, Composition; Fruit and Vegetable, Diseases; Iron; Minerals, Food; Niacin; Nitrate, Vegetables; Phosphorus; Plant Foods, Composition; Potassium; Riboflavin; Riboflavin, Food; Storage; Sugar, Vegetables; Thiamin, Transit Temperature; Vegetable Composition; Vegetable Plants; Vegetables, Classification; Vegetable Storage; Vitamin A

leucine A monoamino-monocarboxylic essential amino acid.

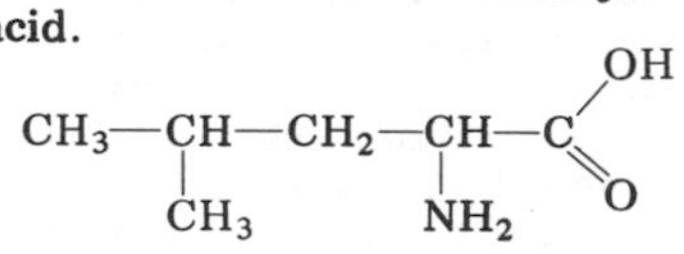

See Part 2: Amino Acids; Amino Acid, Solubilities; Corn, Amino Acids; Egg Products, Nutritive Value; Grain Analysis; Manure Analysis; Milk, Amino Acids; Seed, Chemical Composition; Wheat, Amino Acids; Wheat Products, Amino Acid Compositions

leucocyte *See* **white blood cell**

Leuconostoc *See* Part 2: Spoilage, Carbohydrate Foods

leunasaltpeter A mixture of ammonium nitrate and ammonium sulfate used as a fertilizer.

Levine He developed the Eosin Methylene Blue medium which is used for differentiation of enteric bacilli, including coliform organisms, *Escherichia coli* and *Aerobacter aerogenes.*
See Part 2: Micribiological Examination of Dairy Products; Microbiological Media; Microorganism, Culture Media, Dairy and Food Products

Levine EMB agar *See* Part 2: Microorganism, Culture Media, Water and Sewage, Standard Methods; Microorganism, Media; Microorganism, Selective and Differential Broths and Media, Water Filtration Plant

levorotatory (*l*), (−) The ability of an asymmetric compound to rotate polarized light to the left.

levulans $(C_6H_{10}O_5)_x$ A polysaccharide made up of levulose units and found in many plants.

levulose *See* **fructose**

Leyden cheese *See* **nokkelost cheese**

Li Symbol for the element lithium.

Libbee A variety of clingstone peach.

licanic acid *See* Part 2: Fatty Acids and Their Properties

lice Parasites of several species that live on cattle, horses and swine; may be reddish, bluish or dark gray.

lichen A plant composed of a fungus and an alga in a type of mutually beneficial union called symbiosis; color may be greenish-gray to yellow-brown; found on rocky areas, trees, etc. The chemical indicator litmus is made by fermentation of lichens.

licorice (*Glycyrrhiza glabra*) The dried rhizomes of a perennial herb belonging to the pea family; they are chewed, powdered, extracted with liquid and used to flavor sweets and soft drinks.
See Part 2: Minerals (Trace), Limits; Water Activity, Organisms and Food

licorice extract Rhizomes of the licorice plant are ground into pulp, boiled in water and the extract is concentrated by evaporation.

liederkranz A soft, creamy yellow, dessert cheese slightly less pungent than limburger; ripened by surface bacteria.
Composition: 52% H_2O, 16–17% protein, 28% fat, 1.5% salt, 3.5% ash.
See Part 2: Cheese, Vitamin Content; Vitamin A, Milk and Milk Products

ligament A strip or band of fibrous tissue attaching one bone to another.

ligamentum nuchae Back strap.
See Part 2: Beef Rib Nomenclature; Connective Tissue, Composition

light Radiation of any wavelength of the electromagnetic spectrum; its velocity is 3×10^{10}cm/sec

(186,000 miles/sec). The wavelength range of visible light is from 3.9 to 7.7×10^{-5} cm. Frequency is the ratio of velocity to wavelength in cm. Microwave frequencies are used in cooking; x-rays and gamma rays are used in food preservation. *See also* **radiation.**

light calf skin Calf skin weighing less than 9 lb.

light cow hide A cow hide weighing between 30 and 53 lb.

light steer hide A steer hide weighing between 48 and 58 lb.

lignin A polymer found in wood (25–30%), the balance being cellulose. Its exact chemical composition is unknown; in papermaking it is separated from cellulose in the digestion process.
See Part 2: Histochemical Test

lignite The lowest grade of coal, often called brown coal; it is the next stage above peat in the coal formation cycle.
See Part 2: Fuel, Heating Value

lignoceric acid $CH_3(CH_2)_{22}COOH$ A saturated fatty acid occurring in peanut oil.
See Part 2: Fat and Oils, Fatty Acid Composition; Fatty Acids and Their Properties; Fatty Acids; Fatty Acids, Fats and Oils; Saturated Fatty Acids

liliaceae Botanical name for the lily family.
See Part 2: Vegetables, Classification

lima bean *See* **bean, lima; butter bean**
See Part 2: Potassium

lima bean agar *See* Part 2: Microorganism, Media

limburger cheese (limburg) A soft, creamy white dessert cheese from Belgium with a pungent aroma and a robust, nut-like flavor. It is made from whole or partly skimmed milk and sold in a brick shape with a brownish exterior or packed in jars; ripened 1–2 mo.
Composition: 45–46% H_2O, 21–22% protein, 27–28% fat, 2% carbohydrate, 2% salt, 4% ash.
See Part 2: Cheese Characteristics; Cheese, Vitamin Content; Milk and Cheese Composition; Vitamin A, Milk and Milk Products

lime (fruit) (*Citrus aurantifolia*) A small citrus tree that bears a fruit having a yellowish (Key) or greenish (Persian or Tahitian) skin. It is high in ascorbic and citric acid content and is used to flavor food and drinks, or mixed with water and sugar and sold as a beverage. *See also* **citrus fruit.**
Size: medium = 1½ in. in diameter; 1 box = 80 lb.
Storage: Lime dries out quickly and loses its juiciness; store at 48–50°F, 85–90% relative humidity; storage life, 6 weeks.
Juice composition: 90% H_2O, 0.3% protein, 0.1% fat, 9% carbohydrate, 0.3% ash, pH 1.8–2.2.
See Part 2: Essential Oils; Flavors, Beverage; Fruit and Nut Rootstock; Fruit, Availability; Fruit Classification; Fruit Composition; Fruit Juice Flavors; Fruit Storage; Lime Juice Composition; Lime Oil Composition; Lime Oil Properties; Minerals (Trace), Limits; Organic Acids in Fruits and Vegetables; Storage; Transit Temperature

lime (material) CaO (calcium oxide) The second highest-volume chemical produced in the U.S. Derived from limestone ($CaCO_3$) by heating at high temperature. Aids in hardening of egg shells. Used as a soil conditioner. *See also* **builders lime; caustic lime; hydrated lime; lump lime; precipitated lime; slake; water-slaked lime.**
See Part 2: Fertilizer Materials; Liming Materials

limequat A hybrid between lime and kumquat.

limestone $CaCO_3$ Source of lime; dolomites or dolomitic limestone may contain large quantities of magnesium carbonate; ground limestone weighs 2.4 lb/qt. *See also* **agricultural limestone.**
See Part 2: Fertilizer; Fertilizer Materials; Liming Materials

limestone lettuce *See* **bibb lettuce**

lime-sulfur An inorganic insecticide.

linaloe oil An essential oil obtained by distillation of the Mexican linaloe tree.
See Part 2: Essential Oils

Lincoln A long-wool breed of sheep originating in North-eastern England.
See Part 2: Sheep Breeds

lindane A poisonous chlorinated hydrocarbon insecticide (gamma-benzene hexachloride).

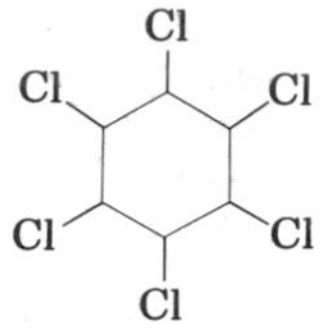

See also **benzene hexachloride.**
See Part 2: Insect Control

line-breeding Mating of related animals, but not as closely related as in in-breeding.

ling *See* **hake; water chestnut**
See Part 2: Vitamin D, Fish

link (1) A measure of length or distance used in surveying.
1 link = 7.92 inches
25 links = 1 rod
(2) To join by interlocking or external attachment; e.g., a linked-chain fence; link sausage; chemical crosslinking.
See Part 2: Sausage Identification

linoleic acid
$CH_3(CH_2)_4CH{=}CHCH_2CH{=}CH(CH_2)_7COOH$
A polyunsaturated 18-carbon fatty acid found in drying oils (cottonseed, linseed, etc.)
See Part 2: Egg Products, Nutritive Value; Fats and Oils Composition; Fat and Oils, Fatty Acid Composition; Fatty Acids; Fatty Acids, Fats and Oils; Fatty Acids and Their Properties; Beans, Peas and Nuts; Dairy Products, Composition; Egg Composition; Fish and Shellfish Composition; Fruit Composition; Grain Products Composition; Meat Composition; Oils, Seed and Fruit; Poultry Composition; Sausage Composition; Seed, Chemical Composition; Soups, Composi-

tion; Sugars and Sweets Composition; Unsaturated Fatty Acids; Vegetable Composition; Wheat, Fatty Acids; Wheat Products Composition

linolenic acid $CH_3(CH_2CH{=}CH)_3(CH_2)_7COOH$ A polyunsaturated 18-carbon (3 double bonds) fatty acid found in many vegetable oils. It is an essential fatty acid in diet.
See Part 2: Fats and Oils Composition; Fatty Acids and Their Properties; Fatty Acids; Fatty Acids, Fats and Oils; Oils, Seed and Fruit; Seed, Chemical Composition; Unsaturated Fatty Acids; Wheat, Fatty Acids; Wheat Products Composition

linseed oil A fatty drying oil obtained from flaxseed. Forms hard film by polymerization on exposure to air. Used as paint base, in linoleum, etc.
1 lb oil = 2.80 lb flaxseed
Acid number 3.42
Specific gravity 20°/4°C 0.9297

	Smoke Point (°F)	Smoke Point (°C)	Flash Point (°F)	Flash Point (°C)	Fire Point (°F)	Fire Point (°C)
Raw	325	163	540	287	667	353
Refined	320	160	588	309	680	360

See Part 2: Fats and Oils, Composition; Fats and Oils, Physical and Chemical Properties; Fatty Acids, Fats and Oils; Iodine and Saponification Values; Oil or Fat, Characteristics; Refractive Indices, Fats and Oils; Specific Gravities; Fats and Oils; Titer, Fats and Oils; Unsaponifiable Matter; Unsaturated Fatty Acids

linseed oil meal A meal made from flaxseed; used as animal feed.
1 lb meal = 1.56 lb flaxseed
new process = 29 lb/bu; 0.9 lb/qt
See Part 2: Oil Meals Composition

linusic acid *See* Part 2: Fatty Acids and Their Properties

lip *See* Part 2: Beef Rib Nomenclature

lipase Enzymes which catalyze hydrolysis of fats to glycerol and fatty acids.
See Part 2: pH Values of Biological Materials

lipid A general term for fats, oils, and similar substances; lipids occur in all living cells. *See also* fat, fatty acid.
See Part 2: Egg Products, Nutritive Value

lipolytic Fat-seeking; descriptive of the action of lipase enzymes.

liqueur *See* **cordial**

liquid cook To cook food in a moist atmosphere.
See Part 2: Beef Cuts; Beef Cuts and Uses; Cooking in Liquid, Time; Lamb Cuts; Lamb Cuts and Uses; Liquid Cooking of Meat; Pork Cookery; Pork Cuts; Pork Cuts and Uses; Pork Loin Cooking; Simmering Meat; Variety Meat, Cooking; Variety Meat Preparation; Veal Chart; Veal Cuts; Veal Cuts and Uses; Vitamin Retention, Meat

liquor (1) A distilled alcoholic beverage (whiskey, gin), as opposed to fermented beverages (wine, beer). Four jiggers contain 6 oz of liquor. (2) A concentrated water solution of sugars (mother liquor). (3) The aqueous solution of juices, fats, and other water-soluble components remaining after a food product is boiled.

listeria *See* Part 2: Microorganism, Media

litchi (litchee, lychee) (*Litchi chinensis*) A medium-size tree that bears bunches of plum-size, warty rind, crimson fruit; the edible pulp (cream to white) surrounds a single brown seed. The pulp has a sweet-acid flavor; it is eaten fresh, canned, preserved in syrup and made into litchi nuts by drying.

Composition	H_2O (%)	Protein (%)	Fat (%)	Carbohydrate (%)	Ash (%)
Raw	82	0.9	0.3	16	0.5
Dried	22	4	1.2	71	2

liter (l) (litre) A measure of volume
1 liter = 16894 minims (Br.)
= 16231 minims (U.S.)
= 1,000.027 cu centimeters (cm^3 or cc)
= 1,000 milliliters (ml)
= 270.5179 drams (U.S. fl.)
= 100 centiliters (cl)
= 61.0234 cubic inches (cu in.)
= 35.196 ounces (Br. fl.)
= 33.814 ounces (U.S. fluid)
= 10 deciliters (dl)
= 2.11336 U.S. fluid pints
= 1.0567 U.S. liquid quarts
= 1 cu decimeter (dm^3)
= 0.9081 U.S. dry quart
= 0.8990 quart (Br.)
= 0.264178 U.S. liquid gallon
= 0.22702 U.S. dry gallon
= 0.21998 gallon (Br.)
= 0.1 decaliter (dkl)
= 0.03531 cubic feet (cu ft)
= 0.02838 U.S. bushel (bu)
= 0.01 hectoliter (hl)
= 8.387×10^{-3} barrel (U.S.)
= 0.001308 cubic yard (cu yd)
= 1×10^{-3} cu meter
See Part 2: Water, Weight and Volume

liter per hectare Volume per unit area.
1 liter/ha = 0.107 gal. (U.S.)/acre
= 0.089 gal. (Imp. or Br.)/acre

liter per minute Rate of flow.
1 liter per min = 4.403×10^{-3} gal./sec
= 3.666×10^{-3} gal. (Br.)/sec
= 5.885×10^{-4} cu ft/sec

lithium (Li) A metallic element; at. no. 3; at. wt. 6.940; Group IA of Periodic Table; oxidation state +1; electron configuration 2–1
orbit K L

litmus An indicator of pH values. In an acid solution it is red, in a basic solution it is blue and in a neutral solution it is lavender; its pH range is 4 to 8. *See also* **lichen.**

litmus milk Medium used for propagating and maintaining stock cultures of lactic acid bacteria

found in dairy products and in determining action of bacteria upon milk; the reduction of litmus is useful in differentiation.
See Part 2: Microorganism, Media

little cabbages Brussels sprouts of large size, which are therefore less desirable.

littleneck Small, hard-shell clams, so named from Little Neck, Long Island. *See also* **quahog.**

little tuna *See* **tuna**

Littman oxgall agar *See* Part 2: Microorganism, Media

livarot A strong-flavored, light terra-cotta colored cheese; it is encased in a girdle of dark chestnut green threads that are made of hollow reeds that keep the cheese in shape while softening.

liver A large glandular, purple organ used as food. The cells of the liver are polygonal in shape with a large central nucleus; the cells are arranged in columns and radiate from a central vein; good source of nutrients.
Storage: Coldest part of refrigerator; use within 1 to 2 days.
Raw composition: 70–72% H_2O, 19–21% protein, 3.5–5% fat, 2.5–5.3% carbohydrate, 1.3–1.5% ash.
See Part 2: Ascorbic Acid; Beef Cuts and Uses; Calories, Daily Recommendations; Food, Composition; Gland Weights; Iron, Daily Recommendations; Lamb Cuts and Uses; Liver; Meat Composition; Meat, Servings per Pound; Minerals, Food; Moisture in Biological Materials; Niacin, Daily Recommendations; Nicotinic Acid, Food; Organ Weights; Pantothenic Acid Content; Pork Cooking Yield; Pork Cuts and Uses; Portion Size; Poultry Dressing Percentage; Riboflavin, Daily Recommendations; Riboflavin, Food; Storage Times; Thiamin, Daily Recommendations; Thiamin, Food; Unsaturated Fatty Acids; Variety Meat, Cooking; Variety Meat Percentage of Daily Recommended Allowances; Variety Meat Preparation; Veal Cuts and Uses; Vitamin A, Daily Recommendations; Vitamin A, Food

liver infusion agar *See* Part 2: Microorganism, Media

liver loaf *See* Part 2: Sausage, Types

liver oil *See* Part 2: Oils and Fats Composition

liver sausage A sausage product made from pork, beef or veal, pork liver and bread; min. 30% liver; internal temperature of 145–165°F (a good grade is often called braunschweiger).
See Part 2: Sausage Identification; Sausage Nutritive Value

liver veal agar *See* Part 2: Microorganism, Media

llama A long-haired ruminant of South America.
See Part 2: Milk, Mammals, Composition

LM agar *See* Part 2: Microorganism, Media

LMM Light meromyosin.

LNF Liquid nitrogen frozen.

load line Highest point at which food should be stacked in a refrigerated case.

loaf (1) The usual unit of size in which bread is produced, normally from 1 to 1.5 lb. (2) A mixture of chopped meat, spices, etc. baked in a definite shape or mold.
See Part 2: Pork, Cooking; Pork Loin Cooking; Portion Size; Sausage Identification

loaf cheese A processed American cheese sold in loaf form.

loam Soil containing clay, sand and humus.
See Part 2: Soil Classes

lobscouse A mixture of meat, vegetables and biscuit.

lobster A lean, marine crustacean; a shellfish; 50% edible (avg. 20% protein)

Types	Where caught
Northern, Maine	New England; Canada
Rock, Rock lobster tail	South Africa; U.S. coast; Australia; New Zealand; Brazil; Ecuador
Spiny	British Honduras; Haiti

Two-claw (*Homarus americanus*)
wt ¾ to 3 lb
2½-lb lobster = 1 lb meat
1-lb lobster = 8 oz tail

Spiny does not have heavy claws; tail avg. 2 to 8 oz
1-lb lobster = 4 to 5 oz cooked lobster meat
= 1 cup cooked meat
= 5 oz canned lobster

Servings:

Form	Amount needed for one serving
Meat (1 cup = 155 g (5.4 oz))	4 oz
Tail	8 oz
Whole	16 oz

As purchased	Oz to purchase/ 1 serving	% yield
In shell	12	22–25
Tails	6	50–66

Tail is about ⅓ of the total weight
Grades of New England lobster

Chicken	¾ to 1 lb
Quarters	1¼ to 1½ lb
Large	1½ to 2½ lb
Jumbo	over 3 lb

Cooking for 1–1½ lb lobster: boil for 15–20 min in 3–4% salt solution
Composition of raw tail meat: 77% H_2O, 20% protein, 2% fat, 1.5% ash.
American lobster—*Homarus americanus*
European lobster—*Homarus vulgaris* or *Homarus gammarus*
Norway lobster—*Nephrops norvegicus*
See Part 2: Fish, Storage; Frozen Food Storage; Lobster; Minerals, Food; Portion Size

lobster paste
Canned composition: 62% H_2O, 21% protein, 9% fat, 1% carbohydrate, 7% ash.

locoweed A plant having a toxic principle.
See Part 2: Poisonous Plants

locules A cell or cavity.
See Part 2: Orange Structure

locust bean gum (carob seed gum); (St. John's bread, gum gatto, jandagum, gum tragon) Refined endosperm of the seed of the carob evergreen tree (*Ceratonia siliqua*); composed of D-mannose and D-galactose units of mol. wt. 310,000; it is used in the food industry as a suspending agent, thickener and to prevent graininess in ice cream; used in cheese.
See Part 2: Gum Characteristics; Gums Physicochemical Properties; Stabilizers, Thickeners

Loeffler blood serum *See* Part 2: Microorganism, Media

loganberry (*Rubus loganobaccus*) A fruit similar to blackberry except that the color is dull red and the acid content higher; 100 lb fresh berries = 17–22 lb dried berries.
Raw berry composition: 83% water, 1% protein, 0.6% fat, 15% carbohydrate, 0.5% ash, pH 3.1.
See Part 2: Fruit Harvest Dates; Fruit Classification; Fruit Frozen Yield; Minerals, Food

logarithm If $a^x = y$; then $x = \log_a y$.
power (x) logarithm (x) base *a*

See also **logarithm, negative.**
Change of base:

$\log_e y = 2.303 \log_{10} y$
$\log_{10} y = 0.4343 \log_e y$

Characteristic is left of decimal—gives position of decimal;
1 is the characteristic in the following example 1.699.
Characteristic changes as follows:
log 8 = 0.9031
log 8000 = 3.9031
log .0008 = $\bar{4}.9031$
Mantissa is right of decimal;
antilogarithm—in table is .699 in above example
Characteristic and Mantissa
log 50 = 1.699

Multiplication:

(a) change numbers to their logs	200 × 4 = 800
(b) add logs	2.3010
(c) find the antilog	0.6021
	2.9031 = 800

Division:

(a) change numbers to their logs	$\frac{900}{45} = 20$
(b) subtract	
(c) find the antilog	2.9542
	1.6532
	1.3010 = 20

Powers:

(a) find log of number	$3^4 = 81$
(b) multiply (a) by the power	log 3 = .4771
(c) find antilog	4
	1.9084 = 81

Roots:

(a) find log of number	$\sqrt[5]{243} = 243^{1/5} = 3$
(b) divide by root	log 243 = 23856 × 1/5
(c) find antilog	= .4771
	= 3

$\log_x x = 1$ and $\log_y 1 = 0$
See Part 2: Constants, Fundamental

logarithm, base 10 (log) In chemistry and algebra (not mathematics), if base is not given it is assumed to be base 10.

logarithm, base e (ln) ($\log_e$) $e = 2.71828$
In mathematics (not algebra) if base is not specified, it is assumed to be *e*.

logarithmic growth phase A stage in bacterial growth following the lag phase in which cells grow and divide at a constant rate.

logarithm, negative *See* **logarithm**; mantissae are always positive in tables.
In multiplication or division, (addition or subtraction of log) no problem

		neg. pos.
Example:	0.05	$\bar{2}.6990$
	0.04	$\bar{2}.6021$
	.0020	$\bar{3}.3011$ = 0.002

neg. pos.

$\bar{x}.xxx$ Form (neg. and pos.) used in multiplication or division (addition & subtraction of log) & looking up in table

$-x.xxx$ Form (all neg.) used in powers and roots (multiplication or division of log)

0.005 = $\bar{3}.699 = -3.000, +0.699$ form used in mult. and div. and table
= $-2.301 = -2.000, -0.301$ form used in powers and roots but *not* in table

All neg. form is obtained as follows:
$-3.000 + 0.699 = -2.301$
To change this back to a form that can be looked up in a table (positive mantissa): Subtract 1 from characteristic and add 1 to mantissa
$-2 - 1 = -3$ characteristic
$-0.301 + 1.000 = +0.699$ mantissa
giving $\bar{3}.699$ can be found in table as 0.005

Example: $\sqrt{0.0016} = 0.04$

$\bar{3}.2041 = -3.000 + .2041 = -2.7959$

$\frac{-2.7959}{2} = -1.39795$

$= \bar{2}.60205 \xrightarrow{\text{table}} 0.04$

loin Backbone and loin eye muscle area of a carcass. For hogs, the trimmed loin is 15% of carcass; for choice steers it is 17%.
See Part 2: Beef, Boneless Cuts; Beef Chart; Beef Cuts and Uses; Beef Retail Yield; Beef Wholesale Cuts; Beef Yields; Bone in Retail Cuts; Broiling Time and Temperature; Lamb Chart; Lamb Cuts; Lamb Cuts and Uses; Lamb, Wholesale Cuts; Meat Identification; Meat Label; Minerals, Food; Pork Carcass, Retail Yield; Pork Chart; Pork Cookery; Pork, Cooking; Pork, Cooking Methods, Pork Cooking Yield; Pork Cuts; Pork Cuts and Uses; Pork Loin Carving; Pork Loin Cooking; Pork Loin Nomenclature; Pork Wholesale Cuts; Pork Yield; Roasting, Time and Temperature; Veal Chart; Veal Cuts; Veal Cuts and Uses; Veal Roasting; Veal Wholesale Cuts

loin chops *See* Part 2: Lamb Yield

loin end The rear area of the loin up to the front of the hip bone; it contains the butt end sirloin, wedge bone sirloin, round bone sirloin, double bone sirloin and pin bone sirloin.

loin eye *See* ***longissimus dorsi***
See Part 2: Meat Identification

loin strip The top muscle found in the short loin; often cut into strip steaks.

long fed Cattle fed 6 months or longer.

longhorn cheese A version of cheddar cheese, usually in a foot-long cylinder about 8 inches in diameter; also made in small 2-pound cylinder sizes.

longissimus costarum A long muscle of the back running from the spinous processes of the lumbar vertebra to the ribs; it is located between the spinous and transverse processes and from lateral to ventral of the *longissimus dorsi* as it proceeds from lumbar to rib section.

longissimus dorsi **(loin eye)** A long muscle of the back running from the neck area to the sacrum and ilium; it is located between the spinous and transverse processes.
See Part 2: Beef Rib Nomenclature

long saddle A wholesale cut of veal or lamb consisting of all the area in back of the 4th rib; the quarters are not split.

long tails Sheep with tails.

longus colli A muscle of the neck area that lies under the cervical and first 4 thoracic vertebrae; the trachea lies below its lower surface.

long-wool mutton type sheep Classification of sheep which includes the following breeds: Cotswold, Leicester, Lincoln, and Romney.
See Part 2: Sheep Breeds

long yearling Cattle almost 2 years old.

loquat (Japanese medlar) A small evergreen that produces a yellow, pear-shaped fruit the size of crab apples; the fruit has a sweetish acid flavor; it is eaten fresh, stewed, as jam or jelly or made into liquor.
Raw fruit composition: 86% H_2O, 0.4% protein, 0.2% fat, 12% carbohydrate, 0.5% ash.

loss leader An item sold at less than cost in order to attract customers.

lotus (*Nelumbium nuciferum*) A water plant used as food.

Part	Prepared
rhizome	roasted steamed pickled arrowroot-like substance prepared
seed embryo removed (bitter)	the remainder is boiled, roasted or eaten raw
fruit	after removal of seed
flower stem & leaves	salad

See Part 2: Seed, Chemical Composition

Lou Gim Gong A variety of late Florida orange.

loupiac A high-quality, medium-rich, white wine.

love apple *See* **tomato**

lovell A variety of freestone peach.

Lovibond color Proprietary name for an official color scale of the American Oil Chemists' Society; a series of yellow and red glass discs are used to match the color (Tintometer).

low-acid food A food in which pH 4.4 is highest permissible for processing at 100°C.
See Part 2: Canned Spoilage Manifestations; Canned Spoilage Related to pH

Lowenstein *See* Part 2: Microorganism, Media

low fat *See* Part 2: Dairy Terms

low-fat soy flour A soy flour having 5–6% fat and 50% protein.

low-grade flour A grade of flour lower than second clear flour; used primarily as stock feed. *See also* **clear flour**.

low-set An animal with short legs.

LSD *See* **least significant difference**

LSM Low-sodium milk.

L/S ratio (L over S ratio) Ratio of linoleic acid to saturated acid in a fat.

LTL Less-than-truckload lot.

Lu Symbol for the element lutetium.

lubia *See* **lablab**

lug (1) A metal or plastic container which will contain 50 to 75 lb of meat. (2) A box used for transporting orchard crops during harvesting.

lumbar vertebrae Backbone area between the ribs and the slip joint.
See Part 2: Bone

lumen (1) Light intensity; 1 lumen = 0.0796 spherical candle power. (2) A measure of power.
1 lumen = 1.496×10^4 erg/sec
= 6.6204×10^{-2} ft lb/min
= 0.001496 watt
= 1.0034×10^{-3} ft lb/sec
= 8.5096×10^{-5} Btu/min
= 1.496×10^{-6} kilowatt

luminous meat A phenomenon caused by phosphorescent bacteria; not a form of food poisoning.

lump lime A liming material composed of 85% CaO; each pound has the neutralizing equivalent of 1.5 to 1.75 lb of $CaCO_3$ (or approximately this quantity of dolomitic limestone).

lumpy jaw A disease caused by fungus (found on grasses) that affects the jaws of cattle and the udders of hogs; noncommunicable.

luncheon meat *See* Part 2: Calories, Daily Recommendations; Iron, Daily Recommendations; Meat and Meat Products Composition; Meat Composition; Meat Storage; Niacin, Daily Recommendations; Pork Storage; Riboflavin, Daily Recommendations; Sausage, Types; Thiamin, Daily Recommendations

lung *See* Part 2: Gland Weights; Organ Weights; Pork Cuts and Uses

lupine A plant having a toxic principle.
See Part 2: Poisonous Plants; Seed, Germination

luster Glistening of a fiber in light.

lutein *See* **xanthophyll**

luteol *See* **xanthophyll**

lutetium (Lu) A rare earth element of the lanthanide series; at. no. 71; Group IIIB of Periodic Table; at. wt. 174.99; oxidation state +3; electron configuration 2-8-18-32-9-2
orbit K L M N O P

lux Unit of illumination.
1 lux = 1 lumen/sq meter

lychee *See* **litchi**
See Part 2: Fruit Storage

lycopene $C_{40}H_{56}$ A red pigment found in tomatoes.

lye Potassium or sodium hydroxide.
See Part 2: Detergent Properties

lymph A fluid that is taken from the body tissues and returned to the blood stream.

lymph node *See* Part 2: Lymph Nodes, Ox; Lymph Nodes, Ox, Lateral; Lymph Nodes, Pig; Lymph Nodes, Sheep

lymphoid *See* Part 2: Organ Weights

lyophilic Solvent-loving.

lyophilization Freezing a product and then changing the ice directly to a vapor, and then removing the vapor. *See also* **freeze-drying**.

lysine An essential amino acid

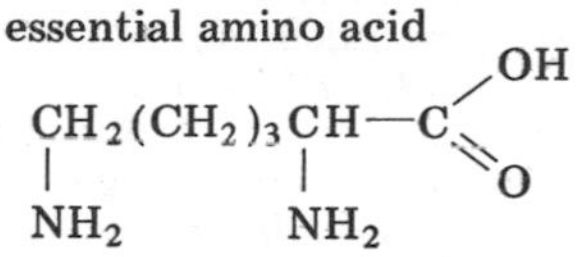

See Part 2: Amino Acids; Corn, Amino Acids; Egg Products, Nutritive Value; Grain Analysis; Manure Analysis; Microorganism, Media; Milk, Amino Acids; Seed, Chemical Composition; Wheat, Amino Acids; Wheat Products, Amino Acid Composition; Wheat Products Composition

lyxose *See* Part 2: Sugar, D-aldehydo

M

M *See* **molar**

m *See* **molal**

ma *See* **milliampere**

macaroni A mixture of wheat flour (semolina, durum flour, farina, or flour) and water (sometimes also milk and eggs) that has been dried into tubes (0.11 to 0.27 inch diameter).

Other varieties:

ditali lisci: small elbow pieces

ditali rigati: grooved small elbow pieces

tubetti: thinnest elbow shaped

rigatoni: large fluted elbow pieces

fovantini (or maccaroncelli): 3/32-inch diameter tubes

zitoni: 1/2-inch diameter tubes

zitoni rigati: 1/2-inch diameter fluted tubes

Optional ingredients: Egg white, min. 0.5%, max. 2.0% solids; disodium phosphate, min. 0.5%, max. 1.0%; seasoning; salt; gum gluten, max. 13% protein; total solids min. 87%; glyceryl monostearate, max. 2%.

4 cups = 1 lb

1 cup = 125 g (4.3 oz)

1 cup broken uncooked = 2 to 2 2/3 cups cooked

1 lb yields 8 to 12 cups cooked

1 cup cooked = 140 g (4.9 oz)

Dry composition: 10% H_2O, 12.5% protein, 1% fat, 75% carbohydrate, 0.7% ash.

See Part 2: Calories, Daily Recommendations; Cereal Composition; Cereal Enrichment; Food, Composition; Grain Products Composition; Macaroni and Noodles Composition; Microwave Processing Time; Minerals, Food; Storage, Dry; Thiamin, Food

macaroni and cheese A baked mixture of small-diameter macaroni and a cheddar cheese.

See Part 2: Portion Size

macaroni wheat *See* **wheat**

macaroon A sweet cake made with almond paste, sugar and egg white.

macassar nut fat *See* Part 2: Saturated Fatty Acids

maccaroncelli *See* **macaroni**

MacConkey agar *See* Part 2: Intestinal Microorganisms; Microorganism, Culture Media, Dairy and Food Products; Microorganism, Media; Microorganism, Selective and Differential Broths and Media, Water Filtration Plant

MacConkey broth *See* Part 2: Microorganism, Selective and Differential Broths and Media, Water Filtration Plant

mace (*Myristica fragrans Houtt*) A spice consisting of the whole or ground aril (external covering) of the seed of nutmeg; it is flattened and dried; used for seasoning sauces and ketchups. *See also* **nutmeg**.

Not less than 20% or more than 30% nonvolatile ether extract

Not more than 10% crude fiber

Not more than 3% total ash

Not more than 0.5% ash insoluble in HCl

See Part 2: Flavoring Agents, Natural

macédoine A mixture of vegetables or fruit.

macerate To soften by steeping in a liquid preparation at room temperature or slightly higher; to soften and wear away by steeping.

macin A protease enzyme found in the osage orange.

mackerel A spiny-finned fat fish; *see also* **pelagic fish**.

Other Names	Where Caught
Blue (American)	New England, Norway
Spanish	South Atlantic, Gulf
King (cero, kingfish)	South Atlantic, Gulf

Maturity Designation

Name	Size in Inches	When Caught
Blink	6 1/2	Aug.: 1st summer
Tacks or spikes	7–8	Oct.: 1st summer
Tinkers	12–14	2nd summer

4 oz per serving

1 cup = 180 g (6.4 oz)

See Part 2: Fish and Shellfish Composition; Fish, Storage; Glutamate; Minerals, Food; Vitamin D, Fish; Vitamin D, Food

macon Mutton bacon.

macromolecule A molecule of a protein or other high molecular weight substance (usually a polymer) whose size extends into the range of colloidal dimensions (diameter more than 1 micron). Some proteins have a molecular weight in excess of 10^6 (viruses).

Madagascar A variety of bean. *See also* **butter bean**.

Madeira A full-bodied, fragrant fortified wine (20% alcohol by volume) similar to sherry.

Types:

Malmsey: dessert, full-bodied and sweet

Bual (boal): a sweet, delicate, dessert

Verdelho: a before or after meal wine

Sercial: a dry, bitter flavor, aperitif

magma (massecuite) A mixture of sugar syrup and crystals in the form of a thin paste.

magnesia MgO Magnesium oxide, a component of insulating board.
See Part 2: Insulation

magnesium (Mg) A metallic element; at. no. 12; at. wt. 24.32; Group IIA of Periodic Table; oxidation state +2; electron configuration 2-8-2
orbit K L M
Occurs in sea water in recoverable concentration. It is the characteristic element in chlorophyll.
See Part 2: Beef Percentages of Daily Recommended Allowances; Cereal Fortification; Cereals, Vitamin and Mineral Content; Egg Products, Nutritive Value; Grain Analysis; Lamb Percentages of Daily Recommended Allowances; Lemon Juice Composition; Macaroni and Noodles Composition; Manure Analysis; Meat, Nutritive Value; Minerals, Food; Minerals, Plant or Animal Tissue; Normal Solutions; Nutrients in Crops; pH and Availability of Plant Nutrients; Pork, Percentages of Daily Recommended Allowances; Recommended Daily Dietary Allowance; Variety Meat Percentage of Daily Recommended Allowances; Water Drinking Standards; Wheat, Minerals; Wheat Products Composition

magnesium carbonate $MgCO_3$ A light fluffy solid, used as an anticaking agent and in insulation.
See Part 2: Liming Materials; Normal Solutions

magnesium chloride ($MgCl_2$) Component of fireproofing agents and refrigeration brines.
See Part 2: Normal Solutions

magnesium hydrate *See* Part 2: Liming Materials

magnesium hydroxide $Mg(OH)_2$ Used in frozen desserts and drying agent in foods.
See Part 2: Liming Materials; Normal Solutions

magnesium sulfate $MgSO_4$ Epsom salts; a neutral fertilizer material, 33% MgO; 0-0-0.
See Part 2: Fertilizer Materials

mahewu A fermented corn and wheat product.

Maiden Blush A variety of apples in season in August and September that makes excellent sauce but only fair eating.

Maillard reaction *See* **browning reaction**

maize (Indian corn) *See* **corn**

maize oil *See* **corn oil**

makopa *See* Part 2: Fruit Classification

Malaga A variety of grape.

malathion (malathon) A poisonous insecticide of the organic phosphate ester type.

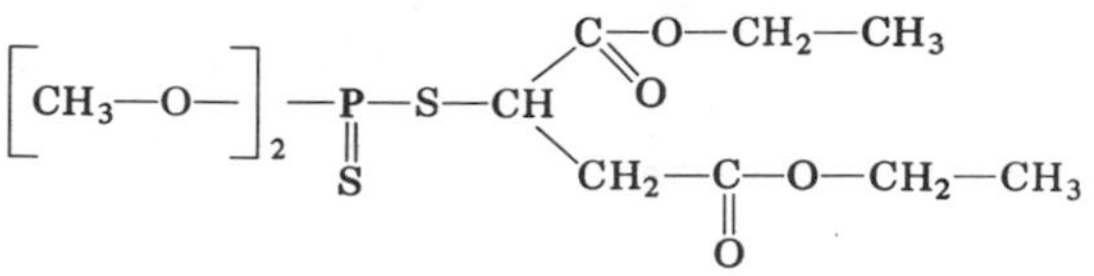

See Part 2: Insect Control

male (♂) The impregnating sex. *See also* **sex**.

malic acid (apple acid) An acid found in fruit.

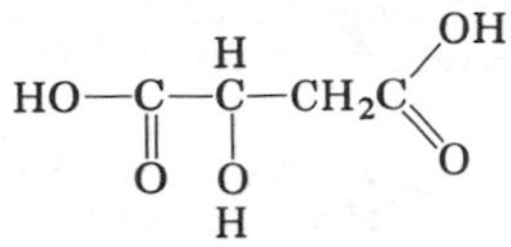

The naturally distributed acid occurs in many foods and is used as an acidulant; in citrus flavors, it is 89-94% as tart as anhydrous citric acid (in fruit flavors 78-83%).
See Part 2: Acidulants; Maple Syrup Composition; Normal Solutions; Organic Acids in Fruits and Vegetables

malonate broth *See* Part 2: Microorganism, Media

malt Barley is germinated and the young seedlings are dried to produce malt, which is used in brewing beer; it contains enzymes which hydrolyze starch to fermentable sugars. *See also* **malted barley**.
1 bu (34-38 lb) malt = 1 bu barley (48 lb)
Dry composition: 5% H_2O, 13% protein, 2% fat, 77% carbohydrate, 2% ash.

malt agar *See* Part 2: Microorganism, Culture Media, Dairy and Food Products; Microorganism, Media

maltase A carbohydrate digestive enzyme that hydrolyzes maltose into 2 glucose units:

$$\text{maltose} \longrightarrow \text{glucose} + \text{glucose}$$

See Part 2: pH Values of Biological Materials

malted barley A product made by allowing the barley to sprout; in this process the starch is changed to maltose; it is used in production of beer, malted milk and malt syrup.

malted milk A product made by combining milk with the liquid separated from a mash of ground barley malt and wheat flour and then removing the water.

	Chocolate type (%)
Min. 7.5% butter fat (avg. 7.8%)	5.8
Max. 3.5% moisture (avg. 2.6%)	1.8
Avg. 27% milk solids	
Avg. 73% malt flour solids	
Avg. 0.7% salt	
Avg. 71% carbohydrates	80.2
Avg. 15% protein	9.4
Avg. 3.7% ash	2.4
Avg. 0.3% fiber	0.4

See Part 2: Milk and Milk Products, Vitamin Content; Milk, Dry Products; Vitamin A, Milk and Milk Products

Malthus, Thomas Robert (1766-1834) A British economist whose "Essay on the Principle of Population" stated that population increases geometrically and the food supply arithmetically.

This principle is much discussed today in view of the population explosion.

malting The wetting (steeping), germination, drying and removal of malt sprouts from barley. *See also* malt.

maltose (malt sugar) (maltobiose) $C_{12}H_{22}O_{11}$ A sugar composed of 2 molecules of glucose. It is dextrorotatory and 30% as sweet as sucrose.

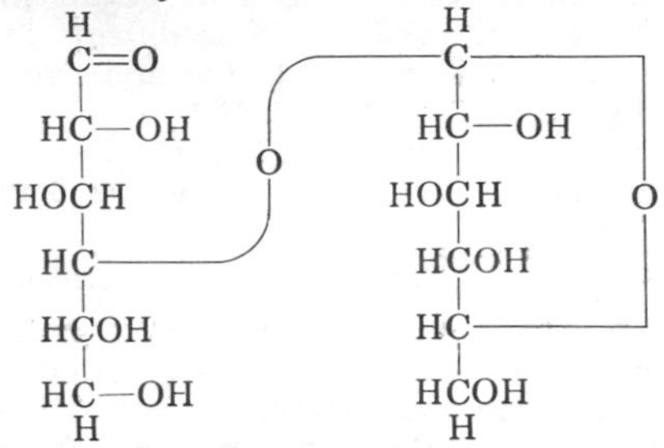

See Part 2: Sugar, Fruit; Sweetening Agents; Sweetening Compounds

malt vinegar A vinegar made by fermentation of malted cereals.
Min.: 4% acetic acid, 2% solids, 0.2% ash (min. 0.009% of phosphoric acid (P_2O_5) in water-soluble ash)

malvaceae *See* Part 2: Vegetables, Classification

mandarin *See* **tangerine**

mandible A jaw of an animal.
See Part 2: Fish Nomenclature

manganese (Mn) A metallic element; at. no. 25; at. wt. 54.94; Group VIIB of Periodic Table; oxidation states +2, +3, +4, +7; electron configuration 2-8-13-2
orbit K L M N
Body function: in reproduction.
See Part 2: Egg Products, Nutritive Value; Grain Analysis; Maple Syrup Composition; Minerals, Food; Normal Solutions; Nutrients in Crops; pH and Availability of Plant Nutrients; Water Drinking Standards; Wheat, Minerals; Wheat Products Composition

manganese sulfate $MnSO_4$ A fertilizer material; source of soluble manganese on land that has been over-limed.
See Part 2: Fertilizer Materials; Normal Solutions

mange A parasite (mite) that affects the skin of dogs, hogs, horses and mules (also man), causing loss of hair. Contagious.

mangetout *See* **sugar pea**

mango Fruit of *Mangifera indica* tree, a medium-size subtropical tree that produces a yellow-green fruit (6 oz-1½ lb); the orange flesh surrounds a central flat, oval stone which is 7 to 20% of its weight.
Storage: 50°F, 85-90% relative humidity, 2 weeks storage life.
Composition: 82% water, 0.7% protein, 0.4% fat, av. 17% carbohydrate (10-20% sugar), 0.4% ash, pH 3.9-4.6.
High in vitamin A; also contains medium amount of vitamins B and C; eaten fresh, canned, or made into preserves; unripe fruit is made into mango chutney.
See Part 2: Fruit, Availability; Fruit Classification; Fruit Composition; Fruit Storage; Minerals, Food; Plant Foods, Composition; Tocopherols

mangosteen A large tree that produces a smooth rind and brownish-purple berry; beneath the tough rind, the white pulp is segmented and contains a few seeds; the fruit is consumed fresh.
See Part 2: Fruit Classification; Fruit Storage

manioc A woody South American tropical plant. *See also* **cassava; tapioca flour.**

manisan A brown sugar made from the coconut.

mannitol $C_6H_8(OH)_6$ A hexahydric alcohol used in dietetic foods.
See Part 2: Microbiological Media

mannose $C_6H_{12}O_6$ A 6-carbon monosaccharide (hexose) found in orange rind, seeds and sugar cane. Has a sweet taste, but bitter aftertaste.

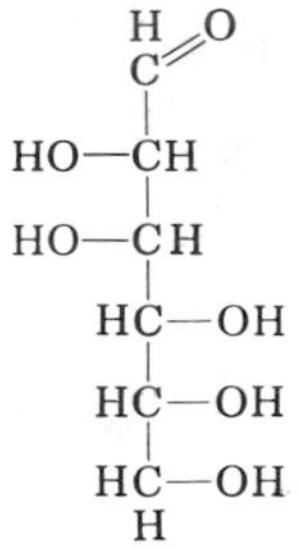

See Part 2: Sugar, D-aldehydo

mantecha A delicately seasoned cheese filled with a rich butter center.

mantissa *See* **logarithm**

manufacturer's sugar *See* **confectioner's sugar**

manure Excrement of animals; used for fertilizer and source of hydrocarbon gases for fuel.

	Production Tons/year			Percent	
	solid	liquid	N	P_2O_5	K_2O
Average	—	—	0.7	0.4	0.5
Cattle	9	4	0.5	0.3	0.5
Chickens	0.07	—	0.9	0.5	0.8
Horses	7	1	0.6	0.3	0.6
Sheep	0.5	0.3	0.9	0.5	0.8
Swine	1	0.6	0.6	0.5	0.4

See Part 2: Fertilizer Materials; Manure Analysis; Wastes, Agricultural and Industrial

manure, green Crops that are plowed under for fertilizer.

manyplies *See* **omasum**

manzanilla A pale, dry, low-alcoholic sherry.

maple cream Maple syrup boiled to 232°F, cooled without stirring to 70°F, and scraped into cream consistency.

maple sap The sap of the sugar maple, which contains sucrose, invert sugar, malic acid, mineral matter, and albuminoids; avg. 3% sucrose; 3 lb/tree/year.

maple sugar *See* **sugar, maple**

maple syrup (sirup) Concentrated sap of the sugar maple (*Acer saccharinum*) made by evaporation of maple sap, which is collected in early spring.
Max. water content, 35%; min. 11 lb/gal. (231 cu in.).
Specific gravity 1.325
66.5% sugar
35.75° Baumé at 60°F
66.5° Brix at 60°F
1 cup = 312 g (11 oz)
1 gal. syrup = 8 lb maple sugar = 34 gal. sap.
pH 6.5-7.0
Storage: 40-45°F.
See Part 2: Maple Syrup Composition; Sugars and Syrups Composition; Sweetening Agents

maraschino cherries Unripe cherries that are cooked in syrup, colored, and flavored. Brined cherries are pitted, SO_2 leached out with water, boiled, dyed, boiled, held in dye, washed in hot water and then citric acid solution, rinsed; some are sweetened and flavored (bitter almond oil, neroli oil and vanilla extract). The colorant formerly used has been prohibited by FDA (1976).

marble $CaCO_3$ with admixed impurities (iron oxide and other metallic oxides) giving a mottled or streaky appearance.

marbling Fat intermingled in the muscle.

marchpane *See* **marzipan**

mare A female horse (generally of breeding age); gestation period 340 days (range 307-412); duration of heat period 5-7 days; normal recurrence of heat, approx. 21 days.

mare mule A female mule.

marengo, à la Fowl in a sauce made of tomato, white wine, butter, mushrooms and garlic.

margaric acid (heptadecanoic acid)
$CH_3(CH_2)_{15}COOH$ Rarely found in natural oils and fats.
See Part 2: Fatty Acids and Their Properties

margarine A manufactured food resembling butter except the fat is derived from vegetable or animal fat (usually not milk); it contains at least 80% of one or more of the following fats, which may be hydrogenated:
(a) rendered animal fat
(b) vegetable fat or oil
(c) stearin or oil derived from above fats or oils
(d) milk fat
Can also contain:
(1) milk products
(2) flavorings
(3) butter
(4) salt
(5) coloring (carotene or other vegetable color approved by USDA)
(6) emulsifying agents
(7) vitamins
(8) preservatives
Vitamin A, min. 15,000 U.S.P. units/lb
D, min. 2,000 U.S.P. units/lb
lecithin, monoglyceride, diglyceride — max. 0.5% total wt
sodium benzoate, benzoic acid, potassium sorbate — max. 0.1% total wt
Artificial flavoring, diacetyl or acetyl methyl carbinoli.
1 cup = 225 g (7.9 oz)
2 cups = 1 lb
3 cups whipped = 1 lb
1 cup whipped = 150 g (5.3 oz)
2 tablespoons = 1 oz
75-84% fat
max. 16% moisture
Storage: Refrigerate (32-35°F), tightly covered, use within 2 weeks.
Composition: 15% H_2O, 0.6% protein, 81% fat, 0.4% carbohydrate, 2.5% ash. *See also* **oleomargarine.**
See Part 2: Butter and Butter Products, Composition; Calories, Daily Recommendations; Fats and Oils, Composition; Margarine Formulae; Margarine Production; Oils and Fats Composition; Spoilage, Fat in Food; Vitamin A, Daily Recommendations; Vitamin D, Food

Margarinomyces Bacteria that cause food spoilage.
See Part 2: Spoilage, Fat in Food

marigold Flowers and the green parts of sweet-scented marigold sometimes used as seasoning.

marinade A seasoned liquid in which food is allowed to stand before cooking.

marinate To let food stand in a liquid such as acetic acid, vinegar, olive oil, lemon juice, or brine.

marine oil An oil obtained from fish or marine mammals.
See Part 2: Oils and Fats Composition; Unsaturated Fatty Acids

marjoram (*Majorana hortensis*), (*Origanum majorana*) A fragrant and very popular herb made from the dried green leaves and flowering tops of a mint family plant found both whole and dried; used as flavoring; leaves are gathered or whole plant is cut and sold in bunches; leaves are cut or powdered; used in soup, stuffing, pies.
See Part 2: Flavoring Agents, Natural

market class *See* Part 2: Sheep Market Classes and Grades

marl (merl) A liming material composed of 60% $CaCO_3$ and clay; each pound has the neutralizing

equivalent of 0.5 to 0.9 lb of $CaCO_3$ (or approx. this quantity of dolomitic limestone).
See Part 2: Liming Materials

marmalade Small pieces of pulpy fruit (*e.g.*, citrus fruit) suspended in a clear smooth jelly-like mixture (1 lb or more sugar/lb of fruit). A preserve made from thinly sliced or chopped citrus fruit, combined with sugar, sometimes combined with pectin and cooked to a jelly consistency; sealed for storage.
See Part 2: Standards, Processed Fruit and Vegetable Products

marmelo *See* **quince**

marrow (1) A soft substance found in the medulla (spaces) in spongy bone; the building site of red blood cells.
See Part 2: Organ Weights
(2) A climbing herb that produces a pepo; the varieties yield fruit of many colors and shapes.
Varieties:
Vegetable Marrow: an oval cylinder with a rind that may be green or white striped; vegetable may weigh up to several pounds; it is boiled or parboiled and baked.
Courgette, zucchini: picked when immature and only a few inches long or when about 9 in. long; when mature they are similar to the vegetable type.
Custard marrow: scalloped summer squash; shape of a flattened sphere, white or yellow in color.
Use: cooked vegetable, jams, chutneys, soups, wine.
pH 4.7–5.6

marsala A fortified Italian dessert wine.

marshmallow A confection of soft, creamy consistency made from egg albumin or gelatin and sugar or starch syrup; originally made from the root of the Althea plant.
1 oz = 3–4 regular marshmallows
¼ lb = 15 regular marshmallows
7–10 oz = 40 regular marshmallows = 3 cups miniature marshmallows = 2 cups marshmallow creme
1 lb = 4 cups marshmallows
See Part 2: Sugars and Sweets Composition; Water Activity, Organisms and Food

Marsh Seedless A variety of grapefruit.

martinique A type of salad dressing.
See Part 2: French Dressing Variations

Maryland *See* Swine Breeds

Maryland No. 1 A breed of hogs produced by crossing Berkshire (38%) and Landrace (62%) breeds; it is black and white in color and has erect ears.

marzipan An almond and sugar paste confection.
See Part 2: Water Activity, Organisms and Food

mascarpone *See* Part 2: Cheese, Vitamin Content

masculinity Possession of secondary male sex characteristics, such as heavy head, neck and shoulders.

mashing Ground grain and a small amount of malt is heated with water and then cooled; malt is added and brought to 140–150°F, at which time the starch is converted to maltose.

Masonite Proprietary name for an insulating board made by steam-treating wood chips at high pressure.
See Part 2: Insulation

mass The amount of matter contained in a body, regardless of its location in space, i.e., it is the same on the moon as on the earth. Weight involves the concept of gravity; thus the weight of an object on earth differs from its weight on the moon.

massecuite *See* **magma**

mass number The sum of the protons and neutrons in an atomic nucleus. *See also* **atomic number.**

mass unit An arbitrary value of mass; the proton has a mass of 1, and is therefore the basic mass unit. Neutrons have a mass of 1.008.
See Part 2: Constants, Fundamental

mastication The grinding, reduction in size, mixing, and addition of saliva that takes place in the mouth.

mastitis A disease of the udder caused by bacteria producing tissue changes.

maté (yerba de maté); (*Ilex paraguaariensis*) A tropical beverage crop whose leaves are picked, dried and ground; used to make a tea-like drink.

mature duck A bird of either sex over 6 months old.

mature turkey A bird of either sex over 15 months old.

maurette A sauce of wine, butter, flour and spices.

maxilla The upper jawbone.
See Part 2: Fish Nomenclature

Maxwell disc *See* **color wheel**

mayonnaise A semi-solid permanent emulsion in which oil is held in water suspension by egg yolk. *See also* **emulsion.**
Min. 75% vegetable oil; the only emulsifying ingredient is egg yolk (cholesterol); the acid ingredient is vinegar or lemon juice (citric acid to ¼ acetic acid in vinegar); vinegar and salt are the principal bacteriological agents.
Typical ingredients:

2 egg yolks	1 tsp dry mustard	1 tbsp vinegar
	1 tsp salt	1½ cups salad oil
	1 tsp sugar	1 tbsp lemon juice
	dash of cayenne	

1 cup = 245 g (8.6 oz)
Storage: Refrigerate after opening.
Composition: 15% H_2O, 1% protein, 80% fat, 2% carbohydrate, 2% ash; pH 4.2–4.5.
See Part 2: Calories, Daily Recommendations; Fats and Oils, Composition; Food, Composition;

Mayonnaise; Mayonnaise and Salad Dressing; Salad Dressing and Mayonnaise Variations

mazola oil Corn oil.

MB-BCP medium *See* Part 2: Microorganism, Selective and Differential Broths and Media, Water Filtration Plant

M broth *See* Part 2: Microorganism, Media

Mc Megacycles per second; millicurie.

McCallum's macerating fluid A mixture composed of nitric acid 1 part, glycerin 2 parts, water 2 parts.

McClung Toabe agar *See* Part 2: Microorganism, Media

McIntosh red A variety of apples that is in season from Sept. to March; makes excellent sauce and good eating and cooking apples.

M coliform broth *See* Part 2: Microbiological Media

Md Symbol for the element mendelevium.

MDR *See* **minimum daily requirement**

mead A drink made from alcoholic fermentation of honey.

mead agar *See* Part 2: Microbiological Media

mean (μ) Center of a distribution.

Estimated by sample mean $\bar{x} = \dfrac{\Sigma X}{n}$

Interval estimate of μ

$\bar{x} - t_{.05}\, S_{\bar{x}} \leqslant \mu \leqslant \bar{x} + t_{.05}\, S_{\bar{x}}$

Probability is 95% that above area will include μ

$t_{.05}$ = table t value at probability desired (95% used here)

$t(df) = n - 1$

$S_{\bar{x}}$ = standard error

See also **randomized group comparisons** for confidence limits on the difference of means.

mean error *See* **mean square**

mean lethal dose (Do) Radiation dosage that will kill 63% of the population.

mean square (s^2)

Variation of observations: it is the square of the sample standard deviation:

$$s^2 = \frac{\Sigma x^2}{n - 1} \qquad x = \text{deviations from mean} \quad n = \text{sample size}$$

Pooled mean square for equal size randomized groups:

$$s^2 = \frac{\text{pooled } \Sigma x^2}{2(n - 1)} \qquad n = \text{no. in 1st group}$$

Pooled mean square for unequal size randomized groups:

$$s^2 = \frac{\text{pooled } x^2}{(n_1 - 1) + (n_2 - 1)}$$

Test for homogeneity of variance: Ho: $\sigma_1^2 = \sigma_1^2$

$$F = \frac{\text{larger } s^2}{\text{smaller } s^2} \qquad s^2 = df = n - 1$$

See Part 2: *F*-Distribution

means test A test of the difference between 2 or more means; a = no. of treatments; n = obs. per treatment.

Turkey: In a means there are $a(a - 1)/2$ comparisons

$D = Q\, s\bar{x}$

$$s\bar{x} = \left(\frac{\text{mean square of individuals or error}}{n = \text{observations in the mean}}\right)^{1/2}$$

Q = table value a = no. of treatments; $df = df$ for individuals or error $(n - 1)\, a$

Treatment	Treatment mean $\bar{x}$	$\bar{x}_1 - \bar{x}_a$	$\bar{x}_1 - \bar{x}_{a-1}$	. . .	$\bar{x}_1 - \bar{x}_2$
1	—	—	—	. . .	—
2	—	—	—		
3	—	—			
.	.				
.	.				
.	.				
a	—	—			

D compared with differences

C.L. i = 1 through a

$(\bar{x}_i - \bar{x}_i) + D \leqslant \mu_i - \mu_i \leqslant (\bar{x}_i - \bar{x}_i) - D$

Keuls test: (more powerful): uses different Q depending on how far in sequence the means are apart.

Q from table $df = (n - 1)\, a$ does not change
a = 2: adjacent means
3: means with one between them
4: etc.
.
.
.
a: extreme means

measuring cup A container having a capacity of ¼ quart (236.6 cc). *See also* **cup.**

meat Meat inspection definition: all edible parts of muscle of cattle, sheep, swine, or goats which is skeletal; includes tongue, diaphragm, heart, esophagus; also bone, skin, sinew, nerve, and blood vessels which normally occur in muscle tissue. Does not include: lips, snout, or ears.

2 cups chopped uncooked/pound
4 cups ground cooked meat/pound
5 cups diced cooked meat/pound
1 lb uncooked = 2¾ cups cooked and ground

Storage: Coldest part of refrigerator; original wrapper, 1 to 2 days; unwrap and cover loosely (roast, chops, steaks), 3 to 5 days.

See Part 2: Animal Foods, Composition; Braising Meat; Broiling Meat; Broiling Griddle, Meat; Calories, Daily Recommendations; Cooking in Liquid, Time; Defrosting Time; Food, Composition; Frozen Food Storage; Frozen Meat Storage Time; Glutamate; Grades, Meat; Liquid Cooking of Meat; Meat and Meat Products Composition; Meat Curing Ingredients; Meat, Frozen Storage; Meat Grade Stamps; Meat Identification; Meat Inspection Stamp; Meat, Nutritive Value; Meat Pigment; Meat, Servings per Pound; Meat Storage; Microwave Processing Time; Minerals, Plant or Animal Tissue; Minerals (Trace), Limits; Moisture in Biological Materials; Nicotinic Acid, Food; Nitrate, Meat Curing; Pan Broiling Meat; Pan Frying Meat; Portion Size; Potassium-Rich Foods; Poultry Yield; Protein Factors; Riboflavin, Food; Roasting Meat; Roasting, Time and Temperature; Simmering Meat; Spoilage, Protein Foods; Stabilizers, Thickeners; Storage Times; Thiamin, Food; Vitamin A, Food; Vitamin Retention, Meat; Yield Grade Meat

meat and bone meal *See* **meat scrap**

meat and bone meal digester tankage *See* **meat meal tankage**

meat and bone meal tankage *See* **meat meal tankage**

meat and bone scrap *See* **meat scrap**

meat balls Max. of 12% singly or collectively of farinaceous material, soya flour, soy-protein concentrate, non-fat dry milk, calcium reduced dried skim milk, and similar materials with ground meat.

meat color *See* Part 2: Color, Meat; Meat Pigment; Nitrate, Meat Curing

meat fat *See* Part 2: Fat and Oil Composition

meat grade Denotes the degree of conformation, finish and quality of a carcass of meat; beef grades are Prime, Choice, Good, Standard, Commercial, Utility, Cutter, Canner.

Meat Inspection Division of the Bureau of Animal Production Former name for Animal and Plant Health Inspection Service (APHIS) which is the agency responsible for Federal meat inspection; its duties include (a) elimination of bad meat, (b) enforcement of sanitary preparation, (c) checking for harmful ingredients, (d) guarding against false or misleading labels.

meat loaf *See* **loaf** (2)

meat meal *See* **meat scrap**

meat meal tankage Live steam- or dry-rendered, finely ground, dried residue from animal tissues, exclusive of hair, hoof, horn, manure and stomach contents; when it contains more than 4.4% phosphorus, the word "bone" must also be included in the name; approx. 1.6 lb/qt; 51 lbs/bu.

meat scrap Dry-rendered finely ground residue from animal tissue, exclusive of hair, hoof, horn, hide trimmings, blood meal, manure and stomach contents; when it contains more than 4.4% phosphorus, the words "and bone" must be added to the name; feed 1.3 lb/qt; 42 lb/bu.
See Part 2: Packinghouse By-Products Composition

meat stamp ink A vegetable dye (food color) certified by Food and Drug Administration. It is combined with water, alcohol and sugar and used by federal inspectors to stamp grades of fresh meat; it is an edible product. *See also* **ink (meat inspection)**.

meat type A classification of hogs that usually includes the following breeds: Berkshire, Chester White, Duroc, Hamprace, Hampshire, Hereford, Kentucky Red Berkshire, Minnesota No. 1, Minesota No. 2, Ohio Improved Chester, Poland China, and Spotted Poland China.

media *See* **medium (1)**

medial The mid-line, middle or middle plane.

median The value of the middle item of an array if n = odd; it is the average value of the two center items of an array if n = even.

median plane Middle plane, where carcass is split, divides into right and left sides.

medic *See* Part 2: Seed, Germination

medium (1) A solid liquid nutrient material that is suitable for the reproduction and growth of microorganisms; often called culture medium. The plural form is "media."
See Part 2: Culture Media, Specific Groups of Microorganisms; Microbiological Media; Microorganism, Culture Media, Dairy and Food Products; Microorganism, Culture Media, Water and Sewage, Standard Methods; Microorganism, Media; Microorganism, Selective and Differential Broths and Media, Water Filtration Plant; Microorganism on Differential Tube Media
(2) A degree of doneness in meat cookery; e.g., internal temperature of beef cooked to medium doneness is 160°F.
See Part 2: Beef Degrees of Doneness; Beef Roasting; Broiling Time and Temperature; Casings, Hog; Casings, Sheep

medium acid *See* Part 2: Canned Spoilage Manifestations; Canned Spoilage Related to pH

medium aged cheese *See* **cured cheese**

medium-wool mutton type sheep Classification of sheep which includes the following breeds: Cheviot, Columbia, Corriedale, Dorset, Hampshire, Oxford, Panama, Shropshire, Southdown, and Suffolk.
See Part 2: Sheep Breeds

medlar (*Mespilus germanica*) A fruit similar to the quince, except that the eye is open; it may be eaten off the tree or made into jam.

medoc A table wine.

medulla Inner portion. *See also* **marrow**.

medulla oblongata Lower portion of the brain that attaches it to the spinal cord.

medullary cavities Hollow tubes in long bones.

mega- Prefix for quantities one million times larger than the base unit.

megaton (mt) 1 mt = energy released by 1,000,000 tons of TNT.

megohm (meg) 1,000,000 ohms.

meitauza *See* Part 2: Fungi Food Products

melba A crisp, thin, crunchy toast.

melezitose $C_{18}H_{32}O_{16}$ A trisaccharide made up of 2 molecules of glucose and one of fructose; found in the exudate of the fir and other trees.

melissic acid (triacontanoic acid) $CH_3(CH_2)_{28}COOH$ A saturated fatty acid occurring in montan and other waxes.
See Part 2: Saturated Fatty Acids

melitose *See* **raffinose**

melitriose *See* **raffinose**

melon (*Cucumis melo*) An annual trailing herb (vine) of many varieties which produces fruit that is variable in size, shape, color, thickness and smoothness of rind, and color of flesh; 60% edible.
Chief types are:
cantaloupe: warty or scaly rind; not netted; deep grooved, orange colored flesh.
musk melon (netted melon; nutmeg melon): smooth rind (or broad ribs) which is yellow or green, covered with a raised, lighter colored prominant net.
winter melon (i.e., honey dew): smooth or shallow corrugated; not netted, hard skin, rind color white to dark green, flesh pale green to yellow; stores well. Flesh is consumed raw, pickled or used in soup. Hard covering of seed is removed and eaten; also yields an edible oil on extraction.
Storage: Unwrapped (85-90% relative humidity); cool room temperature (45-50°F); use within a week.
Raw composition: 90-93% H_2O, 0.5-1.2% protein, 0.1-0.3% fat, 6-8% carbohydrate, 0.3-0.8% ash, pH 5.5-6.7. *See also* **watermelon.**
See Part 2: Ascorbic Acid; Calories, Daily Recommendations; Flavor Ingredients, Taste and Flavor Type; Fruit and Vegetable, Diseases; Fruit Classification; Fruit Composition; Fruit Storage; Storage; Sugar, Vegetables

melon pickle worm *See* Part 2: Insect Control

melt (1) spleen. (2) To change from solid to liquid by heat.

melting point Temperature at which a solid becomes a liquid; impurities lower the melting point. *See also* **freezing point.**
See Part 2: Melting Points, Fats and Oils

menadione *See* Part 2: Vitamins

mendelevium (Md) A synthetic radioactive element of the actinide series; at. no. 101; Group IIIB of Periodic Table; mass number of most stable isotope 256;
electron configuration 2-8-18-32-31-8-2
orbit K L M N O P Q

M endo agar *See* Part 2: Microbiological Media

menhaden oil A drying oil obtained by expressing the flesh of the menhaden fish. In hydrogenated form it is used in cooking fats; also in margarine and in animal feeds.
See Part 2: Fats and Oils, Physical and Chemical Properties; Fats and Oils, Characteristics; Iodine and Saponification Values; Vitamin A, Fish

menthol $CH_3C_6H_9(C_3H_7)OH$ A solid alcohol obtained from oil of peppermint; also occurs naturally; characteristic cool taste; used in cough syrups and cigarettes.

mercaptan RSH. *See also* **thiol.**

mercury (quicksilver) (Hg) A liquid metallic element; at. no. 80; at. wt. 200.61; Group IIB of Periodic Table; oxidation states +1, +2; electron configuration 2-8-18-32-18-2
orbit K L M N O P
All mercury compounds are poisonous!

meringue A topping used for pies and other baked desserts; it is made of well-beaten egg whites plus sugar and vanilla or other flavoring.

Merino A fine-wool breed of sheep originating in Spain; three types are:
A: skin is wrinkled over entire body;
B: skin folds around neck, dock, flanks and thigh;
C: (or Delaine Merinos) most popular type and has practically no wrinkling; has white nostrils, lips and hooves; rams have horns (polled strain does exist) and ewes are hornless; they will breed in almost any season.
See Part 2: Sheep Breeds

merl *See* **marl**

meromyosin *See* Part 2: Myofibrillar Proteins of Muscle

Mertaste A proprietary flavor enhancer containing a mixture of disodium inosinate and disodium guanylate.

mescal bean A plant having a toxic principle.
See Part 2: Poisonous Plants

mesentery *See* Part 2: Intestine, Cross Section

mesh Coarseness or fineness of screens, indicated by number of openings per linear inch, i.e., 200-mesh, 300-mesh, etc.
See Part 2: Mesh Sizes

mesocarp The intermediate layer or fleshy portion of a fruit lying below the pericarp.
See Part 2: Corn Kernel; Orange Structure; Rice Kernel

meso compound Inactive or has no effect on polarized light.

mesophilic bacteria Bacteria that can grow at a medium temperature; minimum growth temp., 10 to 15°C; optimum, 35 to 40°C; maximum, 40 to 50°C.

mesquite A plant having a poisonous principle.
See Part 2: Gum Distribution; Poisonous Plants

metabolic water Water formed from the oxidation of food.

metabolism The biochemical and physicochemical reactions that occur from the time a nutrient enters the body of an organism to the time the waste products are excreted. Digestion and absorption of nutrients and their oxidation and degradation are major aspects. These processes yield the energy necessary for maintenance of the organism. They are distinctive for each class of nutrients (fats, carbohydrates, proteins).

metabolite An active nutrient factor such as a vitamin, protein or enzyme, including numerous combinations of these. Substances that reduce or impair the activity of metabolites are called antimetabolites.

metacarpal bones Fore foot bones located above the phalangeal bones.
See Part 2: Bone

metaphosphate *See* Part 2: Phosphate

metatarsal bones Hind foot bones located between the phalangeal bones and tarsal bones.

meter (m) A measure of length.
1 meter = 1000 millimeters (mm)
= 100 centimeters (cm)
= 39.3700 inches (in.) (U.S.)
= 10 decimeters (dm)
= 3.280843 feet (British)
= 3.280833 feet (ft) (U.S.)
= 1.093611 yard (yd) (U.S.)
= 0.198838 rod (rd) (U.S.)
= 0.001 kilometer (km)
= 0.0006214 mile (statute)
= 0.0005396 mile (U.S. nautical)
0.9144 m = 1 yard

meter columns of water A measure of pressure.
1 = 204.817 lb per sq foot (psf)
= 73.5514 millimeters (columns of mercury, Hg)
= 3.28083 feet (columns of water, max. density at 4°C, 39°F)
= 2.89572 inches (columns of mercury, Hg)
= 1.42234 lb per sq inch (psi)
= 0.10 kilogram per sq centimeter (kg/cm^2)
= 0.09678 atmosphere, standard (760 mm Hg)

meter per minute A measure of velocity.
1 m/min = 3.281 feet/min
= 1.667 centimeters/sec
= 0.06 kilometer/hr
= 0.05468 foot/sec
= 0.03728 mile/hr

meter per second (mps) A measure of velocity.
1 mps = 196.8 feet/min
= 3.6 kilometers per hr
= 3.28083 feet per second (fps)
= 2.23693 miles per hour (mph)
= 1.94254 knots (U.S.)

meter per sec/sec (mps^2) A measure of acceleration.
1 mps^2 = 3.28083 feet per sec/sec (fps^2)
= 2.23693 miles per hour/sec (mph-s)

methanol *See* **methyl alcohol**

methionine

$$CH_3—S—CH_2—CH_2—\underset{NH_2}{\underset{|}{CH}}—COOH$$

An essential amino acid.
See Part 2: Amino Acids; Amino Acid, Solubilities; Corn, Amino Acids; Egg Products, Nutritive Value; Grain Analysis; Manure Analysis; Milk, Amino Acids; Seed, Chemical Composition; Wheat, Amino Acids; Wheat Products, Amino Acids; Wheat Products, Amino Acid Compositions; Wheat Products Composition

methoxychlor (methoxy DDT) A chlorinated organic insecticide, especially useful in dairy barns; it is less toxic than DDT.

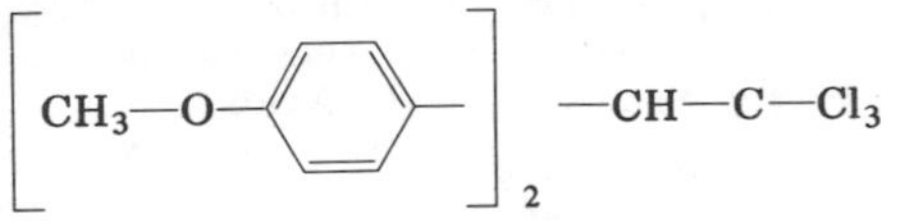

methylal (formal) $CH_2(OCH_3)_2$ An aldehyde used as extraction solvent in perfumery.

methyl alcohol (methanol; wood alcohol) CH_3OH Commercial product is about 90% methyl alcohol; it is poisonous, causing blindness; used as solvent and as denaturant for ethyl alcohol.

methylamine CH_3NH_2 A flammable gas.
See Part 2: Refrigerant

β-methyl-α-amino valeric acid *See* **isoleucine**

methyl bromide CH_3Br An alkyl halide used as an insecticide and fumigant.
See Part 2: Fumigants

methylcellulose A modified cellulose; aqueous solutions form viscous colloidal suspensions; used as a thickener or emulsifier, and to greaseproof paper.

methyl chloride CH_3Cl Flammable gas, or liquid when compressed. Used as extraction solvent and refrigerant.
See Part 2: Refrigerant

methylene chloride CH_2Cl_2 A volatile, nonflammable liquid used as a refrigerant and extraction solvent.
See Part 2: Refrigerant

methyl formate $HCOOCH_3$ Flammable and explosive liquid used as fumigant and larvicide.
See Part 2: Refrigerant

methyl group $—CH_3$ The simplest alkyl group; occurs in aliphatic compounds. Formed by dropping one H atom from methane.

methyl orange An indicator used when titrating weak bases; its pH range is 3–4.5; its color in acid is orange, pink in neutral, and yellow in alkaline solutions. Mix 0.1 g of the Na salt/100 ml water.

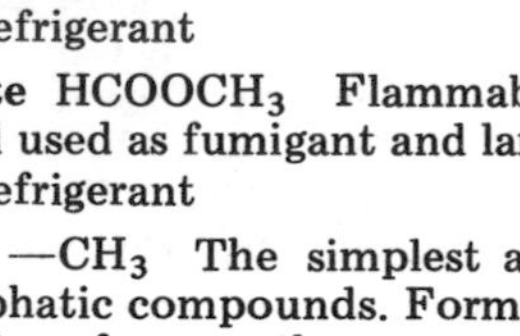

methyl polysilicone An anti-foaming agent used in food; 10 parts/million.

methyl red An indicator used when titrating strong acids, strong bases or weak bases; its pH range is 4–6. Its color in acid is red, or neutral-yellowish red; in alkaline solutions, yellow. Mix 0.1 g in 60 ml of alcohol and 40 ml water.

methyl violet An indicator which is green when the pH is less than 2, blue between pH 2 and 3, and violet for pH above 3; mix 0.1 g/100 ml water.

metmyoglobin Oxidized form of myoglobin, the brown-colored pigment of stale meat.
See Part 2: Meat Pigment; Nitrate, Meat Curing

mett A semi-dry pork sausage.

mettwurst ("smearwurst") A soft pork sausage that is processed at low temperature and tied in 2-3 inch lengths.
See Part 2: Sausage Identification; Sausage, Types

meunière, à la Dipped in flour, heated in butter, and served with brown butter, parsley and lemon.

Mexican altura, coatepec A fairly mild coffee with a fresh taste, delicate aroma and a slight nutty flavor.

Mexican black bean A bean with yellow pods and black seeds.

Mexican squash A summer variety of squash.

mf *See* **microfarad**

Mg Symbol for the element magnesium.

mg *See* **milligram**

M green yeast and mold broth *See* Part 2: Microbiological Media

micro- (1) Prefix for quantities one million times smaller than the base unit. (2) Prefix meaning "very small," e.g., microorganism.

microampere (μa) One millionth of an ampere.

micro assay culture agar *See* Part 2: Microorganism, Culture Media, Dairy and Food Products; Microorganism, Media

microbiology The study of bacteria and other microorganisms (yeasts, molds, etc.).
See Part 2: Microbiological Standards, Dairy

Micrococcus *See* Part 2: Spoilage, Protein Foods

microfarad (μf) (mf) One millionth of a farad.

microgram (μg) (γ) (mcg) A measure of mass; one millionth of a gram, sometimes called a gamma (γ).

1 μg = 0.001 mg
= 0.000,001 g = 1/1,000,000 g
= 3.53×10^{-8} oz (av.)

micro inoculum broth *See* Part 2: Microorganism, Culture Media, Dairy and Food Products; Microorganism, Media

microliter (μl) (λ) A measure of volume.

1 microliter = 1 cubic millimeter
= 0.27×10^{-3} dram
= 6.1×10^{-5} cubic inch
= 1×10^{-6} liter

micrometer *See* **micron**

micromicron ($\mu\mu$) A measure of length.

1 $\mu\mu$ = 0.001 millimicron
= 0.000,000,001 mm
= 1×10^{-12} meter

micron A measure of length. (μm, new designation; μ, old designation).

1 micron = 1×10^4 angstrom units
= 1,000 millimicrons, micromillimeter
= 0.039370 mil
= 0.001 millimeter
= 1×10^{-4} centimeter
= 3.937×10^{-5} inch
= 10^{-6} meter

micronutrient *See* **mineral; trace element**

microorganism A living organism consisting of a single cell, which reproduces asexually; while some types are infective, many others are not; some (such as nitrogen-fixing bacteria) are beneficial. Various forms include bacteria, algae, yeasts, molds, etc.
See Part 2: Bacteria on Chickens at Various Holding Temperatures; Culture Media; Intestinal Microorganisms; Intestinal Microorganisms in Triple-sugar Agar; Microbial Toxins; Microbiological Examination of Dairy Products; Microbiological Media; Microorganism, Culture Media, Dairy and Food Products; Microorganism, Culture Media, Water and Sewage, Standard Methods; Microorganism, Media; Microorganism, Selective and Differential Broths and Media, Water Filtration Plant; Microorganism Reactions on Differential Tube Media; Most Probable Number; Most Probable Number, Bacterial; Rot Spoilage; Spices, Microbial Content; Water Activity, Organisms and Food

microscope An optical instrument used to view small objects by means of glass or magnetic lens systems.

microtome An instrument for cutting thin sections for microscopic observations.

microvolt 1×10^{-6} volt; one-millionth volt.

microwave High-frequency electromagnetic energy (300 to 30,000 megahertz, MH_2); frequencies assigned for cooking are 915 MH_2 and 2450 MH_2.
See Part 2: Microwave Cooking, Frozen Vegetables; Microwave Cooking, Fresh Vegetables; Microwave Cooking, Fruit; Microwave Processing Time; Waves, Energy-producing

Middlebrook *See* Part 2: Microorganism, Media

middles Natural casings used in the meat trade; made from the middle part of the large intestine of pork. *See also* **narrow casings; wide-end middle; fat-end middle.**
See Part 2: Casings, Animal; Casings, Hog and Beef; Casings, Terms

middlings *See* Part 2: Cereal By-products Composition

midriff *See* **diaphragm**

mignonette *See* Part 2: Essential Oils

mil A unit of linear measure usually in reference to thickness; 1 mil = 0.001 inch.

mild cheese *See* **cured cheese**

mile A measure of distance.
British
1 mile = 1.60934 kilometers
U.S. statute
1 mile = 1.609×10^5 centimeters
= 63,360 inches (in.)
= 5,280 feet (ft)
= 1,760 yards (yd)
= 1,609.35 meters (m)
= 320 rods (rd)
= 80 chains (Gunther's)
= 8 furlongs
= 1.60935 kilometers (km)
= 0.86836 U.S. nautical mile
U.S. nautical
1 mile = 72,962.5 inches (in.)
= 6,080.20 feet (ft)
= 2,026.73 yards (yd)
= 1,853.25 meters (m)
= 368.497 rods (rd)
= 1.85325 kilometers (km)
= 1.15155 statute miles

mile per hour (mph) A measure of velocity.
1 mph = 88 feet/min
= 44.7041 centimeters per second
= 26.82 meters/min
= 1.60935 kilometers per hour
= 1.46667 feet per second (fps)
= 0.86839 knot U.S.
= 0.44704 meter per second (mps)
= 0.016667 mile/min

mile per hour/sec (mph-s) A measure of acceleration.
1 = 1.46667 feet per sec/sec (fps^2)
= 0.44704 meter per sec/sec (mps^2)

milk A nutritive liquid secreted by the mammary gland. The following data apply to cow's milk. Min. 3.25% milk-fat and 8.25% nonfat milk solids.
1 cup = 245 g (8.5 oz)
1 cup milk = 3 tbsp sifted nonfat dry milk + (1 cup - 1 tbsp water)
= ⅓ cup instant nonfat dry milk + (1 cup - 1 tbsp water)

Specific gravity,	
whole milk	1.032
skim milk	1.035
milk fat	0.9

1 gal. = 8.6 lb
46½ qts = 100 lb
1 gal. cream = 8.4 lb
Storage: Store at 40°F; f.p.-0.530°C (a rise indicates adulteration); keep out of sunlight; use within 3 to 5 days.

Composition:	Average (%)	Range (%)
Water	87	—
Carbohydrates	5	4.3- 5.3
Fat	4	3.2- 6.0
Protein	3.3	2.5- 4.0
Minerals	0.7	0.7- 0.8
Solids not fat	—	8.0- 9.5
Total solids	—	11.8-15.0

	H_2O (%)	Protein (%)	Fat (%)	Carbohydrate (%)	Ash (%)	pH
3.5%	87	3.5	3.25 3.5	4.9	0.7	6.3-6.9
2%	87	4.2	2	6	0.8	
Skim	90	3.6	0.1	5.1	0.7	

Pasteurized	Min. Temp (°F)	Min. Time (min)	Remarks
	145	30	—
	161	0.25	Promptly cooled to 40°F

Homogenized milk is mechanically treated to reduce size of fat globules and thus stabilize the emulsion so that cream does not rise to top.
Vitamin D milk contains 400 U.S.P. units/qt.
See also **lactic acid.**
See Part 2: Animal Foods, Composition; Calcium, Daily Recommendations; Calories, Daily Recommendations; Canned Spoilage Related to pH; Dairy Products, Composition; Dairy Terms; Fluid and Fermented Milks, Composition; Food, Composition; Glutamate; Microbiological Media; Microbiological Standards, Dairy; Milk, Amino Acids; Milk and Cheese Composition; Milk and Milk Products, Vitamin Content; Milk Breeds, Composition; Milk Composition; Milk, Concentrated Products; Milk, Dry Products; Milk, Fatty Acids, Seasonal; Milk, Mammals, Composition; Milk, Physical Properties; Milk, Species; Milk, Total Solids; Minerals, Food; Minerals, Plant or Animal Tissue; Minerals (Trace), Limits; Moisture in Biological Materials, Nicotinic Acid, Food; Pantothenic Acid Content; pH Values of Biological Materials; Portion Size; Protein Factors; Riboflavin, Daily Recommendations; Riboflavin, Food; Saturated Fatty Acids; Spoilage, Carbohydrate Foods; Spoilage, Fat in Foods; Spoilage, Protein Foods; Storage Times; Thermophiles; Thiamin, Daily Recommendations; Thiamin, Food; Vitamin A, Daily Recommendations; Vitamin A, Food; Vitamin A, Milk and Milk Products

milk chocolate (candy bar chocolate) A mixture of chocolate and condensed milk or dry milk powder; contains not less than 12% milk solids.

milk drink *See* Part 2: Cultured Dairy Products, Composition

milker A cow sold for dairy use.

milk fat Fat obtained from milk; cows' milk ranges from 3.3 to 5.4%.

Fatty Acid

Saturated Carbon Atoms	% of Total	
4	3	Iodine No. 25-45
6	2	
8	1	Saponification value 210-240
10	3	

Fatty Acid Saturated Carbon Atoms	% of Total
12	3
14	9
16	24
18	13
20	tr
Odd No.	2
Branched Chain	1
Monounsaturated	
10	tr
12	tr
14	1
16	2
18	30
Polyunsaturated	
18-2	2
Others	2

Melting point 28-36°C
Specific gravity 0.930-0.940 at 15.5°C
Refractive index 1.460 at 25°C
Titer 33-38°C

Milk fat tests vary with the following:
1. Breed: Jersey and Guernsey are usually higher
2. Stage of lactation: increases with lactation
3. Season: higher in fall and winter
4. When drawn: first milk test lower than stripping
5. Interval between milking: longer intervals give lower test values
6. Number of lactations: after several lactations, milk fat decreases
7. Feed has little effect

See Part 2: Butter and Butter Products, Composition

milk fever A condition in cattle which causes loss of consciousness, head resting on right flank; usually occurs after calving; treatment involves a calcium preparation.

milk, filled *See* **filled milk**

Milking Shorthorn A dual-purpose type of cattle. *See* Part 2: Beef and Dual-purpose Cattle

milk, lowfat Milk containing between 0.5 and 2% milk fat.

milk, nonfat Skim milk with no more than 0.1% fat.

milk powder A powder prepared by spray-drying whole milk.
See Part 2: Microbiological Standards, Dairy; Riboflavin, Food

milk serum *See* **whey**

milk shake A mixture of milk, ice cream, flavoring and sometimes eggs.

milk, skim *See* **skimmed milk**

milk solids nonfat The content of carbohydrates, proteins and minerals in milk.
See Part 2: Cultured Dairy Products, Composition

milk stone Deposits of calcium and magnesium phosphates, proteins and other components precipitated when milk is heated above 140°F.

milk sugar *See* **lactose**

milkweed A plant having a toxic principle.
See Part 2: Poisonous Plants

millet An annual plant often used for grazing and hay; a tropical small-grained cereal that is very drought-resistant and used for food. Varieties: foxtail, gahi, Japanese, pearl, starr; approx. nutrient used for 2 tons of hay: 53 lb N, 14 lb P_2O_5, 86 lb K_2O.
Tropical types:
Sorghum (*Sorghum vulgare*) green millet, kaffir corn, guinea corn, giant millet: white grain (human food and livestock feed); red grain (beer); sweet (stems are crushed for syrup).
Finger millet (*Eleusine coracana*) ragi: human food, stores well.
Bulrush millet (*Pennisetum typhoideum*): pearl millet
Temperate types:
Common millet (*Panicum miliaceum*) proso, Indian, broom-corn, hog millet: food for man and livestock; contains carbohydrates, 10% protein and 4% fat.
Little millet (*Panicum miliare*): like common millet except smaller and will produce a moderate yield on poor soils and in dry or wet weather.
Foxtail millet (*Setaria italica*): human food, hay, silage, beer.
Japanese millet (*Echinochloa frumentacea*): food and forage.
Whole grain composition: 12% H_2O, 10-12% protein (finger millet, 5-7% protein; newer varieties, 8-20% protein), 2-5% fat, 73% carbohydrate, 2-7% fiber, 2-3.5% ash; seed = 45-50 lb/bu. Lysine is the first limiting amino acid and threonine is the second.
See Part 2: Cereal Composition; Cereal Fortification; Cereal Nutrient Content; Cereals, Vitamin and Mineral Content; Seed, Germination; Tocopherols

millet, cracked Size between whole millet and millet meal.

milli- Prefix for quantities 1000 times smaller than the base unit.

milliampere (ma) 10^{-3} ampere; one-thousandth ampere.

millier (metric ton) (tonne) = 10^3 kilograms.

milligram (mg) A measure of mass.
1 milligram = 0.015432356 grain
= 0.005 carat (metric)
= 0.001 gram (10^{-3} g)
= 0.000,771,618 scruples (apoth.)
= 0.000,643,014,8 pennyweight (dwt)
= 0.000,564,383,3 dram (av.)
= 0.000,257,205,9 dram (troy) (apoth.)

1 milligram = 3.527396×10^{-5} ounce (av.)
= 3.215074×10^{-5} ounce (troy) (apoth.)
= 2.67923×10^{-6} pound (troy) (apoth.)
= 2.20462×10^{-6} pound (av.)
= 1×10^{-6} kilogram

milliliter (ml) A measure of volume.
1 ml = 16.894 minims (Br.)
= 16.231 minims (U.S.)
= 1.000027 cu cm (cc)
= 0.2705 dram (U.S. apoth.) (U.S. fl.)
= 0.061024 cu in.
= 0.03520 ounce (Br. fl.)
= 0.03382 ounce (U.S. liquid)
= 0.0084538 gill (U.S.)
= 0.00211 pint (U.S. liquid)
= 0.001 liter
= 2.6418×10^{-4} gallon (U.S.)
= 2.199×10^{-4} gallon (Br.)
= 3.5316×10^{-5} cu ft
= 8.387×10^{-6} barrel (U.S.)
29.6 ml = 1 fluid ounce
See Part 2: Volume

millimeter (mm) A measure of length.
1 mm = 1,000 microns
= 39.37 mils
= 0.1 centimeter
= 0.0393701 inch (British)
= 0.0393700 inch (U.S.) (3.9×10^{-2} in.)
= 0.001 meter

millimeter-columns of mercury (Hg 13.59593 sp. g.) A measure of pressure.
1 = 2.78468 pounds per sq foot (psf)
= 0.04461 foot (columns of water, max. density at 4°C, 39°F)
= 0.03937 inch (columns of mercury, Hg)
= 0.01934 pound per sq inch (psi)
= 0.01360 meter (columns of water, max. density at 4°C, 39°F)
= 0.001360 kilogram per sq centimeter (kg/cm^2)
= 0.001316 atmosphere, standard (760 mm Hg)

millimicrogram ($m\gamma$) ($m\mu g$) A unit of weight.
1 $m\gamma$ = 0.000001 mg
= 10^{-3} microgram
= 3.53×10^{-11} ounce (av.)

millimicron (nanometer) (micro-millimeter) A measure of length ($m\mu$, old designation; nm, new designation)
1 millimicron = 10 Å
= 0.001 micron
= 0.000001 mm
= 1×10^{-7} cm
= 3.9×10^{-8} inch
= 1×10^{-9} meter

milling Separation of the endosperm of a grain from the germ and bran.

Millon test A test for tyrosine or proteins containing tyrosine; a red color is produced when protein is heated with mercury dissolved in nitric acid (Millon reagent). Protein (no tyrosine), negative test; gelatin, faint; carbolic and salicylic acid (phenol group), positive test.
See Part 2: Protein and Amino Acid, Color Reactions

milo A type of grain. *See also* **sorghum.**
See Part 2: Poisonous Plants

milt (1) Roe of male fish. (2) Animal spleen.

mimae *See* Part 2: Intestinal Microorganisms in Triple-sugar Agar

mima-herellea *See* Part 2: Microorganism, Media

mince meat A mixture of chopped meat and beef fat seasoned with various spices, and used as the essential ingredient of mince pie.

mineral In food technology, such elements as iron, calcium, chlorine, copper, iodine, phosphorus, etc., which occur in foods in extremely low concentrations; they are often called trace elements.
See Part 2: Egg Products, Nutritive Value; Cereal Enrichment; Cereal Fortification; Cereals, Vitamin and Mineral Content; Lemon Juice Composition; Minerals, Plant or Animal Tissue; Minerals (Trace), Limits; Wheat, Minerals; Wheat Products Composition

mineral mixtures (livestock) Free choice.
Mixture #1:
100 lb salt
100 lb ground limestone or oyster shell flour
100 lb phosphatic limestone (not over 0.5% fluorine)
Mixture #2:
80 lb steamed bone meal
20 lb salt

mineral wool A fibrous insulation made by blowing air through hot slag.
See Part 2: Insulation

minestrone (minestra) A soup made from beef, bacon and ham, vegetables and spaghetti, macaroni or rice.

minim A measure of volume. British = 0.059 ml; U.S. = 0.062 ml.

minimum daily requirement (MDR) Minimum quantities of specified vitamins and minerals necessary to avoid dietary deficiencies; established by Food and Drug Administration.

Minnesota No. 1 An inbred breed of hogs developed from a cross of Danish Landrace (48%) and English Tamworth (52%); it is red with occasional black spots.
See Part 2: Swine Breeds

Minnesota No. 2 An inbred breed of hogs produced by crossing a Yorkshire (40%) boar with Poland China (60%) sows; the hog is black and white with semi-erect ears.
See Part 2: Swine Breeds

Minorca A Mediterranean class of chickens, with white skin which lays a white-shelled egg. Varieties: *Single-comb black; rose-comb black; single-comb white; rose-comb white; single-comb buff. *Bantam variety also.

mint (*Mentha piperita L.* and *Mentha spicata L.*) A perennial herb; many types: peppermint, spearmint (Our Lady's mint and Erba Santa Maria), and applemint.

mint sauce *See* **spearmint**

minute steak A cube steak.
See Part 2: Portion Size

MIO medium *See* Part 2: Microorganism, Media

mish A dry, salty cheese made from goat's milk.

miso A dark paste food produced by fermentation and aging of mold, rice, barley, soybeans and salt in wooden barrels for 3 years.

mite *See* **cheese mite**

mitral valve Heart value which allows one-way flow of blood from the left auricle to the left ventricle.

M.I.U. Moisture, insolubles and unsaponifiable.

mixed fruit *See* Part 2: Fruit, Dried, Simmering; Fruit Servings Per Pound

mixed glyceride A triglyceride in which more than one type of acid is present.

mixed rot (addled egg) An egg in which the membrane of the yolk breaks, allowing the yolk and white to blend.

mixed vegetables A mixture containing 3 or more
beans, green or wax (½ in. to 1½ in. cuts);
beans, lima (large whole green limas or baby limas);
carrots (⅜ to ½ in. cubes);
corn, sweet (whole kernel, yellow);
peas (sieve size 3 through 5).
When 3 vegetables are used, no one more than 40%; when 4 vegetables are used, no one more than 35% or less than 8%; when 5 vegetables are used, no one more than 30% or less than 8%.
1 cup = 180 g (6.3 oz)

mixture A combination or blend of two or more substances which may be either uniformly or randomly dispersed. The components of a mixture can be separated by mechanical means (gravity, filtration, distillation, etc.). Mixtures are heterogeneous, and thus differ from chemical compounds, which are homogeneous. Milk is an example of a nonuniform mixture; a sugar solution is a uniformly dispersed mixture. *See also* **heterogeneous; compound.**

mizithra *See* Part 2: Milk and Cheese Composition

ml *See* **milliliter**

M-line A dark line bisecting the H-band in muscle fiber.

mm *See* **millimeter**

Mn Symbol for the element manganese.

Mo Symbol for the element molybdenum.

mocha A coffee-chocolate flavoring.

mocha yemen A sharp sweet coffee.

mock chicken *See* Part 2: Veal Chart; Veal Cuts

mock duck A specialty cut of lamb made from the outside of the shoulder.
See Part 2: Lamb Cuts

mode The class which has the greatest frequency.

modified starch A chemically treated starch. *See also* **starch.**

modified wine A wine made by alcoholic fermentation of grapes and sugar or sirup (min. 65% sucrose); max. 11% alcohol (by volume).

mohair Coarse wool sheared from Angora goats.

moist heat cooking A method of cooking the less tender cuts of meat by surrounding them with hot liquid or vapor; this includes braising and cooking in water.

moisture The water content of foods; also steam or atmospheric water vapor. *See also* **humidity.**
See Part 2: Bananas, Composition; Beans, Peas and Nuts; Cereal Nutrient Content; Cheese Composition; Composition of Food; Concentrated and Dried Milk Products; Connective Tissue, Composition; Creams, Butter and Frozen Desserts; Cultured Dairy Products, Composition; Dairy Products, Composition; Egg Composition; Egg Specifications; Fats and Oils, Composition; Fish and Shellfish Composition; Fluid and Fermented Milks, Composition; Food, Composition; Fruit Composition; Grain Analysis; Grain Products Composition; Hide, Layers; Honey Composition; Macaroni and Noodles Composition; Maple Syrup Composition; Meat and Meat Products Composition; Meat Composition; Milk and Cheese Composition; Milk Breeds, Composition; Milk Composition; Milk, Concentrated Products; Milk, Dry Products; Moisture, Drying; Moisture in Biological Materials; Oil Meals Composition; Oils and Fats Composition; Packinghouse By-Products Composition; Plant Foods, Composition; Poultry Composition; Pulses, Nuts and Seeds Composition; Sausage Composition; Seed, Chemical Composition; Seed Composition; Soups, Composition; Soybean Composition; Starches and Starchy Roots Composition; Sugars and Sweets Composition; Sugars and Syrups Composition; Sweetening Agents; Tomato and Tomato Products, Composition; Turkey Composition; Vegetable Composition; Wastes, Agricultural and Industrial

moisture analysis Determination of water content by drying at a specific elevated temperature, with or without vacuum, for a specific time and reporting the loss in weight as moisture; distillation as an azeotropic mixture is sometimes used.

molal (m) The concentration of a solution that contains one mole of solute in 1,000 g of solvent; sometimes called a formal solution.

molar (M) A solution of a concentration such that 1 liter of the *solution* contains one mole of the solute. A 1 molar solution of sodium hydroxide (m.w. = 40) contains 40 g of NaOH dissolved in 960 g of water, the total volume being 1 liter.

molasses Liquid remaining after the sugar has been removed from the concentrated sugar solution; contains not more than 25% water, and not more than 5% ash; wt 3 lb/qt.

Types:

table: light in color, high % sugar, low % ash

cooking (blackstrap): dark, lower % sugar, higher % ash. *See also* **blackstrap molasses.**

barbados: resembles syrup more than molasses.

refiners syrup: residual product from refining sugar cane or sugar beet; it is clarified and decolorized; max. 28% H_2O; used in flavoring corn syrup.

1⅓ cups = 1 lb

1 cup = 330 g (10.9 oz)

pH 5.0–5.5

feed 0.8 lb/qt; 26 lb/bu.

Grades for cane molasses:

	Min. Brix Solids (%)	Total Sugar (%)	Ash (%)
A (U.S. Fancy)	79	63.5	Max. 5
B (U.S. Choice)	79		
C (U.S. Standard)	79		
D (Substandard)	79	under 58	over 9

See Part 2: Calcium, Daily Requirements; Calories, Daily Recommendations; Food, Composition; Iron, Daily Recommendations; Minerals, Food; Minerals (Trace), Limits; Sugars and Sweets Composition; Sugars and Syrups Composition; Sweetness of Sweeteners; Sweetening Agents

molasses feeds 0.8 lb/qt; 75 lb of molasses is equivalent to 1 bu of corn in feeding value; max. amount of molasses to feed: 20% of ration.

mold (mould) A type of fungal growth comprised of microorganisms.

See Part 2: Bacteria, Molds and Yeasts; Canned Spoilage Manifestations; Canned Spoilage Related to pH; Culture Media; Egg Specifications; Microbiological Media; Microbiological Standards, Dairy; Microorganism, Culture Media, Dairy and Food Products; Mold, Food; Molds, Mycotoxins; Spices, Microbial Content; Spoilage, Protein Foods; Water Activity, Organisms and Food

mold inhibitor (For dry or semi-dry sausage):

Apply to outer surface:

1. Clear mineral oil
2. Edible vegetable oil
3. 2½% potassium sorbate

mole (mol) An amount of substance containing the same number of chemical units (atoms, ions, molecules, electrons, etc.) as there are atoms in 12 grams of the 12 isotope of carbon, namely, Avogadro's number of such units, or 6.023×10^{23}. This meaning has replaced the earlier definition of mole as the gram-molecular weight or gram-atomic weight of a substance. *See also* **Avogadro's number; atomic weight.**

molecular formula A chemical formula that states the number and kind of atoms in a molecule, but does not indicate their arrangement.

molecular weight The sum of the weights of all the atoms present in a molecule. In the case of many high polymers such as proteins, this may be several million.

molecule The smallest unit of a chemical *compound* that can retain the properties of the compound. A number of *elements* exist in molecular form, for example, helium (monatomic), oxygen, fluorine, bromine, chlorine, hydrogen (diatomic), and ozone (triatomic).

mollusk (mollusc) A class of shellfish that has a soft unsegmented body and a calcareous shell, i.e., clams, mussels, oysters, scallops.

See Part 2: Fish and Shellfish Composition

moltose *See* Part 2: Honey Composition

molybdenum (Mo) A metallic element; at. no. 42; at. wt. 95.95; Group VIB of Periodic Table; oxidation states +2, +3, +4, +5, +6;
electron configuration 2–8–18–13–1
orbit K L M N O

See Part 2: pH and Availability of Plant Nutrients; Wheat, Minerals

mongrel An animal of nondescript breeding; (usually derogatory), e.g., "son and heir of a mongrel bitch").

Monilia *See* Part 2: Spoilage, Carbohydrate Foods; Spoilage, Fat in Foods; Spoilage, Protein Foods

Monkey Foundation sire of the Santa Gertrudis breed.

monkey fruit *See* Part 2: Fruit Composition

monkey nut *See* **peanut**

Monk's beard *See* **French endive**

mono- A prefix meaning one.

monoammonium phosphate A fertilizer material; 20–66–0.

monogastric Single-stomach animals, e.g., swine, chickens.

monoglyceride Glycerol esterified with one molecule of an acid; has good emulsifying properties.

monohydric Containing one replaceable hydrogen or hydroxyl group per molecule.

monosodium glutamate (MSG) A product derived by hydrolysis of vegetable protein or waste liquor from beet sugar refining; used to enhance the natural flavors of food; 0.2 to 0.5% concentration on salted food.

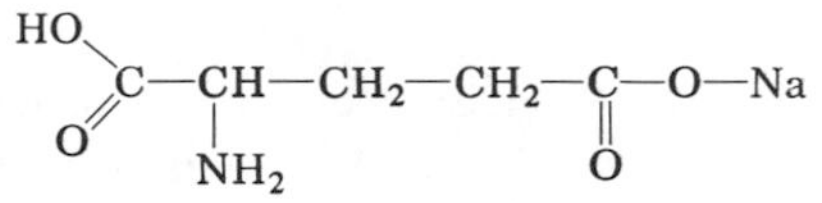

See Part 2: Glutamate; Glutamate Addition

Montadale *See* Part 2: Sheep Breeds

montan An earth wax obtained from lignite.
See Part 2: Wax

Montana No. 1 A breed of hogs developed by crossing solid black Hampshire (45%) boars with Danish Landrace (55%) sows; it is solid black in color.
See Part 2: Swine Breeds

montanic acid *See* Part 2: Saturated Fatty Acids

Monterey Jack (Jack) A mild to mellow-flavored semi-hard American cheese made from whole milk; white to light cream interior and sold in wheel shape; ripened 2–6 weeks for table use, 6–9 mo. for grating.

moon blindness A condition in which blue scum covers the pupil.

mordant Coagulant used to bind dye to cloth fiber; e.g., aluminum hydroxide, stannic acid.

morel (*Morchella esculenta*) An edible fungus that has a top with networklike light brown ridges; valleys are darker brown.

Mornay A sauce made with butter, egg yolks, milk, cream, and parmesan cheese.

mortadella A semi-dry sausage made mostly of pork (75%) mixed with beef (25%) or veal; after curing it is mixed with pork fat cubes; it is then smoked gradually until the internal temperature reaches 140°F.
See Part 2: Sausage Identification; Sausage, Types

moselle A wine having a clean fresh flavor, often natural effervescence, and low alcoholic content; it is generally dry, with a fine bouquet.

mosto *See* **must**

most probable number *See* Part 2: Most Probable Number; Most Probable Number, Bacterial

mother (1) In vinegar, a mold that contains microorganisms that can be used as a starter. (2) A solution that remains after separation of a precipitate, e.g., mother liquor. (3) A secretion of the oyster from which pearls are formed (mother-of-pearl).

motility medium *See* Part 2: Microorganism, Media

mould *See* **mold**

mountain cranberry *See* **cowberry**

mountain laurel A plant having a toxic principle.
See Part 2: Poisonous Plants

mountain oysters *See* **fries**

mousse A frozen whipped cream to which sugar, flavor and ice cream mix have been added.

moyashi Soybean sprouts.

mozzarella A sliced or shredded, mild, delicate, semi-hard cheese made from milk and used for pizza or lasagna; creamy white interior, mild and delicate flavor, firm but elastic texture; when heated becomes stringy or stretchy. Sold in rectangular or spherical shape; made from whole or partly skimmed cow's milk and is not ripened.
Composition: 50% H_2O, 22% protein, 18% fat, 1% salt.
See Part 2: Cheese Characteristics; Cheese, Vitamin Content

MPN *See* **most probable number**

MR-VP medium *See* Part 2: Microorganism, Culture Media, Dairy and Food Products; Microorganism, Media; Microorganism, Selective and Differential Broths and Media, Water Filtration Plant

MSG *See* **monosodium glutamate**

mu (μ) Greek letter with an English equivalent of m.

mucin A mixture of amino sugars, glucuronic acid and sulfuric acid.
See Part 2: Histochemical Test

Mucor A type of fungus which grows on dead or decaying vegetable matter.
See Part 2: Molds, Mycotoxins; Rot Spoilage

mucous Descriptive of a type of lining membrane that secretes a viscid liquid (mucus).
See Part 2: Intestine, Cross Section

Mueller hinton agar *See* Part 2: Microbiological Examination of Dairy Products

Mueller tellurite base *See* Part 2: Microorganism, Media

muenster cheese A semi-hard, rich, appetizer cheese made from whole milk with mellow to sharp flavor (between brick and limburger); it has a yellow-orange, tan or white surface with creamy white to light yellow interior and is sold in small wheels or blocks; ripened 2–8 weeks by bacteria surface growth.
Composition: 44% H_2O, 25% protein, 28% fat, 2% salt.
See Part 2: Cheese Characteristics; Cheese, Vitamin Content; Milk and Milk Products, Vitamin Content

muffin A small unsweetened cake made from wheat or corn flour.
See Part 2: Grain Products Composition; Portion Size

Muir A variety of freestone peaches.

mulberry (*Morus*) A tree that produces black or white, or pink or purplish berries; when they are ripe they are juicy but difficult to store; they are eaten fresh or made into wine or jam; white mulberry leaves are used as food for silkworms.
See Part 2: Fruit Classification

mule A hybrid from the mating of a Jack and a mare.

muley (mulley) Naturally hornless.

mullet (striped, white, jumping, silver) A fat fish with 2 barbels on the chin; caught in the south Atlantic coast and Gulf coast areas. *See also* **pelagic fish.**
See Part 2: Frozen Food Storage

multifidus dorsi Back muscle that connects the transverse process to the spinous process of the vertebra in front of it; in cross section, it is medial and ventral to the *longissimus dorsi* and lies close to the spinous processes.
See Part 2: Beef Rib Nomenclature

multiple fruit Fruit formed from several flowers which combined during ripening, e.g., pineapple.
See Part 2: Fruit Classification

multiple pairs *See* Part 2: Taste Panel, Difference Tests

multiple standard *See* Part 2: Taste Panel, Difference Tests

mung bean A small bean (green) from which sprouts can be obtained or unsprouted bean can be used as other dried legumes.
See Part 2: Vegetable Composition.

munster A cow's milk cheese with a strong flavor; 45–50% fat.

muriate of potash Obsolete term for potassium chloride (KCl); a neutral fertilizer material; 0–0–50 or 0–0–60.
See Part 2: Fertilizer; Fertilizer Materials

murrain wool Wool from decomposed sheep.

Muscat A variety of grape.

muscatel (American) wine A golden dessert wine made from muscat grapes.

muscle (1) A fibrous, dense tissue attached to the bony structure of the body, which contracts to permit movement of the limbs. *See also* **gastrocnemius.** (2) Lean meat.
See Part 2: Gland Weights; Muscle and Body Weight; Organ Weights; pH Values of Biological Materials

muscovado *See* **sugar cane**

mush A soft food product made from cornmeal, soybean flour or hominy; it may be boiled and eaten as a breakfast cereal or fried and served with butter, syrup, etc. *See also* **grits.**

mushroom Any edible fungus of the orders *Agaricales* or *Lycoperdales*; e.g., *Agaricus campestris*; they may be white, pink or brown.

1 lb fresh = 12 large
= 18–20 medium
= 30–40 small
= 2–5 cups sliced
= 6 cups chopped
= 1¾ cups sliced cooked
= 2 cups diced cooked

½ lb fresh = 1 can (6–8 oz)
= 1 cup canned sliced drained
= 18 whole canned

¼ lb fresh = 1 can (3–4 oz)
= ½ can canned, drained, sliced
= ⅓ cup canned, drained stems and pieces

Storage: 32–35°F.
Raw composition: 90% H_2O, 3% protein, 0.3% fat, 4% carbohydrate, 1% ash.
See also **oyster mushroom.**
See Part 2: Flavor Ingredients, Taste and Flavor Type; Frozen Food Storage; Minerals, Food; Plant and Animal Poisoning; Plant Foods, Composition; Soups, Composition; Standards, Processed Fruit and Vegetable Products; Storage; Vegetable Composition; Vegetable Cooking, Frozen; Vegetable Storage

musk An odorant of animal origin (deer), or made synthetically; used as an ingredient of perfumes and fragrances. Contains muscone, $CH_3C_{15}H_{27}O$. *See also* **musk ox.**

musk melon (*Cucumis melo*) A variety of melon similar to canteloupe. *See also* **melon.**
See Part 2: Fruit Classification; Fruit Composition; Minerals, Food; Storage; Sugar, Vegetables; Tocopherols; Vegetable Plants; Vegetable Storage

musk ox Artic North American ruminant that exudes a characteristic odor; odor does not affect meat.

mussel A bivalve mollusk; 20% of its weight is meat.
See Part 2: Minerals, Food; Plant and Animal Poisoning

must Crushed grapes (juice, seeds and skin) or the juice from pressed grapes.

mustard A vegetable whose ground seed is used for spices.
Yellow mustard (*Brassica juncea L.*)
White mustard (*Brassica hirta*)
Black mustard (*Brassica nigra*)
Max. 1.5% starch; max. 6% total ash; may be obtained as: prepared form (hot dog); powdered (ground mustard, mustard flour); whole (a vegetable whose leaf is used as food). *See also* **mustard sauce** and following entries.
Seed is ground and used for spice.
Leaves are eaten raw in salads and sandwiches.
Storage: Wash and drain; refrigerator crisper or plastic bag; use within 1 to 2 days.
See Part 2: Essential Oils; Flavoring Agents, Natural; Flavor Ingredients, Taste and Flavor Type; Minerals, Plant or Animal Tissue; Minerals (Trace), Limits; Mustard, French; Nitrate, Vegetables; Spices, Microbial Content; Unsaponifiable Matter; Vegetables, Classification; Vegetable Plants

mustard flour Ground seed of the mustard plant from which some of the oil and most of the hulls have been removed.

mustard greens Leaves of the mustard plant.
See Part 2: Food, Composition; Minerals, Food; Plant Foods, Composition; Vegetable Composition; Vegetable Cooking, Frozen

mustard oil An essential oil obtained from mustard seed (allyl isothiocyanate).

specific gravity	0.915–0.919
refractive index (15.5°C)	1.474–1.477
saponification number	171–176
iodine number	94–113

See Part 2: Fat or Oil, Physical and Chemical Properties; Fatty Acids, Fats and Oils; Iodine and Saponification Values; Refractive Indices, Fats and Oils; Saturated Fatty Acids; Titer, Fats and Oils; Tocopherols; Unsaturated Fatty Acids

mustard sauce A table sauce with a sharp aromatic flavor.
French mustard: vinegar, white mustard, flour, salt, tumeric, cayenne pepper, clove buds and pimento.
English mustard: vinegar, white mustard, flour, salt, tumeric, cayenne pepper, clove buds and pimento, sugar, tapioca, black mustard and white pepper.
German mustard: vinegar, white mustard, flour, salt, tumeric, cayenne pepper, clove buds and pimento, sugar, tapioca, black mustard and white pepper, plus wine.

mutton Flesh from an ovine animal (sheep) that is older than the lamb age (12 to 14 months).
See Part 2: Bone Age; Meat and Meat Products Composition; Minerals, Food; Riboflavin, Food; Specific Heat, Meat; Thiamin, Food; Vitamin A, Food

mutton fat *See* Part 2: Fats and Oils, Fatty Acid Composition; Fats and Oils, Physical and Chemical Properties; Fatty Acids, Fats and Oils; Unsaturated Fatty Acids

mutton grade Same as beef grades, except not eligible for prime.

muzzle Lower part of face and nose of a quadruped.

Mv Symbol for the element mendelevium.

Mycobacterium tuberculosis *See* Part 2: Microorganism, Media

mycobiotic agar *See* Part 2: Microorganism, Media

mycological agar *See* Part 2: Microorganism, Media

mycophil agar *See* Part 2: Microbiological Media

mycoplasma *See* Part 2: Microorganism, Media

mycostat A mold inhibitor.

mycotoxicosis A disease caused by ingesting poisonous compounds produced by molds.

mycotoxin A poisonous compound produced by molds.
See Part 2: Molds, Mycotoxins

myoblast An embryonic cell that will be transformed into muscle fiber.

myofibril A sub-unit of a muscle fiber.
See Part 2: Myofibrillar Proteins of Muscle

myofilament The contractile element of a muscle; sub-unit of a myofibril.

myoglobin A respiratory pigment responsible for the color of muscle.
See Part 2: Meat Pigment; Nitrate, Meat Curing

myology The study of muscles.

myosin *See* **actomyosin**
See Part 2: Myofibrillar Proteins of Muscle

myotome A fish muscle segment located between the vertebrae.

myrcia Oil of bay, used in manufacturing bay rum.

myristic acid $CH_3(CH_2)_{12}C(=O)OH$ A 14-carbon saturated acid found in butter and wool fat.
See Part 2: Fats and Oils, Fatty Acid Composition; Fatty Acids and Their Properties; Fatty Acids; Fatty Acids, Fats and Oils; Milk, Fatty Acids, Seasonal; Oils, Seed and Fruit; Saturated Fatty Acids; Wheat, Fatty Acids

myristica oil Nutmeg oil.

myristoleic acid $CH_3(CH_2)_3CH{=}CH(CH_2)_7COOH$ An unsaturated fatty acid occurring in some seed fats and fish oil.
See Part 2: Fatty Acids, Fats and Oils; Fatty Acids and Their Properties; Unsaturated Fatty Acids

myrrh An odorous resin found in an Arabian plant.
See Part 2: Essential Oils

myrtle oil An essential oil distilled from myrrh.
See Part 2: Essential Oils

mysost cheese (primost) A cheese having a light tan color, soft, creamy, mild flavor, and a distinctive sweet taste; made from whole milk or cream; it is unripened and sold in cubical or cylindrical shape.
Composition: 14% H_2O, 11% protein, 30% fat.
See Part 2: Cheese Characteristics; Milk and Cheese Composition

N

N Symbol for the element nitrogen and for Avogadro's number.

N *See* **normal**

Na Symbol for the element sodium (Latin *natrium*).

naartje *See* **tangerine**

nacre *See* **cultured pearl; mother (3)**

namage *See* **tofu**

nam plah A condiment which is a salty fish sauce made from cured fish.

Nancy Hall A moist sweet variety of sweet potato.

nanny goat A female goat.

nano- Prefix for a quantity one billionth the size of the base unit.

nanogram (ng) A measure of weight. 1 ng = 10^{-9} g (1 billionth gram).

nanometer *See* **millimicron**

naphtha A low-boiling fraction of petroleum; used as a solvent and source of synthetic natural gas.

naphthalene $C_{10}H_8$ A bicyclic hydrogen derived from coal tar and petroleum fractions; used as an antiseptic and insecticide, especially for moths.

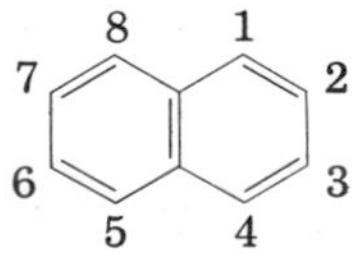

Napierian logarithm *See* **logarithm, base e**

Narragansett A variety of alfalfa.

narrow casings Sausage casings of specific widths taken from hogs, beef, sheep, etc.
- (a) narrow-end middle: natural casings used in the meat trade, from the first part of the large intestine of beef.
- (b) narrow hog casing: 29 to 32 mm in width.
- (c) narrow medium hog casing: 32 to 35 mm in width.

See Part 2: Casings, Hog; Casings, Hog and Beef; Casings, Sheep; Casings, Terms.

National Formulary (N.F. grade) A designation of a grade of chemical purity that meets specifications of the National Formulary. *See also* **grade.**

National Livestock and Meat Board An organization to promote use of livestock and meat (444 N. Michigan Ave., Chicago, Ill. 60611).

native (1) An unbranded hide. (2) Animals from corn belt or northern farms. (3) Of vegetables, grown in U.S.

native protein A protein that is not denatured.

natto A fermented cheese-like soybean product.

natural cheese Unblended cheese whose flavor depends on type of milk, bacteria, seasoning, and ripening technique. It is made from milk solids (curd) that have been separated from milk (liquid portion, whey) by rennet and/or bacterial culture.

natural gas Hydrocarbon gas associated with petroleum; used as fuel and manufacture of ammonia and other petrochemicals. Typical analysis: 83.4% by volume of methane (CH_4); 15.8% by volume of ethane (C_2H_6); 0.8% by volume of nitrogen (N_2).
See Part 2: Fuel, Heating Value.

natural logarithm *See* **logarithm, base e**

natural pearl A pearl produced without artificial addition of a foreign substance to the oyster.

naval stores *See* **spirit of turpentine; rosin**

Navel orange A variety of seedless California orange that has a navel end and is strongly segmented; has poor juice but excellent eating properties; in season November to May.

Nb Symbol for the element niobium.

N broth *See* Part 2: Microorganism, Media

Nd Symbol for the element neodymium.

NDGA *See* **nordihydroguaiaretic acid**

Ne Symbol for the element neon.

neat (1) An animal of the bovine type. (2) Of a material, undiluted or unmodified, e.g., neat whiskey.

neats-foot oil An oil obtained by pressing shin bones and feet of cattle; used for waterproofing and fatliquoring leather.

iodine number	45–75
acid number	13.35
specific gravity 20°/4°C	0.9158

See Part 2: Fats and Oils, Physical and Chemical Properties; Iodine and Saponification Values; Specific Gravities, Fats and Oils; Unsaponifiable Matter

neck bone *See* **cervical vertebrae**
See Part 2: Beef Chuck; Bone; Lamb, Wholesale Cuts; Pork Carcass, Retail Yield; Pork Wholesale Cuts; Pork Yield; Veal Wholesale Cuts

neck slice *See* Part 2: Lamb Cuts

necropsy Postmorten examination.

nectarine (*nectarina*) A small cling or freestone peach, having yellow or white flesh, a smooth-skin, and a rich flavor.
Ripening: Open air; room temperature; out of sun.
Storage: When ripe, refrigerate uncovered; use in 3 to 5 days; pH 3.9.
See Part 2: Fruit, Availability; Fruit Classification; Fruit Storage; Minerals, Food

neem oil *See* Part 2: Fats and Oils, Physical and Chemical Properties; Tocopherols

neisseriae *See* Part 2: Microorganism, Media

Nellore A strain of Brahman cattle.

neodymium (Nd) A rare earth element of the lauthanide series; Group IIIB of Periodic Table; at. no. 60; at. wt. 144.27; oxidation state +3; electron configuration 2-8-18-22-8-2
orbit K L M N O P

neon (Ne) An inert gaseous element; at. no. 10; at. wt. 20.183; oxidation state 0;
electron configuration 2-8
orbit K L

neoplasm A new and abnormal growth of tissue, e.g., a tumor.

nepeta oil *See* Part 2: Essential Oils

nephelometric analysis An optical analysis in which concentration is determined by comparing the intensity of light reflected from suspended particles with that of a known concentration of the same particles.

neptunium (Np) A synthetic radioactive element of the actinide series; Group IIIB of Periodic Table; at. no. 93; mass number of most stable isotope 237; oxidation states +3, +4, +5, +6; electron configuration 2-8-18-32-22-9-2
orbit K L M N O P Q

neroli oil (orange flower oil) An essential oil distilled from citrus flowers and used in flavorings.
See Part 2: Essential Oils

netted melon *See* **melon**

neufchatel cheese (boudart, bondore, coeur de bray) A soft, white, mild, creamy cheese made from whole milk that is higher in moisture and lower in fat than cream cheese; it is foil-wrapped in rectangular portions; a soft, white cheese from France that may be eaten fresh or ripened; *See also* **cream cheese.**
Composition: 55% H_2O, 16-18% protein, 23-25% fat, 2-3% ash, 1% salt; cannot be frozen.
See Part 2: Cheese Characteristics; Cheese, Vitamin Content; Vitamin A, Milk and Milk Products

neurospora culture agar *See* Part 2: Microorganism, Media

neutral (1) Neither acidic nor basic, i.e., pH 7.0. (2) Having neither positive nor negative electric charge, e.g., a neutron.

neutralization A reaction between an acid and a base which yields a salt and water product, e.g., $H_2SO_4 + CaO \rightarrow CaSO_4 + H_2O$.
See Part 2: Margarine Production

neutralizing value *See* Part 2: Liming Materials

neutral lard Lard rendered slowly (at 126°F) from back and leaf fat.

neutral spirit *See* **silent spirit**

neutron A neutral particle in all atomic nuclei except (common) hydrogen; charge 0; weight 1.675×10^{-24} gram; mass 1.0086; diameter 2.8×10^{-13} cm.
See Part 2: Constants, Fundamental

new cocoyam *See* **tannia**

New England (Berliner) A coarse-cut sausage of pork and a little beef.

New Hampshire An American class of chickens that lays a brown-shelled egg; plumage color: chestnut red.
Male (head) reddish; (neck and back) golden; (tail feathers) black (some edged in red).
Female (neck) chestnut red; (tail feathers) black and red.
See Part 2: Poultry Breeds and Varieties

new potatoes Potatoes dug before they reach full maturity.

New York lettuce A variety of head lettuce that is larger and greener than iceberg. *See also* **lettuce.**

New York round A wholesale cut of beef round from which steaks are cut.
See Part 2: Beef Rounds

New York style *See* **Eastern style**
See Part 2: Beef Rounds

New York style shoulder A pork shoulder that is trimmed, skinned and had the neck bone and back removed; about 16% of pork carcass (head and leaf fat on).

N.F. *See* **National Formulary**

NFE *See* **nitrogen-free extract**

Ni Symbol for the element nickel.

niacin (nicotinic acid) (p-p factor) A water-soluble (B-group) vitamin; deficiency causes a disease called pellagra (man) or black tongue (dog). Niacin functions in the oxidation-reduction system in cells. Sources: liver, kidney, meat, yeast, cereals, legumes, wheat germ, enriched foods, green and leaf vegetables; deficiency symptoms: loss of appetite and weight; skin eruptions.

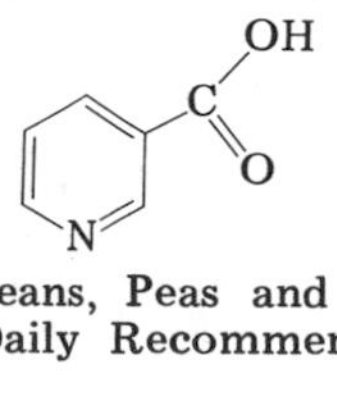

See Part 2: Beans, Peas and Nuts; Beef Percentages of Daily Recommended Allowances;

Cereal Enrichment; Cereal Nutrient Content; Composition of Food; Dairy Products, Composition; Egg Composition; Egg Products, Nutritive Value; Fats and Oils, Composition; Fish and Shellfish Composition; Food, Composition; Fruit Composition; Grain Analysis; Grain Products Composition; Lamb Percentages of Daily Recommended Allowances; Lemon Juice Composition; Lime Juice Composition; Macaroni and Noodles Composition; Meat Composition; Meat, Nutritive Value; Niacin; Niacin, Daily Recommendations; Plant Foods, Composition; Pork, Percentages of Daily Recommended Allowances; Poultry Composition; Sausage Composition; Sausage Nutritive Value; Seed, Chemical Composition; Soups, Composition; Sugars and Sweets Composition; Tomato and Tomato Products, Composition; Variety Meat Percentage of Daily Recommended Allowances; Vegetable Composition; Vitamin Retention, Meat; Vitamins; Vitamin Sources, Functions, and Stability; Wheat Products Composition; Wheat, Vitamins

nickel (Ni) A metallic element; at. no. 28; at. wt. 58.71; Group VIII of Periodic Table; oxidation states +2, +3; electron configuration 2-8-16-2
orbit K L M N
Used as catalyst in hydrogenation of vegetable oils.
See Part 2: Normal Solutions

nicotinamide (niacinamide) Has same function as niacin.
See Part 2: Cereal Fortification; Cereals, Vitamin and Mineral Content; Vitamins

nicotine $C_{10}H_{14}N_2$ An alkaloid derived from tobacco and used as an insecticide and fumigant; it is poisonous.

nicotinic acid *See* **niacin**
See Part 2: Cheese Composition; Cheese, Vitamin Content; Flour, Extraction Rates; Milk and Milk Products, Vitamin Content; Milk Composition; Nicotinic Acid, Food; Vitamins; Wheat, Parts of Grain, Vitamins

niger-seed oil *See* Part 2: Fats and Oils, Physical and Chemical Properties

night-blindness Difficulty in seeing in dim light, due to vitamin A deficiency.

nightshade A poisonous plant.
See Part 2: Poisonous Plants

ninhydrin test A test for amino acids with a free amino and a free carboxyl group; this includes all amino acids except proline and hydroxyproline; a deep blue color appears when ninhydrin is added to these amino acids.
See Part 2: Protein and Amino Acid, Color Reactions

niobium (Nb) (columbium) A metallic element; at. no. 41; at. wt. 92.91; Group VB of Periodic Table; oxidation states +3, +5;
electron configuration 2-8-18-12-1
orbit K L M N O

nisin A naturally-occurring antibiotic which may be added to food in some countries.

nisinic acid *See* Part 2: Fatty Acids and Their Properties

niter (1) Insoluble residue of maple sap. (2) Potassium nitrate.

nitrate A salt of nitric acid; used in meat curing; should not exceed 500 ppm (0.05%) in finished product; sodium or potassium nitrate; 7 lb/100 gal. pickle (10% pump). Levels currently (1978) being reviewed.
See Part 2: Nitrate, Meat Curing; Nitrate, Vegetables; Water Drinking Standards

nitrate of soda (sodium nitrate) $NaNO_3$ A fertilizer material; 16-0-0; basic in nature; each pound is equivalent to 0.29 lb of dolomitic limestone.
See Part 2: Fertilizer Materials

nitre cake $NaHSO_4$ **(sodium bisulfate; sodium acid sulfate; sodium hydrogen sulfate)** Food and feed additive.

nitric acid (aqua fortis) HNO_3 Mol. wt. 63.02; b.p. 86°C.
Commercial strength:

Mole/l	g/l	% by Wt	Sp. Gr.	Normality
15.99	1008	71	1.42	—
—	—	69	1.409	15.4
14.9	938	67	1.40	—
13.3	837	61	1.37	—

ml of 71% HNO_3 to dilute to 10 l	Approx normality
630	1.00

See Part 2: Concentration of Commercial Strengths of Acids and Bases; Nitric Acid Solution; Normal Solutions

nitric oxide NO Reduction product of nitrite; reacts with myoglobin in meat to form nitrosomyoglobin.
See Part 2: Meat Pigment

nitric oxide myoglobin *See* **nitrosomyoglobin**

nitric phosphate *See* Part 2: Fertilizer Materials

nitrification Bacterial conversion of plant and animal waste into soil nitrates.

$$2NH_3 + 3O_2 \longrightarrow 2HNO_2 + 2H_2O$$

$$2HNO_2 + O_2 \longrightarrow 2HNO_3$$

$$2HNO_3 + CaCO_3 \longrightarrow Ca(NO_3)_2 + H_2O + CO_2$$

nitrite A salt of nitrous acid; used in meat curing; both sodium and potassium nitrite can be used; max. amount
¼ oz sodium nitrite or potassium nitrite/100 lb meat;
finished product cannot contain over 200 ppm;
2 lb in 100 gal. of pickle (10% pump);
1 oz/100 lb of meat in dry cure;
200 ppm (0.02%) in finished product

A reduction or elimination is being considered (1978) because of formation of potentially toxic nitrosamine compounds.

Nitrite content is determined by extracting the sample with water and developing a color by using Griess reagent and then measuring this color spectrophotometrically; results can be obtained by comparing the value received with a known standard curve.

See Part 2: Chemical Poisoning

nitrite test strip *See* Part 2: Microorganism, Media

nitroalkane (nitroparaffin) R—NO_2 A paraffinic hydrocarbon in which one hydrogen atom has been replaced by a nitro group. Used as solvents for cellulose derivatives.

nitrogen N_2 A diatomic gaseous element; at. no. 7 at. wt. 14.008; Group VA of Periodic Table; oxidation states +1, +2, +3, +4, +5, −1, −2, −3; electron configuration 2-5

orbit K L

It is nonflammable and nontoxic; present in air (78% by volume); essential element in proteins and amino acids; also essential in soils and fertilizers.

Boiling point: −320.5°F (−195.8°C)
Freezing point: −345.9°F (−209.9°C)
Critical temperature: −232.9°F (−147.1°C) (critical pressure 492.1 psia)
Liquid nitrogen: 50.46 lb/cu ft or 6.7 lb/gal
Latent heat of vaporization (−320°F): 85.7 Btu/lb
Heat absorbed from −320 to 0°F: 85 Btu/lb
Heat absorbed from 0 to 70°F: 17 Btu/lb
Heat absorbed from liquid at −320°F to vapor at 35°F: 174 Btu/lb

See Part 2: Fertilizer; Fertilizer Materials; Honey Composition; Manure Analysis; Normal Solutions; Nutrients in Crops; pH and Availability of Plant Nutrients; Sugar Beet Yield; Wastes, Agricultural and Industrial

nitrogen determination *See* Kjeldahl determination

nitrogen-free extract (NFE) More soluble carbohydrate and cellulose;

% NFE = 100 − (% H_2O + % ash + % protein + % fiber + % fat)

nitrogenous ratio (N.R.) (albuminoid ratio) The ratio by which the body-building power of diet is judged; should be between 1:4 and 1:8

N.R. = ratio of % protein to % carb. + % fat (2.5) + % indigestible matter.

nitrogen pentoxide *See* Part 2: Normal Solutions

nitroparaffin *See* **nitroalkane**

nitrosamine An organic compound in which NNO is attached to an alkyl or aryl group; may be formed from nitrites. Some nitrosamines may be carcinogenic.

nitrosohemochrome *See* Part 2: Meat Pigment; Nitrate, Meat Curing

nitrosomyoglobin (nitric oxide myoglobin) The red cured meat pigment prior to heating.

See Part 2: Meat Pigment; Nitrate, Meat Curing

nitrous acid HNO_2 Aqueous solution of nitrogen trioxide, N_2O_3.

See Part 2: Nitrate, Meat Curing

nitrous oxide N_2O Noncombustible gas used as aerosol propellant, refrigerant, and general anesthetic.

See Part 2: Nitrate, Meat Curing; Refrigerant

No Symbol for the element nobelium.

nobelium (No) Synthetic radioactive element of the actinide series; at. no. 102; mass number of most stable isotope 254; Group IIIB of the Periodic Table; electron configuration 2-8-18-32-32-8-2

orbit K L M N O P Q

noble An element that is chemically unreactive and forms few compounds. Refers especially to the gases of the zero-valent group of the Periodic Table, the first three of which (helium, neon and argon) are completely inert. The term also refers to some metals of low combining power.

node A stem joint where a leaf is or was attached.

See Part 2: Corn

noggin (quartern) A measure of liquor. 1 noggin = ¼ pint = 1 gill.

noil Short wool fibers removed during the process of combining.

nokkelost cheese (Leyden, spiced Leyden) A cheese similar to Edam except it contains caraway seeds.

non-electrolyte A substance that is not a good electrical conductor when in aqueous solution.

non-essential An amino acid or fatty acid that is synthesized in the body and thus need not be obtained from external sources.

nonfat dry milk solids Skim milk that has been dehydrated by spray drying or vacuum drying; max. 1.5% milk-fat; max. 5% moisture. Used as a binder in sausages. *See also* **binder**.

	1 lb	wt per cup
Instant	6 cups	75 g (2.6 oz)
Non-instant	3½ cups	131 g (4.6 oz)

11 lb skim milk required to produce 1 lb nonfat dry milk solids.

¾ cup nonfat dry milk and 4 cups water = 1 qt liquid skim milk.

Instant form: coarse, creamy white, free flowing particles that dissolve easily in water.

Grades: Extra and Standard.

See Part 2: Food, Composition

nonfat milk Milk from which over 95% of the fat has been removed.

See Part 2: Dairy Terms; Milk, Amino Acids

non-polar Liquids having a low dielectric constant and thus poor electrical conductors, e.g., hexane (C_6H_{14}).

non-protein nitrogen (NPN) Nitrogen obtained from sources other than protein, e.g., atmospheric nitrogen.

non-reducing sugar A sugar which is very slowly or not at all oxidized by weak oxidizing agents (silver, mercuric or cupric salts); contains no free aldehyde or ketone groups; e.g., sucrose.

nonsaponifiable Free from fatty acids.
See Part 2: Wheat Products Composition

noodles (1) A mixture of wheat flour and water (sometimes also milk and eggs) that has been dried into flat strips.
Other varieties: reginette (wavy strips); tagliarine (1/3 noodle width); tagliati (irregular shapes).
1 lb broken = 6–8 cups
1 cup = 75 g (2.6 oz)
1 lb broken = 8 cups cooked
Dry composition: 10% H_2O, 13% protein, 5% fat, 72% carbohydrate, 0.8% ash.
(2) Slices of a sugar beet root.
See Part 2: Cereal Enrichment; Grain Products Composition; Macaroni and Noodles Composition; Soups, Composition

nor- A chemical prefix meaning "minus one methyl group."

nordihydroguaiaretic acid (NDGA) $C_{18}H_{22}O_4$ An antioxidant used to retard rancidity in fat; 0.01% in fat (total antioxidant; 0.02% in combination).
See Part 2: Antioxidants, Formula

nori (amanori) A Japanese seaweed used as a garnish.

norleucine A monoamino-monocarboxylic amino acid.

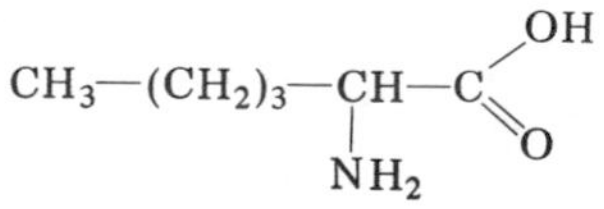

normal (N) A solution of a concentration such that one liter of the solution contains one gram equivalent weight of the solute.
See Part 2: Normal Solutions; pH, Standard Solutions; Reagents, Normal Solutions; Sodium Hydroxide Solution

normal distribution Equation for the distribution.

$$\gamma = \frac{1}{\sigma\sqrt{2\pi}}\, e^{-(x-u)^2/2\sigma^2}$$

If $T = (x - u)/\sigma$

$$\gamma = \frac{1}{\sqrt{2\pi}}\, e^{-T^2/2}$$

This type of frequency distribution is found when the data are measured on a continuous scale (may have fractional components of the unit 1).
See Part 2: Normal Curve

Northern Spy A variety of apples that is in season from Sept. to Dec.; excellent sauce and pie apples and good eating apples.

No Tail A breed of sheep.
See Part 2: Sheep Breeds

nougat A confection made of condensed and skim milk, chopped nuts, sugar and flavoring, often coated with chocolate.

Novocaine Proprietary name for procaine hydrochloride; a nerve block anesthetic used in dentistry.

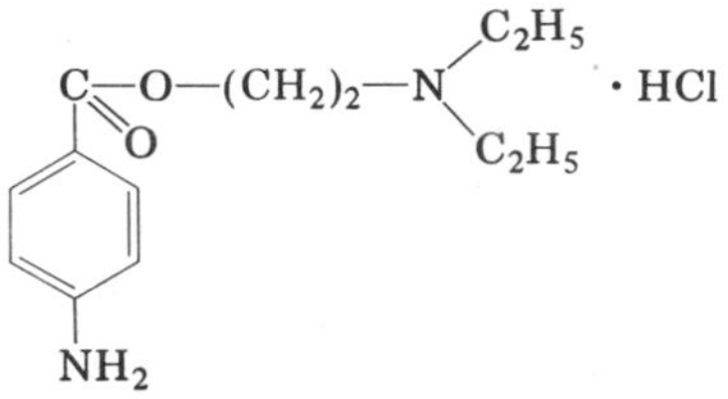

Np Symbol for the element neptunium.

NPN *See* non-protein nitrogen

nu (N, ν) Greek letter with an English equivalent of n; used as a symbol of frequency of light and refractive index.

Nubian A breed of goats.
See Part 2: Goats, Milk Breeds

nucleic acid A complex compound which on hydrolysis yields phosphoric acid, sugars and one or more bases (purines and pyrimidines).

nucleoprotein A combination of proteins and nucleic acids; occurs in animal glands and wheat germ.

nucleotide A molecule consisting of one molecule of phosphoric acid, one molecule of sugar and one molecule of a base.

nucleus (1) The center of an atom that contains the mass made up of protons (positively charged particles) and neutrons (neutral particles). (2) The central portion of a living cell containing the chromosomes. (3) The benzene ring.

nuoc mam A condiment which is a salty fish sauce made from cured fish.

nurse cow A cow used to furnish milk for another cow's calf.

nut One-seeded fruit contained in a shell.
2 lb in shell = 1 lb nut meats
1 cup chopped = 1/3 to 1/4 lb
Storage: Air-tight container (65–75% relative humidity), refrigerate (32°F: 8 mo. storage life) or freeze (−10°F); (freezing point, 13–25°F).
See Part 2: Beans, Peas and Nuts; Calories, Daily Recommendations; Fruit and Nut Rootstock; Fruit Classification; Iron, Daily Recommendations; Nicotinic Acid, Food; Nut, Grades; Oils, Seed and Fruit; Pulses, Nuts and Seeds Composition; Riboflavin, Food; Storage; Thiamin, Daily Recommendations; Thiamin, Food; Tocopherols

nutmeg (*Myristica fragrans Houtt*) Tan fruit (kernel) of nutmeg tree is used as a spice; may be whole or ground. The fruit contains a red fleshy network called an aril which is the spice, mace; the nutmeg is the seed which is dried before use. It may have a coating of lime.

Not less than 25% non-volatile ether extract
Not more than 10% crude fiber
5% total ash
0.5% acid-insoluble ash
6% volatile oil.

Used in sweet and milk dishes. *See also* mace.
See Part 2: Flavoring Agents, Natural; Spices, Microbial Content; Wastes, Agricultural and Industrial

nutmeg fat *See* Part 2: Saturated Fatty Acids

nutrient Any substance that contributes to the growth and health of a living organism.
See Part 2: Nutrients in Crops; pH and Availability of Plant Nutrients

nutrient agar An agar used as a culture medium for bacteria. *See also* agar-agar.
See Part 2: Microbiological Examination of Dairy Products; Microbiological Media; Microorganism, Culture Media, Dairy and Food Products; Microorganism, Culture Media, Water and Sewage, Standard Methods; Microorganism, Media

nutrient broth A protein-rich liquid used as a culture medium for bacteria.
See Part 2: Microbiological Examination of Dairy Products; Microbiological Media

nutrient gelatin A gelatin used as a culture medium for bacteria.
See Part 2: Microorganism, Culture Media, Water and Sewage, Standard Methods; Microorganism, Media

nutrition Maintenance of an organism (plants or animals) by absorption of nourishment from nutrients.

nutrition labeling A statement of nutrient content in terms of stated serving or portion displayed on the container or package.
(a) Caloric content (nearest 5 Calories).
(b) Number of grams of protein, fat and available carbohydrate (nearest gram).
(c) Vitamins: 5% increments of RDA up to 20%; 10% increments above 20%; must include vitamin A, vitamin C, thiamin, riboflavin, niacin; others optional.
(d) Minerals: 5% increments of RDA up to 20% and 10% increments above 20%; must include calcium and iron; others optional.

nutritive value *See* Part 2: Meat, Nutritive Value

nylon *See* polyamide
See Part 2: Mesh Sizes

nystatin A polyene, antifungal antibiotic added to food in some countries.

O

o *See* **ortho-**

O Symbol for the element oxygen.

oak A hardwood tree of which there are over 300 species; used for lumber, vegetable tanning; seeds (acorns) used for animal feed.
See Part 2: Poisonous Plants; Insulation

Oakite Proprietary name for a tribasic sodium phosphate ($Na_3PO_4 \cdot 12H_2O$) used as a cleaning compound.

oak leaf gland The pancreas.

oak leaf lettuce A leaf lettuce with deeply notched leaves.

oarweed (***Laminaria digitata***) A seaweed used for food, livestock feed and the production of alginates used for thickening, emulsification, and food film formation.

oat (***Avena sativa*****, a white oat;** ***Avena byzantina*****, a red oat)** An annual temperate zone grain crop used for livestock (ripe grain as food; green stage as fodder, hay or pellets) and human food (porridge, grits, oat meal and rolled oats). Oat flour has antioxidant properties and is mixed with other flours to retard rancidity. Oat husk (removed during milling) has been used for fuel, packing material and as a raw material for the production of furfural.
Weight of dried products:

	lb/qt	lb/bu
oat	1	32
ground	0.7	22
middling	1.5	48

Strains: *Avena sativa*, *Avena steritis*, *Avena strigosa*; pH 6.0; approx nutrients required to produce:

	N (lb)	P_2O_5 (lb)	K_2O (lb)
50 bu grain	32	13	9
2 tons straw	24	12	70
1 ton cover crop	30	12	50

Plant 50 to 80 lb/acre; 145 to 155 days to maturity.
Composition: 8% H_2O, 13–22% protein, 65–86% starch, 5–10% fat.
See Part 2: Cereal Composition; Cereal Nutrient Content; Minerals, Food; Nicotinic Acid, Food; Nutrients in Crops; Plant Foods, Composition; Protein Factors; Seed, Chemical Composition; Seed Composition; Seed, Germination; Spoilage, Fat in Food; Tocopherols

oat cereal *See* Part 2: Grain Products Composition

oat flour Ground oats with bran removed.

oatgrass *See* Part 2: Seed, Germination

oat, groats Whole, uncut, uncrushed kernel of oatmeal; oats with hull removed.

oatmeal ("oats") Ground or cut and rolled oats made by rolling the groats to form flakes.
Quick-cooking: the groats are cut and then rolled to produce thin small flakes used as a breakfast cereal and in cooking. *See also* **steel cut oatmeal, Scotch oatmeal** and **rolled oats.**
2⅔ cups = 1 lb
100 lb oatmeal = 7.6 bu oats
See Part 2: Food, Composition; Grain Products Composition; Minerals, Food; Thiamin, Food; Vitamin A, Food

objective (1) A test recorded by a physical instrument and thus independent of an individual's judgment; (2) The lens nearest the object of a compound microscope.

obligate aerobes Bacteria that must have oxygen for growth. *See also* **aerobic.**

obligate anaerobes Bacteria which can grow in the absence of oxygen. *See also* **anaerobic.**

obturator A thigh muscle that covers the obturator foramen and runs to the femur.

obturator foramen A hole in the pelvic bone.

oca (***Oxalis tuberosa***) A plant that produces a white, yellow or red edible tuber; the tubers are usually semidried before eating and the leaves and shoots may be eaten as a salad.

ocean catfish *See* **catfish**

ocean perch (rosefish, redfish) A lean fish caught off the North Atlantic and North Pacific coasts.

octacosanoic acid *See* Part 2: Saturated Fatty Acids

octadecadienoic acid Linoleic acid; occurs in vegetable oils. It is polyunsaturated.
See Part 2: Milk, Fatty Acids, Seasonal; Unsaturated Fatty Acids

octadecanoic acid *See* **stearic acid**

octadecatrienoic acid Linolenic acid, a polyunsaturated fatty acid essential in the diet.
See Part 2: Unsaturated Fatty Acids

octadecenoic acid *See* **oleic acid**

octanoic acid $CH_3(CH_2)_6COOH$ A saturated fatty acid found in coconut oil.
See Part 2: Saturated Fatty Acids

odor A sensation caused by stimulation of olfactory receptors in the nasal cavity.

See Part 2: Bacteria on Chickens at Various Holding Temperatures

OF basal medium *See* Part 2: Microorganism, Media

offal Parts removed from carcass in dressing; also the bran and germ removed in milling. *See also* **variety meat.**
See Part 2: Meat and Meat Products Composition

Ogden A variety of soybean.

Ohio Improved Chester A meat-type breed of hogs with early breeding similar to the Chester White; it was later crossed with hogs known as Todd hogs; it is solid white with drooping ears.
See Part 2: Swine Breeds

ohm (Ω) A measure of resistance (R) to current flow
100 ohms = 1 kilohm
1,000,000 ohms = 1 megohm
1 ohm (absolute) = 0.999505 International ohm

Ohm's law $I = \frac{E}{R}$, where I = current in amps, E = potential in volts, and R = resistance in ohms

$P = I^2R = EI = \frac{E^2}{R}$

P = power = watts = joule/sec

OIC *See* **Ohio Improved Chester**

oie farcie Stuffed goose.

oil cake The solid residue remaining after extraction of oil from seeds.

oil, fuel Equivalent to No. 2 fuel oil or diesel oil. 1 gal. = approx 8 lb.
See Part 2: Fuel, Heating Value

oil immersion Microscope examination in which oil with the same refractive index as glass is placed between the objective lens and the specimen.

oil meal Oil cake which has been pulverized; used as cattle feed.
See Part 2: Oil Meals Composition

oil of frankincense Olibanum oil, distilled from a vegetable gum (thus) native to northeast Africa.

oil of shaddock Expressed grapefruit oil.

oil palm (*Elaeis guineensis*) A subtropical palm that grows in fairly poor soil but requires moderate rainfall; grows chiefly in western Africa. *See also* **palm oil; palm kernel oil.**

Parts of fruit	Source	Use
Mesocarp or pericarp	Fibrous pulp beneath outer skin	Palm oil of commerce
Outer black shell of nut	Seed shell	Fuel
Inner kernel	Center of seed	Palm kernel oil
Extracted kernel	Inner kernel extracted	Oil cake for livestock feed
Sap	Tapping tree	Fermented for wine

oils, vegetable Glycerides of fatty acids obtained from seeds, nuts, fruits, etc., of plants. The generalized formula of a triglyceride is:

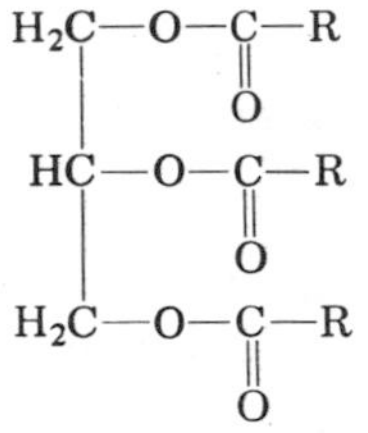

Vegetable oils are liquid at room temperature (18–25°C). *See also* **fat.**
2 tbsp = 1 oz
1 cup = 220 g
Storage: 35°F will yield 8 months' storage life.
Salad or cooking composition: 0% H_2O, 0% protein, 100% fat, 0% carbohydrate, 0% ash.
See Part 2: Fats and Oils, Composition; Fats and Oils, Fatty Acid Composition; Fats and Oils, Physical and Chemical Properties; Melting Points, Fats and Oils; Minerals (Trace), Limits; Oil or Fat, Characteristics; Oils and Fats Composition; Oils, Seed and Fruit; Oil, Triglyceride Mole Percent Composition; Orange Essence Oils; Orange Oil Composition; Orange Oil Properties; Refractive Indices, Fats and Oils; Specific Gravities, Fats and Oils; Titer, Fats and Oils; Vitamin A, Fish; Vitamin D, Fish

oiticica oil A drying oil obtained from a Brazilian tree; used in paints.
See Part 2: Fats and Oils, Physical and Chemical Properties; Iodine and Saponification Values; Refractive Indices, Fats and Oils

oka A light, creamy yellow, semihard to soft cheese made in Canada. *See also* **port du salut.**

Oklahoma Common A variety of alfalfa.

okra (okro, lady's fingers, gumbo) (*Hibiscus esculentus*) An annual of the cotton family that produces pods that may be eaten if picked in the immature stage; they may be eaten fresh, cooked, canned or dried, and are often used to thicken other dishes.
1 lb fresh = 2¼ cups cooked
1 cup cooked = 180 g (6.2 oz)
1½ lb fresh = 1 qt canned
100 lb fresh = 10–11 lb dry
To plant: 30 lb/bu; space 16 in. apart in 3½-ft rows; seed 4 lb/acre.
Weight: 30 lb/bu.
Storage: 50°F, 85–95% relative humidity, 7 days storage life.
Raw composition: 89% H_2O, 3% protein, 0.3% fat, 8% carbohydrate, 0.8% ash.
See Part 2: Minerals, Food; Plant Foods, Composition; Standards, Processed Fruit and Vege-

table Products; Storage; Sugar, Vegetables; Vegetable Boiling; Vegetable Composition; Vegetable Cooking, Frozen; Vegetable Plants; Vegetables, Boiling Time, Frozen; Vegetables, Canning Dates; Vegetables, Classification; Vegetable Servings; Vegetable Storage; Vegetable Yield, Canned and Frozen; Vegetable Yield, Frozen, Canned and Fresh

okro *See* **okra**

old cocogam *See* **taro**

Old Norfolk A breed of wild, horned sheep having long bodies and legs.

oleander A plant having a toxic principle.
See Part 2: Poisonous Plants

olecranon process *See* Part 2: Bone

olefin *See* **alkene**

oleic acid (*cis*-9-octadecenoic acid) $CH_3(CH_2)_7CH{=}CH(CH_2)_7COOH$ An 18-carbon unsaturated fatty acid widely distributed in nature; iodine number 90; m.p. 14°C.
See Part 2: Beans, Peas and Nuts; Dairy Products, Composition; Egg Composition; Egg Products, Nutritive Value; Fats and Oils, Composition; Fat and Oils, Fatty Acid Composition; Fatty Acids and Their Properties; Fatty Acids; Fatty Acids, Fats and Oils; Fish and Shellfish Composition; Fruit Composition; Grain Products Composition; Meat Composition; Milk, Fatty Acids, Seasonal; Oils, Seed and Fruit; Poultry Composition; Sausage Composition; Seed, Chemical Composition; Soups, Composition; Sugars and Sweets Composition; Unsaturated Fatty Acids; Vegetable Composition; Wheat, Fatty Acids; Wheat Products Composition

oleomargarine A term originally applied to margarine; made from oleo oils of beef fat. A plastic food made of animal and/or vegetable fat; minimum 80% fat; citric acid (preservative); isopropyl citrates maximum 0.02% (preservative); stearyl citrate maximum 0.15% (preservative). *See also* **margarine.**
See Part 2: Fats and Oils, Characteristic; Margarine Formulae; Minerals, Food

oleo oil The liquid fraction separated from animal fats and used in making margarine.

oleoresin A viscous, sticky product obtained from softwood trees by extraction with organic solvents; contains essential oils and dissolved resin. *See also* **turpentine.**

olfactory Referring to bodily organs and nerve responses responsible for the sense of smell. *See also* **odor.**

olibanum oil *See* **oil of frankincense**

olive (*Olea europaea*) Grows in subtropical, fairly arid regions in well-drained soil. The drupe (fruit) is green and turns dark blue or purplish when ripe; it contains a single seed and may be picked green or ripe and is usually packed in brine. Stuffed olives are green, pickled with seed removed and pimiento, sweet red pepper, onion, almonds or anchovies inserted in seed area. *See also* **olive oil.**

1 lug (5.75 × 13.5 × 16.1 in.) = 25–30 lb
3 pt = 50 servings

Storage (fresh): 45–50°F, 85–90% relative humidity, storage life, 4 weeks.

Composition of green: 78% H_2O, 1.4% protein, 13% fat, 1.3% carbohydrate, 6.4% ash.

Composition of ripe: 73–84% H_2O, 1.1% protein, 9–20% fat, 2.5–3.5% carbohydrate, 2.5% ash.

U.S. grades, ripe or green olives:
Grade A (fancy); B (choice); C (standard); substandard.

Green and ripe olive sizes:

No. 1 (small)	128–140/lb
No. 2 (medium)	106–127/lb
No. 3 (large)	91–105/lb
No. 4 (extra large)	76–90/lb
No. 5 (mammoth)	65–75/lb
No. 6 (giant)	53–64/lb
No. 7 (jumbo)	46–52/lb
No. 8 (colossal)	33–45/lb
No. 9 (supercolossal)	32 max.

Weight and composition of ripe fruit:
fruit, 1.5–13 g
pit, 15–30% of wt of ripe fruit
Soluble solids, 6–10%
oil, 15–35%
seed kernel, 5% of the oil

Types:
Spanish: fermented, unripe yellowish-green olives.
American: ½ ripe reddish fruit.
Greek: preserved after fully ripe and dark purple in color.

See Part 2: Calories, Daily Recommendations; Food, Composition; Fruit Canning Dates; Fruit Classification; Fruit Composition; Minerals, Food; Oils and Fats Composition; Standards, Processed Fruit and Vegetable Products; Storage; Unsaponifiable Matter

olive loaf *See* Part 2: Sausage Identification

olive oil A nondrying oil obtained by pressing or extracting the fruit of the olive tree (*Olea europea sativa*); color varies from pale gold (highest grade) to greenish-gold to light green; yield 26–60%; oil yield avg 200 kg/ton of olives.
Composition:

	(%)		(%)
palmitic	7–17	linoleic	5–15
palmitoleic	2	linolenic	1
stearic	2–3	arachidic	0.5–0.9
oleic	62–84		

Free fatty acid in edible oil: 0.3–2.8% (1.41% maximum desirable level).

Properties:

Saponification value	185–196
Unsaponifiable	0.5–1.8%
Iodine number	78–90
Specific gravity	0.9158 at 20°/4°C
Titer	17°–26°C
Saturated fatty acids	9–18%

Melting point -6°C
Refractive index (15.5°C) 1.470-1.472
Fresh olive oil:

Smoke point	391°F	199°C
Flash point	435°-610°F	225°-321°C
Fire point	650°-682°F	343°-361°C

Stored olive oil

Smoke point	300°-315°F	149°-157°C

Storage: 35°-40°F (it thickens and changes color at lower temperatures).
Volume:
1 qt = 4 cups
1 cup = 210 g (7.4 oz)
Virgin olive oil grades (oil obtained by pressing):
extra: oleic acid does not exceed 1 g/100 g
fine: oleic acid does not exceed 1.5 g/100 g
ordinary: oleic acid may be up to 3 g/100 g
lampante: off-flavor
Refined olive oil grades:
pure (refined from virgin oil)
second (refined from solvent-extracted oil)
Blended olive oil grades:
pure (blend of virgin and refined)
blended (blend of virgin and second quality refined)
Industrial olive oil:
solvent extraction of olive residues.
Uses: Salad dressings; cooking oil; Castile soap; ointments and cosmetics.
See Part 2: Fats and Oils, Composition; Fats and Oils, Physical and Chemical Properties; Fatty Acids, Fats and Oils; Fats and Oils, Characteristic; Fats and Oils, Composition; Free Fatty Acid, Smoke, Flash, Fire Points; Iodine and Saponification Values; Oil or Fat, Characteristics; Oils, Seed and Fruit; Refractive Indices, Fats and Oils; Specific Gravities, Fats and Oils; Spoilage, Fat in Food; Titer, Fats and Oils; Tocopherols; Unsaturated Fatty Acids

oloroso Sherry that has never developed flavor; full golden-colored wine with more body than amontillado.

omasum The third stomach of a ruminant animal located on its right side and often called the "manyplies"; it reduces the water content of foodstuffs entering it; a bovine omasum may contain from 2 to 5 gal.

omega (Ω, ω) Greek letter with an English equivalent of a long o.

omicron (O, o) Greek letter with an English equivalent of a short o.

onion (*Allium cepa* L.) A bulb of condimental vegetable used as food. A biennial plant whose bulb is composed of enlarged leaf-bases. The shape may be flattened globose to oval; the color may be white, dark brown or red. Onions may be eaten as a vegetable or used to flavor other foods; they may be eaten raw, fried, boiled, roasted, in sauces, stews, curries, pickles and chutneys. When eaten by cattle will cause off-flavors in milk. *See also* **shallot**; **leek**.

Types:
Spanish: large and mild.
Spring: harvested young and eaten raw or in salads.
Welsh: Japanese bunching onion, ciboule; bulbs are elongated and only slightly swollen.
Storage: Mature onions: 32°-40°F; store in loosely woven or open mesh container (70-75% relative humidity); will keep for several months; freezing point, 30°F.
Green onions: refrigerate in plastic bags; keep moist; use in 2-3 days.
Volume
1 oz raw = ⅓ oz onion juice
= ⅛ to ¹⁄₁₀ oz onion powder
1 lb fresh = 3 large onions
= 2-2½ cups chopped
= 1.6 oz onion powder
1 cup chopped = 135 g (4.8 oz)
1 cup cooked = 200 g (6.9 oz)
1 cup dried = 64 g (2.3 oz)
1 bu raw = 57 lb
1 sack = 50 lb
1 crate (13 × 18 × 21.6 in.) green onions = 50-55 lb
100 lb fresh = 9-11 lb dehydrated
Composition:

	H_2O (%)	Protein (%)	Fat (%)	Carbohydrate (%)	Ash (%)
Raw dry	89	1.5	0.1	9	0.6
Raw green + white part of root	88	1	0.2	10	0.6
Dehydrated	4	9	1.3	82	4

pH 5.3-6.0
See Part 2: Fruit and Vegetable, Diseases; Frying Time; Glutamate; Microwave Cooking, Fresh Vegetables; Minerals, Food; Minerals, Plant or Animal Tissue; Minerals (Trace), Limits; Nutrients in Crops; Phosphorus; Plant Foods, Composition; Riboflavin, Food; Spices, Microbial Content; Storage; Storage, Dry; Storage Times; Sugar, Vegetables; Transit Temperature; Vegetable Boiling; Vegetable Composition; Vegetable Plants; Vegetables, Classification; Vegetable Servings; Vegetable Storage

ontjom *See* Part 2: Fungi Food Products

oölogy The study of birds' eggs. *See also* **egg**.

oolong tea Tea made from leaves that have been semifermented before steaming, rolling and drying (between black and green tea); semifermented has a fruity aroma, less sharp than green tea, less body than black tea.
Types:
Taiwan (Formosa): evenly colored leaves, fruity in cup, subtle, fine taste;
Mainland China: brash oolong flavor.

Oospora *See* Part 2: Mold, Food

open Not bred.

open chain Carbon atoms arranged in a straight or branched chain. Characteristic of aliphatic compounds.

open loin The left-hand beef loin.

open shoulder Shoulder blades too far apart at top.

open side (beef) The left side.

operculum *See* Part 2: Fish Nomenclature

opoponax oil *See* Part 2: Essential Oils

optical density Logarithmic scale used to measure opacity

$$D = \log_{10} \frac{1}{T}$$

$$D = xDo$$

$$D = \log \frac{100}{\% T}$$

D = density
T = transmission factor
x = thickness
Do = density of unit thickness

optical isomers Isomers which are mirror-images of each other (enantiomorphs) occurring in compounds containing one or more asymmetric carbon atoms (sugars, amino acids). The number of enantiomorphs is the *n*th power of 2, where *n* is the number of asymmetric carbon atoms. One enantiomorph has a left-handed configuration (levo-) and the other a right-handed or dextro-configuration. Such structures cause the plane of polarized light to be deflected to the left or right as it passes through them; however, the direction of rotation is not always the same as the structure itself. The small cap letters D and L indicate the *structure* of the isomers, while + and − are used for the direction of rotation. *See also* **stereoisomer; enantiomer.**

optical rotation α The ability of a substance to rotate the plane of polarized light to the right or left to an extent characteristic of the substance.

orache (*Atriplex hortensis*) A plant that has green, yellow or red leaves which are used as a boiled vegetable.

orange (*Citrus*) A citrus fruit; 75% edible; a medium size evergreen that produces a globose fruit that contains 10 or more pulpy carpels; the pulp is yellow or red.

- 1 medium orange is 3 in. in diameter, weighs 210 g, and yields 6 to 8 tbsp of juice and 1 tbsp grated peel.
- 6 lb or 1 doz fresh yields 12 cups sectioned (1 cup = 215 g or 7.5 oz) or 4 cups juice (1 cup = 250 g or 8.7 oz).
- 1 case juice (24) No. 2 cans = 0.63 box fresh oranges
- 1 box (12 × 12 × 24 in.) Fla., Tex. = 90 lb
- 1 box (11.5 × 11.5 × 24 in.) Calif., Ariz. = 75 lb
- 1 bu = 36 lb

Storage (unwrapped): Keep dry, cool, and in the dark at 85–90% relative humidity, or refrigerate (32°–34°F); 8 weeks storage life; freezing point 28°F.

Composition	Peeled Fruit	Juice	Peel
H_2O (%)	82–86	87–88	72
Protein (%)	0.7–1.3	0.5–1.0	1.5
Fat (%)	0.1–0.3	0.1–0.3	0.2
Carbohydrate (%)	12–16	9–13	25
Ash (%)	0.5–0.7	0.4	0.8
pH	3.1–4.1	2.7–4.4	

Varieties	Area Produced
Hamlin	Florida, Texas
Parson Brown	Florida, Texas
Pineapple	Florida, Texas
Temple	Florida
Valencia	West, Southwest, Florida
Washington Navel	West

See also **blood orange; citrus fruit; sour orange; sweet orange.**

See Part 2: Ascorbic Acid; Calcium, Daily Recommendations; Calories, Daily Recommendations; Essential Oils; Flavor Ingredients, Taste and Flavor Type; Flavors, Beverage; Food, Composition; Frozen Food Storage; Fruit and Nut Rootstock; Fruit, Availability; Fruit Harvest Dates; Fruit Classification; Fruit Composition; Fruit Juice Flavors; Fruit Storage; Iron; Minerals, Food; Niacin; Nutrients in Crops; Orange Essence Oils; Orange Oil Composition; Orange Oil Properties; Orange Structure; Phosphorus; pH Values of Biological Materials; Plant Foods, Composition; Potassium; Potassium-Rich Foods; Riboflavin; Rot Spoilage; Standards, Processed Fruit and Vegetable Products; Storage; Storage, Dry; Thiamin, Daily Recommendations; Thiamin; Transit Temperature; Vitamin A; Vitamin A, Daily Recommendations; Vitamin C

orange pekoe Black tea made from the first-opened leaves. *See also* **black tea.**

orangequat Hybrid between orange and kumquat.

orange serum agar *See* Part 2: Microbiological Media

orchard grass A perennial grass used for pasture or hay; seed weighs 14 lbs/bu; harvest when it begins flowering; pH 5–5.5; variety, Potomac; plant 5 lb per acre.
See Part 2: Seed, Germination

ordinate (y-axis) The vertical axis on rectangular coordinates.

oregano (*Origanum spp.*) **(joy of the mountain; wild marjoram; winter sweet; origany; origan; pizza herb)** An herb of the mint family; its light green dried leaves (⅝ in. in length) in whole or ground form are used in seasoning.

organ A functional unit of the body, e.g., heart, liver, stomach, etc.
See Part 2: Organ Weights

organic acid A carbon-containing acid with one or more carboxyl groups.
See Part 2: Organic Acids in Fruits and Vegetables

organic chemistry Study of carbon-containing compounds, except oxides of carbons and metallic carbonates.

organoleptic A test of a food product evaluated by a sense perception (feeling, hearing, sight, smell or taste). *See also* **sensory.**

organology A microscopic study of body organs.

organophosphate A group of insecticides that are phosphoric acid esters. They are highly toxic but not persistent. *See also* **parathion.**

origan *See* **oregano**

origany *See* **oregano**

origin Stationary (or fixed bone) attachment of a muscle.

ornithosis (psittacosis) Parrot fever, which can infect other fowl and be transmitted to humans.

Orpington An English class of chickens with white skin which lays a brown-shelled egg. Varieties: Buff, Black, White, Blue.

orris oil A semisolid oil distilled from the Iris plant.
See Part 2: Essential Oils; Flavoring Agents, Natural

ortanique An orange hybrid with flattened fruit; a cross between orange and tangerine.

ortho- (1) In organic compounds, the number 2 position on the benzene ring. (2) In inorganic compounds indicates maximum state of hydration.

orthophosphate A phosphate in maximum state of hydration.
See Part 2: Phosphate

orvieto A dry or sweet white wine.

Os Symbol for the element osmium.

os Bone; mouth.

os calcis *See* **tuber calcis**

os coxae *See* **ossa coxarum**

osmium (Os) A metallic element; at. no. 76; at. wt. 190.2; Group VIII of Periodic Table; oxidation states +3, +4; electron configuration 2-8-18-32-14-2
orbit K L M N O P

Osmophilic *See* Part 2: Spoilage, Carbohydrate Foods

osmosis The passage of fluid (usually water) through a semipermeable membrane into a solution of higher concentration to equalize the concentration on both sides of the membrane.

ossa coxarum The pelvic bone.

ossein Bone collagen produced by decalcifying the bone.

ossify To become bone-like.
See Part 2: Bone Age

osteology The study of bones.

osteomalacia A disease caused by the removal of calcium and phosphorus from mature bones; caused by a deficiency of calcium, phosphorus or vitamin D.

Ottotan A variety of soybean.

ounce (apoth.) A measure of weight (same as troy ounce).

ounce (av.)/acre Weight per unit area.
1 ounce (av.)/acre = 70.063 g/ha

ounce (av.)/square yard Weight per unit area.
1 ounce (av.) sq yd = 33.910 g/m^2

ounce (Br. fl.) (Imp. fl.) A measure of volume.
1 ounce (Br. fl.) = 480 minims (Br.)
= 461.160 minims (U.S.)
= 28.4121 ml
= 8 drachms (Br. fluid)
= 7.6860 drams (U.S. fl.)
= 1.73457 cu. in.
= 0.9607 ounce (U.S. fl.)
= 0.07506 gallon (U.S.)
= 6.250×10^{-3} gallon (Br.)
= 1.0033×10^{-3} cu ft
= 2.3828×10^{-4} barrel (U.S.)

ounce (oz apoth.) (avoirdupois or av.) A measure of weight.
1 av. ounce (oz av.) = 2.8350×10^4 milligrams
= 437.5 grains (gr)
= 28.349527 grams (g)
= 21.875 scruples (apoth.)
= 18.22917 pennyweight
= 16 drams (av.)
= 7.29167 drams (troy) (apoth.)
= 0.911,458,3 troy or apoth. ounce (oz troy) (apoth.)
= 0.075954861 troy or apoth. pound (lb troy) (apoth.)
= 0.06250 av. pound (lb/av.)
= 0.028350 kilogram (kg)
= 0.00003125 net-short ton (2000 lb)
= 0.00002835 metric ton (1000 kg)
= 0.00002790 gross-long ton (2240 lb)
16 oz = 1 pound
See Part 2: Volume; Weight

ounce (U.S. apoth. measure) (oz) (U.S. fluid) (fl. oz) A measure of volume.
1 fl. ounce = 499.61 minims (Br.)
= 480 minims (U.S.)
= 29.574 cu. cm
= 29.5729 milliliters
= 8 fl. drams (U.S.)
= 1.80469 cu in.
= 1.0409 ounces (Br. fl.)
= 0.0625 pint (liquid)
= 0.03125 quart (U.S. liquid)
= 0.029573 liter
= 7.8125×10^{-3} gallon (U.S.)
= 6.5053×10^{-3} gallon (Br.)
= 1.0443×10^{-3} cu ft
= 2.48×10^{-4} barrel (U.S.)

ounce troy (oz troy), same as apoth. A measure of weight used for weighing gold, silver and jewels.

1 troy ounce (oz troy) = 3.1104×10^4 milligrams
= 480 grains (gr)
= 31.103481 grams (g)
= 24 scruples (apoth.)
= 20 pennyweight (dwt) (troy)
= 17.55428 drams (av.)
= 8 drams (troy apoth.)
= 1.0971429 av. ounces (oz av.)
= 0.08333333 troy or apoth. pound (lb troy) (apoth.)
= 0.06857143 av. pound (lb av.)
= 0.03110 kilogram (kg)
= 0.00003429 net short ton (2000 lb)
= 0.00003110 metric ton (1000 kg)
= 0.00003061 gross long ton (2240 lb)

12 oz (troy) = 1 pound (troy)

ouri-curi wax A brown vegetable wax from South America.
See Part 2: Fat and Oils, Fatty Acid Composition

outside chuck (top chuck) Muscles lateral to the scapula; the major ones are triceps brachii (long head), infraspinatus, supraspinatus. *See also* **top chuck.**

outside round (bottom round) A cut of beef consisting of the semitendinosus and biceps femoris muscles.
See Part 2: Beef, Boneless Cuts; Beef Round Cuts; Meat Identification

ovary Site of egg formation in the female.
See Part 2: Flower, Perfect; Gland Weights

oven An enclosed chamber for baking or roasting. Temperature ranges are:

	(°F)	(°C)
Very slow	250–275	121–135
Slow	300–325	149–163
Moderate	350–375	177–191
Hot	400–425	204–218
Very hot	450–475	232–246
Extremely hot	500–525	260–274

overhaul Redistribution of the cure on a curing meat product.

overreach Placing the hind foot ahead of the spot from which the front foot was just removed.

overweight kip skin A calf skin weighing between 25 and 30 lb.

ovule *See* Part 2: Flower, Perfect

ox A castrated bull.
See Part 2: Teeth Eruption

oxalate A salt of oxalic acid. Na oxalate combines with Ca and prevents blood from clotting; 160 mg Na oxalate/100 ml blood.

oxalic acid $(COOH)_2$ A dicarboxylic acid; poisonous; used as a cleaning agent.
See Part 2: Normal Solutions; Organic Acids in Fruits and Vegetables; Reagents, Normal Solutions

Oxford A medium-wool mutton-type breed of sheep originating in south central England by crossing of Cotswold rams on Hampshire ewes; it has a medium brown-to-gray face, no horns and its fleece will grade about ¼.
See Part 2: Sheep Breeds

Oxford Down Former name of Oxford sheep.

oxidase An enzyme which can cause oxidation of a substrate by atmospheric oxygen.

oxidation Loss of one or more electrons by an element or group; addition of oxygen; removal of hydrogen.
See Part 2: Enzymes, Food Industry; Meat Pigment

oxidation number The number of electrons an element can transfer to another element with which it combines; also the number of electrons that must be added to or subtracted from a combined atom to restore it to its elemental state. Thus an oxidation number can be either positive or negative, e.g., that of oxygen is -2. *See also* **valence.**

oxidizing agent An element which gains electrons and is reduced.

oxtail The skinned tail of ox used for food.
See Part 2: Beef Cuts and Uses

ox warbles Eggs laid by adult heel flies on the hair of cattle legs in June; these eggs hatch into larvae that enter the skin and travel through the body to the animal's back; they emerge from the animal's back in February to June and drop to the ground to hatch into heel flies.

oxygen (O) A gaseous element; at. no. 8; at. wt. 15.9994; Group VIA of Periodic Table; oxidation state -2; electron configuration 2–6
orbit K L
Noncombustible, but actively supports combustion.

oxygenation Uptake of oxygen.
See Part 2: Meat Pigment

oxymyoglobin Bright red (desirable retail color) meat pigment formed by oxygenation of myoglobin.
See Part 2: Meat Pigment

oxytetracycline (Terramycin) $C_{22}H_{24}N_2O_9 \cdot 2H_2O$ A broad spectrum antibiotic; mol. wt. 496.46.

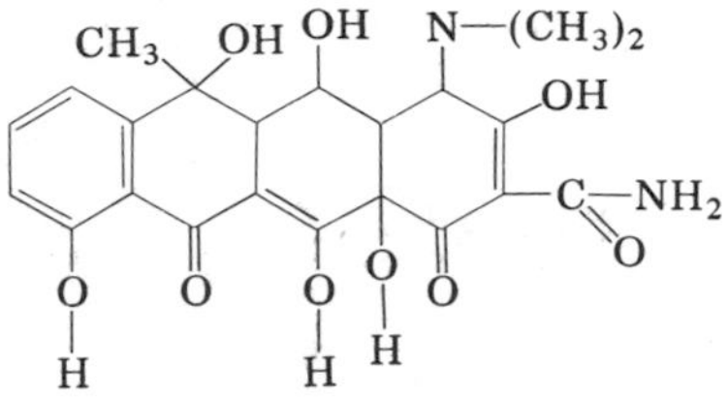

See Part 2: Antibiotic Standards

oyster [*Ostrea virginica* (East Coast) or *O. lurida* (West Coast)] A shellfish; 10–15% weight is meat (10–12% protein); a lean, marine bivalve mollusk.

Types	Where caught
Eastern	U.S. east coast
Pacific, Japanese	Pacific coast; Japan
Olympia, Western	Pacific coast

1 serving = ½ doz shell oysters
= ⅙ qt shucked oysters
= ½ lb shucked oysters
= 3.5 oz breaded
1 cup shucked = 13–19 medium select
= 235 g (8.3 oz)
1 pt shucked = 24 oysters in shell

As Purchased	% Yield	Ounces to Purchase for One Serving
In shell	12	25
Shucked	50	6½

Meat composition: 79–85% H_2O, 8–11% protein, 1.5–2.5% fat, 3–6.5% carbohydrate, 1.7% ash, pH 4.8–6.3. There is a 10–14% fat absorption during frying.

Size:

	Count/gal.	Count/lb
Eastern or Gulf		
Extra large	160 or less	20 or less
Large (extra selects)	161–210	21–26
Medium (selects)	211–300	27–37
Small (standard)	301–500	38–62
Very small	over 500	over 62
Pacific		
Large	65 or less	8 or less
Medium	65–96	9–12
Small	97–144	13–18
Extra small	more than 144	over 18
Olympia	avg. 1600	275–300

See Part 2: Calories, Daily Recommendations; Fish and Shellfish Composition; Fish, Storage; Frozen Food Storage; Frying Time; Iron, Daily Recommendations; Minerals, Food; Portion Size; Riboflavin, Daily Recommendations; Thiamin, Daily Recommendations

oyster mushroom (*Pleurotus osteatus*) An edible fungus whose cap varies from blue-gray to brown and has a very short stem.

oyster plant *See* salsify

oyster shells *See* burned oyster shells; baked oyster shells
See Part 2: Liming Materials

ozokerite An earth wax.
See Part 2: Wax

ozone (O_3) An unstable, blue gas with a penetrating odor; it is a toxic germicide and oxidizing agent. Used for industrial waste treatment and for water purification.

P

p *See* **para-**

P Symbol for the element phosphorus.

P_1 Parental generation (genetics).

Pa Symbol for the element protactinium.

PABA *See* **para-aminobenzoic acid**

Pablum Proprietary name for prepared cereal made especially for infant feeding.

Pacific herring *See* **sea herring**

packaging Placement of foodstuffs in individual containers suitable for distribution and which also preserves them from bacterial contamination, moisture, and oxidative deterioration; materials most widely used are glass, metal, and plastic films.

pack date Date of manufacturing, processing, or final packaging.

packer hide A hide removed by using a uniform pattern and a minimum of cuts, and stored under standard conditions.

packer's style hog carcass A carcass split, with jowls on carcass but head and leaf fat removed.

packinghouse A plant for the slaughter, processing and packing of meat.
See Part 2: Packinghouse By-Products Composition

packing sow A hog that has been a brood sow.

padding Swinging forefeet outward in a trot or walk.

paddock Enclosed outdoor area for exercising horses.

paddy *See* **rice**

paddy whack *See* **back strap**

Paecilomyces A type of mold.
See Part 2: Molds, Mycotoxins; Spoilage, Fat in Food

paella A Spanish fish and seafood dish.

pagano levin agar *See* Part 2: Microorganism, Media

pai egg medium *See* Part 2: Microorganism, Media

paired analysis An analysis in which 2 treatments can be made on essentially the same objects; less original variation between the 2 treatment areas on the same object than there is between adjacent objects.

$D = X_1 - X_2$ $\quad X_1$ = observation of treatment 1 on object 1

$\bar{d} = \frac{\Sigma D}{n}$ $\quad X_2$ = observation of treatment 2 on object 1

$d = D - \bar{d}$ $\quad n$ = number of objects

$d^2 = d \times d$ $\quad \Sigma d = 0$

$s_D^2 = \frac{\Sigma d^2}{n - 1}$

$s_D = \sqrt{s_D^2}$

$s\frac{2}{d} = \frac{s_D^2}{n}$ $\quad Ho: u_D = 0$

$s\bar{d} = \sqrt{s_{\bar{d}}^2}$ $\quad t = \frac{\bar{d} - u_D}{s\bar{d}}$ $\quad df = n - 1$

or

$\bar{d} - [t_{.05 \text{ or } .01}]\, s_{\bar{d}} \leqslant uD \leqslant \bar{d} + [t_{.05 \text{ or } .01}]\, s_{\bar{d}}$

See Part 2: Paired Comparisons; Paired Taste Tests; Taste Panel, Difference Tests

paired comparison *See* Part 2: Paired Comparisons; Paired Taste Tests; Taste Panel, Difference Tests

pak-choi (Chinese cabbage; *Brassica chinensis*) Leaves of this plant are eaten raw in salads, or cooked.
See Part 2: Vegetable Plants

palate The roof of the mouth, comprised of bony hard palate (front) and muscular soft palate (rear). Erroneously said to be a taste organ, hence the term palatable.

palladium (Pd) A metallic element; at. no. 46; at. wt. 106.4; electron configuration 2–8–18–18;
orbit K L M N
oxidation states +2, +4; Group VIII of Periodic Table.

pallet A wooden platform or skid, elevated at least 3 in. from the floor; used for stacking cartons, paper stock, books, etc.

palm (*Elaeis guineensis*) A hard shell nut.

palmitic acid $CH_3(CH_2)_{14}C(=O)OH$ A 16-carbon saturated acid found in all animal and vegetable fats, especially in swine.
See Part 2: Fat and Oils, Fatty Acid Composition; Fatty Acids and Their Properties; Fatty Acids; Fatty Acids, Fats and Oils; Milk, Fatty Acids, Seasonal; Oils, Seed and Fruit; Saturated Fatty Acids; Seed, Chemical Composition; Wheat, Fatty Acids

palmitoleic acid $CH_3(CH_2)_5CH{=}CH(CH_2)_7COOH$ A 16-carbon unsaturated fatty acid found in liver and animal fats.
See Part 2: Fatty Acids and Their Properties; Fatty Acids; Fatty Acids, Fats and Oils; Unsaturated Fatty Acids; Wheat, Fatty Acids

palm kernel oil An oil extracted from kernel of the palm nut or seed. *See also* **oil palm.**
Composition:

caprylic	1-3%	palmitic	9%
capric	3-7%	stearic	1-2%
lauric	47-51%	oleic	16-19%
myristic	14-18%	linoleic	1%

Properties:

acid number	9.0
specific gravity 20°/4°C	0.9190
saponification value	220-255
iodine value	14-37
unsaponifiable	<1%
titer	20-28°C
saturated fatty acid	81-87%
melting point	24-26°C

See Part 2: Fats and Oils, Composition; Fat and Oils, Fatty Acid Composition; Fats and Oils, Physical and Chemical Properties; Fatty Acids, Fats and Oils; Fats and Oils, Characteristics; Melting Points, Fats and Oils; Refractive Indices, Fats and Oils; Specific Gravities, Fats and Oils; Titer, Fats and Oils; Unsaponifiable Matter

palm oil (palm butter) Oil extracted from the pulp (pericarp) of the palm nut (fruit). A soft solid; liquefies at about 80°F. *See also* **oil palm.**
Composition:

myristic	1%
palmitic	40-47%
stearic	4-6%
oleic	38-43%
linoleic	10%

Properties:

saponification value	195-205
iodine value	45-60
unsaponifiable	<1%
titer	40-47°C
saturated fatty acid	41-50%
melting point	27-50°C
specific gravity 15°C	0.915
refractive index (60°C)	1.450-1.452

See Part 2: Fats and Oils, Composition; Fat and Oils, Fatty Acid Composition; Fats and Oils, Physical and Chemical Properties; Fatty Acids, Fats and Oils; Fats and Oils, Characteristics; Iodine and Saponification Values; Melting Points, Fats and Oils; Oils, Seed and Fruit; Refractive Indices, Fats and Oils; Saturated Fatty Acids; Specific Gravities, Fats and Oils; Spoilage, Fat in Food; Titer, Fats and Oils; Tocopherols; Unsaponifiable Matter

palm wine *See* **date palm**

palmyra Borassus palm; a tall tree that produces about 200 nuts per year.
Parts of plant:
nut sap: a drink;
soft kernel of young fruit: eaten;
germinated nut: used as a vegetable;
palm sap: sugar, toddy;
trunk: building material

Palouse *See* Part 2: Swine Breeds

pameras *See* Part 2: Insect Control

pamir tura *See* **black tea**

pampas Grassland of the temperate region of South America.

panada A thick paste made of bread or bread crumbs boiled in milk or water and sometimes flavored with sugar or spices; used as a binder for stuffing.

Panama A medium-wool breed of sheep originating in America by crossing Rambouillet rams on Lincoln ewes; this is the same cross that produced the Columbia, with the sexes reversed.
See Part 2: Sheep Breeds

pan-broiling A dry-heat method of cooking used for the more tender cuts; the meat is placed in a heavy container through which the heat is transferred. The fat is drained off during cooking.
See Part 2: Beef, Cooking; Beef Cuts; Lamb Cuts; Pan Broiling Meat; Pork Cuts

pancake A thin fried cake made from flour, egg and milk, plus shortening and leavening agent.
See Part 2: Grain Products Composition

pancreas A gland attached to the gut whose secretions affect digestion. One of its secretions (insulin) regulates sugar metabolism; sometimes known as gut sweetbread (chest sweetbread is the thymus).
See Part 2: Gland Weights; Organ Weights

pan-dressed *See* Part 2: Fish Yields

panela *See* **sugar cane**

pan-fired Formosa *See* **green tea**

pan-fired Japan *See* **green tea**

panfry To cook with a small quantity of fat.
See Part 2: Beef Cuts; Lamb Cuts; Pan Frying Meat; Pork Cuts; Pork Loin Cooking; Veal Chart; Veal Cuts

panned *See* Part 2: Vegetables, Panned

panocha A confection made from brown sugar, milk, butter and nuts.

pantothenic acid (filtrate factor) A vitamin; deficiency causes chick dermatitis and loss of hair color; sources are yeast, variety meats, egg yolk, rice polishings, dairy products, muscle meats and green leafy vegetables.

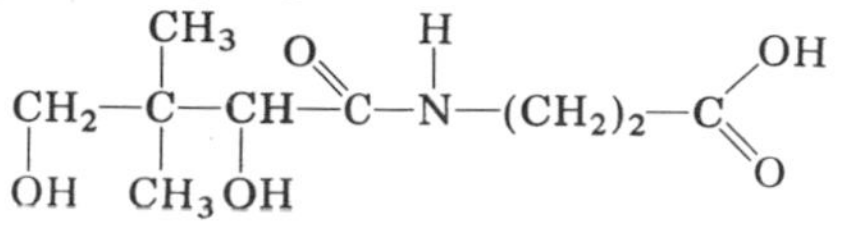

See Part 2: Cheese, Vitamin Content; Egg Products, Nutritive Value; Grain Analysis; Milk and Milk Products, Vitamin Content; Milk Composition; Pantothenic Acid Content; Seed, Chemical Composition; Vitamins; Vitamin Sources, Functions, and Stability; Wheat, Parts of Grain, Vitamins; Wheat Products Composition; Wheat, Vitamins

pap Soft food; baby food.

papain (***Carica papaya***) A plant enzyme (latex of pawpaw) used as a tenderizing agent for meat; activity is slow at room temperature, increases at 55°–57°C, is optimum at 65°–80°C, and ceases at 90°C.

papaya (**pawpaw, papaw;** ***Carica papaya***) An herbaceous tree (tropical evergreen) that has a large, elongated fruit that is green or yellow or orange; the flesh is pink to orange and seeds are enclosed in a central cavity.

Parts of plant:

- ripe fruit: eaten raw (7–9% sugar);
- unripe fruit: boiled as a vegetable;
- white latex obtained by cutting the surface of the fruit: dried to yield enzyme papain;
- leaves: wrapping meat for tenderization;
- mountain pawpaw fruit: cooked before eating; jam.

Storage: 45°F, 85–90% relative humidity, 2–3 weeks' storage life, pH 5.2–5.7.

See Part 2: Fruit, Availability; Fruit Classification; Fruit Composition; Fruit Storage; Plant Foods, Composition

papeda A citrus fruit with a thick skin and a sour pulp.

paperflower A plant having a toxic principle. *See* Part 2: Poisonous Plants

papilla Connective tissue at the base of and projecting into the hair follicle; finger-like projections in the inside of the rumen.

papillote Baked in white parchment paper.

paprika (***Capsicum annum*** **L.**) Whole or ground fruit pods (usually red) of the capsicum group used in seasoning and as garnish; red in color and sweet to the taste; 2 types: (1) mild, sweet (Spanish) and (2) pungent (Hungarian). European types of sweet, mild pepper (*Capsicum*); Spanish paprika is called pimiento. *See also* **pimiento.**

See Part 2: Colors Permanently Listed; Spices, Microbial Content

para- In organic compounds, the number 4 position on the benzene ring.

para-aminobenzoic acid (PABA) A dietary factor that prevents development of gray hair in mice, dogs, and foxes on purified diets.

$$NH_2 \cdot C_6H_4C(=O)OH$$

paraben *See* **para-hydroxybenzoic acid**

Paracolobactrum *See* Part 2: Microorganism Reactions on Differential Tube Media

Paracolon *See* Part 2: Intestinal Microorganisms; Intestinal Microorganisms in Triple-Sugar Agar

paraffin *See* **alkane**

paraffin wax A solid mixture of aliphatic hydrocarbon residues obtained from petroleum; average melting range 50°–57°C. Used as protective coating for cheeses and for waxed paper. *See* Part 2: Wax

para-hydroxybenzoic acid (and esters, paraben) Antimicrobial agents used in food, cosmetic and pharmaceutical products.

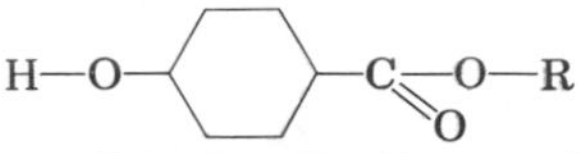

R = alkyl group

parallel circuits Potential is the same across *R* current for each resistor.

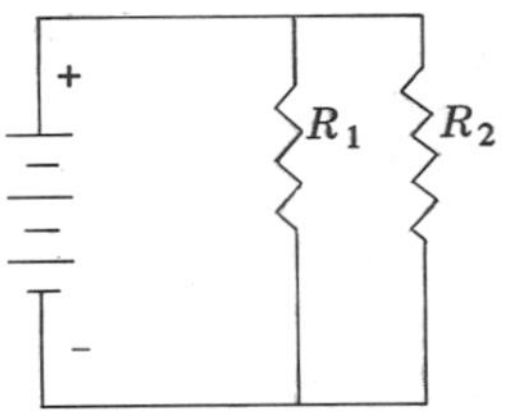

$I_1 = \frac{E}{R_1}$

R_1 = resistance in ohms or 1st resistor

E = voltage

I_1 = ampere in 1st resistor

I_T = total amperes

R_T = resistance total

Total amperage

$$I_T = I_1 + I_2 + \cdots I_n$$

$$R_T = \frac{E}{I_1 + I_2 + \cdots I_n}$$

$$= \frac{E}{E/R_1 + E/R_2 + \cdots E/R_n}$$

$$\frac{1}{R_T} = \frac{1}{R_1} + \frac{1}{R_2} + \cdots \frac{1}{R_n}$$

$$R_T = \frac{(R_1)(R_2)}{R_1 + R_2}$$

Potential sources can be connected in parallel to increase the current; however, they must be of equal voltage.

parathion A poisonous organic phosphorus agricultural insecticide. Inhibits the enzyme cholinesterase, but is biodegradable.

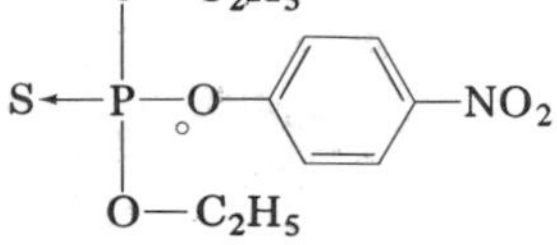

parathyroid glands Four small glands located close to the thyroid gland; their secretions regulate the blood and nervous systems.

paratyphoid A food poison.
See Part 2: Illness from Food; Infectious Diseases, Food-Borne

parboil To boil food until partially cooked. *See also* **precook.**

parboiled rice Rice that is heat-treated or steamed under pressure and dried prior to hulling and milling; it has greater retention of vitamins and minerals than polished rice.

parboiled wheat *See* **bulgur**

pare To cut off outer covering or skin of a fruit or vegetable. *See also* **peel.**

parenchyma Tissue which makes up the pulp of fruits and the pith of stems.
See Part 2: Wheat Kernel Parts

pareve (parve) Jewish cooking term describing a product made without milk, meat or their derivatives. A neutral food; vegetables, fruit, eggs, fish and all other nonmeat and nonmilk foods.

parfait A frozen egg and whipped dessert or ice cream topped with syrup and whipped cream; a combination of well-beaten egg yolks or whites, heavy syrup and whipped cream, frozen without agitation.

Paris green (Schweinfurt green) (copper aceto-arsenite) $(CuO)_3As_2O_3 \cdot Cu(C_2H_3O_2)_2$ A poisonous insecticide.

parity Ratio between the prices farmers receive and the prices they paid in some base period (may be a specific year or a moving base such as average of the last 10 years).

Parker A variety of birdsfoot trefoil.

parmentier Potato soup.

parmesan cheese (reggiano) An aged (1-4 years) hard grating cheese from Italy, made from skimmed milk using starter of *Streptococcus thermophilus* and *Lactobacillus bulgaricus* or *L. lactis*; used in cooking and salads; it is dark green to black on the outside and has a creamy white to light-yellow interior. It is sold in a cylindrical shape and has a mild to sharp, piquant, nutty flavor; it is grated for use. 1 cup grated = 3-3.3 oz (90 g).
Storage: Refrigerate, tightly wrapped.
Composition: 30-31% H_2O, 36-38% protein, 26-28% fat, 3% carbohydrate, 5% ash, 1.8% salt, pH 5.2-5.3.
Other similar cheeses include: bagozzo or bresciano, emiliano, lodigiano, lombardy, parmigiano, reggiano, veneto, and venezza.
See Part 2: Cheese Characteristics; Cheese, Vitamin Content; Glutamate; Milk and Cheese Composition; Milk and Milk Products, Vitamin Content; Vitamin A, Milk and Milk Products

parmigiano A semi-hard cheese with mellow flavor.

parrot mouth A mouth formation in which the upper teeth extend over lower teeth.

parsley (*Petroselinum crispum Mansf.*) A plant whose leaves are used for garnishing and seasoning foods; a cool-season glabrous biennial. It may be chopped fresh or dried and added to sauces, soups, salads, potatoes, omelets, or stuffing.
Raw composition: 85% H_2O, 3.6% protein, 0.6% fat, 8% carbohydrate, 2% ash; pH 5.7-6.0.
See Part 2: Essential Oils; Minerals, Food; Sugar, Vegetables; Unsaturated Fatty Acids; Vegetable Composition; Vegetable Plants; Vegetables, Classification

parsnip (*Pastinaca sativa*) A vegetable whose root is used as food; a plant with a yellow-white fleshy root which contains sugar and starch; also used for livestock feed and for making wine. Has a peculiar and distinctive taste.
1 lb fresh = 4 medium-size parsnips
1 lb fresh = 2 cups cooked
1 cup cooked = 210 g (7.4 oz)
100 lb fresh = 20-22 lb dry.
Storage: Remove tops and store covered (90-95% relative humidity) in refrigerator (32°F); use within 1 to 4 weeks.
Raw composition: 79% H_2O, 2% protein, 0.5% fat, 17% carbohydrate, 1% ash; pH 5.3.
See Part 2: Essential Oils; Microwave Cooking, Fresh Vegetables; Minerals, Food; Plant Foods, Composition; Storage; Sugar, Vegetables; Vegetable Boiling; Vegetable Composition; Vegetable Plants; Vegetable Servings; Vegetable Storage

Parson Brown A variety of early Florida orange.

partition coefficient (K) (gas chromatography)

$$K = \frac{\text{wt of solute/ml of stationary phase}}{\text{wt of solute/ml of mobile phase}}$$

parts per million (ppm) (γ/g) (γ/ml) (mg/kg) A measure of very low concentrations.
1 ppm = 0.058 grain/gallon (U.S.)
= 0.070 grain/gallon (Br.)
= 8.345 pounds/million gallons

w/w	w/v
mg per kilo	mg per liter
0.001 mg per gram	0.001 mg per milliliter
gamma per gram	gamma per milliliter
microgram per gram	microgram per milliliter

ppm	%	Approx. Household* Measure per 1000 lb	Household* Measure per 1000 gal.
1	0.0001	—	1 tsp
10	0.001	1 tsp	8 tsp
100	0.01	3 tbsp	1⅔ cups

*Products with specific gravity of 1.000.

parturition The act of giving birth.

passion fruit (purple granadilla) (*Passiflora*) A climbing plant that produces an egg-size fruit that is purple and wrinkled when ripe; the sweet

juicy pulp contains many black seeds; may be eaten fresh or used as a drink.
Pulp composition: 88–89% H_2O, 0.5% protein, 0.1% fat, 10–12% carbohydrate, 0.4% ash.
See Part 2: Fruit Classification; Fruit Composition; Fruit Storage

paste A thick sauce made from fish or vegetable products, e.g., anchovy paste, tomato paste.
See Part 2: Tomato and Tomato Products, Composition

pastern The area on legs below fetlock and above hoof head.

pasteurella *See* Part 2: Microorganism, Media

pasteurization Mild heat treatment used to kill or inhibit the vegetative forms of many bacteria in liquid or semiliquid food products.

	30 min	15 sec	3 sec
Milk or skim milk	142°–143°F	162°F	205°–207°F
Cream and other milk products	150°F (min)	175°F (min)	
Cream for butter making	165°F (min)	185°F (min)	

Products are cooled immediately to 50°F or lower.
Eggs: 140°F for 3½–4 min.
Beer: 140°F for 20 min; 158°F for 30 sec.
Fruit juices: 170°–200°F for 1–3 min.
Wine: 145°F, flashing; 120°F, several days.
See Part 2: Radiation Preservation; Thermophiles

pasteurization test (milk) A test for absence of phosphatase enzyme; the temperature of enzyme inactivation is high enough to destroy undesirable microorganisms.

pasteurized process cheese A blend of fresh and aged natural cheese that has been heated; may also be mixed with fruits, vegetables, meats, pimientos; may have a smoked flavor; can be frozen for 4 months.

pasteurized process cheese food Similar to pasteurized processed cheese except the fat content is lower and moisture content higher; it is softer and more bland.

pasteurized process cheese spread Made like pasteurized process cheese food, but has a higher moisture and lower milk fat content.

pastry A baked product made of flour, shortening and water. Sometimes eggs and/or milk may be used as the liquid ingredient. Used as crust for pies, turnovers, etc.

pastry flour *See* **soft-wheat flour**

pasture Land used for grazing animals to supplement their regular food supply.
Winter: crimson clover, rye, oats, barley.
Summer: millet, sudan grass, soybeans, kudzu, lespedeza.

patchouli oil An essential oil from steam distillation of plant leaves. Used as a flavoring.
See Part 2: Essential Oils; Wastes, Agricultural and Industrial; Flavoring Agents, Natural

patchy Having lumps of exterior fat.

pâté A meat or fish pie or patty; a spread of finely-mashed, seasoned meat.

pâté de foie gras A rich goose liver paste.

patella Kneecap.
See Part 2: Bone

patent barley *See* **barley**

patent flour A grade of white flour which may be made from the best 40 to 95% of all the white flour milled (the best subdivision of straight grade flour); it may be subdivided into:

extra short patent	highest grade
short family or first patent	↓
short patent	
medium patent	
long patent	lowest grade

See Part 2: Flour, Extraction Rates; Wheat and Flour Composition

pathogenic Disease-producing.

patola *See* Part 2: Vegetable Storage

patty A small unit of slightly compressed chopped meat, usually fried, e.g., hamburger.
See Part 2: Broiling Griddle, Meat; Broiling Meat; Broiling Time and Temperature; Pork, Cooking

Pattypan A summer variety of squash.

paugy *See* **scup**

paunch *See* **rumen**

paunchy Too large a belly.

paw-paw *See* **papaya**

paw-tsay A type of vegetable preserved by salting and fermentation of its juices similar to the production of sauerkraut.

Pb Symbol for the element lead (Latin *plumbum*).

Pd Symbol for the element palladium.

PDQ Peeled, deveined and quick-frozen shrimp.

pea (*Pisum sativum*) A leguminous vegetable whose seed is used as food; a cool-season plant requiring a well-drained soil.
Type:

	Use
Field pea	Livestock feed and green manure; Seeds: human food as pea meal or split peas
Garden pea	Pea picked green: human food; Dried pea: human food; Frozen and canned: human food

1 lb shelled green peas = 2½ lb unshelled
1 case (24) No. 2 cans = 1/100 ton unshelled
Pod:
1 lb fresh = 1 cup shelled
2–3 lb fresh = 1 pt canned
4–4½ lb fresh = 1 qt frozen
1 bu fresh = 28–32 lb = 12–18 pt canned

Shelled:
½–1 lb fresh = 1 pt canned
1 cup shelled = 140 g (4.9 oz)
1 cup shelled, cooked = 165 g (5.7 oz)
1 bu fresh = 30 lb
1 bu dry = 60 lb = 12–16 pt canned
Dried, split:
1 lb = 2.25 cups
1 cup = 200 g (7.1 oz)
1 lb = 5 cups cooked
1 cup cooked = 195 g (6.8 oz)
Storage:
Fresh: Leave in pod; refrigerate (32°F); 85–90% relative humidity; use within 1 to 2 days.
Frozen: 0°F; storage, 1 year.
Composition:

	H_2O (%)	Protein (%)	Fat (%)	Carbohydrate (%)	Ash (%)	pH
Raw podded	83	3.5	0.2	12	1	
Raw green	78	6.3	0.4	14	1	5.4–7.0
Mature dry	12	24	1	60	3	6.5–6.8

See Part 2: Ascorbic Acid; Beans Dry, Cooking; Beans, Peas and Nuts; Calories, Daily Recommendations; Canned Spoilage Related to pH; Canned Yield; Frozen Food Storage; Fruit and Vegetables Composition; Glutamate; Glutamate Addition; Iron; Iron, Daily Recommendations; Microwave Cooking, Fresh Vegetables; Microwave Cooking, Frozen Vegetables; Microwave Processing Time; Niacin; Niacin, Daily Recommendations; Nicotinic Acid, Food; Pentosans; Phosphorus; pH Values of Biological Materials; Plant Foods, Composition; Portion Size; Pulses, Nuts and Seeds Composition; Riboflavin; Riboflavin, Food; Seed, Chemical Composition; Seed, Germination; Soups, Composition; Standards, Processed Fruit and Vegetable Products; Storage; Storage, Dry; Sugar, Legumes; Thiamin, Daily Recommendations; Thiamin; Thiamin, Food; Tocopherols; Vegetable Boiling; Vegetable Composition; Vegetable Cooking, Frozen; Vegetable Frozen Yield; Vegetable Plants; Vegetables, Boiling Time, Frozen; Vegetables, Canning Dates; Vegetables, Classification; Vegetables, Cooking Frozen; Vegetable Servings; Vegetable Storage; Vegetable Yield; Vegetable Yield, Canned and Frozen; Vegetable Yield, Frozen, Canned and Fresh; Vitamin A, Daily Recommendations; Vitamin A, Food

pea, black-eye
1 cup = 145 g (5.1 oz)
1 lb fresh = 2.33 cups cooked
1 cup cooked = 160 g (5.7 oz)
1 cup dried = 200 g (7.1 oz)
1 cup dried, cooked = 250 g (8.7 oz)

peach (*Prunus persica*) A small tree that produces a greenish, white or yellow flesh, single-seeded, dessert fruit that grows well in the temperate regions; the fruit is eaten fresh, canned, dried, frozen, or made into jam.
Size:
medium = 2 in. diameter.
1 lb = 4 medium-size peaches
= 2 cups fresh sliced (1 cup = 175 g or 6.2 oz)
= 3 cups dried whole
1 qt canned = 2 to 3 lb fresh
1 case (24) No. 2½ can = 1 bu fresh
1 bu fresh = 48–50 lb
= 16–25 qt canned
1 lb dried = 6–7½ lb fresh
= 3 cups dried (1 cup = 160 g or 5.6 oz)
= 6 cups cooked (1 cup = 245 g or 8.6 oz)
Ripen: unwrapped, room temperature, out of sun.
Storage: Refrigerate (31°–32°F), uncovered (85–90% relative humidity); freezing point 29°F. Peaches bruise easily; when ripe, use in 3 to 5 days. Frozen (0°F) storage life, 1 year.
Composition:

	H_2O (%)	Protein (%)	Fat (%)	Carbohydrate (%)	Ash (%)	pH
Raw	89	0.6	0.1	10	0.5	3.4–3.6
Dried	25	3	0.7	68	3	

Freestone: flesh separates from stone easily; preferred for eating, freezing; may be canned.
Clingstone: flesh does not separate from stone easily; preferred for canning (firmer flesh).
Peeling: 2–2.5% lye solution or 1 to 2-min scald.
Freezing: 40° Brix and 0.1% ascorbic acid.
See Part 2: Calories, Daily Recommendations; Canned Yield; Flavor Ingredients, Taste and Flavor Type; Food, Composition; Frozen Food Storage; Fruit and Nut Rootstock; Fruit and Vegetable, Diseases; Fruit and Vegetables Composition; Fruit, Availability; Fruit Harvest Dates; Fruit Classification; Fruit Composition; Fruit, Cooking; Fruit, Dried, Simmering; Fruit Frozen Yield; Fruit, Growing Season, Storage Life; Fruit Per Pound; Fruit Sauces; Fruit, Simmering; Fruit Storage; Microwave Cooking, Fruit; Minerals, Food; Niacin; Nutrients in Crops; Plant Foods, Composition; Poisonous Plants; Potassium; Riboflavin; Standards, Processed Fruit and Vegetable Products; Storage; Storage Times; Sugar, Fruit; Vitamin A; Vitamin A, Daily Recommendations; Vitamin A, Food

pea grade (dry edible) U.S. Grades 1, 2, and 3.

Peak A variety of clingstone peaches.

peak (gas chromatography) The portion of the chromatogram that indicates that something is going through the detector. The **peak area** is the area enclosed by peak and peak base. The **peak base** is the interpolation of the base line under peak. The **peak height** is the distance from peak base to maximum of peak measured perpendicular to base line. The peak width portion of peak base that is enclosed by straight lines drawn tangent to the sides of the peak. The peak width at half height is a line drawn tangent to the peak sides at one-half the peak height and perpendicular to it.

peanut (groundnut *Arachis hypogaea*; monkey-nut, earth nut, pinda, Manila nut) A tropical and subtropical plant in which the young pods develop underground; a legume (nut) which after roasting is used as food. Approx nutrient required for:

	1 ton (nuts)	1 ton (vine)
nitrogen (lb)	60	39
P_2O_5 (lb)	14	5
K_2O (lb)	20	41

Types	Kernels per pod
Spanish	2
Virginia	2
Valencia	3-4

Composition: 21-29% shell; 2-3% skin; 71-75% kernel and germ. 4-13% H_2O, 21-36% protein, 36-54% fat, 12-43% carbohydrate, 2-3% ash.

Residue (oil cake) remaining after oil extraction is used for livestock feed.

1.5 lb unshelled = 1 lb shelled
1.75 cups unshelled = 1 lb
3 cups shelled = 1 lb
1 cup shelled = 145 g (5.1 oz)

Type	Unshelled lb per/bu
Virginia	17
Runners	21
Spanish	25

See Part 2: Beans, Peas and Nuts; Minerals, Food; Nicotinic Acid, Food; Nutrients in Crops; Oils, Seed and Fruit; Pantothenic Acid Content; Plant Foods, Composition; Protein Factors; Pulses, Nuts and Seeds Composition; Seed, Chemical Composition; Seed Composition; Seed, Germination; Tocopherols; Unsaponifiable Matter

peanut butter A soft paste made from peanuts by removing skin and germ and grinding the roasted and blanched kernels; separation is prevented by hydrogenation and added emulsifiers.

1 lb = 1.8 cups
1 cup = 250 g (8.9 oz)

Storage: Refrigerate after opening; hold at room temperature shortly before using.

Composition: 1.8% H_2O, 27% protein, 49% fat, 17% carbohydrate, 2% fiber; 4% ash.

See Part 2: Beans, Peas and Nuts; Calories, Daily Recommendations; Niacin, Daily Recommendations; Nut, Grades; Salad Dressing and Mayonnaise Variations; Standards, Processed Fruit and Vegetable Products; Storage, Dry

peanut meal Ground peanut press-cake that can be used as a fertilizer material; 7.2-1.5-1.2.

Dry: 1 lb/qt; 32 lb/bu.

See Part 2: Oil Meals Composition

peanut oil (*Arachis oil*) Oil extracted from the peanut; peanuts contain 47-50% oil.

1 qt = 4 cups
1 cup = 210 g (7.4 oz)

Composition:

palmitic	8-11%	arachidic	1-3%
stearic	2-3%	behenic	2%
oleic	40-56%	lignoceric	1%
linoleic	26-35%		

Properties:

saponification value	185-195
iodine value	85-105
refractive index (15.5°C)	1.471-1.474
unsaponifiable	$<$1%
titer	26-32°C
saturated fatty acid	15-23%
smoke point	230°C
free fatty acid (as oleic)	0.12%
melting point	-2°C
specific gravity 15°C	0.914

See Part 2: Fats and Oils, Composition; Fat and Oils, Fatty Acid Composition; Fats and Oils, Physical and Chemical Properties; Fatty Acids, Fats and Oils; Fats and Oils, Characteristic; Iodine and Saponification Values; Oil or Fat, Characteristics; Oil, Triglyceride Mole Percent Composition; Refractive Indices, Fats and Oils; Saturated Fatty Acids; Specific Gravities, Fats and Oils; Spoilage, Fat in Food; Titer, Fats and Oils; Tocopherols

pear An elongated fleshy fruit (pome) from the tree of the genus *Pyrus*; it often has a gritty texture; 70-80% edible.

Type	Use	Variety
Summer	eaten fresh and canned	Bartlett
Winter	cold storage	Anjou
		Bosc
		Comice
		Winter Nellis

Size:

1 lb fresh whole = 3-4 medium
= 2 cups fresh sliced (1 cup = 160 g or 5.6 oz)
1 qt canned = 2 to 3 lb fresh
= 5 to 6 medium
1 case (24) No. 2½ cans = 1.1 bu fresh
1 bu fresh = 48-50 lb
= 18-27 qt canned
1 box (8.5 × 11.5 × 18 in.) Western = 46 lb
1 lb dried = 5.5 fresh

Storage: Ripen at room temperature, unwrapped, out of sun; store cool (29°-31°F), in a dark, dry place (85-90% relative humidity); when ripe, use in 3 to 5 days.

Raw composition: 83% water, 1% protein, 0.4% fat, 15% carbohydrate, 0.4% ash; pH 3.9-4.9.

See Part 2: Canned Spoilage Related to pH; Canned Yield; Flavor Ingredients, Taste and Flavor Type; Fruit and Nut Rootstock; Fruit, Availability; Fruit Harvest Dates; Fruit Classification; Fruit Composition; Fruit Harvest; Fruit Dried, Simmering; Fruit Frozen Yield; Fruit,

Growing Season, Storage Life; Fruit Servings Per Pound; Fruit, Simmering; Fruit Storage; Minerals, Food; Minerals (Trace), Limits; Organic Acids in Fruits and Vegetables; Plant Foods, Composition; Rot Spoilage; Standards, Processed Fruit and Vegetable Products; Storage; Storage, Dry; Storage Times; Sugar, Fruit

pear cheese A light, creamy tan, pear-shaped cheese; sometimes fried in olive oil before eating.

Pearl A variety of millet.

pearl barley Polished barley grain without the bran and lacking in gluten; processed by dehusking and grinding the barley; used in soups and stews. *See also* **barley.**

pearl hominy Coarse hominy grits. *See also* **hominy.**

pearling *See* **rice**

pearl tapioca Dough made from tapioca flour, forced through a sieve and then heated to high temperature; usually made in 3 sizes—coarse, medium, or fine.

pear tomato *See* **tomato**

peas and carrots A mixture of 50–75% peas and 25–50% sliced or diced carrots.

peat Carbonized vegetable matter; precursor of coal. Used as fuel.

pea weevil *See* Part 2: Insect Control

pecan (*Carya illinoensis*) A large North American tree that produces a hard-shelled nut that may be eaten as a snack or used in many confectionery and cooked items; the nut has a mild, sweet walnut-like flavor.

1 lb shelled = 3–4 cups halves
1 cup halves = 110 g (3.8 oz)
1 lb shelled = 3.5–4 cups chopped
1 cup chopped = 120 g (4.2 oz)
1 lb shelled = 200–225 Mammoth size halves
1 lb in shell = 2 cups in shell
2½ lb in shell = 1 lb shelled

Storage: Store in dry, cool, place protected from insects and odors. Times and temperatures as follows:

	70°-90°F	38°-40°F	0°F
Unshelled	4 mo.	18 mo.	4 years
Halves	2 mo.	9 mo.	2 years
Pieces	20 days	3 mo.	9 mo.

Composition: 3% H_2O, 9% protein, 71% fat, 15% carbohydrate, 2% ash.

See Part 2: Beans, Peas and Nuts; Food, Composition; Minerals, Food; Nut, Grades; Plant Foods, Composition; Tocopherols

peck (pk) (Imperial (Br.) A dry measure of volume.

1 peck = 554.6 cubic inches
= 9.092 liters
= 8 Br. quarts

peck (pk) (U.S.) A dry measure of volume used chiefly for raw vegetables, e.g., potatoes.

1 peck = 537.6 cubic inches
= 16 pints
= 8.809 liters
= 8 quarts
= 0.25 bushel
4 pecks = 1 bushel

pecorino di tavola A sharp, semi-hard table cheese.

pectic acid $C_{17}H_{24}O_{16}$ A dibasic organic acid derived from pectin by chemical treatment; used as a food acidulant.
See Part 2: Pectic Acid Formula

pectin A water-soluble carbohydrate (pectinic acid) polymer made up of varying numbers of the 1 and 4 linked methyl esters of β-galacturonic acid.

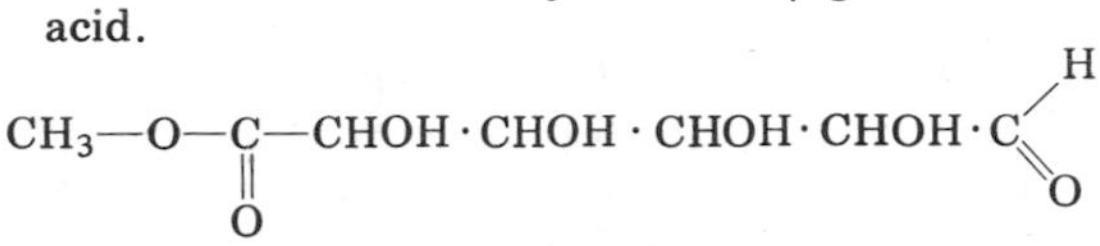

A hydrophilic colloidal carbohydrate (polysaccharide triad) obtained by acid extraction of citrus fruit rinds (20–30%) or apple pomace (10–15%); it is found in just-ripe fruits and has strong gelling properties which are used in cooking. It is used as a gelling agent because of its swelling power at concentrations of less than 1% (0.1–0.4 in jams and jellies); gel power is usually standardized with sugar.
See Part 2: Bananas, Composition; Gums and Gelling Agents; Gums and Gelling Agents, Characteristics; Minerals (Trace), Limits; Pectin; Pectin Content; Pectin Formula

pectinic acid Colloidal polygalacturonic acid containing some methyl ester groups; capable of forming gels (jellies) with sugar and acid. *See also* **pectin.**

pectorals Muscles that attach the ventral end of the scapula and the dorsal end of the humerus to the sternum; they make up most of the brisket.

pedigree A written record of an animal's ancestry for at least three generations.

peduncle *See* Part 2: Fish Nomenclature

peel To remove outer covering or rind of a fruit or vegetable by hand or by 2% lye solution. *See also* **pare.**
See Part 2: Orange Structure

peelability (sausage) Acidification with (1) vinegar (35–40 grains) or (2) 5% citric acid. Spray prior to or after smoking.

peeled shrimp Shrimp from which the shells have been removed.

peewee A small lamb.

Peizer TB medium *See* Part 2: Microorganism, Media

Peking duck *See* Part 2: Poultry Dressing Percentage; Poultry Yield

pelagic fish Fish that live near the surface of the sea; 55% of such fish is edible; examples are herring, mackerel, mullet. Edible portion has 16% avg. protein; 15% avg. fat for herring and mackerel.

pellagra A disease in humans caused by deficiency of niacin (nicotinic acid); the skin becomes rough and irritated; the mouth becomes sore and the tongue becomes red, sore and swollen. In dogs this disease is called black tongue.

pelt The skin of a wool- or fur-bearing animal, with hair attached.

pelvis The hip bone, which is attached to the femur and is made up of the ischium and ilium areas.
See Part 2: Bone; Lamb, Wholesale Cuts; Pork Wholesale Cuts; Veal Wholesale Cuts

pemmican Lean meat dried in the sun and then ground with fat to form a paste or a mixture of dried meat, fruits and vegetables.

penholder An animal left in a pen to keep other animals from being placed in the pen.

penicillin An antibiotic agent produced by the mold *Penicillium notatum* which is effective against Gram-positive and a few Gram-negative bacteria; there are a number of different types. Many individuals are allergic to it, and such reactions can be serious.
See Part 2: Antibiotic Standards; Mold, Food; Molds, Mycotoxins; Rot Spoilage; Spoilage, Carbohydrate Foods; Spoilage, Protein Foods; Wastes, Agricultural and Industrial

pennyroyal oil A reddish-yellow essential oil, used in perfumery and flavoring.
See Part 2: Essential Oils

pentadecanoic acid $CH_3(CH_2)_{13}COOH$ A saturated fatty acid made synthetically.
See Part 2: Fatty Acids and Their Properties

pentosan A carbohydrate mixture (hemicellulose) occurring in cereal plants, brans, etc.
See Part 2: Pentosans; Wheat and Flour Composition; Wheat, Carbohydrate Composition; Wheat, Parts of Grain

pentose A 5-carbon sugar ($C_5H_{10}O_5$).

penuche *See* **panocha**

pepato A sharp, table and grating cheese containing whole black peppercorns.

pepitos Seeds that are deep fat-fried and salted.

pepo A subdivision of simple fruit; it has a fleshy ovary wall enclosing one or more seeds, attached to a fleshy placenta and has a hard rind covering. Examples are cantaloupe, cucumber, squash, pumpkin, watermelon.
See Part 2: Fruit Classification; Vegetables, Classification

pepper A term used to define two different types of plants and fruits. (1) Red, cayenne: bushy plants of genus *Capsicum*. (2) White and black pepper: climbing vine, *Piper nigrum*.
See Part 2: Ascorbic Acid; Calories, Daily Recommendations; Essential Oils; Flavoring Agents, Natural; Fruit and Vegetable, Diseases; Minerals, Food; Plant Foods, Composition; Riboflavin; Spices, Microbial Content; Storage; Sugar, Vegetables; Transit Temperature; Vegetable Composition; Vegetable Frozen Yield; Vegetable Plants; Vegetables, Classification; Vegetable Storage; Vitamin A; Vitamin C

pepper (*Capsicum*) **(red; cayenne)** A bushy plant with a wide range of varieties; pungency due to capsicin.

Types	Immature color	Mature color	Shape	Pungency	Use
Sweet pepper	Green	Red, yellow, brown	Long & narrow to spherical	Mild to med. hot	To make paprika, salads, vegetable, pickled
Red pepper	Green	Bright red	Variable but smaller than above	Med. hot to hot	Dried
Chili				Very hot	Dried, curry powder, pickles, tobasco sauce

Sweet pepper: 25 lb per bushel; 1 crate (13.4 × 11 × 22 in.) = 50 lb; spacing 18 in. in rows 3 ft apart; $1\frac{1}{3}$ lb = 1 qt frozen.

Storage:	Temp. (°F)	RH (%)	Storage Life
Dry chili	32–40	65–75	6 mo.
Sweet	45–50	85–90	8 days

pennyweight (dwt) (Troy) A measure of weight.
1 pennyweight = 24 grains
= 1.555,174,0 grams
= 1.2 scruples (apoth.)
= 0.877,714,3 dram (av.)
= 0.4 dram (apoth.)
= 0.054,857,1 ounce (av.)
= 0.05 ounce (apoth.) (troy)
= 0.004,166,667 pound (apoth.) (troy)
= 0.003,428,571 pound (av.)

pepper (*Piper nigrum*) A whole or ground spice made from the berries of the pepper vine (a

climbing perennial) and used in seasoning. Black pepper: unripe fruit, entire berry is used. White pepper: ripened fruit, outside covering is removed. Fruit (peppercorn) is red when ripe. Country of origin is usually specified:
- Malabar: Indian
- Lampong: Indonesian
- Saigon: Vietnamese and Cambodian

Standards:
- Black: not less than 6.75% nonvolatile ether extract; not less than 30% starch; not more than 7% total ash; not more than 1.5% acid-insoluble ash.
- White: not less than 7% nonvolatile ether extract; not less than 52% starch; not more than 5% crude fiber; not more than 3.5% total ash; not more than 0.3% acid-insoluble ash.

peppercorn Seed or berry of pepper vine; whole pepper.

peppered loaf A type of sausage.
See Part 2: Sausage Identification

peppermint (***Mentha piperita***) Dried leaves of peppermint plant cultivated in Washington. Oil of peppermint is obtained by distillation of the leaves and flowers. Chief constituent is menthol. Used for flavoring liquor, confectionery chewing gum, etc.
See Part 2: Essential Oils

pepperoni A sausage made of dried pork and beef, medium-chopped; the predominant spice is Italian red pepper; it is dried but not smoked.
See Part 2: Sausage, Types

pepsin An enzyme contained in the gastric juices which acts upon proteins; it is secreted in the inactive form pepsinogen (activated by acid); its optimum pH is 1.5 to 2.5; it can be extracted from the pyloric end of a pig's stomach.
See Part 2: pH Values of Biological Materials

pepsinogen The inactive form of pepsin and the form in which it is secreted; it is converted to the active form by hydrochloric acid and pepsin itself.

peptide Combinations of 2 or more amino acids joined by a $-\underset{\underset{O}{\|}}{C}-\underset{\underset{H}{|}}{N}-$ linkage to form a protein.
See also **protein.**

peptizing The ability of some substances to attack, break down and disperse a protein.

peptone A polypeptide of low molecular weight which is water-soluble, is not coagulated by heat, and is not precipitated by saturated ammonium sulfate.

peptone colloid medium *See* Part 2: Microorganism, Media

peptonized milk *See* Part 2: Microorganism, Culture Media, Dairy and Food Products; Microorganism, Media

percentage dilution problems (approximate results)

I. Dilute with H_2O.
Subtract percentage desired from percentage of original; this will give the portion of water that must be added to the portion (same as the desired %) of original.

Examples: Have 95% alcohol
Want 35% alcohol $95 - 35 = 60$

Solution: 60 parts water to 35 parts 95% alcohol = 95 parts of 35% alcohol.

II. Dilute with lower percentage.
(a) Subtract percentage wanted from percentage of original (higher); this equals the parts of lower percentage to be added.
(b) Next subtract lower percentage from percentage wanted; this equals parts of higher percentage to be added.

Examples: Make 35% from 95% and 20%:
$95 - 35 = 60$ parts of 20% to add
$35 - 20 = 15$ parts of 95% to add
} to give 75 parts of 35%

perch A small fresh-water spiny-finned fish. *See also* **rod.**
See Part 2: Fish and Shellfish Composition; Fish, Storage; Frozen Food Storage; Minerals, Food

perchloric acid $HClO_4$ A hygroscopic liquid; strong oxidizing agent. Use care in handling.
See Part 2: Concentration of Commercial Strengths of Acids and Bases

pericarp The outer layer of grain next to the husk; major part of bran.
See Part 2: Wheat Grain; Wheat Kernel; Wheat Kernel Parts; Wheat, Parts of Grain; Wheat, Parts of Grain, Vitamins

perichondrium The connective tissue covering of cartilage.

perilla oil A yellow, edible drying oil obtained from a Japanese plant seed.
See Part 2: Essential Oils; Fats and Oils, Physical and Chemical Properties; Fatty Acids, Fats and Oils; Iodine and Saponification Values; Oil or Fat, Characteristics; Refractive Indices, Fats and Oils; Unsaponifiable Matter

perimysium Connective tissue enclosing bundles of primary muscle fiber.

periodic ophthalmia *See* **moon blindness**

Periodic Table A classification of the chemical elements devised by the Russian chemist Mendeleef in 1869, in which the elements are listed in order of increasing atomic weight. Thus a recurring similarity of properties (periodicity) is revealed, which depends on the atomic number of the element. The table contains seven horizontal divisions, or periods, and nine major vertical divisions (groups).
See Part 2: Elements

periosteum External connective tissue covering of a bone.

peripheral *See* **superficial**

permutations The different orders in which objects can be arranged. *See also* combinations.

$P_r^n = n(n-1)(n-2)(n-3)(n-4)\cdots(n-r+1)$

P = no. of permutations

n = total number of objects

r = no. taken at a time

Example: Letters X, Y, Z can be arranged in how many orders, using 2 letters at a time?

$n = 3$ $P = 3 \cdot 2 = 6$ XY, XZ, YX, YZ, ZX, ZY

$r = 2$

Permutit Proprietary name for a group of ion-exchange resins used to soften water. *See also* **hardness (water)**.

peroxide A compound containing an —O—O— group in which the oxygen atoms are univalent and in a negative oxidation state, e.g., hydrogen peroxide H—O—O—H. Peroxides are strong oxidizing agents.
See Part 2: Antioxidant Activity

peroxide value analysis An indication of oxidation that has taken place by measuring the substances in fat that will oxidize potassium iodide and is expressed as the milliequivalents of peroxide per kilogram of fat; it is determined by adding saturated potassium iodide to a solution of fat, chloroform, glacial acetic acid and HCl; the liberated iodide is titrated with a standardized sodium thiosulfate solution; during oxidation, the peroxide value increases, reaches a peak and then decreases.

perry Pear juice.

persimmon A date plum.
Species:
Japanese (*Diospyros kaki* L.): deciduous tree producing a 2 to 3 in. diameter red fruit that looks like a tomato; it is eaten fresh, cooked and candied.
American (*D. Virginiana* L.): fruit is smaller than Japanese and dark red to maroon in color.
Storage: 30°F; 85–90% relative humidity.
Composition: 64–78% water, 0.8% protein, 0.4% fat, 20–34% carbohydrate, 1% ash; pH 5.4–5.8.
See Part 2: Fruit Composition; Fruit Storage; Minerals, Food

peruvian apple *See* **tomato**

pesticide Any substance used to kill pests; includes fungicides, herbicides, insecticides and rodenticides; some types are toxic to man.

petal One of the leaves of the corolla of a flower.
See Part 2: Flower, Perfect

petit four A small decorated tea cake.

petitgrain oil An essential oil from the leaves of the bitter orange tree (Paraguay); used in flavoring, perfumery, etc.
See Part 2: Essential Oils

petits pois Small-seeded peas which have a good flavor when young and fresh.

petit suisse A soft creamy, nonsalted cheese.
See Part 2: Cheese, Vitamin Content; Milk and Cheese Composition

Petragnani medium *See* Part 2: Microorganism, Media

petrale sole *See* **sole**

petri dish Two shallow dishes (bottom and cover) used for growing bacterial cultures.

petrochemical A chemical derived from petroleum or natural gas, except those used for fuel. Thus benzene and ethylene oxide are petrochemicals, but gasoline and fuel oil are not.

petroselinic acid *See* Part 2: Unsaturated Fatty Acids

petsai (wong bok, chihli; *Brassica pekinensis*) Autumn and winter vegetable used for greens.
See Part 2: Vegetables, Classification; Vegetable Storage

pH Degree of acidity or alkalinity. It is the negative logarithm (base 10) of the H-ion concentration; the range is from 1 to 14, with 7 being neutral; pH values greater than 7 indicate an alkaline solution, while values less than 7 indicate an acid solution.

$$\text{pH} = \log_{10} \frac{1}{[H^+]} = -\log_{(10)} [H^+]$$

Fresh meat 5.3 to 6.0; normal human blood 7.3 to 7.5; pure water 7.0.
See Part 2: Egg Specifications; Indicators: pH and Acid Base; Lemon Juice Composition; Lime Juice Composition; Milk, Physical Properties; pH and Availability of Plant Nutrients; pH, Buffer Solutions; pH, Post Mortem; pH, Standard Solutions; pH, Universal Indicators; pH Values of Biological Materials; Water Drinking Standards

phalangeal bone Foot bones just above the toes.
See Part 2: Bone

pheasant A game bird.
See Part 2: Poultry Dressing Percentage; Poultry Yield

phenol (carbolic acid) An organic compound in which one of the hydrogen atoms in the aromatic ring has been replaced by a hydroxyl group in the ortho position.

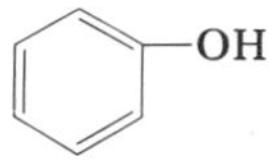

See Part 2: Water Drinking Standards

phenolphthalein $C_{20}H_{14}O_4$ An indicator used when titrating weak acids; its pH range is 8–10; it is colorless in an acid solution; pink to red at pH 9 and above; 0.2g/100 ml alcohol.

phenol red An acid-base indicator.

phenol red broth *See* Part 2: Microorganism, Media

phenomenal berry A fruit similar to loganberry.

phenothiazine An anthelmintic for livestock.

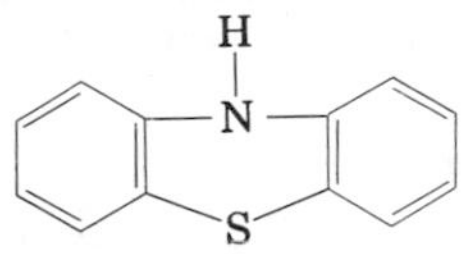

Recommended treatment for internal parasites:
1 part to 12 parts with salt (continuous administration).
For sheep: 15 to 25 g (approx ⅗ to 1 oz);
For cattle: 10 g/100 lb body weight (maximum 60 g); must be done when cattle are dry (causes red discoloration of milk).
For swine: 12–30 g.

phenylalanine An aromatic amino acid.

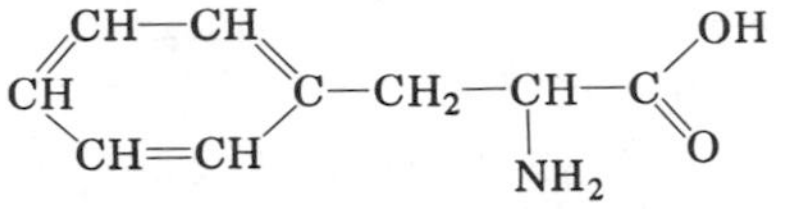

See Part 2: Amino Acids; Amino Acid, Solubilities; Corn, Amino Acids; Egg Products, Nutritive Value; Grain Analysis; Manure Analysis; Microorganism, Media; Milk, Amino Acids; Seed, Chemical Composition; Wheat, Amino Acids; Wheat Products, Amino Acid Compositions

phenylalanine agar *See* Part 2: Microorganism, Media

phenylethanol *See* Part 2: Microorganism, Media

phenyl group An organic group based on the benzene ring, in which one or more substituent atoms or groups have replaced H atoms. Thus a phenyl group may be C_6H_5-, -C_6H_4-, etc.

phi (Φ, ϕ) Greek letter with an English equivalent of ph.

Phillipps A variety of clingstone peaches.

Phoma A type of mold.
See Part 2: Mold, Food

phosphate Any salt of phosphoric acid; 0.5% permitted in finished products such as cured hams and shoulders and canned chopped ham.
- sodium tripolyphosphate: $Na_5P_3O_{10}$
- sodium hexmetaphosphate (Grahams salt): $(NaPO_3)_6$
- sodium acid pyrophosphate: $Na_2H_2P_2O_7$
- sodium pyrophosphate (tetrasodium pyrophosphate): $Na_4P_2O_7$
- disodium phosphate (sodium phosphate dibasic): Na_2HPO_4
- monosodium phosphate (sodium phosphate monobasic): NaH_2PO_4

No more than 5% of such phosphates may be in pickle; 50 lb/100 gal. pickle (10% pump); canned chopped hams, 8 oz/100 lb of fresh uncured ham. Not permitted in beef products. *See also* **fertilizer.**
See Part 2: Fertilizer Materials; Minerals (Trace), Limits; Phosphate; pH, Post Mortem

phosphate rock A fertilizer material composed largely of calcium phosphate; 33% total P_2O_5; occurs widely in U.S., especially Florida.

phosphatide *See* **phospholipid**

phospholipid (phosphatide) Fat-like compounds which also contain phosphorus and nitrogen; when subjected to hydrolysis phospholipids yield glycerol, fatty acids, phosphoric acid and a nitrogenous base; two of the best known examples are lecithin and cephalin.

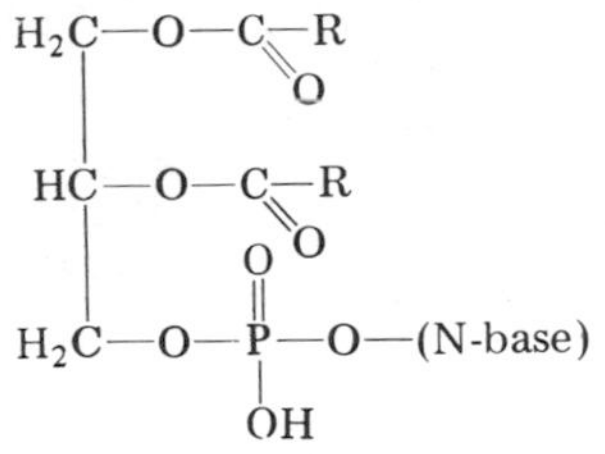

See Part 2: Egg Products, Nutritive Value

phosphoprotein A phosphoric acid ester linked to a protein through a hydroxy amino acid; e.g., casein, vitellin.

phosphoric acid H_3PO_4 An inorganic acid derived from phosphate rock by treatment with HCl or H_2SO_4. Mol. wt. 98; m.p., 41°C.
Commercial strength:

% by wt	Sp Gr	M.	Normality
85	1.689	14.7	41.1
87	1.711	15.2	

ml of 85% H_3PO_4 to dilute to 10 liters	approx normality
230	1.00

Used as an acidulant and flavor in soft drinks and in fertilizers.
85% acid is 55–60% as tart as anhydrous citric acid.
Types:
orthophosphoric acid (H_3PO_4)
metaphosphoric acid (HPO_3)
pyrophosphoric acid ($H_4P_2O_7$)
See Part 2: Concentration of Commercial Strengths of Acids and Bases; Fertilizer Materials; Normal Solutions; Reagents, Normal Solutions

phosphorus P A nonmetallic element; at. no. 15; at. wt. 30.975; Group V-A of Periodic

Table; oxidation states +3, +5, −3; electron configuration 2−8−5
orbit K L M
Body function: in bones (as calcium phosphate Ca_3PO_4); buffer action, lecithins, proteins, and nucleic acids.

High P content	Low P content
Cereals, legumes	
Meat and milk products	Fruit
Eggs, fish	

See Part 2: Beef Percentages of Daily Recommended Allowances; Cereal Fortification; Cereals, Vitamin and Mineral Content; Composition of Food; Concentrated and Dried Milk Products; Creams, Butter and Frozen Desserts; Egg Products, Nutritive Value; Fluid and Fermented Milks, Composition; Food, Composition; Grain Analysis; Lamb Percentages of Daily Recommended Allowances; Lemon Juice Composition; Lime Juice Composition; Macaroni and Noodles Composition; Manure Analysis; Meat, Nutritive Value; Minerals, Food; Minerals, Plant or Animal Tissue; Nutrients in Crops; pH and Availability of Plant Nutrients; Phosphorus; Plant Foods, Composition; Pork, Percentages of Daily Recommended Allowances; Recommended Daily Dietary Allowance; Tomato and Tomato Products, Composition; Variety Meat Percentage of Daily Recommended Allowances; Wastes, Agricultural and Industrial; Wheat, Minerals; Wheat Products Composition

photon The massless unit of electromagnetic energy moving at the speed of light.

photosynthesis Conversion of radiant energy to chemical energy by plants. The generally accepted reaction is:

$$6CO_2 + 6H_2O + 672\text{ kcal} \xrightarrow[\text{chlorophyll}]{\text{light}} C_6H_{12}O_6 + 6O_2$$

The chlorophyll acts as catalyst. Virtually all atmospheric oxygen is due to this reaction. The stored energy is released as heat on combustion.

phycocolloid A hydrophilic colloidal substance derived from seaweed, for example, carrageenan, algin. *See also* **polysaccharide**.

Physalospora A type of mold.
See Part 2: Mold, Food

physiological saline 0.9% sodium chloride in water; used as an isotonic solution of NaCl when dealing with mammals.

phytonadione (K_1) *See* Part 2: Vitamins

Phytophthora A type of mold.
See Part 2: Mold, Food

pi (Π, π) Greek letter with an English equivalent of p; in math $\pi = 3.14159$ (ratio of circumference to diameter of a circle).
See Part 2: Constants, Fundamental

pica Desire for unnatural food, such as chalk, clay, etc., by those affected with chlorosis.

pickerel A lean, fresh-water fish.
See Part 2: Minerals, Food

pickle (1) A brine or vinegar solution; in relation to meat the common ingredients are salt, sugar, sodium nitrate, sodium nitrite (not acid or vinegar). (2) A relish made from vegetables or fruits. Vegetables may be pickled by treatment with salt, vinegar, or both salt and vinegar. Fruits may be pickled with vinegar, sugar and spices.
Types of pickle:

	pH
Dill	2.6−3.8
Sour	3.0−3.5
Sweet	2.5−3.0

See Part 2: Calories, Daily Recommendations; Food, Composition; Meat Curing Ingredients; Vegetables, Canning Dates

pickle and pimento loaf *See* Part 2: Sausage Identification

pickled pigs' feet Clean pigs' feet; submerge in 75°; pickle for several weeks; cook; chill and remove meat; place in hot vinegar solution of 50% vinegar, 50% water, 1 teaspoon salt/pint; seal in jars.
See Part 2: Pork Chart; Pork Cuts; Pork Cuts and Uses; Pork Yield

picnic The lower area of the pork shoulder; it may or may not be cured and smoked.
See Part 2: Cooking in Liquid, Time; Meat, Servings per Pound; Pork Carcass, Retail Yield; Pork Chart; Pork, Cooking; Pork, Cooking Methods; Pork Cooking Yield; Pork Cuts; Pork Cuts and Uses; Pork Shoulder; Pork Wholesale Cuts; Pork Yield; Roasting, Time and Temperature; Simmering Meat

pico- Prefix for a quantity one trillion times smaller than the base unit, i.e., 1 picogram (pg) = 10^{-12} g.

pidan A pickled egg; a thousand-year egg.
Procedure:

Time	Solution	Temp
10 days	20% NaCl	25°C
7−9 days	5% NaOH	
	10% NaCl	
	2% black tea	

Cover with paraffin and they will keep for several months.

pie A baked dish consisting of a filling (fruit, custard, pudding, Bavarian cream, meat, etc.) and a lower or upper crust or both.
See Part 2: Calories, Daily Recommendations; Frozen Food Storage; Grain Products Composition; Portion Size; Storage Times

piecrust *See* **pie shell; pastry**

pie shell Pastry portion of a pie.

Cups of Pastry Mix for:

	Single Crust	Double Crust
8-in.	1 -1¼ cups	2 -2¼ cups
9-in.	1¼-1½ cups	2¼-2½ cups
10-in.	1½-1¾ cups	2½-2¾ cups

For piecrust: ⅛ in. thick with ½ in. over edge of pan.
See Part 2: Grain Products Composition

pig Young swine, 120 lb or under, either sex; *Sus scrofa* (European); *Sus vittatus* (Eastern Asiatic).
See Part 2: Gestation Periods; Muscle and Body Weight; Swine Breeds; Swine Market Classes and Grades; Teeth Eruption

pigeon pea (red gram; *Cajanus cajan*) A tropical legume that has good draught resistance; the pea is cooked to produce "dhal" for human consumption and the pods and foliage are used for livestock feed.
Green seed composition: 69% H_2O, 7% protein, 0.6% fat, 21% carbohydrate, 1% ash.

pigment A substance that absorbs radiant energy in the visible spectrum; a colorant.
See Part 2: Meat Pigment

pigs' feet, pickled *See* **pickled pigs' feet**

pig's-foot jell A jell made by cooking pigs feet, hearts, tongues, and hocks in water, removing the bones and letting product jell.

pig souse *See* **pig's-foot jell**

pike *See* Part 2: Minerals, Food

Pike's Peak Muscles of the hind shank.

pilau (pilaf, pilaw) A dish of rice, raisins, meat and spices.

pilchard A small fish related to the herring family found off the coast of southern Europe and California.
See Part 2: Fats and Oils, Characteristics; Unsaturated Fatty Acids; Vitamin A, Fish; Vitamin D, Fish

pimaricin An antibiotic added to food in some countries.

pimento Spanish paprika or pimiento; allspice; pH 4.6–5.2. *See also* **pimiento.**
See Part 2: Essential Oils; Minerals, Food

pimento cheese *See* Part 2: Cheese, Vitamin Content; Vitamin A, Milk and Milk Products

pimienta *See* **paprika**

pimiento Spanish sweet pepper; used as a stuffing for olives and as flavoring agent in cream sauces. *See also* **paprika.**
See Part 2: Standards, Processed Fruit and Vegetable Products; Vegetable Composition; Vegetables, Canning Dates

pinbone (on carcass) Crest of the ilium.
See Part 2: Bone in Retail Cuts

pinbone (on live animals) Bony structure on each side of the tail head (ischial tuberosity).

pinbone (sirloin) A sirloin steak found in the loin end wholesale cut; it is located in front of the double bone sirloin; it is the first sirloin on the short loin end of the loin end cut.

pinch As used in recipes, less than ⅛ tsp.

pineal gland Reddish gland located behind and above the pituitary; it regulates child growth, puberty and maturity.
See Part 2: Gland Weights

pineapple (*Ananas comosus*) (1) A tropical fruit which is a multiple organ formed from more than a hundred flowers; pineapples are produced by planting (1) crown of leaves; (2) small leaves below fruit (slips); (3) small leaves from base of stem (suckers). Harvest in 15–20 months; will bear for many years with fruit becoming smaller; replant every 2–3 years; 50% edible. High in sugar and in vitamins A and C; eaten fresh or canned; juice used as a drink.
Composition:

	H_2O (%)	Protein (%)	Fat (%)	Carbohydrate (%)	Ash (%)	pH
Raw	85	0.4	0.2	14	0.4	3.5–5.2
Juice	86	0.4	0.1	14	0.4	3.4–3.6

Storage:

	Temp. (°F)	Relative humidity (%)	Storage life (weeks)
Green	50–60	85–90	3–4
Ripe	40–45	85–90	2–3

1 medium fresh = 2 lb
= 3 cups (1 cup = 145 g or 5.2 oz)
2 pineapples (fresh) = 1 qt canned
20 oz canned = 10 slices
1 crate (12 X 10.5 X 33 in.) = 70 lb
1 crate (fresh) = 30 pineapples = 12–16 qt canned

(2) A variety of midsummer Florida orange. (3) An American hard cheese. *See also* **pineapple cheese.**
See Part 2: Calories, Daily Recommendations; Flavor Ingredients, Taste and Flavor Type; Fruit, Availability; Fruit Canning Dates; Fruit Classification; Fruit Composition; Fruit Frozen Yield; Fruit Storage; Minerals, Food; Plant Foods, Composition; Potassium-rich Foods; Standards, Processed Fruit and Vegetable Products; Storage; Vegetable Storage

pineapple cheese A smooth, hard, yellow, tangy-flavored sandwich and dessert cheese; it is shaped like a pineapple and diamond-scored, and rubbed with edible oil during ripening.

Pineau Blanc *See* **Chardonnay**

Pineau Noir A variety of purplish black grapes that are fermented to yield red burgundy.

pine kernels Pine seeds that are eaten as nuts, and used in cooking and confectionery.

Common name	Scientific name	Area
Stone	*Pinus pinea*	Mediterranean
Arolla	*Pinus cembra*	Switzerland
Pine	*Pinus sibirica*	Russia
Mexican nut	*Pinus cembroides*	Mexico
Gerard's	*Pinus gerardiana*	Himalayan
Chile or Monkey-puzzle	*Araucaria araucana*	Chile
Parana-Bunya	*Araucaria bidwillii*	Queensland

pine tar A viscous, sticky liquid or soft solid with a pleasant odor; made by distillation of pine wood, and used as a fly repellent.

pingue *See* Part 2: Poisonous Plants

pink champagne A rose pink wine with a fruity flavor.

pinkelwurst An imitation cooked sausage made of beef fat, oat groats, water and onions.

pink eye A disease of cattle which results in red and irritated eyes and eyelids; it forms a white scum over the eye and often causes blindness.

pink salmon *See* **salmon**

pint A measure of liquid volume.
1 pt (Br.) (Imp.) = 568.25 ml
= 20 ounces (Br. fl.)
= 1.20094 pints (U.S.)
= 0.568 liter
1 pt (U.S.) = 473.179 cubic centimeters
= 473.167 milliliters
= 28.875 cubic inches
= 16 U.S. fluid ounces
= 4 gills (U.S.)
= 0.83268 pint (Br.)
= 0.4732 liter
2 pints = 1 quart
4 qt = 1 gal.
1 cup (U.S.) = 2/5 pint (British)
See Part 2: Volume; Water, Weight and Volume

pinworm A nemotode worm infesting the intestines.
See Part 2: Insect Control

pipe A 105-Imperial-gallon cask for wine.
1 pipe = 2 hogsheads
2 pipes = 1 tun

pipette A glass tube used in the laboratory to measure volume; an opaque band at top of pipette (calibrated for blowout) indicates pipette should be blown out to get calibrated quantity. *See also* TC and TD.

pistachio (***Pistacia vera***) A small tree that produces an edible nut; the nut may be eaten salted or used in confectionery and in decorating and flavoring.
1 lb shelled = 2 lb unshelled
1 lb shelled = 3.2–4 cups
1 cup shelled = 125 g (4.4 oz)
Nut composition: 5% H_2O, 19% protein, 54% fat, 19% carbohydrate, 3% ash.
See Part 2: Minerals, Food

pistil The part of a flower that contains the ovary.
See Part 2: Flower, Imperfect; Flower, Perfect

pit The stone (seed) of a fruit, e.g., cherry, date, etc.

pithing Destroying the medulla oblongata of the brain with a metal rod during slaughter.

Pithomyces A type of mold.
See Part 2: Molds, Mycotoxins

pi-tsi *See* **Chinese water chestnut**

pituitary gland Grayish yellow gland located at the base of the brain; it is made up of 2 sections:
(1) Anterior lobe
(a) thyroid-stimulating hormone
(b) growth-promoting hormone
(c) mammary stimulating
(d) adrenal cortex stimulating
(e) gonad-stimulating
(2) Posterior lobe
(a) regulates energy metabolism
(b) controls blood pressure and pulse rate
(c) regulates contractile organs
See Part 2: Gland Weights

pizza A bread-like crust topped with tomato sauce and one or more of the following: cheese, sausage, beef, anchovies, onions, green peppers or other vegetables.
See Part 2: Grain Products Composition

pK value The logarithm (to base 10) of the reciprocal of the equilibrium constant;

$$pK = \log_{10} \frac{1}{K_{eq}}$$

Pl Private label.

placenta The ovule-bearing portion of the plant ovary.
See Part 2: Orange Structure

plaice *See* Part 2: Fish, Storage

plain chocolate (bitter chocolate) *See* **chocolate.**

plain condensed milk Condensed milk that contains min. 7.9% milk fat, min. 25.9% total milk solids.

plain condensed skim milk Condensed skim milk that contains min. 20% milk solids-not-fat.

planimeter An instrument used to measure irregular areas.

plant (1) A chlorophyll-bearing organism that synthesizes carbohydrates and proteins; composed of root, stem, flower and fruit (seeds). (2) To sow seeds or insert cuttings in the ground.
See Part 2: Acre, Plants; Acre, Trees

plantain A tropical tree bearing a banana-like fruit.
See Part 2: Plant Foods, Composition

plasma Liquid or noncellular portion of the blood, lymph or milk; serum is plasma from which the fibrinogen has not been removed.

plaster A paste composed of lime or gypsum and water which hardens on drying.
See Part 2: Liming Materials

plastic A high-polymer film used for food packaging.
See Part 2: Plastic Permeability

plastic range Temperature range within which a shortening or fat is readily workable or softened.

plastification *See* Part 2: Margarine Production

plate About 12% of a choice steer carcass.
See Part 2: Beef Chart; Beef Cuts; Beef Cuts and Uses; Meat Identification

plate count A procedure for estimating the number of bacteria by growing the cell into a colony which can be seen by the eye. The nutrient medium is often plate count agar.
See Part 2: Microorganism, Culture Media, Dairy and Food Products; Microorganism, Culture Media, Water and Sewage, Standard Methods; Microorganism, Media

platelet Disc-shaped cells in the blood; average 50,000/cu mm of blood.

platinum (Pt) A metallic element; at. no. 78; at. wt. 195.09; Group VIII of Periodic Table; electron configuration 2-8-18-32-16-2
orbit K L M N O P
oxidation states +2, +4.

pleuropneumonia *See* Part 2: Microorganism, Media

Pliofilm Trademark for rubber hydrochloride; clear plastic used for food packaging.

pluck Organs in the thoracic cavity consisting of heart, lungs, gullet and windpipe.

plum (*Prunus*) A tree that yields a short-stalked fruit that may be red, green or yellow; 91% edible; dried plums are called prunes.

Varieties	Use
Sloe	wine and gin
Bullace	cooked
Damson	cooked and jam
Gage	jam and canning
Cherry	cooking
European	stewed, pie, preserved and canned
Pond's seedling	preserving and drying
Prune d'Agen	dried prunes
Victoria	dessert
Coe's Golden Drop	dessert
Kirke's Blue	dessert
Laxton's Delicious	dessert
Jefferson	dessert

Size:
Medium = 2 in. diameter
1 lb = 8–20 medium size
= 2 cups halved (1 cup = 185 g or 6.5 oz)
1 qt canned = 1½ to 2½ lb, fresh
10 lb canned = 10–14 plums
1 bu fresh = 50 to 56 lb
= 20–30 qt canned
½ basket = 28 lb
4-basket crate = 20–29 lb

Ripen: Uncovered, room temperature, out of sun.

Storage: Refrigerate (31°–32°F), uncovered (80–85% relative humidity); when ripe, use in 3 to 5 days.

Composition: 79–87% H_2O, 0.5–0.8% protein, 0–0.2% fat, 12–20% carbohydrate, 0.5% ash; pH 2.8–3.0.

See Part 2: Canned Yield; Flavor Ingredients, Taste and Flavor Type; Fruit and Nut Rootstock; Fruit, Availability; Fruit Harvest Dates; Fruit Classification; Fruit Composition; Fruit, Cooking; Fruit Frozen Yield; Fruit Servings per Pound; Fruit, Simmering; Fruit Storage; Minerals, Food; Organic Acids in Fruits and Vegetables; Plant Foods, Composition; Rot Spoilage; Standards, Processed Fruit and Vegetable Products; Storage; Storage Times; Sugar, Fruit

plumule A plant bud within the embryo.
See Part 2: Corn Kernel; Wheat Kernel; Wheat Kernel Parts

plutonium (Pu) A synthetic radioactive element of the actinide series; at. no. 94; mass number of most stable isotope 242; electron configuration 2-8-18-32-23-9-2
orbit K L M N O P Q
oxidation states +3, +4, +5, +6. Highly toxic and fissionable.

Plymouth Rock An American class of chicken that lays a light-brown egg.

Varieties	Plumage color	Shank	Beak
Barred	gray white with a dark bar across each feather	yellow	yellow
(Also Bantam)			
White	white	dark yellow	yellow
(Also Bantam)			
Buff	buff (golden)	dark yellow	yellow
Silver-penciled	Male neck & back white with black edging of feather; rest of body black with some white	yellow	yellow
	Female gray with black penciling; gives lacy appearance	light yellow	yellow
Partridge	Male neck & back feathers green black with red edging, rest of body darker slate	yellow	yellow
	Female neck & back feathers black with red lacing, rest of body slate	light yellow	yellow

Columbian	mostly white, neck & tail feathers are black with white lacing	yellow	yellow with a dark stripe
Blue	Male primarily slate blue with feathers laced with black, upper sections dark appearance	yellow	yellow
	Female primarily even shade of slate blue with narrow black lacing	light yellow	yellow

See Part 2: Poultry Breeds and Varieties

Pm Symbol for the element promethium.

pneumococci The spherical bacteria that cause pneumonia.
See Part 2: Microorganism, Media

pneumonia Inflammation of the lungs.

Po Symbol for the element polonium.

poach To cook in water just below the boiling point (fish or eggs).

poi Fresh or fermented taro tubers.

point-of-sales material Advertising to be used by a retailer.

point of shoulder Lower end of shoulder blade.

poise Measurement of viscosity of a liquid; number of grams/centimeter/second.

1 poise = 100 centipoise
= 2.089×10^{-3} pound (weight) second/sq ft
= 0.067 pound (mass) foot-second

poison Any substance which coming in contact with the body (in a variety of routes) in small amounts may cause damage to structures, disruption of function, or death.
See Part 2: Food Poisoning, Bacteria; Plant and Animal Poisoning; Poisonous Plants

poison vetch A plant having a toxic principle.
See Part 2: Poisonous Plants

Poisson distribution A frequency distribution in which the variables are counted rather than measured. Information available: the number of times an event occurs, for example, number of "heads" when a coin is tossed 10 times.

poivrade A brown sauce with pepper.

pokeweed A plant having a toxic principle.
See Part 2: Poisonous Plants

Poland China A meat-type breed of hogs originating in south-western Ohio with much the same early breeding as the Spotted Poland China; the Berkshire and Irish Grazier were then used to improve the type; these contributed the solid color, which is black preferably with 6 white points, and a drooping ear.
See Part 2: Swine Breeds

polar A liquid with a high dielectric constant, e.g., water.

polarimetry An optical analysis based upon the rotation of polarized light when it passes through a solution.

policeman A stirring rod made of glass and fitted with a rubber tip; used for loosening precipitates from glassware.

poliomyelitis A crippling disease caused by a virus which attacks motor nerve centers in the spine.
See Part 2: Infectious Diseases, Food-Borne

polished rice Rice grain with husk and bran removed. *See also* **rice.**

Polish sausage Coarsely chopped beef and pork that is normally made into 6-in. lengths.
See Part 2: Sausage, Types

poll The top of the head; cut horns.

pollack *See* **pollock**

polled (muley) Naturally hornless; absence of horns.
Inheritance of horns:
(1) Horned cattle $(xx) \times$ homozygous polled cattle $(yy) \rightarrow$ offspring heterozygous polled (xy).
(2) Horned cattle $(xx) \times$ heterozygous polled cattle $(xy) \rightarrow \frac{1}{2}$ offspring horned (xx) and $\frac{1}{2}$ offspring heterozygous polled cattle (xy).

x = gene for horned
y = gene for polled
xy = heterozygous polled

Polled Cattle Herdbook Early name of Aberdeen Angus Cattle Society.

Polled Hereford Similar to Hereford cattle except that they have no horns; the cattle can be registered as both Hereford and as Polled Hereford. Warren Gammon of Des Moines, Iowa, started the breed from polled mutants of registered Herefords; polled characteristic is a dominant trait. *See also* **Double Standard Polled Hereford** and **Single Standard Polled Hereford.**
See Part 2: Beef and Dual-Purpose Cattle

Polled Shorthorn Shorthorn cattle without horns; registered in Shorthorn Herdbook. *See also* **Single Standard Polled Durham** and **Double Standard Polled Shorthorn.**
See Part 2: Beef and Dual-Purpose Cattle

poll evil A running sore behind the ears.

pollock (pollack, deep-sea fillet, Boston bluefish) A lean fish caught from Cape Cod to Cape Breton.
Composition: 77% H_2O, 20% protein, 1% fat, 1.3% ash.
See Part 2: Fish, Storage; Frozen Food Storage

polonium (Po) A radioactive element; at. no. 84; Group VIA of Periodic Table; mass number of most stable isotope, 210; electron configuration 2-8-18-32-18-6
orbit K L M N O P
oxidation state +2, +4

polyamide A natural or synthetic high polymer containing a $CONH_2$ group; among the natural products of this type are the proteins casein (milk) and zein (corn). Nylon is an example of a synthetic polyamide.

polybasic acid An acid having more than one replaceable hydrogen. *See also* **dibasic acid; tribasic acid.**

polyester A condensation reaction product of a dihydric alcohol and a dicarboxylic acid. Polyester films will remain flexible through a wide range of temperature; hard to seal on conventional equipment; coating with polyethylene provides heat-sealing properties; it is shrinkable, clear and has low O_2 and water permeability; base film for cooking directly in package; generally used in thicknesses of 0.0005 in. or less laminated to less expensive material.

polyethylene An addition polymer of ethylene $(C_2H_4)_n$ having various molecular weights; it may be either linear (amorphous) or crosslinked (crystalline). The linear type may be either high-density or low-density. One of the major uses of linear polyethylene is as packaging film and as a bonding agent in laminates. Film is available in several densities: it has good strength and heat-sealing properties, transparency, low water vapor transmission rate, and high gas transmission rate; low-density type is flexible, tough, transparent; medium-density is slightly stiffer; and high-density is stiff. Laminated polyethylene gives a film that is relatively impermeable to air and moisture; used for vacuum inert gas packaging.
See Part 2: Plastic Permeability; Wax

polyhydric Containing more than two replaceable hydrogens or hydroxyl groups per molecule.

polymorphism The property of a substance that enables it to solidify in different crystal forms; i.e., fat.

polyol General name for polyhydroxy compounds.

polypeptide *See* **peptide; protein**

polyphosphate *See* **phosphate; sodium phosphate**
See Part 2: Phosphate

polypropylene An addition polymer of propylene, from which are made films of high tensile strength and high grease resistance that are transparent, brittle at low temperatures and have medium O_2 and low water permeability. Used as packaging film; can be heat-sealed.

polysaccharide A large class of natural carbohydrate polymers, which includes cellulose, starches, water-soluble gums and seaweed products (phycocolloids).

polysorbate Nonionic surface-active agent made by esterifying sorbitol $(C_6H_8(OH)_6)$ with a fatty acid. They are called polyoxyethylene fatty acid esters. Used as emulsifiers, dispersing agents and as shortening in baked products. The various types are:
20: (polyoxyethylene, 20, sorbitan monolaurate) A mixture of laurate partial esters of sorbitol and sorbitol anhydrides (one mole) condensed with 20 moles of ethylene oxide.
60: (polyoxyethylene, 20, sorbitan monostearate) A mixture of stearate and palmitate partial esters of sorbitol anhydrides (one mole) condensed with 20 moles of ethylene oxide.
65: (polyoxyethylene, 20, sorbitan tristearate) A mixture of stearate and palmitate partial esters of sorbitol and its anhydrides (one mole) condensed with 20 moles of ethylene oxide.
80: (polyoxyethylene, 20, sorbitan monooleate) A mixture of oleate partial esters of sorbitol and sorbitol anhydrides (one mole) condensed with 20 moles of ethylene oxide.

polystyrene An addition polymer of styrene, $(C_6H_5CH{=}CH_2)_n$. It gives transparent, stiff films of high permeability and moderate temperature resistance.
See Part 2: Insulating Value; Insulation, Conductivity Values; Plastic Permeability

polyunsaturated fatty acid A fatty acid containing two or more double bonds.
See Part 2: Fats and Oils, Characteristics

polyurethane A high polymer made by a condensation reaction of a diisocyanate and a hydroxyl-containing molecule (alcohol or drying oil). Foams are used for building insulation.
See Part 2: Insulating Value

polyvinyl butyral (polyvinyl acetal) A high polymer made by a condensation reaction of polyvinyl alcohol and an aldehyde. Used as films for packaging and in glass laminates.
See Part 2: Plastic Permeability

polyvinyl chloride (PVC) A polymer of vinyl chloride $(CH_2{=}CHCl)_n$. Transparent film; good grease and solvent resistance; low to medium gas permeability; moderate temperature range; stretchable: can be heat-sealed.
See Part 2: Plastic Permeability

polyvinylidene chloride (Saran) A high polymer made by polymerization of vinylidene chloride $(CH_2{=}CCl_2)_n$. Film for packaging meats and poultry.
See Part 2: Plastic Permeability

pomace (pummace) Ground apples or fruit; residue left after extracting the oil from the castor bean or fish.
See Part 2: Fertilizer Materials

pomace wine A wine made by extracting marc or pomace with sugar solutions and fermenting the extract.

pome A subdivision of simple fruit; its ovary is a paper-like inner portion, around which is the fleshy part of the plant, e.g., apple, pear.
See Part 2: Fruit Classification

pomegranate (apple of Carthage; *Punica granatum*) A small tree that bears a hard, thick-skinned orange-red berry, divided into cells by walls of pith or juicy flesh; each cell contains a large quantity of seeds encased in a pink acid-sweet pulp; it may be eaten raw; juice used for drinks or wine; seeds are used for conserves or syrup.
Storage: 34°F, 85–90% relative humidity, 2 mo. storage life.

Raw composition: 82% H_2O, 0.6% protein, 0.3% fat, 16% carbohydrate, 0.5% ash; pH 3.0.
See Part 2: Fruit Composition; Fruit Storage

pomelo (pummelo, shaddock) A tree that has the largest fruit of the citrus species; it has a thick skin and a bitter pulp.
See Part 2: Fruit Storage

pomerol A mellow wine having a good color and bouquet.

pon-haws *See* **scrapple**

pont-l'-evêque A soft, somewhat compact curd, square-shaped, thin yellow rind cheese packed in a wooden chip box.

popcorn (*Zea mays everta*) Indian corn that explodes when exposed to dry heat. *See also* **corn.**
56 lb shelled/bu
70 lb on ear/bu
plant 4 to 6 lb per acre.
Unpopped storage: 32°F, 85% relative humidity.
Unpopped composition: 10% H_2O, 11–12% protein, 5% fat, 72% carbohydrate, 1.5% ash.
Popped composition: 4% H_2O, 11% protein, 5% fat, 79% carbohydrate, 1.3% ash.
See Part 2: Grain Products Composition; Seed, Chemical Composition

Pope's Eye Lymphatic gland in leg of mutton and beef.

popliteal *See* Part 2: Lymph Nodes, Ox, Lateral; Lymph Nodes, Pig; Lymph Nodes, Sheep

popover A thin batter baked into a hollow shell.

poppy seed (*Papaver somniferum* L.) Tiny blue seed of poppy plant used as seasoning; no narcotic content. The oil is obtained by pressing the seed.
Properties (oil):

specific gravity	0.924–0.927
refractive index (15.5°C)	1.476–1.478
saponification number	189–197
iodine number	133–158
solidifies	minus 18°C

See Part 2: Fats and Oils, Physical and Chemical Properties; Tocopherols

porcine Pertaining to swine.

porc salé aux choux Salt pork and cabbage.

porgy *See* **scup**

pork Flesh of swine; 1 barrel = 220 lb.
See Part 2: Animal Foods, Composition; Bone; Braising Time; Broiling Time and Temperature; Calories, Daily Recommendations; Food, Composition; Frozen Food Storage; Frozen Meat Storage Time; Glutamate; Glutamate Addition; Grades, Meat; Iron, Daily Recommendations; Liver; Meat and Meat Products Composition; Meat Composition; Meat, Frozen Storage; Meat Identification; Meat Label; Meat, Nutritive Value; Meat, Servings Per Pound; Meat Storage; Minerals, Food; Minerals, Plant or Animal Tissue; Niacin, Daily Recommendations; Pork Carcass, Retail Yield; Pork, Chart; Pork Cookery; Pork, Cooking; Pork Cooking Methods; Pork Cooking Yield; Pork Cuts; Pork Cuts and Uses; Pork Loin Carving; Pork Loin Cooking; Pork Loin Nomenclature; Pork, Percentages of Daily Recommended Allowances; Pork Storage; Pork Wholesale Cuts; Pork Yield; Riboflavin, Daily Recommendations; Roasting Meat; Roasting, Time and Temperature; Sausage Composition; Simmering Meat; Specific Heat, Meat; Thiamin, Daily Recommendations; Thiamin, Food; Vitamin A, Food

pork and beans *See* Part 2: Beans, Peas and Nuts

pork chop A single section of pork loin.
See Part 2: Braising Meat; Braising Time

pork fat *See* Part 2: Oils and Fats Composition; Unsaturated Fatty Acids

porklet *See* Part 2: Pork Loin Cooking

pork loaf *See* Part 2: Pork, Cooking

pork roll Chopped pork is cured and placed in a muslin container; it is then held until a tangy flavor develops; it is normally cooked but not smoked.

pork sausage A sausage made from ground fresh pork with seasoning added. Meat ground through the 3/16-in. plate. Max: 50% trimmable fat. Min: 9.4% protein. Max: 3% added water. May be fresh or smoked pork. Country-style: 75% lean, ground through the 1/4-in. plate. Storage temp: 28°–30°F.
Seasoning: 30 oz salt, 6 oz black pepper, and 2 oz sage per 100 lb of meat; for hot sausage, add 6 oz of red pepper.
See Part 2: Niacin, Daily Recommendations; Sausage Identification; Sausage Nutritive Value; Thiamin, Daily Recommendations

pork trimmings Regular: 50% lean, 50% trimmable fat; lean: 80% lean, 20% trimmable fat.

pork with barbecue sauce Min: 50% meat (weight of cooked and trimmed meat) or 72% uncooked meat.

porridge A hot breakfast cereal. *See also* **oat.**

port A fortified and blended red wine with a sweet, rich flavor; alcoholic content, 20% by volume.

port du salut (oka) A dessert cheese with a soft, creamy, buttery, yellow interior; it has a golden crust and a full rich, robust flavor. Made from whole or sour cows' milk and ripened 6–8 weeks.
See Part 2: Cheese Characteristics; Cheese, Vitamin Content; Vitamin A, Milk and Milk Products

porter English beer having 4.0% alcohol by volume.

porterhouse First steaks taken from the hip end of the short loin.
See Part 2: Beef Cuts; Beef Cuts and Uses; Beef Retail Yield; Broiling Meat; Broiling Time and Temperature; Meat Identification; Portion Size

Porto Rico A moist, sweet variety of sweet potato.

posterior *See* **dorsal (back)**; in comparative anatomy, *see* **caudal (tail)**.

posterior pituitary *See* **pituitary gland**

postmortem After death or slaughter.
See Part 2: pH, Post Mortem

potable Drinkable, e.g., potable water, pure enough to drink.

potage A thick soup.

potash Potassium carbonate, sulfate, or hydroxide.
See also **potassium**.
See Part 2: Fertilizer Materials

potassium (K) An alkali metal element; at. no. 19; at. wt. 39.100; Group IA of Periodic Table; electron configuration 2–8–8–1; oxidation state, +1
orbit K L M N
Body function: in all vegetable and animal cells.
See Part 2: Egg Products, Nutritive Value; Fruit and Vegetables Composition; Grain Analysis; Lemon Juice Composition; Macaroni and Noodles Composition; Manure Analysis; Meat, Nutritive Value; Minerals, Food; Minerals, Plant or Animal Tissue; Normal Solutions; Nutrients in Crops; pH and Availability of Plant Nutrients; Potassium; Potassium-Rich Foods; Tomato and Tomato Products, Composition; Wastes, Agricultural and Industrial; Wheat, Minerals; Wheat Products Composition

potassium alginate *See* **algin**

potassium alum *See* **aluminum potassium sulfate**

potassium bicarbonate ($KHCO_3$) Substitute for sodium carbonate in baking soda.
See Part 2: Normal Solutions

potassium bisulfite ($KHSO_3$) Used as preservative in foods (except meats). *See also* **sulfur dioxide**.

potassium carbonate K_2CO_3 A general-purpose food additive.
See Part 2: Normal Solutions

potassium chloride KCl Used as nutrient and dietary supplement.
See Part 2: Fertilizer Materials; Normal Solutions

potassium cyanide KCN Poisonous compound used as insecticide and fumigant.
See Part 2: Normal Solutions

potassium dichloroisocyanurate $Cl_2K(NCO)_3$ Used as sanitizer in dishwashing compounds, etc.
See Part 2: Chlorine Availability; Sanitizers

potassium hydrogen tartrate *See* Part 2: Reagents, Normal Solutions

potassium hydroxide KOH Food additive and bleaching agent.
See Part 2: Concentration of Commercial Strengths of Acids and Bases; Normal Solutions

potassium magnesium sulfate $K_2SO_4 \cdot 2MgSO_4$ Used as a fertilizer ingredient.
See Part 2: Fertilizer Materials

potassium metabisulfite $K_2S_2O_5$ Used as sanitizer and food preservative. *See also* **sulfur dioxide**.

potassium metaphosphate KPO_3 A fertilizer material 0–58–35.

potassium nitrate KNO_3 (saltpeter) (niter) Used in meat curing and as fertilizer ingredient.
See Part 2: Fertilizer Materials; Nitrate, Meat Curing

potassium nitrite KNO_2 Used in meat curing.
See Part 2: Nitrate, Meat Curing

potassium oxide K_2O A chemical reagent and intermediate.
See Part 2: Normal Solutions

potassium permanganate $KMnO_4$ An oxidizing agent.
Gram equivalent wt $KMnO_4$ (oxidizing agent in acidic solution) = 158/5 = 31.6 g
Gram equivalent wt $KMnO_4$ (oxidizing agent in nonacidic solution) = 158/3 = 52.7 g.
See Part 2: Normal Solutions

potassium phosphates (1) Dibasic (dipotassium monophosphate; dipotassium phosphate) K_2HPO_4. (2) Monobasic (potassium biphosphate; potassium dihydrogen phosphate; monopotassium phosphate) KH_2PO_4. (3) Tribasic (tripotassium phosphate) K_3PO_4. (4) Polymetaphosphate (potassium metaphosphate; potassium Kurrol's salt) $(KPO_3)_x$. (5) Pyrophosphate; (tetrapotassium pyrophosphate) $K_4P_2O_7$. (6) Tripolyphosphate (pentapotassium triphosphate; potassium triphosphate) $K_5P_3O_{10}$.

potassium sulfate K_2SO_4 A neutral fertilizer material; 0–0–48; a potassium fertilizer that can be used where chlorine is harmful.
See Part 2: Fertilizer Materials

potassium sulfite K_2SO_3 Sulfite salt. *See also* **sulfur dioxide**.

potassium tartrate $K_2C_4H_4O_6$.
See Part 2: Normal Solutions; Reagents, Normal Solutions

potato (Irish; *Solanum tuberosum*) A tuberous root eaten as a vegetable; a perennial herb with rhizomes which become swollen at the tip to produce the edible tubers. Classified according to maturity date and skin color (brown to white); yield more food value per acre than cereal. Used as a cooked vegetable, for making chips, flour, dehydrated potatoes, starch, dextrose, liquor and livestock feed; 110 to 125 days to maturity (Irish); 60 lb/bu; seed 1500 to 2000 lb/acre; size of seed approx. 1½ oz; spacing 10 in. in rows 3 ft apart; yield 15–17 ton/acre.
Approximate nutrient used to grow:

	200 lb tubers	tops
N (lb)	43	60
P_2O_5 (lb)	17	10
K_2O (lb)	77	55

Storage: In darkness, well ventilated (85–90% relative humidity), cool room (early crop 50°–55°F, late crop 38°–50°F); use within 1 to 4 weeks.

Freezing pt. 28°F.
1 lb = 3 medium sized
1 cup = 165 g (5.8 oz)
1 lb fresh = 2¼ cups cooked
1 cup cooked = 165 g (5.7 oz)
1 lb fresh = 1.75 cup mashed
1 cup mashed = 210 g (7.3 oz)
1 lb dried granules = 2¼ cups
1 cup dried granules = 200 g (7.1 oz)
1 lb dried granules = 10.5 cups reconstituted
1 cup dried granules reconstituted = 210 g (7.5 oz)
1 peck = 15 lb
1 bu = 60 lb
1 barrel = 165 lb
1 bag = 50 lb
100 lb fresh = 23–25 lb dried

Composition:

	H_2O (%)	Protein (%)	Fat (%)	Carbohydrate (%)	Ash (%)	pH
Raw	78–80	2	0.1	17–18	1	5.5–6.0
Dried	7	7	0.7	82	3	

See Part 2: Ascorbic Acid; Calcium, Daily Recommendations; Calories, Daily Recommendations; Canned Spoilage Related to pH; Food, Composition; Fruit and Vegetables Composition; Fruit and Vegetables, Disease; Frying Time; Iron; Iron, Daily Recommendations; Microwave Cooking, Fresh Vegetables; Microwave Processing Time; Minerals, Food; Niacin; Niacin, Daily Recommendations; Nicotinic Acid, Food; Nutrients in Crops; Pectin Content; Phosphorus; pH Values of Biological Materials; Plant Foods, Composition; Poisonous Plants; Portion Size; Potassium; Riboflavin; Riboflavin, Food; Starches and Starchy Roots Composition; Starch, Microappearance; Standards, Processed Fruit and Vegetable Products; Storage; Storage, Dry; Storage Times; Sugar, Vegetables; Sweet Potato and Irish Potato; Thiamin, Daily Recommendations; Thiamin; Thiamin, Food; Transit Temperature; Vegetable Boiling; Vegetable Composition; Vegetable Plants; Vegetables, Classification; Vegetable Servings; Vegetable Storage; Vegetable Yield, Canned and Frozen; Vegetable Yield, Frozen, Canned and Fresh; Vitamin A, Food; Vitamin C

potato (sweet) (*Ipomoea batatas*) A tuberous root eaten as a vegetable; 56 lb/bu, green; 47 lb/bu, cured; spacing, 6 to 12 inches in rows 3½ feet apart; curing, 5–8 days at 85°F and 90% relative humidity; storage 55°F.

potato beetle *See* Part 2: Insect Control

potato chips Thin slices of deep fat-fried potato; max. 3% H_2O; 32–40% fat absorption during cooking.
Composition: 2% H_2O, 5% protein, 40% fat, 50% carbohydrate, 3% ash.
See Part 2: Calories, Daily Recommendations; Vegetable Composition

potato flour A fine powder made from cooked potatoes which have been dried and ground.
Composition: 8% H_2O, 8% protein, 1% fat, 80% carbohydrate, 4% ash.

potato glucose (dextrose) agar *See* Part 2: Microbiological Examination of Dairy Products; Microbiological Media; Microorganism, Culture Media, Dairy and Food Products; Microorganism, Media

potato grades (USDA) U. S. Fancy; No. 1; U.S. Commercial.

potato infusion agar *See* Part 2: Microorganism, Media

potato maltose agar *See* Part 2: Microorganism, Media

potato peeling (1) Mechanical (abrasive); 20% loss. (2) Flame (boiling saturated soft brine, 2000°F for 30 sec, washing). (3) Lye or caustic soda solution.

potato starch (farina) A carbohydrate derived from potato and used as a stabilizing agent.

pot cheese *See* **farmers cheese**

potential Volts are the unit of measurement of electrical potential.

potentiator A substance that imparts flavor to a food product to a much greater extent than an enhancer. Effective in concentrations of parts per billion, compared with parts per thousand for enhancers. The so-called 5′-nucleotides, e.g., riboflavin 5′-phosphate, are typical potentiators.

Potomac A variety of orchard grass.

potpie *See* Part 2: Meat Composition

pot roast A meat (usually beef) cooked by braising. *See also* **braise.**
See Part 2: Beef Cuts; Beef Cuts and Uses; Beef Retail Yield; Braising Meat; Braising Time; Meat Composition

poultry Birds domesticated for their food value.
Meat storage: Coldest part of refrigerator (32°F); use within 1 to 4 days; frozen (−10°F), storage life, 6 months.
Styles:
(1) Ready to cook (RTC), giblets and neck in body cavity.
(2) RTC halves.
(3) RTC quarters.
(4) RTC cut-up, carcass less the back, neck and giblets; remainder is same proportion as carcass.
(5) RTC parts.
Types:
(1) Fresh chilled but not frozen.
(2) Frozen less than 60 days.
(3) Frozen more than 60 days.
(4) Special Frozen.
See Part 2: Animal Foods, Composition; Bacteria on Chickens at Various Holding Temperatures; Bone; Bone Age; Calories, Daily Recommendations; Egg Incubation Periods; Frozen Food Storage; Glutamate; Meat and Meat Products Composition; Meat, Frozen Storage; Meat, Servings per Pound; Microwave Processing Time;

Molds, Mycotoxins; Niacin, Daily Recommendations; pH, Post Mortem; Portion Size; Poultry Breeds and Varieties; Poultry Class; Poultry Composition; Poultry Cooking, Frozen; Poultry Dressing Percentage; Poultry Grade Stamp; Poultry Inspection and Grade Stamp; Poultry Inspection Stamp; Poultry Roasting; Poultry Yield; Riboflavin, Daily Recommendations; Specific Heat, Meat; Storage Times; Tenderness of Poultry; Thiamin, Daily Recommendations

poultry by-product meal Dry-rendered, ground tissue of poultry exclusive of feathers, gizzard and intestinal contents.

poultry dressing percentage

$$\frac{\text{ready to cook wt}}{\text{live weight}} = \%\ \text{dressing}$$

	(%)
broilers-fryers	70
hens	74
turkey fryers	74
turkey hens and toms:	
small	76
large	80

poultry giblets The gizzard, heart, liver, etc., of a chicken or other poultry, usually chopped and and added to gravy after long boiling. *See also* **giblet.**

Storage: Remove from bag and rewrap; place in coldest part of refrigerator; use within 1 to 2 days.

poultry grades U.S. Grade A; U.S. Grade B; U.S. Grade C.

poultry in sausage Chicken and turkey may be added to a maximum of 15% of comminuted cooked product (excluding water) without using a poultry name. If poultry is used in the name of the product there is no limit to the quantity used, but must be declared in ingredients. Ratio of poultry skin to muscle must be in same proportions as in the whole bird. Kidney and sex glands cannot be included. All-meat product must have the poultry skin removed. All-beef product can contain no poultry.

pound (apoth.) A measure of weight; same as troy pound.

pound (avoirdupois) (U.S. or Br.) A measure of weight.

1 av. lb = 4,5359 × 10^5 milligrams (mg)
= 7,000 grains (gr)
= 453.592,427,7 grams (g)
= 350 scruples (apoth.)
= 291.666,7 pennyweight (dwt)
= 256.00 drams (av.)
= 116.666,7 drams (troy) (apoth.)
= 16 avoir ounces (oz avoir.)
= 14.583,333 troy ounces (oz troy) (apoth.)
= 1.215,277,8 troy pounds (lb troy) (apoth).
= 0.45359 kilogram (kg)
= 0.00050 net-short ton (2,000 lb)
= 0.0004536 metric ton (1,000 kg)
= 0.0004464 gross-long ton (2,240 lb)

See Part 2: Weight

pound (av.) per acre Weight per unit area.

1 pound (av.)/acre = 1.121 kg/ha

pound (troy) (apoth.) (U.S. or Br.) A measure of weight used for weighing gold, silver and jewels (same as apothecaries pound)

1 troy lb = 3.7324 × 10^5 milligrams (mg)
= 5,760 grains (gr)
= 373.241,77 grams
= 288 scruples (℈) (apoth.)
= 240 pennyweight (dwt) (troy)
= 210.651,4 drams (av.)
= 96 drams (ʒ) (troy) (apoth.)
= 13.165,714 av. ounces (oz av.)
= 12 troy ounces (oz troy) (apoth.)
= 0.822,857,1 av. pounds (lb av.)
= 0.37324 kilogram (kg)
= 0.0004114 net-short ton (2,000 lb)
= 0.0003732 metric ton (1,000 kg)
= 0.0003674 gross-long ton (2,240 lb)

pound cake A cake consisting of one pound each of flour, butter, whole eggs, sugar.

pound per bushel (U.S.) A measure of density—specific weights.

1 lb/bu = 21.6962 pounds per cubic yard (lb/yd^3)
= 12.8718 kilograms per cu. meter (kg/m^3)
= 0.80356 pound per cubic foot (lb/ft^3)
= 0.125 pound per gallon, dry (U.S.)
= 0.10742 pound per gallon, liquid (U.S.)
= 0.01287 gram per cubic centimeter (g/cm^3)
= 0.0004650 pound per cubic inch (lb/in^3)

pound per cubic foot (lb/ft^3) A measure of density.

1 lb/cu ft = 27 pounds per cubic yard (lb/yd^3)
= 16.0184 kilograms per cubic meter (kg/m^3)
= 1.24446 pounds per bushel (U.S.)
= 0.15556 pound per gallon dry (U.S.)
= 0.13368 pound per gallon, liquid (U.S.)
= 0.01602 gram per cubic centimeter (g/cm^3)
= 0.0005787 pound per cubic inch (lb/in^3)

pound per cubic inch (lb/in^3) A measure of density.

1 lb/cu in. = 46,656 pounds per cubic yard (lb/yd^3)
= 27,679.7 kilograms per cu meter (kg/m^3)
= 2,150.42 pounds per bushel (U.S.)
= 1,728 pounds per cubic foot (lb/ft^3)

1 lb/cu in. = 268.803 pounds per gallon dry (U.S.)
= 231 pounds per gallon, liquid (U.S.)
= 27.6797 grams per cu centimeter (g/cm^3)

pound per cubic yard (lb/yd^3) A measure of density.
1 lb/cu yd = 0.59327 kilograms per cu. meter (kg/m^3)
= 0.04609 pound per bushel (U.S.)
= 0.03704 pound per cubic foot (lb/ft^3)
= 0.005762 pound per gallon, dry (U.S.)
= 0.004951 pound per gallon, liquid (U.S.)
= 0.0005933 gram per cubic centimeter (g/cm^3)
= 0.00002143 pound per cubic inch (lb/in^3)

pound per foot Mass (weight) per length.
1 lb/ft = 14.88 grams/centimeter
= 1.488 kilograms/meter

pound per gallon (dry) (U.S.) A measure of density—specific weights.
1 lb/gal = 173.570 pounds per cubic yard (lb/yd^3)
= 102.974 kilograms per cubic meter (kg/m^3)
= 8 pounds per bushel (U.S.)
= 6.42851 pounds per cubic foot (lb/ft^3)
= 0.85937 pound per gallon, liquid (U.S.)
= 0.010297 gram per cu centimeter (g/cm^3)
= 0.003720 pound per cu inch (lb/in^3)

pound per gallon (liquid) (U.S.) A measure of density.
1 lb/gal = 201.974 pounds per cu yard (lb/yd^3)
= 119.826 kilograms per cu meter (kg/m^3)
= 9.30920 pound per bushel (U.S.)
= 7.48052 pound per cu foot (lb/ft^3)
= 1.16365 pound per gallon, dry (U.S.)
= 0.11983 gram per cu centimeter (g/cm^3)
= 0.004329 pound per cu inch (lb/in^3)

pound per square foot A measure of pressure.
1 lb/sq ft (psf) = 0.35911 millimeter (columns of Hg 13.59593 sp. g.)
= 0.01602 foot (columns of water, max. density at 4°C, 39°F)
= 0.01414 inch (columns of Hg)
= 0.006944 pound per sq inch (psi)
= 0.004882 meter (columns of water)
= 0.0004882 kilogram per sq centimeter (kg/cm^2)
= 0.0004725 atmosphere, standard (760 mm Hg)

pound per square inch (psi) A measure of pressure.
1 lb/sq inch (psi) = 144 pounds per sq foot (psf)
= 51.7116 millimeters (columns of Hg 13.59593 sp. g.)
= 2.30665 feet (columns of water, max. density at 4°C, 39°F)
= 2.03588 inches (columns of Hg)
= 0.70307 meter (columns of water)
= 0.07031 kilogram per sq centimeter (kg/cm^2)
= 0.070 kilogram per sq centimeter

powdered cream Dried cream; 19 lb milk = 1 lb powdered cream.

powdered milk Dried milk; 7.6 lb milk = 1 lb powdered milk.

powdered sugar Pulverized granulated sugar.
XX powdered = coarse
XXXX powdered = fine

PPC *See* Part 2: Blood

P.P. factor *See* **niacin**

PPLO *See* Part 2: Microorganism, Media

ppm *See* **parts per million**

Pr Symbol for the element praseodymium.

practical (pract.) A designation of a grade of chemical purity; a medium purity grade that is suitable for most syntheses. *See also* **grade.**

praline A burnt almond or a brown sugar-pecan candy.

praseodymium (Pr) A rare-earth element; at. no. 59; Group IIIB of Periodic Table; at. wt. 140.92; electron configuration 2-8-18-20-9-2;
orbit K L M N O P
oxidation state +3

prawn A shell fish; 50% edible (avg. 20% protein). *See also* **shrimp.**

precipitate Separation by gravity of heavy particles from a suspension.

precipitated lime A liming material composed of 80-95% $CaCO_3$; each pound has the neutralizing equivalent of 0.85 to 1 pound of $CaCO_3$ (or approximately this quantity of dolomitic limestone).

precook To simmer for a short time preliminary to cooking.

precrural Near or in front of the thighs.
See Part 2: Lymph Nodes, Ox, Lateral; Lymph Nodes, Pig; Lymph Nodes, Sheep

pregelatinized starch Cooked and dried starch which will form a paste with cold water.

pregnancy Being with young; time from conception to birth. *See also* **gestation period.**
See Part 2: Food, Water Intake

premiéres côtes de Bordeaux Medium-sweet white wine.

prepectoral *See* Part 2: Lymph Nodes, Ox; Lymph Nodes, Pig

prepotency Unusual ability of an animal to make its young resemble the parent.

prescapular *See* Part 2: Lymph Nodes, Ox, Lateral; Lymph Nodes, Pig; Lymph Nodes, Sheep

preservation Maintaining food in edible condition over long periods of time.
See Part 2: Radiation Preservation

preservative A substance that protects against spoilage, discoloration, or decay. *See also* **antioxidant.**

preserves A fruit in its original or cut shape packed in a heavy syrup; a semisolid product made by combining 45 parts of fruit with 55 parts of sugar and cooking until final soluble solids content is 68% (65% some fruits).
Storage: After opening, cover and refrigerate.

pressed cheese *See* **farmers cheese**

pressure (water)
0.433 lb/sq in. of base in a column of water 1 foot high.
1 lb/sq in. of base is a column of water 2.31 ft high.
Feet of Head (water) = (2.31) (lb pressure/sq in.).
lb pressure/sq in. = (0.433) (feet of head of water).
See Part 2: Steam, Properties; Temperatures Corresponding to Gauge Pressure at Various Altitudes

pressure cooker An air-tight vessel used to cook by means of superheated water under pressure.

presternal *See* Part 2: Lymph Nodes, Ox; Lymph Nodes, Pig

pretzel (bretzel) A crisp brittle snack food with a cracker and salt taste; its shape is a 2-looped ring, a single ring, and thin or thick rods; they may be either hard or soft.
Composition: 3.5–5% H_2O, 10% protein, 5% fat, 76% carbohydrate, 5% ash, 3–7% salt.
See Part 2: Fermented Ingredients; Grain Products Composition

primal cuts (hog carcass) Boston butt, picnic, loin, ham, belly; 43 to 55% of live hog weight.

primary Constant composition and high purity; principal; carbon atom which is united by a single valence to chain or ring, $CH_3(CH_2)_nCH_2-$.

primary muscle fiber bundles Bundles made up of muscle fibers bound together by perimysium.

primary root *See* Part 2: Corn Kernel; Wheat Kernel; Wheat Kernel Parts

primary standards (Pri. Std.) A designation of a grade of chemical purity; this is the highest grade of purity and can be used for direct preparation of standard solutions. *See also* **grade.**

prime Usual meaning is first, or highest quality.
See Part 2: Casings, Hog Bungs; Grades, Meat; Meat Grade Stamps

prime-steam lard Lard rendered in a closed container with steam.

primost cheese *See* **mysost cheese**
See Part 2: Cheese Characteristics

prince's plume A plant having a toxic principle.
See Part 2: Poisonous Plants

Pri. Std. *See* **primary standards**

pritch stick A stick sharp on both ends used to hold a beef carcass on its back while removing the hide; one end is secured in the floor and the other end in the brisket.

Prize head lettuce A variety having green leaves tinged with a reddish bronze color.

probability The likelihood of an event taking place.

$$\text{Probability of } a = \frac{a}{a+b}$$

a = number of ways event "a" can occur
b = number of ways event "b" can occur

p = probability of success
$1 - p$ = probability of failure

Probability (P) of 2 independent events occurring simultaneously

$P = q \times r$
q = probability of first event
r = probability of second event

Probability (P) that 2 mutually exclusive (if one happens, the other cannot happen) events will occur;

$P = q + r$
q = probability of 1st event
r = probability of 2nd event

Probability that an event will occur r times in n trials is:

$$P = \frac{n(n-1)(n-2)\cdots(n-r+1)p^r(1-p)^{n-r}}{r!}$$

p = probability of its occurring on a single trial.
See Part 2: Defectives in Lot; Normal Curve; Paired Comparisons; Paired Taste Tests; Taste Panel, Difference Tests; Triangular Taste Test + Preference; Triangular Taste Test Probability

probable error (r) (R) A method of expressing error for a single observation and an average of a series of observations such that the numbers of errors greater than the probable error is equal to the number of errors less than the probable error.

Probable error of a single observation

$$r = \pm 0.6745 \sqrt{\frac{\Sigma(V^2)}{n-1}}$$

$\Sigma(V^2)$ = sum of squares of deviation from the average
n = number of observations

Probable error of an average of measurements (R)

$$R = \pm .6745 \sqrt{\frac{\Sigma(V^2)}{n(n-1)}}$$

Probable error = 0.6745 mean square error
Probable error = 0.8453 average error

process cheddar A cheddar cheese having the composition 39–40% H_2O, 22% protein, 31% fat, 4% ash, 1.7% salt.

process cheese A mixture of fresh and aged natural cheese that has been pasteurized; may have added flavors. A cheese made by melting various types of cheese together and adding butter, milk or cream.
Composition: 40% H_2O, 23–26% protein, 26–30% fat, 1–2% carbohydrate, 4–5% ash.

process cheese food Similar to process cheese but may have added nonfat dry milk, whey solids, and water.
Composition: 43% H_2O, 20% protein, 24% fat, 1% salt.

process cheese spread Similar to process cheese foods but with higher moisture and lower milk-fat content.
Composition: 47–48% H_2O, 16% protein, 21–22% fat, 1% salt.

processing Subjecting a material to a sequence of treatments, e.g., mixing, heating, forming, packaging, etc.
See Part 2: Microwave Processing Time

progesterone $C_{21}H_{30}O_2$ A hormone isolated from bovine ovaries which can be used in treatment of potential abortion and severe dysmenorrhea.

prolamin A simple protein that is insoluble in water, dilute salt solutions or absolute alcohol but soluble in 70–80% alcohol.

prolific Bearing many young.

proline (2-pyrrolidine carboxylic acid) A heterocyclic amino acid. A dietary supplement and culture medium obtained by hydrolysis of protein.

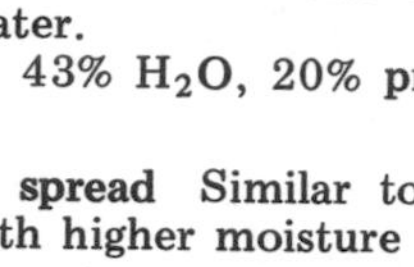

See Part 2: Amino Acids; Amino Acid, Solubilities; Corn, Amino Acids; Grain Analysis; Manure Analysis; Wheat, Amino Acids; Wheat Products, Amino Acid Compositions

promethium (Pm) A radioactive rare-earth element of the lanthanide series; at. no. 61; mass number of most stable isotope 147; oxidation state +3; Group IIIB of Periodic Table;
electron configuration 2-8-18-23-8-2
orbit K L M N O P

promoter A substance which enhances the activity of a catalyst.

proof (U.S.) A measurement of alcoholic strength; 1 degree of proof = ½ of the percentage of alcohol (by volume), e.g., 90 proof = 45% alcohol content.

proof spirit *See* **proof; British Proof Spirit**

pro-oxidant A substance which accelerates oxidation.

propagate To reproduce; to have young.

propane C_3H_8 A flammable hydrocarbon gas used as a fuel and refrigerant.
See Part 2: Refrigerant

propionic acid 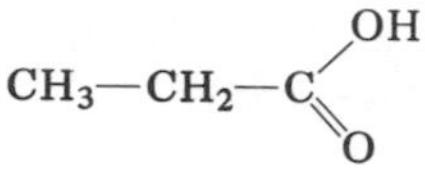

A saturated acid sometimes found as a free fatty acid in natural fat. The acid and its sodium and calcium salts are antimicrobial agents used in food to prevent mold and rope in bakery products and mold in milk products.
Levels used are 0.32% of flour in white bread and rolls, 0.38% of flour in whole wheat products, and 0.3% in cheese products.

propylene glycol $CH_3CHOHCH_2OH$ An emulsifier and preservative in food products.
See Part 2: Antioxidant Mixtures

propylene glycol alginate *See* **algin**

propylene oxide CH_3CHCH_2O A gas used for the sterilization of food, particularly dried and glacéd fruit, cocoa, gums, spices, starch, nut meats. It is flammable.

propyl gallate An antioxidant used to retard rancidity in fat; 0.01% in fat (total antioxidant 0.02% in combination).

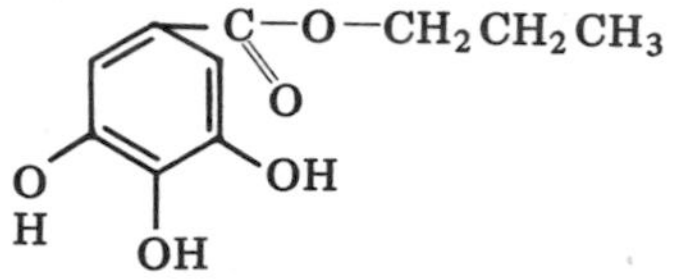

See Part 2: Antioxidants, Formulas; Antioxidant Mixtures; Antioxidant Structure

prosciutti A dry-cured ham coated with black pepper and originating in Italy.

prosciuttini Similar to a prosciutto except it is cooked, and ground black pepper is used as the principal seasoning.

prosciutto ham Italian style ham in which the skin is left on; it is dry-cured under pressure, given a mild heating process, and smoked, it is sliced very thin for eating.

Proskauer Beck medium *See* Part 2: Microorganism, Media

proso *See* **millet**

prosthetic group An active chemical group such as an enzyme or vitamin which promotes essential chemical transformation within the body. Such groups are sometimes called metabolites.

protactinium (Pa) A radioactive element of the actinide series; at. no. 91; at. wt. 231; Group IIIB of Periodic Table; oxidation states +5, +4; electron configuration 2-8-18-32-20-9-2
orbit K L M N O P Q

protamine Any of several simple natural proteins which contain only a few amino acids (mostly arginine); they are basic, water-soluble and not coagulated by heat; found in sperm cells.

protective coating A thin layer of a material which protects the substrate from oxidation or other chemical attack, e.g., packaging films. Paints. lacquers and electroplated metals also are in this classification.

protective colloid A colloidal substance such as gelatin which coats particles of fats in a mixture and thus keeps them from coalescing. This function is performed by lactalbumin in milk.

protein Any large complex polymer of α-amino acids linked through peptide bonds; m.w. may be up to several million. Essential in nutrition.
See Part 2: Bananas, Composition; Beans, Peas and Nuts; Beef Percentages of Daily Recommended Allowances; Cereal Nutrient Content; Cheese Composition; Cherry Composition; Composition of Food; Concentrated and Dried Milk Products; Corn Kernel Composition; Creams, Butter and Frozen Desserts; Cultured Dairy Products, Composition; Dairy Products, Composition; Egg Composition; Egg Specifications; Fats and Oils, Composition; Fish and Shellfish Composition; Flour, Extraction Rates; Fluid and Fermented Milks, Composition; Food, Composition; Fruit Composition; Grain Analysis; Grain Products Composition; Histochemical Test; Lamb Percentages of Daily Recommended Allowances; Lemon Juice Composition; Lime Juice Composition; Macaroni and Noodles Composition; Manure Analysis; Meat and Meat Products Composition; Meat Composition; Meat, Nutritive Value; Milk and Cheese Composition; Milk Breeds, Composition; Milk Composition; Milk, Concentrated Products; Milk, Dry Products; Milk, Mammals, Composition; Milk, Species; Minerals, Plant or Animal Tissue; Minerals (Trace), Limits; Myofibrillar Proteins of Muscle; Oils and Fats Composition; Oil Meals Composition; Packinghouse By-Products Composition; Plant Foods, Composition; Pork, Percentages of Daily Recommended Allowances; Poultry Composition; Protein and Amino Acids, Color Reactions; Protein Factors; Pulses, Nuts and Seeds Composition; Recommended Daily Dietary Allowance; Sausage Composition; Sausage Nutritive Value; Seed, Chemical Composition; Seed Composition; Soups, Composition; Soybean Composition; Starches and Starchy Roots Composition; Sugars and Sweets Composition; Sugars and Syrups Composition; Tomato and Tomato Products, Composition; Turkey Composition; Variety Meat Percentage of Daily Recommended Allowances; Vegetable Composition; Wheat and Flour Composition; Wheat, Parts of Grain; Wheat Products Composition

protein determination *See* **Kjeldahl determination**

proteolytic enzyme An enzyme which decomposes proteins to their component amino acids, as occurs in the digestion of foods, e.g., pepsin. *See also* **enzyme.**

proteose A hydrolytic product of proteins that is water-soluble, not coagulated by heat, and is precipitated by saturated ammonium sulfate.

proteose agar *See* Part 2: Microorganism, Media

proteose tryptone agar *See* Part 2: Microorganism, Culture Media, Dairy and Food Products

Proteus An intestinal microorganism.
See Part 2: Intestinal Microorganisms; Intestinal Microorganisms in Triple-Sugar Agar; Microorganism, Media; Microorganism Reactions on Differential Tube Media; Spoilage, Protein Foods

proton A positively charged particle in all atomic nuclei; it has a mass of 1 and is identical with the hydrogen ion H^+; charge, 4.802×10^{-10} absolute electrostatic units (esu); diameter, 2.8×10^{-13} cm.
See Part 2: Constants, Fundamental

protoplasm The basic material of all plant and animal cells; a complex mixture of proteins, amino acids, phosphorus, and ribose sugars.
See Part 2: Moisture in Biological Materials

protozoa Animal organisms consisting of a single cell, e.g., amoeba, paramecium.
See Part 2: Culture Media

provascular *See* Part 2: Wheat Kernel Parts

provolette cheese *See* **Italian cheese**

provoloncini *See* **Italian cheese**

provolone (provolette) (provoloncini) (salami provolone) An Italian hard cheese; a Pasta Filata cheese.
Shapes: Pear, ball, sausage; stretch cheese; may be smoked
Composition: 38% H_2O, 28% protein, 28% fat, 4% ash, 3% salt.
Similar types of cheese are mozzarella and scamorza. *See also* **Italian cheese.**
See Part 2: Cheese Characteristics; Cheese, Vitamin Content

provoloni A hard, white, mellow-to-sharp, piquant, smokey, tangy, cheese made from whole milk; it has a golden yellow to brown shiny surface bound with a cord, and a light, creamy to yellowish-white interior; pear to sausage shape. *See also* **Italian cheese.**

proximate analysis Chemical analysis showing content of water, protein, fat, carbohydrate and ash.

prune (*Prunus domestica*) A fruit that is 83% edible; the primary sugar is dextrose; a plum that can be dried whole, without fermentation of the pit; dried plums; usually a dried plum that is purplish black. *See also* **plum.**
Composition:

	H_2O (%)	Protein (%)	Fat (%)	Carbohydrate (%)	Ash (%)	pH
Dry prune	3-24	2-3	0.5	71-91	2	3.1-5.4
Juice	80	0.4	0.1	19	0.5	3.7-4.3

1 lb dried = 2½ lb California fresh
= 3-4 lb others, fresh

1 lb dried, whole = 2½ cups (1 cup = 175 g or 6.2 oz)
= 4–4½ cups cooked (230 g or 8.1 oz).
1 lb canned = 10–14 prunes
Prune size:
French: 30 to excess of 120/lb
Italian: 25 to 100/lb
Imperial or sugar: 15 to 70/lb
See Part 2: Food, Composition; Fruit, Availability; Fruit Canning Dates; Fruit Classification; Fruit Composition; Fruit, Dried, Simmering; Fruit Frozen Yield; Fruit Servings; Microwave Cooking, Fruit; Minerals, Food; Plant Foods, Composition; Potassium-Rich Foods; Standards, Processed Fruit and Vegetable Products

PSE Pale, soft, exudative pork.
See Part 2: pH, Post Mortem

Pseudomonas An intestinal microorganism.
See Part 2: Intestinal Microorganisms; Intestinal Microorganisms in Triple-Sugar Agar; Microbiological Media; Microorganism Reactions on Differential Tube Media; Spoilage, Fat in Food; Spoilage, Protein Foods

pseudosel agar *See* Part 2: Microbiological Media

psi (Ψ, ψ) (1) Greek letter with an English equivalent of ps. (2) Abbreviation for pounds per square inch.

psoas major Muscle of the lumbar area that lies under the lumbar vertebrae; in cross section it is larger and more dorsal than the psoas minor; in combination with the psoas minor, it is often called the tenderloin or fillet.

psoas minor Muscle of the lumbar area that lies under the lumbar vertebrae. *See also* ***psoas major***.

psychrophilic bacteria Bacteria that grow at a low temperature; minimum growth temperature -5° to +5°C; optimum growth temperature 20° to 30°C; maximum growth temperature 35° to 45°C.

bacteria genera	mold genera
Achromobacter	*Cladosporium*
Flavobacterium	*Mucor*
Pseudomonas	*Penicillium*
	Thamnidium

psychrotrophic (psychotropic) *See* Part 2: Microbiological Standards, Dairy

psyllium seed (fleaseed) Seeds that can be chewed, used as cereals or in vegetable drinks.

Pt Symbol for the element platinum.

ptomaine poisoning Ptomaine means decarboxylated amino acids; since they are not detrimental to health when eaten, this is a misnomer; as used today, the term is synonymous with staphylococcus food poisoning.

Pu Symbol for the element plutonium.

puberty Age at which organs become capable of reproduction; for the ages of farm animals see gestation period.

pubic symphysis The point at which the two pelvic bones fuse and at which they are separated in splitting of the carcass.

pubis Flat bone forming the floor of the pelvic bone.

pudding A dessert, usually baked or boiled, based on bread, rice, apples, plums, etc., together with milk, flour, sugar and flavoring.
See Part 2: Portion Size; Stabilizers, Thickeners

puff-ball (***Calvatia gigantea***) A large edible fungus (when young and firm fleshed); it is white and turns yellow and brown as it matures.

puffed rice A breakfast cereal made by heating rice under pressure and then rapidly releasing the pressure causing the super-heated steam in the rice to expand the kernel; 1 cup = ½ oz.
Composition: 7% protein, 85% carbohydrate, 7% fat.

puffed wheat A breakfast cereal made by heating wheat in a closed container to a temperature of 288°C; the cylinder is suddenly opened and the super-heated water changes to steam inside the grain, causing it to increase in size; 1 cup = 0.4 oz.
Composition: 14% protein, 71–75% carbohydrate, 2–7% fat.

pull date The last day a retail store may offer an item for sale; the date is designed to offer a reasonable amount of time to store and use product at home.

pullet A young female chicken before it reaches the age of egg laying.

pulley size Formula for calculating the size of pulley:

pulley size (driven machine)

$$= \frac{[\text{D(of driver pulley)}]\ [\text{RPM of driver}]}{\text{Recommended RPM of Driven}}$$

pulley size (driver)

$$= \frac{[\text{D(of driven pulley)}]\ \left[\begin{array}{c}\text{Recommended RPM}\\ \text{of Driven}\end{array}\right]}{\text{RPM of Driver}}$$

speed of driven

$$= \frac{[\text{D(of driver pulley)}]\ [\text{RPM of Driver}]}{\text{D(of driven pulley)}}$$

pulmonary artery The artery which transfers blood from the heart to the lungs.

pulmonary vein A vein that transfers blood from the lungs to the heart.

pulp fed Livestock fed sugar beet pulp.

pulque Fermented juice of the agave plant. *See also* **tequila.**

pulsating d-c Direct current that varies in magnitude.

pulse Leguminous plants' edible seed.
See Part 2: Pulses, Nuts and Seeds Composition; Water Activity, Organisms and Food

pumice A volcanic rock, used as an abrasive in fine-ground form.

pummelo *See* **pomelo**

pumpernickel A hard bread made from rye flour.

pumping Introduction of a pickle into meat under pressure by injection through a needle.

pumpkin (*Cucurbita pepo* and *C. moschata*) A climbing herb producing a large, round, yellow pepo; the fruit is often made into pies; pumpkin seeds are also edible and are rich in protein and fat.

1 lb fresh = 1 cup cooked and mashed
1 cup cooked and mashed = 250 g (8.7 oz)
2 to 4 lb pumpkin in shell = 1 qt canned
100 lb fresh = 6–8 lb dry

Storage: 50–55°F, 70–75% relative humidity, 2 mo. storage life.

Composition:

	H_2O (%)	Protein (%)	Fat (%)	Carbohydrate (%)	Ash (%)	pH
Raw pumpkin	92	1	0.1	6	1	4.8–5.2
Seed dry	4	29	47	15	5	

See Part 2: Frozen Food Storage; Fruit Classification; Minerals, Food; Plant Foods, Composition; Protein Factors; Seed, Chemical Composition; Standards, Processed Fruit and Vegetable Products; Storage; Sugar, Vegetables; Vegetable Composition; Vegetable Frozen Yield; Vegetable Plants; Vegetables, Canning Dates; Vegetable Storage; Vegetable Yield

punch A fruit-flavored drink which may or may not contain liquor.
See Part 2: Flavors, Beverage

purebred Animals that are eligible for registration in any breed.

Purebred Dairy Cattle Association An association made up of representatives of the organizations that sponsor Ayrshire, Brown Swiss, Guernsey, Holstein, and Jersey cattle.

purée Cooked and sieved vegetables, or a soup made from them.
See Part 2: Tomato and Tomato Products, Composition

purified (Purif.) A designation of a grade of chemical purity; a low purity and should not be used for analysis. *See also* **grade**.

purine $C_5N_4H_4$ A derivative of pyrimidine and a component of many end products of animal metabolism including uric acid, adenine, guanine and various alkaloids. Nucleic acids contain purine compounds. The chemical structure is two fused heterocyclic rings *See also* **pyrimidine**.

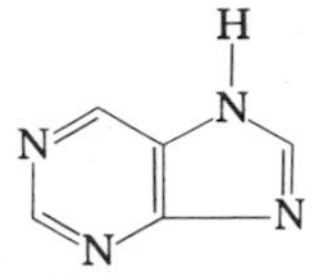

purple broth base *See* Part 2: Microorganism Reactions on Differential Tube Media; Microorganism, Selective and Differential Broths and Media, Water Filtration Plant

purple granadilla *See* **passion fruit**

purple lactose agar *See* Part 2: Microorganism, Media

purple milk *See* Part 2: Microorganism, Media

purse *See* **cod**

PVC *See* Part 2: Blood

Pyrex Brand glass Proprietary name for a heat-resistant borosilicate glass suitable for high baking temperatures. Widely used both in the laboratory and home.

pyridoxine (vitamin B-6) $C_8H_{11}NO_3$ A water-soluble vitamin which if deficient in the diet of the rat will result in dermatitis. Source: yeast, cereal bran, kidney, liver, meats, milk, leafy vegetables, and egg yolk.

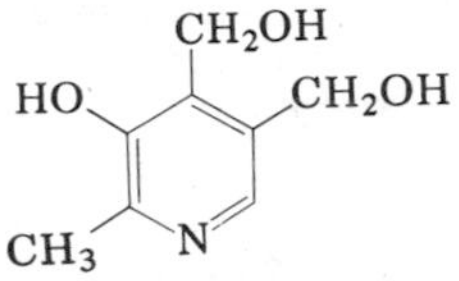

See Part 2: Egg Products, Nutritive Value; Grain Analysis; Vitamins; Vitamin Sources, Functions, and Stability; Wheat, Parts of Grain, Vitamins; Wheat Products Composition

pyrimidine A basic nitrogenous compound from which the purines uracil and thymine are derived. Obtained by hydrolysis of nucleic acids.

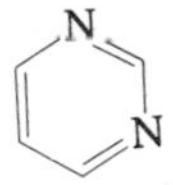

pyrolysis *See* **destructive distillation**

pyrophosphate A cleaning compound that is very stable at high temp. and high alkalinity; slow to dissolve and lacks calcium sequestering power. *See also* **phosphate**.
See Part 2: Phosphate

pyrophyllite $Al_2O_3 \cdot 4SiO_2 \cdot H_2O$ A carrier for insecticides.

pyruvic acid $CH_3CO \cdot COOH$ An intermediate acid formed during metabolism of carbohydrates.

Q

Q fever *See* Part 2: Diseases, Food-Borne

quadratic equation $ax^2 + bx + c = 0$

$$x = \frac{-b \pm \sqrt{b^2 - 4ac}}{2a}$$

quadriceps Four muscles on the anterior section of the thigh, attached to the top of the femur and to the patella and to the tibia. Made up of:
1. *Vastus lateralis* (most lateral)
2. *Vastus medialis* (most medial)
3. *Vastus intermedius* (between 1 & 2 & cranial to the femur)
4. *Rectus femoris* (most cranial of the group)

quahog A New England hard-shelled clam. *See also* **clam.**

quality The degree or grade of excellence of a food product as determined by some objective standard.
See Part 2: Egg Quality; Egg Quality, Broken; Grades, Meat; Meat Grade Stamps

quality assurance date (freshness date) The date at which a product will have the same quality as when it left the processing plant.

quality control The maintenance of a uniform, consistent or predetermined quality. It is usually divided into three categories—raw material control, process control, and finished product inspection. *See also* **sample size; standard deviation.**

quarantine To segregate individuals that have a contagious disease.

quark *See* Part 2: Milk and Cheese Composition

quart (Br. fl.) (Imp.) A measure of volume.
1 qt (Br. fl.) = 1136.49 ml
= 40 fl. ounces (Br. fl.)
= 2 pints (Br. fl.)
= 1.136 liters

quart (dry) (Imp.) (Br.) A measure of volume.
1 dry qt = 40 ounces
= 1.136 liters

quart (U.S.) (dry) (dry qt) A measure of volume.
1 dry qt = 67.2006 cubic inches (cu in.)
= 2 dry pints (pt)
= 1.16365 U.S. liquid quarts (liquid qt)
= 1.10123 cubic decimeters (dm^3)
= 1.101 liters
= 0.29091 U.S. liquid gallon (liquid gal)
= 0.25 U.S. dry gallon (dry gal)
= 0.03889 cubic foot (cu ft)
= 0.03125 U.S. bushel (bu)
= 0.001440 cubic yard (cu yd)

quart (U.S.) (liquid) (liquid qt) (U.S. fluid) A measure of volume.
1 liquid qt = 946.333 milliliters (ml)
= 256.00 drams (fluid)
= 57.749 cubic inches (cu in.)
= 32 fluid ounces
= 2 liquid pints
= 0.94636 liter
= 0.94636 cubic decimeter (dm^3)
= 0.85937 U.S. dry quart (dry qt)
= 0.25 U.S. liquid gallon (liquid gal)
= 0.21484 U.S. dry gallon (dry gal)
= 0.03342 cubic foot (cu ft)
= 0.02686 U.S. bushel (bu)
= 0.001238 cubic yard (cu yd)
See Part 2: Volume

quartern *See* **noggin**

quarters Inside of thighs of a horse or rear fourth of hoof on each side of the foot.

quaternary ammonium compound Any of a group of complex organic compounds comprised of a cation and an anion. They are strong disinfectants and sanitizers. The ionic structure may be represented as

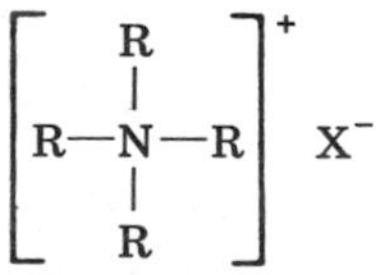

where R is an organic group and X is a negatively charged atom or group.
See Part 2: Sanitizers; Sanitizing Chemicals

Queensland nut (***Macadamia ternifolia***) A thick-shelled nut which can be used as a snack or in confectionery; fat content, 70%.

quenelles A dumpling made of chopped seasoned meat.

quercitron A yellow colorant derived from the bark of the black oak and used to color food.

quick cure A meat-curing pickle containing some nitrite.

quick frozen food A food frozen so rapidly that only small ice crystals have time to form and close to normal flavor is thus retained.
See Part 2: Freezing Rate

quicklime CaO Calcium oxide, made by roasting limestone.

$$CaCO_3 \xrightarrow{\Delta} CaO + CO_2$$

quince (*Cydonia vulgaris*) A tree that produces a fruit similar to an apple or pear but has many ovules in each section; it is hard and acid but makes good jam and jelly; contignac and marmelo candies made from purée and sugar.
1 basket = 48 lbs;
Storage: 32°F, 90–95% relative humidity, storage life, 2 months.
Raw composition: 84% H_2O, 0.4% protein, 0.1% fat, 15% carbohydrate, 0.5% ash, pH 3.2.
See Part 2: Fruit and Nut Rootstock; Fruit Classification; Fruit Composition; Minerals, Food; Storage

quinic acid $C_6H_7(OH)_4COOH \cdot H_2O$ An organic acid obtained from the bark of the cinchona tree.
See Part 2: Organic Acids in Fruits and Vegetables

quinine $C_{20}H_{24}N_2O_2 \cdot 3H_2O$ An alkaloid drug extracted from the bark of the cinchona tree. Especially useful in treating malaria.
See Part 2: Organic Acids in Fruits and Vegetables

quinoa A plant whose seed is used for broth, cake, salads and livestock feed.
See Part 2: Cereal Composition

quinone (1,4-benzoquinone) A toxic chemical used in dye manufacture; obtained by oxidation of aniline with chromic acid.

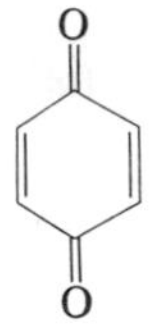

quintal (metric) A measure of weight.
1 quintal = 220.46 lb
= 129.54 lb (Brazil)
= 101.47 lb (Mexico)
= 101.43 lb (Peru)
= 101.41 lb (Chile)
= 101.28 lb (Argentina)
= 100 kilograms

R

R (1) Symbol used in formulas for any organic group (aryl or alkyl). (2) Symbol for degrees Rankine and degrees Réaumur. (3) Symbol for electrical resistance. *See also* **ohm.**

R · Symbol for a free radical.

R_x Pharmacists symbol for ingredients of a prescription (recipe).

Ra Symbol for the element radium.

rabbit A small rodent. Its meat is edible.
See Part 2: Animal Foods, Composition; Bone; Liver; Meat and Meat Products Composition; Minerals, Food; Reproductive Cycle

racemic An equal mixture of two optically active isomers that has no optical activity.

rack *See* Part 2: Lamb Chart; Lamb Cuts; Lamb Cuts and Uses; Lamb Roasting; Lamb, Wholesale Cuts; Roasting, Time and Temperature; Veal Roasting

rad Unit of ionizing radiation; it is a dosage that results in absorption of 100 ergs of energy per gram of tissue.
See Part 2: Constants, Fundamental

radar Microwave frequencies used in cooking; wavelength from 0.1 to 1.0 cm.
See Part 2: Waves, Energy-Producing

radian An arc whose length is equal to the radius.
1 radian = 57.296°

radian per second A measure of velocity and acceleration.
1 = 57.2958 degrees per sec
= 0.159155 revolution per sec

radiation (1) Energy emanating from the unstable nuclei of certain elements (radium, uranium) in the form of alpha particles (helium nuclei), beta particles (electrons), and gamma rays. Such elements are said to be radioactive. (2) Radiant energy comprising the electromagnetic spectrum and consisting of photons.
See Part 2: Radiation Preservation

radical A charged group of connected atoms that maintains this connection through chemical changes, i.e., OH^-, SO_4^{--}. *See also* **group.**

radicle root *See* Part 2: Corn Kernel

radioactivity *See* **radiation**

radioisotope An isotope, either natural or artificial, which emits radiation. Carbon-14 is naturally radioactive, but many artificial radioisotopes are made by neutron bombardment of such elements as sodium, iodine and cobalt and are used as curative agents in medicine.

radio waves Electromagnetic energy in the form of waves from 7000 to 2×10^6 cm in length; also called Hertzian waves.
See Part 2: Waves, Energy-Producing

radish (*Raphanus sativus*) A salad root plant that is usually eaten raw; has sharp, biting taste.
Shape: round, cylindrical, tapered (icicle), turnip-shape.
Color: red, red and white, white, dark brown.
Storage: Remove tops and store covered (90–95% relative humidity) in refrigerator (32°F); use in 1 to 2 weeks (spring) or 2 mo. (winter).
1 bu = 35 lb
Raw Composition: 95% H_2O, 1% protein, 0.1% fat, 4% carbohydrate, 1% ash, pH (red) 5.8–6.5, pH (white) 5.5–5.7.
See Part 2: Minerals, Food; Minerals, Plant or Animal Tissue; Nitrate, Vegetables; Plant Foods, Composition; Storage; Sugar, Vegetables; Vegetables, Classification; Vegetable Composition; Vegetable Plants; Vegetable Storage

radium (Ra) A radioactive metallic element; at. no. 88; mass number of most stable isotope 226; isotopes 223, 224, 226, 228; Group IIA of Periodic Table; electron configuration 2–8–18–32–18–8–2
orbit K L M N O P Q
oxidation state +2.

radius (1) One of the fore shank bones. (2) Distance from the center of a circle to its circumference, i.e., one-half the diameter, or from the center of a sphere to its surface.
See Part 2: Bone

radon (Rn) A gaseous radioactive element; at. no. 86; mass number of most stable isotope 222; noble gas group of Periodic Table; electron configuration 2–8–18–32–18–8
orbit K L M N O P
oxidation state 0.

raffinose (melitose, melitriose) $C_{18}H_{32}O_{16}$ A trisaccharide made up of fructose, glucose and galactose; found in cottonseed, beets and cereals.
See Part 2: Sugar, Legumes

ragôut A thick savory stew of meat, vegetables and spices.

ragusano A type of caciocavallo cheese.

rails (meat) Minimum of 2 ft from fixed portion of building (3 ft for heavier traffic); height: sausage cages, 7½ ft; headless hog and calves, 9 ft (12-in. trolleys); beef quarters, 7½ ft.

rainbow trout A lean game fish; also raised commercially in fish farms in northwestern United States, Denmark and Japan.

raisin A dried (mostly sun-dried) grape; may be dried on the vine, or ripe bunches are cut and dried; grapes used are usually wine grapes because of high sugar content and firm flesh. *See also* **currant; sultana.**

1 lb raisins = 4 lb fresh grapes
1-lb package = 2½ to 2¾ cups seedless (1 cup = 150 g or 5.2 oz)
= 2 cups chopped seedless (190 g or 6.7 oz)
= 3¼ cups seeded (1 cup = 140 g or 5 oz)
= 2½ cups chopped seeded (1 cup = 180 g or 6.4 oz)

Raw composition: 17-24% H_2O, 1-3% protein, 0.2-0.5% fat, 64-77% carbohydrate, 2% ash; pH 3.8-4.0.

See Part 2: Food, Composition; Fruit Composition; Minerals, Food; Plant Foods, Composition; Potassium-Rich Foods; Water Activity, Organisms and Food

raisin bran A breakfast cereal made from wheat bran, flake and other wheat products and containing raisins; 1 cup = 2 oz.

Composition: 7-8% protein, 74-80% carbohydrate, 1-4% fat.

raisin bread A bread containing a minimum of 50 parts by weight of raisins per 100 parts of flour.

ram An uncastrated male ovine animal (sheep) of any age.

See Part 2: Sheep, Market Classes and Grades

Rambouillet A fine-wool breed of sheep developed in France and Germany but originating from the Spanish Merinos; they have white lips and hooves and the rams have horns (also a polled strain); ewes are without horns.

See Part 2: Sheep Breeds

rambutan (*Nephelium lappaceum*) A large tree that produces clusters of plum-size fruit covered with red or yellow soft, long, hair-like spines; the edible part is a fleshy aril, in the center of which is a single seed; the fruit has a sweet-acid taste and may be eaten raw or stewed.

See Part 2: Fruit Classification; Fruit Storage; Saturated Fatty Acids

rancid Having a foul odor or taste similar to that of an old oil, due to degradation caused by oxidation or bacteria.

See Part 2: Spoilage, Fat in Food; Spoilage, Protein Foods

randomization Interesterification of fat.

randomized group comparisons Two groups of equal size (approximately equal variance).

Pooled $\Sigma x^2 = \Sigma x^2$ (1st group) + Σx^2 (2nd group)

Ho: $\mu_1 - \mu_2 = 0$ or $\mu_1 = \mu_2$

$$t = (\bar{x}_1 - \bar{x}_2)\sqrt{\frac{n(n-1)}{\text{pooled } \Sigma x^2}}$$

n = # in a group
$\bar{x}_1$ = mean of group 1
μ_1 = mean of population 1
$df = 2(n-1)$

Confidence limits on the difference

$$\bar{x}_1 - \bar{x}_2 - t_{.05}(s_{\bar{x}_1-\bar{x}_2}) \leqslant \mu_1 - \mu_2 \leqslant \bar{x}_1 - \bar{x}_2 + t_{.05}(s_{\bar{x}_1-\bar{x}_2})$$

$$(s_{\bar{x}_1-\bar{x}_2}) = \sqrt{\frac{\text{pooled } \Sigma x^2}{(n-1)n}}$$ s^2 = *See* **mean square**

Unequal numbers per group

$$t = (\bar{x}_1 - \bar{x}_2)\sqrt{\frac{n_1 n_2(n_1 + n_2 - 2)}{(n_1 + n_2) \text{ pooled } \Sigma x^2}}$$

$$s_{\bar{x}_1-\bar{x}_2} = \frac{\text{pooled } \Sigma x^2 (n_1 + n_2)}{n_1 n_2 (n_1 + n_2 - 2)}$$

$df = n_1 + n_2 - 2$
n_1 = # in group 1
$\bar{x}_1$ = mean in group 1

range Difference between upper and lower limits of a variable.

rangy Body too long.

Rankine (R) A temperature scale based on the absolute zero of the Fahrenheit scale; 0° Rankine = −460°F. *See also* **absolute temperature.**

rape (cole, coleseed); (*Brassica napus, B. campestris*) An herb belonging to the wallflower family; an annual grass of the mustard family used for hog pasture.

Part of plant	Use
seed	oil (35-50%)
stem and leaves	livestock feed
stem and leaves	salad or greens
seed cake	livestock feed

Composition of seed cake: 35-40% protein, 20-25% carbohydrate, 12-16% fiber, 5-7% ash
weight: 50-60 lb/bu
seeding: 3 to 8 lb/acre
pH: 5.5-6.0.

See Part 2: Seed, Chemical Composition; Seed, Germination; Unsaponifiable Matter

rapeseed oil (colza oil) Called mustard oil in India. A vegetable oil expressed or solvent-extracted from rapeseed.

Composition and properties

Palmitic	1-4%
Stearic	1%
Oleic	17-32%
Linoleic	13-15%
Linolenic	1-6%
Arachidic	1%
Eicosenoic	10%
Behenic	1%
Erucic	40-50%
Tetracosenoic	0.5%
Saponification Value	165-180
Iodine Value	81-110
Refractive Index (15.5°C)	1.474-1.476

Titer	10–18°C
Acid number	0.34
Specific gravity 20°/4°C	0.9114
Unsaponifiable	1.5%
Saturated fatty acids	3–8%
Melting point	-9°C

See Part 2: Fats and Oils, Composition; Fats and Oils, Fatty Acid Composition; Fats and Oils, Physical and Chemical Properties; Fatty Acids, Fats and Oils; Iodine and Saponification Values; Oil or Fat, Characteristics; Rapeseed Oil, Triglyceride Mole Percent Composition; Saturated Fatty Acids; Spoilage, Fat in Food; Titer, Fats and Oils; Tocopherols; Unsaturated Fatty Acids

rare (meat) A state of "doneness" at which the internal beef temperature is 140°F.
See Part 2: Beef Degrees of Doneness; Beef Roasting; Broiling Time and Temperature

rare earth element An element with atomic number from 58 through 71, which comprise the lanthanide series of Group IIIB of the Periodic Table.

raspberry (***Rubus idaeus*** **or** ***R. stigosus***) An aggregate fruit used for food; the canes produce a berry comprised of numerous round one-seeded drupelets which are contained close together in a small core. The fruit may be red, yellow (white raspberries), black or purple (black-red raspberries). They are consumed fresh, cooked, canned, frozen or made into jams, jellies, and drinks.
24-qt crate = 36 lb
100 lb fresh = 17–23 lb dry
Storage: Short term (7 days), 31°F, 85–90% relative humidity; long term (1 year), -10°F.
Raw composition: 82% H_2O, 1% protein, 1% fat, 15% carbohydrate, 0.5% ash; pH 3.2–3.7.
See Part 2: Canned Yield; Flavor Ingredients, Taste and Flavor Type; Flavors, Beverage; Frozen Food Storage; Fruit Harvest Dates; Fruit Classification; Fruit Composition; Fruit Frozen Yield; Fruit Servings Per Pound; Minerals, Food; Rot Spoilage; Standards, Processed Fruit and Vegetable Products; Storage; Sugar, Fruit

rat (*Mus*) A destructive and disease-carrying rodent. Types in U.S. are:
Brown rat (Norway rat, barn rat, gray rat); (*Rattus norvegicus*); in northern U.S.
Black rat (ship rat); (*Rattus rattus*); in southern U.S.
Alexandrian rat (roof rat); (*Rattus r.* alexandrinus); in Gulf states, seaport.

rat acrodynia *See* **pyridoxine**

ratio The quotient of a value divided by another of the same type.

ration A fixed amount of food and water for individual consumption.

ratoons *See* **sugar cane**

rattle Part of forequarter of cattle consisting of the arm, shank, brisket and short plate; in veal and lamb it consists of shoulder, breast and shank.

rattlebox A plant having a toxic principle.
See Part 2: Poisonous Plants

raven's beak *See* Part 2: Bone

ravioli A mixture of meat and cheese cooked inside noodle pasta.
See Part 2: Microwave Processing Time

ravison oil A type of rapeseed oil from Black Sea area.
See Part 2: Fatty Acids, Fats and Oils; Iodine and Saponification Values; Oil or Fat, Characteristics

rawboned Underfinished.

rawhide Untanned skin.

rayless goldenrod A plant having a toxic principle.
See Part 2: Poisonous Plants

rayon Fiber made from regenerated cellulose, usually by the viscose process.

razorback Thin, narrow-back hogs.

Rb Symbol for the element rubidium.

RBC Red blood cells.
See Part 2: Blood

RDA See recommended dietary allowance.

Re Symbol for the element rhenium.

reactant One of the original chemicals in a chemical reaction.

reactor Cattle reacting to tuberculin test.

ready-to-eat ham A ham that has reached an internal temperature of 148°F and held to at least this temperature for 2 hr. *See also* **smoked meat.**

ready-to-serve *See* **smoked meat; cooked**

ready-to-slice ham A ham that has been tenderized but must be cooked further before eating; internal temperature has reached approximately 142°F.

reagent (1) A chemical compound used in laboratory analysis to identify specific constituents of the material being analyzed. (2) Designation of a grade of chemical purity; a purity suitable for analytical use; it will show lot analysis or maximum limits of impurities. *See also* **grade.**
See Part 2: Reagents, Normal Solutions

rearrangement *See* **interesterification**

Réaumur (R) A measure of temperature.
$°R = °C \cdot 4/5$
$°R = (°F - 32)\ 4/9$
$°C = °R \cdot 5/4$
$°F = (°R \cdot 9/4) + 32$

reblochon A cheese of soft, buttery consistency with a mild nutty flavor.
See Part 2: Cheese, Vitamin Content; Milk and Milk Products, Vitamin Content

recommended daily dietary allowance *See* Part 2: Beef Percentages of Daily Recommended Allowances; Calcium, Daily Recommendations; Calories, Daily Recommendations; Iron, Daily Recommendations; Lamb Percentages of Daily Recommended Allowances; Niacin, Daily

Recommendations; Pork, Percentages of Daily Recommended Allowances; Recommended Daily Dietary Allowance; Riboflavin, Daily Recommendations; Thiamin, Daily Recommendations; Variety Meat Percentage of Daily Recommended Allowances; Vitamin A, Daily Recommendations

recommended dietary allowance (RDA) Specified vitamins, minerals and protein adequate for maintenance of good nutrition of a healthy person in the U.S. population; developed by NAS-NRC; they are generally higher than minimum daily requirements.
See Part 2: Ascorbic Acid; Cereals, Vitamin and Mineral Content; Recommended Daily Dietary Allowance

recovery *See* Part 2: Food, Water Intake

rectification Purification of an alcoholic product by repeated contact of the liquid distillate with the vapor formed in the first evaporation.

rectified spirit In the United States, 91% alcohol (84% in England).

rectified whiskey Straight whiskey mixed with silent spirit or water and/or caramel.

Rectus abdominis Flank steak.

Rectus femoris *See* **quadriceps**

Red Angus *See* Part 2: Beef and Dual-Purpose Cattle

red blood cell An erythrocyte comprising 1/3 of blood volume; 5 million per cubic millimeter; contains hemoglobin; cell is 8.8 × 1.9 microns. *See also* **erythrocyte.**

Red Brangus *See* Part 2: Beef and Dual-Purpose Cattle

red caviar *See* **caviar**

red clover A biennial clover used for hay; weight 60 lb/bu; seeding, 8–12 lb/acre; harvest, half to full bloom; pH 6.5; varieties: Cumberland, Kenland.
See Part 2: Nutrients in Crops

Red Danish A dairy breed of cattle that originated in Denmark.

Red Delicious A variety of apple that is in season from October to March; excellent for eating and fair for cooking.

red dog flour *See* **low-grade flour**
See Part 2: Wheat and Flour Composition; Wheat, Carbohydrate Composition; Wheat Products Composition

red dressing A type of salad dressing.
See Part 2: Salad Dressing and Mayonnaise Variations

redfish *See* **ocean perch**

red gram *See* **pigeon pea**

red grouper *See* **grouper**

red hake *See* **hake**

red herring Herring cured with saltpeter and heavy salt and smoked about 10 days.

red hot Colloquial term for frankfurter.

redox An oxidation-reduction reaction; a measure of the oxidizing or reducing power of a system.

red pepper (cayenne) (*Capsicum frutescens* L.) Ripe pods of fresh peppers or dried ripe fruit of capsicum; very hot to the taste.

Red Poll An English dual-purpose type of cattle that is hornless.
See Part 2: Beef and Dual-Purpose Cattle; Gestation Periods

reds *See* Part 2: Fish, Smoke-Cured; Salmon and Trout

red salmon *See* **salmon**

red snapper A lean fish caught in the Gulf of Mexico off the middle Atlantic coast of the United States, and off Taiwan.
See Part 2: Minerals, Food

red spider An insect that infests certain evergreen trees.
See Part 2: Insect Control

red tide Red algae which periodically "bloom" in such numbers as to make the ocean surface appear red. They produce a strong toxin which is absorbed by shellfish in shallow waters (paralytic shellfish poison). Often occurs along North Atlantic coast. *See also* **algae.**

redtop (herds grass) (*Agrostis stolonifera*) A perennial grass; weight: 14 lb uncleaned/bu, 30–38 lb cleaned/bu; seeding, 5 lb/acre; pH 5–5.5.
See Part 2: Seed, Germination

reducing agent A substance which loses electrons and is oxidized.

reducing sugar A sugar which is easily oxidized by weak oxidizing agents (silver, mercuric, or cupric salts); it will reduce Fehling's solution and form cuprous oxide. These sugars contain a free aldehyde or ketone group (includes mono- and some di-saccharides); examples are glucose, fructose, maltose and lactose.

reduction A gain of electrons; the loss of a positive charge or the gain of a negative charge; loss of oxygen or gain of hydrogen.

redwood bark *See* Part 2: Insulation

refined lard Lard that has been bleached using fuller's earth.

refiner's sugar *See* **molasses**

refiner's syrup A syrup obtained as a by-product of refining brown sugar.

refining (1) Removal of fatty acids and impurities from fat; processes used: caustic soda, steaming, water-wash, liquid-liquid extraction. (2) Removal of impurities from sugarcane or beet syrup by filtration, crystallization, adsorption on charcoal, etc. (3) Fine-grinding and bolting of cereal grains for white flour.

Refinite Trade mark for silicates used to soften water. *See also* **hardness (water).**

reflux A technique used in distillation in which condensed vapor (liquid) flows back downward through the tower, thus mixing intimately with the rising vapor; this gives greater separation efficiency. Also called countercurrent flow.

refractive index A number that indicates how much the direction of light is deflected when it passes through a substance; n_D^{20} is n at 20°C using the D-line of sodium as light source.
See Part 2: Refractive Indices, Fats and Oils

refrigerant A chemical used in artificial refrigeration. Examples: ammonia (NH_3), carbon dioxide (CO_2), sulfur dioxide (SO_2), ethane (C_2H_6), propane (C_3H_8), butane (C_4H_{10}), isobutane ($(CH_3)_3CH$), methyl chloride (CH_3Cl), ethyl chloride (C_2H_5Cl), and various fluorocarbons.
See Part 2: Refrigerant

reggiano cheese *See* **parmesan cheese**
See Part 2: Cheese Characteristics

reginette *See* **noodles**

regression (multiple)

$$\Sigma x_1^2 = \Sigma X_1^2 - \frac{(\Sigma X_1)^2}{n}$$

$$\Sigma x_2^2 = \Sigma X_2^2 - \frac{(\Sigma X_2)^2}{n}$$

$$\Sigma x_1 x_2 = \Sigma X_1 X_2 - \frac{(\Sigma X_1)(\Sigma X_2)}{n}$$

$$\Sigma x_2 y = \Sigma X_2 Y - \frac{(\Sigma X_2)(\Sigma Y)}{n}$$

$$\Sigma x_1 y = \Sigma X_1 Y - \frac{(\Sigma X_1)(\Sigma Y)}{n}$$

$$\Sigma y^2 = \Sigma Y^2 - \frac{(\Sigma Y)^2}{n}$$

$$D = (\Sigma x_1^2)(\Sigma x_2^2) - (\Sigma x_1 x_2)^2$$

$$b_{y_{1.2}} = \frac{(\Sigma x_2^2)(\Sigma x_1 y) - (\Sigma x_1 x_2)(\Sigma x_2 y)}{D}$$

$$b_{y_{2.1}} = \frac{(\Sigma x_1^2)(\Sigma x_2 y) - (\Sigma x_1 x_2)(\Sigma x_1 y)}{D}$$

$$a = \bar{y} - (b_{1.2})(\bar{x}_1) - (b_{2.1})(\bar{x}_2)$$

$$\hat{Y} = a + b_{1.2} X_1 + b_{2.1} X_2$$

regression coefficient (sample) (b) Unit change in the dependent variable (Y) per each unit of the independent variable (X):

$$b = \frac{\Sigma xy}{\Sigma x^2} = \frac{\Sigma XY - \frac{(\Sigma X)(\Sigma Y)}{n}}{\Sigma X^2 - \frac{(\Sigma X)^2}{n}}$$

x = deviation from mean of X's
y = deviation from mean of Y's
n = # of X *or* Y values

$+b$ upward slope,
$-b$ downward slope
See also **regression equation** for significant test.

regression equation (linear)

$\hat{Y} = \bar{y} + b(X - \bar{x})$ $\quad$ $\bar{y}$ = mean of Y's
$\hat{Y} = a + bX$ $\quad$ $\bar{x}$ = mean of X's
b = see "regression coefficient"
$a = \bar{y} - b\bar{x}$
n = # of X's or Y's

Sum of squares of deviation:

$$\Sigma d_{y.x^2} = \Sigma Y^2 - \frac{(\Sigma Y)^2}{n} - \frac{\left[\Sigma XY - \frac{(\Sigma X)(\Sigma Y)}{n}\right]^2}{\Sigma X^2 - \frac{(\Sigma X)^2}{n}}$$

Mean square deviation from regression:

$$s_{y.x^2} = \Sigma d_{y.x^2}/n-2$$

Sample standard deviation from regression:

$$s_{y.x} = \sqrt{s_{y.x^2}}$$

Sample standard deviation of regression coefficient:

$$s_b = s_{y.x}/\sqrt{\Sigma x^2 - (\Sigma X)^2/n}$$

Test of significance of b

$t = b/s_b \quad df = n - 2$

or test Ho: $b = 0$

$t = \frac{b - \beta}{s_b}$ $\quad$ CL on b

$$b - t_{.05} s_b \leqslant \beta \leqslant b + t_{.05} s_b$$

$df = n - 2$

CL for regression line:

(A) CL for *an average* on Y's for each X

$$\hat{Y} - t_{.05} s_{\hat{y}} \leqslant \mu \leqslant \hat{Y} + t_{.05} s_{\hat{y}}$$

$x = X - \bar{x}$ (calculated for each value of X)

$$s_{\hat{y}} = s_{y.x}\sqrt{1/n + x^2/\Sigma x^2}$$

$$\Sigma x^2 = \Sigma X^2 - \frac{(\Sigma X)^2}{n}$$

(B) CL for individual Y's for each X

$$\hat{Y} - t_{.05} s_y \leqslant \mu \leqslant \hat{Y} + t_{.05} s_y$$

$$s_y = s_{y.x}\sqrt{1 + (1/n) + x^2/\Sigma x^2}$$

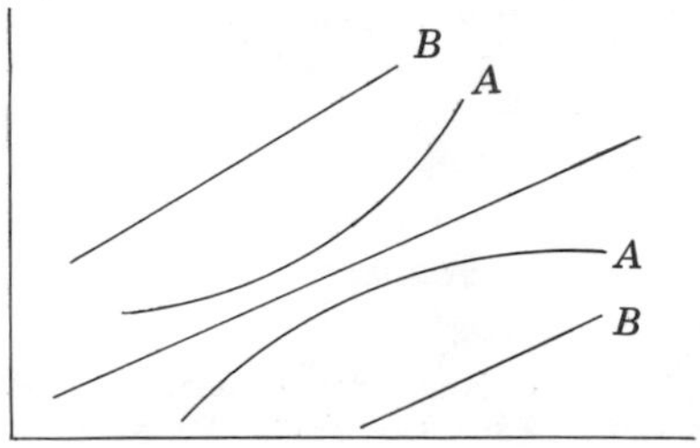

regular grind Medium particle size for boiled coffee.
See Part 2: Coffee Granule Designation; Coffee Particle Size

regular plate *See* Part 2: Pork Shoulder

regular pork trimmings Consists of 50% fat.

regular roll (rib eye) *Longissimus dorsi* and *multifidus dorsi* in the rib area.

reindeer A species of large deer with antlers inhabiting northern latitudes.
See Part 2: Milk, Mammals, Composition

relative humidity Ratio of water vapor present in the air to the quantity that would be present if the air were saturated at the same temperature.
See Part 2: Relative Humidity

relative standard deviation *See* **coefficient of variation**

relish (1) Sweet mixed pickles, usually chopped or ground. (2) Olives, celery, etc., served with a meal as appetizer.
See Part 2: Stabilizers, Thickeners

rem *See* Part 2: Constants, Fundamental

renal Of or pertaining to the kidney.
See Part 2: Lymph Nodes, Ox; Lymph Nodes, Pig

rendering Freeing fat from cells by means of heat. Animals unfit for human food are rendered to obtain their fat values.

rennet Concentrated extract of rennin.
See Part 2: Casings, Terms

rennin (chymosin) An enzyme produced by gastric glands and found in the gastric juices of young mammals. It is extracted from the 4th stomach of suckling calves and is used to coagulate milk in making cheese, rennet casein, junket and rennet custards.

rep (1) Unit of dosage equivalent to 93 ergs of energy absorption per gram of material of unit density. (2) A silk or wool fabric having a ribbed surface.

residue The unusable portion of a product that remains after refining and separation of the valuable portion. In soap making it is called "foots," in wine technology "lees" and in flour milling "tailings."

resin A water-insoluble (organic-soluble) mixture of terpenes and fatty acids found in coniferous trees. Synthetic resins are man-made high polymers.

resistance (R) Opposition to current flow measured in ohms. Power given off by resistance:

$$P = I^2 R = EI = \frac{E^2}{R}$$

P = power = watts = joules/sec
I = current in amps
R = resistance in ohms
E = potential in volts

restoration Addition of selected nutrients to food to provide the same level of these nutrients naturally present in the raw material.

retail cut *See* Part 2: Meat Label

retention time (t_r) In gas chromatography, time from injection to peak maximum.

retention volume In gas chromatography, the gas volume required to elute.

$V_R = (t_r)(F_c)$
t_r = retention time
F_c = flow of carrier gas

reticulin Connective tissue of meat closely related to collagen but highly branched.
See Part 2: Connective Tissue Proteins

reticulum (1) The second stomach of a ruminant animal located on its left side and often called the "honeycomb"; acts as a screening device letting only small particles into the omasum; a bovine reticulum may contain from 1 to 3 gallons. (2) The network of protoplasm in most cells.

retinal *See* **vitamin A aldehyde**

retinene $C_{20}H_{28}O$ The aldehyde form of vitamin A; a component of rhodopsin, a pigment of the eye. *See also* **rhodopsin**; **vitamin A aldehyde**

retinoic *See* **vitamin A acid**

retinol *See* **vitamin A**
See Part 2: Vitamins

retort A vessel used for distillation of heavy oils or for cooking by heat; autoclave. Retort water-treatment agents used to prevent staining of cans:

disodium phosphate Na_2HPO_4
dioctyl sodium sulfosuccinate $C_{20}H_{37}NaO_7S$
sodium bicarbonate $NaHCO_3$
sodium carbonate Na_2CO_3
calcium chloride $CaCl_2$
sodium dodecylbenzenesulfonate $C_{18}H_{29}NaO_3S$
sodium hexametaphosphate (Graham's salt) $(NaPO_3)_6$
sodium lauryl sulfate $C_{12}H_{25}NaO_4S$
sodium metasilicate Na_2SiO_3
sodium tripolyphosphate $Na_5P_3O_{10}$
zinc oxide ZnO
zinc sulfate $ZnSO_4$
propylene glycol $C_3H_8O_2$

retropharyngeal *See* Part 2: Lymph Nodes, Pig

reversion An undesirable change in flavor or other property.

rex sole *See* **sole**

Rh Symbol for the element rhodium.

rhamnose $C_6H_{12}O_5$ Methyl pentose sugar, ⅓ as sweet as sucrose.

rhenium (Re) Metallic element; at. no. 75; at. wt. 186.22; Group VIIB of Periodic Table; electron configuration 2-8-18-32-13-2;
orbit K L M N O P
oxidation states +2, +3, +4, +5, +6, +7.

rheostat A variable resistor.

Rhine wine A dry white table wine.

Rhizoctonia A type of mold.
See Part 2: Mold, Food

rhizome A swollen root-like stem partially or wholly underground.
See Part 2: Vegetables, Classification

Rhizopus A type of mold.
See Part 2: Mold, Food; Molds, Mycotoxins; Rot Spoilage; Spoilage, Carbohydrate Foods

rho (P, ρ) Greek letter with an English equivalent of p.

Rhode Island Red An American class of chicken that lays a brown-shelled egg.

Varieties	Plumage	Shank	Beak
Single comb	red, some black in tail feathers	dark yellow	reddish
Rose comb	(same)	(same)	(same)

Also a bantam variety

See Part 2: Poultry Breeds and Varieties

Rhode Island White An American class of chicken that lays a brown-shelled egg.

Variety	Plumage	Shank	Beak
Rose comb	white	yellow	yellow

rhodesgrass *See* Part 2: Seed, Germination

rhodium (Rh) A metallic element; at. no. 45; at. wt. 102.91; Group VIII of Periodic Table; electron configuration 2-8-18-16-1;
orbit K L M N O
oxidation state +3.

rhodopsin (visual purple) The pigment of the eye which is sensitive to red light; comprised of opsin (a protein) and retinene.

rhomboid muscle A muscle attached to the medial surface of the scapula and to the thoracic spinous processes.

rhubarb (*Rheum rhaponticum; R. hybridum; R. undulatum*) A cool-weather plant whose red (sometimes green) leaf-stalks (66% edible) are used like fruit in pies, preserves, and wine making.
1 lb fresh = 4–8 pieces
= 2 cups cooked (240 g or 8.5 oz)
2 to 3 lb fresh = 1 qt canned
1 bu fresh = 50–55 lb
= 24 to 28 qt canned.
Ripen: Uncovered, room temperature, out of sun.
Storage: Uncovered (90–95% relative humidity), refrigerated (32°F); when ripe use in 3 to 5 days.
Raw composition: 95% H_2O, 0.5% protein, 0.1% fat, 4% carbohydrate, 0.7% ash; pH 3.1–3.4.
See Part 2: Fruit Composition; Fruit, Cooking; Fruit Frozen Yield; Fruit Sauces; Microwave Cooking, Fruit; Minerals (Trace), Food; Organic Acids in Fruits and Vegetables; pH Values of Biological Materials; Storage; Sugar, Vegetables; Vegetables, Cooking Frozen; Vegetable Plants; Vegetables, Canning Dates; Vegetable Yield

rib (1) An area of the forequarter of beef usually consisting of the thick portion of the 6th through 12th rib; about 9% of a Choice carcass. (2) Cattle, goats, sheep, deer normally have 13 ribs (8-sternal, 5-asternal), sometimes 14 (14th usually floating).
Camel: 12 ribs (8-sternal, 4-asternal).
Swine: 14–16 ribs (7-sternal, 7-asternal, and the rest floating).
Horses: 18 ribs (10-sternal, 8-asternal).
See Part 2: Beef Chart; Beef Chuck; Beef Cuts; Beef Cuts and Uses; Beef Retail Yield; Beef Rib Carving; Beef Rib Nomenclature; Beef Roasting; Beef Wholesale Cuts; Beef Yields; Bone; Bone in Retail Cuts; Lamb, Wholesale Cuts; Meat Identification; Meat Label; Meat, Servings per Pound; Microwave Processing Time; Pork Cookery; Pork Cuts; Pork Loin Cooking; Pork Wholesale Cuts; Potassium-Rich Foods; Roasting, Time and Temperature; Veal Chart; Veal Cuts; Veal Cuts and Uses; Veal Wholesale Cuts

rib cap *See* Part 2: Beef Rib Nomenclature

rib chop *See* Part 2: Lamb Yield; Pork Loin Cooking

rib eye *See* Part 2: Beef, Boneless Cuts; Beef Rib Nomenclature; Roasting, Time and Temperature

rib fingers Tissue between the ribs.

riblets *See* Part 2: Lamb Cuts; Veal Chart; Veal Cuts

riboflavin (B_2) $C_{17}H_{20}N_4O_6$ A water-soluble vitamin which functions in the oxidative processes which take place in the cell; it is also the growth-promoting factor of the B complex. Sources: green leafy vegetables, brewer's yeast, liver, kidney, muscle, milk, eggs, meat and legumes. Deficiency Symptoms: redness and scaling of skin in face area, loss of hair, stunted growth.

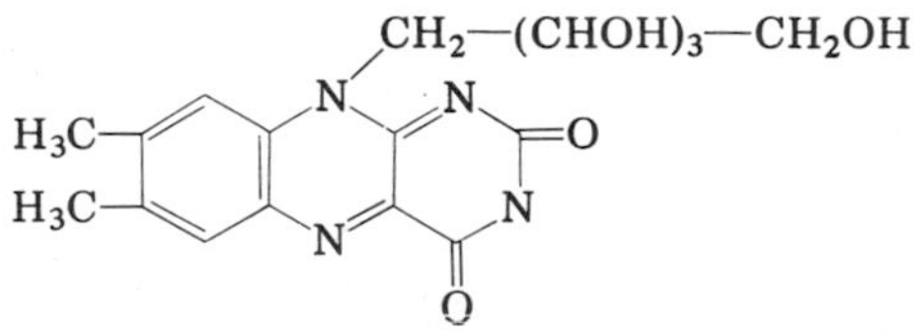

See Part 2: Beans, Peas and Nuts; Beef Percentages of Daily Recommended Allowances; Cereal Enrichment; Cereal Fortification; Cereal Nutrient Content; Cereals, Vitamin and Mineral Content; Cheese Composition; Cheese, Vitamin Content; Colors Permanently Listed; Composition of Food; Dairy Products, Composition; Egg Composition; Egg Products, Nutritive Value; Fats and Oils, Composition; Fish and Shellfish Composition; Flour, Extraction Rates; Food, Composition; Fruit and Vegetables Composition; Fruit Composition; Grain Analysis; Grain Products Composition; Lamb Percentages of Daily Recommended Allowances; Lemon Juice Composition; Lime Juice Composition; Macaroni and Noodles Composition; Meat Composition; Meat, Nutritive Value; Milk and Milk Products, Vitamin Content; Milk Composition; Plant Foods, Composition; Pork, Percentages of Daily Recommended Allowances; Poultry Composition; Recommended Daily Dietary Allowance; Riboflavin; Riboflavin, Daily Recommendations; Riboflavin, Food; Sausage Composition; Sausage Nutritive Value; Seed, Chemical Composition; Soups, Composition; Sugars and Sweets Composition; Tomato and Tomato Products, Composition; Variety Meat Percentage of Daily Recommended Allowances; Vegetable Composition; Vitamin Retention, Meat; Vitamins; Vitamin Sources, Functions, and Stability; Wheat, Parts of Grain, Vitamins; Wheat Products Composition; Wheat, Vitamins

riboflavin phosphate A mononucleotide containing riboflavin and phosphoric acid.

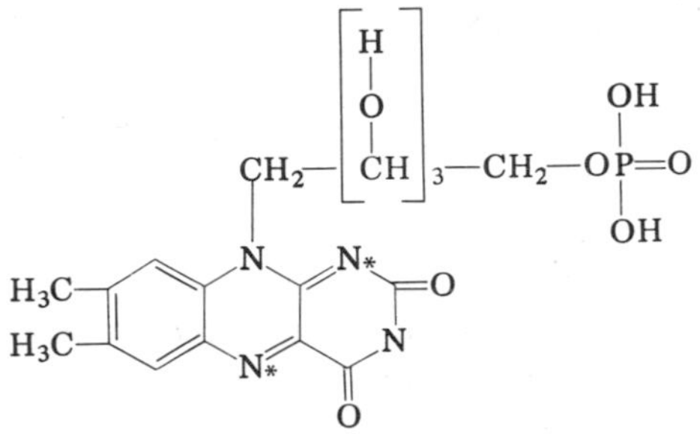

*Take on H here.

ribonucleic acid (RNA) A nucleotide which acts on the instructions of DNA in cells in carrying out the mechanisms of the genetic code. There are several types, namely messenger RNA, ribosomal RNA and transfer RNA. *See also* **deoxyribonucleic acid; ribosome.**

ribose $CH_2OH(CHOH)_3CHO$ A 5-carbon monosaccharide (pentose) found in nucleic acids.
See Part 2: Sugar, D-aldehydo

ribosome A particle in a cell composed of ribonucleic acid and the site of protein synthesis.

rib rack A wholesale cut of lamb consisting of the 5th through 12th ribs.

rib roast *See* Part 2: Beef Cuts and Uses; Beef Rib Carving; Beef Rib Nomenclature; Pork Loin Cooking

rib roll A boned and tied rolled rib.

rib steak *See* Part 2: Broiling Meat; Broiling Time and Temperature

rib wing *See* Part 2: Beef, Boneless Cuts

rice (*Oryza sativa*) An important grain crop particularly in Asia; an annual cereal whose seed is used for food. Maturity: 4 weeks in nursery and 4 months in field.

Growing systems

Standing water: hollow stem allows oxygen to reach roots; water drained a few weeks before harvest; water is used for weed and insect control.

Dry land (upland rice); (*Zizania aquatica*); (Indian rice, Tuscarora rice) Has higher protein content but is difficult to harvest.

Rice Name	Processing Procedure
Paddy	threshed (contains 40% fibrous husk)
Brown	removal of husk
White or polished	removal of bran layers

Processing: Milling removes outer husk; pearling removes outer brownish layer (bran) and yields white grain (polished); does not have to be ground.

Food value: Excellent source of starch; protein content lower than most grains; thiamine present in bran; parboiling before milling causes some of thiamine to diffuse through the grain; lysine is the first limiting amino acid and threonine is the second.

100 lb milled rice = 152 lb rough or unhulled rice
45 lb rough or unhulled rice = 1 bu
1⅞-2⅛ cups of uncooked rice = 1 lb
1 cup raw rice = 2½-4 cups cooked rice
brown rice, hulled rice: only hull removed

Varieties: Long grain, medium grain, short grain.

Size: Head rice: whole and some ¾ grains; 2nd head: ⅓ & ¾ grains; screenings: ¼-⅓ grains; brewers: small particles.

Composition:

	H_2O (%)	Protein (%)	Fat (%)	Carbohydrate (%)	Ash (%)
Rice	12	7	1	79	1
Bran	10	13	16	51	10

Moisture content for storage should be 12.5%
Precooked: cooked and dried.
Parboiled: steamed and dried before hulling and milling; improved nutritive value and keeping quality

Composition:

Rough Rice	(%)
Hull	17-21
Bran	8-14
Polish	1.8-4
Head rice	37-65
Second heads	3-12
Screening	3-11
Brewer's	2-5
Loss and trash	1-3

See Part 2: Calories, Daily Recommendations; Cereal Composition; Cereal Enrichment; Cereal Fortification; Cereal Nutrient Content; Cereals, Vitamin and Mineral Content; Food, Composition; Grain Products Composition; Microwave Processing Time; Minerals, Food; Nicotinic Acid, Food; Nutrients in Crops; Plant Foods, Composition; Portion Size; Protein Factors; Rice Kernel; Seed, Chemical Composition; Seed, Germination; Soups, Composition; Starch, Microappearance; Storage, Dry; Storage Times; Thiamin, Food; Tocopherols; Vitamin A, Food; Water Activity, Organisms and Food

rice bran Bran, germ and some hulls of rice; 0.8 lb/qt; 26 lb/bu. *See also* **bran.**
See Part 2: Fat and Oils, Fatty Acid Composition; Iodine and Saponification Values; Titer, Fats and Oils; Unsaponifiable Matter

rice extract agar *See* Part 2: Microorganism, Media

rice flakes *See* Part 2: Grain Products Composition

rice flour A starchy flour made from white rice; waxy rice flour is made from waxy rice and contains amylopectin, which is useful in frozen products.

rice, glutinous (sweet rice) A dessert rice low in starch.

rice grade Milled white rice: U.S. Grades 1,2,3,4,5,6; brown rice: U.S. Grades 1,2,3,4,5.

rice, grits Coarsely ground brown rice grains. *See also* **grits.**

rice polish The inner bran layers and some endosperm of the rice grain.

rice, puffed A breakfast cereal made of exploded rice kernels.
See Part 2: Grain Products Composition

rice, wild (*Zizonia aquatica*) *See* **wild rice**

ricing Cutting or sieving into small particles, e.g., potatoes.

ricinoleic acid An unsaturated fatty acid found in castor oil.
See Part 2: Fatty Acids, Fats and Oils; Fatty Acids and Their Properties; Oils, Seed and Fruit

rickets (rachitis) A bone condition in growing animals caused by a shortage of phosphorus and/or calcium and/or vitamin D. *See also* **osteomalacia.**

ricotta A soft, moist and grainy white cheese that is bland, semisweet, and saltier in flavor than cottage cheese; made from whey and whole or skimmed milk, or whole or part-skimmed milk; packaged in containers; unripened; some varieties are aged and dried and used for grating.
Composition: 72% H_2O, 12-13% protein, 10% fat, 4% ash, 1.2% salt.
See Part 2: Cheese Characteristics

ridge bone The raised area of the scapula (blade bone in shoulder).

ridgling A male with one or more testicles in the body cavity or with only one testis.

riesling A collective term for the varieties of white grapes that are fermented to yield Rhine wine.

rigatoni *See* **macaroni**

rigor mortis Stiffening of muscles after death.

rigs Cryptorchids.

riksost (farmer's cheese) A Swedish hard cheese.

rillette A fried pork preparation.

rind The outer coating of a fruit, vegetable or cheese; the skin on fat tissue. Removal is called rinding.

rinderpest An infectious disease of cattle, sheep, etc., caused by a virus, and often fatal.

ring bologna A sausage product made from beef and pork; it is placed in a casing and the ends tied together.

ringbone An unsoundness in horses.

ring compound An organic compound in which the carbon atoms are arranged in the form of closed rings of various shapes, i.e., hexagonal (benzene), pentagonal (heterocyclic compounds) or "boat" or "chair"-shaped (alicyclic compounds).

Ringer's solution In 100 cc of boiled, purified water:
820-900 mg NaCl
25-35 mg KCl
30-36 mg $CaCl_2$

ringworm A fungus infecting the skin of domestic animals and man.

ripe Mature; ready for use.

ripening *See* **ethylene; cured cheese**

rippled Variegated flavors in ice cream.

risotto Italian rice mixed with vegetables.

rivet wheat *See* **wheat**

rms Root-mean-square; a value used to measure the amount of a-c current that will produce the same amount of heating in a resistance as will an identical d-c current.

Rn Symbol for the element radon.

RNA Ribonucleic acid.
See Part 2: Histochemical Test

roadster A horse usually of the standard-bred breed shown only at the trot or walk; the trot has 3 speeds: jog, road gait, and trot at speed; either pulls a bike or buggy.

Roanoke A variety of soybean.

roast (1) To cook meat by dry heat, uncovered in an oven, or on a spit over open flame; the term applies specifically to meats, whereas "bake" refers to bread, cake, etc. as well as to meat. (2) A thick cut of meat.
Storage: Refrigerate in coldest part of refrigerator; original wrapper for 1 to 2 days' storage; unwrap and cover loosely for 3 to 5 days' storage.
See Part 2: Animal Foods, Composition; Beef Chart; Beef, Cooking; Beef Cuts; Beef Degrees of Doneness; Beef Roasting; Beef Yields; Braising Time; Frozen Food Storage; Lamb Cuts; Lamb Cuts and Uses; Lamb Roasting; Meat

Composition; Meat, Frozen Storage; Meat, Servings per Pound; Pork Chart; Pork Cookery; Pork, Cooking; Pork, Cooking Methods; Pork Cooking Yield; Pork Cuts; Pork Cuts and Uses; Pork Loin Cooking; Pork Storage; Portion Size; Potassium-Rich Foods; Poultry Class; Poultry Roasting; Roasting Meat; Roasting, Time and Temperature; Veal Chart; Veal Cuts; Veal Cuts and Uses; Veal Roasting; Vitamin Retention, Meat

roast beef *See* Part 2: Meat and Meat Products Composition

roaster Poultry of size suitable for roasting.
Chicken: Bird of either sex, 3 to 6 months old; weighing above $4\frac{1}{4}$ lb.
Duck: Bird of either sex, about 16 weeks old.

robbiole *See* Part 2: Cheese, Vitamin Content

roccal A quaternary ammonium detergent that is quite effective as a disinfectant. Concentrations usually used are 1 to 1000 and 1 to 5000.

Rochelle salt Sodium potassium tartrate used as buffer and sequestering agent.

Rock Alpine A breed of goats.
See Part 2: Goats, Milk Breeds

rock bass *See* **striped bass**

rock candy Large hard crystals of sugar made by slow evaporation.

rock cork *See* Part 2: Insulation

rock fish *See* **striped bass**
See Part 2: Vitamin A, Fish; Vitamin D, Fish

rock phosphate Mined phosphate rock containing from 20 to 34% P_2O_5; may contain toxic amounts of fluorine (avg. 3.5%).

rock salmon Skinned dogfish.

rock salt Large crystals of sodium chloride.

rock wool (mineral wool) An insulating material made by blowing air through molten slag or rock.
See Part 2: Insulation

rod (rd) (pole) (perch) (1) A unit of measurement of length:
1 rd = 198 inches (in.)
= 25 links (Gunther's)
= 16.5 feet (ft)
= 5.5 yards (yd)
= 5.02921 meters (m)
= 0.005029 kilometer (km)
= 0.003125 statute mile
= 0.002714 U.S. nautical mile
4 rd = chain (Gunther's)
40 rd = furlong
(2) A cylindrical-shaped microorganism.
See Part 2: Bacteria, Molds and Yeasts

rodent (***Rodentia***) A gnawing mammal, e.g., rat, mouse, squirrel.

rodenticide A poison used to kill rodents.
See Part 2: Chemical Poisoning

roe A solid mass of fish eggs; roe of some female fish are used for food, e.g., shad, salmon, sturgeon.
Roe of male: soft roe or milt.
Roe of female: hard roe or spawn.
See Part 2: Fish Cross Section; Plant and Animal Poisoning

roentgen *See* **X-ray**
See Part 2: Constants, Fundamental

roentgen equivalent physical *See* **rep (1)**

rogosa agar *See* Part 2: Microorganism, Media

rojak A salad made of cooked vegetable (cabbage, carrot, bean, bean sprout) and raw fruit (pineapple) and served with a sauce.

roll A small bread-like baked product, usually served hot.
See Part 2: Calories, Daily Recommendations; Frozen Food Storage; Grain Products Composition; Portion Size

rolled oats A breakfast cereal made by steaming oat kernels, crushing them on rollers, and then drying; the cereal is heated just before serving. *See also* **oat.**
Regular rolled oats: dehulled, steamed, flattened and dried oats.
Quick oatmeal: made from oat groats that are steel-cut into pieces after dehulling and flattened thinner than regular rolled oats.
Instant or cook-in-the-bowl: prepared like quick oatmeal except
0.1–1.0% of a gum is placed on surface to speed up hydration.

rolling Excessive side shoulder motion in horses.

romaine lettuce (cos) Lettuce with strong nutty flavor, coarse spoon-shaped leaves; has an elongated head. *See also* **cos; lettuce.**

romano A hard cheese made from skim milk and similar to parmesan but with a saltier flavor; it has a yellowish white interior and black coating; shape is round with flat ends; flavor is sharp, piquant. 1 cup grated = 3 oz.
Composition: 32% H_2O, 30% fat, 5% ash, 4.6% salt.
See Part 2: Cheese Characteristics; Cheese, Vitamin Content

Rome Beauty A variety of apples that is in season from December to April; is an excellent-to-good cooking apple, and a fair eating apple.

Romeldale A breed of sheep originating in the western United States by crossing a Rambouillet ewe with a Romney ram.

Romney A long-wool breed of sheep originating in southern England.
See Part 2: Sheep Breeds

rooster A mature male chicken one year or older which has developed spurs and comb. *See also* **cock.**
See Part 2: Poultry Cooking, Frozen; Poultry Roasting

root That part of a plant which grows downward into the soil and furnishes nourishment by absorbing water, nitrogen, etc. Many types are food sources (potato, beet, etc.)
See Part 2: Corn; Storage, Dry; Storage Times; Sweet Potato and Irish Potato; Vegetable Composition; Vegetables, Classification; Wastes, Agricultural and Industrial

root beer A beverage flavored with oil of sassafras and wintergreen.
See Part 2: Beverage Carbonated, Ingredients; Flavors, Beverage

root mean square *See* **rms; mean square**

ropy A slimy condition in bread caused by spore-forming bacilli of the subtilis-mesentericus group.

Roquefort A white, semisoft cheese with green mold (*Penicillium roquefortii*) throughout made from sheep's milk, matured in caves, and used as a dessert, dressing or cooking cheese; it has a sharp, rich, pungent, salty flavor and a creamy but crumbly texture. Sold in cylindrical shape; ripened 2–5 months by internal molds.
Composition: 39–40% H_2O, 21–22% protein, 30–33% fat, 2% carbohydrate, 5–6% ash, 4% salt; pH 4.7–5.9.
See Part 2: Cheese Characteristics; Cheese Composition; Cheese, Vitamin Content; Milk and Cheese Composition; Milk and Milk Products, Vitamin Content; Vitamin A, Milk and Milk Products

Roquefort dressing A temporary emulsion of oil, seasoning, vinegar, and crumbled Roquefort cheese.
See Part 2: French Dressing Variations; Salad Dressing and Mayonnaise Variations

rosa rugosa *See* **dog rose**

rosefish *See* **ocean perch**
See Part 2: Vitamin A, Fish

rose hip Urn-shaped seed receptable at the base of the blossom, used to make tea, jam, syrup and soup. *See also* **dog rose.**

Rosemary (Rosa Maria) (*Rosmarinus officinalis* L.) The fresh or dried leaf of an evergreen shrub of the mint family; leaf looks like a 1-inch pine needle. Used as a spice for flavoring meat, savoury dishes, and salads.
See Part 2: Essential Oils; Flavoring Agents, Natural

rose oil An essential oil used as a flavoring agent.
See Part 2: Essential Oils; Flavor Ingredients, Taste and Flavor Type

rose water A flavoring distilled from rose petals and used in cooking.

rose wine An all-occasion pink wine made from French-American hybrid grapes.

rosin *See* **gum rosin; wood rosin; resin**

rot *See* Part 2: Mold, Food; Rot Spoilage; Spoilage, Protein Foods

Rotbunte German red and white cattle.

rotenone ($C_{23}H_{22}O_6$) A moderately toxic insecticide extracted from derris root; it is extremely poisonous to fish.

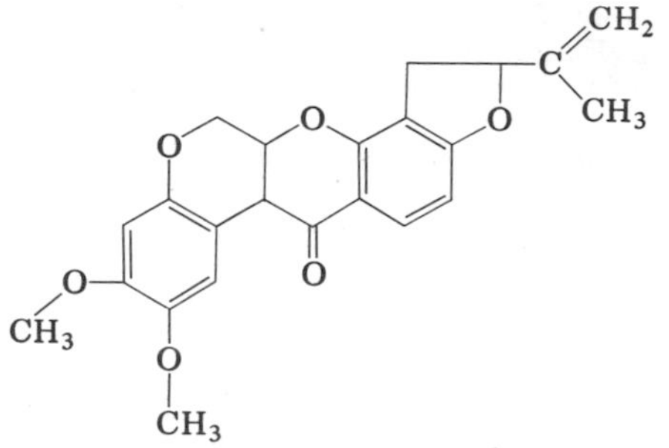

See Part 2: Insect Control

rotisserie An oven equipped with a rotating spit on which meat is roasted.

roughage Indigestible (nonruminant) material in the diet.

round The area of a hind quarter of beef located to the rear of the rump and loin area; its major muscles consist of the tip, top, eye and bottom; about 20% of a choice carcass is round; if rump is included this would add about 5%.
See Part 2: Beef Chart; Beef Cuts; Beef Cuts and Uses; Beef Retail Yield; Beef Roasting; Beef Round, Bone Structure; Beef Round Cuts; Beef Rounds; Beef Wholesale Cuts; Beef Yields; Bone in Retail Cuts; Meat Identification; Meat Label; Potassium-Rich Foods; Veal Chart; Veal Cuts; Veal Roasting

round bone sirloin A sirloin steak found in the loin end wholesale cut; it is located between the wedge bone sirloin and the double bone sirloin.

round fish Fish as it comes from water.

rounding Anything above 50,000, etc., round up, and below round down; at 5,000, etc., round to the nearest even number.

Example: No.	Rounded
9.50	10.00
10.50	10.00
11.50	12.00
12.49	12.00
12.50	12.00
12.51	13.00

rounds Beef and pork small intestine used as natural casings in the meat trade.
See Part 2: Casings, Animal; Casings, Hog and Beef; Casings, Terms

round steak *See* Part 2: Braising Meat; Braising Time

round tip *See* **sirloin**

round worm *See* ***Ascaris suis***

roux A paste made from shortening (various types) and flour for thickening.

Rowan A variety of lespedeza.

royaled A variegated flavor in ice cream.

RSP cherries Red, sour, pitted cherries.

Ru Symbol for the element ruthenium.

rubber $(C_5H_8)_n$ A natural high polymer useful for insulation, vibration damping, etc.
See Part 2: Insulating Value

rubber hydrochloride A stretchable film used in food packaging.

rubber stopper

Size No.	Approx Diam in mm of Large End of Stopper (mm)
00	15
0	17
1	19
2	20
3	23
4	26
5	27
5½	28
6	32
6½	34
7	37
8	41
9	45
10	50
11	51
12	64
13	69
13½	75
14	90
15	103

rubberweed A plant having a toxic principle.
See Part 2: Poisonous Plants

rubidium (Rb) A metallic element; at. no. 37; at. wt. 85.48; Group IA of Periodic Table; oxidation state +1
electron configuration 2-8-18-8-1;
orbit K L M N O

rudimentary shoot (leaves) *See* Part 2: Corn Kernel

rue oil An essential oil used for flavoring.
See Part 2: Essential Oils

rum An alcoholic distillate from fermented juice of sugar cane or sugar cane by-products (molasses) distilled at less than 190° proof. *See also* **sugar cane.**
See Part 2: Flavor Ingredients, Taste and Flavor Type; Minerals (Trace), Limits

rumen (paunch) The first and largest stomach of a ruminant animal located on its left side; this compartment breaks feed down into smaller particles, and is where microorganisms digest most of the cellulose; a bovine rumen may contain from 20 to 50 gal.

ruminant A cud-chewing four-stomach animal which can utilize roughage as a source of food. Examples: cattle, sheep, goats, buffalo, camel, deer, and antelope.

rumination A digestive process which takes place in ruminant animals in which the food in the rumen and reticulum is regurgitated, rechewed and again swallowed.

rump On a live animal, the part between the hips and the tail head.
See Part 2: Beef Cuts; Beef Cuts and Uses; Beef Retail Yield; Beef Roasting; Bone; Roasting, Time and Temperature; Veal Chart; Veal Cuts; Veal Cuts and Uses; Veal Roasting

rump knuckle bone Superior extremity of femur.

rump roast An unboned rump contains the pelvic bone, the sacrum and rump knuckle bone; however, it is usually retailed as a boneless, rolled and tied roast.

runner *See* Part 2: Casings, Animal

Rural New Yorker A variety of potato.

rusk A biscuit; 6% protein, 8% fat, 82% carbohydrate.

Russett Burbank A variety of potato used for baking and frying.

Russian dressing A salad dressing that usually contains the following: corn syrup, tomato, sugar, vinegar, oil, lemon juice, garlic, spices, onion, sweet pepper.
See Part 2: French Dressing Variations; Salad Dressing and Mayonnaise Variations

rust A disease of plants, especially cereal grasses, characterized by the appearance of reddish discoloration of the leaves; caused by virus infestation. *See also* **smut.**

rutabaga (**Swede**); (***Brassica napus*** **var.** ***napobrassica***) A vegetable whose root is used as food; a turnip with a long yellow root.
1 lb fresh = 2.5 cups cubed
1 cup cubed = 140 g (4.9 oz)
1 lb fresh = 2 cups cooked
1 cup cooked = 165 g (5.7 oz)
1 bu = 56 lb
Storage: Cool room temperature or refrigerate (32°F), relative humidity 90–95%; will keep 2 months at 60°F.
Raw composition: 87% H_2O, 1% protein, 0.1% fat, 11% carbohydrate, 1% ash.
See Part 2: Minerals, Food; Plant Foods, Composition; Storage; Sugar, Vegetables; Vegetable Composition; Vegetable Plants; Vegetable Storage

ruthenium (Ru) A metallic element; at. no. 44; at. wt. 101.1; Group VIII of Periodic Table. oxidation states +3, +4, +5, +6, +8
electron configuration 2-8-18-15-1;
orbit K L M N O

Rutherford *See* Part 2: Constants, Fundamental

rye (*Secale cereale*) An annual grass used for grazing; a grain that can withstand cold climate and poor soil; similar in composition to wheat;

used to make black bread (schwartzbrot), whiskey, gin and beer. Young plants used as fodder and older plants for bedding, thatching, paper-making and straw products. Rye sometimes contains a parasitic fungus called ergot (*Claviceps purpurea*) which is poisonous to man and animals.

1.7 lb rye seed/qt
56 lb rye seed/bu
1.5 lb ground rye/qt
Plant 48 to 112 lb/acre
pH 5-5.5
Variety: Abruzzi

Approximate nutrient used for growth of

	20 bu grain	1 ton straw
N	21	10 lb
P_2O_5	8	6 lb
K_2O	6	16 lb

Whole grain composition: 11% H_2O, 12-15% protein, 2% fat, 73% carbohydrate, 2% ash.

Grades of rye flour: Light flour, dark flour, rye bran, red dog.

See Part 2: Cereal Composition; Cereal Nutrient Content; Minerals, Food; Minerals, Plant or Animal Tissue; Nutrients in Crops; Plant Foods, Composition; Protein Factors; Seed, Chemical Composition; Seed, Germination; Vitamin A, Food

rye flour Flour from rye grain low in gluten and elasticity; available in white, medium and dark; 100 lb rye flour = 2.23 bu rye.

Composition: 11% H_2O, 9-16% protein, 1-3% fat, 68-78% carbohydrate, 1-2% ash.

ryegrass An annual and perennial grass. When eaten by cattle, it will sometimes give an off-flavor to milk.

Seeding: 40 lb/acre; 24 lb/bu.
Variety: Italian.

rye meal 4⅓ cups = 1 lb

rye wafer *See* Part 2: Grain Products Composition

rye whiskey Whiskey made from a mixture of rye or barley malt and unmalted rye.

S

S Symbol for the element sulfur.

Saanen *See* Part 2: Goats, Milk Breeds

sabayon A dessert made of egg yolk, vanilla, sugar, and white and sherry wine.

SABHI agar *See* Part 2: Microorganism, Media

sablefish *See* Part 2: Vitamin A, Fish; Vitamin D, Fish

sabouraud medium *See* Part 2: Microorganism, Media

sacahuista A plant having a toxic principle.
See Part 2: Poisonous Plants

saccharase An enzyme that uses sugars as a substrate.

saccharide One of a series of carbohydrates.

saccharimeter (saccharometer, sometimes reserved for density measurements) Instrument for determining the concentration of sugar by measuring the angle of rotation of polarized light.

saccharin A non-nutritive sweetener 500 times as sweet as cane sugar (sucrose); m.p. 227°C. Substitute for sugar used by diabetics. A known carcinogen.

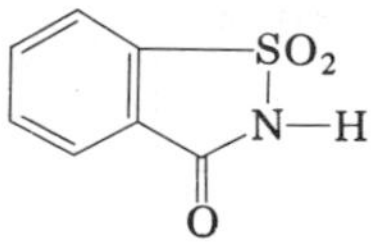

See Part 2: Sweetness of Sweeteners; Sweetening Agents; Sweetening Compounds

Saccharomyces A type of mold.
See Part 2: Spoilage, Carbohydrate Foods

saccharose *See* sucrose

sack A strong, dry, light-colored wine.

sacral vertebrae Backbone behind the slip joint and before the tail bone (loin end area); beef, 5; lamb, 4; pork, 4; chicken, fused; rabbit, 3 or 4.
See Part 2: Bone

sacro iliac The joint in which the sacrum meets the iliac.
See Part 2: Bone

sacrum *See* sacral vertebrae

saffian Leather made from goat or sheep skin.

safflower (*Carthamus tinctorius*) A plant grown for its seed which produces a polyunsaturated oil and protein feed. The light-yellow oil is sometimes used for coloring food. *See also* safflower oil.

Yield from seed:

	(%)
Hull (1% oil, 4% protein)	35–40
Oil	40
Protein	15

See Part 2: Seed, Chemical Composition; Unsaponifiable Matter

safflower meal The ground presscake of safflower seed from which the oil has been expressed. Contains 1% oil and 20–42% protein.
See Part 2: Oil Meals Composition

safflower oil A highly unsaturated oil obtained from pressing and/or solvent-extraction of safflower seed.

Composition:

myristic	0.1	linoleic	70–78
palmitic	5–7	arachidic	0.4
stearic	3	eicosenic	0.6
oleic	13–19	linolenic	3

Properties:

iodine value	143–145
melting point	-18 to -15°C
saponification value	190–192
specific gravity 60°C	0.90

1 qt = 4 cups; 1 cup = 210 g (7.4 oz)

See Part 2: Fats and Oils, Composition; Fats and Oils, Fatty Acid Composition; Fats and Oils, Physical and Chemical Properties; Fatty Acids, Fats and Oils; Free Fatty Acid, Smoke, Flash, Fire Points; Iodine and Saponification Values; Oil, Triglyceride Mole Percent Composition; Refractive Indices, Fats and Oils; Specific Gravities, Fats and Oils; Titer, Fats and Oils; Tocopherols

saffron (*Crocus sativis* L.) Dried orange-yellow stigma of saffron flower used as seasoning; a yellow-red color from the saffron plant used to color food.

Dye: saffron yellow.

Spice: orange red, 3-branched style; bitter, aromatic odor.

See Part 2: Colors Permanently Listed

safranin counterstain *See* Part 2: Gram Stain

sagamite Mush made from hominy.

sage (*Salvia officinalis* L.) A low-growing shrub; sold in fresh or dried bunches; leaf is the only part used. The fresh or dried leaf of a shrubby plant used as an herb; available in whole, rubbed (fluffy) and ground form. The dried product contains:

not less than 1% volatile ether extract
not more than 25% crude fiber
not more than 10% total ash
not more than 1% acid-insoluble ash
not more than 12% stems (excluding petioles) or foreign matter
See Part 2: Essential Oils; Flavoring Agents, Natural; Spices, Microbial Content

sage cheese A cheddar-like cheese containing sage leaves, which give it a green appearance.

sago Refined starch from the pith of the sago palm.

sago palm (*Metroxylon sagu; M. rumphii*) A subtropical tree that contains starch in the pith of the trunk; the trunk is split and the pith scooped out; it is then ground, the starch washed out and dried to form sago flour. A similar flour is also manufactured from other plants such as palm fern, tapioca, potato, sweet potato and maize.
Composition: 0.2% protein, 0.2% fat, 94% carbohydrate.
See Part 2: Starch, Microappearance; Vitamin A, Food

saguero Palm wine.

Saigon cinnamon *See* **cassia**

saim Fat or lard.

sainfoin *See* Part 2: Seed, Germination

Sainte Croix du Mont A high-quality, medium-rich white wine.

Saint-John's bread The carob bean. *See also* **carob pod.**

Saint-Paulin A slightly pressed, large, round cheese with a thin rind; made from cow's milk.

Sakaguchi *See* Part 2: Protein and Amino Acids, Color Reactions

sake (saki) (Samshu) An alcoholic drink made from rice; 13–15% alcohol; rice wine.

sal Pharmacist's term for a salt, e.g., sal ammoniac = ammonium chloride.

salad Uncooked vegetables and sometimes meat which are cut up, mixed, and seasoned; usually served as a side dish, but may be a separate course.
See Part 2: Portion Size

salad berry A berry of *Gaultheria Shallon*.

salad cream A dressing made from olive oil and eggs.

salad dressing A combination of mayonnaise and a cooked paste base with a minimum of 30% vegetable oil. *See also* **cooked salad dressing, French dressing; mayonnaise; Russian dressing.**
Emulsifying ingredient: A minimum of 4% liquid egg yolk.
Acid: Vinegar or lemon juice (citric acid permitted to ¼ acetic acid in vinegar).
Starch paste: Tapioca, wheat or rye flour is required.
Storage: Refrigerate after opening.
Composition: 40% H_2O,. 1% protein, 42% fat, 14% carbohydrate, 2% ash.
See Part 2: Mayonnaise and Salad Dressing; Salad Dressing and Mayonnaise Variations; Stabilizers, Thickeners

salad oil A refined, bleached, deodorized, and winterized (if needed) edible oil, e.g., olive oil; it remains unclouded and pourable at 40°–50°F and will remain clear for 5.5 hr at 32°F. Made from cooking oil by removal of fractions that crystallize at low temperature (winterization).
Storage: Short-term: room temperature; long-term: refrigerate. If it becomes cloudy or solid, this is not harmful, and will clear upon warming.

salame cheese *See* **Italian cheese**

salami A coarse-ground cooked Italian sausage of many varieties; normally 60% beef and 40% pork.
Meats used:

(%)	
50–80	beef
20–60	pork
0–20	hearts
0–25	pork cheek meat
0–35	beef fat plate

Ingredients used:

0–24%	ice
8 oz	sugar/100 lb*
1 oz	cardamon/100 lb*
2–6 oz	cracked black pepper/100 lb*
1 oz	garlic powder/100 lb*
2 oz	$NaNO_3$/100 lb*
¼ oz	$NaNO_2$/100 lb*
0–3 oz	coriander/100 lb
0–1 oz	mace/100 lb
0–1 oz	paprika/100 lb

*Combination used in some formulations.

Processing procedure:
1. Grind with ⅛-in. plate.
2. Mix; add cure and spices.
3. Stuff into casings.
4. Hang until dry.
5. Smoke 80°–90°F for 14 hr then at 150°–160°F until internal temperature reaches 142°F.
6. Rinse with hot water.
7. Shower for 10 min.
8. Hang at room temperature for 2 hr.
9. Store in cooler.

See Part 2: Sausage Identification; Sausage Nutritive Value; Sausage, Types; Water Activity, Organisms and Food

salami (dry) A dry sausage made from predominantly pork with some beef; it is allowed to cure 2 days before stuffing; it is then dried without smoking.
Types:
B.C. salami (German type) stuffed in beef middle casings 11–15 in. long and smoked.

Genoa is stuffed in sewed hog bungs 16–20 in. long.
Milano is stuffed in hog bungs 18–30 in. long.

salami cotto (cooked salami) A coarsely chopped mixture, predominantly pork with some beef; it is held 3 days prior to cooking to allow curing; the internal temperature is raised to above 137°F.

salep (salop) Dried tubers of *Orchis mascula* used to make a drink or jelly.

saleratus Baking soda (Na or K bicarbonate).

salicylage Preserving food with salicylic acid.

saligot Water chestnut.

salimeter (salinometer) (salometer) A floating (specific gravity) instrument used to test the strength or salinity (salt) of a pickle or brine. Pure water = 0°, saturated salt solution at 38°F = 100°.
See Part 2: Brine, Meat Curing; Salt Brine; Salt, Brine Table

saline *See* **physiological saline; salty**

salinometer *See* **salimeter**

Salisbury steak Ground beef mixed with bread and seasoning and fried.
See Part 2: Portion Size

saliva Fluid secreted by glands in the mouth which provides lubrication for swallowing; contains ptyalin, potassium thiocyanate, and albumin; assists in carbohydrate breakdown.
See Part 2: Moisture in Biological Materials; pH Values of Biological Materials

salivary glands *See* Part 2: Organ Weights

salmagundi A mixture of meat, eggs, and pickled vegetables served as a salad.

salmi Birds or game stewed in wine.

salmon (*Oncorhynchus*) A large, soft-finned, fat fish; flesh color, reddish to red yellow. Atlantic salmon are true salmon; percentage of fat varies from 0 to 14% depending on when caught. Pacific salmon are different species from Atlantic salmon. *See also* **fresh-water fish.**
Types, Where Caught, Composition:
Sockeye (*O. nerka*) also called red and blueback; Pacific Coast; 66% H_2O, 21% protein, 10% fat, 1.4% ash.
Chinook (*O. tshawytscha*) also called spring and king; Alaska; 64% H_2O, 19% protein, 16% fat, 1.1% ash.
Silver (*O. kisutch*) also called silversides, coho, and red; North Atlantic; 75% H_2O, 20% protein, 5% fat, 1.2% ash.
Pink (*O. gorbuscha*) also called humpback; Great Lakes; 76% H_2O, 20% protein, 4% fat, 1.2% ash.
Chum (*O. keta*) also called fall and keta salmon; 76% H_2O, 21% protein, 4% fat, 1.2% ash.
See Part 2: Fish and Shellfish Composition; Fish, Smoke-Cured; Fish, Storage; Food, Composition; Frozen Food Storage; Glutamate; Minerals, Food; Salmon and Trout; Vitamin D, Fish; Vitamin D, Food

salmonella A group of pathogens causing gastroenteritis (and a variety of other illnesses); there are about 1500 different serotypes. The second most common type of food-poisoning bacteria; gram-negative rods, facultative anaerobes and nonspore former; salmonella death rate for infected people is low; optimum temperature for growth, 98°–100°F; bacteria killed by heating to 150°–180°F for 15 min.
See Part 2: Egg Specifications; Food Poisoning, Bacteria; Illness from Food; Infectious Agents; Infectious Diseases, Food-Borne; Intestinal Microorganisms; Intestinal Microorganisms in Triple-Sugar Agar; Microbiological Media; Microbiological Standards, Dairy; Microorganism Reactions on Differential Tube Media

salmonellosis *See* Part 2: Diseases, Food-Borne

salmon fry A smolt.

salmon oil *See* Part 2: Iodine and Saponification Values

salmon trout *See* **fresh water fish**

salometer *See* **salimeter**

salpicon A stuffing.

salsify (vegetable oyster); (oyster plant); (*Tragopogon porrifolius*) A biennial plant grown for its cylindrical white root; the root is used as a cooked vegetable and the leaves are used as a salad.
Storage: 32°F, 90–95% relative humidity, 2 months storage life.
See Part 2: Minerals, Food; Storage; Vegetable Composition; Vegetable Plants

salt A chemical compound formed when the hydrogen of an acid is replaced by a metal, e.g., $CaO + 2HCl \rightarrow CaCl_2 + H_2O$.
(1) Inorganic: Common salt is sodium chloride (NaCl); it is used to flavor food, and for food preservation and curing hides; 1 barrel = 280 lb; 1 qt = 2.6 lb. Iodized salt has 1% potassium iodine added.
(2) Organic: Generalized formula is $R{-}\overset{\overset{\displaystyle O}{\|}}{C}{-}O{-}M$, where M is a metal, e.g.,

$$\underset{\text{acetic acid}}{2CH_3COOH} + CuO \longrightarrow \underset{\text{copper acetate}}{Cu(C_2H_3O_2)_2} + H_2O$$

A metallic salt of a fatty acid is called a soap.
1 tbsp = 1 oz
1 lb = 1½ cups
1 cup = 290 g (10.2 oz)
50 lb = 1 bu
Salt added to water lowers its freezing point and raises its boiling point; freezing point is reduced about 2°F for every 1% of salt added. *See also* **brine.**
See Part 2: Boiling Points, Sodium Chloride, Calcium Chloride; Brine, Meat Curing; Chloride Salt,

Injury; Fish, Smoke-Cured; Ham, Curing; Hide Curing; Hide, Layers; Hides, Salt Absorption; Meat Curing Ingredients; Normal Solutions; Reagents, Normal Solutions; Salt Brine; Salt, Brine Table; Salt Penetration Rate; Salt Solution, Freezing; Water Activity, Organisms and Food

salt analysis Determined by digesting the sample with nitric acid in the presence of excess silver nitrate; the silver ion precipitates the chlorides, and the amount of silver nitrate used can be determined by titrating the excess with ammonium thiocyanate; the quantity of chloride can thus be calculated and the results reported as sodium chloride.

salt cake Sodium sulfate (Na_2SO_4) A salt of sulfuric acid found naturally in western U.S. Made by the reaction

$$2NaCl + H_2SO_4 \rightarrow 2HCl + Na_2SO_4$$

salt-free diet A diet that contains 150–500 mg sodium/day.

saltpeter Can be any of the following: (1) Chile saltpeter (cubic nitre, sodium nitrate). (2) Ordinary saltpeter; Bengal saltpeter; nitre; potassium nitrate. (3) Wall saltpeter; Norway saltpeter; calcium nitrate. (1) and (2) are used in meat curing.

saltpeter, Chile As mined 48–75% sodium nitrate ($NaNO_3$) and 20–40% sodium chloride (NaCl).

saltpeter, ordinary Potassium nitrate (KNO_3).

salty (saline) The taste sensation of sodium chloride.

salvia Sage.

Salway A variety of freestone peaches.

samarium (Sm) A rare earth element of the lanthanide series; Group IIIB of Periodic Table; at. no. 62; at. wt. 105.35; electron configuration 2-8-18-24-8-2
orbit K L M N O P
oxidation states +2, +3.

samneh Rendered butterfat.

samp Corn ground larger than meal and smaller than hominy.
See Part 2: Cereal Composition

samphire Leaves used to make pickles.

samp hominy Coarse hominy grits. *See also* hominy.

sample A part taken to represent the whole of a production run or shipment of raw material.

sample size Determination of appropriate size of a sample.
Paired analysis:
With a given size sample the odds are 1:1 that a difference of δ could be detected at the 5% level:

$$\delta = \frac{s_D\, t_{.05}}{\sqrt{n}}$$

δ = difference to be detected
s_D = sample standard deviation
df = degrees of freedom $(n - 1)$
n = sample size in each group
t = student t at .05

To determine sample size, state difference to be detected, since t changes with n, guess at n and solve, adjust n size, resolve until desired value is obtained.

Group analysis (difference between means):

$$\delta = \frac{\sqrt{2}\, s\, t}{n} \quad \text{or} \quad n = \frac{2\, t^2 s^2}{\delta^2}$$

n = sample size in each group
s = estimate of standard deviation
t = table value; $df = 2(n - 1)$
δ = difference to be detected

Analysis of variance:

$$\delta = \frac{(Q_{a,f})\,(s_0)\,F_{f,f_0}}{n}$$

s_0 = estimate of standard deviation
f_0 = df in s_0
a = treatments in new experiment
n = individuals per treatment
$f = a(n - 1)$ of new experiment
δ = difference to be detected
$Q_{a,f}$ = table value
F_{f,f_0} = table value; $f = f_1$; $f_0 = f_2$

Probability = (1 − prob. of success or probability of detecting δ if it exists)

sample standard deviation (s_D) A measure of sample variability.
In paired analysis:

$$s_D = \sqrt{\frac{\Sigma d^2}{n - 1}}$$

$D = X_1 - X_2$

$\bar{d} = \frac{\Sigma D}{n}$

$d = D - \bar{d}$

n = number of pairs
X_x = observations

samshu *See* sake

sand (silica) SiO_2 Granules of impure silicon dioxide; 1 cu ft dry sand = 110 lb.
See Part 2: Fertilizer; Insulation; Insulation, Conductivity Values; Soil Classes

sandalwood oil An East Indian essential oil used in flavoring.
See Part 2: Essential Oils

sanders agar *See* Part 2: Microorganism, Media

Sandhill cattle Cattle from the sandhills of western Nebraska.

sand sole *See* sole

sand trout *See* sea trout

sandwich Two pieces of bread with a filling of meat, jelly, peanut butter, etc. between them. Named for the Earl of Sandwich.
See Part 2: Portion Size

sangaree A spiced drink made of wine, sugar and water.

sanitary Hygienic, pertaining to health.

sanitizer A cleaning preparation, e.g., chlorinated trisodium phosphate.
See Part 2: Sanitizing Chemicals; Sanitizers

Sanka Proprietary name for a coffee from which most of the caffeine has been removed.

San Pierre No. 1 A breed of hogs produced from a Berkshire and Chester White cross; black and white in color.

sansa Residue from olives after removing oil.

Santa Gertrudis First breed of beef cattle originating in the United States developed by R. J. Kleberg of King Ranch, Kingsville, Texas; they originated from Brahman bulls of the Nellore strain and Shorthorn cows and are approximately 5/8 Shorthorn and 3/8 Brahman; they have almost no hump and are deep red in color. *See also* **Monkey.**
See Part 2: Beef and Dual-Purpose Cattle

santol *See* Part 2: Fruit Classification; Fruit Storage

santos *See* **Brazilian santos**

S.A.P. Subject to approval of price.

sap The natural circulating juice in a plant or tree. It is primarily a sugar solution. A few species also contain latex, which is different from sap.

sapo Soap; sodium salt of a fatty acid.

sapodilla (*Achras sapota*) A medium-sized tree that produces a brown fruit with delicious pulp and black seed; flavor somewhat like brown sugar; cuts in bark also yield a latex called chicle, the base for chewing gum.
See Part 2: Fruit Composition

saponification The reaction of a fatty acid ester and an alkali-metal compound; the products are a soap and an alcohol.

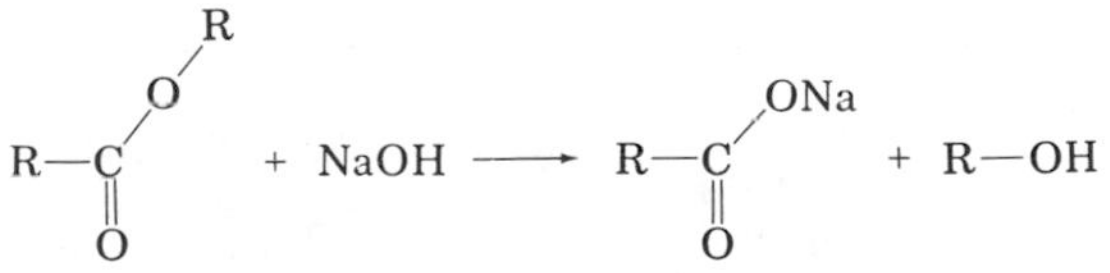

saponification value (or number) analysis The milligrams of potassium hydroxide required to saponify 1 g of fat. It is determined by adding an excess of potassium hydroxide to fat, saponifying the fat, and then titrating the excess potassium hydroxide with a standard acid; from this value it is possible to calculate the mean molecular weight.
See Part 2: Fat and Oils, Fatty Acid Composition; Fats and Oils, Physical and Chemical Properties; Iodine and Saponification Values; Wheat Products Composition

sapor Taste.

sapota *See* Part 2: Fruit Composition; Fruit Storage

sapro- A prefix meaning rotten or putrid.

sap sago cheese A hard, light, sweet, greenish dessert cheese; a clover supplies the unique color and flavor. Made from skimmed and soured cow's milk, buttermilk and whey; ripened for 5 months, sold in small cone shapes.
Composition: 37% H_2O, 41% protein, 7–8% fat, 4.5% salt.
See Part 2: Cheese Characteristics

saracen Buckwheat.

Saran *See* **polyvinylidene chloride**

Saratoga chop Lamb chops made from the shoulder muscle that has been rolled and skewered.
See Part 2: Lamb Cuts

Sarcina *See* Part 2: Spoilage, Protein Foods

sarco- A prefix meaning flesh.

sarcocystis A parasite found in the skeletal muscle fibers of all classes of livestock and man.

sarcolemma A membranous envelope approximately 100 Å thick surrounding the muscle fiber; the cell nuclei are just inside this covering.

sarcomere Area between 2 adjacent Z lines of a muscle fiber.

sarcoplasm The cytoplasm of muscle cells which surrounds the myofibrils.

sarcoplasmic reticulum A network surrounding the myofibrils of a muscle.

sardine Small salt water food fish of the herring family, canned in salted oil.

Country of Origin	Fish Used
France	young pilchard
Norway	sprats (bristling)
Portugal	young pilchard
Spain	young pilchard

Small sea herring (*Clupea harengus*): 3¾ to 6¾ in. long; packed in natural oil, tomato sauce or mustard sauce.
European pilchard *Sardina pilchardus* or *Clupea pilchardus*.
Brisling (brisling sardines) or sprat (*Clupea sprattus*): 3½ to 4¾ in. long; packed in olive oil.
Canned solid composition: 62% H_2O, 24% protein, 11% fat, 3% ash.
Usual serving: 3.5 oz
1 cup = 160 g (5.6 oz)

Type Pack	No. of Sardines
1 layer	6-12
mustard sauce	6-12
2 layers	14-26
cross pack	30-38

See Part 2: Calcium, Daily Recommendations; Fish and Shellfish Composition; Minerals, Food; Riboflavin, Food; Unsaturated Fatty Acids; Vitamin D, Food

sardine oil The fatty oil obtained from pressing sardines.

	No. of Carbons	%
Saturated:	14	5-6
	16	10-15
	18	2-3
Unsaturated:	16	13
	18	24
Polyunsaturated:	20	26
	22	19

Properties:

acid number,	0.57
specific gravity 20°/4°C	0.9384
iodine value	170-193
saponification value	191

See Part 2: Fats and Oils, Physical and Chemical Properties; Fats and Oils, Characteristics; Iodine and Saponification Values; Titer, Fats and Oils

sarrazin Buckwheat.

sarsaparilla A beverage flavor made from the root of several species of *Smilax*.

sassafras An extract of the bark or root of a tree of the laurel family, used as flavoring in food.
See Part 2: Essential Oils

satay Beef, chicken or mutton marinated in soy sauce, garlic, sugar and tamarind juice and broiled on skewers.

sation Planting or sowing.

satsuma *See* **tangerine**

saturated (1) A carbon atom each of whose valences forms a single bond with another atom, which may or may not be carbon. *See also* **alkane.** (2) The maximum amount of a substance that can be held in solution in a given solvent at a given temperature. *See also* **saturated solution.**
See Part 2: Beans, Peas and Nuts; Dairy Products, Composition; Egg Composition; Egg Products, Nutritive Value; Fats and Oils, Composition; Fats and Oils, Characteristic; Fish and Shellfish Composition; Fruit Composition; Fuel, Heating Value; Grain Products Composition; Meat Composition; Poultry Composition; Saturated Fatty Acids; Sausage Composition; Soups, Composition; Sugars and Sweets Composition; Tallow, Beef, Triglyceride Mole Percent Composition; Vegetable Composition

saturated fatty acid $C_nH_{2n+1}COOH$ A fatty acid containing carbon atoms joined together by single bonds. They have a higher melting point and are harder than unsaturated acids of the same chain length. The principal natural saturated fatty acids are:

Name	No. of Carbons
Butyric	4
Caproic	6
Caprylic	8
Capric	10
Lauric	12
Myristic	14
Palmitic	16
Stearic	18
Arachidic	20

saturated hydrocarbon *See* **alkane**

saturated solution A solution which has dissolved all of a given product that is capable of dissolving under normal conditions; there is an equilibrium reached between the saturated solution and the undissolved solute which is a function of the temperature.

saturnism Lead poisoning.

satvic *See* Part 2: Fatty Acids and Their Properties

sauce A liquid mixture placed over a food to alter its flavor.
See Part 2: Fruit Sauces; Sauce, Barbecue; Sauce, Beef Steak; Sauce, Thick; Sauce, Tomato; Sauce, Worcester; Storage Times; White Sauce

saucealone Garlic mustard.

sauerbraten Beef soaked in water, vinegar, onion, salt, pepper, and bay leaves; cooked with soaking liquid and sour cream.

sauerkraut Shredded cabbage leaves preserved by lactic acid fermentation by *Lactobacillus* organisms; major acid produced is lactic acid; air should at least be partially excluded; 2.25% salt is used and sometimes vinegar. 1 cup = 190 g (6.6 oz).
Canned solid and liquid composition: 93% H_2O, 1% protein, 0.2% fat, 4% carbohydrate, 2% ash; 3.1-3.7 pH.
Storage: 34-38°F.
See Part 2: Spoilage, Carbohydrate Foods; Standards, Processed Fruit and Vegetable Products; Vegetable Composition

Saumon du Rhin Grilled or baked salmon.

sausage Meat mixed with salt and spices and often stuffed into casings, natural or artificial.
See Part 2: Animal Foods, Composition; Frozen Food Storage; Frozen Meat Storage Time; Meat, Frozen Storage; Meat Storage; Pork Carcass, Retail Yield; Pork Storage; Pork Yield; Portion Size; Riboflavin, Daily Recommendations; Sausage Composition; Sausage Identification; Sausage, Types; Thiamin, Food; Water Activity, Organisms and Food

sausage bulls Lean, aged male cattle.

sausage casing The covering of a sausage, made of natural or synthetic materials. *See also* **casing.**
Storage: 40°-45°F, 85-90% relative humidity.

sausage dough A sausage emulsion.

sausage seasoning *See* **pork sausage**

sausage trimmings Approximately 12% of a normal hog carcass.

sauté Cooked in a small amount of fat.

sauterne (Barsac) A full, sweet white wine.

saveloy A dried, highly seasoned, smoked pork sausage.

savor Taste or flavor; also the odor of prepared food.

savory Dried brown-green leaf (3/8-in. in length) and flowering tops of a mint family plant used as an herb; sold whole or ground; the leaves and young shoots are used to flavor stuffing, meat pies, sausage, sauces, vegetables.

Type	Name
Summer	*Satureja hortensis*
Winter	*Satureja montana*

See Part 2: Spices, Microbial Content

sawdust Small particles of wood produced by sawing.
See Part 2: Insulation; Wastes, Agricultural and Industrial

Sb Symbol for the element antimony.

SBG *See* Part 2: Microorganism, Media

Sc Symbol for the element scandium.

scald (1) To rinse with boiling water, or to heat just below boiling. (2) A defect of stored apples.

scaldberry Blackberry.

scalding Hog and chicken scalding water temperature 150° to 160°F; packing plants (hog) with long tanks often use lower temperatures; birds, 60 to 90 sec. *See also* **semi-scalding.**

Type	Temp (°F)
Semiscald	125–130
Subscald	131–140
Hardscald	140

scalding water additives Compounds used to aid in hair removal of a hog carcass; must be rinsed from carcass: caustic soda, dioctyl sodium sulfosuccinate, lime, methyl polysilicone, sodium carbonate, sodium dodecylbenzene sulfonate, sodium hexametaphosphate, sodium lauryl sulfate, sodium metasilicate, sodium tripolyphosphate, trisodium phosphate.

scale (1) A thin layer of hard material firmly attached to a substrate, e.g., boiler scale. (2) A standard set of values (degrees) established for measuring temperature, etc. (3) A device for measuring weight.

scalenus Muscle in the neck area between the first rib and the last 4 cervical vertebrae.

scallion A member of the onion family.

scallop A lean, bivalve mollusk; shellfish; the large (1/2–2 in. thick) adductor muscle that controls shell movement is used as food; meat may be white, tan, orange or pink; 20% edible (avg. 20% protein).

Types	Where Caught
Bay (*Aequipecten irradians*)	Middle and south Atlantic
Calico (*Argopecten gibbus*)	New England, Gulf
Sea (*Placopectan megallanicus*)	Canada, New England, middle Atlantic, Australia, Alaska

Purchased as	Ounces per serving
Shucked (63% yield)	5
Breaded	4

Raw composition: 80% H_2O, 15% protein, 0.2% fat, 3% carbohydrate, 1% ash.
See Part 2: Fish, Storage; Frozen Food Storage; Frying Time; Minerals, Food

scalloped summer squash *See* **marrow**

scamorze A semihard cheese packaged in small rolls; has a creamy white interior, and is mild and slightly firm. It has an elastic texture and when heated, becomes stringy.
See Part 2: Cheese Characteristics

scamp *See* **grouper**

scandium (Sc) A metallic element; at. no. 21; at. wt. 44.96; oxidation state +3
electron configuration 2-8-9-2;
orbit K L M N
Group IIIB of Periodic Table.

scapula Shoulder blade bone; spine is lateral, bone is attached only to the humerus.
See Part 2: Beef Rib Nomenclature; Bone

scapular cartilage Cartilage on the bladebone on the end opposite the area where this bone is attached to the humerus.

scarlet fever A viral disease of children accompanied by high fever.
See Part 2: Illness from Food

Scarlet Runner (*Phaseolus coccineus*) A variety of green bean (usually a climber, but there are a few non-climbing varieties) with a pod 8 to 24 in. in length.

scavenge To search for and retrieve small amounts of a usable material after the major part has been removed, e.g., to scavenge a corn field.

scent A light, usually pleasant odor or smell.

Schaal test *See* Part 2: Antioxidant Activity

schenk beer A young beer.

Schiedam Holland gin.

schnapps A liquor manufactured by fermenting cooked potatoes; a strong alcoholic drink; vodka.

schou oil An emulsifying agent.

schrock A plant having a toxic principle.
See Part 2: Poisonous Plants

schwartzbrot *See* **rye**

Schwarzbunte German Friesian cattle.

sclerotin *See* **pectin**

Sclerotinia A type of mold.
See Part 2: Mold, Food; Rot Spoilage; Spoilage, Carbohydrate Foods

Schlerotiorum *See* Part 2: Mold, Food

scone A small cake made of wheat, barley, or oatmeal; used chiefly in England and Scotland as a tea cake.

scoop A utensil used to measure volume.

Scoop No.	Volume
40	1⅗ tbsp
30	2⅕ tsp
24	2⅔+ tsp
16	¼ cup
12	5+ tbsp
10	6+ tbsp
8	½ cup
6	10+ tbsp

See Part 2: Scoop Size

score To cut into the outer hard surface of a material.

scorzonera (black salsify); (*Scorzonera hispanica*) A plant of the daisy family. The cylindrical root has a black skin and white flesh and is eaten as a cooked vegetable. Root contains inulin, a coffee substitute; leaves are used as salad greens.

Scotch cap Wild raspberry.

Scotch Highland *See* Part 2: Beef and Dual-Purpose Cattle

Scotch oatmeal Ground oatmeal.

Scotch tender (chuck tender) Supraspinatus muscle that ties lateral to the scapula and dorsal to its spine.

Scottish Black Face *See* Part 2: Sheep Breeds

scoured wool Greasy wool that has been subjected to a cleaning process before manufacturing.

scouse Seaman's term for vegetables and biscuit.

scrabbed eggs Hard-boiled eggs mixed with butter, salt and pepper.

scran Food scraps.

scrapple Sausage consisting of pork and pork by-products, meal or flour of grain and seasoning; head meat, feet, hearts, tongues, and pork trimmings are cooked in water; bones are removed and meat is ground and cereal (usually corn meal) added.

scribe *See* Part 2: Beef Rib Nomenclature

scrod A young codfish. *See also* **cod; haddock.**

scrotum The skin holding the testicles.

scrow Small bits of hide used to make glue.

scrub Livestock of mixed or unknown breeding; inferior.

scruple (apothecary) (s) A measure of weight.
1 scruple = 20 grains
= 1.295,978,4 grams
= 0.833,333,3 pennyweight
= 0.731,428,6 dram (av.)
= 0.333,333 dram (apoth.)
= 0.045,714,3 oz (av.)
= 0.041,666,7 oz (apoth.) (troy)
= 0.003,472,222 lb (apoth.) (troy)
= 0.002,857,143 lb (av.)

scudding A process in cleaning hides prior to tanning; the hides are placed over a wooden beam and cleaned with a special knife.

scup (porgy, paugy) A lean, sea-bream type of fish caught along the middle Atlantic coast.

scuppernong Muscadine, a wine grape.

scurfs In polled animals small horning "buttons" attached to the skin but not to the skull in the area where horns are normally found.

scurvy A disease caused by deficiency of Vitamin C in the diet; symptoms are loss of weight, fatigue, shortness of breath; gums become swollen and bleed and bruise easily.

scutellum A layer that separates the embryo and endosperm of a seed; part of the germ.
See Part 2: Corn Kernel; Wheat Kernel; Wheat Kernel Parts; Wheat, Parts of Grain; Wheat, Parts of Grain, Vitamins

Se Symbol for the element selenium.

sea bass A lean spiny-finned fish caught off both the Pacific and Atlantic coasts.

Types	Where Caught
Black and white	Pacific coast
Common (blackfish, black sea bass)	Atlantic coast

Composition: 76–78% H_2O, 19–21% protein, 0.5–2% fat, 0% carbohydrate, 1–2% ash.

sea bread Hardtack.

seafood Food from the sea, including all types of vertebrate fish, shellfish, oysters, clams, etc.
Storage: Store in coldest part of refrigerator; use within 1 to 2 days.
See Part 2: Frying Time; Microwave Processing Time; Portion Size

sea herring (Atlantic or Pacific herring) A fat, soft-finned fish caught almost worldwide.

seakale (*Crambe maritima*) A plant whose blanched leaf-stalks are used like asparagus.

seakale beet (chard); (*Beta vulgaris*) A plant that resembles a beet but is grown for its leaves and leaf-stalk which are boiled and consumed as a vegetable.
Storage: Wash and drain; store in refrigerator crisper or plastic bag; use within 1 to 2 days.

seal *See* Part 2: Animal Foods, Composition; Glass Jar Tops

seam *See* Part 2: Can

seam out To separate muscles at the natural seam.

sear To brown a meat surface by a short application of intense heat.

sea salt Sodium chloride obtained by evaporation of sea water. This salt is high in trace minerals.

seasoning A condiment, spice or herb added to food to enhance its flavor.

sea trout A lean, sharp-tooth fish.

Types	Where Caught
Gray (weakfish, squeteagues)	Middle and south Atlantic
Spotted (speckled)	Middle and south Atlantic and the Gulf
White (sand)	Gulf

sea water Water from the ocean. ("Sea" and "ocean" are not exact synonyms, as there are many enclosed bodies of water called seas, some of which are more saline than the ocean.)
Composition: 96.4% H_2O, 2.6% NaCl, 0.4% $MgCl_2$, 0.2% $MgSO_4$, 0.1% $CaSO_4$, 0.1% KCl; trace percentages of bromine and many metals.

seaweed Kelp (marine algae); Irish moss (carreeganan).
See Part 2: Minerals (Trace), Limits; Wastes, Agricultural and Industrial

sebaceous Glands which secrete fatty, tallow-like matter on the skin.

secant A trigonometric function: secant = $\frac{\text{hypotenuse}}{\text{abscissa}}$; also a straight line cutting through the circumference of a circle.

secondary Carbon atom which is united by two valences to chain or ring, $CH_3(CH_2)_nCH(CH_2)_nCH_3$.

section-comb honey *See* **comb honey**

seed Mature ovula, composed of an external skin (perisperm or testa) and a nucleus (kernel).
See Part 2: Fruit and Nut Rootstock; Moisture in Biological Materials; Oils, Seed and Fruit; Orange Structure; Pulses, Nuts and Seeds Composition; Saturated Fatty Acids; Seed Composition; Seed, Germination; Unsaturated Fatty Acids; Wheat Grain; Wheat Kernel; Wheat Kernel Parts

seed cake (1) A sweet cake containing seeds. (2) Oil cake.

seed coat The perisperm or outer skin of a seed.
See Part 2: Corn Kernel; Wheat Grain; Wheat Kernel; Wheat Kernel Parts

seedling A young plant.

seethe To exhibit surface agitation, as boiling water.

segment A geometrical portion of a circle or sphere.
See Part 2: Orange Structure

sego A plant of the lily family that has an edible root.

selamatans Special meals eaten at celebrations.

selective agar *See* Part 2: Microorganism, Selective and Differential Broths and Media, Water Filtration Plant

selenite broth *See* Part 2: Microorganism, Media; Microorganism, Selective and Differential Broths and Media, Water Filtration Plant

selenite F broth *See* Part 2: Microbiological Media

selenium (Se) A nonmetallic element; at. no. 34; at. wt. 78.96; Group VIA of Periodic Table; electron configuration 2-8-18-6;
orbit K L M N
oxidation states +4, +6, -2
Vegetation grown on soils that contain it may cause alkali disease in animals; some evidence seems to indicate that small quantities may be an essential dietary factors.
See Part 2: Grain Analysis; Water Drinking Standards; Wheat Products Composition

self-feeder A trough which is automatically kept full of feed so animals can eat as much and as often as they please.

self-rising flour A mixture of flour, salt and baking powder.

semen The fluid produced by males carrying the spermatozoa; the average volume of semen introduced in one service is: boar, 200 cc, stallion 100 cc, bull 5 cc, ram 1 cc.

semiboiled soap *See* **cold soap**

semibright wool Wool that is soil-stained but that can be scoured white; produced primarily in eastern part of Kansas, Nebraska, North and South Dakota, Oklahoma, Missouri, Iowa, Minnesota and Wisconsin.

semimembranosus A broad medial muscle of the thigh that runs from the ischium to the back of the tibia; the most medial and caudal muscle of the round.

semipermeable membrane A membrane which permits passage of some substances but not others, depending on the size of their molecules.

semiscalding Using 125° to 132°F water to scald poultry followed by a mechanical picker.

semisweet chocolate Sold in bar-shaped package containing 1-oz squares; it is slightly sweet and melts easily.

semisweet chocolate pieces Unsweetened chocolate plus cocoa butter, sugar and a vanilla-type flavoring.

semitendinosus (eye of round) A round-shaped muscle of the thigh that runs from the ischium to the back of the tibia; it is caudal to the biceps femoris and caudal and lateral to the semimembranosus.

semitendinous Composed in part of tendinous structure. *See also* **eye of round; semitendinosus.**

semolina Coarse flour; fine starchy endosperm of hard wheat.

semolina meal A pale yellow meal made from the middlings of hard durum wheat; milled endosperm of durum wheat that contains less than 3% flour; used in macaroni products.
See Part 2: Cereal Composition; Thiamin, Food

senecio A plant having a toxic principle.
See Part 2: Poisonous Plants

sense To perceive objectively by stimulation of organs of the body.

sensitive Ability to receive impressions from external forces.

sensory Examination by taste, smell, feeling and appearance.

sepal The calyx of a flower.
See Part 2: Flower, Perfect

sepsis Poisoning caused by products of putrefaction.

septum A partition between two cavities of the body.

sequestrant (chelating agent) A chemical compound which reacts with metals to form a complex, thus minimizing the effect of the metal; also a food additive that will separate or segregate, usually in the inactive form, ingredients that will interfere with processing.

serial Arranged in a series.

sericin (silk gelatin) A protein cement used to hold the principal constituent (fibroin) together in silk fiber.

series circuit

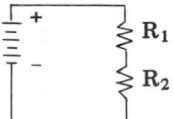

R_T = Resistance total
R_1 = Resistance in Resistor #1
Current (or amp) in each component is the same
$R_T = R_1 + R_2 + \cdots R_n$

The total potential = algebraic sum of the potentials.

serine A nonessential monoamino-monocarboxylic-monohydroxy amino acid.

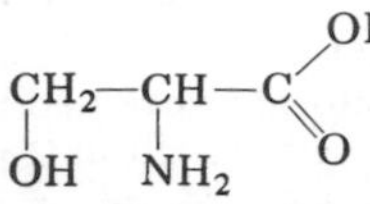

See Part 2: Amino Acids; Amino Acid, Solubilities; Corn, Amino Acids; Egg Products, Nutritive Value; Grain Analysis; Manure Analysis; Wheat, Amino Acids; Wheat Products, Amino Acid Compositions

serous A thin watery body fluid; pertaining to serum. *See also* **serum.**
See Part 2: Intestine, Cross Section

Serratia *See* Part 2: Spoilage, Carbohydrate Foods; Spoilage, Fat in Food

serratus dorsalis A back muscle that runs from the spinous processes of the thoracic vertebrae over the *longissimus dorsi* to the rib; in cross-section it is most prominent on the lateral side of the *longissimus dorsi*.

serum (blood) That part of the plasma remaining after clot, blood corpuscles and fibrin have been removed (defibrinated); it contains: 90% water, 1% glucose, 1% fat, 0.85% NaCl, 0.15% Na bicarbonate and salts, and 7% protein. Serum of milk is whey.

serum test A test to indicate species of meat used and to detect adulteration. Rabbits are injected with solution of X-protein; the rabbit builds up antibodies against X-protein; if a meat is suspected of containing X-protein it is mixed with serum obtained from the rabbit and if X-protein is present it will be destroyed by the serum and if it is not present, the serum will be unaffected.

serving A portion of food sufficient for one person.
See Part 2: Fruit, Cooking; Fruit Servings Per Pound; Meat, Servings Per Pound; Vegetable Servings

Servings Per Pound (Meat)

	Servings per lb	Price Per Pound .29	.39	.49	.59	.69	.79	.89	.99	1.09
		Cost Per Serving								
Beef										
Sirloin steak	2½	.12	.16	.20	.24	.28	.32	.36	.40	.44
Porterhouse, T-bone, rib steak	2	.15	.20	.25	.30	.35	.40	.45	.50	.55
Round steak	3½	.08	.11	.14	.17	.20	.23	.25	.28	.31
Chuck roast (bone in)	2	.15	.20	.25	.30	.35	.40	.45	.50	.55
Rib roast (boneless)	2½	.12	.16	.20	.24	.28	.32	.36	.40	.44
Rib roast (bone in)	2	.15	.20	.25	.30	.35	.40	.45	.50	.55
Rump, sirloin roast	3	.10	.13	.16	.20	.23	.26	.30	.33	.36
Ground beef	4	.07	.10	.12	.15	.17	.20	.22	.25	.27
Short ribs	2	.15	.20	.25	.30	.35	.40	.45	.50	.55
Heart, liver, kidney	5	.06	.08	.10	.12	.14	.16	.18	.20	.22
Frankfurters	4	.07	.10	.12	.15	.17	.20	.22	.25	.27
Stew meat (boneless)	5	.06	.08	.10	.12	.14	.16	.18	.20	.22

	Servings per lb	.29	.39	.49	.59	.69	.79	.89	.99	1.09
		Price Per Pound / Cost Per Serving								
Lamb										
Loin, rib, shoulder (chops)	3	.10	.13	.16	.20	.23	.26	.30	.33	.36
Breast, shank	2	.15	.20	.25	.30	.35	.40	.45	.50	.55
Shoulder roast	2½	.12	.16	.20	.24	.28	.32	.36	.40	.44
Leg of lamb	3	.10	.13	.16	.20	.23	.26	.30	.33	.36
Pork, fresh										
Center cut or rib (chops)	4	.07	.10	.12	.15	.17	.20	.22	.25	.27
Loin or rib roast	2½	.12	.16	.20	.24	.28	.32	.36	.40	.44
Boston butt (bone in)	3	.10	.13	.16	.20	.23	.26	.30	.33	.36
Blade steak	3	.10	.13	.16	.20	.23	.26	.30	.33	.36
Spare ribs	1⅓	.22	.29	.37	.44	.52	.59	.67	.74	.82
Pork, cured										
Picnic (bone in)	2	.15	.20	.25	.30	.35	.40	.45	.50	.55
Ham, fully cooked										
Bone in	3½	.08	.11	.14	.17	.20	.23	.25	.28	.31
Boneless & canned	5	.06	.08	.10	.12	.14	.16	.18	.20	.22
Shankless	4¼	.07	.09	.12	.14	.16	.19	.21	.23	.26
Center slice	5	.06	.08	.10	.12	.14	.16	.18	.20	.22
Poultry										
Broiler, or ready-to-cook chicken	1⅓	.22	.29	.37	.44	.52	.59	.67	.74	.82
Legs, thighs	3	.10	.13	.16	.20	.23	.26	.30	.33	.36
Breast	4	.07	.10	.12	.15	.17	.20	.22	.25	.27
Turkey, ready-to-cook										
Under 12 lb	1	.29	.39	.49	.59	.69	.79	.89	.99	1.09
12 lb & over	1⅓	.22	.29	.37	.44	.52	.59	.67	.74	.82

	Servings per lb	1.19	1.29	1.39	1.49	1.59	1.69	1.79	1.89	1.99	2.09
		Price Per Pound / Cost Per Serving									
Beef											
Sirloin steak	2½	.48	.52	.56	.60	.64	.68	.72	.76	.80	.84
Porterhouse, T-bone, rib steak	2	.60	.65	.70	.75	.80	.85	.90	.95	1.00	1.05
Round steak	3½	.34	.37	.40	.43	.46	.49	.52	.54	.57	.60
Chuck roast (bone in)	2	.60	.65	.70	.75	.80	.85	.90	.95	1.00	1.05
Rib roast (boneless)	2½	.48	.52	.56	.60	.64	.68	.72	.76	.80	.84
Rib roast (bone in)	2	.60	.65	.70	.75	.80	.85	.90	.95	1.00	1.05
Rump, sirloin roast	3	.40	.43	.46	.50	.53	.57	.60	.63	.67	.70
Ground beef	4	.30	.32	.35	.38	.40	.43	.45	.48	.50	.53
Short ribs	2	.60	.65	.70	.75	.80	.85	.90	.95	1.00	1.05
Heart, liver, kidney	5	.24	.26	.28	.30	.32	.34	.36	.38	.40	.42
Frankfurters	4	.30	.32	.35	.38	.40	.43	.45	.48	.50	.53
Stew meat (boneless)	5	.24	.26	.28	.30	.32	.34	.36	.38	.40	.42
Lamb											
Loin, rib, shoulder (chops)	3	.40	.43	.46	.50	.53	.57	.60	.63	.67	.70
Breast, shank	2	.60	.65	.70	.75	.80	.85	.90	.95	1.00	1.05
Shoulder roast	2½	.48	.52	.56	.60	.64	.68	.72	.76	.80	.84
Leg of lamb	3	.40	.43	.46	.50	.53	.57	.60	.63	.67	.70
Pork, fresh											
Center cut or rib (chops)	4	.30	.32	.35	.38	.40	.43	.45	.48	.50	.53
Loin or rib roast	2½	.48	.52	.56	.60	.64	.68	.72	.76	.80	.84
Boston butt (bone in)	3	.40	.43	.46	.50	.53	.57	.60	.63	.67	.70
Blade steak	3	.40	.43	.46	.50	.53	.57	.60	.63	.67	.70
Spare ribs	1⅓	.89	.97	1.04	1.12	1.20	1.27	1.35	1.43	1.50	1.58
Pork, cured											
Picnic (bone in)	2	.60	.65	.70	.75	.80	.85	.90	.95	1.00	1.05
Ham, fully cooked											
Bone in	3½	.34	.37	.40	.43	.46	.49	.52	.54	.57	.60
Boneless & canned	5	.24	.26	.28	.30	.32	.34	.36	.38	.40	.42

	Servings per lb	Price Per Pound / Cost Per Serving									
		1.19	1.29	1.39	1.49	1.59	1.69	1.79	1.89	1.99	2.09
Pork, cured (*Cont.*)											
Ham, fully cooked (*Cont.*)											
Shankless	4¼	.28	.30	.33	.35	.38	.40	.43	.45	.47	.50
Center slice	5	.24	.26	.28	.30	.32	.34	.36	.38	.40	.42
Poultry											
Broiler, or ready-to-cook chicken	1⅓	.89	.97	1.04	1.12	1.20	1.27	1.35	1.43	1.50	1.59
Legs, thighs	3	.40	.43	.46	.50	.54	.57	.60	.63	.67	.70
Breast	4	.30	.32	.35	.38	.40	.43	.45	.48	.50	.53
Turkey, ready-to-cook											
Under 12 lb	1	1.19	1.29	1.39	1.49	1.59	1.69	1.79	1.89	1.99	2.09
12 lb & over	1⅓	.89	.97	1.04	1.12	1.20	1.27	1.35	1.43	1.50	1.59

	Servings per lb	Price Per Pound / Cost Per Serving									
		2.19	2.29	2.39	2.49	2.59	2.69	2.79	2.89	2.99	3.09
Beef											
Sirloin steak	2½	.88	.92	.96	1.00	1.04	1.08	1.12	1.16	1.20	1.24
Porterhouse, T-bone, rib steak	2	1.10	1.15	1.20	1.25	1.30	1.35	1.40	1.45	1.50	1.55
Round steak	3½	.63	.65	.68	.71	.74	.77	.80	.83	.85	.88
Chuck roast (bone in)	2	1.10	1.15	1.20	1.25	1.30	1.35	1.40	1.45	1.50	1.55
Rib roast (boneless)	2½	.88	.92	.96	1.00	1.04	1.08	1.12	1.16	1.20	1.24
Rib roast (bone in)	2	1.10	1.15	1.20	1.25	1.30	1.35	1.40	1.45	1.50	1.55
Rump, sirloin roast	3	.73	.76	.80	.83	.86	.90	.93	.96	1.00	1.03
Ground beef	4	.55	.57	.60	.62	.65	.67	.70	.72	.75	.77
Short ribs	2	1.10	1.15	1.20	1.25	1.30	1.35	1.40	1.45	1.50	1.55
Heart, liver, kidney	5	.44	.46	.48	.50	.52	.54	.56	.58	.60	.62
Frankfurters	4	.55	.57	.60	.62	.65	.67	.70	.72	.75	.77
Stew meat (boneless)	5	.44	.46	.48	.50	.52	.54	.56	.58	.60	.62
Lamb											
Loin, rib, shoulder (chops)	3	.73	.76	.80	.83	.86	.90	.93	.96	1.00	1.03
Breast, shank	2	1.10	1.15	1.20	1.25	1.30	1.35	1.40	1.45	1.50	1.55
Shoulder roast	2½	.88	.92	.96	1.00	1.04	1.08	1.12	1.16	1.20	1.24
Leg of lamb	3	.73	.76	.80	.83	.86	.90	.93	.96	1.00	1.03
Pork, fresh											
Center cut or rib (chops)	4	.55	.57	.60	.62	.65	.67	.70	.72	.75	.77
Loin or rib roast	2½	.88	.92	.96	1.00	1.04	1.08	1.12	1.16	1.20	1.24
Boston butt (bone in)	3	.73	.76	.80	.83	.86	.90	.93	.96	1.00	1.03
Blade steak	3	.73	.76	.80	.83	.86	.90	.93	.96	1.00	1.03
Spare ribs	1⅓	1.64	1.72	1.79	1.87	1.94	2.02	2.09	2.17	2.24	2.32
Pork, cured											
Picnic (bone in)	2	1.10	1.15	1.20	1.25	1.30	1.35	1.40	1.45	1.50	1.55
Ham, fully cooked											
Bone in	3½	.63	.65	.68	.71	.74	.77	.80	.83	.85	.88
Boneless & canned	5	.44	.46	.48	.50	.52	.54	.56	.58	.60	.62
Shankless	4¼	.52	.54	.56	.59	.61	.63	.66	.68	.70	.73
Center slice	5	.44	.46	.48	.50	.52	.54	.56	.58	.60	.62
Poultry											
Broiler, or ready-to-cook chicken	1⅓	1.64	1.72	1.79	1.87	1.94	2.02	2.09	2.17	2.24	2.32
Legs, thighs	3	.73	.76	.80	.83	.86	.90	.93	.96	1.00	1.03
Breast	4	.55	.57	.60	.62	.65	.67	.70	.72	.75	.77
Turkey, ready-to-cook											
Under 12 lb	1	2.19	2.29	2.39	2.49	2.59	2.69	2.79	2.89	2.99	3.09
12 lb & over	1⅓	1.64	1.72	1.79	1.87	1.94	2.02	2.09	2.17	2.24	2.32

sesame (sim-sim, benniseed); (*Sesamum indicum*) A tropical or subtropical plant that produces a small white seed; seed may be used as food or the oil extracted (45–55%); the cake left after extraction is used as a protein-rich livestock feed; 46 lb sesame seed = 1 bu.
Dry seed composition: 5% H_2O, 18–19% protein, 49–55% fat, 17–22% carbohydrate, 5% ash.
See Part 2: Oils and Fats Composition; Protein Factors; Pulses, Nuts and Seeds Composition; Seed, Chemical Composition; Unsaponifiable Matter

sesame oil An oil obtained from the seed of the sesame plant (*Sesamum indicum*).
Properties:

Refractive Index (15.5°C)	1.474–1.476
Saponification no.	188–193
Iodine no.	103–112
Melting Point	−6°C
Specific Gravity 25°C	0.919

Composition:

Palmitic	9%
Stearic	4%
Arachidic	1%
Oleic	45%
Linoleic	40%

See Part 2: Fats and Oils, Composition; Fats and Oils, Physical and Chemical Properties; Fatty Acids, Fats and Oils; Fats and Oils, Characteristics; Iodine and Saponification Values; Oil or Fat, Characteristics; Oil, Triglyceride Mole Percent Composition; Refractive Indices, Fats and Oils; Specific Gravities, Fats and Oils; Titer, Fats and Oils; Tocopherols

sesame seed (*Sesamum indicum* L.) White seed (1/8 in. in length (benne seed) (bene seed) used in flavoring food and as an oil crop.

sesbane A plant having a toxic principle.
See Part 2: Poisonous Plants

sesbania *See* Part 2: Seed, Germination

set point *See* **congealing point**

setting out Mechanical extraction of surplus water from leather after tanning.

setting the hair Occurs when hog carcasses are over-scalded and the hair becomes extremely hard to remove.

Seville orange *See* **sour orange**

Sevin Trademark for a toxic carboxyl insecticide.
See Part 2: Insect Control

sewage Municipal waste. *See also* **sludge.**
See Part 2: Fertilizer Materials; Microorganism, Culture Media, Water and Sewage, Standard Methods; Wastes, Agricultural and Industrial

sex The state of a plant (or part of a plant) or animal that is expressed in the production of ova in the female, or sperm in the male.

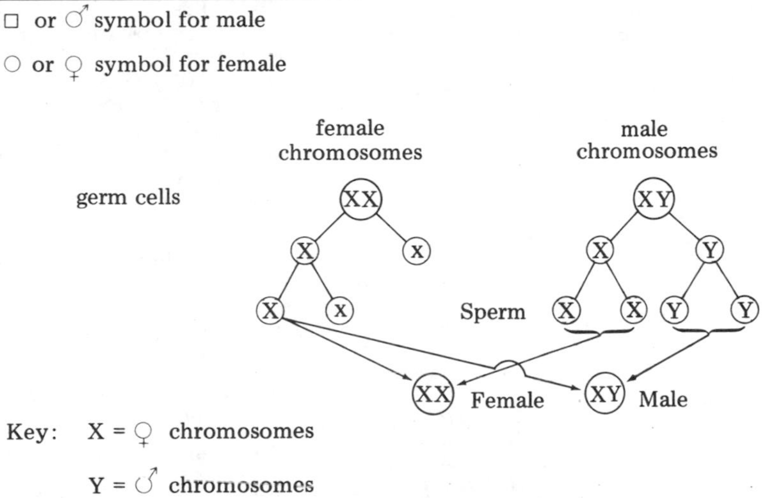

S F broth *See* Part 2: Microbiological Media

SFP agar *See* Part 2: Microorganism, Media

shack To feed upon stubble or fallen grain after harvest.

shad (buck, roe, white) A fat, very bony fish similar to a herring but with a deeper body; caught in U.S. coastal rivers.
See Part 2: Fish and Shellfish Composition

shaddock *See* **pomelo**
See Part 2: Essential Oils

shaggy parasol (*Lepiota rhacodes*) A large (3–7 inch cap) edible fungus with yellow-brown scales on the cap.

shallot (*Allium ascalonicum*) A vegetable whose bulb is used as food; a variety of onion; mild and used for flavoring and as a pickle.
Raw bulb composition: 80% H_2O, 2–3% protein, 0.1% fat, 17% carbohydrate, 1% ash.

shandygaff A mixture of ale and beer.

shank (fore) bone The metacarpal bone.
See Part 2: Beef Chart; Beef Cuts; Beef Cuts and Uses; Beef Retail Yield; Beef Wholesale Cuts; Braising Meat; Braising Time; Cooking in Liquid, Time; Lamb Cuts; Lamb, Wholesale Cuts; Meat, Servings Per Pound; Pork Wholesale Cuts; Veal Chart; Veal Cuts; Veal Cuts and Uses; Veal Wholesale Cuts

shank knuckle bone The inferior extremity of the femur.
See Part 2: Beef Cuts

shark liver oil *See* Part 2: Unsaponifiable Matter; Unsaturated Fatty Acids

shark oil *See* Part 2: Iodine and Saponification Values; Vitamin A, Fish; Vitamin D, Fish

sharp cheese *See* **cured cheese**

sharp freezing Reducing a portion of the interior food temperature to 10°F or less in 5 hours or less; room should be −10°F or lower; tolerance of −10°F for a reasonable length of time after entry of fresh food.

shashlik Cubes of seasoned meat, onions, tomatoes and vegetables cooked on a skewer.

shaw A stem and leaves.

sheal To remove pod, shell or husk.

shea oil *See* Part 2: Fats and Oils, Characteristics; Iodine and Saponification Values; Refractive Indices, Fats and Oils

shear (1) A lateral stress applied to one of the faces of a body. (2) To clip or cut (of hair or wool).

shearer An ovine animal (sheep) any age to be sheared before slaughter.

sheep (*Ovis aries*) Ovine animals of all ages and sex; in common practice one year or older in age; mature sheep is 3 years or older. *Ovis laticauda*, broad tailed; *Ovis montana*, bighorn. Dressing percentage, 48%.
See Part 2: Bone Age; Gestation Periods; Milk and Cheese Composition; Milk, Species; Muscle and Body Weight; Reproductive Cycle; Sheep Breeds; Sheep Market Classes and Grades; Teeth Eruption

sheep casing *See* **casing**

shehitah Jewish method of slaughter.

shelf curing Applying dry cure to meat and placing it so the juices will drain from the product while curing.

shelf-life The storage time of a canned or packaged food product; it is greatly lengthened by use of antioxidants and other preservatives.

shell (1) The hard external coating of a nut, composed chiefly of cellulose. (2) The body covering of lobsters, clams, oysters, etc., composed largely of calcium carbonate. *See also* **shellfish**. (3) The hard, friable coating of avian eggs, composed of lime and calcium carbonate. (4) A pastry container for creamed meats, fish or custard fillings; a patty shell. (5) Emaciated cattle. (6) An electron orbit of an atom, designated by letters K, L, M, etc.
See Part 2: Egg Structure

shellfish Mollusks and crustaceans which have a hard outer covering composed chiefly of calcium carbonate.
See Part 2: Animal Foods, Composition; Fish and Shellfish Composition; Fish, Storage; Frozen Food Storage; Plant and Animal Poisoning; Storage Times

shelling Removing corn kernels from the cob; removing peas from pods or shells from nuts. *See also* **shuck**.

sherbet A sweetened, flavored water ice; sweetened, diluted fruit juice.
More often, a frozen dessert made from sugar, milk solids, stabilizer, food acid, flavoring and water; contains from 1 to 2% milk fat and 2 to 5% total milk solids. 1 qt = 4 cups; 1 cup = 195 g (6.8 oz)
Composition: 67% H_2O, 1% protein, 1.2% fat, 31% carbohydrate, 0.1% ash.
See Part 2: Calories, Daily Recommendations; Creams, Butter and Frozen Desserts; Dairy Terms; Frozen Food Storage; Stabilizers, Thickeners

sherry A wine that is full-bodied, fragrant, fortified and blended (15.5–20% alcohol by volume); it is made from the juice of white grapes and sold in three grades: pale dry, regular, and cream, the last being the sweetest.

sherry cobbler A cold beverage made of sherry, lemon juice, etc.

shield Heavy skin on the shoulder of some boars.

shigellosis *See* Part 2: Illness from Food; Infectious Agents; Infectious Diseases, Food-Borne; Intestinal Microorganisms; Intestinal Microorganisms in Triple-Sugar Agar; Microorganism, Media; Microorganism Reactions on Differential Tube Media

shikar Hunting.

ship biscuit Hard bread that has good keeping qualities.

shipper style hog carcass A carcass that is not split, and the head and leaf fat is left with the carcass.

shipping fever A high fever and general depression in cattle after shipping; to reduce this condition, avoid overexposure during shipping; there is also a preventive vaccination.

shishkebab Meat and vegetables broiled and served on a skewer.

shoat (shote) A young hog, between 100 and 150 lb that will be sent to market.

shochet A cutter (inspector) who manually examines thoracic organs for kosher foods; one who slaughters animals to be eaten by Jews.

shonti annam A fermented rice product.

shood Chaff.

shoot *See* **sprout**

shortcake A cake or biscuit made with a substantial proportion of shortening; served with sweetened fruit (strawberries, peaches, etc.).

short circuit A no resistance connection.

shortening A fatty substance (lard, butter, hydrogenated oil) used in baked products to give a light, crisp texture. This results from formation by the shortening agent of a lubricant layer between the particles of flour, giving the cooked product a less resistant, flaky structure. 2-2⅓ cups/lb. Alteration for altitude, *see* **altitude**.
See Part 2: Fats and Oils, Composition; Oils and Fats Composition

shortening value (shortness) The force required to break a standard crust or cracker; the less the force, the higher the shortening value and the flakier and lighter the pastry.

short-fed Cattle on feed 60–120 days; below choice finish.

Shorthorn A breed of beef cattle that may be red, roan, white, or red and white; horns curve downward and forward. Origin, northeast England; imported to America by Gough and Miller of Virginia. *See also* **Polled Shorthorn**; **Single Standard Polled Durham**; **Double Standard Polled Shorthorn.**
Color determination: white cattle (xx) × red cattle $(yy) \rightarrow$ roan offspring (xy); roan cattle (xy) × red cattle $(yy) \rightarrow \frac{1}{2}$ roan offspring $(xy) + \frac{1}{2}$ red offspring (yy).

Key: x = gene for white
y = gene for red

See Part 2: Beef and Dual-Purpose Cattle; Gestation Periods; Milk Breeds, Composition

short loin The front area of the loin extending from the flat edge of the hip bone to the last rib; it contains the porterhouse, T-bone and club steaks (back to front).
See Part 2: Beef Cuts; Beef Cuts and Uses

shortness *See* **shortening value**

short plate A cut of beef.
See Part 2: Beef, Boneless Cuts; Beef Retail Yield; Beef Rib Nomenclature; Beef Wholesale Cuts

short ribs A cut of beef made from 2- to 3-in. strips removed across the ribs of the plate.
See Part 2: Beef Cuts; Beef Cuts and Uses; Beef Retail Yield; Braising Meat; Braising Time; Portion Size

shorts *See* Part 2: Casings, Hog Bungs; Wheat and Flour Composition; Wheat Products Composition

shote *See* **shoat**

shoulder The forearm area of a pork carcass; about 16% of hog carcasses (head and leaf fat on). *See also* **New York style shoulder.**
See Part 2: Bone in Retail Cuts; Braising Time; Cooking in Liquid, Time; Lamb Cuts; Lamb Cuts and Uses; Lamb Roasting; Lamb, Wholesale Cuts; Lamb Yield; Meat and Meat Products Composition; Meat Composition; Pork Cookery; Pork, Cooking; Pork, Cooking Method; Pork Cooking Yield; Pork Cuts; Pork Shoulder; Pork Yield; Roasting Meat; Roasting, Time and Temperature; Veal Chart; Veal Cuts; Veal Cuts and Uses; Veal Roasting

shoulder arm roast A beef roast made from muscles on the fore shank in front of the arm bone.

shoulder clod *See* **clear cut shoulder**

shoulder roll *See* Part 2: Pork Cookery

shoulder vein Junction of the neck and shoulder.

showbread Bread placed in a Jewish sanctuary.

shoyu *See* **ketjap**
See Part 2: Fungi Food Products

shred To cut into long narrow strips.

shredded coconut Made by shredding ripe coconut meat, mixing with salt and sugar and partially drying.

shredded wheat A breakfast cereal prepared from cooked, dried and tempered whole wheat grain; the grain is passed between grooved rollers; the resulting strands are pinched into biscuits which are then baked. 1 cup (spoon size) = 1.5 oz.
Composition: 10% protein, 79–81% carbohydrate, 4% fat.

shrimp A lean, marine crustacean; a shellfish; (*Crangonidae*): 50% edible.

Types	Where Caught
white, brown, pink prawn	South Atlantic, Gulf of Mexico
Alaska pink	Alaska
California	Maine and world-wide imports

Size (Note: Other size systems are also used):
Jumbo = less than 25/lb
Large = 25–30/lb
Large medium = 28–30/lb
Medium = 30–35/lb
Small = 35 or more/lb

As purchased	Yield (%)
Headless	50
Peeled and cleaned	60

Breaded: 50% flesh content
1 cup canned = 130 g (4.6 oz)
Amount needed per serving:

In shells	6 large or 6 oz
Shelled	4 oz
Cooked, peeled, cleaned	3 oz
Breaded	3.5 oz
Canned	3 oz

12 large raw shrimp in shell = 7-8 oz raw shelled shrimp = 4½-5 oz canned shrimp = 1 cup cooked, shelled, shrimp.
Raw composition: 78% H_2O, 18% protein, 0.8% fat, 2% carbohydrate, 1% ash; pH 6.8-7.0; 12-17% fat absorption during frying.
Shrimp paste composition (canned): 61% H_2O, 20% protein, 9% fat, 2% carbohydrate, 7% ash.
See Part 2: Fish and Shellfish Composition; Fish, Storage; Frozen Food Storage; Frying Time; Minerals, Food; Portion Size; Shrimp

shrink Loss of weight; loss in weight of grease wool in the cleaning process.

shrinkage (drift) Loss in livestock weight from farm to market.

Shropshire A medium-wool mutton type breed of sheep that originated in west central England from several native types of sheep; its face is covered with wool except the mouth and nose area, which is usually brown to black; it has no horns and approximately ⅜ grade fleece.
See Part 2: Sheep Breeds

shroud Unbleached cotton duck cloth used on beef carcasses.

shrouding Placing wet shrouds on a warm beef carcass to absorb the blood and smooth the fat while the carcass is cooling.

shuck To remove covering (pod, husk, or shell) from corn, peas, shellfish, etc.

shungiku (*Chrysanthemum spatiosum*) Young plants that are used as cooked green vegetables.

shunt To provide an alternate pathway.

shuring Pleating and compressing sausage casings to shorter length.

Si Symbol for the element silicon.

sibling Offspring having one or both parents in common.

sicharon Skin and a thin layer of fat that is salted, fried, and stored in lard.

sickle hock A hock that has too much bend in it when viewed from the side.

side A half-carcass of pork or beef.
See Part 2: Pork Cuts; Pork Wholesale Cuts; Pork Yield

side bone (1) An unsoundness in horses. (2) Hip bone.

side chain A straight chain attached to one of the atoms of a ring.

sierra rice Fermented rice.

sieve A perforated device for separating fine from coarser particles; a metal screen from 100 to 400-mesh.

sift To put through a sieve (e.g., flour).

sigma (Σ, σ) Greek letter with an English equivalent of s.

significance (statistical) States that differences between samples are real and not due to chance variation. Significant difference (.05) (*) is a difference which has a 5% probability of occurring by chance alone; a highly significant difference (.01) (**) is a difference which has a 1% probability of occurring by chance alone.
See Part 2: Correlation Significance; F-Distribution

significant figures The number of digits in a value which differentiates this value from the one next to it; it is independent of decimal points and zeros;

$$\left.\begin{array}{r}231\\.00231\\2.31\\23100\end{array}\right\}\text{ all have 3 significant figures}$$

← If next number that could be read is 23200

silage Stored cattle fodder produced by fermentation of green fodder with the production of lactic acid; wt/cu ft 30 to 45 lb depending on depth in the silo, packing, and the substance from which the silage is made. Trench type, whole corn 50 to 60 cu ft per ton; upright (16 to 24 ft diam) 45 to 55 cu ft per ton.

sild Young herring.

silent spirit Distilled spirit with most of the products removed except ethyl alcohol and water.

silica *See* **sand**
See Part 2: Maple Syrup Composition

silica gel A dehydrated form of sodium silicate, used as a dehumidifying agent in food packaging because of its highly porous structure which enables it to absorb water molecules from the air.

silicle Pericarp or seed vessel.

silicon (Si) A nonmetallic element; at. no. 14; at. wt. 28.09; Group IVA of Periodic Table; electron configuration 2-8-4
orbit K L M
oxidation states +2, +4, -4

siliqua Fruit of cabbage or related plants; pods of mustard family.

silk fiber An animal protein fiber constructed of the protein fibroin cemented together by the protein sericin. Processed silk fiber (yarn) is almost pure fibroin.

silo A large cylindrical chamber or a trench in which silage is fermented and stored.

silt Fine soil material.
See Part 2: Soil Classes

silver (Ag) A metallic element; at. no. 47; at. wt. 107.880; Group IB of the Periodic Table; electron configuration 2-8-18-18-1
orbit K L M N O
oxidation state +1; highest electrical conductivity of any metal.
See Part 2: Normal Solutions; Salmon and Trout; Water Drinking Standards

silver hake *See* **hake; whiting**

silverling A plant having a toxic principle.
See Part 2: Poisonous Plants

silver mullet *See* **mullet**

silver nitrate $AgNO_3$ May be used as a germicide and antiseptic.
See Part 2: Normal Solutions

silver salmon *See* **salmon**

silverside Outside or upper part of a beef round. *See also* **salmon; smelt.**

silver skin Thin membrane on an onion.

SIM medium *See* Part 2: Microorganism, Media; Microorganism Reactions on Differential Tube Media; Microorganism, Selective and Differential Broths and Media, Water Filtration Plant

Simmental European red and white cattle; mature bull wt, 2300 lb.
See Part 2: Gestation Periods

simmer To cook in a liquid at a temperature of approximately 185°F.
See Part 2: Fruit, Dried, Simmering; Fruit, Simmering; Lamb Simmering; Meat Composition; Simmering Meat

Simmons citrate agar *See* Part 2: Microorganism, Media; Microorganism Reactions on Differential Tube Media; Microorganism, Selective and Differential Broths and Media, Water Filtration Plant

simple fruit Fruit formed from a simple ovary; e.g., plum, apple, peach, and pear.

simple glyceride A glyceride in which all three acids of the triglyceride are alike.

simple protein A naturally-occurring protein made up primarily of amino acids.

simple syrup Solutions of sugar and water of various concentrations; used in confectionery, soda fountain syrups, etc.

sim-sim *See* **sesame**

sine (sin) A trigonometric function; $\sin = \frac{\text{ordinate}}{\text{hypotenuse}}$.

sinew The tendon of a muscle.

singhara nut *See* **water chestnut**

Single Standard Polled Durham Cross of native polled cows with horned Shorthorn bulls; since 1905 all cattle must be traced to recorded stock; in 1919, Shorthorn was substituted for Durham in the name; in 1923 the association was disbanded and the pure polled Shorthorn was registered in the Shorthorn herdbook.

Single Standard Polled Hereford Registered from 1900 to 1907 and are a cross between a polled breed sire (e.g., Angus or Red Poll) and a horned Hereford cow; never were registered in American Hereford Record; since 1949 all lines must be traced to registered Hereford.

single stimulus *See* Part 2: Taste Panel, Difference Tests

sintered glass *See* fritted glass

sinus A cavity in the bone structure; a blood channel.

sinus node An area in the right auricle which is stimulated by a nerve and causes the auricles to contract.

siphon A U-tube used to transfer liquid from an upper level to a lower level.

sire A male parent.

sirloin A cut of meat. (1) Steak, (back to front) wedge bone, round bone, double bone (flat bone), pin bone (hip bone). (2) Strip (New York cut) (KC steak), the dorsal muscles to the lateral processes of the vertebrae in the porterhouse, T-bone, and club steak area. (3) Tip, a cut of beef obtained when the hind quarter of beef is cut national style; it is located adjacent to the round and the sirloin and before the rump. *See also* **top sirloin.**
See Part 2: Beef Retail Yield; Beef Wholesale Cuts; Bone in Retail Cuts; Broiling Meat; Broiling Time and Temperature; Lamb Cuts; Meat Identification; Pork Cookery; Pork Cuts; Pork Loin Cooking; Pork Loin Nomenclature; Pork Yield; Roasting, Time and Temperature; Veal Chart; Veal Cuts

sirup (syrup) A solution of sugar in water. *See also* **candy.**
See Part 2: Minerals, Food; Sugars and Sweets Composition

sito- Pertaining to food.

sitology Study of food, diet and nutrition.

sitophobia Refusal to eat; fear of food.

sitosterol $C_{29}H_{48}O$ A sterol that is found in the unsaponifiable fraction of vegetable oils such as corn, wheat, cottonseed, and linseed.

skaddon Larva of bee.

skate A type of ray.
See Part 2: Vitamin D, Fish

skeel A vessel for milk.

skeletal muscle Voluntary striped muscle.

skeleton The bony system of an animal or human body.
See Part 2: Organ Weights

skep Straw hive for bees.

skewer (skiver) A pin for fastening meat.

skim To remove the top layer, e.g., of fat from a liquid.
See Part 2: Dairy Terms; Milk and Cheese Composition; Milk Composition; Milk, Concentrated Products; Nicotinic Acid, Food; Riboflavin, Food; Vitamin A, Milk and Milk Products

skimmed milk Milk containing less than 0.5% milk fat and at least 8% nonfat milk solids; 1 cup = 245 g (8.5 oz).
See Part 2: Calories, Daily Recommendations; Microorganism, Culture Media, Dairy and Food

Products; Microorganism, Media; Milk and Milk Products, Vitamin Content

skimmer *See* **clam**

skin (1) The exterior coating of the body, composed of epidermis, corium and the subcutis as the major layers. (2) A small hide (in cattle, weighing under 30 lb after curing). (3) A pelt of a small wild or domestic animal. (4) Animal hide used for holding liquids, e.g., wine.
See Part 2: Gland Weights; Organ Weights; Poultry Yield; Turkey Composition

skinless wiener A wiener that is cooked and smoked in an artificial casing, which is then removed.

skip Light common pig or lamb.
See Part 2: Casings, Hog Bungs

skipjack *See* **tuna**

skirt The nonmuscle membrane of the diaphragm.
See Part 2: Beef Rib Nomenclature

skiver (1) The outer layer (wool side) of a split sheep skin made into leather and used to line shoes. (2) A skewer.

slack *See* **slake**

slack scalding *See* **semiscalding**

slag Waste material resulting from reduction of a metallic ore.
See Part 2: Fertilizer Materials; Liming Materials

slake (slack) To add water to CaO (calcium oxide), thus producing calcium hydroxide, or slaked lime;

$$CaO + H_2O \longrightarrow Ca(OH)_2$$

$$Ca(OH)_2 + \underset{\substack{\text{calcium}\\\text{bicarbonate}\\\text{in hard water}}}{Ca(HCO_3)_2} \longrightarrow \underset{\substack{\text{ppt}\\\text{limestone}}}{2CaCO_3} + 2H_2O$$

slant A sloping surface of agar used for microbiological growth.

slapjack A large pancake (also called flapjack).

slaughterhouse A building in which animals are killed for market; an abattoir.

slaw Cabbage served as a salad or relish, usually shredded and dressed with vinegar, etc.

slice To cut into thin pieces or sections.

slime A thin mucilaginous mixture of proteins, molds, etc.
See Part 2: Bacteria on Chickens at Various Holding Temperatures; Spoilage, Protein Foods

slinkweed A plant having a toxic principle.
See Part 2: Poisonous Plants

slip joint A joint between ilium and vertebrae.
See Part 2: Beef Wholesale Cuts; Bone; Lamb, Wholesale Cuts; Pork Wholesale Cuts; Veal Wholesale Cuts

sliwowitz Plum brandy.

slop Dealcoholized beer.

slop-fed Fed on distillers slop.

sludge A thick mixture of solids and water, especially in reference to municipal wastes (sewage sludge).
See Part 2: Wastes, Agricultural and Industrial

slunk A prematurely born or unborn animal.

slunk skin Skin of an unborn or stillborn calf.

Sm Symbol for the element samarium.

small casings Pork casings, often called rounds.
See also **rounds.**

small packers hides Hides taken off by relatively unskilled labor.

smear A specimen of a body fluid placed on a glass slide for microscopic study.

smearwurst *See* **mettwurst**

smell To detect a scent or odor by the olfactory nerves.

smelt (whitebait, surf smelt, grunion eulachon smelt, Columbia river smelt, silverside, jacksmelt, bay smelt) A number of small trout-like fish caught in North Atlantic, Pacific coast, Columbia river, and bays from Mexico to Canada and Great Lakes. Fat-to-lean composition changes with type.
Raw composition: 79% H_2O, 19% protein, 2% fat, 1% ash.
American smelt (*Osmerus mordax*) 5% fat.
Eulachon or candlefish (*Thaleichtys pacificus*) 10% fat.
See Part 2: Fish, Storage

smiggins Barley soup.

Smithfield ham Ham cured with salt, saltpeter and pepper and smoked with hickory and applewood; it is then aged from 7 to 18 months.

smoke (1) A colloidal suspension of a solid in air (or other gas). (2) To hang in smoke and apply smoke to food, e.g., meats or fish.
See Part 2: Fish, Smoke-Cured; Free Fatty Acid, Smoke, Flash, Fire Points

smoked meat Meat which has been dried or cured and then wood smoke deposited on it; any hardwood makes a satisfactory smoke.

Smoked Product	Min. Internal Temp. 137°F	Recommended Internal Temp. 140°F
Tender	140°F and a process leading to tenderizing.	
Cooked Fully Cooked Ready-to-Eat Ready-to-Serve	148°F and a description of the process which ensures partial separation of meat from bone, easy separation of tissue; and cooked color, flavor and texture throughout.	

smokehouse A building or container in which food is smoked.

smoke point Temperature at which fat starts to smoke.

Fat	°C	
Leaf lard	220	varies with fatty acid content
Average lard	195	
Old lard	190	
Crisco	230	

See also **flash point.**

smokies *See* Part 2: Fish, Smoke-Cured

smooth (involuntary) muscle A muscle constructed of cells with a single nucleus found in the visceral area and the walls of most tubes in the body; it has slow rhythmic contractions.

smorgasbord Appetizers; table with a variety of food, chiefly cold fish of several kinds. Originated in Sweden.

smorrebrod Open sandwich.

smut *See* **rust**

Sn Symbol for the element tin.

snail Edible type (*Helix pomatia*) called escargot. Raw composition: 79% H_2O, 16% protein, 1% fat, 2% carbohydrate, 1% ash.

snake gourd A tropical gourd that may be up to 6 ft in length, used as food; picked when immature, sliced and boiled.

snakeweed A plant having a toxic principle.
See Part 2: Poisonous Plants

sneezeweed A plant having a toxic principle.
See Part 2: Poisonous Plants

snet Deer fat.

snoek *See* Part 2: Vitamin D, Fish

snout Muzzle or nose in swine.
See Part 2: Pork Cuts and Uses

snow *See* **carbon dioxide; Dry Ice**

Snyder test agar *See* Part 2: Microorganism, Culture Media, Dairy and Food Products; Microorganism, Media

soap A detergent obtained by alkaline hydrolysis of animal or vegetable fats or oils; the alkali is either sodium hydroxide (hard soap) or potassium hydroxide (soft soap). *See also* **saponification.**

soapstock (foots) Alkali soaps, made from fatty acids, that settle to the bottom during the refining of oils. *See also* **residue.**
See Part 2: Margarine Production

soapstone (talc) Hydrated magnesium silicate (steatite) used in laboratory table tops. Clean with solvents; dressing: 1 lb paraffin, 1 qt kerosene, 2 qt raw linseed oil. Apply hot and buff in 2 hr.

soba Buckwheat noodles.

sockeye *See* **salmon**
See Part 2: Salmon and Trout

soda A general term for various sodium compounds. *See also* **baking soda; caustic soda, sodium carbonate; soda alum.**

soda alum (sodium alum) Aluminum sodium sulfate; used as a food additive and in baking powders.

soda ash *See* **sodium carbonate**

soda cracker A cracker made with cream of tartar.
See Part 2: Fermented Ingredients

soda glass Glass with a low melting point, a high coefficient of expansion which breaks easily under thermal shock.

soda water Carbon dioxide in water under pressure (a misnomer).

sodium (Na) An alkali metal element; at. no. 11; at. wt. 22.997; Group IA of the Periodic Table; electron configuration 2-8-1
orbit K L M
oxidation state +1.
Body function: in buffer system, in saliva, pancreatic and intestinal juices.
See Part 2: Egg Products, Nutritive Value; Fruit and Vegetables Composition; Grain Analysis; Lemon Juice Composition; Macaroni and Noodles Composition; Manure Analysis; Maple Syrup Composition; Minerals, Food; Normal Solutions; Sodium-Restricted Diet; Tomato and Tomato Products, Composition; Wheat, Minerals

sodium acetate, hydrous $CH_3COONa \cdot 3H_2O$ Can be used as a source of acetic acid.

sodium alginate A carbohydrate extracted from seaweed and used as an emulsifying and thickening agent and to prevent growth of ice crystals in ice cream. *See also* **algin.**

sodium alum *See* **soda alum**

sodium ascorbate $C_6H_7O_6Na$ *See* **ascorbic acid**

sodium benzoate $C_7H_5NaO_2$ A food preservative and antimicrobial additive used in acid foods (pH 2.5–4.0); in use, it is converted to benzoic acid, the active form. *See also* **benzoic acid.**

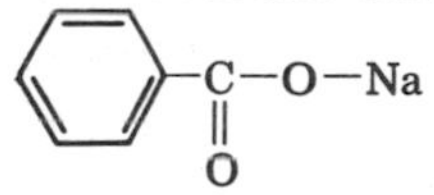

sodium bicarbonate $NaHCO_3$ *See* **baking soda**

sodium bisulfite $NaHSO_3$ *See* **sulfur dioxide**

sodium carbonate (soda ash, washing soda) Na_2CO_3 An alkaline cleaner with good buffer capacity; poor water softener, fair emulsifier and deflocculant.
See Part 2: Concentration of Commercial Strengths of Acids and Bases; Detergent Properties; Normal Solutions

sodium carboxymethylcellulose *See* **carboxymethylcellulose**

sodium chloride (NaCl) *See* **salt** (1)

sodium citrate $C_6H_5Na_3O_7 \cdot 2H_2O$ Complexing agent for iron and calcium in food; prevents coagulation of blood. *See also* **citrate.**

sodium cyclamate $C_6H_{12}O_3NSNa$ A non-nutritive artificial sweetener; prohibited for use in foods by FDA due to possible carcinogenicity.

sodium decaphosphate *See* Part 2: Detergent Properties

sodium diacetate $CH_3COONa \cdot CH_3COOH \cdot ½H_2O$ Can be used as a source of acetic acid.

sodium dichloroisocyanurate NaNC(O)NClC(O)NClCO Used as sanitizer and cleaning agent.
See Part 2: Chlorine Availability; Sanitizers

sodium fluoride NaF An inorganic insecticide; an antiferment; fluoridation of drinking water (1 ppm). It is poisonous.

sodium hexametaphosphate A detergent sold under the trade mark of Calgon.
See Part 2: Detergent Properties; Phosphate

sodium hydrogen carbonate *See* Part 2: Reagents, Normal Solutions

sodium hydroxide NaOH *See* **caustic soda**

sodium hypochlorite (NaClO) A disinfectant and deodorant used on food-handling material and for chlorination of water. Proprietary forms include Clorox and Purex. Household use should contain 2–6% chlorine and industrial use should contain 10–18% chlorine.
See Part 2: Chlorine Availability; Chlorine Compounds; Sanitizers

sodium iso-ascorbate *See* **ascorbic acid**

sodium metabisulfite $Na_2S_2O_5$ A preservative for silage. *See also* **sulfur dioxide.**

sodium metasilicate Na_2SiO_3 An alkaline cleaner that has good deflocculating and emulsifying properties; it is a fair water softener.
See Part 2: Detergent Properties

sodium nitrate (Chilean saltpeter) $NaNO_3$ Used in meat curing and fertilizers; fertilizer notation 16–0–0.2.
See Part 2: Fertilizer Materials; Nitrate, Meat Curing

sodium nitrite $NaNO_2$ Used in meat curing; content restricted to 200 ppm and may be further restricted due to the possible formation of nitrosamines.

sodium orthosilicate $Na_2SiO_3 \cdot 2NaOH$ A heavy-duty cleaner.
See Part 2: Detergent Properties

sodium oxide *See* Part 2: Normal Solutions

sodium phosphate (sodium metaphosphate; sodium polyphosphate; glassy sodium phosphate; sodium hexametaphosphate; sodium tetraphosphate; Graham's salt; Kurrol's salt, sodium trimetaphosphate, sodium tetrametaphosphate; insoluble sodium metaphosphate) Range of composition from $(NaPO_3)_x$ through $Na_xH_2P_xO_{3x+1}$ to $Na_{x+2}P_xO_{3x+1}$.
Sodium phosphate, dibasic (disodium monohydrogen phosphate; disodium phosphate) Na_2HPO_4
Sodium phosphate, monobasic (monosodium phosphate; sodium biphosphate; monosodium dihydrogen phosphate) NaH_2PO_4
Sodium phosphate (trisodium phosphate) Na_3PO_4
Sodium pyrophosphate (tetrasodium diphosphate; tetrasodium pyrophosphate) $Na_4P_2O_7$
Sodium tripolyphosphate (pentasodium triphosphate; triphosphate; sodium triphosphate) $Na_5P_3O_{10}$
See Part 2: Phosphate

sodium sesquisilicate *See* Part 2: Detergent Properties

sodium silicate (water-glass) Na_2SiO_3 Used as a preservative for eggs; in dried form as silica gel.

sodium sulfide Na_2S An ingredient of sheep dips.
See Part 2: Normal Solutions

sodium sulfite Na_2SO_3 Used as food preservative and antioxidant. *See also* **sulfur dioxide.**

sodium tetraphosphate A heavy-duty detergent and cleaner.
See Part 2: Detergent Properties

sodium tripolyphosphate Sequestering agent and detergent builder.
See Part 2: Detergent Properties

soft cider *See* **cider**

soft drink A nonalcoholic beverage of many flavors (pH 2 to 4).
Includes (1) any fruit drink, squash, crush or cordial; (2) soda water, Indian or quinine tonic water and any sweetened, artificially carbonated water; (3) ginger beer and any herbal or botanical beverage.
Does not include (1) natural spring water; (2) fruit juice; (3) tomato or vegetable juice; (4) any drink based on milk, egg, meat, yeast, vegetable extract, tea, coffee, cocoa.
See Part 2: Minerals (Trace), Limits; Portion Size; Stabilizers, Thickeners

soft glass *See* **soda glass**

soft hog A hog fed on acorns or peanuts.

soft soap Potassium soap.

soft water Water that is low in mineral salts; i.e. $CaCO_3$ or $CaSO_4$.

soft-wheat flour Dough made from this flour tends to break rather than stretch, giving a light, porous structure to the baked product.

softwood Wood from all species of coniferous trees (evergreens).
See Part 2: Fuel, Heating Value

soil The layer of weathered rock, silica, clay, etc., that covers much of the earth's land area.

Classification	Size (mm)
Gravel	Over 2
Sand, coarse	0.2–2.0
Sand, fine	0.02–0.2
Silt	0.002–0.02
Clay	less than 0.002

See Part 2: Soil Classes

soja *See* **soybean**

solanaceae *See* Part 2: Vegetables Classification

solanine A toxic glycoside in potato sprouts (0.04%).

solder A low-melting alloy (98% lead, 2% tin) used for joining metals. *See also* **tin can.**

sole A lean, flat fish that has small mouth and gill openings, and eyes placed close together. *See also* **demersal fish; flounder.**

Types	Where Caught
Rex, petrale, sand, gray, lemon	Pacific and Atlantic coasts, Canada, central and northern Europe
Dover, English	England

See Part 2: Fish, Storage; Vitamin A, Fish; Vitamin D, Fish

solid fat index Proportion of solid to liquid in a fat. *See also* **dilatometry.**

solid foam A colloidal system in which a gas is dispersed in a solid, e.g., pumice.

solidifying point The temperature at which an oil hardens to a soft solid.
See Part 2: Margarine Production

solids The nonliquid portion of a food.
See Part 2: Cherry Composition; Lemon Juice Composition; Lime Juice Composition; Milk Breeds, Composition; Milk Composition; Milk, Mammals, Composition; Milk, Species; Milk, Total Solids

solids-not-fat The solids in milk excluding fat, e.g., casein, calcium.

solubility The amount of a product (solute) that will dissolve in a given solvent at a given temperature.

solubility product (K_{sp})
When AB (solid) $\rightleftarrows A^+ + B^-$

$$K_{sp} = (A^+)\ (B^-)$$

soluble Capable of being dissolved; sugar and salt are among the many compounds that are soluble in water.

solute A substance dissolved in a solvent.

solution A uniformly dispersed mixture of two or more substances which may be either liquids or solids.

solvent A substance having the power to dissolve other substances, e.g., alcohol, benzene, water.

soncoya *See* **anonaceous fruit**

sop Food dipped in a liquid.

soppresata *See* **frizzie**

sopressata Sausage placed in wrinkling hog middles.

sorbet A water, ice, and liquor mixture.

sorbic acid (hexadienoic acid)

$$CH_3—CH=CH—CH=CH—COOH$$

An unsaturated fatty acid with two double bonds in the alkyl chain used as a fungistatic agent in some foods; it is a harmless substance that can be metabolized by humans. The acid and its sodium and potassium salts are antimicrobial agents used in food for protection against molds and yeasts and some bacteria at levels from 1000 to 3000 ppm.

sorbitan monostearate A food additive and emulsifier.
See Part 2: Antioxidant Mixtures

sorbitol $C_6H_8(OH)_6$ A 6-carbon alcohol found in food; used in ascorbic acid fermentation and to sweeten diabetic food; 60% as sweet as sucrose.

sorbitol agar *See* Part 2: Microorganism, Media

sorbose (ketohexose) $CH_2OH(CHOH)_3CO \cdot CH_2OH$ A 6-carbon sugar used in manufacture of ascorbic acid and in special diets.

sorghum grain (millet; millo maize, gyp corn, grain, higear, kafir corn) An annual grass plant that can be used for grain, syrup, or ensilage (56 lb/bu); grain harvest, grain 14% moisture; grain storage, grain 12% moisture; pH 5–5.5.
Approximate nutrient used for:

	40 bu of Grain	2 tons of Fodder
N (lb)	33	41
P_2O_5 (lb)	20	13
K_2O (lb)	7	63

Grain can be wet-milled (starch, edible oil, and gluten feed) or dry-milled (flour, and a number of industrial products).
Composition: 8–20% H_2O, 6–16% protein, 2–6% fat, 60–77% starch, 2% ash. Lysine is the first limiting amino acid and threonine is the second.
Sudangrass: 40–50 lb/bu; plant 25 to 40 lb/acre.
Grain: 56 lb/bu; plant 5 to 8 lb/acre.
Forage: 50 lb/bu; plant 5 to 10 lb/acre.
See Part 2: Cereal Composition; Cereal Fortification; Cereal Nutrient Content; Cereals, Vitamin and Mineral Content; Nutrients in Crops; Poisonous Plants; Seed, Chemical Composition; Seed, Germination; Sugars and Syrups Composition; Sweetness of Sweeteners; Sweetening Agents

sorghum syrup Made by concentrating juice of sugar sorghum (*Sorghum bicolor*); max 30% water; max 6¼% ash (dry wt basis); 36% sucrose; 27% glucose.
1⅓ cups = 1 lb
1 cup = 330 g (11.6 oz)

sorosis *See* Part 2: Fruit Classification

sorrel (***Rumex acetosa***) **(sour grass)** A greens "vegetable" similar to dock; reddish in color.
See Part 2: Organic Acids in Fruits and Vegetables; Vegetable Plants

soufflé A fluffy beaten egg-white dish; a fluffy sherbet with eggs (2 per gal.); a light pudding; made light by beating and cooking.

sound Free from disease and with no abnormality of structure that will interfere with usefulness.

soup A liquid food made by boiling meat and/or vegetables in water and various seasoning agents.
See Part 2: Portion Size; Soups, Composition

sour cherries *See* **cherry**

sour cream A cultured cream product made by adding *Streptococcus lactis* (lactic acid-producing) and *Leuconostoc citrovorum* (flavor) to pasteurized coffee cream; 18% fat content.
See Part 2: Cultured Dairy Products, Composition; Fluid and Fermented Milks, Composition; Sour Cream Dressing

sour grass *See* **sorrel**

sour half-and-half Made like sour cream except half-and-half is the starting product; 10.5–11.5% fat.

souring (milk) The action induced by bacteria on lactose (milk sugar), producing lactic acid, which gives the sour taste and causes coagulation (curd formation). Optimum temperature for souring is 40°C.

1 cup sour milk = 1⅓ tbsp vinegar + 1 cup sweet milk
= 1½ tbsp lemon juice + 1 cup sweet milk
= 1 cup buttermilk.

See also **curd; lactic acid; whey.**

sour orange (Seville, bitters); (*Citrus aurantium*) An orange that has a bitter taste and is used to make marmalade; also has been used for root stock for other citrus plants. *See also* **citrus fruit.**

sour rot Decomposition of eggs in which the egg white becomes thin and yolk thickens; when broken, the egg has an ammonia odor.

sour sop *See* **anonaceous fruit**
See Part 2: Fruit Classification; Fruit Composition

souse (sulze) A jelled product made from pork (snouts, cheeks, skins). Vinegar and commercial gelatin are added and it is then cooked.
See Part 2: Sausage, Types

Southdale A breed of sheep originated by USDA by crossing Southdown and Corriedale.

Southdown A medium-wool mutton-type breed of sheep that originated in southeastern England from native Sussex sheep; face is brown to gray-brown in color; body is small and compact; no horns; fleece grades from ⅜ to ½.
See Part 2: Sheep Breeds

southern corn rootworm An insect which bores into corn stalks just below the ground; bud of young plant wilts; worse after a heavy green manure crop.

sow (1) A female hog that has or soon will farrow a litter of pigs. Average gestation period: 114 days (range 110–120); average duration of heat: 2–4 days; normal recurrence of heat: 21 days. (2) To scatter seeds; to plant.
See Part 2: Liver; Swine Market Classes and Grades

Soxhlet A device used for extraction in chemical laboratories.

soy *See* **soybean; soy sauce**

soya *See* **soybean**

soybean (soy, soyabean, soja bean; Chinese pea, Manchurian bean, boyabean); (*Glycine max, Soja hispida*) An annual leguminous herb of the pea family grown for its oil (20%) and protein content (40%). It contains a trypsin inhibitor that is inactivated by heat. Contains 25% carbohydrate. Used for hay, flour, meal, oil, soy sauce, meat substitutes.
Plant in rows 30–60 lb per acre; drilling 90–120 lb per acre; 110 to 130 days to maturity. Harvest hay when beans are fully developed and lower leaves yellowing.

Varieties:		
	Dorman	Ogden
	Jackson	Ottolan
	Laredo	Roanoke
	Lee	Wabash

Parts of plant used for:
Fresh bean, vegetable, human food
Fermented bean, vegetable, human food
Dried bean, vegetable, human food
Young bean sprouts, vegetable, human food
Flour, baking
Milk (extracted from seed), cooking
Soy sauce, flavoring
Soy plant, livestock feed
Oilseed cake, livestock feed
1.8 lb/qt
1 lb = 2 cups
1 cup = 210 g (7.4 oz)
60 lb per bu
Moisture content for storage should be 11–12%.

Composition:	H_2O (%)	Protein (%)	Fat (%)	Carbohydrate (%)	Ash (%)
Raw seed	69	11	5	13	2
Dry seed	10–12	34–40	13–26	33–34	5
Hull (8%)	moisture-free	9	1	85	4
Cotyledon	moisture-free	43	23	29	5
Hypocotyl (2%)	moisture-free	40	11	44	4

See Part 2: Beans Dry, Cooking; Minerals, Food; Nutrients in Crops; Oils, Seed and Fruit; Plant Foods, Composition; Pulses, Nuts and Seeds Composition; Seed, Chemical Composition; Seed Composition; Seed, Germination; Soybean Composition; Sugar, Legumes; Unsaponifiable

Matter; Vegetable Composition; Vegetable Plants; Wastes, Agricultural and Industrial

soybean curd *See* **tofu**

soybean flour (soy flour) A high-protein, low-carbohydrate flour (100-mesh or finer) made from ground, dried soybeans; it lacks gluten-forming properties.

Types:

Full fat: soybean ground with only hull removed.

Low fat: made from presscake after removal of oil.

Defatted.

Composition:

	H_2O (%)	Protein (%)	Fat (%)	Carbohydrate (%)	Ash (%)
Full fat	8	37	20	30	5
Defatted	8	47	1	38	6

soybean grits (soy grits) A cooked, mush-like product made from soybean presscake. *See also* **grits**.

Particle size	U.S. screen mesh
Coarse	10-20
Medium	20-40
Fine	40-80

soybean meal Ground presscake (oil-free) made from the cotyledons of the soybean; used as cattle feed and fertilizer (7-1.2-1.5).

1.28 lb soybeans = 1 lb soybean meal

41, 44 or 49% protein meal. 1.4 lb/qt.

See Part 2: Oil Meals Composition

soybean milk Extract of soybean used for people allergic to cow's milk.

Composition:	H_2O (%)	Protein (%)	Fat (%)	Carbohydrate (%)	Ash (%)
Liquid	92	3.5	1.5	2	0.5
Dry	4	42	20	28	6

soybean mill feed Soybean hulls used as feed; 13% protein, not more than 32% crude fiber.

soybean mill run Soybean hulls used as feed; 11% protein, not more than 32% crude fiber.

soybean oil Oil extracted from soybean with hexane or pressure; 5.45 lb soybeans yields 1 lb soybean oil.

Composition:

Myristic	0.1%
Palmitic	10%
Stearic	3%
Oleic	22-29%
Linoleic	51-55%
Linolenic	6-8 %
Arachidic	0.2%
Eicosenoic	0.8%

Properties:

Melting point	-16°C
Saponification value	185-195
Iodine value	120-141
Titer	20-27°C
Acid number	3.50
Phospholipids	1.8-3.2%
Specific gravity 20°/4°C	0.9228
Unsaponifiable	0.5-2.0
Saturated fatty acids	10-18%

	Smoke Point (°F)	Smoke Point (°C)	Flash Point (°F)	Flash Point (°C)	Fire Point (°F)	Fire Point (°C)
Expeller	357	181	564	296	664	351
Extracted, crude	410	210	603	317	670	354
Refined	492	265	618	326	673	356

See Part 2: Fats and Oils, Composition; Fat and Oils, Fatty Acid Composition; Fats and Oils, Physical and Chemical Properties; Fatty Acids, Fats and Oils; Fats and Oils, Characteristics; Free Fatty Acid, Smoke, Flash, Fire Points; Iodine and Saponification Values; Oil or Fat, Characteristics; Oil, Triglyceride Mole Percent Composition; Refractive Indices, Fats and Oils; Specific Gravities, Fats and Oils; Titer, Fats and Oils; Tocopherols; Unsaturated Fatty Acids

soybean proteinate Water-soluble soybean protein made by washing precipitated globin (pH 4.6) with water and neutralizing with NaOH and spray-drying; contains no sugar or fiber.

soybean protein concentrate A product made from defatted soybean flakes or flour by removing water-soluble sugars.

Composition: 70-74% protein (dry basis); 5.8% ash; 3.6% crude fiber; 0.5% fat.

soybean protein isolate A soybean derivative containing 97% average protein on a dry basis (min 90%). Used as a binder in meat products (up to 2%); insoluble in water at its isoelectric point. Ash 4.5%; sodium 1.7%; crude fiber 0.3%.

soy cheese *See* **tofu**

soy sauce A spicy sauce made from fermented and hydrolyzed soybeans. *See also* **ketjap**.

spacing The distance allowed between plants in a row or between rows.

See Part 2: Acre, Plants; Acre, Trees

spadic Leaves of the coca shrub (narcotic).

spaghetti A mixture of wheat flour and water (sometimes also milk and eggs) that has been dried into a 3/32-in. diameter solid rod (0.06 to 0.11 in. diameter range); may be but seldom is tubular. Other variations:

fedelini: less than 1/32 inch diameter solid rod
vermicelli: 1/32 inch diameter solid rod
forati: 1/8 inch diameter solid rod
fidelini (fettuccelle): flat strips
trenette: flat strips 1/2 as wide as fidelini
1 lb broken = 4-5 cups
1 cup broken = 95 g (3.3 oz)
1 lb makes 8 to 12 cups cooked
1 cup cooked = 160 g (5.6 oz)
1 cup broken uncooked = 2 cups cooked

Dry composition: 10% H_2O, 12% protein, 1% fat, 75% carbohydrate, 1% ash.
With meat and sauce: has minimum of 12% meat.
With meat balls and sauce: has minimum of 12% meat.
See Part 2: Cereal Composition; Grain Products Composition; Microwave Processing Time; Minerals, Food; Portion Size

Spanish A Mediterranean class of chickens that lays a white-shelled egg. Variety: White-Faced Black.

Spanish leaves Tart and tangy salad greens.

Spanish mackerel *See* **mackerel**

Spanish olives Green olives stuffed with pimiento.

Spanish omelet (1) American version is a mixture of eggs and tomato sauce with onions, green peppers, etc. (2) Spanish version (tortilla) is a mixture of eggs with potatoes, onions, olive oil and optional ingredients such as mushrooms, spinach, anchovies, etc.

Spanish paprika *See* **paprika**

Spanish sheep Merino sheep.

spareribs Ribs removed from the belly area of a hog (sometimes beef) carcass. Spareribs are 2½ to 4% of hog carcass.
See Part 2: Braising Meat; Braising Time; Meat Label; Meat, Servings per Pound; Pork Carcass, Retail Yield; Pork Chart; Pork Cookery; Pork, Cooking; Pork, Cooking Methods; Pork Cooking Yield; Pork Cuts; Pork Cuts and Uses; Pork Wholesale Cuts; Pork Yield; Roasting Meat; Roasting, Time and Temperature

sparkling burgundy A coralline-red, dry wine with a vinous flavor but not the robustness of other burgundies.

sparkling wine A wine with an excess of carbon dioxide (several atmospheres pressure at room temperature).

spätlese Grapes gathered later than the normal vintage; they will be riper, and have a higher sugar content.

spatula An implement with a thin, flexible blade designed for spreading thick mixtures, turning foods during frying, and detaching baked products from pans. The smaller sizes are used in pharmacies and chemical laboratories, and the larger ones in cooking.

spay To remove the ovaries from a female animal to prevent conception. Leaves a scar in front of left hip of a heifer.

spearmint A flavoring agent containing carvone, linalol, and pinene obtained from leaves and tops of *Mentha spicata* L. Used to make mint sauce that is served with lamb. Oil of spearmint is distilled from the flowering plants; used for flavoring liquor, confectionery, chewing gum, etc.
See Part 2: Essential Oils

species A taxonomic category below a genus and above a variety.

specific gravity Ratio of the density of a given substance compared to that of a standard (usually air or water).

$$\text{sp gr} = \frac{\text{density of substance}}{\text{density of standard}}$$

The temperature is usually also given; it is often in the form of a fraction; temperature of substance/temperature of standard.
See Part 2: Brine, Meat Curing; Specific Gravities, Fats and Oils

specific heat Amount of heat expressed in BTU required to raise the temperature of one pound of a substance 1°F, or heat required to raise the temperature of 1 gram 1°C; apparent specific heat = 0.20 + (0.008 × % water); specific heat in BTU's = apparent specific heat × wt in lb × temp in °F; specific heat in calories = apparent specific heat × wt in g × temp in °C.
See Part 2: Specific Heat, Meat

specific rotation $[\alpha]$; $[\alpha]_D^{20}$ The angle of rotation produced by a cubic centimeter of a material at 20°C using a sodium light.

specific volume The volume that 1 g will occupy at a specific temperature and pressure; reciprocal of density.

speckled hind *See* **grouper**

speckled trout *See* **sea trout**

spectro grade The designation of a standard of chemical purity; a high grade solvent that will provide low absorption. *See also* **grade.**

spectrophotometric analysis An optical analysis based upon the intensity of light (at known wavelength) transmitted through a sample.

spectrum The wavelengths of electromagnetic energy (i.e. radiant energy, light). They range from gamma to radio frequencies. *See also* **radiation.**
See Part 2: Waves, Energy-Producing

spelt A German species of grain; coarse wheat.

sperm oil Oil obtained from the head cavity of the sperm whale. Its use is now prohibited in U.S.
See Part 2: Fats and Oils, Physical and Chemical Properties; Iodine and Saponification Values; Titer, Fats and Oils; Unsaturated Fatty Acids

spermaceti A waxy substance obtained from whale and used in soap; iodine number 3–5; saponification number 120–135.

spermatozoa Reproductive cells of the male, present in semen.

sphingosine $C_{18}H_{33}(OH)_2 \cdot NH_2$ A nitrogenous base.

spice A plant having a fragrant or aromatic odor and a pungent flavor used to season food; usually contains essential oils.

See Part 2: Flavoring Agents, Natural; Minerals (Trace), Limits; Spices, Microbial Content; Storage, Dry; Storage Times; Vinegar, Spiced; Wastes, Agricultural and Industrial

spider mite An insect which has the following characteristics: less than ⅛-in. long; 8 legs; wingless; soft; round body; green, yellow or red color. They suck sap from cotton leaves and produce webbing causing leaves to become yellow or red.

spikenard A fragrant oil used in perfumes.
See Part 2: Essential Oils

spinach (***Spinacia oleracea***) An annual whose leaves are used as a boiled vegetable or in salads and soups; can be frozen or canned.
1 lb fresh = 4 cups
1 lb fresh = 1.5 cups cooked
1 cup fresh = 55 g (1.9 oz)
1 cup cooked = 200 g (7.1 oz)
2½ cups cooked = 1 lb
2-6 lb fresh = 1 qt canned
2-2½ lb fresh = 1 qt frozen
1 bu fresh = 20 lb
100 lb fresh = 8–16 lb dry
Storage: Wash, dry, store in refrigerator (32°F) in crisper or plastic bags (90–95% relative humidity); use in 1 to 4 days; frozen (0°F) storage, 1 yr.
Raw composition: 91% H_2O, 3% protein, 0.3% fat, 4% carbohydrate, 1–2% ash; pH 5.1–5.7.
See Part 2: Canned Spoilage Related to pH; Food, Composition; Frozen Food Storage; Glutamate; Iron; Microwave Cooking, Fresh Vegetables; Microwave Cooking, Frozen Vegetables; Microwave Processing Time; Minerals, Food; Nicotinic Acid, Food; Nitrate, Vegetables; Nutrients in Crops; Pentosans; Plant Foods, Composition; Portion Size; Potassium; Riboflavin; Riboflavin, Daily Recommendations; Riboflavin, Food; Standards, Processed Fruit and Vegetable Products; Storage; Sugar, Vegetables; Thiamin; Vegetable Boiling; Vegetable Composition; Vegetable Cooking, Frozen; Vegetable Frozen Yield; Vegetable Plants; Vegetables, Boiling Time, Frozen; Vegetables, Canning Dates; Vegetables, Cooking Frozen; Vegetable Servings; Vegetables, Panned; Vegetable Yield; Vegetable Yield, Canned and Frozen; Vegetable Yield, Frozen, Canned and Fresh; Vitamin A; Vitamin A, Daily Recommendations; Vitamin C; Wastes, Agricultural and Industrial

spinach beet (***Beta vulgaris***) A plant that resembles a beet but is grown for its leaves and stalks which are used as a cooked vegetable.

spinach juice A green coloring material often used to color food.

Spinalis dorsi *See* Part 2: Beef Rib Nomenclature

spine The backbone of a vertebrate.
See Part 2: Beef Wholesale Cuts; Bone; Bone Age

spinous processes *See* **feather bone**

spirilla A subdivision of bacteria indicating their shape, resembling that of a corkscrew (Latin, coil shaped).

spirit Volatile or distilled liquid or volatile material.

spirit of orange Alcohol containing oil of orange peel.

spirit of turpentine Volatile oil of turpentine. *See also* **gum spirits of turpentine; wood turpentine.**

spirit of wine Ethyl alcohol solution.

spit A skewer on which meat is placed and rotated while roasting.

spleen (milt) A ductless gland near the gullet end of the stomach.
See Part 2: Gland Weights; Organ Weights

splenius A triangular muscle in the neck area that lies dorsal and lateral to the complexus.

splint A bony growth occurring on the cannon bone.

spoilage Decay; loss of valuable qualities; rancidity; rot.
See Part 2: Canned Spoilage Manifestations; Canned Spoilage Related to pH; pH, Post Mortem; Rot Spoilage; Spoilage, Carbohydrate Foods; Spoilage, Fat in Food

sponge Fibrous skeleton of *Euspongia officinalis.*

sponge cake A light sweet cake made without shortening; air is added by whipping egg whites and yolks.

spongy bone tissue *See* **cancellated bone tissue**

spool joint *See* Part 2: Bone Age

spore Reproductive element of lower organisms that are in the resting state and are highly resistant to heat.
See Part 2: Sanitizing Chemicals; Thermal-Death-Time Curve; Thermophiles

sport A mutant; e.g., polled.

spot (Goody, Lafayette) A lean fish caught from New Jersey to Florida.

Spotted Poland China A meat-type breed of hogs originating in Ohio from the blending of several strains (Bedfordshire, Big China, Big Spotted China, Byfield, Irish Grazier and Russian strains); their color is black and white (20–80% white) spotted and they have drooping ears.
See Part 2: Swine Breeds

Spotted trout *See* **sea trout**

sprat A fish related to herring.
See Part 2: Fish, Storage

spray drying A method of drying of a liquid-solid mixture, such as milk, by spraying it into a hot, tall chamber; the solids are quickly dried and moisture removed while product falls through the chamber.

sprayed cracker *See* Part 2: Fermented Ingredients

spread A soft mixture, often containing cheese, used for sandwiches.
See Part 2: Stabilizers, Thickeners

springer That which is a source of supply: (1) young plants, (2) due to freshen (usually cow), (3) salmon that has finished a run, (4) a defective tin can, (5) various animals. *See also* **fryer.**

spring salmon *See* **salmon**

spring wheat Wheat planted in the spring and harvested in the fall.

spritzig A natural effervescence of wine.

sprout A young growing shoot or bud. Isopropyl N-(3-chlorophenyl) carbamate is used to inhibit sprouting in potatoes.
See Part 2: Vegetable Composition; Vitamin A, Food

sprout-depressing *See* Part 2: Radiation Preservation

SPS agar *See* Part 2: Microorganism, Media

spud (1) Bread boiled in oil. (2) Slang for potato.

squab Young poultry, particularly pigeon. *See also* **poultry grades.**
See Part 2: Animal Foods, Composition

square centimeter (cm^2) A measure of area. 1 cm^2 = 0.1550 square inch = 10^{-4} sq meters.

square chain A measure of area. 10 sq chains = 1 acre.

square foot (sq ft) A measure of surface area.
1 sq ft = 929.0 sq centimeters (cm^2)
= 144 sq inches (sq in.)
= 0.11111 sq yard (sq yd)
= 0.09290 sq meter (m^2)
= 0.000,022,96 acre (A)
= 0.000,009,290 hectare (ha)
= 0.000,000,092,90 sq kilometer (km^2)
= 0.000,000,035,87 sq mile (statute)
9 sq ft = 1 sq yard

square inch (sq in.) A measure of surface area.
1 sq in. = 6.452 sq centimeters (cm^2)
= 0.006,944 sq foot (sq ft)
= 0.000,771,6 sq yard (sq yd)
= 0.000,645,2 sq meter (m^2)
= 0.000,000,159,4 acre (A)
= 0.000,000,064,52 hectare (ha)
= 0.000,000,000,645,2 sq kilometer (km^2)
= 0.000,000,000,249,1 sq mile (statute)
144 sq in. = 1 sq foot
0.155 sq in. = 1 sq centimeter (cm^2)

square kilometer (km^2) A measure of surface area.
1 km^2 = 10,763,867 sq feet (sq ft)
= 1,195,985 sq yards (sq yd)
= 1,000,000 sq meters (m^2)
= 247.104 acres (A)
= 100 hectares (ha)
= 0.38610 sq mile (statute)

square meter (m^2) A measure of surface area.
1 m^2 = 10,000 sq centimeters (cm^2)
= 1,549.99 sq inches (sq in.)
= 100 sq decimeters (dm^2)
= 10.7639 sq feet (sq ft)
= 1.195,99 sq yards (sq yd)
= 0.000,247,1 acre (A)
= 0.000,1 hectare (ha)
= 0.000,001 sq kilometer (km^2)
= 0.000,000,386,1 sq mile (statute)

square mile (statute) A measure of surface area.
1 sq mile = 27,878,400 sq feet (sq ft)
= 3,097,600 sq yards (sq yd)
= 2,589,999 sq meters (m^2)
= 640 acres (A)
= 259.000 hectares (ha)
= 2.59000 sq kilometers (km^2)

square millimeter (mm^2) A measure of surface area.
1 mm^2 = 1,973.5 circular mils
= 0.01 cm^2
= 0.001,55 sq in.

square perch *See* **square rod**

square rod A measure of surface area.
1 sq rod = 625 sq links
= 30.25 sq yds
= 25.29 sq meters
= 1 sq perch
= 1/160 acre
160 sq rods = 1 acre
40 sq rods = 1 rood = 1/4 acre

square root The factor of a number which if squared will yield the number. To determine (long hand):
(1) Start at decimal and mark off every 2nd place on both sides of decimal.
(2) Start with 1 or 2 numbers to the left of the last mark on the left.
(3) First number of answer is the largest sq root that will go into this number.
(4) Write this number squared under the number and subtract.
(5) Bring down next 2 numbers.
(6) Multiply by 2 the number(s) in the answer to this point and write it to the left of the subtracted answer.
(7) The next number in the answer will be determined by dividing the value (6) into the remainder. This number is written to the right of the (6) value and also in the answer. The number just placed in the answer is multiplied by the new (6) value, and written under the remainder.
(8) Subtract and bring down next 2 numbers and repeat (6), (7) and (8) for as many decimals as required.

Example: Sq root of 20507013.0

```
              4  5  2  8. 4  6  7
            √20 50 70 13.00 00 00
(6)          16
   85 /       4 50
              4 25
   902 /        25 70
                18 04
   9048 /        7 66 13
                 7 23 84
   90504 /         42 29 00
                   36 22 56
   905680 /          6 06 44 00
                     5 43 41 10
   9056927 /           63 02 84 00
                       63 39 84 89
```

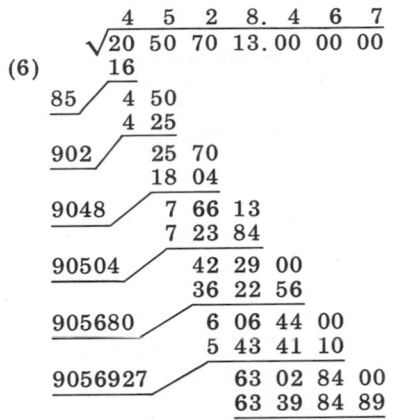

square yard (sq yd) A measure of surface area.

1 sq yd = 1,296 sq inches (sq in.)
= 9 sq feet (sq ft)
= 0.83613 sq meter (m^2)
= 0.000,206,6 acre (A)
= 0.000,083,61 hectare (ha)
= 0.000,000,836,1 sq kilometer (km^2)
= 0.000,000,322,8 sq mile (statute)

30.25 sq yd = 1 sq rod
1.196 sq yd = 1 sq meter

squash (*Cucurbita pepo, C. moschata, C. maxima*) A climbing herb of the gourd family that produces a pepo which is used as food; there are many varieties of different shapes and colors; they are eaten as cooked vegetables, jams, chutneys, soups and fermented into wines. Seed 3 lb/acre; space 3 ft apart in 4-ft rows.

Winter squash:
- 1 lb fresh = 1 cup cooked and mashed
- 1 cup cooked and mashed = 245 g (8.6 oz)
- 1½- to 3-lb winter squash in shell = 1 qt canned
- 3 lb winter squash in shell = 1 qt frozen

Summer squash:
- 1 lb fresh = 1.7 cups cooked and mashed
- 1 cup cooked and mashed = 240 g (8.4 oz)
- 2- to 4-lb summer squash in shell = 1 qt canned
- 2- to 2½-lb summer squash in shell = 1 qt frozen
- 40 lb per bushel
- 100 lb fresh = 7–9 lb dry

Storage:
Winter type: Low room temperature (50°–55°F; 70–75% relative humidity); keeps several months at 60°F; keeps 1 week at higher temp. Summer type: 32°–40°F; 85–95% relative humidity; 2 weeks' storage life.

Composition:

	H_2O (%)	Protein (%)	Fat (%)	Carbohydrate (%)	Ash (%)
Summer	94	1	0.1	4	0.6
Winter	85	1.4	0.3	12	1
Seed dry	4	29	46	15	5

pH 5.0–5.4

See Part 2: Calories, Daily Recommendations; Frozen Food Storage; Fruit Classification; Microwave Cooking, Fresh Vegetables; Microwave Cooking, Frozen Vegetables; Minerals, Food; Nitrate, Vegetables; Plant Foods, Composition; Portion Size; Protein Factors; Pulses, Nuts and Seeds Composition; Riboflavin, Daily Recommendations; Standards, Processed Fruit and Vegetable Products; Storage; Sugar, Vegetables; Vegetable Boiling; Vegetable Composition; Vegetable Cooking, Frozen; Vegetable Frozen Yield; Vegetable Plants; Vegetables, Boiling Time, Frozen; Vegetables, Canning Dates; Vegetables, Classification; Vegetables, Cooking Frozen; Vegetable Servings; Vegetables, Panned; Vegetable Storage; Vegetable Yield; Vegetable Yield, Canned and Frozen; Vegetable Yield, Frozen, Canned and Fresh; Vitamin A, Daily Recommendations

squeteagues *See* **sea trout**

squid Cephalopod with 10 arms used as food and fish bait.
Raw composition: 80% H_2O, 16% protein, 1% fat, 1–2% carbohydrate, 1% ash.

squirrel *See* **hake**

Sr Symbol for the element strontium.

SR medium base *See* Part 2: Microorganism, Media

SS agar *See* Part 2: Intestinal Microorganisms; Microorganism, Media

stabilizer A food additive that thickens, prevents separation, prevents flavor deterioration, retards oxidation by increasing the viscosity and gives a smoother product. Examples: pectin, gelatin, and gums.
See Part 2: Stabilizers, Thickeners

Stachyobotrys A type of mold.
See Part 2: Molds, Mycotoxins

stachyose *See* Part 2: Sugar, Legumes

stag (1) A male animal of several species castrated after reaching the age to develop a masculine character; compared to an animal castrated early in life the stag will have a thicker neck and shoulders, coarse hair and bones, and considerable hardening of breastbone. (2) A young male chicken 9–12 months old and beginning to develop spurs. (3) The uncastrated male of several wild animals (particularly deer).
See Part 2: Swine Market Classes and Grades

staggergrass A plant having a toxic principle.
See Part 2: Poisonous Plants

stain A chemical used to color tissue for microscopic study.

stainless steel An alloy steel containing a high percentage of chromium and often nickel also. A well-known type has 18% Cr and 8% Ni. Used in corrosion-resistant food-processing equipment.
See Part 2: Stainless Steel

staking Flexing a tanned hide over a metal blade to make the fibers pliable.

stale Of food, dried out, not fresh; of carbonated beverages, flat; of animals, to urinate.

stalk *See* **stem**

stallion A male horse (not castrated).

stamen Male part of a flower that bears the pollen.
See Part 2: Flower, Imperfect; Flower, Perfect

standard A stated quality or performance requirement or specification.
See Part 2: Grades, Meat; Meat Grade Stamps; Microbiological Standards, Dairy; Standards, Processed Fruit and Vegetable Products; Water Drinking Standards

standard deviation (σ) Variation of observations; a σ of one population cannot be compared with the σ of another population because the σ is somewhat dependent on the sample magnitude.

$u \pm 1\sigma$ = point of inflection in a normal distribution.

$u \pm 1\sigma$ = ⅔ of observations in normal distribution.

$u \pm 2\sigma$ = 95% of observations in normal distribution.

$u \pm 3\sigma$ = 99.74% of observations in normal distribution.

Estimated by sample standard deviation(s)

$$s = \sqrt{\frac{\Sigma x^2}{n-1}} = \text{(same units as original data)}$$

x = deviations from mean
n = sample size

A quick but inefficient estimation of σ

$$\text{rough estimation of } \sigma = \frac{\text{Largest value of } X - \text{smallest value of } X}{C}$$

n	C
5	2
10	3
25	4
100	5

Interval estimate of σ (95% level)

$$\frac{\Sigma x^2}{\chi^2 0.025} \leqslant \sigma^2 \leqslant \frac{\Sigma x^2}{\chi^2 0.975}$$

Test of σ^2

$$\chi^2 = \frac{\Sigma x^2}{\sigma_0^2}$$

σ_0^2 = Value is assigned according to your HO; (Example: comparing with known σ of another sample) $df = n - 1$

standard error ($\sigma/\sqrt{n}$) Approximated by estimator of standard error ($S\bar{x}$)

$$S\bar{x} = \frac{s}{\sqrt{n}} \qquad s = \text{estimation of standard deviation}$$

$$= \sqrt{\frac{s^2}{n}} \qquad s^2 = \text{estimation of mean square}$$

standard method *See* Part 2: Microorganism, Culture Media, Water and Sewage, Standard Methods

standard methods agar *See* Part 2: Microbiological Examination of Dairy Products; Microbiological Media

standard plate count *See* Part 2: Microbiological Standards, Dairy

standard solution *See* Part 2: pH, Standard Solutions; Reagents, Normal Solutions

standing rib roast A roast made from the fore quarter of beef that comes from the 7th to 12th rib area; the inside portion of the backbone is removed and the ribs are cut at the end of the rib eye muscle.

Staphylococcus A spherical type of infectious bacteria (cocci).
See Part 2: Diseases, Food-Borne; Food Poisoning, Bacteria; Illness from Food; Infectious Diseases, Food-Borne; Intestinal Microorganisms in Triple-Sugar Agar; Microbial Toxins; Microbiological Media; Microbiological Standards, Dairy; Microorganism, Media; Water Activity, Organisms and Food

Staphylococcus aureus The bacteria often found in grape-like clusters of which some strains produce a toxin responsible for the most frequently occurring type of food poisoning; they are Gram-positive cocci, facultative anaerobes, and are easily destroyed by elevated temperature; people having this type of food poisoning usually recover in 1 to 3 days. Heating to 60°C will kill this bacteria but the toxin is stable to boiling temperature for extended periods.

Staphylococcus enterotoxin A heat-resistant toxin produced by *Staphylococcus aureus*.

staple (1) Food products that are essential for daily consumption. (2) A vegetable fiber.

starch $(C_6H_{10}O_5)_x$ A carbohydrate made up of many glucose units (1 and 4 α linkage). Most starches are a mixture of two polysaccharides. Found in seeds and roots; major source of food and feed energy. Amylose content: corn 25–30%; potato 20–29%; rice 15–18%; wheat 25–35%. *See also* **amylose; amylopectin; binder; sago palm.**

See Part 2: Amylose and Amylopectin; Bananas, Composition; Corn Kernel; Corn Kernel Composition; Grain Analysis; Gums and Gelling Agents; Gums and Gelling Agents, Characteristics; Minerals (Trace), Limits; Starches and Starchy Roots Composition; Starch, Microappearance; Starch, Modified; Starch; Wheat and Flour Composition; Wheat, Carbohydrate Composition; Wheat Kernel; Wheat Kernel Parts; Wheat, Parts of Grain; Wheat Products Composition

starch gum Dextrin, formed by hydrolysis of starch; a thickening agent.

starch sugar *See* **glucose**

Starr A variety of millet.

starter culture A bacterial culture added to meat, milk (cheese, butter) or other fermentations. In meat, *Pediococcus cerevisiae* can be used; not more than 0.5% used in cervelat, salami, and thuringer.

stationary phase A stage in bacterial growth following the logarithmic growth phase in which the number of bacteria do not change.

statutory *See* Part 2: Minerals (Trace), Limits

stave Wooden pieces that make the side of a barrel, cask or bucket.

Stayman Winesap A variety of apples that is in season from November to February; excellent cooking and sauce apples; good eating apples.

steak A large, thick, slice of meat; also a cross-section cut of large fish.

Storage: Coldest part of refrigerator; original wrapper for 1 to 2 days' storage; unwrap and cover loosely for 3 to 5 days' storage.

See Part 2: Animal Foods, Composition; Beef Chart; Beef Yields; Broiling Griddle, Meat; Broiling Meat; Broiling Time and Temperature; Fish Forms; Fish Steaks; Fish Yields; Frozen Food Storage; Lamb Cuts; Lamb Cuts and Uses; Meat Composition; Meat, Frozen Storage; Meat Identification; Meat, Servings Per Pound; Minerals, Food; Pork Chart; Pork, Cooking; Pork Cooking Methods; Pork Cuts; Pork Cuts and Uses; Pork Loin Cooking; Portion Size; Sauce, Beef Steak

steam (1) Water in a vapor state at 212°F and 1 atm pressure. (2) To cook in steam.

See Part 2: Steam, Properties

steam bone meal A dried, ground product obtained from cooking bones with steam under pressure.

steam-distilled wood turpentine Wood turpentine distilled with steam from the oleoresin in wood or extracted from wood.

steam jacket A double walled cooking vessel in which steam between the walls is used for heating.

steam-rendered lard Live steam under 30 to 50 lb pressure is introduced into a container with the fat.

stearic acid (octadecanoic acid)

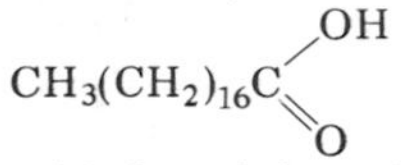

A 18-carbon saturated fatty acid found in animal and vegetable fats, expecially beef; m.p. 69°C; titer 54–55°C; saponification value 207–210; acidic value 206–210; iodine value 3–7.

See Part 2: Fat and Oils, Fatty Acid Composition; Fatty Acids; Fatty Acids, Fats and Oils; Fatty Acids and Their Properties; Milk, Fatty Acids, Seasonal; Oils, Seed and Fruit; Saturated Fatty Acids; Seed, Chemical Composition; Wheat, Fatty Acids; Wheat Products Composition

stearine A hard hydrogenated fat (tristearate); iodine value below 20; m.p. 135–155°F.

steatite *See* **soapstone**

steel (1) A hand tool (smooth or ribbed) used to straighten the wire edge of a knife and to keep it sharp. (2) Purified iron containing 0.1–1.5% carbon.

steel cut oatmeal Cut oatmeal.

steelhead *See* Part 2: Salmon and Trout

steep To extract in liquid just below the boiling point, e.g., tea.

steer A male bovine that has been castrated before developing any masculine characteristics.

steer-bull Cryptorchid.

stem The principal body of a plant; a stalk.

See Part 2: Corn; Vegetables, Classification; Wastes, Agricultural and Industrial

stem correction Temperature correction applied to a thermometer reading to correct for the thermometer liquid that is above the sample being measured, and consequently at a different temperature.

St. Emilion A deep-colored, full-bodied wine having a fine bouquet.

sterculia gum *See* **gum karaya**

stere A solid measure; 1 stere = 1 cu meter or 35.316 cu feet.

stereoisomer A chemical compound having two three-dimensional structural configurations, but the same molecular formula. Two types exist: (1) geometric isomers, which have *cis* and *trans* configurations and (2) optical isomers, which have right-handed (dextro) and left-handed (levo) configurations.

sterile (1) A substance that contains no microorganisms. (2) An animal unable to reproduce.

sterile-male technique A method of controlling pests by producing and releasing sterile males of the species.

sterilization (1) The process of destroying microorganisms by dry heat (320°F for 1 hr) or by radiation. (2) An operation which renders an animal incapable of reproduction.

See Part 2: Radiation Preservation

sterling silver (solid silver) An alloy that must be 925/1000 pure silver; balance usually copper.

sternal rib A rib which articulates directly with the sternum. *See also* **rib**.

sternebrae *See* Part 2: Bone

sternum The breast bone.
See Part 2: Bone; Bone Age

sternum sternebrae Breast bone that attaches first ribs together (hog has 6).

steroid A compound that contains the ring structure:

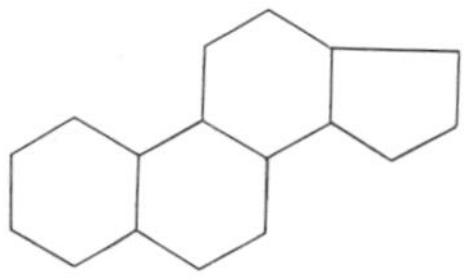

Examples: bile acids, vitamin D, and sex hormones.
See Part 2: Steroids

sterol An alcohol derived from a steroid; a group of cyclic alcohols of complex structure with a base consisting of 3 six-membered rings and 1 five-membered ring; secondary alcohol and various side chains are also in the structures; cholesterol is best known.

stew (1) To cook slowly in liquid. (2) A dish containing a minimum of 25% meat on a fresh meat weight basis, cooked in gravy or meat sauce; small pieces of meat and/or vegetables simmered in water.
See Part 2: Meat Composition; Meat, Servings Per Pound; Microwave Processing Time; Portion Size; Poultry Class; Simmering Meat; Veal Chart; Veal Cuts; Veal Cuts and Uses

stick Tankwater collected in evaporators.

sticking knife A knife with a 6–7 in. blade, sharpened on both sides.

stiffs *See* **osteomalacia**

stifle joint The joint between hind shank and leg bone (femero-tibis-patello joint); in live animals just behind rear flank.
See Part 2: Beef Rounds, Bone Structure; Beef Wholesale Cuts; Bone; Lamb, Wholesale Cuts; Pork Wholesale Cuts; Veal Wholesale Cuts

stigma That portion of the pistil of a plant where pollen is applied.
See Part 2: Flower, Perfect

stilbestrol (diethylstilbestrol) A synthetic estrogen (female sex hormone) that was implanted and fed to cattle. Because of its possible carcinogenic effects, the federal government has published (1976) an "intent to ban" and permits no residues in the tissues of slaughtered animals.

still Equipment used for separating liquids by distillation, i.e., boiling with subsequent condensation.

stillingia *See* Part 2: Iodine and Saponification Values

Stilton cheese A semihard cheese from England; it is similar to Roquefort (milder) or blue (more crumbly). Made from cow's milk and ripened 2–6 months.
See Part 2: Cheese Characteristics; Cheese, Vitamin Content; Milk and Milk Products, Vitamin Content; Vitamin A, Milk and Milk Products

stimulus An energy change in the environment which affects one of the senses.

stink bug *See* Part 2: Insect Control

Stirling's approximation formula *See* **factorial**

stitches Individual injections of a pickle into meat about to be cured.

St. John's bread *See* **locust bean gum**

St. Johnswort A plant having a toxic principle.
See Part 2: Poisonous Plants

stock (1) Short name for livestock. (2) A solution of water-soluble food components, i.e., soup stock.

stockfish *See* Part 2: Vitamin D, Fish

Stoddard oat agar *See* Part 2: Microorganism, Media

stoichiometry Study of the laws governing the quantities of substances that enter into and are produced by chemical reactions; determination of the proportions in which elements combine.

Stokes' law An equation defining the rate of settling of particles from a suspension.

stollen German coffee cake, made with unbleached flour, citrus fruits and raisins.

stomach A pouch between the esophagus and the intestine in which most of the digestive process occurs.
See Part 2: Casings, Animal; Casings, Hog and Beef; Gland Weights; Organ Weights

stomach poison A pesticide that kills an insect that ingests it.

stomata Pores located on the under side of leaves.

stone *See* Part 2: Insulation

storage *See* **controlled atmosphere storage**; **shelf-life**
See Part 2: Fruit, Growing Season, Storage Life; Fruit Storage; Meat, Frozen Storage; Meat Storage; Pork Storage; Vegetable Storage

storax (styrax) A balsamic resin.
See Part 2: Essential Oils

stout A strong, dark beer; an English beer with 3.9–5.3% alcohol by volume.

STP Abbreviation for standard temperature and pressure, i.e., 0°C and 760 mmHg.

straight-grade flour A grade of white flour which comprises from 97 to 100% of all the white flour milled.

straight whiskey *See* **bottled in bond**

strain To pass through a filter.

strained honey Honey separated from comb by straining after the comb has been crushed.

straw The stem of grain after threshing.

strawberry Fruit of the species *Fragaria*; a perennial herb that sends out runners that will root into new plants. The edible fruit is an enlarged receptacle and the seeds are imbedded on its surface. This dessert fruit is very perishable and may be consumed fresh, canned, frozen or made into jam.
Volume:
1½ lb fresh = 4 cups (1 cup = 145 g or 5.1 oz)
= 4 cups sliced
1½ to 4 qt fresh = 1 qt canned
1 bu fresh = 40–50 lb
= 10–16 qt canned
24-qt crate = 36 lb
= 24 pt canned
Storage: Short term (fresh) (4 days): 31°F, 85–90% relative humidity; long term (frozen) (1 year): -10°F.
Raw composition: 90% H_2O, 1% protein, 0.5% fat, 8% carbohydrate, 0.5% ash; pH 2.3–3.8 (lowest acidity for jelly is pH 3.4).
See Part 2: Ascorbic Acid; Canned Yield; Flavor Ingredients, Taste and Flavor Type; Flavors, Beverage; Food, Composition; Frozen Food Storage; Fruit, Availability; Fruit Harvest Dates; Fruit Classification; Fruit Composition; Fruit Frozen Yield; Fruit, Growing Season, Storage Life; Fruit Servings Per Pound; Iron; Minerals, Food; Plant Foods, Composition; Potassium-Rich Foods; Rot Spoilage; Storage; Sugar, Fruit; Vitamin C

strawberry guava A reddish-purple fruit smaller than ordinary guava.

strawberry tomato *See* **gooseberry**

strawberry tree *See* **arbutus**

Streptococcus A type of spherical bacteria.
See Part 2: Bacteria, Molds and Yeasts; Food Poisoning, Bacteria; Illness from Food; Infectious Agents; Infectious Diseases, Food-Borne; Intestinal Microorganisms, in Triple-Sugar Agar; Microbiological Media; Microorganism, Culture Media, Dairy and Food Products; Microorganism, Media; Spoilage, Carbohydrate Foods; Spoilage, Fat in Food; Spoilage, Protein Foods; Thermophiles

streptomycin An antibiotic agent obtained from *Actinomyces griseus* and active against a variety of Gram-negative and some Gram-positive bacteria. It is very useful in controlling fire blight in pome fruit.
See Part 2: Antibiotic Standards; Wastes, Agricultural and Industrial

streptosel agar *See* Part 2: Microbiological Media

stress *See* Part 2: pH, Post Mortem

striated (voluntary) muscle A skeletal muscle tissue that has parallel cross stripes (striations) that may be seen under a microscope. There are two types:
(a) White (based on gross color); shorter twitch time-faster; can be extremely active but fatigues rapidly
(b) Dark or red (based on gross color); contracts slowly but can sustain activity; has greater oxygen uptake; higher sarcoplasmic-myofibril ratio; more myoglobin; large energy phosphate supply; higher glycolytic capacity.

strip *See* Part 2: Meat Identification; Pork Loin Cooking

striped bass (rock, rock bass, rock fish) A lean fish caught on the Atlantic and Pacific coasts.

striped mullet *See* **mullet**

strip steak A steak from the loin strip.

stroganoff A dish of beef sautéed with onion, prepared with a sour cream sauce, mushrooms and seasoning. Originated in Russia.

stroma Framework connective tissue of an organ.

strontium (Sr) A metallic element; at. no. 38; at. wt. 87.63; Group IIA of Periodic Table; electron configuration 2–8–18–8–2
orbit K L M N O
oxidation state +2.
See Part 2: Grain Analysis

structural formula A chemical formula that indicates the geometric contour of an organic compound and the relationship of its constituent atoms.

strychnine $C_{21}H_{22}N_2O_2$ A highly toxic alkaloid used as a pest exterminator; derived from strychnos nuts.

Stuart medium base *See* Part 2: Microorganism, Media

stubble The stalk of grain left in the ground after cutting.

stuck yolk An egg yolk that adheres to the shell membrane.

stuffed chops *See* Part 2: Pork Loin Cooking

stuffing Dressing placed in meat, usually a fowl.

sturgeon (*Acipenser*) A fish used for food; its eggs are called caviar.
Raw composition: 79% H_2O, 18% protein, 2% fat, 1% ash.
See Part 2: Unsaturated Fatty Acids

style A thread-like extension of the ovary of a flower terminating in the stigma.
See Part 2: Flower, Perfect

styrax *See* **storax**

Styrofoam Proprietary name for a rigid polystyrene foam used for insulation.
See Part 2: Insulation

sub- Prefix meaning under or below.

sub clover A winter annual grass.

subcutaneous Injected beneath the skin.

subcutis The 3rd layer of the skin which attaches it to the lower structures; it consists of collagenous and elastin fibers and fatty deposits.

subjective Affected by personal bias or individual preference, as in a taste panel; a value that cannot be precisely measured.

sublime (1) To pass from the solid to the gaseous state without formation of liquid. (2) To purify.

sublime olive oil *See* **virgin olive oil**

sublumbar *See* Part 2: Lymph Nodes, Ox; Lymph Nodes, Pig

submaxillary *See* Part 2: Lymph Nodes, Pig

submucous *See* Part 2: Intestine, Cross Section

subscapularis A muscle of the chuck located medial to the scapula.

substance An element or a compound; broad definition also includes mixtures.

substitution Replacement of one atom or group by another in a chemical reaction; e.g., in phenol a hydroxyl group is substituted for the ortho hydrogen atom of benzene.

substrate A substance acted upon by an enzyme or ferment; media on which microorganisms may be grown.

succinic acid $HOOC{-}CH_2{-}CH_2{-}COOH$ An organic acid found in food and sometimes used as an additive. *See also* **acidulant.**
See Part 2: Acidulants; Maple Syrup Composition; Normal Solutions; Organic Acids in Fruits and Vegetables

succinic anhydride *See* Part 2: Acidulants

succotash A mixture of 50-75% whole kernel corn and 25-50% lima or green beans.

sucrase A carbohydrate digestion enzyme which converts sucrose into glucose and fructose. *See also* **invertase.**

sucrose $C_{12}H_{22}O_{11}$ A carbohydrate made up of a molecule of glucose and a molecule of fructose; used as a sweetening agent and food.

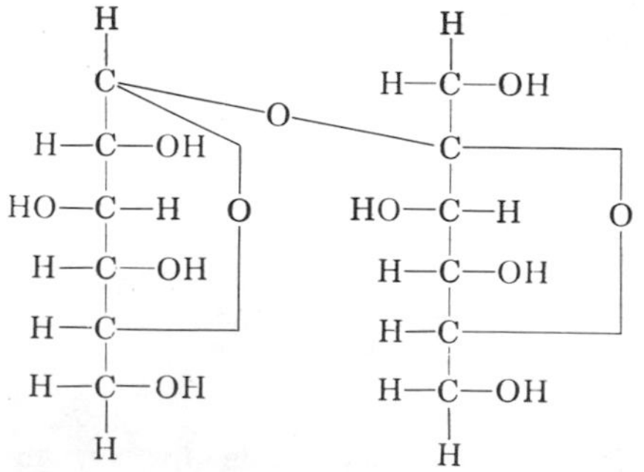

Found in sugar cane (15-20%), sugar beet (10-17%), sugar maple and some palm trees; often called cane sugar or sugar; does not reduce Fehling's solution. *See also* **sugar.**
See Part 2: Concentrated and Dried Milk Products; Honey Composition; Lemon Juice Composition; Maple Syrup Composition; Milk, Concentrated Products; Sugar, Fruit; Sugar, Legumes; Sugar Solutions; Sugar, Vegetables; Sweetness of Sweeteners; Sweetening Compounds; Water Activity, Organisms and Food

Sudan grass An annual grass used for grazing and hay; seeding 32-40 lb per bu; 10-40 lb/acre; pH 5-5.5. Harvest when heading out.
See Part 2: Poisonous Plants; Seed, Germination

suede Leather made from the inner layer of sheep skin.

suet Fatty tissue, about 4% of a choice steer carcass; when rendered it yields tallow; m.p. 45°-50°C; iodine number 30-45; saponification number 190-195. Beef suet smoke point: 235°-245°F.
Volume: Chopped medium fine: 1 lb = 3¾ cups
1 cup = 120 g (4.2 oz)
Beef kidney fat raw composition: 4% H_2O, 1.5% protein, 94% fat.
See Part 2: Beef Retail Yield; Beef Wholesale Cuts; Oils and Fats Composition

Suffolk A medium-wool mutton-type breed of sheep originating in southeastern England; it was started by crossing the Southdown with the Old Norfolk; they have a jet black face with no wool on face or ears and no horns; their fleece grade is approximately ⅜.
See Part 2: Sheep Breeds

sufu *See* **tofu**

sugar (sucrose) Cane and beet sugar are chemically the same; 1 ton of raw sugar = 0.93 ton refined sugar. *See also* **sucrose; sweeteners.**
2¼-3 cups granulated sugar = 1 lb
2 tbsp = 1 oz
2-2¼ cups brown sugar = 1 lb
3½ cups confectioners' sugar = 1 lb
1 barrel = 350 lb
Substitution:
1 cup granulated sugar = 1⅓ cups (lightly packed) brown sugar
= 1½ cups confectioners' sugar
Alteration for altitude, *see also* **altitude.**
See Part 2: Altitude Adjustments for Baking; Bananas, Composition; Brix Table; Calories, Daily Recommendations; Food, Composition; Fruit, Dried, Simmering; Fruit Sauces; Fruit, Simmering; Honey Composition; Lemon Juice Composition; Lime Juice Composition; Microbiological Media; Minerals (Trace), Limits; pH, Post Mortem; Storage, Dry; Storage Times; Sugar Cane Composition; Sugar, D-Aldehydo; Sugar, Fruit; Sugar, Legumes; Sugars and Sweets Composition; Sugars and Syrups Composition; Sugar Solutions; Sugar, Vegetables; Sweetness of Sweeteners; Sweetening Agents; Sweetening Compounds; Brix, Temperature Correction; Wheat and Flour Composition; Wheat, Carbohydrate Composition; Wheat, Parts of Grain

sugar agar *See* Part 2: Microorganism, Media; Microorganism Reactions on Differential Tube Media

sugar apple *See* Part 2: Fruit Storage

sugar beet (***Beta vulgaris subsp. cicla***) A beet (avg. 2 lb) that grows in temperate climates and yields 15–20% sugar; matures in 130–140 days; tops and pulp used for cattle feed; molasses is also used for cattle feed and manufacture of industrial alcohol; filter cake used as a fertilizer.
Composition: 3.7% H_2O, 86.5% sucrose, 8.8% invert sugar, 1% ash; pH 4.2–4.4.
See Part 2: Minerals, Food; Nutrients in Crops; Pectin Content; Sugar Beet Yield

sugar, brown Semirefined sugar that contains molasses, ash and moisture; adds color and flavor to cooked items.
Types:
Less intense molasses flavor:
yellow
golden brown
light brown
brownulated-granulated
dark (old-fashioned)
More intense molasses flavor:
light: 2¼ cups = 1 lb
1 cup = 200 g (7.1 oz)
dark: 2 cups = 1 lb
1 cup (packed) = 210 g (7.5 oz)
Composition: 2% H_2O, 96% carbohydrate, 1.5% ash.

sugar cane (***Saccharum officinarum***) A perennial grass (Cuba, Puerto Rico, Hawaii, Louisiana) which produces sap from which sugar is made; planted by stem cuttings or sets and can be harvested in approximately 1 year; new stems called ratoons grow from the cut root and can be harvested in 1 year; yield decreases and new plantings are made about every 4 years; stem contains 65–80% juice (pH 5.2–6.2), which contains 20–21% sucrose; 1 gal. cane syrup = 5 lb sugar. Waste is used as insulating board (Celotex) and fuel.
Composition

	Stems	Juice	Sugar
Water (%)	75	85	0.9
Protein (%)	0.6	0.1	—
Fat (%)	0.4	0	—
Sugar (%)	13	14	97 (sucrose) 1% invert
Cellulose, lignin, pentosans (%)	10	0.6	—
Ash (%)	0.6	0.4	0.6

See Part 2: Nutrients in Crops; Sugar Cane Composition; Wax

sugar cane fiberboard *See* Part 2: Insulation

sugar cane syrup A syrup made by concentrating sap of the sugar cane; max, 4.5% ash in unsulfured; 6% ash in sulfured. *See also* **top syrup.**

sugar, confectioners' *See* **sugar, powdered**

sugar, corn (dextrose or glucose) Obtained by hydrolyzing corn starch.

sugar, cube Moist sugar placed in molds and dried; 80 to 200/pound.

sugar, cut tablets Sugar molded in slabs and cut.

sugar-free agar *See* Part 2: Microbiological Media

sugar, granulated Most common type of white sugar.
1 cup = 200 g (7.1 oz)
2¼–3 cups = 1 lb
Composition: 0.5% H_2O, 99.5% carbohydrate.
Storage: 50°–80°F, relative humidity below 60%, storage life 1–2 years.

sugar, maple (***Acer saccharum***) Maple sap is concentrated into syrup and sugar by long boiling; the average tap hole produces 8–15 gal. of sap that averages 2.5% sugar; tapping time Feb. 15 to Mar. 25. Produced in New York, Vermont, New Hampshire. *See also* **maple syrup, sugar.**
Composition: 4% H_2O, 86–99% sucrose, 0–9% invert sugar, 1% ash.

Types	Boiling Point (°F)
Sugar on snow	234
Soft sugar	235
Hard sugar	239
Indian or crumb	250–252

sugar millet *See* **sorghum grain**

sugar palm (***Arenga saccharifera***) A palm that produces sugary sap (3 pts/day for 7 weeks) when it is tapped; the sap is concentrated by boiling to produce a dark brown sugar.

sugar pea (mangetout, edible-podded pea) Peas that have tender pods and can be eaten whole when young and still flat.

sugar, powdered (confectioners' sugar) Pulverized sugar used for icings and pastries; contains a small amount of cornstarch as anti-caking agent.
Unsifted: 3–4 cups = 1 lb
1 cup = 125 g (4.3 oz)
Sifted: 4½ cups = 1 lb
1 cup = 95 g (3.4 oz)
Composition: 0.5% H_2O, 99.5% carbohydrate.

sugar, pressed tablets Moist sugar placed in molds and dried.

sugar, raw Unrefined crystalline sugar; contains the molasses portion which makes it dark and sticky; 1 ton = 0.93 ton refined sugar.

sugar syrup *See* **simple syrup**

suint A substance found in wool; it is associated with wool grease but is water-soluble.

sulfate group The SO_4 group; when ionized it becomes the sulfate ion or radical SO_4^{--}.
See Part 2: Water Drinking Standards

sulfate of potash-magnesia A neutral fertilizer material; K_2SO_4; $MgSO_4$; 0-0-22; 11% available magnesia (MgO).

sulfhydryl group SH group, characteristic of thiol (mercaptan) compounds.

sulfite agar *See* Part 2: Microbiological Media

sulfonic acid (R—SO_2OH) A hydrocarbon in which a hydrogen atom has been replaced by the sulfonic acid group $-S(\rightarrow O)_2OH$.

sulfur (S) A nonmetallic element; at. no. 16; at. wt. 32.066; Group VIA of Periodic Table; electron configuration 2-8-6
orbit K L M
oxidation states +4, +6, -2
Body function: necessary for growth and reproduction; occurs in methionine, cystine and glutathione. An ingredient of health tonics; present in eggs and cabbage.
See Part 2: Egg Products, Nutritive Value; Fertilizer Materials; Lemon Juice Composition; Manure Analysis; Minerals, Food; Minerals, Plant or Animal Tissue; Nutrients in Crops; pH and Availability of Plants Nutrients

sulfur dioxide SO_2 A toxic gas used as a preservative, disinfectant or bleaching agent in some foods; is dissipated during boiling. Not permitted in meats or other sources of vitamin B-1. It is obtained by burning sulfur or from the compressed liquid; in water, produces sulfurous acid (H_2SO_3), bisulfite ion (HSO_3^-) and sulfite ion (SO_3^{--}); inhibits yeast, molds and bacteria. Campden tablets yield SO_2 in the presence of fruit juice. Used as a sanitizing agent in wine making; to preserve color and flavor of dried fruit; sulfites restore bright color to stale meat products. Maximum permissible concentration of SO_2 in air is 5 ppm; causes photochemical smog.
See Part 2: Fumigants; Refrigerant

sulfuric acid H_2SO_4 The highest-volume chemical produced in U.S. Mol. wt. 89.08; eq. wt. 49.04.
Commercial strength

Mole/liter	g/liter	% by wt	Specific gravity	Normality
18.0	1766	96	1.84	36.0
—	—	94	1.831	35.1

Ml of 94% H_2SO_4 to dilute to 10 liter	Approx Normality
2.8	0.01
5.7	0.02
28.4	0.10
141.8	0.50
283.5	1.00

See Part 2: Concentration of Commercial Strengths of Acids and Bases; Normal Solutions; Reagents, Normal Solutions; Sulfuric Acid Solution

sulfuric acid, fuming H_2SO_4 Containing various percentages (10–70%) of free SO_3.

sulfurous acid H_2SO_3 Aqueous solution of sulfur dioxide.
See Part 2: Concentration of Commercial Strengths of Acids and Bases

sulfur trioxide SO_3 The anhydride of sulfuric acid. Toxic.
See Part 2: Normal Solutions

Sullivan *See* Part 2: Protein and Amino Acid, Color Reactions

Sultana A small seedless raisin.
Dry composition: 1.7% protein, 65% available carbohydrate.

sulze *See* souse

sumac A plant used in tanning and dyeing.

summation To add; the sign, Σ, is used in statistics to indicate the addition of quantities.

summer sausage A finely chopped sausage that is either "semidry" or "fresh-out-of-smoke"; it was originally produced in winter for summer use. A dry sausage originating in Germany made from pork and beef: it is seasoned (2½ lbs salt/100 lb meat), reground and cured in thin trays for several days; it is stuffed in casings, smoked and aged in a cool place for several weeks. *See also* cervalat.
See Part 2: Sausage Identification; Sausage Nutritive Value

summer savory Fresh or dried leaves of an annual plant used in flavoring.

sum of squares (ΣX^2); values are squared and then summed; sum of squares (corrected) of deviations from sample mean (Σx^2).

$$\Sigma x^2 = \Sigma X^2 - \frac{(\Sigma X)^2}{n}$$

or

$$\Sigma x^2 = \Sigma X^2 - \bar{X}(\Sigma X)$$

or

$$\Sigma x^2 = \Sigma X^2 - n\bar{X}^2$$

sun-dried food A food dried without the use of artificial heat, e.g., raisins, fish, apricots.

sunflower A plant (*Helianthus annuus*) grown for seed, animal feed and oil; a member of the daisy family.
Part of plant and its use
Seed: human food, oil, poultry feed
Oil cake: livestock feed
Stems and leaves: fodder and silage
24–32 lb sunflower seed/bu.
Dry seed composition: 6% H_2O, 19–24% protein, 47–59% fat, 12–20% carbohydrate, 4% ash.
See Part 2: Fat and Oils, Fatty Acid Composition; Fats and Oils, Physical and Chemical Properties; Fatty Acids, Fats and Oils; Fats and Oils, Characteristics; Iodine and Saponification Values; Oil Meals Composition; Oil, Triglyceride Mole Percent Composition; Pectin Content; Protein Factors; Pulses, Nuts and Seeds Composition; Refractive Indices, Fats and Oils; Seed, Chemical Composition; Seed, Germination; Specific Gravities, Fats and Oils; Titer, Fats and Oils; Tocopherols; Unsaponifiable Matter

sunflower oil Oil extracted from sunflower seed (30–45%); used as food, salad oil and in making candy and margarine.

Composition:

Palmitic	5–7%
Stearic	2–3%
Oleic	14–25%
Linoleic	66–75%

Properties:

Saponification value	185–195
Iodine value	125–136
Titer	16–20°C
Acid number	2.76
Specific gravity 20°/4°C	0.9207
Unsaponifiable	1.5%
Saturated fatty acids	8–14%
Melting point	-18 to -16°C
Refractive index (15.5°C)	1.474–1.478

sunshine vitamin *See* **vitamin D**

supercarbonate Bicarbonate.

superficial Near the surface.

superheated A liquid or gas heated above the liquid state boiling point; e.g., water, steam; overheated.

superior Above; higher than. *See also* **cranial.**

superphosphate A neutral fertilizer material; primarily calcium dihydrogen phosphate; $Ca(H_2PO_4)_2$; 0–18–0 or 0–20–0; rock phosphate that has been treated with sulfuric acid.
See Part 2: Fertilizer; Fertilizer Materials

supersaturated solution A solution which contains a greater concentration of a substance than would be present in a saturated solution; (unstable system).

supra- Above or over, e.g., suprarenal.

supramammary *See* Part 2: Lymph Nodes, Pig

suprarenal *See* Part 2: Gland Weights

supraspinatus A muscle of the chuck located lateral to the scapula and above the spine of the scapula.

suprasternal *See* Part 2: Lymph Nodes, Ox

surface The boundary of a geometric solid; of a sphere = $4\pi r^2 = D^2\pi$ (π = 3.1416); Lateral surface of right cylinder = $2\pi rh$; Total surface of right cylinder = $2\pi rh + 2\pi r^2$; Lateral surface of a right cone = πrs; s = slant height; Total surface of right cone = $\pi rs + \pi r^2$.

surface-active agent A molecule one portion of which is hydrophobic and another portion of which is hydrophilic. Such a substance is active at the interface, reducing the surface tension and increasing spreading and wetting properties. *See also* **detergent.**

surface tension A phenomenon resulting from the attraction exerted by the interior molecules of a liquid upon its surface (sometimes called internal pressure). This reduces the tendency of the liquid to flow. Water has rather high surface tension compared to organic liquids such as alcohols. Mercury has the highest surface tension of any liquid. Detergents act by reducing surface tension.

surf smelt *See* **smelt**

suspension A colloidal system in which a solid is dispersed in a liquid; example: muddy water.

Sussex An English class of chickens with white skin, single comb, white shanks; lays a brown-shelled egg; varieties: Speckled, Red, Light.

sweat Exudation from body pores.
See Part 2: pH Values of Biological Materials

swede (*Brassica napus*) The root of a plant (Swedish turnip) used for food; a biennial turnip-like plant grown for its root which consists of both the hypocotyl and the base of the swollen leaf stem; it may be purple-white, or yellow with yellow or white flesh; used in stews; mashed; or used as livestock feed.
Composition: 1% protein, 0.01% fat, 4.3% carbohydrate.
See Part 2: Nicotinic Acid, Food; Vegetable Composition

Swedish sausage *See* **goteborg**

sweet Taste sensation of sucrose (sugar) or honey.
See Part 2: Flavor Ingredients, Taste and Flavor Type; Sugars and Sweets Composition; Sweetness of Sweeteners; Sweetening Agents; Sweetening Compounds; Water Activity, Organisms and Food

sweet basil *See* **basil**

sweet biscuit An English cookie.

sweetbread The thymus gland of calves; (pancreas is also sometimes referred to as sweetbread).
See Part 2: Minerals, Food; Variety Meat, Cooking; Variety Meat Percentage of Daily Recommended Allowances; Variety Meat Preparation; Veal Cuts and Uses

sweet cayenne pepper *See* **paprika**

sweet cherries *See* **cherry**

sweet chestnut (*Castanea sativa*) A large tree grown for nuts and timber; nuts are used for human and livestock feed; nuts may be ground into flour, used in soups, stuffings, eaten whole, boiled or roasted, and preserved in sugar or syrup. 1 lb shelled chestnuts = 1.2 lb unshelled.

Composition	H_2O (%)	Protein (%)	Fat (%)	Carbohydrate (%)	Ash (%)
Fresh	53	3	1	42	1
Dried	8	7	4	79	2

sweet chocolate A mixture of powdered sugar, vanilla, and warm chocolate paste.

sweet clover A biennial used for hay; seeding 60 lb hulled/bu; 32 lb unhulled/bu; plant 8 to

10 lb per acre; pH 6.5–6.8. Harvest at start of bloom. *See also* **dicoumarol.**

sweet cooking chocolate Sold in a 4-oz bar containing 18 squares; rich and light flavor.

sweet dough *See* Part 2: Fermented Ingredients

sweetened condensed milk A product made by evaporating about half the water from whole milk and adding sugar or corn sugar so that it contains 40–45% sugar (by weight); will keep without sterilization. Contains a minimum of 8.5% milkfat, 28% total milk solids, and 27% moisture. Sugar is added as a preservative. Marketed in 14 oz cans.
1 cup = 305 g (10.8 oz)

sweetened condensed skimmed milk Condensed skimmed milk sweetened with sucrose or dextrose; min. 24% milk solids.

sweeteners (sausage) Maximum 2%: maple sugar, invert sugar, corn syrup solids, corn syrup. Sucrose (cane or beet sugar) is self-limiting.

sweetening agents

Comparative Sweetness Ratings
Using Sucrose as 100%

Sugars %		Synthetic (Non-nutritive) %		Others %	
Sucrose	100	Saccharin	55000	Glycerin	70
Fructose	173	Dulain	25000	Glycine	70
Glucose	74	Sucaryl	3000		
Xylose	40				
Maltose	33				
Lactose	16				

sweetmeat Confectionery made with sugar; fruit preserved with sugar.

sweet oil *See* **olive oil**

sweet orange (***Citrus sinensis***) A medium-size tree that bears a citrus fruit that is green to orange in color when ripe and has a sugary pulp; used as fresh fruit or as an orange drink. *See also* **citrus fruit.**

sweet pickle cure A pickle which contains sodium chloride and sugar dissolved in water and is used to cure meat; it will usually contain some nitrite and nitrate and often other ingredients.

sweet potato (***Ipomoea batatas***) A tropical plant that produces elongated to spherical tubers; the outer skin may be white to red and the flesh white to yellow (vitamin A); the tubers contain starch, small amount of protein, some sugar and are usually boiled and mashed for food; vines may be used as livestock feed. The word "yam" is used interchangeably with sweet potato in U.S., but in other countries it is reserved for plants of the genus *Dioscorea*.
Approx. nutrients used

	200 bu root	1 ton vine
N (lb)	30	40
P_2O_5 (lb)	10	11
K_2O (lb)	50	33

1 lb fresh = 3 medium potatoes
1 cup cooked, sliced = 230 g (8.2 oz)
1 bu = 50–55 lb
1 crate = 24 qt = 12 qt canned
2–3 lb fresh = 1 qt canned
1½ lb fresh = 1 qt frozen
100 lb fresh = 23–25 lb dry potatoes

Storage: Low room temperature (55° to 60°F; relative humidity 90–95%); keep several months below 60°F; keep 1 week at higher temperatures.
Raw composition: 71% H_2O, 2% protein, 0.5% fat, 22–26% carbohydrate, 1% ash; pH 5.3–5.6.
See Part 2: Calcium, Daily Recommendations; Calories, Daily Recommendations; Minerals, Food; Niacin, Daily Recommendations; Nutrients in Crops; Plant Foods, Composition; Stabilizers, Thickeners; Standards, Processed Fruit and Vegetable Products; Starches and Starchy Roots Composition; Storage; Sugar, Vegetables; Sweet Potato and Irish Potato; Thiamin; Vegetable Boiling; Vegetable Composition; Vegetable Frozen Yield; Vegetable Plants; Vegetables, Canning Dates; Vegetables, Classification; Vegetable Servings; Vegetable Storage; Vitamin A; Vitamin A, Daily Recommendations; Wastes, Agricultural and Industrial

sweet rice *See* **rice, glutinous**

sweet sop *See* **anonaceous fruit**
See Part 2: Fruit Composition

sweet vermouth A smooth wine with a trace of herbs and aromatics in its flavor.

sweet wine A wine having sufficient sugar in the end product to give a sweet taste; in 100 cc (20°C): not less than 1 g sugar; not less than 0.16 g of ash in sweet red wine; not less than 0.13 g of ash in sweet white wine.

swells A tin can in which gas production has caused expansion.
hard swell: permanently extended ends
soft swell: ends can be moved but not back to original position
springer: end can be forced back, but opposite end will bulge
flipper: end will bulge when can is struck.

swine Inclusive term for hogs, pigs, sows (domestic).
See Part 2: Gestation Periods; Gland Weights; Molds, Mycotoxins; Muscle and Body Weight; Reproductive Cycle; Swine Breeds; Swine Market Classes and Grades; Teeth Eruption

swing churn A churn which functions by swinging rather than rotation.

Swiss Alpine *See* Part 2: Goats, Milk Breeds

Swiss chard (***Beta vulgaris*** **var.** ***cicla***) A beet with a green leafy top that is used in salads.

Swiss cheese (Emmentaler) A hard cheese that is creamy colored, with large holes or eyes and a sweet, salty, nutlike flavor; it is made from skimmed milk and sold as rindless blocks and large wheels with rind; ripened 2–9 mo.

Steps in making:

1. Milk passed through a separator, used as a clarifier.
2. Warmed and stirred.
3. Starters added:

1st starter: produces lactic acid from lactose; acid aids in expelling whey from cheese.

2nd starter: responsible for flavor and eye formation.

3rd starter: aids in acid production and ripening.

Bacteria used are *Streptococcus thermophilus* (lactic acid, flavor, breakdown of curd); *Lactobacillus bulgaricus* or *L. lactis* (lactic acid, flavor, breakdown of curd); and *Propionibacterium shermanii* (flavor, eye formation).

4. Warmed to setting temperature, 88-94°F.
5. Set with rennet extract.
6. Curd cut to ⅛ in. in diameter.
7. Cooked for 25 min at 120°-128°F.
8. Press and knit to a compact mass.
9. Placed in 23% salt brine tank for 3 days; room temp. 55°F and relative humidity 85%.
10. Stored in cold room 10 days.
11. Stored in warm room 68°-74°F (ripening process, eyes begin to form in 2-3 weeks).
12. Returned to cold room (slower curing).
13. Cured for 6 months at 40°F.

Other types of Swiss cheese:

Allguar Emmentaler	Fontine d'Aosta
Bellunese	Traanen
Formaggio	Gruyere
Dolce	Samso
Fontina	

1 cup shredded = 4 oz

Storage: Refrigerate, tightly wrapped.

Composition: 37-39% H_2O, 27-28% protein, 28% fat, (43% milk fat in solids), 2% carbohydrate, 1.3% salt, 4% ash; pH 5.1-6.6.

Grades: U.S. Grade A, B, C, D.

See Part 2: Cheese Characteristics; Cheese, Vitamin Content; Milk and Milk Products, Vitamin Content; Thermophiles; Vitamin A, Milk and Milk Products

Swiss steak *See* Part 2: Braising Meat

swordfish (Broadbill) A lean, large fish with a swordlike beak which is an extension of the upper jaw bone.

See Part 2: Fish and Shellfish Composition; Vitamin A, Fish; Vitamin D, Fish

syn- Prefix meaning with or together.

synergism A phenomenon in which the properties of a mixture are affected to a much greater extent than the sum of the components taken individually would indicate. For example, a copolymer may exhibit much greater strength than the strengths of the individual polymers. Such cooperative materials are called synergists, as in certain antioxidants.

synovial An area where two bones meet and movement is required.

synthetic Man-made; artificial. Synthetic products may be superior to their natural counterparts.

synthetic broth *See* Part 2: Microbiological Media

syrian gum *See* **gum tragacanth**

syrup A mixture of sugar and water.

Strength	%	Cups of Sugar	Cups of Water	Will Make (Cups)
Thin	—	1⅓	4	—
Medium	30	2	4	5
Medium-Heavy	40	3	4	5½
Heavy	50	4¾	4	6½
Extra-Heavy	60	7	4	7¾

Storage: Unopened: room temperature; opened: refrigerate; if crystals form, dissolve by putting container in hot water.

See Part 2: Brix Table; Brix, Temperature Correction; Calories, Daily Recommendations; Cherry Brix; Microbiological Media; Stabilizers, Thickeners; Sugars and Syrups Composition; Sweetness of Sweeteners; Sweetening Agents

systemic insecticide A pesticide that is absorbed into the plant or animal that it is protecting.

systole Muscle contraction.

T

Ta Symbol for the element tantalum.

tabanus A genus of biting flies (e.g., horse fly, botfly, gadfly, seroot).

Tabasco sauce Pepper sauce made from capsicum berries.

table d'hote (1) A complete restaurant meal at a fixed price. (2) A common table for guests at a restaurant.

table salt Sodium chloride (NaCl). *See also* **salt.**

tablespoon A large spoon used at the table; 1/16th of a measuring cup.

1 tbsp = 3 tsp
= 15 milliliters
= 4 fluid drams
= 2 dessert spoons
2 tbsp = 1 fluid ounce
16 tbsp = 1 cupful
32 tbsp = 1 pint
64 tbsp = 1 quart
256 tbsp = 1 gallon

See Part 2: Volume

table wine A wine usually containing less than 14% alcohol, served with food.

tachyphagia Rapid consumption of food.

tack Food of a breadlike nature, e.g., hardtack.

Taenia saginata A parasite found in cattle; the life cycle takes it from ingestion by cattle to the duodenum, through the intestinal wall to the intramuscular connective tissue; as the meat is eaten by man, the tapeworm grows in the intestine to maturity; thorough cooking of meat ensures protection for man.

Taenia solium A parasite found in hogs with a life cycle similar to the *Taenia saginata* in cattle.

taette Fermented milk.

taffy A confection made from brown sugar or molasses and repeatedly stretched or pulled until porous and light-colored.

tafia An alcoholic drink made from sugar cane.

taginette *See* **noodles**

tagliati *See* **noodles**

tail bone *See* **caudal vertebrae**
See Part 2: Bone; Lamb, Wholesale Cuts; Pork Cuts and Uses; Pork Wholesale Cuts; Pork Yield; Veal Wholesale Cuts

taleggio A creamy, soft-textured, snow-white Italian cheese having a mellow, slightly piquant flavor.

tallow An animal fat separated from connective tissue (particularly cattle and sheep) with a titer of 40°C or higher (usually up to 46°C).
Composition:

	Mutton (%)	Beef (%)
Myristic	5	3-6
Palmitic	25	27-29
Palmitoleic	—	3
Margaric	—	0.5
Stearic	30	14-19
Oleic	36	44-49
Linoleic	4	2

Properties:

Melting point	42-47°C	43-48°C
Refractive index (60°C)	1.451	1.449-1.452
Iodine value	32-45	35-55
Specific gravity (99°/15.5°)	0.858-0.860	0.862
Saponification value	192-195	190-200

See Part 2: Fats and Oils, Composition; Fat and Oils, Fatty Acid Composition; Fats and Oils, Physical and Chemical Properties; Fatty Acids, Fats and Oils; Fats and Oils, Characteristics; Free Fatty Acid, Smoke, Flash, Fire Points; Iodine and Saponification Values; Melting Points, Fats and Oils; Oils and Fats Composition; Refractive Indices, Fats and Oils; Saturated Fatty Acids; Specific Gravities, Fats and Oils; Tallow, Beef, Triglyceride Mole Percent Composition; Titer, Fats and Oils; Unsaponifiable Matter; Unsaturated Fatty Acids

tallow (cutting) Tallow from retail store will yield 58% tallow (fat), 22% moisture, 20% meat scraps.

talose *See* Part 2: Sugar, D-aldehydo

tamale (tamal, tamalli) Minced meat and red pepper, rolled in corn and wrapped in corn husks; corn, meat and oil cooked by steaming or baking in a corn shuck (or paper).

tamara A mixture of anise seed, cinnamon, cloves, coriander and fennel.

tammy To strain through cloth.

Tamworth A bacon-type breed of hogs originating in central England; it is solid red in color, has erect ears and a long body.
See Part 2: Swine Breeds

tanbark Shredded tree bark used as a source of tannic acid. *See also* **tannic acid.**

tangelo A citrus fruit that is a hybrid cross between tangerine and grapefruit; is easy to peel.
Juice composition: 90% H_2O, 0.5% protein, 0.1% fat, 10% carbohydrate, 0.3% ash.
See Part 2: Fruit and Nut Rootstock; Fruit, Availability

tangent (1) A straight line that touches the circumference of a circle at one point and is perpendicular to the radius at that point. (2) A trigonometric function:

$$\tan = \frac{\text{ordinate}}{\text{abscissa}}$$

tangerine (mandarin, king orange, satsuma, naartje); (*Citrus reticulata*) A citrus fruit similar to the orange but smaller, with a deeper orange color, and much easier to peel; pulp is very sweet. Used as dessert fruit; segments are canned and the root stock used for other citrus plants.
½ box (Fla.) = 45 lb; medium 2½ in. diameter; 4 per pound.
Storage: 31–35°F, 90–95% relative humidity; storage life 3 weeks.
Composition:

	H_2O (%)	Protein (%)	Fat (%)	Carbohydrate (%)	Ash (%)	pH
Raw	87	0.8	0.2	12	0.4	4.0
Juice	89	0.5	0.2	10	0.3	

See Part 2: Fruit and Nut Rootstock; Fruit, Availability; Fruit Classification; Fruit Composition; Minerals, Food; Plant Foods, Composition; Tangerine Oil Composition; Tangerine Oil Properties

tangor A hybrid between tangerine and sweet orange, i.e., temple.

tankage Residue from rendering used for livestock feed and fertilizer. *See also* **meat meal.**
See Part 2: Fertilizer; Fertilizer Materials; Packinghouse By-Products Composition

tankard A tall one-handled vessel used to hold a liquid for drinking (usually beer or ale).

tanked Steam-pressure cooked.

tannia (yautia, new cocoyam); (*Xanthosoma sagittifolium*) A plant similar to taro.

tannic acid (tannin) $C_{76}H_{52}O_{46}$ An organic acid occurring in the bark of some species of trees; it is extracted by leaching with water. It has the property of converting the proteins in animal hides and skins into the flexible poromeric material called leather—a physicochemical reaction known as tanning. The trees from which it is obtained are:

1. American chestnut
2. Chinese or Turkish nutgal
3. gambier
4. hemlock
5. mangrove
6. myrobalan
7. red oak
8. quebracho
9. spruce
10. sumac
11. valonia
12. water bark
13. wattle (Australia)
14. mimosa (So. Africa)
15. quercitron

It also occurs in some plants and is responsible for the astringent taste of some foods (e.g., tea, nuts, apples).

tanning Making leather from hides by immersing them in a solution of tannic acid. *See also* **tannic acid; vegetable tanning.**

tansy oil An essential oil containing camphor and borneal.
See Part 2: Essential Oils

tantalum (Ta) A metallic element; at. no. 73; at. wt. 180.95; Group VB of Periodic Table; oxidation state +5;
electron configuration 2-8-18-32-11-2
orbit K L M N O P

taotjo A paste made from fermented soybean products.

tapa Salted, and sometimes spiced and sun-dried, beef and pork.

tapai A cake made from eggs, rice flour, sugar, grated coconut and manisan.

tapeworm *See* ***Taenia saginata; Taenia solium***

tapioca *See* **cassava**

tapioca flour Starch obtained from the root of a South American tropical woody plant called the cassava or manioc; used in puddings and as a thickening agent. 3 cups = 1 lb. *See also* **pearl tapioca; flake tapioca.**
See Part 2: Cornstarch Pudding Variations; Minerals, Food; Starch; Starch, Microappearance; Vegetable storage

tare (1) Weight of a container. (2) A fodder plant of the vetch family. (3) Weeds among corn.

Targhee A breed of sheep originated by USDA; they carry about ¾ Rambouillet blood, the remainder being Lincoln and Corriedale.
See Part 2: Sheep Breeds

taro (eddo, dasheen, old cocoyam); (*Colocasia esculenta*) A tropical plant that produces a starchy corm which is formed underground by thickening of the stem; the starch from this plant is very digestible.
Corm composition: 73% H_2O, 2% protein, 0.2% fat, 24% carbohydrate, 1% ash.

tarragon (taragona, estragon); (*Artemisia dracunculus* L.) The dark green leaves of an aster plant used as a flavoring; it is a bushy perennial herb whose leaves are used in fish sauces, salads, vinegar, and French mustard.

tarsal bones Hind foot bones located above the metatarsal bones.
See Part 2: Bone

tart (1) Descriptive of a biting, sour taste. (2) A pastry filled with fruit, jam, etc.
See Part 2: Salad Dressing and Mayonnaise Variations

tartar (tartare) sauce A sauce used with seafood and made from mayonnaise, pickles and herbs, e.g., tarragon.

tartaric acid ($C_4H_6O_6$) An organic acid derived from fruits; 80-85% as sour as anhydrous citric acid.

% W/W at 15°C	d_4^{15}
1	1.0045
10	1.0469
20	1.0969
30	1.1505
40	1.2078
50	1.2696

See Part 2: Acidulants; Normal Solutions; Organic Acids in Fruits and Vegetables; Reagents, Normal Solutions

tassel The flowering portion of the corn plant, *Zea mays*.
See Part 2: Corn

taste A sensation produced by sensory receptors located on the tongue. There are four taste categories:

	Organoleptic Threshold Value (g/100 ml)
Saline	0.25 NaCl
Sweet	0.5 sugar
Sour	0.007 HCl
	0.0002 vanilla (coumarin)
Bitter	0.00005 quinine

See Part 2: Flavor Ingredients, Taste and Flavor Type

taste-bud A receptor end-organ for taste perception. About 9000 are located on the tongue.

taste panel A selected group of people who perform organoleptic tests on food products.
See Part 2: Taste Panel, Difference Tests; Triangular Taste Test + Preference; Triangular Taste Test Probability

taster One who tastes; a device for sampling food or drink.

tau (Τ, τ) Greek letter with an English equivalent of t.

taxonomy The science of arranging and classifying plants and animals.

Tb Symbol for the element terbium.

TB *See* Part 2: Microorganism, Media

TB cattle Cattle that react to the tuberculin test.

TBHQ *See* **tertiary butylated hydroquinone**

T-bone steak A steak that has a T-shaped bone and is cut from the short loin; located between porterhouse and club steaks.
See Part 2: Beef Cuts; Beef Cuts and Uses; Beef Retail Yield; Bone in Retail Cuts; Broiling Meat; Meat Identification; Portion Size

Tc Symbol for the element technetium.

TC Symbol used on volumetric apparatus which means "to contain."

TCA cycle *See* **Krebs cycle; citric acid; tricarboxylic acid cycle.**

TD Symbol used on volumetric apparatus which means "to deliver".

TDE A toxic chlorinated organic insecticide (tetrachlorodiphenylethane):

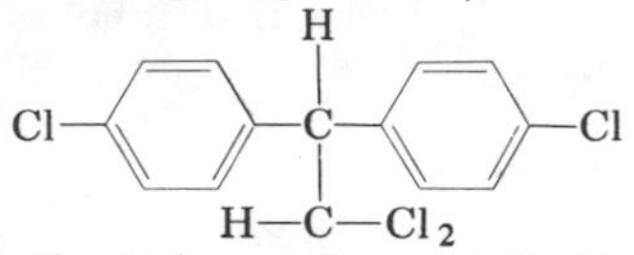

t-distribution A sampling distribution for samples less than 30; at 30 it approaches the normal distribution; it has a higher peak and tails than the normal distribution. $t = 1.96$ ($n = \infty$) means that if a large sample was drawn from a normal population, 2.5% would have a t value greater than 1.96 and 2.5% would have a t value less than −1.96.

$$t = \frac{\bar{x} - \mu}{s/\sqrt{n}}$$

$\bar{x}$ = estimation of mean

μ = population mean or a hypothetical mean to be tested (e.g., difference in mean value $Ho: \mu = 0$)

s = estimation of standard deviation

n = sample number (or number of pairs)

$df = n - 1$

One-tailed test can be used when, by knowledge of the problem, values on one side of μ do not exist or have no meaning.

For a 2-tail table, use ½ of probability indicated in table; all the factors are the same.

Randomized groups:

$$t = \frac{(\bar{x}_1 - \bar{x}_2) - (\mu_1 - \mu_2)}{s_{\bar{x}_1 - \bar{x}_2}}$$

$Ho: \mu_1 - \mu_2 = 0$

$s_{\bar{x}_1 - \bar{x}_2} = \sqrt{2s^2/n}$

$$\text{pooled } s^2 = \frac{\text{pooled } \Sigma x^2}{2(n-1)}$$

n = no. in one group

$df = 2(n - 1)$

TDN *See* **total digestible nutrients**

TDT *See* **thermal death time**

Te Symbol for the element tellurium.

tea (***Camellia*** **or** ***Thea sinensis***) A low bush whose leaves are used to produce the beverage; processing includes: withering, rolling, fermentation, drying, sifting and grading.

Types

Black: leaves oxidized (fermented) before drying.

- Flowering pekoe (highest quality; top leaf buds).
- Orange pekoe (next highest quality, first-opened leaves).
- Pekoe (next highest quality; third leaves).
- Souchong (lower quality, next leaves).

Green: unoxidized (unfermented); made by heating the leaf early in processing to prevent fermentation; light in color; has more tannin than black tea.

Tea contains: 2.5-5% caffein (a stimulant); 5-6% ash; 5-10% water; 7-14% tannin (gives body); 33% extractives; 30-60% fiber; 5% nitrogen; 38-45% soluble matter.

Leaves	Instant
1 lb = 6½ cups	1 lb = 13 cups
1 cup = 70 g (2.5 oz)	1 cup = 35 g (1.2 oz)
1 lb = 300 cups brewed	1 lb = 65 cups brewed

See also **black tea; green tea; oolong tea.**

See Part 2: Essential Oils; Minerals, Food; Minerals (Trace), Limits; Nicotinic Acid, Food; Portion Size; Riboflavin, Food; Wastes, Agricultural and Industrial

tea bag A porous cloth or fiber bag containing one serving of tea.

teacup A measure of volume, usually less than 8 oz.
1 teacup = approx 120 ml

tease (1) To disentangle fibers; card (wool). (2) To tear a tissue into small units for microscopic examination.

teaseed *See* Part 2: Fatty Acids, Fats and Oils; Iodine and Saponification Values; Oil or Fat, Characteristics; Refractive Indices, Fats and Oils; Titer, Fats and Oils; Unsaponifiable Matter

teaspoon A measure of volume.
1 tsp = 120 drops of water
= 60 drops of thick fluid
= approx 3.5-4 milliliters
= approx. 1 to 1⅓ fluid drams
= ⅓ tablespoon
= 1/48 cup
6 tsp = 1 fluid ounce
2 tsp = 1 dessert spoon
See Part 2: Volume

tech. *See* **technical or commercial**

technetium (Tc) An element; at. no. 43; Group VIIB of Periodic Table; mass number of most stable isotope 99; electron configuration 2-8-18-13-2
orbit K L M N O
oxidation states +4, +6, +7.

technical or commercial (tech.) Designation of a grade of chemical purity; it is the lowest chemical grade and is not refined for laboratory use. *See also* **grade.**

teeth A number of bony structures in the mouth embedded in the jawbone and designed for chewing food. Ruminants have teeth in only one jaw. Data for cattle are:

Age (mo)	Teeth
12	all calf teeth in
15	center incisors in
18	center incisors wearing
24	first intermediates through the gum
30	6 incisors in
36	6 incisors wearing
39	corners through the gum
42	8 incisors wearing

See Part 2: Teeth Eruption

teff A cereal grain similar to millet.

Teflon Proprietary name for polytetrafluoroethylene, a chemically inert plastic used as nonstick coating on kitchen utensils.

Telautograph Proprietary name for a device for transcribing information over short distances, for example, from a restaurant counter to the kitchen. The order is written by the counter attendant with a stylus on a special tablet. This activates an electromagnetically controlled slave stylus at the other end, which duplicates the inscription.

tellurite glycine agar *See* Part 2: Microorganism, Media

tellurium (Te) A nonmetallic element; at. no. 52; at. wt. 127.61; Group VIA of Periodic Table; electron configuration 2-8-18-18-6;
orbit K L M N O
oxidation states +4, +6, -2.

tempeh A fermented soybean product (can also be made from coconuts and peanuts).
See Part 2: Fungi Food Products

temperature (1) The thermal state of a solid, liquid or gas considered in terms of its ability to communicate heat to other substances. (2) Body heat as measured by a thermometer. *See also* **candy.**

Rectum Temperature

Animal	Avg. (F°)	Range (F°)	Avg. (C°)	Range (C°)
Bird	—	105-107	—	40.6-41.7
Cat	—	98.9-102.2	—	37.2-39
Cattle	101.5	100-102.4	38.6	38-39
Chicken	—	104-107.6	—	40-42
Dog	101.5	101-102.5	39	38-39.1
Goat	103	—	39.4	—
Guinea pig	—	101.3-103.8	—	38.5-39.9
Horse	100.5	—	38	—
Man	98.6	—	37	—
Pig	102.6	—	39.2	—
Sheep	103	102-104	39.4	38.9-40.0

See Part 2: Altitude Adjustments for Baking; Bacteria on Chickens at Various Holding Temperatures; Beef Degrees of Doneness; Beef Roasting; Broiling Time and Temperature; Ice, Vapor Pressure; Lamb Roasting; Meat Storage; Pork Cookery; Relative Humidity; Roasting Meat; Steam, Properties; Temperature; Temperature of Vaporization, Latent Heat of Vaporization, Boiling Point; Temperatures Corresponding to Gauge Pressure at Various Altitudes; Thermal-arrest Time; Thermal-death-time Curve; Thermophiles; Transit Temperature; Volumetric Solutions, Temperature Corrections

tempering Holding a metal (e.g., steel) at a given temperature for a specific time to achieve stability of crystal form.

temple orange *See* **tangor**

tender On a meat label this term means internal temperature of at least 140°F.

Tenderay Process A process for tenderizing meat by aging it for a short time at high temperature; bacterial growth is kept down by using ultraviolet light and shrinkage is reduced by using high humidity. Example of possible conditions: temp: 60°F, humidity: 85 to 90%, time: 3 days.

tenderizer An enzyme (e.g., papain) or weak acid or salt used to reduce toughness of meat.

tenderloin The muscle located below the backbone; lower muscle in the short loin. *See also* ***psoas major.***
See Part 2: Beef, Boneless Cuts; Beef Cuts; Braising Time; Broiling Meat; Meat Identification; Pork Chart; Pork Cookery; Pork, Cooking; Pork, Cooking Methods; Pork Cuts; Pork Cuts and Uses; Pork Loin Cooking; Roasting, Time and Temperature

tenderness State of being soft and readily chewed and digested.
See Part 2: Tenderness of Poultry

tendon The connective tissue that attaches muscle to bone.

Tenox II Proprietary name for an antioxidant which contains 70 parts propylene glycol, 6 parts propyl gallate, 4 parts citric acid, 20 parts butylated hydroxyanisole.
See Part 2: Antioxidant Activity

tensor fascia lata A muscle of the thigh that tuns from the ilium to the patella; in cross section of the round, it is the most cranial muscle.

teosinte An annual grass similar to Indian corn, and used for fodder.

teou-fu *See* **tofu**

TEPP Tetraethylpyrophosphate; a toxic organic phosphorus insecticide.

$$(C_2H_5O)_2{-}\overset{\overset{O}{/\!/}}{P}{-}O{-}\overset{\overset{O}{/\!/}}{P}{-}(OC_2H_5)_2$$

tequila Distilled pulque (maguey juice), an alcoholic beverage made from fermented juice of heads of cactus; 90-160 proof.

tera- Prefix for quantities one trillion times larger than the base unit.

terbium (Tb) A rare-earth element of the lanthanide series; at. no. 65; at. wt. 158.93; Group IIIB of Periodic Table; oxidation state +3; electron configuration 2-8-18-26-9-2
orbit K L M N O P

teres major A muscle of the chuck, filling the angle between the scapula and the humerus; it lies medial to the triceps and is attached to the upper part of the humerus.

tergitol agar *See* Part 2: Microorganism, Media

termite A white ant that burrows into wood; its stomach contains an enzyme that enables it to digest cellulose.

terpene $(C_5H_8)_n$ One of a series of unsaturated hydrocarbons found in the essential oils of citrus fruits; they are usually removed to reduce oxidative spoilage.

Terramycin Proprietary name for the antibiotic oxytetracycline.

tertiary Carbon atom which is united by three valences to a chain or ring,

$$[CH_3(CH_2)_n]_3C{-}$$

tertiary butylated hydroquinone *See* Part 2: Antioxidant Mixtures

testa The protective covering of the seed embryo.
See Part 2: Rice Kernel; Wheat, Parts of Grain; Wheat, Parts of Grain, Vitamins

testis Male reproductive organ. Plural: testes.
See Part 2: Gland Weights; Organ Weights

testosterone $(C_{19}H_{28}O_2)$ A steroid androgen, produced by the testis.

tetra- Prefix meaning "four."

tetracosanoic acid (lignoceric acid)
$CH_3(CH_2)_{22}COOH$ A saturated fatty acid found in peanut oil.
See Part 2: Saturated Fatty Acids

tetracosenoic acid *See* Part 2: Fatty Acids and Their Properties

tetracycline $C_{22}H_{24}N_2O_8$ An antibiotic added to food in some countries.
See Part 2: Antibiotic Standards

tetradecanoic acid (myristic acid)
$CH_3(CH_2)_{12}COOH$ A saturated fatty acid found in coconut oil.
See Part 2: Saturated Fatty Acids

tetradecenoic acid (myristoleic acid)
$CH_3(CH_2)_3CH{=}CH(CH_2)_7COOH$ An unsaturated fatty acid found in certain plant seeds.
See Part 2: Milk, Fatty Acids, Seasonal; Unsaturated Fatty Acids

tetra pack Four-sided cartons used for milk and beverages.

tetraphosphate A cleaning compound that has good calcium-sequestering power; it is readily soluble in warm water but unstable at high temperature or in highly alkaline solutions. *See also* **phosphate.**

tetrasodium pyrophosphate (sodium pyrophosphate; sodium polyphosphate) *See* Part 2: Detergent Properties

tetrathionate broth *See* Part 2: Microorganism, Selective and Differential Broths and Media, Water Filtration Plant; Microorganism, Media

Texas hide A hide branded on rump or side that is plump and close-grained.

Th Symbol for the element thorium.

thallium (Tl) A metallic element; at. no. 81; at. wt. 204.39; Group IIIA of Periodic Table; electron configuration 2-8-18-32-18-3
orbit K L M N O P
oxidation states +1, +3

thallus A plant not differentiated into root, stem and leaf, e.g., seaweed, algae.

Thayer Martin medium *See* Part 2: Microorganism, Media

theine *See* **caffeine**

theoretical plate (n) (gas chromatography)

$$n = 16\left(\frac{\text{retention volume}}{\text{peak width}}\right)^2$$

therm- Prefix meaning "relating to heat."

thermal arrest *See* Part 2: Thermal-Arrest Time

thermal capacity The amount of heat required to raise the temperature one degree C.

thermal death point The temperature required to kill bacteria in 10 min.

thermal death time (TDT) The time required to completely sterilize a product at a given temperature. *See also* **decimal reduction time.**
See Part 2: Thermal-Death-Time Curve

thermoacidurans agar *See* Part 2: Microorganism, Culture Media, Dairy and Food Products

thermocouple A thermoelectric instrument used to measure interior temperatures by electromotive force; constructed of two wires of different electrically conductive metals joined at one end, i.e., copper and constantan (25.54 mv).

thermoduric *See* Part 2: Sanitizing Chemicals

thermograph An instrument that automatically records temperature.

thermometer An instrument used for measuring temperature, usually by expansion of mercury or alcohol.

thermophile A heat-loving organism.
See Part 2: Microbiological Media; Microorganism, Culture Media, Dairy and Food Products; Microorganism, Media; Thermophiles

thermophilic bacteria Bacteria that can grow at a high temperature; minimum growth temperature 35°-40°C; optimum growth temperature 55°-60°C; maximum growth temperature 65°-75°C.

Thermos Proprietary name for a vacuum bottle used for maintaining the desired temperature of a food or drink.

thermostat An instrument that automatically regulates temperature by means of a feedback mechanism.

theta (Θ, θ) Greek letter with an English equivalent of th. The symbol usually used for an angle in mathematics.

thiamin (vitamin B-1) A water-soluble vitamin often known as vitamin B-1; it functions in carbohydrate metabolism and if deficient in the diet, the visible symptoms of beriberi or polyneuritis develop. Source: brewer's yeast, pork muscle, rice polishings, bran (of grains), fortified foods, peanuts, peas, lima beans and liver. 3 micrograms of pure vitamin = 1 international unit. Functions: promotes appetite, growth and reproduction. Usually sold as the hydrochloride; made synthetically.

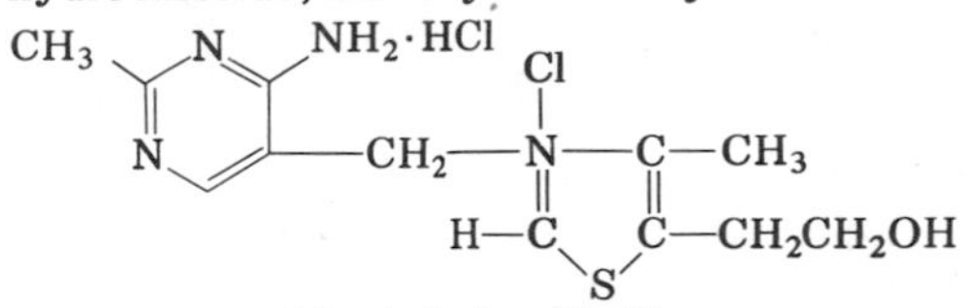

thiamin hydrochloride

See Part 2: Beans, Peas and Nuts; Beef Percentages of Daily Recommended Allowances; Cereal Enrichment; Cereal Fortification; Cereal Nutrient Content; Cereals, Vitamin and Mineral Content; Cheese Composition; Cheese, Vitamin Content; Composition of Food; Dairy Products, Composition; Egg Composition; Egg Products, Nutritive Value; Fats and Oils, Composition; Fish and Shellfish Composition; Flour, Extraction Rates; Food, Composition; Fruit and Vegetables Composition; Fruit Composition; Grain Analysis; Grain Products Composition; Lamb Percentages of Daily Recommended Allowances; Lemon Juice Composition; Lime Juice Composition; Macaroni and Noodles Composition; Meat Composition; Meat, Nutritive Value; Milk and Milk Products, Vitamin Content; Milk Composition; Plant Foods, Composition; Pork, Percentages of Daily Recommended Allowances; Poultry Composition; Recommended Daily Dietary Allowance; Sausage Composition; Sausage Nutritive Value; Seed, Chemical Composition; Soups, Composition; Sugars and Sweets Composition; Thiamin, Daily Recommendations; Thiamin; Thiamin, Food; Tomato and Tomato Products, Composition; Variety Meat Percentage of Daily Recommended Allowances; Vegetable Composition; Vitamin Retention, Meat; Vitamins; Vitamin Sources, Functions, and Stability; Wheat, Parts of Grain, Vitamins; Wheat Products Composition; Wheat, Vitamins

thiamin pyrophosphate A coenzyme which usually functions in a reaction where CO_2 is split out of the substrate:

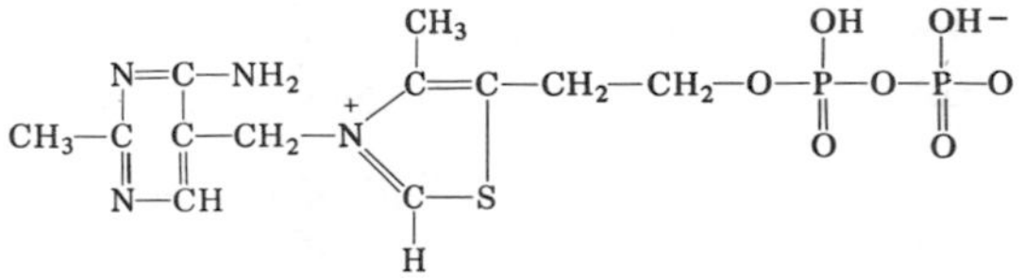

thickener A hydrophilic colloid which increases the viscosity and smoothness of such foods as ice cream, gravies, custards, etc; e.g., gelatin.
See Part 2: Stabilizers, Thickeners

thick filament *See* Part 2: Myofibrillar Proteins of Muscle

thickness (1) Vertical dimension of a solid; sometimes called gauge. (2) Viscosity of a liquid, e.g., oil.
See Part 2: Film Gauge

thin filament *See* Part 2: Myofibrillar Proteins of Muscle

thio- A prefix that indicates presence of divalent sulfur in an organic compound:

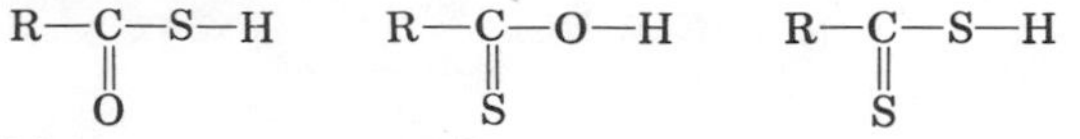

thiocyanate ion CNS^-

thiodipropionic acid $(CH_2CH_2COOH)_2S$ A food preservative and antioxidant.
See Part 2: Antioxidant Structure

thioether R′—S—R A group of compounds similar to ethers but with oxygen atom replaced by sulfur. *See also* **alkylthioalkane.**

thioglycollate *See* Part 2: Microbiological Media; Microorganism, Media

thiol (mercaptan) A group of organic compounds similar to alcohols but having a sulfhydryl group (—SH) instead of a hydroxyl group (—OH). Formerly called mercaptan.

β-thiolalanine *See* **cysteine**

thiol medium *See* Part 2: Microorganism, Media

thixotropic gel A colloidal gel which will liquefy when slight pressure is applied and return to its original form after release of pressure.

Thompson A variety of late Florida grapefruit.

Thompson Seedless A variety of grapes.

thoracic vertebrae Area of the backbone to which the ribs are attached; number of thoracic vertebrae for meat animals: beef, 13; chicken, 7; hog, 14–15; lamb, 12–14; rabbit, 12.
See Part 2: Bone

thorium (Th) A radioactive metallic element of the actinide series; at. no. 90; at. wt. 232.15; Group IIIB of Periodic Table; electron configuration 2-8-18-32-19-9-2
orbit K L M N O P Q
oxidation state +4

thoroughly cooked *See* **smoked meat**

Thousand Island dressing A salad dressing made with mayonnaise, chopped eggs, chili sauce, green pepper, onions or chives and pimento.
See Part 2: Fats and Oils, Composition; Salad Dressing and Mayonnaise Variations

thrash (thresh) To separate grain or seed from straw by beating.

threonine An essential monoamino, monocarboxylic, monohydroxy amino acid:

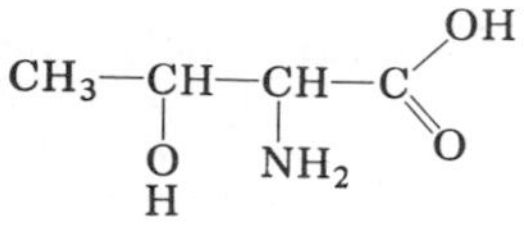

See Part 2: Amino Acids; Corn, Amino Acids; Egg Products, Nutritive Value; Grain Analysis; Manure Analysis; Milk, Amino Acids; Seed, Chemical Composition; Wheat, Amino Acids; Wheat Products, Amino Acid Compositions; Wheat Products Composition

threose *See* Part 2: Sugar, D-aldehydo

threshold The level below which there is no response to a stimulus.

thrip An insect with the following characteristics: less than ⅛-in. long; wings; slender body; yellow, orange or black. They suck sap from leaves and buds and cause leaves to curl upward.
See Part 2: Insect Control

throatlatch The point at which the throat joins the jaw.

thrombin An enzyme in blood that converts fibrinogen to fibrin, which aids clotting.

thrush A disease affecting the feet of certain animals.

thulium (Tm) A rare earth element of the lanthanide group; at. no. 69; at. wt. 168.94; Group IIIB of Periodic Table;
electron configuration 2-8-18-31-8-2
orbit K L M N O P
oxidation state +3

thuringer A finely chopped German summer (semidry) sausage containing mostly beef and some pork with heavy smoke; the beef is never warmed above 95°–110°F and retains most of the nutritive properties of the raw product; contains lactobacilli bacteria.
See Part 2: Sausage Identification; Sausage Nutritive Value; Sausage, Types

thyme (***Thymus vulgaris*** **L.**) Gray-green dried leaves (¼-in. long) and flowering tops of a shrub of the mint family used as an herb; sold in green or dried bunches. There are more than 60 known types. It may be in whole or ground form; used in soups, stuffings, sauces. Not more than 14% total ash; not more than 4% acid-insoluble ash.
See Part 2: Essential Oils; Flavoring Agents, Natural; Spices, Microbial Content

thymine A constituent (pyrimidine base) of nucleic acid:

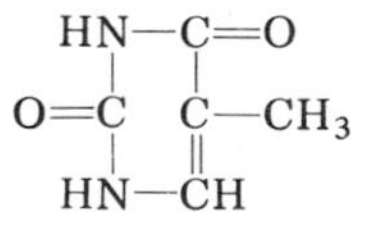

thymol blue $C_{27}H_{30}O_5S$ A pH indicator that is pink at pH 1.5, yellow between 2.8 and 8, and blue at 9.6 and above.

thymol phthalein $C_{28}H_{30}O_4$ A pH indicator that is colorless below a pH of 9.8 and blue at higher values.

thymus A cream-colored lobed and ductless gland located in the neck near the chest; in the

young it inhibits the activity of the sex glands and atrophies after puberty. *See also* **sweetbread**.
See Part 2: Gland Weights; Organ Weights

thyroid A dark-colored ductless gland located on both sides of the windpipe and below the larynx; a deficiency of dietary iodine will cause enlargement of the gland (goiter).
See Part 2: Gland Weights

thyroxine (thyroxin) An iodine-containing amino acid hormone secreted from the thyroid gland that controls the rate of metabolism.

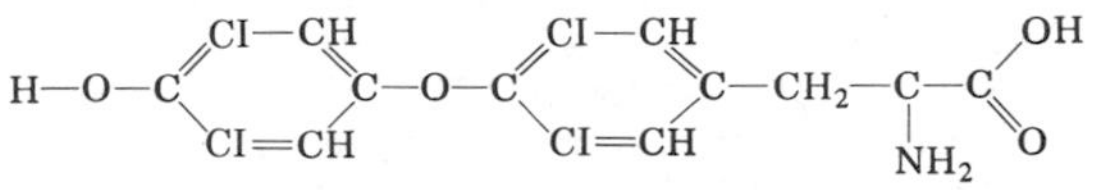

Ti Symbol for the element titanium.

tibia Large hind shank bone that articulates with the femur; larger than its sometimes parallel partner the fibula.
See Part 2: Bone

tierce A measure of volume equal to 42 wine gallons; a cask or container holding this amount.

tiffin A light lunch or afternoon tea (British).

tikitiki Rice polishings.

til Sesame seed.

tillage Plowing and cultivating soil for growing crops and keeping it free of weeds.

tilsit A mild semihard Danish cheese.

tilsiter *See* Part 2: Cheese, Vitamin Content; Vitamin A, Milk and Milk Products

timothy (***Phleum pratense***) A grass with long cylindrical spikes used for hay; 45 lb timothy seed/bu; plant 5 lb/acre; approx nutrient used for 1 ton hay; N 20 lb, P_2O_5 6 lb, K_2O 27 lb.
See Part 2: Nutrients in Crops; Seed, Germination

tin (Sn) A metallic element; at. no. 50; at. wt. 118.70; Group IVA of Periodic Table; electron configuration 2-8-18-18-4;
orbit K L M N O
oxidation states +2, +4;
See Part 2: Minerals (Trace), Limits

tin can Mild steel plate with a thin (1.5% of total) coat of pure tin; tin resists corrosion in the absence of oxygen. Sealing compound: rubber (or synthetic rubber) in benzene, dusted with asbestos powder. Solder: 2% tin and 98% lead solder (evaporated milk cans, 30% tin and 70% lead solder). *See also* **canning**.

tinfoil A thin sheet of tin-lead alloy used for packaging.

tinplate Steel or other metal coated with tin, either by dipping or electroplating.
See Part 2: Cans, Construction

Tinsdale base *See* Part 2: Microorganism, Media

tintometer An instrument for measuring color by comparison with colored glass or standard solutions.

tip *See* **knuckle; top sirloin**
See Part 2: Beef Cuts; Beef Round Cuts; Meat Identification; Roasting, Time and Temperature

tip cap *See* Part 2: Corn Kernel Composition

tissue A group of similar cells that perform a particular function, e.g., muscle, blood.
See Part 2: Gland Weights

tissue culture Technique of keeping parts of animal or plant tissue alive after removal from the organism.

titanium (Ti) A metallic element; at. no. 22; at. wt. 47.90; Group IVB of Periodic Table; electron configuration 2-8-10-2
orbit K L M N
oxidation states +2, +3, +4

titanium dioxide (TiO_2) A white pigment used in paints, paper, plastics, etc.

titer (1) The amount of substance A that will correspond to a given amount of substance B. (2) The solidification point of a saponified fatty acid.
See Part 2: Titer, Fats and Oils

titration The operation of determining the concentration of a given volume of solution by reacting it with a measured volume of a solution of known concentration in the presence of an indicator.

Tl Symbol for the element thallium.

Tm Symbol for the element thulium.

TMM broth *See* Part 2: Microorganism, Media

Tobasco sauce A hot sauce made of fermented tobasco peppers and vinegar.

tocol Precursor of vitamin E.

tocopherol (vitamin E) An antioxidant (alpha better than gamma) found naturally in vegetable oil that retards the development of rancidity; added at the rate of 0.03% to fat. *See also* **alpha-tocopherol.**
See Part 2: Antioxidant Activity; Antioxidant Structure; Grain Analysis; Tocopherols; Vitamins; Wheat Products Composition

tod A measure of weight; 1 tod = 28 lb.

Todd Hewitt broth *See* Part 2: Microorganism, Media

toffee (toffy) A candy made of butter, sugar, milk; similar to caramels but cooked at higher temperatures.
See Part 2: Water Activity, Organisms and Food

tofu (sufu, teou-fu, soy cheese, soybean curd) A fermented soybean product resembling cottage cheese; kori todu or koya dofu: frozen and dried tofu; aburage: french-fried tofu; namage: surface-dried tofu; sufu or to-sufu: tofu on which a special mucor mold is grown.

Composition: 85% H_2O, 8% protein, 4% fat, 2% carbohydrate, 1% ash.
See Part 2: Fungi Food Products; Pulses, Nuts and Seeds Composition

tofukasu A food made from beans.

Toggenburg *See* Part 2: Goats, Milk Breeds

togue *See* lake trout

Tokay A variety of white grapes; a golden dessert wine made from them.

toke Dry bread.

toluene A liquid aromatic hydrocarbon of the benzene series:

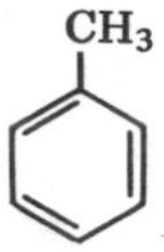

tom A young male turkey before it becomes "staggy;" usually less than 1 year old. *See also* turkey.

tomatillo *See* gooseberry

tomato (*Lycopersicum esculentum*) (golden apple, love apple, Peruvian apple) A vegetable whose fruit is used as food; a weak-stemmed, herbaceous plant that produces a fruit (fleshy, juicy berry) widely different in size (some up to 1 lb.); shape (subglobose, egg-shaped, pear-shaped, or irregularly globose with bulges and ridges); color: red, yellow and, in a few cases, purple. The tomato contains sugar, vitamins A and C and acid which influences flavor and desirability for canning. It is eaten fresh, fried, baked, stuffed and in soups, sauces and ketchup; it is also canned—whole, purée or juice.

Types:
Cherry tomato: small size
Pear tomato: pear-shaped
Tree tomato: egg-shaped fruit on short-lived tree
Approx. 3 medium-size/pound
1 lug box (5.75 × 13.5 × 16.1 in.) = 32 lb
1 lb fresh = 3 to 4 small tomatoes = 1½ cups cooked
2½ to 3½ lb fresh = 1 qt canned
1 bu fresh = 50 to 60 lb = 14 to 22 qt canned
0.027 ton fresh = 1 case (24) No. 2 cans
100 lb fresh = 6–9 lb dry
75–90 days to maturity; seed 2 oz/acre; spacing 2 ft in 4-ft rows.
Ripen: room temp (55°–70°F; relative humidity 85–90%), away from sunlight.
Storage (ripe): Uncovered (85–90% relative humidity); refrigerate (32°F); use within 1 week.
Composition

	H_2O (%)	Protein (%)	Fat (%)	Carbohydrate (%)	Ash (%)	pH
Green	93	1.2	0.2	5	0.5	
Ripe	93	1.1	0.2	5	0.5	4.0–4.9
Dried flakes	3	11	1	77	6	

See Part 2: Ascorbic Acid; Calories, Daily Recommendations; Canned Yield; Food, Composition; Fruit and Vegetable, Diseases; Fruit Classification; Fruit Storage; Glutamate; Iron; Minerals, Food; Minerals (Trace), Limits; Mold, Food; Niacin; Nicotinic Acid, Food; Nitrate, Vegetables; Nutrients in Crops; Pectin Content; Phosphorous; pH Values of Biological Materials; Plant Foods, Composition; Portion Size; Potassium; Potassium-Rich Foods; Riboflavin; Riboflavin, Food; Rot Spoilage; Sauce, Tomato; Soups, Composition; Canned Spoilage Related to pH; Standards, Processed Fruit and Vegetable Products; Storage; Sugar, Vegetables; Thermophiles; Thiamin, Tocopherols; Tomato and Tomato Products, Composition; Tomato Grades; Vegetable Boiling; Vegetable Composition; Vegetable Plants; Vegetables, Canning Dates; Vegetables, Classification; Vegetable Servings; Vegetable Storage; Vegetable Yield, Canned and Frozen; Vegetable Yield, Frozen, Canned and Fresh; Vitamin A; Vitamin A, Daily Recommendations; Vitamin A, Food; Vitamin C

tomato chutney Tomato concentrate, tomato pulp, sugar, water, vinegar, onion, salt, spices (i.e., coriander, cayenne pepper, cinnamon, cardamom, pimento, celery) and essential oils (i.e., garlic, clove, etc.)

tomato juice The juice obtained from fresh ripe tomatoes, usually canned.
1 bu fresh = 50 lb
= 30 pints canned
Canned composition: 94% H_2O, 1% protein, 0.1% fat, 4% carbohydrate, 1% ash; pH 4.1–4.2.
See Part 2: Tomato and Tomato Products, Composition; Vegetable Composition

tomato juice agar *See* Part 2: Microorganism, Culture Media, Dairy and Food Products; Microorganism, Media

tomato ketchup (catsup) Tomato concentrate, sugar, water, vinegar, onion, salt, tragacanth gum, and spices (i.e., nutmeg, cardamom, cinnamon, cloves, and coriander).

ton (gross-long, 2,240 lb) A measure of weight.
1 ton (2,240 lb) = 15,680,000 grains (gr)
= 1.016 × 10^6 grams
= 35,840 av. ounces (oz av.)
= 32,666.7 troy ounces (oz troy) (apoth.)
= 2,722.22 troy pounds (lb troy) (apoth.)
= 2,240 av. pounds (lb av.)
= 1,016.05 kilograms (kg)
= 1.12 net-short tons (2,000 lb)
= 1.01605 metric tons (1,000 kg)

ton (metric, 1,000 kg) (t) A measure of weight.
1 ton (1,000 kg) = 15,432,356 grains (gr)
= 35,274.0 av. ounces (oz av.)
= 32,150.7 troy ounces (oz troy)

= 2,679.23 troy pounds (lb troy)
= 2,204.62 av. pounds (lb av.)
= 1,000 kilograms (kg); 10^3 kg
= 1.10231 net-short tons (2,000 lb)
= 1 cubic meter water at 4°C
= 0.98421 gross-long tons (2,240 lb)

ton (net short, 2,000 lb) (tn) A measure of weight.
1 ton (2,000 lb) = 14,000,000 grains (gr)
= 9.072×10^5 grams
= 32,000 av. ounces (oz av.)
= 29,166.7 troy ounces (oz troy) (apoth.)
= 2,430.56 troy pounds (lb troy) (av.)
= 2,000 av. pounds (lb av.)
= 907.185 kilograms (kg)
= 20 hundredweight (cwt) (av.)
= 0.90719 metric ton (1,000 kg)
= 0.89286 gross-long ton (2,240 lb)
1 ton = 8 sacks of flour
= 10 barrels of flour
= 10 to 36 bushels potatoes
= 20 bushels of wheat

tongue A muscular organ in the mouth; the tongue of some animals is used for food.
See Part 2: Beef Cuts and Uses; Calories, Daily Recommendations; Lamb Cuts and Uses; Meat Composition; Meat, Servings Per Pound; Nicotinic Acid, Food; Pork Cuts and Uses; Riboflavin, Daily Recommendations; Sausage, Types; Storage Times; Variety Meat, Cooking; Variety Meat Percentage of Daily Recommended Allowances; Variety Meat Preparation; Veal Cuts and Uses

tonneau A measure of wine volume; 1 tonneau = approx. 200 gal.

ton of water/24 hr Measure of a rate of flow.
1 ton of water/24 hr = 83.33 lb/hr
= 0.166 gal./min
= 1.335 cu ft/hr

ton, refrigeration The heat required to melt 2,000 lb ice at 32°F = 288,000 Btu.

top (1) The extreme high price of the market. (2) Part of the beef round or chuck. (3) Glass jar closure.
See Part 2: Beef Round Cuts; Glass Jar Tops; Meat Identification

top chuck The outside area of a beef chuck when it is divided along the blade bone. *See also* **outside chuck.**

topfen *See* Part 2: Milk and Cheese Composition

topping *See* Part 2: Stabilizers, Thickeners

top round (*semimembranosus*) The inside muscle of the round; a more tender cut than the eye or bottom round muscles. *See also* **inside round.**
See Part 2: Beef, Boneless Cuts

top sirloin (sirloin tip) Ventral muscles of the sirloin; includes *tensor fasciae latae, vastus medialis, rectus femoris,* and *vastus lateralis.*

top soil Top layer or surface of soil which contains organic matter (humus).

top syrup Syrup obtained by concentrating the entire juice of sugar cane.

tor *See* **torr**

torfu A food prepared from soy beans.

tori seed oil Oil extracted from mustard seed.

torr (tor) International pressure unit approximating one millimeter of mercury.
1 torr = 1/760 standard atmosphere
= 1,013,250/760 dyne/cm^2
= 1333.22 microbars

torte A round cake made with eggs and sugar and sometimes covered with frosting.

tortilla (1) Mexican version: A circular cake made from corn meal. (2) Spanish version: A potato-egg omelet.

to-sufu *See* **tofu**

total digestible nutrients (TDN) Sum of protein, fiber, NFE and fat (2¼); represents approximate heat or energy value.

total nitrogen *See* **Kjeldahl determination**

totuava *See* Part 2: Vitamin A, Fish

tourshi Pickled food.

toxaphene A poisonous insecticide; approx. formula $C_{10}H_{10}Cl_8$.

toxin A poisonous albumin produced by microorganisms.
See Part 2: Microbial Toxins; Plant and Animal Poisoning

TPEY agar *See* Part 2: Microorganism, Media

TPN *See* **triphosphopyridine nucleotide**

trace A small and barely detectable quantity; less than 5×10^{-6} g/g.

trace element An element or its salts needed by the body in very small amounts. *See also* **mineral; trace.**
See Part 2: Minerals (Trace), Limits

trademark A word or distinguishing mark which identifies a proprietary product; if registered, it is protected by law.

tragacanth (gum dragon) *See* **gum tragacanth**

training table Meals planned to aid athletes in their conditioning program.

train oil Oil produced from sea animals (i.e., whale).

trans *See* ***cis-trans*** **isomers.**

transaminase The enzyme responsible for transamination.

transamination Transfer of an amino group ($-NH_2$) from one compound to another, catalyzed by the enzyme transaminase.

Example:

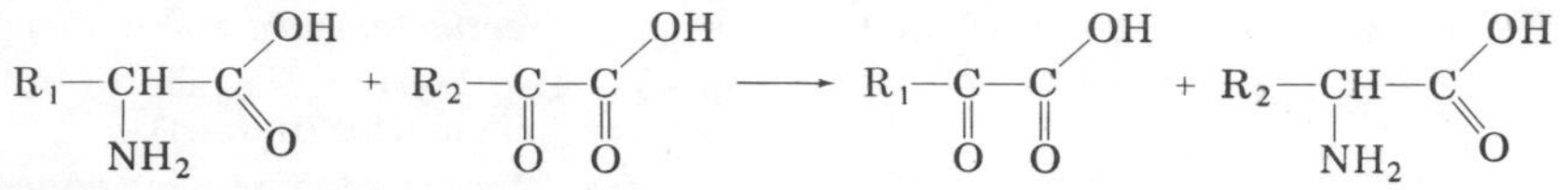

transformer An electrical device used to change the voltage of A.C. power; it contains 2 coils; when current is applied to the primary coil it generates a magnetic field which produces a current in the secondary coil.

transgrow medium *See* Part 2: Microorganism, Media

transit Movement of goods from one location to another.
See Part 2: Transit Temperature

transparent Permitting the passage of light. *See also* Yellow Transparent.

transplant To remove a seedling from the ground and plant it in another place.

transverse plane Crosswise; right angles to long axis; ribbed carcass into fore and hind quarters.

transverse process Lateral projection on vertebra.

trapezius muscle A muscle that is attached to the lateral surface of the scapula and to the thoracic spinous processes.

trappist *See* Part 2: Cheese, Vitamin Content; Vitamin A, Milk and Milk Products

trasi Fermented paste of prawns or shrimp.

trawl A long line with hooks or net used in deep-sea fishing.

treacle British term for molasses.

tree molasses *See* **maple syrup**

tree nuts *See* Part 2: Pulses, Nuts and Seeds Composition

tree sugar *See* **maple sugar**

tree tomato *See* **tomato**

T'refah (trepha) Opposite of kosher; food considered objectionable by Jewish tradition.

trefoil (big trefoil) A shallow-rooted perennial grass used in wet soil; seeding 60 lb/bu; 2-3 lb/acre; variety: Columbia. *See also* Viking.
See Part 2: Seed, Germination

trenette *See* **spaghetti**

trepha *See* **T'refah**

triacontanoic acid (melissic acid) $CH_3(CH_2)_{28}COOH$ A saturated fatty acid found in some plant waxes.
See Part 2: Saturated Fatty Acids

triangle A 3-sided figure. *See also* **rattle.**
See Part 2: Taste Panel, Difference Tests; Triangular Taste Test + Preference; Triangular Taste Test Probability

tribasic acid An acid with 3 replaceable hydrogens.
Examples:

$$H_3PO_4 \rightleftharpoons H_2PO_4^- + H^+$$

$$H_2PO_4^- \rightleftharpoons HPO_4^{=} + H^+$$

$$HPO_4^{2-} \rightleftharpoons PO_4^{\equiv} + H^+$$

tricarboxylic acid cycle *See* **citric acid; Krebs cycle**

triceps Three-headed; small muscle that extends the fore limb. *See also* ***triceps brachii.***

triceps brachii A large muscle of the chuck filling the angle between the scapula and the humerus; it is attached to the head of the ulna.

trichina Trichinella; a parasite found in pork and other animal tissue. *See also* ***Trichinella spiralis;*** trichina destruction.

trichina destruction A technique recommended for destroying trichina.
Heating: 137°F
Refrigerating:

Max Temp (°F)	Meat Samples (separated & not over 6 in. thick) (days)	Meat Samples (6-27 in. thick & separated) (days)
5	20	30
-10	10	20
-20	6	12

Curing:

Method	Max Diam. Meat (in.)	Min salt/100 lb Fresh (lb)	Holding Time: Min Time (Days)	Holding Time: Min Temp (°F)	Max Diam. (In.)	Drying Room: Min Days	Drying Room: Min Temp (°F)	Smoking: Min Time (Hr)	Smoking: Min Temp (°F)	Min Total Days in Cure: Time	Min Total Days in Cure: Min Temp (°F)
1	3/4	3 1/3			3 1/2	20	45			25	
					1 3/8	15	45			20	
					3 1/2-4	35	45			40	
2	3/4	3 1/3			3 1/2	10	45	40	80	18	
					3 1/2-4	25	45	40	80	33	
3	3/4	3 1/3	1 1/2	34	3 1/2			12	90	144 hr	34

Curing:

			Holding Time			Drying Room		Smoking		Min Total Days in Cure	
Method	Max Diam. Meat (in.)	Min salt/100 lb Fresh (lb)	Min Time (Days)	Min Temp (°F)	Max Diam. (In.)	Min Days	Min Temp (°F)	Min Time (Hr)	Min Temp (°F)	Time	Min Temp (°F)
								4 cont.	128		
			50° pickle	44	3½–4			15	90		
								7 cont.	128		
								4 hr to obtain	128		
4	¼	2½	6 in. in depth		3½			3 hr water bath	85	35	45
			10	36				or smoke	80	35	45
5	¾	3⅓				65	45	Coat with paraffin			
Capocollo (Boneless Boston Butts)	—	4½	25	36	washed	20	45	30	80		
Coppa (Boneless Boston Butts)	—	4½	18	36		35	45				
Hams											
1	—	4 + overhaul	40	36	washed			10 days	95		
2	—	4 + 8 oz 100° pickle + overhaul	3 per lb green wt	36	washed	20	45	48	80		
Boneless loins											
1	—	5	25	36				12	100		
2	—	80° pickle, 60 lb pickle/100 lb	25	36	washed			4 cont.	125	12	45
3	—	#1 + #2	25	36							

trichinella *See* trichina

Trichinella spiralis A parasite found in the skeletal muscle fibers of swine, bear, walrus, cat, dog, the rodent family and man; heating to 137°F will kill this parasite.

trichinoscope An instrument used in the inspection of meat for trichina.

trichinosis An infection caused by the parasite *Trichinella spiralis*.
See Part 2: Diseases, Food-Borne; Illness from Food; Infectious Diseases, Food-Borne; Trichinosis

trichloroacetic acid CCl_3COOH An organic acid used to precipitate protein.

trichlorocyanuric acid *See* Part 2: Chlorine Compounds

trichloroethylene $CHCl{=}CCl_2$ A toxic solvent and refrigerant.
See Part 2: Refrigerant

trichloroisocyanuric acid $C_3N_3Cl_3O_3$ An organic acid used as a cleaner and sanitizer.
See Part 2: Chlorine Availability; Sanitizer

trichloromonofluoromethane CCl_3F A chlorofluorocarbon refrigerant.
See Part 2: Refrigerant

trichlorotrifluoroethane CCl_2FCClF_2 A chlorofluorocarbon refrigerant.
See Part 2: Refrigerant

tricho- Resembling a hair (of bacteria).

Trichoderma *See* Part 2: Molds, Mycotoxins

trichomonas A type of bacteria.
See Part 2: Microorganism, Media

trichophyton agar *See* Part 2: Microorganism, Media

tricuspid valve A heart valve which allows one-way flow of blood from the right auricle to the right ventricle.

trier A long flat stainless steel instrument used to inspect the internal area of meat for off-odors.

triethylamine $N(C_2H_5)_3$ A wetting agent with odor of decaying fish.

triglyceride Glycerol esterified with three molecules of an acid.

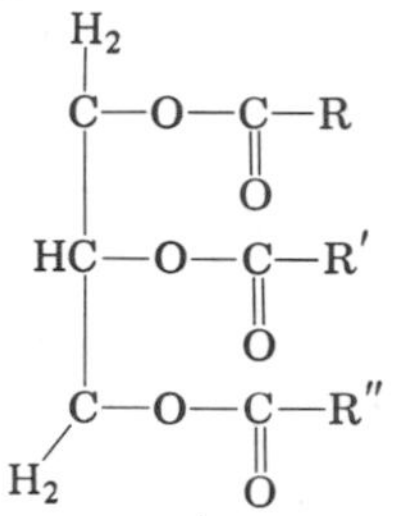

See also **fatty acid.**
See Part 2: Lard, Triglyceride Mole Percent Composition; Oil, Triglyceride Mole Percent Composition; Rapeseed Oil, Triglyceride Mole Percent Composition; Tallow, Beef, Triglyceride Mole Percent Composition

trihydric An alcohol containing three hydroxyl groups, e.g., glycerol.

2,4,5-trihydroxy butyrophenone $C_6H_2(OH)_3COC_3H_7$ A food additive with antioxidant properties.
See Part 2: Antioxidant Structure

trillion American and French 10^{12}
English and German 10^{18}

trimmed lamb A lamb whose tail has been cut; also, an unsexed male lamb.

trinitrobenzene An indicator which is colorless below a pH of 12, orange from 12 to 13, and red-orange above 13.

triose $C_3H_6O_3$ A 3-carbon sugar.

tripe Cleaned, scalded and cooked first and second stomach (with the inside wall removed) from healthy cattle.
Kinds (depends on part of stomach used): blanket; honeycomb; book; monk's hood; reed.
Composition: 79% H_2O, 19% protein, 2% fat, 0.5% ash.
See Part 2: Beef Cuts and Uses; Variety Meat, Cooking; Variety Meat Percentage of Daily Recommended Allowances; Variety Meat Preparation

tripeptide A compound made up of 3 amino acids joined by 2 peptide bonds.

triphosphopyridine nucleotide (TPN) A coenzyme that differs from coenzyme 1 (DPN) only in having one more phosphoric radical in the molecule; used by the cell in many oxidation reactions.

triple bond An unsaturated carbon linkage characteristic of acetylene and its derivatives: $HC{\equiv}CH$.

triple crème A soft-textured, creamy-flavored cheese.

triple-sugar iron agar *See* Part 2: Intestinal Microorganisms in Triple-Sugar Agar

triple superphosphate A fertilizer ingredient made by addition of phosphoric acid to phosphate rock; contains 50% available phosphate (P_2O_5).
See Part 2: Fertilizer

tripolyphosphate A cleaning compound (sodium tripolyphosphate) that has good calcium sequestering power; it is readily soluble in warm water but unstable at high temperature or in solutions high in alkali. *See also* **phosphate.**
See Part 2: Phosphate

trisodium orthophosphate *See* **trisodium phosphate**

trisodium phosphate (trisodium orthophosphate; sodium phosphate, tribasic $Na_3PO_4 \cdot 12H_2O$ An alkaline cleaner that has good solubility, deflocculating and emulsifying properties; it is a fair water softener and quite corrosive.
See Part 2: Detergent Properties

tri sugar agar *See* Part 2: Microorganism, Media

Triumph (1) A variety of potato (white) which is best used in salads. (2) A dry, mealy variety of sweet potato.

trockenbeeren-auslese Made from over-ripe, half-dried grapes affected by the edelfaule or "noble rot."

tropaeolum *See* Part 2: Essential Oils

tropical fruit A fruit grown in the tropics, i.e., avocado, banana, date, fig, guava, mango, papaya, pineapple, pomegranate.

tropics The area between 23° 27′ north and south of the equator.

tropocollagen *See* Part 2: Connective Tissue Proteins

tropomyosin *See* Part 2: Myofibrillar Proteins of Muscle

troponin *See* Part 2: Myofibrillar Proteins of Muscle

trotter A lamb shank.

trout A lean fresh-water fish.
See Part 2: Fish, Storage; Frozen Food Storage; Minerals, Food; Salmon and Trout

troy U.S. and English weight used for gold and silver; based on a pound that contains 12 ounces.

truck farm Land used for raising garden produce.

true stomach *See* **abomasum**

truffle An edible fungus: black or perigord (*Tuber melanospermum*); white (*T. album* or *T. niveum*); dark brown (*T. aestivum*).
Composition: 75% H_2O, 9% protein, 0.3% fat.

truss To tie a roast or fowl to hold shape during cooking.

truttine A protein found in the trout family.

trypsin A proteolytic enzyme which hydrolyzes native proteins to amino acids; it is found in the pancreatic juice in the small intestine; it is secreted in the inactive form called trypsinogen.
See Part 2: pH Values of Biological Materials

trypsin digest agar *See* Part 2: Microorganism, Culture Media, Dairy and Food Products; Microorganism, Media

trypsinogen The inactive form of trypsin in which trypsin is secreted; it is initially activated by enterokinase after which time activation proceeds through the action of trypsin. *See also* **trypsin**.

tryptic digest agar *See* Part 2: Microorganism, Media

tryptic soy agar *See* Part 2: Microbiological Media; Microorganism, Media

tryptic tellurite agar base *See* Part 2: Microorganism, Media

tryptone *See* Part 2: Microorganism, Media

tryptone glucose extract agar *See* Part 2: Microorganism, Culture Media, Dairy and Food Products; Microorganism, Culture Media, Water and Sewage, Standard Methods; Microorganism, Media

tryptophan A heterocylic essential amino acid obtained by hydrolysis of proteins or made synthetically.

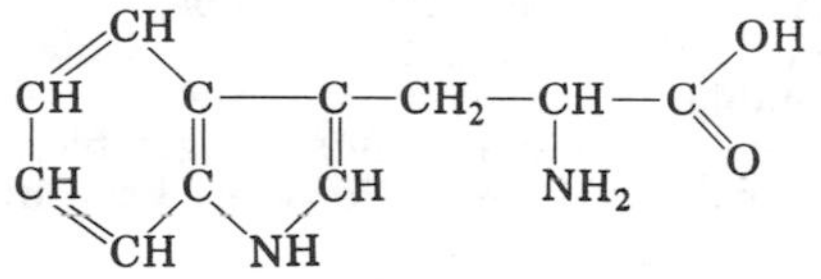

See Part 2: Amino Acids; Amino Acids, Solubilities; Corn, Amino Acids; Egg Products, Nutritive Value; Manure Analysis; Milk, Amino Acids; Seed, Chemical Composition; Wheat, Amino Acids; Wheat Products, Amino Acid Compositions

tryptose agar *See* Part 2: Microorganism, Culture Media, Dairy and Food Products; Microorganism, Media

tryptose blood agar base *See* Part 2: Microorganism, Media

TSH Abbreviation for thyroid-stimulating hormone.

TSI *See* Part 2: Microorganism, Selective and Differential Broths and Media, Water Filtration Plant

T S N agar *See* Part 2: Microbiological Media

TSU agar *See* Part 2: Microorganism, Media

T.T. Tuberculin-tested.

t-table To get a 1 tail value from a 2 tail table, multiply α (prob.) by 2 and look this ($\alpha \times 2$) up in a 2 tail table; To get a 2 tail value from a 1 tail table, divide α by 2 and look this up in a 1 tail table.

TT broth *See* Part 2: Microorganism, Media

tube cell *See* Part 2: Corn Kernel; Wheat Kernel Parts

tuber A short, fleshy, usually underground, stem or root (e.g., potato); usually starchy.
See Part 2: Sweet Potato and Irish Potato; Vegetable Composition; Vegetables, Classification

tuber (os) calcis (point of hock) A bone in the rear leg pointing backward and upward to which the achilles tendon is attached.

tuberculosis A communicable disease of cattle, hogs and chickens; it can be detected by the tuberculin test.
See Part 2: Illness from Food; Infectious Diseases, Food-Borne; Microorganism, Media

tuberose oil An essential oil used as a flavoring agent.
See Part 2: Essential Oils

tubetti *See* **macaroni**

tuck To eat heartily, especially of sweets (British).

tucket Steak; a small green ear of corn.

tularemia An infectious disease of wild rabbits which is communicable to man.
See Part 2: Diseases, Food-Borne; Illness from Food; Infectious Diseases, Food-Borne

tun A wine measure.
1 tun = 252 gallons (U.S.)
= 210 gallons (Imperial)

tuna A fat, large fish caught in warm water.

Type	Where caught	H_2O (%)	Protein (%)	Fat (%)	Ash (%)
Albacore	Pacific coast	66	25	8	1.3
Bluefin	Atlantic & Pacific coast	70	25	4	1.3
Little	Atlantic				
Skipjack	Southern waters				
Yellow fin	Pacific coast	71	25	3	1.4
Canned					
(in oil)	solid & liquid	53	24	20	2.4
(in water)	solid & liquid	70	28	0.8	1.2

pH 5.2–6.1.
3 oz per serving.
1 cup = 170 g (6 oz).

Albacore	*Thunnus germo*
Big-eyed tuna	*Parathunnus mebachi*
Bluefin tuna	*Thunnus thynnus*
Kawakawa	*Euthynnus yaito*
Little tunny	*Euthynnus alletteratus* or *E. lineatus*
Northern bluefin tuna	*Neothunnus raus*
Oriental tuna	*Thunnus orientalis*
Skipjack	*Katsuwonus pelamis*
Southern bluefin tuna	*Thunnus maccoyii*
Yellowfin tuna	*Neothunnus macropterus*

See Part 2: Fish and Shellfish Composition; Frozen Food Storage; Minerals, Food; Niacin, Daily Recommendations; Vitamin A, Fish; Vitamin D, Fish

tung oil (China wood oil) A pale yellow drying oil from nuts of *Aleurites cordata* and *A. fordii*; used in paints. sp. gr. 0.94; iodine number 168; saponification number 194.
See Part 2: Fat or Oils, Physical and Chemical Properties; Fatty Acids, Fats and Oils; Fruit and Nut Rootstock; Iodine and Saponification Values; Oils, Seed and Fruit; Refractive Indices, Fats and Oils; Unsaponifiable Matter; Unsaturated Fatty Acids

tungsten (W) (wolfram) A metallic element; at. no. 74; at. wt. 183.86; electron configuration 2-8-18-32-12-2
orbit K L M N O P
oxidation state +6; has highest melting point of any metal.

Tunis A fat-tailed breed of sheep originating in Northern Africa.
See Part 2: Sheep Breeds

tunol Cod liver oil.

tup hog *See* **hogget**

turbary Land where sod or peat is obtained.

turbidimetric analysis An optical analysis in which concentration is determined by the intensity of light transmitted through a turbid suspension as compared with that of a standard suspension.

turbot A species of fish.
See Part 2: Riboflavin, Food

turkey (*Meleagris gallo-pavo*) A large American bird that has been domesticated; ½ pound of a ready-to-cook bird = 1 serving; 80% dressing percentage.
See Part 2: Animal Foods, Composition; Calories, Daily Recommendations; Egg Incubation Periods; Frozen Food Storage; Meat and Meat Products Composition; Minerals, Food; Portion Size; Potassium-Rich Foods; Poultry Class; Poultry Cooking, Frozen; Poultry Dressing Percentage; Poultry Roasting; Poultry Yield; Spoilage, Protein Foods; Turkey Composition; Turkey Varieties

turkey cock A male turkey.

turkey grade *See* **poultry grades**

turkey hen Female turkey.

Turkey test *See* **means test**

Turkish coffee A sweetened drink made from pulverized coffee.

Turkish delight (Turkish paste) A chewy confection dusted with sugar.

Turkish paste *See* **Turkish delight**

turmeric (*Curcuma longa* L.) Rhizome of a perennial plant used as food, in flavoring food and as a yellow dye; used in curry powder and mustard; yellow pigment is curcumin; rhizomes are washed, peeled and dried and contain 30–40% starch.

turnip (*Brassica rapa*) A biennial with a swollen root; a vegetable whose root is used as food.
Parts of plant:
root: cooked vegetable; livestock feed
tops: spring greens
1 lb fresh = 3 medium sized turnips
= 2 cups cooked
1 cup cooked = 195 g (6.9 oz)
1 bu topped = 54 lb
100 lb fresh topped = 7–8 lb dry
Storage (roots): Remove tops and store covered (90–95% relative humidity) in refrigerator (32°F); use in 1 to 4 weeks.
Storage (greens): Remove root, wash and drain; store in refrigerator crisper or plastic bags; use within 1 to 2 days.
Composition:

	H_2O (%)	Protein (%)	Fat (%)	Carbohydrate (%)	Ash (%)	pH
Root	91	1	0.2	4–7	1	5.2–5.6
Greens	90	3	0.3	5	1	

See Part 2: Microwave Cooking, Fresh Vegetables; Minerals, Food; Minerals, Plant or Animal Tissue; Nitrate, Vegetables; Plant Foods, Composition; Storage; Sugar, Vegetables; Vegetable Boiling; Vegetable Composition; Vegetable Cooking, Frozen; Vegetable Plants; Vegetables, Classification; Vegetables, Cooking Frozen; Vegetable Storage

turnip-rooted celery *See* **celeriac**

turnover *See* Part 2: Frying Time

turpentine An oleoresinous liquid extracted from the *Pinus* species of trees; used as a solvent; b.p. 155–165°C; 1 barrel = 432 lb; 1 gallon = 7.2 lb.
See Part 2: Essential Oils

turpentine weed A plant having a toxic principle.
See Part 2: Poisonous Plants

Tuscarora rice *See* **rice**

tuttifrutti Ice cream containing fruit; a combination of fruits.

Tween Proprietary name for a series of emulsifiers, detergents, and surface active agents.

two-toned beef Meat tissue where neighboring muscles or areas of one muscle are of different shades.

tylosin A macrolide antibiotic which is added to food in some countries.

type I error Rejection of a true hypothesis.

type II error Acceptance of a false hypothesis.

typhoid fever A contagious disease caused by impure water supply.
See Part 2: Diseases, Food-Borne; Illness from Food; Infectious Agents; Infectious Diseases, Food-Borne

typhosa *See* Part 2: Microorganism, Media

tyro Cheese.

tyrosinase An oxidase enzyme which is widely distributed; it is responsible for the darkening of the cut surface of a potato which has been exposed to air; oxidizes tyrosine to homogentisic acid and melanin pigments.

tyrosine A nonessential aromatic amino acid.

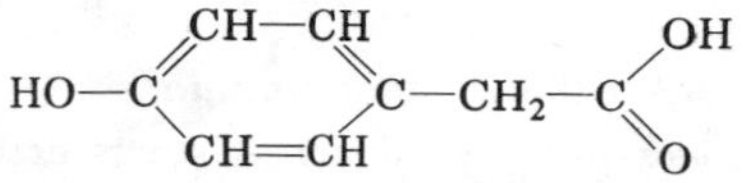

See Part 2: Amino Acids; Amino Acid, Solubilities; Corn, Amino Acids; Egg Products, Nutritive Value; Grain Analysis; Manure Analysis; Milk, Amino Acids; Seed, Chemical Composition; Wheat, Amino Acids; Wheat Products, Amino Acid Compositions

U

U Symbol for the element uranium.

udo A salad of crisp blanched stems eaten with salt.

ugli A hybrid between grapefruit and tangerine; it looks like and is used like a small grapefruit. *See also* **tangelo.**

UHT sterilization Ultra-high-temperature sterilization (96°–153°C for 3 sec or less).

ulna Caudal of 2 bones in fore shank; in ruminants it is smaller than the radius and often fused to it; in swine it is often larger than the radius and not fused to it.
See Part 2: Bone

Ulrich milk *See* Part 2: Microorganism, Media

ultramicroscope An optical microscope equipped with a device for admitting a beam of light at right angles to the sample being studied, which is usually a colloidal solution. The suspended solid particles in the liquid reflect the light as they turn end over end, thus indicating their presence, even if the particles themselves are below the resolution range of the microscope.

ultrasonic High-frequency sound waves of approximately 200,000 cps; 20,000 H_2 to several thousand MH_2.

ultraviolet Wavelength of radiation of approx 1850 to 4 000 angstroms; shorter than visible violet and longer than X-rays. Most effective germicidal wavelength is 2600 angstroms. Used for sterilization, microorganism control during meat aging, and vitamin D activation in milk.
See Part 2: Waves, Energy-Producing

umbelliferae The parsley family.
See Part 2: Vegetables, Classification

undrawn poultry Dressed poultry which has been picked but has not had the entrails removed.

undulant fever Human brucellosis; contracted from animals or animal products.
See Part 2: Illness from Food

unequal to Not equal to indicated by symbol $\neq$.

uni- One; single.

unit cell The smallest group of atoms having the same composition and arrangement in space that can be selected in a crystal.

univalent Having a valence of one.

universal indicator *See* Part 2: pH, Universal Indicators

unpolished rice Whole rice grain with only the husk removed.

unsaponifiable That portion of a mixture that will not react with an alkali to form a soap.

unsaponifiable matter analysis Determined by saponifying the fat with alcoholic potassium hydroxide and then extracting the unsaponifiable matter with ether, and evaporating the ether; the residue is unsaponifiable matter.
See Part 2: Unsaponifiable Matter

unsaturated An organic compound in which one or more double or triple bonds is present between C atoms.
See Part 2: Fuel, Heating Value; Poultry Composition; Rapeseed Oil, Triglyceride Mole Percent Composition; Sausage Composition; Soups, Composition; Sugars and Sweets Composition

unsaturated fatty acid A fatty acid containing one or more carbon-to-carbon double bonds;

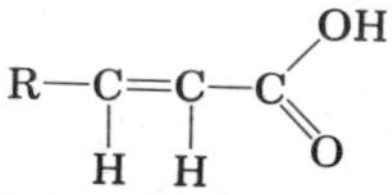

Such acids have a lower melting point and are softer than saturated acids of the same chain length.
See Part 2: Egg Products, Nutritive Value; Beans, Peas and Nuts; Dairy Products, Composition; Egg Composition; Fats and Oils, Characteristics; Fats and Oils, Composition; Fish and Shellfish Composition; Fruit Composition; Grain Products Composition; Meat Composition; Tallow, Beef, Triglyceride Mole Percent Composition; Unsaturated Fatty Acids; Vegetable Composition

unsaturation *See* **unsaturated**
See Part 2: Lard, Triglyceride Mole Percent Composition

unsweetened chocolate Chocolate sold in bar-shaped package containing 1-ounce squares or in liquid form; flavor is deep, rich and bitter; 1 square = 1 envelope of liquid = ¼ cup dry cocoa powder.

upland cress *See* **garden cress**

upside-down cake A cake baked with batter above fruit and turned over for serving.

upsilon (Υ, υ) Greek letter with an English equivalent of u.

uracil A biochemical compound used in research and obtained by hydrolysis of nucleic acids;

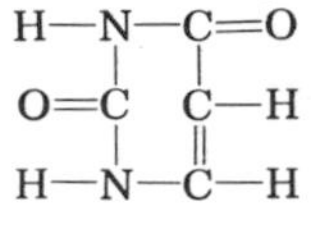

uranium (U) A radioactive metal of the actinide series; element; at. no. 92; at. wt. 238.07; Group IIIB of the Periodic Table;
electron configuration 2-8-18-32-21-9-2
orbit K L M N O P Q
oxidation states +3, +4, +5, +6

urea $NH_2—C(=O)—NH_2$ The chief excretory nitrogenous product of mammals, amphibia and fish; has weak basic properties. It can be utilized as food by ruminant animals; 3 lb to 100 lb grain is maximum; 1 lb urea + 6 lb ground corn equivalent in feeding value to 7 lb oil meal. It can also be used as fertilizer; 45-0-0; hydrolyzes to ammonium in soil; it is acid in nature and would require 0.75 lb of dolomitic limestone to neutralize each pound applied.
See Part 2: Fertilizer Materials; Microorganism, Media; Microorganism Reactions on Differential Tube Media

urease An enzyme that converts urea to ammonia and carbon dioxide; source: soybeans.

uric acid The chief excretory nitrogenous product of birds and reptiles:

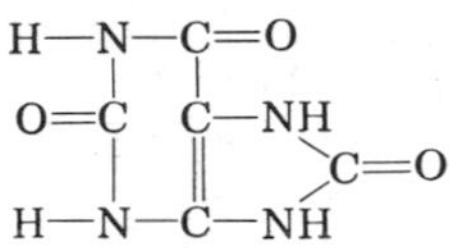

urine The excretory fluid of the body via kidneys and bladder.
See Part 2: pH Values of Biological Materials

U.S. Army Natick Laboratories Center of food and materials research for the Department of Defense, located in Natick, Mass.

U.S. Department of Agriculture (USDA) The government department responsible for all matters relating to agriculture and food quality. It establishes grades and standards for food products, meat inspection, plant sanitation, toxicity, etc. It maintains four Regional Research Laboratories for food-related research; these are located at Philadelphia, Peoria, Albany, California, and New Orleans.

U.S. Pharmacopeia (U.S.P.) The standard compendium of drugs and medicines; the 18th edition was published in 1970. The U.S.P. grade is a standard of chemical purity that meets U.S.P. specifications. *See also* **grade.**

U.S. Recommended Daily Allowances (U.S. RDA) A standard of specified vitamins, minerals and proteins essential for humans as listed by U.S. Food and Drug Administration.

utility *See* Part 2: Grades, Meat

UV Abbreviation for ultraviolet.

UV absorber A substance that prevents the ultraviolet radiation in sunlight from attacking the skin; used in suntan lotions, ointments, and cosmetic preparations.

V

V *See* **vanadium; volt**

vaccenic *See* Part 2: Unsaturated Fatty Acids

vacuole A cavity or fluid-filled space in a cell.

vacuum A space from which virtually all the air has been removed.
See Part 2: Temperature of Vaporization, Latent Heat of Vaporization, Boiling Point

vacuum-packing Removing air from a container before hermetically sealing.

valence Combining power of an element or group; number of hydrogen atoms it can combine with or replace. *See also* **oxidation number.**

Valencia A variety of California orange that is oblong in shape; in season from May to November; a variety of late Florida orange that is often used in frozen concentrate.

valerian An essential oil containing binene, camphene and borneol.
See Part 2: Essential Oils

valine Monoamino-monocarboxylic essential amino acid obtained by hydrolysis of proteins, or made synthetically.

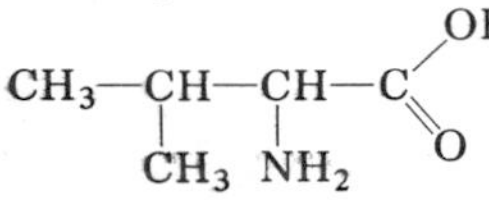

See Part 2: Amino Acids; Amino Acid, Solubilities; Corn, Amino Acids; Egg Products, Nutritive Value; Grain Analysis; Manure Analysis; Milk, Amino Acids; Seed, Chemical Composition; Wheat, Amino Acids; Wheat Products, Amino Acid Compositions

valpolicella A light red wine.

vanadium (V) A metallic element; at. no. 23; at. wt. 50.95; Group VB of the Periodic Table; electron configuration 2-8-11-2
orbit K L M N
oxidation states +2, +3, +4, +5

vanaspati A hydrogenated vegetable oil; a 100% fat type margarine.

vanilla (***Vanilla planifolia, V. tahitensis, V. pompona* and *V. aromatica***) A bean or its alcoholic extract used in flavoring food. *See also* **vanillin.**
Pod Curing: 1. dipping in boiling water
2. slow drying (black in color)
3. packed in foil-lined boxes
Vanillin (2–3%): main flavoring component; 2 tbsp. of extract = 1 ounce.
See Part 2: Flavor Ingredients, Taste and Flavor Type

vanilla extract A product made by chopping vanilla beans in 50% alcohol and subsequent percolation; in 100 cc must be the soluble matter from at least 10 g of vanilla bean; 0.10–0.35% vanillin, 0.20–0.43% ash.

vanilla wafer A cookie.
1 cup = 20 coarsely crumbled = 30 finely crumbled.

vanillin The primary flavoring ingredient in vanilla. Obtained by extraction from vanilla beans or from lignin in sulfite waste liquor.

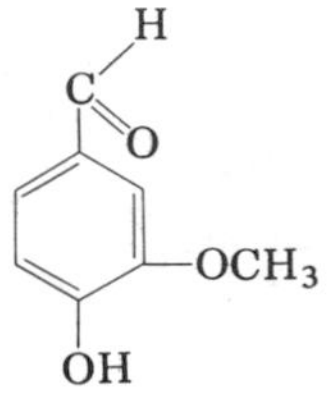

1 part = 400 parts vanilla pods
2-3 parts = 500 parts tincture vanilla. *See also* **vanilla.**

vaporization Conversion of a liquid to a vapor by heat; for water latent heat of vaporization is 540 cal/gram.
See Part 2: Temperature of Vaporization, Latent Heat of Vaporization, Boiling Point

vaporization point The temperature at which a liquid turns to a vapor. *See also* **boiling point.**

vapor pressure Pressure exerted by the evaporation of molecules from a liquid at a given temperature; when the vapor pressure reaches the atmospheric pressure the liquid boils.
See Part 2: Ice, Vapor Pressure

varec (kelp) Ash obtained from a seaweed from which iodine is extracted.

variance (σ^2) Variation of observations; it is the square of the standard deviation estimation; estimated by mean square.

variety meat An edible organ or gland including brain, heart, kidney, liver, pancreas, spleen, tongue, thymus, walls of stomach.
Storage: Coldest part of refrigerator; use within 1 to 2 days.
See Part 2: Animal Foods, Composition; Meat Storage; Pork Storage; Storage Times; Variety Meat, Cooking; Variety Meat Percentage of Daily Recommended Allowances; Variety Meat Preparation; Vitamin A, Food

Vaseline (petroleum jelly) Proprietary name for a purified mixture of hydrocarbons distilled from petroleum.

vaso- Prefix for structures such as a vessel or a duct.

vasoconstrictor A chemical or mixture that reduces the diameter of certain blood vessels, thus restricting proper circulation.

vasodilator The reverse of vasoconstrictor.

vastus intermedius *See* **quadriceps**

vastus lateralis *See* **quadriceps**

vastus medialis *See* **quadriceps**

veal Young bovine flesh from 3 to 14 weeks old at slaughter; flesh is light in color and contains little marbling; high in moisture.
See Part 2: Animal Foods, Composition; Braising Time; Bone; Calories, Daily Recommendations; Cattle; Cooking in Liquid, Time; Food, Composition; Frozen Food Storage; Grades, Meat; Iron, Daily Recommendations; Liver; Meat and Meat Products Composition; Meat Composition; Meat, Frozen Storage; Meat Identification; Meat Label; Meat, Nutritive Value; Meat Storage; Minerals, Food; Niacin, Daily Recommendations; Riboflavin, Daily Recommendations; Roasting, Time and Temperature; Roasting Meat; Sausage Identification; Simmering Meat; Thiamin, Daily Recommendations; Thiamin, Food; Veal Chart; Veal Cuts; Veal Cuts and Uses; Veal Roasting; Veal Wholesale Cuts; Vitamin A, Food

veal back A wholesale cut of veal from the 4th rib to the hip bone.

veal chuck A wholesale cut of veal consisting of all in front of the 4th rib; sides may be split or unsplit.

veal cutlet A veal round steak.
See Part 2: Braising Meat

veal infusion medium *See* Part 2: Microorganism, Media

veal leg A wholesale cut of veal consisting of the area to the rear of the hip; sides may be split or unsplit.

veal rib back A wholesale cut of veal consisting of the unsplit ribs (4th through 12th rib).

veal shoulder *See* **veal chuck**

veal steak *See* Part 2: Braising Meat

vegans A strict vegetarian diet.

vegetable A botanical organism or species of any type, including trees, shrubs, grasses, etc. In common usage, any plant used for food by humans or animals.
See Part 2: Ascorbic Acid; Calcium; Calcium, Daily Recommendations; Calories, Daily Recommendations; Food, Composition; Frozen Food Storage; Fruit and Vegetables Composition; Fruit and Vegetable, Diseases; Frying Time; Glutamate; Iron, Daily Recommendations; Microwave Cooking, Fresh Vegetables; Microwave Cooking, Frozen Vegetables; Microwave Processing Time; Minerals, Plant or Animal Tissue; Minerals (Trace), Limits; Moisture in Biological Materials; Mold, Food; Nicotinic Acid, Food; Nitrate, Vegetables; Nutrients in Crops; Organic Acids in Fruit and Vegetables; Portion Size; Potassium-Rich Foods; Riboflavin, Food; Rot Spoilage; Soups, Composition; Standards, Processed Fruit and Vegetable Products; Storage Times; Thiamin, Daily Recommendations; Thiamin, Food; Vegetable Boiling; Vegetables, Canned Grade; Vegetable Composition; Vegetable Cooking, Frozen; Vegetable Frozen Yield; Vegetable Plants; Vegetables, Boiling Time, Frozen; Vegetables, Canning Dates; Vegetables, Classification; Vegetables, Cooking Frozen; Vegetable Servings; Vegetables, Panned; Vegetable Storage; Vegetable Yield; Vegetable Yield, Canned and Frozen; Vegetable Yield, Frozen, Canned and Fresh; Vitamin A, Daily Recommendations; Vitamin A, Food

vegetable fat *See* Part 2: Fats and Oils' Composition; Oils and Fats Composition; Saturated Fatty Acids

vegetable gelatin *See* **agar-agar**

vegetable grade *See* **fruit grade**

vegetable marrow A summer variety of squash. *See also* **marrow**.

vegetable oil An oil obtained from plants containing one or more fatty acids; many types are edible and are used as food and for cooking; 440°-460°F smoke point for hydrogenated oil.
See Part 2: Tocopherols

vegetable oyster *See* **salsify**

vegetable seed Kernel of plant that can be sowed to reproduce the plant; storage: 32°-40°F, 50-65% R.H.

vegetable shortening A fat from plants used for cooking; 420°-440°F smoke point.

vegetable tanning Converting hides and skins into leather by treatment with tannins derived from plants, e.g., quebracho, wattle, etc. *See also* **tanning.**

vegetarian A person who does not eat any animal food and consumes only products of the vegetable kingdom; some will eat butter, eggs and milk, since these involve no slaughter.

vegetative cell *See* Part 2: Thermal-Death-Time Curve

veitchberry A fruit similar to loganberry.

velvet bean An annual legume used for animal feed and green manure; 1.8 lb/qt; 60 lb/bu; varieties: bunch, osceola, speckle.

velvet bean caterpillar A worm which eats the top leaves of soybean plants.

velvetgrass *See* Part 2: Seed, Germination

velvet spirit *See* **silent spirit**

venison The flesh of deer.
See Part 2: Animal Foods, Composition; Minerals, Food

ventral Belly; stomach; opposite of dorsal.

ventricle Lower chambers of the heart, called right and left ventricle.

verbena *See* Part 2: Essential Oils

verjuice Acid juice from crab apples or unripe grapes used as a drink or for culinary purposes.

vermicelli A macaroni product, cord-shaped, not tubular and not more than 0.06 in. in diameter. *See also* **spaghetti.**

vermiculite A hydrated metallic silicate which expands on strong heating. Used as feed additive, insulation, and soil conditioner.
See Part 2: Insulation

vermouth (vermuth) An alcoholic beverage; wine base; sweetened with sugar syrup (3-20% sugar); fortified with brandy; flavored with aromatic herbs; 14-20% alcohol by volume.

vernier An auxiliary scale used to obtain fine adjustment or measurement.

vertebrae The bones of the spinal column.

	Cervical	Thoracic	Lumbar	Sacral	Coccygeal or Caudal
Cattle	7	13	6	5	18-20
Sheep	7	13	6-7	4-5	16-20
Goats	7	13	6	5	18-20
Camel	7	12	7	4	15-18
Deer	7	13-14	6	5	18-20
Horse	7	18	6	5	18-20
Pig	7	14-16	6-7	4	14-23
Rabbit	7	12	7	3	7

See Part 2: Bone

vetch An annual leguminous grass; seeding 60 lb/bu, 25 lb/acre; varieties: common, hairy.
See Part 2: Seed, Germination

vetiver oil (vetivert) A thick essential oil obtained from roots of East Indian grass.
See Part 2: Essential Oils

Vibrio *See* Part 2: Spoilage, Protein Foods

vibriosis An infective organism causing abortion during first 6 months of gestation.

vichyssoise A potato soup containing chicken broth and onions, served cold.

victus Diet, food.

vicugna (vicuna) A ruminant animal similar to the llama that measures about 2½ feet to the shoulder; native to South America.

vidonia A tart white wine.

Vienna sausage *See* **frankfurter**
See Part 2: Sausage Identification; Sausage, Types

Viking A variety of birdsfoot trefoil. *See also* **trefoil.**

vinaigrous Sour.

vinasse Residue of beet sugar or wine manufacturing.

vinegar A sour solution produced by exposing an alcoholic liquid to air; a surface film appears, and the alcohol is oxidized to acetic acid by *Acetobacter* organisms. Film is a viscous gelatinous Zooglea containing a large number of organisms. Dilute acetic acid solution (3.24 to 9.96 g/100 ml); made from fruit or grain (in United States from cider only); min 4% by wt of absolute acetic acid; made by double fermentation.

$$\underset{\text{sugar}}{C_6H_{12}O_6} \xrightarrow{\text{yeast (type depends on sugar)}} \underset{\text{alcohol}}{2CH_3CH_2OH} + \underset{\text{carbon dioxide}}{2CO_2}$$

$$\underset{\text{alcohol}}{2CH_3CH_2OH} + \underset{\text{oxygen}}{2O_2} \xrightarrow{Acetobacter} \underset{\text{acetic acid}}{2CH_3COOH} + \underset{\text{water}}{2H_2O}$$

Min. 4 g acetic acid in 100 ml solution
100 grains = 10% acetic acid
125 grains = 12.5% acetic acid
Types: (a) cider; (b) wine (from distilled grain alcohol); (c) malt; (d) sugar; (e) glucose; (f) spirit.
Composition: 94-95% H_2O, trace protein, 0% fat, 5-6% carbohydrate, 0.3% ash; pH 2-3.4. *See also* **apple vinegar, grape vinegar, malt vinegar, distilled vinegar, fermented vinegar, acetic acid, grain (vinegar), mother.**
See Part 2: Herb Vinegars; Minerals, Food; Spoilage, Carbohydrate Foods; Vinegar, Spiced

vinometer An instrument used to measure alcohol in wine.

vintage Fruit or wine of any given season.

vinyl The $CH_2{=}CH{-}$ group.

vinylidene chloride $CH_2{=}CCl_2$ The monomer from which polyvinylidene chloride is made. The latter is used as a plastic film in heat-shrinkable bags and as an oxygen barrier in food packaging.

Violet No. 1 An FD&C dye formerly used for meat inspection stamps; FDA prohibited its use in 1973.

violet red bile agar *See* Part 2: Microbiological Examination of Dairy Products; Microorganism, Culture Media, Dairy and Food Products; Microorganism, Selective and Differential Broths and Media, Water Filtration Plant

Virginia ham *See* **Smithfield ham**

virgin olive oil (sublime olive oil) Edible olive oil made from hand-picked ripe olives and extracted by using moderate pressure.

virgin wool Wool that has never been used in fabrics.

virus A parasitic type of infectious agent composed of proteins and nucleic acids. They are not actual organisms, as they do not metabolize nutrients or utilize oxygen.

viscera The internal organs of slaughtered animals.

visceral muscle Involuntary, nonstriated muscle of the intestinal tract type.

viscogen A mixture of lime (CaO), sugar and water used as a thickening agent for whipping cream.

viscometer An instrument for measuring viscosity.

viscosity A measure of the tendency for relative motion of the molecules within a fluid, or its internal resistance to flow.

viscous Sticky; gummy; resistant to deformation or flow.

visible light That portion of the electromagnetic spectrum that is perceived as light.
See Part 2: Waves, Energy-Producing

vitamin An organic compound that is necessary in the diet but is required only in minute amounts for normal functioning of the body. They are produced by plants and animals in nature, and most have been synthesized.
See Part 2: Cereal Enrichment; Cereal Fortification; Cereals, Vitamin and Mineral Content; Cheese, Vitamin Content; Egg Products, Nutritive Value; Vitamin Retention, Meat; Vitamins; Vitamin Sources, Functions, and Stability; Wheat, Parts of Grain, Vitamins; Wheat Products Composition; Wheat, Vitamins

vitamin A (retinol) $C_{20}H_{29}OH$ A fat-soluble vitamin; a high molecular weight alcohol; physiological function: growth-promoting, prevents drying of mucous membranes, essential to reproduction, plays a role in night vision; young mammals are born with limited amounts of vitamin A.

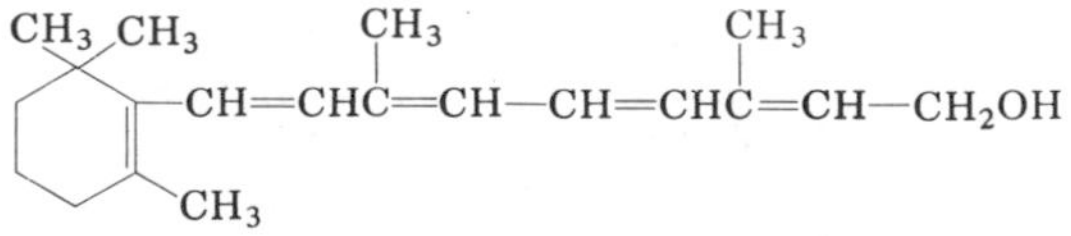

Good sources:	Poor sources:
Fish liver oil	Cereal grain (except yellow corn).
Milk and milk products	
Egg yolk	
Liver	
Green and yellow vegetables	
Oranges	
Peaches	
Sweet potatoes	
Tomatoes	

Vitamin A usually occurs in nature as a provitamin in the form of α-, β-, γ-carotene or cryptoxanthin which is converted in the animal body to vitamin A. 1 mg of carotene = 400 I.U. of vitamin A.
See Part 2: Beans, Peas and Nuts; Cereal Fortification; Cereals, Vitamin and Mineral Content; Cheese Composition; Composition of Food; Dairy Products, Composition; Egg Composition; Egg Products, Nutritive Value; Fats and Oils, Composition; Fish and Shellfish Composition; Food, Composition; Fruit and Vegetables Composition; Fruit Composition; Grain Products Composition; Lemon Juice Composition; Macaroni and Noodles Composition; Plant Foods, Composition; Poultry Composition; Recommended Daily Dietary Allowance; Sausage Composition; Soups, Composition; Sugars and Sweets Composition; Tomato and Tomato Products, Composition; Variety Meat Percentage of Daily Recommended Allowances; Vegetable Composition; Vitamin A; Vitamin A, Daily Recommendations; Vitamin A, Fish; Vitamin A, Food; Vitamin A, Milk and Milk Products; Vitamins; Vitamin Sources, Functions, and Stability; Meat Composition; Meat, Nutritive Value; Milk Composition

vitamin A acid A compound in which an acid group replaces the alcohol group on the common vitamin A formula:

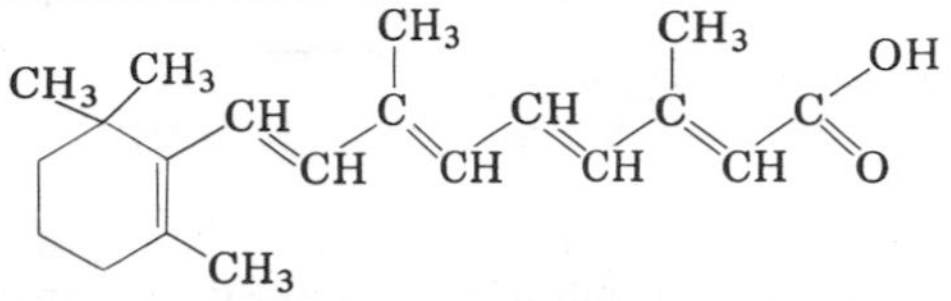

vitamin A aldehyde A compound in which an aldehyde group replaces the alcohol group on the common vitamin A formula:

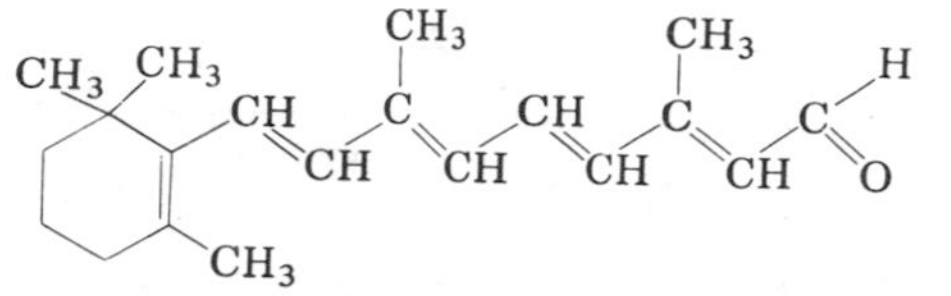

vitamin B-1 *See* **thiamin**

vitamin B-2 *See* **riboflavin**

vitamin B-6 *See* **pyridoxine**
See Part 2: Beef Percentages of Daily Recommended Allowances; Cereal Fortification; Cereals, Vitamin and Mineral Content; Cheese, Vitamin Content; Lamb Percentages of Daily Recommended Allowances; Meat, Nutritive Value; Milk and Milk Products, Vitamin Content; Milk Composition; Pork, Percentages of Daily Recommended Allowances; Recommended Daily Dietary Allowance; Variety Meat Percentage of Daily Recommended Allowances; Vitamins

vitamin B-12 (cyanocobalamin; animal protein factor) $C_{63}H_{90}CoN_{14}O_{14}P$ A cobalt-containing member of the B complex; it is involved in anemia and growth; used in treatment of nerve disorders, e.g., tic douloureux. Sources: variety and muscle meats.
See Part 2: Beef Percentages of Daily Recommended Allowances; Cereal Fortification; Cereals, Vitamin and Mineral Content; Cheese, Vitamin Content; Egg Products, Nutritive Value; Lamb Percentages of Daily Recommended Allowances; Meat, Nutritive Value; Milk and Milk Products, Vitamin Content; Milk Composition; Pork, Percentages of Daily Recommended Allowances; Recommended Daily Dietary Allowances; Variety Meat Percentage of Daily Recom-

mended Allowances; Vitamins; Vitamin Sources, Functions, and Stability

vitamin B_c *See* **folic acid**

vitamin B complex A large and closely interrelated group of water-soluble vitamins, each of which is different from the others; no one member of the group can replace any other. Among them are: thiamin, riboflavin, pyridoxine, nicotinic acid, B-12.

vitamin F Name once applied to essential unsaturated fatty acids (linoleic, linolenic, arachidonic); also applied to vitamin B-1.

vitamin G *See* **riboflavin**

vitamin H *See* **biotin**

vitamin K A fat-soluble vitamin which functions in the clotting of blood. Sources; green plant tissues, soybeans, vegetable oils.
vitamin K_1 ($C_{31}H_{46}O_2$)

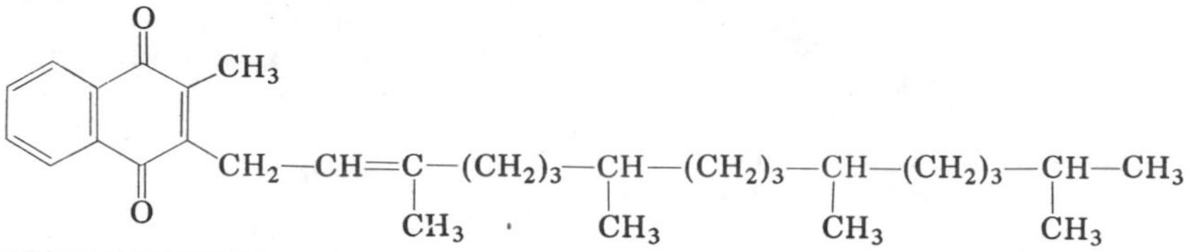

vitamin C *See* **ascorbic acid**
See Part 2: Ascorbic Acid; Meat, Nutritive Value; Vitamin C

vitamin D A fat-soluble vitamin; it regulates calcium and phosphorus metabolism and therefore protects against a disease of the bones called rickets. Essential in bone and teeth building.

ergosterol ($C_{28}H_{43}OH$) $\xrightarrow{\text{ultraviolet light}}$ calciferol ($C_{28}H_{43}OH$) (vitamin D_2)

7-dehydrocholesterol $\xrightarrow{\text{ultraviolet light}}$ (vitamin D_3)

Food sources: fish liver oils, egg yolk, butter, vitamin D-fortified foods, sunshine; 0.025 microgram = 1 I.U.
See Part 2: Cereals, Vitamin and Mineral Content; Dairy Terms; Egg Products, Nutritive Value; Milk Composition; Recommended Daily Dietary Allowance; Vitamin D, Fish; Vitamin D, Food; Vitamins; Vitamin Sources, Functions, and Stability

Vitamin E (X) Tocopherol; a fat-soluble vitamin which functions in promoting reproduction and growth; vitamin E activity in food is in the form of alpha-, beta-, gamma-tocopherol. Sources; wheat germ oil, embryos of most seeds; spinach, lettuce, egg yolk, vegetable oils, meat and milk.

See Part 2: Vitamins; Vitamin Sources, Functions, and Stability

vitamin L *See* **folic acid**

vitamin M *See* **folic acid**

vitamin U *See* **folic acid**

vitellin A phosphoprotein found in egg yolk.

vitelline membrane *See* Part 2: Egg Structure

VJ agar *See* Part 2: Microorganism, Media

vodka An alcoholic beverage made from rye (or grain) or potatoes; it has no aroma or taste and therefore can be mixed with any flavor.

Vogel and Johnson agar *See* Part 2: Microbiological Media

volatile fatty acid A fatty acid which can be removed from solution by steam distillation; these include acids through capric.

vol-au-vent A pastry shell filled with a stew of meat and eggs and often other ingredients.

volt (V or v); E, emf; measurement of electrical potential (E) (pressure); a potential of 1 volt will cause a current of 1 amp in a resistance of 1 ohm.
Voltage between 2 points = $R_T I$ (R_T = total resistance, I = amperes).

voltmeter An instrument for measuring voltage; should be connected in parallel.

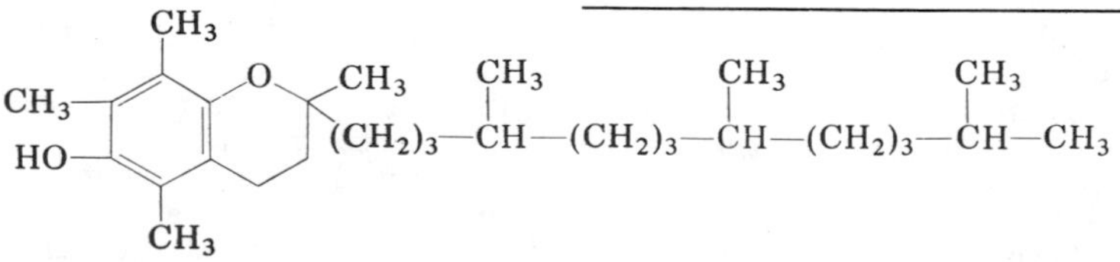

See Part 2: Cereal Fortification; Cereals, Vitamin and Mineral Content; Egg Products, Nutritive Value; Milk and Milk Products, Vitamin Content; Recommended Daily Dietary Allowance; Vitamins; Vitamin Sources, Functions, and Stability

volume The space occupied by a body.
Volume of a sphere = $\frac{4}{3}\pi r^3$
or = D^3 (0.5236)
Volume of right cylinder = $\pi r^2 h$
Volume of right cone = $\frac{1}{3}\pi r^2 h$;

Gram molecular volume = 22,412 cc at 0°C and 760 mm.

See Part 2: Volume; Volumetric Solutions, Temperature Corrections

volumetric analysis An analysis in which results are based upon volume (usually the volume of a solution of known strength that reacts with the substance being analyzed).

voluntary muscle *See* **striated muscle**

Votator Proprietary name for a heat-exchanger; in fat processing, a chilling machine that solidifies fat that is subsequently removed by scraper blades.

Vycor glass Proprietary name for a heat-resistant glass made of pure silica. *See also* **hard glass.**

W

W Symbol for the element tungsten.

Wabash A variety of soybean.

wafer A thin cake, cracker or pastry.

waffle A thin cake made with pancake batter and cooked in a heated mold.
See Part 2: Grain Products Composition

Waldorf salad A salad made with diced apples, celery, nuts and mayonnaise.
See Part 2: Portion Size

wolfram *See* **tungsten**

wallflower *See* Part 2: Essential Oils

walnut A tall tree raised for timber and nuts; walnut oil is extracted from the nuts; nuts are used for desserts, baking and confectionery. *See also* **black walnut.**

English walnut, European walnut: *Juglans regia.*
Black walnut: *Juglans nigra.*
White walnut, butternut: *Juglans cinerea.*
1 lb English shelled = 2.6 lb unshelled
1 lb English shelled halves = 3½ cups
1 cup English shelled halves = 100 g (3.5 oz)
1 lb English shelled chopped = 3.5 cups
1 cup English shelled chopped = 120 g (4.2 oz)
English walnut composition: 3-4% H_2O, 15-21% protein, 59-64% fat, 15-16% carbohydrate, 2-3% ash.
See Part 2: Beans, Peas and Nuts; Fatty Acids, Fats and Oils; Flavor Ingredients, Taste and Flavor Type; Fruit and Nut Rootstock; Iodine and Saponification Values; Minerals, Food; Nut, Grades; Plant Foods, Composition; Protein Factors; Refractive Indices, Fats and Oils; Titer, Fats and Oils; Tocopherols; Unsaturated Fatty Acids

walnut oil A highly unsaturated oil obtained by hot-pressing dried walnut kernels; $d_{25°}$ = 0.923. *See also* **walnut.**

Warburg apparatus A small container and a manometer used to measure gas exchange during a reaction.

Warden A pear that keeps well and is used in cooking.

warfarin $C_{19}H_{16}O_4$ An anticoagulant rodent poison.

warmed-up Cattle on feed just long enough to begin to show effects of feed.

warp (1) Threads that run lengthwise in a fabric. (2) A rich substance deposited on land by flood water.

wash Liquid obtained by fermenting wort with yeast.

washing soda Hydrated sodium carbonate.

washy Animals on new grass which does not make hard flesh.

waste Unwanted or useless residue materials.
See Part 2: Wastes, Agricultural and Industrial

wasty Too much fat, or a paunchy animal.

water (H_2O or HOH) Inorganic liquid essential to life and growth and contained in all living cells. It is colorless, tasteless and odorless. *See also* **moisture.**

Sources for body: (1) water consumed; (2) water in food eaten; (3) water from breakdown of food.
Water content in: human body 65%, blood 80%, bone 10 to 40%, milk 87%, seeds 10-20%.
Purification: liquid chlorine.
Dissociation constant (K_w) = 1×10^{-14}
B.p.: 100°C or 212°F.
F.p.: 0°C or 32°F.
Very slightly compressible.
Heat of Vaporization 539 calories per g.
Specific gravity 1.00
Dielectric constant 81
Specific heat 1 calorie/gram-degree.
Cold water: 8.33 pounds/gal.
Hot water: 8 pounds/gal.
Cold water: 1 cu ft = 62½ lb = 7.48 gal.
= 1728 cu in.
1 gal = 231 cubic inches.
1 cup = 240 g (8.4 oz).
1 acre-inch = 27,154 gal. = 226,193 lb.

Average requirement for livestock:

horse:	10–12 gal/day
beef cattle:	8–12 gal/day
dairy cattle (dry):	8–12 gal/day
dairy cattle (in milk):	35–40 gal/day
sheep:	1–2 gal/day
swine:	1–2 gal/day

Avg. human water intake	Avg. human water loss
1-1.5 liter drinking	0.4–0.6 liter lungs
0.4–0.5 liter part of food	0.4–0.7 liter skin
0.3–0.5 liter oxidation of food	0.08–0.1 liter feces
	0.3–1.8 liter urine
1.7-2.5 liters (total)	1.13–3.2 liters (total)

See Part 2: Food, Water Intake; Ingestion and Inhalation; Microbiological Media; Microorganism, Culture Media, Water and Sewage, Standard

Methods; Microorganism, Selective and Differential Broths and Media, Water Filtration Plant; Milk, Mammals, Composition; Water Drinking Standards; Water, Hardness; Water, Weight and Volume

water (sausage) Added to sausage:
Uncooked, not over 3% of total ingredients
% water = 4 × protein + 3
Cooked, not over 10% of total product in finished product
% water = 4 × protein +10
Canned hams = not over 8% above green wt; bone, fat, and skin that were removed must be included in wt so that total does not exceed 108%.

water activity (a_w) A function defined by the ratio of the vapor pressure of the solution to the vapor pressure of pure solvent. It is inversely proportional to the number of solute molecules.
See Part 2: Water Activity, Organisms and Food

water added (ham) *See* **ham, cured; water (sausage)**

water-binding properties A term used in sausage manufacturing to indicate the ability of a product to retain moisture under elevated temperatures.

water biscuit A cracker made of flour, water and sometimes fat.

water buffalo (*Bubalus bubalis*) An Asiatic buffalo often used for draft purposes.

water chestnut (*Caltrop*) (*Trapa natans*) A water plant of which the edible seeds are used as food (raw, roasted, boiled); the seed has a floury texture and an agreeable flavor.

Species:

Common name	Scientific name	Used for food
Ling	*Trapa bicornis*	seed flour
Singhara nut	*Trapa bispinosa*	seed

See also **Chinese water chestnut.**

watercress (*Radicula nasturtium-aquaticum*) A solid dark green lacy sprig with small ovid leaves that are grown in water, has a pungent flavor and used as garnish or as a salad.
Composition:

H_2O	91–93%
protein	2–3%
fat	0.3%
carbohydrate	1–3%
ash	1%

See Part 2: Minerals, Food

water, demineralized Water from which the minerals have been removed by passing the water through an ion-exchange medium.

water, distilled Water from which minerals have been removed by distillation.

water, drinking Water that contains no pathogenic organisms and little organic matter; pH 6.5–8.0. *See also* **water.**

Max. 1000 ppm total solids
250 ppm Cl^-
250 ppm SO_4^{--}
100 ppm Mg
0.5 ppm Zn
0.3 ppm Fe
0.2 ppm Cu
0.1 ppm Pb

water glass (1) Sodium silicate; eggs are sometimes stored in a solution of this compound. (2) A container for holding drinking water.

water-ground cornmeal *See* **corn meal (old process)**

water hardness Water containing minerals, e.g., calcium carbonate or calcium sulfate.

Class	ppm
Soft	0–60
Moderately hard	60–120
Hard	120–180
Very hard	180–up

water hemlock (*Cicula*) A poisonous plant.
See Part 2: Poisonous Plants

water ice *See* Part 2: Minerals (Trace), Limits

watermelon (*Citrullus vulgaris*) An annual climbing plant that produces a large fruit; different varieties produce different shapes (large, oblong to round) and rind coloring (green and often green and white striped or variegated). The sweet watery flesh may be white, yellow, pink or red; seeds are also various colors and may also be eaten.
Storage: 70°F to ripen; refrigerate (36°–40°F, 85–90% R.H.) before eating; storage life 2–3 weeks.
Varieties: Blackstone, Charleston Gray, Congo, Dixie Queen, Florida Grant.
See Part 2: Fruit, Availability; Fruit Classification; Fruit Composition; Iron; Minerals, Food; Niacin; Organic Acids in Fruits and Vegetables; Phosphorus; Plant Foods, Composition; Potassium; Potassium-Rich Foods; Pulses, Nuts and Seeds Composition; Storage; Sugar, Vegetables; Thiamin; Vegetable Plants; Vegetable Storage

water oats *See* **wild rice**

water, potable Water that is suitable to drink.

water rice (Indian rice) *See* **wild rice**

water, sea Water in the oceans; 3.6% dissolved solids, including 2.6% sodium chloride.

water-slaked lime A liming material composed of 65% CaO; each pound has the neutralizing equivalent of 1.2 to 1.35 lb of $CaCO_3$ (or approx. this quantity of dolomitic limestone). *See also* **lime.**

water-soluble vitamins
ascorbic acid (vit. C), B_{12}, biotin (vit. H), choline, folic acid, inositol, nicotinic acid, pantothenic acid, paraminobenzoic acid, pyridoxine (vit. B-6), riboflavin, thiamin (vit. B-1)

watt A measure of power, rate of energy and heat (10^7 ergs/sec); an electrical measurement; x volt multiplied by y ampere = xy watts.

1 watt = 1×10^7 ergs/sec
= 668 lumens
= 44.254 ft-lb/min
= 3.41304 Btu/hr
= 1 joule per sec
= 0.73761 ft-lb per second (ft-lb/sec)
= 0.10198 kilogram meter per second (kg-m/sec)
= 0.056884 Btu/min
= 0.01433 kg-cal/min
= 0.001360 metric horsepower (75 kg-m/sec)
= 0.001341 U.S. horsepower (550 ft-lb/sec)
= 0.001 kilowatt (kw)
= 0.0009480 Btu/sec (thermal unit per sec)
= 0.0002389 kg-cal/sec (thermal unit per sec)

watt-hour (whr) A rate of power, energy or heat.

1 watt-hour = 2655 foot-pounds
= 367.1 kilogram-meters
= 3.413 Btu
= 1.341×10^{-3} horsepower (U.S.)-hours
= 0.860 kilogram-calorie

wattle The bark of an Australian tree containing tannin; used in the vegetable tanning of leather.

wax An ester of a long-chain fatty acid and a monohydric or dihydric alcohol; material of plant or animal origin that is harder than fat; a substance secreted by bees and used to construct honeycomb; paraffin wax is composed of higher hydrocarbons of petroleum origin.
See Part 2: Saturated Fatty Acids; Wax

wax bean A kidney bean with yellow pods.

waxed paper Paper coated with paraffin wax and impervious to water and grease.
See Part 2: Frozen Food Containers

wax gourd *See* **gourd**

WB agar *See* Part 2: Intestinal Microorganisms

weak electrolyte A substance whose dissociation value lies between nonelectrolytes and electrolytes (strong). Example: organic acids and bases.

weakfish *See* **sea trout**

Wealthy A variety of apples that is in season Aug. to Nov. and which make good pies and sauce, but have only fair eating quality.

weanling An animal that has just been removed from its mother's milk and is eating solid food.

weasand Muscle tissue surrounding the esophagus (passage to the stomach) which is used in sausage.
See Part 2: Casings, Animal; Casings, Terms

web fat Fat covering of paunch and intestines.

wedge bone sirloin A sirloin steak found in the loin end wholesale cut; it is located between the butt end sirloin (first sirloin from rump end) and the round bone sirloin.
See Part 2: Bone in Retail Cuts

weighing bottle A glass vessel with a glass stoppered top used in weighing samples which should not be exposed to air.

weight *See* Part 2: Weight; Weight, Human

welchii *See* Part 2: Illness from Food; Microbial Toxins

well-done Internal beef temperature of 170°F.
See Part 2: Beef Degrees of Doneness; Beef Roasting

Welsh rabbit (Welsh rarebit) A cooked mixture of cheddar cheese, milk, ale or beer served on toast or crackers.

Wessex Saddleback *See* Part 2: Swine Breeds

West Country Down Sheep Early name (1840) of the Hampshire breed of sheep.

Western style *See* **Chicago style**

wet bulb *See* Part 2: Relative Humidity

wether A male ovine animal (sheep) that was castrated before attaining sexual maturity.
See Part 2: Sheep Market Classes and Grades

wether hog A castrated hoggett.

wetting agent A surface-active agent; average concentration of 0.15% will normally reduce surface tension by ½; increased concentrations do not lower this value appreciably; used when mixing solids with liquids and spreading liquids on a surface.

whale (*Cetacea*) An aquatic mammal used for oil, flesh and whalebone; meat composition: 71–78% H_2O, 20–21% protein, 2–8% fat, 0% carbohydrate, 1% ash. Use of such materials has been restricted in the United States for animal conservation reasons.
See Part 2: Meat and Meat Products Composition; Vitamin D, Fish

whale oil Oil obtained from whale blubber.

	No. of C	%
Saturated		
	14	8-9
	16	12-16
	18	2-3
Unsaturated		
	14	2
	16	15
	18	33-35
Polyunsaturated		
	18	9
	20	8
	22	11

Refined oil:

Saponification value	180–205
Unsaponifiable	1–4%
Acid number	0.73
Specific gravity 20°/4°C	0.9227
Iodine value	100–140

See Part 2: Fats and Oils, Physical and Chemical Properties; Fats and Oils, Characteristics; Iodine and Saponification Values; Saturated Fatty Acids; Titer, Fats and Oils; Unsaponifiable Matter; Unsaturated Fatty Acids

wheat The most important cereal grain of the temperate climate; flour is made from wheat by grinding and separating out the chaff.

Type	Name	Sub types and Characteristics	Color	Use
Bread	*Triticum aestivum*, *T. vulgare*	Spring: sown in spring; harvested in late summer. Winter: sown in autumn; harvested in early summer. Hard: high in protein. Soft: mealy in texture, high in starch.	Whitish, amber, reddish, purple, bluish	Bread flour
Durum, Macaroni	*Triticum durum*	High in gluten	White, amber, red, purple	Semolina, pasta
Emmer	*Triticum dicoccum*	Important in early historic times		Fodder
Rivet, cone, English	*Triticum turgidum*	Important in early historic England		Food for livestock

Whole grain wheat is 13% bran, 85% endosperm, 2% germ.

Composition	Bran (%)	Endo-sperm (%)	Germ (%)	Whole grain average (%)
Water	8	13	8	11–13
Protein	11	13	32	8–15
Fat	4	1	8	1–3
Carbohydrate	54	72	38	64–76
Ash			4	1–2

Lysine is the first limiting amino acid and threonine is the second.
Moisture content for storage should be 12–14%.
An annual grain: 60 lb/bu or 1.9 lb/qt.
Seeding: 1–3 bu/acre; 280–300 days to maturity.
Ground wheat 1.7 lb/qt; pH 6.0.
Approx nutrient used for:

	30 bu grain	1 ton straw
N (lb)	34	10
P_2O_5 (lb)	15	3
K_2O (lb)	9	15

See Part 2: Cereal Composition; Cereal Fortification; Cereal Nutrient Content; Cereals, Vitamin and Mineral Content; Grain Analysis; Grain Products Composition; Minerals, Food; Minerals, Plant or Animal Tissue; Nutrients in Crops; Pantothenic Acid Content; Pentosans; Plant Foods, Composition; Protein Factors; Seed, Chemical Composition; Seed Composition; Seed, Germination; Spoilage, Fat in Food; Starch, Microappearance; Tocopherols; Wheat, Amino Acids; Wheat and Flour Composition; Wheat, Carbohydrate Composition; Wheat, Fatty Acids; Wheat Grades; Wheat Grain; Wheat Kernel; Wheat Kernel Parts; Wheat, Minerals; Wheat, Parts of Grain; Wheat, Parts of Grain, Vitamins; Wheat Products, Amino Acid Compositions; Wheat Products Composition; Wheat, Vitamins

wheat bran Husk of grain and some attached endosperm; 0.5 lb/qt; 16 lb/bu.

Composition: 11% H_2O, 15–16% protein, 3–5% fat, 60–70% carbohydrate, 6% ash.
See Part 2: Cereal By-Products Composition

wheat, cracked A product made by cutting or cracking cleaned wheat into small pieces. Durum is not used for cracking wheat.

wheat germ The part of the kernel necessary for new plant life (embryo); it is the oil-containing portion of the kernel and is flattened and sifted out as a yellow oil flake. *See also* **wheat germ oil.**
Composition: 8–11% H_2O, 27–32% protein, 8–11% fat, 38–47% carbohydrate, 4% ash.
See Part 2: Grain Products Composition

wheat germ oil A bland yellow oil obtained from wheat germ.
Composition: saturated fatty acids 15–16%; oleic acid 29–30%; linoleic acid 44–52%; linolenic acid 4–11%.
Properties:

Acid value	6–20
Iodine value	115–125
Unsaponifiable	5%
I.U. of vitamin E/g	2
d_{25}^{25}	0.925–0.933
Saponification value	180–190

See Part 2: Fats and Oils, Physical and Chemical Properties; Tocopherols

wheatgrass *See* Part 2: Seed, Germination

wheatings Wheat middlings with a maximum of 5.75% fiber.

wheatings, superfine Wheat middlings with a maximum of 4.5% fiber.

wheat middlings Particles with less husk and more endosperm than bran; 0.8 lb/qt; 26 lb/bu.

wheat screening Residue left from screening of wheat grain; 1 lb/qt; 32 lb/bu.

whey (milk serum, lacto-serum) The liquid portion of milk separated from solid portion (curd) by action of rennet or lactic acid; obtained when making cheese or manufacturing casein. *See also* **cottage cheese.**

Composition:

	H_2O (%)	Protein (%)	Fat (%)	Carbohydrate (%)	Lactose (%)	Ash (%)
Liquid	92–93	1	0.2–0.3	5		1
Dry	4–5	12–13	1	74	65	8

Acid whey: pH 4.7 from cottage cheese; 100 lb skimmed milk = 16 lb cottage cheese + 84 lb whey.

Sweet whey: pH 6.2 from cheddar and Swiss and other cheeses; 100 lb whole milk = 10 lb cheddar cheese + 90 lb whey.

Casein whey: contains precipitating acid; 100 lb skimmed milk = 2.8 lb casein + 91 lb whey.

See Part 2: Dairy Products, Composition; Milk, Amino Acids; Milk and Milk Products, Vitamin Content; Milk, Concentrated Products; Milk, Dry Products; Vitamin A, Milk and Milk Products

whey agar *See* Part 2: Microorganism, Media

Whipperwill A variety of cowpeas.

whipping cream A cream capable of being beaten to a froth; min 30% milkfat; ½ pt whipping cream = 2 cups whipped cream.

whiskey (Irish, American, Scotch and Canadian) A liquor made by the distillation of fermented grain (rye, corn, barley, wheat), mash of malt or of cereal grains saccharified by diastase of malt and stored in wood for at least 4 years; not less than 80 proof; 37 to 53% alcohol by volume; specific gravity 0.923–0.935 at 25°C; bourbon is from barley or wheat malt and corn; rye is from rye or barley malt and unmalted rye.

See Part 2: Minerals (Trace), Limits

whisky *See* **whiskey**

white The albuminous portion of an egg (cytoplasm).

See Part 2: Egg Structure; Egg Volume

whitebait Young herring (*Culpea harengus*) and sprats (*C. sprattus*). *See also* **smelt.**

white bass (*Lepidema chrysops*) A fresh-water food fish.

white blood cell (leukocyte) A blood cell that contains no hemoglobin; 5000/cu mm of blood; 1/3000 of blood volume.

whitefish A fat fresh-water fish caught in northern lakes of United States and Canada. *See also* **demersal fish.**

See Part 2: Minerals, Food; Nicotinic Acid, Food; Unsaturated Fatty Acids

white flour The starch and gluten of the endosperm of a kernel of wheat. *See also* **flour.**

white hake *See* **hake**

White Holland *See* Part 2: Turkey Varieties

white mullet *See* **mullet**

white mustard (*Brassica hirta* or *Sinapis alba*) A plant grown for mustard and mustard oil.

white pepper Mature peppercorn with outer black skin removed from dried fruit. *See also* **pepper.**

white pine lumber *See* Part 2: Insulation

white rice *See* **rice**

white rot Threadlike shadows in the thin white of an egg.

white sauce A sauce made with flour, thickener, milk and seasoning.

See Part 2: White Sauce

white scours A microbial infection in newborn calves that is often fatal.

white shad *See* **shad**

white snakeroot A plant having a toxic principle.

See Part 2: Poisonous Plants

white tokay wine A dessert wine with nectar-like flavor made from sweet Catawba grapes.

white trout *See* **sea trout**

white walnut *See* **butternut**

whitewash A liquid for whitening and disinfecting a surface.

1. Combine 38 lb quicklime or 50 lb hydrated lime (protected from air) with 7 gal. water.
2. Strain paste through fly screen.
3. Add 4 gal. water and allow to cool.
4. (a) Dissolve 3 lb borax or trisodium phosphate (preferred) in 3 gal. of skimmed milk; or (b) Better method is to dissolve the borax or trisodium phosphate in 1 gal. of water and then add the following solution (5 lb casein softened for 2 hr in 2 gal. hot water).
5. Dissolve 3 pt formaldehyde in 3 gal. of water.
6. When the lime paste in Step No. 3 and milk or casein solution in Step No. 4 are cool, slowly mix by stirring.
7. Just before using, *slowly* add formaldehyde solution with stirring (adding it too fast will cause casein to gel).

NOTE: Mix only as much as can be used in one day.

whiting (frostfish, silver hake) A lean cod-like fish caught in New England and England. *See also* **demersal fish.**

See Part 2: Fish, Smoke-Cured; Frozen Food Storage

whole dry milk (dry milk solids) A product made by removing water from fluid whole milk; max 4–5% moisture; at least 26–28% milkfat; 1 lb = 3⅔ cups; 1 cup = 120 g (4.3 oz). U.S. Grades: Premium, Extra, Standard.

whole fish Fish as it comes from water.
See Part 2: Fish Yields

whole grain Containing all parts of the kernel.

wholesale cut *See* Part 2: Lamb, Wholesale Cuts; Meat Label

whole wheat flour Flour made from the entire kernel of wheat; flavor deteriorates with storage and maximum shelf life is approx 1 month. *See also* **graham flour.**

whortleberry *See* **bilberry**
See Part 2: Flavor Ingredients, Taste and Flavor Type

wide casing *See* Part 2: Casings, Hog; Casings, Hog and Beef; Casings, Sheep; Casings, Terms

wide-end middle Natural beef casings used in the meat trade; they come from the middle part of the large intestine.

wide hog casing A casing that is 38 to 43 mm in width.

wiener Short for wienerwurst; a sausage product made from beef, pork and sometimes veal; same as frankfurter in the United States.
See Part 2: Sausage Identification

wiener schnitzel Breaded veal cutlet with garnish.

wienerwurst Vienna sausage; frankfurter. *See also* **wiener.**

wild cherry When wilted, a poisonous plant.
See Part 2: Poisonous Plants

wild date palm A tropical tree whose sap is obtained and converted into sugar; 3 qt sap = 1 lb sugar.

wild marjoram *See* **oregano**

wild rice (water oats, water rice) (*Zizania aquatica*) The seed of a reed-like water plant and not true rice; it has a dark-colored kernel which is narrow and cylindrical in shape; it is hulled but not milled.

Wiley melting point The temperature at which a solid disk of fat placed in a water-alcohol mixture becomes a sphere as the temperature of the mixture is slowly increased.

Wilson Blair base *See* Part 2: Microorganism, Media

Wiltshire A large, slow-maturing, horned breed of sheep.

Wiltshire side Half a hog carcass with the head, feet, aitch bone, back bone, tenderloin and skirt removed; it is cured and smoked before retailing.

wind (1) Natural movement of the air due to variations in barometric pressure from one area to another.

	(mph)
calm	less than 1
light air	1–3
light breeze	4–7
gentle breeze	8–12
moderate breeze	13–18
fresh breeze	19–24
strong breeze	25–31
near gale	32–38
gale	39–46
strong gale	47–54
storm	55–63
violent storm	64–73
hurricane	74 and over

(2) Breathing capacity of a horse or other large animal.

winding Placing one front or hind foot directly in front of the opposite one in action.

wine An alcoholic drink produced by fermentation of fruit juice by yeast (*Saccharomyces ellipsoideus*) under anaerobic conditions; 30°C and 25% sugar will yield 7–16% alcohol (by volume); alcohol by volume ranges from 7 to 22%;

$$\text{sugar} \xrightarrow{\text{yeast}} \text{alcohol} + \text{carbon dioxide}$$

The carbon dioxide is usually allowed to escape, but in sparkling wines it is retained. Flavor is affected by (1) type of grape; (2) climate; (3) soil; (4) winemaker.

Types:
Dry: low sugar
Fortified: alcohol added
Medicated: medicament added
Sour: ferment to acetic acid
Sweet: high sugar
Red: fermented with grape skins
White: juice is separated from grape skins prior to fermentation; pleasant to drink at an earlier stage than red
Rosé: juice remains in contact with skins a few hours; wine should be consumed when it is young
Sparkling: sugar is added to wine causing fermentation to begin again and more alcohol and bubbles are produced

Content per 100 cc (20°C):
not more than 0.1 g NaCl
not more than 0.2 g potassium sulfate,
not more than 0.14 g volatile acids (calculated as acetic) in red wine,
not more than 0.12 g volatile acids (calculated as acetic) in white wine,
4.5–10.0 g alcohol in unfortified wine
Max 14.5 g alcohol in unfortified wine
0.4–1.0 g glycerin in unfortified wine
0.11–0.44 g ash
0.5–0.9 g total acidity (calculated as tartaric acid)
0.007–0.009 g nitrogen
2.3–3.8 pH.

See Part 2: Flavor Ingredients, Taste and Flavor Type; Minerals (Trace), Limits; Spoilage, Carbohydrate Foods

wineberry (*Rubus phoenicolasius*) A berry that is similar to the common raspberry except it is a clump-forming plant and the canes are covered with red hair rather than prickles; the fruit is golden, orange, shiny and translucent.

wine bottle size Capacity of wine containers.

			Servings per Bottle	
Size	Fl. oz	Cups	Dinner and Sparkling Wines (4 oz)	Dessert Wines (3 oz)
Fifth, 4/5 qt, most popular	25.6	3 1/8	6	8
Tenth, 4/5 pt, 1/2 bottle	12.8	1 1/2	3	4
Half-gallon bottle or jug	64	8	16	21
Gallon bottle or jug	128	16	32	42

wine glass A measure of volume.
1 wine glass = 4 tbsp
= 2 fl oz
= 60 ml
2 wine glasses = 1 gill

Winesap A variety of apple in season from January to June; it is a good cooking and eating apple. *See also* **Stayman Winesap.**

wine spirits Distillation product of fermented grape juice.

wine vinegar *See* **grape (wine) vinegar**

winkle A shellfish; 20% edible (avg. 20% protein).

winter apple An apple that keeps well or ripens late.

winter barley Barley sown in autumn.

wintergreen A flavoring material in confectionery. *See* Part 2: Essential Oils; Flavor Ingredients, Taste and Flavor Type

winterization A method of treating fats and oils in which the higher-melting fractions are removed by cooling, crystallization and filtering; the resulting oil remains clear at low temperatures.

winter melon *See* **melon**

winter pear A pear that keeps well or ripens late.

winter sweet *See* **oregano**

winter wheat Wheat sown in autumn and harvested in the summer.

wire *See* Part 2: Mesh Sizes

wire grass *See* **Bermuda grass**

wireworm Light brown, wiry-looking insect that bores into seed or stem of corn and causes failure to germinate; older plants may wilt and die.

wishbone Furcula bone of the fowl that supports the crop.
See Part 2: Bone

wither (1) Top of a horse's shoulder. (2) Of a plant, to lose sap or juice.

witloof chicory *See* **French endive**

W L differential agar *See* Part 2: Microbiological Media

W L nutrient agar *See* Part 2: Microbiological Media

wok A shallow oriental cooking pan.

wolf fish *See* **catfish**

wolfram *See* **tungsten**

wolin bevis agar *See* Part 2: Microorganism, Media

wong bok *See* **petsai**

wood A mixture of cellulose and lignin. Cells called xylem make up the major portion of a tree stem and branches.
1 cord = 128 cu ft
= 3.625 cu meters
See also **xylem.**

wood alcohol *See* **methyl alcohol**

wood almond (*Hippocratea comosa*) A plant yielding an edible seed and oil.

wood ashes A material that can be used for liming and contains 45% $CaCO_3$; each pound has the neutralizing equivalent of 0.4 to 0.5 lb of $CaCO_3$ (or approx this quantity of dolomitic limestone).
See Part 2: Fertilizer Materials; Liming Materials

wood fiber board *See* Part 2: Insulation

wood nut Filbert.

wood rosin Rosin remaining after the distillation of steam-distilled wood turpentine.

wood spirits *See* **methyl alcohol**

wood sugar *See* **xylose**

wood tar Tar obtained by destructive distillation of wood.

wood turpentine Turpentine produced from wood; it includes steam-distilled wood turpentine and destructively distilled wood turpentine.

wool Crimped fiber produced primarily by sheep; it is principally keratin protein; 1 lb greasy domestic shorn wool = 0.45 lb scoured wool.
See Part 2: Insulation; Insulation, Conductivity Values; Moisture in Biological Materials; Titer, Fats and Oils

wool grease *See* **lanolin; yolk (2)**

wool yield

$$\text{Yield} = \frac{\text{clean (scoured) wool wt}}{\text{grease wool wt}} \times 100$$

$$\text{Yield} = 100 - \%\ \text{shrink}$$

$$\text{Scoured value} = \frac{\text{grease wool price}}{\text{yield}}$$

$$\text{Grease wool value} = \text{scoured value} \times \text{yield}$$

Worcestershire A meat sauce; a fermented, strained, pasteurized product containing anchovies, eschalots, garlic, molasses, onions, salt, soy, spices, sugar, tamarinds, vinegar.
See Part 2: Sauce, Worcester

Worfel Ferguson agar *See* Part 2: Microorganism, Media

wormwood (*Artemisia absinthium*) A perennial herb of the daisy family that is used in flavoring liqueurs and vermouth wine.

wort In beer manufacture, the clear liquid left after straining the mashed grain and malt; infusion of plant to be fermented; contains maltose.

wort agar *See* Part 2: Microorganism, Media

wrapping material *See* Part 2: Plastic Permeability

wurld wheat Wheat in which the bran is chemically (sodium hydroxide and steam) peeled, scoured, acid-neutralized and dried; it is lighter in color, higher in cost and less nutritious than bulgur.

wurst Sausage.

Wyandotte An American class of chickens that lays a light-brown egg, and has a rose comb. Varieties:

	Plumage Color	Shank	Beak
*Silver-laced			
Male	Back white; neck is black with white lacing; body white edged in black; tail feathers black and undercolor slate.	Yellow	Yellow
Female	Black and white lacing over most of body; tail and undercoat is darker.	Yellow	Yellow
Golden-laced	Same as Silver with white replaced by golden.	Yellow	Yellow
*Buffe	Even buff color.	Yellow	Yellow
*White	White	Deep yellow	Yellow
*Partridge			
Male	Neck and back feathers green black with red edging; rest of body slate.	Yellow	Yellow
Female	Neck and back feathers black with red lacing; rest of body slate.	Light yellow	Yellow
*Silver-penciled			
Male	Neck and back white with black edging of feathers; rest of body black with some white.	Yellow	Yellow
Female	Gray with black penciling, gives lacy appearance.	Light yellow	Yellow
*Columbian	Mostly white; neck and tail feathers black with white lacing.	Yellow	Yellow
*Black	Greenish black to slate.	Male, yellow; Female, light yellow	Yellow

*Have bantam varieties

See Part 2: Poultry Breeds and Varieties

X Y Z

χ^2 **(chi-square)** A skewed distribution that shows the lack of agreement between data and hypothesis; sum of (deviation squared/expected number).

xanthine oxidase (Schardinger's enzyme) An oxidative enzyme found in milk and liver.

xanthophyll (lutein, luteol) $C_{40}H_{56}O_2$ A yellow pigment found in plants, egg yolk and butter; an hydroxy carotene derivative.

xanthoproteic test A general but not very sensitive test for protein; a yellow color is formed when concentrated nitric acid comes in contact with tyrosine and tryptophan; all common proteins if present in large quantities give a positive test.
See Part 2: Protein and Amino Acid, Color Reactions

xarque *See* **jerked beef**

X-axis *See* **abscissa**

X chromosome A sex chromosome that carries the female characteristics.

Xe Symbol for the element xenon.

xenon (Xe) A relatively inert gaseous element; at. no. 54; at. wt. 131.30; noble gas group of Periodic Table;
electron configuration 2-8-18-18-8;
orbit K L M N O
oxidation state 0

xerophagia Consuming dry food.

xi (Ξ, ξ) Greek letter with an English equivalent of x.

xiphoid cartilage Tip of breastbone.

XL agar *See* Part 2: Microorganism, Media

X L D agar *See* Part 2: Microbiological Media; Microorganism, Media; Microorganism, Selective and Differential Broths and Media, Water Filtration Plant

x-ray Electromagnetic radiation with a wavelength of 5×10^{-7} to 6×10^{-10} cm.

xylan $(C_5H_8O_4)_n$ A hemicellulose found in many plants; it will hydrolyze to xylose.

xylem Cells from which wood is developed. *See also* **wood.**

xylose (wood sugar) $C_5H_{10}O_5$ A 5-carbon monosaccharide (pentose) found in fibrous materials; a sugar 40% as sweet as sucrose; used as a diabetic food.
See Part 2: Sugar, D-aldehydo

Y Symbol for the element yttrium.

yam (*Dioscorea*) A term sometimes used to describe any tropical root crop; in the United States, same as sweet potato; the *Dioscorea* produces a tuber with a white or yellow flesh; the tuber is cooked and usually mashed; it is high in starch and low in protein.
Composition: 74% H_2O, 2% protein, 0.2% fat, 15-25% carbohydrate, 1% ash. *See also* **sweet potato.**
See Part 2: Minerals, Food; Starches and Starchy Roots Composition; Vegetable Storage

yam bean (*Pachyrrhizus tuberosus*) A plant that produces both edible tubers and seed or pods.

yaourt, yourt A fermented milk. *See also* **yogurt.**

yarbs Ancient term for herbs.

yard (yd) A measure of length.
1 yd = 91.440183 centimeters
= 36 inches (in.)
= 3 feet (ft)
= 0.91440183 meter (m)
= 0.18182 rod (rd)
= 0.0009144 kilometer (km)
= 0.0005682 statute mile
= 0.0004934 U.S. nautical mile
5½ yards = 1 rod

yaro *See* Part 2: Starches and Starchy Roots Composition

yautia *See* **tannia**
See Part 2: Starches and Starchy Roots Composition

Y-axis *See* **ordinate**

Yb Symbol for the element ytterbium.

Y-chromosome A sex chromosome that carries the male characteristics.

yean To lamb.

yearling An ovine animal (sheep) from 1 to 2 years of age which has two permanent incisor teeth; an animal in 2nd year of age.
See Part 2: Bone Age; Sheep Market Classes and Grades

yearling hen Female turkey between 7 and 15 months old.

yearling tom Male turkey between 7 and 15 months old.

yeast A microscopic plant that can convert sugar to carbon dioxide; it is used as a leavening agent in foods and to induce alcoholic fermentation; optimum temp. for reaction (not storage), 82°F. *See also* **compressed yeast; dry yeast.**

See Part 2: Bacteria, Molds and Yeasts; Canned Spoilage Manifestations; Canned Spoilage Related to pH; Culture Media; Egg Specifications; Microbiological Media; Microbiological Standards, Dairy; Microorganism, Culture Media, Dairy and Food Products; Microorganism, Media; Minerals, Plant or Animal Tissue; Minerals (Trace), Limits; Nicotinic Acid, Food; Pantothenic Acid Content; Riboflavin, Food; Rot Spoilage; Thiamin, Food; Water Activity, Organisms and Food

yellowfin *See* **grouper; tuna**

yellowhammer Small, mixed-breed of yellow cattle.

Yellow Jersey A dry, mealy variety of sweet potato.

yellow perch *See* **lake perch**

yellow pine *See* Part 2: Poisonous Plants

yellow prussiate of soda Sodium ferrocyanide; $Na_4Fe(CN)_6 \cdot 10\,H_2O$.

yellow star thistle *See* Part 2: Poisonous Plants

yellowtail *See* **flounder**
See Part 2: Vitamin D, Fish

Yellow Transparent A variety of apple which is in season in July and August that makes excellent sauce, good pies but is only fair for eating.

yerba de maté *See* **maté**

yerba-de-pasmo *See* Part 2: Poisonous Plants

yield The amount of useful product obtained from a planting or growing operation or quantity remaining after treatment. *See also* **wool yield.**
See Part 2: Beef Retail Yield; Fish Yields; Fruit, Dried, Simmering; Fruit Frozen Yield; Fruit Sauces; Fruit, Simmering; Lamb Yield; Nutrients in Crops; Pork Carcass, Retail Yield; Pork Cooking Yield; Pork Yield; Poultry Yield; Sugar Beet Yield; Vegetable Frozen Yield; Vegetable Yield; Vegetable Yield, Canned and Frozen; Vegetable Yield, Frozen, Canned and Fresh; Yield Grade Meat

yield grade *See* Part 2: Beef Carcasses, Yield Grade

ylang-ylang oil An essential oil obtained from a plant grown in the Philippines.
See Part 2: Essential Oils; Flavoring Agents, Natural

YM agar *See* Part 2: Microorganism, Media

yogurt (yoghurt, yogourt, yoghourt) A custard-like product made by fermenting (*Lactobacillus acidophilus, Lactobacillus bulgaricus* and *Streptococcus thermophilus*) concentrated whole or skimmed milk; fruits or flavors are often added.
1 pt = 2 cups; 1 cup = 250 g (8.7 oz)

Composition:

	H_2O (%)	Protein (%)	Fat (%)	Carbohydrate (%)	Ash (%)
Made from skimmed milk	89	3	2	5	1
Made from whole milk	88	3	3.4	5	1

See Part 2: Cultured Dairy Products, Composition; Dairy Terms; Fluid and Fermented Milks, Composition; Milk and Milk Products, Vitamin Content; Vitamin A, Milk and Milk Products

yolk (1) Yellow mass of stored food found in the inner portion of an egg of a bird; the cellular nucleus of an egg.
(2) (wool grease) A natural oil or grease found on sheep fleece which helps to preserve it; source of lanolin.
See Part 2: Egg Structure; Egg Volume

York Imperial A variety of apple that is in season in November to March; is a good sauce apple; a fair to good cooking and eating apple.

Yorkshire A bacon type hog originating in northern England by crossing the Large Yorkshire with Leicester and later crossing with Middle and Small Yorkshire; its color is solid white and has an erect ear and a long body.
See Part 2: Swine Breeds

Yorkshire pudding A batter of eggs, flour and milk baked in meat fat.

youngberry Hybrid between blackberry and dewberry.
See Part 2: Fruit Frozen Yield

young hen Female turkey 5 to 7 months old.

young tom Male turkey 5 to 7 months old.

YPC broth *See* Part 2: Microorganism, Media

ytterbium (Yb) A rare earth element of the lanthanide series; at. no. 70; at. wt. 173.04; Group IIIB of Periodic Table; electron configuration 2-8-18-32-8-2;
orbit K L M N O P
oxidation states +2, +3

yttrium (Y) A metallic element; at. no. 39; at. wt. 88.91; Group IIIB of Periodic Table; electron configuration 2-8-18-9-2;
orbit K L M N O
oxidation state +3

zabaglione A thick, light drink made from eggs, sugar and wine or fruit juice.

zarf Metal holder for coffee cup.

zeaxanthin A carotenoid pigment used in food coloring.

zebu (*Bos indicus*) An Asiatic ox with one or two humps of fat on the shoulder. *See also* **Brahman.**
See Part 2: Beef and Dual-Purpose Cattle

zein An alcohol-soluble protein obtained from corn (2.5–10%) (*Zea mais*); contains little lysine or tryptophan.

Zenker's fixing fluid A fixative.

Mix: bichromate of potassium 2.5 g, bichloride of mercury (corrosive sublimate) (handle with glass) 5.0 g, sodium sulfate 1.0 g.

Dissolve in 100 ml of water with aid of heat; add 5 ml of glacial acetic acid when ready to use.

Use:

1. 90 times as much fluid as tissue.
2. Fixing time 30 min to 36 hr depending on density of tissue.
3. Wash in running water 12 to 24 hr.
4. In alcohol:
   35%–20 minutes
   50%–20 minutes
   70%–20 minutes
5. Remove mercuric crystals; (may be done now or after cutting tissue—by treating with dilute iodized alcohol for 30 minutes and then washed in 70% alcohol).
   (a) add iodine to alcohol to port wine color.
   (b) renew iodine when color disappears (usually 12–36 hr).
   (c) wash in 70% alcohol until no more I_2 is extracted.

zeolite An ion-exchange medium.
$Na_2O \cdot 2Al_2O_3 \cdot 5SiO_2$ or $CaO \cdot 2Al_2O_3 \cdot 5SiO_2$.

zephiran (benzalkonium chloride) An ammonium detergent that is effective as a disinfectant; a cationic surface-active agent; 1:1,000 to 1:5000 concentrations are often used.

zero milk Milk produced on protein-free feed using urea and ammonium salts as the nitrogen sources.

zest Outer peel of citrus fruit.

zeta (Z, ζ) Greek letter with an English equivalent of z.

ziega Curd made by adding rennet and acetic acid to milk.

ziger *See* Part 2: Milk and Cheese Composition

zinc (Zn) A metallic element; at. no. 30; at. wt. 65.38; Group IIB of Periodic Table; electron configuration 2–8–18–2;
orbit K L M N
oxidation state +2
See Part 2: Chemical Poisoning; Egg Products, Nutritive Value; Grain Analysis; Meat, Nutritive Value; Minerals, Food; Minerals, Plant or Animal Tissue; Minerals (Trace), Limits; Normal Solutions; Nutrients in Crops; pH and Availability of Plant Nutrients; Recommended Daily Dietary Allowance; Water Drinking Standards; Wheat, Minerals; Wheat Products Composition

zinc oxide ZnO *See* Part 2: Fertilizer Materials

zinc sulfate $ZnSO_4$ *See* Part 2: Fertilizer Materials; Normal Solutions

zingiberaceae *See* Part 2: Vegetables, Classification

zirconium (Zr) A metallic element; at. no. 40; at. wt. 91.22; Group IVA of Periodic Table; electron configuration 2–8–18–10–2;
orbit K L M N O
oxidation state +4

zitoni *See* **macaroni**

zitoni rigati *See* **macaroni**

Z-line Dark line that bisects the I-band in muscle fibers.

Zn Symbol for the element zinc.

Zr Symbol for the element zirconium.

zucchini A summer variety of squash. *See also* **marrow**.

***z*-value** The slope of the curve when the log of decimal reduction time is plotted against degrees Fahrenheit. *See also* **decimal reduction time.**
See Part 2: Thermal-Death-Time Curve

zwieback A loaf that is baked, sliced and toasted.
1 cup = 4 coarsely crumbled slices = 9 finely crumbled slices.

zymase A yeast enzyme that splits sugar into alcohol and CO_2.

zymogen A precursor of active enzymes.

PART 2

FOOD COMPOSITION, PROPERTIES, AND GENERAL DATA

A

ACIDULANTS

TABLE 2.A.1

PROPERTIES OF SOME COMMON FOOD ACIDULANTS

Property	POMALUS® Malic Acid HOCHCOOH | CH_2COOH	Fumaric Acid HOOCCH ‖ HCCOOH	Adipic Acid CH_2CH_2COOH | CH_2CH_2COOH	Succinic Acid CH_2COOH | CH_2COOH	Succinic Anhydride CH_2CO | O CH_2CO	Citric Acid CH_2COOH | HOCCOOH | CH_2COOH	Tartaric Acid HOCHCOOH | HOCHCOOH
Appearance	White crystal. powder	White crystal. powder	White crystal. powder	White crystal. powder	White crystals	White crystals	White crystals
Crystal system	Triclinic crystal	Monoclinic prisms	Monoclinic prisms	Monoclinic prisms	Ortho-rhombic prisms	Monoclinic holohedra	Monoclinic sphenoidal prisms
Taste	Smooth tart	Tart	Tart	Tart	Burning tart	Tart	Bitter tart
Empirical formula	$C_4H_6O_5$	$C_4H_4O_4$	$C_6H_{10}O_4$	$C_4H_6O_4$	$C_4H_4O_3$	$C_6H_8O_7$	$C_4H_6O_6$
Melting point, °C	130°-132°	286°-287°	153°	188°	118.3°-119°[1]	153°	168°-170°
Specific gravity	1.601 (20°/4°)	1.635 (20°/4°)	1.380 (25°/4°)	1.564 (15°/4°)	1.503 (20°/4°)	1.542 (18°/4°)	1.7598 (20°/4°)
Bulk density, lb/ft³	57.3	32.6	40.5	55.0	47.2	56.2	50.2
Solubility in ethanol gm/100 ml @ 25°C	39.16	4.3	16.10	9.0	2.56	58.9	19.6
Solubility in ether gm/100 ml @ 25°C	1.41	0.56	0.92	0.66	0.64	1.84	0.59
Solubility in chloroform gm/100 ml @ 25°C	0.04	0.02	<0.01	0.02	0.87	<0.01	0.04
Ionization constant K_1	4×10^{-4}	1×10^{-3}	3.7×10^{-5}	6.5×10^{-5}	(See succinic acid)	8.2×10^{-4}	1.04×10^{-3}
K_2	9×10^{-6}	3×10^{-5}	2.4×10^{-6}	2.3×10^{-6}		1.8×10^{-5}	4.55×10^{-5}
K_3	—	—	—	—		3.9×10^{-6}	—
Heat of combustion, kcal/mole, 20°C	-320.1	-320.0	-669.0	357.1	-369.6	-474.5	-257.1
Heat of solution, kcal/mole solute	4.9	—	—	—	—	3.9	3.3
Viscosity 50% aqueous solutions, cps, @ 25°C	6.5	[2]	[2]	[2]	[2]	6.5	6.6
Standard free energy of anion formation, ΔF°_f, kcal, @ 25°C, aqueous solutions	-201.98	-144.41	—	-164.97	—	-278.8	—
Sp gr saturated aqueous solutions, @ 5°	1.210	1.000	1.002	1.012	(See succinic acid)	1.24	1.26
25°	1.250	1.000	1.005	1.024	"	1.28	1.27
75°	1.310	0.989	1.032	1.076	"	1.31	1.31

[1] Solidification point.
[2] Solubility too limited.

SOURCE: SAUSVILLE, T. J. 1975. Acidulants. *In* Encyclopedia of Food Technology. A. H. Johnson and M. S. Peterson (Editors). AVI Publishing Co., Westport, Conn.

ACRE, PLANTS

TABLE 2.A.2

NUMBER OF PLANTS PER ACRE AT GIVEN SPACINGS

Inches	No. of Plants	Inches	No. of Plants	Inches	No. of Plants
12 × 1	522,720	24 × 6	43,560	40 × 30	5,227
12 × 3	174,240	24 × 9	29,040	40 × 36	4,356
12 × 4	130,680	24 × 12	21,780		
12 × 6	87,120	24 × 15	17,424	42 × 3	49,782
12 × 9	58,080	24 × 18	14,520	42 × 6	24,891
12 × 12	43,560	24 × 24	10,890	42 × 12	12,445
				42 × 18	8,297
15 × 1	418,176	30 × 3	69,696	42 × 24	6,223
15 × 3	139,382	30 × 4	52,272	42 × 30	4,978
15 × 4	104,544	30 × 6	34,848	42 × 36	4,148
15 × 6	69,696	30 × 9	23,232		
15 × 9	48,484	30 × 12	17,424	48 × 3	43,560
15 × 12	34,848	30 × 15	13,939	48 × 6	21,780
		30 × 18	11,616	48 × 12	10,890
18 × 1	348,390	30 × 24	8,712	48 × 18	7,260
18 × 3	116,160	30 × 30	6,969	48 × 24	5,445
18 × 4	87,120			48 × 30	4,356
18 × 6	58,080	36 × 3	58,080	48 × 36	3,630
18 × 9	38,720	36 × 4	43,560	48 × 42	3,111
18 × 12	29,040	36 × 6	29,040	48 × 48	2,722
18 × 15	23,232	36 × 9	19,360		
18 × 18	19,360	36 × 12	14,520	60 × 3	34,848
		36 × 15	11,616	60 × 6	17,424
20 × 3	104,544	36 × 18	9,680	60 × 12	8,712
20 × 4	78,408	36 × 24	7,260	60 × 18	5,808
20 × 6	52,272	36 × 30	5,808	60 × 24	4,356
20 × 9	34,848	36 × 36	4,840	60 × 30	3,484
20 × 12	26,136			60 × 36	2,904
20 × 15	20,909	40 × 3	52,272	60 × 42	2,489
20 × 18	17,426	40 × 6	26,136	60 × 48	2,178
		40 × 12	13,068	60 × 54	1,936
24 × 3	87,120	40 × 18	8,709	60 × 60	1,742
24 × 4	65,340	40 × 24	6,534		

SOURCE: MORTENSEN, E. and BULLARD, E. T. 1969. Handbook of Tropical and Sub-Tropical Horticulture. Agency for International Development, U.S. Department of State.

ACRE, TREES

TABLE 2.A.3

NUMBER OF TREES PER ACRE AT GIVEN SPACINGS

Feet	No. of Plants
6 × 1	7,260
6 × 2	3,630
6 × 3	2,420
6 × 4	1,815
6 × 5	1,452
6 × 6	1,210
7 × 1	6,223
7 × 2	3,111
7 × 3	2,074
7 × 4	1,556
7 × 5	1,244
7 × 6	1,037
7 × 7	889
8 × 1	5,445
8 × 2	2,722
8 × 3	1,815
8 × 4	1,361
8 × 5	1,089
8 × 6	907
8 × 7	778
8 × 8	680
9 × 1	4,840
9 × 2	2,420
9 × 3	1,613
9 × 4	1,210
9 × 5	968
9 × 6	807
9 × 7	691
9 × 8	605
9 × 9	528

Feet	No. of Plants
10 × 1	4,356
10 × 2	2,178
10 × 3	1,452
10 × 4	1,089
10 × 5	871
10 × 6	726
10 × 7	622
10 × 8	544
10 × 9	484
10 × 10	435
12 × 2	1,815
12 × 4	907
12 × 6	605
12 × 7	454
12 × 10	363
12 × 12	302
14 × 2	1,556
14 × 4	778
14 × 6	518
14 × 8	389
14 × 10	311
14 × 12	259
14 × 14	222
16 × 2	1,361
16 × 4	680
16 × 6	454
16 × 8	340
16 × 10	272
16 × 12	227

Feet	No. of Plants
16 × 14	194
16 × 16	170
18 × 4	605
18 × 6	404
18 × 8	303
18 × 10	242
18 × 12	202
18 × 14	173
18 × 16	152
18 × 18	132
20 × 8	272
20 × 10	218
20 × 12	184
20 × 14	156
20 × 16	136
20 × 18	121
20 × 20	109
24 × 12	151
24 × 16	114
24 × 20	92
24 × 24	76
30 × 20	72
30 × 30	48
30 × 40	36
40 × 40	27

SOURCE: MORTENSEN, E. and BULLARD, E. T. 1969. Handbook of Tropical and Sub-Tropical Horticulture. Agency for International Development, U.S. Department of State.

ALCOHOLIC SOLUTIONS

TABLE 2.A.4

VARIOUS STRENGTHS OF ALCOHOLIC SOLUTIONS

Alcohol, Strength Desired Ml per Liter	Alcohol Required Grams	Ml
50	42.63	52.6
100	85.26	105.3
150	127.89	157.9
200	170.52	210.5
250	213.16	263.2
300	255.78	315.9
400	341.04	421.1
500	426.32 (proof)	526.3
700	596.84	736.8

NOTE: Alcoholic solutions: Specification requires 95% C_2H_5OH by vol. Sp gr = 0.810 at 25°. Mix and dil. to 1 liter.

Alcohol of any desired strength may be obtained by taking number of ml 95% alcohol equiv. to desired strength and dil. soln. to 95 ml. For example, to obtain soln. of 70% alcohol, take 70 ml 95% alcohol and dil. to 95 ml.

SOURCE: EDITORIAL BOARD, AOAC. 1975. Official Methods of Analysis of the Association of Official Analytical Chemists, 12th Edition. Association of Official Analytical Chemists, Washington, D.C.

ALTITUDE ADJUSTMENTS FOR BAKING

TABLE 2.A.5

ADJUSTMENTS FOR HIGH ALTITUDE BAKING

	3000 ft	5000 ft	7000 ft
Reduce Baking Powder			
For each teaspoon, decrease	⅛ tsp	⅛-¼ tsp	¼-½ tsp
Reduce Sugar			
For each cup, decrease	no change	usually no change	1-2 tbsp
Reduce Lard			
For each cup, decrease	1-2 tbsp	2 tbsp	2-3 tbsp
Increase Liquid			
For each cup, add	1-2 tbsp	2-3 tbsp	3-4 tbsp
Increase Baking Temperature	6-10°F	10-15°F	15-25°F
Decrease Baking Time 5 to 10 minutes when recipes have been tested at sea level.			

NOTE: When two amounts are given, try the smaller adjustment first; then if cake still needs improvement, use the larger adjustment the next time you make the cake.

SOURCE: Kitchen Classics. National Live Stock and Meat Board, Chicago.

AMINO ACID, SOLUBILITIES

TABLE 2.A.6

SOLUBILITIES OF THE AMINO ACIDS IN GRAMS PER 100 GRAMS OF WATER

Amino Acid	Temperature, °C 0°	25°	50°	75°	100°	Ref. No.
DL-Alanine	12.11	16.72	23.09	31.89	44.04	1
L-Alanine	12.73	16.65	21.79	28.51	37.30	1
DL-Aspartic acid	0.262	0.778	2.000	4.456	8.594	1
L-Aspartic acid	0.209	0.500	1.199	2.875	6.893	1
L-Cystine‡ × 10^2	0.502	1.096	2.394	5.229	11.42	2
Diiodo-DL-tyrosine × 10	0.149	0.340	0.773	—	—	3
Diiodo-L-tyrosine × 10	0.204	0.617	1.862	5.62	17.00	1
DL-Glutamic acid	0.855	2.054	4.934	11.86	28.49	1
L-Glutamic acid	0.341	0.864	2.186	5.532	14.00	1
Glycine	14.18	24.99	39.10	54.39	67.17	1
L-Histidine	—	4.19	—	—	—	4
Hydroxy-L-Proline	28.86	36.11	45.18	51.67*	—	5
DL-Isoleucine	1.826	2.229	3.034	4.607	7.802	1
L-Isoleucine	3.791	4.117	4.818	6.076	8.255	2
DL-Leucine	0.797	0.991	1.406	2.276	4.206	1
L-Leucine	2.270	2.426†	2.887†	3.823	5.638	1
DL-Methionine	1.818	3.381	6.070	10.52	17.60	2
DL-Phenylalanine	0.997	1.411	2.187	3.708	6.886	1
L-Phenylalanine	1.983	2.965	4.431	6.624	9.900	2
L-Proline × 10^{-1}	12.74	16.23	20.67	23.90*	—	3
DL-Serine	2.204	5.023	10.34	19.21	32.24	2
L-Tryptophan	0.823	1.136	1.706	2.795	4.987	2
DL-Tyrosine × 10	0.147	0.351	0.836	—	—	3
L-Tyrosine × 10	0.196	0.453	1.052	2.438	5.650	1
D-Tyrosine × 10	0.196	0.453	1.052	—	—	3
DL-Valine	5.98	7.09	9.11	12.61	18.81	1
L-Valine	8.34	8.85	9.62	10.24*	—	6

*Value at 65°.

†Dunn and Stoddard (7) report 2.19 g at 25° for L-leucine rendered methionine-free by repeated recrystallization from 6 *N* HCl. Hlynka (8) found 2.20 g at 25° and 2.66 g at 50° for L-leucine rendered methionine-free [by S. W. Fox (9)] by fractional crystallization of the formyl derivative and identical values for D-leucine obtained by resolution of the DL form.

‡The following values were found by Loring and Du Vigneaud (10): DL-cystine (0.0049 g), D-cystine (0.0108 g), and *meso*-cystine (0.0056 g) at 25°.

References

1. Dalton, J. B., and Schmidt, C. L. A., J. Biol. Chem., 103, 549 (1933).
2. Dalton, J. B., and Schmidt, C. L. A., J. Biol. Chem., 109, 241 (1935).
3. Winnek, P. S., and Schmidt, C. L. A., J. Gen. Physiol., 18, 889 (1934-35).
4. Dunn, M. S., Frieden, E. H., and Brown, H. V., unpublished data.
5. Tomiyama, T., and Schmidt, C. L. A., J. Gen. Physiol., 19, 379 (1935-36).
6. Dalton, J. B., and Schmidt, C. L. A., J. Gen. Physiol., 19, 767 (1935-36).
7. Dunn, M. S., and Stoddard, M. P., unpublished data.
8. Hlynka, I., Thesis (1939), California Institute of Technology, Pasadena, California.
9. Fox, S. W., Science, 84, 163 (1936).
10. Loring, H. S., and du Vigneaud, V., J. Biol. Chem., 107, 270 (1934).

SOURCE: WEAST, R. C. (EDITOR). 1974–1975. Handbook of Chemistry and Physics, 55th Edition. CRC Press, Cleveland. Used by permission of CRC Press.

AMINO ACIDS I

TABLE 2.A.7

PHYSICAL PROPERTIES

Melting Point: Most amino acids decompose when melting. **Specific Rotation:** Values are for the D-line of sodium (589 nm). **Solubility:** sol. = soluble; insol. = insoluble; deliq. = deliquescent; sl. = slightly; v. = very; dil. = dilute; h. = hot; a. = acid; ac. = acetic; acet. = acetone; alc. = alcohol (ethanol, unless otherwise specified); alk. = alkali; aq. = aqueous; et. = ethyl; eth. = ether; me. = methyl.

	Amino Acid	Chemical Formula	Molecular Weight	Melting Point	Specific Rotation				Isoelectric Point	Solubility g/100 ml solvent
					Solvent	g/100 ml	Temp °C	Value		
1	L-Alanine	$C_3H_7NO_2$	89.09	297	1.0 *N* HCl	5.79	15	+14.7	6.11[1/]	sl.sol.alc.; insol.acet., eth.; 16.51, w.
2	β-Alanine	$C_3H_7NO_2$	89.09	196	....	....	......	0	6.90	v.sol.w.; v.sl.sol.alc.; insol. eth.
3	L-α-Aminobutyric acid	$C_4H_9NO_2$	103.12	285	20% HCl	....	20	+14.1	5.98	insol.eth.; 0.18, alc.; 28, w.
4	L-Anserine	$C_{10}H_{16}N_4O_3$	240.26	238-239	H_2O	5.0	20	+12.2	8.27	sol.me.alc., w.; sl.sol. alc.
5	L-Arginine	$C_6H_{14}N_4O_2$	174.20	238	6.0 *N* HCl	1.65	23	+26.9	10.76	v.sol.w.; insol.alc., eth.
6	L-Asparagine	$C_4H_8N_2O_3$	132.12	236	3.4 *N* HCl	2.24	20	+34.3	5.41	sol.dil.NH_4OH; v.sl.sol. alc.; insol.eth.; 2.46, w.
7	L-Aspartic acid	$C_4H_7NO_4$	133.10	269-271	6.0 *N* HCl	2.0	24	+24.6	2.98	sol.dil.HCl; v.sl.sol.alc.; insol.eth.; 0.50, w.
8	L-Canaline	$C_4H_{10}N_2O_3$	134.14	214	H_2O	1.6	21	−8.1	....	sol.w.
9	L-Canavanine	$C_5H_{12}N_4O_3$	176.18	184	H_2O	3.2	20	+8.1	8.2	sol.w.
10	L-Carnosine	$C_9H_{14}N_4O_3$	226.23	246-250	H_2O	2.0	20	+20.5	8.17	sol.w.
11	L-Citrulline	$C_6H_{13}N_3O_3$	175.19	222	1.0 *N* HCl	2.0	27	+24.3	5.92	v.sl.sol.w.; insol.alc.
12	L-Cystathionine	$C_7H_{14}N_2O_4S$	222.26	270-312	1.0 *N* HCl	1.0	22	+23.7	....	sol.HCl
13	L-Cysteic acid	$C_3H_7NO_5S$	169.17	289	H_2O	....	......	+8.7	1.6	sol.a., alk., w.; insol.alc.
14	L-Cysteine	$C_3H_7NO_2S$	121.16	175-178	H_2O	2.0	21	−10.1	5.07	v.sol.w.; sol.a., alk.
15	L-Cystine	$C_6H_{12}N_2O_4S_2$	240.30	258-261	1.0 *N* HCl	1.0	24	−214.4	5.02	sol.a.[2/], NH_4OH; insol. alc., eth.; 0.011 w.
16	L-3,5-Dibromotyrosine	$C_9H_9NO_3Br_2$	338.99	245[3/]	0.3 *N* HCl	....	20	−2.4	4.30	....
17	L-3,4-Dihydroxyphenylalanine	$C_9H_{11}NO_4$	197.19	280	4% HCl	1.0	25	−12.0	....	sol.a., alk.; insol.alc., eth.; 0.50, w.
18	L-3,5-Diiodotyrosine	$C_9H_9NO_3I_2$	432.99	194	1.1 *N* HCl	5.1	20	+2.9	4.29[1/]	0.62, w.
19	L-Djenkolic acid	$C_7H_{14}N_2O_4S_2$	254.33	300-350	1% HCl	2.0	26	−44.5	....	0.10, w.
20	L-Ergothioneine	$C_9H_{15}N_3O_2S$	229.30	290	H_2O	5.0	21	+116.0	....	....
21	L-Ethionine	$C_6H_{13}NO_2S$	163.24	272-284	0.2 *N* HCl	0.8	25	+23.5	....	sol.w.
22	L-Glutamic acid	$C_5H_9NO_4$	147.13	247	6.0 *N* HCl	1.0	22	+31.2	3.22[1/]	0.86, w.
23	L-Glutamine	$C_5H_{10}N_2O_3$	146.15	185-186	H_2O	....	19	+8.0	5.65	v.sl.sol.alc.; insol.eth.; 4.25, w.
24	Glycine	$C_2H_5NO_2$	75.07	290	....	....	......	0	6.20	0.43, 90% alc.; 24.99, w.
25	L-Histidine	$C_6H_9N_3O_2$	155.16	277	H_2O	1.1	25	−39.0	7.64	v.sl.sol.alc.; insol.eth.; 4.19, w.
26	L-Homocysteine	$C_4H_9NO_2S$	135.19	232-233[1/]	....	....	......	....	....	sol.w.

	Amino Acid	Chemical Formula	Molecular Weight	Melting Point	Specific Rotation Solvent	g/100 ml	Temp °C	Value	Isoelectric Point	Solubility g/100 ml solvent
27	L-Homocystine	$C_8H_{16}N_2O_4S_2$	268.36	282	1.0 *N* HCl	1.0	26	+77	5.53	v.sl.sol.w.
28	L-δ-Hydroxylysine	$C_6H_{14}N_2O_3$	162.20	220	6.0 *N* HCl	....	25	+17.8	9.15	sol.a., w.; insol.alc.
29	L-4-Hydroxyproline	$C_5H_9NO_3$	131.13	273-274	H_2O	1.0	22	−75.2	5.82	v.sl.sol.alc.; insol.eth.; 36.11, w.
30	L-Isoleucine	$C_6H_{13}NO_2$	131.18	283-284	6.1 *N* HCl	5.1	20	+40.6 1/	6.04 1/	sol.h.ac.a.; insol.eth.; 0.09, alc.; 3.45 4/, w.; 4.12, w.
31	L-Lanthionine	$C_6H_{12}N_2O_4S$	208.24	270-295	2.4 *N* NaOH	5.0	22	+8.6	....	sol.NH_4OH, aq.HCl; insol.w.
32	L-Leucine	$C_6H_{13}NO_2$	131.18	337	6.0 *N* HCl	2.0	26	+15.1	6.04 1/	sol.ac.a.; insol.eth.; 0.022, alc.; 2.17 4/, w.; 2.19, w.
33	L-Lysine	$C_6H_{14}N_2O_2$	146.19	224	6.0 *N* HCl	2.0	23	+25.9	9.47	v.sol.w.; v.sl.sol.alc.; insol.eth.
34	L-Methionine	$C_5H_{11}NO_2S$	149.21	283	0.2 *N* HCl	0.8	25	+21.2	5.74 1/	insol.eth.; 5.75, w.; 5.62 4/, w.
35	L-Norleucine	$C_6H_{13}NO_2$	131.18	301	6.0 *N* HCl	4.3	20	+21.3	6.08 1/	0.017 1/, alc.; 1.149 1/, w.
36	L-Norvaline	$C_5H_{11}NO_2$	117.15	291-292	20% HCl	5	20	+22.8	6.04	sl.sol.alc.; insol.eth.; 10.7 5/, w.
37	D-Octapine	$C_9H_{18}N_4O_4$	246.27	229-230	H_2O	....	17	+20.9	5.51	sol.w.
38	L-Ornithine	$C_5H_{12}N_2O_2$	132.16	225	H_2O	4.0	27	+16.5 3/	9.70	v.sol.alc.; sl.sol.eth.; v. deliq.w.
39	L-Phenylalanine	$C_9H_{11}NO_2$	165.19	283	H_2O	1.9	20	−35.1	5.91 1/	sl.sol.alc.; insol.eth.; 2.76 4/, w.; 2.96, w.
40	L-Proline	$C_5H_9NO_2$	115.13	220-222	0.5 *N* HCl	0.6	20	−52.6	6.3	insol.eth.; 1.55, alc.; 162.3, w.
41	Sarcosine	$C_3H_7NO_2$	89.1	210	....	....	......	0	6.12	v.sol.w.; sl.sol.alc.; insol.eth.
42	L-Serine	$C_3H_7NO_3$	105.09	228	1.0 *N* HCl	9.3	25	+14.5	5.68 1/	insol.alc., eth.; 4.22 4/, w.; 5.023 1/, w.
43	L-Thiolhistidine	$C_6H_9N_3O_2S$	187.2	310 6/	1.0 *N* HCl	1.0	25	−9.5	5.16	sol.a., w.; insol.alc., organic solvents
44	L-Threonine	$C_4H_9NO_3$	119.12	253	H_2O	1.0	26	−28.4	5.59	insol.alc., eth.; 20.1 1/, w.
45	L-Thyroxine	$C_{15}H_{11}NO_4I_4$	776.88	235-236	0.13 *N* NaOH in 70% ethanol	3	......	−4.4	....	insol.alc., eth.; 0.001, w.
46	L-Tryptophan	$C_{11}H_{12}N_2O_2$	204.23	282	H_2O	1.0	20	−31.5	5.88	sl.sol.alc.; insol.eth.; 1.14, w.; 1.36 1/, w.
47	L-Tyrosine	$C_9H_{11}NO_3$	181.19	344	6.3 *N* HCl	4.4	20	−8.6	5.63	sol.alk.; insol.acet., eth.; 0.01, alc.; 0.0454, w.
48	L-Valine	$C_5H_{11}NO_2$	117.15	293	6.0 *N* HCl	3.4	20	+28.8	6.00 1/	0.019 1/, alc.; 5.81 4/, w.; 8.85, w.

1/ Value for the racemic (DL) mixture. 2/ Mixture of acetonitrile and perchloric acid. 3/ Value for the dihydrate. 4/ Value from reference 1. 5/ Value at 50°C. 6/ Decomposes without melting.

Contributors: Evans, Robert John; Ward, Wilfred H.; Sauberlich, H. E.

(Continued)

Specific Reference

[1] Sober, H. A., ed. 1970. Handbook of Biochemistry. Ed. 2. Chemical Rubber, Cleveland.

General References

[2] Andrews, S., and C. L. A. Schmidt. 1927. J. Biol. Chem. 73:651.

[3] Ashley, J. N., and C. B. Harington. 1930. J. Chem. Soc. London, p. 2586.

[4] Bergel, F. 1948. Biochem. Soc. Symp. 1:78.

[5] Block, R. J., et al. 1958. A Manual of Paper Chromatography and Paper Electrophoresis. Ed. 2. Academic Press, New York.

[6] California Foundation for Biochemical Research. 1958. Properties of the L- (Natural) Amino Acids. Rev. ed. Los Angeles.

[7] Cohn, E. J., and J. T. Edsall. 1943. Proteins, Amino Acids and Peptides. Reinhold, New York.

[8] Du Vigneaud, V., et al. 1942. J. Biol. Chem. 143:59.

[9] Dyer, H. M. 1938. Ibid. 124:519.

[10] Greenstein, J. P., and M. Winitz. 1961. Chemistry of the Amino Acids. J. Wiley, New York. v. 1-3.

[11] Howe, E. E. 1951. Amino Acids and Proteins. C. C. Thomas, Springfield, Ill. p. 3.

[12] Pollock, J. R. A., and R. Stevens, ed. 1965. Dictionary of Organic Compounds. Ed. 4. Oxford Univ. Press, New York.

[13] Riegel, B., and V. du Vigneaud. 1935. J. Biol. Chem. 112:149.

[14] Schmidt, C. L. A. 1945. The Chemistry of the Amino Acids and Proteins. C. C. Thomas, Springfield, Ill.

[15] Weast, R. C., ed. 1971-72. Handbook of Chemistry and Physics. Ed. 52. Chemical Rubber, Cleveland.

[16] West, E. S., et al. 1966. Textbook of Biochemistry. Ed. 4. Macmillan, New York.

[17] Wichers, E. 1952. J. Amer. Chem. Soc. 74:2447.

SOURCE: ALTMAN, P. L., and DITTMER, D. S. (EDITORS). 1972. Biology Data Book, Vol. 1. Federation of American Societies for Experimental Biology, Bethesda, Maryland.

AMINO ACIDS II

TABLE 2.A.8

STRUCTURE OF AMINO ACIDS

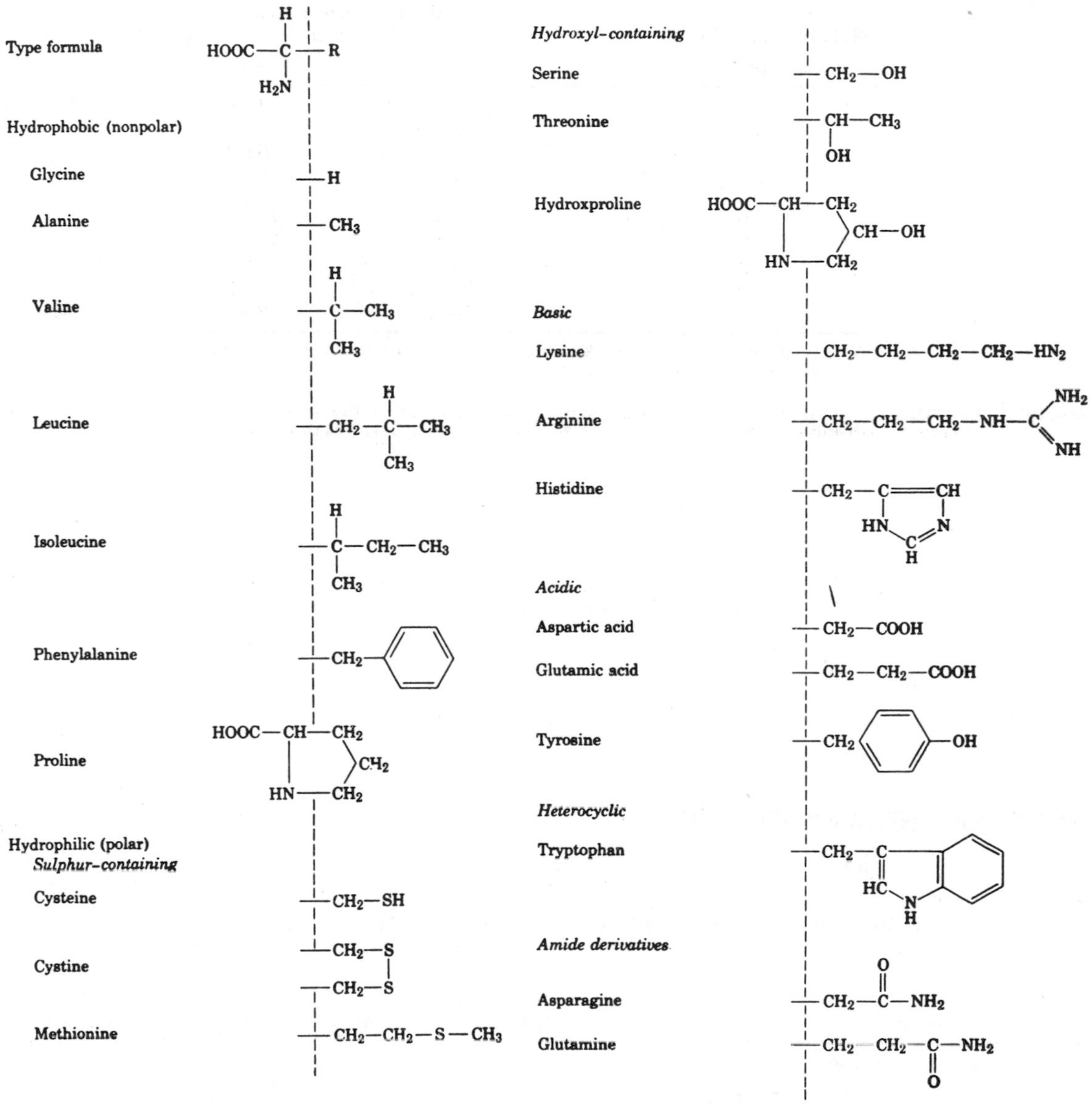

SOURCE: PAUL, P. C. and PALMER, H. H. 1972. Food Theory and Applications. John Wiley & Sons, New York.

AMMONIA SOLUTIONS

TABLE 2.A.9

VARIOUS STRENGTHS OF AMMONIA SOLUTIONS

NH_3 Strength Desired	Reagent Ammonia Required	
Grams per Liter	Grams	Ml
5	18.52	20.6
10	37.04	41.1
15	55.55	61.7
20	74.07	82.3
25	92.59	102.9
50	185.18	205.8
75	277.77	308.6
100	370.37	411.5
150	555.55	617.3
200	740.74	823.0

NOTE: Ammonia solutions: Specification requires not $<27\%$ NH_3 by wt. Sp gr = 0.9. Mix and dil. to 1 liter.

SOURCE: EDITORIAL BOARD. 1975. Official Methods of Analysis of the Association of Official Analytical Chemists, 12th Edition. Association of Official Analytical Chemists, Washington, D.C.

AMYLOSE AND AMYLOPECTIN

TABLE 2.A.10

SIZE AND PROPORTION OF AMYLOSE AND AMYLOPECTIN IN SOME STARCHES

Plant Species	Amylose (%)	Glucose Residues per Molecule	Amylopectin (%)	Glucose Residues per Molecule
Tubers, roots or rhizome				
Tapioca	17	980	83	18,600
Potato	22	980	78	—
Lily	34	640	66	18,600
Seeds				
Corn, hybrid	22	490	78	30,850
Corn, waxy	0	—	100	—
Wheat	24	540	76	24,700
Rice	17	—	83	—

SOURCE: MALLETTE, M. F., ALTHOUSE, P. M., and CLAGETT, C. O. Biochemistry of Plants and Animals. John Wiley & Sons, New York.

AMYLOPECTIN I

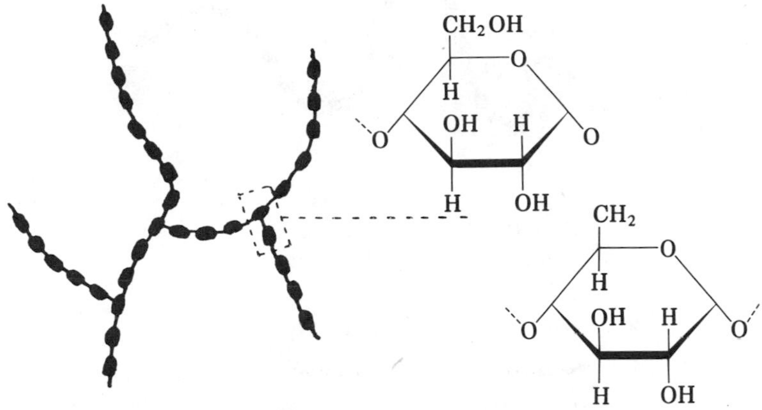

FIG. 2.A.1. CONFORMATION AND STRUCTURE OF AMYLOPECTIN

SOURCE: SONE, T. 1972. Consistency of Foodstuffs. D. Reidel Publishing Co., Boston.

AMYLOPECTIN II

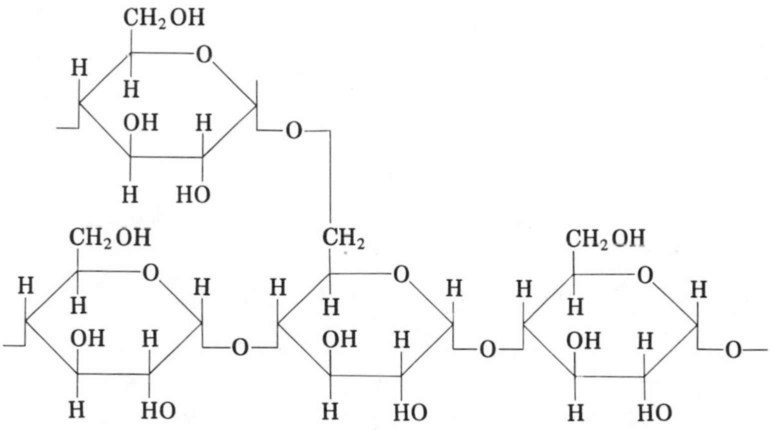

FIG. 2.A.2. POINT OF BRANCHING OF AMYLOPECTIN MOLECULE

SOURCE: POMERANZ, Y. (EDITOR). 1971. Wheat Chemistry and Technology, 2nd Edition. American Association of Cereal Chemists, St. Paul.

AMYLOSE I

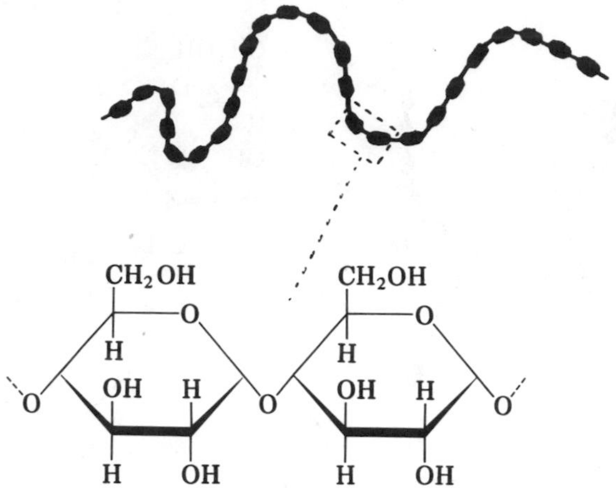

FIG. 2.A.3. CONFORMATION AND STRUCTURE OF AMYLOSE

SOURCE: SONE, T. 1972. Consistency of Foodstuffs. D. Reidel Publishing Co., Boston.

AMYLOSE II

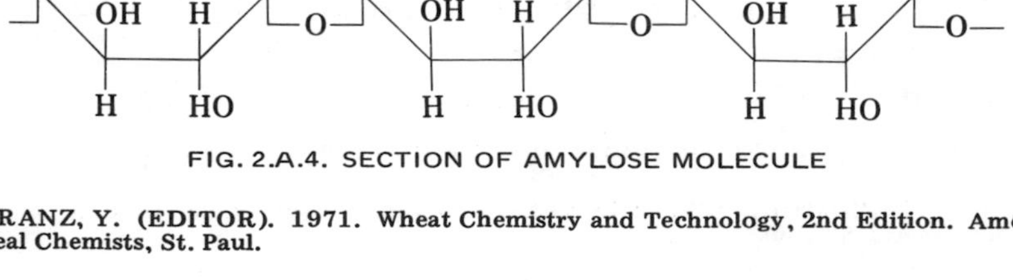

FIG. 2.A.4. SECTION OF AMYLOSE MOLECULE

SOURCE: POMERANZ, Y. (EDITOR). 1971. Wheat Chemistry and Technology, 2nd Edition. American Association of Cereal Chemists, St. Paul.

ANIMAL FOODS, COMPOSITION

TABLE 2.A.11

FOODS OF ANIMAL ORIGIN: COMPOSITION

(Values are per 100 g of Edible Portion of Fresh, Uncooked Food, Unless Otherwise Specified; Values Based on Inadequate Evidence are Enclosed in Parentheses)

	Food	Water	Food Energy	Protein	Fat	Carbohydrate Total	Carbohydrate Fiber	Ash	Ca	Fe	P	Vitamin A	Ascorbic acid	Niacin	Riboflavin	Thiamine
		g	Cal	g	g	g	g	g	mg	mg	mg	I. U.	mg	mg	mg	mg
	Dairy Products															
1	Butter	15.5	716	0.6	81	0.4	0	2.5	20	0	16	3300[1]	0	0.1	0.01	Trace
2	Buttermilk	90.5	36	3.5	0.1	5.1	0	0.8	(118)	0.1	93	Trace	1	0.1	0.18	0.04
3	Cheese: Cheddar	37	398	25.0	32.2	2.1	0	3.7	725	1.0	495	1400	(0)	Trace	0.42	0.02
4	Cottage	76.5	95	19.5	0.5	2.0	0	1.5	96	0.3	189	(20)	(0)	(0.1)	0.31	0.02
5	Cream	51	371	9.0	37.0	2.0	0	1.0	68	0.2	97	(1450)	(0)	0.1	0.22	(0.01)
6	Swiss	39	370	27.5	28.0	1.7	0	3.8	925	0.9	563	1450	(0)	(0.1)	0.40	0.01
7	Cream, light	72.5	204	2.9	20.0	4.0	0	0.6	97	0.1	77	830	1	0.1	0.14	0.03
8	Milk, cow: whole	87	68	3.5	3.9	4.9	0	0.7	118	0.1	93	(160)	1	0.1	0.17	0.04
9	Skimmed	90.5	36	3.5	0.1	5.1	0	0.8	123	0.1	97	Trace	1	0.1	0.18	0.04
10	Milk, goat	87.4	67	3.3	4.0	4.6	0	0.7	129	0.1	106	(160)	1	0.3	0.11	0.04
	Meats															
11	Beef: chuck	65	224	18.6	16	0	0	0.9	11	2.8	167	(0)	0	4.5	0.17	0.08
12	Flank	61	247	19.9	18	0	0	0.9	12	3.0	186	(0)	0	4.8	0.18	0.09
13	Hamburger	55	321	16.0	28	0	0	0.8	9	2.4	128	(0)	0	3.8	0.14	0.07
14	Heart	77.6	108	16.9	3.7	0.7	0	1.1	9	4.6	203	30	6	7.8	0.89	0.58
15	Kidney	74.9	141	15.0	8.1	0.9	0	1.1	9	7.9	221	1150	13	6.4	2.55	0.37
16	Liver	69.7	136	19.7	3.2	6.0	0	1.4	7	6.6	358	43,900	31	13.7	3.33	0.26
17	Porterhouse	58	296	16.4	25	0	0	0.8	10	2.5	134	(0)	0	3.9	0.15	0.07
18	Rib roast	59	282	17.4	23	0	0	0.8	10	2.6	149	(0)	0	4.2	0.15	0.07
19	Round	69	182	19.5	11	0	0	1.0	11	2.9	180	(0)	0	4.7	0.17	0.08
20	Rump	55	322	16.2	28	0	0	0.8	9	2.4	131	(0)	0	3.9	0.14	0.07
21	Sirloin	62	254	17.3	20	0	0	0.9	10	2.6	147	(0)	0	4.2	0.15	0.07
22	Tongue	68	207	16.4	15.0	0.4	(0)	0.9	9	2.8	187	(0)	(0)	5.0	0.29	0.12
23	Brains	78.9	125	10.4	8.6	0.8	0	1.4	16	3.6	330	0	18	4.4	0.26	0.23
24	Lamb: leg roast	63.7	235	18.0	17.5	0	0	0.9	10	2.7	213	(0)	0	5.2	0.22	0.16
25	Liver	70.8	136	21.0	3.9	2.9	0	1.4	8	12.6	364	50,500	33	16.9	3.28	0.40
26	Kidney	77.8	105	16.6	3.3	1.0	0	1.3	13	9.2	237	(1150)	13	7.4	2.42	0.51
27	Shoulder roast	58.3	295	15.6	25.3	0	0	0.8	9	2.3	155	(0)	0	4.5	0.19	0.14
28	Pork: bacon	20	630	9.1	65	1.1	0	4.3	13	0.8	108	(0)	0	1.9	0.12	0.38
29	Ham, fresh	53	344	15.2	31.0	0	0	0.8	9	2.3	168	(0)	0	4.0	0.18	0.74
30	Ham, smoked	42	389	16.9	35.0	(0.3)	0	5.4	10	2.5	136	(0)	0	4.0	0.19	0.70
31	Heart	76.8	117	16.9	4.8	0.4	0	1.1	35	2.7	132	30	6	6.0	1.24	0.43
32	Kidney	77.1	114	16.3	4.6	0.8	0	1.2	11	8.0	246	130	13	9.8	1.74	0.58
33	Liver	72.3	134	19.7	4.8	1.7	0	1.5	10	18.0	362	14,200	23	16.7	2.98	0.40
34	Loin or chops	58	296	16.4	25	0	0	0.9	10	2.5	186	(0)	0	4.3	0.19	0.80
35	Salt pork, fat	8	783	3.9	85	0	(0)	3.5	Trace	0.6	Trace	(0)	0	(0.9)	(0.04)	(0.18)
36	Sausage	41.9	450	10.8	44.8	0	0	2.1	6	1.6	100	(0)	0	2.3	0.17	0.43
37	Spare rib, medium	53	351	14.6	32	0	0	0.8	8	2.2	158	(0)	0	3.8	0.17	0.71
38	Rabbit, domesticated	54	122	16	6	0	0	0.8	15	1.0	271			9.9	0.04	0.06
39	Seal, canned	66	183	19.1	10.6	1.4				11.4				4.9	0.09	0.04
40	Veal: cutlet	70	164	19.5	9.0	0	0	1.0	11	2.9	200	(0)	0	6.5	0.26	0.14
41	Leg roast	68	186	19.1	12.2	0	0	1.0	11	2.9	206	0	0	6.3	0.27	0.17
42	Liver	71	141	19.0	4.9	4	0	1.3	6	10.6	343	22,500	36	16.1	3.12	0.21
43	Shoulder roast	70	173	19.4	10.0	0	0	1.0	11	2.9	199	(0)	0	6.5	0.26	0.14
44	Stew meat	64	231	18.3	17.0	0	0	0.9	11	2.7	182	(0)	0	6.1	0.24	0.13
45	Venison	73	140	20	6.0	0	0	1.0	12	3.0	216					0.14
	Poultry and Eggs															
46	Chicken: broiler	71.2	151	20.2	7.2	0	0	1.1	14	1.5	200	(0)	(0)	10.2	0.16	0.08
47	Heart	69.6	157	20.5	7.0	1.6	0	1.3	23	1.7	142	30	6	5.2	0.91	0.12
48	Liver	69.6	141	22.1	4.0	2.6	0	1.7	16	7.4	240	32,200	20	11.8	2.46	0.20
49	Roaster	66.0	200	20.2	12.6	0	0	1.0	14	1.5	200	(0)	(0)	8.0	0.16	0.08
50	Egg, whole	74.0	162	12.8	11.5	0.7	0	1.0	54	2.7	210	1140	0	0.1	0.29	0.10
51	Egg white	87.8	50	10.8	0	0.8	0	0.6	6	0.2	17	(0)	0	0.1	0.26	0
52	Egg yolk	49.4	361	16.3	31.9	0.7	0	1.7	147	7.2	586	3210	0	Trace	0.35	0.27
53	Duck	54	326	16.1	29	0	0	1.3	9	2.4	172	0	0	6.0	0.23	0.16
54	Goose	50	354	16.4	32	0	0	0.9	9	2.4	176		9	5.6		0.15
55	Squab	58	279	18.6	22.1	0	0	1.5	12	3.0	217					
56	Turkey	58.3	268	20.1	20.2	0	0	1.0	23	3.8	320	Trace	(0)	8.0	0.14	0.09
	Fish and Shellfish															
57	Bluefish	74.6	124	20.5	4.0	0	0	1.2	23	0.6	243			1.9	(0.09)	(0.12)
58	Clam	80.3	81	12.8	1.4	3.4		2.1	(96)	(7.0)	(139)	110		(1.6)	0.18	0.10
59	Cod	82.6	74	16.5	0.4	0	0	1.2	10	0.4	194	0	2	2.2	0.09	0.06
60	Crab	80.0	86	16.1	1.6	0.6		1.7	(39)	(0.8)	(160)			2.7	0.06	0.14
61	Eel	71.6	162	18.6	9.1	0	0	1.0	18	0.7	202	1800		1.4	0.37	0.28
62	Flounder	82.7	68	14.9	0.5	0	0	1.3	61	0.8	195			1.7	0.05	0.06
63	Haddock	80.7	79	18.2	0.1	0	0	1.4	23	0.7	197			2.4	0.08	0.05
64	Halibut	75.4	126	18.6	5.2	0	0	1.0	13	0.7	211	440		9.2	0.06	0.07
65	Herring, Atlantic	67.2	191	18.3	12.5	0	0	2.7		1.1	256	110		3.4	0.15	0.02
66	Herring, Pacific	79.6	94	16.6	2.6	0	0	1.3				100		(2.2)	0.22	0.02
67	Lobster	79.2	88	16.2	1.9	0.5	0	2.2	61	0.6	184			(1.9)	0.06	(0.13)
68	Mackerel	68.1	188	18.7	12.0	0	0	1.2	5	1.0	239	(450)		8.4	0.35	0.15
69	Oyster	80.5	84	9.8	2.1	5.6		2.0	94	5.6	143	320		1.2	0.20	0.15
70	Perch, yellow	80	88	18.7	0.9	0	0	1.2	20	1.0	215			1.7	0.07	0.09
71	Salmon	63.4	223	17.4	16.5	0	0	1.0		(0.9)	(289)	310	9	7.2	0.23	0.10
72	Sardine, canned	57.4	214	25.7	11.0	1.2		(4.7)	386	2.7	586	220	(0)	4.8	0.17	0.02
73	Scallop	80.3	78	14.8	0.1	3.4	0	1.4	26	1.8	208	0		1.4	0.10	(0.04)
74	Shad	70.2	168	18.7	9.8	0	0	1.4		0.5	260			(8.4)	0.24	(0.15)
75	Shrimp, canned	66.2	127	26.8	1.4	0		5.8	115	3.1	263	60	(0)	2.2	0.03	0.01
76	Swordfish	75.8	118	19.2	4.0	0	0	1.3	19	0.9	195	1580		9.1	0.05	0.05
77	Tuna, canned	60.0	198	29.0	8.2	0	0	2.7	(8)	1.4	(351)	80	(0)	12.8	0.12	0.05
78	Whitefish	70	156	22.9	6.5	0	0	1.6	25	1.3	263			(4.2)	(0.09)	(0.09)

/1/ Year-round average.

SOURCE: SPECTOR, W. S. (EDITOR). Handbook of Biological Data. Federation of American Societies for Experimental Biology, Bethesda, Maryland.

ANTIBIOTIC STANDARDS

TABLE 2.A.11

INTERNATIONAL STANDARDS FOR ANTIBIOTICS

Substance	Defined Potency, IU/mg	Equivalence of 1 IU to American μg	Calculated Purity of Standard on Basis of American μg%
Penicillin (sodium salt)	1670	Not used	99[1]
Phenoxymethylpenicillin (free acid)	1695	Not used	99[1]
Streptomycin (sulfate)	780	1 μg of base	97.5
Dihydrostreptomycin (sulfate)	760	1 μg of base	95.1
Bacitracin	55	Not used	Not known
Tetracycline (hydrochloride)	990	1 μg hydrochloride	99.0
Chlortetracycline (hydrochloride)	1000	1 μg hydrochloride	100
Oxytetracycline (base dehydrate)	900	1 μg anhydrous base	97.1
Erythromycin (base)	950	1 μg anhydrous base	95
Polymixin B	7874	Not used	Not known

[1]Independent estimate (Lightbown 1961).

SOURCE: GRANT, J. (EDITOR). 1969. Hackh's Chemical Dictionary, 4th Edition. McGraw-Hill Book Co., New York.

ANTIOXIDANT ACTIVITY

TABLE 2.A.12

COMPARATIVE ANTIOXIDANT ACTIVITY

Additive	(%)	Schaal Oven, Thin Layer, 45°C (Days to Reach 20 Meq Peroxides) Chicken Fat	Pork Fat
None		8	3
BHA	0.01	14	14
BHA	0.02	20	28
BHT	0.02	15	18
Tenox 2	0.05	28	32
α-Tocopherol	0.02	13	15
α-Tocopherol	0.05	13	15
α-Tocopherol	0.2	10	15
α-Tocopherol } Ascorbyl Palmitate }	0.02 0.02	28	28
γ-Tocopherol	0.02	29	37
γ-Tocopherol	0.05	40	58
γ-Tocopherol	0.2	46	61
γ-Tocopherol } Ascorbyl Palmitate }	0.02 0.02	53	67
Ascorbyl Palmitate	0.02	10	9

SOURCE: BAUERNFEIND, J. C. 1975. Tocopherols. *In* Encyclopedia of Food Technology. A. H. Johnson and M. S. Peterson (Editors). AVI Publishing Co., Westport, Conn.

ANTIOXIDANT MIXTURES

TABLE 2.A.13

SOME TYPICAL COMMERCIAL ANTIOXIDANT PREPARATIONS

	BHA[1] (%)	BHT[2] (%)	Propyl Gallate (%)	TBHQ[3] (%)	Propylene Glycol (%)	Citric Acid (%)	Vegetable Oil (%)	Glyceryl Mono-oleate (%)	Sorbitan Mono-stearate (%)	Water (%)	Ethyl Alcohol (%)	Citrate Mono-glyceride (%)
Eastman Tenox BHT		X										
Eastman Tenox BHA	X											
Eastman Tenox 2	20		6		70	4						
Eastman Tenox 4	20	20					60					
Eastman Tenox 6	10	10	6		12	6	28	20	8			
Eastman Tenox 7	28		12		34	6		20				
Eastman Tenox 20				20	70	10						
Eastman Tenox 22	20			6	70	4						
Eastman Tenox 26	10	10		6	12	6	28	28				
Eastman Tenox R	20				60	20						
Eastman Tenox S-1			20		70	10						
UOP-BHA	X											
UOP Sustane		X										
UOP-Sustane 3F	66.7		20			13.3						
UOP-Sustane 6	18	22					60					
UOP-Sustane E	10						40		2.5	47.5		
UOP-Sustane W	10	10	6		8	6	28	30				
UOP-Sustane P	20	20									60	
Shell Ionol		X										
Griffiths G-16	6	13.5	5.5		X	2						X

[1] Butylated Hydroxy Anisole.
[2] Butylated Hydroxy Toluene.
[3] Tertiary Butylated Hydroquinone.

NOTE: Monotertiary butylhydroquinone has recently been introduced as a food grade antioxidant. Its advantages are claimed to be low odor, good fat solubility, and no discoloration in the presence of iron.

SOURCE: MORSE, R. E. 1975. Antioxidants. *In* Encyclopedia of Food Technology. A. H. Johnson and M. S. Peterson (Editors). AVI Publishing Co., Westport, Conn.

ANTIOXIDANT STRUCTURE

TABLE 2.A.14

LIPID ANTIOXIDANTS ACCEPTABLE FOR USE IN HUMAN FOOD IN THE UNITED STATES

Name	Use Limit	Structure
Butylated hydroxyanisole	0.02% of fat content	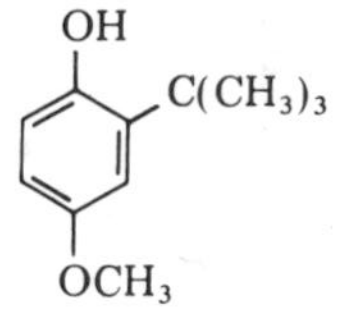
Butylated hydroxytoluene	0.02% of fat content	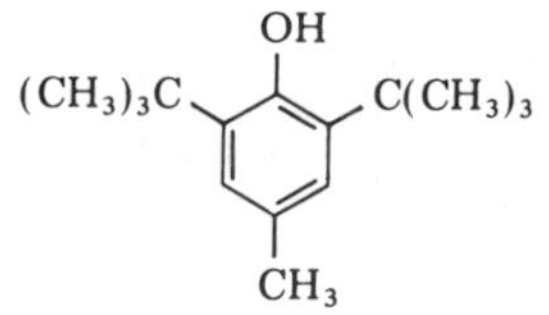
Dilauryl thiodipropionate	0.02% of fat content	$CH_2-CH_2-COO-CH_2-(CH_2)_{10}-CH_3$ S $CH_2-CH_2-COO-CH_2-(CH_2)_{10}-CH_3$
Thiodipropionic acid	0.02% of fat content	CH_2-CH_2-COOH S CH_2-CH_2-COOH
Propyl gallate	0.02% of fat content	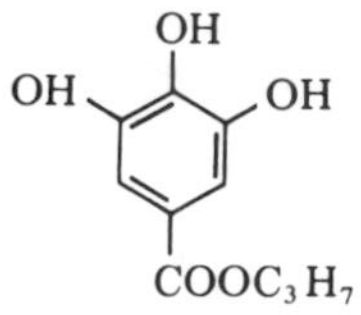

Gum guaiacol	0.1% in fat	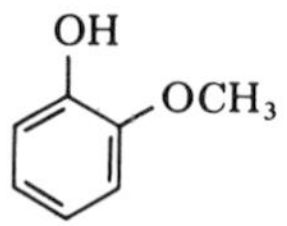
Tocopherols	GMP[1]	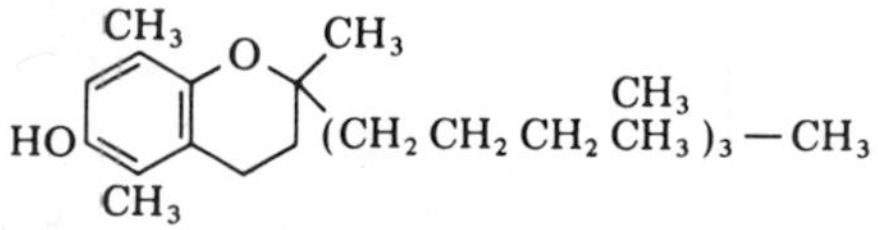
Ethoxyquin	100 ppm in paprika and chili	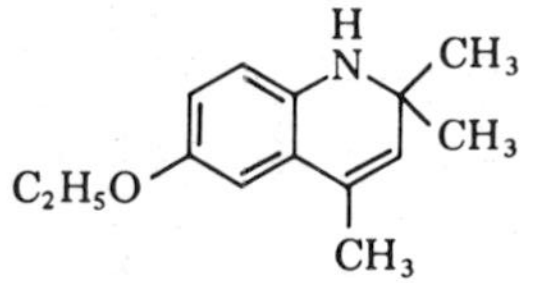
2,4,5 Trihydroxy butyrophenone	0.02% of fat content	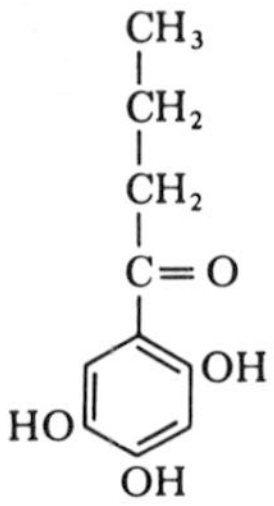
4 hydroxy methyl-2, 6-di tert-butylphenone	0.02% of fat content	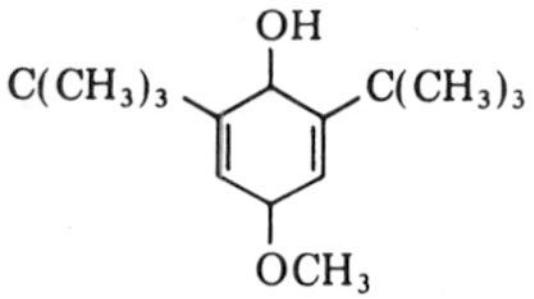

[1] In accordance with good manufacturing practices.

SOURCE: MORSE, R. E. 1975. Antioxidants. *In* Encyclopedia of Food Technology. A. H. Johnson and M. S. Peterson (Editors). AVI Publishing Co., Westport, Conn.

ANTIOXIDANTS, FORMULAS

TABLE 2.A.15

COMPOSITION AND STRUCTURE OF SEVERAL ANTIOXIDANTS

Compound	Common Designation	Structure Formula
Propyl gallate	PG	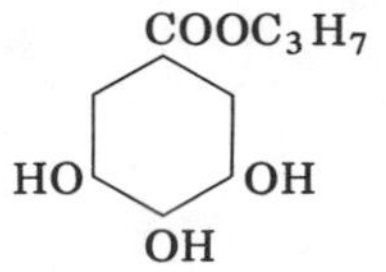
		Commercial BHA is a mixture of two isomers: 2-*tert*-butyl-4-hydroxyanisole 3-*tert*-butyl-4-hydroxyanisole
Butylated hydroxyanisole (3-isomer)	BHA	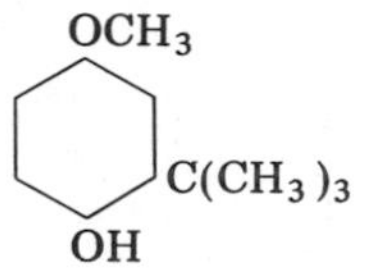
Butylated hydroxytoluene 2-6-*tert*-butyl-p-cresol	BHT	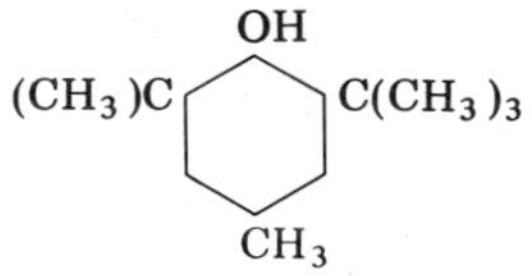
Citric acid	—	CH_2COOH | $HOC-COOH$ | CH_2COOH
Nordihydroguaiaretic acid	NDGA	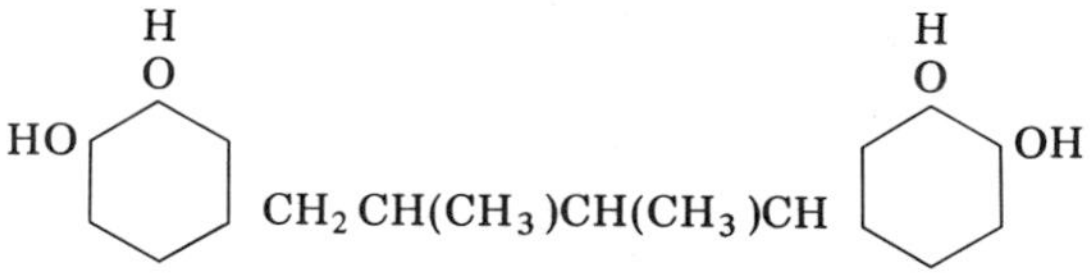

SOURCE: MAHLENBACHER, C. V. 1960. The Analysis of Fats and Oils. Garrard Publishing Co., Champaign, Illinois.

ASCORBIC ACID (REQUIREMENTS AND SOURCES)

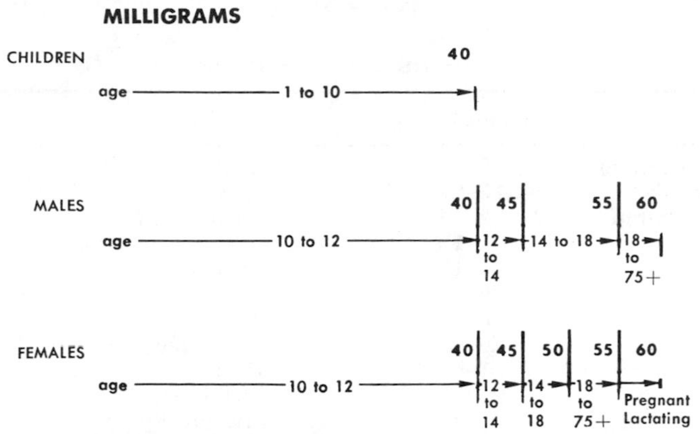

GOOD SOURCES†

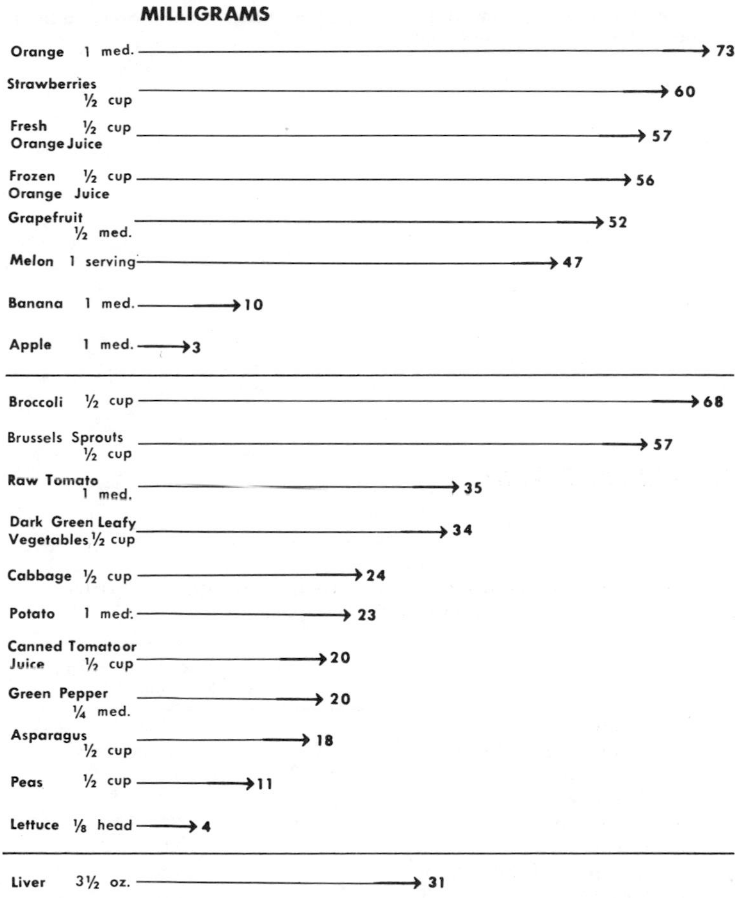

†Average nutrient content as food is served. (Note 3½ oz equals approximately 100 g.)

SOURCE: Lessons on Meat. (1974). National Live Stock and Meat Board, Chicago.

ASCORBIC ACID, FOOD

TABLE 2.A.16

ASCORBIC ACID IN FRUITS

	(mg per 100 g)		(mg per 100 g)
Apple, Blenheim Orange	3	Lemon	14-66
Bramley Seedling	16-22	Lime	32-58
Cox's Orange Pippin	2-14	Loganberry	20-48
Banana	1-15	Melon, Cantaloupe	15-53
Cherry	3-17	Orange	16-99
Currant (black)	136-353	Orange Juice	28-89
(red)	50	Pear	1-10
Gooseberry	28-47	Pineapple	10-63
Grape	1-4	Plum	0.5-5
Grapefruit	26-65	Raspberry	30
Greengage	0.5-7	Strawberry	46-77
Haw	49-500	Tangerine	10-36
Hip	10-1870	Tomato	13-39

SOURCE: SINCLAIR, H. M. and HOLLINGSWORTH, D. F. 1969. Hutchison's Food and the Principles of Nutrition. Edward Arnold (Publishers), London, England.

ASCORBIC ACID, FRUIT JUICES

TABLE 2.A.17

ASCORBIC ACID SUPPLIED BY FOUR OUNCES OF VARIOUS CANNED FRUIT JUICES

Fruit	Ascorbic Acid Mg
Apple	1.5
Apricot nectar	1.5
Pineapple	10
Tomato	20
Tangerine	32
Grapefruit	34
Orange and grapefruit	48
Orange	53

SOURCE: WOODROOF, J. G. and PHILLIPS, G. F. (EDITORS). 1974. Modified Fruit Juice Beverages. *In* Beverages: Carbonated and Noncarbonated. AVI Publishing Co., Westport, Conn.

ASPARAGUS TERMS

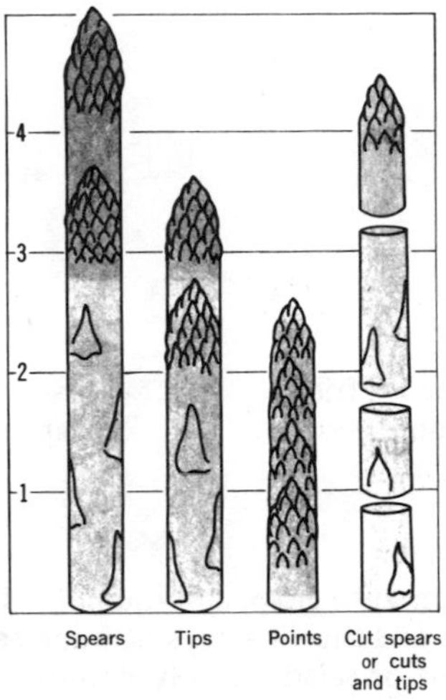

FIG. 2.A.5. IDENTIFICATION OF CUTS OF ASPARAGUS USED FOR PROCESSING CANNED AND FROZEN PRODUCTS

SOURCE: How to Buy Canned and Frozen Vegetables. (1969) USDA Home and Garden Bull. *167*.

B

BACON DRESSING

Ingredients

2 slices of bacon, fried
Bacon fat from bacon
¼ cup vinegar
2 tbsp sugar (optional)
½ tsp salt

Procedure

Fry the bacon until crisp, and crumble. Into the same pan (with the fat) add the vinegar, sugar and salt. Stir and pour hot over greens or salad. Finely chopped onions often are added to this type of salad dressing.

SOURCE: KINTNER, T. C. and MANGEL, M. Vinegars and salad dressings. Univ. Missouri. Agric. Exp. Sta. Bull. *631*.

BACTERIA ON CHICKENS AT VARIOUS HOLDING TEMPERATURES

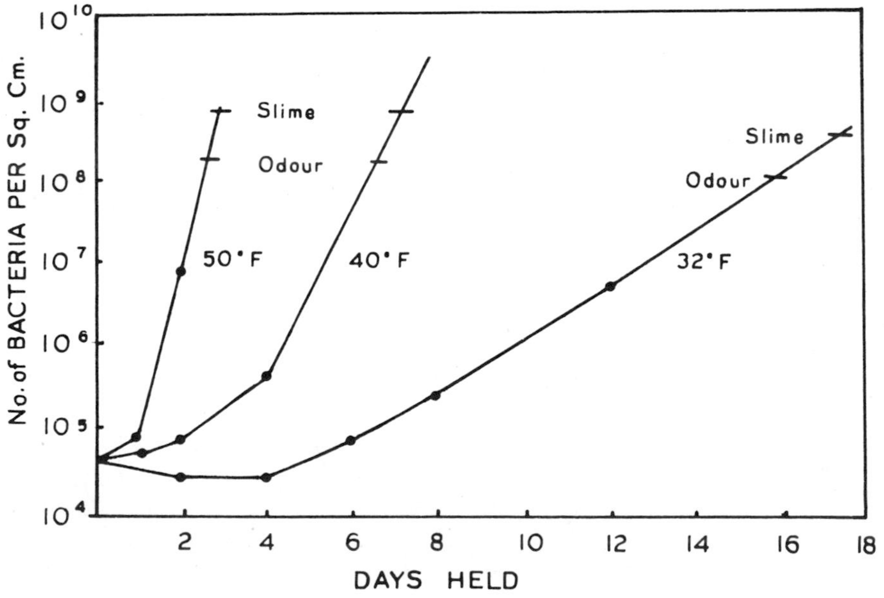

FIG. 2.B.1. GROWTH OF BACTERIA ON CHICKENS AT 32°, 40° AND 50°F

SOURCE: SNYDER, E. S., and ORR, H. L. Poultry Meat. Publ. *9*, Ontario Department of Agriculture, Canada.

BACTERIA, MOLDS AND YEASTS

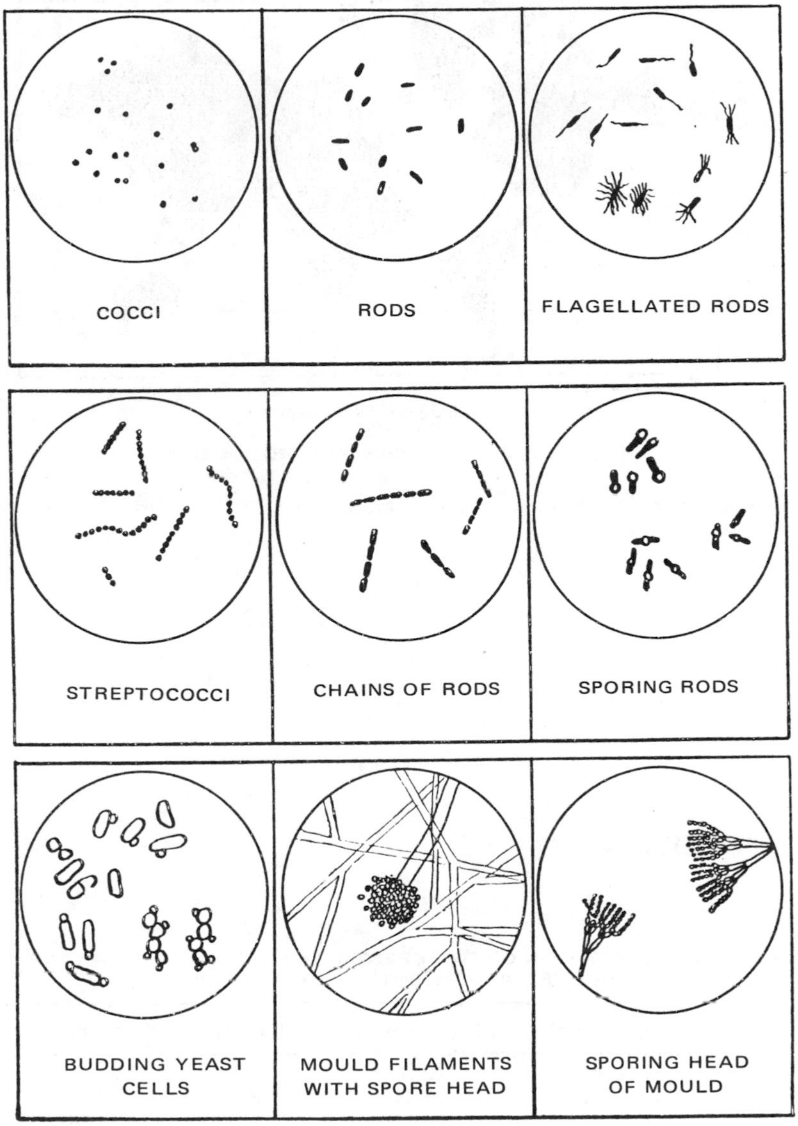

FIG. 2.B.2. MICROSCOPIC APPEARANCE AND IDENTIFICATION OF MOLDS AND YEASTS

SOURCE: GRAHAM-RACK, B. and BINSTED, R. Hygiene in Food Manufacturing and Handling. Food Trade Press, London, England.

BANANA, AREAS OF PRODUCTION

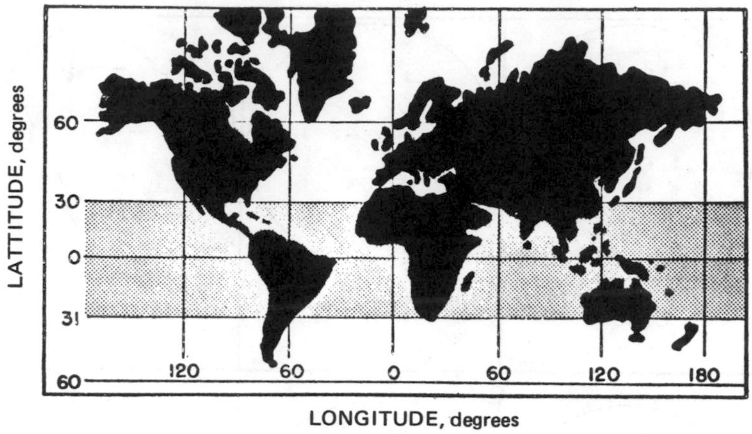

FIG. 2.B.3. ZONE OF BANANA PRODUCTION.

SOURCE: Von Loesecke, H. W. Bananas. *In* Economic Crops, Vol. *1*. Z. I. Kertesz (Editor). John Wiley & Sons, New York.

BANANAS, COMPOSITION

TABLE 2.B.1

CHEMICAL COMPOSITION OF DIFFERENT VARIETIES OF RIPE BANANAS[1] EXPRESSED AS PERCENTAGE OF FRESH PULP

Constituent	Gros Michel	Lady Finger	Lacatan	Plantain	Red[3] Banana
Moisture	75.9	70.6	71.6	63.8	73.3
Reducing sugars	10.73	6.19	8.15	18.89	4.10
Nonreducing sugars	6.12	13.38	10.01	0.00	16.08
Starch	2.93	4.13	6.54	11.69	4.12
Total carbohydrates	19.78	23.70	24.70	30.58	24.30
Protein	0.81	1.49	1.04	1.16	0.48
Crude fat	0.47	0.30	0.40	0.30	0.24
Pectin	0.34	0.57	0.41	0.43	0.62
Protopectin	0.34	0.29	0.35	0.37	0.43
Ash	0.76	0.70	0.77	0.85	0.84
Acidity, cc.[2]	4.46	4.27	4.06	9.00	4.05

[1] These analyses are for fruit the peel of which had developed a full yellow color.
[2] Cubic centimeters of *N* NaOH required to neutralize 100 g of pulp.
[3] Unpublished data, J. T. Manion, United Fruit Co., Research Dept., 1933.

SOURCE: VON LOESECKE, H. W. Bananas. *In* Economic Crops, Vol. *1*. Z. I. Kertesz (Editor). John Wiley & Sons, New York.

BARREL SIZE

TABLE 2.B.2

CONVERSION TABLE FOR BARRELS

Compute Gallons for Liquids, Pounds for Solids	
Wine	31
Ale	36
Petroleum	42
Rosin	180
Flour	196
Butter	224
Pork, beef	200
Cement	376

SOURCE: GRANT, J. (EDITOR). 1969. Hackh's Chemical Dictionary, 4th Edition. McGraw-Hill Book Co., New York.

BEANS DRY, COOKING

TABLE 2.B.3

BOILING GUIDE FOR DRY BEANS, PEAS, AND LENTILS[1]

Vegetable (1 cup)	Amount of water	Approximate boiling time	Yield
	Cups	*Hours*	*Cups*
Black beans	3	2	2
Blackeye beans (blackeye peas, cowpeas)	2½	½	2½
Cranberry beans	3	2	2
Great Northern beans	2½	1 to 1½	2½
Kidney beans	3	2	2¾
Lentils	2	½	2½
Lima beans, large	2½	1	2½
Lima beans, small	2½	1	2
Navy (pea) beans	3	1½ to 2	2½
Peas, whole	2½	1	2½
Pinto beans	3	2	2½
Soybeans	4	2½	2½
Split peas	2	⅓	2½

[1] Soak before cooking.

SOURCE: Vegetables in Family Meals, USDA Home and Garden Bull. *105*, 1975.

BEANS, PEAS AND NUTS

TABLE 2.B.4

COMPOSITION OF BEANS, PEAS AND NUTS

Food, Approximate Measure, and Weight (in Grams)		Water (%)	Food Energy (Cal)	Protein (g)	Fat (Total Lipid) (g)
Mature Dry Beans and Peas, Nuts, Peanuts; Related Products					
Almonds, shelled	1 cup (142 g)	5	850	26	77
Beans, dry:					
Common varieties, such as Great Northern, navy, and others, canned:					
Red	1 cup (256 g)	76	230	15	1
White, with tomato or molasses:					
With pork	1 cup (261 g)	69	330	16	7
Without pork	1 cup (261 g)	69	315	16	1
Lima, cooked	1 cup (192 g)	64	260	16	1
Brazil nuts, broken pieces	1 cup (140 g)	5	905	20	92
Cashew nuts, roasted	1 cup (135 g)	5	770	25	65
Coconut:					
Fresh, shredded	1 cup (97 g)	50	330	3	31
Dried, shredded, sweetened	1 cup (62 g)	3	345	2	24
Cowpeas or blackeye peas, dry, cooked	1 cup (248 g)	80	190	13	1
Peanuts, roasted, shelled:					
Halves	1 cup (144 g)	2	840	30	71
Chopped	1 tbsp (9 g)	2	50	2	4
Peanut butter	1 tbsp (16 g)	2	90	4	8
Peas, split, dry, cooked	1 cup (250 g)	70	290	20	1
Pecans:					
Halves	1 cup (108 g)	3	740	10	77
Chopped	1 tbsp (7.5 g)	3	50	1	5
Walnuts, shelled:					
Black or native, chopped	1 cup (126 g)	3	790	26	75
English or Persian:					
Halves	1 cup (100 g)	4	650	15	64
Chopped	1 tbsp (8 g)	4	50	1	5

SOURCE: INSTITUTE OF HOME ECONOMICS. Nutritive Value of Foods. USDA Home and Garden Bull. *72*.

Fatty Acids										
Saturated (Total) (g)	Unsaturated Oleic (g)	Unsaturated Linoleic (g)	Carbo-hydrate (g)	Cal-cium (mg)	Iron (mg)	Vitamin A Value (IU)	Thia-min (mg)	Ribo-flavin (mg)	Niacin (mg)	Ascorbic Acid (mg)
6	52	15	28	332	6.7	0	0.34	1.31	5.0	Tr
—	—	—	42	74	4.6	0	0.13	0.13	1.5	Tr
3	3	1	54	172	4.4	140	0.13	0.10	1.3	5
—	—	—	60	183	5.2	140	0.13	0.10	1.3	5
—	—	—	48	56	5.6	Tr	0.26	0.12	1.3	Tr
18	44	24	15	260	4.8	Tr	1.21	—	—	—
11	46	5	35	51	5.1	—	0.49	0.46	1.9	—
27	2	—	13	15	1.7	0	0.06	0.03	0.5	4
21	2	—	33	13	1.6	0	0.04	0.02	0.4	0
—	—	—	34	42	3.2	20	0.41	0.11	1.1	Tr
16	31	21	28	104	3.2	0	0.47	0.19	24.6	0
1	2	1	2	6	0.2	0	0.03	0.01	1.5	0
2	4	2	3	12	0.4	0	0.02	0.02	2.8	0
—	—	—	52	28	4.2	120	0.36	0.22	2.2	Tr
5	49	15	16	79	2.6	140	0.93	0.14	1.0	2
Tr	3	1	1	5	0.2	10	0.06	0.01	0.1	Tr
4	26	36	19	Tr	7.6	380	0.28	0.14	0.9	—
4	10	40	16	99	3.1	30	0.33	0.13	0.9	3
Tr	1	3	1	8	0.2	Tr	0.03	0.01	0.1	Tr

BEEF AND DUAL-PURPOSE CATTLE

TABLE 2.B.5

BREEDS AND THEIR CHARACTERISTICS

Breed	Place of Origin	Color	Distinctive Head Characteristics	Other Distinguishing Characteristics	Disqualifications; Comments
Beef Breeds:					
Angus	Scotland; in the northeastern counties of Aberdeen, Angus, Kincardine, and Forfar.	Black	Polled	Comparatively smooth coat of hair. Somewhat cyclindrical body.	Horns, scurs, or buttons. Red color. A noticeable amount of white above the underline, or in front of the navel, or on one or more legs. Calves from females less than 18 mo. of age when calf was dropped, or from bulls less than 6 mo. of age at the time of service.
Beefmasters (approx. ½ Brahman, and ¼ each Shorthorn and Hereford)	United States; on the Lasater Ranch, Falfurrias, Texas.	Red is the dominant color, but color is variable and is disregarded in selection.	The majority are horned, although a few are naturally polled.	Good milk producers under range conditions; heavy weaning and mature weights.	In order that each Beefmaster may be permanently identified with the breeder thereof, the breeds must use a prefix name such as "Jones Beefmaster," "Smith Beefmaster," etc., to designate his cattle. Thus, in a unique way, the responsibility for the continued improvement of the breed is placed squarely upon the individual breeder.
Belted Galloway	Scotland; in the southwestern district of Galloway.	Black with a brownish tinge, or dun; with a white belt completely encircling the body between the shoulders and the hooks.	Polled	Heavy coat of hair.	Red color, incomplete belt, other white marks, or scurs.

Brahman	India (but a distinct American breed has been created through the amalgamation of several Indian types, probably with a small infusion of European breeding).	Gray or red preferred; either solid color, or a gradual blending of the two. However, there are brown, black, white, and spotted Brahmans.	Drooping ears. A long face.	Prominent hump over the shoulders. An abundance of loose, pendulous skin under the throat and along the dewlap. A voice that resembles a grunt rather than a low.	Brindle, gruella (a smutty or blackish red), or albino color. Cryptorchid bull. Freemartin heifer. Inherited lameness. Dwarf or midget characteristics.
Brangus (3/8 Brahman 5/8 Angus)	United States; on Clear Creek Ranch, Welch, Okla., owned by Frank Buttram, beginning in 1942.	Black	Polled	Slight crest over the neck. Smooth, sleek coat.	Horns. Off-color. White on underline or legs.
Charbray (¾ Charolais, ¼ Brahman to 7/8 Charolais, 1/8 Brahman, solid color, golden to white are registered)	United States; in the Rio Grande Valley of Texas.	Light tan at birth, but usually change to a cream white in a few weeks.	Horned	A slight hint of the Brahman dewlap remains.	To qualify for registration, Charbray cattle must have at least ¼ Brahman. Charolais-Brahman of lesser percentages are recorded but not considered registered.
Charolais (usually spelled Charollais in France)	France; in the province of Charolles in Central France.	White or cream	Horned	Pink skin and mucus membranes.	The association disqualifies any animal that (1) has a black nose, (2) is spotted, or (3) has excessive dark skin pigmentation.
Devon	England; in the county of Devon.	Red; rich dark red is preferred.	Creamy white horns with black tips.	Yellow skin.	White other than in the switch or on small areas on the udder and belly.
Dexter	Ireland, in the southern and southwestern parts. They were named after their founder, a Mr. Dexter.	Black or red.	Head is rather long.	Small size and short legs. Mature bulls should not exceed 900 lbs. and mature cows 800 lbs. Some mature animals are less than 40 inches high.	Animals having white other than on the belly, switch, udder, or scrotum are disqualified for registry.

TABLE 2.B.5 (*Continued*)

Breed	Place of Origin	Color	Distinctive Head Characteristics	Other Distinguishing Characteristics	Disqualifications; Comments
Galloway	Scotland; in the southwestern province of Galloway.	Black; sometimes with a brownish or reddish tint; or dun.	Polled	Long curly hair.	White markings on feet or legs or above the underline.
Hereford	England; in the county of Hereford.	Red with white markings; white face and white on the underline, flank, crest, switch, breast, and below the knees and hocks. White back of the crops, high on the flanks, or too high on the legs is objectionable. Likewise, dark or smutty noses and red necks are frowned upon.			Calves from females less than 24 mo. of age when calf was dropped, or from bulls less than 12 mo. of age when service producing the calf occurred, cannot be registered.
Indu Brazil (Zebu)	Brazil	Light grey to silver grey; dun to red.	Prominent forehead and long drooping ears. Symmetrical horns drawing upward and to the rear.	Prominent hump over the shoulders. An abundance of loose, pendulous skin under the throat and along the dewlap. A voice that resembles a grunt rather than a low.	Brindle color combinations. White markings on the nose or switch. Absence of loose, thick, mellow skin. Weak and improperly formed hump.

Polled Hereford	United States; in Iowa.	Red with white markings, white face and white on underline, flank, crest, switch, breast, and below the knees and hocks. White back of the crops, high on the flanks, or too high on the legs is objectionable. Likewise, dark or smutty noses are frowned upon.	Polled		No calf is eligible for registration unless its sire was at least 12 mo. of age at the time of conception, and its dam at least 24 mo. of age at the time of calving. Horned animals.
Polled Shorthorn	United States; in the north central states, chiefly Ohio and Indiana.	Red, white or any combination of red and white. A "smutty nose" or dark nose is objectionable.	Polled		Horned animals.
Red Angus	British Isles[1]	Red	Polled	Similar to black Angus, except for recessive red color.	Any color other than red.
Red Brangus	United States; from Brahman Angus cross, made in 1946. Registry chartered in 1956.	Red	Broad head with slightly curved forehead and straight profile; with medium sized, moderately drooping ears.	Males have crest immediately forward of the shoulders. Smooth, sleek coat.	White spotting other than on the underline, brindling or roan on the body, or black skin or mucus membrane. Long hair, or tight hide. Undersized; too rangy or too compact. Mature females with underdeveloped teats or udders. Mature males with an excessive or pendulous sheath, or the absence of a sheath.

TABLE 2.B.5 (*Continued*)

Breed	Place of Origin	Color	Distinctive Head Characteristics	Other Distinguishing Characteristics	Disqualifications; Comments
Santa Gertrudis (5/8 Shorthorn and 3/8 Brahman)	United States; on the King Ranch in Texas.	Red or cherry red.		Hair should be short, straight, and slick. Hide should be loose, with surface area increased by neck folds and sheath or navel flap.	White or other spotting; fawn, cream, or brindle color; black skin; long wavy hair; absence of neck folds.
Scotch Highland (or Highland)	Scotland	Silver, golden, light red, brindle, black, or dun.	Long, widespread horns and heavy foretop.	Long, shaggy hair, short head and short legs.	Mottled or spotted with white (white permissible on tip of tail or on udder), or polled.
Shorthorn	England; in the northeastern counties of Durham, Northumberland, York, and Lincoln.	Red, white or any combination of red and white. A "smutty nose" or dark nose is objectionable.	Rather short, refined, incurving horns.		No calf is eligible for registration unless its sire and dam were each at least 18 mo. of age at the birth date of the calf.
Dual-Purpose Breeds:					
Milking Shorthorn	England	Red, white, or any combination of red and white.	Fine horns that are rather short.		No calf is eligible for registration unless its sire and dam were each at least 18 mo. of age at the birth date of the calf.
Red Poll	England; in the eastern middle coastal counties of Norfolk and Suffolk.	Red, varying from light to dark red. Any white except in the switch is discriminated against. Also a smoky nose or dark spots on the nose are objectionable.	Polled		White above underline, above switch of tail, or on legs. Bulls with white on underline forward of the navel region; or with only one testicle. Solid black or blue nose. Scurs or any horny growth. Total blindness.

[1]In England and Scotland, both reds and blacks are registered in same association, without distinction. In the U.S., however, red colored animals have been barred from registry in the American Angus Association since 1917. Red Angus Association of America was organized in 1954.

SOURCE: ENSMINGER, M. E. 1969. Animal Science. Interstate Printers & Publishers, Danville, Illinois. Reproduced with permission of the publisher.

BEEF, BONELESS CUTS

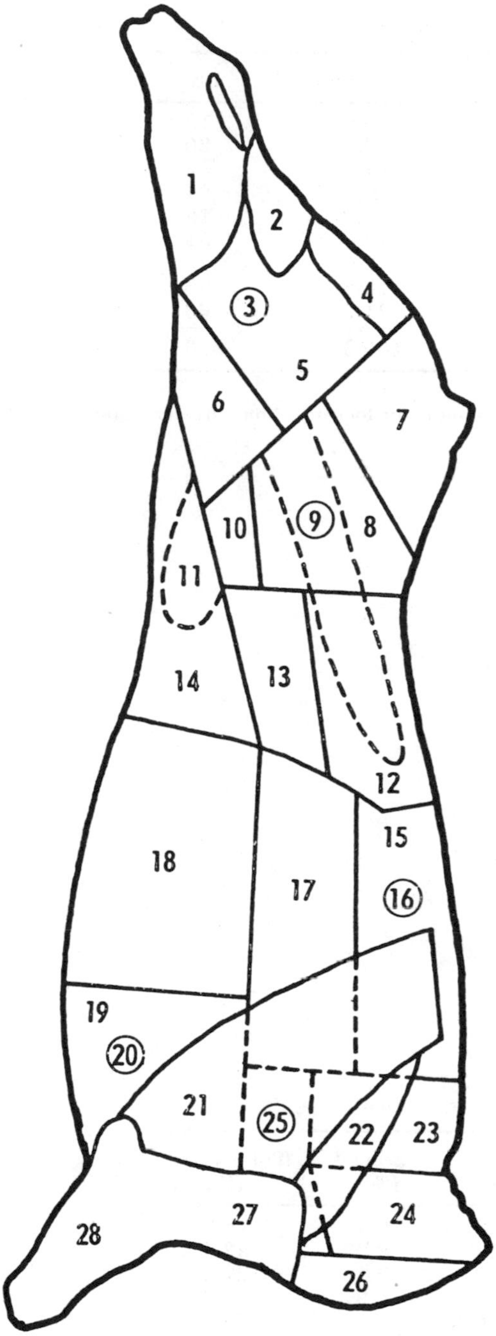

1. HINDSHANK MEAT
2. HEEL
3. TOP ROUND (INSIDE)
4. EYE OF ROUND
5. BOTTOM ROUND (OUTSIDE)
6. KNUCKLE
7. SIRLOIN RUMP
8. TOP SIRLOIN BUTT
9. TENDERLOIN
10. BOTTOM SIRLOIN BUTT
11. FLANK STEAK
12. LOIN STRIP
13. LOIN WING
14. FLANK MEAT
15. RIBEYE COVER
16. RIBEYE
17. RIB WING
18. SHORT PLATE
19. BRISKET
20. DECKLE
21. SHOULDER CLOD
22. CHUCK TENDER
23. CHUCK ROLL (BLADE END)
24. CHUCK ROLL (NECK END)
25. INSIDE CHUCK
26. NECK MEAT
27. ARMBONE MUSCLE
28. FORESHANK MEAT

RIB FINGERS
SKIRT
HANGING TENDER
TRIMMINGS

NOTE: Circled Numbers Lie Deeply

SOURCE: Food Inspection Specialist, Department of the Army, *TM 8-451*, 1969.

BEEF CARCASS, CUTTING YIELD

TABLE 2.B.6

BEEF CARCASS HALF (300 LB)

Retail Cut	% of Carcass	Lb
Porterhouse, T-bone & club steak	6.0	18
Sirloin steak	6.7	20
Round steak	11.0	33
Rib roast	8.0	24
Boneless rump	4.2	12
Chuck roast	17.0	51
Ground beef	7.5	23
Stew meat and miscellaneous	18.6	56
Bone, trimming and cutting loss	21.0	63
	100.0	300

SOURCE: SIMONDS, L. A. and VANSTAVERN, B. D. Buying meat for locker or home freezer. Coop. Ext. Serv., Ohio State Univ.

BEEF CARCASSES, YIELD GRADE

TABLE 2.B.7

RELATIVE COMPOSITION OF BEEF CARCASSES[1]

Yield Grade	Retail Cuts (%)	Fat (%)	Bone (%)	Total Waste (%)
1	82.0	7.6	10.4	18.0
2	77.4	12.7	9.9	22.6
3	72.8	17.8	9.4	27.2
4	68.2	22.9	8.9	31.8
5	63.6	28.0	8.4	36.4

[1] Examples only—individual carcasses will show minor variations.

SOURCE: SIMONDS, L. A. and VANSTAVERN, B. D. Buying meat for locker or home freezer. Coop. Ext. Serv., Ohio State Univ.

BEEF CHART

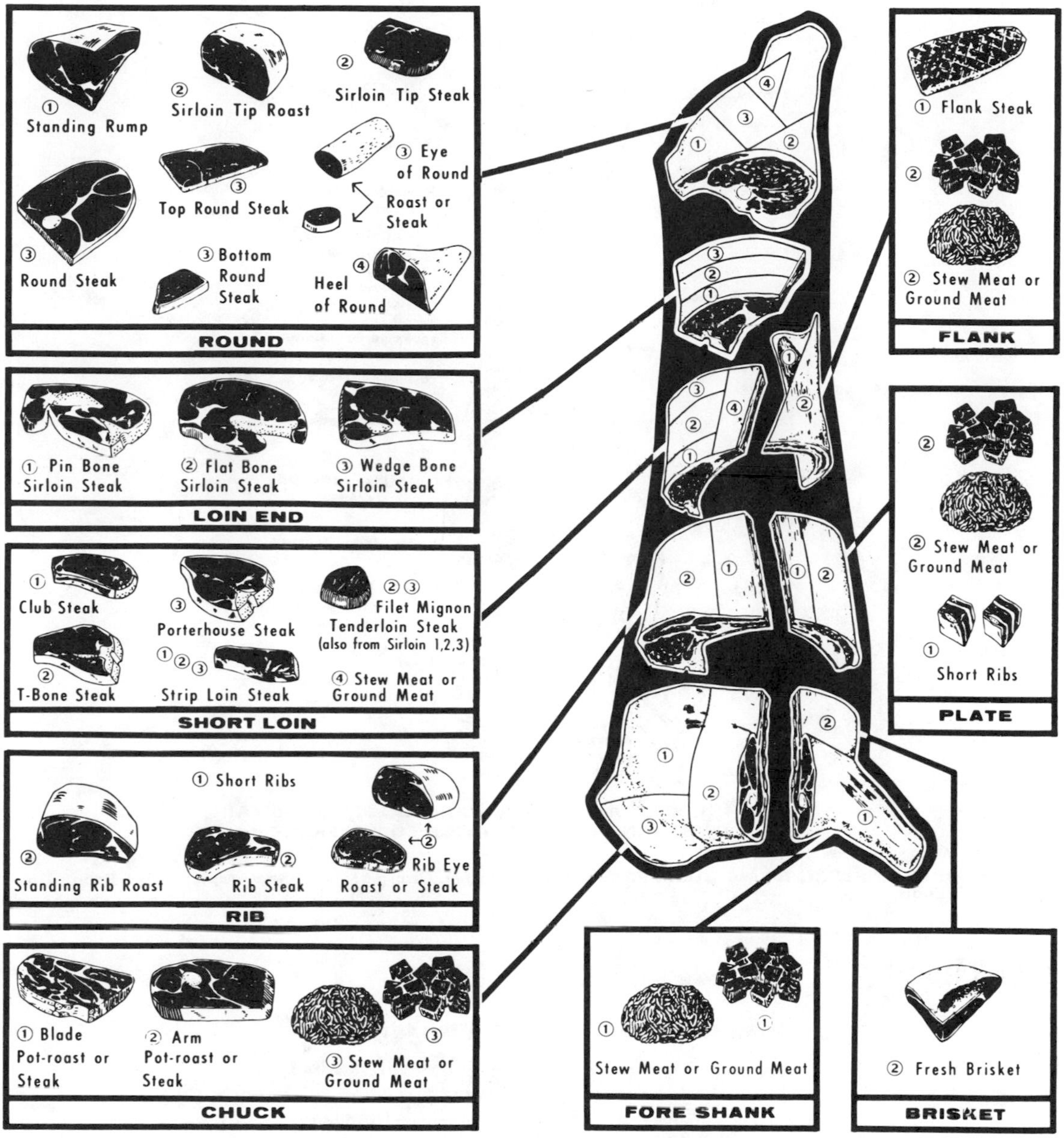

SOURCE: How to Buy Meat for Your Freezer, USDA Home and Garden Bull. *166*, 1969.

BEEF, CHICAGO-STYLE CUTTING

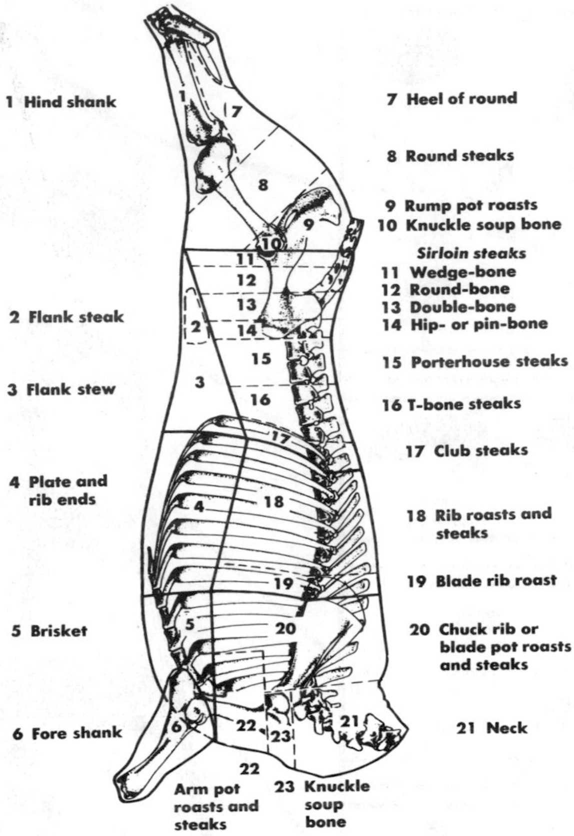

FIG. 2.B.4. LOCATION OF THE CHICAGO-STYLE RETAIL CUTS OF BEEF AND THEIR RELATION TO THE SKELETON

SOURCE: BREIDENSTEIN, B., and BULL, S. Beef for the Table, Circ. *585*, Ext. Serv. Agric. Home Econ., Univ. Illinois.

BEEF CHUCK

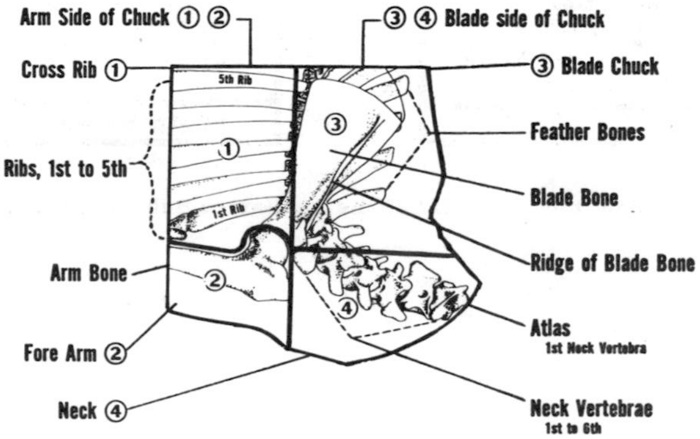

FIG. 2.B.5. BONE STRUCTURE OF A BEEF CHUCK

SOURCE: Muscle Boning the Chuck. National Live Stock and Meat Board, Chicago.

BEEF, COOKING

TABLE 2.B.8

TIME-TABLE FOR COOKING BEEF

	Roasted at 300°F Oven Temp		Broiled[1]		Braised	Cooked in Liquid
Cut	Meat Thermometer Reading (°F)	Time (min per lb)	Meat Thermometer Reading (°F)	Total Time (min)	Total Time (hr)	Total Time (hr)
Standing ribs	140 (rare)	18-20				
Standing ribs	160 (med)	22-25				
Standing ribs	170 (well)	27-30				
Rolled ribs	Same as above	Add 10-15				
Blade, 3rd to 5th rib (high quality only)	150-170	25-30				
Rump (high quality only)	150-170	25-30				
Tenderloin	140-170	20-25				
Beef loaf	160-170	25-30				
Steaks (1 in.)			140 (rare)	15-20		
			160 (med)	20-30		
Steaks (1½ in.)			140 (rare)	25-35		
			160 (med)	35-50		
Steaks (2 in.)			140 (rare)	30-40		
			160 (med)	50-70		
Beef patties (1 in.)			140 (rare)	12-15		
			160 (med)	18-20		
Pot roasts						
Arm or blade					3-4	
Rump					3-4	
Swiss steak					2-3	
Corned beef						3½-5
Fresh beef					3-4	3-4
Stew						2-3

[1] Panbroiling or griddle-broiling requires approximately one-half the time for broiling.

SOURCE: POTTS, B., SIMONDS, L., and VANSTAVERN, B. D. Meat Specials Really are Special. Ohio State Univ. Coop. Ext. Serv. Bull. *574*.

BEEF CUTS

TABLE 2.B.9

CHARACTERISTICS AND COOKING METHODS OF BEEF CUTS

WHOLESALE CUTS	RETAIL CUTS	CHARACTERISTICS	COOKING METHODS
Round (and Rump)	Round Steak (*full cut*)	Round or oval in shape with small round bone. One large muscle, three smaller ones.	*Braise*
	Top Round Steak or Pot-Roast	Most tender portion of round. Is one large muscle.	*Braise; roast; panfry*
	Bottom Round Steak or Pot-Roast	Not so tender as top round. Distinguished from top round by having two muscles.	*Braise*
	Tip Roast or Steak	Triangular cut; roast may contain kneecap. Steaks are boneless.	*Braise; roast; broil; panbroil; panfry*
	Standing Rump	Triangular in shape; contains portions of aitch (rump) bone and tail bone. Knuckle end of leg (round) bone usually removed.	*Braise; roast (high quality)*
	Rolled Rump	Boneless roll.	*Braise, roast (high quality)*
	Heel of Round	Boneless wedge-shaped cut from lower part of round. Weighs 4 to 8 pounds. Has very little fat and is least tender cut of round.	*Braise; cook in liquid*
	Hind Shank	Bony, considerable connective tissue, rich in extractives.	*Cook in liquid (soup)*
Sirloin	Sirloin Steak	Contains portions of back bone and hip bone. Wide variation in bone and muscle structure of the various steaks.	*Broil; panbroil; panfry*
	Pinbone Sirloin Steak	Lies next to the porterhouse. Contains pin bone which is the forward end of hip bone.	*Broil; panbroil; panfry*
	Boneless Sirloin Steak	Any boneless steak from the sirloin.	*Broil; panbroil; panfry*
Short Loin	Porterhouse Steak	Largest steak in short loin. Loin strip and tenderloin muscles. T-shaped bone. Tenderloin larger in porterhouse than in other short loin steaks.	*Broil; panbroil; panfry*
	T-Bone Steak	Same as porterhouse except tenderloin is smaller (porterhouse and T-bone used more or less interchangeably).	*Broil; panbroil; panfry*
	Club (Delmonico) Steak	Triangular-shaped; smallest steak in short loin. Tenderloin has practically disappeared.	*Broil; panbroil; panfry*
	Tenderloin Roast or Steak	Boneless tapering muscle. Most tender cut beef.	*Roast; broil; panbroil; panfry*

Flank	Flank Steak	Oval-shaped boneless steak weighing ¾ to 1½ pounds. Muscles run lengthwise; usually scored to shorten muscle fibers. Less tender cut.	*Braise*
	Flank Steak Fillets	Sections of flank steak rolled and fastened with skewers.	*Braise*
	Flank Meat	Boneless. Coarse fibers. May be rolled, cut into stew or ground.	*Braise; cook in liquid*
Rib	Standing Rib Roast (Short Cut)	Contains two or more ribs from which short ribs and chine bone have been removed. Comparable to rib roast served in restaurants.	*Roast*
	Rolled Rib Roast	Boneless roll. Outer cover of roll consists largely of thin plate meat wrapped around rib eye.	*Roast*
	Rib Steak	Contains rib eye and may contain rib bone.	*Broil; panbroil; panfry*
	Short Ribs	Cut from ends of ribs; layers of lean and fat.	*Braise; cook in liquid*
Short Plate	Plate "Boiling" Beef	Cut across plate parallel with ribs.	*Braise; cook in liquid*
	Rolled Plate	When rolled the absence of the rib eye distinguishes this cut from the rolled rib.	*Braise; cook in liquid*
	Short Ribs	Cut from ends of ribs; layers of lean and fat.	*Braise; cook in liquid*
Square-Cut Chuck	Arm Pot-roast or Steak	Has a round bone and cross sections of 3–5 ribs. A small round muscle near the round bone is surrounded by connective tissue.	*Braise*
	Blade Pot-roast or Steak	Pot-roast contains portions of rib and blade bones. Steaks cut between ribs will not contain rib bone.	*Braise*
	Boneless Chuck	Any part of the square-cut chuck (except the neck) from which the bones have been removed.	*Braise*
	Boneless Neck	Any part of the neck without the neck bone.	*Braise; cook in liquid*
	English (Boston) Cut	A rectangular piece cut across 2 or 3 chuck ribs.	*Braise*
Brisket	Brisket	Layers of lean and fat. Presence of breast bone sure indication that cut is from the brisket.	*Braise; cook in liquid*
	Boneless Brisket	Same as above with ribs and breast bone removed.	*Braise; cook in liquid*
Fore Shank	Shank Knuckle	Knuckle or upper end of fore shank.	*Cook in liquid, braise*
	Shank Cross-Cuts	Small pieces cut across shank bone.	*Braise; cook in liquid*
Ground Beef	Loaf and Patties	Usually made from flank, shank, plate and chuck.	*Roast (bake); broil; panbroil; panfry; braise*

SOURCE: Meat Manual, 6th Edition. National Live Stock and Meat Board, Chicago.

BEEF CUTS AND USES

TABLE 2.B.10

BEEF CUTS AND THEIR USES

WHOLESALE CUT	DESCRIPTION	RETAIL CUTS	BEEF SPECIALTIES
ROUND	Well-flavored, with rump and hind shank off, has very little bone	Steaks, pot-roasts	Brains— Cream, scramble with eggs, cutlets
RUMP	Well-flavored, contains aitch bone, knuckle joint and tail bone. To facilitate carving some or all of bones are removed	Corn beef, pot-roasts, steaks	Heart— Braise, cook in water
LOIN END	Tender, juicy, varying amounts of bone	Sirloin steaks	Liver— Fry, roast whole or as loaf, braise
SHORT LOIN	Tender, juicy, contains portion of tenderloin	Porterhouse, T-bone, club steaks	Tongue (fresh, pickled or corned)— Cook in water
FLANK	Thin, practically boneless, coarse grained, well-flavored	Flank steak, stew meat	
RIB	Tender, juicy; contains rib bones and "eye" muscle	Roasts, rib steaks	Tripe— Cook in water, cream
CHUCK	Juicy, well-flavored, muscles run in different directions	Pot-roasts, steaks, stew meat	Oxtail— Soup, braise
BRISKET	Layer of fat and lean; contains rib ends and breast bone	Fresh brisket, corned brisket	
PLATE	Rib ends, layers of fat and lean	Short ribs, "boiling" beef, boneless roll	
SHANKS	Considerable bone, connective tissue, varying amounts of lean	Soup bones, cross-cut shanks	

SOURCE: Meat Buying Manual. National Live Stock and Meat Board, Chicago.

BEEF DEGREES OF DONENESS

TABLE 2.B.11

INTERNAL TEMPERATURES OF LARGE BEEF ROASTS FOR THE DIFFERENT DEGREES OF DONENESS

Degree of Doneness	Color of Inside of Roast	Meat Thermometer Reading When Roast Comes from Oven*
Rare	Bright pink	120° to 125° F.
Medium	Pinkish brown	135° to 145° F.
Well done	Greyish or light brown	150° to 160° F.

* The temperatures at which color changes take place in beef as it cooks are considerably higher than the temperatures above indicate; however, large roasts continue cooking for some time after they are removed from the oven. Therefore, to prevent over-cooking, roasts should be removed from the oven when the meat thermometer shows several degrees lower than the temperature at which the actual color change takes place.

SOURCE: Cooking Meat in Quantity. National Live Stock and Meat Board, Chicago.

BEEF, NEW YORK-STYLE CUTTING

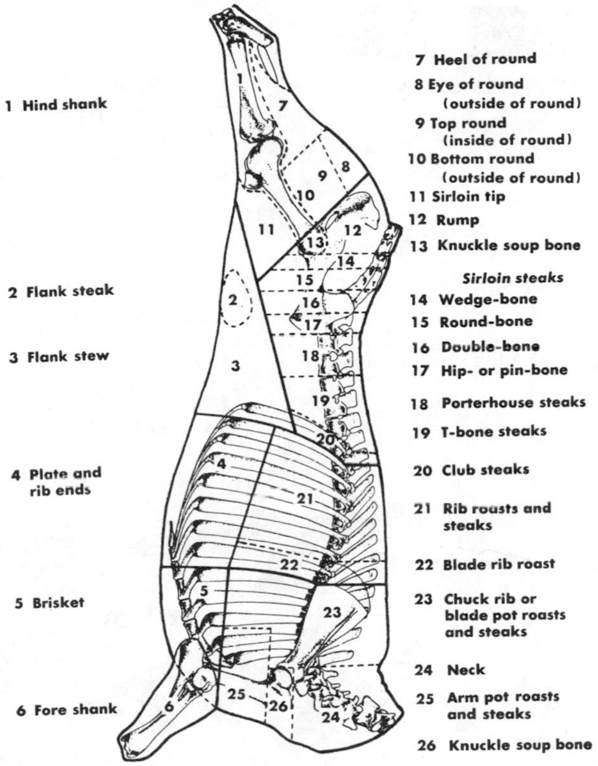

FIG. 2.B.6. LOCATION OF THE NEW YORK-STYLE RETAIL CUTS OF BEEF AND THEIR RELATION TO THE SKELETON

SOURCE: BREIDENSTEIN, B., and BULL, S. Beef for the Table, Circ. *585*, Ext. Serv. Agric. and Home Econ., Univ. Illinois.

BEEF PERCENTAGES OF DAILY RECOMMENDED ALLOWANCES

TABLE 2.B.12

PERCENTAGES OF DAILY RECOMMENDED ALLOWANCES[1]
(Based on 3½ Oz Cooked Lean Beef)

	Age	Protein	Calories	Iron	Phosphorus	Magnesium	Thiamin	Riboflavin	Niacin	Vit. B-6	Vit. B-12
Children	1-3	129	20	25	24	14	14	49	50	61	206
	4-6	99	15	37	24	11	11	35	38	41	137
	7-10	82	11	37	24	9	8	33	28	31	103
Males	11-14	67	9	21	16	6	7	26	25	23	69
	15-18	55	9	21	16	5	7	22	23	18	69
	19-22	55	9	37	24	6	7	22	23	18	69
	23-50	53	10	37	24	6	7	24	25	18	69
	51+	53	11	37	24	6	8	7	28	18	69
Females	11-14	67	11	21	16	7	8	30	28	23	69
	15-18	62	13	21	16	7	9	28	32	18	69
	19-22	64	13	21	24	7	9	28	32	18	69
	23-50	64	13	21	24	7	10	33	35	18	69
	51+	64	15	37	24	7	10	35	38	18	69

[1]Figures based on 1974 National Research Council Recommended Dietary Allowances.

SOURCE: Facts About Beef. 1974. National Live Stock and Meat Board, Chicago.

BEEF RETAIL YIELD

• CHUCK *164.8 lbs (26.8% of total carcass)*

	Saleable Beef—lbs	Other lbs
Blade pot-roast	59.3	
Stew or ground beef	32.1	
Arm pot-roast	22.3	
Cross rib pot-roast	10.7	
Boston cut	9.9	
Fat and bone		30.5
TOTAL	134.3 lbs	30.5 lbs

• BRISKET *23.4 lbs (3.8% of total carcass)*

	Saleable Beef—lbs	Other lbs
Boneless	9.4	
Fat and bone		14.0
TOTAL	9.4 lbs	14.0 lbs

• SHANK *19.1 lbs (3.1% of total carcass)*

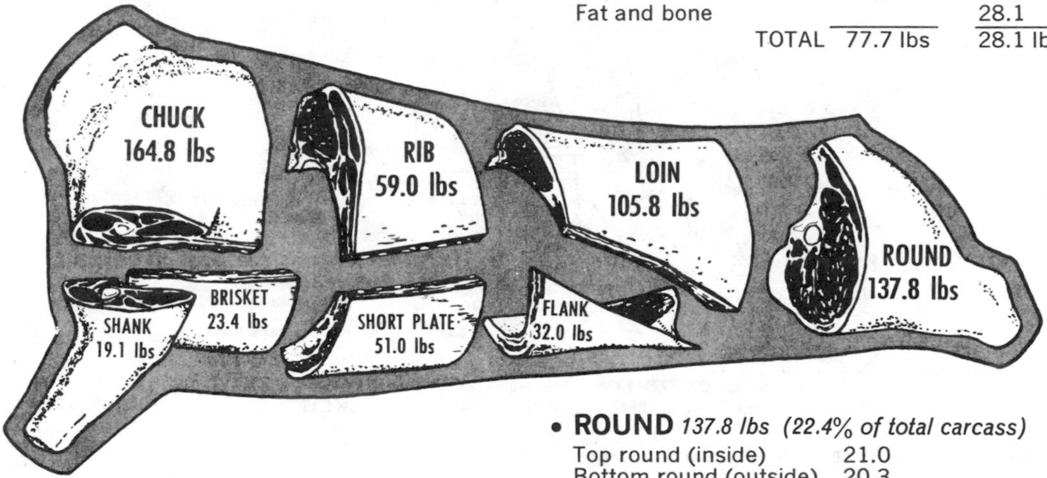

• SHORT PLATE *51.0 lbs (8.3% of total carcass)*

	Saleable Beef—lbs	Other lbs
Plate, stew, short ribs	40.8	
Fat and bone		10.2
TOTAL	40.8 lbs	10.2 lbs

• FLANK *32.0 lbs (5.2% of total carcass)*

	Saleable Beef—lbs	Other lbs
Flank	3.2	
Ground beef	12.6	
Fat		16.2
TOTAL	15.8 lbs	16.2 lbs

MISC. *22.1 lbs (3.6% of total carcass)*

	Saleable Beef—lbs	Other lbs
Kidney, hanging tender	3.6	
Fat, suet, cutting losses		18.5
TOTAL	3.6 lbs	18.5 lbs

• RIB *59.0 lbs (9.6% of total carcass)*

	Saleable Beef—lbs	Other lbs
Standing rib roast	24.2	
Rib steak	12.4	
Short ribs	4.7	
Braising beef	2.7	
Ground beef	3.5	
Fat and bone		11.5
TOTAL	47.5 lbs	11.5 lbs

• LOIN *105.8 lbs (17.2% of total carcass)*

	Saleable Beef—lbs	Other lbs
Porterhouse steak	18.7	
T-bone steak	9.5	
Club steak	5.2	
Sirloin steak	41.4	
Ground beef	2.9	
Fat and bone		28.1
TOTAL	77.7 lbs	28.1 lbs

• ROUND *137.8 lbs (22.4% of total carcass)*

	Saleable Beef—lbs	Other lbs
Top round (inside)	21.0	
Bottom round (outside)	20.3	
Tip	13.1	
Stew	8.3	
Rump	4.8	
Kabobs or cubes	2.1	
Ground beef	14.2	
Fat and bone		54.0
TOTAL	83.8 lbs	54.0 lbs

SUMMARY
(1000 lb choice steer)

Dresses out 61.5%	615 lbs
Less fat, bone and loss	183 lbs
Saleable beef	432 lbs

SOURCE: A Steer's Not All Steak. National Live Stock and Meat Board, Chicago.

BEEF RIB CARVING (STANDING ROAST)

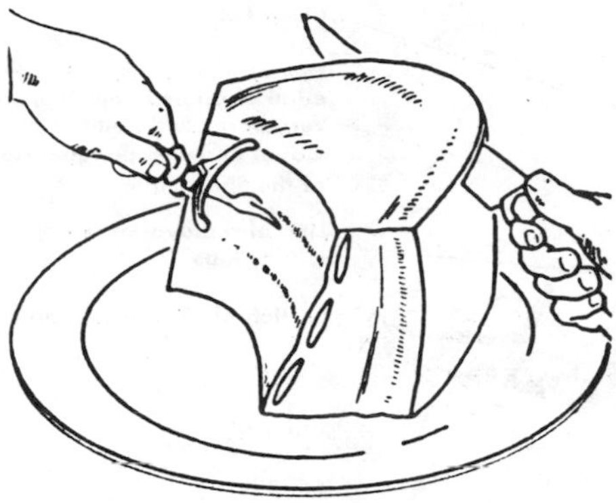

Place the roast on the platter with the largest end down to form a solid base. Insert the fork between the two top ribs. Starting on the fat side, carve across the grain to the rib bone.

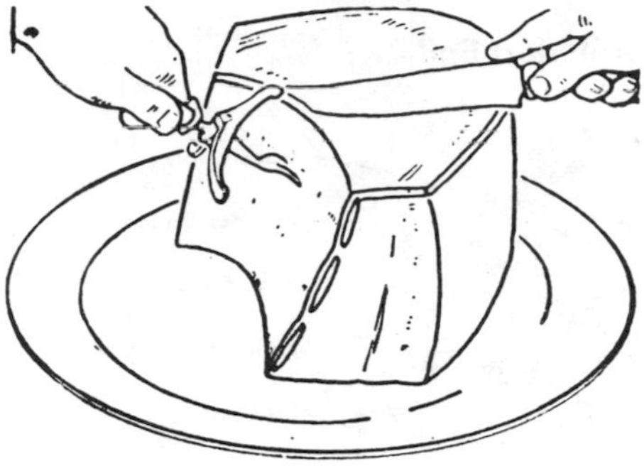

Use the tip of the knife to cut along the rib bone to loosen the slice. Be sure to keep close to the bone, to make the largest servings possible.

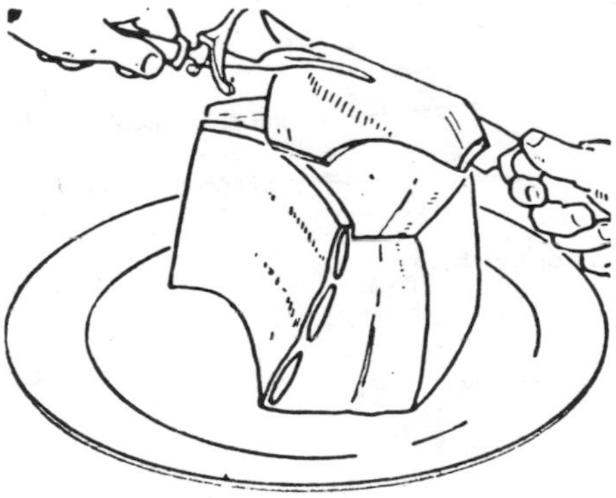

Slide the knife back under the slice and, steadying it with the fork, lift the slice to the side of the platter. If the platter is not large enough, place the slices on a heated platter close by.

SOURCE: Carving Meat. National Live Stock and Meat Board, Chicago.

BEEF RIB NOMENCLATURE

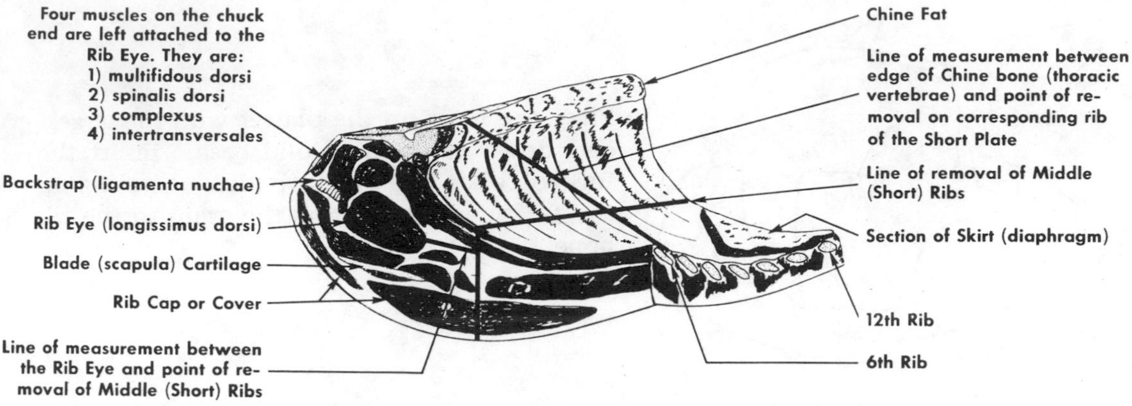

View of Beef Rib from Chuck (Anterior) End

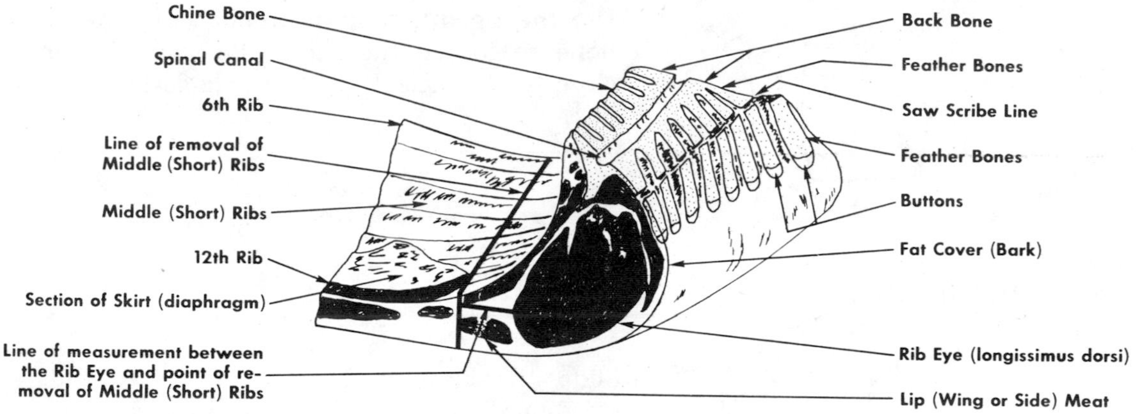

View of Beef Rib from Loin (Posterior) End

FIG. 2.B.7. COMMONLY-USED NAMES FOR BEEF RIB

SOURCE: Merchandising Beef Ribs. National Live Stock and Meat Board, Chicago.

BEEF ROASTING

TABLE 2.B.13

TIME-TABLE FOR ROASTING BEEF

Cut	Approx. Wt. of Single Roast	No. of Roasts in Oven	Approx. Total Wt. of Roasts in Oven	Oven Temperature	Interior Temperature of Roast When Removed from Oven	Minutes per Pound Based on One Roast	Minutes per Pound Based on Total Wt. of Roasts in Oven	Approximate Total Time
	pounds		*pounds*					
Standing rib (3-rib)	6 to 8	1		300° F.	140° F. (rare) 160° F. (medium) 170° F. (well)	18 to 20 22 to 25 27 to 30		2 to 3 hours 2½ to 3 hours 3 to 4 hours
Standing rib (7-rib)	20 to 25	1		250° F.	125° F. (rare) 140° F. (medium) 150° F. (well)	13 15 17		4½ hours 5 hours 6 hours
Standing rib (7-rib)	23	1		300° F.	125° F. (rare) 140° F. (medium) 150° F. (well)	11 12 13		4 hours 4½ hours 5 hours
Rolled rib (7-rib)	16 to 18	1		250° F.	150° F. (well)	26		7 to 8 hours
Rolled rib (7-rib)	17	1		300° F.	150° F. (well)	24		6 hours
Standing rib (7-rib)		2	56	300° F.	140° F. (medium) 160° F. (well)		6 7 to 8	6 hours 7 hours
Chuck rib	5 to 8	1		300° F.	150° to 170° F.	25 to 30		2½ to 4 hours
Rump	5 to 7	1		300° F.	150° to 170° F.	25 to 30		2½ to 3½ hours
Round (rump and shank off)	50	1		250° F.	140° F. (medium) 154° F. (well)	12 14		10 hours 11 to 12 hours

SOURCE: Cooking Meat in Quantity. National Live Stock and Meat Board, Chicago.

BEEF ROUND, BONE STRUCTURE

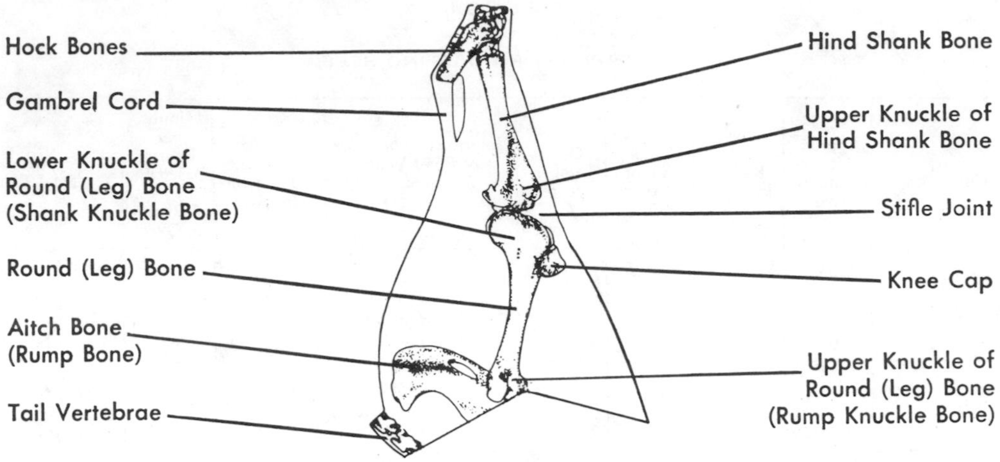

FIG. 2.B.8. BONE STRUCTURE OF A DIAMOND ROUND

SOURCE: Merchandising Beef Rounds. National Live Stock and Meat Board, Chicago.

BEEF ROUND CUTS

Cut through natural seam to split boneless round into two pieces . . . Top Round and Outside Round.

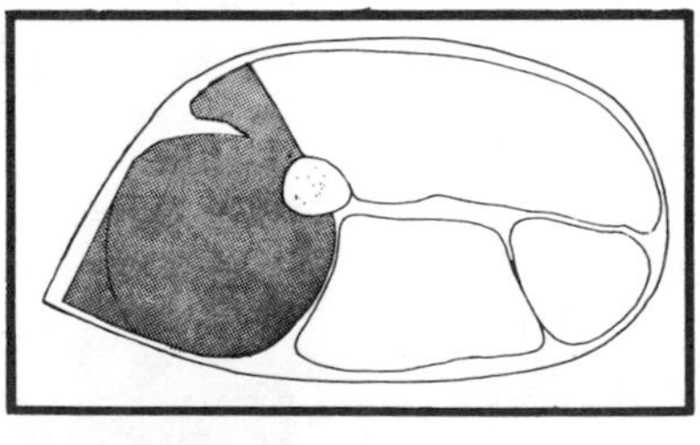

Shaded area indicates location of tip (knuckle)

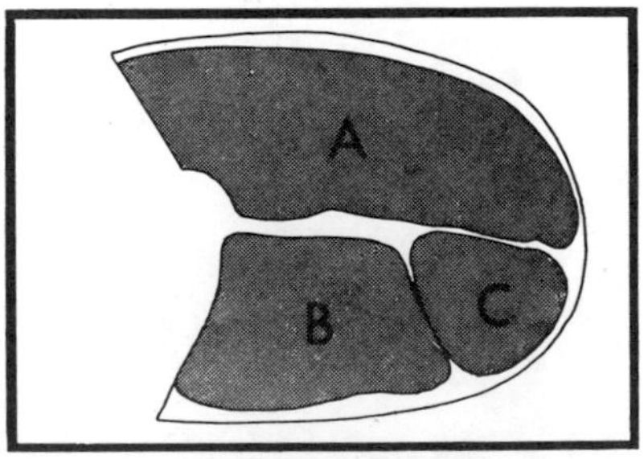

A Top (Inside) Round
B & C Outside (Bottom) Round
B Outside Round
C Eye of Round

SOURCE: Merchandising Beef Rounds. National Live Stock and Meat Board, Chicago.

BEEF ROUNDS

THREE POPULAR BEEF ROUNDS

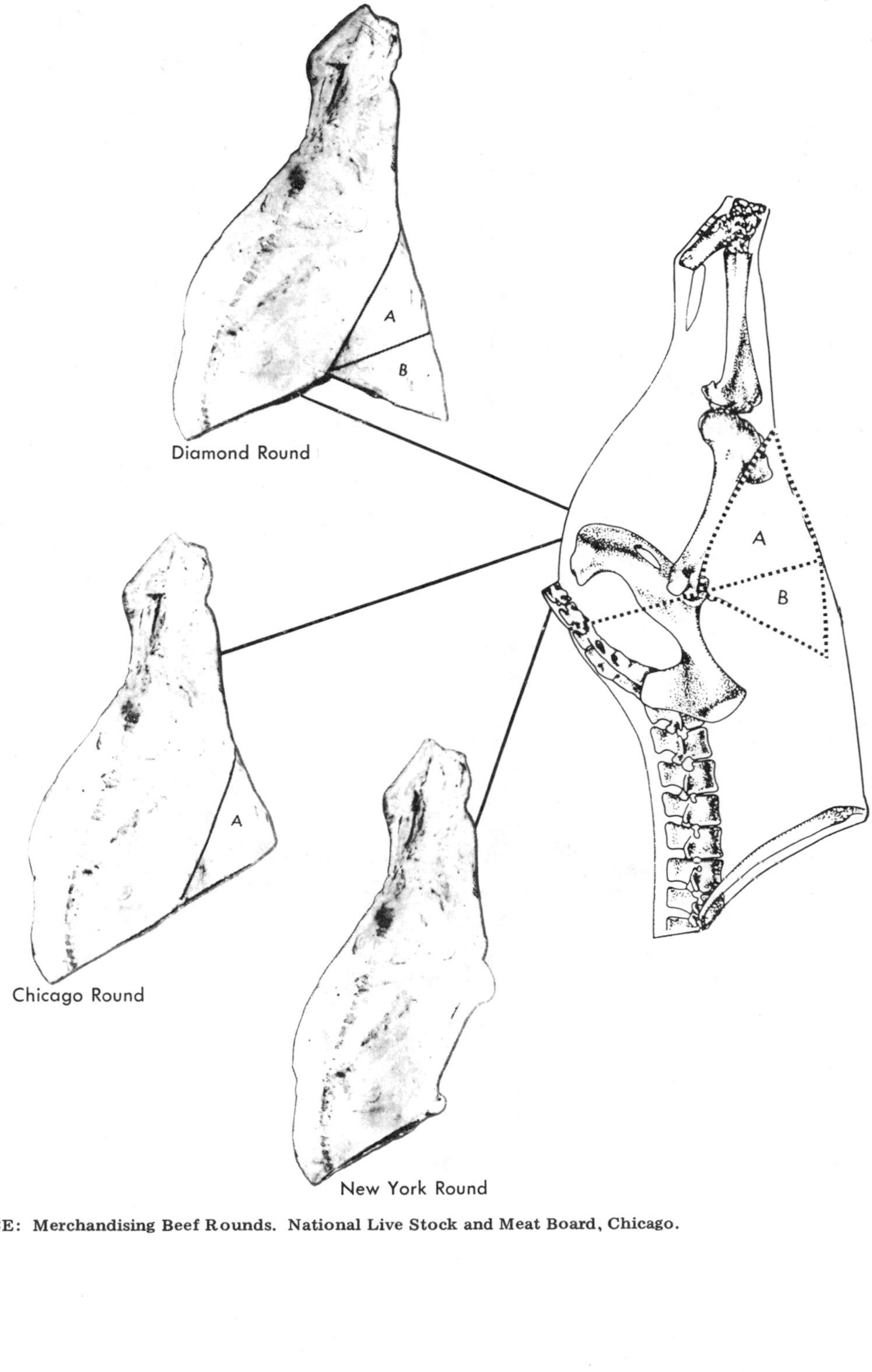

SOURCE: Merchandising Beef Rounds. National Live Stock and Meat Board, Chicago.

BEEF WHOLESALE CUTS

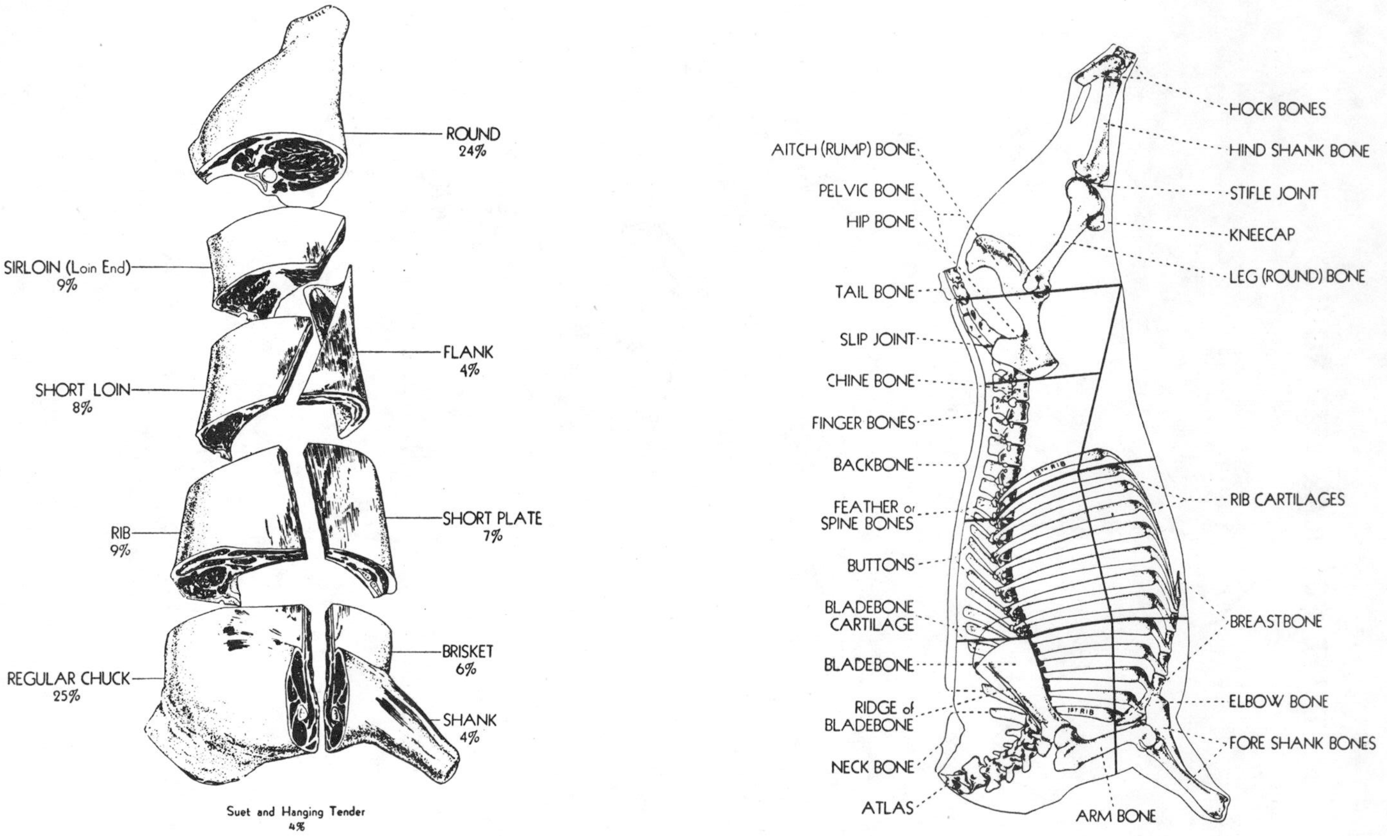

FIG. 2.B.9. BEEF CARCASS SHOWING WHOLESALE CUTS (LEFT) AND LOCATION, STRUCTURE, AND NAMES OF BONES (RIGHT)

SOURCE: Cooking Meat in Quantity. National Live Stock and Meat Board, Chicago.

BEEF YIELDS

TABLE 2.B.14

APPROXIMATE YIELDS FROM WHOLESALE CUTS OF BEEF
(300-LB SIDE, YIELD GRADE 3)

	% of Wholesale Cut	Pounds		% of Wholesale Cut	Pounds
Round (68 lbs.)			**Rib (27 lbs.)**		
Round Steak	39.7	27.0	Rib Roast (7″ cut)	67.8	18.3
Rump Roast (Boneless)	14.6	9.9	Lean Trim	12.6	3.4
Lean Trim	17.9	12.2	Waste (fat, bone, and shrinkage)	19.6	5.3
Waste (fat, bone, and shrinkage)	27.8	18.9	Total Rib	100.0	27.0
Total Round	100.0	68.0			
Trimmed Loin (50 lbs.)*			**Square-Cut Chuck (81 lbs.)**		
Porterhouse, T-Bone, Club Steaks	30.6	15.3	Blade Chuck Roast	33.0	26.7
Sirloin Steak	49.8	24.9	Arm Chuck Roast (Boneless)	21.5	17.4
Lean Trim	6.4	3.2	Lean Trim	25.9	21.0
Waste (fat, bone, and shrinkage)	13.2	6.6	Waste (fat, bone, and shrinkage)	19.6	15.9
Total Loin	100.0	50.0	Total Chuck	100.0	81.0

* Does not include Kidney knob and flank.

SOURCE: How to Buy Meat for Your Freezer. (1969). USDA Home and Garden Bull. *166*.

BEVERAGE CARBONATED, INGREDIENTS

TABLE 2.B.15

PRIMARY INGREDIENTS COMMONLY DETECTED IN CARBONATED BEVERAGES

Ingredients	Cola	Orange	Grape	Lemon-Lime	Root Beer
Water	x	x	x	x	x
Sugar	x	x	x	x	x
Phosphoric acid	x				
Citric acid		x	x	x	x
Caffeine	x				
Sodium benzoate		x	x		x
Carbon dioxide	x	x	x	x	x
Gum acacia	x	x			x
Caramel color	x				x
FDC colors		x	x		
Nutmeg oil	x				x
Methyl anthranilate			x		
Orange oil	x	x			
Lemon oil	x			x	x
Vanilla/vanillin	x				x
Lime oil	x			x	
Cinnamon oil	x				x
Ethyl acetate			x		
Ethyl alcohol			x	x	
Citral		x		x	
Kola nut extract	x				
Ascorbic acid		x			
Cassia oil	x				x
Clove oil	x				x
Ethyl butyrate			x		
Methyl salicylate					x

SOURCE: WOODROOF, J. G. and PHILLIPS, G. F. (EDITORS). 1974. Beverage Acids, Flavors, Colors, and Emulsifiers. *In* Beverages; Carbonated and Noncarbonated. AVI Publishing Co., Westport, Conn.

BIOTIN CONTENT

TABLE 2.B.16

BIOTIN CONTENT OF SOME SELECTED FOODS

	γ/g
Royal jelly	1.70
Liver	0.96
Chocolate	0.32
Roasted peanuts	0.34
Peas	0.21
Cauliflower	0.17
Lima beans	0.098
Whole wheat	0.052
Sea foods	0.080

SOURCE: BRAVERMAN, J. B. S. Introduction to the Biochemistry of Foods. ASP Biological and Medical Press (Elsevier Division), New York.

BITTER FLAVORS

TABLE 2.B.17

CLASSIFICATION OF BITTER FLAVORS

Bitter Flavors		Complementary Flavors		
Aromatic-bitter	Bitter	Aromatic	Pungent	Sweet
Angelica	Aloe	Ambrette	Cardamom	Anise
Balm	Angostura	Clary sage	Cinnamon, Ceylon	Licorice
Calamus	Artichoke	Coriander	Clove buds	Star anise
Camomile, Hungarian	Blessed thistle	Imperatoria	Ginger	Vanilla
Camomile, Roman	Calumba	Lemon	Grains of paradise	
Cascarilla	Centaury	Liatris	Juniper	
Catmint	Chicory	(wild vanilla)	Mace	
Chinotti	Chirata	Melilotus	Nutmeg	
Condurango	Cinchona	Myrrh	Peppermint	
Dittany of Crete	Dandelion	Orange, sweet	Thyme	
Elder	Gentian	Orris		
Elecampane	Gentian, stemless	Saffron		
Galanga	Larch agaric	St. Johnswort		
Genepi	Quassia	Savory, summer		
Germander	Rhubarb	Tonka bean		
Hyssop	Southernwood	Valerian		
Marjoram, sweet	Walnut	Woodruff, sweet		
Mugwort				
Orange, bitter				
Rue				
Wormwood				
Wormwood, mountain				
Yarrow				
Yarrow, musk				
Zedoary				

SOURCE: FURIA, T. E. and BELLANCA, N. (EDITORS). 1971. Fenaroli's Handbook of Flavor Ingredients. CRC Press, Cleveland. Used by permission of CRC Press.

BITTERS, HERBS

TABLE 2.B.18

HERBS AND DERIVATIVES USED TO FORMULATE BITTERS

Common name	Botanical name	Parts of plant used
Aloe	*Aloe* species	Concentrated leaf juice
Ambrette	*Hibiscus abelmoschus* L.	Seeds
Angelica	*Angelica archangelica* L.	Roots
Angostura	*Galipea cusparia* DC.	Bark
Anise	*Pimpinella anisum* L.	Fruits
Artichoke	*Cynara scolymus* L.	Leaves
Balm (lemon balm)	*Melissa officinalis* L.	Leaves and flowering tops
Blessed thistle	*Cnicus benedictus* L.	Leaves and flowers
Calamus	*Acorus calamus* L.	Rhizomes
Calumba	*Jatrorrhiza palmata* (Lam.) Miers	Roots
Camomile, Hungarian or German	*Matricaria chamomilla* L.	Flowers
Camomile, Roman or English	*Anthemis nobilis* L.	Flowers
Cardamom	*Elettaria cardamomum* Maton	Fruits
Cascarilla	*Croton eluteria* Benn.	Bark
Catmint	*Nepeta cataria* L.	Flowering tops
Centaury	*Erythraea centaurium* Pers.	Whole plant
Chicory	*Cichorium intybus* L.	Roots
Chinotti	*Citrus myrtifolia* Risso	Peels or the whole fruit
Chirata	*Swertia chirata* (Roxb.) Buch.-Ham.	Whole plant
Cinchona	*Cinchona* species	Bark
Cinnamon, Ceylon	*Cinnamomum zeylanicum* Nees	Bark
Clary sage	*Salvia sclarea* L.	Flowering tops
Clove	*Eugenia caryophyllata* Thunb.	Buds
Condurango	*Marsdenia condurango* Reichenb. f.	Bark
Coriander	*Coriandrum sativum* L.	Fruits
Dandelion	*Taraxacum officinale* Weber	Leaves and roots
Dittany of Crete	*Origanum dictamnus* L.	Leaves and flowering tops
Elder	*Sambucus nigra* L.	Flowers
Elecampane	*Inula helenium* L.	Rhizomes
Galanga	*Alpinia officinarum* Hance	Rhizomes
Genepi	*Artemisia glacialis* L.	Whole plant
Gentian	*Gentiana lutea* L.	Rhizomes and roots
Gentian, stemless	*Gentiana acaulis* L.	Whole plant
Germander	*Teucrium chamaedrys* L.	Flowering tops
Ginger	*Zingiber officinale* Rosc.	Rhizomes
Grains of paradise	*Aframomum melegueta* Rosc.	Seeds
Hyssop	*Hyssopus officinalis* L.	Leaves and flowers
Imperatoria	*Peucedanum osthruthium* (L.) Koch.	Rhizomes
Juniper	*Juniperus communis* L.	Berries
Larch agaric	*Polyporus laricis* Jacq.	Inner portion of the thallus
Lemon	*Citrus limonum* (L.) Risso	Peels
Liatris (wild vanilla)	*Trilisa odoratissima* (Walt.) Cass.	Leaves
Licorice	*Glycyrrhiza glabra* L.	Roots
Mace	*Myristica fragrans* Houtt.	Arillodes
Marjoram, sweet	*Marjorana hortensis* Moench.	Flowering tops
Melilotus	*Melilotus officinalis* (L.) Lam.	Flowers
Mugwort	*Artemisia pontica* L.	Leaves and flowering tops
Myrrh	*Commiphora* species	Gum resin

(Continued)

TABLE 2.B.18 (*Continued*)

Common name	Botanical name	Parts of plant used
Nutmeg	*Myristica fragrans* Houtt.	Fruits
Orange, bitter	*Citrus aurantium* L. subspecies *amara* L.	Peels
Orange, sweet	*Citrus sinensis* L. Osbeck	Peels
Orris	*Iris pallida* L. and *I. germanica* L.	Roots
Peppermint	*Mentha piperita* L.	Flowering tops
Quassia	*Picrasma excelsa* (Sw.) Planch.	Wood
Rhubarb	*Rheum* species	Rhizomes
Rue	*Ruta graveolens* L.	Leaves
Saffron	*Crocus sativus* L.	Stems
St. Johnswort	*Hypericum perforatum* L.	Flowering tops
Savory, summer	*Satureja hortensis* L.	Flowering tops
Southernwood	*Artemisia abrotanum* L.	Leaves and flowering tops
Star anise	*Illicium verum* Hook. f.	Fruits
Thyme	*Thymus vulgaris* L.	Whole flowering plant
Tonka bean	*Dipteryx oppositia folia*	Seeds
Valerian	*Valeriana officinalis* L.	Rhizomes and roots
Vanilla	*Vanilla* species	Pods
Walnut	*Juglans regia* L.	Leaves and green nuts
Woodruff, sweet	*Asperula odorata* L.	Whole plant
Wormwood	*Artemisia absinthium* L.	Leaves and flowering tops
Wormwood, mountain	*Artemisia valesiaca* L.	Leaves and flowering tops
Yarrow	*Achillea millefolium* L.	Whole flowering plant excluding the root
Yarrow, musk	*Achillea moschata* Jacq.	Leaves and flowering tops
Zedoary	*Curcuma zedoaria* Rosc.	Bark

SOURCE: FURIA, T. E., and BELLANCA, N. (EDITORS). 1971. Fenaroli's Handbook of Flavor Ingredients. CRC Press, Cleveland. Used by permission of CRC Press.

BLOOD

TABLE 2.B.19

ANALYSIS OF BLOOD OF ANIMALS AND POULTRY

Animal	PCV %	Hgb g/100 ml	RBC $\times 10^6$/cu mm	MCV ml $\times 10^{-12}$	MCHC %	PPC g/100 ml
Horse Light breeds	30-50	11-19	7-12	34-58	31-37	6-8
Horse Heavy breeds	25-45	8-14	6-9	37-52	32-38	6-8
Ox	25-45	8-15	5-10	40-60	26-36	6-8
Sheep	25-50	9-16	8-16	25-50	30-38	6-7.5
Goat	20-37	8-14	8-18	18-34	30-40	6-7.5
Pig	32-50	10-16	5-8	50-68	30-35	6-8.5
Dog	37-55	12-18	5-9	60-77	30-35	6-7.5
Cat	27-45	8-15	5-10	40-55	30-35	6-7.5
Rabbit	35-45	9-15	5-7	60-68	31-35	5-7
Chicken	30-40	9-13	3	127	29	3-5
Turkey	39	11	2	203	29	3-5

SOURCE: The Merck Veterinary Manual, 4th Edition, Merck & Co., Rahway, N.J., 1973.

BOILING POINT, ALTITUDE

TABLE 2.B.20

BOILING POINT OF WATER AT VARIOUS ALTITUDES

Altitude in Feet	Boiling Point °F.	Altitude in Feet	Boiling Point °F
0	212.0	4500	203.6
500	211.2	5000	202.6
1000	210.2	5500	201.7
1500	209.2	6000	200.7
2000	208.3	6500	199.8
2500	207.4	7000	198.8
3000	206.4	7500	197.9

SOURCE: DESROSIER, N. W. (EDITOR). 1977. *In* The Technology of Food Preservation, 4th Edition. Avi Publishing Co., Westport, Conn.

BOILING POINTS, SODIUM CHLORIDE, CALCIUM CHLORIDE

TABLE 2.B.21

BOILING POINTS OF SODIUM CHLORIDE AND CALCIUM CHLORIDE SOLUTIONS AT STANDARD PRESSURE

Temperature °F.	Per cent Sodium Chloride	Per cent Calcium Chloride
212	0	0
215	9.5	8.5
220	19.0	18.5
225	25.5	24.5
230	..	29.3
240	..	36.3
250	..	42.0
257	..	45.8

SOURCE: DESROSIER, N. W. (EDITOR). 1977. *In* The Technology of Food Preservation, 4th Edition. Avi Publishing Co., Westport, Conn.

BONE

TABLE 2.B.22

COMMON AND TECHNICAL NOMENCLATURE OF BONES

Common name	Technical name						
Neck bone	Cervical vertebrae (7 in beef and veal, lamb, pork, horse, & rabbit; 13–14 in chicken)						
Atlas	First cervical vertebra						
Backbone	Spine (vertebrae)						
Button	Cartilage of spinous process (on all thoracic vertebrae)						
Feather bone	Spinous process (on all thoracic vertebrae)						
Finger bone	Transverse process (on all lumbar vertebrae)						
Chine bone	Body of each vertebra						
Backbone	*Vertebrae*	*beef & veal*	*lamb*	*pork*	*chicken*	*horse*	*rabbit*
	Thoracic	13	12–14	14–15	7	18	12
	Lumbar	6	6–7	6–7	14 fused	6	7–8
	Sacral	5	4	4		5	3–4
Slip joint	Sacro-iliac diathrosis						
Tail bone	Caudal (coccygeal) vertebrae						
	Coccygeal	*beef & veal*	*lamb*	*pork*	*chicken*	*horse*	*rabbit*
	Total	18–20	16–18	20–23	5–6	15–21	14–20
	Carcass	2–3	2–4	20–23	5–6	2–3	0–2
Blade bone	Scapula						
Arm bone	Humerus						
Foreshank bones	Ulna (7U) and radius (7R)						
Forefoot bones	Pork: carpal, metacarpal, and phalangeal bones, dew claws and toes (digits) Lamb: carpal and metacarpal bones Chicken: 1st, 2nd, and 3rd digit and 2nd and 3rd metacarpal						
Elbow bone	Olecranon process						
Breast bone	Sternum, sternebrae (7; 6 in pork; 1 in chicken: keel of sternum)						
Rib cartilages	Costal cartilages						
Ribs	*Ribs*	*beef & veal*	*lamb*	*pork*	*chicken*	*horse*	*rabbit*
	No. of pairs	13	13–14	14–15	7	18	12
Pelvic bone	Pelvis (os coxae)						
Hip bone	Ilium						
Rump (aitch) bone	Ischium						
Leg (round) bone	Femur						
Knee cap	Patella						
Stifle joint	Femorotibial articulation						
Hindshank bones	Tibia (includes fibula in pork, beef, and poultry)						
Hock bones	Parts of tibia, fibula, and tarsal bones; removed in beef, veal, and poultry						
Hindfoot bones	Pork: tarsal, metatarsal, and phalangeal bones, dew claws and toes (digits) Lamb: metatarsal and proximal phalangeal bones						
Wishbone	Clavicle (in chicken)						
Raven's beak	Coracoid (in chicken)						

SOURCE: OCKERMAN, H. W. 1975. Comparative Anatomy of Meat Animals, *In* Meat Hygiene, Libby, J. A., (Editor). Lea and Febiger, Philadelphia.

BONE AGE

TABLE 2.B.23

RELATIONSHIP BETWEEN AGE AND DEVELOPMENT OF BONES

Beef Age	Ischiopubic Symphysis (Aitch Bone)	Cartilage Extension on the Dorsal Spine of the First 5 Thoracic Vertebrae
1 year old	May be cut with a knife	Cartilaginous extensions are soft and pearly white, no ossification; sharply delineated from soft red bone
2 years old	May be cut with a knife	Some evidence of ossification; red islets of bone appearing in cartilage
3 years old	May be cut with a knife with extreme difficulty	Cartilage partly ossified, grayish in color; red areas are more numerous in cartilage
4-5 years old	Must be cut with a saw	Less cartilage than bone; considerable ossification, outline of tip still visible
6 years old	Must be cut with a saw	Cartilage ossified into compact bony tissue but still definable from bone

Sheep Age	Foreleg Ossification
Lamb	Red break joint
Yearling	White break joint
Mutton	White spool joint

Poultry Age	Amount of flexibility (amount of cartilage remaining) in posterior end of keel of sternum
Broiler	Anterior half or less is ossified

SOURCE: OCKERMAN, H. W. 1975. Comparative anatomy of meat animals. *In* Meat Hygiene. J. A. Libby (Editor). Lea & Febiger, Philadelphia.

BONE AND BODY WEIGHT

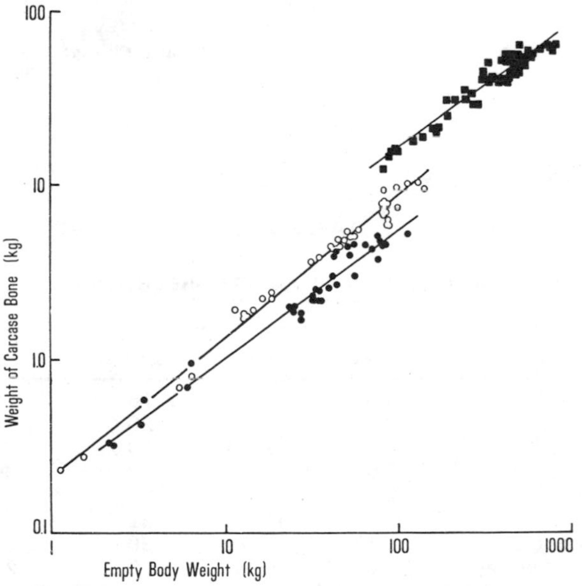

FIG. 2.B.10. WEIGHT OF DISSECTED BONE IN A CARCASS COMPARED WITH EMPTY BODY WEIGHT FOR SHEEP (●), CATTLE (■), AND PIGS (○).

SOURCE: TRIBE, D. E. (EDITOR). Carcass Compositions and Appraisal of Meat Animals. CSIRO, Australia.

BONE IN RETAIL CUTS

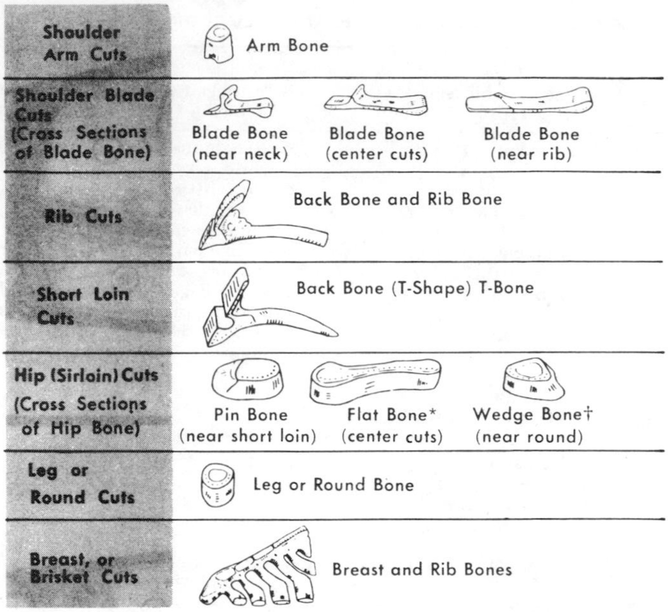

*Formerly part of "double bone" but today the back bone is usually removed leaving only the "flat bone" (sometimes called "pin bone") in the sirloin steak.

†On one side of sirloin steak, this bone may be wedge shaped while on the other side the same bone may be round.

FIG. 2.B.11. BONES THAT IDENTIFY GROUPS OF RETAIL CUTS OF MEAT

SOURCE: Lessons on Meat. (1974). National Live Stock and Meat Board, Chicago.

BONES, COMPOSITION

TABLE 2.B.24

PERCENTAGE COMPOSITION OF ENTIRE SKELETON AND CERTAIN BONES OF CATTLE

Age	Water	Fat	Protein	Ash
At birth	65.31	2.30	16.19	13.76
3 months	49.29	13.30	20.00	16.20
11 months	38.47	18.49	19.25	21.61
2 years	36.08	15.39	20.94	25.78
3 years	32.83	18.05	21.25	25.90
4 years	32.09	17.72	21.00	26.34
Rib bones	28.67	18.02	20.63	28.74
Round bones	26.09	29.96	19.63	23.20

BRAISING MEAT I

The recommended steps for braising meat are:

1. Brown meat on all sides in fat in heavy utensil.
2. Season with salt and pepper if desired.
3. Add small amount of liquid if necessary.
4. Cover tightly.
5. Cook at low temperature until tender.
6. Make gravy from liquid in pan if desired.

SOURCE: Be a Smarter Shopper . . . a Better Cook. (1973). National Live Stock and Meat Board, Chicago.

BRAISING MEAT II

TABLE 2.B.25

TIME-TABLE FOR BRAISING

Cut	Average Weight or Thickness	Approximate Cooking Time
Pot-roast	3 to 5 pounds	3 to 4 hours
Pot-roast	5 to 15 pounds	3 to 5 hours
Swiss steak	1 to 2½ inches	2 to 3 hours
Round steak or flank steak	½ inch (pounded)	45 minutes to 1 hour
Stuffed steak	½ to ¾ inch	1½ hours
Short ribs	Pieces 2 x 2 x 2 inches	1½ to 2 hours
Fricassee	1 to 2 inch pieces	2 to 3 hours
Beef birds	½ x 2 x 4 inches	1½ to 2 hours
Stuffed lamb breast	2 to 3 pounds	1½ to 2 hours
Rolled lamb breast	1½ to 2 pounds	1½ to 2 hours
Lamb shanks	½ pound each	1 to 1½ hours
Lamb neck slices	½ to ¾ inch	1 to 1½ hours
Lamb riblets	¾ x 2½ x 3 inches	2 to 2½ hours
Pork chops or steaks	¾ to 1 inch	45 minutes to 1 hour
Spareribs	2 to 3 pounds	1½ hours
Stuffed veal breast	3 to 4 pounds	1½ to 2 hours
Rolled veal breast	2 to 3 pounds	2 to 3 hours
Veal cutlets	½ x 3 x 5½ inches	45 minutes to 1 hour
Veal steaks or chops	½ to ¾ inch	45 minutes to 1 hour
Veal birds	½ x 2 x 4 inches	45 minutes to 1 hour

SOURCE: Cooking Meat in Quantity. National Live Stock and Meat Board, Chicago.

BRAISING TIME

TABLE 2.B.26

TIME-TABLE FOR BRAISING MEAT

Cut	Average Weight or Thickness	Approximate Total Cooking Time
BEEF		
Pot-Roast		
Arm or blade	3 to 4 pounds	2½-3½ hours
Boneless	3 to 5 pounds	3-4 hours
Cubes	1 to 1½ inches	1½-2½ hours
Short ribs	Pieces (2 in. x 2 in. x 4 in.)	1½-2½ hours
Round steak	¾ to 1 inch	1-1¾ hours
Stuffed steak	½ to ¾ inch	1½ hours
PORK		
Chops	¾ to 1½ inches	45-60 minutes
Spareribs	2 to 3 pounds	1½ hours
Tenderloin		
Whole	¾ to 1 pound	45-60 minutes
Filets	½ inch	30 minutes
Shoulder steaks	¾ inch	45-60 minutes
LAMB		
Breast, stuffed	2 to 3 pounds	1½-2 hours
Breast, boneless	1½ to 2 pounds	1½-2 hours
Riblets		1½-2½ hours
Neck slices	¾ inch	1 hour
Shanks	¾ to 1 pound each	1-1½ hours
Shoulder chops	¾ to 1 inch	45-60 minutes
VEAL		
Breast, stuffed	3 to 4 pounds	1½-2½ hours
Breast, boneless	2 to 3 pounds	1½-2½ hours
Riblets		2-3 hours
Chops	½ to ¾ inch	45-60 minutes
Steaks or cutlets	½ to ¾ inch	45-60 minutes
Cubes	1 to 2 inches	45-60 minutes

SOURCE: Lessons on Meat. (1974). National Live Stock and Meat Board, Chicago.

BREAD AND FLOUR ENRICHMENT

TABLE 2.B.27

FEDERAL STANDARDS FOR FLOUR[1] AND BREAD[2] ENRICHMENT

	Flour		Bread	
	Minimum Mg/Lb	Maximum Mg/Lb	Minimum Mg/Lb	Maximum Mg/Lb
Thiamine	2.0	2.5	1.1	1.8
Riboflavin	1.2	1.5	0.7	1.6
Niacin	16.0	20.0	10.0	15.0
Iron	13.0	16.5	8.0	12.5
Calcium[3]	500	625	300	800
Vitamin D[3] (USP units)	250	1,000	150	750

[1] Anon. (1941).
[2] Anon. (1952).
[3] Optional ingredients.

SOURCE: POTTER, N. N. (EDITOR). 1973. Nutritive Aspects of Food Constituents. *In* Food Science, 2nd Edition. Avi Publishing Co., Westport, Conn.

BRINE, MEAT CURING

TABLE 2.B.28

BRINE, MEAT CURING

Degrees Salinometer	Degrees Baumé	Specific Gravity	Salt (%)	Weight (Lb)	Salt (Lb/Gal.)
20	—	—	5.305	—	0.427
21	—	—	5.570	—	0.453
22	—	—	5.835	—	0.479
23	—	—	6.100	—	0.505
24	—	—	6.365	—	0.531
25	—	—	6.630	—	0.557
26	—	—	6.895	—	0.583
27	—	—	7.160	—	0.609
28	—	—	7.425	—	0.635
29	—	—	7.690	—	0.661
30	—	—	7.955	—	0.687
31	—	—	8.220	—	0.713
32	—	—	8.485	—	0.739
33	—	—	8.745	—	0.765
34	—	—	9.010	—	0.791
35	—	—	9.275	—	0.817
36	—	—	9.540	—	0.843
37	—	—	9.805	—	0.869
38	—	—	10.070	—	0.895
39	—	—	10.335	—	0.921
40	10.40	1.073	10.600	8.939	0.947
41	10.66	1.075	10.865	8.955	0.973
42	10.92	1.077	11.130	8.972	0.998
43	11.18	1.079	11.395	8.989	1.024
44	11.44	1.081	11.660	9.005	1.050
45	11.70	1.083	11.925	9.022	1.075
46	11.96	1.085	12.190	9.039	1.101
47	12.22	1.087	12.455	9.055	1.127
48	12.48	1.089	12.720	9.072	1.154
49	12.74	1.091	12.985	9.089	1.180
50	13.00	1.093	13.250	9.105	1.206
51	13.26	1.095	13.515	9.122	1.232
52	13.52	1.097	13.780	9.139	1.259
53	13.78	1.100	14.045	9.164	1.287
54	14.04	1.102	14.310	9.180	1.313
55	14.30	1.104	14.575	9.197	1.340
56	14.56	1.106	14.840	9.214	1.367
57	14.82	1.108	15.105	9.230	1.394
58	15.08	1.110	15.370	9.247	1.421
59	15.34	1.112	15.635	9.264	1.448
60	15.60	1.114	15.900	9.280	1.475

Degrees Salinometer	Degrees Baumé	Specific Gravity	Salt (%)	Weight (Lb)	Salt (Lb/Gal.)
61	16.86	1.116	16.165	9.297	1.502
62	16.12	1.118	16.430	9.314	1.530
63	16.38	1.121	16.695	9.339	1.559
64	16.64	1.123	16.960	9.355	1.586
65	16.90	1.125	17.225	9.372	1.614
66	17.16	1.127	17.490	9.389	1.642
67	17.42	1.129	17.755	9.405	1.670
68	17.68	1.131	18.020	9.422	1.697
69	17.94	1.133	18.285	9.439	1.725
70	18.20	1.136	18.550	9.464	1.755
71	18.46	1.138	18.815	9.480	1.783
72	18.72	1.140	19.080	9.497	1.812
73	18.98	1.142	19.345	9.514	1.840
74	19.24	1.144	19.610	9.530	1.868
75	19.50	1.147	19.875	9.555	1.899
76	19.76	1.149	20.140	9.572	1.927
77	20.02	1.151	20.405	9.580	1.956
78	20.28	1.154	20.670	9.614	1.987
79	20.54	1.156	20.935	9.630	2.016
80	20.80	1.158	21.200	9.647	2.045
81	21.06	1.160	21.465	9.664	2.074
82	21.32	1.163	21.730	9.689	2.105
83	21.58	1.165	21.995	9.705	2.134
84	21.84	1.167	22.260	9.722	2.164
85	22.10	1.170	22.525	9.747	2.195
86	22.36	1.172	22.790	9.764	2.225
87	22.62	1.175	23.055	9.780	2.256
88	22.88	1.177	23.320	9.805	2.286
89	23.14	1.179	23.585	9.822	2.316
90	23.40	1.182	23.850	9.847	2.348
91	23.66	1.184	23.115	9.864	2.378
92	23.92	1.186	23.380	9.880	2.408
93	24.18	1.189	24.645	9.905	2.441
94	24.44	1.191	24.910	9.922	2.477
95	24.70	1.194	25.175	9.947	2.504
96	24.96	1.196	25.440	9.964	2.534
97	25.22	1.198	25.705	9.980	2.565
98	25.48	1.201	25.970	10.005	2.598
99	25.74	1.203	25.235	10.022	2.629
100	26.00	1.205	26.500	10.039	2.660

SOURCE: KOMARIK, S. L., TRESSLER, D. K., and LONG, L. (EDITORS). 1974. Cured Meats. *In* Food Products Formulary, Vol. 1. Avi Publishing Co., Westport, Conn.

BRIX TABLE

TABLE 2.B.29

SHOWING THE RELATIONSHIP BETWEEN DEGREES BRIX, POUNDS OF SUGAR TO BE ADDED TO 1 GALLON OF WATER, VOLUME OF SYRUP PREPARED FROM 1 GALLON OF WATER, AND WEIGHT OF SUGAR IN 1 GALLON OF SYRUP

Degrees Brix 68°F	Pounds of Sugar to Be Added to Each Gallon of Water (lb)	Volume of Syrup from 1 Gallon of Water (Gal.)	Weight of Sugar Contained in 1 Gallon of Syrup (lb)	Degrees Brix 68°F	Pounds of Sugar to Be Added to Each Gallon of Water (lb)	Volume of Syrup from 1 Gallon of Water (Gal.)	Weight of Sugar Contained in 1 Gallon of Syrup (lb)
10	1.11	1.067	1.04	41	6.97	1.437	4.85
11	1.23	1.076	1.14	42	7.26	1.454	4.99
12	1.36	1.085	1.25	43	7.56	1.474	5.13
13	1.49	1.093	1.36	44	7.88	1.494	5.27
14	1.62	1.101	1.47	45	8.20	1.514	5.42
15	1.76	1.111	1.58	46	8.55	1.536	5.57
16	1.90	1.119	1.70	47	8.90	1.558	5.71
17	2.04	1.127	1.81	48	9.26	1.580	5.86
18	2.19	1.137	1.93	49	9.64	1.604	6.01
19	2.34	1.146	2.04	50	10.03	1.628	6.16
20	2.50	1.157	2.16	51	10.44	1.654	6.31
21	2.66	1.167	2.28	52	10.86	1.681	6.45
22	2.82	1.176	2.40	53	11.31	1.710	6.61
23	3.00	1.187	2.52	54	11.77	1.739	6.77
24	3.17	1.198	2.64	55	12.26	1.770	6.93
25	3.34	1.208	2.76	56	12.77	1.803	7.08
26	3.52	1.220	2.89	57	13.29	1.837	7.23
27	3.70	1.231	3.01	58	13.85	1.871	7.40
28	3.89	1.243	3.13	59	14.43	1.907	7.57
29	4.09	1.256	3.26	60	15.05	1.948	7.73
30	4.30	1.269	3.38	61	15.69	1.988	7.89
31	4.50	1.281	3.51	62	16.37	2.032	8.05
32	4.72	1.294	3.64	63	17.08	2.077	8.21
33	4.94	1.309	3.77	64	17.84	2.124	8.39
34	5.17	1.323	3.90	65	18.62	2.174	8.57
35	5.40	1.338	4.03	66	19.47	2.229	8.75
36	5.64	1.353	4.17	67	20.39	2.287	8.92
37	5.89	1.369	4.30	68	21.32	2.344	9.10
38	6.14	1.384	4.44	69	22.33	2.411	9.27
39	6.41	1.401	4.58	70	23.40	2.480	9.44
40	6.69	1.419	4.71				

Example: Sugar required to add to 50 gal. of water for 45° Brix

Sugar = 50 × 8.2 = 410 lb

Volume of syrup

Volume = 50 × 1.514 = 75.5 gal.

Sugar in 80 gal. of syrup of 40° Brix

Sugar = 80 × 4.71 lb = 376.8 lb

Sugar for 100 gal. of syrup at 45° Brix

Water for 100 gal. of syrup at 45° Brix

Water = 100/1.514 = 66.1 gal.

Sugar = 66 × 8.2 = 542 lb

SOURCE: LOCK, A. 1969. **Practical Canning, 3rd Edition. Food Trade Press, London, England.**

BRIX, TEMPERATURE CORRECTION

TABLE 2.B.30

CORRECTION OF BRIX READINGS FOR TEMPERATURES ABOVE AND BELOW 68°F

	Temperature °F	Degrees Brix, and correction: 10	20	25	30	35	40	45	50	55	60
Subtract correction	40	0.5	0.6	0.7	0.8	0.8	0.9	0.9	0.9	0.9	1.0
	50	0.5	0.5	0.5	0.5	0.6	0.6	0.6	0.6	0.6	0.6
	60	0.2	0.2	0.2	0.2	0.2	0.2	0.2	0.2	0.2	0.2
Add correction	70	0.1	0.2	0.2	0.2	0.2	0.2	0.2	0.2	0.2	0.2
	80	0.5	0.6	0.6	0.6	0.6	0.6	0.6	0.6	0.6	0.6
	90	0.9	1.0	1.0	1.0	1.1	1.1	1.1	1.1	1.1	1.0
	100	1.3	1.4	1.5	1.5	1.5	1.5	1.5	1.5	1.5	1.5
	120	2.5	2.6	2.6	2.6	2.6	2.6	2.6	2.6	2.5	2.5
	140	3.8	3.8	3.8	3.8	3.8	3.8	3.7	3.7	3.6	3.6
	160	4.1	5.1	5.1	5.1	5.1	5.0	5.0	4.9	4.8	4.8
	180	6.7	6.5	6.4	6.3	6.3	6.3	6.2	6.1	6.0	5.9
	212	10.0	9.6	9.4	9.1	9.1	8.9	8.7	8.4	8.2	8.1

Example: Hydrometer reading, 44.4 at 140°F

Corrected reading: 44.4 + 3.7 = 48.1°Brix

SOURCE: LOCK, A. 1969. Practical Canning, 3rd Edition. Food Trade Press, London, England.

BROILING GRIDDLE, MEAT

TABLE 2.B.31

TIME-TABLE FOR GRIDDLE-BROILING

Cut	Approx Thickness	Approx Cooking Time: Rare (min)	Medium (min)	Well-done (min)
Individual servings of beef steaks	¾ in.	4	8	12
	1 in.	6	10	15
	1½ in.	10–12	15–18	20
Ground beef patties	¾ in.	4-5	8–10	12
	1 in. (4 oz)	6-8	10–12	15
Lamb chops	1 in.		10	15
	1½ in.		15	20–25
Ground lamb patties	¾ in.		10	12–15
	1 in. (4 oz)		10–15	15–20
Smoked ham slice	½ in.			6–10
Bacon				2–3

SOURCE: Cooking Meat in Quantity. National Live Stock and Meat Board, Chicago.

BROILING MEAT I

Recommended procedure for broiling meats:

1. Broil in oven or on outdoor grill.
2. If oven is used, set regulator for broiling. Preheat if desired.
3. Place 1-inch steaks, chops or patties 2 to 3 inches from heat . . . 3 to 5 inches for thicker cuts.
4. Whether broiling in oven or on outdoor grill, cook until meat is brown on one side.
5. Season browned side if desired.
6. Broil second side until done. Serve at once.

SOURCE: Be a Smarter Shopper . . . a Better Cook. (1973). National Live Stock and Meat Board, Chicago.

BROILING MEAT II

TABLE 2.B.32

TIME-TABLE FOR BROILING
(For type of broiler which cooks one side of meat at a time)*

Cut	Approximate Thickness	Approximate Cooking Time		
		Rare	Medium	Well-done
		minutes	*minutes*	*minutes*
Rib, club, T-bone, porterhouse, tenderloin or individual servings of sirloin beef steak	1 inch 1½ inches 2 inches	15 25 35	20 35 50	30
Sirloin beef steak (whole steak)	1 inch 1½ inches 2 inches	20 to 30 30 to 40 40 to 55	30 to 40 40 to 50 50 to 65	
Ground beef patties	1 inch (4 oz.)	15	20	
Shoulder, rib, loin and sirloin lamb chops or steaks	1 inch 1½ inches 2 inches		12 to 15 17 to 20 20 to 25	
Ground lamb patties	1 inch (4 oz.)		20	
Smoked ham slice	½ inch 1 inch			10 to 12 16 to 20
Bacon				4 to 5

* There are automatic speed broilers which cook both sides of the meat at once and may, therefore, decrease the time to half or even a third of that given above.

SOURCE: Cooking Meat in Quantity. National Live Stock and Meat Board, Chicago.

BROILING TIME AND TEMPERATURE

TABLE 2.B.33

TIME-TABLE FOR BROILING*

Cut	Weight or Thickness	Approximate Total Cooking Time	
		Rare	Medium
BEEF	Pounds	Minutes	Minutes
Blade steak (high quality)—1 in.	1½ to 2½	24	30
1½ in.	2 to 4	40	45
Rib steak—1 in.	1 to 1½	15	20
1½ in.	1½ to 2	25	30
2 in.	2 to 2½	35	45
Rib eye steak—1 in.	8 to 10 ozs.	15	20
1½ in.	12 to 14 ozs.	25	30
2 in.	16 to 20 ozs.	35	45
Top loin steak—1 in.	1 to 1½	15	20
1½ in.	1½ to 2	25	30
2 in.	2 to 2½	35	45
Sirloin steak—1 in.	1½ to 3	20	25
1½ in.	2¼ to 4	30	35
2 in.	3 to 5	40	45
Porterhouse steak—			
1 in.	1¼ to 2	20	25
1½ in.	2 to 3	30	35
2 in.	2½ to 3½	40	45
Filet Mignon—			
1 in.	4 to 6 ozs.	15	20
1½ in.	6 to 8 ozs.	18	22
Ground beef patties 1 in. thick by 3 in.	4 ozs.	15	25
PORK — SMOKED			
Ham slice—			
½ in.	¾ to 1	Always	10-12
1 in.	1½ to 2	cooked	16-20
Loin Chops—		well done	
¾ to 1 in.			15-20
Canadian-style bacon			
¼ in. slices			6-8
½ in. slices			8-10
Bacon			4-5
PORK — FRESH			
Rib or loin chops	¾ to 1 inch	Always	20-25
Shoulder steaks	½ to ¾ inch	cooked	25-30
		well done	
LAMB			
Shoulder chops—			
1 in.	5 to 8 ozs.	Lamb chops	12
1½ in.	8 to 10 ozs.	are not usually	18
2 in.	10 to 16 ozs.	served rare	22
Rib chops—1 in.	3 to 5 ozs.		12
1½ in.	4 to 7 ozs.		18
2 in.	6 to 10 ozs.		22
Loin chops—1 in.	4 to 7 ozs.		12
1½ in.	6 to 10 ozs.		18
2 in.	8 to 14 ozs.		22
Ground lamb patties 1 in. by 3 in.	4 ozs.		18

*This time-table is based on broiling at a moderate temperature (350° F.). Rare steaks are broiled to an internal temperature of 140°F.; medium to 160°F.; well done to 170°F. Lamb chops are broiled from 170°F. to 175°F. Ham is cooked to 160°F. The time for broiling bacon is influenced by personal preference as to crispness.

SOURCE: Lessons on Meat. (1974). National Live Stock and Meat Board, Chicago.

BUFFER SOLUTIONS

TABLE 2.B.34

COMPOSITION OF STANDARD BUFFER SOLUTIONS

Hydrochloric Acid Buffer		Acid Phthalate Buffer		Neutralized Phthalate Buffer	
To 50.0 ml of 0.2 *M* KCl add the ml of HCl specified		To 50.0 ml of 0.2 *M* $KHC_6H_4(COO)_2$ add the ml of HCl specified		To 50.0 ml of 0.2 *M* $KHC_6H_4(COO)_2$ add the ml of NaOH specified	
pH	0.2 *M* HCl, ml	pH	0.2 *M* HCl, ml	pH	0.2 *M* NaOH, ml
1.2	85.0	2.2	49.5	4.2	3.0
1.3	67.2	2.4	42.2	4.4	6.6
1.4	53.2	2.6	35.4	4.6	11.1
1.5	41.4	2.8	28.9	4.8	16.5
1.6	32.4	3.0	22.3	5.0	22.6
1.7	26.0	3.2	15.7	5.2	28.8
1.8	20.4	3.4	10.4	5.4	34.1
1.9	16.2	3.6	6.3	5.6	38.8
2.0	13.0	3.8	2.9	5.8	42.3
2.1	10.2	4.0	0.1	—	—
2.2	7.8	—	—	—	—

Phosphate Buffer		Alkaline Borate Buffer	
To 50.0 ml of 0.2 *M* KH_2PO_4 add the ml of NaOH specified		To 50.0 ml of 0.2 *M* H_3BO_3-KCl add the ml of NaOH specified	
pH	0.2 *M* NaOH, ml	pH	0.2 *M* NaOH, ml
5.8	3.6	8.0	3.9
6.0	5.6	8.2	6.0
6.2	8.1	8.4	8.6
6.4	11.6	8.6	11.8
6.6	16.4	8.8	15.8
6.8	22.4	9.0	20.8
7.0	29.1	9.2	26.4
7.2	34.7	9.4	32.1
7.4	39.1	9.6	36.9
7.6	42.4	9.8	40.6
7.8	44.5	10.0	43.7
8.0	46.1	—	—

Note: Dilute all final solutions to 200.0 ml. The standard pH values given in this table are considered to be reproducible to within ±0.02 of the pH unit specified at 25°.

SOURCE: Food Chemicals Codex. Committee on Food Protection, National Academy of Sciences—National Research Council.

BUTTER AND BUTTER PRODUCTS, COMPOSITION

TABLE 2.B.35

APPROXIMATE COMPOSITION OF BUTTER AND BUTTER PRODUCTS

Product	Fat (%)	Moisture (%)	Salt (%)	Curd (%)
Salted butter	80.5	15.8	2.4	0.9
Unsalted butter	81.0	18.05	—	0.95
Butter oil	99.0	1.0	—	—
Dry milkfat	99.9	0.1	—	—
Butterfat-vegetable fat blend	82.5	15.0	1.5	1.0
Butterfat-water emulsion	40.0	56.0	2.0	2.0 Emulsifier
Margarine	80.5	15.4	2.4	1.65

SOURCE: ARBUCKLE, W. S. 1973. Dairy Products. *In* Quality Control For The Food Industry, Vol. 2, 3rd Edition. A. Kramer and B. A. Twigg (Editors). Avi Publishing Co., Westport, Conn.

C

CALCIUM

TABLE 2.C.1

CALCIUM CONTENT OF SOME FRESH VEGETABLES AND FRUITS

	mg/100 g		mg/100 g
Broccoli	103	Carrots	37
Spinach	93	Brussels sprouts	36
Snap beans	56	Onions	27
Lima beans	52	Lettuce	20
Artichokes	51	Grapefruit	16
Cabbage	49	Tomatoes	13
Tangerines	40	Oranges	11
Celery	39	Potatoes	7

SOURCE: WHITE, P. L. and SELVEY, N. (EDITORS). 1974. Nutritional Qualities of Fresh Fruits and Vegetables. Futura Publishing Co., Mt. Kisco, N.Y.

CALCIUM, DAILY RECOMMENDATIONS (Requirements and Sources)

MILLIGRAMS

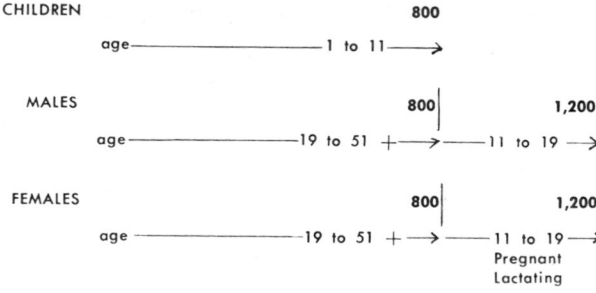

CHILDREN 800
age —— 1 to 11 →

MALES 800 | 1,200
age —— 19 to 51 + → —— 11 to 19 →

FEMALES 800 | 1,200
age —— 19 to 51 + → —— 11 to 19 →
Pregnant
Lactating

GOOD SOURCES†

MILLIGRAMS	
Milk 1 cup	288
Cheese 1 oz.	219
Cottage Cheese	53
Sardines 1¾ oz.	205
Canned Fish 1¾ oz.	80
Fish 3½ oz.	33
Egg 1 med.	27

MILLIGRAMS	
Dark Green Leafy Vegetables ½ cup	99
Broccoli ½ cup	66
Sweet Potato 1 med.	43
Cabbage ½ cup	31
Potato 1 med.	10
Orange 1 med.	58
Canned Figs 3	40

MILLIGRAMS	
Cantaloup ½ med.	27
Dried Fruit ½ cup	27
Grapefruit ½ med.	22
Molasses 1 tblsp.	46
Bread 1 slice	21
Cereal ½ cup	6

*Average nutrient content as food is served. (NOTE: 3½ oz equals approximately 100 g.)

SOURCE: Lessons on Meat. (1974) National Live Stock and Meat Board, Chicago.

CALORIES, BASAL, PER 24 HOURS

BOOTHBY AND SANDIFORD'S NOMOGRAPH

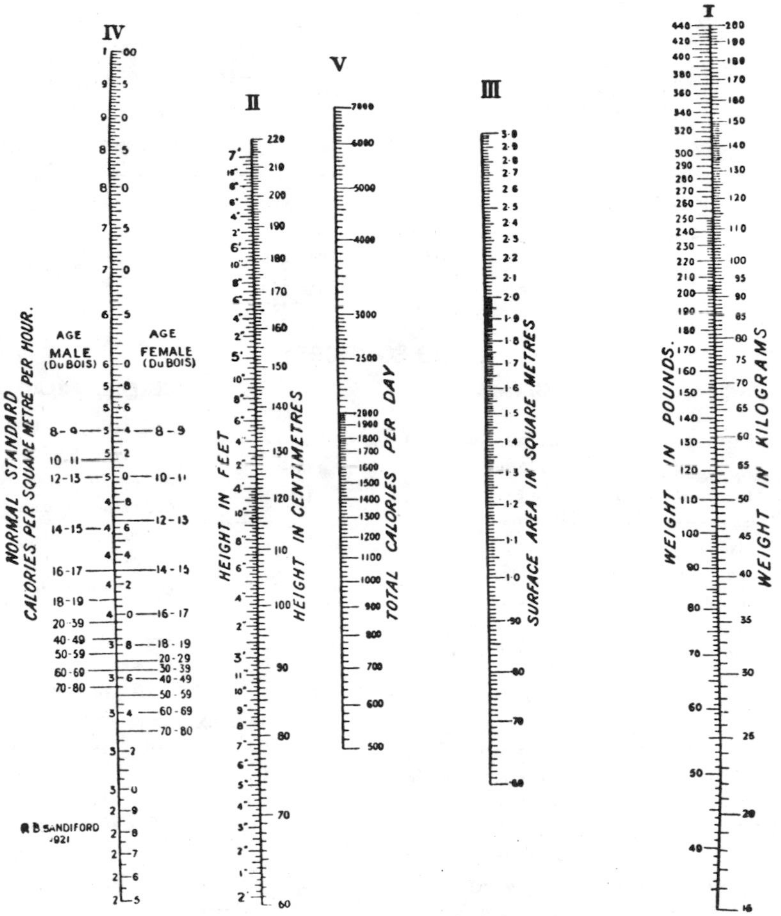

The weight in pounds or kilogrammes is shown on Scale I. The height in inches and centimetres is shown on Scale II. The surface area in square metres is shown on Scale III. The normal standard calories per square metre of body surface per hour are shown on Scale IV. The total calories per diem are shown on Scale V.

Directions.—Keep the chart flat. Use a flexible ruler with a straight edge, or a strip of stiff paper such as a postcard. (A) Locate the position of the weight and height on Scales I and II respectively. Apply the straight edge of the ruler and note where it cuts Scale III. Read the figure on Scale III, which will give the surface area of the body in square metres. (B) Locate the surface area on Scale III, and the normal standard Calories per square metre per hour for the age and sex of the subject on Scale IV. Apply the straight edge of the ruler, and see where it cuts Scale V. Read this figure, which gives the total basal calories per 24 hours.

SOURCE: SINCLAIR, H. M., and HOLLINGSWORTH, D. F. 1969. Hutchison's Food and the Principles of Nutrition. Edward Arnold (Publishers), London, England.

CALORIES, DAILY RECOMMENDATIONS
(Requirements and Sources)

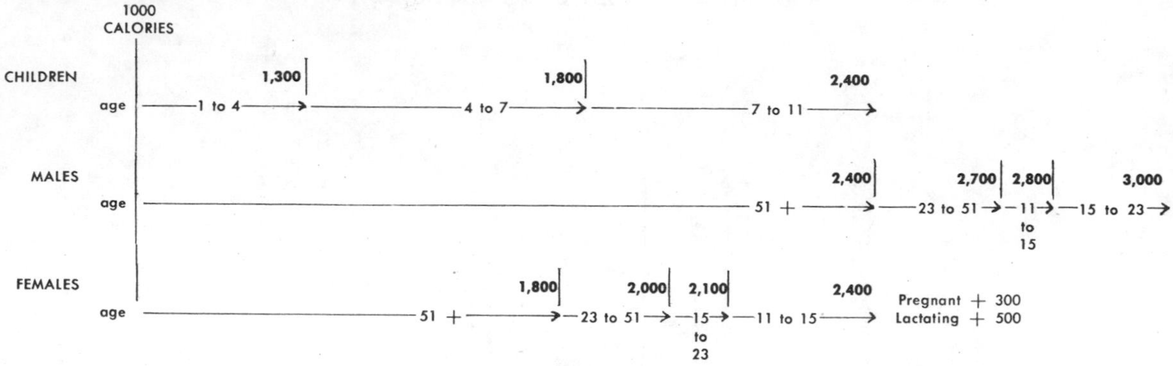

GOOD SOURCES†

MEAT

Frankfurters 2	310 →
Beef 3½ oz.	266 →
Lamb 3½ oz.	258 →
Pork Sausage 2 oz.	253 →
Liver 3½ oz.	248 →
Pork 3½ oz.	240 →
Cured Ham 3½ oz.	219 →
Veal 3½ oz.	213 →
Heart 3½ oz.	192 →
Luncheon Meat 2 oz.	192 →
Tongue 2 oz.	146 →
Bacon 2 slices	68 →

POULTRY, FISH, EGGS

Turkey 3½ oz.	190 →
Chicken 3½ oz.	183 →
Fish 3½ oz.	181 →
Oysters 6-9	80 →
Egg 1	80 →
Canned Fish 1¾ oz.	76 →

DAIRY PRODUCTS

Ice Cream ⅙ qt.	193 →
Custard ⅔ cup	190 →
Hot Chocolate ¾ cup	176 →
Whole Milk 1 cup	160 →
Ice Milk ½ cup	143 →
Cheese 1 oz.	105 →
Skim Milk 1 cup	90 →
Cottage Cheese ¼ cup	59 →
Butter 1 pat	50 →
Coffee Cream 1 tblsp.	30 →

VEGETABLES

Dried Beans and Peas ¾ cup	195 →
Sweet Potato 1 med.	153 →
Potato Chips 10 med.	115 →
Potato 1 med.	85 →
Corn ½ cup	73 →
Winter Squash ½ cup	65 →
Peas ½ cup	64 →
Tomato ½ cup	27 →
Carrots ½ cup	23 →
Broccoli ½ cup	20 →
Dark Green Leafy Vegetables ½ cup	19 →
Asparagus ½ cup	18 →
Summer Squash ½ cup	15 →
Green Beans ½ cup	15 →
Cabbage ½ cup	14 →
Cauliflower ½ cup	13 →
Lettuce ⅛ head	8 →
Green Pepper ¼ med.	4 →

FRUIT

Dried Fruit ½ cup	126 →
Fruit Cocktail ½ cup	98 →
Avocado ¼ med.	93 →
Canned Pineapple 2 sm. slices	90 →
Berries ½ cup	89 →
Melon 1 serving	88 →
Banana 1 med.	85 →
Apple 1 med.	70 →
Orange 1 med.	68 →
Grapefruit ½ med.	55 →
Orange Juice ½ cup	55 →
Cherries ½ cup	40 →
Peach 1 med.	35 →

CEREAL, BREAD, BAKED FOODS

Choc. Cake $\frac{1}{16}$ of 10″	445 →
Layer Cake $\frac{1}{16}$ of 10″	370 →
Apple Pie 1/7 of 9″	345 →
Cup Cake 2¾″ diam.	145 →
Biscuit 2½″ diam.	140 →
Doughnut, Cake Type 1	125 →
Plain Cookie 3″ diam.	120 →
Roll 1 med.	115 →
Angel Cake 2″ sector	110 →
Macaroni ½ cup	95 →
White Rice ½ cup	93 →
Cereal, prepared ¾ cup	71 →
Cereal, cooked ½ cup	65 →
Enriched White Bread 1 slice	60 →
Griddlecake 4″	60 →
Whole Wheat Bread 1 slice	55 →
Soda Cracker 2½″ sq.	50 →

MISCELLANEOUS

Nuts ¼ cup	209 →
Peanut Butter 2 tblsp.	190 →
Sherbet ½ cup	130 →
Lard 1 tblsp.	125 →
Fudge 1 oz.	115 →
Mayonnaise 1 tblsp.	110 →
Soup 1 cup	103 →
Cola Beverage 8 oz.	95 →
Plain Gelatin Dessert ½ cup	70 →
French Dressing 1 tblsp.	60 →
Syrups 1 tblsp.	60 →
Jams, Jellies 1 tblsp.	55 →
Margarine 1 pat	50 →
Molasses 1 tblsp.	48 →
Sweet Pickles 2 sm.	22 →
Sugar 1 tsp.	15 →
Green Olives 2 "Mammoth"/4 med.	15 →

†Average nutrient content as food is served. (Note: 3½ oz equals approximately 100 g.)

SOURCE: Lessons on Meat. (1974) National Live Stock and Meat Board, Chicago.

CANDY STORAGE

TABLE 2.C.2

EXPECTED STORAGE LIFE

Candy			Storage			
			Temperatures, °F. (°C.)			
Name	Moisture Content %	Relative Humidity %	68 (20)	48 (9)	32 (0)	0 (−18)
			Months	Months	Months	Months
Sweet chocolate	0.36	40	3	6	9	12
Milk chocolate	0.52	40	2	4	6	8
Lemon drops	0.76	40	2	4	9	12
Chocolate covered peanuts	0.91	40–45	2	4	6	8
Peanut brittle	1.58	40	1	1½	3	6
Coated nut roll	5.16	45–50	1½	3	6	9
Uncoated peanut roll	5.89	45–50	1	2	3	6
Nougat bar	6.14	50	1½	3	6	9
Hard creams	6.56	50	3	6	12	12
Sugar bonbons	7.53	50	3	6	12	12
Coconut squares	7.70	50	2	3	6	9
Peanut butter taffy kisses	8.00	40	2	3	5	10
Chocolate covered creams	8.09	50	1	3	6	9
Chocolate covered soft creams	8.22	50	1½	3	5	9
Plain caramels	9.04	50	3	6	9	12
Fudge	10.21	65	2½	5	12	12
Gum drops	15.11	65	3	6	12	12
Marshmallows	16.00	65	2	3	6	9

SOURCE: WOODROOF, J. G. 1968. Freezing Candies. *In* The Freezing Preservation of Foods, Vol. 4, 4th Edition. D. K. Tressler, W. B. Van Arsdel and M. J. Copley (Editors). Avi Publishing Co., Westport, Conn.

CANNED FOOD, PROCESSING

TABLE 2.C.3

CLASSIFICATION OF CANNED FOODS ON BASIS OF PROCESSING REQUIREMENTS

Acidity Classification	pH Value	Food Item	Food Groups	Spoilage Agents	Heat and Processing Requirements
	7.0	Lye hominy	Meat	Mesophilic spore-forming anaerobic bacteria	High temperature processing 240°–250 °F.
Low acid		Ripe olives, crabmeat, eggs, oysters, milk, corn, duck, chicken, codfish, beef, sardines	Fish Milk Poultry	Thermophiles	
	6.0	Corned beef, lima beans, peas, carrots, beets, asparagus, potatoes	Vegetables	Naturally occurring enzymes in certain processes	
	5.0	Figs, tomato soup	Soup		
Medium acid	4.5	Ravioli, pimientos	Manufactured foods	Lower limit for growth of *Cl. botulinum*	
Acid		Potato salad		Non-spore forming aciduric bacteria	Boiling water processing (212 °F.)
		Tomatoes, pears, apricots, peaches, oranges	Fruits		
				Acidic spore-forming bacteria	
	3.7	Sauerkraut, pineapple, apple, strawberry, grapefruit	Berries	Natural occurring enzymes	
High acid	3.0	Pickles	High acid foods (pickles)	Yeasts	
		Relish		Molds	
		Cranberry juice Lemon juice Lime juice	High acid-high solids foods (jam-jelly)		
	2.0		Very acid foods		

SOURCE: DESROSIER, N. W. (EDITOR). 1977. Principles of Food Preservation by Canning. *In* The Technology of Food Preservation, 4th Edition. Avi Publishing Co., Westport, Conn.

CANNED SPOILAGE MANIFESTATIONS

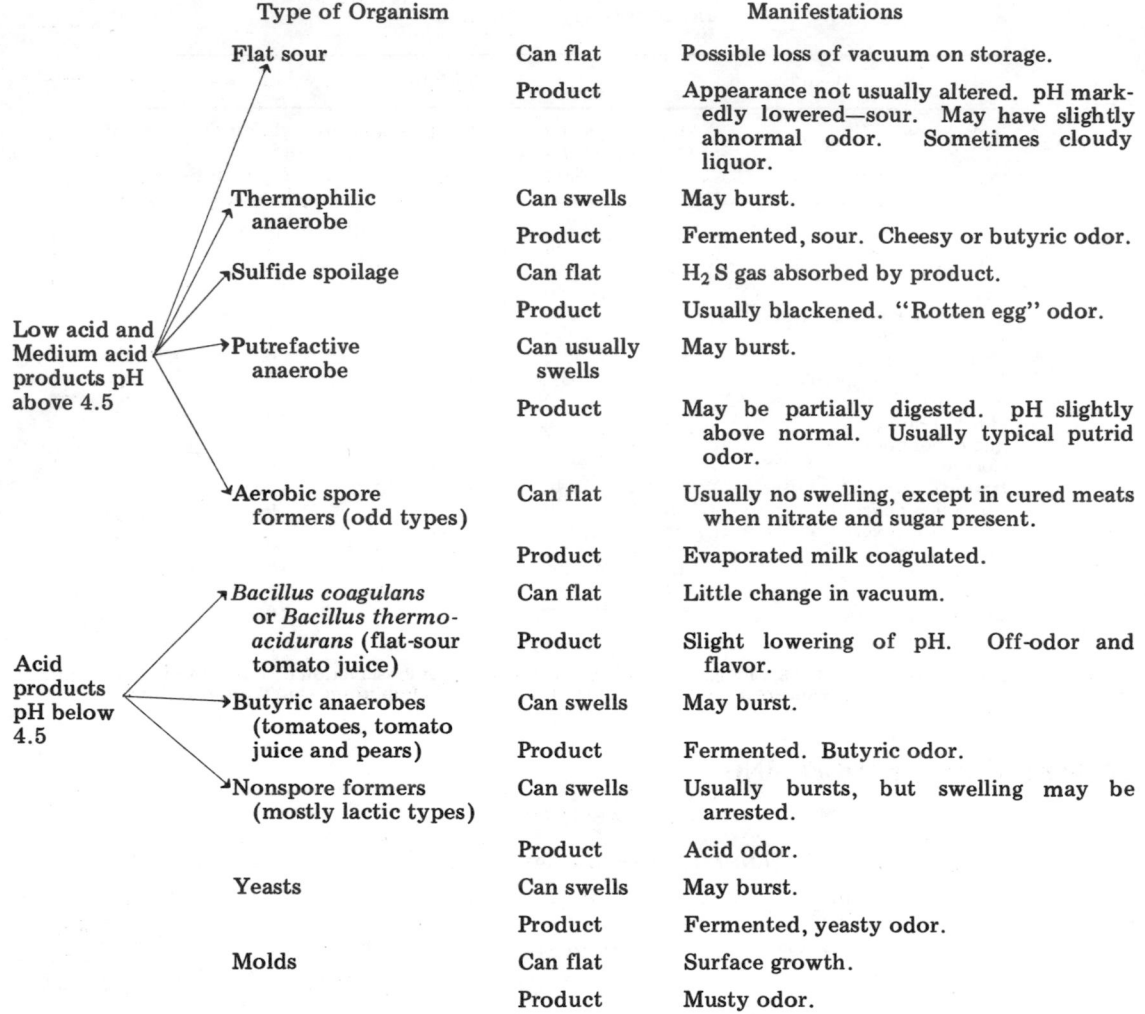

Products	Type of Organism		Manifestations
Low acid and Medium acid products pH above 4.5	Flat sour	Can flat	Possible loss of vacuum on storage.
		Product	Appearance not usually altered. pH markedly lowered—sour. May have slightly abnormal odor. Sometimes cloudy liquor.
Low acid and Medium acid products pH above 4.5	Thermophilic anaerobe	Can swells	May burst.
		Product	Fermented, sour. Cheesy or butyric odor.
Low acid and Medium acid products pH above 4.5	Sulfide spoilage	Can flat	H_2S gas absorbed by product.
		Product	Usually blackened. "Rotten egg" odor.
Low acid and Medium acid products pH above 4.5	Putrefactive anaerobe	Can usually swells	May burst.
		Product	May be partially digested. pH slightly above normal. Usually typical putrid odor.
Low acid and Medium acid products pH above 4.5	Aerobic spore formers (odd types)	Can flat	Usually no swelling, except in cured meats when nitrate and sugar present.
		Product	Evaporated milk coagulated.
Acid products pH below 4.5	*Bacillus coagulans* or *Bacillus thermoacidurans* (flat-sour tomato juice)	Can flat	Little change in vacuum.
		Product	Slight lowering of pH. Off-odor and flavor.
Acid products pH below 4.5	Butyric anaerobes (tomatoes, tomato juice and pears)	Can swells	May burst.
		Product	Fermented. Butyric odor.
Acid products pH below 4.5	Nonspore formers (mostly lactic types)	Can swells	Usually bursts, but swelling may be arrested.
		Product	Acid odor.
	Yeasts	Can swells	May burst.
		Product	Fermented, yeasty odor.
	Molds	Can flat	Surface growth.
		Product	Musty odor.

SOURCE: AMERICAN PUBLIC HEALTH ASSOCIATION. Recommended Methods for the Microbiological Examination of Foods.

CANNED SPOILAGE RELATED TO pH

TABLE 2.C.4

RELATION OF pH TO CANNED FOOD SPOILAGE

Acidity Classification	Typical Foods	Spoilage Organisms
Low acid pH 5.3 and higher	Peas Corn Lima beans Evaporated milk White potatoes	Thermophilic group: Flat-sour types Thermophilic anaerobes, gas producers Sulfide spoilage organism, H_2S gas producers Mesophilic group: Putrefactive anaerobes, gas producers Aerobic formers
Medium acid pH 4.5-5.3	Spinach Green beans Asparagus Sweet potatoes Beets	Same as for low acid products but thermophilic anaerobes assume importance over flat-sour types. Abnormal growth of putrefactive anaerobes.
(A recent study has indicated that a pH of 4.6 may be used as the dividing line between medium acid and acid products.)		
Acid pH 4.5 and lower	Tomato juice Pears Bananas Applesauce Fruit preserves	Spore formers: Aciduric flat-sour types—*Bacillus thermoacidurans* Butyric anaerobes, gas producers Nonspore formers—Lactobacilli Yeasts Molds

SOURCE: AMERICAN PUBLIC HEALTH ASSOCIATION. Recommended Methods for the Microbiological Examination of Foods.

CANNED YIELD

TABLE 2.C.5

APPROXIMATE RATIO OF UNCOOKED TO CANNED PRODUCTS

Product	Amount Fresh Product Needed to Can 1 Qt	No. Quarts Canned Food to 1 Bushel	Approx No. of Pounds of Fresh Food in 1 Bushel
Apples	2-3 lb	20-25 qt	40-45 lb
Cherries	1-1½ qt	12 qt[1] (not pitted)	1 crate or 16 qt = 44 lb
Peaches	2-3 lb	18-20 qt	40-50 lb
Pears	2-3 lb	16-20 qt	50-55 lb
Plums	1½-2 lb	30 qt	50-55 lb
Raspberries	1¼-1½ qt	8-10 qt[1]	1 crate or 24 pt = 16 lb
Strawberries	2-2½ qt	7-8 qt	1 crate or 16 qt = 22 lb
Tomatoes	2½-3½ lb	16 qt	50-60 lb
Beans, green	1½-2 lb	18-22 qt	28 lb
Beets or carrots	2½-3 lb	16-20 qt	50-60 lb
Corn	8-12 ears	7-8 qt	70 lb
Greens	2-3 lb	5-6 qt	12 lb
Peas in pod	3¼-4 lb	7-8 qt	28 lb

[1]Quantities given are for a crate.

SOURCE: JUSTIN, M. M., RUST, L. O., and VAIL, G. E. Foods, Revised Edition. Houghton Mifflin Co., Boston.

CANS, CONSTRUCTION

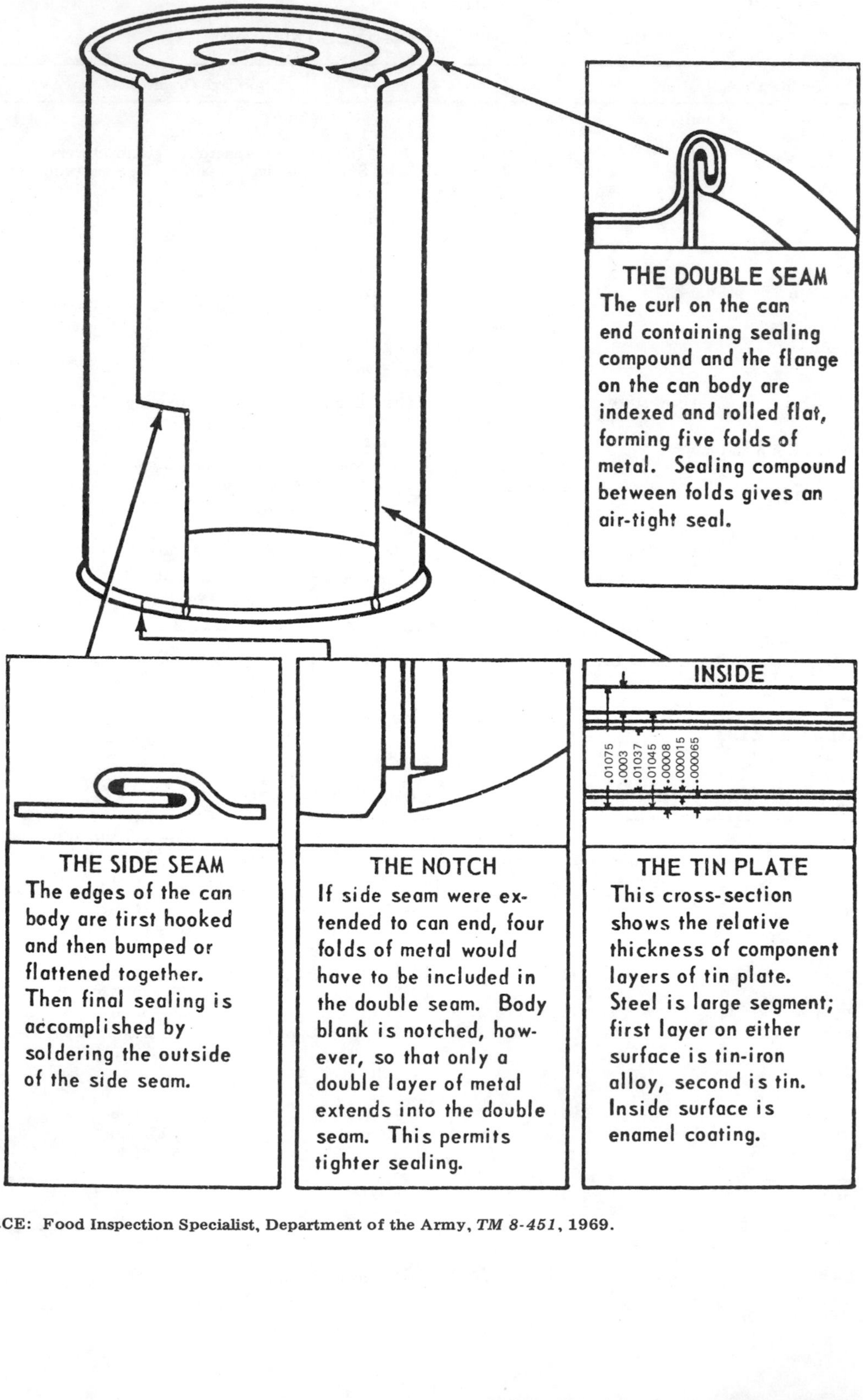
THE DOUBLE SEAM
The curl on the can end containing sealing compound and the flange on the can body are indexed and rolled flat, forming five folds of metal. Sealing compound between folds gives an air-tight seal.
THE SIDE SEAM
The edges of the can body are first hooked and then bumped or flattened together. Then final sealing is accomplished by soldering the outside of the side seam.
THE NOTCH
If side seam were extended to can end, four folds of metal would have to be included in the double seam. Body blank is notched, however, so that only a double layer of metal extends into the double seam. This permits tighter sealing.
INSIDE
.01075
.0003
.01037
.01045
.00008
.000015
.000065
THE TIN PLATE
This cross-section shows the relative thickness of component layers of tin plate. Steel is large segment; first layer on either surface is tin-iron alloy, second is tin. Inside surface is enamel coating.

SOURCE: Food Inspection Specialist, Department of the Army, *TM 8-451*, 1969.

CANS, CONVERSION TABLE

TABLE 2.C.6

CONTAINER SIZE CONVERSION—TIN AND GLASS

				Factors for Converting Stated Size				
Name of Container 1	Diameter X Height 2	Min. Vol. Fil (Cu. In.) 3	Total Capac. Avoir ozs. Water at 68°F 4	No. 303 Can Equiv. 5	No. 2 Can Equiv. 6	No. 2½ Can Equiv. 7	No. 3 Cyl Can Equiv. 8	No. 10 Can Equiv. 9
2z Mushroom	202 X 204	5.45	3.60	0.207	0.170	0.117	0.068	0.032
5z Baby Food	202 X 214	7.63	4.80	.290	.238	.164	.095	.045
6z Jitney	202 X 308	9.42	6.00	.358	.294	.203	.117	.055
6½z	202 X 314	10.62	—	.404	.332	.229	.132	.062
Baby	208 X 211	9.32	6.00	.354	.291	.201	.116	.055
4z Pimento	211 X 200	7.18	4.90	.273	.224	.155	.089	.042
211 Baby Food	211 X 200	10.38	4.90	.395	.324	.223	.129	.061
4z Mushroom	211 X 212	11.19	7.15	.423	.348	.239	.138	.065
8z Short	211 X 300	12.34	7.90	.469	.386	.266	.153	.072
8z Tall	211 X 304	13.48	8.65	.512	.421	.291	.167	.079
No. 1 Picnic	211 X 400	17.06	10.90	.648	.533	.367	.212	.100
211 Cylinder (12r)	211 X 414	21.28	13.55	.809	.665	.455	.264	.125
Pint Olive	211 X 600	26.47	16.95	1.006	.827	.570	.329	.155
4z Flat Pimento	300 X 108	5.59	4.20	.212	.175	.120	.069	.033
7z Pimento	300 X 206	11.37	7.50	.432	.355	.245	.141	.067
	300 X 308	18.03	11.70	.685	.563	.383	.224	.106
No. 1 Square	300 X 308 X 308	26.96	—	1.025	.843	.580	.335	.158
No. 2½ Square	300 X 308 X 604	50.68	—	1.926	1.584	1.091	.629	.297
8z Mushroom	300 X 400	21.11	13.55	.802	.660	.545	.262	.124
No. 300	300 X 407	23.71	15.20	.901	.741	.511	.294	.139
No. 300 Cylinder	300 X 509	30.17	19.40	1.147	.943	.651	.375	.177
No. 1 Tall	301 X 411	25.99	16.60	.988	.812	.561	.323	.152
No. 303	303 X 406	26.31	16.85	1.000	.822	.566	.327	.154
No. 303 Cylinder	303 X 509	34.11	21.85	1.296	1.066	.734	.424	.200
No. 1 Flat	307 X 203	13.21	8.90	.502	.413	.298	.164	.077
No. 2 Flat	307 X 204	14.40	9.20	.547	.450	.310	.179	.084
Kitchenette	307 X 214	19.17	12.25	.729	.599	.413	.238	.112
No. 2 Squat	307 X 302	21.06	13.45	.800	.658	.453	.261	.123
No. 2 Vac. (12z Vac.)	307 X 306	22.90	14.70	.870	.716	.493	.284	.134
No. 95	307 X 400	27.63	17.75	1.050	.863	.595	.343	.162
No. 2	307 X 409	32.00	20.50	1.216	1.000	.689	.397	.187
No. 2 XT	307 X 506	38.30	—	1.456	1.197	.825	.476	.224
Jumbo	307 X 510	40.28	25.70	1.531	1.259	.867	.500	.286
No. 2 Cylinder	307 X 512	40.95	26.35	1.556	1.280	.886	.508	.240
No. 2 Tall	307 X 604	44.99	28.80	1.710	1.406	.969	.559	.264
29z	307 X 700	50.65	32.48	1.925	1.583	1.090	.629	.297
Quart Olive	307 X 704	52.62	33.70	2.000	1.644	1.133	.653	.308
32z (Quart)	307 X 710	55.43	35.54	2.107	1.732	1.193	.688	.325
	312 X 508	47.52	30.45	1.806	1.485	1.023	.590	.278
No. 1¼ (Veg.)	401 X 206	21.51	13.80	.818	.672	.463	.267	.126
No. 1¼ (Pineapple)	401 X 207.5	22.07	—	.839	.690	.475	.274	.129
No. 2½	401 X 411	46.45	29.75	1.765	1.452	1.000	.577	.272
No. 3 Vac	404 X 307	37.19	23.85	1.414	1.162	.801	.462	.218
No. 3	404 X 414	54.09	35.05	2.056	1.690	1.165	.672	.317
	404 X 506	60.80	38.95	2.311	1.900	1.309	.755	.356
No. 3 Cyl. (46z)	404 X 700	80.54	51.70	3.061	2.517	1.735	1.000	.472
No. 5	502 X 510	92.20	59.10	3.504	2.881	1.985	1.145	.540
No. 5 Squat	603 X 408	106.30	68.15	4.040	3.322	2.288	1.320	.623
No. 10	603 X 700	170.71	109.45	6.488	5.335	3.673	2.120	1.000
No. 12 (Gal.)	603 X 812	215.82	138.35	8.203	6.744	4.646	2.680	1.264
GLASS CONTAINERS								
8z		12.12	—	.461	0.379	0.261	.150	0.071
12z		18.18	—	.691	.568	.391	.226	.106
14z		21.21	—	.906	.663	.457	.263	.124
16z (No. 303 or 1 lb. jar)		27.97	—	1.063	.874	.602	.347	.164
30z No. 2½		48.06	—	1.827	1.502	1.035	.597	.282
32z		53.02	—	2.015	1.657	1.143	.658	.312
64z		115.20	—	4.390	3.069	2.487	1.434	.677
128z (1 gal. jug)		231.00	—	8.780	7.219	4.973	2.868	1.353

Instructions: To convert a given quantity of cans, glass jars or bottles of the size listed in column 1 to No. 303's, 2's, 2½'s or 10's *multiply* by corresponding factor in columns 5, 6, 7 and 8. To convert *from* 303's, 2's, 2½'s or 10's to a particular size in column 1, *divide* by corresponding factor. The equivalents are based on a comparison of minimum volume fill in cubic inches.

SOURCE: National Canners Association and Agricultural Marketing Service.

CANS, EQUIVALENT SIZES

TABLE 2.C.7

CASE EQUIVALENTS OF VARIOUS SIZES OF CANS

The following Table gives the equivalent in cases of 24/303's, 24/2's, 24/2½'s and 6/10's of the more commonly used cans.

Case of		No. 303 equiv. cases	No. 2 equiv. cases	No. 2½ equiv. cases	No. 10 equiv. cases	Case of:		No. 303 equiv. cases	No. 2 equiv. cases	No. 2½ equiv. cases	No. 10 equiv. cases
48 6Z	=	.72	.59	.41	.441	24 #303	=	......	.82	.57	.616
48 8Z Tall	=	1.03	.84	.58	.632	36 #303	=	1.50	1.23	.85	.924
24 8Z Tall	=	.512	.421	.290	.316	24 12Z Vac.	=	.87	.72	.49	.536
24 8Z Short	=	.469	.386	.266	.289	24 #2 Vac.	=	.87	.72	.49	.536
48 8Z Short	=	.94	.77	.53	.576	24 #2	=	1.22	......	.69	.748
48 #1 Flat	=	1.05	.87	.60	.619	24 #2 Cyl.	=	1.56	1.284	.89	.960
48 #1 Pic.	=	1.30	1.06	.73	.800	24 #2½	=	1.77	1.45	......	1.088
24 #1 Tall	=	.99	.81	.56	.609	24 #3	=	2.08	1.71	1.16	1.268
48 #1 Tall	=	1.97	1.63	1.12	1.216	24 #3 Vac.	=	1.42	1.16	.80	.871
24 #1 Sqr.	=	1.02	.84	.58	.732	12 #29Z	=	.96	.79	.55	.593
24 #211 Cyl.	=	.80	.66	.46	.499	12 #32Z	=	1.05	.86	.60	.649
48 #211 Cyl.	=	1.61	1.32	.91	1.000	12 #3 Cyl.	=	1.53	1.26	.87	.944
24 #300	=	.90	.74	.51	.556	6 #10	=	1.62	1.33	.92	......
24 #300 Cyl.	=	1.15	.94	.65	.707	6 #5 Squat	=	1.01	.83	.57	.623

The capacity of a 16 oz. and No. 2½ glass jar is approximately the same as the No. 303 and No. 2½ can respectively.

SOURCE: The Almanac of the Canning, Freezing, Preserving Industries, 58th Edition. (1973) E. E. Judge & Son, Baltimore.

CANS, SIZES

TABLE 2.C.8

DIMENSIONS AND CAPACITIES OF CAN SIZES

Name	Dimensions	Total Capacity, avoir. oz. of Water at 68° F	No. 2 Can Equivalent
6Z	202 x 308	6.08	0.295
8Z Short	211 x 300	7.93	0.386
8Z Tall	211 x 304	8.68	0.422
No. 1 (Picnic)	211 x 400	10.94	0.532
No. 211 Cylinder	211 x 414	13.56	0.660
No. 300	300 x 407	15.22	0.741
No. 300 Cylinder	300 x 509	19.4	0.945
No. 1 Tall	301 x 411	16.70	0.813
No. 303	303 x 406	16.88	0.821
No. 303 Cylinder	303 x 509	21.86	1.060
No. 2 Vacuum	307 x 306	14.71	0.716
No. 2	307 x 409	20.55	1.000
Jumbo	307 x 510	25.8	1.2537
No. 2 Cylinder	307 x 512	26.4	1.284
No. 1¼	401 x 206	13.81	0.672
No. 2½	401 x 411	29.79	1.450
No. 3 Vacuum	404 x 307	23.9	1.162
No. 3 Cylinder	404 x 700	51.7	2.515
No. 5	502 x 510	59.1	2.8744
No. 10	603 x 700	109.43	5.325

SOURCE: F. W. GREEN CO. (EDITOR). 1967. Glossary of Packaging Terms, 4th Edition. Packaging Institute, New York.

CARBON DIOXIDE DISSOLVED IN WATER

TABLE 2.C.9

GAS VOLUME TEST CHART (SHOWING VOLUMES OF CARBON DIOXIDE DISSOLVED BY 1 VOLUME OF WATER)

Temp., °F., in bottle	Gage pressures in bottle, lbs. per sq. in.																								
	16[a]	18	20	22	24	26	28	30	32	34	36	38	40	42	44	46	48	50	52	54	56	58	60	62	64
45	2.7	2.9	3.1	3.3	3.4	3.6	3.8	4.0	4.1	4.3	4.5	4.7	4.8	5.0	5.2	5.4	5.6	5.7	5.9	6.1	6.2	6.4	6.6	6.8	6.9
46	2.7	2.8	3.0	3.2	3.4	3.5	3.7	3.9	4.0	4.2	4.4	4.6	4.7	4.9	5.1	5.3	5.4	5.6	5.8	6.0	6.1	6.3	6.4	6.6	6.8
47	2.6	2.8	2.9	3.1	3.3	3.5	3.6	3.8	4.0	4.1	4.3	4.5	4.6	4.8	5.0	5.2	5.3	5.5	5.7	5.9	6.0	6.2	6.3	6.5	6.7
48	2.6	2.7	2.9	3.1	3.2	3.4	3.6	3.7	3.9	4.1	4.2	4.4	4.6	4.7	4.9	5.1	5.2	5.4	5.6	5.7	5.9	6.1	6.2	6.4	6.6
49	2.5	2.7	2.8	3.0	3.2	3.3	3.5	3.7	3.8	4.0	4.1	4.3	4.5	4.6	4.8	5.0	5.1	5.3	5.5	5.6	5.8	6.0	6.1	6.3	6.4
50	2.5	2.6	2.8	2.9	3.1	3.3	3.4	3.6	3.7	3.9	4.0	4.2	4.4	4.5	4.7	4.9	5.0	5.2	5.4	5.5	5.7	5.9	6.0	6.2	6.3
51	2.4	2.6	2.7	2.9	3.1	3.2	3.4	3.5	3.7	3.8	4.0	4.2	4.3	4.5	4.6	4.8	5.0	5.1	5.3	5.4	5.6	5.7	5.9	6.1	6.2
52	2.4	2.5	2.7	2.8	3.0	3.2	3.3	3.5	3.6	3.8	3.9	4.1	4.2	4.4	4.5	4.7	4.9	5.0	5.2	5.3	5.5	5.6	5.8	5.0	6.1
53	2.3	2.5	2.6	2.8	2.9	3.1	3.3	3.4	3.6	3.7	3.8	4.0	4.2	4.3	4.4	4.6	4.8	4.9	5.1	5.2	5.4	5.5	5.7	5.9	6.0
54	2.3	2.4	2.6	2.7	2.9	3.0	3.2	3.3	3.5	3.6	3.8	3.9	4.1	4.2	4.4	4.5	4.7	4.8	5.0	5.2	5.3	5.4	5.6	5.7	5.9
55	2.3	2.4	2.6	2.7	2.8	3.0	3.1	3.3	3.4	3.6	3.7	3.9	4.0	4.1	4.3	4.4	4.6	4.7	4.9	5.1	5.2	5.3	5.5	5.6	5.8
56	2.2	2.4	2.5	2.6	2.8	2.9	3.1	3.2	3.4	3.5	3.7	3.8	3.9	4.1	4.2	4.4	4.5	4.7	4.8	5.0	5.1	5.2	5.4	5.5	5.7
57	2.2	2.3	2.5	2.6	2.7	2.9	3.0	3.2	3.3	3.5	3.6	3.7	3.9	4.0	4.1	4.3	4.4	4.6	4.7	4.9	5.0	5.2	5.3	5.4	5.6
58	2.1	2.3	2.4	2.6	2.7	2.8	3.0	3.1	3.3	3.4	3.5	3.7	3.8	3.9	4.1	4.2	4.4	4.5	4.6	4.7	4.9	5.1	5.2	5.3	5.5
59	2.1	2.2	2.4	2.5	2.7	2.8	2.9	3.1	3.2	3.3	3.5	3.6	3.7	3.9	4.0	4.2	4.3	4.4	4.6	4.7	4.8	5.0	5.1	5.3	5.4
60	2.1	2.2	2.3	2.5	2.6	2.7	2.9	3.0	3.1	3.3	3.4	3.5	3.7	3.8	3.9	4.1	4.2	4.3	4.5	4.6	4.7	4.9	5.0	5.2	5.3
61	2.0	2.2	2.3	2.4	2.6	2.7	2.8	3.0	3.1	3.2	3.3	3.5	3.6	3.7	3.9	4.0	4.1	4.3	4.4	4.5	4.7	4.8	4.9	5.1	5.2
62	2.0	2.1	2.3	2.4	2.5	2.6	2.8	2.9	3.0	3.2	3.3	3.4	3.6	3.7	3.8	4.0	4.1	4.2	4.3	4.4	4.6	4.7	4.8	5.0	5.1
63	2.0	2.1	2.2	2.4	2.5	2.6	2.7	2.9	3.0	3.1	3.2	3.4	3.5	3.6	3.8	3.9	4.0	4.2	4.3	4.4	4.5	4.6	4.8	4.9	5.0
64	1.9	2.1	2.2	2.3	2.4	2.6	2.7	2.8	2.9	3.1	3.2	3.3	3.5	3.6	3.7	3.8	3.9	4.1	4.2	4.3	4.4	4.6	4.7	4.8	4.9
65	1.9	2.0	2.2	2.3	2.4	2.5	2.6	2.8	2.9	3.0	3.1	3.3	3.4	3.5	3.6	3.8	3.9	4.0	4.1	4.2	4.4	4.5	4.6	4.7	4.8
66	1.9	2.0	2.1	2.2	2.4	2.5	2.6	2.7	2.8	3.0	3.1	3.2	3.3	3.5	3.6	3.7	3.8	3.9	4.1	4.2	4.3	4.4	4.5	4.7	4.8
67	1.8	2.0	2.1	2.2	2.3	2.4	2.6	2.7	2.8	2.9	3.0	3.2	3.3	3.4	3.5	3.6	3.7	3.8	4.0	4.1	4.2	4.3	4.4	4.6	4.7
68	1.8	1.9	2.0	2.2	2.3	2.4	2.5	2.6	2.7	2.9	3.0	3.1	3.2	3.3	3.5	3.6	3.7	3.8	3.9	4.0	4.2	4.3	4.4	4.5	4.6
69	1.8	1.9	2.0	2.1	2.2	2.4	2.5	2.6	2.7	2.8	2.9	3.0	3.2	3.3	3.4	3.5	3.6	3.8	3.9	4.0	4.1	4.2	4.3	4.4	4.5
70	1.7	1.9	2.0	2.1	2.2	2.3	2.4	2.5	2.7	2.8	2.9	3.0	3.1	3.2	3.3	3.5	3.6	3.7	3.8	3.9	4.0	4.1	4.2	4.3	4.5
71	1.7	1.8	1.9	2.1	2.2	2.3	2.4	2.5	2.6	2.7	2.8	2.9	3.1	3.2	3.3	3.4	3.5	3.6	3.7	3.9	4.0	4.1	4.2	4.3	4.4
72	1.7	1.8	1.9	2.0	2.1	2.2	2.4	2.5	2.6	2.7	2.8	2.9	3.0	3.1	3.2	3.4	3.5	3.6	3.7	3.8	3.9	4.0	4.1	4.2	4.3
73	1.7	1.8	1.9	2.0	2.1	2.2	2.3	2.4	2.5	2.6	2.8	2.9	3.0	3.1	3.2	3.3	3.4	3.5	3.6	3.7	3.8	3.9	4.0	4.1	4.2
74	1.6	1.8	1.9	2.0	2.1	2.2	2.3	2.4	2.5	2.6	2.7	2.8	2.9	3.0	3.1	3.2	3.3	3.5	3.6	3.7	3.8	3.9	4.0	4.1	4.2
75	1.6	1.7	1.8	1.9	2.0	2.2	2.3	2.4	2.5	2.6	2.7	2.8	2.9	3.0	3.1	3.2	3.3	3.4	3.5	3.6	3.7	3.8	3.9	4.0	4.1
76	1.6	1.7	1.8	1.9	2.0	2.1	2.2	2.4	2.4	2.5	2.6	2.7	2.8	2.9	3.0	3.1	3.3	3.4	3.5	3.6	3.7	3.8	3.9	4.0	4.1
77	1.6	1.7	1.8	1.9	2.0	2.1	2.2	2.3	2.4	2.5	2.6	2.7	2.8	2.9	3.0	3.1	3.2	3.3	3.4	3.5	3.6	3.7	3.8	3.9	4.0
78	1.5	1.6	1.7	1.9	2.0	2.1	2.2	2.3	2.4	2.5	2.5	2.6	2.7	2.8	2.9	3.0	3.1	3.3	3.4	3.5	3.6	3.7	3.8	3.9	4.0
79	1.5	1.6	1.7	1.8	1.9	2.0	2.1	2.2	2.3	2.4	2.5	2.6	2.7	2.8	2.9	3.0	3.1	3.2	3.3	3.4	3.5	3.6	3.7	3.3	3.9

[a]Figures in this column represent the volume of carbon dioxide gas (reduced to 0° and 760 mm.) dissolved by 1 volume of water at the temperatures indicated, if the partial pressure of the carbon dioxide gas is 760 mm. Hg. Solubility data correspond to Bohr and Bock published in Landolt-Börnstein, *Physikalische-Chemische Tabellen*. Figures in the body of the table were calculated for various temperatures and pressures based on the Boyle-Mariotte law for isothermal compression.

SOURCE: JACOBS, M. B. (EDITOR). The Chemistry and Technology of Food and Food Products, 2nd Edition, Vol. 3. John Wiley & Sons, New York.

CARBON DIOXIDE, WEIGHT AND VOLUME

TABLE 2.C.10

CARBON DIOXIDE, WEIGHT AND VOLUME

At Standard Temp and Pressure

One Cubic Foot Equals	0.1227 lb
One Cubic Foot Equals	957.5 oz
One Gram Equals	506 ml
One Liter Equals	1.976 gm
One Liter Equals	0.3532 cu ft
One Milliliter Equals	0.00198 gm
One Ounce Equals	0.0584 gm
One Pound Equals	8.1499 cu ft
One Pound Equals	7803.85 oz

Percent CO_2 by volume x 0.19428 Equals approximate percent by weight.
Percent CO_2 by weight x 5.1470 Equals approximate percent by volume

SOURCE: WOODROOF, J. G. and PHILLIPS, G. F. (EDITORS). 1974. *In* Beverages: Carbonated and Noncarbonated. Avi Publishing Co., Westport, Conn.

CASINGS, ANIMAL

TABLE 2.C.11

ANIMAL CASINGS

Casing	Source
Rounds	Small intestine of cattle, sheep, goats, and pigs
Runners	Small intestines of cattle
Middles	Large intestines of cattle and pigs
Beef bungs	Caecum (blind gut)
Hog bungs	End of the intestinal tract, usually 5 to 6 ft of intestines, starting from the anus
Caps	Caecum or blind gut of the hog
Weasands	Esophagus of cattle
Bladders	Urinary bladder of cattle or hogs
Stomachs	Hog stomach, often called maws
Small casings	Small intestines of hogs, sheep, or goats

SOURCE: KRAMLICH, W. E., PEARSON, A. M., and TAUBER, F. W. (EDITORS). 1973. Sausages. *In* Processed Meats. Avi Publishing Co., Westport, Conn.

CASINGS, HOG

TABLE 2.C.12

HOG CASINGS SIZES

Grades	Millimeters
Extra narrow	Under 28
Narrow medium	28 to 32
Selected medium	32 to 35
English medium	35 to 38
Wides	38 to 42
Extra wides	42 and over

SOURCE: MACKENZIE, D. S. Prepared Meat Product Manufacturing. American Meat Institute, Arlington, Virginia.

CASINGS, HOG AND BEEF

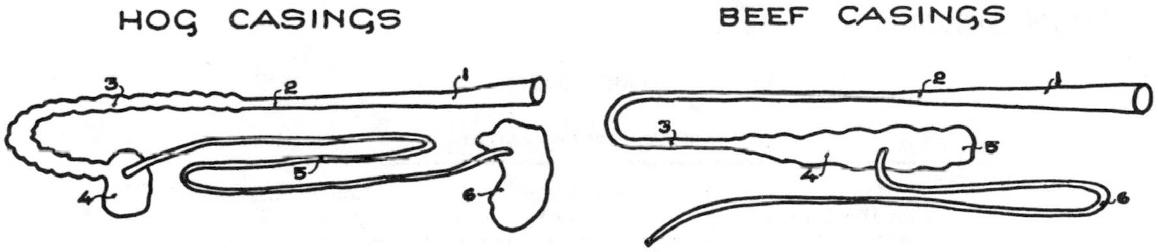

FIG. 2.C.1. HOG CASINGS (LEFT): (1) BUNG, (2) SECOND END, (3) MIDDLE, (4) CAP, (5) SMALL CASING, (6) STOMACH; BEEF CASINGS (RIGHT): (1) FAT END, (2) WIDE MIDDLE, (3) NARROW MIDDLE, (4) BUNG, (5) BLIND END, (6) ROUND

SOURCE: MOULTON, C. R. and LEWIS, W. L. Meat Through The Microscope, Revised Edition. Institute of Meat Packing, The University of Chicago, Chicago.

CASINGS, HOG BUNGS

TABLE 2.C.13

HOG BUNG CASINGS SIZES

Grade	Width, Inches	No. of Pieces to a Tierce
Exports	$2\frac{1}{8}$ and over	400
Large primes	$1\frac{15}{16}$ to $2\frac{1}{8}$	500
Medium primes	$1\frac{12}{16}$ to $1\frac{15}{16}$	550
Special primes	$1\frac{9}{16}$ to $1\frac{12}{16}$	580
Small primes	$1\frac{7}{16}$ to $1\frac{9}{16}$	600
Skips	$1\frac{4}{16}$ to $1\frac{7}{16}$	700
No. 1 broken shorts—large and export primes		800
No. 2 broken shorts—all others except broken skips which are thrown away		1,050

SOURCE: MACKENZIE, D. S. Prepared Meat Product Manufacturing. American Meat Institute, Arlington, Virginia.

CASINGS, SHEEP

TABLE 2.C.14

SHEEP CASINGS SIZES

Classification	Diameter (mm)	Length of Hank (yards)
Narrow	16-18	100
Narrow mediums	18-20	100
Special mediums	20-22	100
Wide	22-24	100
Extra wide	24-26	100

SOURCE: MACKENZIE, D. S. Prepared Meat Product Manufacturing. American Meat Institute, Arlington, Virginia.

CASINGS, TERMS

TABLE 2.C.15

TERMS USED FOR BEEF, HOG, AND SHEEP CASINGS

Packinghouse Terms	Anatomic Terms
Beef:	
Fat end	Rectum, anal end
Wide middle	Rectum, colonic end
Narrow middle Middle	Colon
Bung Bung gut	Cecum
Blind end of bung Cap	Cecum, blind end of, below ileocecal valve
Round	Small intestine, including duodenum, jejunum, and ileum
Weasand	Esophagus
Rennet	Omasum, or true stomach
Bladder	Urinary bladder
Hog:	
Bung	Rectum, anal end
Second end	Rectum, colonic end
Cap	Cecum
Casing Small casing	Small intestine: duodenum, jejunum, and ileum
Middle Black gut Chitterling	Colon
Bladder	Urinary bladder
Rennet	Stomach
Sheep	
Casing	Small intestine: duodenum, jejunum, and ileum

SOURCE: MOULTON, C. R. and LEWIS, W. L. Meat Through the Microscope, Revised Edition. Institute of Meat Packing, University of Chicago, Chicago.

CATTLE

TABLE 2.C.16

MARKET CLASSES AND GRADES

Cattle or Calves	Use Selection	Sex Classes	Age	Weight Divisions Wt. (Group)	Weight Divisions (lbs.)	Weight Divisions (kg)	Commonly Used Grades
Cattle	Slaughter Cattle	Steers	Yearlings	Light	800 down	362.9 down	Prime, Choice, Good, Standard, Commercial, Utility, Cutter, Canner
				Medium	800–1000	362.9–453.6	
				Heavy	1000 up	453.6 up	
			2-year-old and over	Light	1100 down	499.4 down	Prime, Choice, Good, Standard, Commercial, Utility, Cutter, Canner
				Medium	1100–1300	499.4–590.2	
				Heavy	1300 up	590.2 up	
		Heifers	Yearlings	Light	750 down	340.5 down	Prime, Choice, Good, Standard, Utility, Cutter, Canner
				Medium	750–900	340.5–408.6	
				Heavy	900 up	408.6 up	
			2-year-old and over	Light	900 down	408.6 down	Prime, Choice, Good, Standard, Commercial, Cutter, Canner
				Medium	900–1050	408.6–476.7	
				Heavy	1050 up	476.6 up	
		Cows	All ages	All weights			Choice, Good, Standard, Commercial, Utility, Cutter, Canner
		Bullocks (often called "beef" or "butcher" bulls & lower grades bologna bulls)	Yearlings	All weights			Prime, Choice, Good, Standard, Utility
			2-year-old and over	Light	1300 down	590.2 down	Not quality graded but may be yield graded
				Medium	1300–1500	590.2–681.0	
				Heavy	1500 up	681.0 up	
		Stags	All ages	All weights			Choice, Good, Commercial, Utility, Cutter, Canner
	Feeder Cattle[1]	Steers	Yearlings	Light, Medium, Heavy, Mixed			Prime, Choice, Good, Standard, Commercial, Utility, Inferior
			2-year-old and over	Light, Medium, Heavy, Mixed			Prime, Choice, Good, Standard, Commercial, Utility, Inferior
		Heifers	Yearlings	Light, Medium, Heavy, Mixed			Prime, Choice, Good, Standard, Commercial, Utility, Inferior
			2-year-old and over	Light, Hedium, Heavy, Mixed			Prime, Choice, Good, Standard, Commercial, Utility, Inferior
		Cows	All ages	All weights			Prime, Choice, Good, Commercial, Utility, Inferior
		Bullocks	All ages	All weights			Ungraded
		Stags	All ages	All weights			Ungraded
	Milkers & Springers	Cows (milkers or springers)	All ages	All weights			Ungraded
Calves	Vealers	No Sex Class (Sex characteristics of no importance at this age)	Under 3 months	Light	110 down	49.9 down	Prime, Choice, Good, Standard, Utility, Cull
				Medium	110–180	49.9–81.7	
				Heavy	180 up	81.7 up	
	Slaughter Calves	Steers, Heifers, Bullocks	3 months to 1 year	Light	200 down	90.8 down	Prime, Choice, Good Standard, Utility, Cull
				Medium	200–300	90.8–136.2	
				Heavy	300 up	136.2 up	
	Feeder Calves	Steers, Heifers, Bullocks	Usually 6 mo. to 1 year	Light, Medium, Heavy, Mixed			Prime, Choice, Good, Standard, Utility, Inferior

NOTE: In addition to the above quality grades, there are the following yield grades: Yield Grade 1, Yield Grade 2, Yield Grade 3, Yield Grade 4, and Yield Grade 5. Thus, slaughter cattle may be graded for (1) quality alone, (2) yield grade alone, or (3) both quality and yield grades.
[1]Tentative standards proposed by USDA. Not official but widely used for many years and updated by 1977 USDA Grade Standards.

SOURCE: ENSMINGER, M. E. 1969. Animal Science. Interstate Printers & Publishers, Danville, Illinois.

CELLULOSE FORMULA

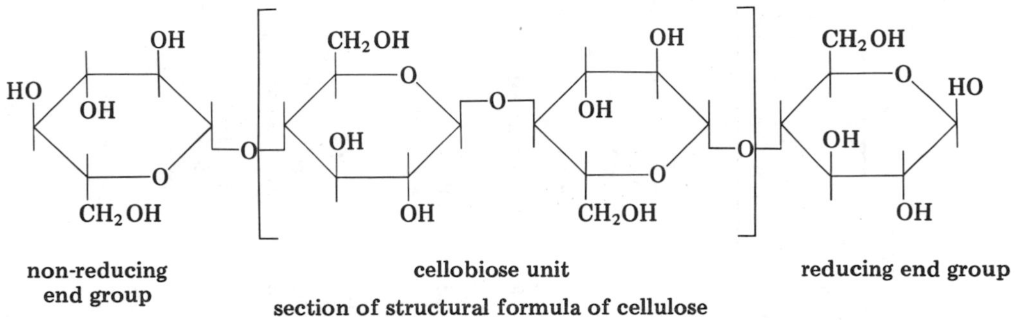

section of structural formula of cellulose

SOURCE: BRAVERMAN, J. B. S. Introduction to the Biochemistry of Foods. ASP Biological and Medical Press (Elsevier Division), London, England.

CEREAL BY-PRODUCTS COMPOSITION

TABLE 2.C.17

PERCENTAGE COMPOSITION OF SOME CEREAL BY-PRODUCTS

Feeding Stuff	Dry Matter	Ash	Crude Protein	Crude Fiber	Crude Lipide	N-free Extract
Brewer's grains	92.9	3.6	27.6	14.3	6.5	40.9
Corn gluten feed	90.9	6.3	25.5	7.6	2.7	48.8
Distiller's corn grains	92.9	2.5	28.3	11.4	8.8	41.9
Distiller's corn solubles	93.0	7.4	26.7	2.6	7.9	48.4
Winter wheat bran	89.9	6.2	15.5	8.9	4.2	55.1
Wheat middlings	89.7	4.5	18.0	7.4	4.7	55.1

SOURCE: MALLETTE, M. F., ALTHOUSE, P. M., and CLAGETT, C. O. 1960. Biochemistry of Plants and Animals. John Wiley & Sons, New York.

CEREAL COMPOSITION

TABLE 2.C.18

COMPOSITION OF THE EDIBLE PORTION (E.P.) AND REFUSE IN THE MATERIAL AS PURCHASED (A.P.)

Commodity and Description	Water	Protein	Fat	Carbohydrate: Total (by Dif.)	Carbohydrate: Fiber	Ash	Calories (No. per 100 g)	Notes: Extraction Rate	Notes: Can Apply to Other Extraction Rates:	Refuse in A.P. (Percent)
CEREALS	Percent of Edible Portion							Percent		
Wheat, Medium[1] (or unspecified)										
Whole meal or flour	12	12.2	2.3	71.8	2.1	1.7	334	100	94 to 100	0
Flour, medium extraction	12	11.7	1.5	74.3	0.5	0.5	350	85	80 to 93	0
Flour, white, low extraction	12	10.9	1.1	75.5	0.3	0.5	370	72	Less than 80	0
Wheat, Hard[1]										
Whole meal or flour	12	13.8	2.0	70.2	2.4	2.0	332	100	94 to 100	0
Flour, medium extraction	12	13.4	1.4	72.7	0.4	0.5	350	85	80 to 93	0
Flour, white, low extraction	12	12.7	1.1	73.7	0.3	0.5	364	72	Less than 80	0
Wheat, Soft[1]										
Whole meal or flour	12	10.5	1.9	73.9	2.1	1.7	333	100	94 to 100	0
Flour, medium extraction	12	9.8	1.3	76.2	0.4	0.7	349	85	80 to 93	0
Flour, white, low extraction	12	8.6	1.1	77.9	0.2	0.4	365	72	Less than 80	0
Rice										
Husked or brown (only hulls removed)	13	7.5	1.8	76.7	0.8	1.0	357	80	75 to 82	0
Home-pounded, undermilled, parboiled	13	7.1	1.1	78.0	0.7	0.8	359	70	68 to 74	0
Milled, white	13	6.7	0.7	78.9	0.4	0.7	360	65	Less than 68	0
Rye										
Whole meal, dark flour	12	11	1.9	73.1	2.0	2.0	319	100	94 to 100	0
Flour, medium extraction	12	9	1.8	76.2	1.5	1.0	341	85	80 to 93	0
Flour, light, low extraction	12	7	1.2	79.1	0.9	0.7	349	70	Less than 80	0
Barley										
Whole seed, except hulls and groats	12	11	1.8	73.4	3.4	1.8	332	[2]65	60 to 70	0
Pearled, light or dark	12	9	1.4	76.5	0.8	1.1	346	[3]55	Less than 60	0
Oats										
Oatmeal, rolled oats	10	13	7.5	67.8	1.9	1.7	385	50	40 to 55	0
Maize (Corn)										
Grain or whole meal	12	9.5	4.3	72.9	2.1	1.3	356	100	97 to 100	0
Meal, coarse, bolted	12	9.3	4.0	73.5	1.4	1.2	360	93	90 to 96	0
Meal, fine, bolted and degerminated	12	8.4	1.2	77.8	0.5	0.6	363	85	Less than 90	0

Buckwheat										
Hulled, groats, dark flour	13	11	2	72.4	1	1.6	330	(90)	85 to 100	0
Light flour	13	6.4	1.2	78.5	0.4	0.9	344	(60)	Less than 85	0
*Quinoa (*Chenopodium quinoa*)										
Whole seeds	12	12	5	68	6	3	342	100	90 to 100	0
Flour	12	11	4	71	3	2	341	(85)	Less than 90	0
Sorghum (*Sorghum vulgare*)	11	10.1	3.3	73.8	1.7	1.8	343	90	All rates	0
Millet										
Ragi (*Eleusine coracana*)	11	6.5	1.7	78.0	2.6	2.8	332	90	All rates	0
Foxtail (*Setaria italica*)	11	9.8	3.0	74.7	2.0	1.5	343	90	All rates	0
Proso (*Panicum miliaceum*)	11	11.8	2.4	72.8	2.2	2.0	338	90	All rates	0
Pearl or bajra (*Pennisetum glaucum*)	11	11.7	4.7	70.5	1.9	2.1	348	90	All rates	0
Unspecified millets	11	9.7	3.0	74.1	2.7	2.2	340	90	All rates	0
Hominy, Samp, Maize Grits	12	8.4	0.7	78.5	0.4	0.4	361	52	All rates	0
Macaroni, Spaghetti, Wheat Pastes	11	11	1.1	76.3	0.5	0.6	367	(69)	All rates	0
Farina, Semolina	Calculate composition from wheat flour, Item No. 3, 6, or 9.									
Mixed Grains, Meslin	Calculate from specific components, each country.									
Spelt	Calculate from wheat, according to extraction used.									

*More information needed.

[1]Medium wheat in this table is considered to have between 13.4% and 15.0% protein (as $N \times 5.83$) on the water-free basis; soft wheat is considered to have less than 13.4% and hard wheat, more than 15.0% on the same basis.

[2]That is, 65% of common varieties. Of the naked or hull-less varieties, the corresponding extraction is 100% and the figures can apply to any extraction over 90%.

[3]That is, 55% of common varieties. Of the naked or hull-less varieties, the corresponding extraction is 85% and the figures can apply to any extraction under 90%.

SOURCE: CHATFIELD, C. Food Composition Tables for International Use. Food and Agriculture Organization, United Nations, Rome.

CEREAL ENRICHMENT

TABLE 2.C.19

REVIEW OF CEREAL ENRICHMENT IN THE UNITED STATES[1]

Product	B-1 Thiamin Min (mg/lb)	B-1 Thiamin Max (mg/lb)	B-2 Riboflavin Min (mg/lb)	B-2 Riboflavin Max (mg/lb)	Niacin Min (mg/lb)	Niacin Max (mg/lb)	Iron Min (mg/lb)	Iron Max (mg/lb)	Code No. Fed. Reg.
Enriched bread, or other baked products	1.1	1.8	0.7	1.6	10.0	15.0	8.0	12.5	17.2
Enriched flour[2]	2.0	2.5	1.2	1.5	16.0	20.0	13.0	16.5	15.1
Enriched farina	2.0	2.5	1.2	1.5	16.0	20.0	13.0	—	15.140
Enriched macaroni products	4.0	5.0	1.7	2.2	27.0	34.0	13.0	16.5	16.9
Enriched noodle products	4.0	5.0	1.7	2.2	27.0	34.0	13.0	16.5	16.10
Enriched corn meals	2.0	3.0	1.2	1.8	16.0	24.0	13.0	26.0	15.513
Enriched corn grits[3]	2.0	3.0	1.2	1.8	16.0	24.0	13.0	26.0	15.514
Enriched milled white rice[3]	2.0	4.0	1.2	2.4	16.0	32.0	13.0	26.0	15.525

[1] Further information, including levels of optional ingredients, are given in Code of Federal Regulations, Title 21, Chapter 1 (1968), Superintendent of Documents, U.S. Government Printing Office, Washington, D.C. 20402.
[2] In enriched self-rising flour, calcium is also required between limits of 500 and 1500 mg per lb.
[3] Levels must not fall below 85% of levels shown after washing and rinsing.

SOURCE: MILNER, M. (EDITOR). 1969. Protein-Enriched Cereal Foods for World Needs. American Association of Cereal Chemists, St. Paul.

CEREAL FORTIFICATION

TABLE 2.C.20

RECOMMENDED[1] FORTIFICATION PER POUND OF CEREAL GRAIN[2]

	Wheat	Flour	Rice	Corn	Millet	Sorghum	Barley	Universal Premix Cereals[3]
Vitamin A (IU)	5,000	5,000	7,600	3,500	5,000	5,000	5,000	5,000
Vitamin E (mg)	26	29	25	18	23	23	23	28
Thiamin (mg)	0	1.0	1.8	—	—	—	0.8	1.0
Riboflavin (mg)	0.8	1.0	2.0	1.0	—	0.7	1.0	1.0
Nicotinamide (mg)	0	10.5	18.0	7.0	6.0	—	3	10.0
Vitamin B-6 (mg)	0.6	1.8	1.4	0.3	1.0	1.1	0.9	1.0
Vitamin B-12 (mcg)	4	4	7.0	4	4	4	4	4.0
Folic acid (mcg)	218	364	400	364	—	—	0	200
Ascorbic acid (mg)	90	90	90	90	90	90	90	90
Calcium (g)	0.8	0.9	1.0	0.9	0.9	0.9	0.9	0.9
Iron (mg)	0	8	16	3	0	0	4	8.0
Iodine (mcg)	75	75	68	75	74	74	60	75
Phosphorus (mg)	0	400	760	0	0	0	200	400
Magnesium (mg)	0	160	270	0	0	0	0	50

[1] For grain-eating nations.
[2] Assume 300 g maximum consumed per day by children and 1 lb maximum by adults for all cereals except rice; assume child eats 200 g and adult 300 g of rice daily.
[3] Excluding rice.

SOURCE: MILNER, M. (EDITOR). 1969. Protein-Enriched Cereal Foods for World Needs. American Association of Cereal Chemists, St. Paul.

CEREAL NUTRIENT CONTENT

TABLE 2.C.21

CALORIE AND NUTRIENT CONTENT OF WHEAT AND OTHER CEREALS[1]

Cereal	Water	Calories	Protein[2]	Fat	Total carbo-hydrate (incl. fibre)	Calcium	Iron	Thiamin	Riboflavin	Nicotinic acid
	Grammes		*Grammes*			*Milligrammes*				
Wheat (hard)	12	332	13.8	2.0	70	37	4.1	0.45	0.13	5.4
Wheat (soft)	12	333	10.5	1.9	74	35	3.9	0.38	0.08	4.3
Rice	13	357	7.5	1.8	77	15	1.4	0.33	0.05	4.6
Maize	12	356	9.5	4.3	73	10	2.3	0.45	0.11	2.0
Barley	12	332	11.0	1.8	73	33	3.6	0.46	0.12	5.5
Rye	12	319	11.0	1.9	73	38	3.7	0.41	0.16	1.3
Oats	9	388	11.2	7.5	70	60	5.0	0.50	0.15	1.0
Sorghum	12	355	9.7	3.4	73	32	4.5	0.50	0.12	3.5
Millet, finger (*Eleusine corocana*)	12	336	5.6	1.5	78	350	5.0	0.30	0.10	1.4
Millet, bulrush (*Pennisetum americana*)	12	363	10.3	5.0	71	25	3.0	0.30	0.15	2.0

[1] Per 100 grammes. — [2] Protein content has been calculated by nitrogen × 5.83.

SOURCE: AYKROYD, W. R. and DOUGHTY, J. 1970. Wheat in Human Nutrition. FAO, United Nations, Rome.

CEREALS, VITAMIN AND MINERAL CONTENT

TABLE 2.C.22

VITAMIN-MINERAL CONTENT OF VARIOUS CEREALS[1]

	Nutrients per 350 g of Cereal Grains[2]							Recommended[3] Dietary Allowances	
	Whole Wheat	Wheat Flour	Rice	Corn	Millet	Sorghum	Barley	(1-3 yr of age)	Adults
Vitamin A (IU)	0	0	0	1,800	0	0	0	2,000	5,000
Vitamin D (IU)	—	—	—	—	—	—	—	400	—
Vitamin E (IU)	3.9	1.2	4.7	12	7.3	—	4.2	10	20-30
Thiamin (mg)	1.8	0.3	0.2	1.3	2.6	1.3	0.4	0.6	1.4
Riboflavin (mg)	0.4	0.2	0.1	0.4	1.3	0.5	0.2	0.7	1.4
Nicotinamide (mg)	15	3.5	6	7	8	14	11	8	17
Vitamin B-6 (mg)	1.4	0.2	1.4	1.7	—	0.9	1.1	0.6	2.0
Vitamin B-12 (mcg)	0.3	—	—	—	—	—	—	2.5	5.0
Folic acid (mcg)	140	28	—	25	—	—	50	100	400
Ascorbic acid (mg)	0	0	0	0	0	0	0	35	60
Calcium (mg)	160	55	85	70	70	100	55	800	800
Phosphorus (mg)	1,240	330	330	900	1,100	1,000	660	800	800
Magnesium (mg)	560	90	180	420	476	500[4]	600	150	350
Iron (mg)	12	3	3	8	24	15	7	10	14
Iodine (mcg)	15	14	14	15	16[4]	16[4]	32	60	100

[1] Data from report of President's Advisory Committee.
[2] Except for B-6 and E values.
[3] RDA reference.
[4] Estimated values.

SOURCE: MILNER, M. (EDITOR). 1969. Protein-Enriched Cereal Foods for World Needs. American Association of Cereal Chemists, St. Paul.

TABLE 2.C.23

CHARACTERISTICS OF SOME POPULAR VARIETIES OF NATURAL CHEESES

Kind or Name Place of Origin	Kind of Milk Used in Manufacture	Ripening or Curing Time	Flavor	Body and Texture	Color	Retail Packaging	Uses
Soft, Unripened Varieties							
Cottage, plain or creamed (Unknown)	Cow's milk skimmed; plain curd or plain curd with cream added.	Unripened	Mild, acid.	Soft, curd particles of varying size.	White to creamy white.	Cup-shaped containers, tumblers, dishes.	Salads, with fruits, vegetables, sandwiches, dips, cheese cake.
Cream, plain (U.S.A.)	Cream from cow's milk.	Unripened	Mild, acid.	Soft and smooth.	White.	3- to 8-oz. packages.	Salads, dips, sandwiches, snacks, cheese cake, desserts.
Neufchatel (Nû-shä-tĕl') (France)	Cow's milk.	Unripened	Mild, acid.	Soft, smooth similar to cream cheese but lower in milkfat.	White.	4- to 8-oz. packages.	Salads, dips, sandwiches, snacks, cheese cake, desserts.
Ricotta (Rĭ-cō'-ta) (Italy)	Cow's milk, whole or partly skimmed, or whey from cow's milk with whole or skim milk added. In Italy, whey from sheep's milk.	Unripened	Sweet, nutlike.	Soft, moist or dry.	White.	Pint and quart paper and plastic containers, 3-lb metal cans.	Appetizers, salads, snacks, lasagne, ravioli, noodles and other cooked dishes, grating, desserts.
Firm, Unripened Varieties							
Gjetost[1] (Yēt'ôst) (Norway)	Whey from goat's milk or a mixture of whey from goat's and cow's milk.	Unripened	Sweetish, caramel.	Firm, buttery consistency.	Golden brown.	Cubical and rectangular.	Snacks, desserts, served with dark breads, crackers, biscuits or muffins.
Mysost (Müs-ôst) also called Primost (Prēm'-ôst) (Norway)	Whey from cow's milk.	Unripened	Sweetish, caramel.	Firm, buttery consistency.	Light brown.	Cubical, cylindrical, pie-shaped wedges.	Snacks, desserts, served with dark breads.

Mozzarella (Mō-tsa-rel′la) also called Scamorza (Italy)	Whole or partly skimmed cow's milk. In Italy, originally made from buffalo's milk.	Unripened	Delicate, mild.	Slightly firm, plastic.	Creamy white.	Small round or braided form, shredded, sliced.	Snacks, toasted sandwiches, cheeseburgers, cooking, as in meat loaf, or topping for lasagne, pizza, and casseroles.
Soft, Ripened Varieties							
Brie (Brē) (France)	Cow's milk.	4 to 8 weeks.	Mild to pungent.	Soft, smooth when ripened.	Creamy yellow interior; edible thin brown and white crust.	Circular, pie-shaped wedges.	Appetizers, sandwiches, snacks, good with crackers and fruit, dessert.
Camembert (Kăm′ĕm-bâr) (France)	Cow's milk.	4 to 8 weeks.	Mild to pungent.	Soft, smooth; very soft when fully ripened.	Creamy yellow interior; edible thin white, or gray-white crust.	Small circular cakes and pie-shaped portions.	Appetizers, sandwiches, snacks, good with crackers, and fruit such as pears, apples, dessert.
Limburger (Belgium)	Cow's milk.	4 to 8 weeks.	Highly pungent, very strong.	Soft, smooth when ripened; usually contains small irregular openings.	Creamy white interior; reddish yellow surface.	Cubical, rectangular.	Appetizers, snacks, good with crackers, rye or other dark breads, dessert.
Semisoft, Ripened Varieties							
Bel Paese[2] (Bĕl Pă-ā′-zĕ) (Italy)	Cow's milk.	6 to 8 weeks.	Mild to moderately robust.	Soft to medium firm, creamy.	Creamy yellow interior; slightly gray or brownish surface sometimes covered with yellow wax coating.	Small wheels, wedges, segments.	Appetizers, good with crackers, snacks, sandwiches, dessert.
Brick (U.S.A.)	Cow's milk.	2 to 4 months.	Mild to moderately sharp.	Semisoft to medium firm, elastic, numerous small mechanical openings.	Creamy yellow.	Loaf, brick, slices, cut portions.	Appetizers, sandwiches, snacks, dessert.

(Continued)

TABLE 2.C.23 (*Continued*)

Kind or Name Place of Origin	Kind of Milk Used in Manufacture	Ripening or Curing Time	Flavor	Body and Texture	Color	Retail Packaging	Uses
Muenster (Mün'stẽr) (Germany)	Cow's milk.	1 to 8 weeks.	Mild to mellow.	Semisoft, numerous small mechanical openings. Contains more moisture than brick.	Creamy white interior; yellow tan surface.	Circular cake, blocks, wedges, segments, slices.	Appetizers, sandwiches, snacks, dessert.
Port du Salut (Por dü Sȧ-lü') (France)	Cow's milk.	6 to 8 weeks.	Mellow to robust.	Semisoft, smooth, buttery, small openings.	Creamy yellow.	Wheels and wedges.	Appetizers, snacks, served with raw fruit, dessert.
Firm Ripened Varieties							
Cheddar (England)	Cow's milk.	1 to 12 months or more.	Mild to very sharp.	Firm, smooth, some mechanical openings.	White to medium-yellow-orange.	Circular, cylindrical loaf, pie-shaped wedges, oblongs, slices, cubes, shredded, grated.	Appetizers, sandwiches, sauces, on vegetables, in hot dishes, toasted sandwiches, grating, cheeseburgers, dessert.
Colby (U.S.A.)	Cow's milk.	1 to 3 months.	Mild to mellow.	Softer and more open than Cheddar.	White to medium-yellow-orange.	Cylindrical, pie-shaped wedges.	Sandwiches, snacks cheeseburgers.
Caciocavallo (Kä'chō-kä-val'lȯ) (Italy)	Cow's milk. In Italy, cow's milk or mixtures of sheep's, goat's, and cow's milk.	3 to 12 months.	Piquant, similar to Provolone but not smoked.	Firm, lower in milkfat and moisture than Provolone.	Light or white interior; clay or tan colored surface.	Spindle or ten-pin shaped, bound with cord, cut pieces.	Snacks, sandwiches, cooking, dessert; suitable for grating after prolonged curing.
Edam (Ē'dăm) (Netherlands.)	Cow's milk, partly skimmed.	2 to 3 months.	Mellow, nutlike.	Semisoft to firm, smooth; small irregularly shaped or round holes; lower milkfat than Gouda.	Creamy yellow or medium yellow-orange interior; surface coated with red wax.	Cannon ball shaped loaf, cut pieces, oblongs.	Appetizers, snacks, salads, sandwiches, seafood sauces, dessert.

Gouda (Gou′-dá) (Netherlands)	Cow's milk, whole or partly skimmed.	2 to 6 months.	Mellow, nutlike.	Semisoft to firm, smooth; small irregularly shaped or round holes; higher milkfat than Edam.	Creamy yellow or medium yellow-orange interior; may or may not have red wax coating.	Ball shaped with flattened top and bottom.	Appetizers, snacks, salads, sandwiches, seafood sauces, dessert.
Provolone (Prō-vō-lō′-nĕ) also smaller sizes and shapes called Provolette, Provoloncini (Italy)	Cow's milk.	2 to 12 months or more	Mellow to sharp, smoky, salty.	Firm, smooth.	Light creamy interior; light brown or golden yellow surface.	Pear shaped, sausage and salami shaped, wedges, slices.	Appetizers, sandwiches, snacks, souffle, macaroni and spaghetti dishes, pizza, suitable for grating when fully cured and dried.
Swiss, also called Emmentaler (Switzerland)	Cow's milk.	3 to 9 months.	Sweet, nutlike.	Firm, smooth with large round eyes.	Light yellow.	Segments, pieces, slices.	Sandwiches, snacks, sauces, fondue, cheeseburgers.
Very Hard Ripened Varieties							
Parmesan (Pär′mē̇-zăn′) also called Reggiano (Italy)	Partly skimmed cow's milk.	14 months to 2 years.	Sharp, piquant.	Very hard, granular, lower moisture and milkfat than Romano.	Creamy white.	Cylindrical, wedges, shredded, grated.	Grated for seasoning in soups, or vegetables, spaghetti, ravioli, breads, popcorn, used extensively in pizza and lasagne.
Romano (Rō̇-mä′-nō) also called Sardo Romano Pecorino Romano (Italy)	Cow's milk. In Italy, sheep's milk (Italian law).	5 to 12 months.	Sharp, piquant.	Very hard granular.	Yellowish-white interior, greenish-black surface.	Round with flat ends, wedges, shredded, grated.	Seasoning in soups, casserole dishes, ravioli, sauces, breads, suitable for grating when cured for about one year.

(Continued)

TABLE 2.C.23 (*Continued*)

Kind or Name Place of Origin	Kind of Milk Used in Manufacture	Ripening or Curing Time	Flavor	Body and Texture	Color	Retail Packaging	Uses
Sap Sago[1] (Săp′-sä-gō) (Switzerland)	Skimmed cow's milk.	5 months or more.	Sharp, pungent cloverlike.	Very hard.	Light green by addition of dried, powdered clover leaves.	Conical, shakers.	Grated to flavor soups, meats, macaroni, spaghetti, hot vegetables; mixed with butter makes a good spread on crackers or bread.
Blue vein Mold-ripened Varieties							
Blue, spelled Bleu on imported cheese (France)	Cow's milk.	2 to 6 months.	Tangy, peppery.	Semisoft, pasty, sometimes crumbly.	White interior, marbled or streaked with blue veins of mold.	Cylindrical, wedges, oblongs, squares, cut portions.	Appetizers, salads, dips, salad dressing, sandwich spreads, good with crackers, dessert.
Gorgonzola (Gôr-gŏn-zō′-lȧ) (Italy)	Cow's milk. In Italy, cow's milk or goat's milk or mixtures of these.	3 to 12 months.	Tangy, peppery.	Semisoft, pasty, sometimes crumbly, lower moisture than Blue.	Creamy white interior, mottled or streaked with blue-green veins of mold. Clay colored surface.	Cylindrical, wedges, oblongs.	Appetizers, snacks, salads, dips, sandwich spread, good with crackers, dessert.
Roquefort[1] (Rōk′-fĕrt) or (Rôk-fôr′) (France)	Sheep's milk.	2 to 5 months or more.	Sharp, slightly peppery.	Semisoft, pasty, sometimes crumbly.	White or creamy white interior, marbled or streaked with blue veins of mold.	Cylindrical, wedges.	Appetizers, snacks, salads, dips, sandwich spreads, good with crackers, dessert.
Stilton[1] (England)	Cow's milk.	2 to 6 months.	Piquant, milder than Gorgonzola or Roquefort.	Semisoft, flaky; slightly more crumbly than Blue.	Creamy white interior, marbled or streaked with blue-green veins of mold.	Circular, wedges, oblongs.	Appetizers, snacks, salads, dessert.

[1] Imported only.
[2] Italian trademark—licensed for manufacture in U.S.A.; also imported.

SOURCE: How to Buy Cheese. (1971) USDA Home and Garden Bull. *193*.

CHEESE COMPOSITION

TABLE 2.C.24

COMPOSITION OF SIX CHEESES REPRESENTING DIFFERENT TYPES

Cheese	Water (%)	Fat (%)	Protein (%)	Calcium (mg)	Vitamin A (Retinol) (μg)	Thiamin (mg)	Riboflavin (mg)	Nicotinic Acid (mg)
				←	per 100 g			→
On the wet basis								
Cheddar	35.1	33.1	25.8	826	410	0.03	0.42	0.09
Emmental	34.9	30.5	27.4	1180	370	0.05	0.33	0.10
Edam	43.4	23.6	26.1	765	180	0.06	0.35	0.07
Camembert	51.3	22.8	18.7	382	420	0.05	0.45	1.45
Cottage cheese	78.3	4.2	13.6	94	51	0.03	0.25	0.10
Roquefort	40.0	30.5	21.5	315	372	0.03	0.70	1.20
On the dry basis								
Cheddar		51.0	39.7	1272	632	0.04	1.00	0.13
Emmental		47.0	42.2	1817	570	0.10	0.50	0.20
Edam		41.8	46.2	1354	319	0.11	0.60	0.12
Camembert		46.7	38.3	783	861	0.10	1.00	2.97
Cottage cheese		19.4	62.7	433	235	0.14	1.15	0.50
Roquefort		50.9	35.9	526	621	0.05	1.16	2.00

SOURCE: KON, S. K. 1972. Milk and Milk Products. *In* Human Nutrition. FAO, United Nations, Rome.

CHEESE GRADE STAMPS

SOURCE: How to Buy Cheese. (1971) USDA Home and Garden Bull. *193*.

CHEESE LABEL

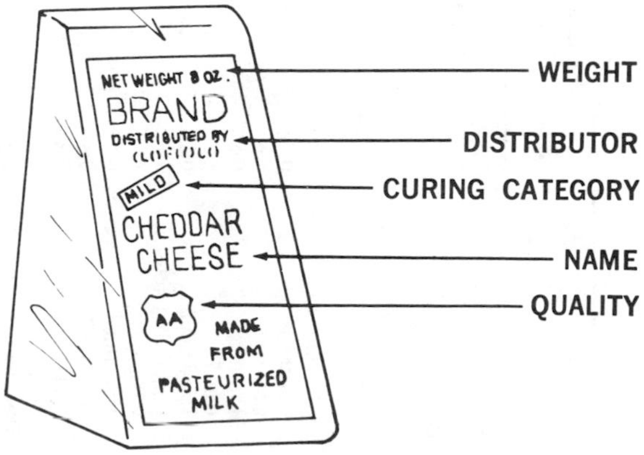

SOURCE: How to Buy Cheese. (1971) USDA Home and Garden Bull. *193*.

CHEESE, VITAMIN CONTENT

TABLE 2.C.25

CONTENT OF THIAMIN, RIBOFLAVIN, NICOTINIC ACID, AND PANTOTHENIC ACID IN VARIOUS CHEESES[a]

Cheese variety [b]	Thiamin Average	Thiamin Range	Riboflavin Average	Riboflavin Range	Nicotinic Acid Average	Nicotinic Acid Range	Pantothenic Acid Average	Pantothenic Acid Range
	(mg/kg)							
Very hard								
Parmesan	0.23	0.20–0.26 (2) [c]	4.8	2.4–7.1 (2)	3.4	1.1 – 7.4 (4)	5.3	... (1)
Romano [d]	...	... ...	...	... ...	0.77	... (1)	...	... ...
Hard								
Ripened by bacteria, without eyes								
Cantal	...	... ...	3.6	2.0–5.2 (2)	0.7	... (1)	2.6	... (1)
Cheddar	0.30	0.12–0.55 (7)	5.0	3.0–8.0 (11)	0.49	0.2 – 0.9 (4)	2.7	1.8– 4.0 (5)
Cheshire	0.38	0.33–0.44 (2)	3.2	... (1)	...	... ...	...	... ...
Colby	...	... ...	5.1	... (1)	0.7	... (1)	2.0	... (1)
Edam	0.83	... (1)	4.1	3.9–4.4 (2)	0.38	0.38– 0.38 (2)	2.8	... (1)
Gouda	...	... ...	4.3	... (1)	0.63	... (1)	3.4	... (1)
Provolone	0.24	... (1)	3.2	... (1)	3.8	1.9 – 5.8 (2)	4.8	... (1)
Ripened by bacteria, with eyes								
Fontina [d]	0.21	... (1)	2.0	... (1)	1.5	... (1)	...	... ...
Gruyère	0.46	0.06–0.86 (2)	3.0	2.4–3.5 (2)	1.4	1.0 – 1.8 (2)	5.2	4.3– 6.1 (2)
Swiss	0.43	0.22–0.72 (3)	3.2	1.9–6.0 (4)	1.7	0.7 – 3.1 (3)	3.0	2.0– 4.4 (3)
Semisoft								
Ripened principally by bacteria								
Brick	...	... ...	4.6	4.2–5.1 (2)	1.0	0.9 – 1.1 (2)	2.9	2.8– 2.9 (2)
Cornhusker	...	... ...	4.7	... (1)	1.0	... (1)	2.4	... (1)
Münster	...	... ...	...	... ...	0.67	... (1)	...	... ...
Ripened by bacteria and surface microorganisms								
Chantelle	...	... ...	4.7	... (1)	0.5	... (1)	3.2	... (1)
Liederkranz	0.80	... (1)	6.1	6.0–6.2 (2)	2.4	0.5 – 4.3 (2)	14.4	9.0–19.9 (2)
Limburger	0.80	0.80–0.80 (2)	4.6	3.6–5.6 (3)	1.3	0.4 – 2.0 (3)	7.9	3.0–12.8 (2)
Port Salut [d]	...	... ...	2.8	... (1)	0.64	0.59– 0.7 (2)	2.1	... (1)
Tilsiter	0.87	... (1)	4.2	... (1)	...	... ...	...	... ...
Trappist [d]	1.18	... (1)	6.6	... (1)	...	... ...	...	... ...

Ripened principally by blue mold in the interior								
Blue [d]	0.27	0.18–0.36 (2)	6.0	4.5–7.2 (4)	7.8	2.8 –12.5 (4)	12.6	7.8–20.5 (3)
Gorgonzola	0.40	0.12–0.68 (2)	4.3	4.3–4.4 (2)	3.2	… (1)	…	… …
Roquefort [e]	0.30	… (1)	6.0	4.1–7.8 (3)	5.9	4.7 – 6.6 (3)	12.9	6.2–19.5 (2)
Stilton	0.50	0.24–0.75 (2)	3.0	… (1)	…	… …	…	… …
Soft								
Ripened								
Bel Paese	0.29	… (1)	2.2	2.0–2.5 (2)	2.6	… (1)	…	… …
Brie	0.60	… (1)	5.9	2.8–9.0 (2)	3.8	0.5 – 7.0 (2)	7.4	0.9–14.0 (2)
Camembert	0.45	0.40–0.50 (2)	6.7	5.0–8.3 (4)	8.2	2.8 –11.6 (5)	7.1	0.4–14.0 (5)
Crescenza	0.39	… (1)	2.7	2.0–3.5 (2)	1.8	… (1)	…	… …
Reblochon	…	… …	4.1	… (1)	1.1	… (1)	2.6	… (1)
Robbiole	0.49	… (1)	3.5	2.4–4.5 (2)	7.8	… (1)	…	… …
Unripened								
Cottage	0.26	0.18–0.34 (3)	3.3	2.8–4.3 (6)	0.92	0.7 – 1.15 (3)	2.2	1.8– 2.8 (3)
Cream	0.24	… (1)	2.6	1.4–5.4 (6)	0.81	0.6 – 1.0 (3)	2.1	1.4– 2.7 (2)
Demisel	…	… …	4.5	… (1)	2.5	… (1)	3.9	… (1)
Mascarpone	0.17	… (1)	1.3	… (1)	…	… …	…	… …
Mozzarella [d]	0.32	… (1)	2.7	… (1)	1.4	0.6 – 2.8 (2)	…	… …
Neufchâtel	…	… …	…	… …	0.86	… (1)	…	… …
Petit Suisse	…	… …	2.6	… (1)	3.0	… (1)	2.0	… (1)
Pimento Cream	…	… …	1.2	… (1)	…	… …	…	… …
Processed								
Brick	…	… …	4.3	… (1)	…	… …	…	… …
Cheddar	0.20	… (1)	5.1	4.3–5.6 (4)	0.88	0.8 – 1.0 (3)	5.7	4.3– 7.9 (2)
Limburger	…	…	3.5	… (1)	1.4	… (1)	5.8	… (1)
Swiss	0.10	… (1)	3.5	3.0–4.0 (2)	0.85	0.7 – 1.0 (2)	2.6	… (1)

[a] Mean and range of average values obtained from publications of various groups of workers.
[b] Classified primarily according to Sanders (935).
[c] Figures in parentheses indicate number of references consulted.
[d] May be made from milk of species other than the cow.
[e] Made from ewe's milk.

SOURCE: HARTMAN, A. M., and DRYDEN, L. P. Vitamins in Milk and Milk Products. J. Dairy Sci., American Dairy Science Association.

TABLE 2.C.26

CONTENT OF VITAMIN B_6, BIOTIN, FOLIC ACID, AND VITAMIN B_{12} IN VARIOUS CHEESES[a]

Cheese variety [b]	Vitamin B_6 Average	Vitamin B_6 Range		Biotin Average	Biotin Range		Folic Acid Average	Folic Acid Range		Vitamin B_{12}[c] Average	Vitamin B_{12}[c] Range	
	(mg/kg)											
Very hard												
Parmesan	0.96	...	(1)[d]	0.030	0.017 –0.043	(2)	0.073	...	(1)	...	...	...
Romano [e]	...	...	...	0.013	...	(1)	0.068	...	(1)	...	...	...
Hard												
Ripened by bacteria, without eyes												
Cantal	...	...	...	...	...	...	0.31	...	(1)	0.020	...	(1)
Cheddar	0.75	0.66–0.84	(2)	0.022	0.017 –0.033	(3)	0.095	0.05 –0.17	(4)	0.013	0.006 –0.028	(6)
Colby	...	...	...	0.016	...	(1)	...	...	...	...	...	...
Edam	0.79	0.74–0.84	(2)	0.015	...	(1)	0.34	0.16 –0.53	(2)	0.014	...	(1)
Gouda	0.80	...	(1)	0.017	...	(1)	0.21	...	(1)	...	...	...
Kachkaval [f]	...	...	...	...	...	...	...	...	...	0.021	...	(1)
Provolone	0.83	...	(1)	0.018	...	(1)	0.104	...	(1)	...	...	...
Svecia	...	...	...	...	...	...	...	...	...	0.011	...	(1)
Ripened by bacteria, with eyes												
Gruyère	0.78	0.76–0.81	(2)	0.013	0.0084–0.017	(2)	0.101	0.098–0.104	(2)	0.016	...	(1)
Swiss	2.33	0.48–5.6	(3)	0.0051	0.0004–0.0094	(3)	0.072	0.064–0.08	(2)	0.018	0.009 –0.028	(4)
Semisoft												
Ripened principally by bacteria												
Brick	0.73	...	(1)	0.022	0.016 –0.028	(2)	0.20	...	(1)	...	...	...
Cornhusker	0.79	...	(1)	0.012	...	(1)	0.104	...	(1)	...	...	...
Münster	0.84	0.76–0.93	(2)	0.012	0.011 –0.014	(2)	0.33	0.12 –0.53	(2)	0.016	...	(1)
Ripened by bacteria and surface microorganisms												
Chantelle	...	...	...	0.036	...	(1)	...	...	...	...	...	...
Liederkranz	1.24	0.60–1.89	(2)	0.030	0.020 –0.041	(2)	1.21	...	(1)	...	...	...
Limburger	0.54	0.2 –0.89	(2)	0.086	0.020 –0.200	(3)	0.58	...	(1)	0.010	...	(1)
Port Salut [e]	0.50	0.40–0.59	(2)	0.012	...	(1)	0.32	0.18 –0.45	(2)	0.015	...	(1)
Tilsiter	...	...	...	0.015	...	(1)	...	...	...	...	...	...
Trappist [e]	...	...	...	...	...	...	...	...	...	0.029	...	(1)

Ripened principally by blue mold in the interior												
Blue [e]	1.81	1.12–2.30	(3)	0.046	0.016 –0.076	(2)	0.48	0.36 –0.59	(2)	0.014	....	(1)
Gorgonzola	1.06	....	(1)	0.019	....	(1)	0.31	....	(1)	0.012	....	(1)
Roquefort [f]	1.00	0.97–1.04	(2)	0.025	0.015 –0.036	(2)	0.46	0.43 –0.49	(2)	0.013	0.006 –0.027	(3)
Soft												
Ripened												
Brie	3.71	1.52–5.9	(2)	0.062	0.045 –0.080	(2)	0.65	....	(1)	0.016	....	(1)
Brinza [e]	......	....	......	......	....	......	......	....	......	0.002	....	(1)
Camembert	2.06	1.3 –2.50	(4)	0.045	0.023 –0.057	(3)	0.62	0.62 –0.62	(2)	0.013	0.012 –0.014	(3)
Coulommiers	0.60	....	(1)	......	....	......	......	....	......	......	....	......
Reblochon	0.75	....	(1)	......	....	......	0.37	....	(1)	0.011	....	(1)
Unripened												
Carré	0.60	....	(1)	......	....	......	......	....	......	......	....	......
Cottage	0.54	....	(1)	0.020	....	(1)	0.30	0.29 –0.33	(3)	0.0085	0.0059–0.0109	(4)
Cream	0.53	....	(1)	0.014	0.012 –0.016	(2)	0.14	....	(1)	0.0021	0.002 –0.0022	(2)
Demisel	0.72	....	(1)	......	....	......	0.29	....	(1)	0.0065	....	(1)
Double Crème	0.56	....	(1)	......	....	......	......	....	......	0.0076 [g]	....	(1)
Mozzarella [e]	0.64	....	(1)	0.016	....	(1)	0.099	....	(1)	......	....	......
Neufchâtel	......	....	......	0.019	....	(1)	0.11	....	(1)	......	....	......
Petit Suisse	0.63	....	(1)	......	....	......	0.19	....	(1)	0.0076 [g]	....	(1)
Processed												
Cheddar	0.82	....	(1)	0.026	0.017 –0.036	(2)	0.089	0.078–0.10	(2)	0.008	....	(1)
Limburger	......	....	......	0.036	....	(1)	......	....	......	......	....	......
Swiss	......	....	......	0.011	....	(1)	......	....	......	0.012	....	(1)

[a] Mean and range of average values obtained from publications of various groups of workers.
[b] Classified primarily according to Sanders (935).
[c] Determined by microbial assay. By a hyperthyroid rat method, Cheddar cheese assayed 0.014 mg/kg (one reference). For values obtained by employment of an assay using the normal rat, see Table 10.
[d] Figures in parentheses indicate number of references consulted.
[e] May be made from milk of species other than the cow.
[f] Made from ewe's milk.
[g] Average includes both Double Crème and Petit Suisse.

SOURCE: HARTMAN, A. M., and DRYDEN, L. P. Vitamins in Milk and Milk Products. J. Dairy Sci., American Dairy Science Association.

CHEMICAL POISONING

TABLE 2.C.27

SOURCES, PREVENTION AND CONTROL OF CHEMICAL POISONING

Disease	Reservoirs	Common Vehicle	Prevention and Control
Lead poisoning	Lead pipe, sprays, oxides, and utensils	Lead-contaminated food or acid drinks	Do not use lead pipe if water is acid; protect food; wash fruits.
Zinc poisoning	Galvanized iron pots	Acid food made in galvanized iron pots	Do not use galvanized utensils in preparation of food; or water with 15.0 ppm.
Sodium nitrite poisoning		Sodium nitrate taken for salt	Use U.S.P. sodium nitrate in curing meat.
Insecticides (rodenticides)			Protected storage.

SOURCE: Reproduced by permission of the U.S. Department of the Army, Food Inspection Specialist, *TM 8-451*, 1969.

CHERRY BRIX

TABLE 2.C.28

PACKING MEDIA AND REQUIRED BRIX MEASUREMENTS FOR CANNED CHERRIES

Media	Brix Measurement Sweet Cherry	Brix Measurement Red Sour Cherry
Water		
Cherry juice		
Slightly sweetened water	Less than 16°	Less than 18°
Light syrup	16–20°	18–23°
Heavy syrup	20–25°	22–28°
Extra heavy syrup	25–35°	28–45°
Slightly sweetened cherry juice	Less than 16°	Less than 18°
Light cherry juice syrup	16–20°	18–22°
Heavy cherry juice syrup	20–25°	22–28°
Extra heavy cherry juice syrup	25–35°	28–45°

SOURCE: MARSHALL, R. E. Cherries and Cherry Products. *In* Economic Crops, Vol. 5. Z. I. Kertesz (Editor). John Wiley & Sons, New York.

CHERRIES, CANNED WEIGHTS

TABLE 2.C.29

RECOMMENDED MINIMUM DRAINED WEIGHTS, IN OUNCES, FOR PITTED AND UNPITTED CANNED SWEET CHERRIES

Container Size or Designation	In Extra Heavy Syrups and in Declared "Dietetic Packs" Whether or Not Packed in Water	In Heavy Syrups	In Light Syrup and in Slightly Sweetened Water or Juice	Other Than Declared "Dietetic Packs" Packed in Water
8Z tall	4¾	5	5¼	5¼
No. 1 tall	9¾	10	10¼	10¼
No. 303	9¾	10	10¼	10¼
No. 2	12	12½	12¾	12¾
No. 2½ metal	17½	18	18½	18½
No. 2½ glass	17¼	17¾	18¼	18¼
No. 10	66	68	70	70

SOURCE: MARSHALL, R. E. Cherries and Cherry Products. *In* Economic Crops, Vol. *5*. Z. I. Kertesz (Editor). John Wiley & Sons, New York.

CHERRY COMPOSITION

TABLE 2.C.30

PROXIMATE COMPOSITION OF SOME CANNED CHERRIES, IN PERCENTAGE

Description[1]	No. of Analyses	Total Solids	Ash	Fat (E.E.)	Protein (N X 6.25)	Crude Fiber	Carbohydrates by Difference	Cal per 100 g
Black, EP, WP	1	19.0	0.4	0.8	0.7	0.2	16.9	78
Black, JP	1	18.9	0.5	0.1	0.5	0.1	17.7	74
Napoleon, WP	2	12.3	0.3	0.3	0.6	0.2	10.8	48
Napoleon, JP	2	16.4	0.6	0.1	0.9	0.2	14.6	63
Napoleon, EP, SP	?	21.9	0.4	0.1	0.6	0.2	20.6	86
Red, pitted, WP	5	13.2	0.4	0.3	0.8	0.1	11.5	50
Red, pitted, JP	2	14.2	0.5	0.9	0.9	0.2	11.8	59
Red, pitted, SP	?	29.8	0.6	0.1	0.6	0.2	28.3	117

[1] The letters are to be interpreted as follows: EP, edible portion ; WP, water pack; JP, juice pack; SP, syrup pack.

SOURCE: MARSHALL, R. E. Cherries and Cherry Products. *In* Economic Crops, Vol. *5*. Z. I. Kertesz (Editor). John Wiley & Sons, New York.

CHLORIDE SALT, INJURY

TABLE 2.C.31

FRUIT ROOTSTOCKS AND VARIETIES

When chloride salts predominate, the Cl^- concentration in the saturation extracts should not exceed the maximum permissible amounts shown below if leaf injury is to be avoided.

	Crop	Specification	Max Permissible Cl^- (mEq/L)		Crop	Specification	Max Permissible Cl^- (mEq/L)
		Rootstocks				Varieties	
1	Avocado	West Indian	8	9	Berries[1]	Boysenberry; Olallie blackberry	10
2		Mexican	5				
3	Citrus	Rangpur lime; Cleopatra mandarin	25	10		Indian Summer raspberry	5
4		Rough lemon; tangelo; sour orange	15	11	Strawberry	Lassen	8
				12		Shasta	5
5		Sweet orange, citrange	10	13	Grape	Thompson Seedless; Perlette	25
6	Stone fruit	Marianna	25	14		Cardinal; Black Rose	10
7		Lovell; Shalil	10				
8		Yunnan	7				

[1] Data available for single variety of each crop only.

SOURCE: ALTMAN, P. L. and DITTMER, D. S. (EDITORS). 1966. Environmental Biology. Federation of American Societies for Experimental Biology, Bethesda, Maryland. Cited from Bernstein, L., 1965, USDA Agric. Inform. Bull. *292*.

CHLORINE AVAILABILITY

TABLE 2.C.32

AVAILABLE CHLORINE IN VARIOUS PREPARATIONS

Chemical	Equivalent Percentage Available Chlorine	Therefore a label stating: This Percentage of Chemical	Contains this Percentage Avg Chlorine
Sodium hypochlorite	100	6.0	6.0
Calcium hypochlorite	100	50.0	50.0
Dichloroisocyanuric acid	70	5.8	4.0
Trichloroisocyanuric acid	90	10.0	9.0
Potassium dichloroisocyanurate	59	25.4	15.0
Sodium dichloroisocyanurate	60	18.0	10.8
Dichlorodimethyl hydantoin	66	25.0	16.5
Chloramine T	25	16.0	4.0

SOURCE: HARPER, W. J. 1972. Sanitation in Dairy Food Plants. *In* Food Sanitation, R. K. Guthrie (Editor). Avi Publishing Co., Westport, Conn.

CHLORINE COMPOUNDS

TABLE 2.C.33

CHLORINE COMPOUNDS
Classes of Available Chlorine Compounds

COMPOUND	STRUCTURE	SOLUBILITY
GASEOUS CHLORINE	Cl : Cl	0.716 GM/100 GM
CALCIUM HYPOCHLORITE	$Ca(OCl)_2$	6.9 GM/100 GM (PRODUCES SLUDGE)
SODIUM HYPOCHLORITE	Na—OCl	
CHLORAMINE T	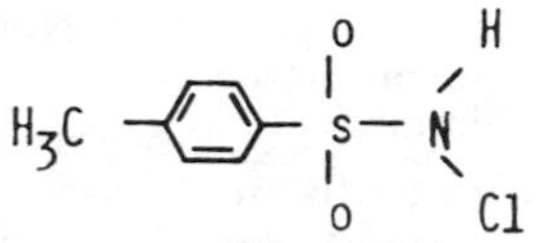	15 GM/100 GM 1.2 GM/100 GM
DICHLORODIMETHYL HYDANTOIN	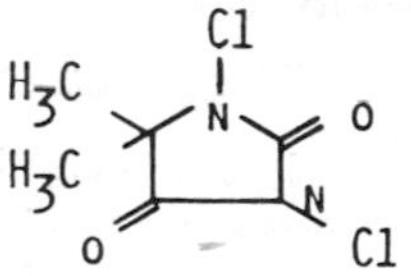	
DICHLOROCYANURIC ACID	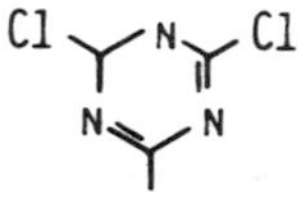	2.6 GM/100 GM (SODIUM SALT IS ABOUT 10 X AS SOLUBLE)
TRICHLOROCYANURIC ACID	(Cl)	1.2 GM/100 GM

SOURCE: HARPER, W. J. 1972. Sanitation in Dairy Food Plants. *In* Food Sanitation, R. K. Guthrie (Editor). Avi Publishing Co., Westport, Conn.

CHLORINE, WATER TREATMENT

TABLE 2.C.34

AMOUNTS OF CHLORINE COMPOUND FOR CHARGING CHEMICAL TANK ON WATER TREATING EQUIPMENT

Ppm Chlorine Desired in Water	Available Chlorine 5%	Available Chlorine 15%	Available Chlorine 50%	Available Chlorine 70%
	Weighed ounces of Compound Required for 1000 gal.			
4	9.6	3.2	1.0	0.7
6	14.0	4.8	1.5	1.0
8	19.2	6.4	2.0	1.4
10	24.0	8.0	2.6	1.8
12	29.0	9.6	3.1	2.2

SOURCE: WOODROOF, J. G. and PHILLIPS, G. F. (EDITORS). 1974. Water in Beverages. *In* Beverages: Carbonated and Noncarbonated. Avi Publishing Co., Westport, Conn.

CLOUDING AGENTS

TABLE 2.C.35

ADVANTAGES AND LIMITATIONS OF CLOUDING AGENTS

Finished Product	Clouding Agent of Choice	Advantages	Limitations	Percentage in Finished Product
Bottled drinks	Neutral or citrus blenders	Improved flavor and shelf-life	Intensity of cloud limited	0.065-0.26
Canned drinks	Neutral or citrus blenders	Improved flavor and shelf-life	Cloud intensity limited if ringing undesirable	0.065-0.26
Dry drink powders	Spray-dried clouds	Easily incorporated in mix	None	0.1-0.25
Liquid alcoholic mixers	Non-stabilized blenders	Greater flavor stability and flexibility	Somewhat less cloud stability	0.1-0.2

SOURCE: WOODROOF, J. G. and PHILLIPS, G. F. (EDITORS). 1974. Beverage Acids, Flavors, Colors, and Emulsifiers. *In* Beverages: Carbonated and Noncarbonated. Avi Publishing Co., Westport, Conn.

COATINGS

TABLE 2.C.36

TYPICAL CONFECTIONERS' COATINGS

	Coating Type, Weight %			
Ingredient	Milk Chocolate	Sweet Chocolate	Compounds	Pastel
Sugar	47.8	48.3	48.0	9.8
Chocolate liquor	16.0	31.0	...	...
Cocoa powder (10% fat)	...	...	8.0	...
Cocoa butter	18.2	19.2	...	...
Hard butter	...	...	30.7	31.7
Whole milk powder (26% fat)	16.5	...	...	...
Msnf	...	...	11.8	18.0
Lecithin	0.3	0.3	0.3	0.3
Sorbitan monostearate	0.6	0.6	0.6	0.6
Polysorbate 60	0.4	0.4	0.4	0.4
Salt	0.2	0.2	0.2	0.2

Flavor: vanillin, ethyl vanillin, heliotropin
Food colors are added to pastel coatings.

SOURCE: WEISS, T. J. (EDITOR). 1970. Confectionery Coatings. *In* Food Oils and Their Uses. Avi Publishing Co., Westport, Conn.

COCOA, COMPOSITION

TABLE 2.C.37

ANALYSES OF UNFERMENTED WEST AFRICAN COCOA

Constituent	Dried Beans (%)	Fat-free Material (%)
Cotyledons	89.60	—
Shell	9.63	—
Germ	0.77	—
Fat	53.05	—
Water	3.65	—
Ash (total)	2.63	6.07
Nitrogen		
Total nitrogen	2.28	5.27
Protein nitrogen	1.50	3.46
Ammonia nitrogen	0.028	0.065
Amide nitrogen	0.188	0.434
Theobromine	1.71	3.95
Caffeine	0.085	0.196
Carbohydrates		
Glucose	0.30	0.69
Sucrose	Nil	Nil
Starch	6.10	14.09
Pectins	2.25	5.20
Fiber	2.09	4.83
Cellulose	1.92	4.43
Pentosans	1.27	2.93
Mucilage and gums	0.38	0.88
Tannins	7.54	17.43
Acids		
Acetic (free)	0.014	0.032
Oxalic	0.29	0.67

SOURCE: ROHAN, T. A. Processing of Raw Cocoa for the Market. FAO, United Nations, Rome.

COCOA CULTIVATION

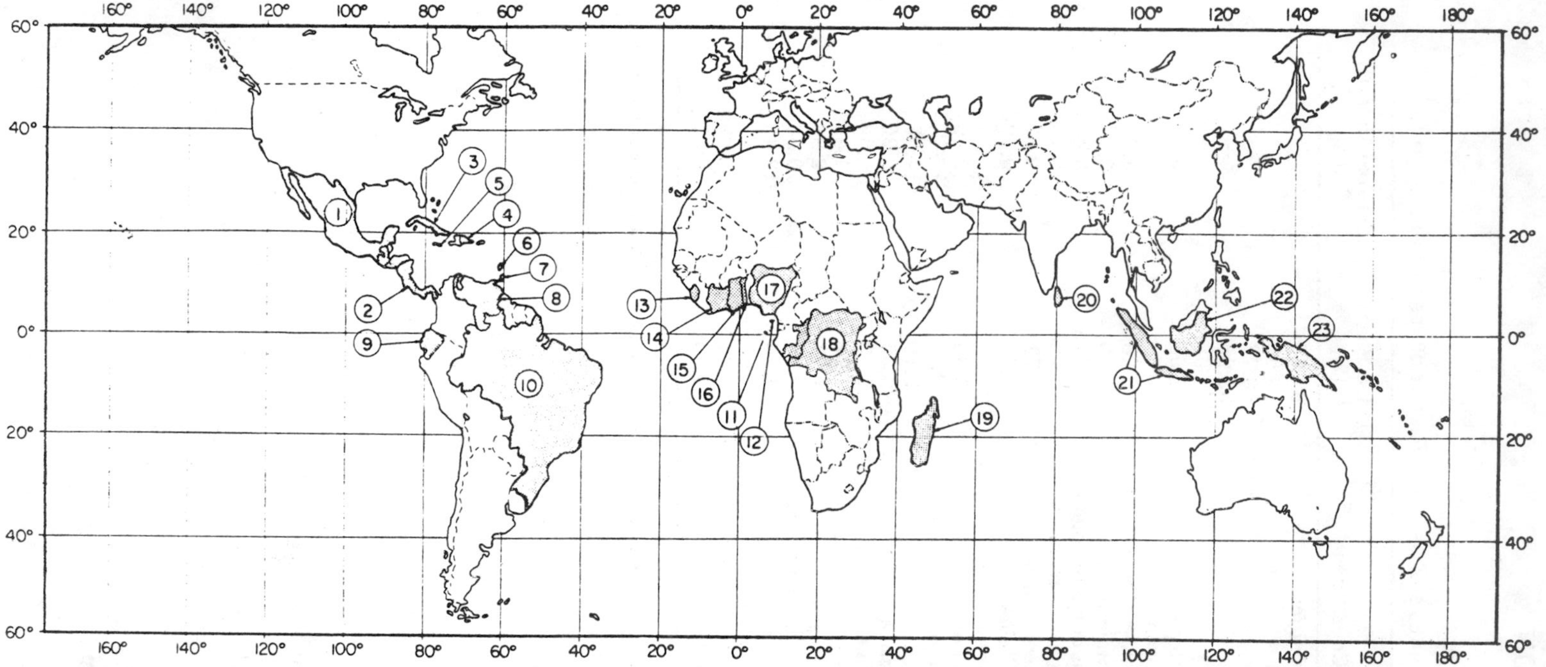

FIG. 2.C.2. GEOGRAPHICAL DISTRIBUTION OF COCOA CULTIVATION, SHOWING ONLY THE MORE IMPORTANT AREAS

1. Mexico. 2. Central America. 3. Cuba. 4. Dominican Republic. 5. Jamaica. 6. Grenada. 7. Trinidad. 8. Venezuela. 9. Equador. 10. Brazil. 11. São Tomé. 12. Fernando Po. 13. Sierra Leone. 14. Ivory Coast. 15. Ghana. 16. Togo. 17. Nigeria. 18. Zaire. 19. Mozambique. 20. Ceylon. 21. Indonesia. 22. Borneo. 23. New Guinea.

SOURCE: ROHAN, T. A. Processing of Raw Cocoa for the Market. Food and Agriculture Organization, United Nations, Rome.

COCONUT, AMINO ACIDS

TABLE 2.C.38

AMINO ACID ANALYSES OF COCONUT PROTEINS
(GRAMS OF AMINO ACID PER 16 G OF N)

Amino Acid	Cocoflour	Purified Protein[1]	Paring Meal
Ala	4.61	4.01	5.35
Arg	15.40	14.40	17.92
Asp	9.16	8.49	9.82
½ Cys	1.46	0.57	2.89
Glu	21.17	17.84	20.05
Gly	5.62	4.10	5.28
His	3.14	2.04	3.52
Iso	3.71	3.83	4.02
Leu	8.37	7.08	7.68
Lys	3.59	3.34	6.31
Met	1.63	2.34	1.57
Phe	5.11	5.13	4.84
Pro	4.10	3.44	4.34
Ser	4.95	5.46	5.22
Thr	3.65	3.32	3.84
Try	1.18	1.12	—
Tyr	3.14	2.93	3.14
Val	5.51	5.54	5.78
Ammonia	—	1.29	—

[1]Average of analyses of four preparations of purified coconut protein that were over 90% protein.

SOURCE: STRENGTH, D. R. 1971. Preparation, Characterization, and Evaluation of Coconut Protein, Proc. 3rd Int. Congr. Food Sci. Technol.

COFFEE BERRY

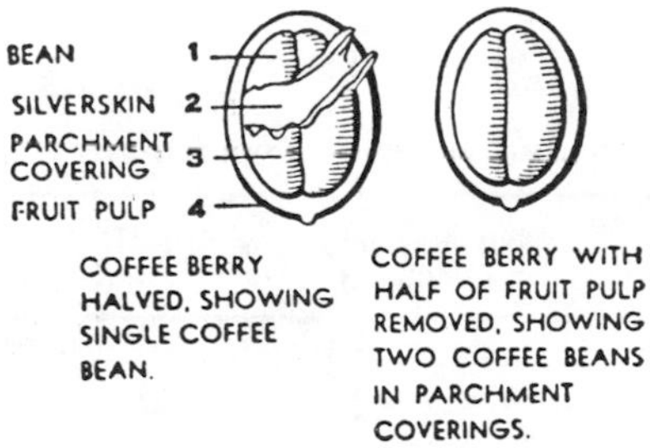

Fig. 2.C.3. STRUCTURE OF THE COFFEE BERRY

SOURCE: JUSTIN, M. M., RUST, L. O. and VAIL, G. E. Foods, Revised Edition. Houghton Mifflin Company, Boston.

COFFEE COMPOSITION

TABLE 2.C.39

CHEMICAL COMPOSITION OF SOLUBLE AND INSOLUBLE PORTIONS OF ROAST COFFEE
(Approximate Dry Basis)

	Solubles (%)	Insolubles (%)
Carbohydrates (53%)		
Reducing sugars	2	—
Caramelized sugars	17	—
Hemicellulose (hydrolyzable)	10	4
Fiber (not hydrolyzable)	—	22
Oils	—	15
Proteins ($N \times 6.25$); amino acids are soluble	2	11
Ash (oxide)	3	1
Acids, nonvolatile		
Chlorogenic	4.5	—
Caffeic	0.5	—
Quinic	0.5	—
Oxalic, malic, citric, tartaric	1.0	—
Volatile acids	0.35	—
Trigonelline	1.0	—
Caffeine (Arabicas 1.0%, Robustas 2.0%)	1.2	—
Phenolics (estimated)	2.0	—
Volatiles		
Carbon dioxide	Trace	2
Essence of aroma and flavor	0.04	—
Total	45	55

SOURCE: SIVETZ, M. 1974. Coffee. *In* Encyclopedia of Food Technology. A. H. Johnson and M. S. Peterson (Editors). Avi Publishing Co., Westport, Conn.

COFFEE GRANULE DESIGNATION

TABLE 2.C.40

GRANULE DESIGNATION: SIZE, NUMBER AND SURFACE AREA PER UNIT WEIGHT

Grind Designation	Approx Mesh (mm)	No. Particles per Gram	Relative No. Particles/Gram	Granule Area Exposed cm^2 per Gram Coffee
Whole bean	4/6.0	6	1 (basis)	8
Cracked bean	8/3.0	48	8	16
Regular grind	12/1.5	400	64	32
Fine grind	24/0.75	3,200	512	64
Vend grind	40/0.375	24,000	4,100	128

SOURCE: SIVETZ, M. 1974. Coffee Origin and Use. Coffee Publications, Corvallis, Oregon.

COFFEE PARTICLE SIZE

TABLE 2.C.41

PARTICLE SIZE ANALYSES OF ROAST AND GROUND COFFEE

Wire Meshes per Inch	Opening in Screen in.	Opening in Screen mm	Weight Percentage on Each Screen Size: Commercial Regular	Commercial Drip	Commercial Fine	Vending Batch	Vending Single Cup
10	0.074	1.84	33 (10–14)	7 (10–14)	0	2	—
14	0.051	1.27					
20	0.034	0.86	55 (20–28)	73 (20–28)	70	33	0
28	0.020	0.51				40	<10
35	0.0176	0.45	—	—	—	15	35
48	0.011	0.28	—	—	—	—	35
Pan	—	—	12	20	30	10	>20
			100	100	100	100	100

SOURCE: SIVETZ, M. 1974. Coffee Origin and Use. Coffee Publications, Corvallis, Oregon.

COFFEE YIELD

TABLE 2.C.42

YIELD OF COFFEE OF DIFFERENT STRENGTHS

Cup Size in Ounces	Usual Portion Ounces	Number of Cups Yield at: 2 Gal. per Lb	2¼ Gal. per Lb	2½ Gal. per Lb	2¾ Gal. per Lb	3 Gal. per Lb
5	4	56	64	72	80	88
6	4½	50	57	64	71	78
6½	5	45	51	57	64	70
7	5½	40	46	52	58	64
½ Gal. Equipment						
Coffee Weight Use		4 Oz	3½ Oz	3⅕ Oz	3 Oz	2¾ Oz
Beverage Yield of		56.0	56.0	57.0	60.0	60.0

SOURCE: SIVETZ, M. 1974. Coffee Origin and Use. Coffee Publications, Corvallis, Oregon.

COFFEE WHITENER, COMPOSITION

TABLE 2.C.43

COFFEE WHITENER FORMULATIONS

Ingredient	Weight % Liquid	Weight % Powder	Ingredient	Weight % Liquid	Weight % Powder
Sugar	1.0–3.0		Carrageenan	0.1–0.2	
Corn syrup solids (42 DE)	1.5–3.0	55.0–60.0	Dipotassium phosphate[2]	0.1–0.3	1.2–1.8
Fat	3.0–18.0	35.0–40.0	Flavor, color		
Sodium caseinate	1.0–3.0	4.5–5.5	Water to make 100%		
Mono-, diglycerides	0.3–0.5	0.2–0.5[1]	(liquid type)		

Source: Anon. (1966).

[1] Mono-, diglycerides 60%, Sorbitan monostearate 20%, Polysorbate 60 20% } 0.3–0.5% or Mono-, diglycerides 75%, Polysorbate 65 25% } 0.2–0.4%

[2] Disodium phosphate or sodium citrate may be substituted.

SOURCE: WEISS, T. J. (EDITOR). 1970. Imitation Dairy Products. *In* Food Oils and Their Uses. Avi Publishing Co., Westport, Conn.

COLOR ADDITIVES

TABLE 2.C.44

FAO/WHO CLASSIFICATION AND ACCEPTABLE DAILY INTAKES OF COLOR ADDITIVES PERMITTED IN THE UNITED STATES, EXEMPT FROM CERTIFICATION

Name	Color Index No.	Toxicological Classification	Maximum Acceptable Daily Intake for Man mg/Kg Body Weight	U.S. Use Limits
Algae meal, dried[d]	—	c	—	Chicken feed only
Annatto extract	75120	A	1.25[a]	GMP
Beta-apo-8′-carotenal	—	A	2.5[f]	May not exceed 15 mg per pound or pint of the food
Beets, dehydrated (beet powder)	—	e	—	GMP
Canthaxanthine	—	A	12.5	May not exceed 30 mg per pound or pint of the food
Caramel	—	D	—	GMP
Carbon black	77266	c	—	g
Carotene (natural)	75130	c	—	GMP
Beta-carotene (synthetic)	—	A	2.5[f]	GMP
Carrot oil	—	e	—	GMP
Cochineal extract; carmine	75470	c	—	GMP
Corn endosperm oil[d]	—	c	—	Chicken feed only
Cottonseed flour, partially defatted, cooked, toasted	—	e	—	GMP
Ferrous gluconate	—	e	—	Ripe olives only
Fruit juice	—	e	—	GMP
Grape skin extract (Enocianina)	—	e	—	Still and carbonated drinks and ades, beverage bases and alcoholic beverages
Iron oxide, synthetic	77492	c	—	May not exceed 0.25% by weight of dog and cat food
Paprika	—	e	—	GMP
Paprika oleoresin	—	e	—	GMP
Riboflavin	—	A	0.5	GMP
Saffron	75100	c	—	GMP
Tagetes meal and extract[d]	—	c	—	Chicken feed only
Titanium dioxide	77891	A	GMP	May not exceed 1% by weight of the food
Turmeric	75300	A	0.5[b]	GMP
Turmeric oleoresin	75300	A	0.5[b]	GMP

Name	Color Index No.	Toxicological Classification	Maximum Acceptable Daily Intake for Man mg/Kg Body Weight	U.S. Use Limits
Ultramarine blue	77007,77013	c	—	May not exceed 0.5% by weight of salt intended for animal feed
Vegetable juice	—	e	—	GMP

[a]Temporary ADI. Further work required by June 1972: metabolic studies on the major carotenoids of annatto.
[b]Temporary ADI. Further work required by June 1974: studies on the metabolism of curcumin and a two-year study in a nonrodent mammalian species.
[c]No attempt was made at toxicological evaluation because the Expert Committee felt that, in the absence of specifications and experimental data, the principles set forth in previous reports precluded the possibility of making such evaluation. Meaningful specifications could not be established.
[d]These products are not listed as such in the FAO/WHO tabulation but are sources of xanthophylls which are listed but not classified toxicologically for the reason given above in footnote *c*.
[e]Not considered by the Expert Committee.
[f]Expressed as total carotenoids by weight.
[g]Provisionally listed.

SOURCE: SCHRAMM, A. T. 1971. Toxicological assessment of food colors. Proc. 3rd Intern. Congr. Food Sci. Technol.

COLOR, MEAT

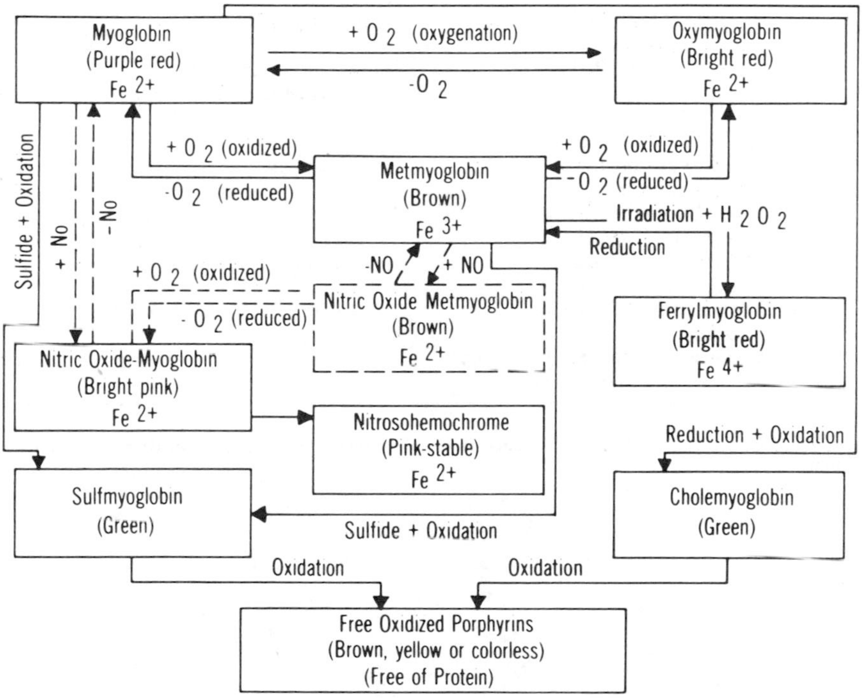

FIG. 2.C.4. HEME PIGMENTS IN MUSCLE IN RELATIONSHIP TO FRESH AND CURED MEATS

Broken lines indicate reactions and compounds possible but not definitely proven. Sulfmyoglobin and cholemyoglobin most frequently occur as a result of bacterial action.

SOURCE: KRAMLICH, W. E., PEARSON, A. M. and TAUBER, F. W. (EDITORS). 1973. Curing. *In* Processed Meats. Avi Publishing Co., Westport, Conn.

COLOR, ORGANIC

TABLE 2.C.45

NATURAL ORGANIC COLORING MATTERS

Name	Source	Color Principle	Color
Alkanet	Root: *Anchusa tinctoria*	Alkannin	Red
Annatto	Fruit of shrub: *Bixa orellana*	Bixin (main color)	Yellow
		Orellin (minor color)	Yellow
Brazilwood	Wood of tree: *Caesalpinia braziliensis*	Brazilin	Reddish-orange
Caramel	Heated sugar	High molecular weight carbohydrate	Reddish-brown
Carotene	Plants, carrots	α, β, γ, and K carotene	Yellow
Chlorophyll	Plant leaves	Chlorophyll α (62% of color)	Greenish-blue
		Chlorophyll β (23% of color)	Green
		Xanthophyll (10% of color)	Yellow
		Carotene (5% of color)	Yellow
Cochineal	Insect: *Coccus cacti*	Carminic acid	Red
Cocoa red	Cocoa beans	Cacaonin	Red
Fustic	Tree: *Morus tinctoria* or *Maclura tinctoria*	Morin (main color)	Yellow
		Maclurin (minor color)	Yellow
Indigo	Plant genus: *Indigofera*	Indigotin	Blue
Lac	Insect: *Coccus lacca*	Laccaic acid	Red
Litmus	Lichens	Azolitmin	Red
Logwood	Wood of tree: *Haematoxylon campechianum*	Haematoxylin	Red-brown
Madder	Root of herb: *Rubia tinctoria*	Alizarin (main color)	Red
		Purpurin (minor color)	Yellow
Orchil and cudbear	Lichens	Orecin	Red
Persian berries	Fruit of *Rhamnus amygdalinus*	Rhamnetin	Yellow
Quercitron	Inner bark of tree: *Quercus nigra* or *Q. tinctoria*	Quercetin	Yellow
Safflower	Flower: *Carthamus tinctoria*	Carthamin	Red
Saffron	Flower petals: *Crocus salivus*	Crocetin	Yellow
Turmeric	Underground stem: *Curcuma longa* or *C. tinctoria*	Curcumin	Yellow

SOURCE: ROE, F. J. C. 1970. Metabolic Aspects of Food Safety. Blackwell Scientific Publications, Osney Media, Oxford, England.

COLORS PERMANENTLY LISTED

TABLE 2.C.46

COLOR ADDITIVES PERMANENTLY LISTED FOR FOOD USE, EXEMPT FROM CERTIFICATION

Color	Use Limitation[1]
Algae meal, dried	For use in chicken feed to enhance the yellow color of chicken skin and eggs
Annatto extract	
β-Apo-8′-carotenal	Not to exceed 15 mg/lb, or pint, of food
Beets, dehydrated (beet powder)	
Canthaxanthine	Not to exceed 30 mg/lb, or pint, of food
Caramel	
β-Carotene	
Carrot oil	
Cochineal extract; carmine	
Corn endosperm oil	For use in chicken feed to enhance the yellow color of chicken skin and eggs
Cottonseed flour, partially defatted, cooked, toasted	
Ferrous gluconate	For coloring ripe olives
Fruit juice	
Grape skin extract	For coloring beverages
Iron oxide (synthetic)	For coloring pet food, not to exceed 0.25 percent by weight of the food
Paprika	
Paprika oleoresin	
Riboflavin	
Saffron	
Tagetes meal and extract (aztec marigold)	For use in chicken feed to enhance the yellow color of chicken skin and eggs
Titanium dioxide	Not to exceed 1% by weight of the food
Turmeric	
Turmeric oleoresin	
Ultramarine blue	For coloring salt intended for animal feed, not to exceed 0.5% by weight of the salt
Vegetable juice	

[1] Unless otherwise indicated, the color may be used for the coloring of food generally in amounts consistent with good manufacturing practice.

SOURCE: ANON. 1971. Food Colors. Food and Nutrition Board, National Academy of Sciences—National Research Council, Washington, D.C.

COMPOSITION OF FOOD

TABLE 2.C.47

CHEMICAL COMPOSITION OF SELECTED HUMAN FOODS
(Nutritive Value of 100 g, Edible Portion)

Food Item	Water, %	Food Energy, Cal	Protein, g	Fat, g	Carbo-hydrate, g	Calcium, mg	Phos-phorus, mg	Iron, mg	Vitamin A Value, I.U.	Thia-min, mg	Ribo-flavin, mg	Niacin, mg	Ascorbic Acid, mg
Milk, cream, ice cream, cheese													
Milk													
Dry whole	3.5	496	25.8	26.7	38.0	949	728	0.58	1,400	0.30	1.46	0.7	6
Evaporated, unsweetened	73.7	139	7.0	7.9	9.9	243	195	0.17	400	0.05	0.36	0.2	1
Fresh skim	90.5	35	3.5	0.1	5.1	118	93	0.07	Tr	0.04	0.18	0.1	1
Fresh whole	87.0	69	3.5	3.9	4.9	118	93	0.07	160	0.04	0.17	0.1	1
Cream, ice cream													
Cream (20%), sweet or sour	72.5	208	2.9	20.0	4.0	97	77	0.06	830	0.03	0.14	0.1	1
Ice cream, plain	62.0	210	4.0	12.3	20.8	132	104	0.10	540	0.04	0.19	0.1	Tr
Cheese													
Cheddar type	39	393	23.9	32.3	1.7	873	610	0.57	1,740	0.04	0.50	0.2	0
Cottage	74.0	101	19.2	0.8	4.3	82	263	0.46	30	0.02	0.29	0.1	0
Fats, oils													
Bacon, medium fat	10	626	9.1	65	1.1	13	108	0.8	0	0.42	0.10	2.1	0
Butter	15.5	733	0.6	81	0.4	16	16	0.2	3,300	Tr	0.01	0.1	0
Lard, other shortening	0	900	0	100	0	0	0	0	0	0	0	0	0
Margarine with vitamin A added	15.5	733	0.6	81	0.4	2	15	0.2	1,980	0	0	0	0
Salt pork, fat	8	781	3.9	85	0	2	42	0.6	0	0.18	0.04	0.9	0
Eggs													
Whole, dried	2	593	48.2	43.3	2.6	187	800	8.7	4,450	0.35	1.23	0.2	0
Whole, fresh	74.0	158	12.8	11.5	0.7	54	210	2.7	1,140	0.12	0.34	0.1	0
Meat, poultry, fish													
Beef													
Loin steaks (wholesale loin)	57	293	16.9	25	0	10	182	2.5	0	0.10	0.13	4.6	0
Round steak (wholesale round)	67	194	19.3	13	0	11	208	2.9	0	0.12	0.15	5.2	0
Lamb													
Leg roast (wholesale leg)	63.7	230	18.0	17.5	0	10	194	2.7	0	0.21	0.26	5.9	0
Sirloin chop (wholesale leg)	63.7	230	18.0	17.5	0	10	194	2.7	0	0.21	0.26	5.9	0
Pork													
Ham, fresh	53	340	15.2	31	0	9	164	2.3	0	0.96	0.19	4.1	0
Ham, smoked	42	384	16.9	35	0.3	10	182	2.5	0	0.78	0.19	3.8	0
Pork links, sausage	41.9	446	10.8	44.8	0	6	116	1.6	0	0.22	0.15	2.3	0
Poultry													
Chicken, roasters	66.0	194	20.2	12.6	0	16	218	1.9	Tr	0.11	0.18	8.6	—
Turkey, medium fat	58.3	262	20.1	20.2	0	23	320	3.8	Tr	0.12	0.19	7.9	—
Fish and shellfish													
Cod	82.6	70	16.5	0.4	0	18	189	0.9	0	0.04	0.05	2.3	2
Salmon, canned	67.4	169	20.6	9.6	0	67	286	1.3	80	0.03	0.18	6.5	0

Dry beans and peas, nuts													
Dry beans and peas													
Beans, canned, baked	71.0	117	5.7	2.0	19.0	40	154	3.4	70	0.05	0.05	0.8	4
Beans, lima, dry seed	12.6	341	20.7	1.3	61.6	68	381	7.5	0	0.60	0.24	2.1	2
Peas, split	10.0	354	24.5	1.0	61.7	73	397	6.0	370	0.87	0.29	3.9	2
Nuts													
Peanut butter	1.7	619	26.1	47.8	21.0	74	393	1.9	0	0.20	0.16	16.2	0
Peanuts, roasted	2.6	600	26.9	44.2	23.6	74	393	1.9	0	0.30	0.16	16.2	0
Fresh vegetables													
Asparagus	93.0	26	2.2	0.2	3.9	21	62	0.9	1,000	0.16	0.17	1.2	33
Beans, snap	88.9	42	2.4	0.2	7.7	65	44	1.1	630	0.08	0.10	0.6	19
Beets	87.6	46	1.6	0.1	9.6	27	43	1.0	20	0.03	0.05	0.4	10
Carrots	88.2	45	1.2	0.3	9.3	39	37	0.8	12,000	0.07	0.06	0.5	6
Corn, sweet, white, or yellow	73.9	108	3.7	1.2	20.5	9	120	0.5	390	0.15	0.14	1.4	12
Cucumbers	96.1	14	.7	0.1	2.7	10	21	0.3	0	0.04	0.09	0.2	8
Lettuce, headed	94.8	18	1.2	0.2	2.9	22	25	0.5	540	0.06	0.07	0.2	8
Onions, mature	87.5	49	1.4	0.2	10.3	32	44	0.5	50	0.03	0.02	0.1	9
Peas, green	74.3	101	6.7	0.4	17.7	22	122	1.9	680	0.36	0.18	2.1	26
Potatoes	77.8	85	2.0	0.1	19.1	11	56	0.7	20	0.11	0.04	1.2	17
Spinach	92.7	25	2.3	0.3	3.2	81	55	3.0	9,420	0.12	0.24	0.7	59
Sweet potatoes	68.5	125	1.8	0.7	27.9	30	49	0.7	7,700	0.10	0.06	0.7	22
Tomatoes	94.1	23	1.0	0.3	4.0	11	27	0.6	1,100	0.06	0.04	0.6	23
Turnips	90.9	35	1.1	0.2	7.1	40	34	0.5	Tr	0.06	0.06	0.5	28
Fresh fruit													
Apples	84.1	64	0.3	0.4	14.9	6	10	0.3	90	0.04	0.002	0.2	5
Bananas	74.8	99	1.2	0.2	23	8	28	0.6	430	0.09	0.06	0.6	10
Strawberries	90.0	41	0.8	0.6	8.1	28	27	0.8	60	0.03	0.07	0.3	60
Grapefruit	88.3	44	0.5	0.2	10.1	17	18	0.3	Tr	0.04	0.02	0.2	40
Lemons	89.3	44	0.9	0.6	8.7	14	10	0.1	0	0.04	Tr	0.1	45
Oranges	87.2	50	0.9	0.2	11.2	33	23	0.4	190	0.08	0.03	0.2	42
Peaches	86.9	51	0.5	0.1	12.0	8	22	0.6	880	0.02	0.05	0.9	8
Rhubarb	94.9	18	0.5	0.1	3.8	51	25	0.5	30	0.01	—	0.1	9
Grain products													
Flour													
Wheat, patent	12	355	10.8	0.9	75.9	19	93	0.7	0	0.07	0.03	0.8	0
Wheat, patent, enriched	12	355	10.8	0.9	75.9	19	93	2.9	0	0.44	0.26	3.5	0
Whole wheat	11	360	13.0	2.0	72.4	38	385	3.8	0	0.56	0.12	5.6	0
Breakfast cereals													
Corn flakes	9.3	359	7.9	0.7	80.3	10	56	1.0	0	0.16	0.08	1.6	0
Oatmeal	8.3	396	14.2	7.4	68.2	54	365	5.2	0	0.55	0.14	1.1	0
Shredded wheat	7.7	369	10.4	1.4	78.7	38	385	3.8	0	0.20	0.14	4.2	0
Other cereals													
Hominy	11.4	357	8.5	0.8	78.9	11	70	1.0	0	0.15	0.05	0.9	0
Macaroni, spaghetti	11	360	13	1.4	73.9	22	144	1.2	0	0.13	0.08	2.1	0
Sugars, sweets													
Honey	20	319	0.3	0	79.5	5	16	0.9	0	Tr	0.04	0.2	4
Sugar, granulated or powdered	0.5	398	0	0	99.5	0	0	0.1	0	0	0	0	0
Miscellaneous													
Cocoa	4.3	329	9.0	18.8	31.0	—	709	2.7	0	Tr	0.39	2.3	0
Yeast, dried, brewers'	7.0	348	46.1	1.6	37.4	106	1,893	18.2	0	9.69	5.45	36.2	0

SOURCE: MALLETTE, M. F., ALTHOUSE, P. M., and CLAGETT, C. O. Biochemistry of Plants and Animals. John Wiley & Sons, New York.

CONCENTRATION OF COMMERCIAL STRENGTHS OF ACIDS AND BASES

TABLE 2.C.48

CONCENTRATION OF ACIDS AND BASES
(Common Commercial Strengths)

	Molecular weight	Moles per liter	Grams per liter	Percent by weight	Specific gravity
acetic acid, glacial	60.05	17.4	1045	99.5	1.05
acetic acid	60.05	6.27	376	36	1.045
butyric acid	88.1	10.3	912	95	0.96
formic acid	46.02	23.4	1080	90	1.20
		5.75	264	25	1.06
hydriodic acid	127.9	7.57	969	57	1.70
		5.51	705	47	1.50
		0.86	110	10	1.1
hydrobromic acid	80.92	8.89	720	48	1.50
		6.82	552	40	1.38
hydrochloric acid	36.5	11.6	424	36	1.18
		2.9	105	10	1.05
hydrocyanic acid	27.03	25	676	97	0.697
		0.74	19.9	2	0.996
hydrofluoric acid	20.01	32.1	642	55	1.167
		28.8	578	50	1.155
hydrofluosilicic acid	144.1	2.65	382	30	1.27
hypophosphorous acid	66.0	9.47	625	50	1.25
		5.14	339	30	1.13
		1.57	104	10	1.04
lactic acid	90.1	11.3	1020	85	1.2
nitric acid	63.02	15.99	1008	71	1.42
		14.9	938	67	1.40
		13.3	837	61	1.37
perchloric acid	100.5	11.65	1172	70	1.67
		9.2	923	60	1.54
phosphoric acid	98	14.7	1445	85	1.70
sulfuric acid	98.1	18.0	1766	96	1.84
sulfurous acid	82.1	0.74	61.2	6	1.02
ammonia water	17.0	14.8	252	28	0.898
potassium hydroxide	56.1	13.5	757	50	1.52
		1.94	109	10	1.09
sodium carbonate	106.0	1.04	110	10	1.10
sodium hydroxide	40.0	19.1	763	50	1.53
		2.75	111	10	1.11

SOURCE: The Merck Index, 8th Edition. (1968) Merck & Co., Rahway, N.J.

CONCENTRATED AND DRIED MILK PRODUCTS

TABLE 2.C.49

TYPICAL ANALYSES OF CONCENTRATED MILKS AND DRIED PRODUCTS

Milk Products	Protein	Fat	Moisture	Carbohydrate Lactose	Carbohydrate Sucrose	Ash	Calcium	Phosphorus	Lactic acid
Concentrated	%	%	%	%	%	%	%	%	%
Evaporated milk	7.0	7.9	73.8	9.7	0	1.6	0.252	0.205	0
Sweetened condensed, whole	8.1	8.7	27.1	11.4	44.3	1.8	0.262	0.206	0
Plain condensed skim	10.0	0.3	73.0	14.7	0	2.3	0.250	0.200	0
Sweetened condensed skim	10.0	0.3	28.4	16.3	42.0	2.3	0.300	0.230	0
Condensed buttermilk (acid)	9.9	1.5	72.0	12.0	0	2.2	—	—	5.7
Condensed skim (acid)	10.19	0.17	72.0	9.43	0	2.13	—	—	6.08
Condensed whey	7.0	2.4	48.1	38.5	0	4.0	—	—	2.4
Sweetened condensed whey	5.0	1.7	24.0	28.5	38.0	2.8	—	—	0
Dried									
Whole milk	26.4	27.5	2.0	38.2	0	5.9	0.909	0.708	0
Skim (conventional)	35.9	0.8	3.0	52.3	0	8.0	1.308	1.016	0
Skim (instant)	35.8	0.7	4.0	51.6	0	7.9	1.293	1.005	0
Buttermilk (sweet)	34.3	5.3	2.8	50.0	0	7.6	1.248	0.970	0
Buttermilk (acid)	37.6	5.7	4.8	38.8	0	7.4	—	—	5.7
Malted milk	14.7	8.3	2.6	20.0	50.5[a]	3.6	0.288	0.380	0
Cream	13.4	65.0	0.8	18.0	0	2.91			0
Whey (sweet) Cheddar	12.9	0.9	4.5	73.5	0	8.0	0.646	0.589	2.3
Whey (acid) cottage	13.0	0	3.2	66.5	0	10.2	1.44	1.17	8.6
Casein (commercial)	88.5	0.2	7.0	0	0	3.8	—	—	—
Casein (co-precipitate)	83.0	1.5	4.0	1.0	0	10.5	2.5	—	—

50.5% = maltose and dextrin.

SOURCE: HARGROVE, ROBERT E. and ALFORD, JOHN A. 1974. Composition of Milk Products. *In* Fundamentals of Dairy Chemistry, 2nd Edition. B. H. Webb, A. H. Johnson and J. A. Alford (Editors). Avi Publishing Co., Westport, Conn.

CONDENSED MILK DRESSING

⅔ cup sweetened milk
¼ cup oil
¼ cup vinegar plus 1 tbsp lemon juice or 5 tbsp vinegar
½ tsp dry mustard
¼ tsp salt
1 tsp minced parsley (optional)

Procedure

Mix the ingredients and stir until the milk is throughly thickened. Refrigerate.

SOURCE: KINTNER, T. C. and MANGEL, M. Vinegars and salad dressings. Univ. Missouri Agric. Expt. Sta. Bull. *631.*

CONNECTIVE TISSUE, COMPOSITION

TABLE 2.C.50

PERCENTAGE COMPOSITION OF WHITE AND YELLOW CONNECTIVE TISSUES

	Tendon of Achilles	Ligamentum Nuchae
Water	62.87	57.57
Ash	0.47	0.47
Fat	1.04	1.12
Albumin-globulin	0.22	0.62
Mucoid	1.28	0.53
Elastin	1.63	31.67
Collagen	31.59	7.23
Extractives	0.90	0.80

SOURCE: MOULTON, C. R. and LEWIS, W. L. Meat Through the Microscope, Revised Edition. Institute of Meat Packing, University of Chicago, Chicago.

CONNECTIVE TISSUE PROTEINS

TABLE 2.C.51

DESCRIPTION OF TISSUE PROTEINS

Name	Shape	Size	Molecular Weight	Distinctive Composition	Reactions and Role
Collagen	Rod, coiled coil of three helices wound together	Polymer of tropocollagen	Indefinite	Hydroxy groups important in H-bonds, proline rings in shape of molecule. Vertebrate collagen contains about 0.5 percent carbohydrate—at least one galactose residue, often a glucose. Probably cross-linked both intra- and intermolecularly. Degree of cross-linking increases with age.	Shrink temperature, T_s, fiber shrinks to about 1/3 length. T_s usually around 60° C—varies with pH, ions, solvent, rate of heating, stretching force. Major component of tissue supporting contractile fibers and connecting muscles to bones.
Tropocollagen	Rod, three chains, each left-handed helix, three wound together in right-handed superhelix	2800 A long, 14 A diameter	300,000–350,000	About 1/3 glycine, 1/8 proline, and 1/10 hydroxyproline. Small amount hydroxylysine. Configuration of single and triple chains determined by H-bonds and by proline rings.	Building blocks of collagen. Soluble in cold neutral salt solution. Heat to 30° C, triple chain separates into gelatin.
Elastin	Cross-linked three-dimensional gel		Indefinite	Very low in amino acids with hydrophilic side chains, small amount of hydroxyproline. Cross-linked by desmocine and isodesmocine.	Elastic component of connective tissue, found in small amounts in muscle. Mainly occurs in walls of blood vessels and in elastic ligaments.
Reticulin				Contains lipid, especially myristic acid.	More found in endomysium than in peri- or epimysium.
Ground substance: Protein, polysaccharides, glycoprotein, and the like				Protein bonded to polysaccharide is noncollagenous. Some glycoproteins—may contain glucose, galactose, mannose, hexosamine, fucose, and sialic acid.	Complexed with mucopolysaccharides.

SOURCE: PAUL, P. C. and PALMER, H. H. 1972. Food Theory and Applications. John Wiley & Sons, New York.

CONSTANTS, FUNDAMENTAL

Name	Value
Avogadro's number	N_0 = 6.023 × 10^{23} molecules/g mole
Base of natural logarithm	e = 2.7183 . . .
Curie	Ci = 3.7 × 10^{10} disintegrations/sec
Electron charge	e = 4.8 × 10^{-10} statcoulomb = 1.6 × 10^{-19} coulomb
Energy equivalent of electron mass	mc^2 = 0.51 Mev
Faraday's constant	F = 96,514 coulombs/g equivalent (physical scale)
Gravitational acceleration	g = 980.665 cm/sec^2
Mass, alpha particle	m_α = 6.64 × 10^{-24} g = 4.002777 *mu*
Mass, electron	m_e = 9.1066 × 10^{-28} g = 0.000548 *mu*
Mass, H atom	m_H = 1.67339 × 10^{-24} g = 1.008142 *mu*
Mass, neutron	m_n = 1.6751 × 10^{-24} g = 1.008982 *mu*
Mass, proton	m_p = 1.67248 × 10^{-24} g = 1.007594 *mu*
Mass unit	*mu* = 1.66035 × 10^{-24} g = 1.000 *mu*
Microcurie	μCi = 10^{-6} curie = 3.7 × 10^4 disintegrations/sec
Micromicrocurie	$\mu\mu$Ci = 10^{-12} curie = 3.7 × 10^{-2} disintegrations/sec
Millicurie	mCi = 10^{-3} curie = 3.7 × 10^7 disintegrations/sec
Pi	π = 3.1416
Planck's constant	h = 6.624 × 10^{27} erg-sec
Rad	rad = 100 ergs/g of tissue
Roentgen	r = 1 esu/0.001293 g of air
Rem	rem = rads × RBE
Rutherford	rd = 10^6 disintegrations/sec

SOURCE: WANG, Y. (EDITOR). 1969. Handbook of Radioactive Nuclides. CRC Press, Cleveland. Reproduced with permission of CRC Press.

COOKED DRESSING

Ingredients

2 tbsp fat	1 egg
2⅓ tbsp flour	¾ tsp salt
2⅓ tbsp sugar	¾ tsp dry mustard
½ cup water	⅛ tsp paprika
½ cup milk	3 tbsp vinegar

Procedure

Melt the fat in the top of the double boiler. Add the flour, and mix. Add the milk and water and cook in the double boiler for 10 min. Beat egg. Add to the starch mixture and cook until thickened. Remove from heat. Add spices and vinegar. Refrigerate.

SOURCE: KINTNER, T. C. and MANGEL, M. Vinegars and salad dressings, Univ. Missouri Agric. Expt. Sta. Bull. *631*.

COOKING IN LIQUID, TIME

TABLE 2.C.52

TIME-TABLE FOR COOKING MEAT IN LIQUID

Cut	Average Weight	Approx. Time Per Pound	Approx. Total Cooking Time
	Pounds	Minutes	Hours
Smoked ham			
(country cured)			
Large	12 to 16	20	
Small	10 to 12	25	
Half	5 to 8	30	
Smoked ham			
Shank or rump half	5 to 8	20-25	
Smoked arm picnic			
shoulder	5 to 8	45	
Fresh or corned beef	4 to 6	40-50	
Beef shank cross cuts	¾ to 1		2½ to 3½
Beef for stew			2½ to 3½
Veal for stew			2 to 3
Lamb for stew			1½ to 2

SOURCE: Lessons on Meat. (1974). National Live Stock and Meat Board, Chicago.

CORN

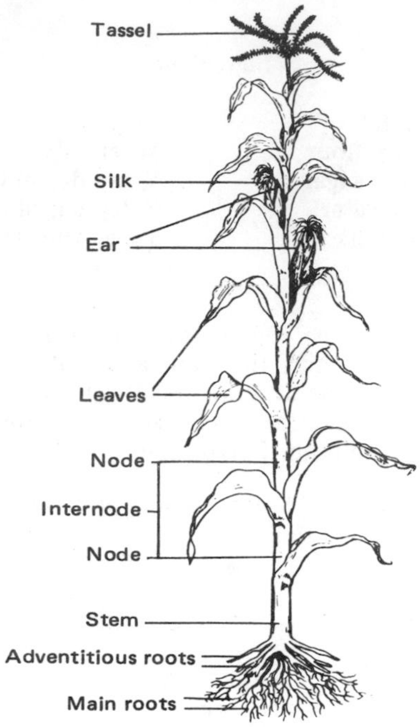

FIG. 2.C.5. NOMENCLATURE OF A CORN STALK

SOURCE: MITTLEIDER, J. R. and NELSON, A. N. 1970. Food for Everyone. Extension Division, Loma Linda University, Cal.

CORN, AMINO ACIDS

TABLE 2.C.53

AMINO ACIDS IN WHOLE KERNELS OF NORMAL AND OPAQUE-2 MAIZE
(grams per 100 g protein)

Amino Acid	Normal	*Opaque-2*
Lysine	3.0	4.8
Tryptophan	0.7	1.3
Histidine	2.6	3.3
Arginine	4.9	8.5
Aspartic acid	9.2	10.8
Glutamic acid	22.6	17.5
Threonine	4.1	4.0
Serine	5.6	4.8
Proline	9.6	7.6
Glycine	4.7	4.8
Alanine	9.2	6.6
Valine	5.7	5.1
Cystine	1.7	1.7
Methionine	1.3	2.1
Isoleucine	4.2	3.4
Leucine	14.6	9.1
Tyrosine	5.2	4.0
Phenylalanine	5.8	4.5
	Percent	Protein
	9.0	11.6

SOURCE: Maize and Maize Diets. FAO Nutritional Studies 9. FAO, United Nations, Rome.

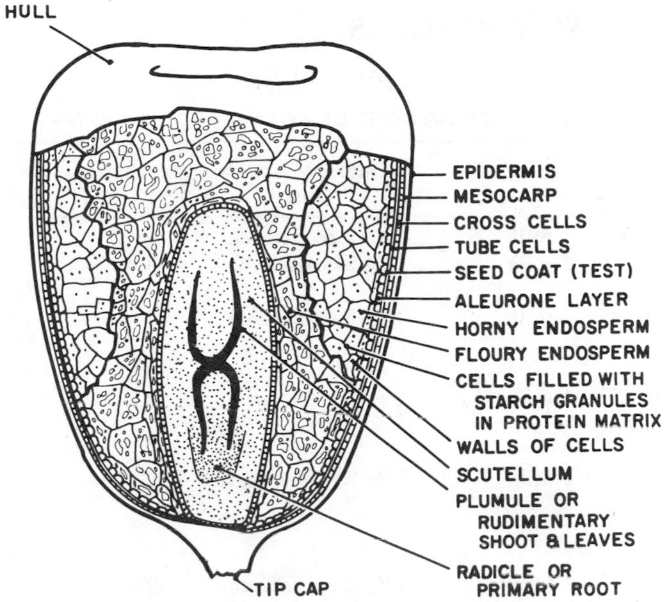

FIG. 2.C.6. CROSS SECTION OF A CORN KERNEL

SOURCE: BROOKER, DONALD B., BAKKER-ARKEMA, FRED W. and HALL, CARL W. (EDITORS). 1974. Principles of Grain Drying. *In* Drying Cereal Grains. Avi Publishing Co., Westport, Conn.

CORN KERNEL COMPOSITION

TABLE 2.C.54

DISTRIBUTION OF PARTS AND CHEMICAL CONSTITUENTS IN THE MAIZE KERNEL
(Moisture-free basis)

FRACTION	Composition of Fraction				% by weight of whole grain	% of Total in whole grain contained in specified fraction			
	Ash %	Protein (N × 6.25) %	Oil %	Carbohydrate (by dif) %		Ash	Protein	Oil	Carbohydrate (by dif.)
1. LOW PROTEIN EAR									
Tip cap	0.91	7.4	1.2	90.6	1.2	0.8	0.9	0.3	1.3
Hulls	0.82	5.0	0.9	93.3	5.5	3.3	2.7	1.2	6.0
Endosperm									
"Horny gluten"	0.92	19.2	4.0	75.9	11.6	8.0	22.6	11.1	10.4
"Horny starch"	0.18	8.1	0.2	91.5	37.1	5.0	30.5	1.4	40.2
"Crown starch" and "tip starch"	0.31	6.8	0.2	92.8	35.0	8.0	24.0	1.9	38.3
Germ	10.5	19.9	36.5	33.1	9.6	74.9	19.3	84.0	3.8
Whole grain, intact	1.4	9.3	4.2	85.1					
Calculated from parts	1.3	9.9	4.2	84.6	100.0	100.0	100.0	99.9	100.0
2. HIGH PROTEIN EAR:									
Tip cap	1.87	4.6	2.0	91.5	1.6	1.8	0.6	0.6	1.8
Hulls	1.10	3.8	0.8	94.3	6.1	3.9	1.8	0.9	7.1
Endosperm									
"Horny gluten"	1.74	24.6	4.6	69.1	13.3	13.5	25.9	12.3	11.4
"Horny starch"	0.21	11.0	0.2	88.6	44.9	5.5	39.0	2.0	49.3
"Crown starch" and "tip starch"	0.46	8.1	0.8	90.5	22.2	5.9	14.2	3.7	24.9
Germ	10.0	19.6	33.7	36.7	11.9	69.5	18.4	80.5	5.4
Whole grain, intact	1.7	12.8	5.4	80.1					
Calculated from parts	1.7	12.6	5.0	80.7	100.0	100.1	99.9	100.0	99.9

NOTE: Results obtained from fractions separated by hand from single ears of low-protein (9.3%) and high-protein (12.8%) maize.

SOURCE: Maize and Maize Diets. FAO Nutritional Studies 9. FAO, United Nations, Rome.

CORNSTARCH PUDDING VARIATIONS

TABLE 2.C.55

COMMON VARIATIONS OF CORNSTARCH PUDDING

Product	Liquid (cup)	Starchy Agent (tbsp)	Sugar (tbsp)	Other Ingredients
Plain blanc mange	1 milk	1½–2 cornstarch	2	½ tsp vanilla
Chocolate blanc mange	1 milk	1½–2 cornstarch	3	½ sq chocolate ¼ tsp vanilla
Chocolate cream pudding	1 milk	1½–2 cornstarch	3	1 stiffly beaten egg white ½ sq chocolate ¼ tsp vanilla
Coconut blanc mange	1 milk	1½–2 cornstarch	2	½ tsp vanilla ½–1 cup shredded coconut
Fruit blanc mange	1 milk	1½–2½ cornstarch	2	½ cup dates, pineapple, bananas, cherries, prunes, or other desired fruit
Nut blanc mange	1 milk	1½–2 cornstarch	2	½ tsp vanilla ¼–½ cup chopped nuts
Caramel blanc mange	1 milk	1½–2 cornstarch	2	½ tsp vanilla 2 tbsp caramel syrup
Maple blanc mange	1 milk	1½–2 cornstarch	2 maple sugar	
Fruit tapioca	1 fruit juice and water	2–2½ minute tapioca	3	½–1 cup fruit
Indian pudding	1 milk	1 cornmeal	1½–2 mo-lasses	¼ tsp ginger

SOURCE: JUSTIN, M. M., RUST, L. O., and VAIL, G. E. Foods, Revised Edition. Houghton Mifflin Co., Boston.

CORRELATION SIGNIFICANCE

TABLE 2.C.56

VALUES OF THE CORRELATION COEFFICIENT FOR DIFFERENT LEVELS OF SIGNIFICANCE

n	P = .1	.05	.02	.01	*n*	P = .1	.05	.02	.01
1	.98769	.996917	.9995066	.9998766	17	.3887	.4555	.5285	.5751
2	.90000	.95000	.98000	.990000	18	.3783	.4438	.5155	.5614
3	.8054	.8783	.93433	.95873	19	.3687	.4329	.5034	.5487
4	.7293	.8114	.8822	.91720	20	.3598	.4227	.4921	.5368
5	.6694	.7545	.8329	.8745					
6	.6215	.7067	.7887	.8343	25	.3233	.3809	.4451	.4869
7	.5822	.6664	.7498	.7977	30	.2960	.3494	.4093	.4487
8	.5494	.6319	.7155	.7646	35	.2746	.3246	.3810	.4182
9	.5214	.6021	.6851	.7348	40	.2573	.3044	.3578	.3932
10	.4973	.5760	.6581	.7079	45	.2428	.2875	.3384	.3721
					50	.2306	.2732	.3218	.3541
11	.4762	.5529	.6339	.6835	60	.2108	.2500	.2948	.3248
12	.4575	.5324	.6120	.6614	70	.1954	.2319	.2737	.3017
13	.4409	.5139	.5923	.6411	80	.1829	.2172	.2565	.2830
14	.4259	.4973	.5742	.6226	90	.1726	.2050	.2422	.2673
15	.4124	.4821	.5577	.6055	100	.1638	.1946	.2301	.2540
16	.4000	.4683	.5425	.5897					

For a total correlation, *n* is 2 less than the number of pairs in the sample; for a partial correlation, the number of eliminated variates also should be subtracted.

SOURCE: FISHER, R. A. 1972. Statistical Methods for Research Workers, 14th Edition. Hafner Press, New York.

CREAMS, BUTTER AND FROZEN DESSERTS

TABLE 2.C.57

TYPICAL COMPOSITION OF MARKET CREAMS, BUTTER, AND FORZEN DESSERTS[a]

	Moisture	Protein	Fat	Lactose	Ash	Calcium	Phosphorus
	%	%	%	%	%	%	%
Market creams							
Half and half	80.0	3.1	11.6	4.5	0.7	0.10	0.08
Light cream	73.0	2.9	19.3	4.2	0.6	0.10	0.08
Whipping, light	62.9	2.5	30.5	3.6	0.5	0.08	0.06
Whipping, heavy	57.3	2.2	36.8	3.2	0.5	0.07	0.05
Plastic	18.2	0.7	80.0	1.0	0.1	0.03	0.02
Butter, butter oil, ghee							
Butter	16.5	0.6	80.5	0.4	2.5	0.02	0.02
Butter oil	0.2	0.3	99.5	0.0	0.0	—	—
Ghee	0.1	0.1	99.8	0.0	0.0	—	—
Frozen desserts							
Ice cream	62.1	4.0	12.5	20.3[b]	0.8	0.12	0.10
Ice cream, low fat	63.2	4.5	10.6	20.8[b]	0.9	0.15	0.12
Ice cream, high fat	62.8	2.6	16.1	18.0[b]	0.5	0.08	0.06
Ice milk	66.7	4.8	5.1	22.4[b]	1.0	0.16	0.12
Sherbet	67.0	0.9	1.2	30.8[b]	0.1	0.02	0.01

[a] Salt concentration in butter ranges from 0.8–2.3%. The lower value is typical of most European countries, the higher value of the United States, New Zealand, and Australia.
[b] Carbohydrate other than lactose added.

SOURCE: HARGROVE, ROBERT E. and ALFORD, JOHN A. (EDITORS). 1974. Composition of Milk Products. *In* Fundamentals of Dairy Chemistry, 2nd Edition. Avi Publishing Co., Westport, Conn.

CULTURED DAIRY PRODUCTS, COMPOSITION

TABLE 2.C.58

APPROXIMATE COMPOSITION OF SOME CULTURED AND SPECIAL DAIRY PRODUCTS

Product	Water (%)	Fat (%)	Msnf (%)	Protein (%)	Carbohydrates (%)	Ash (%)	Lactic Acid (%)
Buttermilk sweet cream	90.83	0.55	8.25	3.45	4.40	0.73	0.04
Sour cream	91.3	0.65	8.25	3.40	3.40	0.65	0.60
Cultured cream	90.5	0.10	8.25	3.6	5.1	0.70	0.75
Plain yogurt	89.0	1.70	8.25	3.4	5.2	0.75	0.95
Flavored yogurt	91.0	1.5	8.25	3.2	12.8	0.70	0.95
Cultured sour cream	74.5	18.0	7.4	2.8	4.1	0.70	0.70
Flavored milk drink	86.0	2.0	8.25	2.8	8.0	0.65	—
Coffee creamer	83.0	5.0	12.00	3.5	5.4	0.80	—
Filled milk	87.0	3.5	8.5	3.5	5.0	0.7	—

SOURCE: ARBUCKLE, W. S. 1973. Dairy Products. *In* Quality Control For The Food Industry, Vol. 2, 3rd Edition. A. Kramer and B. A. Twigg (Editors). Avi Publishing Co., Westport, Conn.

CULTURE MEDIA

TABLE 2.C.59

SUMMARY OF CULTURE MEDIA FOR SPECIFIC GROUPS OF MICROORGANISMS
(NOTE: Those Media Which May Be Expected To Give the Most Efficient Results As Evidenced By Their Ability To Grow More Species, or To Grow Them More Rapidly, Are Indicated By Asterisks)

Organisms	Isolation	Cultivation	Identification	Maintenance
Actinomycetes, aerobic *Nocardia* *Streptomyces*	Blood Agar Base Brain Heart Infusion Agar *Emerson Media ***Eugonagar** ***Mycophil** Media Sabouraud Media *Thioglycollate Medium-135C ***Trypticase** Soy Media	Czapek Dox Media Emerson Media ***Eugonagar** ***Eugonbroth** **Mycophil** Media Sabouraud Media **Trypticase** Soy Media	*C T A Media ***Eugonagar** Indole Nitrite Medium Nutrient Gelatin ***Thiogel**® Medium Carbohydrate **Taxo**® Discs	***C T A Medium** ***Trypticase** Agar Base ***Trypticase** Soy Agar
Anaerobes, exclusive of clostridia, e.g. *A. bovis, israelii* *Bacteroides* Fusiforms *P. anaerobius* *Sphaerophorus*	Actinomyces Broth *Anaerobic Agars ***Eugonagar** *Forget-Fredette Agar *Thioglycollate Medium-135C **Trypticase** Soy Blood Agar **Trypticase** Soy Broth	Anaerobic Agar ***C T A Medium** **Eugonagar** **Eugonbroth** Fluid Thioglycollate Medium *Thioglycollate Medium-135C **Trypticase** Soy Media	*Anaerobic Agar w/o Dextrose ***C T A Medium** with Carbohydrates *Indole Nitrite Medium Loeffler Medium ***Thiogel** Medium Thioglycollate Medium with proteins Carbohydrate **Taxo** Discs	Cooked Meat Medium *Cooked Meat **Phytone** Medium **C T A Medium** Thioglycollate Medium-135C with $CaCO_3$
Bacillus	Nutrient Media Thermoacidurans Agar **Trypticase** Soy Media	A K Agar #2 **Eugonagar** and **Eugonbroth** Nutrient Media **Trypticase** Soy Media **Trypticase** Stratifying Agar 2%	D Nase Test Agar Litmus and other Skim Milk Media **Thiogel** Medium **Trypticase** Agar Base Urease Test Media Carbohydrate **Taxo** Discs	**C T A Medium** **Trypticase** Agar Base **Trypticase** Soy Agar
Bordetella	*Bordet Gengou Agars *Chocolate (**Eugonagar)** Agar ***Trypticase** Soy Agar with Yeast Hemin Extract G C Agar with **IsoVitaleX** and Hemoglobin	*Bordet Gengou Agars ***Eugonagar** with blood **Trypticase** Soy Agar with Yeast Hemin Extract	Litmus Milk	

Brucella	**Biosate** Agar + Crystal Violet Brucella Media ***Eugonagar** **Eugonbroth** *Thioglycollate Medium-135C ***Trypticase** Soy Media	**Biosate** Agar Brucella Agar ***Eugonagar** ***Eugonbroth** Potato Infusion Agar *Thioglycollate Medium-135C ***Trypticase** Soy Media	***C T A Medium** **Thiogel** Medium ***Trypticase** Soy Agar with Fuchsin with Thionin Urease Test Agar *Urease Test Broth Carbohydrate **Taxo** Discs	***C T A Medium**
Clostridium	Anaerobic Agars *Clostrisel Agar Cooked Meat Media Fluid Thioglycollate Medium Forget-Fredette Agar Reinforced Clostridial Media *Thioglycollate Medium-135C **Trypticase** Soy Media S P S Agar *T S N Agar	*Anaerobic Agars **Eugonagar** **Eugonbroth** Fluid Thioglycollate Medium *Thioglycollate Medium-135C with $CaCO_3$ ***Trypticase** Agar Base	*Anaerobic Agar w/o Dextrose *Indole Nitrite Medium Litmus, Purple or Ulrich Milks or Skim Milk Loeffler Medium Sulfite Agar ***Thiogel** Medium Thioglycollate Medium with proteins ***Trypticase** Agar Base **Trypticase** Dextrose Agar ***Trypticase** Lactose Iron Agar Carbohydrate **Taxo** Discs	Cooked Meat Medium *Cooked Meat **Phytone** Medium *Thioglycollate Medium-135C with $CaCO_3$ ***Trypticase** Agar Base
Corynebacterium	Columbia Agar Loeffler Medium *Serum Tellurite Agar Thioglycollate Media Tinsdale Agar ***Trypticase** Soy Media ***Trypticase** Tellurite Agar	Blood Agar Base Brain Heart Infusion Media ***Eugonagar** **Eugonbroth** Infusion Broths Loeffler Medium Thioglycollate Media ***Trypticase** Soy Media	*C T A Media Indole Nitrite Medium **Thiogel** Medium Tinsdale Agar **Trypticase** Agar Base Carbohydrate and N **Taxo** Discs	***C T A Medium** **Trypticase** Soy Agar
Enteric Bacilli	B D G Broth Buffered Glycerol Saline *Cary and Blair Transport Medium ***Desoxycholate Agar** *Desoxycholate Lactose Agar E M B Agars Endo Media **Eugonagar** **Eugonbroth** *G N Broth *MacConkey Agars S B B A Agar *Sorbitol Agar Specimen Preservative Tergitol Media *Thioglycollate Media Transport Media **Trypticase** Soy Media Violet Red Bile Agar	*Blood Agars ***Eugonagar** ***Eugonbroth** Extract Media Infusion Broths Nutrient Agars Nutrient Broths Sanders Media S B B A Agar Thioglycollate Media ***Trypticase** Soy Media	Carlquist Ninhydrin Broth Christensen Citrate Sulfide Agar D L L I Slant Agar D L S I Agar Falkow Lysine Broth Gillies Media H Broth Indole Nitrite Medium *Kliger Iron Agar Koser Citrate Broth Krumwiede Triple Sugar Agar Levine E M B Agars *Lysine Iron Agar Malonate Broth *Moeller Decarboxylase Broths Moeller K C N Broth Motility Test Medium *M R-V P (Clark and Lubs) Broth Nutrient Gelatin O F Medium Carbohydrate and N **Taxo** Discs	**Eugonagar** Infusion Agars Nutrient Agar ***Trypticase** Agar Base ***Trypticase** Soy Agar

(Continued)

TABLE 2.C.59 (*Continued*)

Organisms	Isolation	Cultivation	Identification	Maintenance
Coliforms and *Proteus*	Boric Acid Broth *Brilliant Green Bile Media Crystal Violet Lactose Broth E C and Eijkman Broths Formate Ricinoleate Broth Fuchsin Lactose Broth H D Broth *Lactose Broth *Lauryl Sulfate Broth MacConkey Broth **M*-Coliform Broth *M*-E M B and Endo Broths *M*-Endo Agar L E S *M*-F C Broth Purple Lactose Agar		Phenol Red Media Phenylalanine Media Purple Media Russell Double Sugar Agar Saccharose Mannitol Agar Sanders Agar + **Taxo Discs** Semisolid Medium of Edwards and Bruner Semisolid Medium for Enterics S I M Medium *Simmons Citrate Agar Sorbitol Iron Agar ***Thiogel** Medium ***Trypticase** Agar Base with **Taxo** Discs ***Trypticase** Lactose Iron Agar ***T S I Agar®**	
Salmonella and *Shigella*	*Bismuth Sulfite Agar (Wilson and Blair) Brilliant Green Agars Buffered Glycerol Saline Base **D C L S Agar®** Desoxycholate-Citrate Agars E E Broth G N Broth *M*-Bismuth Sulfite and Brilliant Green Broths Salmonella Shigella Agar Sanders Booster Broth Selenite Media Specimen Preservative Tetrathionate Media Transport Media *X L D Agar		*Tryptophane Broth	
Desulfovibrio	Sulfate Reducer A P I Media			
Erysipelothrix	**Eugonagar** **Trypticase** Soy Media Thioglycollate Medium-135C		**C T A Medium** Indole Nitrite Medium **Thiogel** Medium	**C T A Medium**
Gram-Positive Cocci	*Anaerobic Agar Azide Blood Agar Blood Agar Base Brain Heart Media *B T B Lactose Agar Columbia Agar ***Eugonagar** **Eugonbroth** Mitis Salivarius Agar M N **Trypticase** Soy Agar Thioglycollate Media Transport Medium ***Trypticase** Soy Media	Blood Agar Base Brain Heart Media **Eugonagar** **Eugonbroth** Infusion Media Micro Assay Culture Agar **Trypticase** Soy Media	Ammonium Phosphate Agar *C T A Media *Indole Nitrite Medium ***Thiogel** Medium Litmus and other Milks ***Trypticase** Soy Media Urease Test Broth Carbohydrate **Taxo** Discs	*C T A Media *Thioglycollate Medium-135C with $CaCO_3$ **Trypticase** Agar Base

Diplococcus *Streptococcus*	Columbia C N A Agar *Serum Tellurite Agar ***Streptosel** Agar *Thioglycollate Medium-135C **Trypticase** Tellurite Agar Veal Infusion Media		D Nase Test Agar	
Enterococci	Azide Dextrose Broth B A G G Broth Columbia C N A Agar Enterococcus Presumptive Broth Ethyl Violet Azide Broth K F Streptococcal **Media** MacConkey Agar w/o Crystal Violet Mead Agar **M*-Enterococcus Media *M*-Slanetz Enterococcus Broth *Phenylethyl Alcohol Agar S F Broth ***Streptosel** Agar Thallous Acetate Agar		**C T A Medium** plus Sorbitol Ethyl Violet Azide Broth Infusion or **Trypticase** Soy Broth + 6.5% salt K F Streptococcal Media *M*-Enterococcus Media S F Broth **Thiogel** Medium **Trypticase** Soy Agar Blood Plates	
Staphylococci	Ammonium Phosphate Agar Baird-Parker Agar Chapman Stone Agar Cooked Meat Media *Mannitol Salt Agar Staphylococcus Agar #110 Tellurite Glycine Agar T P E Y Agar Vogel and Johnson Agar	Nutrient Agar Nutrient Broth	Baird-Parker Agar Casein Hydrolysate Broth Coagulase Mannitol Media **C T A Medium** + Mannitol D Nase Test Agar Mannitol Salt Agar Phenol Red Media Staphylococcus Agar #110 T P E Y Agar Carbohydrate **Taxo** Discs	C T A Media
Hemophilus	***Eugonagar** **Eugonbroth** M N **Trypticase** Soy Agar *Thioglycollate Medium-135C Transport Medium ***Trypticase** Soy Agar with Yeast Hemin Extract G C Agar with **IsoVitaleX** and Hemoglobin	**Eugonagar** **Eugonbroth** ***Trypticase** Soy Media	**Taxo** Discs	***C T A Medium** ***Trypticase** Soy Agar
Lactobacillus and *Leuconostoc*	*A P T Media ***Eugonagar** ***L B S** Media *Orange Serum Agar Snycer Agar Tomato Juice Agar	A P T Agar A P T Broth **Eugonagar** L Agar Micro Assay Culture Agar Micro Inoculum Broth Orange Serum Agar Peptonized Milk Agar Thioglycollate Medium-135C Tomato Juice Agar	C T A Media Indole Nitrite Medium L Agar Litmus Milk Purple Milk Skim Milk **Thiogel** Medium Ulrich Milk Carbohydrate **Taxo** Discs	**Eugonagar** *L Agar *Thioglycollate Medium-135C with $CaCO_3$

(Continued)

TABLE 2.C.59 (*Continued*)

Organisms	Isolation	Cultivation	Identification	Maintenance
Leptospira	Fletcher Medium Base or Stuart Broth Base with Leptospira Enrichment	Fletcher Medium Base or Stuart Broth Base with Leptospira Enrichment		
Listeria	*Biosate Agar Eugonagar *Serum Tellurite Agar *Thioglycollate Medium-135C *Trypticase Soy Media	Biosate Agar Eugonagar Eugonbroth Thioglycollate Media Trypticase Soy Media	C T A Media Indole Nitrite Medium Litmus and other Milks Simmons Citrate Agar Thiogel Medium Trypticase Agar Base T S I Agar Urease Test Broth Carbohydrate Taxo Discs	C T A Media Trypticase Soy Agar
Mima	Desoxycholate Lactose Agar Levine E M B Agar MacConkey Agar Trypticase Soy Agar Thioglycollate Medium-135C		Indole Nitrite Medium Litmus Milk Sellers Agar Simmons Citrate Agar Thiogel Medium Urea Agar Taxo Carbohydrate and N Taxo Discs	Trypticase Agar Base Trypticase Soy Agar
Mycobacterium	A T S Medium Blood Agar Base Cary and Blair Transport Medium Chocolate (Eugonagar) Agar *Lowenstein-Jensen Medium *Middlebrook 7H10 Agar Peizer T B Media Petragnani Medium Petroff Medium Tarshis Agar	A T S Medium Dubos Media Lowenstein-Jensen Medium Middlebrook 7H10 Agar Nutrient Agar 1.5% Petragnani Medium Petroff Medium Tarshis Agar T B Broth Media Thioglycollate Medium-135C	Dubos Media *Lowenstein-Jensen Media with Inhibitors MacConkey Agar Middlebrook 7H10 Agar T B Broth Media *Thioglycollate Medium-135C *Wayne Sulfatase Agar	*A T S Medium *Dorset Medium Lowenstein-Jensen Medium Petroff Medium Tarshis Agar
Mycoplasma	B Y E Media *Columbia Agar *Mycoplasma Broth *Mycoplasma Agar *Mycoplasma Enrichment Broth		B Y E Media Columbia Agar C T A Media Mycoplasma Agar *Taxo Mycoplasma Discs	Mycoplasma Media

Neisseria	**Eugonagar** G C Agar with **IsoVitaleX** Enrichment and Hemoglobin Mueller Hinton Media *Thayer-Martin Selective Agar *Thioglycollate Medium-135C **Trypticase** Soy Media	**Eugonagar** and **Eugonbroth** **Trypticase** Soy Media	***C T A Medium** Carbohydrate and N **Taxo** Discs	***C T A Medium**
Pasteurella	*Cary and Blair Transport Medium Cystine Heart Agar Desoxycholate and Desoxycholate-Citrate Agars **Eugonagar** G C A Agar with Thiamine Thioglycollate Medium-135C **Trypticase** Soy Media	**Eugonagar** and **Eugonbroth** Thioglycollate Medium-135C **Trypticase** Soy Media	**C T A Medium** Indole Nitrite Medium **Thiogel** Medium **T S I Agar** Carbohydrate **Taxo** Discs	***C T A Medium**
Pseudomonas	**Eugonagar** **Pseudosel** Agar **Trypticase** Soy Media	**Eugonagar** and **Eugonbroth** Nutrient Media **Trypticase** Soy Media	D Nase Test Agar Flo Agar O F Medium Sabouraud Maltose Agar Tech Agar **T S I Agar**	**Trypticase** Agar Base **Trypticase** Soy Agar
Streptobacillus	Thioglycollate Medium w/o Dextrose **Trypticase** Soy Media	Thioglycollate Medium w/o Dextrose **Trypticase** Soy Media	**C T A Medium**	**C T A Medium**
Treponema	*Spirolate Broth *Thioglycollate Medium-135C	Spirolate Broth Thioglycollate Medium-135C	C T A Media Indole Nitrite Medium **Thiogel** Medium	*Thioglycollate Medium-135C
Vibrio *comma* *fetus* and *bulbulus*	*Cary and Blair Transport Medium Chocolate Agar **D C L S Agar** **Desoxycholate-Citrate Agar**® pH 8.4 **Eugonagar** **Eugonbroth** MacConkey Agar **Selenite-F** Broth T C B S Agar *Thioglycollate Medium-135C **Trypticase** Soy Media	**Eugonagar** **Eugonbroth** Thioglycollate Media **Trypticase** Soy Media	**C T A Medium** Indole Nitrite Medium Litmus Milk **Thiogel** Medium **Trypticase** Lactose Iron Agar **T S I Agar**	**C T A Medium**
Viruses	See Tissue Culture Manual for Media and Cell Lines			

(Continued)

TABLE 2.C.59 (*Continued*)

Organisms	Isolation	Cultivation	Identification	Maintenance
Yeasts and Molds	BiGGY Agar Brain Heart Infusion Agars Dextrose Salt Agar ***Eugonagar** (Chocolate) Agar *Inhibitory Mold Agar Levine E M B Agar Littman Media Malt Media *M*-Yeast Media Mildew Test Agar **M*-Green Yeast and Mold Broth M N **Trypticase** Soy Agar ***Mycophil** Media with Low pH ***Mycosel** Agar Orange Serum Agar ***Phytone** Yeast Extract Agar Potato Dextrose Agar Sabouraud Media *Serum Tellurite Agar Sugar-Free Agar *Thioglycollate Medium-135C ***Trypticase** Soy Media **Trypticase** Tellurite Agar W L Nutrient Agar Wort Media	A A T C C Mineral Salts Agar Antifungal Assay Agar Corn Meal Agar with Dextrose Czapek Dox Media Dextrose Agar **Eugonagar** **Eugonbroth** Malt Media **Mycophil** Agar **Mycophil** Broth Neurospora Culture Agar Sabouraud Media **Trypticase** Soy Media Wort Media	Chlamydospore Agar Corn Meal Agars C T A Media Cystine Heart Agar Levine E M B Agar Liu-Newton Agar **Mycophil** Agar **Mycophil** Broth *Rice Extract Agar ***Trypticase** Agar Media **Trypticase** Soy Broth Urea Agar Yeast Carbon Base Yeast Nitrogen Base Carbohydrate **Taxo** Discs Zein Agar	**C T A Medium** **Eugonagar** ***Mycophil** Agar Sabouraud Agars **Trypticase** Agar Base ***Trypticase** Soy Agar
Protozoa *Entameba* *Trichomonas*	*Hirsch Charcoal Agar with Rice Powder and Locke Solution Thioglycollate Medium-135C ***Trichosel** Broth	**S T S** Medium		

SOURCE: BioQuest, Division of Becton, Dickinson & Company, Cockeysville, Maryland.

D

DAIRY CATTLE BREEDS

TABLE 2.D.1

ORIGIN AND CHARACTERISTICS OF DAIRY CATTLE BREEDS

Breed	Place of Origin	Color	Distinctive Head Characteristics	Other Distinguishing Characteristics	Disqualifications
Ayrshire	County of Ayr, in south-western Scotland.	Light to deep cherry red, mahogany, brown , or a combination of these colors, with white, or white alone. Black or brindle are objectionable.	Horns are wide-spread and tend to curve upward and outward. However, there is a polled strain.	The udders are especially symmetrical and well attached to the body. The breed is noted for its style and animation, good feet and legs, and grazing ability.	
Brown Swiss	The Alps of Switzerland.	Solid brown varying from very light to dark. White markings are objectionable.	The nose and tongue black, and there is a characteristic light-colored band around the muzzle. Medium length horns.	Strong and rugged, with some tendency toward the heavy muscling characteristic of the beef breeds. Calm and unexcitable.	
Guernsey	Isle of Guernsey.	Fawn with white markings clearly defined; preferably a clear (buff) muzzle.	Good length of head; horns incline forward, are refined and medium in length, and taper toward the tips.	The milk is especially yellow in color; golden yellow skin pigmentation; the unhaired portions of the body are light or pinkish in color (whereas in the Jersey they are near black); calves are relatively small at birth.	
Holstein-Friesian	Netherlands and Northern Germany.	Black and white markings, clearly defined.	Clean-cut, broad muzzle, open nostrils, strong jaw, broad and moderately dished forehead, straight bridged nose.	Large angular animal; females should weigh 1,500 lbs. (mature); males in breeding condition 2,200 lbs.	Colors which bar registry: all black or all white, black in switch, black belly, black circling leg and touching hoof, black from hoof to knee or hock, black and white intermixed to give color other than distinct black and white.
Jersey	Island of Jersey.	Jerseys vary greatly in color, but the characteristic color is some shade of fawn, with or without white markings.	Forehead, broad and moderately dished with large, bright eyes. Clean-cut and proportionate to body.	Jerseys are especially known for their well-shaped udders and strong udder attachments. They are also very angular and refined.	Total blindness, permanent lameness that interferes with normal function, blind quarter, freemartin heifers, and animals showing signs of being operated upon or tampered with.

SOURCE: ENSMINGER, M. E. 1969. Animal Science. Interstate Printers & Publishers, Danville, Illinois.

DAIRY PRODUCTS, COMPOSITION I

TABLE 2.D.2

COMPOSITION OF MILK AND MILK PRODUCTS

Material	Protein %	Mineral %	Lactose %	Fat %
Whole Milk	3.3	0.7	4.5	3.75
Evaporated Milk	7.0	1.5	9.9	7.9
Condensed (sweetened)	7.5	1.5	10.5	8.5
Dry Whole Milk	26.5	6.0	38.5	26.75
Malted Milk	7.3	1.6	9.9	8.25
Butter	0.6	0.2	0.4	80.5
Cream	2.9	0.6	4.0	20.0
Dry Cream	13.4	2.9	18.0	65.0
Ice Cream and Ice Cream Mix	3.8	0.9	5.3	12.0
Dry Ice Cream	10.5	2.3	15.0	27.0
Frozen Desserts	1.0	0.2	1.3	1.5
Cheese (fat min., all types)	24.5	3.4	1.8	32.0
Cheese (partially defatted)	39.0	5.4	2.8	15.0
Cheese (cottage, etc.)	19.2	1.7	4.3	0.8
Nonfat Dry Milk Solids	36.9	8.15	50.75	0.88
Dry Buttermilk Solids	34.0	8.0	48.0	5.8
Dry Whey Solids	13.0	8.0	73.0	1.0
Separated Condensed (sweetened)	8.8	2.0	12.7	0.5
Separated Condensed (plain)	7.3	1.6	10.8	0.3
Condensed Buttermilk	10.6	3.3	13.0	2.0
Cultured Buttermilk and Chocolate Drinks	3.5	0.7	4.6	2.0
Casein (commercial)	88.5	3.8	0.0	0.2
Dry Buttermilk	32.0	10.0	46.0	5.0
Dry Skim Milk	35.0	8.2	51.0	0.8
Dry Whey	13.0	9.5	71.0	0.5
Semi-Solid Buttermilk	10.6	3.3	13.0	2.0
Liquid Whey	0.8	0.6	4.5	0.05
Liquid Separated Milk	3.3	0.8	4.8	0.06
Lactose	0.0	0.0	99.5	0.0
Condensed Skim Milk (feed)	11.0	2.6	13.5	0.2
Partially defatted Dry Milk Solids	31.2	7.0	45.3	13.8

SOURCE: COOK, H. L. and DAY, G. H. 1967. The Dry Milk Industry. American Dry Milk Institute, Chicago.

DAIRY PRODUCTS, COMPOSITION II

TABLE 2.D.3

NUTRITIVE VALUES OF THE EDIBLE PART OF DAIRY PRODUCTS

[Dashes in the columns for nutrients show that no suitable value could be found although there is reason to believe that a measurable amount of the nutrient may be present]

	Food, approximate measure, and weight (in grams)			Water	Food energy	Protein	Fat	Fatty acids: Saturated (total)	Fatty acids: Unsaturated: Oleic	Fatty acids: Unsaturated: Linoleic	Carbohydrate	Calcium	Iron	Vitamin A value	Thiamin	Riboflavin	Niacin	Ascorbic acid
	MILK, CHEESE, CREAM, IMITATION CREAM; RELATED PRODUCTS		Grams	Percent	Calories	Grams	Grams	Grams	Grams	Grams	Grams	Milligrams	Milligrams	International units	Milligrams	Milligrams	Milligrams	Milligrams
	Milk:																	
	Fluid:																	
1	Whole, 3.5% fat	1 cup	244	87	160	9	9	5	3	Trace	12	288	0.1	350	0.07	0.41	0.2	2
2	Nonfat (skim)	1 cup	245	90	90	9	Trace	------	------	------	12	296	.1	10	.09	.44	.2	2
3	Partly skimmed, 2% nonfat milk solids added.	1 cup	246	87	145	10	5	3	2	Trace	15	352	.1	200	.10	.52	.2	2
	Canned, concentrated, undiluted:																	
4	Evaporated, unsweetened.	1 cup	252	74	345	18	20	11	7	1	24	635	.3	810	.10	.86	.5	3
5	Condensed, sweetened.	1 cup	306	27	980	25	27	15	9	1	166	802	.3	1,100	.24	1.16	.6	3
	Dry, nonfat instant:																	
6	Low-density (1⅓ cups needed for reconstitution to 1 qt.).	1 cup	68	4	245	24	Trace	------	------	------	35	879	.4	[1]20	.24	1.21	.6	5
7	High-density (⅞ cup needed for reconstitution to 1 qt.).	1 cup	104	4	375	37	1	------	------	------	54	1,345	.6	[1]30	.36	1.85	.9	7
	Buttermilk:																	
8	Fluid, cultured, made from skim milk.	1 cup	245	90	90	9	Trace	------	------	------	12	296	.1	10	.10	.44	.2	2
9	Dried, packaged	1 cup	120	3	465	41	6	3	2	Trace	60	1,498	.7	260	.31	2.06	1.1	------
	Cheese:																	
	Natural:																	
	Blue or Roquefort type:																	
10	Ounce	1 oz.	28	40	105	6	9	5	3	Trace	1	89	.1	350	.01	.17	.3	0
11	Cubic inch	1 cu. in.	17	40	65	4	5	3	2	Trace	Trace	54	.1	210	.01	.11	.2	0

(Continued)

TABLE 2.D.3 (*Continued*)

[Dashes in the columns for nutrients show that no suitable value could be found although there is reason to believe that a measurable amount of the nutrient may be present]

	Food, approximate measure, and weight (in grams)			Water	Food energy	Protein	Fat	Fatty acids: Saturated (total)	Fatty acids: Unsaturated: Oleic	Fatty acids: Unsaturated: Linoleic	Carbohydrate	Calcium	Iron	Vitamin A value	Thiamin	Riboflavin	Niacin	Ascorbic acid
	MILK, CHEESE, CREAM, IMITATION CREAM; RELATED PRODUCTS—Con.																	
	Cheese—Continued																	
	Natural—Continued		*Grams*	*Per-cent*	*Calo-ries*	*Grams*	*Grams*	*Grams*	*Grams*	*Grams*	*Grams*	*Milli-grams*	*Milli-grams*	*Inter-national units*	*Milli-grams*	*Milli-grams*	*Milli-grams*	*Milli-grams*
12	Camembert, packaged in 4-oz. pkg. with 3 wedges per pkg.	1 wedge	38	52	115	7	9	5	3	Trace	1	40	0.2	380	0.02	0.29	0.3	0
	Cheddar:																	
13	Ounce	1 oz.	28	37	115	7	9	5	3	Trace	1	213	.3	370	.01	.13	Trace	0
14	Cubic inch	1 cu. in.	17	37	70	4	6	3	2	Trace	Trace	129	.2	230	.01	.08	Trace	0
	Cottage, large or small curd:																	
	Creamed:																	
15	Package of 12-oz., net wt.	1 pkg.	340	78	360	46	14	8	5	Trace	10	320	1.0	580	.10	.85	.3	0
16	Cup, curd pressed down.	1 cup	245	78	260	33	10	6	3	Trace	7	230	.7	420	.07	.61	.2	0
	Uncreamed:																	
17	Package of 12-oz., net wt.	1 pkg.	340	79	290	58	1	1	Trace	Trace	9	306	1.4	30	.10	.95	.3	0
18	Cup, curd pressed down.	1 cup	200	79	170	34	1	Trace	Trace	Trace	5	180	.8	20	.06	.56	.2	0
	Cream:																	
19	Package of 8-oz., net wt.	1 pkg.	227	51	850	18	86	48	28	3	5	141	.5	3,500	.05	.54	.2	0
20	Package of 3-oz., net wt.	1 pkg.	85	51	320	7	32	18	11	1	2	53	.2	1,310	.02	.20	.1	0
21	Cubic inch	1 cu. in.	16	51	60	1	6	3	2	Trace	Trace	10	Trace	250	Trace	.04	Trace	0
	Parmesan, grated:																	
22	Cup, pressed down	1 cup	140	17	655	60	43	24	14	1	5	1,893	.7	1,760	.03	1.22	.3	0
23	Tablespoon	1 tbsp.	5	17	25	2	2	1	Trace	Trace	Trace	68	Trace	60	Trace	.04	Trace	0
24	Ounce	1 oz.	28	17	130	12	9	5	3	Trace	1	383	.1	360	.01	.25	.1	0
	Swiss:																	
25	Ounce	1 oz.	28	39	105	8	8	4	3	Trace	1	262	.3	320	Trace	.11	Trace	0
26	Cubic inch	1 cu. in.	15	39	55	4	4	2	1	Trace	Trace	139	.1	170	Trace	.06	Trace	0

	Pasteurized processed cheese:																	
	American:																	
27	Ounce	1 oz.	28	40	105	7	9	5	3	Trace	1	198	.3	350	.01	.12	Trace	0
28	Cubic inch	1 cu. in.	18	40	65	4	5	3	2	Trace	Trace	122	.2	210	Trace	.07	Trace	0
	Swiss:																	
29	Ounce	1 oz.	28	40	100	8	8	4	3	Trace	1	251	.3	310	Trace	.11	Trace	0
30	Cubic inch	1 cu. in.	18	40	65	5	5	3	2	Trace	Trace	159	.2	200	Trace	.07	Trace	0
	Pasteurized process cheese food, American:																	
31	Tablespoon	1 tbsp.	14	43	45	3	3	2	1	Trace	1	80	.1	140	Trace	.08	Trace	0
32	Cubic inch	1 cu. in.	18	43	60	4	4	2	1	Trace	1	100	.1	170	Trace	.10	Trace	0
33	Pasteurized process cheese spread, American.	1 oz.	28	49	80	5	6	3	2	Trace	2	160	.2	250	Trace	.15	Trace	0
	Cream:																	
34	Half-and-half (cream and milk).	1 cup	242	80	325	8	28	15	9	1	11	261	.1	1,160	.07	.39	.1	2
35		1 tbsp.	15	80	20	1	2	1	1	Trace	1	16	Trace	70	Trace	.02	Trace	Trace
36	Light, coffee or table	1 cup	240	72	505	7	49	27	16	1	10	245	.1	2,020	.07	.36	.1	2
37		1 tbsp.	15	72	30	1	3	2	1	Trace	1	15	Trace	130	Trace	.02	Trace	Trace
38	Sour	1 cup	230	72	485	7	47	26	16	1	10	235	.1	1,930	.07	.35	.1	2
39		1 tbsp.	12	72	25	Trace	2	1	1	Trace	1	12	Trace	100	Trace	.02	Trace	Trace
40	Whipped topping (pressurized).	1 cup	60	62	155	2	14	8	5	Trace	6	67	-----	570	-----	.04	-----	-----
41		1 tbsp.	3	62	10	Trace	1	Trace	Trace	Trace	Trace	3	-----	30	-----	Trace	-----	-----
	Whipping, unwhipped (volume about double when whipped):																	
42	Light	1 cup	239	62	715	6	75	41	25	2	9	203	.1	3,060	.05	.29	.1	2
43		1 tbsp.	15	62	45	Trace	5	3	2	Trace	1	13	Trace	190	Trace	.02	Trace	Trace
44	Heavy	1 cup	238	57	840	5	90	50	30	3	7	179	.1	3,670	.05	.26	.1	2
45		1 tbsp.	15	57	55	Trace	6	3	2	Trace	1	11	Trace	230	Trace	.02	Trace	Trace
	Imitation cream products (made with vegetable fat):																	
	Creamers:																	
46	Powdered	1 cup	94	2	505	4	33	31	1	0	52	21	.6	[2]200	-----	-----	Trace	-----
47		1 tsp.	2	2	10	Trace	1	Trace	Trace	0	1	1	Trace	[2]Trace	-----	-----	-----	-----
48	Liquid (frozen)	1 cup	245	77	345	3	27	25	1	0	25	29	-----	[2]100	0	0	-----	-----
49		1 tbsp.	15	77	20	Trace	2	1	Trace	0	2	2	-----	[2]10	0	0	-----	-----
50	Sour dressing (imitation sour cream) made with nonfat dry milk.	1 cup	235	72	440	9	38	35	1	Trace	17	277	.1	10	.07	.38	.2	1
51		1 tbsp.	12	72	20	Trace	2	2	Trace	Trace	1	14	Trace	Trace	Trace	Trace	Trace	Trace
	Whipped topping:																	
52	Pressurized	1 cup	70	61	190	1	17	15	1	0	9	5	-----	[2]340	-----	0	-----	-----
53		1 tbsp.	4	61	10	Trace	1	1	Trace	0	Trace	Trace	-----	[2]20	-----	0	-----	-----

(Continued)

TABLE 2.D.3 (*Continued*)

[Dashes in the columns for nutrients show that no suitable value could be found although there is reason to believe that a measurable amount of the nutrient may be present]

	Food, approximate measure, and weight (in grams)			Water	Food energy	Protein	Fat	Fatty acids: Saturated (total)	Fatty acids: Unsaturated: Oleic	Fatty acids: Unsaturated: Linoleic	Carbohydrate	Calcium	Iron	Vitamin A value	Thiamin	Riboflavin	Niacin	Ascorbic acid
	MILK, CHEESE, CREAM, IMITATION CREAM; RELATED PRODUCTS—Con.																	
	Whipped topping—Continued		*Grams*	*Per-cent*	*Calo-ries*	*Grams*	*Grams*	*Grams*	*Grams*	*Grams*	*Grams*	*Milli-grams*	*Milli-grams*	*Inter-national units*	*Milli-grams*	*Milli-grams*	*Milli-grams*	*Milli-grams*
54	Frozen	1 cup	75	52	230	1	20	18	Trace	0	15	5	----	[2]560	----	0	----	----
55		1 tbsp.	4	52	10	Trace	1	1	Trace	0	1	Trace	----	[2]30	----	0	----	----
56	Powdered, made with whole milk.	1 cup	75	58	175	3	12	10	1	Trace	15	62	Trace	[2]330	.02	.08	.1	Trace
57		1 tbsp.	4	58	10	Trace	1	1	Trace	Trace	1	3	Trace	[2]20	Trace	Trace	Trace	Trace
	Milk beverages:																	
58	Cocoa, homemade	1 cup	250	79	245	10	12	7	4	Trace	27	295	1.0	400	.10	.45	.5	3
59	Chocolate-flavored drink made with skim milk and 2% added butterfat.	1 cup	250	83	190	8	6	3	2	Trace	27	270	.5	210	.10	.40	.3	3
	Malted milk:																	
60	Dry powder, approx. 3 heaping teaspoons per ounce.	1 oz.	28	3	115	4	2	----	----	----	20	82	.6	290	.09	.15	.1	0
61	Beverage	1 cup	235	78	245	11	10	----	----	----	28	317	.7	590	.14	.49	.2	2
	Milk desserts:																	
62	Custard, baked	1 cup	265	77	305	14	15	7	5	1	29	297	1.1	930	.11	.50	.3	1
	Ice cream:																	
63	Regular (approx. 10% fat).	½ gal.	1,064	63	2,055	48	113	62	37	3	221	1,553	.5	4,680	.43	2.23	1.1	11
64		1 cup	133	63	255	6	14	8	5	Trace	28	194	.1	590	.05	.28	.1	1
65		3 fl. oz. cup	50	63	95	2	5	3	2	Trace	10	73	Trace	220	.02	.11	.1	1
66	Rich (approx. 16% fat).	½ gal.	1,188	63	2,635	31	191	105	63	6	214	927	.2	7,840	.24	1.31	1.2	12
67		1 cup	148	63	330	4	24	13	8	1	27	115	Trace	980	.03	.16	.1	1
	Ice milk:																	
68	Hardened	½ gal.	1,048	67	1,595	50	53	29	17	2	235	1,635	1.0	2,200	.52	2.31	1.0	10
69		1 cup	131	67	200	6	7	4	2	Trace	29	204	.1	280	.07	.29	.1	1
70	Soft-serve	1 cup	175	67	265	8	9	5	3	Trace	39	273	.2	370	.09	.39	.2	2

	Yoghurt:																	
71	Made from partially skimmed milk.	1 cup	245	89	125	8	4	2	1	Trace	13	294	.1	170	.10	.44	.2	2
72	Made from whole milk	1 cup	245	88	150	7	8	5	3	Trace	12	272	.1	340	.07	.39	.2	2
	EGGS																	
	Eggs, large, 24 ounces per dozen:																	
	Raw or cooked in shell or with nothing added:																	
73	Whole, without shell	1 egg	50	74	80	6	6	2	3	Trace	Trace	27	1.1	590	.05	.15	Trace	0
74	White of egg	1 white	33	88	15	4	Trace	------	------	------	Trace	3	Trace	0	Trace	.09	Trace	0
75	Yolk of egg	1 yolk	17	51	60	3	5	2	2	Trace	Trace	24	.9	580	.04	.07	Trace	0
76	Scrambled with milk and fat.	1 egg	64	72	110	7	8	3	3	Trace	1	51	1.1	690	.05	.18	Trace	0

[1] Value applies to unfortified product; value for fortified low-density product would be 1500 I.U. and the fortified high-density product would be 2290 I.U.

[2] Contributed largely from beta-carotene used for coloring.

SOURCE: ANON. Nutritive Value of Foods. USDA Home and Garden Bull. *72.*

DAIRY TERMS

FRESH WHOLE MILK	Grade A pasturized milk sold for home use.
Whole milk	At least 3.25 percent milkfat and 8.25 percent nonfat milk solids in most States.
Homogenized	Fat uniformly distributed through milk.
Cream-line	Layer of cream at top of container.
Vitamin D	Vitamin D increased to at least 400 U.S.P. or International Units per quart.
Fortified multiple-vitamin and/or mineral	Added vitamin A, vitamin D, riboflavin, thiamin, niacin, and/or iron, iodine.
Concentrated	Fresh milk with two-thirds water removed.
Skim milk	Processed to remove most of the fat.
Skim or nonfat milk	Not more than 0.5 percent milkfat and at least 8.25 percent nonfat milk solids in most States.
Fortified skim	Added vitamin A and vitamin D, less than 0.5 percent milkfat, and at least 10 percent nonfat milk solids.
Lowfat	Between 0.5 and 2 percent milkfat.
2 percent	2 percent milkfat and—usually—10 percent nonfat milk solids.
Flavored milk	Flavoring and stabilizer added.
Chocolate milk	Made from whole milk with chocolate and sweetener.
Chocolate-flavored milk	Made from whole milk with cocoa and sweetener.
Chocolate drink (chocolate lowfat milk)	Made from skim or lowfat milk with chocolate and sweetener. Nonfat milk solids may be added.
Chocolate-flavored drink	Made from skim or lowfat milk with cocoa and sweetener. Nonfat milk solids may be added.
Other	Flavored milk: Strawberry, coffee, maple, or other flavoring combined with whole milk. Flavored drink or flavored lowfat milk: Flavoring combined with skim or lowfat milk.
CULTURED MILK	Made by adding bacterial culture to milk.
Buttermilk	Thick, smooth liquid. Usually made from skim milk; at least 8.25 percent nonfat milk solids.
Yogurt	Semisolid. Made from whole or skim milk. Fruit or other flavorings may be added.
CANNED MILK	Concentrated by removing water from milk.
Evaporated milk	Vitamin D added. Sterilized.
Whole	At least 7.9 percent milkfat and 25.9 percent total milk solids.
Skim	Low milkfat—often 0.2 or 0.3 percent. At least 18 percent total milk solids. Vitamin A may be added.
Sweetened condensed milk	Sugar added to help preserve milk. At least 8.5 percent milkfat and 28 percent total milk solids.
DRY MILK	**Not more than 5 percent of moisture.**
Nonfat dry milk	**Made from fluid skim milk. Usually "instantized." Not more than 1.25 percent milkfat in extra grade dry product. May have vitamins A and D added.**
Whole dry milk	**Made from fluid whole milk. At least 26 percent milkfat in the dry product.**
HALF-AND-HALF	**Mixture of milk and cream. Pasteurized, Grade A.**
Half-and-half	**At least 10.5 percent milkfat; generally homogenized.**
Sour half-and-half	**Made by adding bacterial culture to fresh half-and-half; 0.2 percent acidity. Fluid or semifluid.**
CREAM	**Pasteurized, Grade A.**
Table cream (coffee or light cream)	**At least 18 percent milkfat; generally homogenized.**
Sour cream	**Made by adding bacterial culture to fresh table cream; 0.2 percent acidity. Fluid or semifluid.**
Light whipping cream	**At least 30 percent milkfat.**
Heavy whipping cream	**At least 36 percent milkfat.**
Pressurized whipped cream	**Liquid containing fresh table or whipping cream, sugar, stabilizer, emulsifier in aerosol can.**
FROZEN DESSERTS	**Hard or soft frozen, pasturized during processing.**
Ice cream	**Made from cream, milk, sugar, stabilizers. At least 10 percent milkfat and 20 percent total milk solids.**
Frozen custard (French or New York ice cream)	**Made from the usual ingredients for ice cream, plus egg yolks. At least 10 percent milkfat and 20 percent total milk solids.**
Ice milk	**Made from milk, stabilizers, sweeteners. Between 2 and 7 percent milkfat and at least 11 percent total milk solids.**
Fruit sherbet	**Made from milk, fruit or fruit juice, stabilizers, sweeteners. From 1 to 2 percent milkfat, and between 2 and 5 percent total milk solids.**

Based on recommendations in "Grade 'A' Pasteurized Milk Ordinance," Public Health Service Publication 229 (1967 revision), "Federal and State Standards for the Composition of Milk Products," Agriculture Handbook No. 51 (Jan. 1968), and Federal standards of identity as published in the Federal Register. A few States have set slightly lower minimums than those listed for milkfat and nonfat milk solids for some products.

SOURCE: ANON. 1974. **Milk in family meals. USDA Home and Garden Bull.** *127*.

DEFECTIVES IN LOT

TABLE 2.D.4

PROBABLE DEFECTIVES IN PROCESSED FOOD LOTS

Probabilities for use when the sample size, *n*, is less than 10% of the lot size *N*†

n	*c*	X(%) 1	2	3	4	5	6	7	8	9	10	12	14	16	18	20
		Probability of being right if, based on a sample of *n* which contains *c* defectives, one assumes there is *X*% or less defective in the lot														
3	0	3	6	9	12	14	17	20	22	25	27	32	36	41	45	49
	1	*	*	*	*	1	1	1	2	2	3	4	5	7	9	10
	2				*	*	*	*	*	*	*	*	*	*	1	1
6	0	6	11	17	22	26	31	35	39	43	47	54	60	65	70	74
	1	*	1	1	2	3	5	6	8	10	11	16	20	25	30	34
	2		*	*	*	*	*	1	1	1	2	3	4	6	8	10
	3													1	1	2
	4													*	*	*
13	0	12	23	33	41	49	55	61	66	71	75	81	86	90	92	95
	1	1	3	6	9	14	18	23	28	33	38	47	56	64	71	77
	2	*	*	1	1	2	4	6	8	11	13	20	27	35	42	50
	3		*	*	*	*	1	1	2	2	3	6	10	14	19	25
	4						*	*	*	*	1	1	3	4	7	10
	5										*	*	1	1	2	3
	6												*	*	*	1
	7															*
21	0	19	35	47	58	66	73	78	83	86	89	93	96	97	98	99
	1	2	7	13	20	28	36	44	51	58	64	74	81	87	91	94
	2	*	1	2	5	8	13	18	23	29	35	47	58	68	76	82
	3	*	*	*	1	2	3	6	8	11	15	24	34	44	54	63
	4		*	*	*	*	1	1	2	4	5	10	16	24	32	41
	5						*	*	1	1	1	3	6	11	16	23
	6								*	*	*	1	2	4	7	11
	7											*	1	1	2	4
	8												*	*	1	1
	9														*	*

(Continued)

TABLE 2.D.4 (*Continued*)

		X(%)														
n	*c*	1	2	3	4	5	6	7	8	9	10	12	14	16	18	20
29	0	25	44	59	69	77	83	88	91	94	95	98	99	99	100	100
	1	3	11	22	32	43	53	61	69	75	80	88	93	96	98	99
	2	*	2	6	11	15	25	33	41	49	57	69	79	86	91	95
	3		*	1	3	5	9	14	20	26	33	47	59	70	79	86
	4			*	1	1	3	5	8	11	16	26	38	50	62	72
	5				*	*	1	1	3	4	6	13	21	32	43	54
	6						*	*	1	1	2	5	10	17	26	36
	7								*	*	1	2	4	8	14	21
	8										*	1	1	3	6	11
	9											*	*	1	3	5
	10													*	1	2
	11														*	1
	12															*
38	0	32	54	69	79	86	90	94	96	97	98	99	100	100	100	
	1	5	18	32	45	57	67	76	82	87	90	95	98	99	100	100
	2	1	4	10	19	30	40	50	60	68	75	85	92	96	98	99
	3	*	1	3	6	12	19	27	36	45	54	68	80	88	93	96
	4		*	1	2	4	8	12	18	25	33	49	63	75	84	90
	5			*	*	1	2	5	8	12	17	30	44	58	70	80
	6					*	1	1	3	5	8	16	28	41	54	66
	7						*	*	1	2	3	8	15	26	37	50
	8								*	1	1	3	8	14	23	34
	9									*	*	1	3	7	13	22
	10											*	1	3	7	12
	11												*	1	3	6
	12													*	1	3
	13														*	1
	14															*
48	0	38	62	77	86	91	95	97	98	99	99	100	100	100		
	1	8	25	42	58	70	79	86	91	94	96	98	99	100	100	100
	2	1	7	17	30	43	56	66	75	82	87	94	97	99	100	100
	3	*	2	6	12	22	33	44	54	64	72	84	92	96	98	99
	4		*	1	4	9	16	24	34	44	53	70	82	90	95	98
	5			*	1	3	6	12	18	26	35	52	68	80	89	94
	6				*	1	2	5	9	14	20	35	52	67	78	87
	7					*	1	2	4	6	10	21	36	51	65	77

†When the sample size is more than 10% of the lot size, the probabilities in this table will be changed. The extent of change depends on the value of *n*/*N*.

SOURCE: THATCHER, F. S. and CLARK, D. S. 1968. Microorganisms in Foods. University of Toronto Press, Toronto, Canada.

DEFROSTING TIME

TABLE 2.D.5

TIMETABLE FOR DEFROSTING FROZEN MEAT

Meat	In Refrigerator (36°-40°F)
Large roast	4-7 hr per lb
Small roast	3-5 hr per lb
1-in. steak	12-14 hr

NOTE: Refreezing meat is not a recommended practice because of possible variation in the history and treatment of meat before freezing, during freezing and/or during defrosting prior to refreezing. When refreezing may seem necessary to prevent spoilage, some loss in juiciness can be expected.

SOURCE: Lessons on Meat. (1974). National Live Stock and Meat Board, Chicago.

DETERGENT PROPERTIES

TABLE 2.D.6

PROPERTIES OF VARIOUS DETERGENT MATERIALS

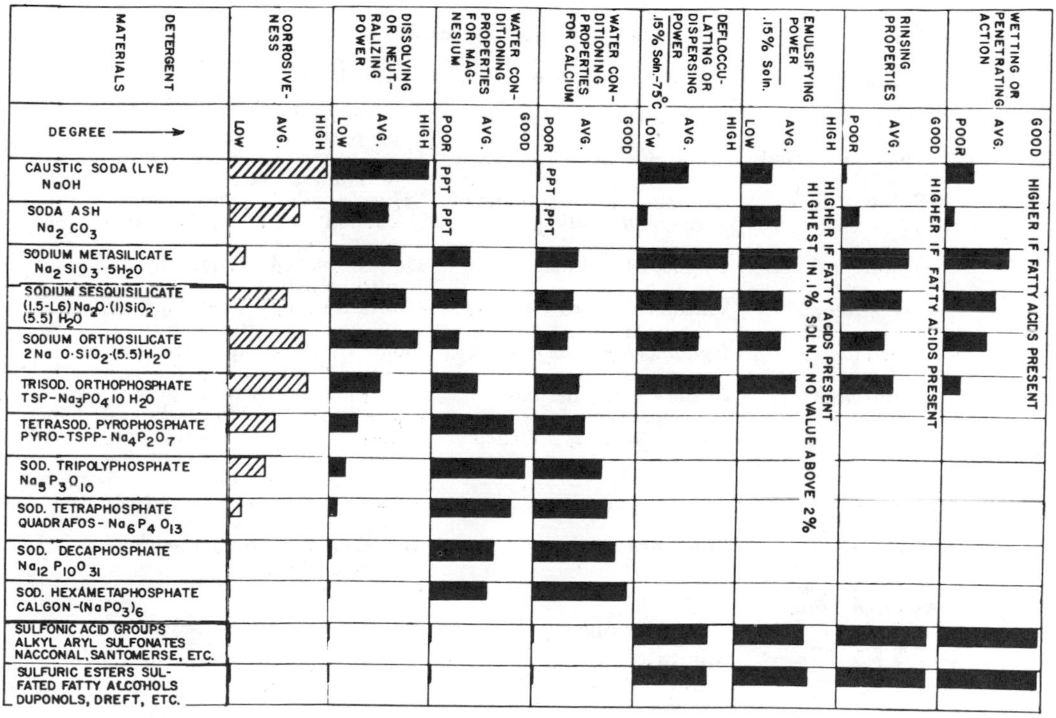
DETERGENT MATERIALS
CORROSIVENESS
DISSOLVING OR NEUTRALIZING POWER
WATER CONDITIONING PROPERTIES FOR MAGNESIUM
WATER CONDITIONING PROPERTIES FOR CALCIUM
DEFLOCCULATING OR DISPERSING POWER .15% Soln.-75°C
EMULSIFYING POWER .15% Soln.
RINSING PROPERTIES
WETTING OR PENETRATING ACTION
DEGREE
LOW AVG. HIGH
POOR AVG. GOOD
CAUSTIC SODA (LYE) NaOH
SODA ASH Na2 CO3
SODIUM METASILICATE Na2 SiO3 · 5H2O
SODIUM SESQUISILICATE (1.5-1.6) Na2O·(1)SiO2·(5.5) H2O
SODIUM ORTHOSILICATE 2Na O·SiO2·(5.5)H2O
TRISOD. ORTHOPHOSPHATE TSP-Na3PO4 10 H2O
TETRASOD. PYROPHOSPHATE PYRO-TSPP-Na4P2O7
SOD. TRIPOLYPHOSPHATE Na5P3O10
SOD. TETRAPHOSPHATE QUADRAFOS-Na6P4O13
SOD. DECAPHOSPHATE Na12P10O31
SOD. HEXAMETAPHOSPHATE CALGON-(NaPO3)6
SULFONIC ACID GROUPS ALKYL ARYL SULFONATES NACCONAL, SANTOMERSE, ETC.
SULFURIC ESTERS SULFATED FATTY ALCOHOLS DUPONOLS, DREFT, ETC.
PPT
HIGHER IF FATTY ACIDS PRESENT
HIGHEST IN .1% SOLN. - NO VALUE ABOVE 2%
HIGHER IF FATTY ACIDS PRESENT
HIGHER IF FATTY ACIDS PRESENT

SOURCE: KRAMER, A. and TWIGG, B. A. (EDITORS). 1973. Sanitation, National Canners Association. *In* Quality Control For The Food Industry, Vol. 2, 3rd Edition. Avi Publishing Co., Westport, Conn.

DETERGENTS

TABLE 2.D.7

PROPERTIES OF DETERGENTS

	Strong Alkalis	Mild Alkalis	Poly-phosphates	Mild Acids	Strong Acids	Sur-factants
Sequestering	0	+	++++	0	0	0
Wetting	+	++	+	+	0	++++
Emulsifying, suspending	+	++	++	0	0	++++
Dissolving	++++	+++	++	+++	++++	+
Saponifying	++++	+++	0	0	0	+
Peptizing	++++	+++	+	++	+++	0
Dispersion	++	+++	+	+	0	+++
Rinsing	+++	+++	++	+	0	++++
Corrosion	++++	++,+++	0	++	++++	0

Degrees of Activity: extreme ++++, high +++, medium ++, low +, none 0.

SOURCE: HARPER, W. J. 1972. Sanitation in Dairy Food Plants. *In* Food Sanitation. R. K. Guthrie (Editor). Avi Publishing Co., Westport, Conn.

DISEASES, FOOD-BORNE

TABLE 2.D.8

FOOD-BORNE DISEASES

Disease	Etiologic Agent	Foods Usually Involved
1. Botulism	*Cl. botulinum* toxins	Canned and bottled food improperly processed
2. *Staphylococcus*	Staphylococci enterotoxin	Custard pastries, cooked ham, hollandaise sauce
3. Salmonellosis	A variety of members of the *Salmonella* group	"Hand-made" salads, sliced cooked meats, "warmed over" foods
4. Typhoid fever	Typhoid bacillus	Contaminated food, water, milk, shellfish
5. Dysentery, Bacillary	Various species of genus *Shigella*	Contaminated food, water, by contact with excreta
6. Dysentery, Amoebic	*Endamoeba histolytica*	Cold moist foods, contaminated drinking water
7. Tularemia	*Pasteurella tularensis*	Wild rabbits (by handling)
8. Brucellosis	*Brucella melitensis, Brucella abortus, Brucella suis*	Ingestion of infected milk and dairy products. Direct contact with infected animals or animal products
9. Q fever	*Coxiella burnetii*	Milk, contact, or exposure to infected livestock
10. Trichinosis	*Trichinella spiralis*	Insufficiently cooked pork or pork products

Average Time of Onset	Symptoms	Preventive Procedure
1. 1–2 days	Difficulty in swallowing and speech, double vision	Careful canning procedure. Cooking to detoxify toxins.
2. 3–6 hours	Nausea, vomiting, abdominal cramps	Prompt refrigeration of foods; pasteurization of custard-filled pastries.

3. 6–18 hours	Diarrhea, abdominal cramps, vomiting	Strict attention to cleanliness of hands of food handlers. Protection of foods during processing and storage. Refrigeration of food.
4. 7–14 days	Fever	Pasteurization of milk, safe water supply; approved source of shellfish; isolation of carrier from food handling.
5. 1–7 days	Diarrhea, fever	Protection of water supply; handwashing.
6. Several days to 4 weeks	Diarrhea	Handwashing. Prevention of cross connections.
7. 1–10 days	Sudden chills and fever	Avoid handling of rabbits or use protective gloves.
8. 6–30 days	Undulating fever; pains in joints and muscles	Pasteurization of milk and dairy products; care in handling meat and meat products.
9. 2–3 weeks	Sudden chills, headaches, severe sweats, malaise	Pasteurization of milk.
10. 2–28 days	Nausea, diarrhea, soreness in muscles, fever	Thorough cooking of pork and pork products. Antigen testings of hogs. Prevent feeding of raw garbage to hogs. Freezing of pork.

SOURCE: WEISER, H. H., MOUNTNEY, G. J. and GOULD, W. A. (EDITORS). 1971. Food Poisoning. *In* Practical Food Microbiology. Avi Publishing Co., Westport, Conn.

DRYER TYPES

TABLE 2.D.9

COMMON DRIER TYPES USED FOR LIQUID AND SOLID FOODS

Drier Type	Usual Food Type
Air Convection Driers	
kiln	pieces
cabinet, tray, or pan	pieces, purées, liquids
tunnel	pieces
continuous conveyor belt	purées, liquids
belt trough	pieces
air lift	small pieces, granules
fluidized bed	small pieces, granules
spray	liquids, purées
Drum or Roller Driers	
atmospheric	purées, liquids
vacuum	purées, liquids
Vacuum Driers	
vacuum shelf	pieces, purées, liquids
vacuum belt	purées, liquids
freeze driers	pieces, liquids

SOURCE: POTTER, NORMAN N. (EDITOR). 1973. Food dehydration and concentration. *In* Food Science, 2nd Edition. Avi Publishing Co., Westport, Conn.

E

EDIBLE MEAT AND CHILLED CARCASS (OR M. BICEPS FEMORIS)

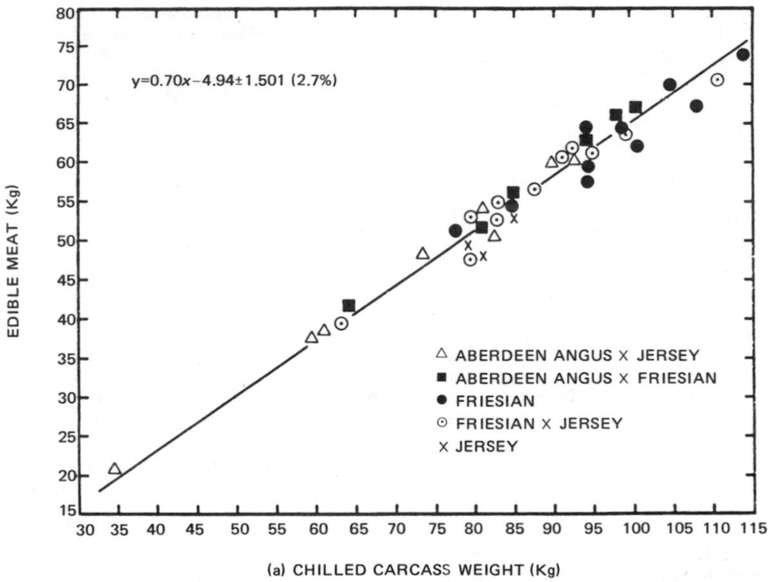

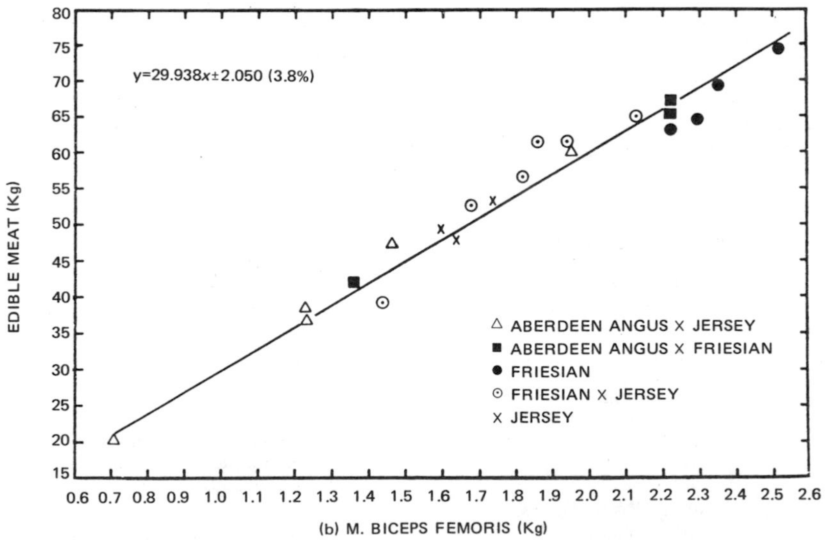

FIG. 2.E.1. THE RELATION OF THE YIELD OF EDIBLE MEAT FROM BREEDS AND CROSSES OF CALVES AT 10 MONTHS OF AGE WITH: (A) CHILLED CARCASS WEIGHT, (B) THE WEIGHT OF THE RIGHT BICEPS FEMORIS MUSCLE

SOURCE: TRIBE, D. E. (EDITOR). Carcass Composition and Appraisal of Meat Animals. CSIRO, Australia.

EGG COMPOSITION I

TABLE 2.E.1

COMPOSITION OF THE EDIBLE PORTION (EP) AND REFUSE IN THE MATERIAL AS PURCHASED (AP)

Commodity and Description	Percent of Edible Portion: Water	Protein	Fat	Carbohydrate: Total (by dif)	Carbohydrate: Fiber	Ash	Calories (No. per 100 g)	Notes	Refuse in AP (%)
EGGS									
Fresh									
Hen	74	12.4	11.7	0.9	—	1.0	163	Refuse: shell	11
—liquid, whole	74	12.4	11.7	0.9	—	1.0	163		0
Duck	71	13	14.5	0.5	—	1.0	189	Refuse: shell	13
Goose	70.5	14	13.6	0.8	—	1.1	187	Refuse: shell	13
Dehydrated, whole	3	47	43	3.2	—	3.8	605		0

SOURCE: CHATFIELD, C. Food Composition Tables for International Use. FAO, United Nations, Rome.

EGG COMPOSITION II

TABLE 2.E.2

COMPOSITION OF EGGS

Approximate Measure, and Weight (in Grams)			Water (%)	Food Energy (Cal)	Protein (g)	Fat (Total Lipid) (g)	Fatty Acids: Saturated (Total) (g)	Fatty Acids: Unsaturated: Oleic (g)	Fatty Acids: Unsaturated: Lin-oleic (g)	Carbo-hydrate (g)	Calcium (mg)	Iron (mg)	Vitamin A Value (IU)	Thiamin (mg)	Riboflavin (mg)	Niacin (mg)	Ascorbic Acid (mg)
Eggs, large, 24 oz per doz:																	
Raw:																	
Whole, without shell	1 egg	(50 g)	74	80	6	6	2	3	Tr	Tr	27	1.1	590	0.05	0.15	Tr	0
White of egg	1 white	(33 g)	88	15	4	Tr	—	—	—	Tr	3	Tr	0	Tr	0.09	Tr	0
Yolk of egg	1 yolk	(17 g)	51	60	3	5	2	2	Tr	Tr	24	0.9	580	0.04	0.07	Tr	0
Cooked:																	
Boiled, shell removed	2 eggs	(100 g)	74	160	13	12	4	5	1	1	54	2.3	1,180	0.09	0.28	0.1	0
Scrambled, with milk and fat	1 egg	(64 g)	72	110	7	8	3	4	1	1	51	1.1	690	0.05	0.18	Tr	0

SOURCE: INSTITUTE OF HOME ECONOMICS. Nutritive Value of Foods. USDA Home and Garden Bull. 72.

EGG, DRIED EQUIVALENTS

TABLE 2.E.3

AMOUNTS OF DRIED EGG PRODUCT AND WATER TO REPLACE SPECIFIED NUMBERS OF WHOLE EGGS, EGG YOLKS, OR EGG WHITES

If a recipe calls for—	You may use—	
	Dried egg product, sifted	Lukewarm water
Whole eggs:[1]		
1	2½ tablespoons.	2½ tablespoons.
6	1 cup.	1 cup.
Egg yolks:		
1	2 tablespoons.	2 teaspoons.
6	¾ cup.	¼ cup.
Egg whites:		
1	2 teaspoons.	2 tablespoons.
6	¼ cup.	¾ cup.

[1] Large eggs weighing 24 ounces per dozen.

SOURCE: Eggs in Family Meals. (1970). USDA Home and Garden Bull. *103*.

EGG EQUIVALENTS

TABLE 2.E.4.

GUIDE FOR USING WHOLE EGGS OF VARIOUS SIZES IN RECIPES

Number of Large Eggs	In Recipe Use Equivalent to:			Approximate Volume
	Extra Large Eggs	Medium Eggs	Small Eggs	
1	1	1	1	3 Tbsp
2	2	2	3	¼ cup + 2 Tbsp
3	3	4	4	½ cup + 2 Tbsp
4	3	5	6	¾ cup
5	4	6	7	1 cup
6	5	7	8	1 cup + 2 Tbsp
8	6	10	11	1½ cups
10	8	12	14	2 cups
12	10	14	17	2½ cups

SOURCE: VAN EGMOND, DOROTHY. (EDITOR). 1974. Food Preparation. *In* School Food Service. Avi Publishing Co., Westport, Conn.

EGG INCUBATION PERIODS

TABLE 2.E.5

INCUBATION PERIODS

Domestic Birds	Days	Caged and Game Birds	Days
Chicken	20–22	Budgerigar	17–31
Duck	26–28	Dove	12–19
Muscovy duck	33–35	Finch	11–14
Goose	30–33	Parrot	17–31
Guinea fowl	26–28	Pheasant	21–28
Turkey	26–28	Pigeon	16–18
		Quail	21–28
		Swan	21–35

SOURCE: The Merck Veterinary Manual, 4th Edition. (1973) Merck & Co., Rahway, N.J.

EGG PRODUCTS, NUTRITIVE VALUE

TABLE 2.E.6

NUTRITIVE VALUE OF EGG PRODUCTS
(Nutrients per 100 Grams of Product)

	Whole Egg		White		Yolk	
	Liquid	Dry	Liquid	Dry	Liquid	Dry
Calories	193	592	51	372	312	664.
Water—gm	75.3	5.0	89.0	8.0	57.0	5.0
Protein—gm	12.0	45.0	10.0	81.0	14.0	32.0
Amino acids						
Alanine—gm	0.64	2.59	0.83	5.34	0.79	1.83
Arginine—gm	0.78	3.03	0.73	5.03	1.08	2.29
Aspartic acid—gm	0.95	2.61	0.75	6.94	1.04	2.43
Cystine—gm	0.27	1.01	0.28	2.35	0.25	0.64
Glutamic acid—gm	1.48	5.73	1.24	10.93	1.75	3.88
Glycine—gm	0.42	1.61	0.42	3.21	0.49	1.05
Histidine—gm	0.30	1.09	0.25	1.94	0.41	0.81
Isoleucine—gm	0.72	2.72	0.61	5.09	0.89	1.88
Leucine—gm	1.01	3.82	0.83	6.94	1.29	2.68
Lysine—gm	0.84	2.17	0.65	5.67	1.11	2.36
Methionine—gm	0.40	1.51	0.40	3.40	0.36	0.85
Phenylalanine—gm	0.61	2.41	0.58	5.00	0.63	1.43
Serine—gm	0.92	3.63	0.66	5.94	1.27	2.82
Threonine—gm	0.63	2.35	0.48	4.03	0.83	1.73
Tryptophane—gm	0.22	0.81	0.18	1.46	0.24	0.49
Tyrosine—gm	0.54	1.94	0.43	3.40	0.68	1.38
Valine—gm	0.88	3.27	0.85	6.38	0.98	2.09
Lipids—gm	10.5	40.0	—	—	28.0	60.7
Total saturated fatty acids—gm	3.0	11.4	—	—	8.0	17.7
Total unsaturated fatty acids—gm	6.0	22.8	—	—	16.0	35.4
Oleic—gm	4.0	15.2	—	—	10.7	23.7
Linoleic—gm	0.9	3.4	—	—	2.4	5.3
Cholesterol—gm	0.42	1.60	—	—	1.12	2.5
Phospholipids—gm	3.3	12.5	—	—	8.6	19.1

	Whole Egg		White		Yolk	
	Liquid	Dry	Liquid	Dry	Liquid	Dry
Minerals (ash)—gm	1.0	3.7	0.7	5.7	1.6	3.4
Calcium—mg	54.0	201.0	6.0	48.4	147.0	309.0
Chlorine—mg	100.0	372.0	131.0	1057.0	67.0	141.0
Copper—mg	0.17	0.63	0.04	0.32	0.25	0.52
Fluorine—mg	0.06	0.22	0.22	0.16	0.12	0.25
Iodine—mg	12.0	45.0	6.8	54.9	16.0	34.0
Iron—mg	2.1	7.8	0.3	0.24	5.6	11.8
Magnesium—mg	9.0	33.5	11.0	89.0	13.0	27.0
Manganese—mg	0.04	0.15	—	—	0.11	0.23
Phosphorous—mg	210.0	731.0	17.0	137.0	586.0	1231.0
Potassium—mg	149.0	554.0	149.0	1202.0	110.0	231.0
Sodium—mg	111.0	413.0	175.0	1412.0	78.0	164.0
Sulfur—mg	233.0	867.0	211.0	1702.0	214.0	449.0
Zinc—mg	1.3	4.8	0.01	0.8	3.8	8.0
Vitamins						
A-IU	1140.0	4240.0	—	—	3210.0	6741.0
B_{12}—mcg	0.28	1.04	0.01	0.08	0.83	1.74
Biotin—mcg	22.5	83.7	7.0	56.5	52.0	109.0
Choline—gm	0.53	1.97	—	—	1.49	3.13
D-IU	50.0	186.0	—	—	150.0	315.0
E—mg	2.0	7.4	—	—	6.0	12.6
Folic acid—mg	9.4	35.0	1.6	12.9	23.2	48.7
Niacin—mg	0.1	0.37	—	—	—	—
Pantothenic acid—mg	2.7	10.0	0.13	1.05	6.0	12.6
Pyridoxine—mg	0.25	0.93	0.22	1.78	0.31	0.65
Riboflavin—mg	0.29	1.08	0.26	2.1	0.35	0.74
Thiamin—mg	0.1	0.37	—	—	0.27	0.57
Inositol—mg	33.0	122.8	—	—	—	—
Carbohydrates—gm	0.7	—	0.8	—	0.7	—

SOURCE: COTTERILL, O. J. 1974. A Scientist Speaks About Egg Products. (Revised). Technical Advisory Committee, American Egg Board, Park Ridge, Illinois.

EGG QUALITY

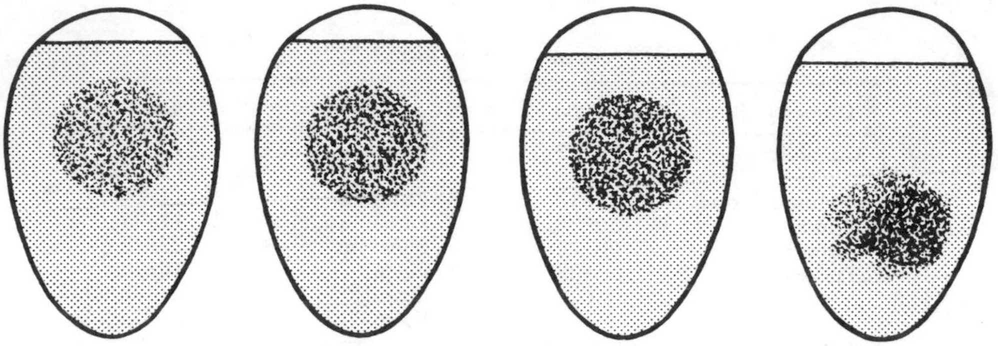

AA QUALITY A QUALITY B QUALITY C QUALITY

FIG. 2.E.2. CANDLED APPEARANCE OF EGGS DENOTING QUALITY

SOURCE: U.S. DEPARTMENT OF THE ARMY. 1969. Food Inspection Specialist. *TM 8-451*. Reproduced with permission of U.S. Department of the Army.

EGG QUALITY, BROKEN

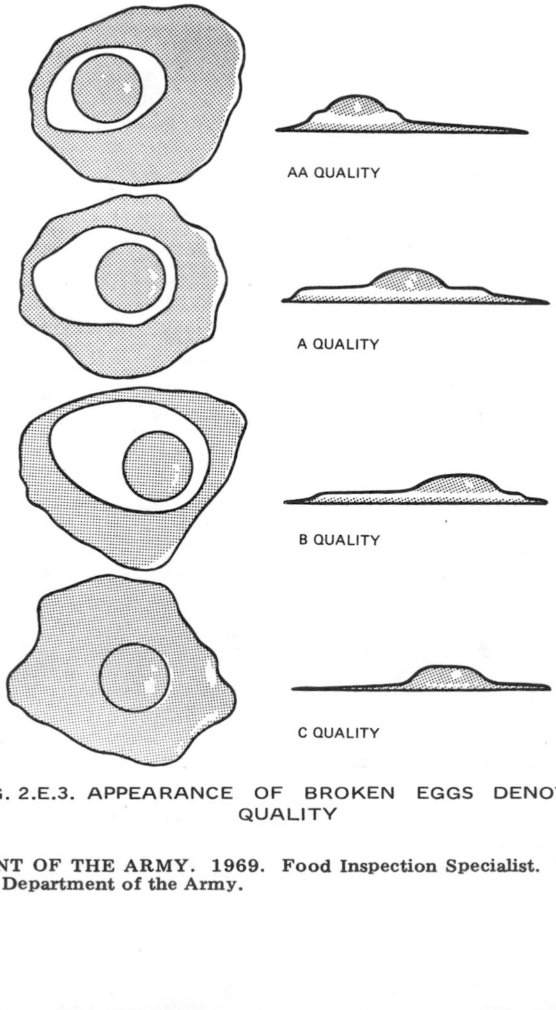

FIG. 2.E.3. APPEARANCE OF BROKEN EGGS DENOTING QUALITY

SOURCE: U.S. DEPARTMENT OF THE ARMY. 1969. Food Inspection Specialist. *TM 8-451*. Reproduced with permission of U.S. Department of the Army.

EGG SPECIFICATIONS

TABLE 2.E.7

SPECIFICATIONS FOR VARIOUS EGG PRODUCTS

	Liquid or frozen			Solids						
				Whites		Whole		Yolk		
Specification	White	Yolk[a]	Whole	Spray Dried	Pan Dried	Plain	Free[b] Flowing	Plain	Free Flowing	Scram. Egg
Moisture—%	—	—	—	8.0	14.0	5.0	3.0	5.0	3.0	2.5
Total solids—%	11.0	43.0	24.7	—	—	—	—	—	—	—
Crude protein—%	10.0	14.0	12.0	80.0	74.0	45.0	45.0	30.0	30.0	34.3
Total lipids—%	nil	28.0	10.5	<.02	nil	40.0	40.0	56.0	56.0	36.5
pH	8.9±.3	6.2±.1	7.3±.3	7.0±.5	5.5±.5	8.3±.3	8.3±.3	6.4±.3	6.4±.3	
Carbohydrates[c] — %	—	—	—	glu. free	glu. free	SOP	SOP	SOP	SOP	17
Total microbial count—gm	<5,000	<5,000	<5,000	<10,000	<10,000	<10,000	<10,000	<10,000	<10,000	<10,000
Yeast—gm	10 max.	10 max.	10 max.	10 max.	10 max.	10 max.	10 max.	10 max.	10 max.	—
Mold—gm	10 max.	10 max.	10 max.	10 max.	10 max.	10 max.	10 max.	10 max.	10 max.	—
Coliform—gm	10 max.	10 max.	10 max.	10 max.	10 max.	10 max.	10 max.	10 max.	10 max.	—
Salmonellae—gm	Neg.[d]	Neg.	Neg.	Neg.	Neg.	Neg.	Neg.	Neg.	Neg.	Neg.
Granulation	—	—	—	100%[e] USBS-60	SOP	100% USBS-16	100% USBS-16	100% USBS-16	100% USBS-16	—
Others[f]	—	—	—	—	—	—	—	—	—	—

a Egg yolk contains 17% egg white; Natural egg yolk contains about 52% solids.
b Free flowing products contain less than 2% sodium silicoaluminate.
c. Most egg white solids are desugared. Whole egg and yolk products are desugared if specified on purchase (SOP).
d Negative by approved testing procedures.
e U. S. Bureau of Standard Screens No. 80.
f Additives and performance specifications may be specified on purchase.

SOURCE: A Scientist Speaks About Egg Products. (1974) American Egg Board.

EGG STRUCTURE

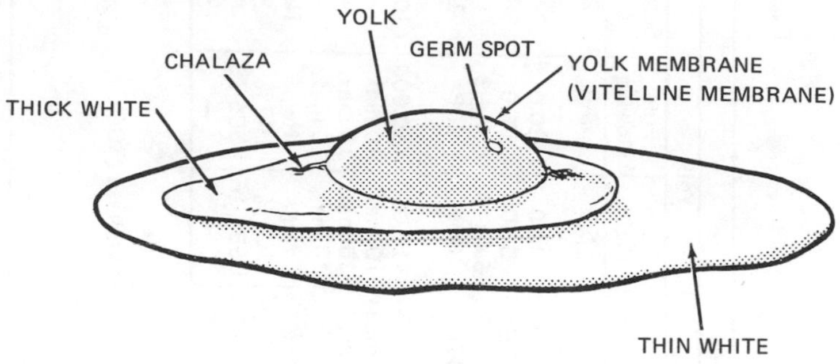

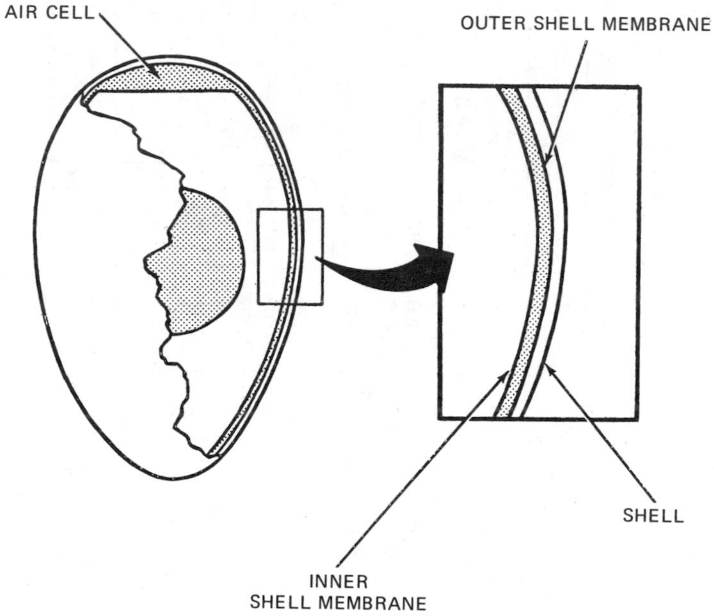

SOURCE: Food Inspection Specialist, Department of the Army, *TM 8-451*, 1969.

EGG VOLUME

The following shows the approximate number of whole eggs needed to make 1 cup:

Egg Size	No. of Whole Eggs
Small	7
Medium	6
Large	5
Extra large	4

The following shows the approximate number of whites or yolks needed to make 1 cup:

Egg Size	Whites	Yolks
Small	10	18
Medium	8	16
Large	7	14
Extra large	6	12

SOURCE: Eggs in Family Meals. (1970) USDA Home and Garden Bull. *103*.

FISHER SCIENTIFIC / PERIODIC CHART OF THE ELEMENTS

IA	IIA	IIIA	IVA	VA	VIA	VIIA	VIIIA			IB	IIB	IIIB	IVB	VB	VIB	VIIB	NOBLE GASES	
1 H 1.0079																1 H 1.0079	2 He 4.00260	2
3 Li 6.941†	4 Be 9.01218											5 B 10.81	6 C 12.011	7 N 14.0067	8 O 15.9994†	9 F 18.998403	10 Ne 20.179†	2 8
11 Na 22.98977	12 Mg 24.305											13 Al 26.98154	14 Si 28.0855†	15 P 30.97376	16 S 32.06	17 Cl 35.453	18 Ar 39.948†	2 8 8
19 K 39.0983†	20 Ca 40.08	21 Sc 44.9559	22 Ti 47.90†	23 V 50.9414†	24 Cr 51.996	25 Mn 54.9380	26 Fe 55.847†	27 Co 58.9332	28 Ni 58.70	29 Cu 63.546†	30 Zn 65.38	31 Ga 69.72	32 Ge 72.59†	33 As 74.9216	34 Se 78.96†	35 Br 79.904	36 Kr 83.80	2 8 18 8
37 Rb 85.4678†	38 Sr 87.62	39 Y 88.9059	40 Zr 91.22	41 Nb 92.9064	42 Mo 95.94	43 Tc (97)	44 Ru 101.07†	45 Rh 102.9055	46 Pd 106.4	47 Ag 107.868	48 Cd 112.41	49 In 114.82	50 Sn 118.69†	51 Sb 121.75†	52 Te 127.60†	53 I 126.9045	54 Xe 131.30	2 8 18 18 8
55 Cs 132.9054	56 Ba 137.33	57 *La 138.9055†	72 Hf 178.49†	73 Ta 180.9479†	74 W 183.85†	75 Re 186.207	76 Os 190.2	77 Ir 192.22†	78 Pt 195.09†	79 Au 196.9665	80 Hg 200.59†	81 Tl 204.37†	82 Pb 207.2	83 Bi 208.9804	84 Po (209)	85 At (210)	86 Rn (222)	2 8 18 32 18 8
87 Fr (223)	88 Ra 226.0254	89 ‡Ac (227)	104 § (260)	105 § (260)														

*Lanthanides

58 Ce 140.12	59 Pr 140.9077	60 Nd 144.24†	61 Pm (145)(147)	62 Sm 150.4	63 Eu 151.96	64 Gd 157.25†	65 Tb 158.9254	66 Dy 162.50†	67 Ho 164.9304	68 Er 167.26†	69 Tm 168.9342	70 Yb 173.04†	71 Lu 174.97	2 8 18 32 9 2

‡Actinides

90 Th 232.0381	91 Pa 231.0359	92 U 238.029	93 Np 237.0482	94 Pu (244)	95 Am (243)	96 Cm (247)	97 Bk (247)	98 Cf (251)	99 Es (254)	100 Fm (257)	101 Md (258)	102 No (259)	103 Lr (260)	2 8 18 32 32 9 2

FISHER SCIENTIFIC COMPANY
CAT. NO 5-702-10

§The International Union for Pure and Applied Chemistry has not adopted official names or symbols for these elements.

†These weights are considered reliable to ±3 in the last place. Other weights are reliable to ±1 in the last place.

Atomic weights corrected to conform to the 1976 values of the Commission on Atomic Weights.

Data in this chart have been checked by the National Bureau of Standards' Office of Standard Reference Data.

Printed in U.S.A.

ENZYMES, FOOD INDUSTRY

TABLE 2.E.8

CLASSIFICATION OF ENZYMES SIGNIFICANT IN FOOD AND IN THE FOOD INDUSTRY

Trivial Name	Systematic Name	Enzyme Commission No.	Reaction (As Significant in Food Material)
Oxidoreductases			
Glucose oxidase	β-D-Glucose: O_2 oxidoreductase	1.1.3.4	β-D-Glucose + O_2 ⟶ D-glucono-δ-lactone + H_2O_2
Phenolase (polyphenol oxidase)	o-Diphenol: O_2 oxidoreductase	1.10.3.1	2 o-Diphenol + O_2 ⟶ 2 o-quinone + 2 H_2O
Ascorbic acid oxidase	L-Ascorbate: O_2 oxidoreductase	1.10.3.3	2 L-ascorbate + O_2 ⟶ 2 dehydroascorbate + 2 H_2O
Catalase	H_2O_2 : H_2O_2 oxidoreductase	1.11.1.6	H_2O_2 + H_2O_2 ⟶ O_2 + 2 H_2O
Peroxidase	Donor: H_2O_2 oxidoreductase	1.11.1.7	Donor + H_2O_2 ⟶ oxidized donor + 2 H_2O
Lipoxidase (lipoxygenase)	—	1.99.2.1	Unsaturated fat + O_2 ⟶ a peroxide of the unsaturated fat
Hydrolases			
Lipase	Glycerol ester hydrolase	3.1.1.3	Triglyceride + H_2O ⟶ glycerol + fatty acids
Pectin methylesterase	Pectin pectyl-hydrolase	3.1.1.11	Pectin + n H_2O ⟶ pectic acid + n MeOH
Chlorophyllase	Chlorophyll chlorophyllido-hydrolase	3.1.1.14	Chlorophyll + H_2O ⟶ phytol + chlorophyllide
Phosphatase (acid or alkaline)	Orthophosphoric monoester phosphohydrolase	3.1.3.(1,2)	An orthophosphoric monoester + H_2O ⟶ an alcohol + H_3PO_4
α-Amylase	α-1,4-Glucan 4-glucanohydrolase	3.2.1.1	Hydrolysis of α-1,4-glucan links: Internal random hydrolysis
β-Amylase	α-1,4-Glucan maltohydrolase	3.2.1.2	Hydrolysis of α-1,4-glucan links: Successive maltose units removed
Glucoamylase	α-1,4-Glucan glucohydrolase	3.2.1.3	Hydrolysis of α-1,4-glucan links: Successive glucose units removed
Cellulase	β-1,4-Glucan 4-glucanohydrolase	3.2.1.4	Hydrolyses β-1,4-glucan links in cellulose
Amylopectin-1,6-glucosidase (R-enzyme)	Amylopectin 6-glucanohydrolase	3.2.1.9	Hydrolyses α-1,6-glucan links in amylopectin
Polygalacturonase	Polygalacturonide glucanohydrolase	3.2.1.15	Pectic acid + (x − 1) H_2O ⟶ x α-D-galacturonic acid
Maltase (α-glucosidase)	α-D-Glucoside glucohydrolase	3.2.1.20	Maltose + H_2O ⟶ 2 α-D-glucose
Lactase	β-D-Galactoside galactohydrolase	3.2.1.23	Lactose + H_2O ⟶ α-D-glucose + β-D-galactose
Invertase (sucrase)	β-D-Fructofuranoside fructohydrolase	3.2.1.26	Sucrose + H_2O ⟶ α-D-glucose + β-D-fructose
Pepsin	—	3.4.4.1	Hydrolysis of peptide linkages
Rennin	—	3.4.4.3	Hydrolysis of peptide linkages
Trypsin	—	3.4.4.4	Hydrolysis of peptide linkages
Chymotrypsin	—	3.4.4.5	Hydrolysis of peptide linkages
Elastase	—	3.4.4.7	Hydrolysis of peptide linkages
Papain	—	3.4.4.10	Hydrolysis of peptide linkages
Chymopapain	—	3.4.4.11	Hydrolysis of peptide linkages
Ficin	—	3.4.4.12	Hydrolysis of peptide linkages
Bromelain	—	3.4.4.c	Hydrolysis of peptide linkages
Bacterial protease	—	3.4.4.16	Hydrolysis of peptide linkages
Fungal protease	—	3.4.4.17	Hydrolysis of peptide linkages
Collagenase	—	3.4.4.19	Hydrolysis of peptide linkages

SOURCE: ESKIN, N. A. M., HENDERSON, H. M., and TOWNSEND, R. J. 1971. Biochemistry of Foods. Academic Press, New York.

EQUIVALENT WEIGHTS

TABLE 2.E.9

EQUIVALENT COMBINING WEIGHTS AND THEIR RECIPROCALS BASED ON INTERNATIONAL ATOMIC WEIGHTS, 1973

Neg. Radicals	Equiv. Combining Wts	Reciprocals of Equiv. Combining Wts	Pos. Radicals	Equiv. Combining Wts	Reciprocals of Equiv. Combining Wts
NO_3	62.0049	0.01613	NH_4	18.0383	0.05544
BO_2	42.81	0.02336	Li	6.941	0.14407
AsO_4	46.3064	0.02160	K	39.098	0.02558
I	126.9045	0.00788	Na	22.98977	0.04350
Br	79.904	0.01252	Mg	12.153	0.08228
PO_4	31.6571	0.03159	Ca	20.04	0.04990
HS	33.07	0.03024	Sr	43.81	0.02283
S	16.03	0.06238	Ba	68.67	0.01456
SiO_3	38.042	0.02629	Mn	27.4690	0.03640
O	7.9997	0.12500	Fe^{++}	27.924	0.03581
Cl	35.453	0.02821	Fe^{+++}	18.616	0.05372
SO_4	48.03	0.02082	Al	8.9938	0.11119
CO_3	30.005	0.03333	Cu	31.773	0.03147
HCO_3	61.017	0.01639			

Salts	Equiv. Combining Wts	Reciprocals of Equiv. Combining Wts	Salts	Equiv. Combining Wts	Reciprocals of Equiv. Combining Wts
NH_4Cl	53.491	0.01869	$MgCl_2$	47.606	0.02101
LiCl	42.394	0.02359	$MgSO_4$	60.18	0.01662
Li_2SO_4	54.97	0.01819	$MgCO_3$	42.157	0.02372
Li_2CO_3	36.946	0.02707	$Mg(HCO_3)_2$	73.170	0.01367
$LiHCO_3$	67.958	0.01471	$Mg(NO_3)_2$	74.157	0.01348
KCl	74.551	0.01341	$CaCl_2$	55.49	0.01802
K_2SO_4	87.13	0.01148	$CaSO_4$	68.07	0.01469
K_2CO_3	69.103	0.01447	$CaCO_3$	50.04	0.01998
$KHCO_3$	100.115	0.00999	$Ca(HCO_3)_2$	81.06	0.01234
KI	166.003	0.00602	$CaSiO_3$	58.08	0.01722
KBr	119.002	0.00840	$Ca_3(PO_4)_2$	51.70	0.01934
NaCl	58.443	0.01711	$SrSO_4$	91.84	0.01089
NaBr	102.894	0.00972	$SrCO_3$	73.81	0.01355
NaI	149.8942	0.00667	$Sr(HCO_3)_2$	104.83	0.00954
Na_2SO_4	71.02	0.01408	$BaSO_4$	116.70	0.00857
Na_2CO_3	52.994	0.01887	$Ba(HCO_3)_2$	129.69	0.00771
$NaHCO_3$	84.007	0.01190	$MnSO_4$	75.50	0.01325
$NaNO_2$	68.9952	0.01449	$MnCO_3$	57.474	0.01740
$NaNO_3$	84.9946	0.01177	$Mn(HCO_3)_2$	88.486	0.01130
$NaBO_2$	65.80	0.01520	$FeSO_4$	75.95	0.01317
Na_3AsO_4	69.2961	0.01443	$Fe_2(SO_4)_3$	66.64	0.01501
NaF	41.9881	0.02382	$FeCO_3$	57.928	0.01726
NaHS	56.06	0.01784	$Fe(HCO_3)_2$	88.941	0.01124
Na_3PO_4	54.6468	0.01830	Fe_2O_3	26.615	0.03757
Na_2S	39.02	0.02563	$Al_2(SO_4)_3$	57.02	0.01754
Na_2SiO_3	61.032	0.01638	Al_2O_3	16.9935	0.05885

SOURCE: AOAC. 1975. Official Methods of Analysis, 12th Edition. Editorial Board (Editors). Association of Official Analytical Chemists.

ESSENTIAL OILS

TABLE 2.E.10

DETAILS OF SOME OF THE ESSENTIAL OILS TO SHOW HOW DIVERSE ODORS AND FLAVORS ARE DERIVED FROM THE VEGETABLE WORLD

Oil of—	Distilled or extracted from—	Chief odorous components	Remarks
Allspice (Pimento)	Fruit of *Pimenta officinalis*, W. Indies	Eugenol, cineol	Odour recalls nutmeg, pepper and cinnamon. Used in bay rum
Angelica	Root or seed of *Angelica Archangelica*, Saxony	Exaltolide and Δ^7 hexadeceno-lactone	Musky odour. Used for liqueurs
Angostura bark	Bark of *Galipea cusparia*, Venezuela	Cadinene	Used for liqueurs
Asafœtida	Gum resin of *Ferula narthex*, Afghanistan	Terpenes, foul sulphur compounds, diallyl sulphide	Foul-smelling
Balsam of Peru	Oleo-resinous exudation of *Myroxylon Balsamum β-Pereiræ*, San Salvador	Benzyl benzoate, benzyl cinnamate	The resin itself is more commonly used than the oil from it
Balsam of Tolu	Exudation of *Myroxylon Balsamum gennimum*, New Granada, Venezuela	Benzyl benzoate, benzyl cinnamate, farnesol	Hyacinth odour
Bay	Leaves of *Pimenta acris*, W. Indies	Eugenol and its methyl ether, pinene, myrcene	Used in preparation of bay rum
Bergamot	Peel of Bergamot, *Citrus aurantium Bergamot*, Calabria	Linalyl acetate, 40 per cent, linalool, limonene, bisabolene, pinene	Perfumes
Bitter almonds	Kernels of bitter almond, *Prunus amygdalis*, all parts of the world	Benzaldehyde, hydrocyanic acid	
Camphor	Twigs of *Cinnamomum Camphora*, Formosa	Camphor, terpenes	Household and medical uses. Also a source of synthetic safrol for art. oil of sassafras
Cananga			Inferior grade of ylang-ylang (*q.v.*)
Caraway	Seeds of *Carum carui* Holland, etc.	*l*-carvone, carveol, *d*-limonene	Medicine. Perfumes. Used in soaps of Brown Windsor type
Carrot seed	Seed of carrot *Daucus carota*	Pinene	
Cassia	Leaves and twigs of *Cinnamomum cassia*, China	Cinnamic aldehyde, 80 to 90 per cent	Spice and perfumery. Used in Brown Windsor type soap
Cedar wood	Pencil shavings of cedar wood, *Juniperus virginiana*, Florida	Cedrene, cedrol, cedrenol	Oil used for fine soap and perfumes. Powdered wood used for incense
Celery seed	Common celery seed, *Apium graveolens*	Selinene, sedanolide (tetrahydrobutyl phthalide)	

TABLE 2.E.10 (*Continued*)

Oil of—	Distilled or extracted from—	Chief odorous components	Remarks
Chamomile	Flowers of *Anthemis nobilis*, Germany	Esters of angelic and tiglic acids	Medicine
Cinnamon	Bark and leaves of *Cinnamomum Zeylanicum*, Ceylon, E. Indies	Bark oil—cinnamic aldehyde; leaf oil—eugenol	Similar to oil of cassia but more delicate in odour. Used for dentifrices and also in Oriental type perfumes
Citronella	Citronella grass, several varieties, Ceylon, Java	Geraniol, citronellol, camphene	Cheap perfumery
Clary sage	Leaves and twigs of *Salvia sclarea*, Dalmatia	Pinene, cineol, linalool	Odour recalls ambergris. Used as a fixative
Cloves	Dried flower-buds of *Eugenia caryophyllata*, E. Indies, Zanzibar	Eugenol, 80 per cent	Source of vanillin (via isoeugenol). Also used for dentifrices and soaps
Coriander	Fruit of *Coriandrum sativum*, many parts of the world	Linalool, pinene	
Cubebs	Dried fruits of *Piper cubeba*, Singapore	*dl*-Limonene, pinene, cadinene	Used in medicine
Dill	Fruit of *Anethum graveolens*, Europe, India	Carvone, limonene	Used as a carminative
Elemi	Exudation of *Canarium luzonicum*, Philippines	Phellandrene, *d*-limonene	
Eucalyptus	Leaves of *Eucalyptus globulus*, Australia, etc.	Cineol, pinene	Used medicinally
Fennel	Fruit of *Fœniculum vulgare*, Mediterranean countries	Anethol; 60 per cent, fenchone	Anethole is a source of Aubepine or anisaldehyde
Frankincense	Exudation of *Boswellia Carterii* and *B. serrata*, India	Pinene, Camphene, *dl*-limonene	Balsamic odour
Gardenia	Flowers of *Gardenia grandiflora*	Benzyl acetate, linalool, methyl anthranilate	
Garlic	Entire plant, *Allium sativum*	Diallyl disulphide	Flavours
Geranium	Leaves of varieties of *Pelargonium*, France, Algeria, etc.	Geraniol, Citronellol	Used for floral bouquets
Ginger	Rhizome of *Zingiber officinale*, Asia, W. Indies	Zingiberene, Zingerone, Camphene, Cineol, Borneol, citral	Flavour
Jasmine	Flowers of *Jasminum grandiflorum*, Asia chiefly	Jasmone, indole, Methyl anthranilate	Perfume
Lavender	Flowers of *Lavandula vera*, England, France	Cineol, limonene, linalyl acetate, linalool, geraniol and esters	Perfumery

(Continued)

TABLE 2.E.10 (*Continued*)

Oil of—	Distilled or extracted from—	Chief odorous components	Remarks
Lemon	Peel of lemon, *Citrus limonum*, Mediterranean countries	*d*-limonene, 90 per cent; citral	
Lemon-grass	Lemon-grass, Varieties of *Cymbopogon*, E. Indies	Citral, 80 per cent	Source of citral from which ionone is made for violet perfumes
Limes	Fruit of *Citrus medica acida*, W. Indies	Citral, limonene	
Linaloe	Wood and fruit of *Bursera Delpechiana*, Mexico	Linalool	Soft sweet odour. Used for perfumes and soaps
Mignonette	Flowers of mignonette, *Reseda odorata*	Aldehydes, eugenol caprylic acid	Yield only 0·002 per cent. Powerful odour. Floral extract generally used instead of oil
Musk-seed	Seeds of *Hibiscus abelmoschus*, Java	Farnesol, Δ^7 hexadecenolactone	Known also as oil of ambrette seeds. Musky odour.
Mustard	Seeds of *Brassica nigra*	Allyl thiocarbimide	
Myrrh	Oleo-resin secreted in the bark of various *Commiphora*, Arabia, Somaliland	Cuminic aldehyde, bisabolene, pinene, *dl*-limonene, eugenol, *m*-cresol	
Myrtle	Leaves of *Myrtus communis*, Mediterranean countries	Pinene, cineol, camphene	
Nepeta	Catmint, *Nepeta cataria*, Sicily	Menthol and its caprylic and valeric esters	
Neroli	Orange-flowers, *Citrus aurantium*, France	Nerol, geraniol, linalool, Phenyl ethyl alcohol methyl anthranilate	Perfumes. Used for eau-de-Cologne
Opoponax	Exudation of varieties of *Commiphora*, Arabia, Somaliland	Bisabolene	Similar to oil of myrrh
Orange	Peel of orange, *Citrus aurantium*, Mediterranean countries	*d*-limonene, 90 per cent; decylic aldehyde	
Orris-root	Iris rhizomes, varieties of *Iris*, Italy	Irone, aldehydes	Odour develops after roots are dried. Powdered roots used in violet powder. Pure oil used in highest quality violet perfumes; as a fixative for ionone in cheaper qualities
Parsley	All parts of common parsley, *Petroselinum sativum*, France, Germany	Pinene, apiol	

TABLE 2.E.10 (*Continued*)

Oil of—	Distilled or extracted from—	Chief odorous components	Remarks
Parsnip	Chiefly parsnip seed, *Pastinaca sativa*	Octyl butyrate, octyl propionate	
Patchouli	Dried leaves of *Pogostemon patchouli*, Singapore, Java	Terpenes, eugenol	Used for face powder and perfumes. Thick liquid with powerful and persistent odour. Good fixative
Pennyroyal	Leaves of *Mentha pulegium*, Europe	Pulegone, 85 per cent	
Pepper	Unripe berries of *Piper nigrum*	Piperine, *dl* - limonene	
Peppermint	Flowering tops of mint herb, *Mentha piperita*, England, America, Japan	Menthol, 50 per cent menthyl acetate, menthone, cadinene, *l*-limonene	Flavouring sweetmeats and dentifrices
Perilla	Leaves of *Perilla nankinensis*, Japan	Perillic aldehyde	Peculiar hay-like odour. Used in perfumes
Petitgrain	Leaves and young shoots of orange, *Citrus aurantium*, Paraguay	Pinene, geraniol, linalool, Methyl anthranilate	Used for making eau-de-Cologne
Roses	Flowers of *Rosa damascena*, Bulgaria, France	Citronellol, 30 per cent, geraniol, 40 per cent, phenylethyl alcohol, nerol	Perfumes
Rose-geranium	Mixture of roses and pelargonium leaves, France		
Rosemary	Flowering tops of *Rosemarina officinalis*, S. Europe	Camphor, borneol, pinene, cineol	Used in cheap perfumes, soaps and hair-washes
Rue	Herb, *Ruta graveolens*, France	Methyl nonyl ketone, methyl heptyl ketone	
Sandalwood	Wood or roots of *Santalum album*, India	Santalenes, santalone, cadinene, diacetyl	Used as a fixative for Oriental type perfumes. Also used in soaps and face powders
Sassafras	Bark and roots of *Sassafras officinale*, N. America	Safrol, 80 per cent, Pinene	Used in soap perfumery
Shaddock	Grape - fruit, *Citrus decumana*, W. Indies	Limonene	
Spearmint	Herb, *Mentha viridis*, America chiefly	*l*-carvone, phellandrene, limonene and esters	Used for flavouring sweetmeats
Spikenard	Root of *Nardostachys jatamansi*, India	Sesquiterpenes	Valued in the East as a perfume. Disliked by Western people as a rule. Largely replaced by oil of valerian.

(Continued)

TABLE 2.E.10 (*Continued*)

Oil of—	Distilled or extracted from—	Chief odorous components	Remarks
Star Aniseed (Badiane)	Fruit of *Illicium verum*, China	Pinene, anethol, phellandrene	Flavouring
Storax	Oleo-resin from bark of *Liquidamber orientale*, Asia Minor	Phenyl ethylene (oil of styrol)	
Sweet Basil	Herb, *Oceum basilicum*, Europe, Algeria	Ocimene, cineol, pinene	Used in mignonette perfumes, etc.
Tansy	Herb, *Tanacetum vulgare*, England, France, America	Thujone, borneol	
Tea	Leaves of tea plant, *Thea chinensis*, China		Yield only 0·006 per cent
Thyme	Herb, *Thymus vulgaris*, France, Spain	Borneol, thymol, carvacrol, bornyl acetate	Used medicinally. Also in soap
Tropæolum	Leaves of nasturtium, *Tropæolum majus*	Benzyl thiocarbimide, 80 per cent (benzyl mustard oil)	
Tuberose	Flowers of *Polyanthus tuberosa*, France	Methyl anthranilate, methyl benzoate	Made by enfleurage
Turpentine	Pine-wood exudations, Europe, India	Pinene, limonene	Ordinary turpentine is a solution of resins, e.g. colophony in the oil of turpentine. Source of terpineol
Valerian	Roots of *Valeriana officinalis*, Europe, Japan	Borneol, bornyl acetate, camphene isovalerianic esters	Used in medicine, also as a soap perfume
Verbena	Herb, *Lippia citriodora*, France, etc.	Citral	Perfumes. Lemongrass oil also consists chiefly of citral and is often called verbena
Vetivert	Roots of Khas-khas grass, *Vetiveria zizanioides*, India	Sesquiterpenes, esters	Heavy liquid used as a fixative. Perfume suggests myrrh
Wallflower	Wallflowers, *Cheiranthus cheiri*	Nerol, geraniol, indol, methyl anthranilate	Yield only 0·06 per cent
Wintergreen	Originally from leaves of *Gaultheria procumbens*, later bark of sweet birch. *Betula lenta*	99 per cent methyl salicylate	Used for flavouring dentifrices, etc.
Ylang-ylang	Flowers of *Cananga odorata*, Philippines	Benzyl benzoate alcohols, esters	Over 30 components already isolated. Used for fine perfumes

SOURCE: MONCRIEFF, R. W. 1967. The Chemical Senses. Leonard Hill Books, London, England.

F

FAT AND BODY WEIGHT

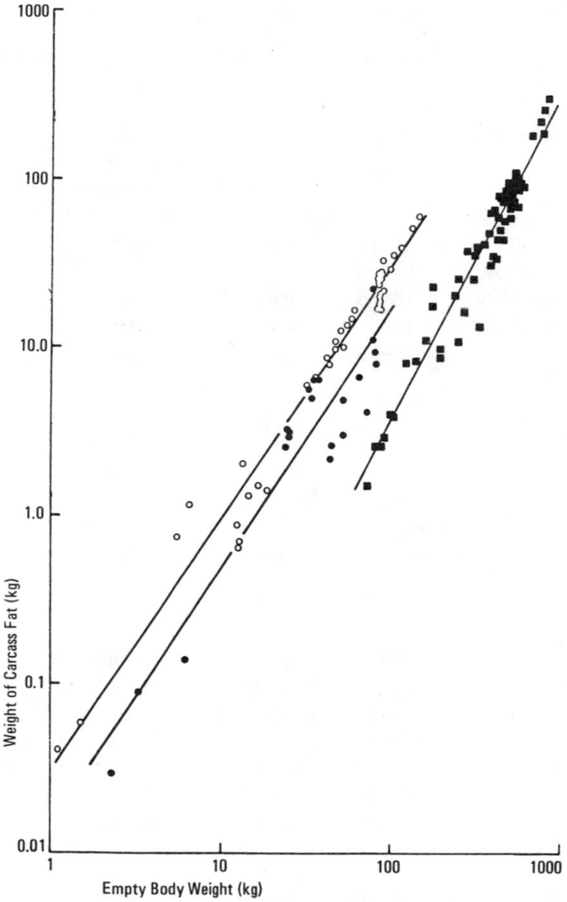

FIG. 2.F.1. WEIGHT OF DISSECTED FAT IN A CARCASS (EXCLUDING KIDNEY FAT) COMPARED WITH EMPTY BODY WEIGHT FOR SHEEP (●), CATTLE (■), AND PIGS (0).

SOURCE: TRIBE, D. E. (EDITOR). Carcass Composition and Appraisal of Meat Animals. CSIRO, Australia.

FATS AND OILS, CHARACTERISTICS

TABLE 2.F.1

MAIN EDIBLE FATS USED AS RAW MATERIALS IN THE MANUFACTURE OF MARGARINE TOGETHER WITH THEIR CHARACTERISTIC FIGURES

Name	Iodine number	Saturated fatty acids %	Unsaturated fatty acids %	Polyunsaturated fatty acids %
Animal fats				
Beef tallow (*premier jus*)	42–8	48	52 especially oleic acid	
Oleomargarine (oleo oil)	44–5	c45	c55	
Pressed tallow (oleostearine)	18–28	c70	c30	
Mutton tallow	40–8	c50	c50	
Lard	52–68	40	60	
Animal oils				
Whale oil	105–20	25	75	
Fish oils				
Herring	135–40			
Sardine	170–90			
Menhaden	160–75	20	80	
Pilchard	180–90			
Vegetable oils				
Olive	85	10–12	83–90	7
Groundnut	85–40	17–20	80–3	20–40
Cottonseed	104–12	25 (palm)	75	45 (linol)
Soya	130–5	12–15	86–8	60
Sunflower	127–37	10–14	86–90	55 (linol)
Sesame	109–14	13–17	83–7	38–48
Maize	115–20	12–18	82–8	40
Vegetable fats				
Coconut	8–10	90–2	8–10	
Palm kernel	15–18	83	17	
Babassu	15	82	18	
Palm	53–60	48	52	
Shea	±60	46	54	

SOURCE: VAN STUYVENBERG, J. H. 1969. Margarine. Liverpool University Press, Liverpool, England.

FATS AND OILS, COMPOSITION I

TABLE 2.F.2

COMPOSITION OF FATS AND OILS

Food, Approximate Measure, and Weight (in Grams)		Water (%)	Food Energy (Cal)	Protein (g)	Fat (Total Lipid) (g)	Fatty Acids: Saturated (Total) (g)	Fatty Acids: Unsaturated: Oleic (g)	Fatty Acids: Unsaturated: Linoleic (g)	Carbohydrate (g)	Calcium (mg)	Iron (mg)	Vitamin A Value (IU)	Thiamin (mg)	Riboflavin (mg)	Niacin (mg)	Ascorbic Acid (mg)
Fats, Oils																
Butter, 4 sticks per lb:																
Sticks, 2	1 cup (224 g)	16	1,605	1	181	100	60	5	1	45	Tr	[1] 7,400	—	—	—	0
Stick, 1/8	1 tbsp (14 g)	16	100	Tr	11	6	4	Tr	Tr	3	Tr	[1] 460	—	—	—	0
Pat or square (64 per lb)	1 pat (7 g)	16	50	Tr	6	3	2	0	Tr	1	Tr	[1] 230	—	—	—	0
Fat, cooking:																
Lard	1 cup (220 g)	0	1,985	0	220	84	101	22	0	0	0	0	0	0	0	0
	1 tbsp (14 g)	0	135	0	14	5	6	1	0	0	0	0	0	0	0	0
Vegetable fats	1 cup (200 g)	0	1,770	0	200	46	130	14	0	0	0	0	0	0	0	0
	1 tbsp (12.5 g)	0	110	0	12	3	8	1	0	0	0	0	0	0	0	0
Margarine, 4 sticks per lb:																
Sticks, 2	1 cup (224 g)	16	1,615	1	181	47	103	16	1	45	Tr	[1] 7,400	—	—	—	0
Stick, 1/8	1 tbsp (14 g)	16	100	Tr	11	3	6	1	Tr	3	Tr	[2] 460	—	—	—	0
Pat or square (64 per lb)	1 pat (7 g)	16	50	Tr	6	1	3	1	Tr	1	Tr	[2] 230	—	—	—	0
Oils, salad or cooking:																
Corn	1 tbsp (14 g)	0	125	0	14	1	4	7	0	0	0	—	0	0	0	0
Cottonseed	1 tbsp (14 g)	0	125	0	14	3	3	7	0	0	0	—	0	0	0	0
Olive	1 tbsp (14 g)	0	125	0	14	2	11	1	0	0	0	—	0	0	0	0
Soybean	1 tbsp (14 g)	0	125	0	14	2	3	7	0	0	0	—	0	0	0	0
Salad dressings:																
Blue cheese	1 tbsp (16 g)	28	90	1	10	2	2	5	1	11	Tr	30	Tr	0.02	Tr	Tr
Commercial, plain; mayonnaise type	1 tbsp (15 g)	48	60	Tr	6	1	1	3	2	2	Tr	30	Tr	Tr	Tr	0
French	1 tbsp (15 g)	42	60	Tr	6	1	1	3	2	3	0.1	0	0	0	0	0
Home cooked, boiled	1 tbsp (17 g)	68	30	1	2	1	1	Tr	3	15	0.1	80	0.01	0.03	Tr	Tr
Mayonnaise	1 tbsp (15 g)	14	110	Tr	12	2	3	6	Tr	2	0.1	40	Tr	Tr	Tr	0
Thousand Island	1 tbsp (15 g)	38	75	Tr	8	1	2	4	1	2	0.1	60	Tr	Tr	Tr	2

[1] Year-round average.
[2] Based on the avg vitamin A content of fortified margarine. Federal specifications for fortified margarine require a minimum of 15,000 IU of vitamin A per lb.

SOURCE: INSTITUTE OF HOME ECONOMICS. Nutritive Value of Foods. USDA Home and Garden Bull. 72.

FATS AND OILS, COMPOSITION II

TABLE 2.F.2-a

COMPOSITION OF PRINCIPAL CLASSES OF FOOD, ANIMAL, AND VEGETABLE FATS AND OILS

Composition and Analytical Characteristics of Principal Classes of Food Fats and Oils of the U.S.A.

	Household Shortenings		Commercial Bulk shortenings		Margarine oils	Cottonseed salad oils	Liquid shortenings
	Vegetable fat	Meat fat and vegetable fat	Vegetable fat	Meat fat and vegetable fat			
Composition							
Oleic acid (%)[a]	53-75	37-57	45-76	40-65	42-79	17-36	18-45
Linoleic acid (%)[b]	3-14	6-13	3-13	3-13	2-18	42-55	30-47
Linolenic acid (%)[b]	0-0.5	0-0.6	0-0.7	0-0.8	0-0.4	0-0.7	0-1.0
Arachidonic acid (%)[b]	0	0-0.5	0	0-0.5	0	0	0
Total saturated acids (%)	16-31	30-50	15-40	28-40	12-24	18-30	17-36
Analytical characteristics							
Iodine value	70-81	54-74	65-90	55-67	68-83	107-117	90-104
Melting point (FAC) (°F)	108-125	114-129	103-124	110-125	96-106	—	86-126
Solids index at 70°F	15-30	16-28	16-26	19-30	11-21	—	2-7
Solids index at 90°F	10-20	10-22	7-21	7-21	1-7	—	0.5-5

[a] Total monounsaturated acids. [b] By spectrophotometric analysis.

Composition and Analytical Characteristics of the Principal Animal and Vegetable Fats and Oils Used in Foods in the U.S.A.

	Beef fat	Butter fat	Coco butter	Coconut oil	Corn oil	Cotton-seed oil	Lard	Olive oil	Peanut oil	Soybean oil
Composition										
Oleic acid (%)[a]	35-45	30-32	34-38	6-9	25-37	17-37	47-83	62-83	30-58	16-47
Linoleic acid (%)[b]	0.5-3	1.0-2.5	3-3.5	1-4	50-56	44-55	7-13	8-15	21-37	39-53
Linolenic acid (%)[b]	0.2-0.6	0.2-0.5	0.1-0.2	0-0.1	0.1-0.7	0-0.6	0.2-1.4	0.5-0.7	0-0.5	4-9
Arachidonic acid (%)[b]	0.05-0.2	0.2-0.4	—	—	—	—	0.2-0.4	—	—	—
Total saturated acids (%)	45-58	63-68	57-61	86-91	9-15	17-31	29-37	9-22	16-26	5-24
Analytical characteristics										
Iodine value	38-44	30-40	37-44	8-15	122-125	103-112	63-69	76-88	90-99	125-131
Melting point (FAC). (°F)	116-121	97-100	86-95	79-82	—	—	99-112	—	—	—
Solids index at 70°F	23-30	11-13	47-49	19-27	—	—	17-21	—	—	—
Solids index at 90°F	18-24	2.5-4	0	0	—	—	4-6	—	—	—

[a] Total monounsaturated acids. [b] By spectrophotometric analysis.

Composition and Analytical Characteristics of Some Other Vegetable Oils Not Normally Used in Foods in the U.S.A.

	Linseed oil	Palm oil	Palm kernel oil	Rape-seed oil	Saf-flower oil	Sesame oil
Composition						
Oleic acid (%)[a]	31-36	34-56	14[c]	59-62[d]	10-23	35-47
Linoleic acid (%)[b]	8-21	10-11	2-3[c]	15	69-78	40-44
Linolenic acid (%)[b]	42-50	0.1-0.4	—	9-10	0-2	0-0.3
Arachidonic acid (%)[b]	—	—	—	—	—	—
Total saturated acids (%)	0-6	34-50	84[c]	14-16	5-13	12-16

	Linseed oil	Palm oil	Palm kernel oil	Rape-seed oil	Saf-flower oil	Sesame oil
Analytical characteristics						
Iodine value	181-192	51-58	16-18	103-109	141-150	109-115
Melting point (FAC)(°F)	—	103-105	84-86	—	—	—
Solids index at 70°F	—	11-13	31-33	—	—	—
Solids index at 90°F	—	6-8	—	—	—	—

[a] Total monounsaturated acids.
[b] By spectrophotometric analysis.
[c] Only one analysis available.
[d] Mostly erucie.

SOURCE: ANON. 1969. The Wecobee Handbook. PVO International, Boonton, New Jersey.

FATTY ACIDS AND THEIR PROPERTIES

TABLE 2.F.6

PROPERTIES OF VARIOUS FATTY ACIDS

Acid	Formula	Molecular Weight	Neutralization Value	Iodine Value	Melting Pt. °C.	Boiling Pt. °C. @ 5 mm Hg	Boiling Pt. °C. @ 10 mm Hg	Number Double Bonds
Butyric	$C_4H_8O_2$	88.10	636.82	0	− 8.0	50.0	—	0
Caproic	$C_6H_{12}O_2$	116.16	483.03	0	− 3.5	86.5	99	0
Caprylic	$C_8H_{16}O_2$	144.21	389.07	0	16.5	113.5	124	0
Capric	$C_{10}H_{20}O_2$	172.26	325.71	0	31.3	137.0	152	0
Lauric	$C_{12}H_{24}O_2$	200.31	280.08	0	43.6	158.0	170	0
Lauroleic	$C_{12}H_{22}O_2$	198.29	282.94	128.01	—	—	—	1
Myristic	$C_{14}H_{28}O_2$	228.36	245.69	0	53.8	178.0	190	0
Myristoleic	$C_{14}H_{26}O_2$	226.34	247.87	112.14	− 4.5	—	—	1
Pentadecanoic	$C_{15}H_{30}O_2$	242.40	231.46	0	52.3	187.0	—	0
Palmitic	$C_{16}H_{32}O_2$	256.42	218.80	0	62.9	197.0	210	0
Palmitoleic	$C_{16}H_{30}O_2$	254.40	220.53	99.78	1.5	—	—	1
Margaric	$C_{17}H_{34}O_2$	270.45	207.45	0	61.3	206.0	—	0
Stearic	$C_{18}H_{36}O_2$	284.47	197.23	0	69.9	214.0	226	0
Oleic	$C_{18}H_{34}O_2$	282.44	198.64	89.87	13.4	209.0	—	1
Linoleic	$C_{18}H_{32}O_2$	280.43	200.07	181.03	− 5.0	—	—	2
Linolenic	$C_{18}H_{30}O_2$	278.40	201.51	273.51	−11.0	—	—	3
Hydnocarpic	$C_{16}H_{28}O_2$	252.22	222.6	100.65	—	—	—	

FATS AND OILS, FATTY ACID COMPOSITION

TABLE 2.F.3

FATTY ACID COMPOSITION OF COMMON FATS AND OILS AS DETERMINED BY GAS CHROMATOGRAPHY

Acid (Commonly referred to ..name of.. predominant specie)	G.C. Common Desig-nation	Babassu	Butter Fat (1)	Cocoa Butter	Coconut	Corn	Cotton-seed	Lard (1)	Ouri-Curi	Palm	Palm Kernel
Caprylic	C8:0	7	1.5	—	8	—	—	—	10	—	4
Capric	C10:0	5	3	—	7	—	0.1	—	9	—	4
Lauric	C12:0	45	4	—	48.2	—	0.1	0.1	46	—	50
Myristic	C14:0	15	12	0.5	18	0.2	0.9	1	9	1	16
Palmitic	C16:0	9	25	25	8.5	12	23.5	23	8	46	8
Stearic	C18:0	3	9	35	2.3	2.2	2.5	9	2	4	2.5
Oleic	C18:1	13	—	37.5	6	27	18	46	13	37	12
Linoleic	C18:2	2	—	2	2	57	54	14	3	10	3
Arachidic	C20:0	0.1	1	—	—	0.3	0.3	0.2	—	0.4	0.1
Linolenic	C18:3	—		—	—	1	0.3	1	—	0.3	0.1
Gadoleic	C20:1	—		—	—				—		
Behenic	C22:0	—	—	—	—	—	—	Trace	—	—	—
Lignoceric	C24:0	—	—	—	—	—	—	—	—	—	—
Others	C4:0		3	—	—	—	—	—	—	—	—
	C6:0		1								
	C12:1		0.4								
	C14:1		1.5								
	C16:1		4								
Iodine No. (Wijs) Typical		16	30	40	9	125	110	73	15	50	17
Iodine No. (Wijs) Range		15-19	25-35	35-43	8-12	120-128	105-116	65-80	12-18	45-55	16-20
Sap. Value Range		247-250	216-240	190-200	254-262	189-193	189-198	190-198	255-260	196-200	244-255
Wiley Melting Pt. °F.		79	82-95	79-99	76	—	—	88-110	—	104-110	80

Acid (Commonly referred to ..name of.. predominant specie)	G.C. Common Desig-nation	Peanut (1)	Rape-seed (1)	Rice-Bran	Safflower	Soybean	Sun-flower	Tallow Beef	Tallow Mutton
Caprylic	C8:0	—	—	—	—	—	—	—	—
Capric	C10:0	—	—	—	—	—	—	—	—
Lauric	C12:0	0.2	—	—	—	—	—	—	—
Myristic	C14:0	0.1	—	0.5	—	—	—	2	1
Palmitic	C16:0	11	3	17	8	11	8	35	21
Stearic	C18:0	3	1.5	2.5	3	4	3	16	30
Oleic	C18:1	46	32	46	13	25	20	44	43
Linoleic	C18:2	31	19	32	75	50	67.8	2	5
Arachidic	C20:0	1.5	—	0.5	trace	0.4	0.5	—	—
Linolenic	C18:3	1.5	10	1	1	8	0.5	0.4	—
Gadoleic	C20:1		10						—
Behenic	C22:0	3.3	0.5	—	—	0.3	0.2		—
Lignoceric	C24:0	1.3	—	—	—	—	—	—	—
Others	C22:1	23.5	—	—	—	—	—	—	—
Iodine No. (Wijs) Typical		100	101	145	132	130	40	40	
Iodine No. (Wijs) Range		90-110	95-108	135-150	127-140	125-140	35-45	35-45	
Sap. Value Range		170-180	183-194	188-192	190-194	188-194	196-200	193-195	
Wiley Melting Pt. °F.		—	—	—	—	—	—	—	

(1) Large variation normally encountered.

SOURCE: ANON. 1969. The Wecobee Handbook. PVO International, Boontoon, New Jersey.

FATS AND OILS, PHYSICAL AND CHEMICAL PROPERTIES

TABLE 2.F.4

PROPERTIES OF LAND AND MARINE ANIMALS AND PLANTS

Specific Gravity was calculated at the specified temperature and referred to water at the same temperature, unless otherwise indicated. **Refractive Index** was measured at 40°C, unless otherwise specified, using the D-line of sodium (589 nm). Data in brackets refer to the column heading in brackets.

	Fat or Oil	Source (Synonym)	Melting [Solidification] Point, °C	Specific Gravity [1] [Temp, °C]	Refractive Index [Temp, °C]	Iodine Value	Saponification Value
	Land Animals						
1	Butterfat	*Bos taurus*	32.2	0.911 [40][2]	1.4548	36.1	227
2	Depot fat	*Homo sapiens*	[15]	0.918 [15]	1.4602	67.6	196.2
3	Lard oil	*Sus scrofa*	[30.5]	0.919 [15]	1.4615	58.6	198.5
4	Neat's-foot oil	*Bos taurus*	....	0.910 [25]	1.464 [25]	69-76	190-199
5	Tallow, beef	*Bos taurus*	....	....	....	49.5	197
6	mutton	*Ovis aries*	[42.0]	0.945 [15]	1.4565	40	194
	Marine Animals						
7	Cod-liver oil	*Gadus morhua*	....	0.925 [25]	1.481 [25]	165	186
8	Herring oil	*Clupea harengus*	....	0.900 [60]	1.4610 [60]	140	192
9	Menhaden oil	*Brevoortia tyrannus*	....	0.903 [60]	1.4645 [60]	170	191
10	Sardine oil	*Sardinops caerulea*	....	0.905 [60]	1.4660 [60]	185	193
11	Sperm oil, body	*Physeter catodon (P. macrocephalus)*	....	....	....	76-88	122-130
12	head	*Physeter catodon (P. macrocephalus)*	....	....	....	70	140-144
13	Whale oil	*Balaena mysticetus*	....	0.892 [60]	1.460 [60]	120	195
	Plants						
14	Babassu oil	*Attalea funifera*	22-26	0.893 [60][3]	1.443 [60]	15.5	247
15	Castor oil	*Ricinus communis*	[−18.0]	0.961 [15]	1.4770	85.5	180.3
16	Cocoa butter	*Theobroma cacao*	34.1	0.964 [15]	1.4568	36.5	195
17	Coconut oil	*Cocos nucifera*	25.1	0.924 [15]	1.4493	10.4	257
18	Corn oil	*Zea mays*	[−20.0]	0.922 [15]	1.4734	122.6	190
19	Cottonseed oil	*Gossypium hirsutum*	[−1.0]	0.917 [25]	1.4735	105.7	194.3
20	Linseed oil	*Linum usitatissimum*	[−24.0]	0.938 [15]	1.4782 [25]	178.7	190.3
21	Mustard oil	*Brassica hirta*	....	0.914 [15]	1.475	102	174
22	Neem oil	*Melia azedarach*	−3	0.917 [15]	1.4615	71	194.5
23	Niger-seed oil	*Guizotia abyssinica*	....	0.925 [15]	1.471	128.5	190
24	Oiticica oil	*Licania rigida*	....	0.974 [25]	1.514 [25]	140-180	190.5
25	Olive oil	*Olea europaea sativa*	[−6.0]	0.918 [15]	1.4679	81.1	192
26	Palm oil	*Elaeis guineensis*	35.0	0.915 [15]	1.4578	54.2	199.1
27	Palm-kernel oil	*Elaeis guineensis*	24.1	0.923 [15]	1.4569	37.0	250
28	Peanut oil	*Arachis hypogaea*	[3.0]	0.914 [15]	1.4691	93.4	192.1
29	Perilla oil	*Perilla frutescens*	....	0.935 [15][3]	1.481 [25]	195	192
30	Poppy-seed oil	*Papaver somniferum*	[−15]	0.925 [15]	1.4685	135	197.5
31	Rapeseed oil	*Brassica campestris*	[−10]	0.915 [15]	1.4706	98.6	174.7
32	Safflower oil	*Carthamus tinctorius*	....	0.900 [60][3]	1.462 [60]	145	192
33	Sesame oil	*Sesamum indicum*	[−6.0]	0.919 [25]	1.4646	106.6	191.5
34	Soybean oil	*Glycine max (G. soja)*	[−16.0]	0.927 [15]	1.4729	130.0	190.6
35	Sunflower-seed oil	*Helianthus annuus*	[−17.0]	0.923 [15]	1.4694	125.5	188.7
36	Tung oil	*Aleurites fordii*	[−2.5]	0.934 [15]	1.5174 [25]	168.2	193.1
37	Wheat-germ oil	*Triticum aestivum*	....	0.929 [25]	1.4745	125	174.5

[1] Unless otherwise indicated. [2] Referred to water at 15°C. [3] Density, measured at the specified temperature.

SOURCE: ALTMAN, P. L., and DITTMER, D. S. (EDITORS). 1972. Biology Data Book, Vol. 1. Federation of American Societies for Experimental Biology, Bethesda, Maryland.

FATTY ACIDS

TABLE 2.F.5

COMMON FATTY ACIDS AND THEIR STRUCTURAL FORMULAS

Common Name	Systematic Name	Structural Formula
	Saturated Acids	
Butyric	*n*-Butanoic	$CH_3(CH_2)_2COOH$
Isovaleric	3-Methyl-*n*-Butanoic	$(CH_3)_2CH\,CH_2COOH$
Caproic	*n*-Hexanoic	$CH_3(CH_2)_4COOH$
Caprylic	*n*-Octanoic	$CH_3(CH_2)_6COOH$
Capric	*n*-Decanoic	$CH_3(CH_2)_8COOH$
Lauric	*n*-Dodecanoic	$CH_3(CH_2)_{10}COOH$
Myristic	*n*-Tetradecanoic	$CH_3(CH_2)_{12}COOH$
Palmitic	*n*-Hexadecanoic	$CH_3(CH_2)_{14}COOH$
Stearic	*n*-Octadecanoic	$CH_3(CH_2)_{16}COOH$
Arachidic	*n*-Eicosanoic	$CH_3(CH_2)_{18}COOH$
Behenic	*n*-Docosanoic	$CH_3(CH_2)_{20}COOH$
Lignoceric	*n*-Tetracosanoic	$CH_3(CH_2)_{22}COOH$
	Unsaturated Acids	
Palmitoleic	Hexadec-9-enoic	$CH_3(CH_2)_5CH{:}CH(CH_2)_7COOH$
Oleic	Octadec-9-enoic	$CH_3(CH_2)_7CH{:}CH(CH_2)_7COOH$
Linoleic	Octadeca-9,12-dienoic	$CH_3(CH_2)_4CH{:}CH\,CH_2CH{:}CH(CH_2)_7COOH$
Linolenic	Octadeca-9,12,15-trienoic	$CH_3CH_2CH{:}CHCH_2CH{:}CHCH_2CH{:}CH(CH_2)_7COOH$
Arachidonic	Eicosa-5,8,11,14-tetraenoic	$CH_3(CH_2)_4CH{:}CHCH_2CH{:}CHCH_2CH{:}CHCH_2CH{:}CH(CH_2)_3COOH$

SOURCE: PAUL, P. C., and PALMER, H. H. 1972. Food Theory and Applications. John Wiley & Sons, New York.

Gorlic	$C_{18}H_{30}O_2$	278.24	201.7	181.16	—	—	—	2
Chaulmoogric	$C_{18}H_{32}O_2$	280.25	200.4	90.58	—	—	—	1
Ricinoleic	$C_{18}H_{34}O_3$	298.44	187.98	85.05	5.0	—	—	1
Satvic	$C_{18}H_{36}O_6$	348.29	161.6	0	—	—	—	0
Linusic	$C_{18}H_{36}O_8$	380.29	147.6	0	—	—	—	0
Dihydroxystearic	$C_{18}H_{36}O_4$	316.47	177.20	0	141.0	—	—	0
Licanic	$C_{18}H_{28}O_3$	292.40	191.87	260.43	99.5	—	—	3
Eleostearic	$C_{18}H_{30}O_2$	278.42	201.51	273.51	48.5	—	—	3
Arachidic	$C_{20}H_{40}O_2$	312.52	179.52	0	75.2	233.0	240	0
Gadoleic	$C_{20}H_{38}O_2$	310.50	180.69	81.75	24.5	—	—	1
Arachidonic	$C_{20}H_{32}O_2$	304.5	185	333.5	−45.5	—	—	4
Behenic	$C_{22}H_{44}O_2$	340.56	164.73	0	80.2	247.0	257	0
Erucic	$C_{22}H_{42}O_2$	338.54	165.72	74.98	34.7	—	—	1
Clupanodonic	$C_{22}H_{34}O_2$	332.5	169	384.0	—	—	—	5
Lignoceric	$C_{24}H_{48}O_2$	368.61	152.22	0	84.2	255.0	272	0
Tetracosenoic	$C_{24}H_{46}O_2$	366.59	153.04	69.24	—	—	—	1
Nisinic	$C_{24}H_{38}O_2$	358.51	156.49	354.02	—	—	—	5

SOURCE: ANON. 1969. The Wecobee Handbook. PVO International, Boonton, New Jersey.

FATTY ACIDS, FATS AND OILS

TABLE 2.F.7

FATTY ACID COMPOSITION OF COMMON ANIMAL AND VEGETABLE FATS AND OILS

SECTION 1

Fatty Acid Systematic Name	Common Name	No. of Carbon Atoms	Cottonseed	Kapok	Soybean	Sesame	Coconut	Palm Kernel	Babassu
n-Tetranoic	Butyric	4							
n-Hexanoic	Caproic	6			↑		0–0.8		0–0.2
n-Octanoic	Caprylic	8					5.5–9.9	3–4	4–6.5
n-Decanoic	Capric	10					4.5–9.5	3–7	2.7–7.6
n-Dodecanoic	Lauric	12					44–52	46–52	44–46
n-Tetradecanoic	Myristic	14	0.5			0.1	13–19	14–17	15–20
n-Hexadecanoic	Palmitic	16	21.9	10.5	14	8.2–9.4	7.5–10.5	6.5–9	6–9
n-Octadecanoic	Stearic	18	1.9	8.6		3.6–5.7	1–3	1–2.5	3–6
n-Eicosanoic	Arachidic	20	0.1	} 1.3		0.8–1.2	0–0.4		0.2–0.7
n-Docosanoic	Behenic	22							
n-Tetracosanoic	Lignoceric	24			↓				
9-Tetradecenoic	Myristoleic	14							
9-Hexadecenoic	Palmitoleic	16				0.5	0–1.3		
9-Octadecenoic	Oleic	18	30.7	46.1	23.0	35–45.4	5–8	13–19	12–18
9-Eicosenoic	Gadoleic	20							
13-Docosenoic	Erucic	22							
9, 12-Octadecadienoic	Linoleic	18	44.9	33.5	55.0	40.4–48.4	1.5–2.5	0.5–2	1.4–2.8
9, 12, 15-Octadecatrienoic	Linolenic	18			8.0				
9, 11, 13-Octadecatrienoic	Eleostearic	18							
5, 8, 11, 14-Eicosatetraenoic	Arachidonic	20							
4, 8, 12, 15, 19-Docosapentaenoic	Clupanodonic	22							
Docosadienoic									

Fatty Acid: Systematic Name	Common Name	No. of Carbon Atoms	Palm	Rapeseed	Mustard: White	Mustard: Black	Ravison	Sunflower	Safflower
n-Tetranoic	Butyric	4							
n-Hexanoic	Caproic	6						↑	
n-Octanoic	Caprylic	8							
n-Decanoic	Capric	10							
n-Dodecanoic	Lauric	12							
n-Tetradecanoic	Myristic	14	1.1–2.5		0.4	0.8		7–14.2	
n-Hexadecanoic	Palmitic	16	40–46	1.9–2.8	1.5	0.7	4.3		6.4
n-Octadecanoic	Stearic	18	3.6–4.7	0.4–3.5	0.4		2.1		3.1
n-Eicosanoic	Arachidic	20		0.5–2.4	0.5	0.5	1.8		0.2
n-Docosanoic	Behenic	22		0.6–2.1	2.0	2.3	0.5	↓	
n-Tetracosanoic	Lignoceric	24		0.5–0.8	1.0	1.8	0.6		
9-Tetradecenoic	Myristoleic	14							
9-Hexadecenoic	Palmitoleic	16	0–1.2	0.1–2.9			0.6		
9-Octadecenoic	Oleic	18	39–45	12.3–16.0	22.0	20.7	15.5	14.1–43.1	13.4
9-Eicosenoic	Gadoleic	20		3.5–6.0	7.0	8.1	4.1		
13-Docosenoic	Erucic	22		45–54	44.2	40.6	38.7		
9, 12-Octadecadienoic	Linoleic	18	7–11	12–16	14.2	18.0	20.9	44.2–75.4	76.9
9, 12, 15-Octadecatrienoic	Linolenic	18		7.0–9.9	6.8	0.5	9.9		
9, 11, 13-Octadecatrienoic	Eleostearic	18							
5, 8, 11, 14-Eicosatetraenoic	Arachidonic	20							
4, 8, 12, 15, 19-Docosapentaenoic	Clupanodonic	22							
Docosadienoic				0.9–2.3			1.0		

(Continued)

SECTION 3

TABLE 2.F.7 (*Continued*)

Fatty Acid: Systematic Name	Common Name	No. of Carbon Atoms	Olive	Teaseed	Walnut	Peanut	Perilla	Linseed	Butter-fat
n-Tetranoic	Butyric	4							3.5-3.7
n-Hexanoic	Caproic	6				↑	↑	↑	1.4-2.0
n-Octanoic	Caprylic	8							0.5-1.7
n-Decanoic	Capric	10							1.9-2.6
n-Dodecanoic	Lauric	12							2.5-4.5
n-Tetradecanoic	Myristic	14	0.5-1.2		0.01-0.4	17.1-21.9	6-12	5.9-16.5	8.1-14.6
n-Hexadecanoic	Palmitic	16	9.7-15.6	4.9	3.5-4.6				25.9-30.2
n-Octadecanoic	Stearic	18	1.0-3.3	1.2	0.9-1.9				9.2-11.2
n-Eicosanoic	Arachidic	20	0.1-0.9						↑
n-Docosanoic	Behenic	22		0.8					1.2-2.4
n-Tetracosanoic	Lignoceric	24				↓	↓	↓	↓
9-Tetradecenoic	Myristoleic	14							
9-Hexadecenoic	Palmitoleic	16				0.9	↑		3.4-5.7
9-Octadecenoic	Oleic	18	64.6-79.8	86.7	17.8-36.4	42.3-71.5		13-28.6	18.7-32.8
9-Eicosenoic	Gadoleic	20							
13-Docosenoic	Erucic	22							
9, 12-Octadecadienoic	Linoleic	18	7.5-15.0	6.8	50-73.4	13.0-33.4	83-88	15.2-22.4	2.1-3.7
9, 12, 15-Octadecatrienoic	Linolenic	18			3.3-7.7			46.8-54	
9, 11, 13-Octadecatrienoic	Eleostearic	18							
5, 8, 11, 14-Eicosatetraenoic	Arachidonic	20						C_{20} & C_{22} }	0.9-1.7
4, 8, 12, 15, 19-Docosapentaenoic	Clupanodonic	22							
Docosadienoic									

SECTION 4

Fatty Acid Systematic Name	Common Name	No. of Carbon Atoms	Lard	Beef Tallow	Mutton Tallow	Corn	Castor	Tung	Cacao Butter
n-Tetranoic	Butyric	4							
n-Hexanoic	Caproic	6	↑	↑			↑		
n-Octanoic	Caprylic	8							
n-Decanoic	Capric	10	Trace to 1.1	2–8.2	1–4		Saturated acids 2.4		
n-Dodecanoic	Lauric	12							
n-Tetradecanoic	Myristic	14	↓	↓		0.2–1.7			
n-Hexadecanoic	Palmitic	16	26–32	24–33	20–28	8–12		5.5	26.2
n-Octadecanoic	Stearic	18	12–16	14–29	25–32	2.5–4.5			34.4
n-Eicosanoic	Arachidic	20							
n-Docosanoic	Behenic	22							
n-Tetracosanoic	Lignoceric	24					↓		
9-Tetradecenoic	Myristoleic	14							
9-Hexadecenoic	Palmitoleic	16	2–5	1.9–2.7		0.2–1.6			
9-Octadecenoic	Oleic	18	41–51	39–50	26–47	19–49	7.4	4.0	37.3
9-Eicosenoic	Gadoleic	20							
13-Docosenoic	Erucic	22							
9, 12-Octadecadienoic	Linoleic	18	3–14	1–4	3–5	34–62	3.1	8.5	2.1
9, 12, 15-Octadecatrienoic	Linolenic	18		Trace to 0.5	0.5				
9, 11, 13-Octadecatrienoic	Eleostearic	18						82	
5, 8, 11, 14-Eicosatetraenoic	Arachidonic	20	0.4–3	Trace to 0.5	1.5				
	Dihydroxy-stearic	18					0.6		
12-OH, 9-octadecanoic	Ricinoleic	18					87.0		

SOURCE: MAHLENBACHER, C. V. The Analysis of Fats and Oils. Garrard Publishing Co., Champaign, Illinois.

F-DISTRIBUTION, UPPER 5% (0.05 or 95% LEVEL)

If a calculated F value is equal to or greater than the Table value the calculated F value is significant.

Degrees of Freedom of Greater Mean Square

Degrees of Freedom of Lesser Mean Square

ν_2 \ ν_1	1	2	3	4	5	6	7	8	9
1	161·45	199·50	215·71	224·58	230·16	233·99	236·77	238·88	240·54
2	18·513	19·000	19·164	19·247	19·296	19·330	19·353	19·371	19·385
3	10·128	9·5521	9·2766	9·1172	9·0135	8·9406	8·8867	8·8452	8·8123
4	7·7086	6·9443	6·5914	6·3882	6·2561	6·1631	6·0942	6·0410	5·9988
5	6·6079	5·7861	5·4095	5·1922	5·0503	4·9503	4·8759	4·8183	4·7725
6	5·9874	5·1433	4·7571	4·5337	4·3874	4·2839	4·2067	4·1468	4·0990
7	5·5914	4·7374	4·3468	4·1203	3·9715	3·8660	3·7870	3·7257	3·6767
8	5·3177	4·4590	4·0662	3·8379	3·6875	3·5806	3·5005	3·4381	3·3881
9	5·1174	4·2565	3·8625	3·6331	3·4817	3·3738	3·2927	3·2296	3·1789
10	4.9646	4·1028	3·7083	3·4780	3·3258	3·2172	3·1355	3·0717	3·0204
11	4·8443	3·9823	3·5874	3·3567	3·2039	3·0946	3·0123	2·9480	2·8962
12	4.7472	3·8853	3·4903	3·2592	3·1059	2·9961	2·9134	2·8486	2·7964
13	4·6672	3·8056	3·4105	3·1791	3·0254	2·9153	2·8321	2·7669	2·7144
14	4·6001	3·7389	3·3439	3·1122	2·9582	2·8477	2·7642	2·6987	2·6458
15	4·5431	3·6823	3·2874	3·0556	2·9013	2·7905	2·7066	2·6408	2·5876
16	4.4940	3·6337	3·2389	3·0069	2·8524	2·7413	2·6572	2·5911	2·5377
17	4·4513	3·5915	3·1968	2·9647	2·8100	2·6987	2·6143	2·5480	2·4943
18	4·4139	3·5546	3·1599	2·9277	2·7729	2·6613	2·5767	2·5102	2·4563
19	4·3807	3·5219	3·1274	2·8951	2·7401	2·6283	2·5435	2·4768	2·4227
20	4·3512	3·4928	3·0984	2·8661	2·7109	2·5990	2·5140	2·4471	2·3928
21	4·3248	3·4668	3·0725	2·8401	2·6848	2·5727	2·4876	2·4205	2·3660
22	4·3009	3·4434	3·0491	2·8167	2·6613	2·5491	2·4638	2·3965	2·3419
23	4.2793	3·4221	3·0280	2·7955	2·6400	2·5277	2·4422	2·3748	2·3201
24	4·2597	3·4028	3·0088	2·7763	2·6207	2·5082	2·4226	2·3551	2·3002
25	4·2417	3·3852	2·9912	2·7587	2·6030	2·4904	2·4047	2·3371	2·2821
26	4·2252	3·3690	2·9752	2·7426	2·5868	2·4741	2·3883	2·3205	2·2655
27	4·2100	3·3541	2·9604	2·7278	2·5719	2·4591	2·3732	2·3053	2·2501
28	4·1960	3·3404	2·9467	2·7141	2·5581	2·4453	2·3593	2·2913	2·2360
29	4·1830	3·3277	2·9340	2·7014	2·5454	2·4324	2·3463	2·2783	2·2229
30	4·1709	3·3158	2·9223	2·6896	2·5336	2·4205	2·3343	2·2662	2·2107
40	4·0847	3·2317	2·8387	2·6060	2·4495	2·3359	2·2490	2·1802	2·1240
60	4·0012	3·1504	2·7581	2·5252	2·3683	2·2541	2·1665	2·0970	2·0401
120	3·9201	3·0718	2·6802	2·4472	2·2899	2·1750	2·0868	2·0164	1·9588
∞	3·8415	2·9957	2·6049	2·3719	2·2141	2·0986	2·0096	1·9384	1·8799

Degrees of Freedom of Greater Mean Square

Degrees of Freedom of Lesser Mean Square

ν_2 \ ν_1	10	12	15	20	24	30	40	60	120	∞
1	241·88	243·91	245·95	248·01	249·05	250·10	251·14	252·20	253·25	254·31
2	19·396	19·413	19·429	19·446	19·454	19·462	19·471	19·479	19·487	19·496
3	8·7855	8·7446	8·7029	8·6602	8·6385	8·6166	8·5944	8·5720	8·5494	8·5264
4	5·9644	5·9117	5·8578	5·8025	5·7744	5·7459	5·7170	5·6877	5·6581	5·6281
5	4·7351	4·6777	4·6188	4·5581	4·5272	4·4957	4·4638	4·4314	4·3985	4·3650
6	4·0600	3·9999	3·9381	3·8742	3·8415	3·8082	3·7743	3·7398	3·7047	3·6689
7	3·6365	3·5747	3·5107	3·4445	3·4105	3·3758	3·3404	3·3043	3·2674	3·2298
8	3·3472	3·2839	3·2184	3·1503	3·1152	3·0794	3·0428	3·0053	2·9669	2·9276
9	3·1373	3·0729	3·0061	2·9365	2·9005	2·8637	2·8259	2·7872	2·7475	2·7067
10	2·9782	2·9130	2·8450	2·7740	2·7372	2·6996	2·6609	2·6211	2·5801	2·5379
11	2·8536	2·7876	2·7186	2·6464	2·6090	2·5705	2·5309	2·4901	2·4480	2·4045
12	2·7534	2·6866	2·6169	2·5436	2·5055	2·4663	2·4259	2·3842	2·3410	2·2962
13	2·6710	2·6037	2·5331	2·4589	2·4202	2·3803	2·3392	2·2966	2·2524	2·2064
14	2·6022	2·5342	2·4630	2·3879	2·3487	2·3082	2·2664	2·2229	2·1778	2·1307
15	2·5437	2·4753	2·4034	2·3275	2·2878	2·2468	2·2043	2·1601	2·1141	2·0658
16	2·4935	2·4247	2·3522	2·2756	2·2354	2·1938	2·1507	2·1058	2·0589	2·0096
17	2·4499	2·3807	2·3077	2·2304	2·1898	2·1477	2·1040	2·0584	2·0107	1·9604
18	2·4117	2·3421	2·2686	2·1906	2·1497	2·1071	2·0629	2·0166	1·9681	1·9168
19	2·3779	2·3080	2·2341	2·1555	2·1141	2·0712	2·0264	1·9795	1·9302	1·8780
20	2·3479	2·2776	2·2033	2·1242	2·0825	2·0391	1·9938	1·9464	1·8963	1·8432
21	2·3210	2·2504	2·1757	2·0960	2·0540	2·0102	1·9645	1·9165	1·8657	1·8117
22	2·2967	2·2258	2·1508	2·0707	2·0283	1·9842	1·9380	1·8894	1·8380	1·7831
23	2·2747	2·2036	2·1282	2·0476	2·0050	1·9605	1·9139	1·8648	1·8128	1·7570
24	2·2547	2·1834	2·1077	2·0267	1·9838	1·9390	1·8920	1·8424	1·7896	1·7330
25	2·2365	2·1649	2·0889	2·0075	1·9643	1·9192	1·8718	1·8217	1·7684	1·7110
26	2·2197	2·1479	2·0716	1·9898	1·9464	1·9010	1·8533	1·8027	1·7488	1·6906
27	2·2043	2·1323	2·0558	1·9736	1·9299	1·8842	1·8361	1·7851	1·7306	1·6717
28	2·1900	2·1179	2·0411	1·9586	1·9147	1·8687	1·8203	1·7689	1·7138	1·6541
29	2·1768	2·1045	2·0275	1·9446	1·9005	1·8543	1·8055	1·7537	1·6981	1·6376
30	2·1646	2·0921	2·0148	1·9317	1·8874	1·8409	1·7918	1·7396	1·6835	1·6223
40	2·0772	2·0035	1·9245	1·8389	1·7929	1·7444	1·6928	1·6373	1·5766	1·5089
60	1·9926	1·9174	1·8364	1·7480	1·7001	1·6491	1·5943	1·5343	1·4673	1·3893
120	1·9105	1·8337	1·7505	1·6587	1·6084	1·5543	1·4952	1·4290	1·3519	1·2539
∞	1·8307	1·7522	1·6664	1·5705	1·5173	1·4591	1·3940	1·3180	1·2214	1·0000

$F = \frac{s_1^2}{s_2^2} = \frac{S_1}{\nu_1} \Big/ \frac{S_2}{\nu_2}$, where $s_1^2 = S_1/\nu_1$ and $s_2^2 = S_2/\nu_2$ are independent mean square estimators of a common variance σ^2, based on ν_1 and ν_2 degrees of freedom, respectively.

SOURCE: PEARSON, E. S., and HARTLEY, H. O. 1972. The Biometrika Tables for Statisticians, Vol. II. University Press, Cambridge, England.

F-DISTRIBUTION, UPPER 0.5% (0.005 or 99.5% LEVEL)

If a calculated F value is equal to or greater than the Table value, the calculated F value is significant.

Degrees of Freedom of Greater Mean Square (ν_1); Degrees of Freedom of Lesser Mean Square (ν_2)

ν_2 \ ν_1	1	2	3	4	5	6	7	8	9
1	16211	20000	21615	22500	23056	23437	23715	23925	24091
2	198·50	199·00	199·17	199·25	199·30	199·33	199·36	199·37	199·39
3	55·552	49·799	47·467	46·195	45·392	44·838	44·434	44·126	43·882
4	31·333	26·284	24·259	23·155	22·456	21·975	21·622	21·352	21·139
5	22·785	18·314	16·530	15·556	14·940	14·513	14·200	13·961	13·772
6	18·635	14·544	12·917	12·028	11·464	11·073	10·786	10·566	10·391
7	16·236	12·404	10·882	10·050	9·5221	9·1553	8·8854	8·6781	8·5138
8	14·688	11.042	9·5965	8·8051	8·3018	7·9520	7·6941	7·4959	7·3386
9	13·614	10·107	8·7171	7·9559	7·4712	7·1339	6·8849	6·6933	6·5411
10	12·826	9·4270	8·0807	7·3428	6·8724	6·5446	6·3025	6·1159	5·9676
11	12·226	8·9122	7·6004	6·8809	6·4217	6·1016	5·8648	5·6821	5·5368
12	11·754	8·5096	7·2258	6·5211	6·0711	5·7570	5·5245	5·3451	5·2021
13	11·374	8·1865	6·9258	6·2335	5·7910	5·4819	5·2529	5·0761	4·9351
14	11·060	7·9216	6·6804	5·9984	5·5623	5·2574	5·0313	4·8566	4·7173
15	10·798	7·7008	6·4760	5·8029	5·3721	5·0708	4·8473	4·6744	4·5364
16	10·575	7·5138	6·3034	5·6378	5·2117	4·9134	4·6920	4·5207	4·3838
17	10·384	7·3536	6·1556	5·4967	5·0746	4·7789	4·5594	4·3894	4·2535
18	10·218	7·2148	6·0278	5·3746	4·9560	4·6627	4·4448	4·2759	4·1410
19	10·073	7·0935	5·9161	5·2681	4·8526	4·5614	4·3448	4·1770	4·0428
20	9·9439	6·9865	5·8177	5·1743	4·7616	4·4721	4·2569	4·0900	3·9564
21	9·8295	6·8914	5·7304	5·0911	4·6809	4·3931	4·1789	4·0128	3·8799
22	9·7271	6·8064	5·6524	5·0168	4·6088	4·3225	4·1094	3·9440	3·8116
23	9·6348	6·7300	5·5823	4·9500	4·5441	4·2591	4·0469	3·8822	3·7502
24	9·5513	6·6609	5·5190	4·8898	4·4857	4·2019	3·9905	3·8264	3·6949
25	9·4753	6·5982	5·4615	4·8351	4·4327	4·1500	3·9394	3·7758	3·6447
26	9·4059	6·5409	5·4091	4·7852	4·3844	4·1027	3·8928	3·7297	3·5989
27	9·3423	6·4885	5·3611	4·7396	4·3402	4·0594	3·8501	3·6875	3·5571
28	9·2838	6·4403	5·3170	4·6977	4·2996	4·0197	3·8110	3·6487	3·5186
29	9·2297	6·3958	5·2764	4·6591	4·2622	3·9831	3·7749	3·6131	3·4832
30	9·1797	6·3547	5·2388	4·6234	4·2276	3·9492	3·7416	3·5801	3·4505
40	8·8279	6·0664	4·9758	4·3738	3·9860	3·7129	3·5088	3·3498	3·2220
60	8·4946	5·7950	4·7290	4·1399	3·7599	3·4918	3·2911	3·1344	3·0083
120	8·1788	5·5393	4·4972	3·9207	3·5482	3·2849	3·0874	2·9330	2·8083
∞	7·8794	5·2983	4·2794	3·7151	3·3499	3·0913	2·8968	2·7444	2·6210

Degrees of Freedom of Greater Mean Square

ν_2 \ ν_1	10	12	15	20	24	30	40	60	120	∞
1	24224	24426	24630	24836	24940	25044	25148	25253	25359	25464
2	199·40	199·42	199·43	199·45	199·46	199·47	199·47	199·48	199·49	199·50
3	43·686	43·387	43·085	42·778	42·622	42·466	42·308	42·149	41·989	41·828
4	20·967	20·705	20·438	20·167	20·030	19·892	19·752	19·611	19·468	19·325
5	13·618	13·384	13·146	12·903	12·780	12·656	12·530	12·402	12·274	12·144
6	10·250	10·034	9·8140	9·5888	9·4742	9·3582	9·2408	9·1219	9·0015	8·8793
7	8·3803	8·1764	7·9678	7·7540	7·6450	7·5345	7·4224	7·3088	7·1933	7·0760
8	7·2106	7·0149	6·8143	6·6082	6·5029	6·3961	6·2875	6·1772	6·0649	5·9506
9	6·4172	6·2274	6·0325	5·8318	5·7292	5·6248	5·5186	5·4104	5·3001	5·1875
10	5·8467	5·6613	5·4707	5·2740	5·1732	5·0706	4·9659	4·8592	4·7501	4·6385
11	5·4183	5·2363	5·0489	4·8552	4·7557	4·6543	4·5508	4·4450	4·3367	4·2255
12	5·0855	4·9062	4·7213	4·5299	4·4314	4·3309	4·2282	4·1229	4·0149	3·9039
13	4·8199	4·6429	4·4600	4·2703	4·1726	4·0727	3·9704	3·8655	3·7577	3·6465
14	4·6034	4·4281	4·2468	4·0585	3·9614	3·8619	3·7600	3·6552	3·5473	3·4359
15	4·4235	4·2497	4·0698	3·8826	3·7859	3·6867	3·5850	3·4803	3·3722	3·2602
16	4·2719	4·0994	3·9205	3·7342	3·6378	3·5389	3·4372	3·3324	3·2240	3·1115
17	4·1424	3·9709	3·7929	3·6073	3·5112	3·4124	3·3108	3·2058	3·0971	2·9839
18	4·0305	3·8599	3·6827	3·4977	3·4017	3·3030	3·2014	3·0962	2·9871	2·8732
19	3·9329	3·7631	3·5866	3·4020	3·3062	3·2075	3·1058	3·0004	2·8908	2·7762
20	3·8470	3·6779	3·5020	3·3178	3·2220	3·1234	3·0215	2·9159	2·8058	2·6904
21	3·7709	3·6024	3·4270	3·2431	3·1474	3·0488	2·9467	2·8408	2·7302	2·6140
22	3·7030	3·5350	3·3600	3·1764	3·0807	2·9821	2·8799	2·7736	2·6625	2·5455
23	3·6420	3·4745	3·2999	3·1165	3·0208	2·9221	2·8197	2·7132	2·6015	2·4837
24	3·5870	3·4199	3·2456	3·0624	2·9667	2·8679	2·7654	2·6585	2·5463	2·4276
25	3·5370	3·3704	3·1963	3·0133	2·9176	2·8187	2·7160	2·6088	2·4961	2·3765
26	3·4916	3·3252	3·1515	2·9685	2·8728	2·7738	2·6709	2·5633	2·4501	2·3297
27	3·4499	3·2839	3·1104	2·9275	2·8318	2·7327	2·6296	2·5217	2·4079	2·2867
28	3·4117	3·2460	3·0727	2·8899	2·7941	2·6949	2·5916	2·4834	2·3690	2·2470
29	3·3765	3·2110	3·0379	2·8551	2·7594	2·6600	2·5565	2·4479	2·3331	2·2102
30	3·3440	3·1787	3·0057	2·8230	2·7272	2·6278	2·5241	2·4151	2·2998	2·1760
40	3·1167	2·9531	2·7811	2·5984	2·5020	2·4015	2·2958	2·1838	2·0636	1·9318
60	2·9042	2·7419	2·5705	2·3872	2·2898	2·1874	2·0789	1·9622	1·8341	1·6885
120	2·7052	2·5439	2·3727	2·1881	2·0890	1·9840	1·8709	1·7469	1·6055	1·4311
∞	2·5188	2·3583	2·1868	1·9998	1·8983	1·7891	1·6691	1·5325	1·3637	1·0000

Degrees of Freedom of Lesser Mean Square (ν_2)

SOURCE: PEARSON, E. S., and HARTLEY, H. O. 1972. The Biometrika Tables for Statisticians, Vol. II. University Press, Cambridge, England.

F-DISTRIBUTION, UPPER 1% (0.01 or 99% LEVEL)

If a calculated F value is equal to or greater than the Table value the calculated F value is significant.

Degrees of Freedom of Greater Mean Square (columns, ν_1); Degrees of Freedom of Lesser Mean Square (rows, ν_2)

ν_2 \ ν_1	1	2	3	4	5	6	7	8	9
1	4052·2	4999·5	5403·4	5624·6	5763·6	5859·0	5928·4	5981·1	6022·5
2	98·503	99·000	99·166	99·249	99·299	99·333	99·356	99·374	99·388
3	34·116	30·817	29·457	28·710	28·237	27·911	27·672	27·489	27·345
4	21·198	18·000	16·694	15·977	15·522	15·207	14·976	14·799	14·659
5	16·258	13·274	12·060	11·392	10·967	10·672	10·456	10·289	10·158
6	13·745	10·925	9·7795	9·1483	8·7459	8·4661	8·2600	8·1017	7·9761
7	12·246	9·5466	8·4513	7·8466	7·4604	7·1914	6·9928	6·8400	6·7188
8	11·259	8·6491	7·5910	7·0061	6·6318	6·3707	6·1776	6·0289	5·9106
9	10·561	8·0215	6·9919	6·4221	6·0569	5·8018	5·6129	5·4671	5·3511
10	10·044	7·5594	6·5523	5·9943	5·6363	5·3858	5·2001	5·0567	4·9424
11	9·6460	7·2057	6·2167	5·6683	5·3160	5·0692	4·8861	4·7445	4·6315
12	9·3302	6·9266	5·9525	5·4120	5·0643	4·8206	4·6395	4·4994	4·3875
13	9·0738	6·7010	5·7394	5·2053	4·8616	4·6204	4·4410	4·3021	4·1911
14	8·8616	6·5149	5·5639	5·0354	4·6950	4·4558	4·2779	4·1399	4·0297
15	8·6831	6·3589	5·4170	4·8932	4·5556	4·3183	4·1415	4·0045	3·8948
16	8·5310	6·2262	5·2922	4·7726	4·4374	4·2016	4·0259	3·8896	3·7804
17	8·3997	6·1121	5·1850	4·6690	4·3359	4·1015	3·9267	3·7910	3·6822
18	8·2854	6·0129	5·0919	4·5790	4·2479	4·0146	3·8406	3·7054	3·5971
19	8·1849	5·9259	5·0103	4·5003	4·1708	3·9386	3·7653	3·6305	3·5225
20	8·0960	5·8489	4·9382	4·4307	4·1027	3·8714	3·6987	3·5644	3·4567
21	8·0166	5·7804	4·8740	4·3688	4·0421	3·8117	3·6396	3·5056	3·3981
22	7·9454	5·7190	4·8166	4·3134	3·9880	3·7583	3·5867	3·4530	3·3458
23	7·8811	5·6637	4·7649	4·2636	3·9392	3·7102	3·5390	3·4057	3·2986
24	7·8229	5·6136	4·7181	4·2184	3·8951	3·6667	3·4959	3·3629	3·2560
25	7·7698	5·5680	4·6755	4·1774	3·8550	3·6272	3·4568	3·3239	3·2172
26	7·7213	5·5263	4·6366	4·1400	3·8183	3·5911	3·4210	3·2884	3·1818
27	7·6767	5·4881	4·6009	4·1056	3·7848	3·5580	3·3882	3·2558	3·1494
28	7·6356	5·4529	4·5681	4·0740	3·7539	3·5276	3·3581	3·2259	3·1195
29	7·5977	5·4204	4·5378	4·0449	3·7254	3·4995	3·3303	3·1982	3·0920
30	7·5625	5·3903	4·5097	4·0179	3·6990	3·4735	3·3045	3·1726	3·0665
40	7·3141	5·1785	4·3126	3·8283	3·5138	3·2910	3·1238	2·9930	2·8876
60	7·0771	4·9774	4·1259	3·6490	3·3389	3·1187	2·9530	2·8233	2·7185
120	6·8509	4·7865	3·9491	3·4795	3·1735	2·9559	2·7918	2·6629	2·5586
∞	6·6349	4·6052	3·7816	3·3192	3·0173	2·8020	2·6393	2·5113	2·4073

Degrees of Freedom of Greater Mean Square

Degrees of Freedom of Lesser Mean Square ν_2 \ ν_1	10	12	15	20	24	30	40	60	120	∞
1	6055·8	6106·3	6157·3	6208·7	6234·6	6260·6	6286·8	6313·0	6339·4	6365·9
2	99·399	99·416	99·433	99·449	99·458	99·466	99·474	99·482	99·491	99·499
3	27·229	27·052	26·872	26·690	26·598	26·505	26·411	26·316	26·221	26·125
4	14·546	14·374	14·198	14·020	13·929	13·838	13·745	13·652	13·558	13·463
5	10·051	9·8883	9·7222	9·5526	9·4665	9·3793	9·2912	9·2020	9·1118	9·0204
6	7·8741	7·7183	7·5590	7·3958	7·3127	7·2285	7·1432	7·0567	6·9690	6·8800
7	6·6201	6·4691	6·3143	6·1554	6·0743	5·9920	5·9084	5·8236	5·7373	5·6495
8	5·8143	5·6667	5·5151	5·3591	5·2793	5·1981	5·1156	5·0316	4·9461	4·8588
9	5·2565	5·1114	4·9621	4·8080	4·7290	4·6486	4·5666	4·4831	4·3978	4·3105
10	4·8491	4·7059	4·5581	4·4054	4·3269	4·2469	4·1653	4·0819	3·9965	3·9090
11	4·5393	4·3974	4·2509	4·0990	4·0209	3·9411	3·8596	3·7761	3·6904	3·6024
12	4·2961	4·1553	4·0096	3·8584	3·7805	3·7008	3·6192	3·5355	3·4494	3·3608
13	4·1003	3·9603	3·8154	3·6646	3·5868	3·5070	3·4253	3·3413	3·2548	3·1654
14	3·9394	3·8001	3·6557	3·5052	3·4274	3·3476	3·2656	3·1813	3·0942	3·0040
15	3·8049	3·6662	3·5222	3·3719	3·2940	3·2141	3·1319	3·0471	2·9595	2·8684
16	3·6909	3·5527	3·4089	3·2587	3·1808	3·1007	3·0182	2·9330	2·8447	2·7528
17	3·5931	3·4552	3·3117	3·1615	3·0835	3·0032	2·9205	2·8348	2·7459	2·6530
18	3·5082	3·3706	3·2273	3·0771	2·9990	2·9185	2·8354	2·7493	2·6597	2·5660
19	3·4338	3·2965	3·1533	3·0031	2·9249	2·8442	2·7608	2·6742	2·5839	2·4893
20	3·3682	3·2311	3·0880	2·9377	2·8594	2·7785	2·6947	2·6077	2·5168	2·4212
21	3·3098	3·1730	3·0300	2·8796	2·8010	2·7200	2·6359	2·5484	2·4568	2·3603
22	3·2576	3·1209	2·9779	2·8274	2·7488	2·6675	2·5831	2·4951	2·4029	2·3055
23	3·2106	3·0740	2·9311	2·7805	2·7017	2·6202	2·5355	2·4471	2·3542	2·2558
24	3·1681	3·0316	2·8887	2·7380	2·6591	2·5773	2·4923	2·4035	2·3100	2·2107
25	3·1294	2·9931	2·8502	2·6993	2·6203	2·5383	2·4530	2·3637	2·2696	2·1694
26	3·0941	2·9578	2·8150	2·6640	2·5848	2·5026	2·4170	2·3273	2·2325	2·1315
27	3·0618	2·9256	2·7827	2·6316	2·5522	2·4699	2·3840	2·2938	2·1985	2·0965
28	3·0320	2·8959	2·7530	2·6017	2·5223	2·4397	2·3535	2·2629	2·1670	2·0642
29	3·0045	2·8685	2·7256	2·5742	2·4946	2·4118	2·3253	2·2344	2·1379	2·0342
30	2·9791	2·8431	2·7002	2·5487	2·4689	2·3860	2·2992	2·2079	2·1108	2·0062
40	2·8005	2·6648	2·5216	2·3689	2·2880	2·2034	2·1142	2·0194	1·9172	1·8047
60	2·6318	2·4961	2·3523	2·1978	2·1154	2·0285	1·9360	1·8363	1·7263	1·6006
120	2·4721	2·3363	2·1915	2·0346	1·9500	1·8600	1·7628	1·6557	1·5330	1·3805
∞	2·3209	2·1847	2·0385	1·8783	1·7908	1·6964	1·5923	1·4730	1·3246	1·0000

$F = \frac{s_1^2}{s_2^2} = \frac{S_1}{\nu_1}\Big/\frac{S_2}{\nu_2}$, where $s_1^2 = S_1/\nu_1$ and $s_2^2 = S_2/\nu_2$ are independent mean square estimators of a common variance σ^2, based on ν_1 and ν_2 degrees of freedom, respectively.

SOURCE: PEARSON, E. S., and HARTLEY H. O. 1972. The Biometrika Tables for Statisticians, Vol. II. University Press, Cambridge, England.

FERMENTED INGREDIENTS

TABLE 2.F.8

EXAMPLES OF FORMULAS FOR FERMENTED FOODS

Ingredient	Pastry		Crackers				Bagel	Pretzel
	Sweet Dough Mellow Br.	Danish Bread	Soda Cracker	Cheese Cracker	Sprayed Cracker	Graham Cracker	H. Glut	Cracker
Flour	46.8	35.8	70.3	66.1	69.0	43.5	64.0	71.6
Water	23.3	18.0	20.5	15.1	20.7	13.3	28.8	25.0
Salt	0.7	0.6	1.1	0.8	1.0	0.9	1.2	1.1
Yeast	2.9	2.2	0.1	0.2	0.1		1.8	0.2
Shortening	8.7	22.5*	7.0	4.0	5.9	7.0		2.1
Yeast food				0.1	0.1			
Malt			0.6	0.3	0.3		4.2	
Sugar	8.7	9.0			1.7	12.1		
Nonfat milk solids	2.9	2.2			0.9			
Whole egg	5.8	9.0						
Sodium bicarbonate			0.4	0.2	0.3	0.7		
Ammonium bicarbonate						0.3		
Cheese				13.2				
Invert syrup						2.9		
Molasses						2.4		
Graham meal						2.4		
Graham flour						14.5		
Mace	0.2							
Vanilla		0.6						
Cardamom		0.1						

***Approximately 80.0% of this shortening is comprised of "roll in" shortening.**

Data based on 100 parts of wet dough or batter.

SOURCE: COTTON, R. H. and PONTE, J. G. 1973. Baking Industry. *In* Wheat: Production and Utilization. G. E. Inglett (Editor). Avi Publishing Co., Westport, Conn.

FERTILIZER

TABLE 2.F.9

EXAMPLES OF GRADE FORMULAS

Pounds	Ingredient	Analysis	Nitrogen (N)	Available phosphoric acid (APA)	Potassium oxide (K_2O)	Pounds input	Ammonia capacity	Water	Residual acidity
5-10-5 (including organic N)									
200	Tankage	8.0 N	0.80	—	—	—	—	0.80	—
424	Sulfate of ammonia	20.8 N	4.41	—	—	—	—	—	458
1,020	Superphosphate	20.0 APA	—	10.20	—	—	61	3.32	—
174	Muriate of potash	60.0 K_2O	—	—	5.22	—	—	—	—
182	Limestone or sand	—	—	—	—	—	—	—	182+
2,000			5.21	10.20	5.22	0	61	4.12	276
5-10-5									
254	Nitrogen solution 410 (22-65-0)	41.0 N	5.21	—	—	56	—	1.59	188
1,020	Superphosphate	20.0 APA	—	10.20	—	—	61	3.32	
174	Muriate of potash	60.0 K_2O	—	—	5.22				

TABLE 2.F.9 (*Continued*)

Pounds	Ingredient	Analysis	Nitrogen (N)	Available phosphoric acid (APA)	Potassium oxide (K_2O)	Pounds input	Ammonia capacity	Water	Residual acidity
552	Limestone or sand	—	—	—	—	—	—	—	552+
2,000			5.21	10.20	5.22	56	61	4.91	364+
		8-16-8							
304	Nitrogen solution 410 (22-65-0)	41.0 N	6.23	—	—	67	—	1.90	224
200	Sulfate of ammonia	20.8 N	2.08	—	—	—	—	—	225
392	Triple superphosphate	46.0 APA	—	9.02	—	—	32	0.88	
730	Superphosphate	20.0 APA	—	7.30	—	—	44	2.37	
274	Muriate of potash	60.0 K_2O	—	—	8.22				
100	Conditioner	—							
2,000			8.31	16.32	8.22	67	76	5.15	449
		10-20-10							
274	Nitrogen solution 410 (19-72-0)	41.0 N	5.62	—	—	52	—	1.16	202
300	Diammonium phosphate	18.0 N 46.0 APA	2.70	6.90	—	—	—	0.30	
200	Sulfate of ammonia	20.8 N	2.08	—	—	—	—		225
434	Triple superphosphate	46.0 APA	—	9.98	—	—	35	0.98	
352	Superphosphate	20.0 APA	—	3.52	—	—	21	1.14	
340	Muriate of potash	60.0 K_2O	—	—	10.20				
100	Conditioner	—							
2,000			10.40	20.40	10.20	52	56	3.59	427
		0-20-20							
570	Triple superphosphate	46.0 APA	—	13.11	—	—	—	1.28	
730	Superphosphate	20.0 APA	—	7.30	—	—	—	2.37	
680	Muriate of potash	60.0 K_2O	—	—	20.40				
20	Hydrated lime (or 5 lb of ammonia)	—							
2,000			0	20.41	20.40	0	0	3.65	0
		20-0-20							
1,220	Ammonium nitrate	33.5 N	20.44	—					
680	Muriate of potash	60.0 K_2O	—	—	20.40				
100	Conditioner	—							
2,000			20.44	0	20.40	0	0	0	0

SOURCE: SAUCHELLI, V. (EDITOR). Chemistry and Technology of Fertilizers. Van Nostrand Reinhold Co., New York.

FERTILIZER MATERIALS

TABLE 2.F.10

COMPOSITION OF PRINCIPAL FERTILIZER MATERIALS[1]

Material	Nitrogen %	Available Phosphate $\%P_2O_5$	Potash $\%K_2O$	Calcium %	Magnesium %	Sulfur %	Chlorine %	Copper %	Manganese %	Zinc %	Boron %	Approximate Calcium Carbonate Equiv.[2] Lb/per Ton
					Nitrogen							
Ammonia, anhydrous	82	—	—	—	—	—	—	—	—	—	—	-2,960
Ammonia, aqua	16-25	—	—	—	—	—	—	—	—	—	—	-720 to -1,080
Ammonium nitrate	33.5	—	—	—	—	—	—	—	—	0.01	—	-1,180
Ammonium nit.-limestone mixtures	20.5	—	—	7.3	4.4	0.4	0.4	—	—	—	—	0
Ammonium sulfate	21	—	—	0.3	—	23.7	0.5	0.3	—	0.1	—	-2,200
Ammonium sulfate-nitrate	26	—	—	—	—	15.1	—	—	—	—	—	-1,700
Calcium cyanamide	21	—	—	38.5	.06	0.3	0.2	0.02	0.04	—	—	+1,260
Calcium nitrate	15	—	—	19.4	1.5	0.02	0.2	—	—	—	—	+400
Nitrogen solutions	21-49	—	—	—	—	—	—	—	—	—	—	-750 to -1,760
Sodium nitrate	16	—	0.2	0.1	0.05	0.07	0.4	0.07	—	—	0.01	+580
Urea	46	—	—	—	—	—	—	—	—	—	—	-1,680
Urea-form	38	—	—	—	—	—	—	—	—	—	—	-1,360
					Organics							
Castor pomace	5	1.8	1.1	0.4	0.3	0.04	0.3	—	0.04	0.05	0.01	-100
Cottonseed meal	6	2.6	1.4	0.2	0.4	0.3	0.06	—	—	0.02	—	-200
Dried cattle manure	2	1.5	2.2	3.3	0.9	0.4	0.6	0.01	0.03	0.03	0.01	+300
Sewage sludge, activated	5-6	2.9	0.6	1.3	0.7	0.5	0.6	0.07	0.07	0.10	—	-200
Sewage sludge, digested	2	1.4	0.8	2.1	0.5	0.1	0.2	0.30	0.3	0.4	—	-100
Tankage, Process	7-9	1	0.1	0.8	0.01	0.9	0.8	—	—	—	0.03	-320

Phosphates												
Basic slag, open hearth	—	8-12[3]	—	29.0	3.4	0.3	—	—	2.2	—	—	+1,000
Bone meal	2-4.5	22-28[4]	0.2	20-25	0.4	0.1	0.2	—	—	0.02	—	+400 to 500
Phosphoric acid	—	52-54[5]	—	—		—	—	—	—	—	—	-1000 to -1400
Rock phosphate	—		—	33.2	0.2	0.3	0.1	—	0.03	—	—	+200
Superphosphate, normal	—	18-20	0.2	20.4	0.2	11.9	0.3	—	—	0.01	—	0
Superphosphate, concentrated	—	42-50	0.4	13.6	0.3	1.4	—	0.01	0.01	—	0.01	0
Superphosphoric acid	—	76	—	—	—	—	—	—	—	—	—	—
Potash												
Potassium chloride (muriate)	—	—	60-62	0.1	0.1	—	47.0	—	—	—	0.03	0
Potassium magnesium sulfate	—	—	22	—	11.2	22.7	1.5	—	—	—	—	0
Potassium sulfate	—	—	50	0.7	1.2	17.6	2.1	0.001	—	—	0.002	0
Tobacco stems	2	0.7	6.0	3.6	0.4	0.4	1.2	0.01	0.03	—	0.02	+400
Multiple Nutrient												
Ammoniated superphosphate	3-6	18-20	—	17.2	—	12	—	—	—	—	—	-140
Ammonium phosphate-nitrate	27	15	—	—	—	—	—	—	—	—	—	-1240
Ammonium phosphate-sulfate	13-16	20-39	0.2	0.3	0.1	15.4	0.1	0.02	0.2	0.02	0.03	-1520 to -2260
Cotton hull ashes	—	4-7	22-30	6.8	3.1	1.0	1.9	0.04	0.06	0.07	—	+
Diammonium phosphate	16-21	48-53	—	—	—	—	—	—	—	—	—	-1250 to -1,550
Monoammonium phosphate	11	48	0.2	1.1	0.3	2.2	0.1	0.02	0.03	0.03	0.02	-1,300
Nitric phosphates	14-22	10-22	—	8-10	0.1	0.2-3.6	1.-12.0	0.02	0.2	0.02	0.03	-300 to -500
Nitrate of soda-potash	15	—	14	—	—	—	0.5	—	—	—	0.13	+550
Potassium nitrate	13	—	45	0.6	0.4	0.2	1.1	—	—	—	0.10	+520
Wood ashes	—	1.8	5.5	23.3	2.2	0.4	0.2	0.12	0.76	0.20	0.16	+

TABLE 2.F.10 (*Continued*)

Material	Nitrogen %	Available Phosphate $\%P_2O_5$	Potash $\%K_2O$	Calcium %	Magnesium %	Sulfur %	Chlorine %	Copper %	Manganese %	Zinc %	Boron %	Approximate Calcium Carbonate Equiv.[2] Lb/per Ton
Secondary Nutrient												
Blast furnace slag	—	1.7	0.6	29.3	3.8	1.4	—	—	1.02	0.001	0.01	+
Chats	—	—	—	21.2	9.3	0.2	—	0.001	0.55	0.2	—	+1,800
Dolomite	—	—	—	21.5	11.4	0.3	—	0.001	0.11	—	0.01	+1,960
Gypsum	—	—	0.5	22.5	0.4	16.8	0.3	—	—	—	—	0
Kieserite (emjeo)	—	—	—	1.6	18.2	—	—	—	—	—	—	0
Limestone	—	—	0.3	31.7	3.4	0.1	—	0.004	0.48	0.05	0.003	+1,800
Lime-sulfur solution	—	—	—	6.7	—	23.8	—	—	—	—	—	—
Magnesium sulfate (epsom salt)	—	—	—	2.2	10.5	14.0	0.4	—	—	—	—	0
Sulfur	—	—	—	—	—	30-99.6	—	—	—	—	—	-1900 to -6,320

[1] Most of the percentages larger than one of N, P_2O_5 and K_2O are the usual guarantees. Where more than one grade is sold, the range is indicated by two numbers separated by a dash. The rest of the percentages are averages compiled by A. L. Mehring from many published analyses.

[2] Ind. Eng. Chem. Anal. Ed. 5, 229-34 and other sources. A minus sign indicates the number of pounds of calcium carbonate needed to neutralize acid formed when 1 ton of the material is added to the soil. A plus sign indicates basic materials, and a zero physiologically neutral materials.

[3] By the 2% citric acid method.

[4] Total P_2O_5. All of the P_2O_5 in natural organics is considered available.

[5] 30–36% total P_2O_5, which is relatively unavailable in some soils.

Micro Nutrient Materials. Some commercial grades have the following average compositions:

Borax	11.6% B
Copper oxide	75% Cu
Copper sulfate	24.9% Cu, 12.8% S, and 0.5% Zn
Hydrated Iron sulfate	19.7% iron
Manganese sulfate	25.1% Mn, 0.5% Cu, 0.08% Zn, 0.3% B, and 14.5% S
White copperas	34.4% iron
Zinc oxide	77.2% Zn
Zinc sulfate	27.8% Zn, 0.02% Cu, and 13.6% S

SOURCE: GARMAN, W. H. (EDITOR). The Fertilizer Handbook, 2nd Edition. Fertilizer Institute.

FILM GAUGE

A film gauge is the number indicative of the thickness of packaging films. (1) For films other than cellophane the gauge number is a numerical prefix and is the last figures of the 5-digit decimal fraction of the thickness in inches, thus 88-gauge = 0.00088 in. (2) Cellophane is designated by the first three digit numbers to indicate yield (square inches per pound). Example: 250 indicates a film with 25,000 sq in. per lb. Typical weights and yields are:

	Approx Thickness, In.	Approx No. Sq In. Per Lb
215 plain	0.0009	21,500
195 plain	0.0010	19,500
150 plain	0.0013	15,000
250 moistureproof	0.0008	25,000
210 moistureproof	0.0009	21,000
195 moistureproof	0.0010	19,500
140 moistureproof	0.0014	14,000

(3) Film thickness is sometimes expressed in mils which is equivalent to 0.001 in.

SOURCE: F. W. GREENE CO. (EDITORS). 1967. Glossary of Packaging Terms, 4th Edition. Packaging Institute, New York.

FISH AND SHELLFISH COMPOSITION I

TABLE 2.F.11

COMPOSITION OF FISH AND SHELLFISH

Food, Approximate Measure, and Weight (in Grams)			Water (%)	Food Energy (Cal)	Protein (g)	Fat (Total Lipid) (g)	Fatty Acids: Saturated (Total) (g)	Fatty Acids: Unsaturated: Oleic (g)	Fatty Acids: Unsaturated: Lin-oleic (g)	Carbohydrate (g)	Calcium (mg)	Iron (mg)	Vitamin A Value (IU)	Thiamin (mg)	Riboflavin (mg)	Niacin (mg)	Ascorbic Acid (mg)
Fish and shellfish:																	
Bluefish, baked or broiled	3 oz	(85 g)	68	135	22	4	—	—	—	0	25	0.6	40	0.09	0.08	1.6	—
Clams:																	
Raw, meat only	3 oz	(85 g)	80	70	11	1	—	—	—	3	82	6.0	90	0.08	0.15	1.4	—
Canned, solids and liquid	3 oz	(85 g)	87	45	7	1	—	—	—	2	74	5.4	70	0.04	0.08	0.9	—
Crabmeat, canned or cooked.	3 oz	(85 g)	77	90	14	2	—	—	—	1	38	0.8	—	0.04	0.05	2.1	—
Fishsticks, breaded, cooked, frozen; stick, 3.8 by 1.0 by 0.5 in.	10 sticks or 8 oz package	(227 g)	66	400	38	20	5	4	10	15	25	0.9	—	0.09	0.16	3.6	—
Haddock, fried	3 oz	(85 g)	67	135	16	5	1	3	Tr	6	15	0.5	50	0.03	0.08	2.2	—
Mackerel:																	
Broiled, Atlantic	3 oz	(85 g)	62	200	19	13	—	—	—	0	5	1.0	450	0.13	0.23	6.5	—
Canned, Pacific, solids and liquid.	3 oz	(85 g)	66	155	18	9	—	—	—	0	221	1.9	20	0.02	0.28	7.4	—
Ocean perch, breaded (egg and breadcrumbs), fried.	3 oz	(85 g)	59	195	16	11	—	—	—	6	14	1.3	50	0.09	0.10	1.7	—
Oysters, meat only: Raw, 13–19 medium selects.	1 cup	(240 g)	85	160	20	4	—	—	—	8	226	13.2	740	0.30	0.39	6.6	—
Oyster stew, 1 part oysters to 3 parts milk by vol, 3–4 oysters	1 cup	(230 g)	84	200	11	12	—	—	—	11	269	3.3	640	0.12	0.40	1.7	—
Salmon, pink, canned	3 oz	(85 g)	70	120	17	5	1	1	—	0	[1]159	0.7	60	0.03	0.16	6.8	—
Sardines, Atlantic type, canned in oil, drained solids.	3 oz	(85 g)	57	180	22	9	2	2	4	1	367	2.5	190	0.02	0.18	4.6	—
Shad, baked	3 oz	(85 g)	64	170	20	10	—	—	—	0	20	0.5	20	0.11	0.22	7.3	—
Shrimp, canned, meat only	3 oz	(85 g)	66	110	23	1	—	—	—	—	98	2.6	50	0.01	0.03	1.9	—
Swordfish, broiled with butter or margarine.	3 oz	(85 g)	65	150	24	5	—	—	—	0	23	1.1	1,750	0.03	0.04	9.3	—
Tuna, canned in oil, drained solids.	3 oz	(85 g)	60	170	25	7	2	1	4	0	7	1.2	70	0.04	0.10	10.9	—

[1] If bones are discarded, calcium content is much lower. Bones equal about 2% by weight of total contents of can.

SOURCE: INSTITUTE OF HOME ECONOMICS. Nutritive Value of Foods. USDA Home and Garden Bull. *72*.

FISH AND SHELLFISH COMPOSITION II

TABLE 2.F.12

COMPOSITION OF THE EDIBLE PORTION (EP) AND REFUSE IN THE MATERIAL AS PURCHASED (AP)

Item No.	Commodity and Description	Water	Protein	Fat	Carbohydrate Total (by dif)	Carbohydrate Fiber	Ash	Calories (No. per 100 g)	Notes	Refuse in AP (%)
		Percent of Edible Portion								
	Fish and Shellfish									
	Fish, fresh									
220	Fat-rich—fillet	68.6	20	10	0	—	1.4	176	Herring and similar sp., tuna, mackerel (all types), salmon, trout, jacks, pompanos	0
221	—round	68.6	20	10	0	—	1.4	176		50
	Fish and shellfish									
222	Cod and related species—fillet	81.8	16.4	0.5	0	—	1.3	75	Hake, haddock, cusk, saithe	0
223	—round	81.8	16.4	0.5	0	—	1.3	75		55
224	Others—fillet	77.2	19	2.5	0	—	1.3	104	Incl flatfish, sharks, barracudas, mullets, perch, bream, fresh-water species	0
225	—round	77.2	19	2.5	0	—	1.3	104		55
226	All, unspecified—fillet	74.1	18.8	5.7	0	—	1.4	132		0
227	—round	74.1	18.8	5.7	0	—	1.4	132		53
	Crustaceans and molluscs, fresh									
228	Crustaceans, in shell	76.0	17.8	2.1	2.0	—	2.1	103	Lobster, crawfish, crab, shrimp, etc.	63
229	Molluscs, in shell	81.0	13.0	1.5	2.9	—	1.6	80	Oysters, mussels, clams, squids, etc.	75
230	Both, unspecified, in shell	79.3	14.6	1.7	2.6	—	1.8	88		72
	Fish, cured—salted, smoked, dried									
	Fat-rich kinds								Herring, sardines, salmon, mackerel	
	Light cure:								Brined: kippers, bloaters	
231	Only flesh considered as edible	58	21	11	0	0	10	189	Refuse: bones	31
232[1]	Eaten whole	58	21	11	0	0	10	189		0
	Medium cure:									
233	Only flesh considered as edible	41	40	10	0	0	9	261		31
234[1]	Eaten whole	41	40	10	0	0	9	261		0

(Continued)

TABLE 2.F.12 (*Continued*)

Item No.	Commodity and Description	Water	Protein	Fat	Carbohydrate Total (by dif)	Carbohydrate Fiber	Ash	Calories (No. per 100 g)	Notes	Refuse in AP (%)
		Percent of Edible Portion								
	Hard, heavy cure:									
235	Only flesh considered as edible	25	55	14	0	0	6	361		31
236[1]	Eaten whole	25	55	14	0	0	6	361		0
237	Dried—fish eaten whole	4	60	21	0	0	15	446	Very dry	0
	Fat-poor kinds								Haddock, cod, sea bream, sapsap, maigre	
	Light cure:								Brined	
238	Only flesh considered as edible	54	27.5	2	0	0	16.5	135	Refuse: bones	45
239[1]	Eaten whole	54	27.5	2	0	0	16.5	135		0
	Medium cure:									
240	Only flesh considered as edible	37	46	3	0	0	14	223	Refuse: bones	45
241[1]	Eaten whole	37	46	3	0	0	14	223		0
	Hard, heavy cure:									
242	Only flesh considered as edible	21	62	5	0	0	12	310	Refuse: bones	45
243[1]	Eaten whole	21	62	5	0	0	12	310		0
244	Fully dried, boneless flesh; fish meal	10	75	5	0	0	10	365	Very dry	0
	Fish, canned									
245	All kinds in oil	51	22	24	1	0	2	314		0
246	Fat-rich kinds, not in oil	65	20	11	1	0	3	188	Refuse: bones	0
247	Fat-poor kinds, not in oil	75	21	2	0	0	1.5	108		0
	Shellfish, canned									
248	Crustaceans, canned	78	17.5	1.5	1	0	2	92	Lobster, crawfish, crab, shrimp, etc.	0
249	Molluscs, canned	88	7	1	2	0	2	47	Oysters, mussels, clams, squid, etc.	0

[1] More information required.

SOURCE: CHATFIELD, C. Food Composition Tables for International Use. FAO, United Nations, Rome.

FISH CROSS SECTION

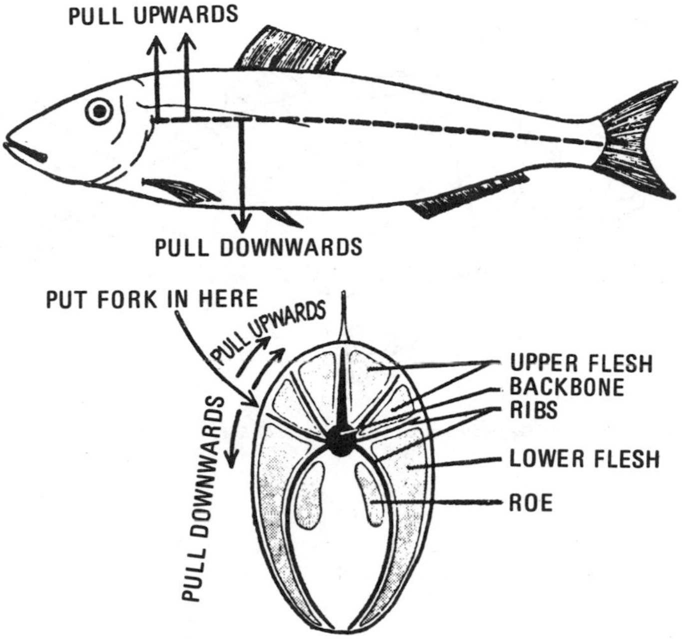

FIG. 2.F.2. CROSS SECTION OF A HERRING

SOURCE: CALLOW, A. B. Cooking and Nutritive Value. Oxford University Press, Fairlawn, New Jersey.

FISH DRAWN (EVISCERATED)

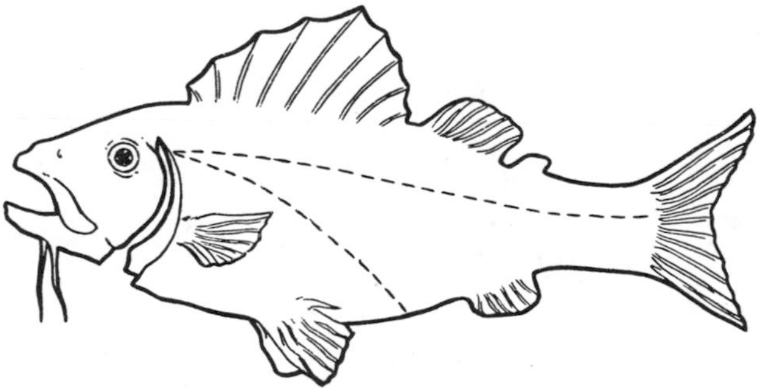

SOURCE: Food Inspection Specialist, Department of the Army, *TM 8-451*, 1969.

FISH DRESSED

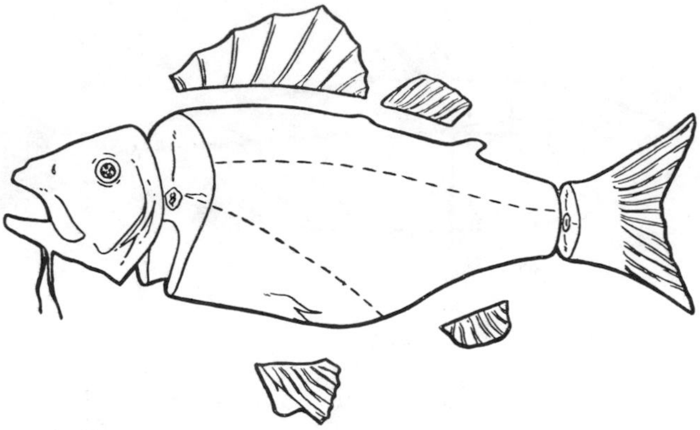

SOURCE: Food Inspection Specialist, Department of the Army, *TM 8-451*, 1969.

FISH FILLETS

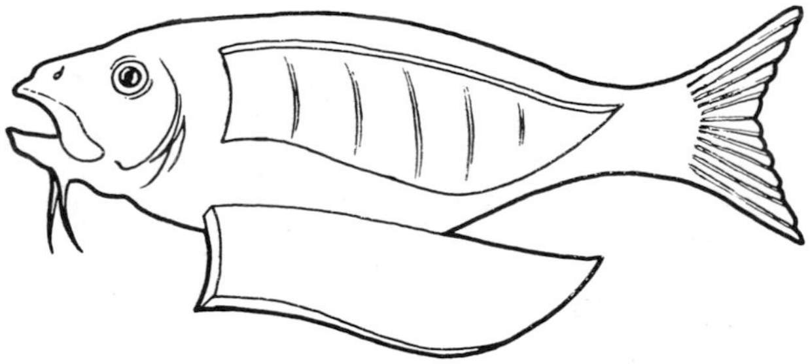

A. SINGLE FILLET

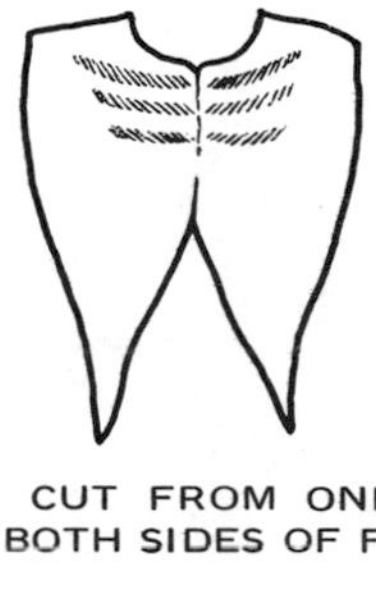

B. BUTTERFLY FILLET

FIG. 2.F.3. SINGLE FILLET (A) IS CUT FROM ONLY ONE SIDE OF FISH; BUTTERFLY FILLET IS CUT F
BOTH SIDES OF FISH AND NOT SEPARATED

SOURCE: Food Inspection Specialist, Department of the Army, *TM 8-451*, 1969.

FISH FORMS

FIG. 2.F.4. MARKET FORMS OF FISH

SOURCE: Food For Us All. Yearbook of Agriculture, 1969, USDA.

FISH NOMENCLATURE

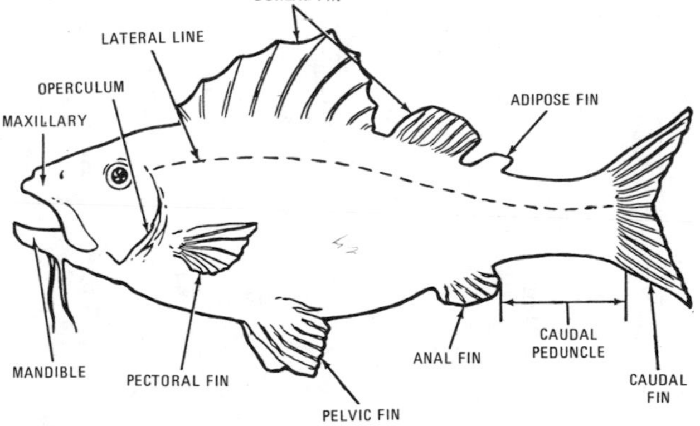

FIG. 2.F.5. SHOWING NAMES AND LOCATION OF VARIOUS PARTS OF FISH

SOURCE: Food Inspection Specialist, Department of the Army, *TM 8-451*, 1969.

FISH, SMOKE-CURED

TABLE 2.F.13

CHIEF TYPES OF SMOKE-CURED FISH

Product	Species Usually Used	Pretreatment	Method of Salting	Smoking: Type	Smoking: Time (hr) Traditional Kilns	Smoking: Time (hr) Torry Kiln	Weight Loss by Drying (%)	Final Salt Concentration (g/100 g Fish)
"Finnans"	Haddocks	Headed, split up belly, second cut made into flesh, blood and black lining removed.	Brined for 10–15 min, depending on size, in 70–80% saturated brine.	Cold-smoked.	6–12	4–6	15–18	2–3
Fillets (single)	Cod, large Haddocks	Cut from the gutted fish, sometimes skinned and "lugs" (belly-walls) removed.	Brined for 10–15 min, according to size; usually with dye.	Cold-smoked.	6–12	4–6	10–15	2–3
Fillets ("block")	Smaller Haddocks or Whiting	Head and bone removed; skin on or off, double fillet.	Brined for about 4 min.	Cold-smoked.	4–6	2–3	12–14	2–3
"Smokies"	Small Haddocks or Whitings	Whole gutted fish headed and cleaned; tied in pairs by tails with string.	Brined for about 1 hr.	Hot-smoked in a dense smoke without excessive drying.	2–3	1½	30	2–3
"Reds"	Herring	Whole, ungutted.	Dry-salted in vats with about 1 salt: 2 fish for 7–8 days (if salted longer, require partial desalting before smoking).	Cold-smoked intermittently.	[a]	[b]	20–25	14
Kippers	Herring	Split along back and gills, and viscera removed and washed.	Brined for 20–25 min, usually with dye.	Cold-smoked.	6–18	4–6	15–20	2–3
Buckling	Herring	Whole, usually ungutted.	Dry-salted overnight.	Hot-smoked in a dense smoke.	3–4	2–3	20–25	2–3
Smoked Salmon	Salmon	Gutted and cleaned and backbone taken out but head left on; flesh scored in order to let salt in.	Dry-salted 16–40 hr, depending on size.	Cold-smoked.	24–36	9–12	10	5

[a] Smoked on alternate nights for a week.
[b] Smoked nightly for 3–4 days.

SOURCE: HERSCHDOERFER, S. M. (EDITOR). 1968. Quality Control in the Food Industry, Vol. 2. Academic Press, New York.

FISH STEAKS

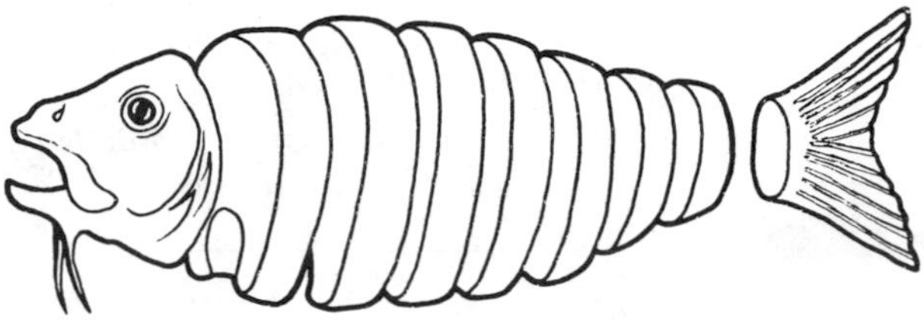

FIG. 2.F.6. STEAKS ARE CUT CROSSWISE FROM FISH AS ILLUSTRATED

SOURCE: Food Inspection Specialist, Department of the Army, *TM-8451*, 1969.

FISH, STORAGE

TABLE 2.F.14

APPROXIMATE STORAGE TIMES FOR PACKAGED AND GLAZED FISH AND SHELLFISH[1]

Product[2]	Storage Time in Months at 0°F. (−18°C.) (A)[3]	(B)[4]
Fatty fish		
Mackerel	2–3	4–6
Salmon	2–3	4–6
Sea herring	2–3	4–6
Smelt	2–3	4–6
Sprat	2–3	4–6
Trout	2–3	4–6
Lean and medium fatty fish		
Cod fillets	3–4	7–10
Haddock fillets	3–4	7–10
Fish sticks	3–4	7–10
Flounder fillets	3–4	7–10
Ocean perch fillets	3–4	7–10
Plaice	3–4	7–10
Pollock fillets	3–4	7–10
Sole	3 4	7–10
Shellfish		
Shrimp	3–4	6–8
Scallops	3–4	6–8
Clams	2–3	4–6
Lobster (cooked)	2–3	4–6
Oysters	2–3	4–6

[1] The storage times at a designated temperature will vary with the quality of the fish prior to freezing.
[2] Values for fish up to three days in ice before freezing.
[3] (A) Hardly detectable changes in quality occur; product is still of good acceptability.
[4] (B) Very significant changes in quality occur, and product is of low acceptability.

SOURCE: SLAVIN, JOSEPH W. 1968. Frozen Fish: Characteristics and Factors Affecting Quality During Freezing and Storage. *In* The Freezing Preservation of Foods, Vol. 2, 4th Edition. D. K. Tressler, W. B. Van Arsdel and M. J. Copley (Editors). Avi Publishing Co., Westport, Conn.

FISH YIELDS

TABLE 2.F.15

FISH YIELDS (APPROX)

		Edible Portion %
	Whole	45
	Drawn	48
	Dressed or pan dressed	67
	Steaks	84
	Fillets	100

SOURCE: Freezing Meat and Fish in the Home, USDA Home and Garden Bull. *93*, 1973.

FLAVORING AGENTS, NATURAL

TABLE 2.F.16

NATURAL FLAVORING AGENTS

Name	*Chemical Component Eliciting Flavor*	*Flavor Contributed*	*Use*
Anise	Anethole	Anise	Licorice-anise flavor
Basil	Methyl chavicol, cineole, linalool	Medicinal, herby, slight licorice	Spicy flavors, meat products
Bergamot	Limonene	Bitter orange	Citrus flavor, orange, cola
Betula	Methyl salicylate	Wintergreen	Mint-type flavors
Caraway	*d*-Carvone	Caraway	Spice flavor, bakery products
Cardamom	Terpineol, cineole	Spicy, slight lemon citrus	Processed meats
Cassia	Cinnamic aldehyde	Cinnamon, bite	Hot, spicy, candy, bakery products
Celery Seed	Limonene, sedenene	Celery, spicy	Spice blends, carbonated beverages, meat products

TABLE 2.F.16 (*Continued*)

Name	*Chemical Component Eliciting Flavor*	*Flavor Contributed*	*Use*
Chamomile		Pungent aromatic	Liqueur flavor
Cinnamon	Cinnamic aldehyde	Spicy, hot	Spice flavors, cola beverages
Clove	Eugenol	Warm, pungent, spicy clove	Spice and medicinal flavors, meat products
Copaiba	Caryophyllene	Bitter balsamic	Medicinal flavor
Coriander	*d*-Linalool	Spicy	General spice flavors, meats
Dill (weed)	Phellandrene, carvone	Herby, bitter	Pickle spice flavors
Fennel	Anethole	Anise	Liqueur, salad dressing
Grapefruit	Limonene	Grapefruit	Citric products (beverages)
Hops	Humulone	Fatty, green, oily	Beverage flavors
Horseradish	Allyl isothiocyanate	Hot, bite, penetrating	Hot sauces
Lavandin	Linalyl acetate	Pungent lavender	Dentrifices, chewing gum
Mace	*d*-Pinene, myristicin, *d*-Camphene	Nutmeg, aromatic, pine	Spice flavors
Marjoram	Terpinene	Spicy, pungent	Spice flavors
Mustard	Allyl isothiocyanate	Pungent, sharp	Relish flavors, salad dressings
Nutmeg	Pinene, myristicin	Spicy, hot, nutmeg	General spice flavors, baked goods
Orris root	Methyl ionone	Violet	Raspberry flavors
Patchouly		Earthy, slight woody	Cola beverages
Pepper	Piperidine	Warm, spicy	General spice flavors, prepared meats
Rosemary	Pinene, borneol, cineole	Slight medicinal, woody	Herb blends, mouthwashes
Sage	Thujone	Spicy, warm, tea-like	Meat flavors, poultry
Thyme	Thymol	Medicinal, burnt	Medicinal flavors
Ylang ylang	Benzyl alcohol, linalool, cresol methyl ether	Fragrant, slight orange	Beverage flavors

SOURCE: BERARDE, M. A. 1971. The Chemicals We Eat. McGraw-Hill Book Co., New York. Published with permission of the publisher.

FLAVOR INGREDIENTS, TASTE AND FLAVOR TYPE

TABLE 2.F.17

CLASSIFICATION OF FLAVOR INGREDIENTS BY PRIMARY TASTE AND FLAVOR TYPE

Flavor ingredient	Taste			Flavor type
	Sweet	Bittersweet	Bitter	
Acetophenone			x	—
Allyl anthranilate		x		Green leaves
Allyl benzoate		x		Cherry
Allyl butyrate		x		Apple, apricot
Allyl caproate		x		Pineapple
Allyl cyclohexylacetate		x		Pineapple
Allyl cyclohexylbutyrate		x		Pineapple
Allyl cyclohexylcaproate		x		Peach, apricot
Allyl cyclohexylpropionate		x		Pineapple
Allyl cyclohexylvalerate		x		Peach, apricot, apple
Allyl formate				Mustard
Allyl isovalerate		x		Apple, cherry
Allyl 2-nonylenate				Pineapple
Allyl pelargonate		x		Cognac, pineapple
Allyl phenoxyacetate		x		Pineapple, honey
Allyl phenylacetate			x	Honey
Allyl propionate		x		Apple, apricot
Allyl salicylate		x		Wintergreen, grape
Allyl undecylate		x		Coconut, peach
n-Amyl butyrate		x		Cherry, apple
Amyl phenylacetate	x			Apricot, peach
Anethol	x			Anise
Anisyl alcohol	x			Peach
Anisyl butyrate		x		Cherry, peach
Anisyl formate	x			Strawberry
Anisyl propionate		x		Cherry
Benzyl acetate			x	—
Benzyl butyrate	x			Pear
Benzyl cinnamate	x			Honey
Benzyl formate	x			Apricot, pineapple
Benzyl isobutyrate	x			Strawberry
Benzyl isovalerate	x			Apple
Benzyl propionate	x			Apricot, peach
Benzyl salicylate	x			Raspberry
Bornyl acetate	x			Pineapple
n-Butyl acetate	x			Pineapple
Butyl formate				Plum
Butyl isobutyrate	x			Pineapple
Butyl isovalerate	x			Apple
Butyl propionate	x			Apricot

TABLE 2.F.17 (*Continued*)

Flavor ingredient	Taste			Flavor type
	Sweet	Bittersweet	Bitter	
Butyl valerate				Apple
Carvacryl acetate		x		Honey
Cinnamaldehyde		x		Cinnamon, melon
Cinnamic acid	x			Apricot
Cinnamyl acetate	x			Pineapple
Cinnamyl alcohol			x	—
Cinnamyl anthranilate		x		Grape
Cinnamyl butyrate	x			Honey
Cinnamyl formate		x		Apple
Cinnamyl isobutyrate	x			Apple
Citral				Lemon
l-Citronellol	x			Peach
Citronellyl acetate	x			Apricot
Citronellyl butyrate	x			Plum
Citronellyl formate	x			Plum
Citronellyl isovalerate	x			Apple
Citronellyl propionate		x		Plum
Coumarin			x	—
p-Cresyl acetate				Honey
p-Cresyl ethyl ether	x			Honey
m-Cresyl phenylacetate	x			Honey
p-Cresyl phenylacetate	x			Honey
Cuminic alcohol		x		Strawberry
Cyclohexyl acetate		x		Apple, banana
Cyclohexyl butyrate		x		Banana, apple, currant
Cyclohexyl caproate		x		Peach, cognac
Cyclohexyl cinnamate				Peach, cherry
Cyclohexyl formate		x		Cherry
Cyclohexyl isovalerate		x		White apple
Cyclohexyl phenylacetate		x		Honey
Cyclohexyl propionate		x		Apple, banana
γ-Decalactone		x		Plum, apricot, peach
Decanal dimethyl acetal			x	Citrus
Decyl acetate	x			Pineapple
Decyl formate	x			Grape
Diacetyl	x			Butter
Dimethylbenzylcarbinol			x	—
Dimethyl hydroquinone			x	—
Dimethyl phenethyl carbinyl acetate			x	—
Dimethyl phenethyl carbinyl propionate	x			Rose-like
Diphenyl ether	x			Black currant
γ-Dodecalactone		x		Apricot, peach
Ethyl acetate		x		Wine

(Continued)

TABLE 2.F.17 (*Continued*)

Flavor ingredient	Taste			Flavor type
	Sweet	Bittersweet	Bitter	
2-Ethylbutyl acetate		x		Pear
Ethyl butyrate	x			Pineapple
Ethyl cinnamate	x			Apricot, peach
Ethyl formate			x	Rum
2-Ethyl-3-furylacrolein		x		Cola
Ethyl heptylate	x			Wine, pear
Ethyl hexadienoate		x		Pineapple, melon
Ethyl isovalerate	x			Apple
Ethyl methylphenylglycidate	x			Strawberry
Ethyl-2-octynoate	x			—
Ethyl phenoxyacetate		x		Pineapple, honey
Ethyl phenylacetate		x		Honey
Ethyl phenylglycidate	x			Strawberry
Ethyl undecylate		x		Coconut
Ethyl undecynoate			x	—
Ethyl valerate		x		Apple, banana
Ethyl vanillin		x		Vanilla
Eugenol			x	Clove buds
Geraniol			x	Rose-like
Geraniol "palmarosa"	x			Peach, apricot
Geranyl acetate			x	—
Geranyl anthranilate			x	—
Geranyl butyrate	x			Apricot
Geranyl formate			x	—
Geranyl isobutyrate	x			Apricot
Geranyl isovalerate	x			Apricot
Geranyl propionate			x	—
Guaiol acetate	x			Black currant, grape
Guaiol butyrate	x			Plum
Guaiol phenylacetate	x			Honey
Heptyl acetate	x			Apricot
Heptyl formate				Plum
Heptyl propionate		x		Apricot
Hexyl acetate		x		Pear
Hexyl butyrate	x			Pineapple
Hexyl formate	x			Plum
Hexyl furan carboxylate		x		Pear, mushroom
α-Ionone	x			Raspberry
Isoamyl acetate		x		Pear
Isoamyl formate	x			Plum
Isoamyl isobutyrate				Pineapple
Isoamyl propionate		x		—

TABLE 2.F.17 (*Continued*)

Flavor ingredient	Taste			Flavor type
	Sweet	Bittersweet	Bitter	
Isoamyl salicylate		x		Strawberry
Isobutyl acetate			x	—
Isobutyl anthranilate		x		Strawberry, grape
Isobutyl butyrate	x			Rum
Isobutyl cinnamate	x			Raspberry
Isobutyl formate	x			Rum
Isobutyl phenylacetate	x			Honey
Isobutyl propionate			x	—
Isobutyl salicylate			x	—
Isopropyl acetate	x			Apple
Isopropyl benzyl carbinol		x		Peach
Isopropyl formate	x			Plum
Isopropyl isovalerate	x			Apple
Isopropyl propionate		x		Plum
Isopropyl valerate		x		Apple
Isovalerophenone		x		Grape
Linalool	x			Plum
Linalyl acetate	x			Black currant
Linalyl anthranilate	x			Orange
Linalyl butyrate	x			Honey
Linalyl formate		x		Pineapple
Linalyl isobutyrate	x			Black currant
Linalyl isovalerate			x	—
Linalyl propionate	x			Black currant
Methyl acetate			x	—
Methylacetophenone	x			Strawberry
2-Methylallyl butyrate		x		Apple, plum
2-Methylallyl caproate		x		Pineapple
Methyl amyl ketone			x	Pear
Methyl anisate	x			Melon
Methyl anthranilate			x	—
Methylbenzyl propionate		x		Cherry
Methyl butyrate	x			Apple
Methyl cinnamate	x			Strawberry
Methyl eugenol			x	Clove
Methylheptenone			x	Pear
Methyl ionone	x			Raspberry, black currant
Methyl isobutyrate	x			Apricot
Methyl isoeugenol			x	Clove
Methyl isovalerate			x	—
Methyl methylanthranilate		x		Peach
Methyl-β-methylpropionate		x		Pineapple
Methyl naphthyl ketone		x		Strawberry

(Continued)

TABLE 2.F.17 (*Continued*)

Flavor ingredient	Taste			Flavor type
	Sweet	Bittersweet	Bitter	
Methyl nonyl ketone	x			Peach
Methyl octine carbonate	x			Peach
Methyl phenylacetate	x			Honey
Methyl phenyl carbinyl acetate				—
Methyl propionate	x			Black currant
Methyl undecylate				Pineapple
Methyl undecyl ketone		x		Coconut
Musk ambrette	x			Peach
Nerol			x	Rose-like
Nerolin	x			Strawberry
Neryl acetate	x			Raspberry
Neryl butyrate	x			Cocoa
Neryl formate			x	—
Neryl isobutyrate	x			Strawberry
Neryl isovalerate			x	—
Neryl propionate	x			Plum
γ-Nonalactone		x		Coconut
Nonyl acetate			x	—
Nonyl alcohol			x	—
γ-Octalactone		x		Peach, coconut, walnut
Octyl acetate	x			Peach
Octyl butyrate	x			Melon
Octyl formate		x		—
Octyl isobutyrate	x			Grape
2-Octynoate	x			—
Phenethyl acetate		x		Honey
Phenethyl alcohol			x	Peach, rose
Phenethyl butyrate	x			Honey
Phenethyl cinnamate			x	—
Phenethyl dimethyl carbinol	x			Apricot
Phenethyl dimethyl carbinyl isovalerate		x		Rose
Phenethyl formate		x		Green plum
Phenethyl isobutyrate		x		Green plum
Phenethyl isovalerate		x		Peach
Phenethyl phenylacetate	x			Honey
Phenethyl propionate				Honey
Phenethyl salicylate	x			Peach
Phenylacetaldehyde dimethyl acetal		x		—
Phenylacetic acid	x			Honey
Phenylallyl alcohol		x		Plum, peach
Phenylglycidate	x			Strawberry
Phenylpropyl acetate		x		Grape
Phenylpropyl alcohol	x			Apricot
Phenylpropyl butyrate	x			Plum

TABLE 2.F.17 (*Continued*)

Flavor ingredient	Taste			Flavor type
	Sweet	Bittersweet	Bitter	
Phenylpropyl cinnamate	x			Cocoa
Phenylpropyl ether		x		Grape
Phenylpropyl isobutyrate		x		Peach
Propenyl guaethol	x			Vanilla
Propyl acetate		x		Pear
Propyl cinnamate		x		Peach, apricot
Propyl formate		x		Plum
Propyl isobutyrate	x			Pineapple
Propyl phenylacetate	x			Honey
Propyl propionate			x	—
Rhodinol			x	Rose
Rhodinyl acetate			x	—
Rhodinyl butyrate	x			Whortleberry
Rhodinyl formate		x		Cherry
Rhodinyl isobutyrate	x			Peach
Rhodinyl isovalerate		x		Cherry
Santalol	x			Woody, raspberry
Santalyl acetate		x		Apricot
Santalyl phenylacetate	x			Honey
Styralyl acetate			x	Grapefruit
Terpenyl acetate	x			Raspberry
Terpenyl anthranilate			x	—
Terpenyl butyrate		x		Plum
Terpenyl cinnamate			x	—
Terpenyl formate				—
Terpenyl isovalerate	x			Apple
Terpenyl propionate		x		—
Terpineol		x		Peach
Tetrahydrofurfuryl propionate		x		Apricot, chocolate
Tetrahydrogeraniol			x	—
Tolualdehyde (*o,m,p*)		x		Cherry, almond
γ-Undecalactone	x			Apricot, peach
Undecynoate			x	—
Vanillin			x	Vanilla
Vanillylidene acetone		x		Vanilla
Yara yara	x			Strawberry

SOURCE: FURIA, T. E., and BELLANCA, N. (EDITORS). 1971. Fenaroli's Handbook of Flavor Ingredients. CRC Press, Cleveland. Used with permission of CRC Press.

FLAVORS, BEVERAGE

TABLE 2.F.18

HANDY GUIDE FOR CHOOSING BEVERAGE FLAVORS

Flavor	Best Type	Best Form	Recommended Strength	Remarks
Birch beer	Natural	Extract or emulsion	1 oz	Because of faint color desired in finished drink, an extract is somewhat better than an emulsion.
Cherry	Natural	Extract-concentrate	4 oz	The 4-oz strength is best for all-round economy and flavor quality. Extract-concentrate gives longest shelf-life.
Cola	Natural	Extract or emulsion	4 oz	Necessary flavor and color can be incorporated in a 4-oz strength. Some additional acid may be needed, however. Because of deep color, either extract or emulsion can be used.
Cream soda	Imitation	Extract	1 oz or 2 oz	A very satisfactory product can be made with aromatic chemicals. Extract affords better, easier dispersion.
Ginger ale	Natural	Extract	4 oz or 2 oz	Flavor bouquet composed mainly of citrus oils, with some flower and spice oils. Extract needed to produce a clear beverage.
Grape	Imitation	Extract	2 oz	Combination of grape extractives, juice, wine, and aromatic chemicals gives excellent flavor with 2 oz.
Grapefruit	Natural	Concentrate Emulsion	1-10 1-17 or 2 oz.	Acceptable flavor obtainable without juice, but juices give added appeal.
Lemon (table beverage)	Natural	Concentrate Emulsion	1-17	Should contain juice and show deep cloud.

Lemon mixer ("UP" tang type)	Natural	Extract	2 oz or ½ oz	Due to solubility of lemon and lime oils, a superior product can be produced in the 2 oz strength.
Lemon and lime (table beverage)	Natural	Emulsion	2 oz 1-10	An emulsion necessary to produce deep cloud.
Orange	Natural	Concentrate Emulsion	1-17 or 2 oz	If economy is prime consideration, 2 oz recommended. There is marked difference, however, in flavor quality of a juice orange and one that contains no juice.
Punch	Natural and imitation	Concentrate Emulsion	1-17 2 oz	In general, there are two types—citrus and berry base. Citrus punch should contain juice and be no more conc. than 1-17. Berry punch can be part artificial with conc. as high as 2 oz.
Raspberry	Natural and imitation	Extract-Concentrate	4 oz 2 oz	There are some good imitation raspberry flavors available using natural extractions and imitation fortifiers, but best flavor is obtained with true fruit.
Root beer	Natural and imitation	Extract or emulsion	4 oz	Root beer is made from oils of sassafras, sweet birch, wintergreen, cassia, spice, citrus, vanillin, and other materials. Finished product is deeply colored with caramel, which occupies volume in extract.
Strawberry	Natural and imitation	Extract-Concentrate	2 oz 4 oz	A mixture of true fruit and imitation flavors has a slight edge over straight true fruit flavor.
Tom Collins	Natural	Emulsion Concentrate	1-10 1-17	Best flavor base is made with heavy emulsion of lemon and lime oils in liberal quantity of concentrated juice.

SOURCE: PHILLIPS, G. F. and WOODROOF, J. G. (EDITORS). 1974. Beverage Acids, Flavors, Colors, and Emulsifiers. *In* Beverages: Carbonated and Noncarbonated. Avi Publishing Co., Westport, Conn.

FLOUR, EXTRACTION RATES

TABLE 2.F.19

COMPOSITION OF FLOURS OF DIFFERENT EXTRACTION RATES

Extraction Rate (%)	Protein (g/100g)	Fat (g/100g)	Carbohydrate (g/100g)	Fiber (g/100g)	Calories (per 100g)
100	12.2	2.4	64.1	2.0	327
85	12.1	1.6	69.8	0.40	342
80	11.7	1.4	70.2	0.21	341
70/72	11.3	1.1	72.0	0.10	343
Patent flour (about 40)	10.0	0.8	74.5	Tr	345

	Thiamin (mg/100g)		Riboflavin (mg/100g)		Nicotinic Acid (mg/100g)		Iron (mg/100g)
Extraction Rate (%)	Mean	Range	Mean	Range	Mean	Range	Mean
100	0.37	0.28-0.46	0.12	0.09-0.15	5.70	4.2-7.2	3.50
85	0.29	0.22-0.36	0.07	0.05-0.09	2.00	1.5-2.5	2.10
80	0.24	0.18-0.39	0.06	0.045-0.075	1.60	1.2-2.0	1.65
70/72	0.08	0.06-0.10	0.05	0.04-0.06	0.80	0.6-1.0	1.25
Patent flour (about 40)	0.05	0.04-0.06	0.03	0.02-0.04	0.70	0.5-0.9	0.90

SOURCE: AYKROYD, W. R. and DOUGHTY, J. 1970. Wheat in Human Nutrition. FAO, United Nations, Rome.

FLOWER, IMPERFECT

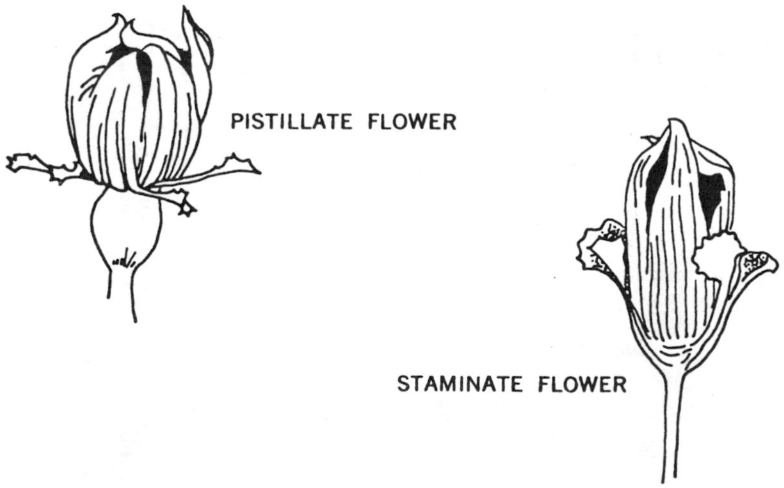

FIG. 2.F.7. THE FLOWERS OF SQUASH, PUMPKINS, CUCUMBERS, MUSKMELONS AND WATERMELONS ARE IMPERFECT, EACH FLOWER HAVING ONLY ONE TYPE OF SEX ORGAN

SOURCE: Handbook for the Home. 1973 Yearbook of Agriculture. USDA.

FLOWER, PERFECT

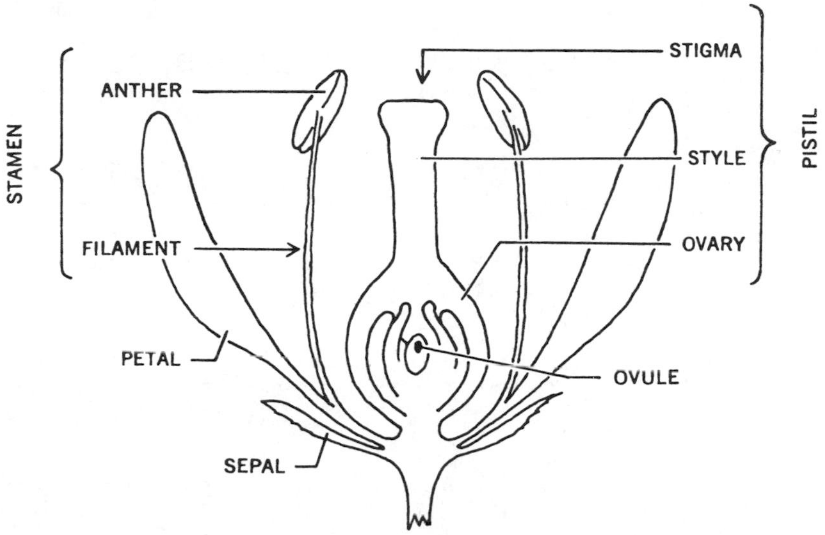

FIG. 2.F.8. SHOWING THE PARTS OF A PERFECT FLOWER WITH BOTH MALE AND FEMALE REPRODUCTIVE ORGANS; STAMEN IS THE MALE ORGAN, PISTIL IS THE FEMALE ORGAN

SOURCE: Handbook for the Home, 1973 Yearbook of Agriculture. USDA.

FLUID AND FERMENTED MILKS, COMPOSITION

TABLE 2.F.20

TYPICAL COMPOSITION OF FLUID AND FERMENTED MILKS

	Moisture	Protein	Fat	Lactose	Ash	Calcium	Phosphorus	Lactic acid	Ethyl alcohol
	%	%	%	%	%	%	%	%	%
Whole milk	87.4	3.5	3.5	4.8	0.7	0.1	0.09		
Chocolate milk	81.5	3.4	3.4	11.0[a]	0.7	0.11	0.09		
Chocolate drink	82.8	3.3	2.3	10.9[a]	0.7	0.11	0.09		
10—2 Milk	87.0	4.2	2.0	6.0	0.8	0.14	0.11		
Low fat, 1%, milk	89.5	3.5	1.0	4.9	0.7	0.12	0.09		
Skim milk	90.5	3.6	0.1	5.1	0.7	0.12	0.09		
Cultured buttermilk	90.5	3.6	0.1[b]	4.3	0.7	0.12	0.10	0.8	
Sour cream	74.5	2.8	18.0	3.4	0.5	0.10	0.08	0.6	
Acidophilus skim milk	90.1	3.5	0.5	4.4	0.7	0.12	0.09	0.7	
Kefir, part skim	89.4	3.5	2.0	4.0	0.7	0.10	0.09	0.6	1.0
Yoghurt, plain	87.2	3.4	3.4	4.1	0.6	0.12	0.09	0.9	
Yoghurt, solids added	83.1	5.0	4.8	6.0	0.8	0.18	—	0.9	
Yoghurt, part skim	89.0	3.4	1.7	5.2	0.7	0.11	0.09	0.9	
Yoghurt, full skim	91.0	3.4	—	4.0	0.7	0.12	0.09	0.9	
Yoghurt, fruit	c	3.4	1.7	12.5[b]	—	0.14	0.10	0.8	

a Carbohydrate other than lactose added. b Additional fat may be added. c Varies with solids content of added fruit.

SOURCE: HARGROVE, ROBERT E and ALFORD, JOHN A. 1974. Composition of Milk Products. *In* Fundamentals of Dairy Chemistry, 2nd Edition. B. H. Webb, A. H. Johnson and J. A. Alford (Editors). Avi Publishing Co., Westport, Conn.

FOOD, COMPOSITION

TABLE 2.F.21

NUTRIENTS IN FOODS PER POUND OF DRY MATTER

Food Item	Water Originally Present (%)	Energy (Cal)	Protein (g)	Fat (g)	Carbo-hydrate (g)	Calcium (mg)	Phos-phorus (mg)	Iron (mg)	Vitamin A (IU)	Thiamin (mg)	Ribo-flavin (mg)	Niacin (mg)
Liquid milk	87.0	2400	122.3	136.1	170.8	4123	3246	2.3	5,538	1.23	6.00	3.84
Nonfat dry milk solids	3.23	1681	173.0	4.3	248.3	6040	4784	2.7	196	1.65	9.58	4.33
Dry whole milk	2.03	2294	123.5	124.5	179.3	4387.7	3619	2.7	6,490	1.32	6.54	3.27
Cottage cheese	74.0	1765	335.4	13.8	75.0	1430	4592	8.0	577	0.31	5.07	1.92
Cheddar cheese	39.0	2924	177.8	240.3	12.6	6496	4539	4.2	12,983	0.33	3.75	1.47
Ice cream, plain	62.0	2507	47.8	146.8	248.4	1576	1242	1.3	6,447	0.45	2.21	1.31
Butter	15.5	3937	3.2	435.1	2.1	86	86	1.1	17,751	0.01	0.06	0.59
Bacon sliced (medium fat)	20.0	3550	51.6	3.7	6.2	74	612	4.5	0	2.38	0.59	11.75
Mayonnaise	16.0	3890	8.1	421.4	16.2	102	323	5.3	1,130	0.19	0.19	0
Eggs, whole fresh	74.0	2446	198.8	178.8	10.7	838	3261	41.9	17,653	1.80	5.19	1.15
Beef, chopped	54.0	3217	158.9	286.9	0	89	1717	23.7	0	0.98	1.26	42.8
Beef, roasting (boned)	67.0	2648	260.0	178.7	0	151	2806	38.4	0	1.60	2.06	70.3
Lamb, leg	63.7	2385	187.0	181.8	0	104	2013	28.0	0	2.20	2.75	61.7
Pork, ham smoked	42.0	2610	115.1	237.9	2.0	69	1239	17.0	0	5.31	1.31	26.0
Pork, loin chops	58.0	2547	143.8	219.0	0	88	1550	21.9	0	9.07	1.78	38.8
Veal, cutlet	70.0	2410	295.0	136.6	0	167	3176	44.0	0	2.66	4.17	97.6
Frankfurters	64.3	2554	193.2	179.3	42.0	115	2087	29.1	0	2.41	2.91	30.0
Liver, fresh	70.9	2051	308.9	65.6	56.0	123	5817	188.6	298,969	4.22	43.74	250.8
Chicken, roaster	66.0	1582	164.7	111.4	0	129	1776	15.6	Trace	0.91	1.44	70.0
Fish, steaks	77.2	1644	317.5	41.6	0	350	3644	16.6	—	1.09	1.09	69.3
Salmon, canned	67.4	2349	286.8	149.0	0	932	3981	18.1	113	0.46	2.45	90.8
Beans, dry	10.5	1774	111.6	7.6	314.9	750	2348	52.3	0	3.03	1.19	10.7
Pecans	3.0	1816	22.8	177.6	31.6	180	788	5.9	124	1.74	0.28	2.2
Beans, snap	88.9	1549	88.3	7.2	283.8	2396	1621	40.5	23,063	2.88	3.69	22.5
Beets	87.6	1250	43.5	2.4	262.9	742	1177	27.4	645	0.88	1.37	11.3
Broccoli	89.9	1020	90.1	5.9	150.5	3564	2089	35.6	96,040	2.57	5.84	24.7

Cabbage	92.4	1250	60.5	9.2	230.2	2000	1355	22.3	3,552	3.02	2.76	11.8
Corn on cob, edible portion	73.9	712	24.5	8.0	136.0	61	796	3.4	2,605	1.03	0.92	9.2
Carrots	88.2	1517	40.6	10.1	315.2	1322	1254	27.1	40,678	2.28	2.20	16.9
Lettuce, head	94.8	1096	73.0	11.5	175.0	1326	1500	30.7	32,884	3.84	4.03	9.6
Mustard greens	92.2	1179	97.4	12.8	169.2	9333	1615	123.0	27,397	3.97	8.71	35.9
Peas, fresh	74.3	801	53.3	3.1	140.4	175	968	15.1	5,408	2.80	1.44	16.3
Potatoes	77.8	1464	34.2	1.8	327.9	189	959	12.1	315	1.80	0.67	19.8
Spinach	92.7	1260	117.8	15.0	163.0	4127	2808	153.4	480,000	6.02	12.30	35.6
Tomatoes	94.1	1542	67.7	20.3	271.1	745	1830	40.6	74,237	4.06	2.70	42.3
Apples	84.1	1622	7.5	10.0	374.8	151	251	7.5	2,264	0.94	0.50	6.3
Bananas	74.8	1186	14.3	2.3	277.3	95	337	7.1	5,158	1.07	0.75	6.7
Strawberries	90.0	1790	35.0	26.0	353.0	1220	1180	35.0	2,500	1.30	2.90	13.0
Grapefruit	88.8	1187	13.3	5.3	270.5	455	482	8.0	625	0.98	0.53	5.3
Oranges	87.2	1281	22.6	5.4	285.9	844	586	10.1	4,840	1.95	0.62	6.2
Peaches	86.9	1557	15.2	3.0	366.4	244	671	18.3	26,946	0.61	1.45	27.4
Cantaloupe	94.0	800	21.6	6.6	163.3	600	566	15.0	121,500	2.00	1.33	28.3
Prunes	24.0	1517	11.7	3.0	360.9	273	431	19.7	9,605	0.50	0.84	8.7
Raisins	24.0	1782	13.7	3.0	425.2	465	771	19.7	302	0.90	0.48	2.9
Corn meal, white	12	1831	38.6	5.6	406.6	51	722	5.1	0	0.82	0.47	4.8
Corn meal, yellow	12	1835	42.8	6.1	402.3	51	722	5.1	1,545	0.77	0.31	4.6
Wheat flour (patent)	12	1831	55.6	4.6	391.6	97	479	15.0	0	2.27	1.36	18.2
Bread, white (enriched)	35.9	1850	60.2	14.2	370.3	396	708	12.8	0	1.71	1.11	15.6
Bread, whole wheat	37	1884	68.4	25.2	345.8	431	2666	18.7	0	2.03	1.11	25.5
Bread, rye	37.6	1913	46.6	24.6	376.1	160	698	5.7	0	1.13	0.29	8.0
Corn flakes	9.3	1798	39.5	3.5	402.0	49	280	4.9	0	0.79	0.43	7.9
Oatmeal	8.3	1962	70.3	36.6	337.6	267	1807	25.7	0	2.71	0.69	5.6
Farina	11	1832	58.6	5.0	388.2	106	638	4.0	0	0.31	0.28	4.9
Whole grain (uncooked)	8.7	1830	58.1	9.9	376.8	189	1914	18.9	0	2.21	0.64	22.6
Macaroni	11	1838	66.3	7.2	376.9	112	734	6.0	0	0.66	0.40	10.6
Rice (white)	12.3	1816	39.3	1.6	411.0	46	476	3.6	0	0.27	0.14	7.2
Molasses	24	1434	0	0	358.4	1630	305	4.0	0	0.47	0.95	16.9
Sugar (Gran.)	0.5	1816	0	0	453.9	0	0	0.5	0	0	0	0
Cocoa	4.3	1562	42.7	89.2	147.0	758	3363	12.8	0	0	1.84	10.8
Olives, green	75.2	2080	21.7	195.5	580.6	1463	217	29.0	6,048	0	0	0
Pickles	95.2	1083	47.9	18.7	179.1	2270	2083	85.4	18,125	0.62	2.29	4.1

SOURCE: COOK, H. L., and DAY, G. H. The Dry Milk Industry. American Dry Milk Institute, Chicago.

FOOD, WATER INTAKE

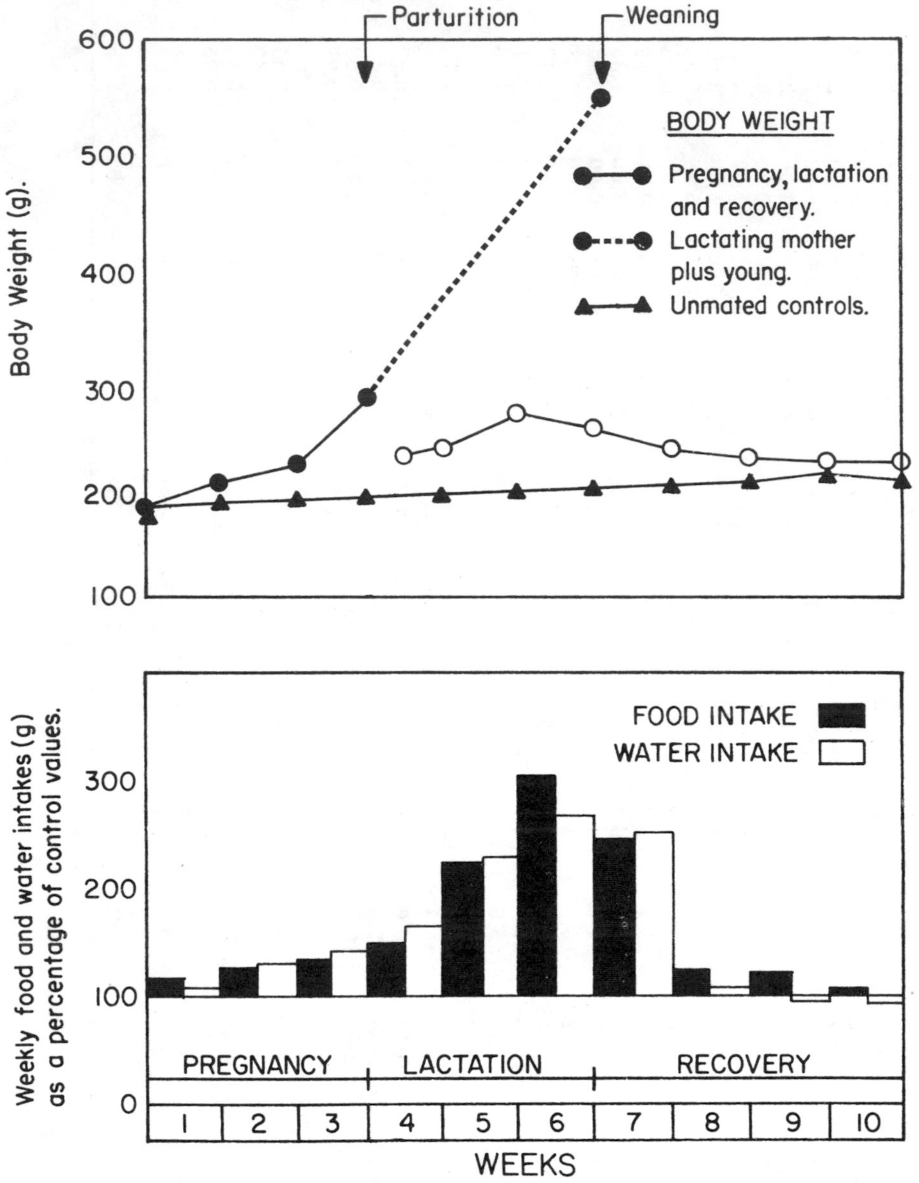

FIG. 2.F.9. MEAN BODY WEIGHT, FOOD AND WATER CONSUMPTION OF FEMALE RATS DURING REPRODUCTION AND SUBSEQUENT RECOVERY

SOURCE: ROE, F. J. C. Metabolic Aspects of Food Safety. Blackwell Scientific Publications, Oxford, England.

FOOD POISONING, BACTERIA

TABLE 2.F.22

CHARACTERISTICS OF FOOD POISONING

Disease	Onset of Symptoms	Type of Food Commonly Involved	Symptoms and Other Characteristics
Botulism	6 hours to 8 days; avg 12-30 hr	Home-canned low-acid vegetables.	Difficulty in swallowing, speech, and respiration; double vision. Death from paralysis of muscles of repiration.
Staphylococcus poisoning	1 to 6 hr; avg $2\frac{1}{2}$-3 hr	Processed meat, potato salad, cream-filled bakery products, dairy products.	Nausea, vomiting, abdominal cramps, diarrhea, and acute prostration and circulatory collapse in occasional severe cases. Usually no fever. No secondary cases.
Salmonellosis	5 to 72 hr	Poultry and poultry products, processed meat.	Abdominal pain, diarrhea, chills, fever, frequent vomiting, and prostration. Secondary cases may occur. Leukocytosis.
Streptococcus faecalis poisoning		Ground meats, dressing.	
Clostridium perfringens poisoning	2 to 18 hr; usually 11-15 hr	Reheated meats, meat pies, and pasties, cold meats, stews, and made-up dishes.	Nausea, seldom vomiting, usually abdominal cramps and diarrhea. Symptoms seldom persist longer than 8-12 hr. No secondary cases. Fever and prostration absent.
Bacillus cereus poisoning		Foods containing cereal products, e.g., vanilla pudding.	

SOURCE: ALBERTSEN, V. E. *et al.* Meat Hygiene. Agricultural Studies *34*, FAO, United Nations.

FREE FATTY ACID, SMOKE, FLASH, FIRE POINTS

TABLE 2.F.23

SMOKE, FLASH AND FIRE POINTS OF SOME FATS AND OILS

Sample	Free Fatty Acids (%)	Smoke (°F)	Flash (°F)	Fire (°F)
Olive oil (edible)	2.1	280	550	670
Safflower oil	1.7	318	603	683
Soybean oil	0.01	443	625	685
Corn oil	0.065	400	618	675
Cottonseed oil	0.04	428	613	680
Tallow (1)	0.34	—	600	650
Tallow (2)	5.3	—	510	650
Tallow (3)	8.0	—	495	615
Tallow (4)	18.0	—	420	500
Tallow (5)	21.0	—	400	475

SOURCE: MAHLENBACHER, C. V. The Analysis of Fats and Oils. Garrard Press, Champaign, Illinois.

FREEZER SIZES

TABLE 2.F.24

SIZE UNIT TO USE ON VARIOUS SIZES OF FREEZERS

Size of Freezer (cu ft)	Min Size Unit to Use (hp)	Size of Freezer (cu ft)	Min Size Unit to Use (hp)
30	1/5 or 1/4	80	1/3 or 1/2
40	1/4 or 1/3	100	1/2 or 3/4
50	1/4 or 1/3	150	3/4
60	1/3		

SOURCE: STOUT, G. J. The Home Freezer Handbook. Van Nostrand Reinhold Co., New York.

FREEZING RATE

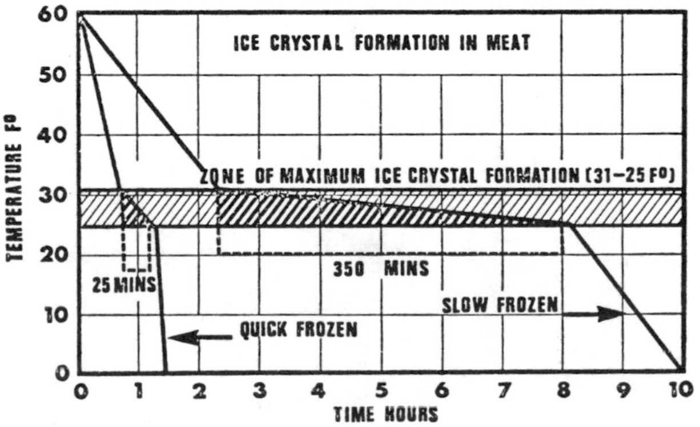

FIG. 2.F.10. ZONE OF MAXIMUM ICE FORMATION

SOURCE: GEARY, D., and GERRARD, F. 1968. Meat and refrigeration. Meat Trades J., London, England.

FRENCH DRESSINGS

French Dressing

½ cup salad oil	1 tsp sugar
2 tbsp vinegar	¼ tsp paprika
1 tsp salt	¼ celery seed

Procedure

Mix the dry ingredients, add vinegar and oil. Shake thoroughly before using. Keep in the refrigerator.

Honey French Dressing

½ cup sugar	1 tsp paprika
⅓ cup strained honey	6 tbsp vinegar or use 3 tbsp vinegar with 3 tbsp lemon juice
1 tsp salt	1 cup salad oil
1 tsp dry mustard	
1 tsp celery seed	

Procedure

Mix the dry ingredients, add the honey, vinegar and oil. Store in refrigerator. Shake well before using. This is a rather sweet dressing.

Red French Dressing

½ small onion	½ tsp salt
½ clove of garlic	½ tsp paprika
2 tbsp vinegar	½ tsp celery salt
¼ cup lemon juice	¼ cup tomato catsup
⅔ cup white corn syrup	½ cup salad oil

Procedure

Chop the garlic and onion and let stand 10 min in the vinegar and lemon juice. Strain. Add the spices, catsup, syrup and oil. Store in the refrigerator. Shake well before using.

Sweet Mustard French Dressing

⅔ cup sugar	1 cup vinegar
2 tsp salt	1 cup oil
2 tsp dry mustard	

Procedure

Mix the dry ingredients, add the oil and vinegar. Shake well before using. This is a good general purpose French dressing. Refrigerate.

Tomato Soup French Dressing

1 can tomato soup	1 tsp paprika
½ cup salad oil	1 chopped green pepper (optional)
¾ cup vinegar	1 chopped onion (optional)
½ cup sugar	
1 tsp dry mustard	

Procedure

Combine all the ingredients in a jar. Shake well before using. Keep refrigerated.

Thick French Dressing (Will Not Separate)

½ cup sugar	1½ cups salad oil
1 pkg prepared pectin	1 tsp Worcestershire sauce
1 tsp paprika	1 tsp minced onion
1 tsp dry mustard	1 can tomato soup
2 tsp salt	1 clove garlic chopped (optional)
⅔ cup vinegar (or less if preferred)	

Procedure

Mix all ingredients and beat with an egg beater. This dressing will not separate. Keep in the refrigerator.

SOURCE: KINTNER, T. C. and MANSEL, M. Vinegars and salad dressings. Univ. Missouri. Agric. Exp. Sta. Bull. *631*.

FRENCH DRESSING VARIATIONS

TABLE 2.F.25

SUGGESTED VARIATIONS TO BE MADE WITH FRENCH DRESSING

Kind	Amount of Dressing	Suggested Additions	Suggested Uses
Cocktail Sauce	1 cup	1 cup chili sauce	Fish sauce
Russian	1 cup	2 tbsp chili sauce 1 tbsp chopped onion	Green or vegetable salads
Red	1 cup	2 tbsp tomato catsup 2 tbsp chopped olives or pickles Sweeten if desired	Green salads Sauces
Roquefort	1 cup	2–4 tbsp crumbled Roquefort or blue cheese Few drops Worcestershire sauce	Green salads
Martinique	1 cup	2 tbsp chopped parsley 2 tbsp green pepper	Green salads
Chiffonade	1 cup	2 tbsp chopped olives 1 tbsp chopped green pepper 1 tbsp chopped onion 1 chopped hard cooked egg	Lettuce or greens
Creamy	1 cup	2–3 tbsp cream (shake well)	Greens
Sweet French	1 cup	4 tbsp confectioner's sugar or 4 tbsp honey	Fruit salads

SOURCE: KINTNER, T. C., and MANGEL, M. Vinegars and salad dressings. Univ. Missouri Agric. Exp. Sta. Bull. *631*.

FROZEN FOOD CONTAINERS

TABLE 2.F.26

FROZEN FOOD CONTAINERS

	Cellophane Bag or Wrapper (Heat Sealed)	Carton with Cellophane Liner (Heat Sealed)	Carton with Thermo-plastic Liner (Heat Sealed)	Carton, No Liner (Thermo-plastic Seal)	Tin-tie Bag (Single)	Tin-tie (Bag) (Double)	Waxed Paper Cup or "Tub"	Round Sealright Paper Container	Tin Can Standard Flange	Tin Can Friction Top	Special Rect "Can" Tin Ends, Paper Sides	Glass Jars
Inexpensive	Yes	No	No	No	Yes	No	No	No	No	No	?	No
Liquid, moisture, and vapor tight	Yes	Yes	Yes	?	No	Yes	Yes	?	Yes	Yes	Yes	Yes
Easily and securely sealed	Yes	Yes	Securely but not easily	No	Easily but not securely	Yes	Yes	Easily, not so securely	?	Yes	No	Yes
Special filling or closing devices required	No	No	?	No	No	No	No	No	Yes	No	Yes	No
Substantial—not broken by usual handling	No	Yes	Yes	Yes	Yes	Yes	Yes	Yes	Yes	Yes	Yes	No
Economical of space	No	Yes	Yes	Yes	No	No	No	No	No	No	Yes	No
Readily emptied without thawing	?	?	Yes	Yes	Yes	Yes	Yes	Yes	Yes	No	Yes	No
Transparent	Yes	Yes	No	No	No	No	No	No	No	No	No	Yes
Easy to mark on or label	No	Yes	Yes	No	Yes	Yes	Yes	Yes	Yes	Yes	Yes	Yes
Readily obtainable	?	?	?	?	Yes	Yes	?	?	Yes	No	No	Yes
Re-usable	No	Carton yes	Carton yes	?	? No	? No	Yes	Yes	Yes	Yes	No	Yes
Heat conductivity good (a question-able virtue)	Yes	No	No	No	No	No	No	No	Yes	Yes	?	Yes
Use: F—fruits V—vege-tables M—meats L—liquids	FVM	FV	VF	V	V	VF	Any-thing	Any-thing	Any-thing	Any-thing	FVM	VFL

SOURCE: STOUT, G. J. The Home Freezer Handbook. Van Nostrand Reinhold Co., New York.

FROZEN FOOD STORAGE I

TABLE 2.F.27

MAXIMUM HOME-STORAGE PERIODS TO MAINTAIN GOOD QUALITY IN PURCHASED FROZEN FOODS

Food	Approximate holding period at 0° F.	Food	Approximate holding period at 0° F.
Fruits and vegetables		*Meat—Continued*	
Fruits:	*Months*	Cooked meat:	*Months*
Cherries	12	Meal dinners	3
Peaches	12	Meat pie	3
Raspberries	12	Swiss steak	3
Strawberries	12	*Poultry*	
Fruit juice concentrates:		Chicken:	
Apple	12	Cut-up	9
Grape	12	Livers	3
Orange	12	Whole	12
Vegetables:		Duck, whole	6
Asparagus	8	Goose, whole	6
Beans	8	Turkey:	
Cauliflower	8	Cut up	6
Corn	8	Whole	12
Peas	8	Cooked chicken and turkey:	
Spinach	8	Chicken or turkey dinners (sliced meat and gravy)	6
Baked goods			
Bread and yeast rolls:			
White bread	3	Chicken or turkey pies	6
Cinnamon rolls	2	Fried chicken	4
Plain rolls	3	Fried chicken dinners	4
Cakes:		*Fish and shellfish*	
Angel	2	Fish:	
Chiffon	2	Fillets:	
Chocolate layer	4	Cod, flounder, haddock, halibut, pollack	6
Fruit	12		
Pound	6		
Yellow	6	Mullet, ocean perch, sea trout, striped bass	3
Danish pastry	3		
Doughnuts:			
Cake type	3	Pacific Ocean perch	2
Yeast raised	3	Salmon steaks	2
Pies (unbaked):		Sea trout, dressed	3
Apple	8	Striped bass, dressed	3
Boysenberry	8	Whiting, drawn	4
Cherry	8	Shellfish:	
Peach	8	Clams, shucked	3
Meat		Crabmeat:	
Beef:		Dungeness	3
Hamburger or chipped (thin) steaks	4	King	10
		Oysters, shucked	4
Roasts	12	Shrimp	12
Steaks	12	Cooked fish and shellfish:	
Lamb:		Fish with cheese sauce	3
Patties (ground meat)	4	Fish with lemon butter sauce	3
Roasts	9		
Pork, cured	2	Fried fish dinner	3
Pork, fresh:		Fried fish sticks, scallops, or shrimp	3
Chops	4		
Roasts	8	Shrimp creole	3
Sausage	2	Tuna pie	3
Veal:		*Frozen desserts*	
Cutlets, chops	9	Ice cream	1
Roasts	9	Sherbet	1

SOURCE: Handbook for the Home. 1973 Yearbook of Agriculture. USDA.

FROZEN FOOD STORAGE II

TABLE 2.F.28

APPROXIMATE STORAGE LIFE OF SOME FROZEN FOODS AT VARIOUS TEMPERATURES[1]

	+10°F Months	0°F Months	-10°F Months
Fish			
Fish, fatty	4	6-8	10-12
Fish, lean	6	10-12	14-16
Fruit			
Apricots, with ascorbic acid	6-8	18-24	24
Apricots, without ascorbic acid	3-4	8-10	12-14
Peaches, with ascorbic acid	6-8	18-24	24
Peaches, without ascorbic acid	3-4	8-10	12-14
Raspberries, sugared	8-10	18	24
Raspberries, without sugar or syrup	6-8	12	18
Strawberries, sliced	8-10	18	24
Meat			
Beef, roasts	6-8	16-18	18-24
Lamb	5-7	14-16	16-18
Pork, roasts	4	8-10	12-15
Pork, sausage	2	4-6	8-10
Poultry			
Poultry, giblets	1	3-5	8-10
Poultry, roasting	4	8-10	12-15
Shellfish			
Lobsters	3-4	8-10	10-12
Shrimp, raw	6	12	16-18
Vegetables			
Asparagus	4-6	8-12	16-18
Beans, snap	4-6	8-12	16-18
Beans, lima	6-8	14-16	24 or longer
Broccoli	6-8	14-16	24 or longer
Brussels sprouts	4-6	8-12	16-18
Cauliflower	6-8	14-16	24 or longer
Corn, on the cob	4-6	8-10	12-14
Corn, cut	12	24	36 or longer
Carrots	12	24	36 or longer
Mushrooms	3-4	8-10	12-14
Peas	6-8	14-16	24 or longer
Pumpkin	12	24	36 or longer
Spinach	6-8	14-16	24 or longer
Squash	12	24	36 or longer

[1] Data compiled by D. K. Tressler (1946A and B) and presented at the First Regional Training Conference, The Refrigeration Research Foundation, Hershey, Pa., 1946. Published in The Refrigeration Research Foundation, Commodity Storage Manual, p. 23, (Appendix C) 1953.

SOURCE: TRESSLER, D. K. and EVERS, C. F. The Freezing Preservation of Foods, 3rd Edition, Vol. *1*. Avi Publishing Co., Westport, Conn.

FROZEN MEAT STORAGE TIME

TABLE 2.F.29

SUGGESTED STORAGE TIMES FOR MEAT AT 0°F

	Months
Beef	8-12
Lamb	8-12
Pork, fresh	4-8
Ground beef and lamb	3-4
Pork Sausage	1-3

SOURCE: How to Buy Meat for Your Freezer. (1969) USDA Home and Garden Bull. *166*.

FRUIT AND NUT ROOTSTOCK

TABLE 2.F.30

DATA FOR ROOTSTOCKS FOR FRUITS AND NUTS

Common Name	Latin Name	Approx Seeds per Ounce	After-ripening Needed for Germination (days)	Speed of Germination at Optimum Temp (days)	Length of Viability (yr)
Almond	*Prunus amygdalus*	12–15	50	15	5
Apple	*Malus domestica*	600–1000	75–100	30	2–3
Apple (crab)	*Malus pumila*	1000	75	30	2–3
Apricot	*Prunus armeniaca*	18–20	60	15	5
Cherry (Mahaleb)	*Prunus mahaleb*	300–350	100	15	1–3 cool-dry
Cherry (sweet) (Mazzard)	*Prunus avium*	150–160	100–120	15	1–2 cool-dry
Cherry (sour)	*Prunus cerasus*	200–250	100–120	15	1–2 cool-dry
Citranges	*Poncirus trifoliata* × *Citrus sinensis*	200–300	None	10–15 at 55°F	Up to 1 yr in polyethylene bag at 45°
Citrus macrophylla	*Citrus macrophylla*	200–300	None	(Same)	(Same)
Fig	*Ficus carica*		Propagated by cuttings		
Filbert	*Corylus maxima*		Propagated by cuttings		
Grapefruit	*Citrus paradisi*	150–200	None	10–15 at 55°F	(Same)
Lemon (rough)	*Citrus limon*	200–300	None	(Same)	(Same)
Lime (sweet)	*Citrus aurantifolia*	300–400	None	(Same)	(Same)
Orange (sweet)	*Citrus sinensis*	200–300	None	(Same)	(Same)
Orange (sour)	*Citrus aurantium*	200–300	None	(Same)	(Same)
Orange (trifoliate)	*Poncirus trifoliata*	200–300	None	(Same)	(Same)
Peach	*Prunus persica*	8–10	100	15	5
Peach (David)	*Prunus davidiana*	10–14	100	15	5
Pear	*Pyrus communis*	750	60–90	45	2–3 dry
Pear (Oriental)	*Pyrus calleryana*	1000	60–90	45	3
Pear (Oriental)	*Pyrus serotina*	1000	60–90	45	3
Pear (Oriental)	*Pyrus ussuriensis*	1000	60–90	45	3
Pecan	*Carya pecan*	8–10	30–90	20	1–3
Plum (American)	*Prunus americana*	50–55	150	30	4–6
Plum (Bessey)	*Prunus besseyi*	160–170	80–100	15	4–6
Plum (Damson)	*Prunus insititia*	100–120	100–120	30	4–6
Plum (Japanese)	*Prunus salicina*	20–40	60–100	15	4–6
Plum (domestic)	*Prunus domestica*	26–30	120	30	4–6
Plum (Myrobalan) (cherry plums)	*Prunus cerasifera*	60–70	80–100	30	4–6
Plum (Marianna)	*Prunus cerasifera*	50–70	100	30	4–6
Plum (Wild Goose)	*Prunus munsoniana*	120–140	80–100	15	4–6
Quince	*Cydonia oblonga*		Propagated by cuttings		
Tangelo	*Citrus reticulata* × *Citrus paradisi*	200–300	None	10–15 at 55°F	Up to 1 yr in polyethylene bag at 45°
Tangerine (Mandarin)	*Citrus reticulata*	300–400	None	(Same)	(Same)
Tung	*Aleurites fordii*	10–15	30–60	10	1–3
Walnut (Eastern black)	*Fuglans nigra*	3	60–120	30	3–5
Walnut (Northern Calif. black)	*Fuglans hindsii*	2–4	60–120	30	3–5
Walnut (Persian)	*Fuglans regia*	2	30–60	20	1–3
Walnut (Paradox hybrid)	*Fuglans hindsii* × *F. regia*	3–4	60–80	25	3–5
Walnut (Royal hybrid)	*Fuglans hindsii* × *F. nigra*	3–5	60–100	25	3–5

SOURCE: Seeds. The Yearbook of Agriculture. USDA.

FRUIT AND VEGETABLES COMPOSITION

TABLE 2.F.31

COMPOSITION OF SELECTED FRUITS AND VEGETABLES, 100 GRAMS EDIBLE PORTION[1]

Food Description	Iron (mg)	Vitamin A Value (IU)	Thiamin (mg)	Ribo-flavin (mg)	Ascorbic Acid (mg)	Sodium (mg)	Potassium (mg)
Apricots							
Raw	0.5	2,700	0.03	0.04	10	1	281
Canned	0.3	1,830	0.02	0.02	4	1	246
Asparagus							
Raw spears	1.0	900	0.18	0.20	33	2	278
Cooked spears, boiled and drained	0.6	900	0.16	0.18	26	1	183
Green, canned spears, regular pack, drained solids	1.9	800	0.06	0.10	15	236	166
Lima beans							
Raw	2.8	290	0.24	0.12	29	2	650
Cooked, boiled, drained	2.5	280	0.18	0.10	17	1	422
Canned, drained solids	2.4	190	0.03	0.05	6	236	222
Frozen, cooked, boiled, drained	1.7	230	0.07	0.05	17	101	426
Green snap beans							
Raw	0.8	600	0.08	0.11	19	7	243
Cooked, boiled and drained	0.6	540	0.07	0.09	12	4	151
Canned, drained solids	1.5	470	0.03	0.05	4	236	95
Frozen, cooked, boiled, drained	0.7	580	0.07	0.09	5	1	152
Cauliflower							
Raw	1.1	60	0.11	0.10	78	13	295
Cooked, boiled, drained	0.7	60	0.09	0.08	55	9	206
Frozen, cooked, boiled, drained	0.5	30	0.04	0.05	41	10	207
Cherries							
Raw, sour, red	0.4	1,000	0.05	0.06	10	2	191
Canned, sour, red, water pack	0.3	680	0.03	0.02	5	2	130
Sweet corn							
Raw	0.7	400	0.15	0.12	12	Tr	280
Cooked, boiled, drained, cut off cob	0.6	400	0.11	0.10	7	Tr	165
Canned, cream style	0.6	330	0.03	0.05	5	Tr	196
Frozen, cooked, boiled, drained	0.8	350	0.09	0.06	5	1	184
Grapefruit							
Raw, all varieties	0.4	20	0.04	0.02	38	1	135
Canned, water pack	0.3	10	0.03	0.02	30	4	144
Peaches							
Raw	0.5	1,330	0.02	0.05	7	1	202
Canned, water pack	0.3	450	0.01	0.03	3	2	137
Peas							
Raw	1.9	640	0.35	0.14	27	2	316
Cooked, boiled, drained	1.8	540	0.28	0.11	20	1	196
Canned, regular pack, drained solids	1.9	690	0.09	0.06	8	236	96
Frozen, cooked, boiled, drained	1.9	600	0.27	0.09	13	115	135
Potatoes							
Raw	0.6	Tr	0.10	0.04	20	3	407
French fried from raw	1.3	Tr	0.13	0.08	21	6	853
Mashed from raw	0.4	170	0.08	0.05	9	331	331
Dehydrated, mashed, prepared	0.5	110	0.04	0.05	3	290	290
Frozen French fries, heated	1.8	Tr	0.14	0.02	21	4	652

[1] The data shown here provide an indication of what may be expected when processed forms are substituted for fresh on an equal weight basis. It is not a measure of the effect of processing on nutritive values. Some differences may be attributed to a difference in the selection of varieties used for the fresh market and for the processed product. In the case of fruit items, the dilution with sirup in the canned product also contributes to the difference between the values for the fresh and canned products.

SOURCE: WHITE, P. L. and SELVEY, N. (EDITORS). 1974. Nutritional Qualities of Fresh Fruits and Vegetables. Futura Publishing Co., Mt. Kisco, N.Y.

FRUIT AND VEGETABLES, COST PER SERVING

The net weight of various foods in the same size can (or glass jar) will vary with the density of the food. Net weight of a No. 10 can of vegetables, for instance, will vary from 6 lb 2 oz for spinach to 6 lb 12 oz for kidney beans. Corn weighs 6 lb 10 oz, peas 6 lb 9 oz, etc. Similarly, No. 10 fruits vary from approximately 6 lb for certain apples to 6 lb 14 oz for peaches in heavy syrup; 7 lb 5 oz for cranberry sauce, all the way up to 7 lb 8 oz for pitted cherries.

Pieces (depends on size) in 1 No. 10 can:
- Can contains 3 qt of juice
- Can contains 12-13 cups
- Can contains 50-60 medium size whole apricots
- Can contains 95-130 medium size apricot halves
- Can contains 45-65 peach or pear halves
- Can contains 28-50 pineapple slices
- Can contains 40-60 plums or prunes
- Can contains 70-90 figs
- Can contains 115-145 asparagus spears
- Can contains 55-65 small whole white potatoes

Approx equivalents of other can sizes:
- 1 No. 10 Can equals 7 No. 303 (1 lb) cans
- 1 No. 10 Can equals 5 No. 2 (1 lb 4 oz) cans
- 1 No. 10 Can equals 4 No. 2-½ (1 lb 13 oz) cans
- 1 No. 10 Can equals 2 No. 3 cyl. (46-50 oz) cans

TABLE 2.F.32

COST PER SERVING CHART FOR NO. 10 CANS OF FRUITS & VEGETABLES

Cost per Case of 6/10	Cost per Can	Number of Servings 20	25[1]	33	50
		⅝ cup 5 fl oz	½ cup 4 fl oz	⅜ cup 3 fl oz	¼ cup 2 fl oz
$2.00	$0.33	0.016	0.013	0.010	0.007
2.25	0.38	0.019	0.015	0.012	0.008
2.50	0.42	0.021	0.017	0.013	0.008
2.75	0.46	0.023	0.018	0.014	0.009
3.00	0.50	0.025	0.020	0.015	0.010
3.25	0.54	0.027	0.022	0.016	0.011
3.50	0.58	0.029	0.023	0.017	0.012
3.75	0.63	0.032	0.025	0.019	0.013
4.00	0.67	0.034	0.027	0.020	0.013
4.25	0.71	0.036	0.028	0.022	0.014
4.50	0.75	0.038	0.030	0.023	0.015
4.75	0.79	0.040	0.032	0.024	0.016
5.00	0.83	0.042	0.033	0.025	0.017
5.25	0.88	0.044	0.035	0.027	0.018
5.50	0.92	0.046	0.037	0.028	0.018
5.75	0.96	0.048	0.038	0.029	0.019
6.00	1.00	0.050	0.040	0.030	0.020
6.25	1.04	0.052	0.042	0.032	0.021
6.50	1.08	0.054	0.043	0.033	0.022
6.75	1.13	0.057	0.045	0.034	0.023
7.00	1.17	0.059	0.047	0.035	0.023
7.50	1.25	0.063	0.050	0.038	0.025
8.00	1.33	0.067	0.053	0.040	0.027
8.50	1.42	0.071	0.057	0.043	0.028
9.00	1.50	0.075	0.060	0.045	0.030

[1] 25 servings per can (½ cup each) is the average serving for most fruits and vegetables.
Source: Wisconsin Canners Association.

SOURCE: The Almanac of the Canning, Freezing, Preserving Industries, 58th Edition. (1973) E. E. Judge & Son, Baltimore.

FRUIT AND VEGETABLES, DISEASE

TABLE 2.F.33

DISEASES AND CONDITIONS COMMON TO FRUITS AND VEGETABLES

Apples

- Internal breakdown
- Internal browning
- Watercore
- Jonathan spot
- Scab (storage)
- Scale
- Blue mold rot
- Bullseye rot

Bananas

- Black rot
- Anthracnose
- Chilling injury
- Scars
- Freeze injury
- Overripe

Cabbage

- Alternaria leaf spot
- Aphids
- Black leaf speck
- Bursting
- Leaf separation from stem
- Yellowing of outer leaves

Cantaloupes

- Coal dust damage
- Fresh cracks
- Ground color
- Low temperature breakdown
- Mold in stem scar
- Surface mold

Carrots

- Broken roots
- Brown, black, or yellow tops
- New top growth
- Wilting and flabbiness of roots
- Wilting of tops

Cauliflower

- Alternaria leaf spot
- Aphids
- Black leaf speck
- Curd discoloration
- Fuzziness
- Riciness
- Ring spot

Celery

- Bacterial soft rot
- Bacterial blight
- Black heart
- Brown stem
- Early blight
- Late blight on leaves or stems
- Pithiness
- Wilting
- Watery soft rot

Citrus

- Stem and rot
- Skin breakdown
- Softness
- Watery breakdown
- Water spot
- Blue and green mold

Cucumbers

- Bacterial spot
- Flabbiness
- Scab

Lettuce

- Bacterial soft rot
- Broken midribs
- Brown blight
- Downy mildew
- Red butts or midribs
- Russet
- Tipburn
- Watery soft rot

Melons (Honeydew and Honeyball)

- Brown discoloration of rind
- Coal dust damage
- Low temperature breakdown
- Cracks, unhealed
- Surface mold
- Free liquid and loose seeds

Onions

- Black mold
- Breakdown
- Gray mold
- Fusarium rot
- Scalding
- Sun scale

Peaches

- California blight
- Discoloration around pit
- Discoloration from brushing injury
- Ground color
- Brown rot

Peppers

- Anthracnose
- Dark discoloration
- Flabbiness
- Shriveling
- Ripe rot

Potatoes

- Greening
- Air cracks
- Black heart
- Late blight
- Southern bacterial wilt
- Ring rot
- Internal browning
- Scald
- Bacterial soft rot
- Sprouts
- Wet breakdown
- Fusarium rot

Tomatoes

- Blossom end rot
- Radial cracks
- Sun scald
- Late blight
- Rhizopus
- Catface
- Alternaria
- Fusarium rot

SOURCE: U.S. Department of the Army, Food Inspection Specialist, *TM 8-451*, 1969.

FRUIT, AVAILABILITY

TABLE 2.F.34

AVAILABILITY OF FRESH FRUIT
G = Good Supply F = Fair Supply S = Small Supply

	January	February	March	April	May	June	July	August	September	October	November	December
Apples	G	G	G	G	F	S	S	S	G	G	G	G
Apricots					S	G	G	S				
Avocados	G	G	G	G	G	F	F	F	F	F	G	G
Bananas	G	G	G	G	G	G	G	G	G	G	G	G
Berries (misc)					S	G	G	G	S	S	S	
Blueberries					S	G	G	G	S			
Cantaloup		S	S	S	F	G	G	G	G	S	S	
Cherries				S	G	G	S	S				
Cranberries	S								F	F	G	G
Dates	G	F	F	S	S	S	S	S	S	G	G	G
Figs						F	G	G	F			
Grapefruit	G	G	G	G	G	F	S	S	S	G	G	G
Grapes	S	S	S	S	S	F	G	G	G	G	G	F
Honeydews		F	G	F	F	G	G	G	G	G	S	S
Lemons	G	G	G	G	G	G	G	G	G	G	G	G
Limes	S	S	S	S	G	G	G	F	F	F	S	G
Mangoes			S	F	G	G	G	F	S			
Nectarines	S	S				F	G	G	G	S		
Oranges	G	G	G	G	G	F	S	S	S	F	G	G
Papayas	S	S	S	S	F	S	S	S	S	F	S	S
Peaches					S	G	G	G	G	S		
Pears	F	F	F	F	F	S	S	G	G	G	G	F
Pineapple	S	F	G	G	G	G	F	F	S	F	F	F
Plums-prunes						G	G	G	G	S		
Strawberries	S	S	F	G	G	G	G	S	S	S	S	S
Tangelos	F	S							S	F	G	G
Tangerines	G	S	S	S	S	S				S	G	G
Watermelons	S	S	S	S	F	G	G	G	S	S	S	S

NOTE: Each year's production will vary. This chart is an estimate of probable availability.

SOURCE: Food For Us All. Yearbook of Agriculture (1969). USDA, Washington, D.C.

FRUIT CLASSIFICATION I

TABLE 2.F.35

CHART SHOWING CLASSIFICATION OF FRUITS

Fleshy							
Simple							
Berry	Pepo	Hesperidium	Drupe	Pome	Multiple	Aggregate	Dry
Cranberry	Cucumber	Orange	Cherry	Apple	Pineapple	Blackberry	Legumes
Blueberry	Squash	Grapefruit	Peach	Pear	Fig	Dewberry	Nuts
Gooseberry	Pumpkin	Lemon	Plum	Quince	Mulberry	Loganberry	Grains
Huckleberry	Muskmelon	Lime	Apricot			Raspberry	
Currant	Watermelon	Tangerine	Nectarine			Strawberry	
Grape		Kumquat	Prune				
Banana			Olive				
Tomato			Coconut[1]				
Eggplant			Date				

[1] The coconut is a somewhat modified fruit, the edible portion being a part of the food storage inside the hard seed, often called the endosperm.

SOURCE: JUSTIN, M. M., RUST, L. O., and VAIL, G. E. Foods, Revised Edition. Houghton Mifflin Co., Boston.

FRUIT CLASSIFICATION, II

TABLE 2.F.36

CLASSIFICATION OF FRUITS AND VEGETABLES ACCORDING TO SYSTEMATIC POSITION, TYPE, AND USE

Family	Fruit/ Vegetable	Scientific Name	Type	Description
			A. Fruits	
Anarcardiaceae	Cashew	*Anacardium occidentale* L.	Nut	The woody achene is borne on a fleshy receptacle.
	Mango	*Mangifera indica* L.	Fleshy drupe	Tough rind, extensive fleshy mesocarp with a stony outer endocarp and inner papyraceous membrane.
Annonaceae	Sugar apple	*Annona squamosa* L.	Aggregate	Each fruitlet is a small berry.
	Soursop	*Annona muricata* L.	Aggregate	Large, fleshy with soft, spiny rind. Multiple accessory fruit. Fruitlets (berries) fused together with associated bracts and floral axis.
Bromeliaceae	Pineapple	*Ananas comosus* Merr.	Sorosis	Multiple accessory fruit.
Bombacaceae	Durian	*Durio zibethinus* L.	Berry	Thick, bony dehiscent rind covered with hard sharp spines.
Caricaceae	Papaya	*Carica papaya* L.	Berry	Fleshy pericarp with large central cavity; derived from superior ovary.
Cucurbitaceae	Watermelon	*Citrullus vulgaris* Schrad	Pepo	Modified berry formed from an inferior ovary with well-developed carpel wall including some receptacle tissue.
	Melon	*Cucumis Melo* L.	Pepo	–ditto–
Guttiferae	Mangosteen	*Garcinia mangostana* L.	Berry	Thick, tough skin with sweet flesh adhering to the seeds.
Lauraceae	Avocado	*Persea americana* Mill	Berry	Thick exocarp, fleshy mesocarp and a very thin layer of endocarp next to the outer seed coat. Testa is hard.
Meliaceae	Lanzones, Langsat	*Lansium domesticum* Correa	Berry	Leathery exocarp, thin mesocarp and fleshy endocarp.
	Santol	*Sandoricum koetjape* M.	Berry	Exocarp fused with mesocarp with fleshy fibrous aril adhering to seeds.
Moraceae	Fig	*Ficus carica* L.	Synconium	Multiple accessory fruit, mainly a fleshy hollow receptacle bearing numerous small achenes.
	Jackfruit	*Artocarpus integra* L.	Multiple	Very large, fruit with sharp protruberances, thick endocarp fused with the mesocarp, aromatic, and rich in latex.
Musaceae	Banana	*Musa paradisiaca* L. var. *sapientum*	Berry	Fruits borne in bunches bearing fingers.
Myrtaceae	Duhat	*Syzygium cumini* Skeels	Drupe	Dark purple fruit, clustered, high in tannins and anthocyanins.
	Guava	*Psidium guajava* L.	Berry	Pericarp is not distinct.
	Makopa	*Eugenia javanica* Lam.	Berry	Cone-shaped fruit with porous pericarp.
Passifloraceae	Passion fruit	*Passiflora edulis* Sims.	Berry	Thick pericarp with shell-like, brittle rind.
Rosaceae	Strawberry	*Fragaria vesca* L.	Etaenio	Aggregate accessory fruit, mainly a large fleshy receptacle bearing externally numerous small achenes.
Rutaceae	Orange	*Citrus sinensis* Osbeck	Hesperidium	Modified berry with well-developed endocarp.
Sapindaceae	Rambutan	*Nephellium lappaceum* L.	Berry	Fruit covered with soft spines, leathery rind and juicy aril.
Sapotaceae	Cainito	*Chrysophyllum cainito* L.	Berry	Very fleshy, juicy endocarp, rich in latex.
	Chico	*Achras sapota* L.	Berry	Mesocarp fused with endocarp.

SOURCE: PANTASTICO, ER. B. (EDITOR). 1975. Structure of Fruits and Vegetables. *In* Postharvest Physiology, Handling and Utilization of Tropical and Subtropical Fruits and Vegetables. Avi Publishing Co., Westport, Conn.

FRUIT COMPOSITION, PART I

TABLE 2.F.37

NUTRITIVE VALUES OF THE EDIBLE PART OF FRUITS AND FRUIT PRODUCTS

[Dashes in the columns for nutrients show that no suitable value could be found although there is reason to believe that a measurable amount of the nutrient may be present]

Food, Approximate Measure, and Weight in Grams		(g)	Water (%)	Food Energy (Cal)	Protein (g)	Fat (g)
Apples, raw (about 3 per lb)[1]	1 apple	150	85	70	Tr	Tr
Apple juice, bottled or canned	1 cup	248	88	120	Tr	Tr
Applesauce, canned:						
Sweetened	1 cup	255	76	230	1	Tr
Unsweetened or artificially sweetened	1 cup	244	88	100	1	Tr
Apricots:						
Raw (about 12 per lb)[1]	3 apricots	114	85	55	1	Tr
Canned in heavy syrup	1 cup	259	77	220	2	Tr
Dried, uncooked (40 halves per cup)	1 cup	150	25	390	8	1
Cooked, unsweetened, fruit and liquid	1 cup	285	76	240	5	1
Apricot nectar, canned	1 cup	251	85	140	1	Tr
Avocados, whole fruit, raw:[1]						
California (mid- and late-winter; diam 3⅛ in.)	1 avocado	284	74	370	5	37
Florida (late summer, fall; diam 3⅝ in.)	1 avocado	454	78	390	4	33
Bananas, raw, medium size[1]	1 banana	175	76	100	1	Tr
Banana flakes	1 cup	100	3	340	4	1
Blackberries, raw	1 cup	144	84	85	2	1
Blueberries, raw	1 cup	140	83	85	1	1
Cantaloup, raw; medium, 5-in. diam about 1⅔ lb[1]	½ melon	385	91	60	1	Tr
Cherries, canned, red, sour, pitted, water pack	1 cup	244	88	105	2	Tr
Cranberry juice cocktail, canned	1 cup	250	83	165	Tr	Tr
Cranberry sauce, sweetened, canned, strained	1 cup	277	62	405	Tr	1
Dates, pitted, cut	1 cup	178	22	490	4	1
Figs, dried, large, 2 × 1 in.	1 fig	21	23	60	1	Tr
Fruit cocktail, canned, in heavy syrup	1 cup	256	80	195	1	Tr
Grapefruit:						
Raw, medium, 3¾-in. diam[1]						
White	½ grapefruit	241	89	45	1	Tr
Pink or red	½ grapefruit	241	89	50	1	Tr
Canned, syrup pack	1 cup	254	81	180	2	Tr
Grapefruit juice:						
Fresh	1 cup	246	90	95	1	Tr
Canned, white:						
Unsweetened	1 cup	247	89	100	1	Tr
Sweetened	1 cup	250	86	130	1	Tr
Frozen, concentrate, unsweetened:						
Undiluted, can, 6 fl oz	1 can	207	62	300	4	1
Diluted with 3 parts water, by volume	1 cup	247	89	100	1	Tr
Dehydrated crystals	4 oz	113	1	410	6	1
Prepared with water (1 lb yields about 1 gal.)	1 cup	247	90	100	1	Tr
Grapes, raw:[1]						
American type (slip skin)	1 cup	153	82	65	1	1
European type (adherent skin)	1 cup	160	81	95	1	Tr

TABLE 2.F.37 (*Continued*)

Fatty Acids										
Saturated (Total) (g)	Unsaturated Oleic (g)	Unsaturated Linoleic (g)	Carbo-hydrate (g)	Cal-cium (mg)	Iron (mg)	Vitamin A Value (IU)	Thia-min (mg)	Ribo-flavin (mg)	Niacin (mg)	Ascorbic Acid (mg)
—	—	—	18	8	0.4	50	0.04	0.02	0.1	3
—	—	—	30	15	1.5	—	0.02	0.05	0.2	2
—	—	—	61	10	1.3	100	0.05	0.03	0.1	3[2]
—	—	—	26	10	1.2	100	0.05	0.02	0.1	2[2]
—	—	—	14	18	0.5	2,890	0.03	0.04	0.7	10
—	—	—	57	28	0.8	4,510	0.05	0.06	0.9	10
—	—	—	100	100	8.2	16,350	0.02	0.23	4.9	19
—	—	—	62	63	5.1	8,550	0.01	0.13	2.8	8
—	—	—	37	23	0.5	2,380	0.03	0.03	0.5	8[2]
7	17	5	13	22	1.3	630	0.24	0.43	3.5	30
7	15	4	27	30	1.8	880	0.33	0.61	4.9	43
—	—	—	26	10	0.8	230	0.06	0.07	0.8	12
—	—	—	89	32	2.8	760	0.18	0.24	2.8	7
—	—	—	19	46	1.3	290	0.05	0.06	0.5	30
—	—	—	21	21	1.4	140	0.04	0.08	0.6	20
—	—	—	14	27	0.8	6,540[3]	0.08	0.06	1.2	63
—	—	—	26	37	0.7	1,660	0.07	0.05	0.5	12
—	—	—	42	13	0.8	Tr	0.03	0.03	0.1	40[4]
—	—	—	104	17	0.6	60	0.03	0.03	0.1	6
—	—	—	130	105	5.3	90	0.16	0.17	3.9	0
—	—	—	15	26	0.6	20	0.02	0.02	0.1	0
—	—	—	50	23	1.0	360	0.05	0.03	1.3	5
—	—	—	12	19	0.5	10	0.05	0.02	0.2	44
—	—	—	13	20	0.5	540	0.05	0.02	0.2	44
—	—	—	45	33	0.8	30	0.08	0.05	0.5	76
—	—	—	23	22	0.5	—[5]	0.09	0.04	0.4	92
—	—	—	24	20	1.0	20	0.07	0.04	0.4	84
—	—	—	32	20	1.0	20	0.07	0.04	0.4	78
—	—	—	72	70	0.8	60	0.29	0.12	1.4	286
—	—	—	24	25	0.2	20	0.10	0.04	0.5	96
—	—	—	102	100	1.2	80	0.40	0.20	2.0	396
—	—	—	24	22	0.2	20	0.10	0.05	0.5	91
—	—	—	15	15	0.4	100	0.05	0.03	0.2	3
—	—	—	25	17	0.6	140	0.07	0.04	0.4	6

(Continued)

TABLE 2.F.37 (*Continued*)

Food, Approximate Measure, and Weight in Grams		(g)	Water (%)	Food Energy (Cal)	Protein (g)	Fat (g)
Grapejuice:						
Canned or bottled	1 cup	253	83	165	1	Tr
Frozen concentrate, sweetened:						
Undiluted, can, 6 fl oz	1 can	216	53	395	1	Tr
Diluted with 3 parts water, by volume	1 cup	250	86	135	1	Tr
Grapejuice drink, canned	1 cup	250	86	135	Tr	Tr
Lemons, raw, 2⅛-in. diam, size 165[1], used for juice	1 lemon	110	90	20	1	Tr
Lemon juice, raw	1 cup	244	91	60	1	Tr
Lemonade concentrate:						
Frozen, 6 fl oz per can	1 can	219	48	430	Tr	Tr
Diluted with 4⅓ parts water, by volume	1 cup	248	88	110	Tr	Tr
Lime juice:						
Fresh	1 cup	246	90	65	1	Tr
Canned, unsweetened	1 cup	246	90	65	1	Tr
Limeade concentrate, frozen:						
Undiluted, can, 6 fl oz	1 can	218	50	410	Tr	Tr
Diluted with 4⅓ parts water, by volume	1 cup	247	90	100	Tr	Tr
Oranges, raw, 2⅝-in. diam, all commercial varieties[1]	1 orange	180	86	65	1	Tr
Orange juice, fresh, all varieties	1 cup	248	88	110	2	1
Canned, unsweetened	1 cup	249	87	120	2	Tr
Frozen concentrate:						
Undiluted, can, 6 fl oz	1 can	213	55	360	5	Tr
Diluted with 3 parts water, by volume	1 cup	249	87	120	2	Tr
Dehydrated crystals	4 oz	113	1	430	6	2
Prepared with water (1 lb yields about 1 gal.)	1 cup	248	88	115	2	1
Orange-apricot juice drink	1 cup	249	87	125	1	Tr
Orange and grapefruit juice:						
Frozen concentrate:						
Undiluted, can, 6 fl oz	1 can	210	59	330	4	1
Diluted with 3 parts water, by volume	1 cup	248	88	110	1	Tr
Papayas, raw, ½-in. cubes	1 cup	182	89	70	1	Tr
Peaches:						
Raw:						
Whole, medium, 2-in. diam, about 4 per lb[1]	1 peach	114	89	35	1	Tr
Sliced	1 cup	168	89	65	1	Tr
Canned, yellow-fleshed, solids and liquid:						
Syrup pack, heavy:						
Halves or slices	1 cup	257	79	200	1	Tr
Water pack	1 cup	245	91	75	1	Tr
Dried, uncooked	1 cup	160	25	420	5	1
Cooked, unsweetened, 10–12 halves and juice	1 cup	270	77	220	3	1
Frozen:						
Carton, 12 oz, not thawed	1 carton	340	76	300	1	Tr

TABLE 2.F.37 *(Continued)*

Fatty Acids Saturated (Total) (g)	Fatty Acids Unsaturated Oleic (g)	Fatty Acids Unsaturated Linoleic (g)	Carbo-hydrate (g)	Cal-cium (mg)	Iron (mg)	Vitamin A Value (IU)	Thia-min (mg)	Ribo-flavin (mg)	Niacin (mg)	Ascorbic Acid (mg)
—	—	—	42	28	0.8	—	0.10	0.05	0.5	Tr
—	—	—	100	22	0.9	40	0.13	0.22	1.5	—[6]
—	—	—	33	8	0.3	10	0.05	0.08	0.5	—[6]
—	—	—	35	8	0.3	—	0.03	0.03	0.3	—[6]
—	—	—	6	19	0.4	10	0.03	0.01	0.1	39
—	—	—	20	17	0.5	50	0.07	0.02	0.2	112
—	—	—	112	9	0.4	40	0.04	0.07	0.7	66
—	—	—	28	2	Tr	Tr	Tr	0.02	0.2	17
—	—	—	22	22	0.5	20	0.05	0.02	0.2	79
—	—	—	22	22	0.5	20	0.05	0.02	0.2	52
—	—	—	108	11	0.2	Tr	0.02	0.02	0.2	26
—	—	—	27	2	Tr	Tr	Tr	Tr	Tr	5
—	—	—	16	54	0.5	260	0.13	0.05	0.5	66
—	—	—	26	27	0.5	500	0.22	0.07	1.0	124
—	—	—	28	25	1.0	500	0.17	0.05	0.7	100
—	—	—	87	75	0.9	1,620	0.68	0.11	2.8	360
—	—	—	29	25	0.2	550	0.22	0.02	1.0	120
—	—	—	100	95	1.9	1,900	0.76	0.24	3.3	408
—	—	—	27	25	0.5	500	0.20	0.07	1.0	109
—	—	—	32	12	0.2	1,440	0.05	0.02	0.5	40[4]
—	—	—	78	61	0.8	800	0.48	0.06	2.3	302
—	—	—	26	20	0.2	270	0.16	0.02	0.8	102
—	—	—	18	36	0.5	3,190	0.07	0.08	0.5	102
—	—	—	10	9	0.5	1,320[7]	0.02	0.05	1.0	7
—	—	—	16	15	0.8	2,230[7]	0.03	0.08	1.6	12
—	—	—	52	10	0.8	1,100	0.02	0.06	1.4	7
—	—	—	20	10	0.7	1,100	0.02	0.06	1.4	7
—	—	—	109	77	9.6	6,240	0.02	0.31	8.5	28
—	—	—	58	41	5.1	3,290	0.01	0.15	4.2	6
—	—	—	77	14	1.7	2,210	0.03	0.14	2.4	135[8]

(Continued)

TABLE 2.F.37 *(Continued)*

Food, Approximate Measure, and Weight in Grams		(g)	Water (%)	Food Energy (Cal)	Protein (g)	Fat (g)
Pears:						
Raw, 3 by 2½-in. diam[1]	1 pear	182	83	100	1	1
Canned, solids and liquid:						
Syrup pack, heavy:						
Halves or slices	1 cup	255	80	195	1	1
Pineapple:						
Raw, diced	1 cup	140	85	75	1	Tr
Canned, heavy syrup pack, solids and liquid:						
Crushed	1 cup	260	80	195	1	Tr
Sliced, slices and juice	2 small or 1 large	122	80	90	Tr	Tr
Pineapple juice, canned	1 cup	249	86	135	1	Tr
Plums, all except prunes:						
Raw, 2-in. diam, about 2 oz[1]	1 plum	60	87	25	Tr	Tr
Canned, syrup pack (Italian prunes):						
Plums (with pits) and juice[1]	1 cup	256	77	205	1	Tr
Prunes, dried, "softenized," medium:						
Uncooked[1]	4 prunes	32	28	70	1	Tr
Cooked, unsweetened, 17-18 prunes and ⅓ cup liquid[1]	1 cup	270	66	295	2	1
Prune juice, canned or bottled	1 cup	256	80	200	1	Tr
Raisins, seedless:						
Packaged, ½ oz or 1½ tbsp per pkg	1 pkg	14	18	40	Tr	Tr
Cup, pressed down	1 cup	165	18	480	4	Tr
Raspberries, red:						
Raw	1 cup	123	84	70	1	1
Frozen, 10-oz carton, not thawed	1 carton	284	74	275	2	1
Rhubarb, cooked, sugar added	1 cup	272	63	385	1	Tr
Strawberries:						
Raw, capped	1 cup	149	90	55	1	1
Frozen, 10-oz carton, not thawed	1 carton	284	71	310	1	1
Tangerines, raw, medium, 2⅜-in. diam, size 176[1]	1 tangerine	116	87	40	1	Tr
Tangerine juice, canned, sweetened	1 cup	249	87	125	1	1
Watermelon, raw, wedge, 4 × 8 in. (1/16 of 10 × 16-in. melon, about 2 lb with rind)[1]	1 wedge	925	93	115	2	1

[1] Measure and weight apply to entire fruit including parts not usually eaten.
[2] This is the amount from the fruit. Additional ascorbic acid may be added by the manufacturer. Refer to the label for this information.
[3] Value for varieties with orange-colored flesh; value for varieties with green flesh would be about 540 IU.
[4] Value listed is based on products with label stating 30 mg per 6 fl oz serving.
[5] For white-fleshed varieties value is about 20 IU per cup; for red-fleshed varieties, 1080 IU per cup.
[6] Present only if added by the manufacturer. Refer to the label for this information.
[7] Based on yellow-fleshed varieties; for white-fleshed varieties value is about 50 IU per 114-g peach and 80 IU per cup of sliced peaches.
[8] This value includes ascorbic acid added by manufacturer.

SOURCE: ANON. Nutritive Value of Foods. USDA Inst. Home Econ., Home Garden Bull. 72.

TABLE 2.F.37 (*Continued*)

Fatty Acids											
Saturated (Total) (g)	Unsaturated Oleic (g)	Unsaturated Linoleic (g)	Carbo-hydrate (g)	Cal-cium (mg)	Iron (mg)	Vitamin A Value (IU)	Thia-min (mg)	Ribo-flavin (mg)	Niacin (mg)	Ascorbic Acid (mg)
—	—	—	25	13	0.5	30	0.04	0.07	0.2	7
—	—	—	50	13	0.5	Tr	0.03	0.05	0.3	4
—	—	—	19	24	0.7	100	0.12	0.04	0.3	24
—	—	—	50	29	0.8	120	0.20	0.06	0.5	17
—	—	—	24	13	0.4	50	0.09	0.03	0.2	8
—	—	—	34	37	0.7	120	0.12	0.04	0.5	22[2]
—	—	—	7	7	0.3	140	0.02	0.02	0.3	3
—	—	—	53	22	2.2	2,970	0.05	0.05	0.9	4
—	—	—	18	14	1.1	440	0.02	0.04	0.4	1
—	—	—	78	60	4.5	1,860	0.08	0.18	1.7	2
—	—	—	49	36	10.5	—	0.03	0.03	1.0	5[2]
—	—	—	11	9	0.5	Tr	0.02	0.01	0.1	Tr
—	—	—	128	102	5.8	30	0.18	0.13	0.8	2
—	—	—	17	27	1.1	160	0.04	0.11	1.1	31
—	—	—	70	37	1.7	200	0.06	0.17	1.7	59
—	—	—	98	212	1.6	220	0.06	0.15	0.7	17
—	—	—	13	31	1.5	90	0.04	0.10	1.0	88
—	—	—	79	40	2.0	90	0.06	0.17	1.5	150
—	—	—	10	34	0.3	360	0.05	0.02	0.1	27
—	—	—	30	45	0.5	1,050	0.15	0.05	0.2	55
—	—	—	27	30	2.1	2,510	0.13	0.13	0.7	30

FRUIT COMPOSITION, PART II

TABLE 2.F.38

COMPOSITION OF THE EDIBLE PORTION (E.P.) AND REFUSE IN THE MATERIAL AS PURCHASED (A.P.)

Commodity and Description	Water	Protein	Fat	Carbohydrate Total (by dif.)	Carbohydrate Fiber	Ash	Calories (per 100 g)	Notes	Refuse in A.P. (%)
	Percent of edible portion								
Bananas and plantains, fresh									
Bananas (*Musa sapientum*)	73.5	1.3	0.4	24.0	0.5	0.8	94	Edible raw when ripe; can apply in all areas	29
Plantains (*Musa paradisiaca*)	68.2	1.2	0.5	29.2	0.4	0.9	113	Require cooking; can apply in producing areas	34
Both, unspecified (*Musa* spp.)	71.0	1.2	0.4	26.5	0.5	0.9	103	Can apply in producing areas	31
Citrus, fresh									
Grapefruit (*Citrus grandis*)	89.0	0.6	0.2	9.8	0.5	0.4	39		36
Lemons (*C. limonia*)	88.7	0.8	0.5	9.5	0.9	0.5	41		38
Limes (*C. aurantifolia*)	86.8	0.9	0.4	11.2	1.3	0.7	47	Juice only	(65)
Oranges (*C. sinensis*)	87.1	0.9	0.2	11.3	0.8	0.5	45		28
Oranges, Mandarin type (*C. nobilis*)	87.4	0.8	0.3	10.9	0.6	0.6	44		29
Other fruits, fresh									
Apples (*Malus sylvestris*)	84.0	0.3	0.4	15.0	0.9	0.3	58		16
Apricots (*Prunus armeniaca*)	85.3	0.9	0.2	12.9	1.0	0.7	51		9
Avocados (*Persea* spp.), all types	75	1.7	16	6.1	1.5	1.2	162		32
Low fat types	82.9	1.4	8.3	6.5	1.5	0.9	98		33
High fat types	67.1	1.8	23.4	6.3	1.7	1.4	225		30
Berries									
Blackberries (*Rubus* spp.)	84.9	1.2	1.0	12.4	3.8	0.5	57		0
Blueberries (*Vaccinium* spp.)	85.0	0.7	0.7	13.3	1.9	0.3	56		0
Cranberries (*Oxycoccus macrocarpus*)	87.3	0.4	0.7	11.4	1.4	0.2	48		0
Currants (*Ribes* spp.)	83.7	1.4	0.4	13.9	3.2	0.6	58		3
Gooseberries (*Ribes* spp.)	88.4	1.0	0.4	9.8	2.0	0.4	42		1
Raspberries (*Rubus* spp.)	82.7	1.3	1.3	14.2	3.9	0.5	66		0
Strawberries (*Fragaria* spp.)	89.9	0.8	0.5	8.3	1.2	0.5	37		4
All, unspecified	86.5	1.0	0.7	11.3	2.4	0.5	50		2
Breadfruit, jackfruit, monkey fruit (*Artocarpus* spp.)	76.2	1.1	0.4	21.3	1.8	1.0	84		45
Cherimoya, custard apple, sweetsop (*Annona cherimola, A. reticulata, A. squamosa*)	73.3	1.9	0.5	23.5	2.9	0.8	95		40
Cherries (*Prunus* spp.)	83.4	1.1	0.4	14.6	0.5	0.5	60		9

Figs (*Ficus carica*)	81.7	1.2	0.4	16.1	1.4	0.6	65		3
Grapes (*Vitis* spp.)	81.5	0.8	0.4	16.8	0.5	0.5	67		8
Guavas (*Psidium* spp.)	80.6	1.0	0.4	17.3	6.2	0.7	69		22
Mangoes (*Mangifera indica*)	81.7	0.7	0.2	17.0	0.8	0.4	65		38
Melons:									
Muskmelons (*Cucumis melo*)	92.6	0.7	0.2	6.0	0.5	0.5	26		44
Watermelons (*Citrullus vulgaris*)	92.9	0.5	0.2	6.1	0.2	0.3	25		47
Both, unspecified	92.8	0.6	0.2	6.0	0.3	0.4	25		46
Papayas (*Carica papaya*)	88.6	0.6	0.1	10.1	0.9	0.6	39		34
Passion fruit or granadillo (*Passiflora* spp.)	80.0	0.6	(0)	18.9	(0)	0.5	70	Juice only	67
Peaches (*Amygdalus persica*)	86.6	0.8	0.2	11.8	0.6	0.6	47		12
Pears (*Pyrus communis*)	83.2	0.5	0.4	15.5	1.5	0.4	61		18
Persimmons, Japanese (*Diospyros kaki*)	79.6	0.8	0.3	18.7	1.2	0.6	73		20
Pineapples (*Ananas sativus*)	86.7	0.5	0.2	12.2	0.5	0.4	47		36
Plums (*Prunus* spp.)	82.0	0.8	0.2	16.5	0.5	0.5	64	Includes fresh prunes	6
Pomegranates (*Punica granatum*)	81.3	0.6	0.3	17.2	0.3	0.6	66		52
Quinces (*Cydonia oblonga*)	83.2	0.7	0.3	14.9	2.4	0.9	59		22
Sapodilla or sapote (*Achras sapota*)	75.8	0.6	1.1	22.0	2.4	0.5	90		23
Sapote or marmalade plum (*Calocarpum mammosum*)	67.9	1.3	0.5	29.3	2.5	1.0	114		26
Soursop (*Annona muricata*)	80.2	0.8	0.4	18.0	1.0	0.6	71		34
Unspecified (group figures)[1]									
Temperate areas	84.6	0.6	0.3	14.1	0.9	0.4	55	Other than citrus fruits, bananas, and plantains	17
Subtropical areas	83.2	0.8	0.9	14.6	1.1	0.5	63		21
Tropical areas	83.4	0.8	1.1	14.1	1.5	0.6	63		35
All regions	84.0	0.7	0.7	14.1	1.1	0.5	59		24
Fruits, canned									
General (excluding sugar)	90	0.5	0.2	9	0.7	0.3	36	Applies to net weight of canned fruit	0
Orange juice, unsweetened	86	0.6	0.1	12.9	—	0.4	49		0
Grapefruit juice, unsweetened	89.4	0.5	0.2	9.4	—	0.5	37		0
Fruits, dried									
Figs, dates, prunes, raisins, jujubes	21.1	3.1	0.8	73.0	3.4	2	280		11
Apples, apricots, peaches, pears	20	3	0.6	73.8	4.5	2.6	281		0
All, unspecified	20.4	3	0.7	73.6	4	2.3			5
Olives									
Processed (green)	75	1	14	4	0.9	6	135	Ordinary cure	20
Greek process (ripe)	43.4	2.1	32.3	14.9	3.8	7.3	331	Heavy brine	27

[1] Group figures are unsatisfactory because the proportions of different kinds vary widely within areas and the fruits are dissimilar in many respects (for example, compare apples, avocados, and watermelons). Thus, group figures should be applied only to quantities of unspecified kinds, i.e., the residual supply, after making separate estimates for the principal kinds.

SOURCE: CHATFIELD, C. Food Composition Tables for International Use. FAO, United Nations, Rome.

FRUIT, COOKING

TABLE 2.F.39

COOKING GUIDE FOR FRESH FRUIT

Kind of Fruit	Amount[1] of Fruit	How to Prepare	Amount of Water	Amount of Sugar	Cooking Time After Adding Fruit
			Cups	Cups	Minutes
Apples	8 medium-size	Pare and slice	½	¼	8-10, for slices 12-15, for sauce
Apricots	15	Halve, pit, peel if desired.	½	¾	5
Cherries	1 qt	Remove pits	1	⅔	5
Cranberries	1 lb	Sort	1 or 2, as desired[2]	2	5
Peaches	6 medium-size	Peel, pit, halve, or slice.	¾	¾	5
Pears	6 medium-size	Pare, core, halve, or slice.	⅔	⅓	10, for soft varieties 20-25, for firm varieties
Plums	8 large	Halve, pit	½	⅔	5
Rhubarb	1½ lb	Slice	¾	⅔	2-5

[1]Makes 6 servings, about ½ cup each.
[2]Cranberries make 6 servings with 1 cup water; 8 servings with 2 cups water.

SOURCE: Food For Us All, Yearbook of Agriculture (1969). USDA, Washington, D. C.

FRUIT DRESSING

Clear Fruit Dressing

½ cup salad oil
2 tbsp vinegar
3 tbsp sugar
½ tsp salt
¼ tsp dry mustard (optional)

Procedure

Mix the dry ingredients, add vinegar and oil and shake thoroughly. Keep refrigerated.

SOURCE: KINTNER, T. C. and MANGEL, M. Vinegars and salad dressings. Univ. Missouri Agric. Exp. Sta. Bull. *631*.

FRUIT, DRIED, SIMMERING

TABLE 2.F.40

GUIDE TO SIMMERING DRIED FRUITS

Kind of fruit	Amount of fruit	Amount of water	Amount of sugar	Cooking time	Approximate number of ½-cup servings
	Ounces	*Cups*	*Cup*	*Minutes*	
Apples	8	3½	⅓	10	8
Apricots	8	2¼	⅓	10	6
	11	3	½	10	8
Mixed fruits	8	2¼	⅓	20	6
	11	3	½	20	8
Peaches	8	3	⅓	25	7
	11	4	½	25	9 or 10
Pears	8	2	⅛	25	4
	11	3	¼	25	6
Prunes	16	4	¼ to ½, if desired.	25	8 or 9

SOURCE: **Fruits in Family Meals. (1972). USDA Home and Garden Bull.** ***125.***

FRUIT FROZEN YIELD

TABLE 2.F.41

APPROXIMATE YIELD OF FROZEN FRUITS FROM FRESH

Fruit	Fresh, as Purchased or Picked	Frozen
Apples	1 bu. (48 lb.)	32 to 40 pt.
	1 box (44 lb.)	29 to 35 pt.
	1 ¼ to 1½ lb.	1 pt.
Apricots	1 bu. (48 lb.)	60 to 72 pt.
	1 crate (22 lb.)	28 to 33 pt.
	⅔ to 4/5 lb.	1 pt.
Berries [1]	1 crate (24 qt.)	32 to 36 pt.
	1⅓ to 1½ pt.	1 pt.
Cantaloups	1 dozen (28 lb.)	22 pt.
	1 to 1¼ lb.	1 pt.
Cherries, sweet or sour	1 bu. (56 lb.)	36 to 44 pt.
	1¼ to 1½ lb.	1 pt.
Cranberries	1 box (25 lb.)	50 pt.
	1 peck (8 lb.)	16 pt.
	½ lb.	1 pt.
Currants	2 qt. (3 lb.)	4 pt.
	¾ lb.	1 pt.

(Continued)

TABLE 2.F.41 (*Continued*)

Fruit	Fresh, as Purchased or Picked	Frozen
Peaches	1 bu. (48 lb.)	32 to 48 pt.
	1 lug box (20 lb.)	13 to 20 pt.
	1 to 1½ lb.	1 pt.
Pears	1 bu. (50 lb.)	40 to 50 pt.
	1 western box (46 lb.)	37 to 46 pt.
	1 to 1¼ lb.	1 pt.
Pineapple	5 lb.	4 pt.
Plums and prunes	1 bu. (56 lb.)	38 to 56 pt.
	1 crate (20 lb.)	13 to 20 pt.
	1 to 1½ lb.	1 pt.
Raspberries	1 crate (24 pt.)	24 pt.
	1 pt.	1 pt.
Rhubarb	15 lb.	15 to 22 pt.
	⅔ to 1 lb.	1 pt.
Strawberries	1 crate (24 qt.)	38 pt.
	⅔ qt.	1 pt.

[1] Includes blackberries, blueberries, boysenberries, dewberries, elderberries, gooseberries, huckleberries, loganberries, and youngberries.

SOURCE: Home Freezing of Fruits and Vegetables. (1971). USDA Home and Garden Bull. *10.*

FRUIT, GROWING SEASON, STORAGE LIFE

TABLE 2.F.42

GROWING SEASON FOR FRUITS IN RELATION TO STORAGE LIFE

Fruit	Full Bloom to Harvest	Normal Storage Life[1]
	Days	Days
Strawberries[2]		
Klondlike and others	24-28	5-7
Cherries[3]		
Black Tartarian	57	14
Bing	71	14
Napoleon	68	14
Apricots[4]		
Royal	100	7-21
Peaches[3]		
Belle of Georgia	122	14
Elberta	128	21-28
Pears[5]		
Bartlett	110-130	75-90
Bosc	130-145	90-105
Anjou	145-150	120-180
Apples[6]		
Yellow Transparent	70-75	0-7
Jonathan	140-145	60-90
Winesap	160-170	150-180

[1] Lutz and Hardenburg (1968)
[2] Wilson and Giamalva (1954)
[3] Tukey (1942)
[4] Brown (1952)
[5] Ryall, *et al* (1941)
[6] Magness (1941)

SOURCE: RYALL, A. LLOYD and PENTZER, W. T. (EDITORS). 1974. Fruit Physiology After Harvest. *In* Handling, Transportation and Storage of Fruits and Vegetables, Vol. 2. Avi Publishing Co., Westport, Conn.

FRUIT HARVEST DATES

TABLE 2.F.42a

OPENING AND CLOSING CANNING DATES

States and Territories	Apples	Apricots	Berries: Black	Blue	Cran	Goose	Logan	Rasp	Straw	Cherries	Figs
Arkansas	Aug. 15 Nov. 15		June 1 July 15						Apr. 1 Oct. 1		
California		June 8 Aug. 15								May 10 July 10	Aug. 15 Oct. 31
Colorado	Oct. 15 Dec. 15	July 10 Aug. 1								June 15 July 15	
Delaware	Oct. 1 Nov. 10										
Kansas	Aug. 1 Nov. 1										
Louisiana			June 1 July 31								May 1 July 31
Maine				Aug. 10 Sept. 15							
Maryland	Aug. 25 Dec. 1										
Massachusetts					Sept. 1 Dec. 31						
Michigan	Aug. 1 Nov. 30		July 25 Aug. 10	July 25 Sept. 15		July 20 Aug. 20		July 5 July 20	June 10 July 10	July 1 Aug. 15	
Mississippi			June 1 July 31								May 1 July 31
Missouri	Aug. 15 Dec. 1		June 20 Aug. 1								
Montana										July 14 Aug. 15	
New Jersey			June 10 July 10	June 20 Aug. 20	Sept. 1 Dec. 31			July 15 Aug. 15	June 10 July 10		
New York	Sept. 15 Dec. 31	Aug. 1 Aug. 15						July 10 Aug. 20	June 14 July 17	June 25 Aug. 15	
Ohio	Sept. 15 Dec. 31									July 5 Aug. 15	
Oklahoma	Aug. 15 Oct. 15		June 1 July 1								
Oregon	Sept. 15 Dec. 31	Aug. 15 Sept. 15	Aug. 1 Oct. 10			May 15 June 15	June 20 Aug. 1	June 25 Aug. 1	May 20 June 25	June 20 July 31	
Pennsylvania	Aug. 15 Dec. 31									June 30 July 31	
Texas			June 10 July 31								May 1 July 1
Utah	Oct. 15 Dec. 15	July 10 Aug. 1						July 1 July 20	June 15 July 15	June 15 July 15	
Virginia	Aug. 15 Dec. 31										
Washington	Sept. 15 Dec. 31	Aug. 25 Sept. 20	Aug. 15 Oct. 15	Oct. 1 Oct. 30		May 15 June 15	June 25 Aug. 1	July 1 Aug. 1	June 1 July 1	June 25 July 31	
West Virginia	Aug. 15 Nov. 30										
Wisconsin				June 10 Aug. 30	Oct. 1 Nov. 20	June 25 Aug. 1			June 10 July 20	June 25 Aug. 20	
Ontario, Canada	Sept. 15 Dec. 31		Aug. 1 Sept. 1					July 10 Aug. 17	June 14 July 17	July 1 Aug. 10	
Quebec, Canada	Sept. 15 Nov. 30			Aug. 15 Sept. 15							
Vancouver, B. C.	Sept. 1 Dec. 1	July 15 Aug. 30	Sept. 1 Oct. 30				July 1 Aug. 30	July 1 Aug. 30	June 1 July 30	July 1 July 30	

(Continued)

TABLE 2.F.42a (*Continued*)

OPENING AND CLOSING CANNING DATES—Continued
FRUITS—Continued

States and Territories	Grapes	Grape-fruit	Lemons	Olives	Oranges	Peaches	Pears	Pineapple	Plums	Prunes
Alabama						June 10 Aug. 1				
Arizona		Nov. 1 May 1								
Arkansas	Aug. 15 Oct. 1					July 10 Sept. 1				
California	Aug. 1 Sept. 25		All Year	Oct. 15 Feb. 15	July 1 Nov. 15	July 10 Sept. 20	July 18 Sept. 15		July 15 Sept. 30	All Year
Colorado						Aug. 25 Sept. 25	Sept. 15 Oct. 20			
Delaware						Aug. 1 Sept. 1	Oct. 1 Nov. 1			
Florida		Oct. 15 June 15			Dec. 1 June 1					
Georgia						June 10 Aug. 1				
Hawaii								Jan. 1– Mar. 15 June 15– Sept. 30		
Idaho										Sept. 15 Oct. 15
Maryland						Aug. 1 Sept. 15	Oct. 1 Nov. 15			
Michigan	Sept. 1 Oct. 30					Sept. 1 Oct. 15	Sept. 1 Dec. 30		Aug. 1 Aug. 30	
Missouri	Aug. 25 Oct. 15					July 25 Sept. 1				
New Jersey						Aug. 1 Sept. 15	Sept. 20 Nov. 15			
New York	Oct. 1 Nov. 1					Sept. 1 Oct. 5	Sept. 15 Nov. 10		Aug. 10 Oct. 7	Sept. 10 Oct. 5
North Carolina						July 15 Aug. 15				
Oregon						Aug. 15 Oct. 1	Aug. 10 Nov. 1		Aug. 15 Sept. 30	Sept. 1 Sept. 30
Pennsylvania	Sept. 20 Nov. 1					Aug. 15 Sept. 15				
Puerto Rico		Nov. 15 Apr. 30						May 1 June 30		
South Carolina						July 15 Aug. 15				
Texas		Dec. 1 May 1				June 10 Aug. 1				
Utah						Aug. 25 Sept. 25	Sept. 15 Oct. 20			Sept. 15 Oct. 15
Washington						Aug. 15 Sept. 20	Aug. 10 Nov. 1		Aug. 15 Sept. 30	Sept. 1 Sept. 30
Ontario, Canada						Sept. 1 Oct. 5	Sept. 15 Dec. 15		Sept. 15 Oct. 7	
Vancouver, B. C.						Aug. 15 Sept. 30	Aug. 15 Oct. 10		Aug. 15 Oct. 15	Aug. 15 Oct. 15

SOURCE: E. E. Judge & Son, Inc., *The Almanac of the Canning, Freezing, Preserving Industries, 58th Edition*, 1973.

FRUIT JUICE FLAVORS

TABLE 2.F.43

RANGES IN PPM OF DIFFERENT FLAVORS USED IN IMITATION FRUIT JUICE DRINKS

Flavor Compound	Usage Level in ppm
Lime oil	10–150
Lemon oil	10–200
Orange oil	10–150
Grapefruit oil	10–150
Allyl heptanoate	1–4
Benzaldehyde	10–30
Benzyl butyrate	1–6
Citral	5–15
Cognac	3–8
Geraniol	1–2
Isoamyl acetate	10–25
Isoamyl butyrate	10–15
Isoamyl formate	5–10
Ethyl acetate	30–50
Ethyl butyrate	10–30
Linalool	1–3
Methyl anthranilate	5–20

SOURCE: PHILLIPS, G. F. 1971. Imitation Fruit Flavored Beverages and Fruit Juice Bases. *In* Fruit and Vegetable Juice Processing Technology. 2nd Edition. Donald K. Tressler and Maynard A. Joslyn (Editors). Avi Publishing Co., Westport, Conn.

FRUIT SALAD DRESSING

Ingredients

2 egg yolks
2 tbsp sugar
1 tbsp butter
2 tbsp vinegar
¼ cup pineapple or other fruit juice

Procedure

Beat the egg until fluffy. Add the other ingredients, and blend. Cook in the top of the double boiler until thick. Cool. Combine with an equal quantity of whipped cream just before using. Refrigerate.

SOURCE: KINTNER, T. C. and MANGEL, M. Vinegars and salad dressings. Univ. Missouri Agric. Exp. Sta. Bull. *631*.

FRUIT SAUCES

TABLE 2.F.44

GUIDE TO MAKING FRESH FRUIT SAUCES

Kind of fruit	Amount of fruit, as purchased	Amount of water	Amount of sugar[1]	Cooking time after adding fruit	Approximate yield
	Pounds	*Cups*	*Cups*	*Minutes*	*Cups*
Apples	2	⅓	¼	12–15	3
Cherries	1	⅔	½	5	2
Cranberries	1	2	2	15	4 (whole) 3 (strained)
Peaches	1	⅔	½	5–8	2
Rhubarb	1½	¾	⅔	2–5	3

[1] For fruits of medium tartness. For very tart fruits, add more sugar.

SOURCE: Fruits in Family Meals. (1972). USDA Home and Garden Bull. *125*.

FRUIT SERVINGS PER POUND (OR PACKAGE)

TABLE 2.F.45

SERVINGS PER POUND OF FRUIT

Fresh Fruit	Servings per Market Unit[1]
Apples, Bananas, Peaches, Pears, Plums	3 or 4 per lb
Apricots, Cherries, sweet, Grapes, seedless	5 or 6 per lb
Blueberries, Raspberries	4 or 5 per pt
Strawberries	8 or 9 per qt

[1]As purchased.

Canned Fruit	Servings per Can (1 lb)
Served with liquid	4
Drained	2 or 3

Dried Fruit	Servings per Package (8 oz)
Apples	8
Apricots	6
Mixed fruits	6
Peaches	7
Pears	4
Prunes	4 or 5

Frozen Fruit	Servings per Package (10 or 12 oz)
Blueberries	3 or 4
Peaches	2 or 3
Raspberries	2 or 3
Strawberries	2 or 3

SOURCE: Nutrition, Food at Work for You, USDA Home and Garden Bull. *1*, Family Fare, Separate 1, 1968.

FRUIT, SIMMERING

TABLE 2.F.46

GUIDE TO SIMMERING FRESH FRUITS

Kind of fruit	Amount of fruit, as purchased	Amount of water	Amount of sugar [1]	Cooking time after adding fruit	Approximate number of ½-cup servings
	Pounds	*Cup*	*Cup*	*Minutes*	
Apples	2	½	¼	8–10	6
Apricots	1½	½	¾	5	6
Peaches	1½	¾	¾	5	6
Pears:					
Soft varieties	2	⅔	⅓	10	6
Firm varieties	2	⅔	⅓	20–25	6
Plums	1	½	⅔	5	6

[1] For fruits of medium tartness. For very tart fruits, add more sugar.

SOURCE: Fruits in Family Meals. (1972). USDA Home and Garden Bull. *125*.

FRUIT STORAGE I

TABLE 2.F.47

RECOMMENDED COLD STORAGE CONDITIONS, HEAT OF RESPIRATION AND LOSS IN WEIGHT OF FRUITS GROWN IN THE TROPICS

Fruits	Temp. °F	Relative Humidity %	Storage Life Wk	Heat Evolution[a] BTU/ton-day	Weight Loss[b] %
Acerola	32	85–90	8		
Avocado, West Indian	55	85–90	2	10,400	6.3
Avocado, Guatemalan	42–45	85–90	4	4,440–7,700	10.0
Banana					
'Lacatan', green	55–60	85–90	4	5,280–6,600	6.2
'Lacatan', ripe	55	85–90	1.5	9,282	
'Latundan', green	58–60	85–90	3–4	5,500–6,600	5.8
'Latundan', ripe	55–58	85–90	1		
'Cavendish', green	55–58	85–90	3–4	6,600	5.2
'Cavendish', ripe	55	85–90	1.5	11,200	
'Plantain', green	50	85–90	5	3,960	6.0
'Plantain', ripe	45–50	85–90	1.5		
'Poovan', green	55	85–90	2–3	3,520–5,500	6.7
Caimito, ripe	37–42	90	3	1,600–4,400	
Cashew	32–35	85–90	5	6,600–7,600	22.0
Citrus					
Calamondin	48–50	90	2	5,500	6.5
'Coorg' mandarin (main crop)	42–45	85–90	8	4,400	13.0
'Coorg' mandarin (rainy season)	42–45	85–90	6	2,200–3,300	15.8
'Valencia' orange	40–43	88–92	5–6	2,545	12.0
'Swikom' orange	48–50	85–90	4–5	3,300	8.0
'Ponkan' orange	40	85–90	3–4	2,200	7.5
'Sathgudi' orange	42–45	85–90	16	1,760–2,229	15.0

(Continued)

TABLE 2.F.47 (*Continued*)

Fruits	Temp. °F	Relative Humidity %	Storage Life Wk	Heat Evolution[a] BTU/ton-day	Weight Loss[b] %
Lime, yellow	52–55	85–90	8	1,760–2,640	15.0
Lime, green	52–55	85–90	7	880–1,760	18.0
Lemon	42–45	85–90	6	1,600–2,680	
Grapefruit	42–45	85–90	8–12	1,200–1,530	
Pomelo	45–48	85–90	12	1,800	
Custard apple	41	85–90	6		
Date	44	85–90	2		
Durian	39–42	85–90	6–8		
Fig	32–35	85–90	7	800–1,400	11.5
Guava	47–50	85–90	2–5	7,040–7,700	14.0
Indian Gooseberry	32–35	85–90	8		
Jackfruit	52–55	85–90	6		15.6
Langsat	52–58	85–90	2	15,400–16,000	24.3
Lychee	35	85–90	8–12		
Mango					
'Carabao'	45–50	85–90	2.5–3.5	6,700	5.1
'Pico'	45–50	85–90	2.5	6,700	6.2
'Badami'	47–50	85–90	4	11,000–13,200	6.8
'Raspuri'	42–45	85–90	6	11,000–13,200	6.8
Mangosteen	39–42	85–90	7		
Papaya, green	50	85–90	3–4	2,500	5.8
Papaya, turning	47	85–90	2–3		
Passion fruit, purple	42–45	85–90	3		32.0
Persimmon	32–35	85–90	7		
Pineapple, all green	47–50	85–90	4–6	1,700	4.0
Pineapple, 25% yellow	40–44	85–90	1–2		
Plum					
'Alu Bokharo'	32–35	85–90	2	1,700–1,920	5.2–9.6
'Gaviotaa' and 'Rubio'	32–35	85–90	3	1,700–1,920	5.2–7.8
'Shiro' and 'Hale'	32–35	85–90	4	1,760–1,920	5.2–12.9
Pomegranate, 'Khandari'	32–35	85–90	11		
Rambutan	50	90–95	1–2.5	13,200	6.0–12.0
Santol, 'Bangkok'	45–48	85–90	3		
Sapota, turning	67–70	85–90	2.5	3,300–5,500	12.0
Sapota, ripe	32–36	85–90	2		
Sugar apple, turning	45	85–90	4		
Sugar apple, ripe	34–37	85–90	2		

Source: Authors' unpublished data.
[a]Represents steady state heat production during storage at indicated temperatures.
[b]Loss in weight upon removal from storage at indicated storage periods.

SOURCE: PANTASTICO, ER. B., CHATTOPADHYAY, T. K., and SUBRAMANYAM, H. 1975. Storage and Commercial Storage Operations. *In* Postharvest Physiology, Handling and Utilization of Tropical and Subtropical Fruits and Vegetables. Er. B. Pantastico (Editor). Avi Publishing Co., Westport, Conn.

FRUIT STORAGE II

Hold at room temperature until ripe; then refrigerate, uncovered:

Apples	Grapes	Peaches
Apricots	Melons, except watermelons	Pears
Avocados	Nectarines	Plums
Berries		Tomatoes
Cherries		

Store in cool room or refrigerate, uncovered:

Grapefruit	Limes
Lemons	Oranges

SOURCE: Nutrition, Food at Work for You. (1968) USDA Home and Garden Bull. *1*.

FRYING TIME

TABLE 2.F.48

APPROXIMATE FRYING TIMES FOR CONVENTIONAL FRYERS

Food Item	Frying Time (Min)
Chicken	
Raw pieces	10–15
Fritters	3–4
Sea foods	
Fish fillets	3–5
Clams	3–4
Scallops	3–5
Shrimp	3–4
Oysters	3–5
Vegetables	
Potatoes, ¼ in. cut	4–6
Potatoes, ⅜ in. cut	5–7
Potatoes, ½ in. cut	6–8
Cauliflower	2–4
Eggplant	5–7
Onions	2–3
Miscellaneous	
Doughnuts	2–3
Corn on the cob	3–4
Meat turnovers	5–7
French toast	2–3

SOURCE: KAZARIAN, E. A. (EDITOR). 1975. Equipment Requirements. *In* Food Service Facilities Planning. Avi Publishing Co., Westport, Conn.

FUEL, HEATING VALUE

TABLE 2.F.49

HEATING VALUE OF TYPICAL FUELS

Fuel	High Heating Value Btu/lb
Coal	11,000 to 14,000
Oil	18,000 to 19,500
Natural gas	700 to 1,000
Saturated hydrocarbons (C_nH_{2n+2})	21,000 to 23,000
Unsaturated hydrocarbons (C_nH_{2n})	18,000 to 21,000
Lignite (dry)	6,000 to 7,000
Bagasse (dry)	8,000 to 9,000
Gasoline	20,200
Kerosene	19,900
Fuel oil	18,500
Hardwoods	8,100 to 8,900
Softwoods	8,400 to 11,000

SOURCE: HALL, C. W., FARRALL, A. W. and RIPPEN, A. L. (EDITORS). 1971. Energy. *In* Encyclopedia of Food Engineering. Avi Publishing Co., Westport, Conn.

FUMIGANTS

TABLE 2.F.50

FUMIGANTS AND AMOUNTS USED PER 1000 CU FT OF AIR SPACE

Fumigant	Amount	Comment
Carbon disulfide	20 lb	Explosive, inflammable
Hydrogen cyanide	8 oz	Very toxic to man, leaves residue
Methyl bromide	1 lb	Toxic to man
Ethylene dichloride–carbon tetrachloride	15–20 lb	Anesthetic to man
Ethylene oxide–ethylene dichloride	10–15 lb	Anesthetic to man
Ethyl formate	5–10 lb	
Ethylene oxide	2–4 lb	
Chloropicrin	1 lb	Lachrymator
Sulfur dioxide	Burning sulfur fumes	Inexpensive

SOURCE: JACOBS, M. B. (EDITOR). The Chemistry and Technology of Food and Food Products, 2nd Edition, Vol. *1*. Interscience Publishers, New York.

FUNGI FOOD PRODUCTS

TABLE 2.F.51

SOME COMMON ORIENTAL FOODS WHICH ARE PRODUCED BY PROCESSES IN WHICH FILAMENTOUS FUNGI ARE USED

Food Type	Consistency	Raw Materials	Fungus Employed
Miso	Paste	Soybeans and rice	*Aspergillus oryzae*
Shoyu	Liquid	Soybeans and rice or wheat	*Aspergillus oryzae*
Tempeh	Solid	Soybeans or coconut meat	*Rhizopus oligosporus*
Ang-khak	Solid	Rice	*Monascus purpureus*
Ontjom	Solid	Peanut press cake	*Neurospora sitophila*
Sufu	Moist solid	Soybean "milk"	*Actinomucor elegans*
Meitauza	Solid	Residuum from preparation of soybean "milk"	*Actinomucor elegans*
Ketjap	Liquid	Black soybeans	*Aspergillus oryzae*
Katsuobushi	Solid	Bonito fish	*Aspergillus glaucus*

SOURCE: GRAY, WILLIAM, D. 1974. Fungi As Food. *In* Encyclopedia of Food Technology. A. H. Johnson and M. S. Peterson (Editors). Avi Publishing Co., Westport, Conn.

G

GESTATION PERIODS

TABLE 2.G.1

GESTATION PERIODS OF DOMESTIC AND WILD ANIMALS

	Days		Days	Months
Domestic Animals		Wild Animals		
Ass	365	Ape, Barbary	210	
Cat	63–65	Bear, black		7
Cattle		Bison		9
Aberdeen-Angus	281	Camel	410	
Ayrshire	279	Coyote	60–64	
Brown Swiss	290	Deer, Virginia	197–220	
Charolais	289	Elephant		20–22
Guernsey	283	Elk, Wapiti		8½
Hereford	285	Giraffe		14–15
Holstein-Friesian	279	Hare	38	
Jersey	279	Hippopotamus	225–250	
Red Poll	285	Kangaroo, red	32–34[1]	
Shorthorn, beef	282	Leopard	92–95	
Shorthorn, milking	282	Lion	108	
Simmental	289	Llama		11
Dog	58–63	Marmoset	140–150	
Goat	151	Moose	240–250	
Horse		Muskrat	28–30	
Heavy	333–345	Otter		9–10
Light	330–337	Panther	90–93	
Pig	112–115	Porcupine	112	
Sheep		Pronghorn	230–240	
Mutton breeds	144–147	Raccoon	63	
Wool breeds	148–151	Reindeer		7–8
Laboratory and Fur Animals		Rhinoceros, African	530–550	
Chinchilla	105–128	Seal		11
Ferret	42	Shrew	20	
Fisher	338–358	Skunk	62–65	
Fox	49–55	Squirrel, gray	44	
Marten, European	236–274	Tapir	390–400	
Pine Marten	220–265	Tiger	105–113	
Mink	40–75	Walrus		12
Monkey, macaque	150–180	Whale, sperm		16
Mouse	18–20	Woodchuck	31–32	
Nutria (coypu)	120–134	Wolf	60–63	

[1] Delayed development as long as a "joey" is in the pouch.

SOURCE: The Merck Veterinary Manual, 4th Edition, Merck & Co., Rahway, N.J., 1973.

GLAND WEIGHTS

TABLE 2.G.2

WEIGHTS OF IMPORTANT GLANDS OR TISSUES OF MEAT-PRODUCING ANIMALS
(Weights in Grams, Ounces, or Pounds)

Portion	Beef Animal	Sheep	Hog
Pineal body	0.32 g	0.04–0.12 g	0.10 g
Pituitary gland	3.0 g	0.37–0.55 g	0.33–0.78 g
Ovary	5.7 g	0.76 g	3.15 g
Testis	$\frac{1}{2}$ lb	2 oz	3–4 oz
Suprarenal	11–15 g	1.5–2 g	3–5 g
Thyroid	$1-1\frac{1}{2}$ oz	2–9 g	4–10 g
Thymus	$\frac{1}{3}-\frac{1}{2}$ lb	15–25 g	9–35 g
Pancreas	$\frac{1}{2}-1$ lb	1 oz	$1\frac{1}{2}-2$ oz
Stomach	16–20 lb	1–2 lb	2–4 lb
Spleen	1–2 lb	$\frac{1}{6}-\frac{1}{2}$ lb	$\frac{1}{3}-\frac{3}{4}$ lb
Kidney	$\frac{1}{2}-1\frac{1}{2}$ lb	3–4 oz	$\frac{1}{3}-\frac{1}{8}$ lb
Heart	$3\frac{1}{2}-4\frac{1}{2}$ lb	$\frac{3}{8}-\frac{5}{8}$ lb	$\frac{1}{2}-\frac{3}{4}$ lb
Lungs	4–5 lb	$\frac{1}{2}-1$ lb	$1-1\frac{1}{2}$ lb
Brain and cord	20–26 oz	6–9 oz	10–16 oz
Liver	10 lb	1–2 lb	2–4 lb
Blood	30–40 lb	3–5 lb	5–10 lb
Skin, vessels, etc.	65–75 lb	12–14 lb	Not Removed
Bones and muscles	560–600 lb	37–43 lb	160–175 lb
Total	1,000 lb	85–90 lb	215–225 lb

SOURCE: MOULTON, C. R. and LEWIS, W. L. Meat Through the Microscope, Revised Edition. Institute of Meat Packaging, University of Chicago, Chicago.

GLASS JAR TOPS

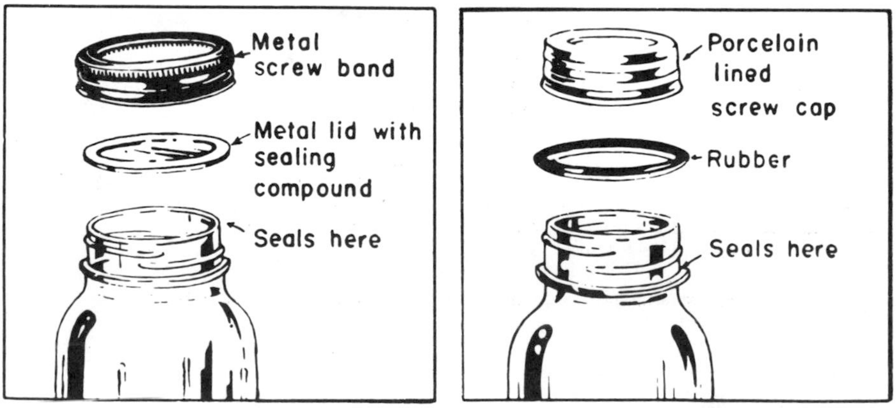

FIG. 2.G.1. COMPONENTS OF TWO KINDS OF TOPS FOR GLASS JARS FOR HOME CANNING

SOURCE: Home Canning of Fruits and Vegetables. (1972) USDA Home and Garden Bull. *8*.

GLUTAMATE

TABLE 2.G.3

THE GLUTAMATE CONTENT OF FOODS

Product	Percentage of Protein[1] in Food	Percentage of Glutamate[1] in Protein	Total Glutamate[1] (g/100 g)	Free Glutamate[2] (g/100 g)
Milk				
Cow	3.5	23.4	0.819	0.004[5]
Human	1.4	16.4	0.229	0.020[5]
Milk Products				
Casein	100.0	23.0	23.052	—
Buttermilk	3.5	17.7	0.620	0.004[6]
Cheese				
Camembert	17.5	27.4	4.787	ca. 0.600[6, 7]
Parmesan	36.0	27.4	9.847	ca. 0.600[6, 7]
Poultry Products				
Eggs	12.8	12.4	1.583	0.023[3]
Chicken	20.6	16.1	3.309	0.044[2]
Duck	21.4	17.0	3.636	0.069[3]
Meat				
Beef	18.8	15.1	2.846	0.033[2]
Lamb	18.0	15.2	2.730	0.020[4]
Pork	15.2	15.3	2.325	0.023[2]
Fish				
Cod	16.5	12.7	2.101	0.009[3]
Mackerel	18.7	12.7	2.382	0.036[2]
Salmon	17.4	12.7	2.216	0.020[4]
Vegetables				
Peas	23.8	23.5	5.583	0.200[4]
Corn	10.0	17.7	1.765	0.130[4]
Beets	1.6	16.0	0.256	0.030[4]
Carrots	1.2	18.2	0.218	0.033[2]
Onions	1.4	14.9	0.208	0.018[2]
Spinach	2.3	12.6	0.289	0.039[2]
Tomatoes	1.0	23.8	0.238	0.140[2]

1-Orr, M. L. and Watt, B. K., "Amino Acid Content of Foods", Home Economics Research Report #4, U.S. Government Printing Office, 1957.

2-Maeda, S., *et al, Journal of Home Economics* (Japan) 9 163 (1968).

3-*Ibid, 12* 105 (1969).

4-Hac, L. R., et al, *Food Technology 3* 351 (1949).

5-Private Communication, Research Laboratories, Ajinomoto Company, Inc., Tokyo, Japan.

6-Private Communication, Research Laboratories, C.O.F.A.G., Paris, France.

7-Müller, H. Z., *Ernährungswissenschaft 10* 83 (1970).

SOURCE: The Remarkable Story of Monosodium Glutamate. International Glutamate Technical Committee (1974).

GLUTAMATE ADDITION

TABLE 2.G.4

COMPARISON OF GLUTAMATE INGESTED IN FOODS WITH GLUTAMATE ADDED TO FOODS AS A FLAVOR ENHANCER

Food	Total Glutamate Naturally Present %	Free Glutamate Naturally Present %	Recommended Addition of MSG* %	MSG in Proportion to Total Glutamate %
Beef	2.846	0.033	0.4	14.1
Chicken	3.309	0.044	0.3	9.1
Pork	2.325	0.023	0.4	17.2
Peas	5.583	0.200	0.2	3.6
Corn	1.765	0.130	0.2	11.3

*General Guideline: Use ½ teaspoon MSG per pound of meat or per 4 to 6 servings of vegetables.

SOURCE: The Remarkable Story of Monosodium Glutamate. International Glutamate Technical Committee (1974).

GLUTEN-FREE DIET

TABLE 2.G.5

FOODS INCLUDED AND EXCLUDED IN GLUTEN-FREE DIET

Type of Food	*Foods Included*	*Foods Excluded*
Beverage	Carbonated beverages, cocoa powder, coffee, tea, whole milk (not > 2½ cups/day)	Cereal beverages; cocoa mixes; malted milks, drinks made with malt or other excluded cereals; ale, beer
Bread	Bread and muffins made with arrowroot, corn, potato, rice, or soybean flour	Any made with wheat, barley, rye, or oat flour; crackers; pretzels; rusk; pancakes; prepared mixes
Cereal	Ready-to-eat corn and rice cereals, cornmeal, rice, hominy	Any made with wheat, oats, rye, bran, malt flavoring, barley, buckwheat; macaroni, noodles, spaghetti
Dessert	Blancmange, custards, and puddings made with allowable flours or starches; gelatin desserts; sherbert; tapioca; home-made ice cream; special cookies made without wheat, rye, or oat flour	Any containing wheat, rye, barley, or oat products, as commercial cakes, cookies, ice cream, pastries, pies, puddings, or those made from commercial mixes

TABLE 2.G.5 (*Continued*)

Type of Food	*Foods Included*	*Foods Excluded*
Fat	Butter, margarine, pure mayonnaise, cooking oils, shortening	Commercial salad dressings, wheat germ oil
Fruit	Any	
Meat, egg, or cheese	Any meat, fish, or fowl except those excluded; natural cheese; eggs	Meat, fish, or chicken loaf or croquettes made with bread or bread crumbs; cheese spreads; canned meat dishes, cold cuts unless pure meat; bread stuffings; gravy thickened with flour
Soup	Broth or bouillon; vegetable soup and cream soups made from allowable foods, thickened with cornstarch or potato flour only	Any containing excluded flours or starches
Sweets	Any except those prepared with excluded grain products	Candy containing wheat, rye, oats, barley
Vegetable	Any except those prepared with excluded grain products	
Miscellaneous	Salt, spices, vinegar, herbs, pickles, baking chocolate, olives, nuts, peanut butter	All gravies or sauces thickened with wheat flour; flavoring syrups, bottled meat sauces, malt extract

SOURCE: HOLVEY, D. N. 1972. The Merck Manual, 12th Edition. Merck & Co., Rahway, New Jersey.

GOATS, MILK BREEDS

TABLE 2.G.6

BREEDS OF MILK GOATS AND THEIR CHARACTERISTICS

Breed	Place of Origin	Color; Face, Ears, and Legs	Head Characteristics	Disqualification
French-Alpine	France; but from Swiss foundation stock.	Multicolored coats, with no standard markings.	Some have horns at birth and are disbudded, others are hornless; erect ears; straight nose.	Pendulous ears.
La Mancha	Spain	Any color or combination of colors.	Short ears; straight nose; hornless or neatly disbudded.	Anything other than gopher ears in males. Ears other than true La Mancha type in females.
Nubian	Nubia, in northeastern Africa.	Black and whites, tan and whites, red and whites are common, but they may be any of these colors without white markings.	Some born with horns and disbudded, others are hornless. Long drooping ears. Roman nose and prominent forehead. Does are beardless.	Upright ears.
Rock Alpine	United States.	Multicolored coats, with no standard markings.	Some have horns at birth and are disbudded, others are hornless; erect ears; straight nose.	
Saanen	Switzerland, in the Saanen Valley.	Pure white or creamy white.	Hornless animals preferred; straight nose; erect ears.	Large (1½" diameter or more) dark spot in hair; pendulous ears.
Swiss Alpine	Switzerland.	Chamoise; solid brown, ranging from light to a deep-red bay. Black points.	Hornless or neatly disbudded. Erect ears.	
Toggenburg	Switzerland, in the Toggenburg Valley.	Brown, with 2 white stripes on the face and white on the legs below the knees.	Hornless or debudded; straight or dished nose; erect ears.	Tricolor or piebald; large (1½" or more) white spot in males; pendulous ears.

In addition to the specific breed disqualifications given in the right-hand column, the American Dairy Goat Association lists the following as disqualifications in any breed: total blindness; permanent lameness or difficulty in walking; blind or non-functioning half of udder; blind teat; double teats; extra teats that interfere with milking; hermaphrodism; navel hernia; crooked face in bucks; and extra teats, teats cut off, or double orifice in bucks.

SOURCE: ENSMINGER, M. E. 1969. Animal Science. Interstate Printers & Publishers, Danville, Illinois. Reproduced with permission of the publisher.

GRADES, MEAT

Government grades for beef, veal, lamb and pork are:

Beef				
Quality	Cutability	Veal	Lamb	Pork
Prime	1	Prime	Prime	U.S. No. 1
Choice	2	Choice	Choice	U.S. No. 2
Good	3	Good	Good	U.S. No. 3
Standard	4	Standard	Utility	U.S. No. 4
Commercial	5	Utility	Cull	Utility
Utility		Cull		
Cutter				
Canner				

SOURCE: Lessons on Meat. (1974) National Live Stock and Meat Board, Chicago.

GRAIN ANALYSIS

TABLE 2.G.7

COMPARATIVE NUTRIENT ANALYSIS OF WHEAT AND CORN

	Wheat		
	Hard	Soft	Corn[1]
Protein, % (N x 5.7)	11.93	10.48	7.84
Ash, %	1.54	1.41	1.03
Moisture, %	12.34	13.88	11.00
Crude fat, %	1.60	1.68	3.78
Crude fiber, %	2.28	1.91	1.89
Starch, %	57.13	57.49	
Gross energy, kcal/kg	3910	3782	3786
Lysine, %	0.33	0.34	0.17
Histidine, %	0.28	0.29	0.17
Arginine, %	0.57	0.59	0.44
Aspartic acid, %	0.63	0.61	
Threonine, %	0.36	0.35	0.34
Serine, %	0.59	0.58	
Glutamic acid, %	4.07	3.86	
Proline, %	1.31	1.21	
Glycine, %	0.53	0.50	
Alanine, %	0.45	0.44	
Cystine, %	0.29	0.32	0.09
Valine, %	0.54	0.52	0.34
Methionine, %	0.20	0.19	0.09
Isoleucine, %	0.45	0.41	0.44
Leucine, %	0.85	0.81	0.95
Tyrosine, %	0.38	0.35	
Phenylalanine, %	0.59	0.56	0.44
Minerals:			
Ca, %	0.035	0.026	
P, %	0.36	0.35	
K, %	0.37	0.39	
Na, %	0.007	0.006	
Mg, %	0.11	0.10	
Zn, ppm	42	31	
Fe, ppm	25	26	
Mn, ppm	30	26	
Cu, ppm	4.2	4.2	
Se, ppm	0.34	0.04	
B, ppm	1.3	2.0	
Sr, ppm	0.64	0.48	
Al, ppm	25.0	>5.0	
Ba, ppm	5.8	4.9	
Co, ppm	0.13	0.12	
Niacin, ppm	54.2	47.5	25.3
Pantothenic acid, ppm	9.3	8.5	3.8
Folic acid, ppm	0.385	0.391	
Thiamine, ppm	3.85	4.11	3.4
Riboflavin, ppm	1.57	1.43	1.3
Pyridoxine, ppm	2.39	1.86	
α-Tocopherol, ppm	13.3	14.9	
Betaine, ppm	716.7	1234.3	
Choline, ppm	1096.5	1060.4	

[1] Yellow U.S. #2

SOURCE: SAUNDERS, R. M., WALKER, JR., H. G. and KOHLER, G. O. 1973. Feed Uses of Wheat and Its Products. *In* Wheat: Production and Utilization. G. E. Inglett (Editor). Avi Publishing Co., Westport, Conn.

GRAIN PRODUCTS COMPOSITION

TABLE 2.G.8

NUTRITIVE VALUES OF THE EDIBLE PART OF GRAIN PRODUCTS

[Dashes in the columns for nutrients show that no suitable value could be found although there is reason to believe that a measurable amount of the nutrient may be present]

Food, Approximate Measure, and Weight (in Grams)		(g)	Water (%)	Food Energy (Cal)	Protein (g)	Fat (g)	Fatty Acids: Saturated (Total) (g)	Fatty Acids: Unsaturated: Oleic (g)	Fatty Acids: Unsaturated: Lin-oleic (g)	Carbohy-drate (g)	Calcium (mg)	Iron (mg)	Vitamin A Value (IU)	Thiamin (mg)	Riboflavin (mg)	Niacin (mg)	Ascorbic Acid (mg)
Bagel, 3-in. diam:																	
Egg	1 bagel	55	32	165	6	2	—	—	—	28	9	1.2	30	0.14	0.10	1.2	0
Water	1 bagel	55	29	165	6	2	—	—	—	30	8	1.2	0	0.15	0.11	1.4	0
Barley, pearled, light, uncooked	1 cup	200	11	700	16	2	Tr	1	1	158	32	4.0	0	0.24	0.10	6.2	0
Biscuits, baking powder from home recipe with enriched flour, 2-in. diam	1 biscuit	28	27	105	2	5	1	2	1	13	34	0.4	Tr	0.06	0.06	0.1	Tr
Biscuits, baking powder from mix, 2-in. diam	1 biscuit	28	28	90	2	3	1	1	1	15	19	0.6	Tr	0.08	0.07	0.6	Tr
Bran flakes (40 % bran), added thiamin and iron	1 cup	35	3	105	4	1	—	—	—	28	25	12.3	0	0.14	0.06	2.2	0
Bran flakes with raisins, added thiamin and iron	1 cup	50	7	145	4	1	—	—	—	40	28	13.5	Tr	0.16	0.07	2.7	0
Breads:																	
Boston brown bread, slice 3 × 3/4 in.	1 slice	48	45	100	3	1	—	—	—	22	43	0.9	0	0.05	0.03	0.6	0
Cracked-wheat bread:																	
Loaf, 1 lb	1 loaf	454	35	1,190	40	10	2	5	2	236	399	5.0	Tr	0.53	0.41	5.9	Tr
Slice, 18 slices per loaf	1 slice	25	35	65	2	1	—	—	—	13	22	0.3	Tr	0.03	0.02	0.3	Tr
French or vienna bread:																	
Enriched, 1-lb loaf	1 loaf	454	31	1,315	41	14	3	8	2	251	195	10.0	Tr	1.27	1.00	11.3	Tr
Unenriched, 1-lb loaf	1 loaf	454	31	1,315	41	14	3	8	2	251	195	3.2	Tr	0.36	0.36	3.6	Tr
Italian bread:																	
Enriched, 1-lb loaf	1 loaf	454	32	1,250	41	4	Tr	1	2	256	77	10.0	0	1.32	0.91	11.8	0
Unenriched, 1-lb loaf	1 loaf	454	32	1,250	41	4	Tr	1	2	256	77	3.2	0	0.41	0.27	3.6	0

Raisin bread:																
Loaf, 1-lb	1 loaf	454	35	1,190	30	13	3	8	2	243	322	5.9	Tr	0.23	0.41	3.2	Tr
Slice, 18 slices per loaf	1 slice	25	35	65	2	1	—	—	—	13	18	0.3	Tr	0.01	0.02	0.2	Tr
Rye bread:																
American, light (1/3 rye, 2/3 wheat):																
Loaf, 1-lb	1 loaf	454	36	1,100	41	5	—	—	—	236	340	7.3	0	0.82	0.32	6.4	0
Slice, 18 slices per loaf	1 slice	25	36	60	2	Tr	—	—	—	13	19	0.4	0	0.05	0.02	0.4	0
Pumpernickel, loaf, 1-lb	1 loaf	454	34	1,115	41	5	—	—	—	241	381	10.9	0	1.04	0.64	5.4	0
White bread, enriched:[1]																
Soft-crumb type:																
Loaf, 1-lb	1 loaf	454	36	1,225	39	15	3	8	2	229	381	11.3	Tr	1.13	0.95	10.9	Tr
Slice, 18 slices per loaf	1 slice	25	36	70	2	1	—	—	—	13	21	0.6	Tr	0.06	0.05	0.6	Tr
Slice, toasted	1 slice	22	25	70	2	1	—	—	—	13	21	0.6	Tr	0.06	0.05	0.6	Tr
Slice, 22 slices per loaf	1 slice	20	36	55	2	1	—	—	—	10	17	0.5	Tr	0.05	0.04	0.5	Tr
Slice, toasted	1 slice	17	25	55	2	1	—	—	—	10	17	0.5	Tr	0.05	0.04	0.5	Tr
Loaf, 1½ lb	1 loaf	680	36	1,835	59	22	5	12	3	343	571	17.0	Tr	1.70	1.43	16.3	Tr
Slice, 24 slices per loaf	1 slice	28	36	75	2	1	—	—	—	14	24	0.7	Tr	0.07	0.06	0.7	Tr
Slice, toasted	1 slice	24	25	75	2	1	—	—	—	14	24	0.7	Tr	0.07	0.06	0.7	Tr
Slice, 28 slices per loaf	1 slice	24	36	65	2	1	—	—	—	12	20	0.6	Tr	0.06	0.05	0.6	Tr
Slice, toasted	1 slice	21	25	65	2	1	—	—	—	12	20	0.6	Tr	0.06	0.05	0.6	Tr
Firm-crumb type:																
Loaf, 1-lb	1 loaf	454	35	1,245	41	17	4	10	2	228	435	11.3	Tr	1.22	0.91	10.9	Tr
Slice, 20 slices per loaf	1 slice	23	35	65	2	1	—	—	—	12	22	0.6	Tr	0.06	0.05	0.6	Tr
Slice, toasted	1 slice	20	24	65	2	1	—	—	—	12	22	0.6	Tr	0.06	0.05	0.6	Tr
Loaf, 2-lb	1 loaf	907	35	2,495	82	34	8	20	4	455	871	22.7	Tr	2.45	1.81	21.8	Tr
Slice, 34 slices per loaf	1 slice	27	35	75	2	1	—	—	—	14	26	0.7	Tr	0.07	0.05	0.6	Tr
Slice, toasted	1 slice	23	35	75	2	1	—	—	—	14	26	0.7	Tr	0.07	0.05	0.6	Tr
Whole-wheat bread, soft-crumb type:																
Loaf, 1-lb	1 loaf	454	36	1,095	41	12	2	6	2	224	381	13.6	Tr	1.36	0.45	12.7	Tr
Slice, 16 slices per loaf	1 slice	28	36	65	3	1	—	—	—	14	24	0.8	Tr	0.09	0.03	0.8	Tr
Slice, toasted	1 slice	24	24	65	3	1	—	—	—	14	24	0.8	Tr	0.09	0.03	0.8	Tr
Whole-wheat bread, firm-crumb type:																
Loaf, 1-lb	1 loaf	454	36	1,100	48	14	3	6	3	216	449	13.6	Tr	1.18	0.54	12.7	Tr
Slice, 18 slices per loaf	1 slice	25	36	60	3	1	—	—	—	12	25	0.8	Tr	0.06	0.03	0.7	Tr
Slice, toasted	1 slice	21	24	60	3	1	—	—	—	12	25	0.8	Tr	0.06	0.03	0.7	Tr
Bread crumbs, dry, grated	1 cup	100	6	390	13	5	1	2	1	73	122	3.6	Tr	0.22	0.30	3.5	Tr
Buckwheat flour, light, sifted	1 cup	98	12	340	6	1	—	—	—	78	11	1.0	0	0.08	0.04	0.4	0
Bulgur, canned, seasoned	1 cup	135	56	245	8	4	—	—	—	44	27	1.9	0	0.08	0.05	4.1	0
Cakes made from cake mixes:																
Angelfood:																
Whole cake	1 cake	635	34	1,645	36	1	—	—	—	377	603	1.9	0	0.03	0.70	0.6	0
Piece, 1/12 of 10-in. diam cake	1 piece	53	34	135	3	Tr	—	—	—	32	50	0.2	0	Tr	0.06	0.1	0

(Continued)

TABLE 2.G.8 (*Continued*)

Food, Approximate Measure, and Weight (in Grams)		(g)	Water (%)	Food Energy (Cal)	Protein (g)	Fat (g)	Fatty Acids: Saturated (Total) (g)	Fatty Acids: Unsaturated: Oleic (g)	Fatty Acids: Unsaturated: Linoleic (g)	Carbohydrate (g)	Calcium (mg)	Iron (mg)	Vitamin A Value (IU)	Thiamin (mg)	Riboflavin (mg)	Niacin (mg)	Ascorbic Acid (mg)
Cupcakes, small, 2½ in. diam:																	
Without icing	1 cupcake	25	26	90	1	3	1	1	1	14	40	0.1	40	0.01	0.03	0.1	Tr
With chocolate icing	1 cupcake	36	22	130	2	5	2	2	1	21	47	0.3	60	0.01	0.04	0.1	Tr
Devil's food, 2-layer, with chocolate icing:																	
Whole cake	1 cake	1,107	24	3,755	49	136	54	58	16	645	653	8.9	1,660	0.33	0.89	3.3	1
Piece, 1/16 of 9-in. diam cake	1 piece	69	24	235	3	9	3	4	1	40	41	0.6	100	0.02	0.06	0.2	Tr
Cupcake, small, 2½ in. diam	1 cupcake	35	24	120	2	4	1	2	Tr	20	21	0.3	50	0.01	0.03	0.1	Tr
Gingerbread:																	
Whole cake	1 cake	570	37	1,575	18	39	10	19	9	291	513	9.1	Tr	0.17	0.51	4.6	2
Piece, 1/9 of 8-in. square cake	1 piece	63	37	175	2	4	1	2	1	32	57	1.0	Tr	0.02	0.06	0.5	Tr
White, 2-layer, with chocolate icing:																	
Whole cake	1 cake	1,140	21	4,000	45	122	45	54	17	716	1,129	5.7	680	0.23	0.91	2.3	2
Piece, 1/16 of 9-in. diam cake	1 piece	71	21	250	3	8	3	3	1	45	70	0.4	40	0.01	0.06	0.1	Tr
Cakes made from home recipes:[2]																	
Boston cream pie:																	
Piece, 1/12 of 8-in. diam	1 piece	69	35	210	4	6	2	3	1	34	46	0.3	140	0.02	0.08	0.1	Tr
Fruitcake, dark, made with enriched flour:																	
Loaf, 1 lb	1 loaf	454	18	1,720	22	69	15	37	13	271	327	11.8	540	0.59	0.64	3.6	2
Slice, 1/30 of 8-in. loaf	1 slice	15	18	55	1	2	Tr	1	Tr	9	11	0.4	20	0.02	0.02	0.1	Tr
Plain sheet cake:																	
Without icing:																	
Whole cake	1 cake	777	25	2,830	35	108	30	52	21	434	497	3.1	1,320	0.16	0.70	1.6	2
Piece, 1/9 of 9-in. square cake	1 piece	86	25	315	4	12	3	6	2	48	55	0.3	150	0.02	0.08	0.2	Tr
With boiled white icing:																	
piece, 1/9 of 9-in. square cake	1 piece	114	23	400	4	12	3	6	2	71	56	0.3	150	0.02	0.08	0.2	Tr

Pound:																	
Loaf, 8½ X 3½ X 3-in.	1 loaf	514	17	2,430	29	152	34	68	17	242	108	4.1	1,440	0.15	0.46	1.0	0
Slice, ½ in. thick	1 slice	30	17	140	2	9	2	4	1	14	6	0.2	80	0.01	0.03	0.1	0
Sponge:																	
Whole cake	1 cake	790	32	2,345	60	45	14	20	4	427	237	9.5	3,560	0.40	1.11	1.6	Tr
Piece, 1/12 of 10-in. diam cake	1 piece	66	32	195	5	4	1	2	Tr	36	20	0.8	300	0.03	0.09	0.1	Tr
Yellow, 2-layer, without icing:																	
Whole cake	1 cake	870	24	3,160	39	111	31	53	22	506	618	3.5	1,310	0.17	0.70	1.7	2
Piece, 1/16 of 9-in. diam cake	1 piece	54	24	200	2	7	2	3	1	32	39	0.2	80	0.01	0.04	0.1	Tr
Yellow, 2-layer, with chocolate icing:																	
Whole cake	1 cake	1,203	21	4,390	51	156	55	69	23	727	818	7.2	1,920	0.24	0.96	2.4	Tr
Piece, 1/16 of 9-in. diam cake	1 piece	75	21	275	3	10	3	4	1	45	51	0.5	120	0.02	0.06	0.2	Tr
Cookies:																	
Brownies with nuts:																	
Made from home recipe with enriched flour	1 brownie	20	10	95	1	6	1	3	1	10	8	0.4	40	0.04	0.02	0.1	Tr
Made from mix	1 brownie	20	11	85	1	4	1	2	1	13	9	0.4	20	0.03	0.02	0.1	Tr
Chocolate chip:																	
Made from home recipe with enriched flour	1 cookie	10	3	50	1	3	1	1	1	6	4	0.2	10	0.01	0.01	0.1	Tr
Commercial	1 cookie	10	3	50	1	2	1	1	Tr	7	4	0.2	10	Tr	Tr	Tr	Tr
Fig bars, commercial	1 cookie	14	14	50	1	1	—	—	—	11	11	0.2	20	Tr	0.01	0.1	Tr
Sandwich, chocolate or vanilla, commercial	1 cookie	10	2	50	1	2	1	1	Tr	7	2	0.1	0	Tr	Tr	0.1	0
Corn flakes, added nutrients:																	
Plain	1 cup	25	4	100	2	Tr	—	—	—	21	4	0.4	0	0.11	0.02	0.5	0
Sugar-covered	1 cup	40	2	155	2	Tr	—	—	—	36	5	0.4	0	0.16	0.02	0.8	0
Corn (hominy) grits, degermed, cooked:																	
Enriched	1 cup	245	87	125	3	Tr	—	—	—	27	2	0.7	150[3]	0.10	0.07	1.0	0
Unenriched	1 cup	245	87	125	3	Tr	—	—	—	27	2	0.2	150[3]	0.05	0.02	0.5	0
Cornmeal:																	
Whole-ground, unbolted, dry	1 cup	122	12	435	11	5	1	2	2	90	24	2.9	620[3]	0.46	0.13	2.4	0
Bolted (nearly whole-grain) dry	1 cup	122	12	440	11	4	Tr	1	2	91	21	2.2	590[3]	0.37	0.10	2.3	0
Degermed, enriched:																	
Dry form	1 cup	138	12	500	11	2	—	—	—	108	8	4.0	610[3]	0.61	0.36	4.8	0
Cooked	1 cup	240	88	120	3	1	—	—	—	26	2	1.0	140[3]	0.14	0.10	1.2	0
Degermed, unenriched:																	
Dry form	1 cup	138	12	500	11	2	—	—	—	108	8	1.5	610[3]	0.19	0.07	1.4	0
Cooked	1 cup	240	88	120	3	1	—	—	—	26	2	0.5	140[3]	0.05	0.02	0.2	0

(Continued)

TABLE 2.G.8 (*Continued*)

Food, Approximate Measure, and Weight (in Grams)		(g)	Water (%)	Food Energy (Cal)	Protein (g)	Fat (g)	Fatty Acids: Saturated (Total) (g)	Fatty Acids: Unsaturated: Oleic (g)	Fatty Acids: Unsaturated: Linoleic (g)	Carbohydrate (g)	Calcium (mg)	Iron (mg)	Vitamin A Value (IU)	Thiamin (mg)	Riboflavin (mg)	Niacin (mg)	Ascorbic Acid (mg)
Corn muffins, made with enriched degermed cornmeal and enriched flour; muffin 2⅜ in. diam	1 muffin	40	33	125	3	4	2	2	Tr	19	42	0.7	120[3]	0.08	0.09	0.6	Tr
Corn muffins, made with mix, egg, and milk; muffin 2⅜ in. diam	1 muffin	40	30	130	3	4	1	2	1	20	96	0.6	100	0.07	0.08	0.6	Tr
Corn, puffed, presweetened, added nutrients	1 cup	30	2	115	1	Tr	—	—	—	27	3	0.5	0	0.13	0.05	0.6	0
Corn, shredded, added nutrients	1 cup	25	3	100	2	Tr	—	—	—	22	1	0.6	0	0.11	0.05	0.5	0
Crackers:																	
Graham, 2½ in. sq.	4 crackers	28	6	110	2	3	—	—	—	21	11	0.4	0	0.01	0.06	0.4	0
Saltines	4 crackers	11	4	50	1	1	—	1	—	8	2	0.1	0	Tr	Tr	0.1	0
Danish pastry, plain (without fruit or nuts):																	
Packaged ring, 12 oz	1 ring	340	22	1,435	25	80	24	37	15	155	170	3.1	1,050	0.24	0.51	2.7	Tr
Round piece, approx 4¼ in. diam by 1 in.	1 pastry	65	22	275	5	15	5	7	3	30	33	0.6	200	0.05	0.10	0.5	Tr
Ounce	1 oz	28	22	120	2	7	2	3	1	13	14	0.3	90	0.02	0.04	0.2	Tr
Doughnuts, cake type	1 doughnut	32	24	125	1	6	1	4	Tr	16	13	0.4[4]	30	0.05[4]	0.05[4]	0.4[4]	Tr
Farina, quick-cooking, enriched, cooked	1 cup	245	89	105	3	Tr	—	—	—	22	147	0.7[5]	0	0.12[5]	0.07[5]	1.0[5]	0
Macaroni, cooked:																	
Enriched:																	
Cooked, firm stage (undergoes additional cooking in a food mixture)	1 cup	130	64	190	6	1	—	—	—	39	14	1.4[5]	0	0.23[5]	0.14[5]	1.8[5]	0
Cooked until tender	1 cup	140	72	155	5	1	—	—	—	32	8	1.3[5]	0	0.20[5]	0.11[5]	1.5[5]	0
Unenriched:																	
Cooked, firm stage (undergoes additional cooking in a food mixture)	1 cup	130	64	190	6	1	—	—	—	39	14	0.7	0	0.03	0.03	0.5	0
Cooked until tender	1 cup	140	72	155	5	1	—	—	—	32	11	0.6	0	0.01	0.01	0.4	0

Macaroni (enriched) and cheese, baked	1 cup	200	58	430	17	22	10	9	2	40	362	1.8	860	0.20	0.40	1.8	Tr
Canned	1 cup	240	80	230	9	10	4	3	1	26	199	1.0	260	0.12	0.24	1.0	Tr
Muffins, with enriched white flour; muffin, 3-in. diam	1 muffin	40	38	120	3	4	1	2	1	17	42	0.6	40	0.07	0.09	0.6	Tr
Noodles (egg noodles), cooked:																	
Enriched	1 cup	160	70	200	7	2	1	1	Tr	37	16	1.4[5]	110	0.22[5]	0.13[5]	1.9[5]	0
Unenriched	1 cup	160	70	200	7	2	1	1	Tr	37	16	1.0	110	0.05	0.03	0.6	0
Oats (with or without corn) puffed, added nutrients	1 cup	25	3	100	3	1	—	—	—	19	44	1.2	0	0.24	0.04	0.5	0
Oatmeal or rolled oats, cooked	1 cup	240	87	130	5	2	—	—	1	23	22	1.4	0	0.19	0.05	0.2	0
Pancakes, 4-in. diam:																	
Wheat, enriched flour (home recipe)	1 cake	27	50	60	2	2	Tr	1	Tr	9	27	0.4	30	0.05	0.06	0.4	Tr
Buckwheat (made from mix with egg and milk)	1 cake	27	58	55	2	2	1	1	Tr	6	59	0.4	60	0.03	0.04	0.2	Tr
Plain or buttermilk (made from mix with egg and milk)	1 cake	27	51	60	2	2	1	1	Tr	9	58	0.3	70	0.04	0.06	0.2	Tr
Pie (piecrust made with unenriched flour):																	
Sector, 4-in., 1/7 of 9-in. diam pie:																	
Apple (2-crust)	1 sector	135	48	350	3	15	4	7	3	51	11	0.4	40	0.03	0.03	0.5	1
Butterscotch (1-crust)	1 sector	130	45	350	6	14	5	6	2	50	98	1.2	340	0.04	0.13	0.3	Tr
Cherry (2-crust)	1 sector	135	47	350	4	15	4	7	3	52	19	0.4	590	0.03	0.03	0.7	Tr
Custard (1-crust)	1 sector	130	58	285	8	14	5	6	2	30	125	0.8	300	0.07	0.21	0.4	0
Lemon meringue (1-crust)	1 sector	120	47	305	4	12	4	6	2	45	17	0.6	200	0.04	0.10	0.2	4
Mince (2-crust)	1 sector	135	43	365	3	16	4	8	3	56	38	1.4	Tr	0.09	0.05	0.5	1
Pecan (1-crust)	1 sector	118	20	490	6	27	4	16	5	60	55	3.3	190	0.19	0.08	0.4	Tr
Pineapple chiffon (1-crust)	1 sector	93	41	265	6	11	3	5	2	36	22	0.8	320	0.04	0.08	0.4	1
Pumpkin (1-crust)	1 sector	130	59	275	5	15	5	6	2	32	66	0.7	3,210	0.04	0.13	0.7	Tr
Piecrust, baked shell for pie made with:																	
Enriched flour	1 shell	180	15	900	11	60	16	28	12	79	25	3.1	0	0.36	0.25	3.2	0
Unenriched flour	1 shell	180	15	900	11	60	16	28	12	79	25	0.9	0	0.05	0.05	0.9	0
Piecrust mix including stick form:																	
Package, 10-oz, for double crust	1 pkg	284	9	1,480	20	93	23	46	21	141	131	1.4	0	0.11	0.11	2.0	0
Pizza (cheese) 5½-in. sector; 1/8 of 14-in. diam pie	1 sector	75	45	185	7	6	2	3	Tr	27	107	0.7	290	0.04	0.12	0.7	4
Popcorn, popped:																	
Plain, large kernel	1 cup	6	4	25	1	Tr	—	—	—	5	1	0.2	—	—	0.01	0.1	0
With oil and salt	1 cup	9	3	40	1	2	1	Tr	Tr	5	1	0.2	—	—	0.01	0.2	0
Sugar coated	1 cup	35	4	135	2	1	—	—	—	30	2	0.5	—	—	0.02	0.4	0

(Continued)

TABLE 2.G.8 (*Continued*)

Food, Approximate Measure, and Weight (in Grams)		(g)	Water (%)	Food Energy (Cal)	Protein (g)	Fat (g)	Fatty Acids: Saturated (Total) (g)	Fatty Acids: Unsaturated: Oleic (g)	Fatty Acids: Unsaturated: Linoleic (g)	Carbohydrate (g)	Calcium (mg)	Iron (mg)	Vitamin A Value (IU)	Thiamin (mg)	Riboflavin (mg)	Niacin (mg)	Ascorbic Acid (mg)
Pretzels:																	
Dutch, twisted	1 pretzel	16	5	60	2	1	—	—	—	12	4	0.2	0	Tr	Tr	0.1	0
Thin, twisted	1 pretzel	6	5	25	1	Tr	—	—	—	5	1	0.1	0	Tr	Tr	Tr	0
Stick, small, 2¼ in.	10 sticks	3	5	10	Tr	Tr	—	—	—	2	1	Tr	0	Tr	Tr	Tr	0
Stick, regular, 3⅛ in.	5 sticks	3	5	10	Tr	Tr	—	—	—	2	1	Tr	0	Tr	Tr	Tr	0
Rice, white:																	
Enriched:																	
Raw	1 cup	185	12	670	12	1	—	—	—	149	44	5.4[6]	0	0.81[6]	0.06[6]	6.5[6]	0
Cooked	1 cup	205	73	225	4	Tr	—	—	—	50	21	1.8[6]	0	0.23[6]	0.02[6]	2.1[6]	0
Instant, ready-to-serve	1 cup	165	73	180	4	Tr	—	—	—	40	5	1.3[6]	0	0.21[6]	—[6]	1.7[6]	0
Unenriched, cooked	1 cup	205	73	225	4	Tr	—	—	—	50	21	0.4	0	0.04	0.02	0.8	0
Parboiled, cooked	1 cup	175	73	185	4	Tr	—	—	—	41	33	1.4[6]	0	0.19[6]	—[6]	2.1[6]	0
Rice, puffed, added nutrients	1 cup	15	4	60	1	Tr	—	—	—	13	3	0.3	0	0.07	0.01	0.7	0
Rolls, enriched:																	
Cloverleaf or pan:																	
Home recipe	1 roll	35	26	120	3	3	1	1	1	20	16	0.7	30	0.09	0.09	0.8	Tr
Commercial	1 roll	28	31	85	2	2	Tr	1	Tr	15	21	0.5	Tr	0.08	0.05	0.6	Tr
Frankfurter or hamburger	1 roll	40	31	120	3	2	1	1	1	21	30	0.8	Tr	0.11	0.07	0.9	Tr
Hard, round or rectangular	1 roll	50	25	155	5	2	Tr	1	Tr	30	24	1.2	Tr	0.13	0.12	1.4	Tr
Rye wafers, whole-grain, 1⅞ × 3½ in.	2 wafers	13	6	45	2	Tr	—	—	—	10	7	0.5	0	0.04	0.03	0.2	0
Spaghetti, cooked, tender stage, enriched	1 cup	140	72	155	5	1	—	—	—	32	11	1.3[5]	0	0.20[5]	0.11[5]	1.5[5]	0
Spaghetti with meat balls, and tomato sauce:																	
Home recipe	1 cup	248	70	330	19	12	4	6	1	39	124	3.7	1,590	0.25	0.30	4.0	22
Canned	1 cup	250	78	260	12	10	2	3	4	28	53	3.3	1,000	0.15	0.18	2.3	5
Spaghetti in tomato sauce with cheese:																	
Home recipe	1 cup	250	77	260	9	9	2	5	1	37	80	2.3	1,080	0.25	0.18	2.3	13
Canned	1 cup	250	80	190	6	2	1	1	1	38	40	2.8	930	0.35	0.28	4.5	10
Waffles, with enriched flour, 7-in. diam	1 waffle	75	41	210	7	7	2	4	1	28	85	1.3	250	0.13	0.19	1.0	Tr
Waffles, made from mix, enriched, egg and milk added, 7-in. diam	1 waffle	75	42	205	7	8	3	3	1	27	179	1.0	170	0.11	0.17	0.7	Tr

Wheat, puffed, added nutrients	1 cup	15	3	55	2	Tr	—	—	—	12	4	0.6	0	0.08	0.03	1.2	0
Wheat, shredded, plain	1 biscuit	25	7	90	2	1	—	—	—	20	11	0.9	0	0.06	0.03	1.1	0
Wheat flakes, added nutrients	1 cup	30	4	105	3	Tr	—	—	—	24	12	1.3	0	0.19	0.04	1.5	0
Wheat flours:																	
Whole-wheat, from hard wheats, stirred	1 cup	120	12	400	16	2	Tr	1	1	85	49	4.0	0	0.66	0.14	5.2	0
All-purpose or family flour, enriched:																	
Sifted	1 cup	115	12	420	12	1	—	—	—	88	18	3.3[6]	0	0.51[6]	0.30[6]	4.0[6]	0
Unsifted	1 cup	125	12	455	13	1	—	—	—	95	20	3.6[6]	0	0.55[6]	0.33[6]	4.4[6]	0
Self-rising, enriched	1 cup	125	12	400	12	1	—	—	—	93	331	3.6[6]	0	0.55[6]	0.33[6]	4.4[6]	0
Cake or pastry flour, sifted	1 cup	96	12	350	7	1	—	—	—	76	16	0.5	0	0.03	0.03	0.7	0

[1] Values for iron, thiamin, riboflavin, and niacin per pound of unenriched white bread would be as follows:

	Iron (mg)	Thiamin (mg)	Riboflavin (mg)	Niacin (mg)
Soft crumb	3.2	0.31	0.39	5.0
Firm crumb	3.2	0.32	0.59	4.1

[2] Unenriched cake flour used unless otherwise specified.

[3] This value is based on product made from yellow varieties of corn; white varieties contain only a trace.

[4] Based on product made with enriched flour. With unenriched flour, approximate values per doughnut are: iron, 0.2 mg; thiamin, 0.01 mg; riboflavin, 0.03 mg; niacin, 0.2 mg.

[5] Iron, thiamin, riboflavin, and niacin are based on the minimum levels of enrichment specified in standards of identity promulgated under the Federal Food, Drug, and Cosmetic Act.

[6] Iron, thiamin, and niacin are based on the minimum levels of enrichment specified in standards of identity promulgated under the Federal Food, Drug, and Cosmetic Act. Riboflavin is based on unenriched rice. When the minimum level of enrichment for riboflavin specified in the standards of identity becomes effective the value will be 0.2 mg per cup of parboiled rice and of white rice.

SOURCE: Nutritive Value of Foods. USDA Inst. Home Econ., Home Garden Bull. 72.

GRAM STAIN

FORMULA

1. Crystal violet stain (Hucker's Modification)	
Solution A:	
Crystal violet (85% dye content)	20 g
Ethyl alcohol (95%)	200 ml
Solution B:	
Ammonium oxalate	8 g
Distilled water	800 ml
Mix Solutions A and B	
Filter	
2. Iodine solution	
a. Resublimed iodine	20 g
b. N 1 Sodium hydroxide solution (4 g per 100 ml distilled H_2O)	100 ml
c. Distilled water	900 ml
Note: Dissolve iodine in NaOH and add water to make 1000 ml	
3. Safranin Counterstain	
a. Ethyl alcohol solution of safranin (Use 3.4 g per 100 ml of 95% alcohol)	10 ml
b. Distilled water	90 ml

SOURCE: BioQuest, Division of Becton, Dickinson and Co., Rutherford, N.J.

GRAPEFRUIT OIL COMPOSITION

TABLE 2.G.9

CHEMICAL COMPOSITION OF COLD-PRESSED GRAPEFRUIT OIL

TERPENES:
α-pinene
sabinene
β-myrcene
d-limonene
γ-α-terpinene
β-ocimene
α-β-cubebene
α-β-copaene
b-elemene
carophyllene
?
α,β-humulene
cadinene
?
Δ-cadinene
$C_{15}H_{24}$
auraptene

ALDEHYDES:
heptanal
octanal
nonanal
citronellal
decanal
undecanal
dodecanal
citral { geranial, neral }

PHENOLS:
o-phenylphenol

ACIDS:
acetic acid
caprylic acid
capric acid

ALCOHOLS:
methyl heptenol
linalool
octanol
nonanol
decanol
α-terpineol
nerol
geraniol
nerolidol
elemol
trans-2-8-p-menthadiene-1-ol
cis-2-8-p-menthadiene-1-ol
citronellol
trans-carveol
cis-carveol
dodecanol
1-8-p-menthadiene-9-ol
8-p-menthene-1,2-diol

TRITERPENOIDS:
b-sitosterol
citrostadienol
campesterol
stigmasterol
cycloartenol
24-methylene cycloartenol
24-methylene lophenol

ESTERS:
octyl acetate
linalyl acetate
nonyl acetate
geranyl acetate
decyl acetate
neryl acetate
citronellyl acetate
geranyl butyrate

OXIDES:
trans-linalool oxide
cis-linalool oxide

COUMARINS & PSORALENS:
bergamottin
7-geranyloxycoumarin
osthol
limettin (citroptene)
bergapten
bergaptol
7-methoxy-8-(2-formyl-2-methylpropyl)-coumarin
7-((6,7-dihydroxy-3,7-dimethyl-2-octenyl)oxy)-coumarin
5-((3,6-dimethyl-6-formyl-2-heptenyl)oxy)-psoralen
Umbelliferone

KETONES:
nootkatone
methyl heptenone
carvone

SOURCE: KESTERSON, J. W., HENDRICKSON, R. and BRADDOCK, R. J. (1971) Florida Citrus Oils. Florida Agric. Exp. Sta. Tech. Bull. *749*.

GUM CHARACTERISTICS

TABLE 2.G.10

CHARACTERISTICS OF EDIBLE GUMS

Popular Name	Raw Material	Chemical Remarks	Main Residue	Viscosity[1]
Agar-agar	Seaweed	Mixture of polysaccharides	D-galactose, sulfate 3,6-anhydro-L-galactose	Gel
Algin	Brown algae	Polyuronic acid	D-mannuronic acid, L-glucuronic acid	1,800
Carrageenan	Red algae	Polysaccharide ester sulfate	D-galactose, sulfate 3,6-anhydro-D-galactose	225
Guar gum	Seed of bean family	Polyhexose	D-mannose, D-galactose	3,000
Gum acacia	Secretion from a tree	Ca, Mg, and K salts of arabic acid	D-galactose, L-arabinose, L-rhamnose, D-glucuronic acid	Low
Gum tragacanth	Secretion from a shrub	Mixture of complex acid, polysaccharide and neutral araban	L-arabinose, D-xylose, L-fucose, D-galactose	3,200
Karaya gum	Secretion from a tree	Complex acid of polysaccharide	D-galacturonic acid, L-rhamnose, D-galactose	2,300
Locust bean gum	Seed of a tree	Galactomannan	D-galactose, D-mannose	2,750

[1]Centipoise in 1% solution at 25°C.

SOURCE: SONE, T. 1972. Consistency of Foodstuffs. D. Reidel Publishing, Co., Dordrecht, The Netherlands.

GUM DISTRIBUTION

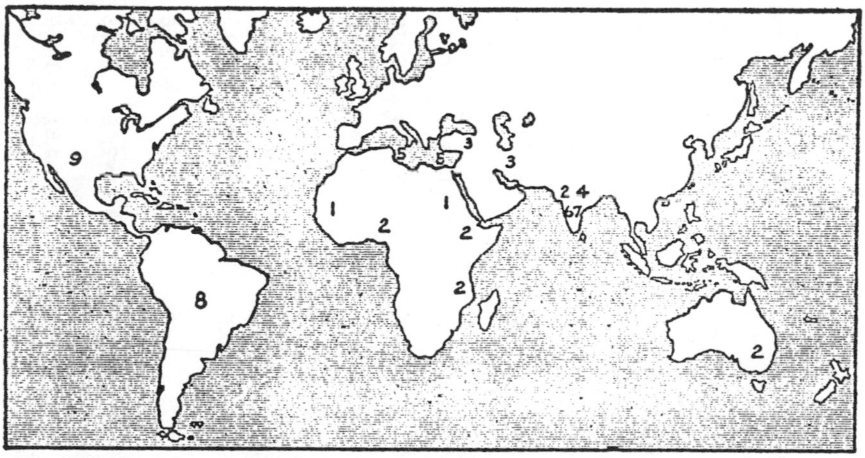

FIG. 2.G.2. MAP SHOWING THE DISTRIBUTION OF THE MORE IMPORTANT VEGETABLE GUMS

(1) Gum Arabic (*Acacia senegal* Willd.); (2) Other Acacia Gums; (3) Gum Tragacanth (*Astragalus* spp.); (4) Indian Tragacanth or Karaya Gum (*Sterculia urens* Roxb.); (5) Carob Seed Gum (*Ceratonia siliqua* L.); (6) Kutira Gum (*Cochlospermum gossypium* DC.); (7) Ghatti Gum (*Anogeissus latifolia* Wall.); (8) Angico Gum (*Piptadenia* spp.); (9) Mesquite Gum (*Prosopis juliflora* DC.).

SOURCE: HOWES, F. N. Vegetable Gums and Resins. Ronald Press Company, New York.

GRAPEFRUIT OIL PROPERTIES

TABLE 2.G.11

MAXIMUM AND MINIMUM VALUES FOR THE PROPERTIES OF COLD-PRESSED GRAPEFRUIT OIL PRODUCED BY VARIOUS METHODS

Method of Extraction	Pipkin Roll		Screw Press		Fraser-Brace		FMC Rotary		FMC In-Line		AMC Scarifier		Brown Shaver	
No. of Samples	4		13		32		5		36		4		6	
Property	Max.	Min.	Max.	Min.	Max.	Min.	Max.	Min.	Max.	Min.	Max.	Min.	Max.	Min.
Sp. grav. 25°C/25°C	0.8537	0.8508	0.8552	0.8483	0.8610	0.8539	0.8649	0.8515	0.8576	0.8476	0.8715	0.8520	0.8583	0.8531
Ref. ind. η_D^{20}	1.4767	1.4746	1.4769	1.4749	1.4785	1.4764	1.4777	1.4752	1.4784	1.4751	1.4836	1.4762	1.4775	1.4766
Ref. ind. 10% dist. η_D^{20}	1.4714	1.4702	1.4721	1.4713	1.4716	1.4706	1.4713	1.4698	1.4722	1.4715	1.4719	1.4714	1.4721	1.4713
Difference	0.0053	0.0038	0.0051	0.0030	0.0072	0.0052	0.0064	0.0054	0.0068	0.0033	0.0117	0.0048	0.0062	0.0047
Opt. rot. α_D^{25}	+92.96	+92.03	+95.56	+91.07	+90.68	+85.14	+91.97	+88.92	+93.95	+90.60	+93.74	+87.02	+93.04	+90.49
Opt. rot. 10% dist. α_D^{25}	+97.77	+96.29	+98.53	+96.60	+98.05	+96.03	+98.14	+95.52	+98.91	+96.55	+98.82	+97.86	+98.28	+97.33
Difference	+4.81	+3.68	+6.10	+2.96	+11.29	+5.99	+6.60	+4.03	+6.40	+3.44	+14.56	+4.12	+6.88	+4.60
Aldehyde content %	1.61	1.49	1.57	1.30	2.06	1.01	1.67	1.12	1.75	0.74	1.91	1.02	1.56	1.17
Ester content %	4.38	2.77	3.68	2.48	5.25	2.91	4.66	2.11	—	—	—	—	—	—
Evaporation residue %	7.72	2.82	8.24	4.57	14.59	9.59	10.12	7.85	9.39	5.22	18.16	7.18	10.45	7.23

SOURCE: KESTERSON, J. W., HENDRICKSON, R., and BRADDOCK, R. J. 1971. Florida Citrus Oils. Florida Agric. Exp. Sta. Tech. Bull. *749*.

GUMS AND GELLING AGENTS

TABLE 2.G.12

PROPERTIES OF GELLING AGENTS AND GUMS

Agent	pH	Solubility Cold	Solubility Hot	Stability Heat	Stability Acid	Storage	Viscosity (aq soln)	Gel Formation
Agar agar	at 1%-:7	Insoluble (swells)	Soluble	Fairly stable	Fairly stable	Weakens	Viscous	Forms firm gel at 0.5% conc. Gels show syneresis. Swell less in acid media.
Alginate	Varies with type	Na salt soluble	Na salt soluble	Fairly stable	Stable	Stable	Very viscous	Compatible with alkalis up to pH 11. Gels formed by divalent salts, the setting time controlled by phosphate.
Arabic gum	at 10%-:4.6	Truly soluble up to 50%	Truly soluble	Degrades	Fairly stable	Weakens	Viscous at at high conc.	Gelling power low. Electrolytes reduce consistency.
Carob gum	at 1%-:5.3	Slightly soluble (swells)	Soluble	Fairly stable	Fairly stable	Stable	Viscous	Useful with agar. Gelling by addition of alkali.
Carrageenan	at 1%-:7.9	Fairly soluble (swells)	Soluble	Stable	Stable	Stable	Viscous	Forms firm gel with added K+ —hence regulation of gel strength by K + salt. Gel thermally reversible.
Gelatin	Varies with type	Insoluble (swells)	Soluble	Degrades	Degrades	Stable	Viscous at low conc.	Gel thermally reversible its rigidity depending on pH, conc., temp, and additives.
Ghatti gum	at 1%-:4.5	Slightly soluble	Soluble	Fairly stable	Fairly stable	Stable	Viscous	Mainly used as an emulsification agent for oil-in-water emulsions.
Guar gum	at 1%-:5.5-6.1	Slightly soluble (swells)	Soluble	Stable	Stable	Stable	Viscous	Gel resistant to heat shock for long periods.
Karaya gum	at 1%-:4.6	Slightly soluble	Soluble	Not very stable	Stable	Stable	Viscous	Normally 3-4% conc. max for uniform gel by cold water hydration.
Pectin	Varies with esterification	Slightly soluble	Soluble	Stable	Stable	Stable	Very viscous	High degree of esterification or methoxylation gives rapid-set gels.

(Continued)

Starch:								
Unmodified	5.0-6.5	Slightly soluble	Soluble	Stable	Degrades	Stable	Viscous	Can be modified for many gels and textures.
Modified	Neutral or adjusted for acid conditions	Slightly soluble	Soluble	Stable	Stable	Stable	Viscosity controlled	Many starches when cooked have a low viscosity but form a rigid gel on cooling.
Tragacanth	at 1%:5.1-5.9	Slightly soluble	Disperses	Highly stable	Stable	Stable	Very viscous	2-4% of gum gives thick gel when thoroughly dispersed.

SOURCE: LEES, R. and JACKSON, E. B. 1973. Sugar Confectionery & Chocolate Manufacture. Leonard Hill Books, International Textbook Co., London, England.

GUMS AND GELLING AGENTS, CHARACTERISTICS

TABLE 2.G.13

CHARACTERISTICS

	Gum Arabic	Starch	Gelatin	Agar	Pectin
Usage Levels for Gelling Agents in Confectionery Products	35%-45%	9%-12%	5%-12½%	1%-1½%	1%-1½%
Percentage of gelling agent to water to effect solution water/agent	50/50	10/1	2/1	50/1	40/1
Temperature of solution required to bring about solution	25°C 77°F	71°-82°C 160°-180°F	60°-65°C 140°-150°F	87°-93°C 190°-200°F	93°-100°C 200°-212°F
Sweetener ratio sucrose/glucose syrup	66/33-50/50	66/33-50/50	66/33-50/50	66/33-60/40	50/50-60/40
Temperature of acid addition	82°C 180°F	93°C 200°F	71°-82°C 160°-180°F	76°C 170°F	93°C 200°F
Depositing temperature	71°-82°C 160°-180°F	82°-93°C 180°-200°F	71°-82°C 160°-180°F	65°-76°C 150°-170°F	82°-93°C 180°-200°F
Setting temperature	20°-37°C 68°-100°F	20°-37°C 68°-100°F	20°-37°C 68°-100°F	35°-37°C 95°-100°F	71°-82°C 160°-180°F
Setting time	24 hr +	12 hr +	4 hr +	3 hr +	1 hr +
Time in starch moulds	36-72 hr	12-36 hr	12-24 hr	12-24 hr	6-12 hr
Starch moisture (%)	5%-8%	5%-8%	5%-8%	5%-8%	5%-10%
Starch temperature	26°-37°C 80°-100°F	37°-49°C 100°-120°F	26°-37°C 80°-100°F	26°-43°C 80°-110°F	37°-49°C 100°-120°F
Total solids: Depositing	68%-70%	72%-78%	72%-78%	76%-80%	76%-78%
Final	85% +	78% +	78% +	80% +	78% +

(Continued)

TABLE 2.G.13 (*Continued*)

	Gum Arabic	Starch	Gelatin	Agar	Pectin
Usage Levels for Gelling Agents in Confectionery Products	35%–45%	9%–12%	5%–12½%	1%–1½%	1%–1½%
Texture	Smooth Malleable Hard bite	Short	Tough, long	Short, soft, some insolubility	Short, ridged, clean bite
Complementary gelling agents	Starch Gelatin	Gum arabic Agar pectin	Agar-starch	Starch Gelatin	Starch
Temperature at final solid atmospheric pressure	124°C 256°F	108°C 228°F	115°C 240°F	107°C 226°F	108°C 228°F
Effect of cooking or holding time on gel strength	Decrease in strength due to extended time and low pH	Prolonged cooking at low pH decreases gel strength	Prolonged time in liquid state and low pH causes loss of gel strength	Lengthy cooking causes weak gel with discoloration	Prolonged boiling causes some degradation
pH during cooking recommended	pH 5.0–6.0	pH 5.0–6.0	pH 5.0–6.0	pH 5.0–6.0	pH 4.0–5.0
Percentage of acid for flavoring	0.3%–0.45%	0.2%–0.4%	0.2%–0.3%	0.2%–0.3%	0.4%–0.7%
Buffer salt recommended	Only required for low pH products	Not normally required	0.1% if acid is added	0.1% to prevent degradation of agar at high temperatures and low pH	0.1%–0.2% to retard setting
Final pH of product	pH 4.2–5.0	pH 4.2–5.0	pH 4.5–5.0	pH 4.8–5.6	pH 3.2–3.5
Shelf-life—Approx	6 months +	5 months +	4 months +	3 months +	5 months +
Flavor carrying performance	Good	Good	Poor	Fair	Very good
Ease of manufacture	Good	Excellent particularly continuous production	Good	Fair	Fair
Preparation of reclaimed waste material for re-use	Good	Fair	Good	Fair	Difficult

SOURCE: LEES, R., and JACKSON, E. B. 1973. Sugar Confectionery and Chocolate Manufacture. Leonard Hill Books, London, England.

GUMS, PHYSICOCHEMICAL PROPERTIES

TABLE 2.G.14

PHYSICOCHEMICAL PROPERTIES OF EDIBLE GUMS

			Effect of Reagents			
Popular Name	pH	Gelation	HCl	NaOH	Salts	Thermal Effect
Agar-agar	7	Yes	Decrease of viscosity	Increase of viscosity up to pH 8.5, then decrease	Little affected	Rigid gel up to 92°C
Carrageenan	7	Yes	Decrease of viscosity	Decrease of viscosity	Prompt gelation	Sol ⇄ Gel at 38°C
Guar gum	7	No	Little affected	Little affected	Gelation	Decrease of viscosity
Gum acacia	5	No	Decrease of viscosity	Increase of viscosity up to pH 7	Gelation	Decrease of viscosity
Gum tragacanth	5.5	Yes	Decrease of viscosity	Increase of viscosity up to pH 8, then decrease	Little affected	Decrease of viscosity
Karaya gum	4.6	No	Decrease of viscosity	Increase of viscosity	Decrease of viscosity	Decrease of viscosity
Locust bean gum	5.3	No	Increase of viscosity	Decrease of viscosity at low concentration Increase of viscosity at high concentration	Gelation	Increase of viscosity up to 70°C

SOURCE: SONE, T. 1972. Consistency of Foodstuffs. D. Reidel Publishing Co., Dordrecht, The Netherlands.

H

HAM CARVING (WHOLE)

Place the ham on the platter with the decorated side up and the shank to the carver's right. Remove several slices from the thin side to form a solid base on which to set the ham.

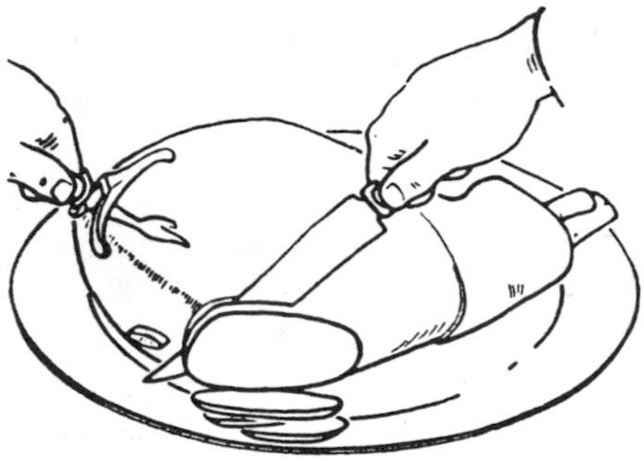

Turn the ham on its base. Starting at the shank end, a small wedge cut is removed; then carve perpendicular to the leg bone as shown at right.

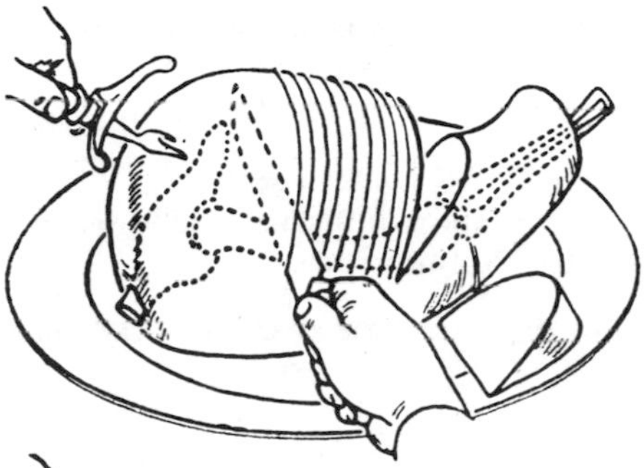

Release slices by cutting under them and along the leg bone, starting at the shank end. For additional servings, turn ham over to the original position and make slices to the bone, release and serve.

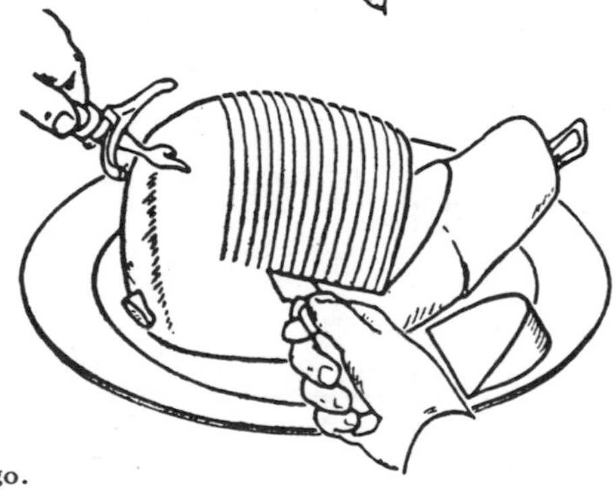

SOURCE: Carving Meat. National Live Stock and Meat Board, Chicago.

HAM, CURING

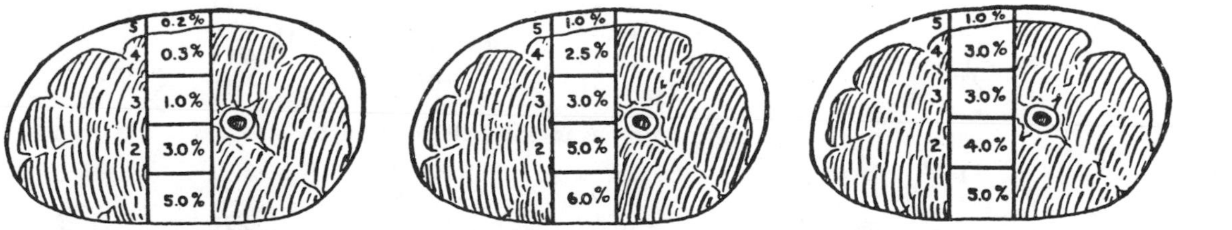

PARTLY CURED | FULLY CURED | AFTER SOAKING AND SMOKING

FIG. 2.H.1. ANALYTICAL CONTROL OF HAM CURING (DRY CURING) SHOWING SECTIONS SAMPLED AND TYPICAL ANALYSIS FOR SALT

SOURCE: MOULTON, C. R. and LEWIS, W. L. Meat Through The Microscope, Revised Edition. Institute of Meat Packaging, The University of Chicago, Chicago.

HERB VINEGARS

Bring to the boiling point 1 pt of cider vinegar and pour it over one of the following:

½ tsp of dried herbs
rosemary tarragon
basil dill seed
2 tbsp of fresh herbs
rosemary sorrel
sage
½ cup of chopped mint leaves
chives
1 head dill seed
1 small clove garlic (slashed)

Some prefer a mixed spice herb vinegar. Here is one combination. To 1 qt of boiling clear vinegar add:

½ tsp clove buds 1 stick cinnamon
½ tsp peppercorn 1 small clove garlic, slashed

Let the above infusion stand for about 10 days, then strain and store covered or bottled for future use.

SOURCE: KINTNER, T. C. and MANGEL, M. Vinegars and salad dressings. Univ. Missouri, Agric. Expt. Sta., Bull. *631*.

HIDE CURING

TABLE 2.H.1

DEHYDRATION AND SALT ABSORPTION

Hours Treatment	Percentage of Shrinkage	Percentage of Dehydration	Percentage of Salt Absorbed	Ratio: Dehydration / Salt Absorbed
		Dry-Salt Treatment		
1	5.37	6.91	+1.54	4.49
3	10.45	13.81	+3.36	4.11
4	12.79	16.69	+3.89	4.29
5	16.45	20.76	+4.31	4.81
24	23.85	30.51	+6.66	4.58
		Brining in 25% Salt Solution		
1	5.76	8.15	+2.39	3.41
2	8.96	11.62	+2.66	4.37
3	9.63	13.12	+3.49	3.76
4	10.90	15.06	+4.16	3.62
5	11.81	16.48	+4.67	3.53
24	13.45	21.21	+7.76	2.74

SOURCE: MOULTON, C. R. and LEWIS, W. L. Meat Through the Microscope, Revised Edition. Institute of Meat Packing, University of Chicago, Chicago.

HIDE, LAYERS

TABLE 2.H.2

PERCENTAGE OF WATER AND SALT IN VARIOUS HIDE LAYERS

Layer		When Fresh	After 1 hr in Salt	After 4.5 hr in Salt	After 24 hr in Salt
Epidermal layer	Water	74.35	74.00	71.75	54.75
	Salt	—	0.42	0.85	1.10
Corium	Water	61.00	57.25	58.85	45.30
	Salt	—	0.80	2.09	3.78
Adipose tissue	Water	54.10	50.00	46.60	22.30
	Salt	—	0.28	0.37	1.03
Total hide	Water	61.66	60.41	57.07	40.78
	Salt	—	1.50	3.31	5.90

SOURCE: MOULTON, C. R. and LEWIS, W. L. Meat Through the Microscope, Revised Edition. Institute of Meat Packing, University of Chicago, Chicago.

HIDES, SALT ABSORPTION

TABLE 2.H.3

ABSORPTION OF SALT FROM FLESH AND HAIR SIDES

Side	Hours	Percentage of Salt Absorbed	Percentage of Total Salt in		
			Epidermis	Corium	Adipose Tissue
Hair side only	1.0	None	—	—	—
	4.5	None	—	—	—
	24.0	0.227	23	59	18
Flesh side only	1.0	1.20	28	62	10
	4.5	2.97	23	66	11
	24.0	5.70	18	67	15
Both sides	1.0	1.05	28	53	19
	4.5	2.86	26	53	11
	24.0	5.45	19	64	17

SOURCE: MOULTON, C. R. and LEWIS, W. L. Meat Through the Microscope, Revised Edition. Institute of Meat Packing, University of Chicago, Chicago.

HISTOCHEMICAL TESTS

TABLE 2.H.4

PREPARATION AND METHODS FOR HISTOCHEMICAL TESTS
Abbreviations: conc. = concentrated; sat. = saturated; sol. = solution.

Substance	Preparation of Tissue	Preparation of Reagents	Test Method	Result
Lipids	Fix in 4% formaldehyde containing 1% calcium chloride. Cut frozen sections, if necessary, after embedding in gelatin.	Digest 1 g Sudan black B in 100 ml 60% triethyl phosphate at 100°C for 5 min with constant agitation. Cool, then filter.	Stain section 2-5 min. Wash in 60% triethyl phosphate. Wash in H_2O and stain carmine-light green. Mount in aqueous medium.	Lipid granules, black; nuclei, red; cytoplasm, green.
Cholesterol	Cut frozen sections of fresh or formaldehyde-fixed material.		Strand section on slide. Drain well. Cover with 2 drops conc. H_2SO_4 for 10 sec. Add 2 drops acetic anhydride, wait 10 sec, then wash thoroughly with acetic anhydride. Place cover slip on section.	Cholesterol shows green, or blue-green. Preparation cannot be preserved.
Glycogen	Fix in ethanol at 0°C. Cut 10-μ paraffin sections and mount on slide; deparaffinize in xylene. Rinse in equal parts ethanol and ether. Dip in collodion U.S.P.	Boil 2 g carmine, 1 g potassium carbonate, and 5 g potassium chloride in 60 ml H_2O for 5 min. Cool, then add 20 ml ammonium hydroxide. For use, dilute 10 ml of this stock sol. with 15 ml ammonium hydroxide and 15 ml ethanol.	Stain collodionized sections in celestin blue B. Wash thoroughly in water. Stain in carmine 15 min. Rinse thoroughly in methanol, dehydrate in acetone, clear in xylene, and mount in balsam.	Nuclei, black; glycogen granules, scarlet.
Starch	Fix in any dichromate--chromic acid--formaldehyde fixative. Cut paraffin sections.	Saturate hot anilin with acid fuchsin. Shake well, separate, and retain water fraction.	Pour acid fuchsin stain on sections; heat to steaming for 1 min. Rinse in H_2O and place in 5% aurantia in ethanol until no color comes away. Rinse in 70% ethanol and transfer to 2% tannic acid for 15 min. Transfer directly to 1% methyl green for 10 min. Differentiate in ethanol until starch grains are sharply distinct.	Plastids, proplastids, and mitochondria, red; starch, green. The standard iodine test for starch does not yield permanent preparations.
Mucin	Cut paraffin sections of material fixed in any mercuric chloride or dichromate fixative.		Stain 10-40 sec in 1% Alcian Blue. Rinse quickly in H_2O and transfer for 2 hr to 0.5% borax in 80% ethanol. Dehydrate and mount in balsam.	Mucin, bright blue. Stained sections may be counterstained in hematoxylin-eosin if further histological detail is desired.
Celluloses	Sections of plant tissues, or teased fibers.	Dissolve 2 g iodine and 5 g potassium iodide in a small amount of H_2O. Dilute to 100 ml. Add 10 ml iodine sol. and 0.25 ml glycerol to 90 ml H_2O.	Cover specimen with iodine sol. for 15 sec. Blot dry. Add 1 drop of sat. aqueous sol. lithium carbonate. Apply cover slip.	Pure cellulose, blue; impure celluloses, various shades of green, yellow, and brown.
Lignin	Sections of plant tissues, or teased fibers.		Place in 1% phloroglucinol for 2 min. Blot and add 1 drop of HCl.	Lignin, red.
Chitin	Sections of tissues.	Dissolve 10 g anilin hydrochloride in 100 ml 1% HCl. Stain sections 5 min.	Transfer to 7.5% potassium dichromate for 1 min. Rinse in H_2O and place in alkaline tap water until color changes from green to blue.	Chitin, blue.

TABLE 2.H.4 (*Continued*)

Substance	Preparation of Tissue	Preparation of Reagents	Test Method	Result
DNA	Sections or smears of either animal or plant material.	Boil 1 g magenta ("basic" fuchsin) in 100 ml H_2O. Add 20 ml *N* HCl. Cool, filter, and add 5 ml 10% sodium bisulfite. Leave in dark 24 hr.	Hydrolyze material 20 min in *N* HCl. Stain 2 hr in dark. Bleach cytoplasm 1-2 min in freshly made 100 ml H_2O, 5 ml 10% sodium bisulfite, 5 ml *N* HCl. Counterstain in light green if desired. Dehydrate, clear, and mount in balsam.	
RNA	10-μ paraffin sections of tissues.	Shake 0.5 g methyl green with successive batches of chloroform until all chloroform-soluble color is removed. Add 13 ml of purified dye sol. to 50 ml pH 4.8 acetate buffer and 37 ml 0.5% pyroam G.	Take sections to H_2O. Blot. Stain 30 min. Blot. Pass to acetone 1 min, and 50:50 acetone-xylene 1 min. Clear in xylene and mount in balsam.	RNA, blue to blue-green; DNA, red.
Proteins	10-μ sections of neutral formaldehyde-fixed material.	Mix 95 ml ethanol with 0.5 ml 0.2 *N* sodium hydroxide. Add 0.5 g 2,4-dinitro-fluorobenzene.	Take sections to H_2O. Stain 24 hr. Rinse thoroughly in ethanol, then H_2O. Bleach in 5% sodium thiosulfate 40 min at 37°C. Rinse in H_2O. Add 5 ml ice-cold 4*N* H_2SO_4 to 100 ml ice-cold 5% sodium nitrate. Soak bleached sections 4-5 min. Rinse in H_2O. Transfer to 2% H-acid in barbitone-acetate pH 9.2 buffer for 15 min. Rinse in H_2O, dehydrate, clear, and mount in balsam.	Protein, purple-red.
Iron	10-μ, or thicker, sections of tissues fixed in iron-free, neutral formaldehyde.		Take sections to H_2O. Place in 2% potassium ferrocyanide with equal volume of 0.2 *N* HCl and stain 20 min. Dehydrate, clear, mount in balsam.	Reactive iron, blue. Non-reactive iron (e.g., in hemoglobin) may be rendered reactive by treating sections for 30 min, before staining, in alkaline H_2O_2.
Hemoglobin	10-μ, or thicker, sections of tissues fixed in neutral formaldehyde.	Dissolve 1-2 g benzidine in 100 ml methanol with 1.2 ml acetic acid. Add 0.12 g sodium nitroprusside.	Deparaffinize sections in xylene. Remove xylene completely in several changes of methanol. Stain 10 min. Wash in 50 ml methanol, 25 ml ether, 25 ml 3% H_2O_2. Dehydrate, clear, and mount in balsam.	Hemoglobin, bright blue.
Carotene	Immerse plant tissues in 20 ml sat. aqueous sol. potassium hydroxide, 15 ml ethanol, 85 ml H_2O in dark until all green removed.		Wash pieces thoroughly in H_2O. Place fragment on slide, blot, and cover with H_2SO_4.	Areas of dark blue crystals indicate carotene locations.

SOURCE: ALTMAN, P. L., and DITTMER, D. S. (EDITORS). Biology Data Book. Federation of American Societies for Experimental Biology, Bethesda, Maryland.

HONEY COMPOSITION

TABLE 2.H.5

AVERAGE COMPOSITION OF US HONEY AND RANGE OF VALUES[1]

Characteristic or constituent		Floral Honey Average values	Range of Values
Color[2]		Dark half of white	Light half of water white to dark
Granulating tendency[3]		Few clumps of crystals, 1/8- to 1/4-inch layer	Liquid to complete hard granulation
Moisture	percent	17.2	13.4 - 22.9
Fructose	,,	38.19	27.45 - 44.26
Glucose	,,	31.28	22.03 - 40.75
Sucrose	,,	1.31	0.25 - 7.57
"Maltose"[4]	,,	7.31	2.74 - 15.98
Higher sugars	,,	1.50	0.13 - 8.49
Undetermined	,,	3.1	0 - 13.2
pH		3.91	3.42 - 6.10
Free acidity[5]		22.03	6.75 - 47.19
Lactone[5]		7.11	0 - 18.76
Total acidity[5]		29.12	8.68 - 59.49
Lactone ÷ free acid		0.335	0 - 0.950
Ash	percent	0.169	0.02 - 1.028
Nitrogen	,,	0.041	0 - 0.133
Diastase[6] (270 samples)		20.8	2.1 - 61.2

[1] Based on 490 samples of floral honey.

[2] Expressed in terms of USDA color classes.

[3] Extent of granulation for heated samples after 6 months' undisturbed storage.

[4] Reducing disaccharides as maltose.

[5] Milliequivalent per kilogram.

[6] Grams of starch converted by enzyme in 100 gm honey in 1 hr under assay conditions.

SOURCE: WHITE, JR., JONATHAN and UNDERWOOD, J. CLYDE. 1974. Maple Syrup and Honey. *In* Symposium: Sweeteners. G. E. Inglett (Editor). Avi Publishing Co., Westport, Conn.

HUMIDITY, SOLUTIONS

A saturated aqueous solution in contact with an excess of the solute when kept in an enclosed space will maintain a constant humidity at a given temperature.

TABLE 2.H.6

CONSTANT HUMIDITY SOLUTIONS

Substance Dissolved and Solid Phase	Temp (°C)	Humidity (%)
Lead nitrate, $Pb(NO_3)_2$	20	98
Dibasic sodium phosphate, $Na_2HPO_4 \cdot 12H_2O$	20	95
Monobasic ammonium phosphate, $NH_4H_2PO_4$	20-25	93
Zinc sulfate, $ZnSO_4 \cdot 7H_2O$	20	90
Potassium chromate, K_2CrO_4	20	88
Potassium bisulfate, $KHSO_4$	20	86
Potassium bromide, KBr	20	84
Ammonium sulfate, $(NH_4)_2SO_4$	20	81
Ammonium chloride, NH_4Cl	20-25	79
Sodium acetate, $NaC_2H_3O_2 \cdot 3H_2O$	20	76
Sodium chlorate, $NaClO_3$	20	75
Sodium nitrite, $NaNO_2$	20	66
Sodium bromide, $NaBr \cdot 2H_2O$	20	58
Magnesium nitrite, $Mg(NO_3)_2 \cdot 6H_2O$	18.5	56
Sodium dichromate, $Na_2Cr_2O_7 \cdot 2H_2O$	20	52
Potassium thiocyanate, KSCN	20	47
Zinc nitrate, $Zn(NO_3)_2 \cdot 6H_2O$	20	42
Chromium trioxide, CrO_3	20	35
Calcium chloride, $CaCl_2 \cdot 6H_2O$	24.5	31
Potassium acetate, $KC_2H_3O_2$	20	20
Lithium chloride, $LiCl \cdot H_2O$	20	15

SOURCE: The Merck Index, 8th Edition. (1968). Merck & Co., Rahway, N.J.

HYDROCHLORIC ACID, SOLUTION

TABLE 2.H.7

VARIOUS STRENGTHS OF HYDROCHLORIC ACID SOLUTIONS
Hydrochloric Acid Solutions: Specification requires not <35% HCl by wt Sp gr = 1.778 at 15°. Mix with H_2O and dil to 1 liter.

HCl Strength Desired	HCl Required		
g per liter	g	ml	
5	14.29	12.13	
10	28.57	24.26	
15	42.85	36.39	
20	57.14	48.52	
36.46	104.17	88.45	1*N* soln
50	142.86	121.29	
100	285.71	242.58	
150	428.57	363.88	
200	571.43	485.17	
222.6	636.00	539.99	Constant boiling
278.4	795.43	675.35	Sp gr 1.125
300	857.14	727.75	

SOURCE: EDITORIAL BOARD, AOAC. 1975. Official Methods of Analysis of the Association of Official Analytical Chemists, 12th Edition. Association of Official Analytical Chemists, Washington, D.C.

I

ICE, VAPOR PRESSURE

TABLE 2.I.1

VAPOR PRESSURE OF ICE

Pressure of Aqueous Vapor over Ice in mm Hg at Various Temperatures							
Temperature		Vapor Pressure		Temperature		Vapor Pressure	
°C	°F	mm Hg	μ	°C	°F	mm Hg	μ
0	32.0	4.579	4579.0	-36	-32.8	0.1507	150.7
-2	28.4	3.880	3880.0	-40	-40.0	0.0966	96.6
-4	24.8	3.280	3280.0	-44	-47.2	0.0609	60.9
-6	21.2	2.765	2765.0	-48	-54.4	0.0378	37.8
-8	17.6	2.326	2326.0	-52	-61.6	0.02300	23.00
-10	14.0	1.950	1950.0	-56	-68.8	0.01380	13.80
-12	10.4	1.632	1632.0	-60	-76.0	0.00808	8.08
-14	6.8	1.361	1361.0	-64	-83.2	0.00464	4.64
-16	3.2	1.132	1132.0	-68	-90.4	0.00261	2.61
-18	-0.4	0.939	939.0	-72	-97.6	0.00143	1.43
-20	-4.0	0.776	776.0	-76	-104.8	0.00077	0.77
-22	-7.6	0.640	640.0	-80	-112.0	0.00040	0.40
-24	-11.2	0.526	526.0	-84	-119.2	0.00020	0.20
-26	-14.8	0.430	430.0	-88	-126.4	0.00010	0.10
-28	-18.4	0.351	351.0	-92	-133.6	0.000048	0.048
-30	-22.0	0.2859	285.9	-96	-140.8	0.000022	0.022
-32	-25.6	0.2318	231.8	-98	-144.4	0.000015	0.015
-34	-29.2	0.1873	187.3	—	—	—	—

SOURCE: COPSON, D. A. (EDITOR). 1975. Derivation of the Theory of Microwave Freeze-Drying. *In* Microwave Heating, 2nd Edition. Avi Publishing Co., Westport, Conn.

ILLNESS FROM FOOD

TABLE 2.1.2

CLASSIFICATION OF ILLNESS ATTRIBUTABLE TO FOODS

Type of Illness	Causative agent	Food Usually Involved	Incubation Period	Symptoms
		A. Bacterial Food Infections		
Shigellosis Bacillary Dysentery	Members of the genus *Shigella*	Moist prepared foods, milk and other dairy products, contaminated with excreta	Usually 2–3 days	Diarrhea, bloody stools, fever in severe cases
Cholera	*Vibrio Comma*	Fecally contaminated food and water	2–5 days	Nausea, vomiting, diarrhea, and abdominal cramps
Brucellosis, Undulant Fever or Bang's Disease	*Brucella abortus, B. melitensis, or B. Suis*	Raw milk or dairy products contaminated with raw milk, animal contact (meat)	3–21 days sometimes several months	Chills, sweats, weakness, malaise, headache, fever, muscle and joint pains, and loss of weight
Diphtheria	*Corynebacterium diphtheriae*	Milk contaminated from human sources	3–7 days	Insidious onset, inflammation of throat and nose
Hemolytic streptococci, scarlet fever and septic sore throat	Beta hemolytic streptococci	Food contaminated with nasal or oral discharges and milk from cows having udder infections	1–7 days	Fever, sore throat, sometimes rash
Streptococcal food infections	*Enterococcus Streptococcus fecalis*	Food contaminated with excreta or human carrier	2–18 days	Nausea, vomiting, pains, and diarrhea
Salmonellosis				
a. Typhoid Fever	*Salmonella typhi*	Any food contaminated with excreta from human case or carrier	Usually 7–21 days	Malaise, lack of appetite, headache, fever
b. Paratyphoid A.	*Salmonella paratyphi* A.	Same as for typhoid fever	1–10 days	Same as for typhoid fever

c. Other Types	*Salmonella typhimurium* *Salmonella enteritis* *Salmonella cholera suis* *Salmonella newport*	Meat, poultry salads, and egg products	12–72 hours	Abdominal pain, diarrhea, chills, fever, vomiting, and prostration
Tuberculosis	*Mycobacterium tuberculosis*, human and bovine types A and B	Raw contaminated milk and other dairy products	Variable	Depends on part of body affected
Tularemia	*Pasteurella tularensis*	Wild game animals	3–10 days	Sudden onset, headache, chills, body pains, fever, vomiting, swollen lymph glands, and loss of appetite
Trichinosis	*Trichinella spiralis*	Raw pork or similar products	36–72 hours	
		B. Bacterial Food Intoxications		
Staphylococcal intoxication	Staphylococcus producing Enterotoxin	Meats, food rich in carbohydrates, especially salads and warmed over foods	2–11 hours	Nausea, vomiting, diarrhea, and abdominal cramps
Botulism	Exotoxin *Clostridium botulinum* and *C. parabotulinum*	Home processed foods and contaminated canned foods with pH over 4.5	12 hours to 6 days	Dizziness, double vision, muscular weakness, difficulty in swallowing, speech and respiration
Clostridium perfringens (welchii)	*Cl. welchii* Type A. Exotoxin Alpha type	Cold and reheated meats, water, milk, salt rising bread. Found in intestinal tract of man and animals	8–22 hours (variable)	Acute abdominal pains, diarrhea, nausea, and vomiting rare

NOTE: *Clostridium perfringens* and *Bacillus cereus* may cause symptoms identical to *Streptococcus fecalis*, providing they are present in the food product in large numbers.

SOURCE: WEISER, H. H., MOUNTNEY, G. J. and GOULD, W. A. (EDITORS). 1971. Food Poisoning. *In* Practical Food Microbiology and Technology, 2nd Edition. Avi Publishing Co., Westport, Conn.

INDICATORS: pH AND ACID BASE

TABLE 2.I.3

ACID BASE INDICATORS

Indicator	Approximate pH range	Color-change	Preparation
Methyl Violet	0.0–1.6	yel to bl	0.01–0.05% in water
Crystal Violet	0.0–1.8	yel to bl	0.02% in water
Ethyl Violet	0.0–2.4	yel to bl	0.1 g in 50 ml of MeOH + 50 ml of water
Malachite Green	0.2–1.8	yel to bl grn	water
Methyl Green	0.2–1.8	yel to bl	0.1% in water
2-(p-dimethylaminophenylazo)pyridine	0.2–1.8 4.4–5.6	yel to bl red to yel	0.1% in EtOH
o-Cresolsulfonephthalein (Cresol Red)	0.4–1.8 7.0–8.8	yel to red yel to red	0.1 g in 26.2 ml 0.01N NaOH + 223.8 ml water
Quinaldine Red	1.0–2.2	col to red	1% in EtOH
p-(p-dimethylaminophenylazo)-benzoic acid, Na-salt (Paramethyl Red)	1.0–3.0	red to yel	EtOH
m-(p-anilnophenylazo)benzene sulfonic acid, Na-salt (Metanil Yellow)	1.2–2.4	red to yel	0.01% in water
4-Phenylazodiphenylamine	1.2–2.6	red to yel	0.01 g in 1 ml 1N HCl + 50 ml EtOH + 49 ml water
Thymolsulfonephthalein (Thymol Blue)	1.2–2.8 8.0–9.6	red to yel yel to bl	0.1 g in 21.5 ml 0.01N NaOH + 229.5 ml water
m-Cresolsulfonephthalein (Metacresol Purple)	1.2–2.8 7.4–9.0	red to yel yel to purp	0.1 g in 26.2 ml 0.01N NaOH + 223.8 ml water
p-(p-anilinophenylazo)benzenesulfonic acid, Na-salt (Orange IV)	1.4–2.8	red to yel	0.01% in water
4-o-Tolylazo-o-toluidine	1.4–2.8	or to yel	water
Erythrosine, disodium salt	2.2–3.6	or to red	0.1% in water
Benzopurpurine 48	2.2–4.2	vt to red	0.1% in water
N,N-dimethyl-p-(m-tolylazo)aniline	2.6–4.8	red to yel	0.1% in water
4,4′-Bix(2-amino-1-naphthylazo)2,2′-stilbenedisulfonic acid	3.0–4.0	purp to red	0.1 g in 5.9 ml 0.05N NaOH + 94.1 ml water
Tetrabromophenolphthaleinethyl ester, K-salt	3.0–4.2	yel to bl	0.1% in EtOH
3′,3″,5′,5″-tetrabromophenolsulfonephthalein (Bromophenol Blue)	3.0–4.6	yel to bl	0.1 g in 14.9 ml 0.01N NaOH + 235.1 ml water
2,4-Dinitrophenol	2.8–4.0	col to yel	saturated water solution
N,N-Dimethyl-p-phenylazoaniline (p-Dimethylaminoazobenzene)	2.8–4.4	red to yel	0.1 g in 90 ml in EtOH + 10 ml water
Congo Red	3.0–5.0	blue to red	0.1% in water
Methyl Orange-Xylene Cyanole solution	3.2–4.2	purp to grn	ready solution
Methyl Orange	3.2–4.4	red to yel	0.01% in water
Ethyl Orange	3.4–4.8	red to yel	0.05–0.2% in water or aqueous EtOH
4-(4-Dimethylamino-1-naphthylazo)-3-methoxybenzenesulfonic acid	3.5–4.8	vt to yel	0.1% in 60% EtOH
3′,3″,5′,5″-Tetrabromo-m-cresolsulfonephthalein (Bromocresol Green)	3.8–5.4	yel to blue	0.1 g in 14.3 ml 0.01N NaOH + 235.7 ml water
Resazurin	3.8–6.4	or to vt	water
4-Phenylazo-1-naphthylamine	4.0–5.6	red to yel	0.1% in EtOH
Ethyl Red	4.0–5.8	col to red	0.1 g in 50 ml MeOH + 50 ml water
2-(p-Dimethylaminophenylazo)-pyridine	0.2–1.8 4.4–5.6	yel to red red to yel	0.1% in EtOH
4-(p-ethoxyphenylazo)-m-phenylenediamine monohydrochloride	4.4–5.8	or to yel	0.1% in water
Lacmoid	4.4–6.2	red to bl	0.2% in EtOH
Alizarin Red S	4.6–6.0	yel to red	dilute solution in water
Methyl Red	4.8–6.0	red to yel	0.02 g in 60 ml EtOH + 40 ml water

TABLE 2.1.3 (*Continued*)

Indicator	Approximate pH range	Color-change	Preparation
Propyl Red	4.8–6.6	red to yel	EtOH
5′,5″-Dibromo-o-cresolsulfone-phthalein (Bromocresol Purple)	5.2–6.8	yel to purp	0.1 g in 18.5 ml 0.01N NaOH + 231.5 ml water
3′,3″-Dichlorophenolsulfonephthalein (Chlorophenol Red)	5.2–6.8	yel to red	0 1 g in 23.6 ml 0.01N NaOH + 226.4 ml water
p-Nitrophenol	5.4–6.6	col to yel	0.1% in water
Alizarin	5.6–7.2	yel to red	0.1% in MeOH
	11.0–12.4	red to purp	
2-(2,4-Dinitrophenylazo)-1-naphthol-3, 6-disulfonic acid, di-Na salt	6.0–7.0	yel to bl	0.1% in water
3′,3″-Dibromothymolsulfonephthalein (Bromothymol Blue)	6.0–7.6	yel to bl	0.1 g in 16 ml 0.01N NaOH + 234 ml water
6,8-Dinitro-2,4-(1H)quinazolinedione (m-Dinitrobenzoylene urea)	6.4–8.0	col to yel	25 g in 115 ml M NaOH + 50 ml boiling water
			0.292 g of NaCl in 100 ml water
Brilliant Yellow	6.6–7.8	yel to or	1% in water
Phenolsulfonephthalein (Phenol Red)	6.6–8.0	yel to red	0.1 g in 28.2 ml 0.01N NaOH + 221.8 ml water
Neutral Red	6.8–8.0	red to amb	0.01 g in 50 ml EtOH + 50 ml water
m-Nitrophenol	6.8–8.6	col to yel	0.3% in water
o-Cresolsulfonephthalein (Cresol Red)	0.0–1.0	red to yel	0.1 g in 26.2 ml 0.01N
	7.0–8.8	yel to red	NaOH + 223.8 ml water
Curcumin	7.4–8.6	yel to red	EtOH
	10.2–11.8		
m-Cresolsulfonephthalein (Metacresol Purple)	1.2–2.8	red to yel	0.1 g in 26.2 ml 0.01N
	7.4–9.0	yel to purp	NaOH + 223.8 ml water
4,4′-Bis(4-amino-1-naphthylazo) 2,2′stilbene disulfonic acid	8.0–9.0	bl to red	0.1 g in 5.9 ml 0.05N NaOH + 94.1 ml water
Thymolsulfonephthalein (Thymol Blue)	1.2–2.8	red to yel	0.1 g in 21.5 ml 0.01N
	8.0–9.6		NaOH + 228.5 ml water
o-Cresolphthalein	8.2–9.8	col to red	0.04% in EtOH
p-Naphtholbenzene	8.2–10.0	or to bl	1% in dil. alkali
Phenolphthalein	8.2 10.0	col to pink	0.05 g in 50 ml EtOH + 50 ml water
Ethyl-bis(2,4-dimethylphenyl)acetate	8.4–9.6	col to bl	saturated solution in 50% acetone alcohol
Thymolphthalein	9.4–10.6	col to bl	0.04 g in 50 ml EtOH + 50 ml water
5-(p-Nitrophenylazo)salicylic acid, Na-salt (Alizarin Yellow R)	10.1–12.0	yel to red	0.01% in water
p-(2,4-Dihydroxyphenylazo)benzenesulfonic acid, Na-salt	11.4–12.6	yel to or	0.1% in water
5,5′-Indigodisulfonic acid, di-Na-salt	11.4–13.0	bl to yel	water
2,4,6-Trinitrotoluene	11.5–13.0	col to or	0.1–0.5% in EtOH
1,3,5-Trinitrobenzene	12.0–14.0	col to or	0.1–0.5% in EtOH
Clayton Yellow	12.2–13.2	yel to amb	0.1% in water

SOURCE: WEAST, R. C. (EDITOR). 1974–1975. Handbook of Chemistry and Physics, 55th Edition. CRC Press, Cleveland. Reproduced with permission of CRC Press.

INFECTIOUS AGENTS

TABLE 2.I.4

DISEASE FROM INGESTION OF INFECTIOUS AGENTS

Disease	Reservoirs	Common Vehicle	Prevention and Control
Salmonellosis (salmonella infection)	Hogs, cattle and other livestock, poultry, pets, eggs, powdered eggs, carriers.	Contaminated cooked meat; infected meats; salads; warmed over foods; milk; milk products.	Thoroughly cook food; eliminate rodents, pets and carriers; similar measures as in staphylococcus, plant sanitation.
Typhoid fever	Feces and urine of typhoid carrier or patient.	Contaminated water; milk and milk products; shellfish and foods; flies.	Protect and purify water supply; pasteurize milk and milk products; educate food handlers; provide food, fly, shellfish control, and sanitary sewage disposal; supervise carriers; immunize.
Streptococcal infections	Human mouth, nose, throat, respiratory tract.	Contaminated meats; milk; croquettes; cheese; dressing.	Provide control measures similar to those for Staphylococcus; pasteurize milk and milk products.
Shigellosis (bacillary dysentery)	Bowel discharges of carriers and infected persons.	Contaminated water or foods; milk and milk products; flies.	Provide food, water, sewage sanitation as in typhoid; pasteurize milk (boil for infants); control flies; supervise carriers.

SOURCE: U.S. Department of the Army, Food Inspection Specialist, *TM 8-451*, 1969.

INFECTIOUS DISEASES, FOOD-BORNE

TABLE 2.I.5

SOME COMMON INFECTIOUS DISEASES ACCORDING TO MOST USUAL MODE OF TRANSMISSION
(Common Food-borne)

Disease	Synonym	Causative Agent	Mode of Transmission	Methods of Prevention	Treatments Available
Food poisoning	Staph food poisoning	Soluble enterotoxin produced by the growth of *Staphylococcus aureus* in foods	Ingestion of contaminated foods	1. Prevent contamination 2. Refrigeration	Supportive
Food poisoning		Growth of *Clostridium perfringens* in foods, most often meats	Ingestion of contaminated foods	1. Prevent contamination 2. Serve foods hot without delay 3. Adequate cooking 4. Refrigeration	Supportive

TABLE 2.1.5 (*Continued*)

Disease	Synonym	Causative Agent	Mode of Transmission	Methods of Prevention	Treatments Available
Botulism		Soluble toxins produced by growth of *Clostridium botulinum* in anaerobic nonacid foods	Ingestion of contaminated foods	1. Prevent contamination 2. Proper heat preservation 3. Heat to boiling for 15 min before eating	Specific antitoxin
Salmonellosis	Food poisoning	Anyone of many species or types of *Salmonella*	Ingestion of live organisms in contaminated foods	1. Prevent contamination 2. Cleaning raw foods 3. Thorough cooking 4. Refrigeration 5. Detect and eliminate carriers	Antibiotic treatment has irregular success
Typhoid fever, Paratyphoid fever	Enteric fever	*Salmonella typhi*, *Salmonella paratyphi* A, *Salmonella paratyphi* B, *Salmonella paratyphi* C	Ingestion of live organisms in contaminated foods or water	1. Chlorination of water 2. Detection and elimination of carriers 3. Proper cooking of foods 4. Immunization 5. General sanitation	Antibiotic treatment
Shigellosis	Bacillary dysentery	Any one of many species or types of *Shigella*	Ingestion of live organisms in contaminated foods or water	1. Chlorination of water 2. Proper cooking and handling of foods 3. General sanitation	Antibiotic treatment plus fluid maintenance
Streptococcal Pharangitis	Strep throat Septic sore throat	*Streptococcus pyogenes*, many types	Ingestion of live organisms in contaminated food or milk. Also contact and respiratory	1. General sanitation 2. Pasteurization of milk 3. Proper food cooking, handling, storage	Antibiotic treatment
Diphtheria		*Corynebacterium diphtheriae*	Ingestion of live organisms in milk or food. Also contact and respiratory	1. Immunization 2. Pasteurization of milk 3. Proper food handling and refrigeration 4. General sanitation	Antibiotic treatment and antitoxin treatment
Brucellosis	Undulant fever, milk fever, malta fever	*Brucella abortus B. melitensis* or *B. suis*	Ingestion of live organisms in milk or meat products. Also contact	1. Pasteurization of milk 2. Proper cooking of milk and meat products 3. General sanitation	Antibiotic treatment
Infectious hepatitis	Epidemic jaundice Catarrhal jaundice	Virus	Ingestion of virus in contaminated water, milk and food. Also direct contact	1. General sanitation 2. Isolation of cases	Gamma globulin

(Continued)

TABLE 2.1.5 (*Continued*)

Disease	Synonym	Causative Agent	Mode of Transmission	Methods of Prevention	Treatments Available
Amebiasis	Amebic dysentery	*Entamoeba histolytica*	Ingested cysts of organism in contaminated water, food	1. General sanitation 2. Water filtration	Antibiotic and chemical therapy
Trichinosis	Trichiniasis Trichinellosis	Larva of *Trichinella spiralis*	Ingested meat containing viable larva of organisms	1. Adequate processing of pork 2. Adequate cooking of pork	
Acute diarrheal disease	Summer complaint Travelers diarrhea Infant diarrhea	*Escherichia coli, Shigella* sp., *Salmonella* sp., *Giardia lamblia, Staphylococcus* sp., *Pseudomonas aeruginosa, Proteus vulgaris,* others	Ingestion of live organisms in contaminated water, food. Also direct contact	1. Chlorination of water 2. General sanitation	Antibiotic and supportive therapy. Especially fluid balance in children.
Epidemic gastroenteritis	The Virus	One of several viruses	Ingestion of virus in contaminated water, food. Also contact	1. Treatment of water 2. General sanitation	Supportive therapy
Poliomyelitis	Infantile paralysis Polio	One of three types of poliovirus	Direct contact. Contaminated water. Foods possible but not proven	1. General sanitation 2. Immunization	Supportive therapy
Tularemia		*Pasteurella tularensis*	Direct contact. Bite of insects. Ingestion of organisms.	1. Properly cooking meat, especially rabbit	Antibiotic therapy
Tuberculosis	TB	*Mycobacterium tuberculosis*	Contact. Respiratory. Consumption of organism in milk from infected cows.	1. General sanitation 2. Pasteurization of milk and milk products 3. Elimination of infected cattle	Antibiotic and supportive therapy

SOURCE: GUTHRIE, R. K. (EDITOR). 1972. *In* Food Sanitation. Avi Publishing Co., Westport, Conn.

INGESTION AND INHALATION

TABLE 2.1.6

DAILY RATES OF INGESTION AND INHALATION OF WATER AND AIR

Water intake in food	700 cm^3
Water intake in fluids	1,500 cm^3
Water of oxidation	300 cm^3
Total water consumption	2,500 cm^3
Air inhaled during 8-hr working day	10^7 cm^3
Air inhaled during 16 hr not at work	10^7 cm^3
Total air inhaled	2×10^7 cm^3

SOURCE: WANG, Y. (EDITOR). 1969. Handbook of Radioactive Nuclides. CRC Press, Cleveland. Reproduced with permission of CRC Press.

INSECT CONTROL

TABLE 2.1.7

INSECTICIDES FOR INSECT CONTROL

	5% Sevin	4% or 5% Malathion	1.5% Lindane	1% Rotenone
Aphids		X	X	
Armyworms	X			X
Budworms	X			
Cabbage worms	X	X		X
Col. potato beetle	X			
Cucumber beetle		X	X	
Earworms	X			
Fleabeetle	X			X
Fruit, horn, pinworms	X			X
Leaf-hopper	X	X	X	X
Leaf-roller	X	X		X
Melon pickle worms		X	X	X
Mexican bean beetle	X	X		X
Pameras	X	X		
Pea weevils	X	X	X	
Red spiders		X		
Stink bugs	X	X	X	
Thrips	X	X	X	Diazinon 2%
Leafminers			X	Diazinon 2%

SOURCE: Vegetable Gardening Guide. 1975. Florida Coop. Ext. Serv. Circ. *104K*, Gainesville.

INSULATING VALUE

TABLE 2.1.8

INSULATING SLABS OR BOARDS

Material	Density Lb per Cu Ft	Average Btu Passing per Hr Through a Plate of Material 1 Sq Ft in Area, 1 In. Thick, per °F Difference in the Two Faces
Cellular glass	9	0.41
Glass fiber	7	0.21
Polyurethane (exp.)	3	0.17
Rubber (exp.)	4.5	0.22
Polystyrene (extruded)	1.9	0.22
Expandable polystyrene	1.0	0.24

SOURCE: WOOLRICH, W. R. and HALLOWELL, E. R. (EDITORS). 1970. Insulation for, and Heat Transfer through Cold and Freezer Storage Walls and Ceilings. *In* Cold and Freezer Storage Manual. Avi Publishing Co., Westport, Conn.

INSULATION

TABLE 2.I.9

THERMAL CONDUCTIVITIES AND DENSITIES

Insulating Materials	Density, lb/cu. ft.	Thermal Conductivity[1] for Thickness of 1 in., B.t.u./sq ft/hr. per °F.
Air cell 1/2 in.	8.80	0.458
Asbestos fibers packed	44	1.6
Asphalt roofing	55	0.70
Balsa wood	7–9	0.31–0.38
Balsam-wool	3.6	0.250
Brick, soft	87	5.0
Brick, hard	140	9.2
Concrete, 1:2:5[2]	170	6.3
Concrete, cinder aggregate	97	4.9
Celotex	13.8	0.300
Corkboard, various grades	8–10	0.28–0.32
Cork, granulated	5	0.32
Cotton	5	0.42
Cottonseed hulls	5	0.31
Dry-Zero	2.0	0.250
Eel brass mats	14	0.34
Ferro-Therm (steel)	—	0.226
Foamglas	—	0.450
Glass wool	4	0.29
Hair felt	17	0.25
Insulite	11.9	0.296
Kapok fibers	1	0.24
Magnesia, 85%	17	0.50
Masonite	15.0	0.330
Mineral wool (slag or rock wool)	12	0.26
Mineral wool board, asphaltic binder	16	0.33
Oak lumber, cross grain	38	1.0
Redwood bark, fiber	6	0.28
Rock cork	14.5	0.326
Rock wool	14	0.28
Sand, river dried	95	2.3
Sawdust, pine	12	0.40
Stone masonry	170	12.0
Styrofoam	1.7	0.250
Sugar cane fiberboard	15	0.33
Tar roofing	55.0	0.707
Vermiculite	6.2	0.32
White pine lumber, cross grain	31	0.78
Wood fiber board	14	0.33
Wool, pure	5	0.26

[1] British thermal units per hr, passing through 1 sq. ft. of a plate of material 1 in. thick, per °F difference in temperature between the two faces.

[2] Mix 1 part Portland cement, 2 parts sand, 5 parts limestone.

SOURCE: WOOLRICH, W. R. 1968. Design of Above Ground Refrigerated Storages. *In* The Freezing Preservation of Foods, Vol. 1, 4th Edition. D. K. Tressler, W. B. Van Arsdel, M. J. Copley and W. R. Woolrich (Editors). Avi Publishing Co., Westport, Conn.

INSULATION, CONDUCTIVITY VALUES

TABLE 2.I.10

COMPARISON OF HEAT CONDUCTIVITY VALUES

	Btu
Expanded ebonite	0.20
Regranulated cork	0.238
Cork slab	0.25
Slag wool	0.25-0.28
Granulated cork	0.328-0.345
Charcoal	0.369
Polystyrene	0.23
Alfol	0.22-0.36
Glass wool	0.26-0.40
Expanded slate concrete	1.9
Bricks (Flettons)	6.3
Concrete;	
Gravel (4), sand (2), cement (1)	7.0

Based upon the above, the equivalent thickness in inches to give a similar insulating effect would be:

Expanded ebonite 1 in.
Cork slab 1.25 in.
Expanded polystyrene 1.15 in.
Bricks 31.5 in. and concrete 35 in.

SOURCE: GEARY, D. and GERRARD, F. 1968. Meat and Refrigeration. Meat Trades J., London, England.

INSULATION, THICKNESS

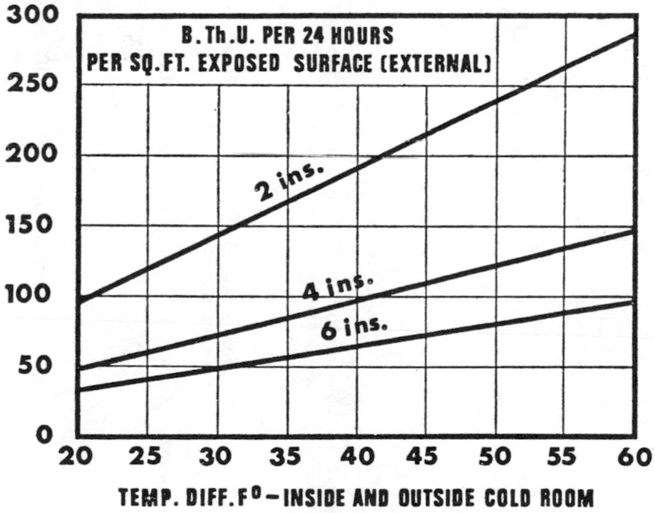

FIG. 2.I.1. EFFECT OF INSULATION THICKNESS ON COLD ROOM TEMPERATURE

SOURCE: GEARY, D. and GERRARD, F. 1968. Meat and Refrigeration. Meat Trades J., London, England.

INTESTINAL MICROORGANISMS

TABLE 2.I.11

CHARACTER OF GROWTH OF ENTERIC ORGANISMS ON SELECTIVE PLATING MEDIA

Group of Microorganisms	Shigella Salmonella (SS) Agar	Plain Desoxycholate, MacConkey's, or Eosin Methylene-blue Agar (EMB)	Bismuth Sulfite Wilson-Blair (WB) Agar	Brilliant-green (BG) Agar
Shigella	Colorless, some slightly pink; translucent, varying to transparent or to mode-rate opacity; round; raised; 1- to 5-mm diameter, some larger. *S. sonnei* may be large, flat, and irregular.	Colorless; transparent, 2- to 7-mm diameter; generally round. *S. sonnei* may be large, flat, and irregular.	Large, inhibited, occasionally develop as small colorless or greenish colonies with depressed centers.	No significant growth.
Salmonella typhosa	Similar to *Shigella*.	Similar to *Shigella*.	Isolated surface colonies; black, with surrounding brownish-black zone; a characteristic metallic sheen by reflected light. With congested growth; small, light green, often with darker center. Sub-surface colonies; jet black, well-defined; no sheen. Size 1-4 mm.	Largely inhibited.
Salmonella group (other than *S. typhosa*)	Similar to *Shigella*; occasionally some darkening of center of colonies.	Similar to *Shigella*.	Variable; many types markedly inhibited, a few simulate *S. typhosa*, others develop as flat greenish to brownish colonies.	Isolated surface colonies, pink to fuchsia surrounded by red medium, occasionally brownish with little change in medium.
Alkalescens-dispar group	Similar to *Shigella*; tend to be more opaque.	Similar to *Shigella*.	Light to dark green, smooth, glistening.	Largely inhibited; rarely may simulate *Salmonella* group.
"Coliform-aerogenes groups"	Largely inhibited; pink to red; opaque; may be mucoid; size variable.	On desoxycholate and MacConkey's: red; opaque; on EMB: characteristic sheen by reflected light; 2- to 7-mm diameter; may be mucoid with dark centers.	Quite marked inhibition; some develop as dark, brown, or greenish colonies.	Largely inhibited; may be yellowish-green.
Proteus group	Growth in discrete colonies; colorless, some with black centers, transparent to water-clear; irregular edge.	Often a spreading growth on EMB or MacConkey's; usually discrete colonies on plain desoxycholate; may simulate *Shigella* or *Salmonella*.	Marked inhibition; some green with darker centers.	Largely inhibited; may be small reddish colony.
Paracolon groups	Variable; may be similar to *Shigella* or may approach coli-aerogenes group.	Variable; may be similar to *Shigella* or may approach coliforms.	Similar to coliform group.	Similar to coliform.
Pseudomonas group	Variable; usually colorless, often greyish-brown.	Variable; may simulate *Proteus*.	Variable.	Pink to purplish; irregular edges; may closely simulate *Salmonella* group.

SOURCE: ALBERTSON, V. E. *et al.* Meat Hygiene. FAO Agricultural Studies *34*, United Nations, Rome.

INTESTINAL MICROORGANISMS IN TRIPLE-SUGAR AGAR

TABLE 2.I.12

REACTIONS AND SUGGESTED MICROORGANISMS INDICATED

Reaction on Slant[1]	Reaction on Butt[2]	H_2S Production	Abbreviated Recording	Microorganisms Suggested	Indicated Procedure for Organisms Isolated from Faeces
Alk	Acid	–	A–	*Shigella*, *S. typhosa*, *Proteus*, paracolon, alkalescens-dispar group	Screen and identify as indicated
Alk	Acid	+	A+	*S. typhosa*, *Proteus*, paracolon, anaerogenic *Salmonella*	Screen and identify as indicated
Alk	Acid and gas	+	AG+	*Salmonella*, *Proteus*, paracolon (including Arizona)	Screen and identify as indicated (ordinarily many pathogens)
Alk	Acid and gas	–	AG–	Paracolon, *Proteus*, occasionally *Salmonella*	Screen and identify as indicated (ordinarily very few pathogens)
Acid	Acid	–	A/A–	Streptococci, staphylococci, occasionally *S. typhosa*, other Gram-negative rods	Screen and identify as indicated if a Gram-negative rod; discard others
Alk (spreading growth)	Acid and gas	+ or –	Sp[3]	*Proteus*	Discard
Acid	Acid and gas	–	–	"Coli-aerogenes"	Examine serologically for entero-pathogenic *E. coli* when indicated; otherwise discard
Alk	Alk	–	–	*Alcaligenes*, *Mimae*, *Pseudomonas*	Discard
Purplish	Alk	–	–	*Pseudomonas* species	Discard

[1] Alk slant indicates lactose and sucrose not fermented; acid slant indicates lactose and or sucrose fermented.
[2] Alk butt indicates dextrose not fermented; acid butt indicates dextrose fermented.
[3] Sp indicates spreader.

SOURCE: ALBERTSON, V. E. *et al.* Meat Hygiene. FAO Agricultural Studies *34*, United Nations, Rome.

INTESTINE, CROSS SECTION

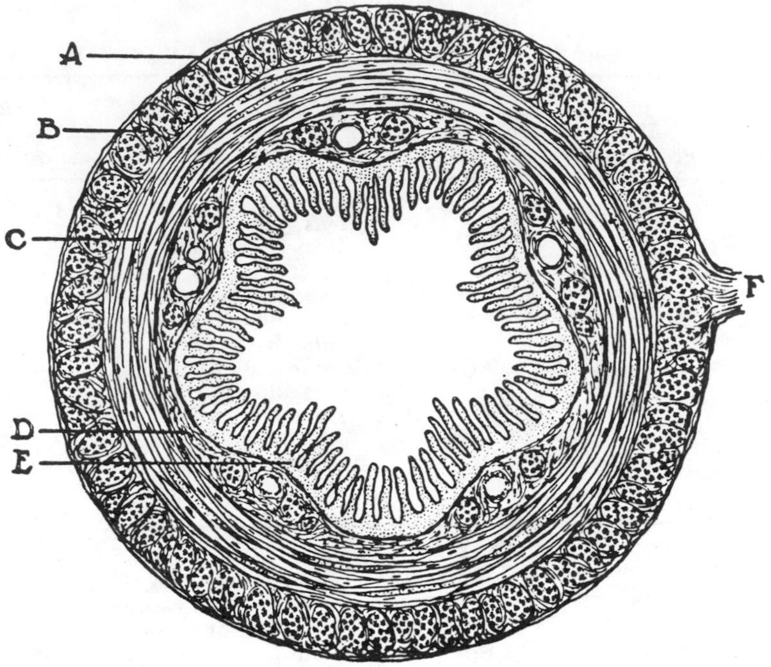

FIG. 2.1.2. DIAGRAMMATIC CROSS SECTION OF SMALL INTESTINE (AFTER SOBOTTA). (A) SEROUS COAT, (B) LONGITUDINAL MUSCLE LAYER, (C) CIRCULAR MUSCLE LAYER, (D) SUBMUCOUS LAYER, (E) MUCOUS MEMBRANE, (F) MESENTERY ATTACHMENT

SOURCE: MOULTON, C. R. and LEWIS, W. L. Meat Through the Microscope, Revised Edition. Institute of Meat Packing, The University of Chicago, Chicago.

IODINE AND SAPONIFICATION VALUES

TABLE 2.I.13

IODINE VALUES AND SAPONIFICATION VALUES OF NATURAL FATS AND OILS

Fat	Saponification Value	Iodine Value	Fat	Saponification Value	Iodine Value
Babassu kernel oil	247-251	14-18	Rice bran oil	183-194	92-109
Borneo tallow	189-200	29-38	Safflower oil	188-194	140-150
Cacao butter	190-200	35-40	Sesame oil	188-195	103-116
Cashew nut oil	187-195	79-85	Sheanut butter oil	178-190	56-67
Castor oil	176-187	81-91	Soybean oil	189-195	120-141
Chinese vegetable tallow	200-209	20-29	Stillingia oil	203-212	169-187
Coconut oil	250-264	7.5-10.5	Sunflower oil	188-194	125-136
Cohune nut oil	252-260	9-14	Teaseed oil	188-196	80-90
Corn oil	187-193	103-128	Tung oil	189-195	160-175
Cottonseed oil	189-198	99-113	Walnut oil	189-198	140-152
Hempseed oil	190-193	150-166	Butterfat	210-233	26-42
Illipe butter	188-204	53-70	Bone grease	186-198	48-56
Jaboty tallow	228-236	5-9	Chicken fat	194-204	64-76
Kapok oil	189-197	86-110	Horse fat	195-199	72-86
Linseed oil	188-196	170-204	Lard	190-202	52-77
Mustard seed oil—black	176-184	106-113	Neatsfoot oil	190-199	69-76
			Tallow (beef)	190-199	40-48
			Tallow (mutton)	192-197	35-46
Mustard seed oil—white	170-178	94-106	Ghee	225-235	28-32
			Cod-liver oil	180-190	140-170
Oiticica oil	186-193	140-160	Herring oil	179-194	124-128
Olive oil	188-196	80-88	Menhaden oil	189-193	148-160
Palm oil	195-205	44-54	Salmon oil	183-186	141-166
Peanut oil	188-195	84-100	Sardine oil	189-193	170-193
Perilla oil	188-197	193-208	Shark oil	158-164	115-139
Rapeseed oil (Calza)	170-180	97-108	Shark-liver oil	160-196	112-136
			Whale oil	185-194	110-135
Ravison oil	173-181	109-122	Sperm oil (wax)	120-129	76-88

SOURCE: MAHLENBACHER, C. W. The Analysis of Fats and Oils. Garrard Press, Champaign, Illinois.

IRON

TABLE 2.I.14

IRON CONTENT OF FOODS

	mg/100 g		mg/100 g
Spinach	3.1	Snap beans	0.8
Lima beans	2.8	Corn	0.7
Peas	1.9	Bananas	0.7
Brussels sprouts	1.5	Potatoes	0.6
Artichokes	1.3	Watermelon	0.6
Broccoli	1.1	Tomatoes	0.5
Cauliflower	1.1	Lettuce	0.5
Strawberries	1.0	Apples	0.3
Asparagus	1.0	Oranges	0.2

SOURCE: WHITE, P. L. and SELVEY, N. (EDITORS). 1974. Nutritional Qualities of Fresh Fruits and Vegetables. Futura Publishing Co., Mt. Kisco, N.Y.

IRON, DAILY RECOMMENDATIONS

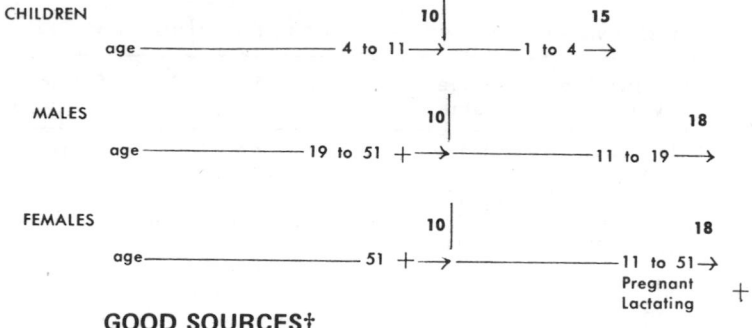

MILLIGRAMS

	Age	Milligrams
CHILDREN	4 to 11	10
	1 to 4	15
MALES	19 to 51 +	10
	11 to 19	18
FEMALES	51 +	10
	11 to 51, Pregnant, Lactating	18 +

GOOD SOURCES†

MILLIGRAMS

		Milligrams
Liver	3½ oz.	18
Heart	3½ oz.	5.4
Beef	3½ oz.	3.7
Pork	3½ oz.	3.5
Veal	3½ oz.	3.3
Lamb	3½ oz.	2.0
Luncheon Meat	2 oz.	2.0

		Milligrams
Oysters	6-9 med.	6.6
Chicken	3½ oz.	1.5
Egg	1 med.	1.1
Fish	3½ oz.	1.1
Canned Fish	1¾ oz.	1.0

		Milligrams
Dried Beans and Peas	¾ cup	3.6
Dried Fruit	½ cup	2.5
Dark Green Leafy Vegetables	½ cup	1.0
Potato	1 med.	0.8

		Milligrams
Molasses	1 tblsp.	1.1
Nuts	¼ cup	1.1

		Milligrams
Cereal	½ cup	0.6
Bread	1 slice	0.6

†Average nutrient content as food is served. (Note: 3½ oz equals approximately 100 g.)

SOURCE: Lessons on Meat. (1974). National Live Stock and Meat Board, Chicago.

Note: There are no entries for the letters J and K in this Section.

L

LADLE SIZE

TABLE 2.L.1

LADLE SIZES

Ladles (Oz)	Approximate Measure (Cup)
2	1/4
4	1/2
6	3/4
8	1

SOURCE: VAN EGMOND, DOROTHY (EDITOR). 1974. Cost Management. *In* School Food Service. Avi Publishing Co., Westport, Conn.

LAMB BRAISING

Brown meat on all sides in hot fat in heavy utensil. Season with salt and pepper. Add small amount of liquid, if necessary. Cover tightly. Cook at simmering temperature until tender.

Cut	Time (hr)
Neck slices	
3/4 in.	1
Shanks	1½ to 2
Cubes	1½ to 2
Breast	
Stuffed	1½ to 2
Rolled	1½ to 2
Riblets	1½ to 2

SOURCE: How to Identify and Prepare Cuts of Lamb. (1971). American Lamb Council.

LAMB BROILING

Lamb should be broiled 3 to 4 in. from the source of heat. Broil until top of meat is nicely browned. Season with salt and pepper. Turn and brown on the other side. Use the following as a guide to total cooking time.

Cut	Total Time in Minutes
Loin Chops, Rib Chops, Shoulder Chops	
1 in.	12
1½ in.	18
2 in.	22
Lamb Patties	
1 in. × 3 in.	18

SOURCE: How to Identify and Prepare Cuts of Lamb. (1971). American Lamb Council.

LAMB CHART

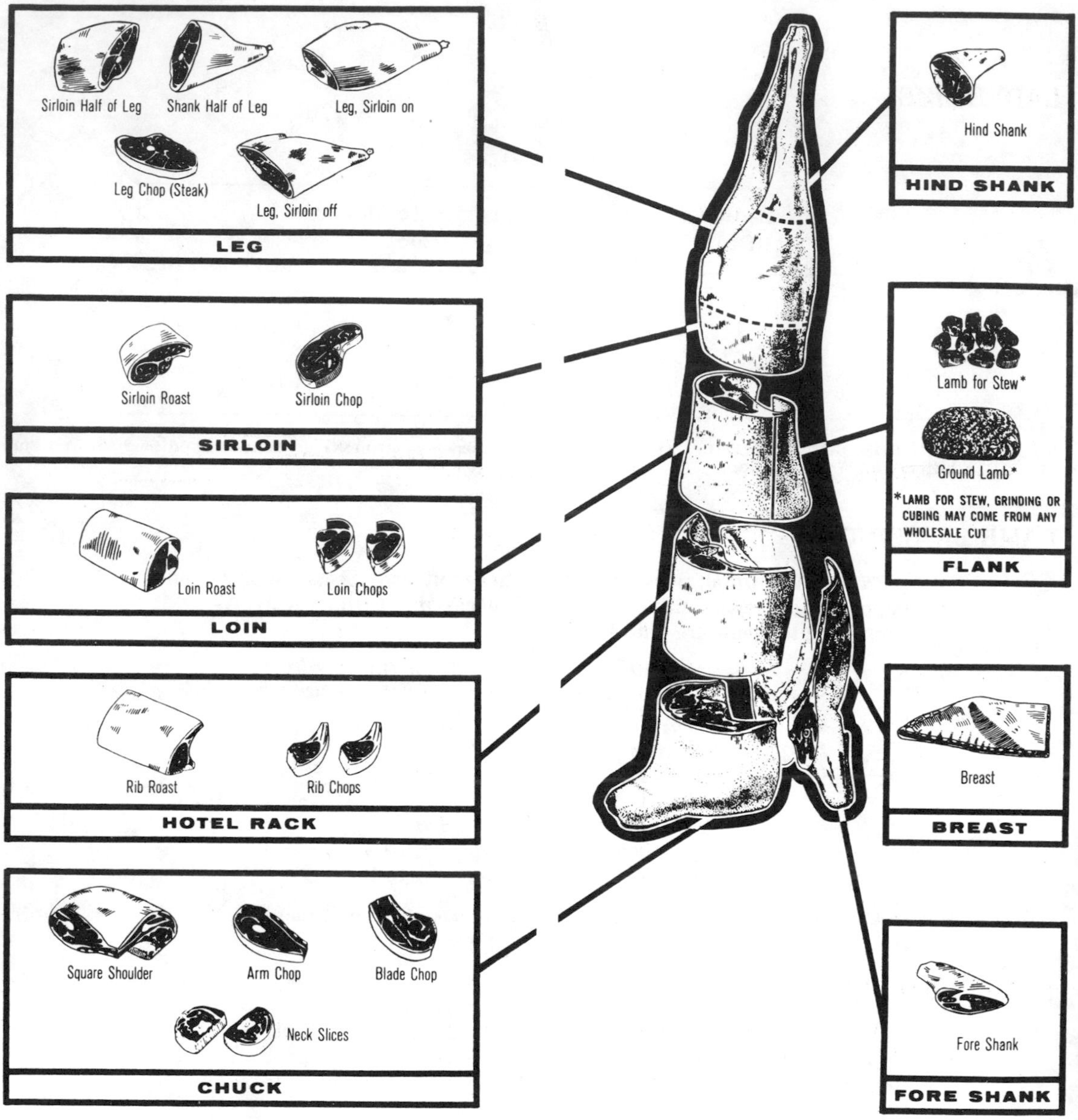

SOURCE: How to Buy Meat for Your Freezer, USDA Home and Garden Bull. *166*, 1969.

LAMB CROWN ROAST CARVING

Remove any garnish in the center of the roast that might interfere with carving. Steady roast by placing fork firmly between the ribs. Start carving at one of the two ends where ribs are tied together.

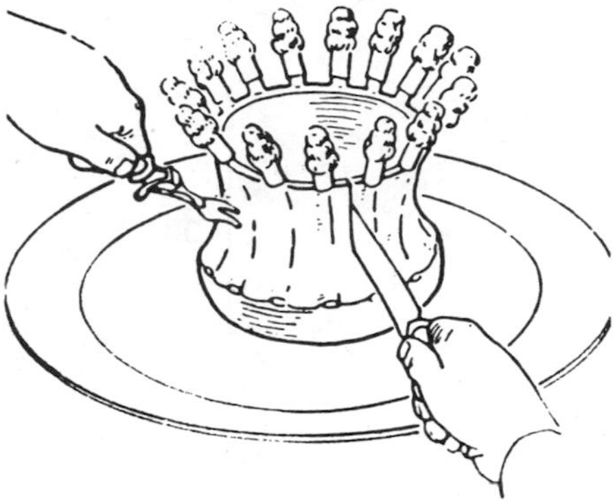

Cut down between the ribs, allowing one or more ribs for each serving. Using the fork to steady it, lift the slice on the knife blade to the platter. Dressing can be cut and served with the slices.

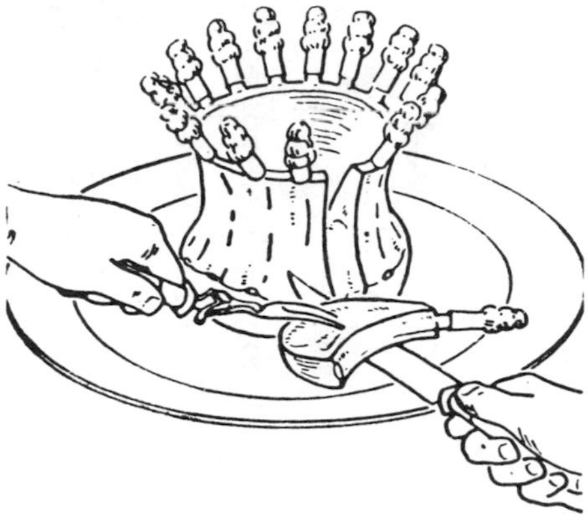

SOURCE: Carving Meat. National Live Stock and Meat Board, Chicago.

LAMB CUTS

TABLE 2.L.2

CHARACTERISTICS AND COOKING METHODS FOR LAMB CUTS

WHOLESALE CUTS	RETAIL CUTS	CHARACTERISTICS	COOKING METHODS
Leg	Frenched Leg	Shank bone is "frenched", that is, meat is removed to expose one inch or more of lower end of shank bone.	*Roast*
	American Leg	Shank meat is removed at stifle joint. Shank meat is tucked into pocket under fell and pinned into place	*Roast*
	Half of Leg	Either the shank half or the loin half.	*Roast*
	Leg Chops (*Steaks*)	May contain cross section of back bone and aitch bone. Center cut steaks look like miniature beef round steaks.	*Broil; panbroil; panfry*
	Sirloin Chops	Correspond to beef sirloin steaks. Pinbone chops have considerable bone.	*Broil; panbroil; panfry*
	Boneless Sirloin Roast	Small boneless roll weighing from 2 to 3½ pounds.	*Roast*
Loin	Loin Roast	Corresponds to beef short loin. It can be the unsplit loin but is usually one side of the split loin.	*Roast*
	Rolled Loin Roast	Boned and rolled loin.	*Roast*
	Loin Chops	Contain T-shaped bones; correspond to porterhouse, T-bone, and club beef steaks.	*Broil; panbroil; panfry*
	English Chops	Cut across the unsplit loin. Back bone removed and boneless chop skewered into shape.	*Broil; panbroil; panfry*
Rack	Rib (Rack) Roast	Contains rib bones and rib eye muscle.	*Roast*
	Crown Roast	Ribs are "frenched," that is, meat is removed from rib ends, then two or more rib sections are shaped and tied into a "crown".	*Roast*
	Rib Chops	Contain rib bone and rib eye muscle.	*Broil; panbroil; panfry*
	Frenched Chops	Same as rib chops except meat is removed from ends of ribs.	*Broil; panbroil; panfry*

Shoulder	Square Cut Shoulder	Thickest part of forequarter, with shank, breast, rib (rack), and neck removed.	*Roast*
	Cushion Shoulder	Boned and left flat. Sewed on two sides. One side may be left open for stuffing, then skewered or sewed.	*Roast*
	Rolled Shoulder	Boneless roll made from square cut shoulder.	*Roast*
	Boneless Shoulder Chops	Cut from boneless rolled shoulder.	*Broil; panbroil; panfry; braise*
	Mock Duck	Made from outside of shoulder. Shaped like a duck.	*Roast*
	Arm Chops	Contain small round bone and usually the cross sections of 4 or 5 rib bones.	*Broil; panbroil; panfry; braise*
	Blade Chops	Contain portions of rib, back and blade bones.	*Broil; panbroil; panfry; braise*
	Saratoga Chops	Boneless chops made fron. the inside shoulder muscle.	*Broil; panbroil; panfry; braise*
	Neck Slices	Round slice with neck vertebrae in center.	*Braise; cook in liquid*
Breast	Breast	Corresponds to veal breast and to short plate and brisket of beef. Narrow strip of meat containing breast bone and ends of 12 ribs.	*Roast; braise; cook in liquid*
	Breast with Pocket	Same as above but with pocket between ribs and lean.	*Roast; braise*
	Rolled Breast	Small boneless roll. Alternating layers of lean and fat.	*Roast; braise*
	Riblets	Breast bone removed and breast cut between ribs. Each small piece contains part of a rib bone.	*Braise; cook in liquid*
Shank	Shank	Contains shank and elbow bones.	*Braise; cook in liquid*
Ground Lamb	Loaf	Usually made from flank, breast, shank, and neck. May be straight ground lamb or combined with varying amounts of beef, pork or veal.	*Roast (bake)*
	Patties	Ground lamb formed into patties. May be encircled with sliced bacon.	*Broil; panbroil; panfry*

SOURCE: ***Meat Manual, 6th Edition.*** **National Live Stock and Meat Board, Chicago.**

LAMB CUTS AND USES

TABLE 2.L.3

LAMB CUTS AND HOW TO USE THEM

CUT	DESCRIPTION	RETAIL CUTS	LAMB SPECIALTIES
LEG	Solid meat, fine quality	Roasts, steaks	Brains— Cream, braise, scramble with eggs
LOIN	Tender, high quality, small amount of bone	Chops, English chops, roast	Heart— Braise, cook in water
RACK	Tender, high quality; contains rib bones	Chops, roasts, crown roast	Kidney— Fry, broil, cook in water
SHOULDER	Tender, well-flavored; often boned and rolled or made into cushion style roast	Roasts, chops, stews, loaf	Liver— Fry, broil, braise
BREAST (Including flank)	Meat tender, but not so fine in grain as other sections	Stews; boned and rolled for roast; pocket for stuffing	Tongue— Cook in water

SOURCE: Meat Buying Manual. National Live Stock and Meat Board, Chicago.

LAMB LEG CARVING

Place the roast on the platter with the shank to the carver's right and the tip section on the near side. From this, remove two or three slices lengthwise to form a base.

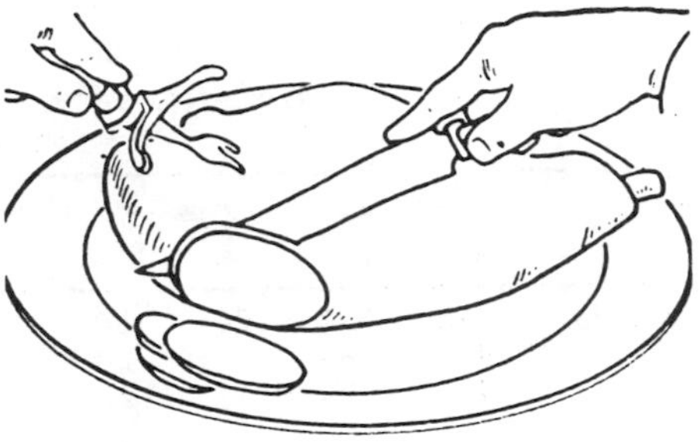

Turn the roast up on the base and, starting at the shank end, make slices perpendicular to the leg bone as shown in the illustration.

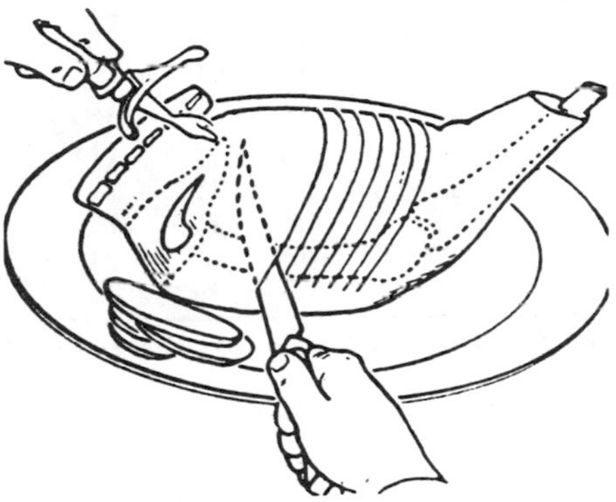

After reaching the aitch bone, loosen the slices by cutting under them, following the top of the leg bone. Remove slices to platter and then serve.

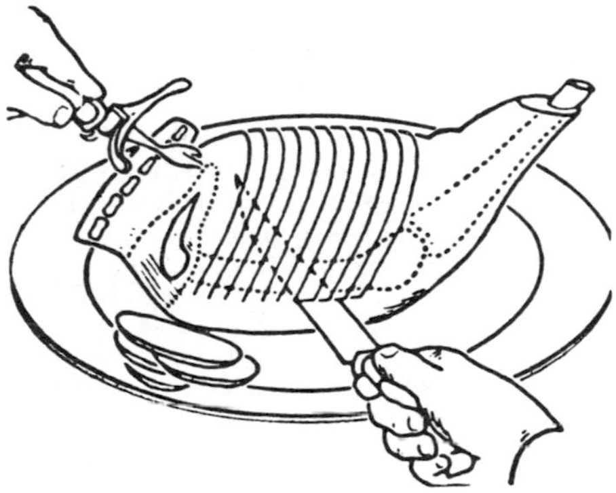

SOURCE: Carving Meat. National Live Stock and Meat Board, Chicago.

LAMB PERCENTAGES OF DAILY RECOMMENDED ALLOWANCES

TABLE 2.L.4

PERCENTAGES OF DAILY RECOMMENDED ALLOWANCES[1]
(Based on $3^1/_2$ Oz Cooked Lean Lamb)

	Age	Protein	Calories	Iron	Phosphorus	Magnesium	Thiamin	Riboflavin	Niacin	Vit. B-6	Vit. B-12
Children	1-3	116	20	13	26	15	31	40	84	53	280
	4-6	87	14	20	26	11	24	29	63	36	187
	7-10	74	11	20	26	9	18	27	48	27	140
Males	11-14	60	9	11	18	6	16	21	42	20	93
	15-18	49	9	11	18	6	15	18	38	16	93
	19-22	49	9	20	26	6	15	18	38	16	93
	23-50	47	10	20	26	6	16	20	42	16	93
	51+	47	11	20	26	6	18	21	48	16	93
Females	11-14	60	11	11	18	8	18	25	48	20	93
	15-18	55	12	11	18	8	20	23	54	16	93
	19-22	58	12	11	26	8	20	23	54	16	93
	23-50	58	13	11	26	8	22	27	58	16	93
	51+	58	14	20	26	8	22	29	63	16	93

[1] Figures based on 1974 National Research Council Recommended Dietary Allowances.

SOURCE: Facts About Lamb. 1974. National Live Stock and Meat Board, Chicago.

LAMB ROASTING I

To roast lamb, place fat side up on a rack in an open roasting pan. Add no water. Do not cover. Baste only if a glaze or flavor-adding sauce is used. Lamb is best when it roasts at an oven temperature of 325°F. The meat is well done when it reaches an internal temperature of 175°-180°F.

Tip: Try lamb a little rare—slightly pink and extra juicy in the middle.

Cut	Min per Lb
Leg	
Bone-in	30 to 35
Boneless, rolled or netted	35 to 40
Shoulder	
Bone-in	30 to 35
Boneless, rolled or netted	40 to 45
Cushion roast	30 to 35
Breast	
Stuffed	30 to 35
Rolled	30 to 35
Lamb loaf	30 to 35
Crown roast	40 to 45
Rack	40 to 45

SOURCE: How to Identify and Prepare Cuts of Lamb. (1971). American Lamb Council.

LAMB ROASTING II

TABLE 2.L.5

TIME-TABLE FOR ROASTING LAMB

Cut	Approx. Wt. of Single Roasts	No. of Roasts in Oven	Approx. Total Wt. of Roasts in Oven	Oven Temperature	Interior Temperature of Roast When Removed from Oven	Minutes per Pound Based on One Roast	Minutes per Pound Based on Total Wt. of Roasts in Oven	Approximate Total Time
	pounds		*pounds*					
Leg		2	16	300° F.	180° F.		15	4 hours
Leg	6½ to 7½	1		300° F.	180° F.	30 to 35		3 to 4 hours
Cushion shoulder (with stuffing)	4½ to 5½	1		300° F.	180° F.	30 to 35		2 to 3 hours
Rolled shoulder	3 to 4	1		300° F.	180° F.	40 to 45		2½ to 3 hours
Rolled shoulder		5	29	300° F.	180° F.		10	5 hours
Square cut shoulder		8	40	300° F.	180° F.		7	4 to 5 hours

SOURCE: Cooking Meat in Quantity. National Live Stock and Meat Board, Chicago.

LAMB SIMMERING

Brown meat on all sides in hot fat. Season with salt and pepper. Cover with water, then cover kettle tightly. Cook slowly. Allow meat to simmer, not boil, until tender. Add vegetables just long enough before serving to be cooked.

Cut	Time (hr)
Cubes	
1 to 1½ in.	1½ to 2
Larger cuts	
Riblets, neck, shanks	1½ to 2

SOURCE: How to Identify and Prepare Cuts of Lamb. (1971). American Lamb Council.

LAMB, WHOLESALE CUTS

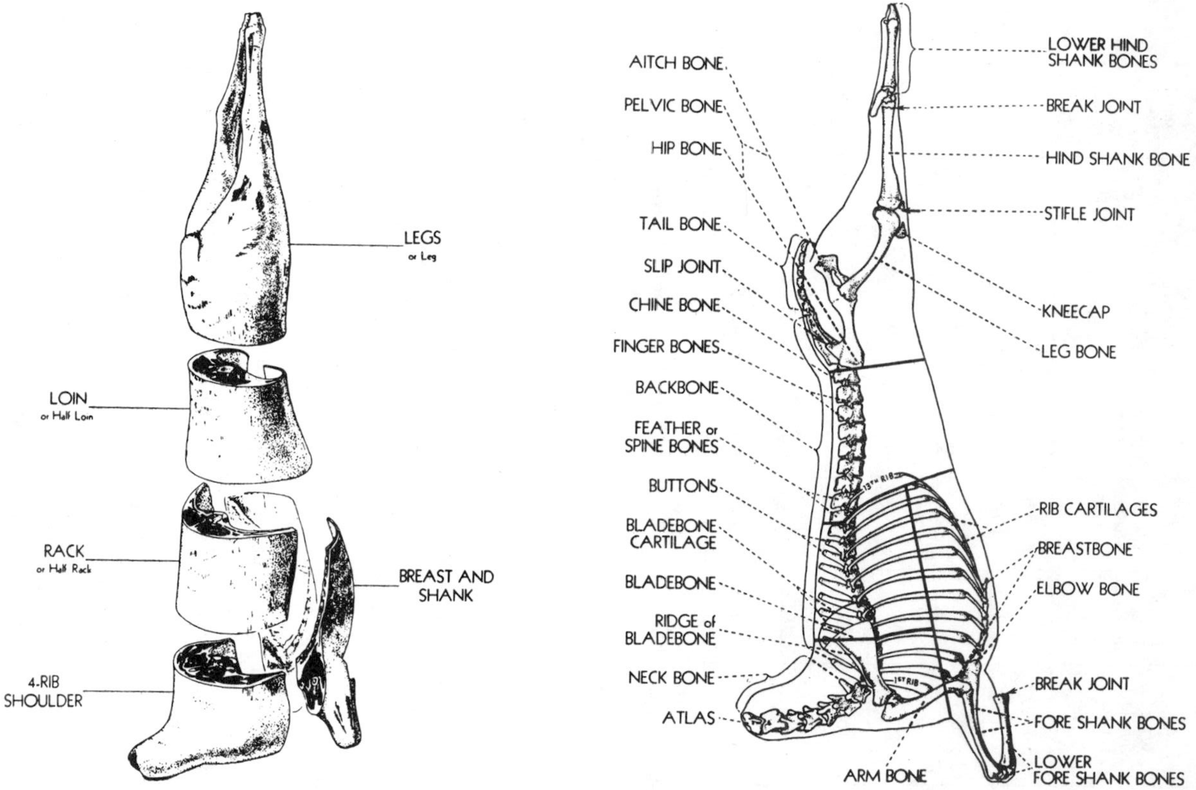

FIG. 2.L.1. WHOLESALE CUTS OF LAMB (LEFT); STRUCTURE, LOCATION, AND NAMES OF CARCASS BONES (RIGHT)

SOURCE: Cooking Meat In Quantity, National Live Stock and Meat Board, Chicago.

LAMB YIELD

TABLE 2.L.6

YIELD OF CUTS FROM YIELD GRADE 3 LAMB CARCASSES

Retail Cuts	Percent of Carcass	Pounds
Loin Chops	16.5	8.25
Rib Chops	8.2	4.10
Legs (Short Cut)	20.5	10.25
Shoulder Roast ...	22.3	11.15
Foreshanks	3.1	1.55
Breast	7.9	3.95
Flank	2.9	1.45
Stew Meat	1.9	.95
Kidney	.5	.25
Total Usable Retail Cuts	83.8	41.90
Waste (fat, bone, shrinkage)	16.2	8.10
TOTAL	100.0	50.00

SOURCE: How to Buy Meat for Your Freezer. (1969). USDA Home and Garden Bull. *166*.

LARD, TRIGLYCERIDE MOLE PERCENT COMPOSITION

TABLE 2.L.7

PERCENTAGE OF MOLES OF TRIGLYCERIDES IN LARD

Triglyceride	Mole %
0 Double Bonds	
PMP	0.1
PMSt	0.4
StMSt	0.4
PPP	0.5
PPSt	2.0
StPSt	2.0
PStP	0.1
PStSt	0.4
StStSt	0.4
Remaining ones	0.3
1 Double Bond	
POP	0.6
POSt	1.9
StOSt	1.5
PMO	0.4
StMO	0.7
MPO	0.8
PPO	7.9
StPO	12.8
PStO	0.9
StStO	1.6
Remaining ones	0.6
2 Double Bonds	
POO	5.2
StOO	6.1
OMO	1.6
OPO	18.4
OStO	1.2
PPL	1.8
StPL	2.1
Remaining ones	1.5
3 Double Bonds	
OOO	11.7
PLO	0.2
StLO	0.6
OML	0.6
OPL	7.2
OStL	1.2
Remaining ones	0.3
4 or More Double Bonds	
OLL	1.4
OLO	1.5
LPL	0.5
LStL	0.1
OPLe	0.3
Remaining ones	0.2

SOURCE: BOEKENOOGEN, H. A. (EDITOR). 1968. Oil, Fats and Fat Products, Vol. *2*. John Wiley & Sons, New York.

LEMON JUICE COMPOSITION

TABLE 2.L.8

COMPOSITION OF LEMON JUICE

Constituent	Source of Juice[1]	Number of Samples	Content per 100 Grams			
			Range		Average	
Protein (total N × 6.25)	C, X	26	0.26–0.77	gm	0.42	gm
Amino nitrogen	C	31	0.019–0.046	gm	0.035	gm
Fat (ether extract)	C, X	...	None—0.6	gm	0.2	gm
Soluble solids, total (°Brix)	C	2746	7.1–11.9	gm	9.3	gm
Acid, total, as anhyd. citric	C	3123	4.20–8.33	gm	5.97	gm
Malic acid	C	15	0.15–0.41	gm	0.26	gm
Sugar, total, as invert	C, X	368	0.77–4.08	gm	2.16	gm
Reducing sugar	C	95	0.78–2.63	gm	1.67	gm
Sucrose	C	47	0.03–0.63	gm	0.18	gm
Minerals, total ash	C, X	50	0.15–0.35	gm	0.25	gm
Calcium	C, X	26	5.6–27.9	mg	9.88	mg
Phosphorus	C, X	27	5.3–16.6	mg	9.35	mg
Iron	C, X	20	0.14–0.69	mg	0.23	mg
Magnesium	C, X	19	5.8–11.3	mg	6.7	mg
Potassium	C	24	99–128	mg	103	mg
Sodium	C, X	19	1.0–5.0	mg	1.3	mg
Sulfur	C, X	20	2.0–8.0	mg	3.36	mg
Chlorine	C, X	4	2.3–4.0	mg	3	mg
Vitamin A (as carotene)	C, X	...	None or trace		None	
Thiamine (B_1)	C, X	34[2]	0.004–0.125	mg	0.043	mg
Riboflavin (B_2)	C, X	30[3]	0.005–0.073	mg	0.0183	mg
Niacin	C, X	26	0.056–0.196	mg	0.089	mg
Inositol	C	17	56–76	mg	66.5	mg
Folic acid	C	17	0.00082–0.00094	mg	0.00091	mg
Flavanones	C	2	46–54	mg	50	mg
Ascorbic acid (vitamin C)	C	357	31–61	mg	45	mg
pH	C	93	2.11–2.48		2.30[4]	

[1] C denotes juice from California-Arizona fruit; X, juice from fruit of other or unknown sources.
[2] Includes 8 samples of edible portion (excluding peel and seeds).
[3] Includes 6 samples of edible portion.
[4] Representative value.
Note: Original references used, weighted with data from the Wisconsin Alumni Research Foundation, W.A.R.F.

SOURCE: SWISHER, H. E. and SWISHER, L. H. 1971. Lemon and Lime Juices. *In* Fruit and Vegetable Juice Processing Technology, 2nd Edition. Donald K. Tressler and Maynard A. Joslyn (Editors). Avi Publishing Co., Westport, Conn.

LEMON OIL COMPOSITION

TABLE 2.L.9

THE CHEMICAL COMPOSITION OF COLD-PRESSED LEMON OIL

TERPENES:	**ACIDS:**	**KETONES:**
α-terpinene	acetic acid	methyl heptenone
α-pinene	caprylic acid	d-carvone
β-pinene	capric acid	
β-myrcene		**ESTERS:**
d-limonene	**ALCOHOLS:**	citronellyl acetate
γ-terpinene	octanol	neryl acetate
p-cymene	nonanol	geranyl acetate
α-terpinolene	linalool	n-propyl benzoate
sabinene	terpinene-1-ol	octyl acetate
camphene	terpinene-4-ol	decyl acetate
β-phellandrene	α-terpineol	nonyl acetate
α-phellandrene	citronellol	geranyl butyrate
tetradecane	nerol	
?	geraniol	
?	decanol	
pentadecane	1,8-methadiene-9-ol	**COUMARINS:**
$C_{15}H_{24}$		5-geranoxy psoralen
α-bergamotene	**ALDEHYDES:**	7-methoxy-5-geranoxy-coumarin
caryophyllene	hexanal	5-allyloxypsoralen
?	heptanal	7-methoxy-5-allyloxy-psoralen
$C_{15}H_{24}$	octanal	
α, β-humulene	nonanal	8-geranoxy psoralen
β-bisabolene	decanal	5,7-dimethoxy coumarin (limettin)
$C_{15}H_{24}$	undecanal	
$C_{15}H_{24}$	citral {neral	
α-thujene	citral {geranial	5-methoxy-8-psoralen (byakangelicin)
Δ-3-carene	citronellal	
p-isopropenyltoluene	dodecanal	Bergamotene

SOURCE: KESTERSON, J. W., HENDRICKSON, R. and BRADDOCK, R. J. 1971. Florida Citrus Oils. Florida Agric. Expt. Sta. Tech. Bull. *749*.

LEMON OIL PROPERTIES

TABLE 2.L.10

PHYSICAL AND CHEMICAL PROPERTIES USED AS A CRITERION OF PURITY FOR COLD-PRESSED LEMON OIL

Property	U.S.P. xvii		Italian		California	
	Min.	Max.	Min.	Max.	Min.	Max.
Specific gravity 25C°/25°C	0.849	0.855	0.849	0.855	0.849	0.855
Refractive index η^{20}_{D}	1.4739	1.4755	1.4742	1.4755	1.4742	1.4755
Difference	Not less than 0.0010 and not more than 0.0027 lower than original oil.		—	—	—	—
Optical rotation α^{25}_{D}	+57°	+65.6°	+57°	+65.36°	+57°	+65.36°
Difference	Not more than 6° less than original oil.		—	—	—	—
Aldehyde content % Calif.	2.2	3.8				
Aldehyde content % Italian	3.0	5.5	3.7	5.0	2.3	2.8
Evaporation residue %	—	—	1.5	2.2	1.5	1.8
U. V. spectrum 315 mμ log E $\frac{0.25g}{100\ cc}$						
CD Calif.	0.20	—				
CD Italian	0.49	—	0.49	0.96	0.23	0.74
Peak	—	—	1.00	1.70	0.53	1.50

SOURCE: KESTERSON, J. W., HENDRICKSON, R., and BRADDOCK, R. J. 1971. Florida Citrus Oils. Florida Agric. Expt. Sta. Tech. Bull. *749*.

LIME JUICE COMPOSITION

TABLE 2.L.11

COMPOSITION OF LIME JUICE

Constituent	Number of Samples	Content per 100 Grams	
		Range	Average
Protein (total N × 6.25)	11	0.3–0.7 gm	0.4 gm
Fat	...	0.0–0.11 gm	Trace
Soluble solids, total (°Brix)	93	8.3–14.1 gm	10.0 gm
Acid, total, as anhyd. citric	129	4.94–8.32 gm	5.97 gm
Sugar, total, as invert	13	0.0–1.74 gm	0.72 gm
Non-reducing sugar	7	0.02–0.26 gm	0.14 gm
Ash, total	5	0.25–0.4 gm	0.35 gm
Calcium	2	4.5–10.4 mg	7 mg
Phosphorus	2	9.3–11.2 mg	10 mg
Iron	2	0.19–0.92 mg	0.6 mg
Carotene	2	0.003–0.005 mg	0.004 mg
Thiamine (B_1)	2	0.011–0.028 mg	0.020 mg
Riboflavin (B_2)	2	0.011–0.018 mg	0.015 mg
Niacin	5	0.090–0.275 mg	0.19 mg
Ascorbic acid (vitamin C)	13	23.6–32.7 mg	29 mg
pH	20	1.7–3.2	...
Food energy (calories)	...	24–33	...

SOURCE: SWISHER, H. E. and SWISHER, L. H. 1971. Lemon and Lime Juices. *In* Fruit and Vegetable Juice Processing Technology, 2nd Edition. Donald K. Tressler and Maynard A. Joslyn (Editors). Avi Publishing Co., Westport, Conn.

LIME OIL COMPOSITION

TABLE 2.L.12

CHEMICAL COMPOSITION OF COLD-PRESSED "PERSIAN" LIME OIL

TERPENES:

α-pinene
β-pinene
β-myrcene
d-limonene
γ-terpinene
p-cymene
camphene
terpinolene
tetradecane
△-elemene
$C_{15}H_{24}$
pentadecane
$C_{15}H_{24}$
α-bergamotene
caryophyllene
α-elemene
$C_{15}H_{24}$
α,β-humulene
$C_{15}H_{24}$
β-bisabolene
$C_{15}H_{24}$
$C_{15}H_{24}$

ALCOHOLS:

octanol
nonanol
α-terpineol
linalool
β-terpineol
borneol
geraniol
bergaptol
decanol

OXIDE:

(2) monoterpene-oxides $C_{10}H_{17}O$

ALDEHYDES:

nonanal
decanal
dodecanal
citral {neral, geranial}

PHENOLS:

1,4-cineole
1,8-cineole

ESTERS:

Methyl anthranilate

ACIDS:

acetic
octylic
decylic

COUMARINS:

5,7-dimethoxy coumarin (limettin)
5,8-dimethoxyfurano-2',3',6,7-coumarin (isopimpinellin)
7-methoxy-5-geranoxy coumarin
5-hydroxy-7-methoxy coumarin
4,6-dimethoxy-2-geranoxycinnamic acid
5,-Hydroxyfurano-2',3',6,7-coumarin (Bergaptol)

SOURCE: KESTERSON, J. W., HENDRICKSON, R., and BRADDOCK, R. J. 1971. Florida Citrus Oils. Florida Agric. Expt. Sta. Tech. Bull. *749*.

LIME OIL PROPERTIES

TABLE 2.L.13

COMPARISON OF COMMERCIAL COLD-PRESSED 'PERSIAN' LIME OILS MADE BY THREE DIFFERENT PROCESSES

Property	Pipkin roll (11)*		Fraser-Brace (4)		FMC in-line (15)	
	Max.	Min.	Max.	Min.	Max.	Min.
Sp. grav. 20°C/20°C	0.8823	0.8769	0.8792	0.8786	0.8947	0.8533
Ref. ind. η^{20}_{D}	1.4853	1.4834	1.4849	1.4841	1.4907	1.4744
Ref. ind. 10% dist. η^{20}_{D}	1.4732	1.4729	1.4734	1.4724	1.4734	1.4730
Difference	0.0122	0.0103	0.0122	0.0110	0.0177	0.0053
Opt. rot. α^{20}_{D}	+43.36	+38.60	**	**	+49.01	+39.85
Opt. rot. 10% dist. α^{20}_{D}	+52.20	+47.60	+54.60	+49.32	+51.71	+48.33
Difference	+9.88	+6.20	**	**	+10.27	+689
Aldehyde (citral), %	6.14	3.66	5.20	4.46	6.66	4.30
Ester content, %	8.08	4.95	7.28	6.78	—	—
Evap. res., %	14.67	11.01	13.24	12.62	16.67	11.50

* No. of samples.
**Too dark to read in 25 mm tube.

SOURCE: KESTERSON, J. W., HENDRICKSON, R., and BRADDOCK, R. J. 1971. Florida Citrus Oils, Florida Agric. Expt. Sta. Tech. Bull. *749*.

LIMING MATERIALS I

TABLE 2.L.14

RELATIVE NEUTRALIZING VALUES OF PURE LIMING MATERIALS

Liming Materials	Relative Neutralizing Values	Pounds of Liming Materials Equivalent to 1 Ton Calcium Carbonate	Pounds of Liming Materials Equivalent to 1 Ton Calcium Oxide
Calcium carbonate	100	2,000	3,570
Magnesium carbonate	119	1,680	3,000
Calcium oxide	178	1,120	2,000
Magnesium oxide	250	800	1,430
Calcium hydrate	135	1,480	2,640
Magnesium hydrate	172	1,160	2,070
Dolomite	108	1,850	3,330
Dolomitic hydrate	175	1,145	2,040

SOURCE: SAUCHELLI, V. (EDITOR). Chemistry and Technology of Fertilizers. Van Nostrand Reinhold Co., New York.

LIMING MATERIALS II

TABLE 2.L.15

COMMON LIMING MATERIALS

Common Names	Neut[1] Equiv	Approx Analyses	Pounds of Liming Material Equiv to 1 Ton Calcium Carbonate
Ground dolomitic limestone[2]	95-108	52% $CaCO_3$ 42% $MgCO_3$	2105-1852
Ground agricultural limestone[2] Air slacked lime	85-100	80-95% $CaCO_3$	2353-2000
Precipitated lime Lump lime Builders lime Caustic lime	150-175	85% CaO	1333-1143
Hydrated lime Water slacked lime	120-135	65% CaO	1667-1481
Burned oyster shells	90-110	55% CaO; 5% MgO	2222-1818
Baked oyster shells	80-90	85% $CaCO_3$	2500-2222
Marl	50-90	60% $CaCO_3$	4000-2222
Basic Slag 8-10% P_2O_5	50-70	45% CaO; 6% MgO	4000-2857
Wood Ashes	40-50	45% $CaCO_3$	5000-4000
Land Plaster	None	70-75% $CaSO_4$	None

[1] Neutralizing equivalent given is percent in comparison to $CaCO_3$ as 100.
[2] Fineness of grinding is important. For practical purposes a limestone ground so that 65 to 80% passes a 48 mesh screen is satisfactory providing the 100 mesh and finer materials have not been removed.

SOURCE: Agronomy Extension Handbook of N.C. and Bulletin A-60 University of Maryland, and reproduced in *The Fertilizer Handbook, 2nd Edition*. Fertilizer Institute, Washington, D.C.

LIQUID COOKING OF MEAT

Recommended procedure for cooking meats in liquid are:

1. If you prefer, brown meat on all sides in own fat or lard.
2. Season with salt and pepper if desired.
3. Cover with liquid, cover kettle, cook below boiling point until tender.
4. Add vegetables just long enough before serving to be cooked.

SOURCE: Be a Smarter Shopper . . . a Better Cook. (1973). National Live Stock and Meat Board, Chicago.

LIVER

TABLE 2.L.16

THE AVERAGE WEIGHT AND COLOR OF THE LIVER AND THE LENGTH OF THE GALLBLADDER IN MEAT ANIMALS

Animal (Market Weight)	Liver				
	Weight of Liver	Percentage of Body Weight	Color	Lobes	Gallbladder
Beef	10-14 lb	1.1	Reddish brown	2	4-6 in. long
Veal	2-2½ lb	1.5	Reddish brown	2	3-4 in. long
Lamb	1½ lb	1.5	Reddish brown	2	4 in. long
Pork	2 lb	1.7	Reddish brown	4	3 in. long
Sow	7 lb	1.7	Reddish brown	4	3-5 in. long
Horse	10-12 lb	0.8-1.5	Purplish brown	3	Absent
Chicken (3-4 lb)	31-50 g	1.6-2.3	Chocolate	2	0.8 in. long
Rabbit (3¾ lb)	95 g	5.5	Reddish brown	4-5	1 in. long

SOURCE: OCKERMAN, H. W. 1975. Comparative anatomy of meat animals. *In* Meat Hygiene. J. A. Libby (Editor). Lea & Febiger, Philadelphia.

LOBSTER

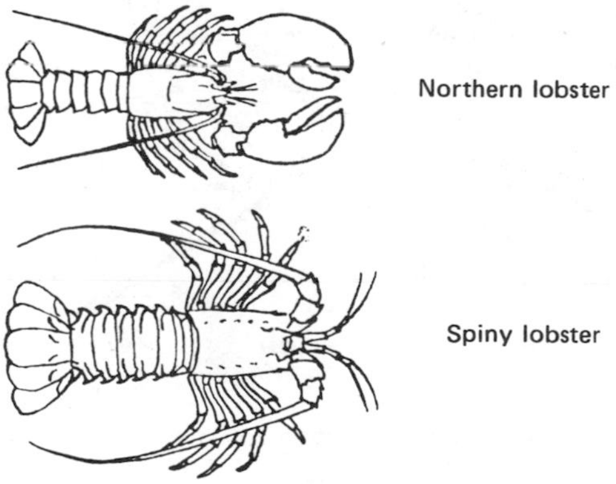

FIG. 2.L.2. HOW TO IDENTIFY NORTHERN AND SPINY LOBSTERS

SOURCE: Food For Us All. Yearbook of Agriculture, 1969. USDA.

LYMPH NODES, OX

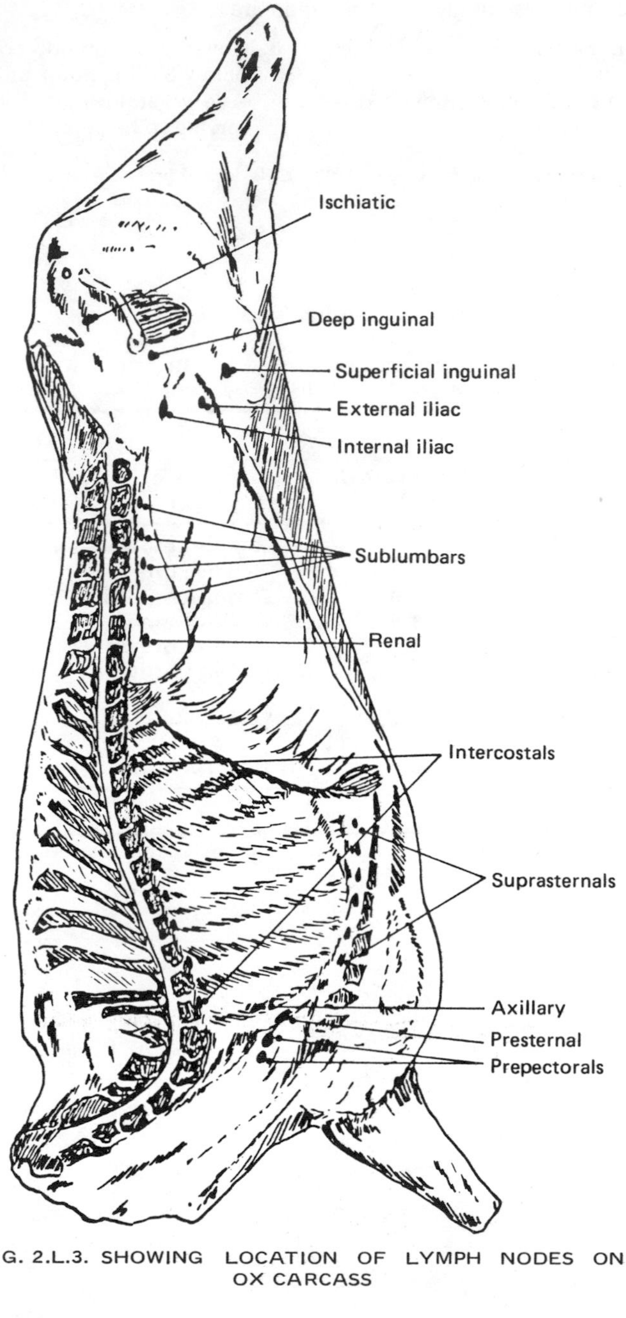

FIG. 2.L.3. SHOWING LOCATION OF LYMPH NODES ON OX CARCASS

SOURCE: WILSON, A. 1968. Practical Meat Inspection. Blackwell Scientific Publications, Ltd., Osney Media, Oxford, England.

LYMPH NODES, OX, LATERAL

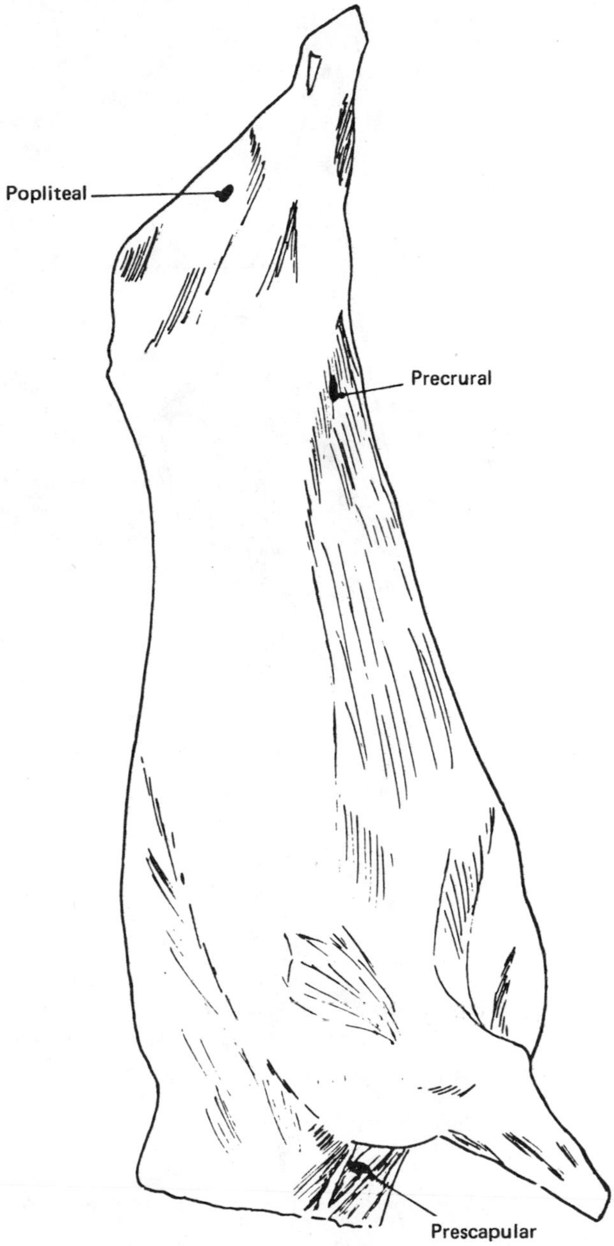

FIG. 2.L.4. SHOWING LOCATION OF LYMPH NODES ON EXTERIOR OF OX CARCASS

SOURCE: WILSON, A. 1968. Practical Meat Inspection. Blackwell Scientific Publications, Ltd., Osney Media, Oxford, England.

LYMPH NODES, PIG

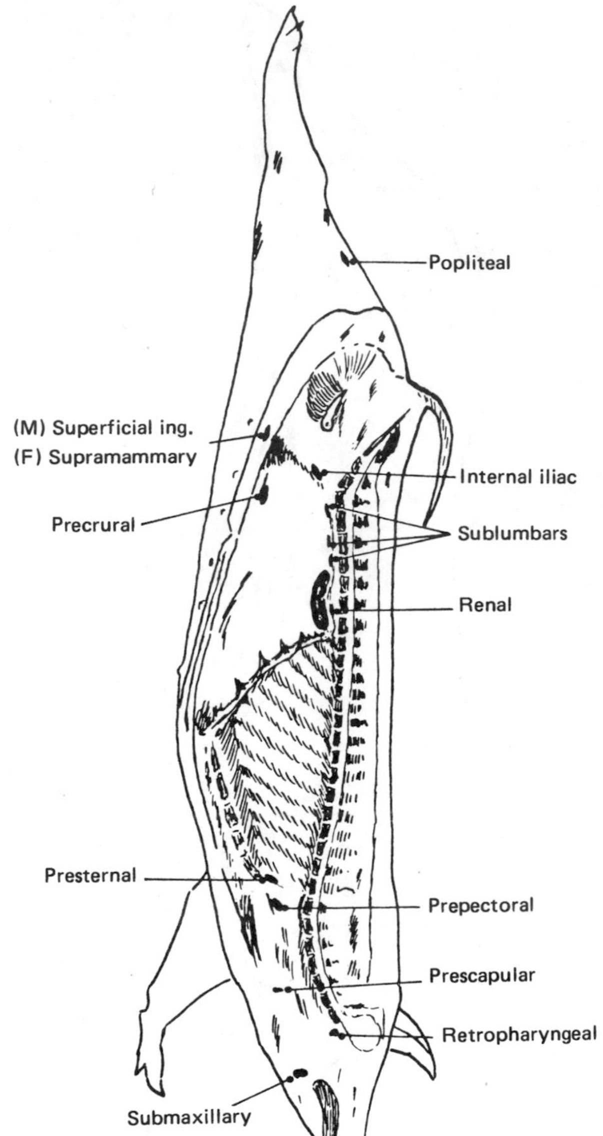

FIG. 2.L.5. SHOWING LOCATION OF LYMPH NODES ON HOG CARCASS

SOURCE: WILSON, A. 1968. Practical Meat Inspection. Blackwell Scientific Publications, Ltd., Osney Media, Oxford, England.

LYMPH NODES, SHEEP

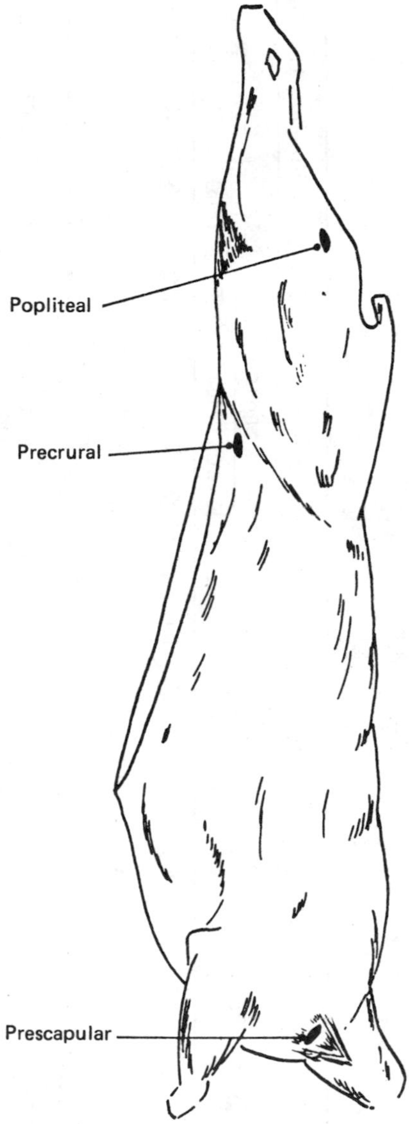

FIG. 2.L.6. SHOWING LOCATION OF LYMPH NODES ON SHEEP CARCASS

SOURCE: WILSON, A. 1968. Practical Meat Inspection. Blackwell Scientific Publications, Ltd., Osney Media, Oxford, England.

M

MACARONI AND NOODLES COMPOSITION

TABLE 2.M.1

COMPOSITION OF MACARONI AND NOODLES

Food[1]	Energy, Cal/100 Gm	Major Constituents[2]					Minerals, Mg/100 Gm						Vitamins/100 Gm			
		Proteins (%)	Carbo-hydrates (%)	Crude Fiber (%)	Fat (%)	Mois-ture (%)	Na	K	Ca	Mg	P	Fe	Thiamin (Mg)	Ribo-flavin (Mg)	Niacin (Mg)	A (IU)
Macaroni, enriched dry	368	12.5	74.0	0.3	1.2	12.0	2.0	197	27	48	161	2.9	0.88	0.37	6.0	0
Macaroni, enriched cooked	107	3.4	23.0	0.1	0.4	73.1	0.7	60	8	18	50	0.9	0.14	0.08	1.1	0
Macaroni, not enriched dry	386	12.5	74.0	0.3	1.2	12.0	2.0	197	27	48	161	1.3	0.09	0.06	1.7	0
Macaroni, not enriched cooked	107	3.4	23.0	0.1	0.4	73.1	0.7	60	8	18	50	0.4	0.01	0.01	0.3	0
Egg noodles, enriched dry	388	15.5	67.8	0.3	4.4	12.0	6.0	133	33	48	183	2.8	0.89	0.39	6.1	220
Egg noodles, enriched cooked	125	4.1	23.3	0.1	1.5	71.0	2.0	44	10	14	59	0.9	0.14	0.08	1.2	70

[1] All products as defined by FDA Definitions and Standards, no optional ingredients included.
[2] All data reported on an "as is" basis.

SOURCE: **WALSH, D. E. and GILLES, K. A. 1974. Macaroni Products. *In* Encyclopedia of Food Technology. A. H. Johnson and M. S. Peterson (Editors). Avi Publishing Co., Westport, Conn.**

MANURE ANALYSIS

TABLE 2.M.2

ANALYSIS OF TYPICAL MANURE
(Dry Matter Basis)

Proximate Analysis	%	lb/ton
Crude protein	12.9	258
Fat	1.0	20
Fiber	33.1	662
NFE	47.8	956
Ash	5.2	104
Minerals		
Carbon	50.0	1,000
Nitrogen (organic)	2.1	42
Phosphorus	0.4	8
Potassium	1.0	20
Calcium	1.0	20
Magnesium	0.4	8
Sodium	1.0	20
Sulfur	0.3	6
Iron	0.4	8
Amino Acids		
Alanine	0.47	9.4
Valine	0.27	5.4
Glycine	0.32	6.4
Isoleucine	0.20	4.0
Leucine	0.48	9.6
Proline	0.32	6.4
Threonine	0.26	5.2
Serine	0.25	5.0
Methionine	0.12	2.4
Hydroxyproline	0.03	0.6
Phenylalanine	0.27	5.4
Aspartic acid	0.53	10.6
Glutamic acid	0.82	16.4
Tyrosine	0.18	3.6
Lysine	0.18	3.6
Histidine	0.10	2.0
Arginine	0.15	3.0
Tryptophan	—	—
Cystine/2	0.05	1.0
Diaminopimelic acid	—	—
Total Amino Acid	5.00	100.0
Amino Acid/Crude Protein	0.39	—

SOURCE: COE, WARREN B. and TURK, MICHAEL. 1973. Processing Animal Waste by Anaerobic Fermentation. *In* Processing Agricultural and Municipal Wastes. G. E. Inglett (Editor). Avi Publishing Co., Westport, Conn.

MAPLE SYRUP COMPOSITION

TABLE 2.M.3

COMPOSITION OF MAPLE SYRUP[1]

Component	Amount %	Component	Amount %
Water	34.0	Soluble ash	0.30-0.81
Sucrose	58.2-65.5	Insoluble ash	0.08-0.67
Hexoses	0.0-7.9	Calcium	0.07
Malic acid	0.093	Silica	0.02
Citric acid	0.010	Manganese	0.005
Succinic acid	0.008	Sodium	0.003
Fumaric acid	0.004		

[1] Willits 1965; Hart and Fisher 1971.

SOURCE: WHITE, JR., JONATHAN W. and UNDERWOOD, J. CLYDE. 1974. Maple Syrup and Honey. *In* Symposium: Sweeteners. G. E. Inglett (Editor). Avi Publishing Co., Westport, Conn.

MARGARINE FORMULAE

The composition of the fatty phase of margarine may be varied *ad infinitum* and allows for the properties required of the product as well as the raw materials available. The formulae below were collected from the literature from the late 19th Century up to 1967.

1. Formulae for animal fats (table margarine)

	%		%
Oleomargarine	60	Oleomargarine	40
Lard	30	Premier jus	20
Liquid oil	10	Lard	15
		Liquid oil	25

2. Formulae for coconut and palm kernel oils

	%		%
Coconut oil	50	Palm oil	50
Vegetable oil hydrogenated (P.F. 42°C.)	25	Palm oil hydrogenated (P.F. 44°C.)	20
Liquid oil	25	Liquid oil	30

3. Formulae for hydrogenated oils

	%		%
Groundnut hydrogenated (P.F. 32-4°C.)	70	Palm kernel hydrogenated (P.F. 34°C.)	70
Coconut	10	Coconut	15
Liquid oil	20	Liquid oil	15

4. 'Single oil' formulae

	%		%
Cottonseed hydrogenated (P.F. 28°C.)	85	Sunflower hydrogenated (P.F. 44°C.)	20
Cottonseed hydrogenated (P.F. 42-4°C.)	15	Sunflower hydrogenated (P.F. 32°C.)	60
		Sunflower liquid	20

5. Formulae for bakery margarines

	%		%
Premier jus	25	Groundnut hydrogenated (P.F. 42°C.)	30
Palm oil hydrogenated (P.F. 46°C.)	25	Coconut oil	20
Groundnut hydrogenated (P.F. 34°C.)	10	Palm kernel oil	20
Liquid oil	40	Liquid oil	30
(For puff pastry)		(For biscuits and raised pastry)	

6. Standard margarine made in the United Kingdom during the 1939-45 war

	%
Coconut oil, Palm kernel oil	40
Palm oil	7
Groundnut oil hydrogenated (P.F. 34°C.)	13
Whale oil hydrogenated (P.F. 46-8°C.)	20
Groundnut oil	20

7. Recent formulae for products with special characteristics

(a) Margarine rich in essential fatty acids

	%
Coconut oil	30
Palm oil	10
Palm kernel oil	15
Palm oil hydrogenated (P.F. 42°C.)	10
Liquid sunflower oil hydrogenated	35

(b) Margarine very rich in polyunsaturated fatty acids

	%
Liquid sunflower oil	88
Palm kernel oil hydrogenated	6
Palm oil hydrogenated	6

(c) Margarine using a mixture of interesterified oils

(i)	%	
Liquid sunflower oil	20	
Sunflower oil hydrogenated (P.F. 33°C.)	40	interesterified
Sunflower oil hydrogenated (P.F. 42°C.)	20	interesterified
Liquid sunflower oil	20	interesterified

(ii)	%	
Cottonseed oil	20	interesterified
Sunflower oil hydrogenated (P.F. 33°C.)	32	interesterified
Soya bean oil hydrogenated (33°C.)	8	interesterified
Sunflower oil hydrogenated (42°C.)	20	interesterified
Liquid sunflower oil	20	

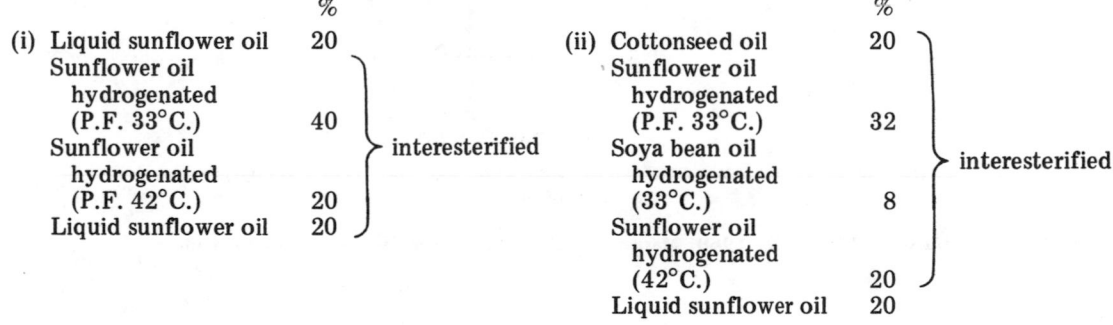

SOURCE: STUYVENBERG, J. H. 1969. Margarine. Liverpool University Press, United Kingdom.

MARGARINE PRODUCTION

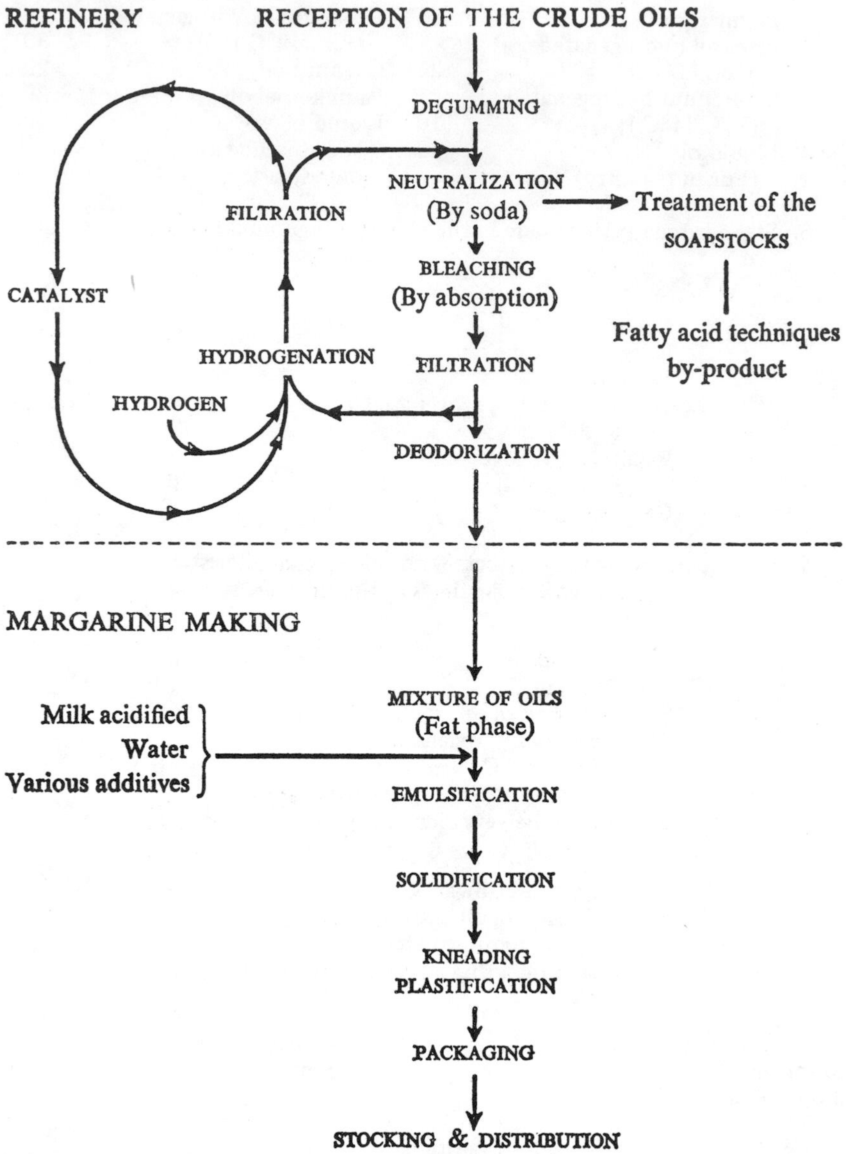

FIG. 2.M.1. FLOW SHEET SHOWING STAGES IN THE PRODUCTION OF MARGARINE

SOURCE: STUYVENBERG, J. H. 1969. Margarine. Liverpool University Press, United Kingdom.

MAYONNAISE

Ingredients

½ tsp paprika	1 egg yolk
½ tsp salt	2 tbsp vinegar
1 tsp sugar	1 cup salad oil
1 tsp dry mustard	

Procedure

Mix the dry ingredients. Add the egg yolk and stir thoroughly. Add 1 tbsp vinegar. Add the oil a tsp at a time, beating thoroughly after each addition until the mixture has thickened. Add more vinegar. Add oil in increasing amounts and thin the mixture with vinegar whenever it becomes very stiff. Cover, store in a cool place but do not freeze.

SOURCE: KINTNER, T. C. and MANGEL, M. Vinegars and Salad Dressings. Univ. Missouri Agric. Expt. Sta., Bull. *631.*

MAYONNAISE AND SALAD DRESSING

Mayonnaise

	Consistency		
	Light (%)	Medium (%)	Heavy (%)
Egg yolk	9.0	8.5	6.3
Oil	77.3	78.8	81.2
Spice mix	3.2	3.2	3.2
Vinegar and water	10.5	9.5	9.3

Salad Dressing

	Low Oil (%)	Medium Oil (%)	High Oil (%)
Egg yolk	4.0	5.0	6.0
Oil	30.0	35.0	40.0
Spice mix	6.0	5.0	4.0
Sugar	10.0	9.0	8.0
Starch paste	50.0	46.0	42.0

SOURCE: BINSTED, R., DEVEY, J. D., and DAKIN, J. C. 1971. Pickle & Sauce Making, 3rd Edition. Food Trade Press, London, England.

MEAT AND MEAT PRODUCTS COMPOSITION

TABLE 2.M.4

COMPOSITION OF THE EDIBLE PORTION (EP) AND REFUSE IN THE MATERIAL AS PURCHASED (AP)

Item No.	Commodity and Description	Water	Protein	Fat	Carbohydrate Total (by dif)	Carbohydrate Fiber	Ash	Calories No. per 100 g	Notes Wt (kg) Live	Notes Wt (kg) Carc	Notes Corres U.S. Grade	Refuse in AP (%)
	Meat and Meat Products		*(Percent of edible portion)*									
	Beef, carcasses[1]											
172	Thin—incl kidney fat	66	18.8	14	0	0	1.0	207	375	119	Utility	19
173	—excl kidney fat (0.9%)	67	19.0	13	0	0	1.0	198				19
174	Medium—incl kidney fat	60	17.5	22	0	0	0.9	273	408	220	Commercial	16
175	—excl kidney fat (1.8%)	61	17.8	20	0	0	0.9	256				16
176	Fat—incl kidney fat	55	16.3	28	0	0	0.8	322	446	250	Good	15
177	—excl kidney fat (2.5%)	56	16.8	26	0	0	0.8	306				15
178	Very fat—incl kidney fat	47	13.7	39	0	0	0.7	410	487	290	Choice and Prime	12
179	—excl kidney fat (3.4%)	48	14.2	37	0	0	0.7	394				
180	Beef, or veal, very thin carcasses[1]	69	19.6	10	0	0	1.0	174	Use in exceptional cases only			20
	Veal, carcasses[1]											
181	Thin—incl kidney fat	70	19.4	10	0	0	1.0	173				22
182	—excl kidney fat (2.3%)	71	19.7	8	0	0	1.0	156				23
183	Medium—incl kidney fat	66	18.8	14	0	0	1.0	207				21
184	—excl kidney fat (2.4%)	68	19.1	12	0	0	1.0	190				21
185	Fat—incl kidney fat	62	18.0	19	0	0	0.9	248				19
186	—excl kidney fat (2.7%)	65	18.5	16	0	0	0.9	223				19
	Pork, carcasses[2]											
187	Thin—shipper's carcass (head on)	50	14.1	35	0	0	0.8	376	75	54		22.6
188	—packer's carcass (head off)	50	14.1	35	0	0	0.8	376	75	50		16.4
189	Medium—shipper's carcass (head on)	42	11.9	45	0	0	0.6	457	100	74		17.5
190	—packer's carcass (head off)	42	11.9	45	0	0	0.6	457	100	70		12.5
191	Fat—shipper's carcass (head on)	35	9.8	55	0	0	0.5	538	125	96		14.5
192	—packer's carcass (head off)	35	9.8	55	0	0	0.5	538	125	92		10.5

	Mutton and Lamb, carcasses[2]											
193	Thin, young, incl kidney fat	71.1	18.0	10.0	0	0	0.9	167	20	9	Cull and Utility	29
194	Medium, incl kidney fat	56	15.7	27.7	0	0	0.8	317	32	15	Commercial and Good	24
195	Fat, incl kidney fat	46.5	13.0	39.8	0	0	0.7	415	46	22.5	Choice and Prime	19
196	Offal, all species	74	16.0	7.8	1	0	1.2	143			Liver, heart, kidney, tongue, brains, pancreas, etc.	0
	Other Meats											
197	Horsemeat, carcass	74	20	4	1		1	125				25
198	Goat meat, carcass	71	18.7	9.4	0		0.9	165				25
199[2]	Buffalo, carcass, very lean; Carabao, carcass, very lean	74	20	4	1		1	125				36
	*Camel—use No. 172											
	*Reindeer—use No. 172											
200	Rabbit, domestic, dressed and drawn	71	21.8	6.1	0		1.2	148			1.2 kg (drawn weight) AP	20
201	Whale meat, lean only, edible portion	74	20	4	1		1	125				0
	Game											
202	Mammals, dressed	73.8	21.4	3.6	0		1.2	124			Deer, wild rabbit, wild boar, etc.	16
203	Birds, dressed, not drawn	71.3	22.4	5.2	0		1.1	143			Wt dressed, not drawn (AP) (Kilograms)	42
	Poultry (total edible—flesh, skin, giblets, and fat)											
204	Chickens	66	20.2	12.6	0		1.0	200			1.4	39
205	Ducks; Geese	52.8	16.2	30	0		1.0	340			(2.2) (5.3)	39
206	Turkeys	58.3	20.1	20.2	0		1.0	268			7.5	33
207	Poultry, unspecified, group figure	65	20	14	1		1.0	212			1.5	39
	Meats, canned											
208	Roast beef, corned beef	58	25	14	0		3	233				0
209	Luncheon meats (chiefly pork)	57	16	22	1		4	271				0
	Meats, cured											
210	Corned beef	57	22	17	0		4	247				0
211	Pork (ham, shoulder)	44	17.2	33	0		5.3	371				13
212	Bacon (smoked belly)	21	9	65	1		4	629				6
	Meats, dehydrated											
213	Beef or pork (lean with some fat)	9	60	28	0		3	509				0
214	Lean beef	9	82	5	0		4	395				0

[1] These factors are for the edible portion of the entire *untrimmed* carcass, except for Nos. 173, 175, 177, 179, 182, 184, and 186 where allowances have been made for the removal of small proportions of fat. When fat has been trimmed in excess of the indicated percentages separate calculations are needed.

[2] These factors are for the edible portion of the entire *untrimmed* carcass, *including kidney fat*. When meat fat has been removed (domestic production of pork or mutton fat), these figures are not directly applicable; separate calculations are required.

[3] More information required.

SOURCE: CHATFIELD, C. Food Composition Tables for International Use. FAO, United Nations, Rome.

MEAT COMPOSITION

TABLE 2.M.5

COMPOSITION OF MEAT

Food, Approximate Measure, and Weight (in Grams)		Water (%)	Food Energy (Cal)	Protein (g)	Fat (Total Lipid) (g)	Fatty Acids: Saturated (Total) (g)	Fatty Acids: Unsaturated: Oleic (g)	Fatty Acids: Unsaturated: Lin-oleic (g)	Carbohy-drate (g)	Calcium (mg)	Iron (mg)	Vitamin A Value (IU)	Thiamin (mg)	Riboflavin (mg)	Niacin (mg)	Ascorbic Acid (mg)
Bacon, broiled or fried crisp	2 slices (16 g)	8	95	5	8	3	4	1	1	2	0.5	0	0.08	0.05	0.8	
Beef, trimmed to retail basis,[1] cooked:																
Cuts braised, simmered, or pot-roasted:																
Lean and fat	3 oz (85 g)	53	245	23	16	8	7	Tr	0	10	2.9	30	0.04	0.18	3.5	
Lean only	2.5 oz (72 g)	62	140	22	5	2	2	Tr	0	10	2.7	10	0.04	0.16	3.3	
Hamburger, broiled:																
Market ground	3 oz (85 g)	54	245	21	17	8	7	Tr	0	9	2.7	30	0.07	0.02	4.6	
Ground lean	3 oz (85 g)	60	185	23	10	5	4	Tr	0	10	3.0	20	0.08	0.20	5.1	
Roast, oven-cooked, no liquid added:																
Relatively fat, such as rib:																
Lean and fat	3 oz (85 g)	38	390	16	36	17	16	1	0	7	2.1	70	0.04	0.13	3.0	
Lean only	1.8 oz (51 g)	57	120	14	7	3	3	Tr	0	6	1.8	10	0.04	0.11	2.6	
Relatively lean, such as round:																
Lean and fat	3 oz (85 g)	56	220	23	14	7	6	Tr	0	10	3.0	30	0.06	0.18	4.2	
Lean only	2.5 oz (71 g)	63	130	21	4	2	2	Tr	0	9	2.7	10	0.05	0.16	3.8	
Steak, broiled:																
Relatively fat, such as sirloin:																
Lean and fat	3 oz (85 g)	44	330	20	27	13	12	1	0	8	2.5	50	0.05	0.16	4.0	
Lean only	2 oz (56 g)	59	115	18	4	2	2	Tr	0	7	2.2	10	0.05	0.14	3.6	
Relatively lean, such as round:																
Lean and fat	3 oz (85 g)	55	220	24	13	6	6	Tr	0	11	3.0	20	0.07	0.19	4.8	
Lean only	2.4 oz (69 g)	61	130	22	4	2	2	Tr	0	9	2.6	10	0.06	0.16	4.2	
Beef, canned:																
Corned beef	3 oz (85 g)	59	180	22	10	5	4	Tr	0	17	3.7	20	0.01	0.20	2.9	
Corned beef hash	3 oz (85 g)	70	120	12	5	2	2	Tr	6	22	1.1	10	0.02	0.11	2.4	
Beef, dried or chipped	2 oz (57 g)	48	115	19	4	2	2	Tr	0	11	2.9		0.04	0.18	2.2	
Beef and vegetable stew	1 c (235 g)	82	185	15	10	5	4	Tr	15	31	2.8	2,530	0.13	0.18	4.4	14
Beef potpie, baked: Individual pie, 4 1/4-in.-diam, wt before baking about 8 oz	1 pie (227 g)	63	460	18	28	10	15	1	32	20	2.5	2,830	0.07	0.14	3.0	Tr

Chile con carne, canned:															
With beans	1 c (250 g)	72	335	19	15	7	7	Tr	30	98	4.2	150	0.08	0.20	3.5	
Without beans	1 c (255 g)	67	510	26	38	18	17	1	15	97	3.6	380	0.05	0.31	5.6	
Heart, beef, trimmed of fat, braised	3 oz (85 g)	61	160	26	5	2	2	Tr	1	14	5.9	30	0.23	1.05	6.8	3
Lamb, trimmed to retail basis,[1] cooked:															
Chop, thick, with bone, broiled	1 chop, 4.8 oz (137 g)	47	405	25	33	18	12	1	0	10	3.1		0.14	0.25	4.5	
Lean and fat	4 oz (112 g)	47	405	25	33	18	12	1	0	10	3.1		0.14	0.25	5.6	
Lean only	2.6 oz (74 g)	62	140	21	6	3	2	Tr	0	9	2.5		0.11	0.20	4.5	
Leg, roasted:															
Lean and fat	3 oz (85 g)	54	235	22	16	9	6	Tr	0	9	2.8		0.13	0.23	4.7	
Lean only	2.5 oz (71 g)	62	130	20	5	3	2	Tr	0	9	2.6		0.12	0.21	4.4	
Shoulder, roasted:															
Lean and fat	3 oz (85 g)	50	285	18	23	13	8	1	0	8	2.4		0.11	0.20	4.0	
Lean only	2.3 oz (64 g)	61	130	17	6	3	2	Tr	0	8	2.2		0.10	0.18	3.7	
Liver, beef, fried	2 oz (57 g)	57	120	13	4	2	2	Tr	6	5	4.4	30,330	0.15	2.25	8.4	18
Pork, fresh, trimmed to retail basis,[1] cooked:															
Chop, thick, with bone	1 chop, 3.5 oz (98 g)	42	260	16	21	8	9	2	0	8	2.2	0	0.63	0.18	3.8	
Lean and fat	2.3 oz (66 g)	42	260	16	21	8	9	2	0	8	2.2	0	0.63	0.18	3.8	
Lean only	1.7 oz (48 g)	53	130	15	7	3	3	1	0	7	1.9	0	0.54	0.16	3.3	
Roast, oven-cooked, no liquid added:															
Lean and fat	3 oz (85 g)	46	310	21	24	9	10	2	0	9	2.7	0	0.78	0.22	4.7	
Lean only	2.4 oz (68 g)	55	175	20	10	4	4	1	0	9	2.6	0	0.73	0.21	4.4	
Cuts simmered:															
Lean and fat	3 oz (85 g)	46	320	20	26	9	11	2	0	8	2.5	0	0.46	0.21	4.1	
Lean only	2.2 oz (63 g)	60	135	18	6	2	3	1	0	8	2.3	0	0.42	0.19	3.7	
Pork, cured, cooked:															
Ham, smoked, lean and fat	3 oz (85 g)	48	290	18	24	9	10	2	1	8	2.2	0	0.39	0.15	3.1	
Luncheon meat:															
Cooked ham, sliced	2 oz (57 g)	48	170	13	13	5	5	1	0	5	1.5	0	0.57	0.15	2.9	
Canned, spiced or unspiced	2 oz (57 g)	55	165	8	14	5	6	1	1	5	1.2	0	0.18	0.12	1.6	
Tongue, beef, simmered	3 oz (85 g)	61	205	18	14	7	6	Tr	Tr	7	2.5		0.04	0.26	3.1	
Veal, cooked:															
Cutlet, broiled	3 oz without bone. (85 g)	60	185	23	9	4	4	Tr	0	9	2.7		0.06	0.21	4.6	
Roast, medium fat, medium done: lean and fat.	3 oz (85 g)	55	305	23	14	7	6	Tr	0	10	2.9		0.11	0.26	6.6	

[1] Outer layer of fat on the cut was removed to within approximately 1/2 in. of the lean. Deposits of fat within the cut were not removed.

SOURCE: INSTITUTE OF HOME ECONOMICS. Nutritive Value of Foods. USDA Home and Garden Bull. *72*.

MEAT CURING INGREDIENTS

TABLE 2.M.6

LIQUID PICKLE FOR CURING LARGE PIECES OF MEATS USING EITHER SALT OR BRINE

Ingredients	Quantity To Be Used When Various Percentages are To Be Pumped 10%	12%	14%	16%	18%	20%
When using salt (lb)	167	140	130	111	95	83.50
Bring volume up to 100 gal. with water						
or						
When using 100° salinometer brine (gal.)	63	53	49	42	36	31.50
Bring volume up to 100 gal. with water						
Make up pickle with these ingredients:						
Sodium nitrite (lb)	2.0	1.67	1.43	1.25	1.11	1.0
Sodium nitrate (lb)	2.0	1.67	1.43	1.25	1.11	1.0
Food grade phosphate (lb)[1]	50.0	41.66	35.71	31.25	27.78	25.0
Sodium erythorbate (lb)	5.51	4.55	3.90	3.42	3.04	2.75
Sodium carbonate or bicarbonate	Use sufficient amount to stabilize sodium erythorbate and sodium nitrite to pH of 7.6 at pickle temperature of 40°F					
Cane sugar (lb)	30.0	25.0	21.5	18.75	16.5	15.0
If flavoring ingredients are desired add:						
Monosodium glutamate (oz)	24.0	24.0	20.0	20.0	16.0	16.0
Plant protein hydrolyzate (oz)	15.0	12.50	10.75	9.50	8.25	7.50
Smoke flavor (optional)		Depending on the concentrate desired				

[1] It is now permissible to use sodium hydroxide in combination with food grade phosphate. It may be used only in combination with food grade phosphate in the ratio of 4 parts of phosphate to 1 part of sodium hydroxide. The combination should not exceed 5% pickle at 10% pump, or 0.5% to products. Instead of using the quantities indicated above of the food grade phosphate, the following combined percentages may be used:

	10%	12%	14%	16%	18%	20%
Food grade phosphate (lb)	40.0	33.33	28.57	25.00	22.23	20.0
Sodium hydroxide (lb)	10.0	8.33	7.14	6.25	5.55	5.0

SOURCE: KOMARIK, STEPHAN L., TRESSLER, DONALD K. and LONG, LUCY (EDITORS). 1974. Cured Meats. *In* Food Products Formulary, Vol. 1. Avi Publishing Co., Westport, Conn.

MEAT, FROZEN STORAGE

TABLE 2.M.7

RECOMMENDED LENGTH OF STORAGE FOR FROZEN MEATS

Meat	Maximum Number of Months at 0°F
Beef	
Roasts, steaks	6-12
Ground	2-3
Veal	
Roasts	4-8
Cutlets, chops	3-4
Ground meat	2-3
Lamb	
Chops	3-4
Roasts	6-12
Pork	
Roasts	4-6
Chops	3-4
Sausage, without salt	1-2
Ham, cured	1-2
Bacon	Less than 1
Poultry	6-12

SOURCE: SIMONDS, L. A. and VANSTAVERN, B. D. 1975. Buying Meat for Locker or Home Freezer. Ohio State Univ. Coop. Ext. Serv.

MEAT GRADE (QUALITY) STAMPS

USDA Prime

Prime grade beef is the ultimate in tenderness, juiciness, and flavor. It has abundant marbling —flecks of fat within the lean— which enhances both flavor and juiciness. Steaks of this grade are the best for broiling.

USDA Choice

Most USDA Choice steaks are good for broiling and pan-broiling, too—they will be very tender, juicy, and flavorful. Choice grade beef has slightly less marbling than Prime, but still is of very high quality.

USDA Good

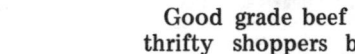

Good grade beef often pleases thrifty shoppers because it is somewhat more lean than the higher grades. It is relatively tender, but because it has less marbling it lacks some of the juiciness and flavor of the higher grades. Some stores sell this quality of beef under a "house" brand name rather than under the USDA grade name.

USDA Standard

Standard grade beef has a high proportion of lean meat and very little fat. Because it comes from young animals, beef of this grade is fairly tender. But because it lacks marbling, it is mild in flavor and most cuts will be somewhat dry unless prepared with moist heat.

USDA Commercial

Commercial grade beef is produced only from mature animals —the top four grades are restricted to young animals. It has abundant marbling (compare it with the Prime grade), and will have the rich, full flavor characteristic of mature beef. However, Commercial grade beef requires long, slow cooking with moist heat to make it tender. When prepared in this manner it can provide delicious and economical meat dishes.

SOURCE: How to Buy Beef Steaks. (1968). USDA Home and Garden Bull. *145*.

MEAT IDENTIFICATION

TABLE 2.M.8

CHARACTERISTICS AND TYPICAL CUTS OF MEATS

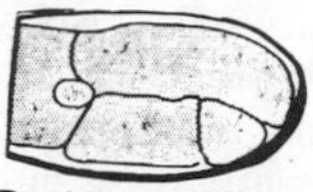

Beef Round Steak

Veal Round Steak (Cutlet)

Pork Ham Slice, Center Cut
(Fresh or Smoked)

Lamb Leg Steak, Center Cut

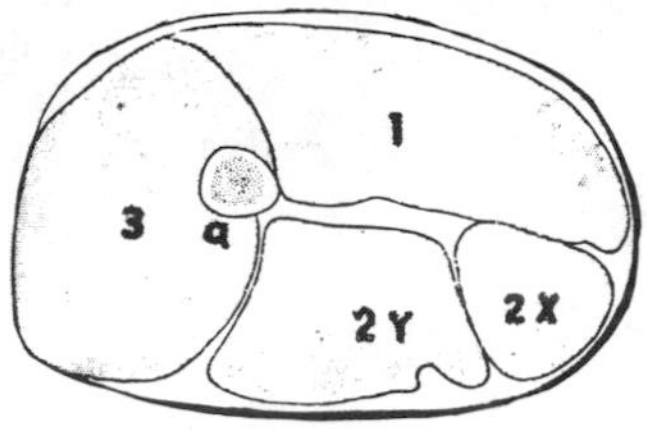

Bone
- a. Round or leg (smallest in center cuts)

Muscles
1. Top (inside) round or leg
2. Bottom (outside) round or leg
   - (X) Eye of round or leg
   - (Y) Bottom round or leg
3. Tip (knuckle)

Other Features
- Oval shape
- Separating lines of connective tissue and fat between muscles.

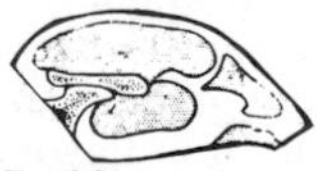

Beef Sirloin Steak

Veal Sirloin Steak

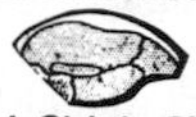

Pork Sirloin Chop

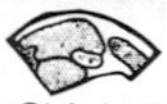

Lamb Sirloin Chop

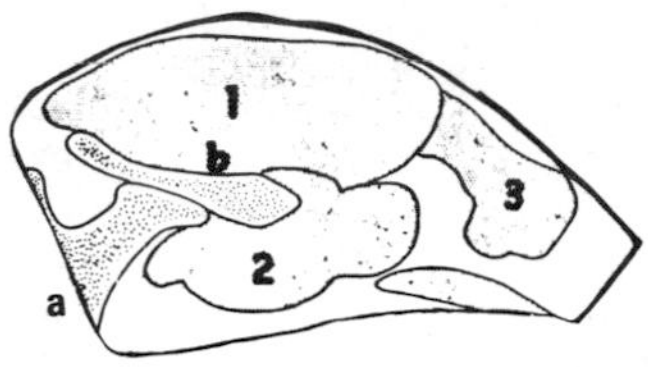

Bones
- a. Back } wide variation in shape
- b. Hip }

Muscles
1. Top sirloin }
2. Tenderloin } wide variation in shape
3. Tip (knuckle) }

Tip muscle (3) is replaced by flank in steaks and chops cut across forward end of hip bone.

Other Features

Muscles in area (3), in some steaks and chops, appear to have been cut with grain of meat.

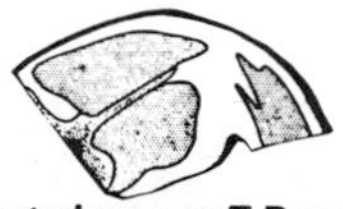

Beef Porterhouse or T-Bone Steak

Veal Loin Chop

Pork Loin Chop

Lamb Loin Chop

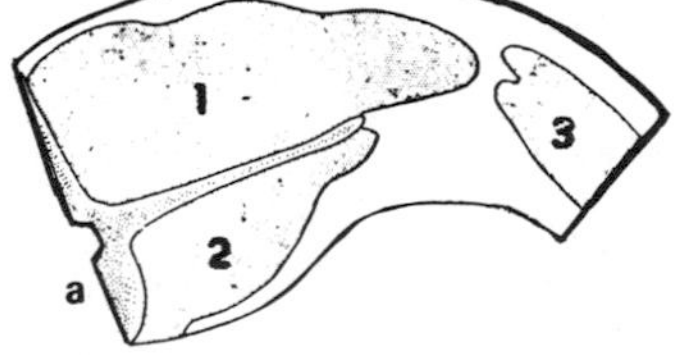

Bone
- a. Back (T shape)

Muscles
1. Loin eye or strip
2. Tenderloin (larger in Porterhouse than in T-Bone)
3. Flank (tail of steaks and chops)

Other Features

Beef club steak looks very much like Porterhouse or T-Bone except that it contains no tenderloin.

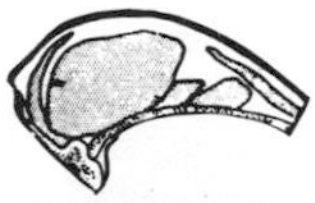

Beef Rib Steak

Veal Rib Chop

Pork Rib (Loin) Chop

Lamb Rib Chop

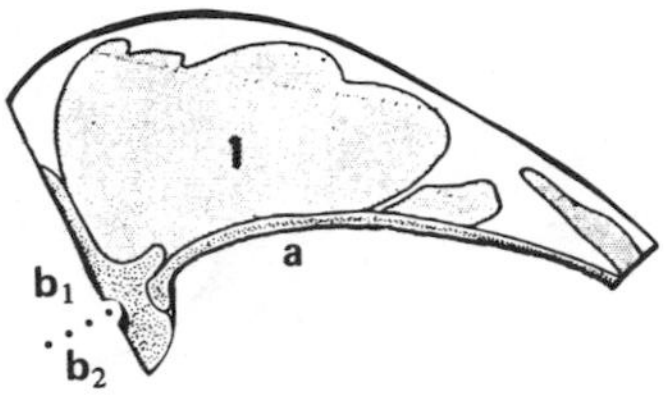

Bones

a. Rib (steaks and chops cut between ribs do not have this bone).

b. Back

(b_1) Feather

(b_2) Chine

Muscles

1. Rib eye (continuation of loin eye muscle.)

Other Features

Steaks and chops near chuck or shoulder have thin layer of meat over rib eye called rib cover.

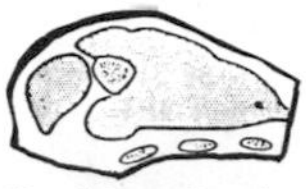

Beef Arm Steak

Veal Arm Steak (Chop)

Pork Arm Steak (Chop)

Lamb Arm Chop

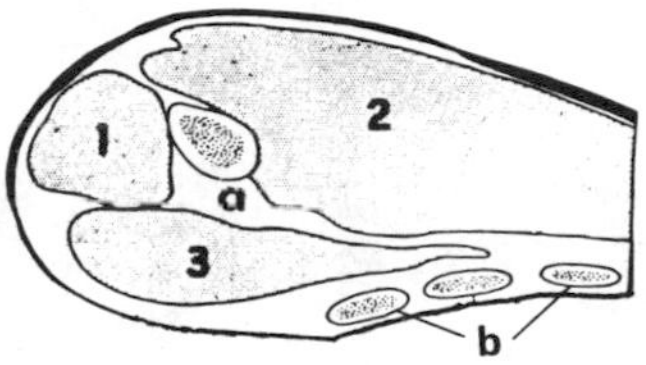

Bones

a. Arm

b. Rib cross cuts (in all cuts except pork)

Muscles

1. Small round forearm muscle completely surrounded with connective tissue
2. Arm (thick end of clod or outside shoulder)
3. Brisket or middle rib

Other Features

Although cuts from round and arm look somewhat alike, a close comparison shows a wide difference in muscle structure. Cuts from round contain no cross cut rib bones.

Beef Blade Steak

Veal Blade Steak

Pork Blade Steak

Lamb Blade Chop

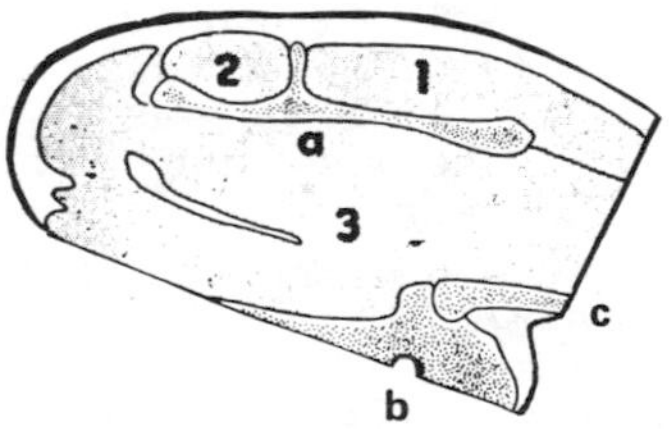

Bones

a. Blade

b. Back (in all cuts except pork)

c. Rib (in all cuts except pork, unless made between ribs)

Muscles

1. Outside chuck (thin end of clod or outside shoulder)
2. Chuck tender
3. Inside chuck

Other Features

Muscles of inside chuck (3) run in different directions.

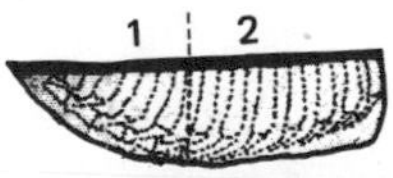

Beef Brisket (1) and Short Plate (2)

Veal Breast

Pork (Side Pork and Bacon)

Lamb Breast

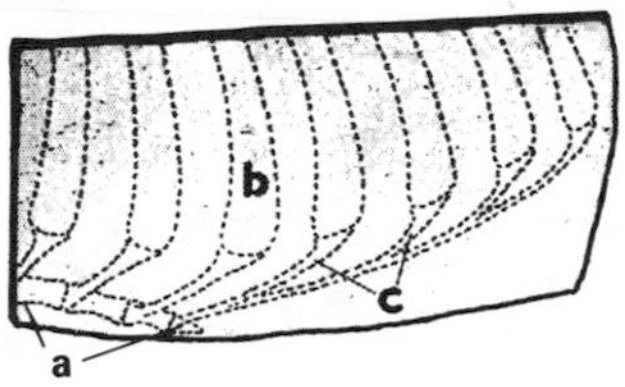

Bones

a. Breast (except in pork)

b. Ribs (except in pork)

c. Rib cartilages (except in pork)

Muscles

1. Alternating layers of lean and fat.

Other Features

Breasts of veal and lamb are comparable to plate and brisket sections of beef.

Side pork (bacon before curing and smoking) comes from same area in pork as preceding cuts come from in beef, lamb and veal.

Side pork and bacon are sold boneless. Bones (spareribs) were removed in packing plant.

SOURCE: Meat Manual, 6th Edition, National Live Stock and Meat Board, Chicago.

MEAT INSPECTION (WHOLESOMENESS) STAMP

SOURCE: How to Buy Beef Steaks. (1968). USDA Home and Garden Bull. *145*.

MEAT LABEL

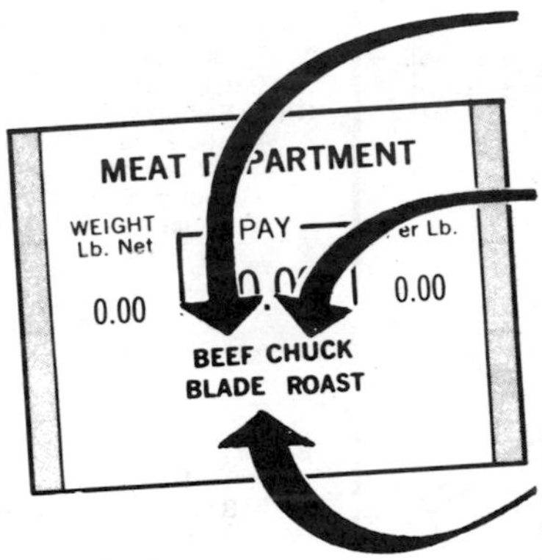

1 The kind of meat — BEEF, PORK, LAMB or VEAL. It's listed first on every label.

2 The primal (wholesale) cut —CHUCK, RIB, LOIN or ROUND —tells where the meat comes from on the animal.

3 The retail cut — BLADE ROAST, SPARERIBS, LOIN CHOPS, etc.—tells what part of the primal cut the meat comes from.

FIG. 2.M.2. HOW TO IDENTIFY THE LABEL ON RETAIL MEAT PACKAGES

SOURCE: Be a Smarter Shopper . . . a Better Cook. (1973). National Live Stock and Meat Board, Chicago.

MEAT, NUTRITIVE VALUE

TABLE 2.M.9

NUTRITIVE VALUE OF COOKED MEATS

	Beef[1]	Veal[1]	Lamb[1]	Pork[1]
	(3½ oz Cooked Lean Meat)			
Protein (g)	29.6	32.7	26.6	28.5
Calories/100 g	265.8	213	258	240
Fat (g)	15.4	8.1	16.1	13.1
Carbohydrate (gm)	0	0	0	0
Iron (mg)[2]	3.7	3.3	2.0	3.5
Calcium (mg)	9.6	9.7	8.2	8.1
Phosphorus (mg)	191.1	260	210.8	228
Potassium (mg)	442	543	499	496
Magnesium (mg)	21.3	21.7	22.6	22.7
Zinc (mg)[3]	5.8[4] (6.2)[5]	4.1[4] (4.2)[5]	4.3[4] (5)[5]	3.8[4]
Thiamin (mg)	0.10	0.18	0.22	1.03
Riboflavin (mg)	0.39	0.35	0.32	0.29
Niacin (mg)	4.5	7.2	7.6	4.4
B-6 (mg)	0.37	0.48	0.32	0.46
B-12 (mcg)	2.056	2.53	2.8	1.2
Vitamin A (IU)	0	0	0	0
Vitamin C (mg)	0	0	0	0

[1]LEVERTON, RUTH M. and ODELL, G. V. 1958. The nutritive value of cooked meat. Stillwater, Oklahoma: Oklahoma Agric. Expt. Sta., Misc. Publ. *MP-49*, Oklahoma State Univ.
[2]WATT, BERNICE K. and MERRILL, ANNABEL L. Revised 1963. Composition of Foods—Raw, Processed, Prepared. USDA Agriculture Handbook *8*.
[3]MURPHY, E. W., WILLIS, B. W. and WATT, BERNICE K. 1975. Provisional tables on zinc content of foods. J. Am. Diet. Assoc. *66*, 345.
[4]Dry heat.
[5]Moist heat.

SOURCE: National Live Stock and Meat Board, Chicago, 1975.

MEAT PIGMENT

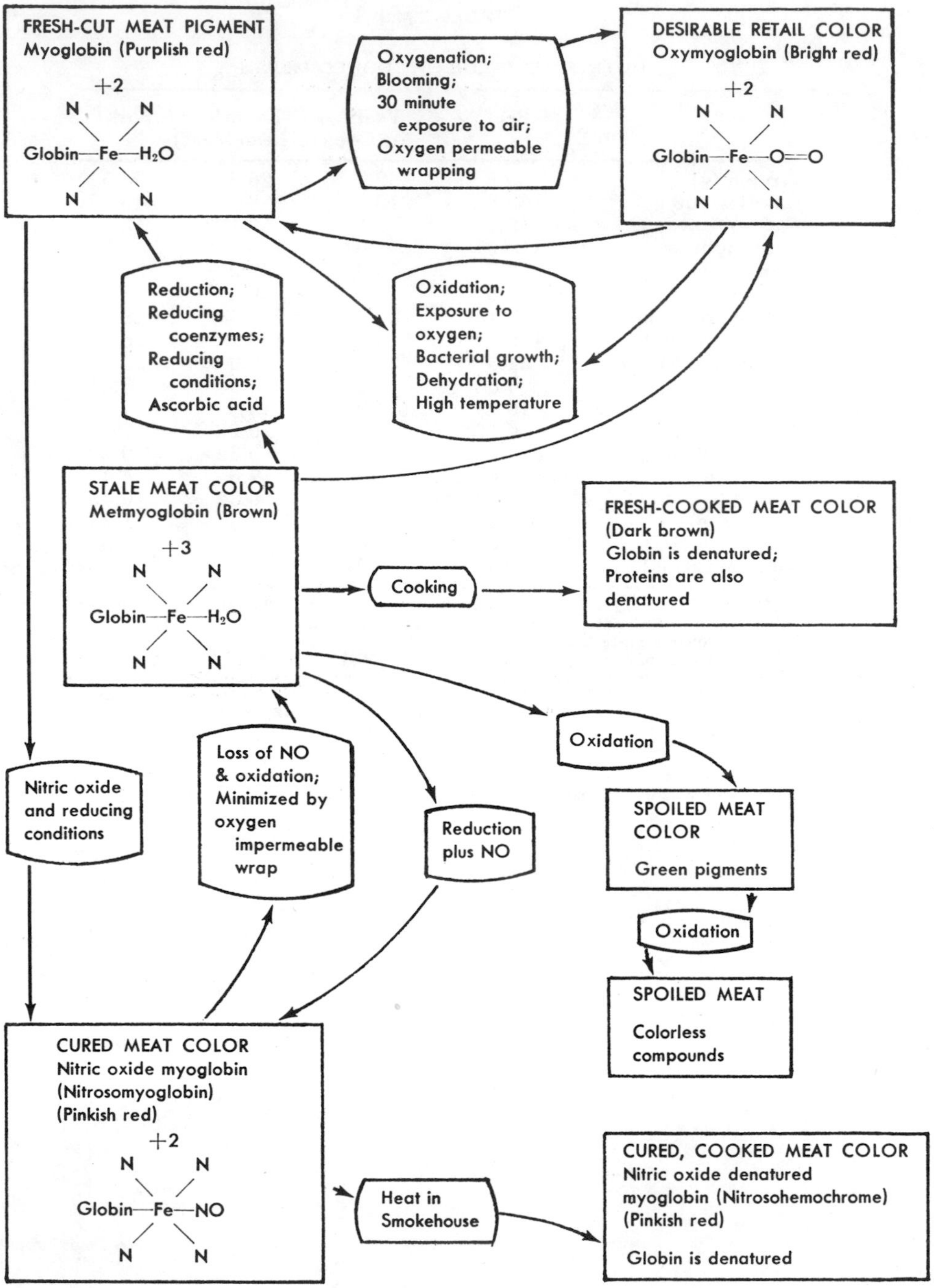

FIG. 2.M.3. FRESH AND CURED MEAT PIGMENT ALTERATIONS

SOURCE: OCKERMAN, H. W. 1975. Chemistry of Muscle and Major Organs. *In* Meat Hygiene. J. A. Libby (Editor). Lea & Febiger, Philadelphia.

MEAT, SERVINGS PER POUND I

TABLE 2.M.10

AVERAGE NUMBER OF SERVINGS FROM ONE POUND OF DIFFERENT RETAIL CUTS OF MEAT AND POULTRY[1]

Meat Cut	Servings Per Pound	Meat Cut	Servings Per Pound
Beef		Pork, fresh	
Sirloin steak	2½	Center cut or rib chops	4
Porterhouse, T-bone, rib steak	2	Loin or rib roasts	2½
Round steak	3½	Ham roast	2½
Flank steak	4	Boston butt, bone in	3
Chuck steak	2	Boston butt, boneless	4
Chuck roast, bone in	2	Blade steak	3
Rib roast, boneless	2½	Spareribs	1-⅓
Chuck roast, boneless	3	Liver	5
Rib roast, bone in	2	Pork, cured	
Rump roast, sirloin roast	3	Picnic:	
Ground beef	4	Bone in	2
Short ribs	2	Boneless	3
Heart, liver or kidney	5	Canned	5
Tongue	3	Center slice	3
Frankfurters	4	Ham, ready-to-eat:	
Stew meat, boneless	5	Bone in	3½
Dried, chipped	8	Boneless	5
Lamb		Shankless	4½
Loin, rib or shoulder chops	3	Center slice	5
Breast and shank	2	Ham, cook-before-eating:	
Shoulder roast	2½	Bone in	2½
Leg of lamb	3	Boneless	3½
Stew meat, boneless	5	Shankless	3

[1]From 2½ to 3½ oz of cooked, lean meat is considered a standard serving.

SOURCE: POTTS, B. 1975. Meat Buying "Know-How." Ohio State Univ. Coop. Ext. Serv.

MEAT, SERVINGS PER POUND II

TABLE 2.M.11

MEAT, POULTRY, AND FISH

	Servings per Lb[1]
Meat	
Much bone or gristle	1-2
Medium amounts of bone	2-3
Little or no bone	3-4
Poultry (Ready-To-Cook)	
Chicken	2-3
Turkey	2-3
Duck and goose	2
Fish	
Whole	1-2
Dressed or pan-dressed	2-3
Portions or steaks	3
Fillets	3-4

[1]Three ounces of cooked lean meat, poultry, or fish per serving.

SOURCE: Nutrition, Food at Work for You. (1968). USDA Home and Garden Bull. *1*.

MEAT STORAGE

TABLE 2.M.12

MAXIMUM MEAT STORAGE TIME

Meat	Refrigerator (36°-40°F)	Freezer (at 0°F or lower)
Beef (fresh)	2-4 days	6-12 months
Veal (fresh)	2-4 days	6-9 months
Pork (fresh)	2-4 days	3-6 months
Lamb (fresh)	2-4 days	6-9 months
Ground beef, veal and lamb	1-2 days	3-4 months
Ground pork	1-2 days	1-3 months
Variety meats	1-2 days	3-4 months
Luncheon meats	1 week	Not recommended
Sausage, fresh pork	1 week	60 days
Sausage, smoked	3-7 days	
Sausage, dry and semi-dry (unsliced)	2-3 weeks	
Frankfurters	4-5 days	1 month
Bacon	5-7 days	1 month
Smoked ham, whole	1 week	60 days
Ham slices	3-4 days	60 days
Beef, corned	1 week	2 weeks
Leftover cooked meat	4-5 days	2-3 months

SOURCE: Be a Smarter Shopper . . . a Better Cook. 1973. National Live Stock and Meat Board, Chicago.

MELTING POINTS, FATS AND OILS

TABLE 2.M.13

MELTING POINTS OF SOME FATS AND OILS[1]

Oil or Fat	Melting Point (°C)
Coconut	23-26
Palm	27-43
Palm kernel	24-26
Babassu	24-26
Butter	28-35
Tallow (beef)	43-48
Tallow (mutton)	44-47
Lard	36-45
Horse fat	36-43
Cacao butter	28-36
Borneo tallow	34-39

[1] Closed capillary tube method.

SOURCE: MAHLENBACHER, C. V. The Analysis of Fats and Oils. Garrard Press, Champaign, Illinois.

MESH SIZES

Below are some of the most widely used mesh sizes. British and U.S. standard sizes differ only slightly. Special metal meshes with fine wires which provide greater percentage open area are available for higher outputs.

TABLE 2.M.14

MESH REFERENCE: WIRE AND NYLON CLOTH

Mesh No.	Size of Opening (in.)	Open Area (%)	Wire Diam (in.)	Closest Equiv Nylon Cloth (No.)	Aperture Size (μ)	Open Area (%)
20	.0340	46.2	.016	860	860	57
30	.0198	35.3	.0135	505	505	51
40	.0150	36.0	.010	390	390	47
60	.0087	27.2	.008	223	223	45
80	.0070	31.4	.0055	183	183	47
100	.0055	30.3	.0045	130	130	44
120	.0046	30.7	.0037	116	116	43
150	.0041	37.4	.0026	102	102	39
180	.0033	34.7	.0023	86	86	35
200	.0029	33.6	.0021	73	73	33
250	.0024	36.0	.0016	64	64	30
325	.0017	30.0	.0014	44	44	17

SOURCE: SLADE, F. H. 1967. Food Processing Plant, Vol. *1*. International Textbook Co., London, England.

MICROBIAL TOXINS

TABLE 2.M.15

INTOXICATION FROM MICROBIAL TOXINS

Disease	Reservoirs	Common Vehicle	Prevention and Control
Clostridial intoxication (Botulism).	Soil, dust, fruits, vegetables, and other foods.	Improperly processed canned and bottled foods containing toxin.	Boil home-canned nonacid food 5 minutes; thoroughly cook meat, fish and dried foods held over; do not taste suspected food.
Staphylococcal intoxication.	Skin, mucous membranes, pus, dust, air, sputum, and throat.	Contaminated custard pastries, cooked or processed meats, poultry, dairy products, hollandaise sauce, salads, and milk.	Refrigerate prepared food in shallow container at a temperature below 45°F; avoid handling food; educate food handlers in personal hygiene and sanitation.
Clostridium welchii type A.	Meat animal species, soil, and man.	Meat and meat products.	Avoid storage of large pieces of cooked meat; refrigerate so that temperature at the center of the meat cut is below 45°F; reheat thoroughly meat cuts or gravy immediately prior to serving.

SOURCE: Reproduced by permission of the Department of the Army, TM 8-451, Food Inspection Specialist (1969).

MICROBIOLOGICAL EXAMINATION OF DAIRY PRODUCTS

TABLE 2.M.16

MICROBIOLOGICAL EXAMINATION OF DAIRY PRODUCTS

APHA Designation	Used For
AK medium No. 2	Spore production
Antibiotic medium No. 1	Detection of inhibitory substances
Aureomycin-rose Bengal agar	Yeast and mold counts
Brilliant green lactose Bile broth, 2%	Detection of coliforms
Casein soy peptone agar	Quantitative surface sampling by the RODAC® plate method
Casein soy peptone agar with Polysorbate 80[1] and lecithin	Surface sampling by the RODAC plate method
Citrate azide agar	Enterococcus count for butter
Endo agar	Isolation of coliforms
Eosine methylene blue agar, levine	Isolation of coliforms
Lactose broth	Detection of coliforms
MF-endo broth	Coliform determination with membrane filters
Mueller hinton agar	Detection of inhibitory substances in milk
Nutrient agar Nutrient broth	Surface sampling by the Rinse Solution Method
Potato glucose agar (acidified)	Yeast and mold counts
Standard methods agar	Standard plate count
Standard methods agar with Polysorbate 80[1] and lecithin	Surface sampling by the RODAC plate method
Violet red bile agar	Isolation of coliforms

[1] TWEEN 80® Atlas Chemical Industries.

SOURCE: BioQuest, Division of Becton, Dickinson and Co., Rutherford, N.J.

MICROBIOLOGICAL MEDIA

TABLE 2.M.17

ORGANISMS AND MEDIA FOR EXAMINATION OF FOODS, WATER, AND OTHER MATERIALS OF SANITARY AND PUBLIC HEALTH IMPORTANCE

(NOTE: Those Media Which May Be Expected to Give the Most Efficient Results as Evidenced by Their Ability to Grow More Species, or to Grow Them More Rapidly, are Indicated by Asterisks)

Organisms	Media
CANNED FOODS	
Clostridia	Clostrisel Agar
C. perfringens	T S N Agar
Enteric Bacilli	Desoxycholate Lactose Agar
	E E Broth
Lactobacilli	A P T Agar and Eugonagar
	L Agar
	Thioglycollate Medium-135C
Pseudomonas	Pseudosel Agar
Thermophiles	Dextrose Tryptone Agar
Total Aerobes	Eugonagar or Standard Methods Agar
Yeasts and Molds	Mycophil Agar with Low pH or Potato Dextrose Agar
FROZEN FOODS	
These present new problems in evaluation of sanitary quality and safety.	
Total Aerobes	Eugonagar
	Trypticase Soy Agar
Staphylococci	
Total	Mannitol Salt Agar
Coagulase +	Vogel and Johnson Agar
Streptococci	Azide Blood Agar Base
especially enterococci	*M*-Enterococcus Agar
Total	Streptosel Agar
Yeasts and Molds	Mycophil Agar with Low pH or Potato Dextrose Agar
MILK AND OTHER DAIRY PRODUCTS	
Total Aerobes	Standard Methods Agar
	Dextrose Salt Agar
Brucella	Trypticase Soy Agar
	Brucella or Biosate Agars
Coliforms	Brilliant Green Bile Broth 2%
	Desoxycholate Lactose Agar or
	Levine E M B Agar
Plant Contaminants	Eugonagar
Salmonella	Desoxycholate Lactose Agar
	D C L S Agar® or
	Brilliant Green Agar
	E E Broth
	Selenite-F Broth
	X L D Agar
Staphylococci	
Total	Mannitol Salt Agar
Coagulase +	Vogel and Johnson Agar
Streptococci	Trypticase Soy Media
Yeasts and Molds	Mycophil Agar with Low pH or
	Potato Dextrose Agar
	Sugar-Free Agar

(Continued)

TABLE 2.M.17 (*Continued*)

Organisms	Media
SUGARS, SYRUPS, CITRUS, CARBONATED AND OTHER BEVERAGES	
Aerobes—Total Also for plant control studies	*Eugonagar or Standard Methods Agar
Coliforms	*Desoxycholate Lactose or Levine E M B Agar
Lactobacilli, etc.	*Orange Serum Agar
Thermophiles—Aerobic	*Dextrose Tryptone Agar
Anaerobic	Sulfite Agar
Yeasts and Molds	**M*-Green Yeast and Mold Broth *Mycophil Agar with Low pH or Potato Dextrose Agar
(For BEER, the above media may be used; the bracketed media are particularly recommended.)	{ Eugonagar W L Differential Agar W L Nutrient Agar
WATER AND WASTEWATER	
Clostridia	Clostrisel Agar
Coliforms	Brilliant Green Bile Broth 2% *Desoxycholate Lactose or Levine E M B Agars *Lauryl Sulfate Broth or Lactose Broth *M*-Coliform Broth **M*-Endo Agar L E S
Enterococci	*Azide Dextrose Broth *Ethyl Violet Azide Broth Mead Agar **M*-Enterococcus Agar *S F Broth
DISINFECTANT TESTING	
AOAC NAME	BBL NAME
Nutrient Broth	F D A Broth
Synthetic Broth	Wright and Mundy Broth
Nutrient Agar	F D A Agar
Letheen Broth	Letheen Broth
Cystine Trypticase Agar	C T A Medium
Fluid Thioglycollate Medium	Fluid Thioglycollate Medium

SOURCE: BioQuest, Division of Becton, Dickinson and Company, Cockeysville, Maryland.

MICROBIOLOGICAL STANDARDS, DAIRY

TABLE 2.M.18

QUALITY CONTROL GUIDELINES FOR MICROBIOLOGICAL STANDARDS IN DAIRY FOODS

Product	SPC	Coliform	Psychrotrophic SPC After (5 Days at 70°C)	Yeast and Mold	*Staphylococci*	*Salmonella*
Raw milk–bulk tankers	<1000-50,000	<100-<1000	<10,000-<100,000			
Comingled raw milk at pasteurizer	<50,000-30,000	<100-<1000	<100,000-<800,000		<5,000-<100,000	
Pasteurized milk	<1,000-<10,000	<1-<5	<20,000-<6000			
Cottage cheese (dry)	<1,000-<20,000	<1-<5	<10,000-<100,000	<5-<10	<1	<1
Butter	<5,000-<20,000		<50,000	<5-<10	<1	<1
Milk powder	<20,000-<50,000	NS	NS	<10	<1	<1

SOURCE: HARPER, W. J. 1972. Sanitation in Dairy Food Plants. *In* Food Sanitation. R. K. Guthrie (Editor). Avi Publishing Co., Westport, Conn.

MICROORGANISM, CULTURE MEDIA, DAIRY AND FOOD PRODUCTS

Culture media used for the examination of dairy and other food products:

Plate Counts
- Tryptone Glucose Extract Agar
- Proteose Tryptone Agar
- Beef Lactose Agar
- Nutritive Caseinate Agar
- Heart Infusion Agar
- Plate Count Agar
- Antibiotic Medium No. 1
- Nutrient Agar

Brucella
- Tryptose Agar

Lactobacilli
- Tomato Juice Agar
- Trypsin Digest Agar
- Peptonized Milk
- Skim Milk
- Micro Assay Culture Agar
- Micro Inoculum Broth
- Snyder Test Agar

Hemolytic Streptococci
- Heart Infusion Agar

Coliform Organisms
- Brilliant Green Bile 2%
- Formate Ricinoleate Broth
- Violet Red Bile Agar
- Desoxycholate Agar
- Desoxycholate Lactose Agar
- MacConkey Agar
- Lactose Broth
- Endo Agar
- Levine EMB Agar
- Bacto—Tryptone
- MR-VP Medium
- Koser Citrate Medium

Thermophiles
- Dextrose Tryptone Agar
- Thermoacidurans Agar

Molds and Yeasts
- Potato Dextrose Agar
- Malt Agar

SOURCE: Difco Laboratories, Detroit.

MICROORGANISM, CULTURE MEDIA, WATER AND SEWAGE, STANDARD METHODS

Culture Media used for the examination of water and sewage "Standard Methods" procedures:

Plate Counts	Tests for Coliform Organisms: Presumptive	Confirmed	Completed
Nutrient Agar	Lactose Broth	Endo Agar	Nutrient Agar
Nutrient Gelatin	Lauryl Tryptose Broth	Levine EMB Agar	Lactose Broth
Tryptone Glucose Extract Agar	Azide Dextrose Broth	Brilliant Green Bile 2%	
Plate Count Agar	Ethyl Violet Azide Broth	Formate Ricinoleate Broth	
	m Enterococcus Agar	Lauryl Tryptose Broth	
	KF Streptococcus Agar	EC Medium	
		Boric Acid Broth	
		m Endo Agar LES	
		m Endo Broth MF	
		m FC Broth Base	
		m Coliform Holding Broth	

SOURCE: Difco Laboratories, Detroit.

MICROORGANISM, MEDIA

Media for growth of microorganisms:

	Microorganism			
	Actinomyces (aerobic)		**Algae**	
Isolation	Actinomyces Agar Actinomycete Isolation Agar Casitone Starch Agar	Fluid Sabouraud Medium Sabouraud Dextrose/Maltose Agar Tryptic Soy Agar/Broth	Algae Culture Agar/Broth Chlorella Agar/Broth	Euglena Agar/Broth Euglena Broth BM
Differentiation	Nutrient Gelatin			
Propagation	Actinomyces Agar/Broth/Medium Actinomycete Isolation Agar Fluid Sabouraud Medium	Sabouraud Dextrose Agar Sabouraud Maltose Agar Tryptic Soy Agar	Algae Culture Broth Chlorella Broth Euglena Broth	Euglena Broth BM
	Brucella		**Candida albicans**	
Isolation	Brain Heart Infusion w/PAB & Agar Brucella Agar/Broth Columbia Blood Agar Base Eugon Agar + Supplement B or C	Potato Infusion Agar Tryptose Agar Tryptose Agar w/Crystal Violet Tryptose Broth	BiGGY Agar (Nickerson Medium) Candida BCG Agar Chlamydospore Agar	Levine EMB Agar Rice Extract Agar Wolin Bevis Agar
Differentiation	Tryptic Soy Agar w/Thionin or Basic Fuchsin		ABY Agar BiGGY Agar (Nickerson Medium) Candida BCG Agar	Chlamydospore Agar Corn Meal Agar Pagano Levin Agar Rice Extract Agar Wolin Bevis Agar
Propagation	Brain Heart Infusion w/PAB & Agar Brucella Agar/Broth Liver Infusion Agar/Broth Potato Infusion Agar	Tryptose Agar/Broth	Corn Meal Agar Sabouraud Dextrose Agar Sabouraud Maltose Agar	
Serological Identification	Brucella Abortus Antiserum Brucella AMS Antiserum Poly Brucella Melitensis Antiserum	Brucella Suis Antiserum Corresponding Antigens Also Available FA Brucella Abortus	Candida Albicans Antiserum F A C. Albicans	
	Clostridia		**Coliform Group**	
Isolation	Brewer Anaerobic Agar Columbia Blood Agar Base Cooked Meat Medium Fluid Thioglycollate Medium Forget Fredette Agar LM Agar Liver Veal Agar	Liver Veal Agar w/o Dext. McClung Toabe Agar Base Proteose No. 3 Agar w/Hemoglobin SFP Agar Base w/Egg Yolk Enrichment 50% and Antimicrobic Vials K & P SPS Agar Tryptose Blood Agar Base	BDG Broth m BG Endo Broth Cled Agar Desoxycholate Agar Desoxycholate Lactose Agar Endo Agar m Endo Agar LES m Endo Broth w/BG m Endo Broth MF m FC Broth Base m HD Endo Broth	Hektoen Enteric Agar Levine EMB Agar MacConkey Agar MacConkey Agar w/o Salt Sorbitol Agar (Path. E. Coli) Tergitol 7 Agar Tryptose Blood Agar Base w/Blood XL Agar Base XLD Agar

Differentiation	LM Agar Loeffler Blood Serum Nutrient Gelatin Peptone Colloid Medium Phenol Red Broth Base w/Carbohydrates under anaerobic conditions Sulfite Agar Tryptone	Acetate Differential Agar Christensen Agar Christensen Iron Agar Citrate Mannitol Agar Decarboxylase Base Moeller Decarboxylase Medium Base Differentiation Disks Lysine, ONPG, Ornithine, Urea F35M Hajna H_2S Test Strips Indole Nitrite Medium Indole Test Strips KCN Broth Base Kligler Iron Agar Koscr Citrate Medium Krumweide Tri Sugar Agar Levine EMB Agar Lysine Decarboxylase Broth Lysine Iron Agar Lysine Lactose Broth MIO Medium MR–VP Medium Malonate Broth Motility Medium S Motility Sulfide Medium Motility Test Medium Nitrite Test Strips OF Basal Medium Phenol Red Agar/Broth w/Carbohydrates or w/Diff. Disks, Carbohydrates Phenol Red Tartrate Agar Phenylalanine Agar Phenylalanine Malonate Broth Purple Agar/Broth w/Carbohydrates or w/Diff. Disks, Carbohydrates Purple Lactose Agar Russell Double Sugar Agar Sanders Agar w/Differentiation Disks Carbohydrates Simmons Citrate Agar Sorbitol Iron Agar TSU Agar Triple Sugar Iron Agar Tryptone Solution 1% (Indole Test) Urea Agar/Broth Urea R Broth
Propagation	AC Medium Brain Heart Infusion w/PAB & Agar Columbia Blood Agar Base Cooked Meat Medium Egg Meat Medium Liver Veal Agar w/o Dext. Veal Infusion Medium	Brain Heart Infusion w/PAB & Agar Cooked Meat Medium Nutrient Agar/Broth Plate Count Agar Tryptic Soy Broth Tryptone Glucose Extract Agar
Serological Identification		Arizona Antiserum Poly Monophasic or Diphasic Bethesda–Ballerup Anti-serum Poly (Citrobacter Antiserum) E Coli OB & OK Antisera 20 Serogroups and 3 Polyvalent E Coli O Antisera 51 Serogroups E Coli OB Antigens 11 Serogroups E Coli O Antigens 11 Serogroups Fluorescent E Coli Conjugates 20 F A E Coli Serogroups 3 F A E Coli Polyvalent
	Corynebacterium	**Endamoeba histolytica**
Isolation	Columbia Blood Agar Base w/Tinsdale Enrichment Dextrose Proteose No. 3 Agar w/Tellurite Blood Solution Loeffler Blood Serum Mueller Tellurite Base w/Mueller Tellurite Serum Pai Egg Medium, Tubes Tinsdale Base & Enrichment	Balamuth Medium Endamoeba Medium w/Horse Serum Saline 1:6 & Rice Powder
Differentiation	Columbia Blood Agar Base w/Tinsdale Enrichment Dextrose Proteose No. 3 Agar w/Tellurite Blood Solution Mueller Tellurite Base w/Mueller Tellurite Serum Phenol Red Agar/Broth w/Carbohydrates or w/Diff. Disks, Carbohydrates Tinsdale Base and Enrichment Tryptic Tellurite Agar Base	

(Continued)

MICROORGANISM, MEDIA (Continued)

Corynebacterium (Continued)

Propagation
- Brain Heart Infusion w/PAB & Agar
- Loeffler Blood Serum
- Tryptic Soy Agar
- Tryptose Blood Agar Base

Serological Identification
- C Acnes 554 & 605 Antisera
- FA C Diphtheriae
- KL Antitoxin Strips
- KL Virulence Agar
- KL Virulence Enrichment

Fungi

Isolation
- Actinomycete Isolation Agar
- Brain Heart CC Agar
- Brain Heart Infusion Agar
- Cooke Rose Bengal Agar
- DTM Agar
- Emerson YpSs Agar
- Eugon Agar w/Blood
- Georg Fungus Medium
- Ink Blue Agar
- Littman Oxgall Agar
- Malt Agar
- Mycobiotic Agar
- Potato Dextrose Agar
- SABHI Agar
- Sabouraud Agar Modified
- Sabouraud Dextrose Agar
- Sabouraud Maltose Agar

Differentiation
- Brain Heart CC Agar
- Corn Meal Agar
- SABHI Agar
- Sabouraud Agar Modified
- Sabouraud Dextrose Agar
- Sabouraud Maltose Agar
- Trichophyton Agars 1, 2, 3, 4, 5, 6, 7
- Vitamin Free Yeast Base
- Yeast Carbon Base
- Yeast Morphology Agar
- Yeast Nitrogen Base

Propagation
- Actinomycete Isolation Agar
- Brain Heart Infusion Agar
- Cantino PYG Agar/Broth
- Dextrose Neopeptone Broth
- Fluid Sabouraud Medium
- Lima Bean Agar
- Malt Extract Broth
- Mycological Agar & Broth
- Neurospora Culture Agar
- Potato Dextrose Agar
- Potato Maltose Agar
- SABHI Agar
- Sabouraud Agar Modified
- Sabouraud Dextrose Agar
- Sabouraud Maltose Agar/Broth
- Stoddard Oat Agar
- WL Nutrient Broth
- Wort Agar/Broth (Cult. of yeasts)
- YM Agar/Broth

Serological Identification
- Candida Albicans Antiserum
- FA C. Albicans

Klebsiella

Isolation
- Bismuth Sulfite Agar
- m Bismuth Sulfite Broth
- Brilliant Green Agar
- m Brilliant Green Broth
- EMB Agar
- Endo Agar
- Hektoen Enteric Agar
- MacConkey Agar
- MacConkey Agar w/o CV
- MacConkey Agar w/o Salt
- XL Agar Base
- XLD Agar

Endamoeba histolylica (Continued)

Propagation
- Balamuth Medium
- Endamoeba Medium w/Horse Serum
- Saline 1:6 and Rice Powder

Hemophilus or Bordetella

Isolation
- Bordet Gengou Agar Base w/Fresh Blood (Pertussis only)
- Brain Heart Infusion w/Supp. B, C, or VX
- Casman Medium Base
- Charcoal Agar
- Columbia Blood Agar Base w/Blood (Chocolated) and Supplement B
- Eugon Agar w/Supplement B or C
- Heart Infusion Agar/Broth w/Fildes Enrichment
- Proteose No. 3 Agar or GC Med. Base w/Hemo. and Supp. A, B, C, or VX

Differentiation
- Brain Heart Infusion Agar
- Heart Infusion Agar
- Proteose No. 3 Agar or GC Med. Base w/Hemo. and Supp. A, B, C, or VX
- Tryptic Soy Agar w/Differentiation Disks BV, BVX, BX

Propagation
- Bordet Gengou Agar Base w/Blood
- Brain Heart Infusion w/Supp. B
- Casman Broth Base
- Charcoal Agar
- Eugon Broth w/Supp. A or B
- Proteose No. 3 Agar w/Hemo. and Supp. A, B, or VX

Serological Identification
- B. Parapertussis Antiserum
- B. Pertussis Antiserum
- B. Pertussis Antigen
- FA Bordetella Parapertussis
- FA Bordetella Pertussis
- FA H. Influenzae A, B, C, D, E, F
- H. Influenzae Antisera Type A, B, C, D, E, F. Poly

Lactobacilli

Isolation
- APT Agar/Broth
- Elliker Broth
- Eugon Broth
- Lactobacilli MRS Broth
- Orange Serum Agar
- Orange Serum Broth Conc. 10X
- Rogosa SL Agar/Broth
- Tomato Juice Agar/Broth
- Trypsin Digest Agar
- Whey Agar/Broth

Differentiation	Capsule Ink Decarboxylase Medium Base Differentiation Disks Lysine, ONPG, Ornithine, Urea F35M Hajna H_2S Test Strips Indole Test Strips KCN Broth Base Kligler Iron Agar Lysine Decarboxylase Broth Lysine Iron Agar Lysine Lactose Broth MIO Medium	Nitrite Test Strips Phenol Red Agar/Broth w/Carbohydrates or w/Diff. Disks, Carbohydrates Phenol Red Tartrate Agar Purple Agar/Broth w/Carbohydrates w/Diff. Disks, Carbohydrates Russell Double Sugar Agar SIM Medium Triple Sugar Iron Agar Tryptone Solution 1% (Indole Test) Worfel Ferguson Agar/Broth
Propagation	Brain Heart Infusion w/PAB & Agar Cooked Meat Medium	Nutrient Agar/Broth
Serological Identification	Capsule Ink FA Klebsiella Type 1 FA Klebsiella Type 2 FA Klebsiella Poly (1-6) Klebsiella Antisera Types 1 through 72 and Poly (1-6)	

	Litmus Milk Purple Milk Snyder Test Agar	
	APT Agar/Broth Elliker Broth L Agar Lactobacilli Agar AOAC Litmus Milk Micro Assay Culture Agar Micro Inoculum Broth Orange Serum Agar/Broth	Peptonized Milk Agar Purple Milk Skim Milk Tomato Juice Agar/Broth Tryptic Digest Agar Ulrich Milk Whey Agar/Broth

Leptospira

Isolation	Fletcher Medium Base w/Leptospira Enrichment Leptospira Medium Base EMJH w/Lepto Enrichment EMJH	Stuart Medium Base w/Leptospira Enrichment Stuart Medium Base w/o Phenol Red w/Leptospira Enrichment
Differentiation		
Propagation	Fletcher Medium Base w/Leptospira Enrichment Leptospira Medium EMJH w/Leptospira Enrichment EMJH Stuart Medium Base w/Leptospira Enrichment Stuart Medium Base w/o Phenol Red w/Leptospira Enrichment	
Serological Identification	LEPTOSPIRA ANTIGENS Pool 1 L. Ballum, L. Canicola, L. Icterohemorrhagiae Pool 2 L. Bataviae, L. Grippotyphosa, L. Pyrogenes Pool 3 L. Autumnalis, L. Pomona, L. Wolfii Pool 4 L. Australis, L. Hyos, L. Mini, Georgia (LT 117) Pool 5 L. Cynopteri, L. Ce Iedoni, L. Javanica Pool 6 L. Cynopteri, L. Panama, L. Shermani	Leptospira Ictero Kremastos Antigen Pool Individual Antigens and Antisera Listed in Pools also Available, plus L. Andamana, L. Medanensis, L. Sejroe. L. Biflexa Patoc and L. Hardjo.

Listeria

Isolation	Cystine Heart Agar w/Hemoglobin and Supplement B Eugon Agar/Broth	McBride Listeria Agar Tryptose Blood Agar Base w/Blood
Differentiation	Indole Nitrite Medium Indole Test Strips MR-VP Medium Motility GI Medium Motility Medium S	Phenol Red Broth w/1% Carbohydrates Tryptone Solution 1% (Indole Test) Urea R Broth
Propagation	Brain Heart Infusion Thiol Medium Tryptic Soy Agar/Broth	Tryptose Blood Agar Base Tryptose Agar/Broth
Serological Identification	Listeria O Antiserum Type 1 Listeria O Antiserum Type 4 Listeria O Antiserum Poly Corresponding Slide and Tube Antigens Available	FA Listeria Type 1 FA Listeria Type 4 FA Listeria Poly

(Continued)

MICROORGANISM, MEDIA (Continued)

	Mima-Herellea		Mycobacterium tuberculosis	
Isolation	Blood Agar Base w/Blood Brain Heart Infusion Agar EMB Agar	Hektoen Enteric Agar Herellea Agar Tryptose Blood Agar Base w/Blood	ATS Medium Bovine TB Medium Dubos Oleic Agar IUTM Base Lowenstein Medium Gruft Lowenstein Jensen Medium	Middlebrook 7H9 Agar/7H10 Agar Middlebrook 7H10 Agar w/WR1339 Mycobacteria 7H11 Agar Peizer TB Medium Petragnani Medium
Differentiation	p-Aminodimethylaniline Oxalate (Oxidase Reagent) Differentiation Disks Oxidase F35M Hajna Indole Test Strips Indole Nitrite Medium Motility GI Medium	Motility Medium S Nitrite Test Strips OF Basal Medium Phenol Red Agar/Broth Base w/1% & 10% Carbohydrates Simmons Citrate Agar Tryptone Solution 1% (Indole Test)	Differentiation Disks Auramine Dubos Medium Albumin Lowenstein Medium Gruft Lowenstein Jensen Medium Deeps (for Catalase) Mycobacteria 7H11 Agar	Nitrite Test Strips Proskauer Beck Medium TB Niacin Test Base TB Niacin Test Strips & Control TB Stain Sets K & ZN TB Fluorescent Stain Sets M, & T
Propagation	Brain Heart Infusion Brain Heart Infusion w/PAB & Agar Nutrient Agar/Broth Tryptic Soy Broth		ATS Medium Bovine TB Medium Dubos Media IUTM Base Kirchner Medium Lowenstein Jensen Medium	Middlebrook 7H9 Broth Mycobacteria 7H11 Agar Peizer TB Medium Petragnani Medium TB Egg Agar
Serological Identification	Mima Polymorpha Antiserum Poly Herellea Vaginicola Antiserum		H-37 Ra Antigen & Antiserum	

	Neisseriae		Pasteurella	
Isolation	Brain Heart Infusion w/PAB & Agar Casman Medium Base Chocolate Agar Columbia Blood Agar Base w/Hemoglobin 2% w/Supp. B, C, or VX	Eugon Agar/Broth w/Supp. B, C, or VX GC Med. Base or Proteose No. 3 Agar enriched w/Hemoglobin and Supplement A, B, C, or VX Thayer Martin Medium Transgrow Medium Tryptose Blood Agar Base w/Blood	Civil Defense Agar Cystine Heart Agar w/Hemo. and Supplement B	Eugon Agar/Broth w/Supp. B or C Tryptose Agar Tryptose Blood Agar Base
Differentiation	p-Aminodimethylaniline Oxalate (Oxidase Reagent) Cystine Tryptic Agar w/Carbohydrates Differentiation Disks Oxidase	Phenol Red Agar/Broth Base w/Carbohydrates	Indole Nitrite Medium Indole Test Strips Motility GI Medium Motility Medium S	Phenol Red Broth w/1% Carbohydrates Tryptone Solution 1% (Indole Test)
Propagation	Brain Heart Infusion Agar/Broth Chocolate Agar (tubes) Dextrose Broth Dextrose Starch Agar Eugon Broth w/Supp. B, C, or VX	GC Medium Base or Proteose No. 3 Agar enriched w/Hemoglobin or Hemoglobin Solution 2% and Supplement B, C, or VX Tryptose Phosphate Broth	Brain Heart Infusion w/PAB & Agar Civil Defense Agar	Cystine Heart Agar w/Hemoglobin or Hemoglobin Solution 2% Tryptose Agar/Broth YPC Broth
Serological Identification	FA N. Gonorrhoeae FA Meningococcus Poly	Meningococcus Antisera Groups A, B, C, D, X, Y, Z, Poly & Poly 2	P. Tularensis Antigen (Slide) P. Tularensis Antigen (Tube)	P. Tularensis Antiserum

PPLO Pleuropneumonia-Like Organisms (Mycoplasma)

Isolation

Heart Infusion Agar or Broth w/*
PPLO Agar
PPLO Broth w/CV
PPLO Broth w/o CV
} Enriched with PPLO Serum Fraction or *Mycoplasma Supplement or *Mycoplasma Supplement S

Differentiation

Propagation

Heart Infusion Agar or Broth w/*
PPLO Agar
PPLO Broth w/CV
PPLO Broth w/o CV
} Enriched with PPLO Serum Fraction or *Mycoplasma Supplement or *Mycoplasma Supplement S

Serological Identification

Pneumococci

Isolation

Blood Agar Base w/Blood
Blood Agar Base No. 2 w/Blood
Brain Heart Infusion Agar
Columbia Blood Agar Base w/Blood
Eugon Agar
GC Medium Base w/Hemoglobin
Tryptic Soy Agar w/Blood
Tryptose Blood Agar Base w/Blood

Differentiation

Bile Salts No. 3
Blood Agar Base Media
Differentiation Disks Optochin
Hiss Capsule Stain + Copper Sulfate

Propagation

Brain Heart Infusion Agar/Broth
Brain Veal Agar
Tryptic Soy Agar/Broth

Serological Identification

PNEUMOCOCCUS ANTISERA (Diplococcus Pneumoniae)
Pool A: Types 1, 2, 7
Pool B: Types 3, 4, 5, 6, 8
Pool C: Types 9, 12, 14, 15, 17, 33
Pool D: Types 10, 11, 13, 20, 22, 24
Pool E: Types 16, 18, 19, 21, 28
Pool F: Types 23, 25, 27, 29, 31, 32
Individual Types 1, 2, 3, 4, 5, 6, 7, 8, 14, 18 & 19 Also Available.
FA Pneumococcus Poly

Proteus

Isolation

Bismuth Sulfite Agar
m Bismuth Sulfite Broth
Brilliant Green Agar
m Brilliant Green Broth
Cled Agar
EMB Agar
Endo Agar
Hektoen Enteric Agar
MacConkey Agar
MacConkey Agar w/o CV
MacConkey Agar w/o Salt
XL Agar Base
XLD Agar

Differentiation

Decarboxylase Base Moeller
Decarboxylase Medium Base
Differentiation Disks Lysine ONPG, Ornithine, Urea
F35M Hajna
H_2S Test Strips
Indole Test Strips
Kligler Iron Agar
Lysine Iron Agar
MIO Medium
Motility Medium S
Motility Sulfide Medium
Motility Test Medium
Nitrite Test Strips
Phenol Red Agar/Broth w/Carbohydrates or w/Diff. Disks, Carbohydrates
Phenylalanine Agar
Purple Agar/Broth w/Carbohydrates or w/Diff. Disks, Carbohydrates
Sanders Agar w/Diff. Disks Carbohydrates
TSU Agar
Triple Sugar Iron Agar
Tryptone Solution, 1% (Indole Test)
Urea Agar/Broth
Urea R Broth

Pseudomonas

Isolation

BDG Broth
Bismuth Sulfite Agar
Cetrimide Agar Base
Cled Agar
EMB Agar
Endo Agar
Hektoen Enteric Agar
MacConkey Agar
MacConkey Agar w/o CV
MacConkey Agar w/o Salt
Pseudomonas Isolation Agar
Tryptic Soy Agar
Tryptose Blood Agar Base w/Blood
XL Agar Base
XLD Agar

Differentiation

Decarboxylase Medium Base
Differentiation Disks Lysine, ONPG, Ornithine, Oxidase, Urea
Indole Test Strips
Kligler Iron Agar
Lysine Decarboxylase Broth
Lysine Iron Agar
MIO Medium
Motility GI Medium
Motility Medium S
Motility Sulfide Medium
Motility Test Medium
N Broth
OF Basal Medium
Pseudomonas Agar F & P
SIM Medium
Sellers Differential Agar
TSU Agar
Tryptone Solution 1% (Indole Test)

(Continued)

MICROORGANISM, MEDIA (Continued)

Proteus (Continued)

Propagation

Brain Heart Infusion w/PAB & Agar
Cooked Meat Medium
Nutrient Agar
Nutrient Broth
Tryptic Soy Agar/Broth

Serological Identification

Proteus OX2 Antigen (Slide)
Proteus OX19 Antigen (Slide)
Proteus OXK Antigen (Slide)
Corresponding Antigens Also Available for Tube Test
Corresponding Antisera Also Available

Salmonella typhosa

Isolation

ENRICHMENTS
FAS Broth
GN Broth Hajna
SBG Enrichment
SBG Sulfa Enrichment
Selenite Broth
Selenite Cystine Broth
Tetrathionate Broth Base
m Tetrathionate Broth Base
TT Broth Base

PLATING MEDIA
BCP-D Agar
BG Sulfa Agar
Bismuth Sulfite Agar
m Bismuth Sulfite Broth
Brilliant Green Agar
m Brilliant Green Broth
Cled Agar
Desoxycholate Citrate Agar
EMB Agar
m EMB Broth
Endo Agar
Hektoen Enteric Agar
MacConkey Agar
MacConkey Agar w/o CV
MacConkey Agar w/o Salt
SS Agar
m Urease Test Reagent
XL Agar Base
XLD Agar

Differentiation

Decarboxylase Base Moeller
Decarboxylase Medium Base
Differentiation Disks Lysine, ONPG, Ornithine, Urea
F35M Hajna
H Broth
H_2S Test Strips
Hemmes 7-In Medium
Indole Test Strips
KCN Broth Base
KP Organic Acid Base
Kligler Iron Agar
Lysine Decarboxylase Broth
Lysine Iron Agar
Lysine Lactose Broth
MIO Medium
Motility Test Medium
Nitrite Test Strips
Phenol Red Tartrate Agar
Purple Agar/Broth w/Carbohydrates or w/Diff. Disks, Carbohydrates
Russell Double Sugar Agar
SIM Medium
Sanders Agar w/Diff. Disks, Carbohydrates
TSU Agar
Triple Sugar Iron Agar
Tryptone Solution 1% (Indole Test)
Urea Agar/Broth
Urea R Broth

Pseudomonas (Continued)

Propagation

Brain Heart Infusion w/PAB & Agar
Cooked Meat Medium
Nutrient Agar/Broth
Tryptic Soy Agar/Broth

Serological Identification

FA Pseudomonas Pseudomallei
Pseudomonas Pseudomallei Antiserum

Salmonella other than Typhosa

Isolation

ENRICHMENTS
FAS Broth
GN Broth Hajna
M Broth
SBG Enrichment
SBG Sulfa Enrichment
Selenite Broth
Selenite Cystine Broth
Tetrathionate Broth Base
m Tetrathionate Broth Base
TT Broth Base

PLATING MEDIA
BCP-D Agar
BG Sulfa Agar
Bismuth Sulfite Agar
m Bismuth Sulfite Broth
Brilliant Green Agar
m Brilliant Green Broth
Cled Agar
Desoxycholate Citrate Agar
EMB Agar
m EMB Broth
Endo Agar
Hektoen Enteric Agar
MacConkey Agar
MacConkey Agar w/o CV
MacConkey Agar w/o Salt
SS Agar
m Urease Test Reagent
XL Agar Base
XLD Agar

Differentiation

Decarboxylase Base Moeller
Decarboxylase Medium Base
Differentiation Disks Lysine, ONPG, Ornithine, Urea
F35M Hajna
H Broth
H_2S Test Strips
Hemmes 7-In Medium
Indole Test Strips
KCN Broth Base
KP Organic Acid Base
Kligler Iron Agar
Krumweide Tri Sugar Agar
Lysine Decarboxylase Broth
Lysine Iron Agar
Lysine Lactose Broth
MIO Medium
Motility GI Medium
Motility Medium S
Motility Sulfide Medium
Motility Test Medium
Nitrite Test Strips
OF Basal Medium w/Carbohydrates
Phenol Red Tartrate Agar
Purple Agar/Broth w/Carbohydrates or w/Diff. Disks, Carbohydrates
Russell Double Sugar Agar
SIM Medium
Sanders Agar w/Diff. Disks, Carbohydrates
TSU Agar
Triple Sugar Iron Agar
Tryptone Solution 1% (Indole Test)
Urea Agar/Broth
Urea R Broth
Wilson Blair Base

Propagation	Brain Heart Infusion w/PAB & Agar Cooked Meat Medium	Nutrient Agar/Broth Tryptic Soy Agar/Broth	Brain Heart Infusion w/PAB & Agar Cooked Meat Medium	Nutrient Agar/Broth Tryptic Soy Agar/Broth
Serological Identification	Salmonella H Antiserum Group d Salmonella O Antiserum Group D Salmonella O Antiserum Poly A-I and Vi Salmonella O Antiserum Poly A Corresponding Antigens Also Available		POLYVALENT ANTISERA Salmonella O Antiserum Poly A-I and Vi Salmonella O Antisera Poly A, B, C, D, E, F, and G Salmonella H Antiserum Poly a-z Salmonella H Antisera Poly A, B, C, D, E, and F Salmonella H Antisera Spicer Edwards 1, 2, 3, 4, and EN, Z_4, L and 1 Complexes FA Salmonella Panvalent FA Salmonella Poly	SALMONELLA O ANTISERA Groups A, B, C_1, C_2, D, E, E_1, E_2, E_3, E_4, F, G, H, I, J, K, L, M, N, O, P, Q, R, S, T, U, V, W, X, Y, Z and 51–61 and Salmonella Vi Antiserum SALMONELLA H ANTISERA Salmonella H Antisera a-z SALMONELLA ANTIGENS Salmonella O Antigens A-I and Vi Salmonella H Antigens a, b, c, d, eh, g, i and 1 Complex
	Shigella		**Staphylococci**	
Isolation	BCP-D Agar Cled Agar Desoxycholate Agar Desoxycholate Citrate Agar EMB Agar Hektoen Enteric Agar MacConkey Agar MacConkey Agar w/o CV MacConkey Agar w/o Salt SS Agar XL Agar Base XLD Agar		Baird Parker Agar Base w/EY Tellurite Enrichment Blood Agar Base w/Blood Chapman Stone Medium Coagulase Agar Base Colbeck EY Agar Base/Broth Columbia CNA Agar w/Blood DNase Test Agar DNase Test Agar w/Methyl Green Mannitol Neomycin Agar Mannitol Salt Agar	Mannitol Salt Broth Phenylethanol Agar Staphylococcus Medium 110 Staphylococcus Medium 110 w/Azide m Staphylococcus Broth TMM Broth Tellurite Glycine Agar TPEY Agar w/TPEY Enrichment & Antimicrobic Vial P Tryptose Blood Agar Base
Differentiation	Acetate Differential Agar Decarboxylase Base Moeller Decarboxylase Medium Base Differentiation Disks Lysine, ONPG, Ornithine, Urea H Broth Hemmes 7-In Medium H_2S Test Strips Indole Test Strips KCN Broth Base KP Organic Acid Base Kligler Iron Agar Lysine Decarboxylase Broth Lysine Iron Agar Lysine Lactose Broth MIO Medium Motility GI Medium	Motility Medium S Motility Test Medium Nitrite Test Strips Phenol Red Tartrate Agar Purple Agar/Broth w/Carbohydrates or w/Diff. Disks, Carbohydrates Russell Double Sugar Agar SIM Medium Sanders Agar w/Diff. Disks, Carbohydrates TSU Agar Triple Sugar Iron Agar Tryptone Solution 1% (Indole Test) Urea Agar/Broth Urea R Broth Wilson Blair Base	Blood Agar Base w/Blood Chapman Stone Medium Coagulase Agar Base Coagulase Plasma Coagulase Plasma EDTA Colbeck EY Agar Base/Broth DNase Test Agar DNase Test Agar w/Methyl Green Mannitol Salt Agar Mannitol Salt Broth	OF Basal Medium w/Carbohydrates Staphylococcus Medium 110 Staphylococcus Medium 110 w/Azide Tellurite Glycine Agar TPEY Agar w/TPEY Enrichment and Antimicrobic Vial P Tryptose Blood Agar Base w/Blood VJ Agar
Propagation	Brain Heart Infusion w/PAB & Agar Cooked Meat Medium Nutrient Agar/Broth Tryptic Soy Agar/Broth		Brain Heart Infusion Agar/Broth Cooked Meat Medium Dextrose Starch Agar Phenylethanol Agar	Tryptic Soy Agar/Broth Tryptose Agar Tryptose Phosphate Broth

(Continued)

MICROORGANISM, MEDIA (Continued)

Shigella (Continued)

Serological Identification

Alkalescens–Dispar Antisera Types 1, 2, 3, 4 and Poly
Shigella Antisera Poly Groups A, A_1, B, C_1, C_2, D
Shigella Boydii Antisera Types 1–15
Shigella Dysenteriae Antisera Types 1–10
Shigella Flexneri Antisera Types 1–6

Streptococci including Enterococci

Isolation

Azide Blood Agar Base
Azide Dextrose Broth
m Azide Broth
BAGG Broth
Columbia CNA Agar w/Blood
m Enterococcus Agar
EVA Broth
Heart Infusion Agar
KF Streptococcus Agar/Broth
Mannitol Neomycin Agar
Mitis Salivarius Agar
Phenylethanol Agar
Pike Streptococcal Broth
SF Medium
Tryptose Blood Agar Base w/Blood
Tryptose Blood Agar Base w/Hemo. and Supp. A or B

Differentiation

Bile Esculin Agar (entero)
Bile Esculin Azide Agar (entero)
Blood Agar Base w/Blood
Blood Agar Base No. 2 w/Blood
Differentiation Disks Bacitracin
EVA Broth
Enterococcus Confirmatory Agar
Enterococcus Presumptive Broth
Heart Infusion 6.5% NaCl Broth (entero)
Phenol Red Broth Base w/Carbohydrates
SR Medium Base
Tryptose Blood Agar Base w/Blood

Propagation

AC Medium
Brain Heart Infusion Agar/Broth
Brain Veal Agar
Cooked Meat Medium
Dextrose Agar
Dextrose Broth
Todd Hewitt Broth
Tryptic Soy Agar/Broth
Tryptose Agar
Tryptose Phosphate Broth

Serological Identification

AHT Kit
FA Streptococcus Group A,
Streptolysin O Reagents
Streptococcus Antisera Groups A, B, C, D, E, F, G, H, K, L, M, N, O, P, Q, R, S, T, MG
Streptococcus MG Suspension

Trichomonas

Isolation

Kupferberg Trichomonas Base
Kupferberg Trichomonas Broth
Lash Serum Medium (tubes)

Propagation

Kupferberg Trichomonas Base
Kupferberg Trichomonas Broth
Lash Serum Medium (tubes)

Staphylococci (Continued)

FA Staphylococcus Aureus

Thermophilic Flat Sour Organisms

Isolation

Dextrose Tryptone Agar
m Dextrose Tryptone Broth

Differentiation

Dextrose Tryptone Agar
m Dextrose Tryptone Broth

SOURCE: Difco Product Selection Guide, *0229*. 1974. Difco Laboratories, Detroit.

MICROORGANISM REACTIONS ON DIFFERENTIAL TUBE MEDIA

TABLE 2.M.19

MICROORGANISM REACTIONS ON DIFFERENTIAL TUBE MEDIA

	Bacto-Purple Broth Base Containing:									Bacto S I M Medium			Bacto Urea Broth	Bacto Urea Agar		Bacto Simmons Citrate Agar
Organism[1]	Xylose	Dextrose	Maltose	Saccharose	Lactose	Rhamnose	Mannitol	Dulcitol	Salicin	Indol	Motility	H_2S		Butt	Slant	
Shigella dysenteriae (Shiga)	NC	Y	NC	NC	NC	NC	NC	NC	NC	–	–	–	–	–	–	–
Shigella ambigua (Schmitz)	NC	Y	NC	NC	NC	Y	NC	NC	NC	+	–	–	–	–	–	–
Shigella sonnei	NC or Y	Y	Y	Y	Y slow	Y	Y	NC	NC	–	–	–	–	–	–	–
Shigella paradysenteriae—Boyd and Flexner	NC	Y	NC or Y	NC	NC	NC	Y	NC	NC	±	–	–	–	–	–	–
Shigella paradysenteriae—Newcastle	NC	YG	NC or YG	NC	NC	NC	YG	YG	NC	–	–	–	–	–	–	–
Shigella alkalescens	Y	Y	Y	NC or Y	NC	Y	Y	Y	NC	+	–	–	–	–	–	–
Shigella madampensis	Y	Y	Y	Y	Y	Y	Y	NC	NC	+	–	–	–	–	–	–
Shigella ceylonensis (dispar)	Y	Y	Y	Y	Y	Y	Y	Y	NC	+	–	–	–	–	–	–
Salmonella typhosa (Eberthella typhosa)	Y	Y	Y	NC	NC	NC	Y	NC	NC	–	+	+	–	–	–	–
Salmonella paratyphi	NC	YG	YG	NC	NC	YG	YG	YG	NC	–	+	–	–	–	–	–
Salmonella schottmuelleri	YG	YG	YG	NC	NC	YG	YG	YG	NC	–	+	+	–	–	–	+
Salmonella typhimurium		YG	YG	NC	NC		YG	YG	NC	–	+	+	–	–	–	+
Salmonella choleraesuis	YG	YG	YG	NC	NC	YG	YG	YG	NC	–	+	–	–	–	–	+
Salmonella enteritidis	YG	YG	YG	NC	NC		YG	YG	NC	–	+	+	–	–	–	+
Salmonella pullorum	YG	YG	NC	NC	NC	YG	YG	NC	NC	–	–	+	–	–	–	–
Salmonella gallinarum	Y	Y	Y	NC	NC	NC or Y	Y	Y	NC	–	–	±	–	–	–	–
Aerobacter aerogenes	YG	YG	YG	NC or YG	YG	YG	YG	NC or YG	YG	±	–	–	–	–	R	+
Aerobacter cloacae	YG	YG	YG	YG	YG	NC	YG	NC	YG	–	+	–	–	–	R	+
Escherichia coli	YG	YG	YG	NC or YG	YG	YG	YG	NC or YG	NC or YG	+	+	–	–	–	–	–
Escherichia freundii	YG	YG	YG	NC or YG	YG	YG	YG	NC or YG	NC or YG	±	±	+	–			+
Escherichia intermedium	YG	YG	YG	NC or YG	YG	YG	YG	NC or YG	NC or YG	±	±	–	–			+
Proteus vulgaris		YG	YG	YG	NC		NC		NC or YG	+	+	+	R	R	R	±
Proteus mirabilis		YG	NC	YG	NC		NC		NC	–	+	+	R	R	R	+
Proteus morganii	NC or Y	Y or YG	NC	NC	NC	NC	NC	NC	NC	+	+	–	R	R	R	–
Proteus rettgeri		Y or YG	NC	NC or Y	NC		Y or YG	NC	NC or YG	+	±	–	R	R	R	+
Klebsiella pneumoniae		NC or YG	NC or YG	NC or YG	NC or YG		NC or YG			±	–	–	–	–	–	±
Pseudomonas aeruginosa	NC	NC or Y	NC	NC	NC	NC	NC	NC	NC	–	+	–	–	–	–	+
Alcaligenes faecalis	NC	NC	NC	NC	NC	NC	NC	NC	NC	–	+	–	–	–	–	±

TABLE 2.M.19 (*Continued*)

Organism[1]	Bacto Russell Double Sugar Agar		Bacto-Kligler Iron Agar			Bacto Kramwiede Triple Sugar Agar		Bacto Triple Sugar Iron Agar			Bacto Friewer Shaughnessy Medium		
	Butt	Slant	Butt	Slant	H_2S	Butt	Slant	Butt	Slant	H_2S	Fermentation	Motility	H_2S
Shigella dysenteriae (Shiga)	Y	NC	Y	NC	–	Y	NC	Y	NC	–	NC	–	–
Shigella ambigua (Schmitz)	Y	NC	Y	NC	–	Y	NC	Y	NC	–	NC	–	–
Shigella sonnei	Y	NC	Y	NC	–	Y	NC	Y	NC	–	NC	–	–
Shigella paradysenteriae—Boyd and Flexner	Y	NC	Y	NC	–	Y	NC	Y	NC	–	NC	–	–
Shigella paradysenteriae—Newcastle	Y or YG	NC	Y or YG	NC	–	Y or YG	NC	Y or YG	NC	–	NC	–	–
Shigella alkalescens	Y	NC	Y	NC	–	Y	NC or Y	Y	NC or Y	–	NC	–	–
Shigella madampensis	Y	Y	Y	Y	–	Y	Y	Y	Y	–	Y	–	–
Shigella ceylonensis (dispar)	Y	Y	Y	Y	–	Y	Y	Y	Y	–	Y	–	–
Salmonella typhosa (Eberthella typhosa)	Y	NC	Y	NC	+	Y	NC	Y	NC	+	NC	+	+
Salmonella paratyphi	YG	NC	YG	NC	–	YG	NC	YG	NC	–	NC	+	–
Salmonella schottmuelleri	YG	NC	YG	NC	+	YG	NC	YG	NC	+	NC	+	+
Salmonella typhimurium	YG	NC	YG	NC	+	YG	NC	YG	NC	+	NC	+	+
Salmonella choleraesuis	YG	NC	YG	NC	–	YG	NC	YG	NC	–	NC	+	–
Salmonella enteritidis	YG	NC	YG	NC	+	YG	NC	YG	NC	+	NC	+	+
Salmonella pullorum	YG	NC	YG	NC	+	YG	NC	YG	NC	+	NC	–	+
Salmonella gallinarum	Y	NC	Y	NC	±	Y	NC	Y	NC	±	NC	–	±
Aerobacter aerogenes	YG	Y	YG	Y	–	YG	Y	YG	Y	–	YG	–	–
Aerobacter cloacae	YG	Y	YG	Y	–	YG	Y	YG	Y	–	YG	+	–
Escherichia coli	YG	Y	YG	Y	–	YG	Y	YG	Y	–	YG	±	–
Escherichia freundii	YG	Y	YG	Y	+	YG	Y	YG	Y	+	YG	±	+
Escherichia intermedium	YG	Y	YG	Y	–	YG	Y	YG	Y	–	YG	±	–
Proteus vulgaris	YG	NC	YG	NC	+	YG	Y	YG	Y	+	NC	+	+
Proteus mirabilis	YG	NC	YG	NC	+	YG	NC or Y	YG	NC or Y	+	NC	+	+
Proteus morganii	Y or YG	NC	Y or YG	NC	–	Y or YG	NC	Y or YG	NC	–	NC	+	–
Proteus rettgeri	Y or YG	NC	Y or YG	NC	–	Y or YG	NC	Y or YG	NC	–	NC	±	–
Klebsiella pneumoniae	Y or YG	NC	Y or YG	NC	–	Y or YG	NC	Y or YG	NC	–	NC	–	–
Pseudomonas aeruginosa	NC	NC	NC	NC	–	NC	NC	NC	NC	–	NC	+	–
Alcaligenes faecalis	NC	NC	NC	NC	–	NC	NC	NC	NC	–	NC	+	–
Paracolobactrum aerogenoides	Reactions are the same as those of Aerobacter aerogenes except that the fermentation of lactose is consistently delayed.												
Paracolobactrum intermedium	Reactions are the same as those of Escherichia freundii or E. intermedium except that the fermentation of lactose is consistently delayed.												
Paracolobactrum coliforme	Reactions are the same as those of Escherichia coli except that the fermentation of lactose is consistently delayed.												

NC=No change or alkaline reaction. Y=Yellow—acid formation. YG=Acid and gas formation. R=Red—urea hydrolyzed. +=Positive for a given reaction. –=Negative. ±=Variable.

[1] Names of organisms according to Bergey's "Manual of Determinative Bacteriology," Sixth Edition, 1948.

SOURCE: Difco Manual, 9th Edition. (1973). Difco Laboratories, Detroit.

MICROORGANISM, SELECTIVE AND DIFFERENTIAL BROTHS AND MEDIA, WATER FILTRATION PLANT

Selective and differential broths and media used for control of water filtration plant operation:

Selective Broths	Selective Agars	Differential Test Media
Fuchsin Lactose Broth	MacConkey Agar	Bacto-Tryptone
Brilliant Green Bile 2%	Violet Red Bile Agar	MR-VP Medium
MB-BCP	Desoxycholate Lactose Agar	Koser Citrate Medium
Formate Ricinoleate Broth	Brilliant Green Bile Agar	Simmons Citrate Agar
Crystal Violet Broth	Levine EMB Agar	Decarboxylase w/Lysine
Eijkman Lactose Medium	Brilliant Green Agar	Decarboxylase w/Arginine
EC Medium	Bismuth Sulfite Agar	Decarboxylase w/Ornithine
MacConkey Broth	Desoxycholate Citrate Agar	TSI
Tetrathionate Broth	XLD Agar	KCN Broth
Selenite Broth		SIM Medium
GN Broth, Hajna		m Bismuth Sulfite Broth
		Purple Broth Base w/Carbohydrates

SOURCE: Difco Laboratories, Detroit.

MICROWAVE COOKING, FRESH VEGETABLES

The vegetables in Table 2.M.20 require cooking in a 3-qt casserole with ½ tsp of salt added. Times are average and may need adjustments according to taste. (Power input, 0.8 kw)

TABLE 2.M.20

MICROWAVE COOKING OF FRESH VEGETABLES

Vegetable	Weight (Oz)	Water (Cups)	Cooking Time (Min)	Preparation Notes
Asparagus	16	½	12	—
Beans (green or waxed)	16	1	9	—
Parsnip	16	1	8	Peel and slice
Peas	16	½	6½	Shell
Potatoes	16	None	3½	Skins on
Squash				
Acorn	16	None	6	Halve and remove seeds
Butternut	16	½	6	Peeled 1-in. cubes
Hubbard	16	½	6	Peeled 1-in. cubes
Summer	16	¼	6	Quarter and slice
Turnip	16	1	15	Cut into 8 pieces
Spinach	10	None	4	Wash and drain
Onions	12	2	15	—

SOURCE: COPSON, D. A. (EDITOR). 1975. Guide to Domestic Microwave Cooking. *In* Microwave Heating, 2nd Edition. Avi Publishing Co., Westport, Conn.

MICROWAVE COOKING, FROZEN VEGETABLES

The vegetables in Table 2.M.21 require cooking in a casserole with ½ tsp of salt added. (Power input, 0.8 kw)

TABLE 2.M.21

MICROWAVE COOKING OF FROZEN VEGETABLES

Vegetable	Weight (oz)	Water (Cups)	Cooking Time (Min)
Asparagus	10	⅓	6½
Beans (green)	12	⅔	12-14
Beans (wax)	10	1	12
Broccoli	10	½	9
Brussels sprouts	10	½	10
Cauliflower	10	½	4½
Corn-on-cob	8 (2 ears)	¼	5
Corn (whole kernel)	10	½	4
Lima beans (baby)	10	1½	15
Lima beans (fordhook)	10	1	10
Peas	12	⅓	8
Peas and carrots	10	½	8
Spinach (chopped)	12	None	8
Spinach (whole)	12	⅓	9
Squash	12	None	4

SOURCE: COPSON, D. A. (EDITOR). 1975. Guide to Domestic Microwave Cooking. *In* Microwave Heating, 2nd Edition. Avi Publishing Co., Westport, Conn.

MICROWAVE COOKING, FRUIT

TABLE 2.M.22

PREPARATION AND HEATING TIMES IN MINUTES FOR COOKING FRUIT

Fruit	Amount	Time (min)	Preparation
Apples	4 medium	6	Remove core, pare around top, fill, and sprinkle with sugar.
Apple sauce	6 medium	6-8	Wash and core. Cook with ½ cup water. Strain. Add ¼ cup sugar.
Apricots (dried)	11 oz	9	Cook in 2 cups boiling water. Covered casserole.
Bananas	2 large	1½	Quarter, space well in dish, brush with melted butter. Heat.
Cranberry sauce	1 lb	8	Cook until skins burst in 2 cups sugar, 1½ cups water.
Grapefruit	4 halves	8	Brush fruit with hot mixture of 2 tsp butter, 2 tbsp honey, ⅛ tsp nutmeg. Cook until hot.
Peaches (fresh)	8 medium	5	Mix 2 tbsp lemon juice and ¼ cup water. Pour over sliced, peeled fruit. Make smooth mixture and pour over fruit; ¾ cup flour, 1 cup brown sugar, ¼ tsp salt. Heat.
Prunes	1 lb	8	Place in 2 cups of water and soak over night. Cook.
Rhubarb sauce	2 cups	4	Mix rhubarb with 1 cup sugar, 2 tbsp water and dash of salt.

SOURCE: COPSON, D. A. (EDITOR). 1975. Guide to Domestic Microwave Cooking. *In* Microwave Heating, 2nd Edition. Avi Publishing Co., Westport, Conn.

MICROWAVE PROCESSING TIME

TABLE 2.M.23

APPROXIMATE PROCESSING TIMES FOR MICROWAVE OVENS

Food Item	Processing Time (Min)
Meat, precooked and cooled	
Ham steak	3
Short ribs of beef	2
Poultry, precooked and cooled	
Fried chicken, disjointed	2½
Fried chicken, half	2½
Seafood, raw to done	2
Vegetables, canned	
Corn, green beans, peas	½
Baked beans	¾
Potatoes	1¼
Vegetables, fresh	
Corn on the cob	2
Broccoli	8
Spinach	3
Asparagus	9
Potatoes	5
Vegetables, frozen	
Corn	5
Asparagus	7
Cauliflower	12
Casseroles, precooked and cooled	
Chicken a la king	1½
Stuffed cabbage	2
Macaroni and cheese	1¾
Spanish rice	1½
Spaghetti	1½
Beef Stew	2
Ravioli	2
Chili con carne	1¾
Meat pie	1¾
Chop suey	2

SOURCE: KAZARIAN, E. A. (EDITOR). 1975. Equipment Requirements. *In* Food Service Facilities Planning. Publishing Co., Westport, Conn.

MILK, AMINO ACIDS

TABLE 2.M.24

AMINO ACIDS ESSENTIAL TO MAN IN COW'S MILK PRODUCTS
(gr per 100 gm)

	Casein	Lactalbumin	Dried Nonfat Milk	Dried Whey
Tryptophan	1.3	2.2	0.50	0.15
Threonine	4.3	5.2	1.6	0.68
Isoleucine	6.6	6.2	2.3	0.73
Leucine	10.0	12.3	3.5	1.04
Lysine	8.0	9.1	2.8	0.77
Methionine	3.1	2.3	0.87	0.19
Cystine	0.38	3.4	0.32	0.25
Phenylalanine	5.4	4.4	1.7	0.32
Tyrosine	5.8	3.8	1.8	0.13
Valine	7.4	5.7	2.4	0.64

SOURCE: GORDON, W. G. and KALAN, E. B. 1974. Proteins of Milk. *In* Fundamentals of Dairy Chemistry, : Edition. B. H. Webb, A. H. Johnson and J. A. Alford (Editors). Avi Publishing Co., Westport, Conn.

MILK AND CHEESE COMPOSITION

TABLE 2.M.25

COMPOSITION OF THE EDIBLE PORTION (EP) AND REFUSE IN THE MATERIAL AS PURCHASED (AP)

Item No.	Commodity and Description	Water	Protein	Fat	Carbohydrate Total (by dif)	Carbohydrate Fiber	Ash	Calories (No./100 g)	Notes	Refuse in AP (%)
		(Percent of Edible Portion)								
	Milk and Cheese									
	Milk (cow's)									
250	Whole, fluid—3.5% fat	87.3	3.5	3.5	5.0	0	0.7	65		0
251	3.0% fat	88.0	3.3	3.0	5.0	0	0.7	60		0
252	3.2% fat	87.7	3.4	3.2	5.0	0	0.7	62		0
253	3.9% fat	87.0	3.5	3.9	4.9	0	0.7	68		0
254	Skim, fluid, or buttermilk	90.2	3.6	0.4	5.1	0	0.7	39		0
255	Cream (20% butterfat)	72.4	2.9	20	4.1	0	0.6	204		0
	Other milk									
256	Goat's, whole, fluid	86.4	3.8	4.5	4.5	0	0.8	73		0
257	Sheep's, whole, fluid	82.3	5.8	6.5	4.5	0	0.9	99		0
258	Buffalo's, whole, fluid	83	4	7.5	4.7	0	0.8	101		0
259	Carabao's, whole, fluid	80	5.8	9	4.4	0	0.8	121		0
	Camel's—Use No. 256									
	Processed milk (cow's)									
260	Whole, evaporated, unsweetened	73.7	7	7.9	9.9	0	1.5	138	Use for U.S.A., Canada	0
261	Whole, evaporated, unsweetened	69	8.3	9.0	12.0	0	1.7	161	Use for U.K., prewar (Currently composition is similar to No. 260)	0
262	Whole, condensed, sweetened	27	8.1	8.4	54.8	0	1.7	320	Use for U.S.A., Canada	0
263	Whole, condensed, sweetened	25	8.2	10	55	0	1.8	336	Use for U.K.	0
264	Skim, condensed, sweetened	28	9.6	0.4	59.9	0	2.1	276		0
265	Whole, dried	4	26	27	37	0	6	492	Use for U.S.A., Canada	0
266	Whole, dried	4	26	30	34	0	6	506	Use for Australia	0
267	Skim, dried	4	36	1	51	0	8	360		

	Cheese									
268[1]	Hard, whole milk[1]	37	25	31	2	0	5	387	Cheddar, Gruyere, Roquefort, Gorgonzola, Caciocavallo	0
269[1]	Hard, "¾ fat"[1]	36	34	21	3	0	6	341	Edam, Parmesan	0
270[1]	Hard, skim milk[1]	40	46	4	4	0	6	247		0
271[1]	Semi-soft, whole milk[1]	51	18	24	3	0	4	299	Camembert, Limburger, Feta, and cheeses from buffalo or carabao milk	0
272[1]	Semi-soft, skim milk[1]	55	35	3	3	0	4	187		0
273[1]	Soft, fresh, partly whole milk[1]	70	15	7	5	0	3	145	Topfen, Petit Suisse, fromage à la pie	0
274[1]	Soft, fresh, skim milk[1]	74	19	1	4	0	2	105	Quark, cottage cheese, fromage blanc	0
	Whey cheeses									
275[1]	Hard, low fat type[1]	30	9	3	52	0	6	266	Mysost	0
276[1]	Soft	75	14	3	5	0	3	106	Ziger, Mizithra	0

[1] More information required.

SOURCE: CHATFIELD, C. Food Composition Tables for International Use. FAO, United Nations, Rome.

MILK AND MILK PRODUCTS, VITAMIN CONTENT

TABLE 2.M.26

VITAMIN CONTENT OF MILK AND MILK PRODUCTS
Content of thiamin, riboflavin, nicotinic acid, and pantothenic acid in milk and milk products[a]

Milk or milk product	Thiamin Avg	Thiamin Range	Riboflavin Avg	Riboflavin Range	Nicotinic Acid Avg	Nicotinic Acid Range	Pantothenic Acid Avg	Pantothenic Acid Range
				(mg/kg)[b]				
Whole milk:								
Fluid	0.44	0.20-0.80 (48)[c]	1.75	0.81-2.58 (73)	0.94[d]	0.30-2.00 (34)	3.46	2.60-4.90 (23)
Condensed	1.1	0.8-1.5 (5)	3.6	2.6-4.0 (4)	2.1	1.6-2.4 (3)	8.7	7.5-10.4 (3)
Evaporated	0.56	0.40-0.82 (6)	3.8	2.8-4.8 (6)	2.0	1.8-2.3 (5)	7.0	5.8-8.0 (4)
Dried	3.4	2.5-5.1 (9)	15.5	9.8-25.6 (9)	7.3	6.1-9.0 (7)	27.3	22.7-39.0 (7)
Skimmilk:								
Fluid	0.40	0.20-0.53 (6)	1.7	1.5-1.8 (4)	0.86	0.74-1.1 (4)	3.6	2.8-4.0 (6)
Dried	3.6	2.2-4.6 (14)	18.9	13.0-25.4 (25)	10.6	8.2-18.3 (8)	38.8	22.9-77.0 (12)
Chocolate milk:								
Fluid	0.30	0.28-0.31 (2)	1.7	1.5-1.8 (4)				
Malted milk:								
Dried	3.3	(1)	5.4	(1)				
Buttermilk:								
Fluid	0.42	(1)	1.7	1.6-1.8 (2)	0.55	0.27-0.82 (2)	3.8	2.9-4.7 (2)
Condensed			14.3	(1)				
Dried	3.5	(1)	32.0	29-35 (10)	8.6	(1)	28.0	27.0-30.1 (3)
Kefir			0.7	(1)				
Yoghurt	0.37	(1)	1.4	0.8-1.8 (3)	1.3	0.8-1.9 (2)		
Cream:								
Half and half	0.3	(1)	1.5	(1)	0.4	(1)		
Light table	0.3	(1)	1.4	1.4-1.5 (2)	0.4	(1)		
Medium whipping	0.25	(1)	1.3	(1)	0.4	(1)		
Heavy whipping	0.2	(1)	1.2	(1)	0.4	(1)	2.6	(1)
Butter	0.03	(1)	0.16	0.08-0.37 (4)	0.5	0-1.0 (2)	2.3	0-4.6 (2)
Ice cream	0.48	0.38-0.65 (3)	2.3	2.0-2.6 (6)	1.1	1.0-1.2 (2)		
Whey:								
Fluid	0.4	(1)	1.2	0.5-1.6 (3)	0.85	0.72-1.03 (3)	3.4	2.1-4.1 (5)
Condensed	3.3	(1)	16.3	(1)	3.5	(1)	15.1	(1)
Dried	3.7	1.7-4.9 (5)	23.4	20.0-29.7 (8)	9.6	8.0-11.2 (2)	47.3	42.4-56.0 (4)
Casein, crude	0.82	0.44-1.2 (2)	2.6	1.5-3.6 (2)	2.4	1.3-3.4 (2)	3.6	2.6-4.5 (2)
Milk albumin:								
Dried	0.7	(1)	8.8	(1)	2.0	(1)	7.3	(1)

Content of vitamin B-6, biotin, folic acid, and vitamin B-12 in milk and milk products[a]

Milk or milk product	Vitamin B_6 Avg	Vitamin B_6 Range	Biotin Avg	Biotin Range	Folic Acid Avg	Folic Acid Range	Vitamin B_{12} Avg	Vitamin B_{12} Range
					(*mg/kg*)[b]			
Whole milk								
Fluid	0.64	0.22-1.90[e] (42)[c]	0.031	0.012-0.060 (21)	0.0028	0.0004-0.0062 (12)[f]	0.0043	0.0024-0.0074 (44)
Condensed	0.56	0.52-0.59 (2)	0.040	0.032-0.047 (2)			0.0039	0.0031-0.0054 (3)
Evaporated	0.74	0.55-1.37 (5)	0.056	0.031-0.090 (3)	0.014	(1)	0.0014	0.0010-0.0019 (3)
Dried	3.9	1.7-7.0 (7)	0.30	0.10-0.47 (5)	0.018	0.014-0.022 (2)[g]	0.026	0.018-0.038 (6)
Skimmilk:								
Fluid	0.45	0.26-0.56 (3)	0.016	0.015-0.016 (2)	0.012	0.008-0.016 (2)	0.0038	0.0031-0.0047 (4)
Dried	4.5	2.8-6.8 (6)	0.27	0.14-0.35 (3)	0.044	0.029-0.059 (2)[h]	0.034	0.022-0.045 (9)
Malted milk:								
Dried							0.022	(1)
Buttermilk:								
Fluid	0.39	0.38-0.40 (2)	0.011	(1)	0.11	(1)	0.0023	(1)
Dried	2.4	(1)	0.29	(1)	0.40	(1)[i]	0.019	0.018-0.02 (2)
Kefir							0.0021	0.0017-0.0024 (4)
Yoghurt			0.012	(1)			0.0012	0.0007-0.0018 (5)
Cream:								
Half and half	0.38	(1)						
Light table	0.40	(1)						
Medium whipping	0.35	(1)						
Butter	0.04	(1)						
Whey:								
Fluid	0.42	0.21-0.77 (3)	0.014	0.013-0.015 (2)			0.0020	0.0015-0.0024 (4)
Condensed	1.8	(1)	0.29	(1)				
Dried	4.0	(1)	0.37	(1)	0.89	0.88-0.90 (2)[j]	0.021	0.017-0.025 (3)
Casein, crude	2.7	0.4-7.0 (3)	0.052	0.044-0.060 (2)	0.34	0.16-0.51 (2)	0.071	0.043-0.104 (4)
Milk albumin:								
Dried	1.2	(1)						

(Continued)

MILK AND MILK PRODUCTS, VITAMIN CONTENT (Continued)

Content of choline, vitamin C, and vitamin E in milk and milk products[a]

Milk or milk product	Choline Avg	Choline Range	Vitamin C Avg	Vitamin C Range	Vitamin E Avg	Vitamin E Range
			(mg/kg)[b]			
Whole milk:						
Fluid	121	43-218 (9)[c]	21.1[k]	16.5-27.5 (46)	0.98	0.20-1.84 (14)
Condensed	344	(1)	26	4-58 (7)		
Evaporated	246	(1)	11	4-18 (6)	2.6	2.2-3 (2)
Dried	862	394-1,070 (4)	81	26-120 (7)	7.5	5-10 (2)
Skimmilk:						
Fluid	48	(1)	19	9-25 (4)		
Dried	1,182	410-1,700 (6)	98	53-170 (3)	4.8	0.5-9.1 (2)
Chocolate milk:						
Fluid			13	(1)		
Buttermilk:						
Fluid			12	9-14 (2)		
Dried	2,059	1,808-2,310 (2)	0	(1)		
Kefir			8	(1)		
Yoghurt	6	(1)	6.2	0-10.9 (5)		
Cream:						
Half and half			9	(1)		
Butter	183	20-400 (3)	0	0-0 (4)	24	17-31 (10)
Ice Cream	24	(1)	3	0-11 (4)	3	(1)
Whey:						
Fluid			13	11-15 (2)		
Dried	1,356	700-2,011 (2)				
Casein, crude	210	209-210 (2)				
Cheese:[l]						
Very hard:						
Parmesan	220	(1)				
Hard:						
Cantal			0	(1)		
Cheddar	335	190-480 (2)	0	0-0 (3)	10	(1)
Cheshire			0	(1)		
Edam			0	(1)	3.1	(1)
Gruyère			0	(1)	3.0	(1)
Swiss			0	(1)		
Semisoft:						
Blue[m]			0	(1)		
Münster			8.5	(1)		
Roquefort[n]			0	(1)	6.5	(1)
Stilton			0	(1)		

Soft:				
Ripened:				
Bel Paese			0	(1)
Brie			4.0	(1)
Camembert			4.0	(1)
Reblochon			8.8	(1)
Unripened:				
Cottage			0	(1)
Cream			0	(1)
Processed:				
Cheddar			0	(1)
Gruyère	470	(1)		

[a]Mean and range of average values obtained from publications of various groups of workers.
[b]Milligram per liter for products designated fluid.
[c]Figures in parentheses indicate number of references consulted.
[d]This average is based on determinations made by both microbiological and chemical assays, but some of the early values obtained by chemical means were extremely high (3.0, 4.5, and 8.2 mg per liter) and have been omitted.
[e]Three figures outside this range, one much higher (6.5) and two much lower (each 0.06) have been omitted.
[f]One high value of 0.024 mg per liter has been excluded.
[g]Obtained by microbiological assay; rat assay gave 0.500 (1).
[h]Obtained by microbiological assay; chick assay gave 0.585 (0.570–0.600) (2); other assays of unstated type gave 0.616 (1).
[i]Type of assay not stated.
[j]One value obtained by chick assay; the other, by assay of unstated type.
[k]Fresh milk; average for market milk (18 references); 10.5 (2.4–20.5) mg per liter.
[l]Classified primarily according to Sanders.
[m]May be made from milk of species other than the cow.
[n]Made from ewe's milk.

SOURCE: HARTMAN, A. M. and DRYDEN, L. P. Vitamins in Milk and Milk Products. J. Dairy Sci.

MILK BREEDS, COMPOSITION

TABLE 2.M.27

TYPICAL COMPOSITION (PERCENT) OF THE MILKS OF COWS OF SIX BREEDS

	in Milk							in Total Solids				
Breed	Water	Fat	Protein	Lactose	Ash	Nonfat Solids	Total Solids	Fat	Protein	Lactose	Ash	Nonfat Solids
Guernsey	85.35	5.05	3.90	4.96	0.74	9.60	14.65	34.47	26.62	33.86	5.05	65.53
Jersey	85.47	5.05	3.78	5.00	0.70	9.48	14.53	34.75	26.02	34.41	4.82	65.25
Ayrshire	86.97	4.03	3.51	4.81	0.68	9.00	13.03	30.93	26.94	36.91	5.22	69.07
Brown Swiss	86.87	3.85	3.48	5.08	0.72	9.28	13.13	29.32	26.50	38.69	5.48	70.68
Shorthorn	87.43	3.63	3.32	4.89	0.73	8.94	12.57	28.88	26.41	38.82	5.81	71.12
Holstein	87.72	3.41	3.32	4.87	0.68	8.87	12.28	27.77	27.03	39.66	5.54	72.23

SOURCE: WEBB, B. H., JOHNSON, A. H., and ALFORD, J. A. 1974. Fundamentals of Dairy Chemistry, 2nd Edition. Avi Publishing Co., Westport, Conn.

MILK COMPOSITION I

TABLE 2.M.28

COMPOSITION[1] OF WHOLE AND SKIM COW'S MILK, IN LIQUID, CONCENTRATED AND DRIED FORMS, AND LOSSES IN NUTRIENTS IN TREATMENT

	Water	Protein (N × 6.38)	Fat	Carbo-hydrate	Calcium	Vitamin A (retinol) activity		Vitamin D		Thiamine	
						Amount (μg/100 g)	Loss (%)	Amount (IU/100 g)	Loss (%)	Amount (μg/100 g)	Loss (%)
	. . . *Percent* . . .										
WHOLE											
Raw	87.6	3.3	3.6	4.7	0.12	50	—	2	—	45	—
HTST treated	87.6	3.3	3.6	4.7	0.12	50	None	2	None	42	<10
Sterilized (in-bottle process)	87.6	3.3	3.6	4.7	0.12	50	None	2	None	30	35
UHT treated	87.6	3.3	3.6	4.7	0.12	50	None	2	None	42	<10
Evaporated											
(1)	68.5	8.4	9.2	12.0	0.30	125	None	5	None	67	40
(2)	73.0	7.0	8.0	10.0	0.26	105	None	4	None	57	40
Sweetened condensed											
(1)	25.0	8.4	9.2	55.4	0.30	125	None	5	None	103	10
(2)	29.0	7.3	8.0	53.9	0.27	110	None	4	None	90	10
Dried											
Roller	3.0	25.0	27.5	37.5	0.91	383	None	15	None	290	15
Spray	3.0	25.0	27.5	37.5	0.91	383	None	15	None	310	10
SKIM											
Raw	90.8	3.4	0.1	4.9	0.12	1	—	0	—	47	—
Evaporated	80.0	7.4	0.2	10.7	0.26	3	None	0	—	61	40
Sweetened condensed	29.0	9.6	0.3	58.8	0.34	4	None	0	—	120	10
Dried	3.0	36.0	1.0	50.5	1.26	13	None	1	None	450	10

? indicates possible slight loss.

[1] For simplicity, rounded-off values have been taken for raw milk and all other forms are assumed to sweetened condensed whole milk to represent two different degrees of concentration current on the raw milk: 2 mg/100 g is for milk as it leaves the udder. — [3] Appreciable loss of biological availability.

SOURCE: KON, S. K. 1972. Milk and Milk Products in Human Nutrition, FAO, United Nations, Rome.

Riboflavin		Pantothenic acid		Nicotinic acid		Vitamin B_6		Biotin		Vitamin B_{12}		Vitamin C [2]	
Amount (µg/ 100 g)	Loss (%)	Amount (µg/ 100 g)	Loss (%)	Amount (µg/ 100 g)	Loss (%)	Amount (µg/ 100 g)	Loss (%)	Amount (µg/ 100 g)	Loss (%)	Amount (µg/ 100 g)	Loss (%)	Amount (µg/ 100 g)	Loss (%)
150	—	350	—	100	—	25	—	1.5	—	0.30	—	2.0	—
150	None	350	?	100	None	25	None	1.5	None	0.30	<10	1.8	10
150	None	350	?	100	None	25	[3]	1.5	None	Trace	>90	1.0	50
150	None	350	?	100	None	25	None	1.5	None	0.24	20	1.8	10
375	None	875	?	250	?	63	[3]	3.4	10	<0.10	90	2.0	60
315	None	735	?	210	?	53	[3]	2.8	10	<0.10	90	1.7	60
375	None	875	?	250	None	63	None	3.4	10	0.53	30	4.3	15
330	None	775	?	220	None	55	None	3.0	10	0.47	30	3.8	15
1 150	None	2 700	?	760	?	190	None	10.0	10	1.60	30	11.0	30
1 150	None	2 700	?	760	?	190	None	10.0	10	1.60	30	13.0	20
145	[4]—	360	—	103	—	26	—	1.5	—	0.30	—	2.0	—
315	None	780	?	225	?	57	[3]	2.9	10	<0.10	90	1.7	60
410	None	1 000	?	290	None	73	None	3.8	10	0.60	30	4.8	15
1 530	None	3 800	?	1 100	?	275	None	14.0	10	2.20	30	17.0	20

have been derived from that particular milk. Two separate values are given for evaporated and for international market. — [2] Survival of vitamin C would depend on the amount originally present in the — [4] Loss of riboflavin in the fat-globule membrane.

MILK COMPOSITION II

TABLE 2.M.29

COMPOSITION OF COW'S MILK

Composition	Mean	Normal Variations	Breed Means: Holstein	Jersey	Guernsey	Ayrshire	Brown Swiss	Minimum Requirements: States	USPH
Fat	4.00	2.60–8.37	3.40	5.37	4.95	4.00	4.01	3.25	3.25
Protein	3.50	2.44–6.48	3.32	3.92	3.91	3.58	3.61	—	—
Casein	2.90	1.60–4.50	2.30	3.00	2.90	2.50	2.60	—	—
Lactose	4.90	2.41–6.11	4.87	4.93	4.93	4.67	5.04	—	—
Ash	0.70	0.56–0.936	0.68	0.71	0.74	0.73	0.68	—	—
Milk-solids-not-fat (msnf)	9.10	7.20–11.90	8.86	9.54	9.66	8.90	9.40	8.50	8.00
Total solids	13.10	10.56–17.90	12.26	14.93	14.61	12.90	13.41	11.75	11.25

SOURCE: ARBUCKLE, W. S. 1973. Dairy Products. *In* Quality Control For The Food Industry, Vol. 2, 3rd Edition. A. Kramer and B. A. Twigg (Editors). Avi Publishing Co., Westport, Conn.

MILK, CONCENTRATED PRODUCTS

TABLE 2.M.30

APPROXIMATE COMPOSITION OF CONCENTRATED MILK PRODUCTS

Product	Water (%)	Fat (%)	Protein (%)	Lactose (%)	Sucrose (%)	Ash (%)
Evaporated milk	73.00	8.30	7.50	9.70	—	1.40
Plain condensed milk	70.00	8.50	7.80	11.90	—	1.80
Condensed skim milk	71.50	0.50	8.80	12.70	—	2.00
Sweetened condensed whole	27.47	9.28	7.42	13.35	40.60	1.88
Sweetened condensed skim	29.00	0.06	10.32	15.60	42.27	2.25
Condensed buttermilk	72.00	1.95	10.61	13.01	—	3.33
Condensed whey	70.00	0.30	3.60	21.60	—	3.33

SOURCE: ARBUCKLE, W. S. 1973. Dairy Products. *In* Quality Control For The Food Industry, Vol. 2, 3rd Edition. A. Kramer and B. A. Twigg (Editors). Avi Publishing Co., Westport, Conn.

MILK, DRY PRODUCTS

TABLE 2.M.31

APPROXIMATE COMPOSITION OF DRY MILK PRODUCTS

Product	Water (%)	Fat (%)	Protein (%)	Lactose (%)	Ash (%)	Lactic Acid (%)
Dried whole milk	2.00	27.00	26.50	38.00	6.05	—
Nonfat dry milk	3.23	0.88	36.89	50.52	8.15	1.40
Dry buttermilk	3.90	4.68	35.88	47.84	7.80	1.55
Dried whey	6.10	0.90	12.50	72.25	8.90	7.00
Dried malted milk	3.29	7.55	13.19	72.40[1]	3.66	—
Dry cream	0.66	65.15	13.42	17.86	2.91	—

[1] Lactose, maltose, and dextrin.

SOURCE: ARBUCKLE, W. S. 1973. Dairy Products. *In* Quality Control For The Food Industry, Vol. 2, 3rd Edition. A. Kramer and B. A. Twigg (Editors). Avi Publishing Co., Westport, Conn.

MILK, FATTY ACIDS, SEASONAL

TABLE 2.M.32

SEASONAL VARIATION (WEIGHT PERCENT) OF COMPONENT ACIDS OF MILKFAT

Acid	Stall-Fed Winter	Silage-Fed Winter	June Pasture	August Pasture
Butyric	3.0	3.6	3.7	3.5
Caproic	1.4	2.0	1.7	1.9
Caprylic	1.5	0.5	1.0	0.7
Capric	2.7	2.3	1.9	2.1
Lauric	3.7	2.5	2.8	1.9
Myristic	12.1	11.1	8.1	7.9
Palmitic	25.3	29.0	25.9	25.8
Stearic	9.2	9.2	11.2	12.7
As Arachidic	1.3	2.4	1.2	1.5
9-Decenoic	0.3	0.1	0.1	0.1
9-Dodecenoic	0.4	0.1	0.2	0.2
9-Tetradecenoic	1.6	0.9	0.6	0.6
9-Hexadecenoic	4.0	4.6	3.4	2.4
Oleic	29.6	26.7	32.8	34.0
As Octadecadienoic	3.6	3.6	3.7	3.7
As C_{20-22} unsaturated	0.3	1.4	1.7	1.0

SOURCE: KURTZ, F. E. 1974. The Lipids of Milk: Composition and Properties. *In* Fundamentals of Dairy Chemistry, 2nd Edition. B. H. Webb, A. H. Johnson and J. A. Alford (Editors). Avi Publishing Co., Westport, Conn.

MILK, MAMMALS, COMPOSITION

TABLE 2.M.33

AVERAGE COMPOSITION (PERCENT) OF MILKS OF VARIOUS MAMMALS[1]

	in Milk							in Total Solids				
Species	Water	Fat	Protein	Lactose	Ash	Nonfat Solids	Total Solids	Fat	Protein	Lactose	Ash	Nonfat Solids
Woman	87.43	3.75	1.63	6.98	0.21	8.82	12.57	29.83	12.97	55.53	1.67	70.17
Cow	87.2	3.7	3.5	4.9	0.7	9.1	12.8	28.9	27.34	38.28	5.47	71.1
Cow	86.61	4.14	3.58	4.96	0.71	9.25	13.39	30.91	26.76	37.04	5.30	69.09
Goat	87.00	4.25	3.52	4.27	0.86	8.75	13.00	32.69	27.08	32.85	6.62	67.31
Ewe	80.71	7.90	5.23	4.81	0.90	11.39	19.29	40.96	27.11	24.94	4.67	59.05
Egyptian buffalo	82.09	7.96	4.16	4.86	0.78	9.95	17.91	44.44	23.23	27.14	4.36	55.56
Chinese buffalo	76.80	12.60	6.04	3.70	0.86	10.60	23.20	54.31	26.03	15.94	3.71	45.69
Philippine carabao	78.46	10.35	5.88	4.32	0.84	11.19	21.54	48.05	27.30	20.06	3.90	51.95
Indian buffalo	82.76	7.38	3.60	5.48	0.78	9.86	17.24	42.81	20.88	31.78	4.52	57.19
Camel	87.61	5.38	2.98	3.26	0.70	7.01	12.39	43.42	24.05	26.31	5.65	56.58
Mare	89.04	1.59	2.69	6.14	0.51	9.37	10.96	14.51	24.54	56.02	4.65	85.49
Ass	89.03	2.53	2.01	6.07	0.41	8.44	10.97	23.06	18.32	55.33	3.74	76.94
Reindeer	63.30	22.46	10.30	2.50	1.44	14.24	36.70	61.20	28.06	6.81	3.92	38.80
Llama	86.55	3.15	3.90	5.60	0.80	10.30	13.45	23.42	29.00	41.63	5.95	76.58

[1] Ed. note. An unpublished survey (1973) of over one million commercial cow milk samples indicates an average composition of: fat 3.68%, nonfat solids 8.48%, protein 3.14%, lactose 4.64%, ash .7%.

SOURCE: JOHNSON, A. H. 1974. The Composition of Milk. *In* Fundamentals of Dairy Chemistry, 2nd Edition. B. H. Webb, A. H. Johnson and J. A. Alford (Editors). Avi Publishing Co., Westport, Conn.

MILK, PHYSICAL PROPERTIES

TABLE 2.M.34

PHYSICAL PROPERTIES OF MILK

Acidity (%)	0.16±0.02
pH	6.6±0.2
Surface tension (dynes)	55.3
Specific gravity	1.032±0.004
Freezing point (°C)	—0.55
Boiling point (°C)	100.17
Specific heat at	
0°C	0.920
15°C	0.938
40°C	0.930
Coefficient of expansion at	
10°C	0.9975
15.6°C	0.9985
21.1°C	1.0000
Viscosity (centipoise)	1.6314
Electrical conductivity (mho)	$45–48 \times 10^{-4}$

SOURCE: ARBUCKLE, W. S. 1973. Dairy Products. *In* Quality Control For The Food Industry, Vol. 2, 3rd Edition. A. Kramer and B. A. Twigg (Editors). Avi Publishing Co., Westport, Conn.

MILK, SPECIES

TABLE 2.M.35

COMPOSITION OF MILK OF DIFFERENT SPECIES

Component	Cow	Human	Goat	Sheep
Fat (%)	4.0	3.7	4.25	7.92
Protein (total %)	3.5	1.6	3.52	5.2
Casein (%)	2.9	0.9	2.8	3.6
Albumin (%)	0.5	0.7	0.7	1.3
Lactose (%)	4.9	7.0	4.2	4.8
Ash (%)	0.7	0.21	0.73	0.93
Specific gravity	1.032	1.029	1.035	1.034
Total solids (%)	13.1	12.5	13.0	19.29

SOURCE: ARBUCKLE, W. S. 1973. Dairy Products. *In* Quality Control For The Food Industry, Vol. 2, 3rd Edition. A. Kramer and B. A. Twigg (Editors). Avi Publishing Co., Westport, Conn.

MILK, TOTAL SOLIDS

The following data show the percentages of total solids in milk corresponding to the percentage of fat and Quevenne lactometer reading.[1]

To use the data, first find in the column at the extreme left the number corresponding to the percentage of butterfat, then in the same line with this and in the same column as the observed lactometer reading as given across the top will be found the percentage of total solids.

Per Cent	Quevenne Lactometer Reading at 15.56°C (60°F)																						
Fat	25.0	25.5	26.0	26.5	27.0	27.5	28.0	28.5	29.0	29.5	30.0	30.5	31.0	31.5	32.0	32.5	33.0	33.5	34.0	34.5	35.0	35.5	36.0
2.6	9.5	9.6	9.8	9.9	10.0	10.1	10.3	10.4	10.5	10.6	10.8	10.9	11.0	11.1	11.3	11.4	11.5	11.6	11.8	11.9	12.0	12.1	12.3
2.7	9.6	9.8	9.9	10.0	10.1	10.3	10.4	10.5	10.6	10.8	10.9	11.0	11.1	11.3	11.4	11.5	11.6	11.8	11.9	12.0	12.1	12.3	12.4
2.8	9.8	9.9	10.0	10.1	10.3	10.4	10.5	10.6	10.8	10.9	11.0	11.1	11.3	11.4	11.5	11.6	11.8	11.9	12.0	12.1	12.3	12.4	12.5
2.9	9.9	10.0	10.1	10.2	10.4	10.5	10.6	10.7	10.9	11.0	11.1	11.2	11.4	11.5	11.6	11.7	11.9	12.0	12.1	12.2	12.4	12.5	12.6
3.0	10.0	10.1	10.2	10.4	10.5	10.6	10.7	10.9	11.0	11.1	11.2	11.4	11.5	11.6	11.7	11.9	12.0	12.1	12.2	12.4	12.5	12.6	12.7
3.1	10.1	10.2	10.4	10.5	10.6	10.7	10.9	11.0	11.1	11.2	11.4	11.5	11.6	11.7	11.9	12.0	12.1	12.2	12.4	12.5	12.6	12.7	12.9
3.2	10.2	10.4	10.5	10.6	10.7	10.9	11.0	11.1	11.2	11.4	11.5	11.6	11.7	11.9	12.0	12.1	12.2	12.4	12.5	12.6	12.7	12.9	13.0
3.3	10.4	10.5	10.6	10.7	10.9	11.0	11.1	11.2	11.4	11.5	11.6	11.7	11.9	12.0	12.1	12.2	12.4	12.5	12.6	12.7	12.9	13.0	13.1
3.4	10.5	10.6	10.7	10.8	11.0	11.1	11.2	11.3	11.5	11.6	11.7	11.8	12.0	12.1	12.2	12.3	12.5	12.6	12.7	12.8	13.0	13.1	13.2
3.5	10.6	10.7	10.8	11.0	11.1	11.2	11.3	11.5	11.6	11.7	11.8	12.0	12.1	12.2	12.3	12.5	12.6	12.7	12.8	13.0	13.1	13.2	13.3
3.6	10.7	10.8	11.0	11.1	11.2	11.3	11.5	11.6	11.7	11.8	12.0	12.1	12.2	12.3	12.5	12.6	12.7	12.8	13.0	13.1	13.2	13.3	13.5
3.7	10.8	11.0	11.1	11.2	11.3	11.5	11.6	11.7	11.8	12.0	12.1	12.2	12.3	12.5	12.6	12.7	12.8	13.0	13.1	13.2	13.3	13.5	13.6
3.8	11.0	11.1	11.2	11.3	11.5	11.6	11.7	11.8	12.0	12.1	12.2	12.3	12.5	12.6	12.7	12.8	13.0	13.1	13.2	13.3	13.5	13.6	13.7
3.9	11.1	11.2	11.3	11.4	11.6	11.7	11.8	11.9	12.1	12.2	12.3	12.4	12.6	12.7	12.8	12.9	13.1	13.2	13.3	13.4	13.6	13.7	13.8
4.0	11.2	11.3	11.4	11.6	11.7	11.8	11.9	12.1	12.2	12.3	12.4	12.6	12.7	12.8	12.9	13.1	13.2	13.3	13.4	13.6	13.7	13.8	13.9
4.1	11.3	11.4	11.6	11.7	11.8	11.9	12.1	12.2	12.3	12.4	12.6	12.7	12.8	12.9	13.1	13.2	13.3	13.4	13.6	13.7	13.8	13.9	14.1
4.2	11.4	11.6	11.7	11.8	11.9	12.1	12.2	12.3	12.4	12.6	12.7	12.8	12.9	13.1	13.2	13.3	13.4	13.6	13.7	13.8	13.9	14.1	14.2
4.3	11.6	11.7	11.8	11.9	12.1	12.2	12.3	12.4	12.6	12.7	12.8	12.9	13.1	13.2	13.3	13.4	13.6	13.7	13.8	13.9	14.1	14.2	14.3
4.4	11.7	11.8	11.9	12.0	12.2	12.3	12.4	12.5	12.7	12.8	12.9	13.0	13.2	13.3	13.4	13.5	13.7	13.8	13.9	14.0	14.2	14.3	14.4
4.5	11.8	11.9	12.0	12.2	12.3	12.4	12.5	12.7	12.8	12.9	13.0	13.2	13.3	13.4	13.5	13.7	13.8	13.9	14.0	14.2	14.3	14.4	14.5
4.6	11.9	12.0	12.2	12.3	12.4	12.5	12.7	12.8	12.9	13.0	13.2	13.3	13.4	13.5	13.7	13.8	13.9	14.0	14.2	14.3	14.4	14.5	14.7
4.7	12.0	12.2	12.3	12.4	12.5	12.7	12.8	12.9	13.0	13.2	13.3	13.4	13.5	13.7	13.8	13.9	14.0	14.2	14.3	14.4	14.5	14.7	14.8
4.8	12.2	12.3	12.4	12.5	12.7	12.8	12.9	13.0	13.2	13.3	13.4	13.5	13.7	13.8	13.9	14.0	14.2	14.3	14.4	14.5	14.7	14.8	14.9
4.9	12.3	12.4	12.5	12.6	12.8	12.9	13.0	13.1	13.3	13.4	13.5	13.6	13.8	13.9	14.0	14.1	14.3	14.4	14.5	14.6	14.8	14.9	15.0
5.0	12.4	12.5	12.6	12.8	12.9	13.0	13.1	13.3	13.4	13.5	13.6	13.8	13.9	14.0	14.1	14.3	14.4	14.5	14.6	14.8	14.9	15.0	15.1
5.1	12.5	12.6	12.8	12.9	13.0	13.1	13.3	13.4	13.5	13.6	13.8	13.9	14.0	14.1	14.3	14.4	14.5	14.6	14.8	14.9	15.0	15.1	15.3
5.2	12.6	12.8	12.9	13.0	13.1	13.3	13.4	13.5	13.6	13.8	13.9	14.0	14.1	14.3	14.4	14.5	14.6	14.8	14.9	15.0	15.1	15.3	15.4
5.3	12.8	12.9	13.0	13.1	13.3	13.4	13.5	13.6	13.8	13.9	14.0	14.1	14.3	14.4	14.5	14.6	14.8	14.9	15.0	15.1	15.3	15.4	15.5
5.4	12.9	13.0	13.1	13.2	13.4	13.5	13.6	13.7	13.9	14.0	14.1	14.2	14.4	14.5	14.6	14.7	14.9	15.0	15.1	15.2	15.4	15.5	15.6
5.5	13.0	13.1	13.2	13.4	13.5	13.6	13.7	13.9	14.0	14.1	14.2	14.4	14.5	14.6	14.7	14.9	15.0	15.1	15.2	15.4	15.5	15.6	15.7
5.6	13.1	13.2	13.4	13.5	13.6	13.7	13.9	14.0	14.1	14.2	14.4	14.5	14.6	14.7	14.9	15.0	15.1	15.2	15.4	15.5	15.6	15.7	15.9
5.7	13.2	13.4	13.5	13.6	13.7	13.9	14.0	14.1	14.2	14.4	14.5	14.6	14.7	14.9	15.0	15.1	15.2	15.4	15.5	15.6	15.7	15.9	16.0
5.8	13.4	13.5	13.6	13.7	13.9	14.0	14.1	14.2	14.4	14.5	14.6	14.7	14.9	15.0	15.1	15.2	15.4	15.5	15.6	15.7	15.9	16.0	16.1
5.9	13.5	13.6	13.7	13.8	14.0	14.1	14.2	14.3	14.5	14.6	14.7	14.8	15.0	15.1	15.2	15.3	15.5	15.6	15.7	15.8	16.0	16.1	16.2
6.0	13.6	13.7	13.8	14.0	14.1	14.2	14.3	14.5	14.6	14.7	14.8	15.0	15.1	15.2	15.3	15.5	15.6	15.7	15.8	16.0	16.1	16.2	16.3

[1] The percentage of total milk solids may be calculated from the following expression: (A + B + 0.14) = % total solids; where A = % butter fat × 1.2; and B = Quevenne lactometer reading × 0.25.

SOURCE: LANGE, N. A. (EDITOR). 1967. Lange's Handbook of Chemistry, 10th Edition. McGraw-Hill Book Co., New York.

MINERALS, PLANT OR ANIMAL TISSUE

TABLE 2.M.36

SOME SPECIFIC ORGANIC COMPOUNDS OF MINERAL ELEMENTS KNOWN TO EXIST IN PLANT OR ANIMAL MATERIALS

Element	Compound		Contained in
	Name	Formula	
Potassium	Acid salt of tartaric acid	$KHC_4H_4O_6$	Grapes, cucumbers
	Salts of citric acid	$K_2HC_6H_5O_7$	Fruits, vegetables
	Salts of malic acid	$KHC_4H_4O_5$	Fruits, vegetables
Calcium	Acid salt of tartaric acid	$Ca(HC_4H_4O_6)_2$	Grapes
	Salts of phytic acid	$C_6H_6(CaPO_4)_6$	Bran of wheat, rye, etc.
	Calcium caseinate	Not known	Milk
Magnesium	Salts of phytic acid	$C_6H_6(MgPO_4)_6$	Bran of wheat, rye, etc.
	Chlorophyll	$C_{55}H_{72}N_4MgO_5$	Green plants
Iron	Hematin	$C_{34}H_{33}N_4FeO_5$	Hemoglobin of blood
Sulfur	Cystine	$C_6H_{12}N_2S_2O_4$	Proteins
	Glutathione	$C_{10}H_{17}N_3SO_6$	Animal tissues
	Insulin	$(C_{45}H_{69}N_{11}SO_{14})_n$	A hormone, secreted by Isles of Langerhans
	Thiamin chloride	$C_{12}H_{17}N_4SCl$	Yeast, pork muscle, etc.
	Allyl isothiocyanate	C_3H_5NCS	Mustard, onions
	Allyl sulfide	$(C_3H_5)_2S$	Garlic, radishes, cabbage, turnips, etc.
Phosphorus	Lecithins	*e.g.*, $C_{44}H_{88}NPO_9$	Egg yolk, brain, nerves, etc.
	Cephalins	*e.g.*, $C_{41}H_{80}NPO_8$	Blood
	Nucleic acids	*e.g.*, $C_{29}H_{45}N_5PO_{26}$	Nuclear tissue, *e.g.*, thymus
	Phosphoproteins	Not known	Egg yolk, milk
	Hexosemonophosphate	$C_6H_{11}O_5(H_2PO_4)$	Yeast, muscle
	Hexosediphosphate	$C_6H_{10}O_4(H_2PO_4)_2$	Yeast
	Phytic acid	$C_6H_6(H_2PO_4)_6$	Bran of wheat, rye, etc.
	Creatine phosphate	$C_4H_{10}N_3PO_5$	Muscle
Iodine	Thyroxine	$C_{15}H_{11}I_4O_4N$	A hormone secreted by thyroid gland
Copper	Hemocyanins	Not known	Respiratory protein in lower animals (*e.g.*, lobster)
Zinc	Carbonic anhydrase	Not known	Red blood cells

SOURCE: PETERSON, W. H., SKINNER, J. T., and STRONG, F. M. Elements of Food Biochemistry. Prentice-Hall, Englewood Cliffs, New Jersey.

MINERALS (MAJOR), FOOD

TABLE 2.M.37

PERCENTAGES OF MAJOR MINERAL ELEMENTS IN THE EDIBLE PORTION OF FOODS (FRESH BASIS)

Food	Calcium	Magnesium	Potassium	Sodium	Phosphorus	Chlorine	Sulfur
Almonds	.228	.275	.756	.024	.465	.037	.164
Apples, fresh	.011	.006	.116	.015	.011	.004	.004
dried	.053	.029	.557	.072	.053	.019	.019
Apricots, fresh	.028	.012	.370	.021	.038	.004	.006
dried	.146	.062	1.924	.109	.198	.021	.031
Asparagus	.020	.015	.200	.008	.055	.047	.051
Bananas	.008	.024	.412	.023	.029	.163	.013
Barley, entire	.058	.126	.495	.070	.343	.139	.152
Beans, dried	.164	.165	1.284	.189	.495	.007	.224
Lima, fresh	.030	.067	.606	.089	.128	.009	.068
dried	.078	.181	1.899	.282	.367	.025	.156
string or green	.066	.032	.288	.012	.050	.045	.024
Beef	.014	.032	.382	.066	.198	.056	.221
Beets	.023	.027	.235	.053	.040	.040	.017
Beet greens	.158	.097	.390	*	.040	*	.035
Brains	.008	.016	.269	.160	.385	.155	.130
Bread, white	.036	.034	.110	.517	.080	.602	.083
Broccoli	.146	.024	.352	.030	.086	.076	.126
Brussels sprouts	.033	.015	.375	*	.051	*	.098
Butter	.022	.002	.019	(a)	.004	(a)	.009
Cabbage	.054	.016	.217	.038	.031	.034	.074
celery	.040	.011	.400	.028	.041	.023	.013
Cantaloupe	.019	.016	.243	.048	.016	.048	.016
Carrots	.044	.020	.219	.050	.037	.035	.019
Cauliflower	.036	.023	.292	.048	.068	.038	.074
Celery	.098	.025	.320	.101	.041	.225	.021
Cheese, hard	.703	.031	.116	.900	.547	.972	.214
Cherries	.016	.012	.125	.015	.031	.004	.018
Chestnuts	.029	.048	.415	.037	.081	.010	.049
Chicken	.015	.047	.402	.054	.218	.034	.303
Chocolate	.067	.082	.400	.019	.285	.009	.114
Cocoa	.065	.192	.534	.060	.476	.050	.197
Coconut, fresh	.020	.040	.360	.040	.118	.120	.044
Collards	.205	.017	*	*	.078	*	*
Corn, field, mature	.013	.142	.300	.110	.341	.041	.124
sweet, fresh	.008	.047	.278	*	.117	*	.037
mature	.021	.121	.415	.148	.349	.050	.146
Cowpeas, dried	.060	.265	1.305	.036	.390	.019	.250
Crabs	.126	.117	.271	.366	.261	.570	.255
Cranberries	.013	.005	.056	.002	.008	.004	.008

TABLE 2.M.37 (*Continued*)

Food	Calcium	Magnesium	Potassium	Sodium	Phosphorus	Chlorine	Sulfur
Cream	.073	.006	.112	.031	.048	.067	.033
Cucumbers	.027	.020	.170	.026	.037	.028	.011
Currants, fresh	.036	.031	.208	.015	.044	.010	.021
dried	.180	.155	1.040	.075	.220	.050	.105
Dates	.065	.065	.580	.040	.059	.253	.048
Eel	.039	.018	.241	.032	.177	.035	.133
Eggplant	.018	.015	.260	.026	.037	.063	.020
Eggs	.059	.009	.149	.111	.166	.100	.233
Egg white	.012	.011	.149	.175	.014	.131	.211
yolk	.146	.013	.110	.078	.577	.067	.214
Figs, fresh	.060	.020	.205	.043	.021	.037	.017
dried	.207	.068	.709	.151	.074	.126	.060
Fish (all kinds)	.031	.024	.375	.064	.221	.137	.199
Flour, wheat, white	.021	.021	.137	.053	.096	.079	.155
Frog	.016	.024	.308	.055	.196	.040	.163
Garlic	.006	.008	.130	.009	.090	.004	.318
Goose	.012	.031	.406	*	.197	*	.326
Gooseberries	.020	.009	.150	.010	.036	.009	.015
Grapefruit	.019	.007	.164	.006	.035	.007	.005
Grapes	.040	.004	.267	.011	.018	.002	.009
Haddock	.022	.017	.334	.099	.137	.241	.225
Heart	.025	.035	.329	.102	.313	.204	.151
Honey	.004	.004	.051	.006	.015	.015	.003
Horseradish	.160	.028	.550	.094	.059	.013	.234
Kale	.340	.055	.486	.050	.089	.120	.160
Kidney	.014	.019	.240	.238	.233	.376	.148
Kohlrabi	.059	.052	.370	.050	.060	.050	.039
Lamb—See mutton							
Leeks	.091	.037	.380	.036	.049	.110	.056
Lemons	.030	.006	.152	.009	.018	.006	.012
Lentils, dried	.064	.082	.662	.754	.392	.062	.123
Lettuce	.047	.015	.256	.028	.032	.085	.014
Liver	.011	.021	.255	.021	.327	.091	.258
Lobster	.027	.022	.258	*	.395	*	*
Macaroni	.027	.038	.054	.010	.130	.077	.119
Milk, cow, fresh	.123	.019	.129	.047	.088	.114	.031
evaporated	.260	.038	.258	.094	.176	.228	.067
powder	.934	.118	.955	.348	.580	1.029	.229
goat	*	*	*	.026	.118	.163	*
human	.032	.005	.055	*	.017	.058	.142
Mushrooms	.008	.012	.280	.013	.083	.026	.025
Mustard greens	.194	.016	.330	.020	.053	.090	.142
Mutton	.020	.033	.260	.070	.212	.069	.187

(Continued)

TABLE 2.M.37 (*Continued*)

Food	Calcium	Magnesium	Potassium	Sodium	Phosphorus	Chlorine	Sulfur
Oatmeal (rolled oats)	.098	.143	.365	.072	.351	.027	.207
Oats, entire	.094	.150	.450	.168	.318	.089	.187
Onions	.040	.016	.200	.020	.039	.053	.065
Oranges	.036	.011	.177	.014	.027	.006	.011
Orange juice	.017	.014	.200	.006	.017	.008	.005
Parsnips	.060	.038	.396	.010	.094	.038	.025
Peaches, fresh	.007	.015	.174	.012	.019	.006	.005
dried	.041	.087	1.009	.070	.110	.035	.029
Peanuts	.111	.169	.706	.052	.394	.040	.276
Pears	.005	.005	.110	.010	.008	.004	.010
Peas, green	.033	.035	.259	.024	.124	.049	.035
mature	.091	.121	.943	.072	.369	.034	.178
Peppers, green	.016	.025	.270	.015	.039	.031	.030
red	.035	.013	.120	.006	.042	.014	.030
Persimmons	.010	.005	.170	.013	.019	.009	.011
Pike	.040	.031	.416	.029	.213	.032	.218
Pineapple	.014	.014	.230	.008	.033	.038	.003
Plums	.007	.010	.212	.003	.022	.002	.004
Pork	.014	.027	.415	.081	.262	.040	.216
Potatoes	.012	.027	.498	.030	.053	.048	.033
Prunes, dried	.047	.032	.845	.101	.068	.004	.024
Pumpkins	.029	.021	.198	.011	.026	.025	.016
Rabbit	.018	.029	.415	.047	.244	.051	.184
Radishes	.035	.014	.166	.083	.032	.056	.038
Raisins	.040	.017	.796	.120	.126	.068	.043
Raspberries	.021	.018	.141	.007	.013	.010	.012
Rhubarb	.066	.015	.392	.010	.044	.070	.008
Rice, entire	.079	.141	.334	.068	.310	.066	.121
polished	.013	.033	.046	.012	.113	.056	.114
Rutabagas	.054	.015	.210	.052	.035	.031	.069
Rye, entire	.104	.136	.477	.060	.333	.043	.152
Sardines, fresh	.900	.035	*	*	.550	*	*
Shrimps, dried, salted	.860	.327	.760	(a)	.480	(a)	.183
Soybeans, mature	.225	.287	1.693	.280	.633	.007	.269
Spaghetti—See macaroni							
Spinach	.098	.048	.416	.093	.053	.118	.027
Squash	.034	.006	.161	.011	.038	.018	.029
Strawberries	.035	.019	.205	*	.020	*	.013
Sugar beets	.030	.041	.440	.130	.049	.180	.021
Sweet potatoes	.024	.035	.381	.031	.039	.022	.014

TABLE 2.M.37 (*Continued*)

Food	Calcium	Magnesium	Potassium	Sodium	Phosphorus	Chlorine	Sulfur
Tomatoes	.012	.016	.277	.013	.033	.048	.017
Turkey	.023	.028	.367	.130	.205	.123	.234
Turnips	.042	.019	.193	.104	.032	.054	.048
Turnip greens	.317	.079	.300	.260	.040	.390	.051
Veal	.014	.030	.380	.086	.235	.073	.199
Venison	.010	.029	.336	.070	.249	.041	.211
Walnuts	.108	.132	.606	.013	.309	.030	.120
Watercress	.072	.010	.100	.031	.044	.059	.071
Watermelon	.008	.006	.071	.012	.010	.006	.005
Wheat, entire	.055	.163	.409	.106	.342	.088	.175
Wheat bran	.065	.420	1.252	.007	1.430	.042	.245
Yams	.041	.015	.290	.015	.042	.037	.013

(a) Variable.

SOURCE: PETERSON, W. H., SKINNER, J. T., and STRONG, F. M. Elements of Food Biochemistry. Prentice-Hall, Englewood Cliffs, New Jersey.

MINERALS (TRACE), FOOD

TABLE 2.M.38

TRACE ELEMENTS IN FOODS
(Fresh Basis)

Food	Milligrams per 100 grams of edible portion				Micrograms per 100 grams of edible portion
	Fe	Cu	Mn	Zn	Iodine
Abalone	*	.08	*	2.5	105.3
Almonds	4.1	1.2	1.2	1.9	*
Apples	.36	.1	.11	.07	6.6
Apricots, fresh	.54	.15	*	.04	*
dried	6.5	.32	.28	*	*
Artichokes	2.2	.32	.38	*	*
Asparagus	1.3	.11	.19	.34	6.9
Avocados	.58	.21	.29	*	*
Bacon	1.7	.41	.08	*	16.0 cooked
Bananas	.62	.21	1.1	.26	20.0
Barley, whole	8.9	1.2	1.6	2.3	9.1
pearled	1.3	.26	*	*	*
Bass	.26	.14	*	*	15.5
Beans, navy, dried	9.9	.98	1.9	3.1	4.8
kidney, dried	7.6	.92	1.6	5.2	1.8
Lima, dried	9.1	.86	1.1	*	*
Lima, fresh	3.2	.53	.6	1.5	*
string	1.3	.13	.37	.09	6.9
Beef, chuck	2.8	.1	*	*	*
heart	4.2	*	*	*	30.0
kidney	11.0	.11	1.	2.4	9.0
liver	7.4	2.0	.32	3.5	14.0
"lean"	4.2	.05	.02	1.5	3.5
loin	2.8	.1	*	*	*
steak	3.7	.11	.02	*	9.1
sweetbreads	6.	.08	.07	2.	*
Beets	1.3	.12	.62	.65	3.3
Beet greens	4.2	.12	1.2	.02	8.0
Blackberries	.89	.15	.57	*	*
Blueberries	.64	.11	3.4	*	*
Bluefish	.9	.23	*	*	26.0
Brazil nuts	3.6	1.3	.94	*	*
Bread, rye	1.8	.28	1.3	*	9.
white	.86	.25	.42	3.3	11.3
whole wheat	2.5	.33	3.2	*	11.
Broccoli	1.8	.20	.26	*	15.
Brussels sprouts	1.9	.11	.30	*	6.2
Butter	.18	.04	.04	*	8.6

TABLE 2.M.38 (*Continued*)

Food	Milligrams per 100 grams of edible portion				Micrograms per 100 grams of edible portion
	Fe	Cu	Mn	Zn	Iodine
Buttermilk	.28	.05	*	*	*
Butternuts	6.8	1.2	*	*	*
Cabbage	.66	.11	.21	.20	2.3
Calf's liver	5.2	6.3	.37	3.0	*
Cantaloupe	.58	.05	.05	.09	2.3
Carrots	.91	.12	.37	.35	4.4
Catfish	.36	.17	*	12.4	9.4
Cauliflower	1.2	.27	.15	.22	1.6
Celery	.68	.12	.17	.21	12.3
Celery cabbage	.6	.06	.12	*	*
Chard	3.7	.11	.8	*	11.0
Cheese, hard	1.	.09	.11	*	10.0
cottage	.98	*	.05	*	6.4
Cherries	.54	.13	.03	.15	.6
Chestnuts	2.2	.39	1.7	.19	*
Chicken	2.0	.54	*	.46	*
Chocolate	3.	2.1	3.2	2.6	*
Citron	5.	.57	*	*	2.1
Clams	4.3	0	*	3.6	124.0
Cocoa	8.2	2.4	3.5	2.6	*
Coconut, dried	2.8	.62	*	*	*
fresh	1.9	.53	1.3	.84	1.8
Codfish	.65	.55	.01	*	31.4
Cod-liver oil	*	*	0	.9	860.
Coffee, beans	5.4	1.3	*	.5	8.6
water extract	.46	*	*	*	4.
Collards	3.1	*	2.0	*	1.
Corn	3.1	.71	1.1	2.2	12.
Corn germ	25.	.91	3.6	9.4	*
Corn meal, yellow	1.1	.19	.22	1.8	*
Corn, sweet	.64	.08	.31	*	3.3
Cow peas	2.7	.17	1.5	*	5.7
Crab	2.	1.3	0.3	2.5	30.2
Cranberries	.57	.11	.38	*	3.3
Cream	.23	.15	*	*	5.7
Cucumber	.31	.13	.13	.12	.83
Currants, dried	3.3	.8	.31	*	*
fresh	.74	.13	*	.2	*
Dandelion greens	5.5	.17	.34	1.2	*
Dates	3.5	.23	2.6	.32	*

(Continued)

TABLE 2.M.38 (*Continued*)

Food	Milligrams per 100 grams of edible portion				Micrograms per 100 grams of edible portion
	Fe	Cu	Mn	Zn	Iodine
Duck	2.0	.46	.03	.34	*
Eggplant	.61	.09	.23	.28	.8
Eggs, hen	2.6	.17	.04	1.3	12.
Egg white	.1	.04	*	.01	6.8
Egg yolk	7.0	.25	.11	3.8	16.
Endive	2.9	.09	.23	.12	3.7
Escarole (chicory)	1.1	.14	*	.19	*
Figs, dried	3.5	.34	.34	.36	*
fresh	.42	.06	*	.12	1.5
Filberts	4.1	1.2	*	1.0	*
Fish, general	.61	.33	.02	.80	66.5 salt water 7.0 fresh water
Flounder	.73	.22	*	.82	30.9
Flour, buckwheat	1.2	.72	2.1	1.	*
graham or whole wheat	3.8	.47	4.3	1.9	*
rye	2.1	.43	2.	*	2.3
white	1.2	.14	.54	1.2	3.6
Garlic	*	.26	.46	.92	2.7
Goose	2.2	.33	.05	*	*
Gooseberries	.49	.10	.05	.1	*
Grapefruit	.28	.45	.01	*	1.3
Grapes	.80	.11	.08	.17	*
Grape juice	.3	.02	*	*	.9
Haddock	.71	.28	.02	*	83.4
Halibut	.97	.23	*	*	27.7
Hazelnuts	4.3	1.2	3.6	.97	1.4
Herring	1.1	.27	*	3.6	21.4
Hickory nuts	2.6	1.4	*	*	*
Hominy	.73	.18	.11	*	*
Honey	.75	.15	.03	*	*
Huckleberries—See blueberries					
Kale	3.1	.52	.86	*	*
Kidney—See beef, lamb					
Kohlrabi	.65	.14	.12	*	*
Kumquats	.55	.09	.07	*	*
Lamb	2.4	.42	*	*	*
chop	3.3	.42	.04	*	15.
kidney	12.	.31	*	1.9	*
Lard	.1	.02	*	*	9.3

TABLE 2.M.38 (*Continued*)

Food	Milligrams per 100 grams of edible portion				Micrograms per 100 grams of edible portion
	Fe	Cu	Mn	Zn	Iodine
Leeks	1.3	.17	*	.23	*
Lemons	.6	.04	.35	*	.5
Lemon juice	.15	.13	*	.17	5.2
Lentils (dried)	8.1	.59	3.3	5.4	*
Lettuce, head	.58	.11	1.0	.39	2.9
leaf	2.	.14	.82	.44	2.7
Liver—See beef, etc.					
Lobster	.67	1.5	.04	.24	80.1
Loganberries	1.4	.14	*	.45	2.7
Macaroni	1.3	.07	*	*	*
Mackerel	.98	.27	.02	*	16.3
Mangoes	.3	.04	*	*	1.6
Milk, cow's	.24	.04	.03	.36	3.8
Milk powder	.64	.34	*	*	32.
Molasses	8.2	1.4	.44	*	*
Mushrooms	1.5	1.	.12	.4	0.0
Muskmelon—See cantaloupe					
Mussels	*	.35	.46	4.5	80.2
Mustard greens	4.9	.12	1.2	*	5.4
Mutton, leg	4.8	.4	*	2.2	1.8
chop	1.	.16	*	*	*
liver	*	1.6	*	4.1	3.3
Nectarines	.46	.06	*	*	*
Oatmeal	4.	.38	3.3	*	4.2
Oats	7.2	1.4	5.	2.9	5.2
Okra	1.2	.14	.56	*	5.6
Oleomargarine	.3	.04	*	*	7.4
Olives	2.	.25	.12	.3	*
Onions	.68	.11	.38	1.3	3.6
Oranges	.42	.18	.03	.17	.6
Orange juice	.24	.05	*	0	1.5
Oysters	5.9	3.4	.13	46.	74.2
Oyster plant—See salsify					
Parsley	13.	.23	1.2	*	*
Parsnips	1.1	.12	.04	*	3.6
Peaches	.38	.07	*	.02	1.3
dried	6.3	.27	.68	*	*
Peanuts	2.2	1.1	.86	1.6	.7
Pears	.47	.16	.05	.16	.4

(Continued)

TABLE 2.M.38 (*Continued*)

Food	Milligrams per 100 grams of edible portion				Micrograms per 100 grams of edible portion
	Fe	Cu	Mn	Zn	Iodine
Peas, dried	5.5	1.1	1.8	4.0	*
fresh	2.	.23	.3	1.1	2.1
Pecans	2.6	1.4	3.5	*	*
Peppers, green	.49	.11	.15	.06	*
red	.6	*	.19	*	2.3
Perch	.74	.37	*	*	5.3
Pickerel	.8	.34	*	*	7.
Pike	.34	.17	*	*	*
Pimentos	*	.60	*	.23	.2
Pineapple	.38	.09	1.5	.28	16.
Pistachio nuts	7.9	1.2	.67	*	*
Plums	.71	.14	.11	.03	4.7
Pork, general	1.5	1.5	*	1.4	7.6
chop	2.	.31	.06	*	*
liver	25.	1.3	.38	.79	14.
Potatoes	1.3	.17	.41	.31	3.9
Prunes, dried	3.6	.29	.16	.05	.12
Pumpkin	.81	.07	.04	.21	1.4
Quinces	.85	.13	.04	*	*
Radishes	1.5	.22	.17	.16	6.4
Raisins	2.7	.23	.34	.20	*
Raspberries	.96	.16	.67	.35	*
Red snapper	.40	.16	.01	.28	31.
Rhubarb	.90	.09	.16	.16	26.
Rice, entire	4.4	.26	1.9	2.1	25.
polished	.93	.2	1.1	.22	5.1
Rutabagas	.64	.12	.12	.30	6.7
Rye, whole	4.2	.63	9.0	1.8	6.7
flour	2.1	.43	2.0	*	6.8
Salsify (oyster plant)	1.4	.3	.41	.22	*
Salmon	1.2	.23	*	.8	29.1
Sardines	3.3	.04	.26	.94	27.
Scallops	3.0	.23	3.9	*	47.5
Shrimp	2.7	1.2	.23	1.4	35.5
Sirup	1.5	.09	*	*	*
Soybeans	7.2	1.1	2.9	1.8	6.3
Soybean flour	7.4	1.2	*	*	*
Spinach	4.7	.11	.73	.62	41.
Squash, summer	.53	.08	.14	*	2.3
winter	.77	.10	.22	.21	*

TABLE 2.M.38 (*Continued*)

Food	Milligrams per 100 grams of edible portion				Micrograms per 100 grams of edible portion
	Fe	Cu	Mn	Zn	Iodine
Strawberries	.75	.07	.23	.09	*
Sweet potatoes	1.0	.15	.3	.23	2.4
Tangerines	.46	.09	.04	*	*
Tapioca	.96	.07	*	.04	*
Tea extract	.72	*	*	*	16.
Tomatoes	.50	.09	.13	.24	1.5
Trout	.89	.33	.06	1.0	3.1
Tuna fish	1.6	.5	*	*	30.5
Turkey	3.0	.17	.03	*	*
Turnips	.61	.08	.16	.08	7.5
Turnip greens	6.1	.08	1.9	.28	2.4
Veal, medium, lean	2.6	.20	.03	3.5	5.0
Vinegar	.47	.04	1.0	*	*
Walnuts, black	6.	3.2	*	*	*
English	2.6	.88	2.4	2.3	*
Watercress	4.4	.1	.42	.56	3.6
Watermelon	.41	.07	.02	*	*
Wheat	6.	.8	4.2	5.4	7.6
Wheat bran	13.7	1.3	10.2	12.	*
Wheat germ	24.0	2.7	13.	14.3	*
Whitefish	.42	.19	*	*	3.0
Yams	8.4	*	.05	*	4.7

SOURCE: PETERSON, W. H., SKINNER, J. T., and STRONG, F. M. Elements of Food Biochemistry. Prentice-Hall, Englewood Cliffs, New Jersey.

MINERALS, TRACE, LIMITS

TABLE 2.M.39

LIMITS FOR TRACE ELEMENTS IN FOODS

General Limits in Parts per Million

(*a*) Statutory—Lead 2 ppm
—Arsenic 1 ppm

(*b*) Recommended—Copper 20 ppm
—Zinc 50 ppm
—Tin 250 ppm (canned foods only)

Specific Limits in Parts per Million

Foods	Lead	Statutory Arsenic	Fluorine	Recommended Copper	Recommended Zinc
Agar	10				
Alcoholic cordials	1.0			7.0	
Alginic acid and alginates	10				
Apples	3.0				
Baking powder			15		
Beer	0.5			7.0	
Beer: black beer *or* black beer and rum		0.5			
Beverages: alcoholic	1.0	0.2			
Beverages: nonalcoholic: prepared from cider				7.0	
Beverages: nonalcoholic: ready-to-drink	0.2	0.1			
Beverages: ready-to-drink				2.0	5.0
Brandy	0.5				
Caramel	5.0				
Carrageen	10				
Chemicals	10				
Chemicals: excluding synthetic colorings		2.0			
Chemicals: for which arsenic limits are specified in the British Pharmacopoeia or the British Pharmaceutical Codex, excluding synthetic colors		2.0[1]			
Chemicals: for which lead limits are specified in the British Pharmacopoeia or the British Pharmaceutical Codex	—[2]				
Chicory: dried and roasted		4.0		30	
Cider	0.5			7.0	
Cocktails	1.0			7.0	
Cocoa nib, mass and liquor				70[3]	
Cocoa powder	5.0[4]			70[3]	
Coffee beans				30	
Colors				30[5]	
Colors: excluding caramel	20[5]				
Colors: excluding synthetic colors		5.0[3]			
Curry powder	20				
Dextrose: anhydrous or monohydrate	0.5				
Fats	0.5				
Finings and clearing agents		5.0			
Fish: canned	5.0				
Fish paste: canned	5.0				
Flavorings	10			30	
Flour: self-rising; containing a farinaceous substance and an acidic phosphate			3.0		
Frozen confections	0.5	0.5			
Fruit juices: concentrated	2.0				
Fruit juices: excluding lime or lemon	0.5				
Fruit juices: undiluted		0.5			
Gelatine: edible	5.0	2.0		30	100
Geneva	0.5				

TABLE 2.M.39 (*Continued*)

Foods	Lead	Statutory Arsenic	Fluorine	Recommended Copper	Zinc
Gin	0.5				
Glucose: liquid or solid; sulphated ash content greater than 1%	5.0				
Golden raising powder			15		
Herbs: dried	10	5.0			
Hop concentrates: excluding those for commercial brewing		5.0			
Hops: dried: excluding those for commercial brewing		2.0			
Ice cream		0.5			
Ice cream: excluding water ices	1.0				
Iron: reduced iron; used in the preparation of flour		5.0			
Lecithin	5.0				
Lemon juice	2.0				
Licorice: dried extract		2.0			
Lime juice	2.0				
Liqueurs	1.0			7.0	
Meat: canned	5.0				
Meat extract	5.0				
Meat paste: canned	5.0				
Milk beverages: ready-to-drink; prepacked	1.0				
Molasses: edible	5.0				
Mustard		5.0			
Mustard: ground	20				
Oils: edible	0.5				
Onions: dehydrated	10	2.0			
Pears	3.0				
Pectin: liquid	10	2.0		30	
Pectin: solid	50	5.0		300	
Perry	0.5				
Phosphates: acidic; for use as food ingredients			30[6]		
Protein: hydrolyzed	5.0				
Rum	0.5				
Seaweed: products derived from seaweed	10				
Soft drink concentrates: for use in the manufacture of soft drinks	2.5	0.5		20	
Soft drinks: concentrated	1.0	0.5		7.0	
Soft drinks: ready-to-drink	0.2				
Spices		5.0			
Spices: excluding ground	10				
Spices: ground	20				
Starch conversion products: sulphated ash content greater than 1%	5.0				
Sugar: raw: for the manufacture of refined sugar	5.0				
Sugar: white: refined; ash content less than 0.03%	0.5				
Sugars and sugar syrups: sulphated ash content greater than 1%	5.0				
Tea	10			150	
Tomato catsup				20	
Tomato juice	1.0			100[7]	
Tomato juice beverages				100[7]	
Tomato juice cocktails	1.0				
Tomato paste				100[7]	
Tomato paste: total solids between 15 and 25%	3.0				
Tomato paste: total solids greater than 25%	5.0				

(Continued)

TABLE 2.M.39 (*Continued*)

Foods	Lead	Statutory Arsenic	Fluorine	Recommended Copper	Zinc
Tomato powder				100[7]	
Tomato powder: total solids between 15 and 25%	3.0[8]				
Tomato powder: total solids greater than 25%	5.0				
Tomato purée				100[7]	
Tomato purée: total solids between 15 and 25%	3.0				
Tomato purée: total solids more than 25%	5.0			6	
Tomato relish				20	
Tomato sauce				20	
Vegetable juices: excluding tomato juice and tomato juice cocktail	0.5				
Vegetables: dehydrated or dried, excluding onions	5.0				
Water ices	0.5				
Whisky	0.5				
Wines				7.0	
Wines: excluding vintage port	1.0				
Yeast: brewers' yeast: for the manufacture of yeast products	10[9]	5.0[9]			
Yeast and yeast products				120[9]	
Yeast and yeast products: excluding brewers' yeast for the manufacture of yeast products	7.0[9]	2.0[9]			

[1]—Note: 2.0 ppm or the limit specified in the BP or the BPC, whichever is the higher.
[2]—Limit specified in the BP or the BPC.
[3]—Calculated on the fat-free substance.
[4]—Calculated on the dry fat-free substance.
[5]—Calculated on the dry coloring matter.
[6]—Of the acidic phosphate present.
[7]—Calculated on dried tomato solids.
[8]—See notes about lead regulations above.
[9]—Calculated on dry matter.

SOURCE: DAVIS, M. S. U. K. Regulations on Trace Elements in Foods. Food Trade Review, Vol. *36*, No. 3. Food Trade Press Ltd., London, England.

MOISTURE, DRYING

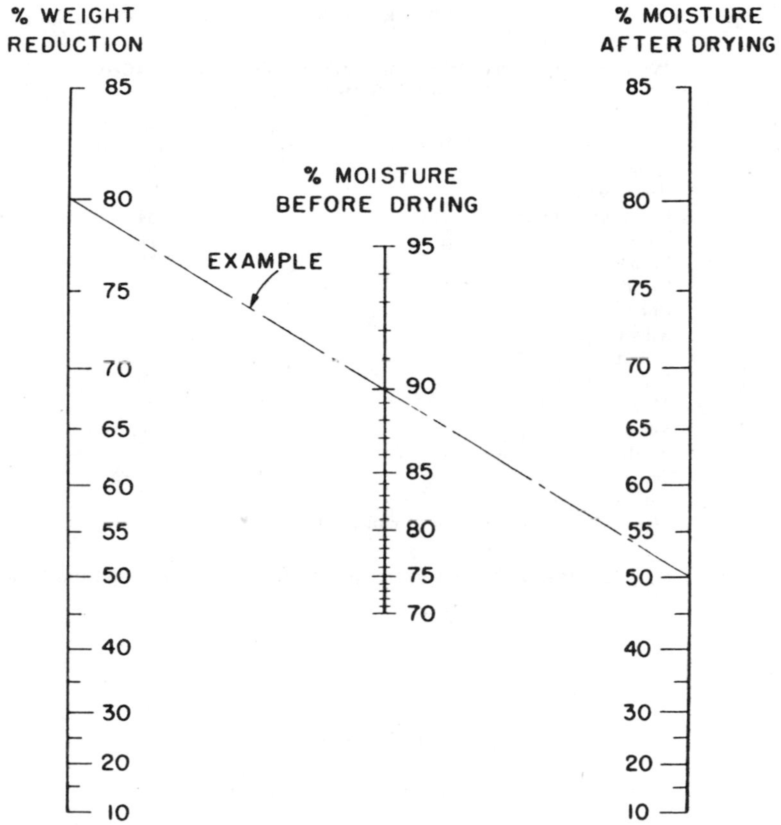

FIG. 2.M.4. MOISTURE AND WEIGHT RELATIONSHIP DUE TO DRYING

SOURCE: TRESSLER, D. K., VanARSDEL, W. B., and COPLEY, M. J. 1968. The Freezing Preservation of Foods, Vol. 3. Avi Publishing Co., Westport, Conn.

MOISTURE IN BIOLOGICAL MATERIALS

TABLE 2.M.40

WATER CONTENT OF SOME IMPORTANT BIOLOGICAL MATERIALS

Material	*Water per cent*
Human body	65
Brain, white matter	68
Brain, gray matter	84
Liver	76
Muscle	73
Blood	80
Bone	10–40
Saliva	99.5
Protoplasm	70–93
Fish, muscle	80
Milk	87
Vegetables	90
Fruits	85
Seeds	10–20
Larvae of clothes-moth	58
Wool, hair (food of larvae of clothes-moth)	4–9

SOURCE: PETERSON, W. H., SKINNER, J. T., and STRONG, F. M. Elements of Food Biochemistry. Prentice-Hall, Englewood Cliffs, N.J.

MOLD, FOOD

TABLE 2.M.41

MOLDS AFFECTING FOODS

Product	Organism	Common Name, or Type of Rot
Dairy products	*Alternaria sp.*	
	Oospora lactis	
	Cladosporium sp.	
	Penicilium sp.	
Stone fruits	*Sclerotinia fructicola*	Brown rot
	Rhizopus nigricans	Soft rot
	Cladosporium sp.	Green mold
	Penicillium sp.	Blue mold rot
	Aspergillus sp.	Black rot
	Botrytis sp.	Gray mold rot
Pome fruits	*Glomerella cingulata*	Bitter rot
	Physalospora cydoniae	Black rot
	Penicillium expansum	Blue mold rot
Tomatoes	*Colletotricum phomoides*	Anthracnose
	Alternaria sp.	Alternaria rot
	Oospora sp.	Machine mold
	Fusarium sp.	
	Phoma destructiva	
	Phytophthora sp.	Buckeye rot
	Rhizopus nigricans	
Other vegetable crops	*Sclerotiorum sp.*	Watery rot
	Rhizopus nigricans	Soft, mushy rot
	Colletotricum lindimuthianum	Anthracnose
	Diaportha batatis	Dry rot
	Sclerotium bataticola	Dry rot
	Botrytis sp.	Gray mold
	Rhizoctonia	Soil rot

SOURCE: KRAMER, A. and TWIGG, B. A. (EDITORS). 1970. Microanalytical and Microbiological Methods. *In* Quality Control For The Food Industry, Vol. 1, 3rd Edition. Avi Publishing Co., Westport, Conn.

MOLDS, MYCOTOXINS

TABLE 2.M.42

MYCOTOXINOGENIC MOLDS

Species	*Clinical effect*	*Susceptible species*
Group 1, Producers of well-defined mycotoxins		
Alternaria tenuis	ATA	man
A. sp.	haemorrhages	mouse
Aspergillus amstelodami	emaciation	poultry
Asp. candidus	cf. *Pen. citrinum*	
Asp. clavatus	haemorrhages	poultry
Asp. flavus	hepatic carcinoma	poultry, man
	tremors	mouse
	haemorrhages	swine
Asp. fumigatus	perirenal oedema	swine
Asp. glaucus	haemorrhages and diarrhoea	poultry
Asp. niger	cf. *Asp. flavus*	
Asp. ochraceus	hepatic injury	poultry
		rat
Asp. oryzae	hepatic necrosis	various
Asp. ostianus	cf. *Asp. ochraceus*	
Asp. parasiticus	cf. *Asp. flavus*	
Asp. ruber	cf. *Asp. flavus*	
Asp. terreus	cf. *Pen. citrinum*	
Asp. wentii	emaciation	poultry
Chaetomium globosum	haemorrhages and paralysis	rat
Cladosporium epiphyllum	ATA	man
Fusarium culmorum	anorexia	bovine
Fus. nivale	emaciation and gangrene	bovine
*Fus. roseum (*Syn. *Gibberella saubinetti)*	hepatic necrosis	swine
Fus. sporotrichioides	ATA	man
Gibberella zeae	oestromimetic response	swine
Mucor hiemalis	ATA	man
Penicillium brevicompactum	ATA	man
Pen. citreoviride	ascending paralyses	various
Pen. citrinum	haemorrhages and	poultry
	renal damage	mouse
Pen. cyclopium	tremors	mouse
Pen. islandicum	hepatic atrophia cirrhosis	various
Pen. puberulum	cf. *Asp. flavus*	
Pen. rubrum	haemorrhages and hepatic injury	swine
Pen rugulosum	cf. *Pen. citrinum*	
Pen. tardum	cf. *Pen. citrinum*	
Pen. variabile	cf. *Asp. flavus*	
Pen. viridicatum	renal damage	swine, rat
Pen. sp.	cf. *Asp. ochraceus*	
Pithomyces chartarum	angiocholecystitis	sheep
	facial oedema	bovine
Rhizopus sp.	cf. *Asp. flavus*	
Stachyobotrys atra	haemorrhages	horse
Group 2. Producers of less well-defined orally active toxins		
Asp. avenaceus, carneus, chevalieri, nidulans and *niveus*		
Cladosporium fragi		
Fusarium moniliforme		
Paecilomyces varioti (Syn. *Byssochlamys fulva)*		
Pen. oxalicum, piceum, purpurogenum, urticae		
Trichoderma lignorum		

SOURCE: MOSSEL, D. A. A. 1970. Microbial Spoilage of Proteinaceous Foods. *In* Proteins as Human Food. R. A. Lawrie (Editor). Avi Publishing Co., Westport, Conn.

MOST PROBABLE NUMBER

MPN index and 95% confidence limits for various combinations of positive and negative results when five 10-ml portions, five 1-ml portions, and five 0.1-ml portions are used.

TABLE 2.M.43

MOST PROBABLE NUMBER CALCULATIONS

Number of tubes giving positive reaction out of			MPN index per 100 ml	95% confidence limits	
5 of 10 ml each	5 of 1 ml each	5 of 0.1 ml each		Lower	Upper
0	0	1	2	<0.5	7
0	1	0	2	<0.5	7
0	2	0	4	<0.5	11
1	0	0	2	<0.5	7
1	0	1	4	<0.5	11
1	1	0	4	<0.5	11
1	1	1	6	<0.5	15
1	2	0	6	<0.5	15
2	0	0	5	<0.5	13
2	0	1	7	1	17
2	1	0	7	1	17
2	1	1	9	2	21
2	2	0	9	2	21
2	3	0	12	3	28
3	0	0	8	1	19
3	0	1	11	2	25
3	1	0	11	2	25
3	1	1	14	4	34
3	2	0	14	4	34
3	2	1	17	5	46
3	3	0	17	5	46
4	0	0	13	3	31
4	0	1	17	5	46
4	1	0	17	5	46
4	1	1	21	7	63
4	1	2	26	9	78
4	2	0	22	7	67
4	2	1	26	9	78
4	3	0	27	9	80
4	3	1	33	11	93
4	4	0	34	12	93
5	0	0	23	7	70
5	0	1	31	11	89
5	0	2	43	15	114
5	1	0	33	11	93
5	1	1	46	16	120
5	1	2	63	21	150
5	2	0	49	17	130
5	2	1	70	23	170
5	2	2	94	28	220
5	3	0	79	25	190
5	3	1	109	31	250
5	3	2	141	37	340
5	3	3	175	44	500
5	4	0	130	35	300
5	4	1	172	43	490
5	4	2	221	57	700
5	4	3	278	90	850
5	4	4	345	120	1000
5	5	0	240	68	750
5	5	1	348	120	1000
5	5	2	542	180	1400
5	5	3	918	300	3200
5	5	4	1609	640	5800

SOURCE: THATCHER, F. S. and CLARK, D. S. 1968. Microorganisms in Foods. University of Toronto Press, Toronto, Canada.

MOST PROBABLE NUMBER, BACTERIAL

TABLE 2.M.44

VALUES FOR THE MOST PROBABLE NUMBER (MPN) FOR 5 TUBES INOCULATED FROM EACH OF 3 SUCCESSIVE 10-FOLD DILUTIONS[1]

No. of Positive Tubes Observed			MPN of Inoculum of First Dilution	No. of Positive Tubes Observed			MPN of Inoculum of First Dilution
0	1	0	0.18	5	0	0	2.3
1	0	0	0.20	5	0	1	3.1
1	1	0	0.40	5	1	0	3.3
2	0	0	0.45	5	1	1	4.6
2	0	1	0.68	5	2	0	4.9
2	1	0	0.68	5	2	1	7.0
2	2	0	0.93	5	2	2	9.5
3	0	0	0.78	5	3	0	7.9
3	0	1	1.1	5	3	1	11.0
3	1	0	1.1	5	3	2	14.0
3	2	0	1.4	5	4	0	13.0
4	0	0	1.3	5	4	1	17.0
4	0	1	1.7	5	4	2	22.0
4	1	0	1.7	5	4	3	28.0
4	1	1	2.1	5	5	0	24.0
4	2	0	2.2	5	5	1	35.0
4	2	1	2.6	5	5	2	54.0
4	3	0	2.7	5	5	3	92.0
				5	5	4	160.0

[1] Example 1. Suppose 1 ml was inoculated from the 10^0, 10^{-1} and 10^{-2} dilutions of culture into 5 tubes for each dilution, and that the numbers of turbid tubes observed after incubation were 4-2-1. The table shows that the MPN = 2.6 per inoculum taken from the 10^0 dilution.

Example 2. Suppose the same results were obtained with tubes inoculated from 10^{-3}, 10^{-4} and 10^{-5} dilutions. The MPN is then 2.6 per inoculum taken from the 10^{-3} dilution, or 2.6×10^{-3} per inoculum of undiluted culture.

SOURCE: SULZBACHER, W. L. 1973. Meat and Meat Products. *In* Quality Control For The Food Industry, Vol. 2, 3rd Edition. A. Kramer and B. A. Twigg (Editors). Avi Publishing Co., Westport, Conn.

MUSCLE AND BODY WEIGHT

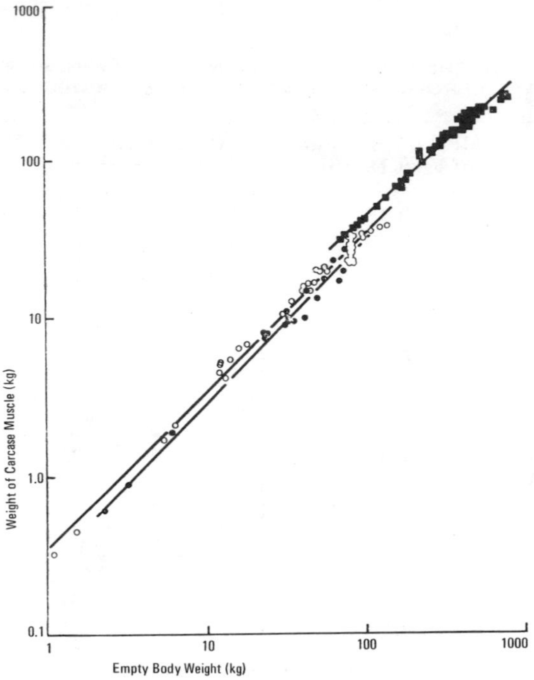

FIG. 2.M.5. WEIGHT OF DISSECTED MUSCLE IN A CARCASS COMPARED WITH EMPTY BODY WEIGHT FOR SHEEP (●), CATTLE (■), AND PIGS (○)

SOURCE: TRIBE, D. E. (EDITOR). Carcass Composition and Appraisal of Meat Animals. CSIRO, Australia.

MUSTARD, FRENCH

Prepared French Mustard

Distilled malt vinegar (4% acetic acid)	60 gal. (U.S.)
White mustard farina	60 lb
Salt	16½ lb
Ground turmeric	2½ lb
Ground cayenne pepper	1 lb
Ground cloves	1 lb
Ground pimiento	½ lb

SOURCE: BINSTED, R., DEVEY, J. D., and DAKIN, J. C. 1971. Pickle & Sauce Making, 3rd Edition. Food Trade Press, London, England.

MYOFIBRILLAR PROTEINS OF MUSCLE

TABLE 2.M.45

DESCRIPTION OF PROTEINS OF MUSCLE

Protein	Shape	Size	Molecular Weight	Makeup and Role
Myosin	Rod with enlarged "head," 57 percent α-helix	1600 Å long, 30Å diameter	About 500,000	Thick filaments of A band; major role in contraction-relaxation; contains about 7-SH groups per 10^5; made up of subunits, LMM + HMM, ratio 2:1; ATPase
Light meromyosin (LMM)	Rod, 76 percent α-helix, probably 2-stranded coiled-coil	850 Å × 15 Å	About 150,000	Major portion of "tail" of myosin molecule; noncovalently bonded to HMM so that two subunits are easily separated
Heavy meromyosin (HMM)	"Tadpole," 43 percent α-helix		About 200,000	ATPase; "head" and part of "tail" of myosin
$HMMS_1$	Globular, 27 percent α-helix	70 Å long	About 120,000	"Head" of myosin; contains four times as much proline as "tail" portion
$HMMS_2$	Rod, 2-stranded coiled-coil, 73 percent α-helix	450 Å long	About 60,000	"Tail" of HMM
Tropomyosin	Rod, 2-chain coiled-coil, 91 percent α-helix	400 Å × 20 Å	About 70,000	Located in Z line and thin filaments; possibly responsible for structure of Z line; highly charged molecule; resistant to denaturation; may act as core for double helix of F-actin
Actin-G form	Globular, about 30 percent helical	55 Å diameter	50,000–60,000	Aggregates into F-actin of thin filaments
Actin-F form	Double chain of spheres coiled together	Length approximates that of thin filaments	Many millions	Primary structural units of thin filaments; major role in contraction-relaxation; sensitive to Ca^{++} when complexed with tropomyosin and troponin, so may be trigger mechanism for contraction
Actomyosin (myosin B)				Complex of myosin +1 actin doublet, formed and broken in contraction-relaxation
Troponin A and B				Found in thin filaments; troponin A binds Ca^{++}
α-actinin				Influences cross linking of actin; found in Z line and in thin filaments adjacent to Z line
β-actinin			6500 to 300,000 depending on solvent used	May occur in thin filaments; may act by influencing natural filament length; deterrent to interaction among actin strands, which otherwise tend to form gel
M-protein				Located in middle of H-zone; accelerates lateral aggregation of myosin; holds thick filaments in position in A band

SOURCE: PAUL, P. C., and PALMER, H. H. 1972. Food Theory and Applications. John Wiley & Sons, New York.

N

NIACIN

TABLE 2.N.1

NIACIN CONTENT OF FOODS

	mg/100 g		mg/100 g
Peas	2.9	Brussels sprouts	0.9
Corn	1.7	Cauliflower	0.7
Potatoes	1.5	Tomatoes	0.7
Asparagus	1.5	Bananas	0.7
Lima beans	1.4	Carrots	0.6
Peaches	1.0	Watermelon	0.5
Artichokes	1.0	Oranges	0.4
Broccoli	0.9	Lettuce	0.3

SOURCE: WHITE, P. L. and SELVEY, N. (EDITORS). 1974. Nutritional Qualities of Fresh Fruits and Vegetables. Futura Publishing Co., Mt. Kisco, N.Y.

NIACIN, DAILY RECOMMENDATIONS

MILLIGRAMS

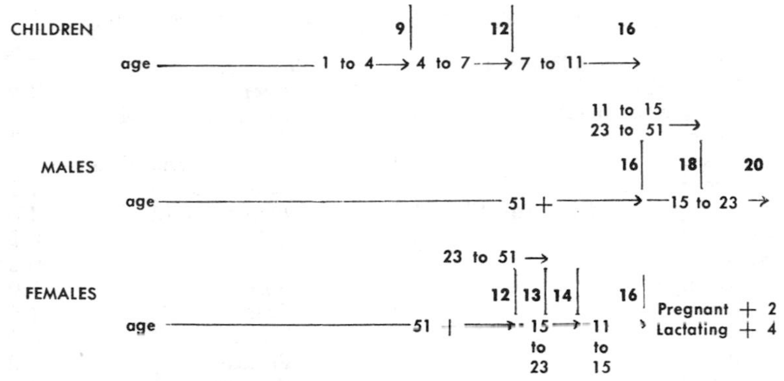

GOOD SOURCES†

MILLIGRAMS

Liver	3½ oz.	20.1
Lamb	3½ oz.	7.6
Veal	3½ oz.	7.2
Beef	3½ oz.	4.5
Pork	3½ oz.	4.4
Luncheon Meat	2 oz.	2.4.
Pork Sausage	2 oz.	2.4
Tuna Fish	3 oz.	10.1
Poultry	3½ oz.	8.1
Fish	3½ oz.	5.5
Peanut Butter	2 tblsp.	4.8
Potato	1 med.	1.8
Dried Fruit	½ cup	1.5
Peas	½ cup	1.3
Dried Beans and Peas	¾ cup	1.3
Corn	½ cup	1.0
Sweet Potato	1 med.	0.8
Banana	1 med.	0.7
Cereal	½ cup	0.7
Bread	1 slice	0.7

†Average nutrient content as food is served. (Note: $3^1/_2$ oz equals approximately 100 g.)

SOURCE: Lessons on Meat. (1974). National Live Stock and Meat Board, Chicago.

NICOTINIC ACID, FOOD

TABLE 2.N.2

NICOTINIC ACID CONTENT OF FOODS (mg per 100 G)

Cereals and Cereal Products		Beverages	
Bread, white	1.7	Beer	0.7
wholemeal	3.5	Chocolate	1.0
Maize	1.0	Tea	6.0
Oats	1.0	Vegetables and Nuts	
Rice, milled	1.5	Asparagus	1.2
parboiled and milled	3.8	Beans, broad	4.0
Eggs	0.07	Cabbage	0.3
Fish		Carrot	0.25
Herring	3.5	Kale	1.0
White	3.0	Peas	2.6
Fruits		Peanut	16.0
Apples	0.1	Potato	1.2
Tomatoes	0.6	Spinach	0.6
Meats		Sprouts	0.7
Beef	5.0	Swede	1.2
Heart	7.0	Yeast	
Kidney	6.0	Baker's moist	10.0
Liver	13.0	Brewer's moist	10.0
Tongue	6.0		
Milk	0.08		
Dried	0.7		
Dried, skimmed	0.8		

SOURCE: SINCLAIR, H. M. and HOLLINGSWORTH, D. F. 1969. Hutchison's Food and the Principles of Nutrition. Edward Arnold (Publishers), London, England.

NITRATE, MEAT CURING

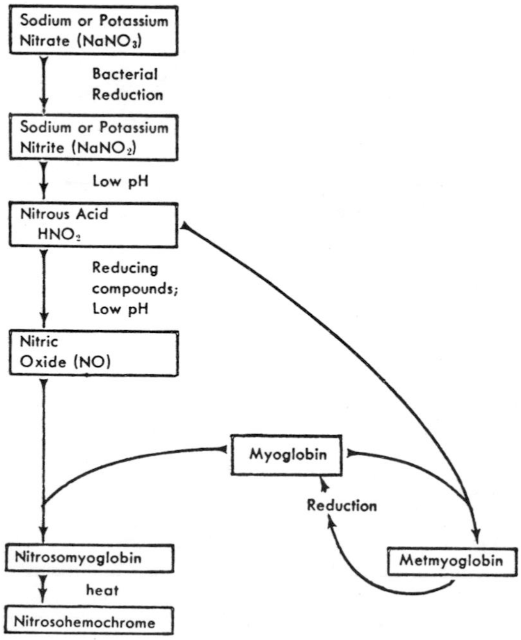

FIG. 2.N.1. NITRATE AND NITRITE PATHWAY IN MEAT CURING

SOURCE: OCKERMAN, H. W. 1975. Comparative Anatomy of Meat Animals. *In* Meat Hygiene. J. A. Libby (Editor). Lea & Febiger, Philadelphia.

NITRATE, VEGETABLES

TABLE 2.N.3

NITRATE CONTENT OF VEGETABLES GROWN IN 1963 AND 1964 AND VEGETABLES PURCHASED IN COLUMBIA, MISSOURI, STORES IN 1964[a]

	NO_3-N Content (% dry weight)		
Vegetable	Field Grown[b] (1963)	Field Grown[b] (1964)	Purchased[c] (1964 range)
Radishes (red)	0.53–1.2	0.8 –1.9	0.39–1.50
Beets (red)	–	0.19–0.78	0.09–0.84[d]
Turnips, tops	0.25–0.85	–	0.03–0.76
Carrots	0.02–0.05	0.02–0.05	0.0 –0.13
Lettuce, leaf	0.08–0.5	0.09–0.60	0.02–1.06
Spinach	–	0.09–0.24	0.07–0.66
Kale	0.30–1.02	–	–
Mustard	0.46–0.98	–	–
Sweet corn	–	–	0.01
Cabbage	–	–	0.01–0.09
Broccoli	–	–	0.01–0.09
Cauliflower	–	–	0.0 –0.31
Celery	–	–	0.11–1.12
Green beans	–	–	0.04–0.25
Squash	–	–	0.09–0.43
Cucumbers	–	–	0.0 –0.16
Tomatoes	–	–	0.0 –0.11

[a] From Brown and Smith (1967).
[b] Low values were from plants grown on soil receiving no nitrogen fertilizer, and high values were from plants grown in soil receiving 400 lb N/acre (450 kg/ha).
[c] Includes both locally grown and shipped-in supplies.
[d] Baby foods.

SOURCE: ANON. 1972. Accumulation of nitrate. Publ. *2038*, Agric. Board, Nat. Acad. Sci.—Nat. Res. Council.

NITRIC ACID SOLUTION

TABLE 2.N.4

VARIOUS STRENGTHS OF NITRIC ACID SOLUTIONS
Nitric Acid Solutions: Specification requires not <68% HNO_3 by wt. Sp gr = 1.4146 at 15°. 1 ml concd HNO_3 contains ca 0.96 gm HNO_3. Mix with H_2O and dil to 1 liter.

HNO_3 Strength Desired	Nitric Acid Required	
Grams per Liter	Grams	Ml
5	7.35	5.2
10	14.71	10.4
20	29.41	20.8
30	44.12	31.2
40	58.82	41.6
50	73.53	52.0
63	92.65	65.5
70	102.94	72.8
100	147.06	104.0
150	220.59	156.0
200	294.12	207.9
300	441.18	312.9

SOURCE: EDITORIAL BOARD, AOAC. 1975. Official Methods of Analysis of the Association of Official Analytical Chemists, 12th Edition. Association of Official Analytical Chemists, Washington, D.C.

NORMAL CURVE

Areas under the Normal Probability Curve
Area to the right of z (or to the left of $-z$), or the probability of a random value of z exceeding the marginal value

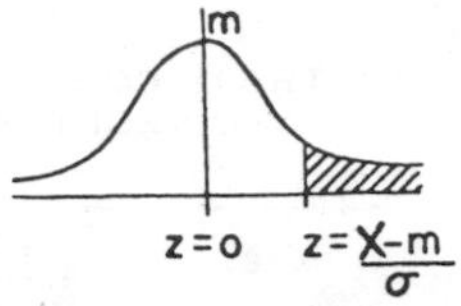

z	.00	.01	.02	.03	.04	.05	.06	.07	.08	.09
.0	.5000	.4960	.4920	.4880	.4840	.4801	.4761	.4721	.4681	.4641
.1	.4602	.4562	.4522	.4483	.4443	.4404	.4364	.4325	.4286	.4247
.2	.4207	.4168	.4129	.4090	.4052	.4013	.3974	.3936	.3897	.3859
.3	.3821	.3783	.3745	.3707	.3669	.3632	.3594	.3557	.3520	.3483
.4	.3446	.3409	.3372	.3336	.3300	.3264	.3228	.3192	.3156	.3121
.5	.3085	.3050	.3015	.2981	.2946	.2912	.2877	.2843	.2810	.2776
.6	.2743	.2709	.2676	.2643	.2611	.2578	.2546	.2514	.2483	.2451
.7	.2420	.2389	.2358	.2327	.2296	.2266	.2236	.2206	.2177	.2148
.8	.2119	.2090	.2061	.2033	.2005	.1977	.1949	.1922	.1894	.1867
.9	.1841	.1814	.1788	.1762	.1736	.1711	.1685	.1660	.1635	.1611
1.0	.1587	.1562	.1539	.1515	.1492	.1469	.1446	.1423	.1401	.1379
1.1	.1357	.1335	.1314	.1292	.1271	.1251	.1230	.1210	.1190	.1170
1.2	.1151	.1131	.1112	.1093	.1075	.1056	.1038	.1020	.1003	.0985
1.3	.0968	.0951	.0934	.0918	.0901	.0885	.0869	.0853	.0838	.0823
1.4	.0808	.0793	.0778	.0764	.0749	.0735	.0721	.0708	.0694	.0681
1.5	.0668	.0655	.0643	.0630	.0618	.0606	.0594	.0582	.0571	.0559
1.6	.0548	.0537	.0526	.0516	.0505	.0495	.0485	.0475	.0465	.0455
1.7	.0446	.0436	.0427	.0418	.0409	.0401	.0392	.0384	.0375	.0367
1.8	.0359	.0351	.0344	.0336	.0329	.0322	.0314	.0307	.0301	.0294
1.9	.0287	.0281	.0274	.0268	.0262	.0256	.0250	.0244	.0239	.0233
2.0	.0228	.0222	.0217	.0212	.0207	.0202	.0197	.0192	.0188	.0183
2.1	.0179	.0174	.0170	.0166	.0162	.0158	.0154	.0150	.0146	.0143
2.2	.0139	.0136	.0132	.0129	.0125	.0122	.0119	.0116	.0113	.0110
2.3	.0107	.0104	.0102	.0099	.0096	.0094	.0091	.0089	.0087	.0084
2.4	.0082	.0080	.0078	.0075	.0073	.0071	.0069	.0068	.0066	.0064
2.5	.0062	.0060	.0059	.0057	.0055	.0054	.0052	.0051	.0049	.0048
2.6	.0047	.0045	.0044	.0043	.0041	.0040	.0039	.0038	.0037	.0036
2.7	.0035	.0034	.0033	.0032	.0031	.0030	.0029	.0028	.0027	.0026
2.8	.0026	.0025	.0024	.0023	.0023	.0022	.0021	.0021	.0020	.0019
2.9	.0019	.0018	.0018	.0017	.0016	.0016	.0015	.0015	.0014	.0014
3.0	.0013	.0013	.0013	.0012	.0012	.0011	.0011	.0011	.0010	.0010
3.1	.0010	.0009	.0009	.0009	.0008	.0008	.0008	.0008	.0007	.0007
3.2	.0007	.0007	.0006	.0006	.0006	.0006	.0006	.0005	.0005	.0005
3.3	.0005	.0005	.0005	.0004	.0004	.0004	.0004	.0004	.0004	.0003
3.4	.0003	.0003	.0003	.0003	.0003	.0003	.0003	.0003	.0003	.0002
3.6	.0002	.0002	.0001	.0001	.0001	.0001	.0001	.0001	.0001	.0001
3.9	.0000									

SOURCE: AMERINE, M. A., PANGBORN, R. M., and ROESSLER, E. B. Principles of Sensory Evaluation of Food. Academic Press, New York.

NORMAL SOLUTIONS

TABLE 2.N.5

DECI-NORMAL SOLUTIONS OF SALTS AND OTHER REAGENTS

Atomic and molecular weights in the following table are based upon the 1965 atomic weight scale and the isotope C-12. The weight in grams of the compound in 1 cc of the following deci-normal solutions is found by dividing the H equivalent in the last column by 1000.

Name	Formula	Atomic or molecular weight	Hydrogen equivalent	0.1 Hydrogen equivalent in g
Acetic acid	$HC_2H_3O_2$	60.0530	$HC_2H_3O_2$	6.0053
Ammonia	NH_3	17.0306	NH_3	1.7031
Ammonium ion	NH_4^+	18.0386	NH_4	1.8039
Ammonium chloride	NH_4Cl	53.4916	NH_4Cl	5.3492
Ammonium sulfate	$(NH_4)_2SO_4$	132.1388	$\frac{1}{2}(NH_4)_2SO_4$	6.6069
Ammonium thiocyanate	NH_4CNS	76.1204	NH_4CNS	7.6120
Barium	Ba	137.34	$\frac{1}{2}Ba$	6.867
Barium carbonate	$BaCO_3$	197.3494	$\frac{1}{2}BaCO_3$	9.8675
Barium chloride hydrate	$BaCl_2{\cdot}2H_2O$	244.2767	$\frac{1}{2}BaCl_2{\cdot}2H_2O$	12.2138
Barium hydroxide	$Ba(OH)_2$	171.3547	$\frac{1}{2}Ba(OH)_2$	8.5677
Barium oxide	BaO	153.3394	$\frac{1}{2}BaO$	7.6670
Bromine	Br	79.909	Br	7.9909
Calcium	Ca	40.08	$\frac{1}{2}Ca$	2.004
Calcium carbonate	$CaCO_3$	100.0894	$\frac{1}{2}CaCO_3$	5.0045
Calcium chloride	$CaCl_2$	110.9860	$\frac{1}{2}CaCl_2$	5.5493
Calcium chloride hydrate	$CaCl_2.6H_2O$	219.0150	$\frac{1}{2}CaCl_2.6H_2O$	10.9508
Calcium hydroxide	$Ca(OH)_2$	74.0947	$\frac{1}{2}Ca(OH)_2$	3.7047
Calcium oxide	CaO	56.0794	$\frac{1}{2}CaO$	2.8040
Chlorine	Cl	35.453	Cl	3.5453
Citric acid	$C_6H_8O_7{\cdot}H_2O$	210.1418	$\frac{1}{3}C_6H_8O_7{\cdot}H_2O$	7.0047
Cobalt	Co	58.9332	$\frac{1}{2}Co$	2.9466
Copper	Cu	63.54	$\frac{1}{2}Cu$	3.177
Copper oxide (cupric)	CuO	79.5394	$\frac{1}{2}CuO$	3.9770
Copper sulfate hydrate	$CuSO_4{\cdot}5H_2O$	249.6783	$\frac{1}{2}CuSO_4{\cdot}5H_2O$	12.4839
Cyanogen	$(CN)_2$	26.0179	CN	2.6018
Hydrochloric acid	HCl	36.4610	HCl	3.6461
Hydrocyanic acid	HCN	27.0258	HCN	2.7026
Iodine	I	126.9044	I	12.6904
Lactic acid	$C_3H_6O_3$	90.0795	$C_3H_6O_3$	9.0080
Malic acid	$C_4H_6O_5$	134.0894	$\frac{1}{2}C_4H_6O_5$	6.7045
Magnesium	Mg	24.312	$\frac{1}{2}Mg$	1.2156
Magnesium carbonate	$MgCO_3$	84.3214	$\frac{1}{2}MgCO_3$	4.2161
Magnesium chloride	$MgCl_2$	95.2180	$\frac{1}{2}MgCl_2$	4.7609
Magnesium chloride hydrate	$MgCl_2{\cdot}6H_2O$	203.2370	$\frac{1}{2}MgCl_2{\cdot}6H_2O$	10.1623
Magnesium oxide	MgO	40.3114	$\frac{1}{2}MgO$	2.0156
Manganese	Mn	54.938	$\frac{1}{2}Mn$	2.7469
Manganese sulfate	$MnSO_4$	150.9996	$\frac{1}{2}MnSO_4$	7.5500
Mercuric chloride	$HgCl_2$	271.4960	$\frac{1}{2}HgCl_2$	13.5748
Nickel	Ni	58.71	$\frac{1}{2}Ni$	2.9356
Nitric acid	HNO_3	63.0129	HNO_3	6.3013
Nitrogen	N	14.0067	N	1.4007
Nitrogen pentoxide	N_2O_5	108.0104	$\frac{1}{2}N_2O_5$	5.4005
Oxalic acid	$H_2C_2O_4$	90.0358	$\frac{1}{2}H_2C_2O_4$	4.5018
Oxalic acid hydrate	$H_2C_2O_4{\cdot}2H_2O$	126.0665	$\frac{1}{2}H_2C_2O_4{\cdot}2H_2O$	6.3033

(Continued)

TABLE 2.N.5 (*Continued*)

Name	Formula	Atomic or molecular weight	Hydrogen equivalent	0.1 Hydrogen equivalent in g
Oxalic acid anhydride	C_2O_3	72.0205	$\frac{1}{2}C_2O_3$	3.6010
Phosphoric acid	H_3PO_4	97.9953	$\frac{1}{3}H_3PO_4$	3.2665
Potassium	K	39.102	K	3.9102
Potassium bicarbonate	$KHCO_3$	100.1193	$KHCO_3$	10.0119
Potassium carbonate	K_2CO_3	138.2134	$\frac{1}{2}K_2CO_3$	6.9106
Potassium chloride	KCl	74.5550	KCl	7.4555
Potassium cyanide	KCN	65.1199	KCN	6.5120
Potassium hydroxide	KOH	56.1094	KOH	5.6109
Potassium oxide	K_2O	94.2034	$\frac{1}{2}K_2O$	4.7102
Potassium permanganate for Co estimation	$KMnO_4$	158.0376	$\frac{1}{6}KMnO_4$	2.6339
Potassium permanganate for Mn estimation	$KMnO_4$	158.0376	$\frac{1}{3}KMnO_4$	5.2678
Potassium tartrate	$K_2H_4C_4O_6$	226.2769	$\frac{1}{2}K_2H_4C_4O_6$	11.3139
Silver	Ag	107.87	Ag	10.787
Silver nitrate	$AgNO_3$	169.8749	$AgNO_3$	16.9875
Sodium	Na	22.9898	Na	2.2990
Sodium bicarbonate	$NaHCO_3$	84.0071	$NaHCO_3$	8.4007
Sodium carbonate	Na_2CO_3	105.9890	$\frac{1}{2}Na_2CO_3$	5.2995
Sodium chloride	NaCl	58.4428	NaCl	5.8443
Sodium hydroxide	NaOH	39.9972	NaOH	3.9997
Sodium oxide	Na_2O	61.9790	$\frac{1}{2}Na_2O$	3.0990
Sodium sulfide	Na_2S	78.0436	$\frac{1}{2}Na_2S$	3.9022
Succinic acid	$H_2C_4H_4O_4$	118.0900	$\frac{1}{2}H_2C_4H_4O_4$	5.9045
Sulfuric acid	H_2SO_4	98.0775	$\frac{1}{2}H_2SO_4$	4.9039
Sulfur trioxide	SO_3	80.0622	$\frac{1}{2}SO_3$	4.0031
Tartaric acid	$C_4H_6O_6$	150.0888	$\frac{1}{2}C_4H_6O_6$	7.5044
Zinc	Zn	65.37	$\frac{1}{2}$Zn	3.269
Zinc sulfate	$ZnSO_4 \cdot 7H_2O$	287.5390	$\frac{1}{2}ZnSO_4 7 \cdot H_2O$	14.3769

SOURCE: WEAST, R. C. (EDITOR). 1974–1975. Handbook of Chemistry and Physics, 55th Edition. CRC Press, Cleveland. Reprinted with the permission of CRC Press.

NUT, GRADES

TABLE 2.N.6

U.S. GRADE STANDARDS FOR NUTS

Kind of Nut	Grade	Description of quality
In-shell		
Almonds	U.S. No. 1	Best quality.
Brazils	"	" "
English walnuts	"	" "
Filberts	"	" "
Pecans	"	" "
Mixed nuts (almonds, brazils, filberts, pecans, and English walnuts).	U.S. Extra Fancy	Best quality and largest sizes. At least 10 percent but not over 40 percent of each kind in the mixture.
	U.S. Fancy	Same quality and mixture, but permits smaller sizes of some kinds.
Shelled, raw		
Almonds	U.S. Fancy	Best quality.
	U.S. Extra No. 1	Almost the best—permits a few doubles and broken.
	U.S. No. 1	Very good quality—permits more doubles and broken.
English walnuts	U.S. No. 1	Best quality.
Pecans	U.S. No. 1	" "
Peanut butter	U.S. Grade A	" "

SOURCE: Food For Us All. Yearbook of Agriculture, 1969. USDA.

NUTRIENTS IN CROPS

TABLE 2.N.7

APPROXIMATE POUNDS PER ACRE OF NUTRIENTS CONTAINED IN PORTION OF THE SIZE OF CROP
(Will Vary with Variety, Soil Type, Season and Fertility of Soil)

Crop: Kind	Crop: Part	Acre Yield: Bushels	Acre Yield: Tons	Nitrogen	Phosphorus as P_2O_5	Potassium as K_2O	Calcium	Magnesium	Sulfur	Boron	Copper	Manganese	Zinc
						Grains							
Barley	Grain	40	0.96	35	15	10	1	2	3	0.04	0.03	0.03	0.06
	Straw		1	15	5	30	8	2	4	—	.01	.32	.05
Corn	Grain	100	3.5	90	36	26	10	14	9	.08	.04	.06	.10
	Stover		3	67	24	96	18	12	7	—	.03	1.00	.20
Oats	Grain	80	1.28	50	20	15	2	3	5	—	.03	.12	.05
	Straw		2	25	15	80	8	8	9	—	.03	—	.29
Rice	Rough grain	100	2.25	60	24	12	4	5	4	—	.01	.10	.08
	Straw		3	36	12	80	11	6	—	—	—	1.89	—
Rye	Grain	30	0.84	35	10	10	2	3	7	—	.02	.22	.03
	Straw		1.5	15	8	25	8	2	3	—	.01	.14	.07
Sorghum	Grain	80	2	65	35	20	4	5	5	—	.01	.04	.04
	Straw		3	85	25	125	29	18	—	—	—	—	—
Wheat	Grain	40	1.2	50	25	15	1	6	3	.04	.03	.09	.14
	Straw		1.5	20	5	35	6	3	5	—	.01	.16	.05
						Hay							
Alfalfa[1]			4	180	40	180	112	21	19	.06	.06	.44	.42
Bluegrass			2	60	20	60	16	7	5	—	.02	.30	.08
Cowpea[1]			2	120	25	80	55	15	13	.21	—	.65	—
Peanut[1]			2	91	22	83	39	15	14	—	—	.20	—
Red Clover[1]			2	80	20	80	55	14	6	.05	.03	.44	.28
Soybean[1]			2	90	20	50	40	18	10	.01	.04	.46	.15
Timothy			2	48	20	76	14	5	4	—	.02	.25	.16
						Fruits and Vegetables							
Apples		500	12	30	10	45	8	5	10	.01	.03	.03	.03
Beans, dry		30	0.9	75	25	25	2	2	5	.12	.02	.03	.06
Cabbage Heads			20	130	35	130	20	8	44	.09	.04	.10	.08
Onions			15	90	40	80	22	4	16	—	.06	.16	.62
Oranges		(800-70-lb. boxes)	28	85	30	140	33	12	9	.14	.20	.06	.24
Peaches		600	14.4	35	20	65	4	8	2	.05	—	—	.01
Potatoes Tubers		400	12	80	30	150	3	6	6	.05	.04	.09	.05
Spinach			5	50	15	30	12	5	4	—	.02	.10	.10
Sweet Potatoes Roots		300	8.25	45	15	75	4	9	6	.05	.03	.06	.03
Tomatoes Fruit			20	120	40	160	7	11	14	.14	.07	.13	.16
						Other Crops							
Cotton	Seed & lint		.75	40	20	15	2	4	2	—	.06	.11	.32
	Stalks, leaves & burs		1	35	10	35	28	8	—	—	—	—	—
Peanuts[1]	Nuts		1	68	8	11	1	2	4	.03	.02	.01	—
Soybeans[1]	Grain	40	1.2	150	35	55	7	7	4	—	.04	.05	.04
Sugar Beets	Roots		20	80	27	66	44	32	13	—	.04	1.00	—
Sugar Cane			30	96	54	270	28	24	24	—	—	—	—
Tobacco	Leaves		1	75	15	120	75	18	14	.05	.03	.55	.07

[1] Legumes normally get the greater part of their nitrogen from the air. Computed from data in USDA Misc. Publ. *369*, *Morrison's Feed and Feeding*, from a Spec. USDA rept. by Lowe. USDA Tech. Bull. *1009*, *Our Land and Its Care*. American Potash Institute, and other sources, by A. L. Mehring.

SOURCE: GARMAN, W. H. (EDITOR). The Fertilizer Handbook, 2nd Edition. Fertilizer Institute.

O

OIL MEALS COMPOSITION

TABLE 2.O.1

COMPOSITION OF THE COMMON OIL MEALS

Feeding Stuff	Dry Matter (%)	Ash (%)	Crude Protein (%)	Crude Fiber (%)	Crude Lipide (%)	N-free Extract (%)
Soybean meal (solvent process)	90.4	6.1	45.7	5.9	1.3	31.4
Cottonseed meal (hydraulic) (Texas analyses)	92.6	5.6	42.1	10.5	6.1	28.3
Linseed meal (solvent process)	91.0	5.8	36.6	9.3	1.0	38.3
Peanut meal (hydraulic) (hulls)	92.3	4.8	41.1	15.0	6.6	24.8
Safflower (hydraulic) (hulled)	90.5	6.4	42.5	8.5	6.7	26.4
Sunflower (hydraulic) (hulled)	94.3	5.9	49.5	5.4	4.9	28.6

SOURCE: MALLETTE, M. F., ALTHOUSE, P. M., and CLAGETT, C. O. Biochemistry of Plants and Animals. John Wiley & Sons, New York.

OIL OR FAT, CHARACTERISTICS

TABLE 2.O.2

CHARACTERISTICS OF OIL OR FAT

Oil or Fat	Identifiable Characteristics
Babassu kernel oil	High saponification value, low iodine value, contains lauric acid
Castor oil	Solubility characteristics, high hydroxyl value, high viscosity
Coconut oil	High saponification value—low iodine value—contains lauric acid
Cottonseed oil	Positive Halphen test—not reliable for heated or hydrogenated oils
Kapok oil	Positive Besson test
Linseed oil	Bromo-derivatives of unsaturated fatty acid
Olive oil	Contains squalene
Peanut oil	Positive Bellier test—contains arachidic acid
Perilla oil	Bromo-derivatives of unsaturated fatty acids
Rape seed oil	Contains erucic acid
Ravison oil	Resembles rapeseed oil—contains erucic acid
Sesame oil	Positive Baudouin and Villavecchia tests—not destroyed by hydrogenation
Soybean oil	Contains linolenic acid but no reliable specific tests available
Teaseed oil	Positive Fitelson test
Butterfat	Contains butyric and other low molecular weight fatty acids
Fish oils	Contain squalene, also bromo-derivatives of unsaturated fatty acids

SOURCE: MAHLENBACHER, C. V. The Analysis of Fats and Oils. Garrard Press, Champaign, Illinois.

OIL, TRIGLYCERIDE MOLE PERCENT COMPOSITION

TABLE 2.O.3

ANALYSIS OF GLYCERIDES
(Triglyceride Composition (Mole %) of Oils)

Triglyceride	Corn Oil	Cottonseed Oil	Groundnut Oil (Argentine)	Safflowerseed Oil	Sesame Oil	Soyabean Oil	Sunflowerseed Oil
0 double bonds							
SSS		0.5					
1 double bond							
SOS	2.5	4.5	2.3	1.7	3.1	1.1	0.3
SSO		0.8	0.7			0.3	0.2
2 double bonds							
SOO	6.0	4.8	8.7	1.2	8.1	2.9	2.3
OSO	0.3	0.3	0.8			0.4	0.1
SLS	5.0	12.4	5.3	2.2	3.4	2.8	2.2
SSL	0.1	0.6	0.6			0.6	0.3
3 double bonds							
OOO	4.0	0.8	6.2	0.2	7.7	1.5	1.3
SOL	6.6	9.4	5.0			4.1	4.4
SLO	7.0	8.4	15.7	8.1	16.7	5.0	5.0
OSL	0.7	0.6	1.0			0.4	0.5
SSLe						0.1	
SLeS							
4 double bonds							
OOL	8.4	4.1	7.8	1.7	21.8	6.7	8.1
OLO	4.2	1.6	8.7			2.5	3.1
SLL	13.8	22.5	10.7	20.1	9.2	13.9	13.2
LSL	0.4	1.1	1.2			0.9	1.3
SOLe						0.2	
SLeO	0.1					0.2	
OSLe							
5 double bonds							
OLL	15.3	6.4	17.8	21.3	19.8	13.5	20.4
LOL	4.8	6.5	2.2			5.1	8.4
OOLe	0.3		0.2			0.2	
OLeO						0.6	
SLeL		0.4				0.4	
SLLe	1.0		0.7			0.3	
LSLe						0.5	
6 double bonds							
LLL	16.3	13.0	3.9	43.5	10.2	35.8	28.1
Remaining with 6 or more double bonds	3.2	1.3	0.5				0.8

SOURCE: BOEKENOOGEN, H. A. 1968. Oils, Fats and Fat Products, Vol. 2. John Wiley & Sons, New York.

OILS AND FATS COMPOSITION

TABLE 2.0.4

COMPOSITION OF THE EDIBLE PORTION (EP) AND REFUSE IN THE MATERIAL AS PURCHASED (AP)

Item No.	Commodity and Description	Water	Protein	Fat	Carbohydrate Total (By Dif)	Carbohydrate Fiber	Ash	Cal (No./100 g)	Notes	Refuse in AP (%)
				Percent of Edible Portion						
	Vegetable									
277	Oils, pure			100	0			884	Cottonseed, sesame, coconut, olive, etc.	0
278	Shortening (hardened)			100	0			884		0
279	Margarine (either vegetable or animal)	15.5	0.6	81	0.4		2.5	720		0
	Marine									
280	Liver oils, body oils			100	0			902		0
	Animal fats									
281	Butter	15.5	0.6	81	0.4		2.5	716		0
282	Ghee			100	0			879	Butter, "fat basis"	0
283	Lard, leaf fat	5	2	93	0		0.1	847		0
284	Pork fat, other	12	4	84	0		0.2	775		0
285	Pork fat, all	8	3	89	0		0.1	816	Fat trimmed from pork carcasses	0
286	Suet, tallow (kidney fat)	5	2	93	0		0.1	847	Fat trimmed from beef, veal, mutton or lamb	0
287	Meat fat, rendered			100	0			902	Lard or tallow, "fat basis"	0

SOURCE: CHATFIELD, C. Food Composition Tables for International Use. FAO, United Nations, Rome.

OILS, SEED AND FRUIT

TABLE 2.0.5

OIL CONTENT AND COMPOSITION OF SOME SEEDS AND FRUITS

Tissue and Species	Fat, %, Dry-weight Basis	Lauric	My-ristic	Pal-mitic	Stearic	Oleic	Lin-oleic	Lin-olenic	α-Eleo-stearic	Ricin-oleic
Nut or seed										
Peanut	45			8.3	3.1	56.0	26.0			
Cotton (whole seed)	20		0.5	21.9	1.9	30.7	44.9			
Soybean	18		0.1	9.8	2.4	28.4	50.7	6.5		
Flaxseed	38		0.2	5.4	3.5	19.0	24.0	47.0		
Palm	50		1.5	42.9	4.7	39.8	11.3			
Coconut (copra)	67	46.4	18.0	9.0	1.0	7.6	1.6			
Castor bean	48					7.4	3.1			87.0
Tung (kernel)	58			5.5		4.0	8.5		82.0	
Seed germ										
Corn	35		0.5	10.0	3.5	33.0	53.0			
Fruit										
Olive	30–65		1.2	15.6	2.0	64.6	15.0			

SOURCE: MALLETTE, M. F., ALTHOUSE, P. M., and CLAGETT, C. O. Biochemistry of Plants and Animals. John Wiley & Sons, New York.

ORANGE ESSENCE OILS

TABLE 2.0.6

PHYSICOCHEMICAL PROPERTIES OF ORANGE ESSENCE OILS

Property	Max	Min	Avg
Sp gr 25°C/25°C	0.8428	0.8403	0.8415
Ref ind η_D^{20}	1.4725	1.4721	1.4723
Opt rot α_D^{25}	+99.16	+97.68	+98.42
Aldehyde (%)	1.86	1.28	1.57
Evap res (%)	1.29	0.34	0.81
Acid No.	0.22	0.11	0.16
Free acid (%)	0.06	0.03	0.04
Ester No. before acetylation	3.08	2.94	3.00
% ester before acetylation	1.08	1.03	1.05
Ester No. after acetylation	6.50	5.43	6.06
% ester after acetylation	2.27	1.90	2.12
Free alcohol (%)	0.97	0.64	0.84
Total alcohol (%)	1.78	1.49	1.66

SOURCE: KESTERSON, J. W., HENDRICKSON, R., and BRADDOCK, R. J. 1971. Florida Citrus Oils. Florida Agric. Exp. Sta. Tech. Bull. *749*.

ORANGE OIL COMPOSITION

TABLE 2.0.7

CHEMICAL COMPOSITION OF COLD-PRESSED VALENCIA ORANGE OIL

TERPENES:

α-thujene
α-pinene
camphene
2,4-p-menthadiene
sabinene
myrcene
δ-3-carene
α-phellandrene
α-terpinene
d-limonene
β-terpinene
p-cymene
α-terpinolene
α-β-cubebene
α-β-copaene
β-elemene
caryophyllene
farnesene
α-β-humulene
valencene
δ-cadinene

ALDEHYDES:

formaldehyde
acetaldehyde
n-hexanal
n-heptanal
n-octanal
n-nonanal
n-decanal
n-undecanal
n-dodecanal
citral { neral, geranial
citronellal
α-sinensal
β-sinensal
trans-hexen-2-al-1
dodecene-2-al-1
furfural
perillyldehyde
Aldehyde A
B
C
D
E

OXIDES:

trans-limonene oxide
cis-limonene oxide

ALCOHOLS:

methyl alcohol
ethyl alcohol
amyl alcohol
n-octanol
n-decanol
linalool
citronellol
α-terpineol
n-nonanol
trans-carveol
geraniol
nerol
heptanol
undecanol
dodecanol
elemol
cis-trans-2,8-p-menthadiene-1-ol
cis-carveol
1-p-methene-9-ol
1,8-p-menthadiene-9-ol
8-p-methene-1,2-diol
isopulegol
borneol
methyl heptenol
hexanol-1
terpinen-4-ol

ESTERS:

perillyl acetate
n-octyl acetate
bornyl acetate
geranyl formate
terpinyl acetate
linalyl acetate
linalyl propionate
geranyl acetate
nonyl acetate
decyl acetate
neryl acetate
citronellyl acetate
ethyl isovalerate
geranyl butyrate
1,8-p-menthadiene-9-yl-acetate

ACIDS:

formic
acetic
caprylic
capric

KETONES:

carvone
methyl heptenone
α-ionone
acetone
piperitenone
6-methyl-5-hepten-2-one
nootkatone

α,β-DIALKYL ACROLEINS:

α-hexyl-β-heptyl acrolein
α-hexyl-β-octyl acrolein
α-heptyl-β-heptyl acrolein
α-octyl-β-heptyl acrolein
α-hexyl-β-nonyl acrolein
α-octyl-β-octyl acrolein
α-heptyl-β-nonyl acrolein

PARAFIN WAXES:

n-$C_{21}H_{44}$
2-methyl-$C_{21}H_{43}$
n-$C_{22}H_{46}$
2-methyl-$C_{22}H_{45}$
n-$C_{23}H_{48}$
3-methyl-$C_{23}H_{47}$
n-$C_{24}H_{30}$
2-methyl-$C_{24}H_{49}$
n-$C_{25}H_{52}$
3-methyl-$C_{25}H_{51}$
n-$C_{26}H_{54}$
2-methyl-$C_{26}H_{53}$
n-$C_{27}H_{56}$
3-methyl-$C_{27}H_{55}$
n-$C_{28}H_{58}$
2-methyl-$C_{28}H_{57}$
n-$C_{29}H_{60}$

SOURCE: KESTERSON, J. W., HENDRICKSON, R., and BRADDOCK, R. J. 1971. Florida Citrus Oils. Florida Agric. Exp. Sta. Tech. Bull. *749*.

ORANGE OIL PROPERTIES

TABLE 2.O.8

MAXIMUM AND MINIMUM VALUES FOR THE PROPERTIES OF COLD-PRESSED ORANGE OIL PRODUCED BY VARIOUS METHODS

Method of Extraction	Pipkin Roll		Screw Press		Fraser-Brace		FMC Rotary		FMC In-Line		AMC Scarifier		Brown Shaver	
No. of Samples	21		123		52		112		237		2		4	
Yield, lbs. oil/ton fruit	0.75 to 1.0		3.5 to 5.0		4.5 to 7.5		2.0 to 3.0		3.0 to 4.5		3.0 to 5.0		3.5 to 6.0	
	Max.	Min.	Max.	Min.	Max.	Min.	Max.	Min.	Max.	Min.	Max.	Min.	Max.	Min.
Property														
Sp. grav. 25° C/25° C	0.8432	0.8420	0.8426	0.8416	0.8458	0.8441	0.8443	0.8420	0.8438	0.8424	0.8449	0.8433	0.8435	0.8427
Ref. ind. η_D^{20}	1.4734	1.4718	1.4733	1.4719	1.4743	1.4730	1.4737	1.4722	1.4731	1.4725	1.4731	1.4728	1.4730	1.4730
Ref. ind. 10% dist. η_D^{20}	1.4722	1.4708	1.4723	1.4707	1.4724	1.4703	1.4727	1.4707	1.4717	1.4715	1.4716	1.4716	1.4723	1.4719
Difference	0.0013	0.0007	0.0015	0.0007	0.0031	0.0016	0.0015	0.0010	0.0014	0.0010	0.0015	0.0012	0.0011	0.0007
Opt. rot. α_D^{25}	+98.05	+96.64	+97.80	+96.53	+96.30	+94.54	+97.57	+94.98	+97.08	+95.32	+96.70	+96.36	+97.32	+97.18
Opt. rot. 10% dist. α_D^{25}	+98.31	+97.30	+98.65	+97.24	+98.70	+96.96	+98.73	+96.49	+97.92	+95.74	+98.16	+97.47	+99.11	+98.09
Difference	+1.28	+0.01	+1.41	+0.03	+3.70	+1.51	+2.00	+0.00	+1.51	+0.11	+1.80	+0.77	+1.89	+0.80
Aldehyde content, %	2.02	1.63	1.85	0.92	1.65	0.93	2.04	1.17	1.96	1.54	1.86	1.86	1.66	0.86
Ester content, %	1.01	0.15	1.09	0.04	1.63	0.35	1.34	0.08	—	—	—	—	—	—
Evaporation residue, %	2.42	1.07	2.23	1.37	4.93	3.12	3.22	1.85	3.08	2.45	4.00	2.80	2.56	2.17

SOURCE: KESTERSON, J. W., HENDRICKSON, R., and BRADDOCK, R. J. 1971. Florida Citrus Oils. Florida Agric. Exp. Sta. Tech. Bull. *749*.

ORANGE STRUCTURE

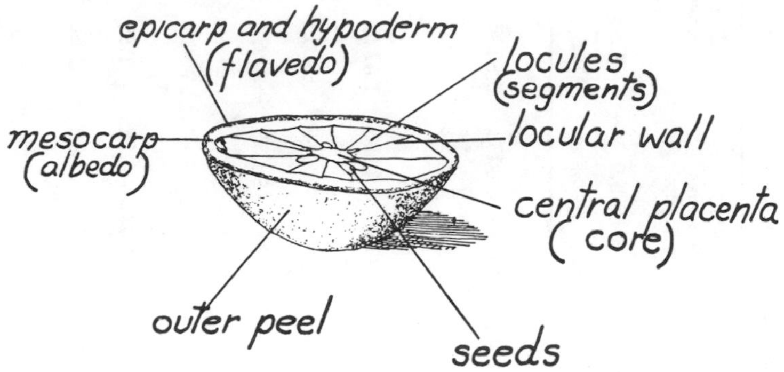

FIG. 2.O.1. MACROSCOPIC STRUCTURE OF HALVED ORANGE

SOURCE: VELDHUIS, MATTHEW, K. 1971. Orange and Tangerine Juices. *In* Fruit and Vegetable Juice Processing Technology, 2nd Edition. Donald K. Tressler and Maynard A. Joslyn (Editors). Avi Publishing Co., Westport, Conn.

ORGAN WEIGHTS

TABLE 2.O.9

WEIGHTS OF ORGANS IN THE HUMAN BODY
(Conventional Standard Man)

Organ	Mass (g)	Organ	Mass (g)
Total body	70,000	Lungs (2)	1,000
Muscle	30,000	Lymphoid tissue	700
Skin and subcutaneous tissue	6,100	Kidneys (2)	200
Skin only	2,000	Heart	300
Fat	10,000	Spleen	150
Skeleton		Urinary bladder	150
Without bone marrow	7,000	Pancreas	70
Red marrow	1,500	Salivary glands (6)	50
Yellow marrow	1,500	Testes (2)	40
Blood	5,400	Spinal cord	30
Gastrointestinal tract	2,000	Eyes (2)	30
Contents of gastrointestinal tract		Thyroid gland	20
Stomach	250	Teeth	20
Small intestine	1,000	Prostate gland	20
Upper large intestine	135	Adrenal glands or suprarenal (2)	20
Lower large intestine	150	Thymus	10
Liver	1,700	Miscellaneous (blood vessels,	
Brain	1,500	cartilage, nerves, etc.)	390

SOURCE: WANG, Y. (EDITOR). 1969. Handbook of Radioactive Nuclides. CRC Press, Cleveland. Reproduced with permission of publisher.

ORGANIC ACIDS IN FRUITS AND VEGETABLES

TABLE 2.0.10

NATURAL ACIDS FOUND IN FRUITS AND VEGETABLES

Acid	*Chemical Formula*	*Product*
Malic	$C_4H_6O_5$	Apples, cherries, plums, cauliflower
Citric	$C_6H_8O_7$	Apricots, bananas, lemons, lima beans
Oxalic	$C_4H_8O_8$	Sorrel, rhubarb, apricots, blueberries
Tartaric	$C_4H_6O_6$	Grapes, apples, cherries
Benzoic	$C_6H_5CO_2HC_7H_6O_2$	Cranberries, benzoin, Peru and Tolu balsams
Succinic	$C_4H_6O_4$	Currants, cranberries
Quinic	$C_7H_{12}O_7$	Cranberries, carrot leaves, quinine, pears
Isocitric	$C_6H_8O_7$	Blueberries
Fumaric	$C_4H_4O_4$	Gooseberries, apples, watermelon

SOURCE: BERARDE, M. A. 1971. The Chemicals We Eat. McGraw-Hill Book Company, New York.

P

PACKING-HOUSE BY-PRODUCTS COMPOSITION

TABLE 2.P.1

COMPOSITION OF SOME TYPICAL PACKING-HOUSE BY-PRODUCTS

Feeding Stuff	Dry Matter (%)	Ash (%)	Crude Protein (%)	Crude Fiber (%)	Crude Lipid (%)	N-free Extract (%)
Blood meal	92.2	4.7	84.7	1.1	1.0	0.7
Fish meal	92.9	17.6	63.9	0.6	6.8	4.0
Meat scraps	93.9	25.4	55.8	2.1	9.3	1.3
No. 1 tankage	93.1	20.2	60.6	2.0	8.5	1.8

SOURCE: MALLETTE, M. F., ALTHOUSE, P. M., and CLAGETT, C. O. Biochemistry of Plants and Animals. John Wiley & Sons, New York.

PAIRED COMPARISONS

TABLE 2.P.2

PAIRED COMPARISON-NUMBER OF CORRECT SELECTIONS REQUIRED TO INDICATE SIGNIFICANT DIFFERENCES

Total Number of Comparisons	Number of Correct Choices for Odds: 19:1 (5 Per cent Level)	99:1 (1 Per cent Level)	999:1 (.1 Per cent Level)
6	6	..	..
8	7	8	..
10	9	10	..
12	10	11	..
14	11	12	14
16	13	14	15
18	14	15	17
20	15	16	18
25	18	20	22
30	21	23	25
35	24	26	28
40	27	29	32
45	30	32	35
50	33	35	38
60	38	41	44
70	44	46	50
80	50	52	56
90	55	58	62
100	60	63	67
200	113	116	121
300	165	169	175
400	218	223	230
500	270	276	284
600	332	338	347
700	374	480	490
800	427	434	445
900	479	487	499
1000	531	539	552

SOURCE: KRAMER, A. and TWIGG, B. A. 1968. Statistical Quality Control. *In* The Freezing Preservation of Foods, Vol. 3, 4th Edition. D. K. Tressler, W. B. Van Arsdel and M. J. Copley (Editors). Avi Publishing Co., Westport, Conn.

PAIRED TASTE TESTS

TABLE 2.P.3

SIGNIFICANCE IN PAIRED TASTE TESTS (p = ½)

No. of Tasters or Tastings	Minimum Agreeing Judgments Necessary to Establish Significant Differentiation (Two-tail Test)			Minimum Correct Answers Necessary to Establish Significant Differentiation (One-tail Test)		
	Probability Level			Probability Level		
	0.05	0.01	0.001	0.05	0.01	0.001
5	—	—	—	5	—	—
6	—	—	—	6	—	—
7	7	—	—	7	7	—
8	8	8	—	7	8	—
9	8	9	—	8	9	—
10	9	10	—	9	10	10
11	10	11	11	9	10	11
12	10	11	12	10	11	12
13	11	12	13	10	12	13
14	12	13	14	11	12	13
15	12	13	14	12	13	14
16	13	14	15	12	14	15
17	13	15	16	13	14	16
18	14	15	17	13	15	16
19	15	16	17	14	15	17
20	15	17	18	15	16	18
21	16	17	19	15	17	18
22	17	18	19	16	17	19
23	17	19	20	16	18	20
24	18	19	21	17	19	20
25	18	20	21	18	19	21
26	19	20	22	18	20	22
27	20	21	23	19	20	22
28	20	22	23	19	21	23
29	21	22	24	20	22	24
30	21	23	25	20	22	24
31	22	24	25	21	23	25
32	23	24	26	22	24	26
33	23	25	27	22	24	26
34	24	25	27	23	25	27
35	24	26	28	23	25	27
36	25	27	29	24	26	28
37	25	27	29	24	27	29
38	26	28	30	25	27	29
39	27	28	31	26	28	30
40	27	29	31	26	28	31
41	28	30	32	27	29	31
42	28	30	32	27	29	32
43	29	31	33	28	30	32
44	29	31	34	28	31	33
45	30	32	34	29	31	34
46	31	33	35	30	32	34
47	31	33	36	30	32	35
48	32	34	36	31	33	36
49	32	34	37	31	34	36
50	33	35	37	32	34	37
60	39	41	44	37	40	43
70	44	47	50	43	46	49
80	50	52	56	48	51	55
90	55	58	61	54	57	61
100	61	64	67	59	63	66

SOURCE: ROESSLER, E. B., BAKER, G. A., and AMERINE, M. A. One-Tailed and Two-Tailed Tests in Organoleptic Comparisons. Food Res. *21*, 117.

PAN BROILING MEAT

Recommendations for pan broiling meats:

1. Place meat in heavy frying pan.
2. Do not add fat or water. Do not cover.
3. Cook slowly, turning occasionally.
4. Pour fat from pan as it accumulates.
5. Brown meat on both sides.
6. Cook to desired doneness. Season if desired. Serve at once.

SOURCE: Be a Smarter Shopper . . . a Better Cook. (1973). National Live Stock and Meat Board, Chicago.

PAN FRYING MEAT

Recommendations for pan frying meats:

1. Brown meat on both sides in small amount of fat.
2. Season with salt and pepper if desired.
3. Do not cover.
4. Cook at moderate temperature until done, turning occasionally
5. Remove from pan and serve at once.

SOURCE: Be a Smarter Shopper . . . a Better Cook. (1973). National Live Stock and Meat Board, Chicago.

PANTOTHENIC ACID CONTENT

The daily amount in a normal diet is more than adequate. The following shows the pantothenic acid content of some foods which are good sources:

Brewer's dry yeast	200 γ/g	Spinach (fresh)	26 γ/g
Beef liver	76 γ/g	Wheat bran	30 γ/g
Egg yolk	63 γ/g	Roasted peanuts	25 γ/g
Kidney	35 γ/g	Whole milk powder	24 γ/g
Buckwheat	26 γ/g	Bread	5 γ/g

SOURCE: BRAVERMAN, J. B. S. Introduction to the Biochemistry of Foods. ASP Biological and Medical Press (Elsevier Division), New York.

PECTIC ACID FORMULA

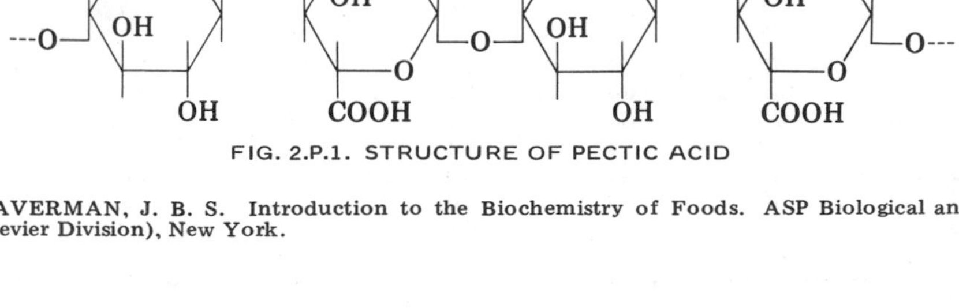

FIG. 2.P.1. STRUCTURE OF PECTIC ACID

SOURCE: BRAVERMAN, J. B. S. Introduction to the Biochemistry of Foods. ASP Biological and Medical Press (Elsevier Division), New York.

PECTIN

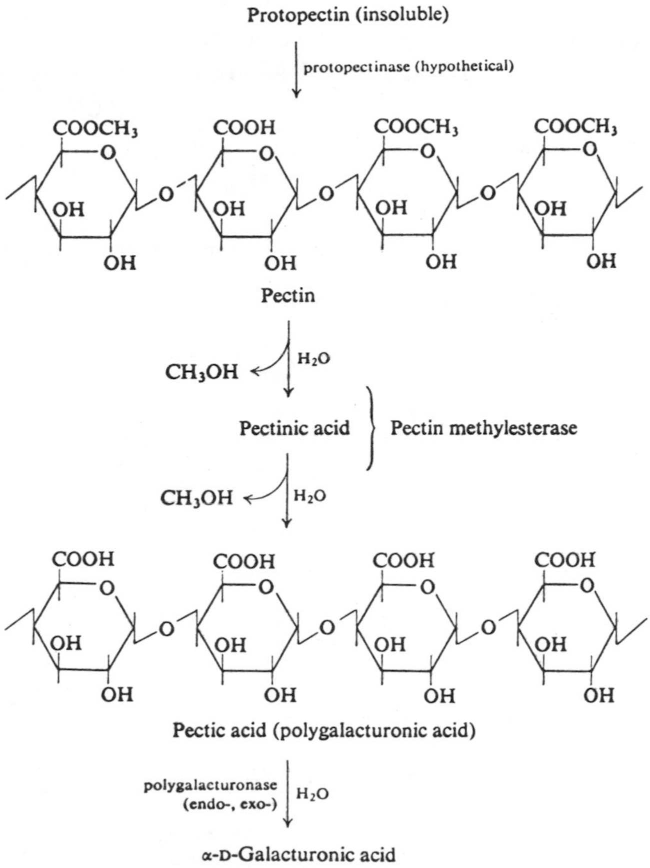

FIG. 2.P.2. STRUCTURE OF PECTIN

SOURCE: ESKIN, N. A. M., HENDERSON, H. M., and TOWNSEND, R. J. 1971. Biochemistry of Foods. Academic Press, New York.

PECTIN CONTENT

TABLE 2.P.4

PECTIN CONTENT OF SEVERAL PLANT TISSUES

Tissue	Pectin (%)
Potato	2.5
Tomato	3
Apple	5-7
Apple pomace	15-20
Carrot	10
Sunflower heads	25
Sugar beet pulp	15-20
Citrus albedo	30-35

SOURCE: SCHULTZ, H. W., CAIN, R. F., and WROLSTAD, R. W. (EDITORS). 1969. Symposium on Foods; Carbohydrates and Their Roles. Avi Publishing Co., Westport, Conn.

PECTIN FORMULA

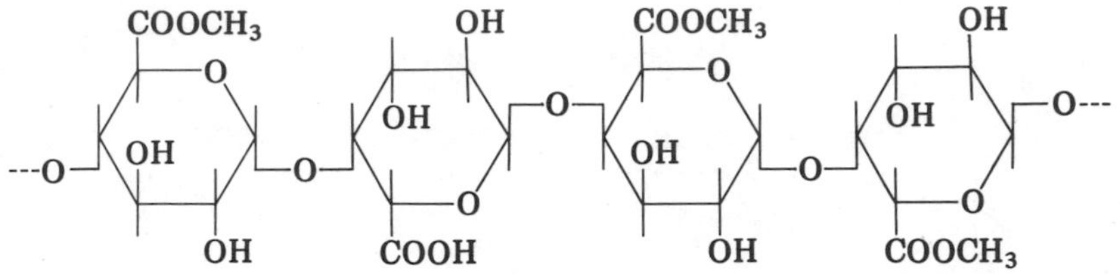

FIG. 2.P.3. STRUCTURE OF A PORTION OF THE PECTIN MOLECULE

SOURCE: BRAVERMAN, J. B. S. Introduction to the Biochemistry of Foods. ASP Biological and Medical Press (Elsevier Division), New York.

PENTOSANS

TABLE 2.P.5

PENTOSANS IN PLANT MATERIALS
(Undried Basis)

	(%)		(%)
Navy bean	8.4	Cabbage	1.0
Corn meal	5.0	Wheat bran	22.0
Corn (whole)	7.4	Wheat straw	27.1
Dried peas	7.2	Corn fodder	21.8
Barley (whole)	11.1	Corn cobs	35.0
Cottonseed flour	5.6	Gum arabic	26.0
Beets	1.7	Cherry gum	52.0
Spinach	1.0		

SOURCE: PETERSON, W. H., SKINNER, J. T., and STRONG, F. M. Elements of Food Biochemistry. Prentice-Hall, Englewood Cliffs, N.J.

pH AND AVAILABILITY OF PLANT NUTRIENTS

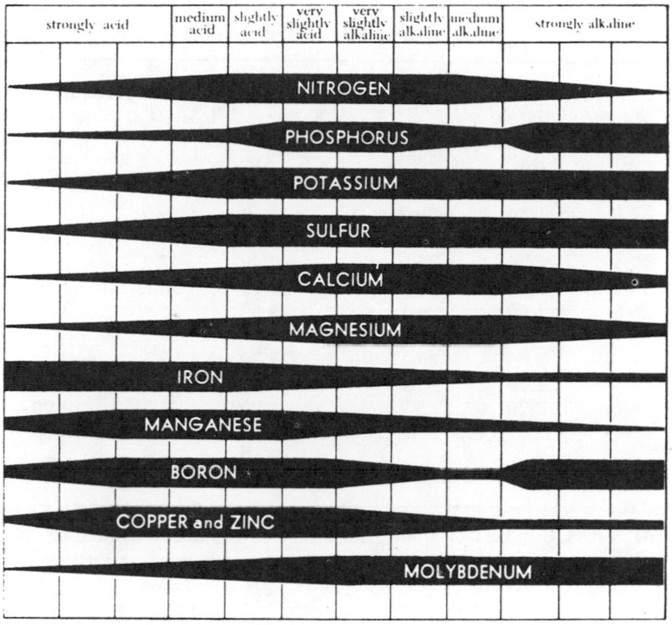

FIG. 2.P.4. HIGH SOIL pH AFFECTS AVAILABILITY OF PLANT NUTRIENTS; THE WIDER THE BAR, THE GREATER THE AVAILABILITY

SOURCE: MITTLEIDER, J. R., and NELSON, A. N. 1970. Food for Everyone. Extension Division, Loma Linda University, Loma Linda, Calif.

pH, BUFFER SOLUTIONS

TABLE 2.P.6

BUFFER SOLUTIONS FOR INDICATOR MEASUREMENTS AND pH CONTROL

25 ml 0.2 *M* KCl, *x* ml 0.2 *M* HCl, diluted to 100 ml

pH	*x*	pH	*x*
1.00	67.0	1.50	20.7
1.10	52.8	1.60	16.2
1.20	42.5	1.70	13.0
1.30	33.6	1.80	10.2
1.40	26.6	1.90	8.1
—	—	2.00	6.5
—	—	2.10	5.1
—	—	2.20	3.9

50 ml 0.1 *M* KH Phthalate, *x* ml 0.1 *M* HCl, diluted to 100 ml

pH	*x*	pH	*x*
2.20	49.5	3.20	15.7
2.30	45.8	3.30	12.9
2.40	42.2	3.40	10.4
2.50	38.8	3.50	8.2
2.60	35.4	3.60	6.3
2.70	32.1	3.70	4.5
2.80	28.9	3.80	2.9
2.90	25.7	3.90	1.4
3.00	22.3	4.00	0.1
3.10	18.8	—	—

50 ml 0.1 *M* KH Phthalate, *x* ml 0.1 *M* NaOH, diluted to 100 ml

pH	*x*	pH	*x*
4.10	1.3	5.10	25.5
4.20	3.0	5.20	28.8
4.30	4.7	5.30	31.6
4.40	6.6	5.40	34.1
4.50	8.7	5.50	36.6
4.60	11.1	5.60	38.8
4.70	13.6	5.70	40.6
4.80	16.5	5.80	42.3
4.90	19.4	5.90	43.7
5.00	22.6	—	—

50 ml 0.1 *M* KH_2PO_4, *x* ml 0.1 *M* NaOH, diluted to 100 ml

pH	*x*	pH	*x*
5.80	3.6	6.80	22.4
5.90	4.6	6.90	25.9
6.00	5.6	7.00	29.1
6.10	6.8	7.10	32.1
6.20	8.1	7.20	34.7
6.30	9.7	7.30	37.0
6.40	11.6	7.40	39.1
6.50	13.9	7.50	41.1
6.60	16.4	7.60	42.8
6.70	19.3	7.70	44.2
—	—	7.80	45.3
—	—	7.90	46.1
—	—	8.00	46.7

50 ml 0.1 *M* Tris(hydroxmethyl)-aminomethane, *x* ml 0.1 *M* HCl, diluted to 100 ml

pH	*x*	pH	*x*
7.00	46.6	8.00	29.2
7.10	45.7	8.10	26.2
7.20	44.7	8.20	22.9
7.30	43.4	8.30	19.9
7.40	42.0	8.40	17.2
7.50	40.3	8.50	14.7
7.60	38.5	8.60	12.4
7.70	36.6	8.70	10.3
7.80	34.5	8.80	8.5
7.90	32.0	8.90	7.0
—	—	9.00	5.7

50 ml of a mixture 0.1 *M* with respect to both KCl and H_3BO_3, *x* ml 0.1 *M* NaOH, diluted to 100 ml

pH	*x*	pH	*x*
8.00	3.9	9.00	20.8
8.10	4.9	9.10	23.6
8.20	6.0	9.20	26.4
8.30	7.2	9.30	29.3
8.40	8.6	9.40	32.1
8.50	10.1	9.50	34.6
8.60	11.8	9.60	36.9
8.70	13.7	9.70	38.9
8.80	15.8	9.80	40.6
8.90	18.1	9.90	42.2
—	—	10.00	43.7
—	—	10.10	45.0
—	—	10.20	46.2

TABLE 2.P.6 (*Continued*)

50 ml 0.025 *M* Borax, *x* ml 0.1 *M* HCl, diluted to 100 ml			
pH	*x*	pH	*x*
8.00	20.5	8.50	15.2
8.10	19.7	8.60	13.5
8.20	18.8	8.70	11.6
8.30	17.7	8.80	9.4
8.40	16.6	8.90	7.1
—	—	9.00	4.6
—	—	9.10	2.0

50 ml 0.025 *M* Borax, *x* ml 0.1 *M* NaOH, diluted to 100 ml			
pH	*x*	pH	*x*
9.20	0.9	10.20	20.5
9.30	3.6	10.30	21.3
9.40	6.2	10.40	22.1
9.50	8.8	10.50	22.7
9.60	11.1	10.60	23.3
9.70	13.1	10.70	23.80
9.80	15.0	10.80	24.25
9.90	16.7	—	—
10.00	18.3		
10.10	19.5		

50 ml 0.05 *M* $NaHCO_3$, *x* ml 0.1 *M* NaOH, diluted to 100 ml			
pH	*x*	pH	*x*
9.60	5.0	10.60	19.1
9.70	6.2	10.70	20.2
9.80	7.6	10.80	21.2
9.90	9.1	10.90	22.0
10.00	10.7	11.00	22.7
10.10	12.2	—	—
10.20	13.8	—	—
10.30	15.2	—	—
10.40	16.5	—	—
10.50	17.8	—	—

50 ml 0.05 *M* Na_2HPO_4, *x* ml 0.1 *M* NaOH, diluted to 100 ml			
pH	*x*	pH	*x*
10.90	3.3	11.40	9.1
11.00	4.1	11.50	11.1
11.10	5.1	11.60	13.5
11.20	6.3	11.70	16.2
11.30	7.6	11.80	19.4
—	—	11.90	23.0
—	—	12.00	26.9

25 ml 0.2 *M* KCl, *x* ml 0.2 *M* NaOH, diluted to 100 ml			
pH	*x*	pH	*x*
12.00	6.0	12.50	20.4
12.10	8.0	12.60	25.6
12.20	10.2	12.70	32.2
12.30	12.8	12.80	41.2
12.40	16.2	12.90	53.0
—	—	13.00	66.0

SOURCE: SOBER, H. A. (EDITOR). 1968. Handbook of Biochemistry: Selected Data for Molecular Biology. CRC Press, Cleveland. Reproduced with permission of CRC Press.

pH, POST MORTEM

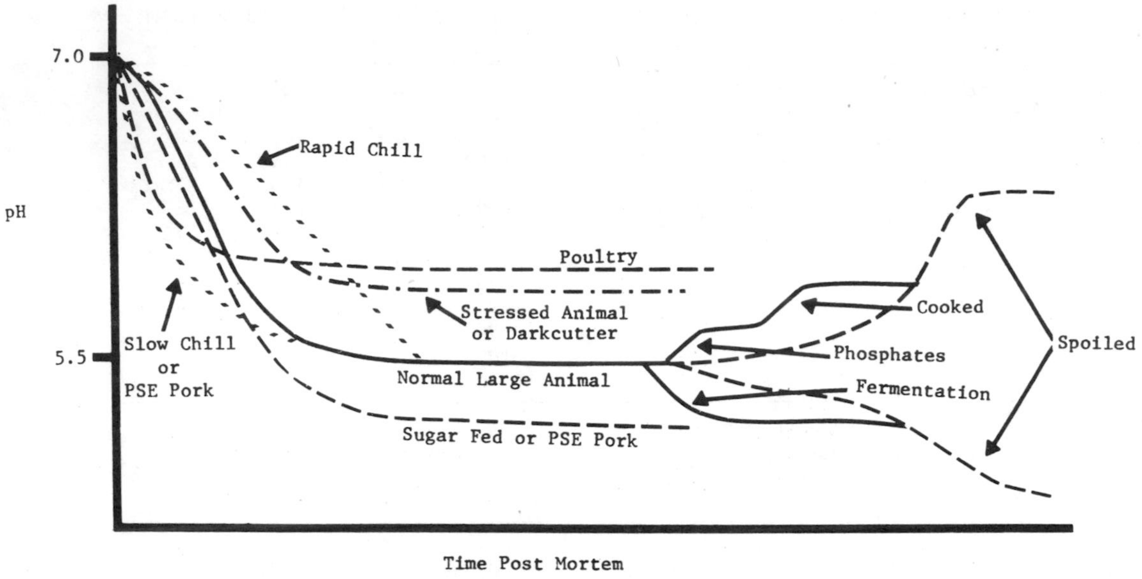

FIG. 2.P.5. ALTERATION OF pH PLOTTED AGAINST TIME POST MORTEM FOR A VARIETY OF TISSUES AND CONDITIONS

SOURCE: OCKERMAN, H. W. 1975. Chemistry of muscle and major organs. *In* Meat Hygiene. J. A. Libby (Editor). Lea & Febiger, Philadelphia.

pH, STANDARD SOLUTIONS

TABLE 2.P.7

pH VALUES OF STANDARD SOLUTIONS

Normality	pH values			
	HCl	CH_3COOH	NaOH	NH_3
1	0.10	2.37	14.05	11.77
0.1	1.07	2.87	13.07	11.27
0.01	2.02	3.37	12.12	10.77
0.001	3.01	3.87	11.13	10.27
0.0001	4.01			

SOURCE: The Merck Index, 8th Edition. (1968). Merck & Co., Rahway, N.J.

pH, UNIVERSAL INDICATORS

TABLE 2.P.8

FOR APPROXIMATE pH DETERMINATIONS

pH	Color		pH	Color	
	No. 1	No. 2		No. 1	No. 2
1	cherry-red	red	7	yellowish-green	greenish-yellow
2	rose	red	8	green	green
3	red-orange	red	9	bluish-green	greenish-blue
4	orange-red	deeper red	10	blue	violet
5	orange	orange-red	11	—	reddish-violet
6	yellow	orange-yellow			

No. 1. Dissolve 60 mg methyl yellow, 40 mg methyl red, 80 mg bromthymol blue, 100 mg thymol blue and 20 mg phenolphthalein in 100 ml of ethanol and add enough 0.1*N* NaOH to produce a yellow color.

No. 2. Dissolve 18.5 mg methyl red, 60 mg bromthymol blue and 64 mg phenolphthalein in 100 ml of 50% ethanol and add enough 0.1*N* NaOH to produce a green color.

SOURCE: The Merck Index, 8th Edition. (1968). Merck & Co., Rahway, N.J.

pH, VALUES OF BIOLOGICAL MATERIALS

TABLE 2.P.9

pH VALUES OF REPRESENTATIVE BIOLOGICAL MATERIALS

Material	pH Value	Material	pH Value
Blood, normal limits	7.3–7.5	Gastric juice, adult	0.9–1.6
Blood, extreme limits	7.0–7.8	Milk, cows, limits	6.2–7.3
Enzymes, activity range of		Milk, human	7.0–7.2
Amylopsin, optimum	7.0	Muscle juice	6.8
Erepsin, optimum	7.8	Plants (extracted juice)	
Invertase, optimum	5.5	Alfalfa tops	5.9
Lipase, pancreatic	7.0–8.0	Carrot	5.2
Maltase, optimum	6.1–6.8	Cucumber	5.1
Pepsin, optimum	1.5–2.4	Peas, field	6.8
Trypsin, optimum	8–9	Potato	6.1
Fruit juices		Rhubarb, stalks	3.4
Apple	3.8	String beans	5.2
Banana	4.6	Saliva	6.2–7.6
Grapefruit	3.0–3.3	Sweat	4.5–7.1
Orange	3.1–4.1	Tears	7.2
Tomato	4.2	Urine, human, limits	4.2–8.0

SOURCE: PETERSON, W. H., SKINNER, J. T., and STRONG, F. M. Elements of Food Biochemistry. Prentice-Hall, Englewood Cliffs, N.J.

PHOSPHATE

TABLE 2.P.10

COMPARISON OF PHOSPHATE NOMENCLATURES

Na_2HPO_4	
Disodium phosphate	Industry
Disodium hydrogen orthophosphate	Scientific
Sodium phosphate, dibasic	FCC
Disodium monophosphate	Codex Alimentarius
$Na_2H_2P_2O_7$	
Sodium acid pyrophosphate	Industry
Disodium dihydrogen phosphate	Scientific
Sodium acid pyrophosphate	FCC
Disodium diphosphate	Codex Alimentarius
$Na_5P_3O_{10}$	
Sodium tripolyphosphate	Industry
Pentasodium triphosphate	Scientific
Sodium tripolyphosphate	FCC
Pentasodium triphosphate	Codex Alimentarius
Glass	
Sodium hexametaphosphate	Industry
Glassy sodium polyphosphate	
$XNa_2O : yP_2O_5$[1]	Scientific
Sodium metaphosphate	FCC
Sodium polyphosphate	Codex Alimentarius

[1] Suggested.

SOURCE: BELL, R. N. 1971. The Nomenclature and Manufacture of Phosphates. *In* Phosphates in Food Processing, Symposium. J. M. deMan and P. Melnychyn (Editors). Avi Publishing Co., Westport, Conn.

PHOSPHORUS

TABLE 2.P.11

PHOSPHORUS CONTENT OF FOODS

	mg/100 g		mg/100 g
Lima beans	142	Cauliflower	56
Peas	116	Potatoes	53
Corn	111	Onions	36
Artichoke	88	Cabbage	29
Brussels sprouts	80	Tomatoes	27
Broccoli	78	Bananas	26
Watermelon	69	Lettuce	22
Asparagus	62	Oranges	17

SOURCE: WHITE, P. L. and SELVEY, N. (EDITORS). 1974. Nutritional Qualities of Fresh Fruits and Vegetables. Futura Publishing Co., Mt. Kisco, N.Y.

PLANT AND ANIMAL POISONING

TABLE 2.P.12

PLANT AND ANIMAL POISONING

Disease	Reservoirs	Common Vehicle	Prevention and Control
Mushroom poisoning		Poisonous mushrooms (*Amanita phalloides*, *Amanita muscaria*, others).	Do not eat wild mushrooms. Amanita very poisonous when raw or cooked.
Fish poisoning	Pike, carp, sturgeon roe in breeding season.	Fish-Tedrodon, Meletta, Clupea, pickerel eggs.	Avoid eating roe during breeding season; heed local warnings concerning edible fish.
Shellfish poisoning	Probably plankton, food of mussels.	Mussels	Avoid eating shellfish during spawning season (July through September); toxin appears to be heat stable.

SOURCE: U.S. Department of the Army, Food Inspection Specialist, *TM 8-451*, 1969.

PLANT FOODS, COMPOSITION

TABLE 2.P.13

FOODS OF PLANT ORIGIN: COMPOSITION

Values are per 100 g of edible portion of fresh, uncooked food, unless otherwise specified. Values based on inadequate evidence are enclosed in parentheses.

	Food	Water	Food Energy	Protein	Fat	Carbohydrate		Ash	Ca	Fe	P	Vitamin A	Ascorbic Acid	Niacin	Riboflavin	Thiamine
						Total	Fiber									
		g	Cal	g	g	g	g	g	mg	mg	mg	I. U.	mg	mg	mg	mg
1	Apple (Pyrus malus)	84.1	58	0.3	0.4	14.9	1.0	0.3	6	0.3	10	90	5	0.2	0.03	0.04
2	Apricot (Prunus armeniaca)	85.4	51	1.0	0.1	12.9	0.6	0.6	16	0.5	23	2790	7	0.8	0.05	0.03
3	Asparagus (Asparagus officinalis)	93.0	21	2.2	0.2	3.9	0.7	0.7	21	0.9	62	1000	33	1.4	0.19	0.16
4	Avocado (Persea gratissima)	65.4	245	1.7	26.4	5.1	1.8	1.4	10	0.6	38	290	16	1.1	0.13	0.06
5	Banana (Musa paradisiaca sapientum)	74.8	88	1.2	0.2	23.0	0.6	0.8	28	8	0.6	430	10	0.7	0.05	0.04
6	Barley, pearled, dry (Hordeum vulgare)	11.1	349	8.2	1.0	78.8	0.5	0.9	189	16	(2.0)	(0)	0	3.1	0.08	0.12
7	Bean, common, dried (Phaseolus vulgaris)	12.2	336	23.1	1.7	59.4	3.5	3.6	163	6.9	437	(0)	2	2.5	0.22	0.57
8	Bean, lima, immature (P. lunatus mac.)	66.5	128	7.5	0.8	23.5	1.5	1.7	63	2.3	158	280	32	1.4	0.11	0.21
9	Bean, lima, mature (P. lunatus macrocarpus)	12.6	333	20.7	1.3	61.6	4.3	3.8	68	7.5	381	0	2	2.0	0.18	0.48
10	Bean, snap, green and yellow (P. vulgaris)	88.9	35	2.4	0.2	7.7	1.4	0.8	65	1.1	44	630[1]	19	0.5	0.11	0.08
11	Beet, garden (Beta vulgaris)	87.6	42	1.6	0.1	9.6	0.9	1.1	27	1.0	43	20	10	0.4	0.05	0.02
12	Blackberry (Rubus spp)	84.8	57	1.2	1.0	12.5	4.2	0.5	32	0.9	32	200	21	0.4	0.04	0.04
13	Blueberry (Vaccinium corymbosum)	83.4	61	0.6	0.6	15.1	1.2	0.3	16	0.8	13	280	16	(0.3)	(0.02)	(0.02)
14	Brazil nut (Bertholletia excelsa)	5.3	646	14.4	65.9	11.0	2.1	3 4	186	3.4	693	Trace				0.86
15	Broccoli (Brassica oleracea botrytis)	89.9	29	3.3	0.2	5.5	1.3	1.1	130	1.3	76	3500	118	1.1	0.2	0.10
16	Brussels sprouts (B. oleracea gemmifera)	84.9	47	4.4	0.5	8.9	1.3	1.3	34	1.3	78	400	94	0.7	0.16	0.08
17	Cabbage (B. oleracea capitata)	92.4	24	1.4	0.2	5.3	1.0	0.8	46	0.5	31	80	50	0.3	0.05	0.06
18	Cantaloupe (Cucumis melo cantalupensis)	94.0	20	0.6	0.2	4.6	0.6	0.6	17	0.4	16	3420	33	0.5	0.04	0.05
19	Carrot (Daucus carota)	88.2	42	1.2	0.3	9.3	1.1	1.0	39	0.8	37	12000		0.5	0.06	0.06
20	Cauliflower (Brassica oleracea botrytis)	91.7	25	2.4	0.2	4.9	0.9	0.8	22	1.1	72	90	69	0.6	0.10	0.11
21	Celery (Apium graveolens)	93.7	18	1.3	0.2	3.7	0.7	1.1	50	0.5	40	0	7	0.4	0.04	0.05
22	Cherry, sour and sweet (Prunus spp)	83.0	61	1.1	0.5	14.8	0.3	0.6	18	0.4	20	620	8	0.4	0.06	0.05
23	Coconut (Cocos nucifera)	46.9	359	3.4	34.7	14.0	3.2	1.0	21	2.0	98	0	2	0.2	0.01	0.10
24	Collard (Brassica acephala)	86.6	40	3.9	0.6	7.2	1.2	1.7	249	1.6	58	6870	100	(2.0)	0.27	0.11
25	Corn, sweet, white and yellow (Zea mays)	73.9	92	3.7	1.2	20.5	0.8	0.7	9	0.5	120	390	12	1.7	0.12	0.15
26	Cranberry (Vaccinium macrocarpon)	87.4	48	0.4	0.7	11.3	1.4	0.2	14	0.6	11	40	12	0.1	(0.02)	(0.03)
27	Cucumber (Cucumis sativus)	96.1	12	0.7	0.1	2.7	0.5	0.4	10	0.3[2]	21	0[2]	8	0.2	0.04	0.03
28	Currant, red (Ribes rubrum)	84.4	55	1.2	0.2	13.6	4.0	0.6	36	0.9	33	120	36			0.04
29	Date, dried (Phoenix dactylifera)	20.0	284	2.2	0.6	75.4	2.4	1.8	72	2.1	60	60	(0)	2.2	0.10	0.09
30	Eggplant (Solanum melongena)	92.7	24	1.1	0.2	5.5	0.9	0.5	15	0.4	37	30	5	0.6	0.05	0.04

(Continued)

TABLE 2.P.13 (*Continued*)

Values are per 100 g of edible portion of fresh, uncooked food, unless otherwise specified. Values based on inadequate evidence are enclosed in parentheses.

	Food	Water	Food Energy	Protein	Fat	Carbohydrate Total	Carbohydrate Fiber	Ash	Ca	Fe	P	Vitamin A	Ascorbic Acid	Niacin	Riboflavin	Thiamine
		g	Cal	g	g	g	g	g	mg	mg	mg	I. U.	mg	mg	mg	mg
31	Fig, dried (Ficus carica)	24.0	270	4.0	1.2	68.4	5.8	2.4	186	3.0	111	80	(0)	1.7	0.12	0.16
32	Grape, American (Vitis spp)[3]	81.9	70	1.4	1.4	14.9	0.5	0.4	17	0.6	21	80	4	0.2	0.04	0.06
33	Grapefruit (Citrus paradisi)	88.8	40	0.5	0.2	10.1	0.3	0.4	22	0.2	18	Trace	40	0.2	0.02	0.04
34	Guava (Psidium guajava)	80.6	70	1.0	0.6	17.1	5.5	0.7	30	0.7	29	250	302	1.2	0.04	0.07
35	Kale (Brassica oleracea acephala)	86.6	40	3.9	0.6	7.2	1.2	1.7	225	2.2	62	7540	115	2.0	0.26	0.10
36	Lemon (Citrus limonia)	89.3	32	0.9	0.6	8.7	0.9	0.5	40	0.6	22	0	50	0.1	Trace	0.04
37	Lettuce (Lactuca sativa)	94.8	15	1.2	0.2	2.9	0.6	0.9	22	0.5	25	540	8	0.2	0.08	0.04
38	Mango (Mangifera indica)	81.4	66	0.7	0.2	17.2	1.0	0.5	9	0.2	13	6350	41	0.9	0.06	0.06
39	Mushroom (Agaricus campestris)	91.1	16	2.4	0.3	4.0	0.9	1.1	9	1.0	115	0	5	4.9	0.44	0.10
40	Mustard greens (Brassica japonica)	92.2	22	2.3	0.3	4.0	0.8	1.2	220	2.9	38	6460	102	0.8	0.20	0.09
41	Oats, rolled (Avena sativa)	8.3	390	14.2	7.4	68.2	1.2	1.9	53	4.5	405	(0)	(0)	1.0	0.14	0.60
42	Okra (Hibiscus esculentus)	89.8	32	1.8	0.2	7.4	1.0	0.8	82	0.7	62	740	30	1.1	0.07	0.08
43	Onion, immature, green (Allium cepa)	87.6	35	1.0	0.2	10.6	1.8	0.6	135	0.9	24	(50)	24	(0.2)	(0.04)	(0.03)
44	Onion, mature (A. cepa)	87.5	45	1.4	0.2	10.3	0.8	0.6	32	0.5	44	50	9	0.2	0.04	0.03
45	Orange (Citrus spp)	87.2	45	0.9	0.2	11.2	0.6	0.5	33	0.4	23	(190)	49	0.2	0.03	0.08
46	Papaya (Carica papaya)	88.7	39	0.6	0.1	10.0	0.9	0.6	20	0.3	16	1750	56	0.3	0.04	0.03
47	Parsnip (Pastinaca sativa)	78.6	78	1.5	0.5	18.2	2.2	1.2	57	0.7	80	0	18	0.2	0.12	0.08
48	Pea, garden, immature (Pisum sativum)	74.3	98	6.7	0.4	17.7	2.2	0.9	22	1.9	122	680	26	2.7	0.16	0.34
49	Pea, garden, mature, dried (P. sativum)	11.6	339	23.8	1.4	60.2	5.4	3.0	57	4.7	388	370	2	3.1	0.28	0.77
50	Peach (Prunus persica)	86.9	46	0.5	0.1	12.0	0.6	0.5	8	0.6	22	880	8	0.9	0.05	0.02
51	Peanut, roasted (Arachis hypogaea)	2.6	559	26.9	44.2	23.6	2.4	2.7	74	1.9	393	0	(0)	16.2	0.13	0.30
52	Pear (Pyrus communis)	82.7	63	0.7	0.4	15.8	1.4	0.4	13	0.3	16	20	4	0.1	0.04	0.02
53	Pecan (Carya illinoensis)	3.0	696	9.4	73.0	13.0	2.2	1.6	74	2.4	324	50	2	0.9	0.11	0.72
54	Pepper, green (Capsicum annuum)	92.4	25	1.2	0.2	5.7	1.4	0.5	11	0.4	25	630	120	0.4	0.07	0.04
55	Pineapple (Ananas sativus)	85.3	52	0.4	0.2	13.7	0.4	0.4	16	0.3	11	130	24	0.2	0.02	0.08
56	Plantain (Musa paradisiaca)	66.4	119	1.1	0.4	31.2	0.4	0.9	7	0.7	30	10[4]	14	0.6	0.04	0.06
57	Plum (Prunus spp)	85.7	50	0.7	0.2	12.9	0.5	0.5	17	0.5	20	350	5	0.5	0.04	0.06
58	Potato (Solanum tuberosum)	77.8	83	2.0	0.1	19.1	0.4	1.0	11	0.7	56	20	17[5]	1.2	0.04	0.11
59	Prune (Prunus spp)	24.0	268	2.3	0.6	71.0	1.6	2.1	54	3.9	85	1890	3	1.7	0.16	0.10
60	Pumpkin (Cucurbita pepo)	90.5	31	1.2	0.2	7.3	1.3	0.8	21	0.8	44	(3400)	8	(0.6)	(0.08)	(0.05)
61	Radish (Raphanus sativus)	93.6	20	1.2	0.1	4.2	0.7	1.0	37	1.0	31	30	24	0.3	0.02	0.03
62	Raisin (Vitis vinifera)	24.0	268	2.3	0.5	71.2		2.0	78	3.3	129	50	Trace	0.5	0.08	0.15
63	Rice, brown (Oryza sativa)	12.0	360	7.5	1.7	77.7	0.6	1.1	39	2.0	303	(0)	(0)	4.6	0.05	0.32
64	Rice, white (O. sativa)	12.3	362	7.6	0.3	79.4	0.2	0.4	24	0.8	136	(0)	(0)	1.6	0.03	0.07
65	Rutabaga (Brassica campestris)	89.1	38	1.1	0.1	8.9	1.3	0.8	55	0.4	41	330	36	0.9	0.08	0.07
66	Rye (Secale cereale)	11.0	321	12.1	1.7	73.4	2.0	1.8	(38)	3.7	376	(0)	(0)	1.6	0.22	0.43
67	Soybean, mature, dried (Glycine soja)	7.5	331	34.9	18.1	34.8	5.0	4.7	227	8.0	586	110	Trace	2.3	0.31	1.07
68	Soybean, sprouts (G. soja)	86.3	46	6.2	1.4	5.3	0.8	0.8	48	1.0	67	180	13	0.8	0.20	0.23
69	Spinach (Spinacia oleracea)	92.7	20	2.3	0.3	3.2	0.6	1.5	81	3.0	55	9420	59	0.6	0.20	0.11
70	Squash, summer (Cucurbita pepo)	95.0	16	0.6	0.1	3.9	0.5	0.4	15	0.4	15	260	17	0.8	0.09	0.05
71	Squash, winter (C. maxima)	88.6	38	1.5	0.3	8.8	1.4	0.8	19	0.6	28	4950	8	0.5	0.12	0.05
72	Strawberry (Fragaria spp)	89.9	37	0.8	0.5	8.3	1.4	0.5	28	0.8	27	60	60	0.3	0.07	0.03
73	Sweetpotato (Ipomoea batatas)	68.5	123	1.8	0.7	27.9	1.0	1.1	30	0.7	49	7700	22	0.6	0.05	0.09
74	Tangerine (Citrus reticulata)	87.3	44	0.8	0.3	10.9	1.0	0.7	(33)	(0.4)	(23)	(420)	31	(0.2)	(0.03)	0.07
75	Tomato (Lycopersicon esculentum)	94.1	20	1.0	0.3	4.0	0.6	0.6	11	0.6	27	1100	23	0.5	0.04	0.06
76	Turnip (Brassica rapa)	90.9	32	1.1	0.2	7.1	1.1	0.7	40	0.5	34	Trace	28	0.5	0.07	0.05
77	Turnip greens (B. rapa)	89.5	30	2.9	0.4	5.4	1.2	1.8	259	2.4	50	9540	136	0.8	0.46	0.09
78	Walnut, English (Juglans regia)	3.3	654	15.0	64.4	15.6	2.1	1.7	83	2.1	380	30	3	1.2	0.13	0.48
79	Watermelon (Citrullus vulgaris)	92.1	28	0.5	0.2	6.9	0.6	0.3	7	0.2	12	590	6	0.2	0.05	0.05
80	Wheat (Triticum aestivum)	12.5	330	12.3	1.8	71.7	2.3	1.7	46	3.4	354	(0)	(0)	4.3	0.12	0.52

/1/ For yellow varieties, 150 I. U. /2/ Applicable to pared cucumber; for unpared, 1.2 mg iron and 260 I. U. vitamin A. /3/ Data also applicable to European grapes with the following modifications; food energy, 66 cal.; protein, 0.8 g; fat, 0.4 g; ash, 0.5 g. /4/ Applicable to white varieties; for yellow varieties, 1200 I. U. /5/ Year-round average. Recently harvested potatoes, 24 mg; after storage of 3 mo, 12 mg; after storage of 6 mo, 8 mg.

SOURCE: SPECTOR (EDITOR). Handbook of Biological Data. Federation of American Societies for Experimental Biology, Bethesda, Maryland.

PLASTIC PERMEABILITY

TABLE 2.P.14

PERMEABILITY OF SELECTED PLASTICS AT INDICATED TEMPERATURES

Material	T (°F)	Permeability Coefficient[a] (cc) (cm^{-2})/(sec) (cm Hg) (cm^{-1})
Cellulose nitrate	68	450
Cellulose acetate	75	6210
Polyvinylbutyral	77	185
Polyvinyl chloride (PVC)	88	15
Polystyrene	77	97
	122	107
Polyethylene (den = 0.922)	75	9
(den = 0.038)	75	2.5
(den = 0.96)	75	1.2
Polyethylene	68	3.2
	104	7.9
	176	50
Polystyrene	75	83.5×10^{-9}
	100	83.0
Polyvinyl chloride	75	11.6–12.3
	95	15.5
	131	20.3
Polyvinylidene chloride	75	0.20
	91	0.52
	100	0.82

[a](cc) (cm^{-2})/(sec) (cm^{-1}) (cm Hg) = (cc) (cm)/(sec) (sq cm) (cm Hg).

SOURCE: HALL, C. W., HARDENBURG, R. E. and PANTASTICO, ER. B. 1975. Principles of Packaging. Part II. Consumer Packaging with Plastics. *In* Postharvest Physiology, Handling and Utilization of Tropical and Subtropical Fruits and Vegetables. Er. B. Pantastico (Editor). Avi Publishing Co., Westport, Conn.

POISONOUS PLANTS

TABLE 2.P.15

POISONOUS PLANTS OF NORTH AMERICA

Dangerous Season	Scientific Name	Common Name	Habitat and Distribution	Affected Animals	Important Characteristics	Toxic Principle and Effects	Remarks and Treatment
SPRING	*Hymenoxys* spp.	Bitterweed, Rubberweed, Pingue	Roadways, lakebeds, flooded areas, overgrazed range; western.	Sheep, also cattle	Much-branched annual or perennial up to 2 ft. high. Yellow flower head. Leaves divided into narrow glandular segments.	Depression, loss of appetite, abdominal pain, green nasal discharge, salivation, prostration.	Fresh or dry. Remove from pasture. Avoid overgrazing.
	Nolina texana	Sacahuista, Beargrass	Open areas on rolling hills and slopes; southwest.	Sheep, cattle and goats	Perennial with many clustered, long, narrowed leaves. Several flower stems with many small white flowers in clusters.	Toxin in buds, flowers and fruit. Photosensitization. Anorexia, icterus, prostration.	Remove animals from range during blooming season. (*See* PHOTOSENSITIZATION, p. 6.)
	Cicuta spp.	Water hemlock	Open, moist to wet situations.	All	White flower, umbels. Veins of leaflets ending at notches. Stems hollow except at nodes. Tuberous roots from chambered rootstock.	A higher alcohol—excessive salivation, violent convulsions, dilation of pupils, diaphragm contractions, pain.	Death usually rapid. Use sedatives to control spasm and heart action. Intestinal evacuation followed by astringents may help.
	Delphinium	Larkspurs	Either cultivated or wild. Usually in open foothills or meadows; mostly western.	All grazing animals, mostly cattle	Annual or perennial herbs. Flowers each with one spur, in racemes. Perennial with tuberous roots. Leaves palmately lobed or divided.	Alkaloid delphinine and others—straddled stance, repeated falling, nausea, rapid pulse and respiration, constipation, bloating.	Use ℞ 486.
	Phytolacca americana	Pokeweed, Poke	Recent clearings, pastures, waste areas; eastern.	Cattle, swine	Tall, glabrous, green, red-purplish perennial herbs. Berries black-purple, staining, in drooping racemes.	More than one—vomiting, spasms, respiratory paralysis, ulcerative gastritis.	Roots most poisonous. 10 ml nikethamide (cattle).
(and occasionally fall)	*Xanthium* spp.	Cocklebur	Fields, waste places, exposed shores of ponds or rivers.	All animals, more common in swine	Coarse annual herb. Fruit one solid mass, 2 beaked, with 2 cavities, armed with hooked spines.	Hydroquinone—anorexia, depression, incoordination, twitching, paralysis, inflammation of mucous membranes.	Only cotyledons poisonous. Eaten after emerging from seed. Milk, vegetable oil and fats may be beneficial.
	Peganum harmala	African rue	Arid to semi-arid ranges; southwest.	Cattle and sheep	Much-branched, leafy, perennial, bright green, succulent herb; leaves divided; flowers white.	Alkaloids—weakness of hind limbs, listlessness, subserous edema and hemorrhage of small intestine.	Unpalatable. Eaten only under drought conditions.
	Sarcobatus vermiculatus	Greasewood	Alkaline or saline bottom soils, not in higher mountains; western.	Sheep	Large shrub with spiny stems; fleshy, alternate cross-section. Flowers inconspicuous.	Oxalates—kidney lesions, weakness, depression, prostration, coma.	Poisoning occurs only on steady diet of greasewood leaves. Provide other forage.
	Veratrum spp.	False hellebore	Low, moist woods and pastures, and high mountain valleys.	Cattle, sheep and fowl	Erect herbs; leafy throughout, leaves large and plaited. Flowers small and white or greenish.	Steroid alkaloids—salivation, prostration, depressed heart action, dyspnea; "Monkey-face" in lambs.	Remove animals from range. Provide other forage.
	Tetradymia spp.	Horsebrush	Arid foothills and higher desert and sagebrush ranges; western.	Sheep	Shrubs with yellow flowers in spring, not later. Leaves spiny, silvery white, early deciduous.	Resinous substances—weakness, "bighead" photosensitization; liver injury, death.	Cumulative. Remove animals from range and light. Antihistaminics. (*See* PHOTOSENSITIZATION, p. 6.)
	Zygadenus spp.	Death camas	Foothill grazing lands, occasionally boggy grasslands, low open woods.	Sheep, cattle and horses	Perennial bulbous herbs with basal flat grass-like leaves; flowers greenish, yellow or pink, in racemes or panicles. No onion odor.	Steroid alkaloids of the veratrum group—salivation, vomiting, staggering or prostration, coma and death.	Hay with dried camas is poisonous. 2 to 3 subcut. injections of 2 mg atropine sulfate and 8 mg picrotoxin in 5 ml of water per 100 lb body wt.

Dangerous Season	Scientific Name	Common Name	Habitat and Distribution	Affected Animals	Important Characteristics	Toxic Principle and Effects	Remarks and Treatment
SPRING and SUMMER	*Aesculus* spp.	Buckeyes	Woods and thickets; Eastern U.S.A. and California.	All grazing animals	Trees or shrubs. Leaves opposite and palmately compound. Seeds large, glossy brown, with large white scar.	Glycoside, aesculin and possibly others—depression, incoordination, twitching, paralysis, inflammation of mucous membranes.	Young shoots and seeds especially poisonous. Use stimulants and purgatives.
	Amianthium muscaetoxicum	Fly-poison, Staggergrass	Open woods, fields, and acid bogs; eastern.	All grazing animals	Bulbous perennial herb. Leaves basal, linear white flowers in a compact raceme, the pedicels subtended by short brownish bracts.	Alkaloid, of the veratrum group—salivation, vomiting, rapid and irregular respiration, weakness, death by respiratory failure.	No practical treatment. Especially dangerous for animals new to pasture. Keep animals well fed.
	Lantana spp.	Lantana	Ornamentals and wild in lower coastal plain of southeast, and southern California.	All grazing animals	Shrubs. Young stems 4-angled. Leaves opposite. Flowers in flat-topped clusters. Berries black.	Lantadene A, a polycyclic triterpenoid—erythema, pruritus, edematous suffusions and usually sloughing of skin, gastroenteritis, bloody watery feces.	Remove plants from pasture. Keep animals out of light sources after eating plant.
	Quercus spp.	Oaks	In most deciduous woods.	All grazing animals	Mostly deciduous trees, rarely shrubs, with 2 to 4 leaves clustered at tips of all twigs.	Tannic acid—anorexia, constipation, dry muzzle, black pelleted feces followed by diarrhea with blood and mucus, frequent urination, thin rapid pulse.	Remove animals from oak source. Treat symptomatically.
SUMMER and FALL	*Prosopis juliflora*	Mesquite	Dry ranges, washes, draws; southwest.	Cattle	Deciduous shrub or small tree with smooth or furrowed gray bark, paired spines; leaves divided. Legume pod long, constricted between seeds.	Malnutrition, excessive salivation, stasis of rumen; sublingual or submaxillary edema, loss of weight.	Believed that high-sucrose content of beans alters bacterial flora to extent that cellulose cannot be digested and B-vitamins synthesized.
	Centaurea solstitialis	Yellow star thistle	Waste areas, roadsides, pastures; mostly western.	Horses	Annual weed. Leaves densely covered with cottony hair. Terminal spreading cluster of bright yellow flowers with spines below. Branches winged.	Involuntary chewing movements, twitching of lips, flicking of tongue. Mouth commonly held open. Unable to eat. Eventual death from starvation or thirst.	Force food far back into mouth.
	Oxytenia acerosa	Copperweed	Arid, alkaline soils in foothills, and sagebrush plains; western.	Cattle, also sheep	Tall, perennial herb with leaflets; flowers in many heads resembling goldenrod.	Stupor, loss of appetite, coma, death without struggling.	Supplement diet.
	Eupatorium rugosum	White snakeroot	Woods, cleared areas, waste places, usually the more moist and richer soils; eastern.	Cattle and sheep	Perennial herb; leaves 3-nerved, taper-pointed, opposite; flowers small, white, many.	An alcohol, tremetol—trembling, depression, vomiting, labored respiration, death.	"Milk sickness." "Trembles." Cathartics and stimulants may help.
	Solanum spp.	Nightshades, Jerusalem cherry, potato, Horsenettle	Fence rows, waste areas, grain and hay fields.	All	Fruits small, when ripe yellow, red, or black; structurally like tomatoes; clustered on stalk arising from stem between leaves.	Glycoalkaloids—weakness, trembling, dyspnea, nausea, constipation or diarrhea, death.	Leaves, shoots and berries may be poisonous. In cattle repeated doses of 2 to 3 mg carbachol or of injection of 15 mg strychnine may be useful.
FALL or WINTER	*Haplopappus heterophyllus*	Rayless goldenrod	Dry plains, grasslands, open woodlands and along irrigation canals; western.	Cattle, sheep and horses	Bushy perennial 2 to 4 ft tall, with many yellow flower heads. Leaves alternate, sticky.	An alcohol, tremetol—trembling, depression, vomiting, labored respiration, coma, death.	"Milk sickness." Keep animals away by fencing.

(Continued)

TABLE 2.P.15 (*Continued*)

Dangerous Season	Scientific Name	Common Name	Habitat and Distribution	Affected Animals	Important Characteristics	Toxic Principle and Effects	Remarks and Treatment
	Halogeton glomeratus	Halogeton	Deserts, overgrazed areas, winter ranges, alkaline soils; western.	Sheep, also cattle	Annual herb. Leaves fleshy, round in cross-section, tip with stiff hair. Axillary flowers inconspicuous. Fruits bracted and conspicuous.	Oxalates—dyspnea followed by rapid death.	Alfalfa hay or dicalcium phosphate, fed free-choice when added to 3 parts salt, is effective preventive in sheep. Avoid dense growths of weeds.
	Sophora secundiflora	Mescal bean	Hills and canyons, limestone soils; southwestern Texas into Mexico.	Cattle, also sheep and goats	Evergreen shrub or small tree. Leaves alternate, divided and leathery; flowers violet-blue, fragrant; seeds large and bright red with hard seed coat, in legume pod.	Alkaloid sophorine—trembling, stiff gait, falling after exercise; recumbent for few minutes, then arise alert and fall again if exercised.	Not cumulative. Provide supplemental feed.
	Notholaena sinuata var. *cochisensis*	Jimmy fern, Cloak fern	Dry rocky slopes and crevices, chiefly limestone areas; southwest.	Sheep, goats and cattle	Evergreen, perennial, erect fern with divided leaves, folding when dry.	After exercise by walking, will have arched back, stilted movement of hind legs, and usually increased respiration. Continued walking induced violent trembling and death if not allowed to rest.	Avoid driving during danger period. Provide ample watering, placed to avoid long walks.
	Glottidium vesicarium, *Sesbania* spp.	Bladder pod, Rattlebox, Sesbane, Coffeebean	Mostly open low ground, abandoned cultivated fields; southeast.	All	Tall annual. Legume pods flat, tapered at both ends, 2-seeded. Leaves pinnate-divided. Flowers yellow.	Saponins—intense inflammation of gastrointestinal tract, yellowish diarrhea, frequent urination, shallow and accelerated respiration, death.	Seeds poisonous. Remove plants from pasture. Keep animals off pasture after seed pods form.
	Daubentonia punicea	Rattlebox, Purple sesbane	Cultivated and escaped in waste places; southeastern coastal plain.	All	Shrub. Flowers orange. Legume pods longitudinally four-winged.	A saponin—rapid pulse, weak respiration, diarrhea, death.	Seeds poisonous. Keep seeds from animals. Use saline purgative followed by stimulants and soft food.
FALL, WINTER and SPRING	*Melia azedarach*	Chinaberry	Fence rows, brush, waste places; southeast.	Swine, cattle	Tree. Leaves 2 to 3 pinnate; fruit cream or yellow with a furrowed globose stone, persisting on tree through winter.	Nausea, constipation, excitement or depression, often weakened heart action and death.	Fruit most poisonous. Use stimulants and cathartics followed by easily digestible diet.
ALL SEASONS	*Baccharis* spp.	Silverling, Baccharis, Yerba-de-pasmo	Open areas, often moist; eastern and southwestern.	All grazing cattle	Shrubs; numerous small, whitish flowers; leaves resin-dotted, and persistent southward.	Glucosidal saponin having digitaloidal properties—paralysis and death soon after ingestion. Depression and weakness in chronic cases.	Most dangerous during new growth in spring or root sprouts in fall.
	Pteridium aquilinum	Bracken fern	Dry poor soil, open woods, sandy ridges.	All grazing animals	Leaves firm, leathery, thrice pinnate.	(*See* BRACKEN FERN POISONING, p. 977.)	
	Prunus spp.	Chokecherries, Wild cherries, Peaches	Waste areas, fence rows, woods, orchards, prairies, dry slopes.	All grazing animals	Large shrubs or trees. Flowers white or pink. Cherries or peach. Crushed twigs with strong odor.	Prussic acid—slobbering, increased respiration rate, dyspnea, rapid weak pulse, convulsions, rapid death.	(*See* CYANIDE POISONING, p. 938.)
	Acacia berlandieri	Guajillo	Semiarid range lands; southwestern Texas into Mexico.	Sheep, also goats	Deciduous shrub or small tree; leaf divided; flowers white to yellowish in dense heads; fruit a legume with margins thickened.	Amine, N-methyl beta phenylethylamine—after eating for 6 to 9 months, may have locomotor ataxia called "limber leg." Mortality as high as 50% in extreme drought.	Dominates vegetation in some areas. Valuable to sheep industry due to high nutritive value and dominance. Supplemental feeding.

Dangerous Season	Scientific Name	Common Name	Habitat and Distribution	Affected Animals	Important Characteristics	Toxic Principle and Effects	Remarks and Treatment
(especially spring)	*Agave lecheguilla*	**Lechuguilla**	Low limestone hills, dry valleys and canyons; southwest.	Sheep and goats, rarely cattle	Perennial stemless, with thick fleshy tapered leaves having sharply serrated margins. Flowering infrequently with tall terminal panicle.	A photodynamic agent; also a saponin that is hepatonephrotoxic—photosensitization, generalized icterus, listlessness, progressive weakness, coma, death.	Remove animals from range and provide shade. (*See* PHOTOSENSITIZATION, p. 6.)
	Asclepias spp.	Milkweeds	Dry areas, usually waste places, roadsides, streambeds.	All	Perennial herbs with milky sap; seeds very silky-hairy from elongated pods.	Resinoid and others—loss of control, spasms, bloating, pulse rapid and weak, rapid breathing, coma, death.	Mainly due to drought or overgrazing.
(especially spring)	*Astragalus* spp. *Oxytropis* spp.	Locoweeds, Poison vetch	Nearly all habitats; mostly western.	All	Perennial stemmed or stemless herbs. Leaves with many small leaflets. Flowers like garden peas, in racemes.	Selenium or "locoine" in different species. Weakness, trembling, ataxia, or paralysis.	Cumulative. (*See* SELENIUM POISONING, p. 947 as one type.)
(especially spring)	*Stanleya pinnata*	Prince's plume	Foothills or deserts; western.	All	Perennial herb, woody at base and coarse; leaves divided; flowers yellow in showy spike.	May not be eaten but does accumulate selenium.	(*See* SELENIUM POISONING, p. 947.)
	Drymaria pachyphylla	Inkweed, Drymary	Heavy alkaline clay soil in low areas or dry overgrazed pastures; southwest.	Cattle. sheep; also goats	Much-branched, succulent, prostrate annual with opposite leaves and small white flowers.	Diarrhea, lack of appetite, arched back, coma, death.	Occurs after rain. Avoid overstocking to improve range.
	Gutierrezia microcephala	Broomweed, Snakeweed, Slinkweed, Turpentine weed	Widespread over dry range and desert; overgrazed lands; western.	Cattle, sheep, goats and swine	Much-branched, perennial, resinous shrub, with many yellow-flowered heads.	Saponin. Loss of appetite, listlessness, hematuria in severe cases. Abortion with retained placenta in cattle.	Supplement diet.
	Psilostrophe spp.	Paperflowers	Open range lands and pastures; southwest.	Sheep	Perennial composite with erect, woolly stems branching from base. Many small heads of yellow flowers.	Sluggishness, stumbling, coughing, vomiting, depression, death.	About 2 weeks of grazing before signs appear. Pasture rotation, or placing animals on other feed.
	Senecio spp.	Groundsel, Senecio	Grassland areas; mostly western.	Cattle, horses and sheep	Perennial or annual herbs; heads of yellow flowers with whorl of bracts below.	Alkaloids—aimless walking, slight staggering, staring expression, and running into fences or other objects. Hepatic cirrhosis, edema of visceral peritoneum and distension of gallbladder.	Cumulative, fresh or dry. Supplemental feeding. Treat symptoms. (*See* SENECIO POISONING, p. 1003.)
(especially dry season)	*Triglochin* spp.	Arrowgrass	Salt marshes, wet alkaline soils, lake shores.	Sheep and cattle	Grass-like, except leaves are thick; heads of fruits globular on erect raceme. Flowers inconspicuous.	Prussic acid in leaves—abnormal breathing, trembling, and jerking, convulsions. Rapid poisoning.	(*See* CYANIDE POISONING, p. 938.)
	Hypericum perforatum	St. Johnswort, Goatweed, Klamath weed	Dry soil, roadsides, pastures, ranges.	Sheep, cattle, horses and goats	Perennial herb or woody below; leaves opposite, dotted; flowers many, yellow, with many stamens.	Primary photosensitizer; skin lesions in white skin, itching, blindness, convulsions, death.	Fresh or dry. Remove animals from infested areas. (*See* PHOTOSENSITIZATION, p. 6.)
	Agrostemma githago	Corn cockle	Weed, grain fields and waste areas.	All	Green winter annual with silky white hairs, opposite leaves, purple flowers, black seeds.	Sapogenin, githagenin—irritation of mucosa, vomiting, vertigo, diarrhea.	Toxin in seeds. Avoid grain screenings containing seed. Give oils, demulcents, cardiac stimulants.

(Continued)

TABLE 2.P.15 (*Continued*)

Dangerous Season	Scientific Name	Common Name	Habitat and Distribution	Affected Animals	Important Characteristics	Toxic Principle and Effects	Remarks and Treatment
	Helenium hoopesii	Sneezeweed	Moist slopes and well-drained mountain meadows; western.	Sheep, also cattle	Perennial herb with orange sunflower-like heads or yellow flowers. Leaves alternate.	Glycoside dugaldin—salivation, "spewing sickness," vomiting, weakness.	Cumulative. Cathartics may help. Avoid dense areas of weed.
	Lupinus spp.	Lupines, Bluebonnet	Dry to moist soils, roadsides, fields, and mountains; mostly western.	Sheep, also cattle, goats, horses and swine	Perennials; leaves simple or palmately divided; flowers in terminal raceme.	Alkaloids D-lupanine, sparteine and others, nervousness, convulsions or coma.	Fresh or dry. Eating of pods with seeds frequent cause of poisoning. Not cumulative. (*See* MYCOTOXIC LUPINOSIS, p. 998.)
	Conium maculatum	Poison hemlock	Roadside ditches, damp waste areas, especially northward.	All	Purple-spotted hollow stem; leaves resemble parsley, parsnip odor when crushed; tap root; flowers white, in umbels.	Alkaloid coniine and others —loss of appetite, salivation, bloating, feeble pulse, paralysis.	Vegetative parts, later the seeds most poisonous. Give stimulants.
	Crotalaria spp.	Crotalaria, Rattlebox	Fields and roadsides; Eastern and Central States.	All	Annual legume with yellow flowers in racemes; pods inflated; bracts at base of pedicels of flowers and fruits persistent; leaves simple or divided.	Alkaloid monocrotaline—diarrhea, abnormally light or dark comb in fowl. Diarrhea, stupor alternating with apparent improvement, walking in circles in horse and mule. Bloody feces, anorexia, weakness in others. In all death.	Cumulative. All parts, especially seeds, poisonous. Seeds often found in combined corn. No treatment known. Keep plant from fields and hay.
	Datura stramonium	Jimsonweed	Fields, barn lots, trampled pastures, and waste places on rich bottom soils.	All	Leaves wavy; flower large (4 in.) white, tubular; fruit a spiny pod, 2 in. long.	Alkaloids atropine, hyoscyamine and hyoscine—nausea, vertigo, thirst, dilated pupils convulsions, death.	Rapid death. KI or tannic acid per os; cardiac and respiratory stimulants.
	Gelsemium sempervirens	Yellow jessamine	Open woods, thickets; eastern.	All	Climbing or trailing vines with evergreen, entire, opposite leaves; yellow tubular flowers, very fragrant.	Alkaloids gelsemine and gelsemine—weakness, convulsions rigid extremities, lowered respiration and temperature, death; "limp-neck" in fowl.	Use relaxing agents, sedatives; repeat as required.
(especially winter and spring)	*Kalmia* spp.	Laurel, Ivybush, Lambkill	Rich moist woods, meadows; or acid bogs; eastern and northwestern.	All, often sheep	Woody shrub with evergreen glossy leaves; flowers pink to rose, showy.	Andromedotoxin—salivation, nasal discharge, emesis paralysis, coma, death.	Laxatives, demulcents nerve stimulants.
	Nerium oleander	Oleander	Common ornamental in southern regions.	All	Evergreen shrub. Leaves whorled and prominently finely pinnately veined beneath. Flowers showy, white to deep pink.	Cardiac glucosides—nausea, depression, increased pulse rate, mydriasis, bloody diarrhea. Later weak and irregular heart beat, death.	Fresh, clipped or dried leaves most dangerous.
(especially winter and spring)	*Prunus caroliniana*	Laurel cherry, Cherrylaurel	Woods, fence rows and often escaped from cultivation; southern regions.	All grazing animals	Leaves evergreen, shiny, leathery. Broken twigs with strong cherry bark odor.	Prussic acid—slobbering, increased respiration rate, dyspnea, rapid weak pulse, convulsions, rapid death.	Wilted parts most poisonous. (*See* CYANIDE POISONING, p. 938.)
	Ricinus communis	Castor bean	Cultivated in southern regions.	All	Large palmately lobed leaves; seeds resembling engorged ticks, usually 3 in somewhat spiny pod.	Ricin, irritant blood poison—nausea, vomiting, diarrhea, thirst, cessation of rumination, death.	Seeds and "press-cakes" most dangerous. Gastric lavage, warmth, sedation.
	Sorghum vulgare	Sorghum, Sudan grass, Kafir, Durra, Milo, Broomcorn, Schrock, etc.			Coarse grasses with terminal flower cluster. Some to 8 ft tall.	Prussic acid—slobbering, increased respiration rate, dyspnea, rapid weak pulse, convulsions, rapid death.	Dark green, short (2 ft) second growth or stunted by dry weather most dangerous. (*See* CYANIDE POISONING, p. 938.)

Dangerous Season	Scientific Name	Common Name	Habitat and Distribution	Affected Animals	Important Characteristics	Toxic Principle and Effects	Remarks and Treatment
	Sorghum halepense	Johnson grass	Weed of open fields and waste places in south; scattered north to New York and Iowa.	All grazing animals	Coarse grass with large rhizomes and white midvein on leaf. Topped by large, open panicle.	Prussic acid—slobbering, dyspnea, increased respiration rate, rapid weak pulse, convulsions, rapid death.	Dark green second growth or stunted by dry weather most dangerous. (*See* CYANIDE POISONING, p. 938.)
ALL SEASONS (especially winter)	*Pinus ponderosa*	Western yellow pine	Coniferous forests of Rocky Mountains at moderate elevations; western.	Cattle	Tree, 150 to 180 ft; leaves in groups of 3, yellowish green, 7 to 11 in. long; barky platy, reddish orange.	Toxin in leaves; browsing cattle predisposed to abortion.	Remove from western yellow pine stands in later stages of gestation.

SOURCE: MERCK & CO. 1973. The Merck Veterinary Manual, 4th Edition. Merck & Company, Rahway, N.J.

PORK CARCASS, RETAIL YIELD

TABLE 2.P.16

RETAIL YIELD OF A SIDE OF PORK CARCASS
Pork Carcass (Side) = 70 Lb

Retail Cut	% of Carcass	Lb
Fresh ham	18–23	13–16
Trimmed loin	14–20	10–14
Fresh picnic	8–11	6–8
Fresh Boston butt	7–9	5–6
Fresh side	11–16	8–11
Spareribs and neckbones	4–6	3–4
Jowl	1½–4	1–3
Sausage	3–7	2–5
Hocks	3–4	2–3
Trimmed fat (for lard)	11–24	8–17

SOURCE: SIMONDS, L. A. and VANSTAVERN, B. D. 1975. Buying Meat for Locker or Home Freezer. Ohio State Univ. Coop. Ext. Serv.

PORK CHART

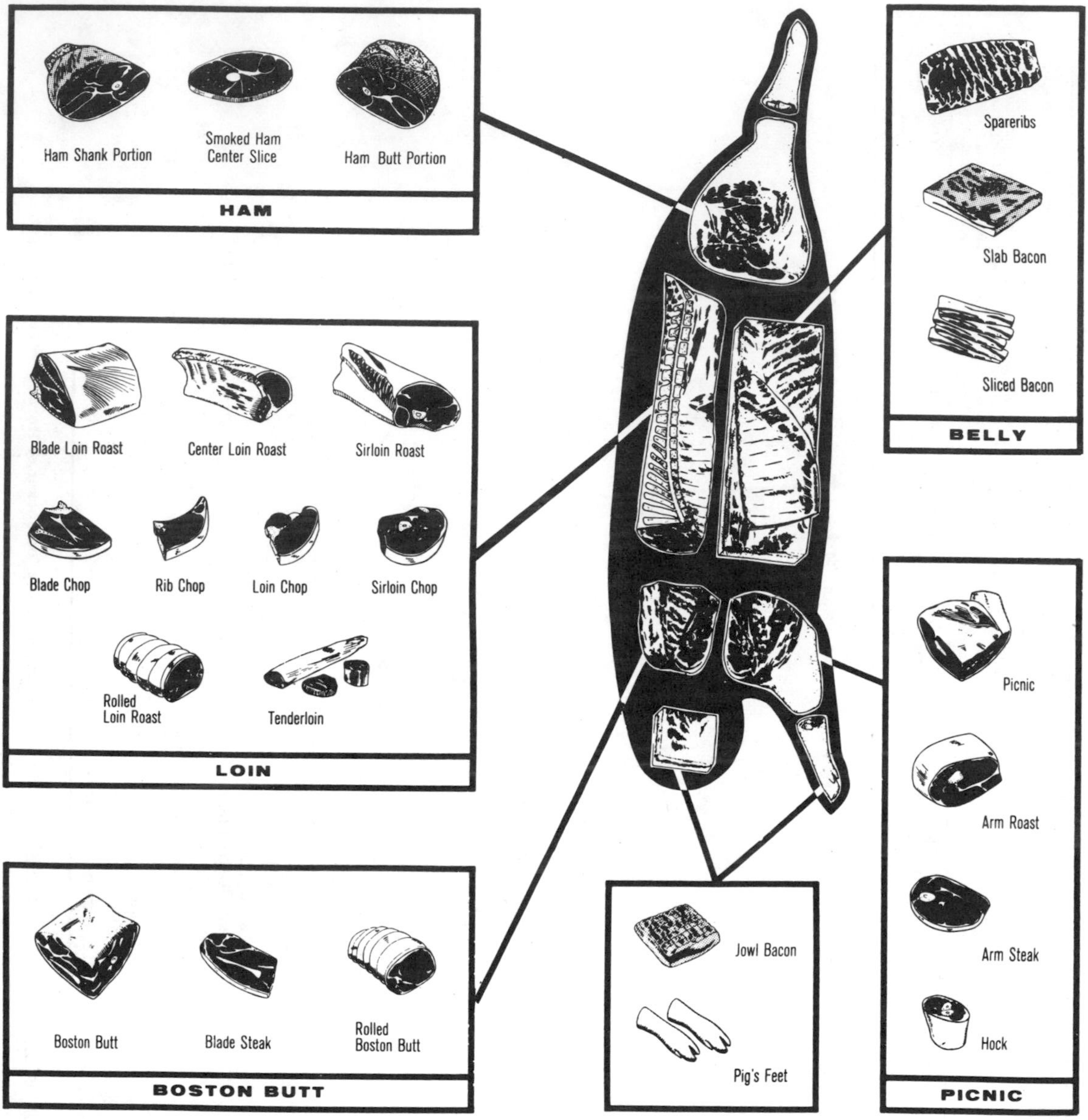

SOURCE: How to Buy Meat for Your Freezer, USDA Home and Garden Bull. *166*, 1969.

PORK, COOKING

TABLE 2.P.17

TIME AND TEMPERATURE TABLES FOR PORK COOKERY

ROASTING AT 300°F.-350°F.* OVEN TEMPERATURE

CUT	Approximate Weight	Meat Thermometer Reading	Approximate[1] Cooking Time
FRESH	Pounds	Degrees F.	Min. Per Lb.
Loin			
Center	3 to 5	170° F.	30 to 35
Half	5 to 7	170° F.	35 to 40
End	3 to 4	170° F.	40 to 45
Roll	3 to 5	170° F.	35 to 40
Boneless Top	2 to 4	170° F.	30 to 35
Crown	4 to 6	170° F.	35 to 40
Picnic Shoulder			
Bone-In	5 to 8	170° F.	30 to 35
Rolled	3 to 5	170° F.	35 to 40
Boston Shoulder	4 to 6	170° F.	40 to 45
Leg (fresh ham)			
Whole (boneless)	10 to 14	170° F.	24 to 28
Whole (bone-in)	12 to 16	170° F.	22 to 26
Half (bone-in)	5 to 8	170° F.	35 to 40
Tenderloin	½ to 1		45 to 60
			Hours
Back ribs		Cooked	1½ to 2½
Country-style		Well	
backbones		Done	1½ to 2½
Spareribs			1½ to 2½
Pork loaf	2		1¾
SMOKED			
Ham			
(cook-before-eating)			
Whole	10 to 14	160° F.	18 to 20
Half	5 to 7	160° F.	22 to 25
Shank Portion	3 to 4	160° F.	35 to 40
Butt Portion	3 to 4	160° F.	35 to 40
Ham (fully-cooked)[2]			
Half	5 to 7	140° F.	18 to 24
Loin	3 to 5	160° F.	25 to 30
Picnic Shoulder			
(cook-before-eating)	5 to 8	170° F.	30 to 35
Picnic Shoulder			
(fully-cooked)	5 to 8	140° F.	25 to 30
Shoulder roll (butt)	2 to 4	170° F.	35 to 40
Canadian-style bacon	2 to 4	160° F.	35 to 40
Ham Kabobs	1" to 1½" cubes		45 to 60
Ham loaf	2	160° F.	1½ hrs.
Ham Patties	1" thick	160° F.	45 to 60

*325°F. to 350°F. oven temperature is recommended for fresh pork and 300°F. to 325°F. oven temperature for smoked pork.

[1] Based on meat taken directly from the refrigerator.

[2] Heat "fully-cooked" whole hams to 140°F. internal temperature. Allow 15 to 18 minutes per pound for heating.

Source: National Livestock and Meat Board.

BROILING AT MODERATE TEMPERATURE

CUT	Approx. Thickness	Approx. Total Cooking Time
SMOKED		Minutes
Ham Slice	½ inch	10 to 12
Ham Slice	1 inch	16 to 20
Loin Chops	½ to ¾ inch	15 to 20
Canadian-Style Bacon		
Sliced	¼ inch	6 to 8
Sliced	½ inch	8 to 10
Bacon		4 to 5
Ham Patties	1 inch	16 to 20
FRESH		
Rib or loin chops	¾ to 1 inch	20 to 25
Shoulder Steaks	½ to ¾ inch	20 to 22
Patties	1 inch	20 to 25
Pork Kabobs	1½x1½x¾ to 1 inch	22 to 25

BRAISING

CUT	Approx. Weight or Thickness	Approx. Total Cooking Time
Chops, fresh	¾ to 1½ inches	45 to 60 min.
Spareribs	2 to 3 pounds	1½ hrs.
Backribs		1½ to 2 hrs.
Country-style backbones		1½ to 2 hrs.
Tenderloin		
Whole	¾ to 1 pound	45 to 60 min.
Fillets	½ inch	30 min.
Shoulder steaks	¾ inch	45 to 60 min.
Cubes	1 to 1¼ inches	45 to 60 min.

COOKING IN LIQUID

CUT	Approx. Weight	Approx. Total Cooking Time
SMOKED	Pounds	Hours
Ham (old style and		
country-cured		
Large	12 to 16	4½ to 5
Small	10 to 12	4½ to 5
Half	5 to 8	3 to 4
Picnic Shoulder	5 to 8	3½ to 4
Shoulder roll	2 to 4	1½ to 2
Hocks		2 to 2½
FRESH		
Spareribs		2 to 2½
Country-style backbones		2 to 2½
Hocks		2½ to 3

SOURCE: POTTS, B., SIMONDS, L., and VANSTAVERN, B. D., Meat Specials are Special. Ohio State Univ. Columbus Coop. Ext. Serv., Bull *574*.

PORK, COOKING CURED PRODUCTS

Label instructions should be followed. When not available, one of the following cooking methods should be used.

Roasting (Baking)

Place meat on a rack in a shallow roasting pan. Insert meat thermometer so the bulb is centered in the thickest part but does not rest in fat or on bone. Do not add water or cover. Roast (bake) in a slow oven (325°F) until done—internal temperature of 140°F is recommended for fully-cooked or canned hams and arm picnic shoulders; 160°F for cook-before-eating hams, loins and Canadian-style bacon; and 170°F for cook-before-eating arm picnic shoulders and shoulder rolls (butts). If ham is to be glazed, brush glaze on the ham 15 to 30 min before the end of the cooking time.

Broiling

Set oven regulator for broiling. Broil meat 2 to 3 in. from heat until meat is lightly browned on one side. Turn meat and cook until done.

Panbroiling

Cuts cooked by broiling can also be panbroiled. Allow about half as much cooking time as for broiling.

Cooking in Liquid

Cook-before-eating arm picnic shoulders and shoulder rolls can also be cooked in liquid. Follow cooking instructions on the package label. In case of no instructions, simmer in water just to cover in a covered utensil, allowing 1½ hr for the shoulder roll and 3½ to 4 hr for the picnic.

TABLE 2.P.18

ROASTING AND BROILING CURED HAM PRODUCTS

Cut	Weight or Approx Thickness	Approx Total Cooking Time[1] at 325°F	Cut	Weight or Approx Thickness	Approx Total Cooking Time[1] at 325°F
For Roasting (Baking)					
	(lb)	(hr)		(lb)	(hr)
Boneless ham, fully-cooked	3-4 (portion)	1½-1¾	Bone-in ham, cook-before-eating	3-4 (portion)	2½-2¾
	5-7 (half)	2-2¼		5-7 (half)	3-3¼
	7-10	2½-3		10-12	3½-4
	10-12	3-3½		12-15	4-4½
	12-14	3½-4		15-18	4½-5
Bone-in ham, fully-cooked	10-13	3-3½		18-22	5-6
	13-16	3½-4			
Semi-boneless ham, fully-cooked	4-6 (half)	1¾-2½	Loin, cook-before-eating	3-5	1-2
	10-12	3-3½			
Canned hams	1½-3	1-1½	Canadian-style bacon	2-4	1¼-2¼
	3-7	1½-2			
	7-10	2-2½			
	10-13	2½-3			
Arm picnic shoulder, fully-cooked	4-8	1¾-2¾	Arm picnic shoulder, cook-before-eating	4-8	2½-4
Boneless ham, cook-before-eating	8-11	2½-3¼	Shoulder roll (butt), cook-before-eating	2-3	1½-2
	11-14	3¼-4			

TABLE 2.P.18 (*Continued*)

Cut	Approx Thickness (in.)	Approx Total Cooking Time (min)
	For Broiling at Moderate Temp[2]	
Ham slice	½	10–12
Ham slice	1	16–20
Smoked loin chops	½–¾	15–20
Canadian-style bacon		
Sliced	¼	6–8
Sliced	½	8–10
Ham kabobs	1–1½	16–20
Ham patties	1	16–20

[1] Cooking times are for (1) heating fully-cooked or canned cuts to 140°F internal temperature as registered on a meat thermometer; (2) cooking cook-before-eating ham and loin cuts to 160°F; and (3) cooking cook-before-eating picnics and shoulder rolls to 170°F.

[2] Temperature that results from broiling ½ to 1-in. thick cuts 2 to 3 in. from the heat.

SOURCE: Pork Industry Group, National Live Stock & Meat Board, Chicago.

PORK, COOKING METHODS

Suggested Cooking Methods

For fresh pork	
Arm or blade shoulder chop or steak	Pan fry, pan broil, or braise
Ham	Roast
Hocks	Simmer
Loin or rib roast	Roast
Loin or rib chops	Pan fry, pan broil, or braise
Shoulder roast (picnic) or shoulder butt roast (Boston butt)	Roast
Spareribs	Roast or braise
Tenderloin	Pan fry, pan broil, or braise
For cured pork	
Bacon	Broil, pan broil, or pan fry
Canadian bacon	Roast, broil, pan broil, or pan fry
Ham, whole or part	Roast or simmer
Ham slices	Broil,[1] pan broil, pan fry, or braise
Ham shanks	Simmer or braise
Shoulder (picnic) or shoulder butt (Boston butt)	Roast or simmer

[1] Thin slices only.

SOURCE: Pork in Family Meals. (1969). USDA Home and Garden Bull. *160*.

PORK COOKING YIELD

TABLE 2.P.19

YIELD OF BONELESS COOKED MEAT FROM RETAIL PORK CUTS

Cut of pork	Approximate yield of cooked lean and some fat from one pound of pork as purchased [1]	
	3-ounce servings	Volume, chopped or diced
	Number	*Cups*
Fresh:		
Ham:		
Bone-in	2½	1½
Boneless	3	2
Heart	2 to 2½	1½ to 2
Liver	3	
Loin chops, bone-in	2½	
Loin roast:		
Bone-in	2 to 2½	1 to 1½
Boneless	3 to 3½	2
Rib chops, bone-in	2 to 2½	
Shoulder roast (picnic):		
Bone-in	2	1 to 1½
Boneless	3	1½ to 2
Shoulder butt roast (Boston butt):		
Bone-in	3	1½ to 2
Boneless	3 to 3½	2
Spareribs	1½ to 2	
Cured (mild):		
Ham:		
Canned, boneless:		
Served cold	4½	2½ to 3
Heated before serving	4	2½
Cook-before-eating:		
Bone-in	3½	2
Boneless	4	2½
Fully cooked:		
Bone-in	3½	2
Boneless	4	2½
Shoulder (picnic):		
Bone-in	2½	1½
Boneless	3 to 3½	2
Shoulder butt (Boston butt):		
Bone-in	3	1½ to 2
Boneless	3½	2

[1] These figures allow no more than 10 percent fat on a cooked bone-in cut and no more than 15 percent fat on a cooked boneless cut.

SOURCE: Pork in Family Meals. (1969). USDA Home and Garden Bull. *160*.

PORK CUTS

TABLE 2.P.20

CHARACTERISTICS AND COOKING METHODS FOR PORK CUTS

WHOLESALE CUTS	RETAIL CUTS	CHARACTERISTICS	COOKING METHODS
Ham Fresh Pickled, or Smoked	Ham, Whole	Corresponds to beef round with tail bone and portion of backbone removed. Outer skin or rind is left on the regular ham but it is removed, with excess fat, from the skinned ham.	*Roast (bake); cook in liquid*
	Ham, Shank Half	Lower half of ham. Includes shank and ½ of center section.	*Roast (bake); cook in liquid*
	Ham Shank	Cone-shaped, rind-covered piece containing shank bones.	*Cook in liquid*
	Ham, Butt Half	Upper half of ham. Includes butt and ½ of center section.	*Roast (bake); cook in liquid*
	Ham Butt	Same as above minus most of center section.	*Roast (bake); cook in liquid*
	Ham, Center Baking Piece	Center section of ham. Both cut surfaces look like center slices.	*Roast (bake); cook in liquid*
	Ham, Center Slice	Oval shape, small round bone, four separate muscles.	*Broil, panbroil, panfry*
	Ham, Boneless	Boneless roll. Fresh, pickled, or smoked.	*Roast (bake); cook in liquid*
Loin Also Tenderloin, Boneless Back Strip and Canadian Style Bacon	Tenderloin	Long tapering round muscle. Weighs ½ to 1 pound.	*Roast; braise*
	Frenched Tenderloin	Piece cut from tenderloin and flattened.	*Braise; panfry*
	Boneless Loin Roast	Boneless back strip. Two pieces sometimes tied together.	*Roast*
	Canadian Style Bacon	Boneless back strip, cured and smoked.	*Roast; broil; panbroil; panfry*
	Butterfly Chop	Double chop, hinged together, cut from boneless loin strip.	*Braise; panfry*
	Sirloin Roast	Ham end of loin containing hip bone.	*Roast*
	Blade Loin Roast	Shoulder end of loin containing rib bones and blade bone.	*Roast*
	Loin Chop	T-shaped bone and two muscles (back strip and tenderloin).	*Braise; panfry*
	Rib Chop	Alternate chops have rib bone. May be "frenched".	*Braise; panfry*
	Crown Roast	Rib sections "frenched" and formed in shape of crown.	*Roast*

(Continued)

TABLE 2.P.20 (*Continued*)

WHOLESALE CUTS	RETAIL CUTS	CHARACTERISTICS	COOKING METHODS
Picnic Shoulder Fresh, Pickled, or Smoked	Picnic Shoulder	Includes arm and shank sections of the shoulder.	*Roast (bake); cook in liquid*
	Rolled Picnic Shoulder	Boneless roll. Fresh, pickled or smoked.	*Roast (bake); cook in liquid*
	Cushion Picnic Shoulder	Arm section of fresh picnic with pocket for stuffing.	*Roast*
	Arm Steak	Oval at one end, squared off at other. Small round bone.	*Braise; panfry*
	Pork Hock	Round, tapering, skin-covered piece containing shank bones.	*Braise; cook in liquid*
Boston Butt Also Smoked Shoulder Butt	Boston Butt	Upper half of shoulder. Contains part of blade bone.	*Roast*
	Blade Steak	Cut from Boston butt. Most steaks have section of blade bone.	*Braise; panfry*
	Smoked Shoulder Butt	Eye of Boston butt. Cured and smoked boneless roll.	*Roast (bake); cook in liquid*
	Sm. Sh. Butt Slices	Round boneless slices. Lean and fat intermixed.	*Broil; panbroil; panfry*
Side (Belly) Fresh, Salt Pickled, or Smoked	Fresh Side Pork	Usually sliced. Alternating layers of lean and fat.	*Braise; panfry*
	Pickled Side Pork	Same as above but cured in a sweet pickle solution.	*Braise; panfry*
	Salt Side Pork	Same as above but cured with dry salt.	*Panfry; cook in liquid*
	Sliced Bacon	Same as above but cured, dry or in pickle, then smoked.	*Broil; panbroil; panfry*
Spareribs	Spareribs	Ribs and breastbone which have been removed from the bacon strip.	*Roast; braise; cook in liquid*
Jowl	Jowl Bacon Square	Jowl, trimmed square, then cured and smoked. High percentage of fat. May be sliced.	*Cook in liquid; broil; panbroil; panfry*
Feet	Pig's Feet, Fresh	Contain bones and tendons of foot and ankle. Little lean meat.	*Cook in liquid*
	Pig's Feet, Pickled	Pickled, cooked and ready to eat.	*No cooking necessary*

SOURCE: Meat Manual, 6th Edition. National Live Stock and Meat Board, Chicago.

PORK CUTS AND USES

TABLE 2.P.21

PORK CUTS AND HOW TO USE THEM

WHOLESALE CUT	DESCRIPTION OF CUT	RETAIL CUTS	PORK SPECIALTIES
FEET	Bone, skin, not much meat, but this is delicate.	Pig's feet	Brains— Fry, scramble with eggs
HAM OR LEG OF PORK	Solid meat, very little bone. Fresh or smoked.	Roasts, steaks	Lungs— Braise
BACON	Cured and smoked, fat streaked with lean.	Breakfast bacon	Head— Head cheese
LOIN	Tender, lean meat. May be boned and cured as Canadian style bacon.	Roasts, chops, tenderloin	Heart— Braise
PICNIC SHOULDER	Well flavored, largely lean meat, fresh or smoked.	Roasts, steaks	Liver— Fry, broil, braise, roast whole or as loaf
BOSTON BUTT	Higher in lean than any pork cut, very little bone	Boston butt, steaks, smoked shoulder butt	Tongue— Cook in water
SPARERIBS	Lean and fat, good flavor.	Spareribs	Tails— Cook in water with vegetables
			Ears and snouts— Cook in water with vegetables

SOURCE: Meat Buying Manual. National Live Stock and Meat Board, Chicago.

PORK LOIN CARVING

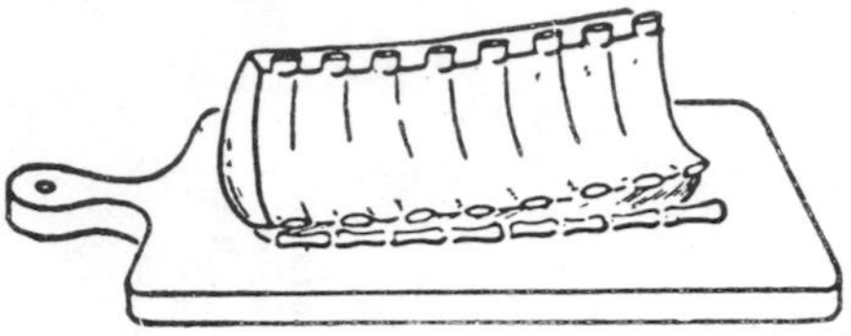

Have retailer saw backbone free from ribs for easier carving. Saw cut should not cut into meaty center.

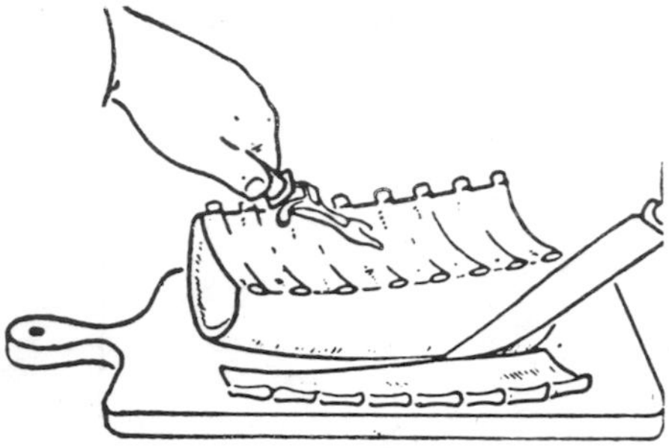

Before the roast is brought to the table, remove the backbone. Do this by cutting close along the bone, leaving as much meat on roast as possible. Place roast with bone side facing carver.

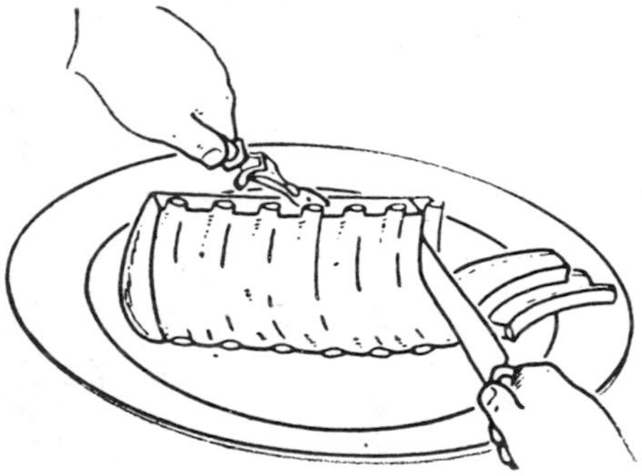

Insert the fork in the top of the roast. Make slices by cutting close along each side of the rib bone. One slice will contain the rib, the next will be boneless.

SOURCE: Carving Meat. National Live Stock and Meat Board, Chicago.

PORK LOIN COOKING

HOW TO COOK CUTS FROM THE PORK LOIN

Back Ribs
Braise, cook in liquid, roast

Back Ribs, Meaty
Braise, roast, cook in liquid

Blade/Bladeless Loin Chops
See "Chops, medium thick, thick, thin, stuffed"

Blade/Bladeless Loin Chops Tied Together
See "Chops tied together"

Blade/Bladeless Loin Roast
Roast

Blade Pieces
Cook in liquid, braise

Boneless Crown Roast
Roast

Brown and Serve (Breakfast) Chops
Panfry

Butterfly Chops
See "Chops, medium thick, thick, thin, stuffed"

Butterfly Cutlets
Braise, Panfry

Butterfly Top Loin
Braise, roast, broil

Canadian Style Bacon, Piece
Roast (Bake)

Canadian Style Bacon, Sliced
Broil, panbroil, panfry

Center Chops (Loin, Rib, Strip, Top Loin)
See "Chops, medium thick, thick, thin, stuffed"

Center Roast (Loin, Rib, Strip, Top Loin)
Roast

Chops, Medium Thick (½" to ¾")
Braise, panfry, broil, panbroil

Chops, Thick (1" to 2")
Braise, roast, broil

Chops, Thin (¼" to ⅜")
Braise, panfry

Chops, Stuffed
Braise, roast

Chops Tied Together
Best results when chops are separated and cooked as regular chops

Combination Loaf (Pork, Beef, Veal)
Roast (Bake)

Country Style Back Bones
Braise, roast, cook in liquid

Cradle Roast
Roast

Crown Roast, Bone-In or Boneless
Roast

Cube Steak (Porklets)
Panfry, braise

Cutlets, Regular (about ¼")
Braise, panfry

Cutlets, Wafer (⅛" to 3/16")
Panfry, braise

Frenched Rib Chops
See "Chops, medium thick, thick, thin, stuffed"

Frenched Rib Roast
Roast

Ground Pork, Individual Loaves (or Pork with Veal/Beef)
Roast (Bake), braise

Ground Pork, Loaf (or Pork with Veal/Beef)
Roast (Bake)

Ground Pork, Patties
Braise, panfry

Loin Back Bones
Cook in liquid

Loin Back Bones, Meaty
Braise, roast, cook in liquid

Loin Chops
See "Chops, medium thick, thick, thin, stuffed"

Loin Eye Fillet
Braise, roast, broil

Loin Eye Fillet Slices
See "Chops, medium thick, thick, thin, stuffed"

Meaty Loin Back Bones/Back Ribs
Braise, roast, cook in liquid

Pork and Ham Loaf
Roast (Bake)

Pork and Veal Cube Steaks
Panfry, braise

Pork and Veal for Chop Suey
Braise

Pork and Veal Individual Loaves
Roast (Bake), braise

Pork and Veal Loaf
Roast (Bake)

Pork and Veal Patties
Braise, panfry

Pork Kabobs
Braise, roast, broil

Pork for Chop Suey
Braise

Porklets (Cube Steaks)
Panfry, braise

Pork Mates
Braise, roast

Pork Patties
Braise, panfry

Rib Back Bones
Cook in liquid

Rib Chops
See "Chops, medium thick, thick, thin, stuffed"

Roasts, Bone-In or Boneless
Roast

Rolled Loin Roast
Roast

Sirloin Chops
See "Chops, medium thick, thick, thin, stuffed"

Sirloin Chops Tied Together
See "Chops tied together"

Sirloin Cutlets
Panfry, braise

Sirloin Roast
Roast

Strip Loin Chops
See "Chops, medium thick, thick, thin, stuffed"

Strip Loin Roast
Roast

Stuffed Chops (All Kinds)
Braise, roast

Tenderloin, Frenched or Butterflied
Braise, panfry

Tenderloin Kabobs
Braise, roast, broil, panfry

Tenderloin Roll
Roast

Tenderloin Roundels
Roast, braise, broil, panfry

Tenderloin Tips
Braise, panfry

Tenderloin, Whole
Braise, roast, broil

Tipless Tenderloin
Braise, roast, broil

Top Loin Chops
See "Chops, medium thick, thick, thin, stuffed"

Top Loin Roast
Roast

Top Loin Wafer Cutlets
Panfry

Wafer Cutlets
Panfry

SOURCE: Merchandising Pork Loins. National Live Stock and Meat Board, Chicago.

PORK LOIN NOMENCLATURE

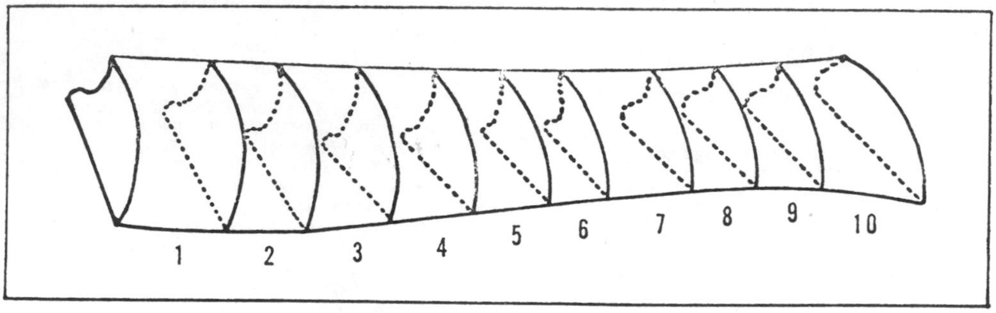

	Recommended Name	Descriptive Information
(1)	Pork loin blade roast	3-rib (blade/bladeless) loin roast
(1-2)	Pork loin blade roast	5-rib (blade/bladeless) loin roast
(1-3)	Pork loin blade roast	7-rib (blade/bladeless) loin roast
(1-4)	Pork loin blade roast	9-rib (blade/bladeless) loin roast
(1-5)	Pork loin blade half	Rib half (blade/bladeless) pork loin
(10)	Pork loin sirloin roast	Pork sirloin (hip only)
(9-10)	Pork loin sirloin roast	7 in. sirloin roast
(8-10)	Pork loin sirloin roast	9 in. sirloin roast (or portion)
(6-10)	Pork loin sirloin half	Loin half of pork loin
(2-9)	Pork loin center loin roast or chops	Pork center loin roast or chops

SOURCE: Uniform Retail Meat Identity Standards. (1973). National Live Stock and Meat Board, Chicago.

PORK, PERCENTAGES OF DAILY RECOMMENDED ALLOWANCES

TABLE 2.P.22

PERCENTAGES OF DAILY RECOMMENDED ALLOWANCES*
(based on $3\frac{1}{2}$ oz cooked lean pork)

	Age	Protein	Calories	Iron	Phosphorus	Magnesium	Thiamin	Riboflavin	Niacin	Vit. B_6	Vit. B_{12}
CHILDREN	1-3	124	18	23	30	16	147	36	49	69	110
	4-6	95	13	35	30	12	114	26	37	46	73
	7-10	79	10	35	30	10	86	24	28	35	55
MALES	11-14	65	9	19	20	7	74	19	24	26	37
	15-18	53	8	19	20	6	69	16	22	21	37
	19-22	53	8	35	30	7	69	16	22	21	37
	23-50	51	9	35	30	7	74	18	24	21	37
	51+	51	10	35	30	7	86	19	28	21	37
FEMALES	11-14	65	10	19	20	8	86	22	28	26	37
	15-18	59	11	19	20	8	94	21	31	21	37
	19-22	62	11	19	30	8	94	21	31	21	37
	23-50	62	12	19	30	8	103	24	34	21	37
	51+	62	13	35	30	8	103	26	37	21	37

*Figures based on 1974 National Research Council Recommended Dietary Allowances.

SOURCE: Facts About Pork. (1974). National Live Stock and Meat Board, Chicago.

PORK SHOULDER

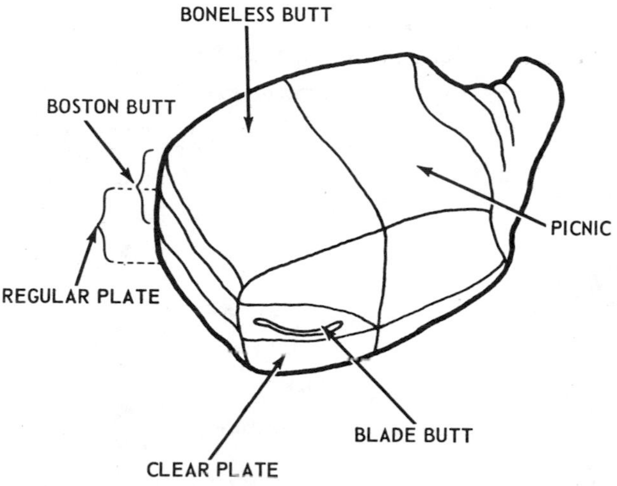

FIG. 2.P.6. BREAKDOWN OF PORK SHOULDER SHOWING RETAIL CUTS

SOURCE: Reproduced with permission of U.S. Department of the Army from Food Inspection Specialist *TM 8-451*.

PORK STORAGE

TABLE 2.P.23

SUGGESTED HOME STORAGE PERIODS TO MAINTAIN HIGH QUALITY IN PORK

Product	Storage period	
	Refrigerator, 35° to 40° F.	Freezer, 0° F.
Fresh raw pork:		
Chops	3 to 5 days	3 to 4 months
Roasts	3 to 5 days	4 to 8 months
Sausage	1 to 2 days	1 to 2 months
Variety meats	1 to 2 days	3 to 4 months
Cured or processed pork:		
Bacon	7 days	1 month or less [1]
Frankfurters	7 days	2 weeks
Ham:		
Whole	7 days	1 to 2 months [1]
Half	3 to 5 days	1 to 2 months [1]
Slices	3 days	1 to 2 months [1]
Large canned, unopened	Several months	
Luncheon meat	3 to 5 days	Not recommended
Sausage:		
Smoked	7 days	Not recommended
Dry and semi-dry	2 to 3 weeks	Not recommended
Cooked pork:		
Cooked pork and pork dishes	1 to 2 days	2 to 3 months
Gravy and meat broth	1 to 2 days	2 to 3 months

[1] Frozen cured meat loses quality rapidly and should be used as soon as possible.

SOURCE: Pork in Family Meals. (1969). USDA Home and Garden Bull. *160*.

PORK WHOLESALE CUTS

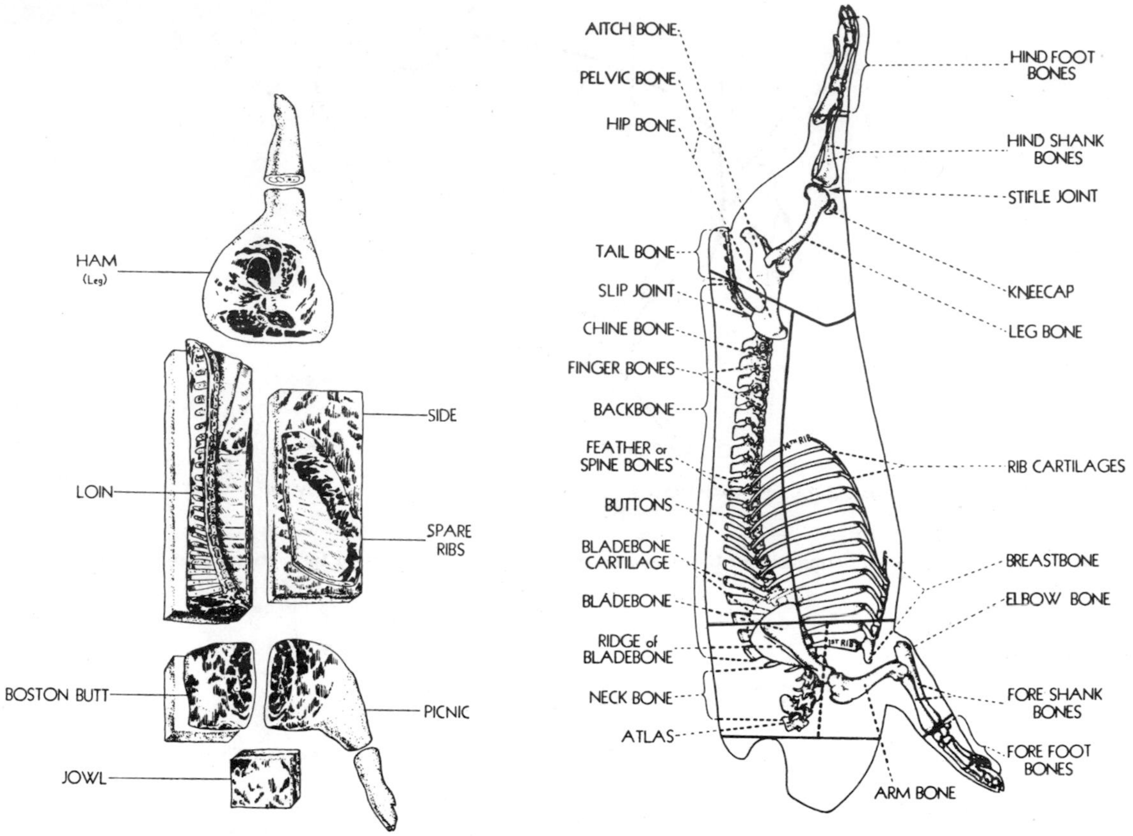

FIG. 2.P.7. WHOLESALE CUTS OF PORK (LEFT); STRUCTURE, LOCATION, AND NAMES OF CARCASS BONES (RIGHT)

SOURCE: Cooking Meat in Quantity. National Live Stock and Meat Board, Chicago.

PORK YIELD

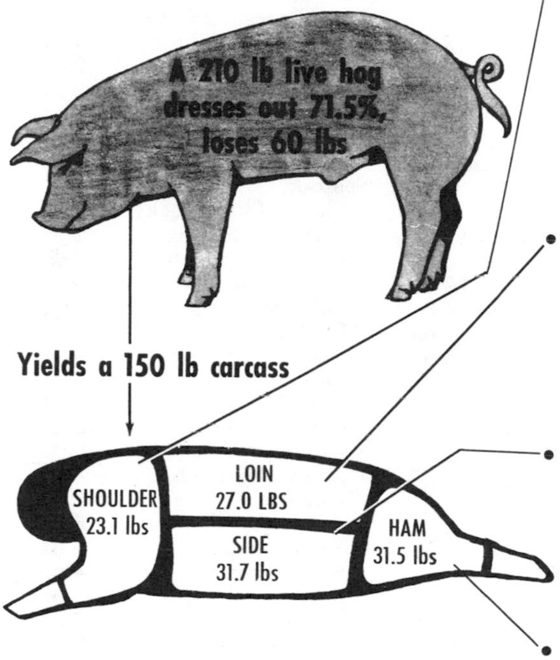

An additional 30 lb of fat for lard, bones and waste further reduces this 150-lb carcass to only 120 lb of saleable retail cuts—chops, hams, bacon, ribs and sausage—that the retailer wraps and puts on display in the meat case.

Figures are averages taken from actual cut-out tests. Carcass data vary, depending on cutting method and type of hog.

Shoulder 23.1 lb (15.4% of total carcass)

	Saleable Pork Cuts (lb)	Other (lb)	(lb)
Boston shoulder	9.4		
Fat for lard		0.5	
Picnic shoulder cubes	7.0		
Bone		2.8	
Hocks	3.4		
Total	19.8	3.3	23.1

Loin 27.0 lb (18.0% of total carcass)

	(lb)	(lb)	(lb)
Blade roast (5 rib)	6.3		
Center chops	13.3		
Sirloin roast	4.2		
Fat for lard		3.2	
Total	23.8	3.2	27.0

Side 31.7 lb (21.1% of total carcass)

	(lb)		(lb)
Bacon, cured	24.0		
Sausage trimmings	2.0		
Spareribs	5.7		
Total	31.7		31.7

Ham 31.5 lb (21.0% of total carcass)

	(lb)	(lb)	(lb)
Rolled leg of pork roast, boneless	19.8		
Sausage trimmings	2.8		
Skin	2.2		
Fat for lard		3.2	
Bone and shrink		3.5	
Total	24.8	6.7	31.5

Miscellaneous 36.7 lb (24.5% of total carcass)

	(lb)	(lb)	(lb)
Jowl, trimmed	4.5		
Feet, tail, neckbones	9.0		
Sausage trimmings	6.4		
Fat for lard		16.8	
Total	19.9	16.8	36.7

	(lb)
Total saleable pork cuts	120.0
Total fat for lard	23.7
Bone and shrink	6.3
Total carcass weight	150.0

SOURCE: A Hog's Not All Chops. (1972). National Live Stock and Meat Board, Chicago.

PORTION SIZE

TABLE 2.P.24

TYPICAL PORTION SIZES FOR MENU ITEMS

Beverages		Beef		Sandwiches (excluding bread)	
Coffee	4 oz	Roasts	6 oz	Beef	4 oz
Tea	4 oz	Steaks		Cheese	2 oz
Milk	½ pt	Chateaubriand	16 oz	Chicken	2 oz
Soft drinks	4–6 oz	Filet mignon	6 oz	Ham	2 oz
Breads, rolls, cereals		Minute	6 oz	Hamburgers	2–4 oz
Bread	2 oz	Porterhouse	16 oz	Turkey	2 oz
Cream of wheat	4 oz	Salisbury	8 oz	Seafood	
Hot rolls	2 oz	Sirloin	8 oz	Clams (Little Neck)	12
Muffins (cakes)	2	T-bone	12 oz	Crabs, soft-shell	2
Cereals, flaked	4 oz	Ham	6 oz	Fish	6–7 oz
Cereals, puffed	2 oz	Lamb chops	10 oz	Frogs' legs	8 oz
Toast	4 oz	Liver	4 oz	Lobster, half	12 oz
Casseroles, stews, etc.		Pork chops	7 oz	Oysters	6
Baked beans	6 oz	Sausage	6 oz	Shrimp	6 oz
Chili con carne	6 oz	Veal chops	8 oz	Soups	
Corned beef	6 oz	Veal cutlets	5 oz	Cup	6 oz
Corned beef hash	6 oz	Pastries, desserts, etc.		Bowl	8 oz
Goulash	6 oz	Cakes	2 oz	Vegetables	
Ham a la king	4 oz	Ice cream	4 oz	Asparagus, fresh pieces	7
Macaroni and cheese	5 oz	Pies, fruit	8 oz	Asparagus, tips	5 oz
Meat loaf	5 oz	Puddings	5 oz	Beans, green	4 oz
Short ribs	12 oz	Poultry		Beans, lima	4 oz
Spaghetti	5 oz	Chicken, fried	8 oz	Beets	5 oz
Spanish rice	5 oz	Chicken, broiled	8 oz	Cauliflower	5 oz
Stews	7 oz	Duck	10 oz	Carrots	5 oz
Stuffed cabbage	4 oz	Turkey	7 oz	Corn, cob (ears)	2
Fruits		Salads		Corn, kernel	5 oz
Canned	4 oz	Cole slaw	3 oz	Potatoes	6 oz
Fresh	4–6 oz	Chicken salad	4 oz	Peas	4 oz
Meats		Mixed vegetable	4 oz	Spinach	6 oz
Bacon	5 oz	Potato	4 oz	Squash	4 oz
		Waldorf	4 oz	Tomatoes	5 oz

SOURCE: KAZARIAN, E. A. 1975. Food Service Facilities Planning. Avi Publishing Co., Westport, Conn.

POTASSIUM

TABLE 2.P.25

POTASSIUM CONTENT OF FOODS

	mg/100 g		mg/100 g
Lima beans	650	Carrots	341
Watermelon	600	Celery	341
Spinach	470	Corn	280
Artichokes	430	Tomatoes	244
Potatoes	407	Peaches	202
Brussels sprouts	390	Oranges	200
Broccoli	382	Lettuce	175
Bananas	370	Apples	110

SOURCE: WHITE, P. L. and SELVEY, N. (EDITORS). 1974. Nutritional Qualities of Fresh Fruits and Vegetables. Futura Publishing Co., Mt. Kisco, N.Y.

POTASSIUM-RICH FOODS

TABLE 2.P.26

FOODS THAT ARE RICH IN POTASSIUM

Foods	*Average Portion*	*Potassium (mg)*	*Calories*
Fruits			
Orange	1 medium	360	95
Grapefruit	1 cup	380	75
Banana	1 medium	630	130
Strawberries	1 cup	270	55
Avocado	½ medium	380	275
Apricots	3 medium	500	55
Dates	1 cup	1390	500
Watermelon	½ slice	380	95
Cantaloupe	½ medium	880	75
Raisins	1 cup	1150	425
Prunes	4 large	240	90
Juices			
Orange	8-oz glass	440	105
Grapefruit	8-oz glass	370	130
Prune	8-oz glass	620	170
Pineapple	8-oz glass	340	120
Meats			
Hamburger	3 oz	290	310
Beef chuck	3 oz	310	260
Beef round	3 oz	340	200
Rib roast	3 oz	290	270
Turkey	4 oz	350	300
Vegetables			
Tomato	1 medium	340	30
Artichoke	1 medium	210	30
Brussels sprouts	1 cup	300	35

SOURCE: HOLVEY, D. N. 1972. The Merck Manual, 12th Edition. Merck & Co., Rahway, New Jersey.

POULTRY BREEDS AND VARIETIES

TABLE 2.P.27

SOME BREEDS AND VARIETIES OF POULTRY AND THEIR CHARACTERISTICS

Breed and Variety	Plumage	Standard Weight Cock (lb)	Standard Weight Hen (lb)	Comb Type	Ear Lobe Color	Skin Color	Shank Color	Shanks Feathered?	Egg Color
American:									
White Plymouth Rock	White	9½	7½	Single	Red	Yellow	Yellow	No	Brown
White Wyandotte	White	8½	6½	Rose	Red	Yellow	Yellow	No	Brown
Rhode Island Red	Red	8½	6½	Single and rose	Red	Yellow	Yellow	No	Brown
New Hampshire	Red	8½	6½	Single	Red	Yellow	Yellow	No	Brown
Asiatic:									
Brahma (light)	Columbian pattern	12	9½	Pea	Red	Yellow	Yellow	Yes	Brown
Cochin (buff)	Buff	11	8½	Single	Red	Yellow	Yellow	Yes	Brown
English:									
Australorp	Black	8½	6½	Single	Red	White	Dark slate	No	Brown
White Cornish	White	10½	8	Pea	Red	Yellow	Yellow	No	Brown
Mediterranean:									
White Leghorn	White	6	4½	Single and rose	White	Yellow	Yellow	No	White

SOURCE: ENSMINGER, M. E. 1969. Animal Science. Interstate Printers & Publishers, Danville, Illinois.

POULTRY CLASS

The following are cooking recommendations and identification labeling for classes of poultry:

Young tender-meated classes are most suitable for barbecuing, frying, broiling, or roasting.

Young chickens may be labeled: young chicken, Rock Cornish game hen, broiler, fryer, roaster, or capon.

Young turkeys may be labeled: young turkey, fryer-roaster, young hen, or young tom.

Young ducks may be labeled: duckling, young duckling, broiler duckling, fryer duckling, or roaster duckling.

Mature, less-tender meated classes may be preferred for stewing, baking, soups, or salads.

Mature chickens may be labeled: mature chicken, old chicken, hen, stewing chicken, or fowl.

Mature turkeys may be labeled: mature turkey, yearling turkey, or old turkey.

Mature ducks, geese, and guineas may be labeled: mature or old.

SOURCE: How to Buy Poultry. (1968). USDA Home and Garden Bull. *157*.

POULTRY COMPOSITION

TABLE 2.P.28

COMPOSITION OF POULTRY PRODUCTS

Food, Approximate Measure, and Weight (in Grams)		Water (%)	Food Energy (Cal)	Protein (g)	Fat (Total Lipid) (g)	Fatty Acids: Saturated (Total) (g)	Fatty Acids: Unsaturated: Oleic (g)	Fatty Acids: Unsaturated: Linoleic (g)	Carbohydrate (g)	Calcium (mg)	Iron (mg)	Vitamin A Value (I.U)	Thiamin (mg)	Riboflavin (mg)	Niacin (mg)	Ascorbic Acid (mg)
Chicken, cooked—																
Breast, fried, ½ breast:																
With bone	3.3 oz (94 g)	52	215	24	12	3	6	2		10	1.1	60	0.03	0.06	9.4	
Flesh and skin only	2.8 oz (79 g)	52	215	24	12	3	6	2		10	1.1	60	0.03	0.06	9.4	
Leg, fried (thigh and drumstick):																
With bone	4.3 oz (121 g)	52	245	27	15	4	7	2		13	1.8	220	0.05	0.18	4.7	
Flesh and skin only	3.1 oz (89 g)	52	245	27	15	4	7	2		13	1.8	220	0.05	0.18	4.7	
Chicken, canned, boneless	3 oz (85 g)	62	170	25	7	2	3	1	0	12	1.5	160	0.03	0.14	5.4	
Chicken, cooked:																
Flesh and skin, broiled	3 oz without bone. (85 g)	61	185	23	9	3	4	2	0	10	1.4	260	0.04	0.15	7.1	
Poultry potpie (chicken or turkey): Individual pie, 4¼-in.-diam, about 8 oz	1 pie (227 g)	60	485	17	28	8	15	3	39	41	1.6	1,860	0.07	0.14	3.2	Tr

SOURCE: INSTITUTE OF HOME ECONOMICS. Nutritive Value of Foods. USDA Home and Garden Bull. 72.

POULTRY DRESSING PERCENTAGE

TABLE 2.P.29

DRESSING PERCENTAGES OF THE SEVERAL KINDS OF POULTRY PROCESSED AT ONTARIO COMMERCIAL PROCESSING PLANTS

		As a Percentage of Live Weight										As a Percentage of Dressed Weight			
						Giblets									
Kind	Sex	Hot Dressed	Heads	Legs	Carcass and Neck	Heart	Liver	Gizzard	Total	Total Ready-to-Cook	Chilled Carcass and Neck	Carcass and Neck	Total Giblets	Total Ready-to-Cook	Chilled Carcass
		%	%	%	%	%	%	%	%	%	%	%	%	%	%
Chicken Broilers	Male	92.1	2.7	5.3	72.2	0.5	2.1	1.9	4.6	76.7	72.8	78.3	4.9	83.3	79.0
	Female	91.8	2.9	4.8	71.5	0.5	2.2	2.3	5.1	76.7	72.9	77.9	5.6	83.5	79.5
	Male	94.5	2.6	4.7	74.2	0.4	1.9	1.6	3.9	78.2	76.4	78.5	4.2	82.7	80.9
	Female	92.6	2.5	3.9	73.8	0.4	1.9	2.3	4.7	78.5	74.8	79.7	5.1	84.8	80.7
Capons		90.3	2.4	3.9	68.9	0.4	1.7	2.0	4.0	75.7	71.5	79.3	4.5	83.8	79.1
Turkeys B.B.W.	Male	92.6	1.8	1.7	77.0	0.4	1.9	1.2	3.6	80.6	80.1	83.2	3.8	87.1	86.6
	Female	92.0	1.5	2.7	75.8	0.4	1.7	1.6	3.6	79.4	78.7	82.4	4.0	86.3	85.5
Turkey Broilers B.B.W.	Male	89.9	3.7	3.1	75.8	0.4	1.3	1.4	3.2	79.0	81.5	84.3	3.5	87.8	89.5
	Female	92.8	2.8	2.6	77.0	1.7[2]		1.5	3.2	80.1	80.5	83.0	3.4	86.3	86.8
Pekin Ducks	Male	85.8	4.3	2.1	64.4	0.7	3.3	1.8	5.7	70.1	67.9	75.1	6.6	81.7	79.1
	Female	84.8	4.0	2.0	64.7	0.6	3.0	1.9	5.5	70.3	64.7	76.3	6.5	82.9	76.3
Pheasants	Male	91.7	3.0	2.4	76.8	0.5	1.9	1.8	4.3	81.1	78.9	83.7	4.7	88.4	86.0
	Female	90.8	2.8	2.1	75.1	0.5	1.8	2.2	4.5	79.6	78.8	82.7	4.9	87.6	86.8

Note:
(2) Hearts and livers

Poultry Products Lab.
Ontario Agricultural College
1962-63

SOURCE: SNYDER, E. S., and ORR, H. L. 1964. Poultry Meat. Dep. Agric. Publ. 9, Can. Dep. Agric., Ottawa.

POULTRY GRADE STAMP

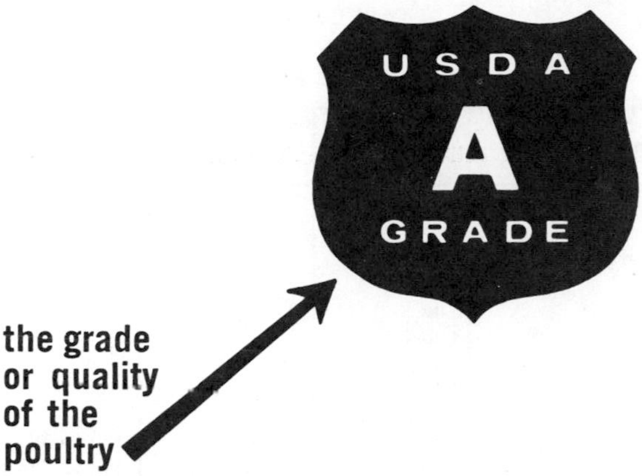

SOURCE: How to Buy Poultry. (1968). USDA Home and Garden Bull. *157*.

POULTRY INSPECTION AND GRADE STAMP

SOURCE: How to Buy Poultry. (1968). USDA Home and Garden Bull. *157*.

POULTRY INSPECTION STAMP

SOURCE: How to Buy Poultry. (1968). USDA Home and Garden Bull. *157*.

POULTRY ROASTING

TABLE 2.P.30

ROASTING GUIDE FOR POULTRY

Kind	Ready-to-cook weight [1]	Approximate total roasting time at 325° F.[2]	Internal temperature of poultry when done
	Pounds	*Hours*	*Degrees F.*
Chickens, whole:			
Broilers, fryers, or roasters	1½ to 2½	1 to 2	
	2½ to 4½	2 to 3½	
Capons	5 to 8	2½ to 3½	
Ducks	4 to 6	2 to 3	
Geese	6 to 8	3 to 3½	
	8 to 12	3½ to 4½	
Turkeys:			
Whole	6 to 8	3 to 3½	180 to 185 in thigh.
	8 to 12	3½ to 4½	180 to 185 in thigh.
	12 to 16	4½ to 5½	180 to 185 in thigh.
	16 to 20	5½ to 6½	180 to 185 in thigh.
	20 to 24	6½ to 7	180 to 185 in thigh.
Halves, quarters, and pieces	3 to 8	2 to 3	
	8 to 12	3 to 4	
Boneless turkey roasts	3 to 10	3 to 4	170 to 175 in center.

[1] Weight of giblets and neck included for whole poultry.

[2] Cooking time suggested is for stuffed poultry (except for turkey parts and boneless roasts). Unstuffed whole poultry may take slightly less time than stuffed poultry.

Cooking time is only approximate; a meat thermometer can be used to help determine doneness of whole turkeys. Stuffing temperature should reach at least 165° F.

Cooking time is based on chilled poultry or poultry that has just been thawed—temperature not above 40° F. Unstuffed poultry cooked from the frozen state will take longer. Do not use this table for frozen commercially stuffed poultry

SOURCE: Poultry in Family Meals. (1974). USDA Home and Garden Bull. *110*.

POULTRY TIME AND TEMPERATURE COOKING (FROZEN)

TABLE 2.P.31

RECOMMENDED COOKING TIMES FOR FROZEN COMMERCIALLY STUFFED POULTRY[1]

Kind and class	Weight as purchased	Approximate time, uncovered, at 325° F.	Approximate time, covered, at 400° F.
	Pounds	*Hours*	*Hours*
Turkeys	5 to 7	4½ to 6	2½ to 3½.
	7 to 9	6 to 6¾	3½ to 4.
	9 to 11	6¾ to 7¼	4 to 4½.
	11 to 13	7¼ to 8	4½ to 5.
	13 to 15	8 to 8½	5 to 5½.
	15 to 17	8½ to 10	5½ to 6.
Chickens:			
Rock Cornish game hens	2 to 2½	2½ to 3½	
Rock Roasters	4 to 5		2¾ to 3.
	5 to 6		3 to 3¼.
	6 and over		3¼ to 3½.

[1] **Do not thaw before cooking.**

SOURCE: Poultry in Family Meals. (1974). USDA Home and Garden Bull. *110*.

POULTRY YIELD

TABLE 2.P.32

PERCENTAGE RELATIONSHIP OF COOKED EDIBLE PORTION, PARTS AND BONES TO LIVE WEIGHT OF VARIOUS KINDS OF POULTRY PROCESSED IN ONTARIO COMMERCIAL PLANTS

Kind	Sex	Method of Cooking	Cooked Carcass[2] and Neck	White Meat	Dark Meat	Skin	Neck Meat	Total Edible Meat	Carcass Bones	Neck Bones	Total Bones	Total Loss[3] in Deboning
			%	%	%	%	%	%	%	%	%	%
Chicken Broilers	Male	Combined	51.9	15.3	13.5	4.2	1.3	36.8	10.9	0.7	11.6	3.5
	Female	Combined	52.7	17.0	13.8	5.1	1.4	37.4	11.0	0.8	11.7	3.6
Chicken Broilers	Male	Combined	51.8	16.9	14.4	4.1	1.2	36.6	11.0	0.7	11.8	3.4
	Female	Combined	51.2	17.2	13.6	4.5	1.4	36.8	10.2	0.7	10.8	2.7
Capons		Combined	47.9	17.6	14.7	3.5		35.8	8.7			3.4
Turkey Broilers	Male	Roasted	54.8	21.8	14.1	3.4	1.4	40.6	11.0	0.7	11.7	2.5
	Female	Roasted	57.7	22.3	15.1	3.5	1.3	42.2	10.7	0.7	11.4	3.6
Pekin Ducks	Male	Roasted	34.2	10.7[4]	9.0	4.3		24.1	7.8			2.6
	Female	Roasted	33.2	10.1	8.7	4.2		23.0	7.1			3.0
Pheasants	Male	Roasted	57.7	26.0	13.7	3.2	1.2	44.1	7.9	0.5	8.4	5.1
	Female	Roasted	52.7	24.0	12.3	3.0	1.0	40.4	6.8	0.4	7.2	5.0

Note
(2) For capons and ducks—carcass only, necks not included
(3) Includes waste + evaporation
(4) Breast meat

Poultry Products Lab.
Ontario Agricultural College
1962-63

SOURCE: SNYDER, E. S., and ORR, H. L. Poultry Meat. Dep. Agric. Publ. 9, Can. Dep. Agric., Ottawa.

PROTEIN AND AMINO ACIDS, COLOR REACTIONS

TABLE 2.P.33

SOME COLOR REACTIONS OF PROTEINS AND AMINO ACIDS

Test	Reagents	Linkage, group, or amino acid giving positive reaction	Color
Biruet reaction	Strong alkali, dilute copper sulfate	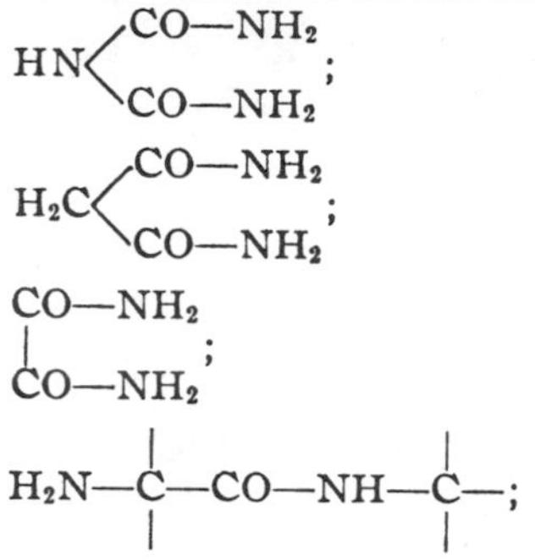 three or more amino acids joined by peptide linkage; histidine	Reddish violet to violet
Millon reaction	Mercurous and mercuric nitrate in a solution of nitric acid	Hydroxyphenyl group; among amino acids specific for tyrosine	Brick-red
Xanthoproteic reaction	Concentrated nitric acid	Phenyl group; among amino acids, tyrosine and tryptophan give test most readily	Yellow, deepens to orange on addition of alkali
Glyoxylic or Hopkins-Cole reaction	Glyoxylic acid	Indole ring; among amino acids specific for tryptophan	Violet
Ninhydrin reaction	Triketohydrindene hydrate	α-Amino acids; proline; hydroxyproline	Blue
Ehrlich benzaldehyde reaction	*p*-Dimethylaminobenzaldehyde	Indole ring	Blue[a]
Sakaguchi reaction	α-Naphthol, sodium hypochlorite	Guanidine group; among amino acids specific for arginine	Red
Sullivan reaction	1,2-Naphthoquinone-4-sodium sulfonate; sodium sulfite; sodium hydrosulfite; sodium cyanide	Cysteine, cystine	Red

[a] Proteins or a mixture of amino acids containing tryptophan yield a blue color when treated with Ehrlich's reagent in the presence of concentrated hydrochloric acid. Indole yields a red color. With *p*-dimethylaminobenzaldehyde in sulfuric acid, tryptophan gives a red-violet color

SOURCE: JACOBS, M. B. (EDITOR). The Chemistry and Technology of Food and Food Products, 2nd Edition, Vol. 1. John Wiley & Sons, New York.

PROTEIN FACTORS

TABLE 2.P.34

FACTORS SUGGESTED FOR USE IN CONVERTING PERCENTAGES OF NITROGEN IN VARIOUS SUBSTANCES INTO PERCENTAGES OF PROTEIN[1]

Substance	Factor Suggested	Substance	Factor Suggested
Cereal grains		Brazil nut	5.46
Wheat, endosperm	5.70	Hazelnut	5.30
Wheat, embryo	5.80	Walnut	5.30
Wheat, bran	6.31	Peanut	5.46
Wheat, whole kernel	5.83	Soybean	5.71
Rye	5.83	Butternut	5.30
Barley	5.83	Castor bean	5.30
Oats	5.83		
Rice	5.95	Substances of animal origin	
Corn (maize)	5.26	Milk	6.38
		Eggs	6.25
Oilseeds and nuts		Meats	6.25
Hempseed	5.30	Gelatin	5.55
Cottonseed	5.30		
Sunflower seed	5.30		
Flaxseed	5.30	Leguminous seeds	
Squash seed	5.30	Navy bean	6.25
Pumpkin seed	5.30	Lima bean	6.25
Sesame seed	5.30	Mung bean	6.25
Cantaloupe seed	5.30	Velvet bean	6.25
Almonds	5.18	Adzuki bean	6.25
Coconut	5.30	Jack bean	6.25

[1] D. B. Jones, *U.S. Dept. Agr., Circ.* 183 (1941).

SOURCE: JACOBS, M. B. (EDITOR). The Chemistry and Technology of Food and Food Products, 2nd Edition, Vol. 1. John Wiley & Sons, New York.

PULSES, NUTS AND SEEDS COMPOSITION

TABLE 2.P.35

COMPOSITION OF THE EDIBLE PORTION AND REFUSE IN THE MATERIAL AS PURCHASED

Commodity and Description Pulses, Nuts, and Seeds	Water	Protein	Fat	Carbohydrate: Total (by Dif.)	Carbohydrate: Fiber	Ash	Calories (No. per 100 g)	Notes	Refuse (%)
	Percent of edible portion								
Groundnuts, peanuts—in shell	5.2	25.6	43.3	23.4	3.3	2.5	546		29
—shelled	5.2	25.6	43.3	23.4	3.3	2.5	546		0
Soybeans and soybean products								Yield from 1 kg soybeans (kg)	
Whole seeds, dry	8	38	18	31.3[1]	4.8	4.7	335	1.0	0
Flour, full fat (seed coat removed)	8	39	21	27.4[1]	2.4	4.6	357	0.95	0
Flour, low fat; grits, flakes (partially defatted)	8	46	5	35.2[1]	2.3	5.8	261	0.84	0
Curd, tofu	87.4	6.3	3.1	2.5	0.1	0.7	58	3.5	0
Fermented beans, Japanese *natto*	61	17	9	11[1]	3	2	153	2.0	0
Fermented beans, Chinese *tsiang*	45	17	10	6[1]	3	22	153	2.0	0
Soybean milk	92	3.2	2.0	2.3	0.4	0.5	37	7.5	0
Paste, miso (made with small amounts of rice or other starchy materials)	52	11.0	5.8	16.5[1]	2.9	14.7	114	2.5	0
Shouyu sauce	67	5.5	0.5	8	(0)	19	56	3.5	0
Other dry beans and peas, unspecified	11	22.2	2.1	61.6	4.4	3.1	345	Beans, grams, peas, chickpea, fava, cowpea, lentils	0
Treenuts									
Coconuts, meat, fresh									
Old, ripe	48	4.2	34	12.8	3.3	1	351	As purchased: in shell, outer husk removed	54
Young, under-ripe	70	4	15	10	3	1	180	As purchased: in shell, outer husk removed	66
Chestnuts									
Fresh	48	3.4	1.9	45.6	1.3	1.1	213		21
Dry	9	6.3	4.0	78.5	2.5	2.2	375		18
Treenuts, other	7	16	58	17	2.6	2	610	Almonds, Brazil nuts, filberts, pecans, pistachios, walnuts	57
Treenuts, other shelled	7	16	58	17	2.6	2	610		0
Seeds									
Squash, watermelon, sunflower	5	27.4	43.0	19.7	2.7	4.9	535		47
Sesame, whole or decorticated	6	18.1	51.3	20.0	3.7	4.6	574		0

[1] In these products, only a small part of the carbohydrate, approximately 40%, is in sugar, starch, and dextrin. In calculating the calories it is assumed that the digestibility quotient is 40%.

SOURCE: CHATFIELD, C. Food Composition Tables for International Use. FAO, United Nations, Rome.

NOTE: There are no entries for the letter Q in this Section.

R

RADIATION PRESERVATION

TABLE 2.R.1

REQUIRED DOSAGES OF RADIATION

Purpose	Dose Range (1000 rad)
Sterilization	1000–5000
Pasteurization	50–1000
Insect disinfestation	5–100
Sprout-depressing	5–100

SOURCE: BORGSTROM, G. 1968. Principles of Food Science, Vol. *1*. Macmillan Publishing Co., New York.

RAPESEED OIL, TRIGLYCERIDE MOLE PERCENT COMPOSITION

1 *Double Bond*	
SOS	0.2
SSEr[1]	0.2
2 *Double Bonds*	
SOO	0.1
SOEr	3.9
SErEr	0.2
ErSEr	1.0
SLS	0.3
3 *Double Bonds*	
OOEr	0.9
ErOEr	18.1
ErErEr	0.9
SOL	0.4
SLO	0.1
SLEr	5.2
ErSL	0.2
SLeS	0.2
4 *Double Bonds*	
OOL	0.1
OLEr	1.2
ErOL	3.4
ErErL	0.2
ErLEr	24.3
SLL	0.5
SLeO	0.1
SOLe	0.2
SLeEr	3.4
ErSLe	0.1
5 *Double Bonds*	
LOL	0.2
OLL	0.1
ErLL	4.5
OOLe	0.1
OLeEr	0.8
ErOLe	2.2
ErErLe	0.1
ErLeEr	16.3
5 *Double Bonds* (Cont.)	
SLLe	0.3
SLeL	0.3
6 *Double Bonds*	
LLL	0.2
OLLe	0.1
OLeL	0.1
LOLe	0.2
ErLLe	3.0
ErLeL	3.0
SLeLe	0.2
7 *Double Bonds*	
LLLe	0.3
LLeL	0.1
OLeLe	0.1
ErLeLe	2.0
LLeLe	0.2
LeLLe	0.2

[1] Er = Erucic acid.

SOURCE: BOEKENOOGEN, H. A. (EDITOR). 1968. Oil, Fats and Fat Products, Vol. *2*. John Wiley & Sons, New York.

REAGENTS, NORMAL SOLUTIONS

TABLE 2.R.2

WEIGHTS OF TYPICAL REAGENTS IN REPRESENTATIVE STANDARD SOLUTIONS

Reagent	Molecular Weight	Hydrogen Equivalent	Equivalent Weight	Grams of Reagent	
				Per Liter of Normal Solution	Per cc of Normal Solution
HCl	36.5	1	36.5	36.5	0.0365
$HC_2H_3O_2$	60	1	60	60	0.060
H_2SO_4	98	2	49	49	0.049
$H_2C_2O_4 \cdot 2H_2O$	126	2	63	63	0.063
$H_2C_4H_4O_6$	150	2	75	75	0.075
H_3PO_4	98	3	32.7	32.7	0.0327
$H_3C_6H_5O_7$	192	3	64	64	0.064
NaOH	40	1	40	40	0.040
$Ca(OH)_2$	74	2	37	37	0.037
NH_4OH	35	1	35	35	0.035
NaCl	58.5	1	58.5	58.5	0.0585
$Ba(NO_3)_2$	261.4	2	130.7	130.7	0.1307
$Al_2(SO_4)_3$	342	6	57	57	0.057
$K_2C_4H_4O_6$	226.2	2	113.1	113.1	0.1131
$KHC_4H_4O_6$	188.1	1	188.1	188.1	0.1881
$NaHCO_3$	84	1	84	84	0.084

SOURCE: PETERSON, W. H., SKINNER, J. T., and STRONG, F. M. Elements of Food Biochemistry. Prentice-Hall, Englewood Cliffs, N.J.

RECOMMENDED DAILY DIETARY ALLOWANCE

TABLE 2.R.3

FOOD AND NUTRITION BOARD, NATIONAL ACADEMY OF SCIENCES—NATIONAL RESEARCH COUNCIL
RECOMMENDED DAILY DIETARY ALLOWANCES, REVISED 1974
Designed for the maintenance of good nutrition of practically all healthy people in the U.S.A.

								Fat-Soluble Vitamins				Water-Soluble Vitamins							Minerals					
	Age (yr)	Weight (kg)	Weight (lb)	Height (cm)	Height (in.)	Energy (kcal)[2]	Protein (gm)	Vitamin A Activity (RE)[3]	Vitamin A Activity (IU)	Vitamin D (IU)	Vitamin E Activity[5] (IU)	Ascorbic Acid (mg)	Folacin[6] (μg)	Niacin[7] (mg)	Riboflavin (mg)	Thiamin (mg)	Vitamin B-6 (mg)	Vitamin B-12 (μg)	Calcium (mg)	Phosphorus (mg)	Iodine (μg)	Iron (mg)	Magnesium (mg)	Zinc (mg)
Infants	0.0–0.5	6	14	60	24	kg X 117	kg X 2.2	420[4]	1400	400	4	35	50	5	0.4	0.3	0.3	0.3	360	240	35	10	60	3
	0.5–1.0	9	20	71	28	kg X 108	kg X 2.0	400	2000	400	5	35	50	8	0.6	0.5	0.4	0.3	540	400	45	15	70	5
Children	1–3	13	28	86	34	1300	23	400	2000	400	7	40	100	9	0.8	0.7	0.6	1.0	800	800	60	15	150	10
	4–6	20	44	110	44	1800	30	500	2500	400	9	40	200	12	1.1	0.9	0.9	1.5	800	800	80	10	200	10
	7–10	30	66	135	54	2400	36	700	3300	400	10	40	300	16	1.2	1.2	1.2	2.0	800	800	110	10	250	10
Males	11–14	44	97	158	63	2800	44	1000	5000	400	12	45	400	18	1.5	1.4	1.6	3.0	1200	1200	130	18	350	15
	15–18	61	134	172	69	3000	54	1000	5000	400	15	45	400	20	1.8	1.5	2.0	3.0	1200	1200	150	18	400	15
	19–22	67	147	172	69	3000	54	1000	5000	400	15	45	400	20	1.8	1.5	2.0	3.0	800	800	140	10	350	15
	23–50	70	154	172	69	2700	56	1000	5000		15	45	400	18	1.6	1.4	2.0	3.0	800	800	130	10	350	15
	51+	70	154	172	69	2400	56	1000	5000		15	45	400	16	1.5	1.2	2.0	3.0	800	800	110	10	350	15
Females	11–14	44	97	155	62	2400	44	800	4000	400	12	45	400	16	1.3	1.2	1.6	3.0	1200	1200	115	18	300	15
	15–18	54	119	162	65	2100	48	800	4000	400	12	45	400	14	1.4	1.1	2.0	3.0	1200	1200	115	18	300	15
	19–22	58	128	162	65	2100	46	800	4000	400	12	45	400	14	1.4	1.1	2.0	3.0	800	800	100	18	300	15
	23–50	58	128	162	65	2000	46	800	4000		12	45	400	13	1.2	1.0	2.0	3.0	800	800	100	18	300	15
	51+	58	128	162	65	1800	46	800	4000		12	45	400	12	1.1	1.0	2.0	3.0	800	800	80	10	300	15
Pregnant						+300	+30	1000	5000	400	15	60	800	+2	+0.3	+0.3	2.5	4.0	1200	1200	125	18+[8]	450	20
Lactating						+500	+20	1200	6000	400	15	80	600	+4	+0.5	+0.3	2.5	4.0	1200	1200	150	18	450	25

[1] The allowances are intended to provide for individual variations among most normal persons as they live in the United States under usual environmental stresses. Diets should be based on a variety of common foods in order to provide other nutrients for which human requirements have been less well defined. See text for more detailed discussion of allowances and of nutrients not tabulated. See Table I (p. 6) for weights and heights by individual year of age.

[2] Kilojoules (kJ) = 4.2 X kcal.

[3] Retinol equivalents.

[4] Assumed to be all as retinol in milk during the first six months of life. All subsequent intakes are assumed to be half as retinol and half as β-carotene when calculated from international units. As retinol equivalents, three fourths are as retinol and one fourth as β-carotene.

[5] Total vitamin E activity, estimated to be 80 percent as α-tocopherol and 20 percent other tocopherols. See text for variation in allowances.

[6] The folacin allowances refer to dietary sources as determined by *Lactobacillus casei* assay. Pure forms of folacin may be effective in doses less than one fourth of the recommended dietary allowance.

[7] Although allowances are expressed as niacin, it is recognized that on the average 1 mg of niacin is derived from each 60 mg of dietary tryptophan.

[8] This increased requirement cannot be met by ordinary diets; therefore, the use of supplemental iron is recommended.

SOURCE: PENNINGTON, J. A. (EDITOR). 1976. A Food Guide Critique. *In* Dietary Nutrient Guide. Avi Publishing Co., Westport, Conn.

REFRACTIVE INDICES, FATS AND OILS

TABLE 2.R.4

REFRACTIVE INDICES OF SOME COMMON FATS AND OILS

Fat or Oil	Refractive Index at 40°C	Fat or Oil	Refractive Index at 40°C
Cottonseed	1.4643-1.4679	Palm	1.4531-1.4580
Coconut	1.4477-1.4495	Palm kernel	1.4492-1.4517
Corn	1.4765-1.4768	Linseed	1.4742-1.4754
Castor	1.4659-1.4730	Walnut	1.469 -1.471-
Kapok	1.4605-1.4657	Mustard seed (white)	1.4704 at 20°C
Peanut	1.4600-1.4643	Mustard seed (black)	1.4720-1.4733
Sunflower	1.4663-1.4680	Tung	1.5100-1.5200 at 20°C
Safflower	1.4679-1.4693		
Perilla	1.4735-1.4785	Oiticica	1.4942-1.5062
Soybean	1.4675-1.4736	Borneo tallow	1.4561-1.4573
Sesame	1.4698-1.4731	Cacao butter	1.4565-1.4570
Teaseed	1.4619-	Shea butter	1.4635-1.4668
Olive	1.4606-1.4633	Illipé butter	1.4577-1.4610

SOURCE: MAHLENBACHER, C. V. The Analysis of Fats and Oils. Garrard Press, Champaign, Illinois.

REFRIGERANT I

TABLE 2.R.5

REFRIGERANT PERFORMANCE PER STANDARD AMERICAN TON AT 86°F (30°C) CONDENSATION, 5°F (−15°C) SUCTION

Refrigerant	No.	Evaporator Pressure, p.s.i.g.	Condensing Pressure, p.s.i.g.	Refrigerant Circulated, lb. / min.	Net Refrigerating Effect B.t.u. lb.	Coefficient of Performance	Horse-Power per Ton	Compressor Discharge Temp., °F.	Compression Ratio	Compressor Discharge Temp., °C.
Ethane	170	221.3	661.1	3.41	58.6	2.41	1.953	1.22	2.86	50
Nitrous oxide	744A	294.3	922.3	2.35	85.2	3.60	1.310	—	3.03	—
Carbon dioxide	744	317.5	1031.0	3.62	55.5	2.56	1.840	151	3.15	66.11
Propane	290	27.2	140.5	1.65	121.0	4.58	1.030	97	3.70	36.11
22/115 azeotrope	502	36.0	175.1	4.38	45.7	4.37	1.079	99	3.75	37.22
Monochlorodifluoromethane	22	28.2	158.2	2.86	70.0	4.66	1.011	128	4.03	53.33
Ammonia	717	19.6	154.5	0.422	474.4	4.76	0.989	210	4.94	98.89
12/152a azeotrope	500	16.4	113.4	3.27	61.1	4.61	1.022	105	4.12	40.56
Dichlorodifluoromethane	12	11.8	93.3	4.00	50.0	4.70	1.002	101	4.08	38.33
Methyl chloride	40	6.5	80.0	1.33	150.2	4.90	0.962	172	4.48	77.78
Isobutane	601	3.3	44.8	1.79	111.5	4.36	1.083	80	4.54	26.67
Sulfur dioxide	764	5.9	51.8	1.41	141.4	4.87	0.968	191	5.63	88.33
Methylamine	630	9.9	46.8	0.66	304.0	4.81	0.978	—	6.13	—
Butane	600	13.2	26.9	1.56	128.6	4.95	0.953	88	5.07	31.11
Dichlorotetrafluoroethane	114	16.1	22.0	4.64	43.1	4.49	1.049	86	5.42	30.00
Dichloromonofluoromethane	21	19.2	16.5	2.24	89.4	5.01	0.941	142	5.96	61.11
Ethyl chloride	160	20.5	12.4	1.45	142.3	5.21	0.906	106	5.83	41.11
Ethylamine	631	23.1	10.0	0.89	225.5	5.52	0.855	—	7.40	—
Trichloromonofluoromethane	11	24.0	3.6	2.98	67.3	5.05	0.933	109	6.24	42.7
Methyl formate	611	26.3	1.6	1.06	189.2	—	—	—	7.74	—
Ethyl ether	610	26.9	4.9	1.58	126.3	5.74	0.822	—	8.20	—
Trichlorotrifluoroethane	113	27.9	13.9	3.73	53.7	4.84	0.973	86	8.02	30.00
Dichloroethylene	1130	28.3	15.8	1.75	114.3	4.83	0.973	—	8.42	—
Trichloroethylene	1120	29.6	26.2	2.18	91.7	4.82	0.980	—	11.65	—

SOURCE: WOOLRICH, W. R. 1968. Principles of Refrigeration. *In* The Freezing Preservation of Foods, Vol. 1, 4th Edition. D. K. Tressler, W. B. Van Arsdel, and M. J. Copley (Editors). Avi Publishing Co., Westport, Conn.

REFRIGERANT II

TABLE 2.R.6

CHEMICAL FORMULAS OF REFRIGERANTS

Group I	
Carbon dioxide (Refrigerant 744)	CO_2
Dichlorodifluoromethane (Refrigerant 12)	CCl_2F_2
Dichlorodifluoromethane, 73.8% and ethylidene, 26.2% (Refrigerant 500)	CCl_2F_2 CH_3CHF_2
Dichloromethane (Methylene Chloride) (Refrigerant 30)	CH_2Cl_2
Dichloromonofluoromethane (Refrigerant 21)	$CHCl_2F$
Dichlorotetrafluoroethane (Refrigerant 114)	$C_2Cl_2F_4$
Monochlorodifluoromethane (Refrigerant 22)	$CHClF_2$
Monochlorotrifluoromethane (Refrigerant 13)	$CClF_3$
Trichloromonofluoromethane (Refrigerant 11)	CCl_3F
Trichlorotrifluoroethane (Refrigerant 113)	$C_2Cl_3F_3$
Group II	
Ammonia	NH_3
Dichloroethylene	$C_2H_2Cl_2$
Ethyl chloride	C_2H_5Cl
Methyl chloride	CH_3Cl
Methyl formate	$HCOOCH_3$
Sulfur dioxide	SO_2
Group III	
Butane	C_4H_{10}
Ethane	C_2H_6
Ethylene	C_2H_4
Isobutane	$(CH_3)_3CH$
Propane	C_3H_8

Group I has the greater usefulness because these refrigerants possess low toxicity, explosiveness and flammability.

Group II is next in preference, while Group III refrigerants must be handled with the most discretion and caution.

SOURCE: WOOLRICH, W. R. and HALLOWELL, E. R. (EDITORS). 1970. Safety of Workmen in Cold and Freezer Storage Rooms. *In* Cold and Freezer Storage Manual. Avi Publishing Co., Westport, Conn.

RELATIVE HUMIDITY

DRY BULB TEMPERATURE °F

WET BULB TEMPERATURE °F	21	22	23	24	25	26	27	28	29	30	31	32	33	34	35	36	37	38	39	40	41	42	43	44	45	46	47	48	49	50	51	52	53	54	55	56	57	58	59	60	WET BULB TEMPERATURE °F
14	1																																								14
15	15	4																																							15
16	28	17	7																																						16
17	42	31	20	10	1																																				17
18	56	44	33	22	13	4																																			18
19	71	58	46	35	25	16	7																																		19
20	85	71	59	47	37	27	18	10	3																																20
21	100	86	72	60	49	39	29	21	13	6																															21
22		100	86	73	62	51	41	32	23	16	8	2																													22
23			100	87	74	63	52	43	34	26	18	11	5																												23
24				100	87	75	64	54	44	36	28	20	14	8	2																										24
25					100	87	76	65	55	46	37	30	23	16	10	5																									25
26						100	88	76	66	56	47	39	32	25	19	13	7	2																							26
27							100	88	77	67	58	49	41	34	27	21	15	10	5																						27
28								100	88	78	68	59	51	43	36	29	23	17	12	7	3																				28
29									100	89	78	69	60	52	45	38	31	25	20	15	10	5																			29
30										100	89	79	70	62	54	46	40	33	27	22	17	12	8	4																	30
31											100	89	80	71	63	55	48	42	35	29	24	19	14	10	6																31
32												100	90	81	72	64	57	50	43	37	31	26	21	16	12	8	5	1													32
33													100	90	81	73	65	58	51	45	39	33	28	23	18	14	10	7	3												33
34														100	91	82	74	66	59	52	46	40	35	30	25	20	16	12	9	5											34
35															100	91	83	75	67	60	54	47	42	36	31	26	22	18	14	10	7	4	1								35
36																100	91	83	75	68	61	55	48	43	38	32	28	23	19	16	12	9	6	3							36
37																	100	91	83	75	69	62	55	49	44	39	34	29	25	21	17	14	10	8	5	2					37
38																		100	92	83	76	69	63	56	51	45	40	35	31	27	23	19	16	12	9	7	4	1			38
39																			100	92	84	77	70	63	57	52	46	41	36	32	28	24	20	17	14	11	8	6	3	1	39
40																				100	92	85	77	71	64	58	52	47	42	38	34	29	26	22	19	16	13	10	7	5	40
41																					100	92	85	78	71	65	59	54	48	43	39	35	31	27	23	20	17	14	11	9	41
42																						100	92	85	78	72	66	60	54	49	45	40	36	32	28	25	22	18	16	13	42
43																							100	93	86	79	72	66	61	55	50	46	41	37	33	30	26	23	20	17	43
44																								100	93	86	79	73	67	61	56	51	47	42	38	34	31	27	24	21	44
45																									100	93	86	79	73	67	62	57	52	48	43	39	35	32	29	26	45
46																										100	93	86	80	74	68	63	58	53	49	44	40	37	33	30	46
47																											100	93	86	80	75	69	63	59	54	50	45	41	38	34	47
48																												100	93	87	81	75	69	64	59	55	50	46	42	39	48
49																													100	93	87	81	75	70	65	60	55	51	47	43	49
50																														100	94	87	81	76	70	65	61	56	52	48	50
51																															100	94	87	82	76	71	66	61	57	53	51
52																																100	94	88	82	76	71	66	62	58	52
53																																	100	94	88	82	77	72	67	63	53
54																																		100	94	88	82	77	72	68	54
	21	22	23	24	25	26	27	28	29	30	31	32	33	34	35	36	37	38	39	40	41	42	43	44	45	46	47	48	49	50	51	52	53	54	55	56	57	58	59	60	

DRY BULB TEMPERATURE °F

Taylor Relative Humidity Tables

These values are correct for air velocity of not less than 600 ft. per minute.

In using wall or standing type hygrometers when greatest accuracy is desired the instrument must be fanned vigorously until the column of the wet-bulb thermometer no longer recedes.

Printed by *Taylor Instrument Companies* Rochester, N. Y.

(Continued)

RELATIVE HUMIDITY (*Continued*)

DRY BULB TEMPERATURE °F

WET BULB TEMPERATURE °F	41	42	43	44	45	46	47	48	49	50	51	52	53	54	55	56	57	58	59	60	61	62	63	64	65	66	67	68	69	70	71	72	73	74	75	76	77	78	79	80	
41	100	92	85	78	71	65	59	54	48	43	39	35	31	27	23	20	17	14	11	9	7	4	2																		41
42		100	92	85	78	72	66	60	54	49	45	40	36	32	28	25	22	18	16	13	10	8	6	4	2																42
43			100	93	86	79	72	66	61	55	50	46	41	37	33	30	26	23	20	17	14	12	10	7	5	3	2														43
44				100	93	86	79	73	67	61	56	51	47	42	38	34	31	27	24	21	18	16	13	11	9	7	5	3	1												44
45					100	93	86	79	73	67	62	57	52	48	43	39	35	32	29	26	22	20	17	15	12	10	8	6	5	3	1										45
46						100	93	86	80	74	68	63	58	53	49	44	40	37	33	30	27	24	21	18	16	14	12	10	8	6	4	3	1								46
47							100	93	86	80	75	69	63	59	54	50	45	41	38	34	31	28	25	22	20	17	15	13	11	9	7	6	4	3	1						47
48								100	93	87	81	75	69	64	59	55	50	46	42	39	35	32	29	26	24	21	19	16	14	12	10	9	7	5	4	3	1				48
49									100	93	87	81	75	70	65	60	55	51	47	43	40	36	33	30	27	25	22	20	18	15	13	12	10	8	7	5	4	3	1		49
50										100	94	87	81	76	70	65	61	56	52	48	44	41	37	34	31	29	26	23	21	19	17	15	13	11	9	8	6	5	4	3	50
51											100	94	87	82	76	71	66	61	57	53	49	45	42	38	35	32	30	25	24	22	20	18	16	14	12	11	9	8	6	5	51
52												100	94	88	82	76	71	66	62	58	54	50	46	43	39	36	33	31	28	25	23	21	19	17	15	13	12	10	9	7	52
53													100	94	88	82	77	72	67	63	58	54	50	47	44	40	37	34	32	29	27	24	22	20	18	16	14	13	11	10	53
54														100	94	88	82	77	72	68	63	59	55	51	48	44	41	38	35	33	30	28	25	23	21	19	17	16	14	12	54
55															100	94	88	83	78	73	68	64	60	56	52	48	45	42	39	36	33	31	29	26	24	22	20	18	17	15	55
56																100	94	88	83	78	73	69	64	60	56	53	49	46	43	40	37	34	32	29	27	25	23	21	19	18	56
57																	100	94	89	83	78	74	69	65	61	57	53	50	47	44	41	38	35	33	30	28	26	24	22	20	57
58																		100	94	89	84	79	74	70	66	61	58	54	51	48	45	42	39	36	34	31	29	27	25	23	58
59																			100	94	89	84	79	74	70	66	62	58	55	51	48	45	42	39	37	34	32	30	28	26	59
60																				100	94	89	84	79	75	71	66	62	59	55	52	49	46	43	40	38	35	33	31	29	60
61																					100	94	89	84	80	75	71	67	63	59	56	53	50	47	44	41	39	36	34	32	61
62																						100	95	90	85	80	75	71	67	64	60	57	53	50	47	44	42	39	37	35	62
63																							100	95	90	85	80	76	72	68	64	61	57	54	51	48	45	43	40	38	63
64																								100	95	90	85	80	76	72	68	65	61	58	54	51	48	46	43	41	64
65																									100	95	90	85	81	77	72	69	65	61	58	55	52	49	46	44	65
66																										100	95	90	85	81	77	73	69	65	62	59	56	53	50	47	66
67																											100	95	90	86	81	77	73	69	66	62	59	56	53	50	67
68																												100	95	90	86	82	78	74	70	66	63	60	57	54	68
69																													100	95	90	86	82	78	74	70	67	63	60	57	69
70																														100	95	91	86	82	78	74	71	67	64	61	70
71																															100	95	91	86	82	78	74	71	68	64	71
72																																100	95	91	86	82	79	75	71	68	72
73																																	100	95	91	87	83	79	75	72	73
74																																		100	96	91	87	83	79	75	74
75																																			100	96	91	87	83	79	75
76																																				100	96	91	87	83	76
77																																					100	96	91	87	77
78																																						100	96	91	78
79																																							100	96	79
80																																								100	80
	41	42	43	44	45	46	47	48	49	50	51	52	53	54	55	56	57	58	59	60	61	62	63	64	65	66	67	68	69	70	71	72	73	74	75	76	77	78	79	80	

DRY BULB TEMPERATURE °F

WET BULB TEMPERATURE °F

Printed by
Taylor Instrument Companies
Rochester, N. Y.

Taylor Relative Humidity Tables

The values on this chart are for air velocity of not less than 600 ft. per minute. It is cautioned that values above 140° (Dry Bulb) are extrapolated.

In using wall or standing type hygrometers when greatest accuracy is desired the instrument must be fanned vigorously until the column of the wet-bulb thermometer no longer recedes.

DRY BULB TEMPERATURE °F (columns); WET BULB TEMPERATURE °F (rows)

Wet \ Dry	82	84	86	88	90	92	94	96	98	100	102	104	106	108	110	112	114	116	118	120
54	10	7	5	3	1															
56	14	12	9	7	5	3														
58	20	16	14	11	9	7	5	3												
60	25	21	18	15	13	11	9	7	5											
62	30	26	23	20	17	15	12	10	8	7	5									
64	36	32	28	25	22	19	16	14	12	10	8	7	5							
66	42	37	33	30	26	23	20	18	15	13	11	10	8	7						
68	48	43	39	35	31	28	24	22	19	17	15	13	11	10	8	7	6			
70	55	49	44	40	36	32	29	26	23	21	18	16	14	12	11	9	8			
72	61	56	50	46	41	37	33	30	27	24	22	20	17	16	14	12	11	9	8	
74	69	62	57	51	47	42	38	35	32	28	26	23	21	19	17	15	13	12	11	9
76	76	69	63	57	52	48	43	39	36	33	30	27	24	22	20	18	16	14	13	12
78	84	76	70	64	58	53	49	44	40	37	34	31	28	25	23	21	19	17	16	14
80	92	84	77	70	65	59	54	50	45	41	38	35	32	29	26	24	22	20	18	17
82	100	92	84	77	71	65	60	55	50	46	42	39	36	33	30	27	25	23	21	19
84		100	92	85	78	72	66	61	55	51	47	43	40	37	34	31	28	26	24	22
86			100	92	85	78	72	66	61	56	52	48	44	41	38	35	32	29	27	25
88				100	92	85	79	73	67	62	57	53	49	45	42	38	35	33	30	28
90					100	92	85	79	73	68	62	58	53	49	46	42	39	36	34	31
92						100	93	86	79	73	68	63	58	54	50	47	43	40	37	34
94							100	93	86	80	74	69	64	59	55	51	47	44	41	38
96								100	93	86	80	74	69	64	60	55	52	48	45	41
98									100	93	86	80	75	70	65	60	56	52	49	45
100										100	93	87	81	75	70	65	61	57	53	49
102											100	93	87	81	75	70	66	61	57	53
104												100	93	87	81	76	71	66	62	58
106													100	93	87	81	76	71	67	62
108														100	93	87	82	76	72	67
110															100	94	88	82	77	72
112																100	94	88	82	77
114																	100	94	88	82
116																		100	94	88
118																			100	94
120																				100
122																				
124																				
126																				
128																				
130																				
132																				

Wet \ Dry	122	124	126	128	130	132	134	136	138	140	142	144	146	148	150	152	154	156	158	160
54																				
56																				
58																				
60																				
62																				
64																				
66																				
68																				
70																				
72																				
74	8																			
76	10	9	8																	
78	13	11	10	9																
80	15	14	12	11	10															
82	18	16	15	13	12	11														
84	20	18	17	16	14	13	12													
86	23	21	19	18	16	15	14	13												
88	26	24	22	20	19	17	16	15	14											
90	29	27	25	23	21	20	18	17	15	14										
92	32	30	27	25	24	21	20	19	17	16	15									
94	35	33	30	28	26	24	22	21	20	18	18	16								
96	39	36	33	31	29	26	25	23	22	21	20	19	16							
98	42	39	37	34	32	30	27	26	24	23	22	21	19	17						
100	16	43	40	37	35	33	30	28	27	25	24	23	21	20	18					
102	50	47	44	41	38	36	33	31	29	27	26	25	23	22	21	18				
104	54	50	47	44	41	39	36	34	32	30	28	27	25	24	23	21	19			
106	58	54	51	48	45	42	39	37	34	32	31	29	27	26	25	23	22	19		
108	63	59	55	52	48	45	43	40	37	35	33	81	29	28	27	25	24	22	20	
110	67	63	59	56	52	49	46	43	40	38	36	34	32	30	28	27	26	24	23	
112	72	68	64	60	56	53	49	46	44	41	39	36	34	32	30	29	28	26	25	23
114	77	73	68	64	60	56	53	50	47	44	42	39	37	35	33	31	30	28	27	25
116	83	78	73	68	64	61	57	54	50	47	45	42	40	37	35	34	32	30	29	27
118	88	83	78	73	69	65	61	57	54	51	48	45	43	40	38	36	34	32	31	29
120	94	88	83	78	73	69	65	61	58	54	52	48	46	43	41	38	36	35	33	31
122	100	94	88	83	78	74	69	65	62	58	55	52	49	46	43	41	39	37	35	33
124		100	94	89	83	79	74	70	66	62	59	55	53	49	46	44	42	39	38	35
126			100	94	89	84	79	74	70	66	63	59	55	53	49	47	44	42	40	38
128				100	94	89	84	79	75	70	67	63	59	56	53	50	47	45	43	40
130					100	94	89	84	79	75	71	67	63	60	56	54	50	47	45	43
132						100	94	89	84	79	75	71	67	64	60	57	54	50	48	46

Printed by
Taylor Instrument Companies
Rochester, N. Y.

(Continued)

RELATIVE HUMIDITY (*Continued*)

DRY BULB TEMPERATURE °F

WET BULB TEMPERATURE °F	134	136	138	140	142	144	146	148	150	152	154	156	158	160	162	164	166	168	170	172	174	176	178	180	182	184	186	188	190	192	194	196	198	200	202	204	206	208	210	212	WET BULB TEMPERATURE °F
112	49	46	44	41	39	36	34	33	30	29	28	26	25	23	22															100	96	92	88	84	81	78	76	73	70	67	192
114	53	50	47	44	42	39	37	35	33	31	30	28	27	25	24	22															100	96	92	88	85	81	79	76	73	70	194
116	57	54	50	47	45	42	40	37	35	34	32	30	29	27	26	24	23															100	96	92	89	86	82	79	76	73	196
118	61	57	54	51	48	45	43	40	38	36	34	32	31	29	28	27	25	23															100	96	92	89	86	82	79	77	198
120	65	61	58	54	52	48	46	43	41	38	36	35	33	31	30	29	27	25	23															100	96	92	90	86	82	79	200
122	69	65	62	58	55	52	49	46	43	41	39	37	35	33	32	31	29	27	25	24															100	96	93	90	86	83	202
124	74	70	66	62	59	55	53	49	46	44	42	39	38	35	34	32	31	29	27	26	24															100	96	93	90	86	204
126	79	74	70	66	63	59	55	53	49	47	44	42	40	38	36	34	33	31	29	28	26	25															100	96	93	90	206
128	84	79	75	70	67	63	59	56	53	50	47	45	43	40	39	37	35	33	31	30	28	27	25															100	96	93	208
130	89	84	79	75	71	67	63	60	56	54	50	47	45	43	41	39	37	35	33	32	30	29	27	26															100	96	210
132	94	89	84	79	75	71	67	64	60	57	54	50	48	46	44	41	40	38	35	34	32	31	29	28	26															100	212
134	100	94	89	84	80	75	71	68	64	60	57	54	51	48	47	44	42	40	38	36	34	33	31	80	28	26															
136		100	94	89	84	80	76	71	68	64	61	57	55	51	49	47	45	42	40	39	36	35	33	31	30	28	27														
138			100	95	90	84	80	76	71	68	65	61	57	55	51	49	48	45	42	41	39	37	35	33	32	30	28	27													
140				100	95	90	85	80	76	72	69	65	61	58	55	52	50	48	45	43	41	40	37	35	34	32	30	29	28												
142					100	95	90	85	80	76	72	69	65	62	58	56	53	50	48	46	43	42	40	37	36	34	32	31	30	28											
144						100	95	90	85	81	76	72	69	65	62	58	56	53	50	49	46	44	42	40	38	36	34	33	32	30	29										
146							100	95	90	85	81	77	72	69	66	62	59	57	53	51	49	47	44	42	41	38	37	35	33	32	31	29									
148								100	95	90	85	81	77	73	70	66	63	59	57	54	51	50	47	44	43	41	39	37	35	34	33	31	30								
150									100	95	90	85	81	77	73	70	66	63	60	58	54	52	50	47	45	43	42	39	37	36	34	33	32	30							
152										100	95	90	85	81	77	73	70	67	63	60	58	55	52	50	48	45	44	42	39	38	36	35	34	32	30						
154											100	95	90	85	82	78	74	70	67	63	61	58	55	52	50	48	46	44	42	40	38	37	35	34	32	30	29				
156												100	95	90	86	82	78	74	70	67	64	61	58	55	53	50	48	46	44	42	40	39	37	36	34	32	31	30			
158													100	95	91	86	82	78	74	71	67	64	61	58	56	53	51	48	46	44	42	40	39	38	36	34	33	82	30		
160														100	95	91	86	82	78	74	71	68	64	61	59	66	54	51	49	47	45	43	41	40	38	36	35	33	32	31	160
162															100	95	91	86	82	79	74	71	68	64	62	59	57	54	51	49	47	45	43	42	40	38	37	35	34	33	162
164																100	96	91	86	83	79	75	72	68	65	62	60	57	54	52	50	47	45	44	42	40	39	37	36	34	164
166																	100	96	91	87	83	79	75	72	69	65	63	60	57	55	52	50	48	46	45	42	41	39	38	36	166
168																		100	96	92	87	83	79	75	72	69	66	63	60	58	55	53	50	48	47	45	43	42	40	38	168
170																			100	96	92	87	83	79	76	72	69	66	63	61	58	55	53	51	49	47	45	44	42	40	170
172																				100	96	92	87	83	79	76	73	69	66	63	61	58	55	53	52	49	48	46	44	42	172
174																					100	96	92	87	83	79	76	73	69	67	63	61	58	56	54	52	50	48	46	44	174
176																						100	96	92	87	83	80	76	73	70	67	64	61	59	57	55	53	50	48	46	176
178																							100	96	92	87	83	80	76	73	70	67	64	62	60	58	55	53	50	48	178
180																								100	96	92	87	83	80	76	73	70	67	65	63	60	58	55	53	51	180
182																									100	96	92	87	83	80	76	74	70	68	66	63	60	58	56	54	182
184																										100	96	92	87	84	80	77	74	72	69	66	63	61	58	56	184
186																											100	96	92	88	84	80	77	75	72	69	66	64	61	58	186
188																												100	96	92	88	84	80	78	75	72	70	67	64	61	188
190																													100	96	92	88	84	80	78	75	73	70	67	64	190
	134	136	138	140	142	144	146	148	150	152	154	156	158	160	162	164	166	168	170	172	174	176	178	180	182	184	186	188	190	192	194	196	198	200	202	204	206	208	210	212	

Printed by
Taylor Instrument Companies
Rochester, N. Y.

DRY BULB TEMPERATURE °F

SOURCE: Relative Humidity Tables. (1933). Taylor Instrument Co., Arden, N. Carolina.

REPRODUCTIVE CYCLE

TABLE 2.R.7

FEATURES OF THE REPRODUCTIVE CYCLE

Species	Age at Puberty	Cycle Type	Cycle Length	Duration of Heat	Best Breeding Time	First Heat after Parturition	Remarks
Cattle*	4 to 8 months. Usually first bred about 15 months.	Polyestrous, all year.	21 days (18 to 24).	18 hours (10 to 24).	Insemination, from mid-heat until 6 hours after end.	Varies,* best to breed at 60 to 90 days.	Ovulation 10 to 12 hours after end of heat. Uterine bleeding about 24 hours after ovulation in most.
Horse	1 year.	Seasonally polyestrous. Early spring on.	Very variable, about 22 days.	6 days (2 to 11).	Last few days; should be bred at 3-day intervals.	4 to 14 days.	Ovulation 1 to 2 days before end of heat. Twins are usually aborted.
Sheep	7 to 8 months.	Seasonally polyestrous. Early fall to winter. Prolonged seasons in Dorsets and Merinos.	16½ days (14 to 19).	30 to 36 hours.	Little significance.	Next fall.	Ovulation near end of heat.
Swine	5 to 8 months.	Polyestrous, all year.	20 to 22 days.	2 to 3 days.	Little significance.	About 7 days after weaning.	Ovulation usually about 36 hours after beginning of heat.
Goat	7 to 8 months.	Seasonally polyestrous from early fall to late winter.	20 to 22 days.	2 to 3 days.		Next fall.	Many intersexes born in hornless strains.
Dog	6 to 8 months or later.	Monestrous. All year, but mostly late winter and summer.		About 1 week.		Several months.	Proestrous bleeding 7 to 10 days. Ovulation usually 1 to 3 days after first acceptance. Ova shed before 1st polar body has been extruded. Pseudopregnancy (pseudocyesis) usually ends between 60 and 70 days.
Cat	6 to 15 months.	Provoked ovulation. Seasonally polyestrous spring and early fall.	15 to 21 days.	9 to 10 days in absence of male. Four days if mated.		4 to 6 weeks.	Ovulation 24 to 56 hours after coitus. Pseudopregnancy lasts 36 days.
Fox	10 months.	Monestrous. December to March, but mostly late January to February.		2 to 4 days.		Next winter.	Ovulation usually on 1st or 2nd day of receptivity. Ova shed before 1st polar body has been extruded. No proestrous bleeding.
Mink	10 months.	Provoked ovulation. Seasonally polyestrous. Mid-February to early April.	Waves of follicles at intervals of a few days.			Next spring.	Ovulation begins 47 hours after coitus which must last ½ hour at least.
Chinchilla	4 months.	Polyestrous, all year.	24 days.	2 days. Mate at night.		12 hours.	
Nutria	5 to 8 months.	Polyestrous, all year.	24 to 29 days.	2 to 4 days.		48 hours.	

(Continued)

TABLE 2.R.7 (*Continued*)

Species	Age at Puberty	Cycle Type	Cycle Length	Duration of Heat	Best Breeding Time	First Heat after Parturition	Remarks
Rabbit	5 to 9 months.	Provoked ovulation. Breed all year, more or less.		To 1 month.	When vulva is enlarged and hyperemic.	Immediately, but blastocysts die if doe suckles large litter.	In United States do not breed well in summer. Ovulation 10½ hours after coitus. Pseudopregnancy lasts 14 to 16 days.
Rhesus Monkey (*Macaca mulatta*)	3 years.	Polyestrous all year; tendency to anovulatory cycles in summer in United States.	27 to 28 days (23 to 33).	Most matings near ovulation time.	Near ovulation.		Menstruation lasts 4 to 6 days. Ovulation usually about 13 days after onset.
Rat	37 to 67 days.	Polyestrous, all year.	4 to 5 days.	About 14 hours (12 to 18). Usually begins about 7 p.m.	Near ovulation.	Within 24 hours.	Ovulation a little after midnight. Cervical stimulation causes pseudopregnancy lasting 12 to 14 days.
Mouse	35 days (28 to 49).	Polyestrous, all year.	4 or 5 days, usually.	A few hours from 10 p.m. on.		Within 24 hours.	Ovulation soon after midnight. Stimulation of cervix causes pseudopregnancy lasting 10 to 12 hours.
Guinea pig	55 to 70 days.	Polyestrous, all year.	16½ days.	6 to 11 hours. Begins usually in evening.	Mid-heat on.	Usually immediately.	Ovulation about 10 hours after onset of heat.
Hamster	7 to 8 weeks.	Polyestrous, all year. Few pregnancies in winter.	4 days.	At night.		After weaning.	Ovulation about 1 a.m. Pseudopregnancy lasts 7 to 13 days.

* Many normal cows ovulate as early as 8 to 12 days after parturition with or without detectable external signs of estrus.

SOURCE: Merck & Co. 1973. The Merck Veterinary Manual, 4th Edition. Merck & Company, Rahway, N.J.

RIBOFLAVIN

TABLE 2.R.8

RIBOFLAVIN CONTENT OF FOODS

	mg/100 g		mg/100 g
Broccoli	0.23	Peppers	0.08
Spinach	0.20	Lettuce	0.06
Asparagus	0.20	Bananas	0.06
Brussels sprouts	0.16	Peaches	0.05
Peas	0.14	Potatoes	0.04
Corn	0.12	Tomatoes	0.04
Lima beans	0.12	Oranges	0.03
Snap beans	0.11	Apples	0.02
Cauliflower	0.10		

SOURCE: WHITE, P. L. and SELVEY, N. (EDITORS). 1974. Nutritional Qualities of Fresh Fruits and Vegetables. Futura Publishing Co., Mt. Kisco, N.Y.

RIBOFLAVIN, DAILY RECOMMENDATIONS

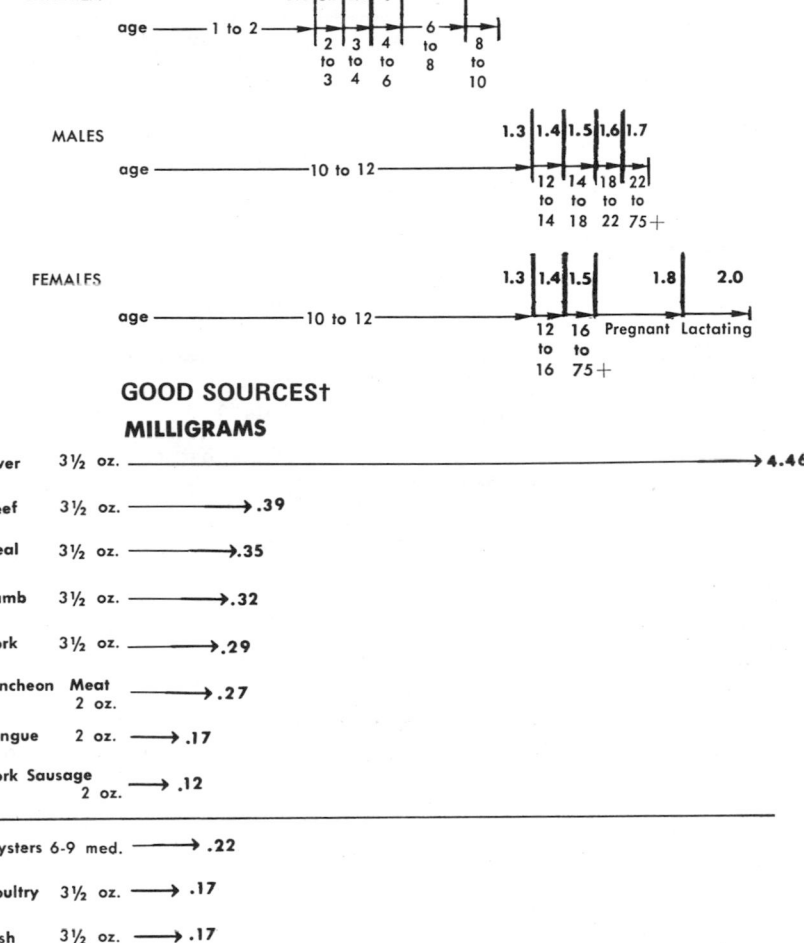

MILLIGRAMS

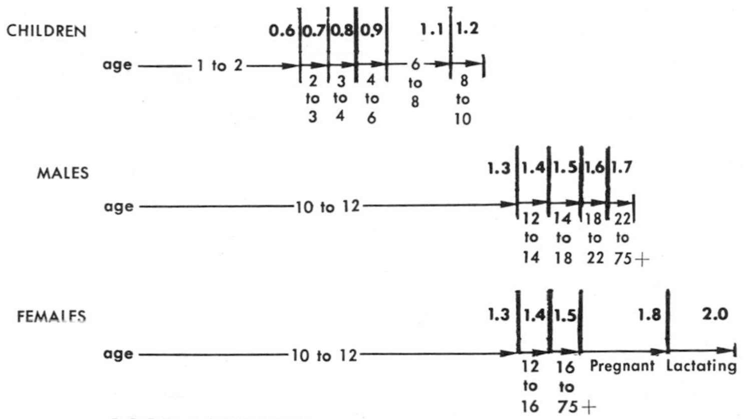

GOOD SOURCES†

MILLIGRAMS

Liver	3½ oz.	4.46
Beef	3½ oz.	.39
Veal	3½ oz.	.35
Lamb	3½ oz.	.32
Pork	3½ oz.	.29
Luncheon Meat	2 oz.	.27
Tongue	2 oz.	.17
Pork Sausage	2 oz.	.12
Oysters	6-9 med.	.22
Poultry	3½ oz.	.17
Fish	3½ oz.	.17
Egg	1 med.	.15
Milk	1 cup	.42
Cottage Cheese	¼ cup	.14
Cheese	1 oz.	.12
Asparagus	½ cup	.13
Spinach	½ cup	.12
Squash	½ cup	.11
Bread	1 slice	.04
Cereal	½ cup	.03

†Average nutrient content as food is served. (*Note: 3½ oz equals approximately 100 g.*)

SOURCE: Lessons on Meat. (1974). National Live Stock and Meat Board, Chicago.

RIBOFLAVIN, FOOD

TABLE 2.R.9

RIBOFLAVIN CONTENT OF FOODS (MG PER 100 G)

Cereals		Dairy Products, etc. (*Cont.*)	
Flour,		Milk	0.15
White	0.04	Milk powder	
Wholemeal	0.16	Skim	1.6
Fish		Whole	1.2
Cod	0.10	Vegetables	
Herring	0.30	Asparagus	0.15
Soft roe	0.50	Beans, broad	0.05
Kipper	0.30	Lettuce	0.08
Sardines in oil	0.20	Onions	0.05
Turbot	0.15	Peas	0.15
Meat		Potatoes	0.04
Beef		Spinach	0.20
Brisket	0.20	Tomatoes	0.04
Corned	0.20	Fruits	
Lean	0.20	Apple	0.02
Ham	0.20	Currants	0.06
Liver		Gooseberries	0.03
Ox	3.0	Nuts	
Pig	3.0	Nuts	0.10
Mutton	0.25	Sundries	
Meat Extract	2.0	Beer	0.05
Juice (conc)	1.5	Honey	0.05
Dairy Products, etc.		Tea	0.90
Cheese		Yeast	
Dutch	0.40	Bakers	3.0
Whole milk	0.50	Brewer's	2.5
Eggs	0.35		

SOURCE: SINCLAIR, H. M. and HOLLINGSWORTH, D. F. 1969. Hutchison's Food and the Principles of Nutrition. Edward Arnold (Publishers), London, England.

RICE KERNEL

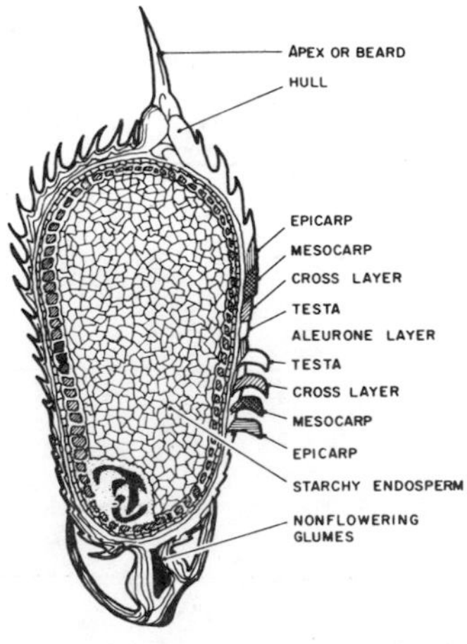

FIG. 2.R.1. CROSS SECTION OF A RICE KERNEL

SOURCE: BROOKER, DONALD B., BAKKER-ARKEMA, FRED W. and HALL, CARL J. (EDITORS). 1974. Principles of Grain Drying. *In* Drying Cereal Grains. Avi Publishing Co., Westport, Conn.

ROASTING MEAT I

Recommendations for roasting procedures for meats:

1. Season with salt and pepper if desired.
2. Place meat fat side up on rack in open roasting pan.
3. Insert meat thermometer.
4. Do not add water. Do not cover. Do not baste.
5. Roast in slow oven (325°F) until done as shown on meat thermometer.

Roasts permitted to stand 15-20 min before carving will carve more easily.

SOURCE: Be a Smarter Shopper . . . aBetter Cook. (1973). National Live Stock and Meat Board, Chicago.

ROASTING MEAT II

TABLE 2.R.10

ESTIMATED TIMES FOR ROASTING MEAT AT 325°F

Kind of meat and cut	Ready-to-cook weight Pounds	Time required for center of meat to reach a given temperature					
		° F.	Hours	° F.	Hours	° F.	Hours
Beef roasts	5	140	2 to 3	160	2½	170	3 to 3¾
Veal roasts	3 to 5					170	2½ to 3½
Lamb roasts	5			150	2½ to 3	180	2¾ to 3¼
Fresh pork roasts	5			170	2¾ to 3½	185	3½ to 4
Spareribs	3						1½
Stuffed pork chops							¾
Mild cured ham	6	130	1½ to 2	160	2½		
Mild cured pork shoulder	6					170	3½

SOURCE: Food For Us All. Yearbook of Agriculture, 1969. USDA.

ROASTING, TIME AND TEMPERATURE

TABLE 2.R.11

ROASTING GUIDE FOR MEATS

Cut	Approx. Wt (lb)	Oven Temp Constant (°F)	Interior Temp When Removed From Oven (°F)	Approx. Cooking Time (Min. per lb.)
Beef				
Rib[1]	6-8	300-325	140 (rare)	23-25
			160 (med)	27-30
			170 (well)	32-35
	4-6	300-325	140 (rare)	26-32
			160 (med)	34-38
			170 (well)	40-42
Rolled rib	5-7	300-325	140 (rare)	32
			160 (med)	38
			170 (well)	48
Rib eye (Delmonico)	4-6	350	140 (rare)	18-20
			160 (med)	20-22
			170 (well)	22-24
Tenderloin, Whole	4-6	425	140 (rare)	45-60 (total)
Tenderloin, Half	2-3	425	140 (rare)	45-60 (total)
Boneless rolled rump (high quality)	4-6	300-325	150-170	25-30
Tip (high quality)	3½-4	300-325	140-170	35-40
	4-6	300-325	140-170	30-35
Veal				
Leg	5-8	300-325	170	25-35
Loin	4-6	300-325	170	30-35
Rib (rack)	3-5	300-325	170	35-40
Boneless shoulder	4-6	300-325	170	40-45
Pork, fresh				
Loin				
Center	3-5	325-350	170	30-35
Half	5-7	325-350	170	35-40
Blade loin or sirloin	3-4	325-350	170	40-45
Boneless double	3-5	325-350	170	35-45
Arm picnic shoulder	5-8	325-350	170	30-35
Boneless	3-5	325-350	170	35-40
Cushion	3-5	325-350	170	30-35
Blade Boston shoulder	4-6	325-350	170	40-45
Leg (fresh ham)				
Whole (bone in)	12-16	325-350	170	22-26
Whole (boneless)	10-14	325-350	170	24-28
Half (bone in)	5-8	325-350	170	35-40
Spareribs		325-350	Well done	1½-2½ (hr total)
Pork, smoked				
Ham (cook before eating)				
Whole	10-14	300-325	160	18-20
Half	5-7	300-325	160	22-25
Shank or rump portion	3-4	300-325	160	35-40
Ham (fully cooked)[2]				
Half	5-7	325	140	18-24
Arm picnic shoulder	5-8	300-325	170	35
Shoulder roll	2-3	300-325	170	35-40
Canadian-style bacon	2-4	325	160	35-40
Lamb				
Leg	5-8	300-325	175-180	30-35
Shoulder	4-6	300-325	175-180	30-35
Boneless	3-5	300-325	175-180	40-45
Cushion	3-5	300-325	175-180	30-35
Rib	1½-3	375	170-180	35-45

[1] Ribs which measure 6 to 7 in. from chine bone to tip of rib.
[2] Allow approximately 15 min per lb for heating whole ham to serve hot.

SOURCE: Lessons on Meat. (1974). National Live Stock and Meat Board, Chicago.

ROT SPOILAGE

TABLE 2.R.12

ORGANISMS ASSOCIATED WITH SOFT ROT SPOILAGE

Fruit or Vegetable	Spoilage	Microorganism
Apples	Soft rot	*Bacillus polymyxa*
Pears	Brown rot	*Penicillium expansum*, *Aspergillus niger*, *A. foetidus*
Oranges	Black rot	*Alternaria* spp.
Lemons	Dry rot	*Penicillium digitatum*
Citrus fruits	Soft rot	*P. italicum*, *P. herbarum*, *P. glaucum*
Grapes	Soft rot	*Rhizopus nigricans*
Raspberries	Soft rot	*R. stolonifer*
Plum	Soft rot	Yeasts
Strawberries	Soft rot	*Bacillus cereus*
Tomato	Soft rot	*Byssochlamys fulva*
Carrots	Soft rot	*Erwinia carotovora*
Cabbage	Soft rot	*Botrytis cinerea*
Celery	Pink rot	*Sclerotinia sclerotiorum*, *Mucor racemosus*

SOURCE: ESKIN, N. A. M., HENDERSON, H. M., and TOWNSEND, R. J. 1971. Biochemistry of Foods. Academic Press, New York.

S

SALAD DRESSING OR MAYONNAISE VARIATIONS

TABLE 2.S.1

VARIATIONS TO BE MADE WITH MAYONNAISE OR SALAD DRESSING

Kind	Amount of Dressing	Suggested Additions	Suggested Uses
Appetizer	1 cup	1 cup French dressing	Vegetable salads
Thousand Island	1 cup	1/3 cup chili sauce 1 T. chopped olives 1 T. chopped pickles 1 chopped hard cooked egg	Lettuce
Russian	1 cup	2 T. chili sauce 1 t. sugar	Lettuce Greens
Roquefort	1 cup	2 T. mashed Roquefort cheese 1 T. lemon juice	Lettuce or Greens
Cream	1 cup	1/3 cup cream or canned milk 1 T. sugar 1/2 t. salt	All types vegetables
Herb	1 cup	2 T. chopped chive 1 T. chopped parsley 2 T. milk	Fish Meat Cabbage
Tart	1 cup	2 T. horseradish 1 T. prepared mustard	Potato or starchy vegetable salads
Red	1 cup	4 T. tomato paste Sugar) to taste Salt)	Fish Salad or sauces
Fluffy	1 cup	2 T. sugar 1/2 cup cream, whipped	Fruit or sweet salads
Fruit	1 cup	1/4 cup fruit juice 1/2 cup cream, whipped	Fruit
Party	1 cup	2 T. Maraschino cherry sirup 4 T. Maraschino cherries 1/4 cup cream, whipped	Fruit
Hawaiian	1 cup	1/2 cup crushed pineapple (slightly drained)	Fruit
Cranberry	1 cup	1/2 cup cranberry jelly 1/4 cup cream, whipped	Turkey, chicken, banana salads
Peanut Butter	1 cup	1/3 cup peanut butter 1 T. sugar 3 T cream	Apple or fruit
Gelatin	1 cup	1/2 cup stiff gelatin - beaten 2 T. sugar	Fruit or gelatin salads
Cream cheese	1 cup	6 oz. cream cheese 1 T. sugar 1/2 t. salt	Fruit or gelatin salads (excellent as spread)

SOURCE: KINTNER, T. C., and MANGEL, M. Vinegars and Salad Dressings, Univ. Missouri Agric. Expt. Sta. Bull. *631.*

SALMON AND TROUT

TABLE 2.S.2

DESCRIPTION OF DIFFERENT SPECIES OF PACIFIC SALMON AND OF STEELHEAD TROUT AFTER CANNING

Common Name	Normal Oil Color	Normal Flesh Color	Normal Flesh Texture	Normal Flake Size	Normal Vertebrae Size	Normal Scale Size
Chinook (King)	Deep red through orange to almost white	Bright red to white	Soft	Large, thick	Large	Large
Red (Sockeye) (Blueback)	Deep red	Deep red	Very firm	Small, thin	Small	Medium
Medium red (Silver) (Coho)	Light red to yellowish pink	Light red w/orange	Very firm	Large, medium, thick	Large	Large
Pink (Humpback)	Deep pink to light yellow	Pink	Tendency to be soft	Small, thin	Small	Small
Chum (Fall), (Dog), or (Keta)	Light pink w/orange shade to yellow	Light pink to grayish white	Firm	Medium	Medium	Medium
Steelhead trout	Light orange to yellow	Pink w/ orange shade	Rather soft	Large, thick	Large	Large

SOURCE: U.S. Department of the Army, Food Inspection Specialist, *TM8-451*, 1969.

SALT, BRINE TABLE

TABLE 2.S.3

SODIUM CHLORIDE BRINE TABLE

Salometer°	Sp Gr	Baume°	Sodium Chloride by Wt (%)	Lb per Gal. Brine NaCl	Lb per Gal. Brine Water	Gal. Water per Gal. Brine	Lb Salt per Gal. Water	Freezing Point (F°)
0	1.000	0.0	.000	.000	8.328	1.000	.0	+32.0
2	1.004	0.6	.528	.044	8.318	.999	.044	+31.5
4	1.007	1.1	1.056	.089	8.297	.996	.089	+31.1
6	1.011	1.6	1.584	.133	8.287	.995	.134	+30.5
8	1.015	2.1	2.112	.178	8.275	.993	.179	+30.0
10	1.019	2.7	2.640	.224	8.262	.992	.226	+29.3
12	1.023	3.3	3.167	.270	8.250	.990	.273	+28.8
14	1.026	3.7	3.695	.316	8.229	.988	.320	+28.2
16	1.030	4.2	4.223	.362	8.216	.987	.367	+27.6
18	1.034	4.8	4.751	.409	8.202	.985	.415	+27.0
20	1.038	5.3	5.279	.456	8.188	.983	.464	+26.4
22	1.042	5.8	5.807	.503	8.175	.982	.512	+25.7
24	1.046	6.4	6.335	.552	8.159	.980	.563	+25.1

(Continued)

TABLE 2.S.3 (*Continued*)

Salometer°	Sp Gr	Baume°	Sodium Chloride by Wt (%)	Lb per Gal. Brine NaCl	Lb per Gal. Brine Water	Gal. Water per Gal. Brine	Lb Salt per Gal. Water	Freezing Point (F°)
26	1.050	6.9	6.863	.600	8.144	.978	.614	+24.4
28	1.054	7.4	7.391	.649	8.129	.976	.665	+23.7
30	1.058	7.9	7.919	.698	8.113	.974	.716	+23.0
32	1.062	8.5	8.446	.747	8.097	.972	.768	+22.3
34	1.066	9.0	8.974	.797	8.081	.970	.821	+21.6
36	1.070	9.5	9.502	.847	8.064	.968	.875	+20.9
38	1.074	10.0	10.030	.897	8.047	.966	.928	+20.2
40	1.078	10.5	10.558	.948	8.030	.964	.983	+19.4
42	1.082	11.0	11.086	.999	8.012	.962	1.039	+18.7
44	1.086	11.5	11.614	1.050	7.994	.960	1.094	+17.9
46	1.090	12.0	12.142	1.102	7.976	.958	1.151	+17.1
48	1.094	12.5	12.670	1.154	7.957	.955	1.208	+16.2
50	1.098	12.9	13.198	1.207	7.937	.953	1.266	+15.4
52	1.102	13.4	13.725	1.260	7.918	.951	1.325	+14.5
54	1.106	13.9	14.253	1.313	7.898	.948	1.385	+13.7
56	1.110	14.4	14.781	1.366	7.878	.946	1.444	+12.8
58	1.114	14.8	15.309	1.420	7.858	.943	1.505	+11.8
60	1.118	15.3	15.837	1.475	7.836	.941	1.568	+10.9
62	1.122	15.8	16.365	1.529	7.815	.938	1.629	+9.9
64	1.126	16.2	16.893	1.584	7.794	.936	1.692	+8.9
66	1.130	16.7	17.421	1.639	7.772	.933	1.756	+7.9
68	1.135	17.2	17.949	1.697	7.755	.931	1.822	+6.8
70	1.139	17.7	18.477	1.753	7.733	.929	1.888	+5.7
72	1.143	18.1	19.004	1.809	7.710	.926	1.954	+4.6
74	1.147	18.6	19.532	1.866	7.686	.923	2.022	+3.4
76	1.152	19.1	20.060	1.925	7.669	.921	2.091	+2.2
78	1.156	19.6	20.588	1.982	7.645	.918	2.159	+1.0
80	1.160	20.0	21.116	2.040	7.620	.915	2.229	-.4
82	1.164	20.4	21.644	2.098	7.596	.912	2.300	-1.6
84	1.169	21.0	22.172	2.158	7.577	.910	2.372	-3.0
86	1.173	21.4	22.700	2.218	7.551	.907	2.446	-4.4
88	1.178	21.9	23.228	2.279	7.531	.904	2.520	-5.8
88.3	1.179	22.0	23.310	2.288	7.528	.904	2.531	-6.0
90	1.182	22.3	23.755	2.338	7.506	.901	2.594	-1.1
92	1.186	22.7	24.283	2.398	7.479	.898	2.670	+4.8
94	1.191	23.3	24.811	2.459	7.460	.896	2.745	+11.1
95	1.193	23.5	25.075	2.491	7.444	.894	2.787	+14.4
96	1.195	23.7	25.339	2.522	7.430	.892	2.827	+18.0
97	1.197	23.9	25.603	2.552	7.417	.891	2.865	+21.6
98	1.200	24.2	25.867	2.585	7.409	.890	2.906	+25.5
99	1.202	24.4	26.131	2.616	7.394	.888	2.947	+29.8
100	1.204	24.6	26.395	2.647	7.380	.886	2.987	

SOURCE: Ion Exchange Calculator, Morton Salt Co., Chicago, 1958.

SALT, BRINE

TABLE 2.S.4

SODIUM CHLORIDE BRINES—GALLON BASIS
Gerlach Salimeter Scale (26.395 g NaCl/100 g Brine)

A	B	C	D	E		F	G
Sp Gr	% Salt by Wt	Degrees Salimeter[1]	Lbs NaCl per Gal. of Brine (BXF)	Water Required to Make 1 Gal. of Brine (Lb)	(Gal.)	Wt per Gal. of Brine in Lbs at 60°/60°F (Sp Gr X 8.32823)	Lbs of Salt per Gal. of Water
1.000	0.00	0	0.00	8.32823	1.000	8.32823	0.000
1.019	2.64	10	0.22	8.27	0.992	8.49	0.226
1.038	5.28	20	0.46	8.18	0.983	8.64	0.464
1.058	7.92	30	0.70	8.11	0.974	8.81	0.716
1.078	10.56	40	0.95	8.03	0.964	8.98	0.983
1.098	13.20	50	1.20	7.94	0.953	9.14	1.266
1.118	15.84	60	1.47	7.84	0.941	9.31	1.568
1.139	18.48	70	1.75	7.74	0.929	9.49	1.888
1.149	19.80	75	1.89	7.68	0.922	9.57	2.057
1.160	21.12	80	2.04	7.62	0.915	9.66	2.229
1.171	22.44	85	2.19	7.56	0.908	9.75	2.409
1.179	23.31	88.3	2.29	7.53	0.904	9.82	2.531
1.182	23.76	90	2.34	7.50	0.901	9.84	2.594
1.193	25.08	95	2.49	7.45	0.894	9.94	2.787
1.204	26.40	100	2.65	7.38	0.886	10.03	2.987

SODIUM CHLORIDE BRINES—LITER BASIS
Gerlach Salimeter Scale (26.395 g NaCl/100 g H_2O)

A	B	C		H	I	J	K
Sp Gr	% Salt by Wt	Degrees Salimeter[1]	Baumé	G NaCl per Liter of Brine (BXJ)	G H_2O Needed to Make 1 Liter of Brine (J-H)	Wt per Liter of Brine at 20°C (or 68°F) (Sp Gr X 997.18 g)	Freezing Point (°F)
1.000	0.00	0	0.00	0.00	997.18	997.18	+32.0
1.019	2.640	10	2.7	26.83	989.30	1016.1	+29.3
1.038	5.279	20	5.3	54.64	980.43	1035.1	+26.4
1.058	7.919	30	7.9	83.55	971.47	1055.0	+23.0
1.078	10.558	40	10.5	113.49	961.47	1075.0	+19.4
1.098	13.197	50	12.9	144.49	950.41	1094.9	+15.4
1.118	15.837	60	15.3	176.57	938.28	1114.9	+10.9
1.139	18.477	70	17.7	209.86	925.93	1135.8	+5.7
1.149	19.796	75	18.9	226.81	918.95	1145.8	+2.8
1.160	21.116	80	20.0	244.26	912.47	1156.7	-0.4
1.171	22.436	85	21.2	261.99	905.71	1167.7	-3.7
1.179	23.307	88.3	22.0	274.02	901.66	1175.7	-6.0
1.182	23.756	90	22.3	280.00	898.67	1178.7	-1.1
1.193	25.075	95	23.5	298.30	891.34	1189.6	+14.4
1.204	26.395	100	24.6	316.90	883.70	1200.6	+60.0

[1] Temperature correction: Subtract 0.116° Salimeter for each degree Fahrenheit below 60°.

SOURCE: OCKERMAN, H. W. 1976. Quality Control of Post-Mortem Muscle Tissue, Vol. II. Ohio State University, Columbus.

SALT PENETRATION RATE

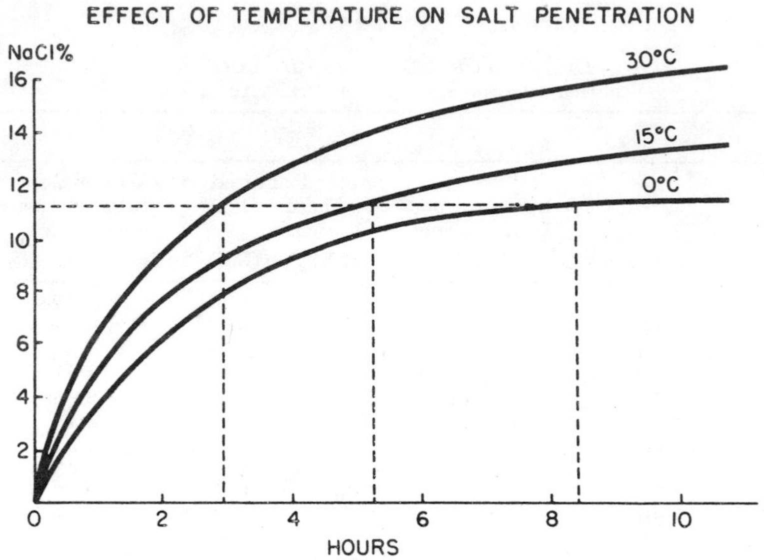

FIG. 2.S.1. RATE OF SALT PENETRATION AS AFFECTED BY TEMPERATURE

SOURCE: BORGSTROM, G. 1968. Principles of Food Science, Vol. *1*. Macmillan Publishing Co., New York.

SALT SOLUTION, FREEZING

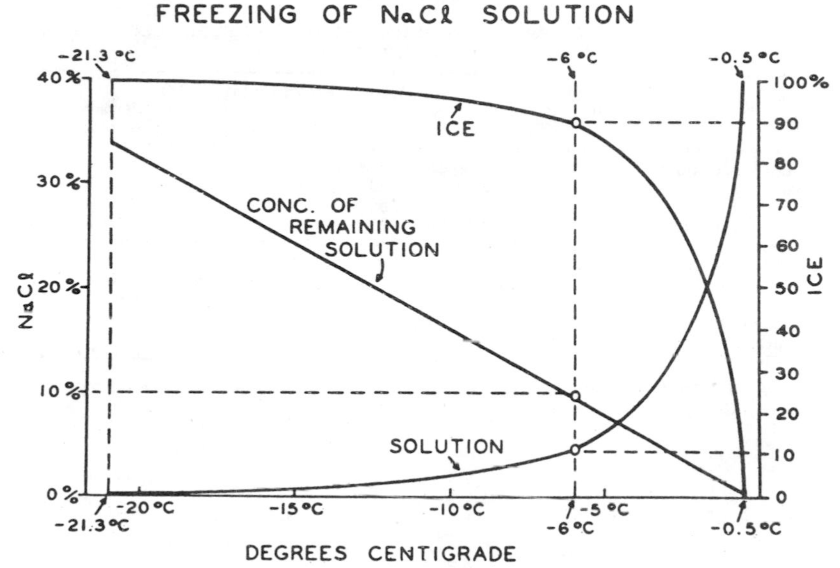

FIG. 2.S.2. FREEZING CURVE FOR SODIUM CHLORIDE SOLUTION—THE EUTECTIC TEMPERATURE: -21.3° C

SOURCE: BORGSTROM, G. 1968. Principles of Food Science, Vol. *1*, Macmillan Publishing Co., New York.

SANITIZERS

TABLE 2.S.5

MANUFACTURERS' RECOMMENDATIONS FOR CONCENTRATION AND TIME OF EXPOSURE

Chemical	Concentration Soak and Circulation (Ppm)	Concentration Spray and Fog (Ppm)	Exposure Time	Exposure Temp (°F)
Chlorine				
Sodium hypochlorite	100	200	1–2	75
Calcium hypochlorite	100	200	1–2	75
Dichloroisocyanuric acid	100	200	1–2	75
Trichloroisocyanuric acid	100	200	1–2	75
Potassium dichloroisocyanurate	100	200	1–2	75
Sodium dichloroisocyanurate	100	200	1–2	75
Chloramine T (pH 7.0)	250	400–500	2	
Chloramine T (pH 8.5)	250	400–500	20	
Hydantoin (acid pH)	200	400	2	
Quaternary Ammonium Compounds				
pH 6.0 or higher at 75°F or higher	200	400	2	
Iodine				
nonionic wetting agents plus iodine	12.5	25	2	
Bromine-chlorine	25	75	2	
Acid-anionic	200	400	2	

SOURCE: HARPER, W. J. 1972. Sanitation in Dairy Food Plants. *In* Food Sanitation. R. K. Guthrie (Editor). Avi Publishing Co., Westport, Conn.

SANITIZING CHEMICALS

TABLE 2.S.6

RELATIVE COMPARATIVE PROPERTIES OF SELECTED CHEMICAL SANITIZING AGENTS

	Relative Effectiveness		
	Chlorine	Iodine	Quaternary Ammonium
Gram + bacteria	2nd in effectiveness	Most effective	3rd in effectiveness
Gram − bacteria	Most effective	2nd in effectiveness	Poor
Spores	Most effective	2nd in effectiveness	Least effective
Thermoduric organisms	2nd in effectiveness	Least effective	Most effective
Bacteriophage	Most effective	2nd in effectiveness	Not effective
Affected by hard water	2nd	Least	Most
Corrosiveness	Most corrosive	Slightly corrosive	Noncorrosive
Cause of off-flavors	+ (10 ppm)	++ (7 ppm)	± (15 ppm)
Affected by organic matter	Most	2nd	Least

SOURCE: HARPER, W. J. 1972. Sanitation in Dairy Food Plants. *In* Food Sanitation. R. K. Guthrie (Editor). Avi Publishing Co., Westport, Conn.

SATURATED FATTY ACIDS

TABLE 2.S.7

NAME, FORMULA, AND SOURCE OF SATURATED FATTY ACIDS

Common Name	Systematic Name	Formula	Source
Butyric	*n*-Butanoic	$CH_3(CH_2)_2COOH$	Butter fat
Caproic	*n*-Hexanoic	$CH_3(CH_2)_4COOH$	Butter fat, coconut oil, babassu fat, palm oil
Caprylic	*n*-Octanoic	$CH_3(CH_2)_6COOH$	Butter fat, coconut oil, palm oil, seed oils
Capric	*n*-Decanoic	$CH_3(CH_2)_8COOH$	Butter fat, head oil of sperm whale, coconut oil
Lauric	*n*-Dodecanoic	$CH_3(CH_2)_{10}COOH$	Laurel kernel oil, seed fats of laurel family and *Palmae*; milk fat, coconut oil
Myristic	*n*-Tetradecanoic	$CH_3(CH_2)_{12}COOH$	Nutmeg fat, most animal and vegetable fats; nutmeg butter, fatty acids of *Myristicaceae*
Palmitic	*n*-Hexadecanoic	$CH_3(CH_2)_{14}COOH$	Lard, in practically all animal and vegetable fats
Stearic	*n*-Octadecanoic	$CH_3(CH_2)_{16}COOH$	Mutton tallow, usually wherever palmitic acid is present
Arachidic	*n*-Eicosanoic	$CH_3(CH_2)_{18}COOH$	Peanut oil, rambutan tallow, macassar nut fat, fish oils
Behenic	*n*-Docosanoic	$CH_3(CH_2)_{20}COOH$	Behen oil from horseradish tree (*Moringa oleifera* Lam.), peanut, rapeseed, and mustard oils
Lignoceric	*n*-Tetracosanoic	$CH_3(CH_2)_{22}COOH$	Beech-tar paraffin, peanut oil; most natural fats in small amounts; seed oil of *Adenanthera pavonina* ("Circassian seeds" from red sandalwood)
Cerotic	*n*-Hexacosanoic	$CH_3(CH_2)_{24}COOH$	Chinese insect wax (*Coccus ceriferus*), beeswax, wool wax, flax wax
Montanic	*n*-Octacosanoic	$CH_3(CH_2)_{26}COOH$	Beeswax, most waxes including montan wax
Melissic	*n*-Triacontanoic	$CH_3(CH_2)_{28}COOH$	Beeswax, various vegetable, insect, and mineral waxes
Lacceroic	*n*-Dotriacontanoic	$CH_3(CH_2)_{30}COOH$	Stick-lac wax (*Tachardia lacca*), natural waxes

SOURCE: MAHLENBACHER, C. V. The Analysis of Fats and Oils. Garrard Publishing Co., Champaign, Illinois.

SAUCE, BARBECUE

Ingredients	Amount
Water	85 gal. (U.S.)
Butter	80 lb
Vinegar (10% acetic acid)	4.8 gal. (U.S.)
Prepared mustard	10 lb
Locust bean gum	10 lb
Sugar	8 lb
Tomato paste	8 lb
Salt	4 lb
Paprika	2½ lb
Worcester sauce	2½ lb
Chilli powder	2½ lb
Tabasco sauce	1½ lb
Red pepper	15 oz
Black pepper	15 oz
Garlic powder	4 oz
Onion powder	4 oz

SOURCE: BINSTED, R., DEVEY, J. D., and DAKIN, J. C. 1971. Pickle & Sauce Making, 3rd Edition. Food Trade Press, London, England.

SAUCE, BEEF STEAK

Ingredients	Amount
Vinegar (2.4% acetic acid)	30 gal. (U.S.)
Soy	5 gal. (U.S.)
Mushroom ketchup	5 gal. (U.S.)
Tamarinds	30 lb
Sugar	10 lb
Salt	5 lb
Onions	4 lb
Horseradish	3 lb
Ground mustard	3 lb
Ground cayenne pepper	½ lb
Garlic	½ lb
Caramel	4 oz

SOURCE: BINSTED, R., DEVEY, J. D., and DAKIN, J. C. 1971. Pickle & Sauce Making, 3rd Edition. Food Trade Press, London, England.

SAUCE, THICK

Ingredients	Amount
Vinegar (20-grain)	43 gal. (U.S.)
Onions	36 lb
Molasses	25 lb
Tapioca	18 lb
Dates	6½ lb
Salt	4½ lb
Garlic (chopped)	4¼ lb
Caramel	4¼ lb
Lemon pulp	2½ lb
Ground ginger	1 lb
Ground coriander	½ lb
Ground nutmeg	½ lb

SOURCE: BINSTED, R., DEVEY, J. D., and DAKIN, J. C. 1971. Pickle & Sauce Making, 3rd Edition. Food Trade Press, London, England.

SAUCE, TOMATO

Ingredients	Amount
Tomato paste (single strength)	120 gal. (U.S.)
Vinegar	14.5 gal. (U.S.)
Acetic acid	1.2 gal. (U.S.)
Sugar	123 to 125 lb
Salt	27 to 29 lb
Onions (chopped)	25 lb
Paprika	2 lb
Cinnamon (bark)	24 oz
Allspice	15 oz
Cloves (ground)	13 oz
Mace (ground)	3½ oz
Cayenne pepper	3 oz
Garlic (chopped)	4 oz

SOURCE: BINSTED, R., DEVEY, J. D., and DAKIN, J. C. 1971. Pickle & Sauce Making, 3rd Edition. Food Trade Press, London, England.

SAUCE, WORCESTER

Ingredients	Amount
Vinegar (20-grain)	21 gal. (U.S.)
Walnut ketchup	13 gal. (U.S.)
Mushroom ketchup	12 gal. (U.S.)
Sherry (or equiv non-alcoholic flavor)	6 gal. (U.S.)
Soy sauce	5.5 gal. (U.S.)
Hogs' livers (ground)	21 lb
Salt	11 lb
Tamarinds	10 lb
Brandy (or equiv essence)	1.2 gal. (U.S.)
Sugar	2½ lb
Ground cayenne pepper	1 lb
Ground black pepper	1 lb
Ground pimiento	1 lb
Ground coriander	1 lb
Ground mace	7 oz

SOURCE: BINSTED, R., DEVEY, J. D., and DAKIN, J. C. 1971. Pickle & Sauce Making, 3rd Edition. Food Trade Press, London, England.

SAUSAGE COMPOSITION

TABLE 2.S.8

COMPOSITION OF SAUSAGE

Food, Approximate Measure, and Weight (in Grams)		Water (%)	Food Energy (Cal)	Protein (g)	Fat (Total Lipid) (g)	Fatty Acids: Saturated (Total) (g)	Fatty Acids: Unsaturated: Oleic (g)	Fatty Acids: Unsaturated: Linoleic (g)	Carbohydrate (g)	Calcium (mg)	Iron (mg)	Vitamin A Value (IU)	Thiamin (mg)	Riboflavin (mg)	Niacin (mg)	Ascorbic Acid (mg)
Sausage:																
Bologna, slice 4.1 by 0.1 in.	8 slices (227 g)	56	690	27	62	26	27	3	2	16	4.1	—	0.36	0.49	6.0	—
Frankfurter, cooked	1 frankfurter (51 g)	58	155	6	14	6	6	1	1	3	0.8	—	0.08	0.10	1.3	—
Pork, bulk, canned	4 oz (113 g)	55	340	18	29	10	12	3	0	10	2.6	0	0.23	0.27	3.4	—

SOURCE: INSTITUTE OF HOME ECONOMICS. Nutritive Value of Foods. USDA Home and Garden Bull. 72.

SAUSAGE IDENTIFICATION

Fresh Sausage

Fresh sausage is made from selected cuts of fresh meats, principally pork and beef that have not previously been cured. Being neither cooked nor smoked, it should be stored under refrigeration and always thoroughly cooked before serving. Some of the varieties of fresh sausage are:

- Fresh Pork Sausage
- Fresh Bockwurst
- Bratwurst
- Italian Pork Sausage
- Fresh Thuringer
- Fresh Beef Sausage
- Fresh Country Style Pork Sausage

Fresh Smoked Sausage

As the name implies, fresh smoked sausage has been smoked, but has not been cooked. Like fresh sausage, it should always be refrigerated and thoroughly cooked before serving. Included in the fresh smoked sausage family are:

- Country-Style Pork Sausage
- Mettwurst
- Roumanian Sausage

Cooked Sausage

Cooked sausages are prepared basically from fresh meats, although occasionally some cured meats are used. They are thoroughly cooked and ready to serve. Like all sausages, this group also must be refrigerated. Examples of the cooked sausage group are:

- Liver Sausage
- Blutwurst
- Beer Salami
- Veal Sausage
- Braunschweiger

Cooked Smoked Sausage

Cooked smoked sausages are prepared from fresh meats and are both cooked and smoked. Although they are ready to eat, some of the products in this group are improved in flavor if heated before serving. The two most popular members of this family are the wiener or frankfurter and bologna. Included in this classification are:

- Knackwurst
- Bologna
- Mortadella
- Berliner
- Wiener or Frankfurter
- Vienna Sausage
- Kielbasa
- Smoked Links

Dry and Semidry Sausage

Made from selected meats and prepared in a complicated and carefully controlled drying process, the dry and semidry sausages are ready to eat. They will keep for a long period of time if refrigerated. Included are:

- Summer Sausage
- Chorizos
- Cappicola
- Frizzes
- Cervelat
- German Salami
- Italian Salami
- Hungarian Salami

Ready-to-Serve Meats

The ready-to-serve meats, commonly called luncheon meats, are fully cooked and most are available in the presliced form. Examples of ready-to-serve meats are:

- Peppered Loaf
- Olive Loaf
- Honey Loaf
- Head Cheese
- Meat Loaf
- Pickle and Pimiento Loaf

SOURCE: Facts About Sausage. (1974). National Live Stock and Meat Board, Chicago.

SAUSAGE NUTRITIVE VALUE

TABLE 2.S.8.A

NUTRITIVE VALUE OF SELECTED SAUSAGES AND READY-TO-SERVE MEATS

TYPE OF SAUSAGE	PROTEIN (gm/100gm)	CALORIES (cal/100gm)	IRON (mg/100gm)	THIAMINE (mg/100gm)	RIBOFLAVIN (mg/100gm)	NIACIN (mg/100gm)
Bologna	14.8	220	0.8	.31	.30	3.1
Braunschweiger	15.2	280	5.9	.13	1.40	8.1
Dutch Loaf	15.0	190	1.8	.31	.17	3.2
Frankfurters	15.2	200	2.3	.23	.24	2.7
Head Cheese	15.1	240	2.3	.08	.12	1.1
Kolbassie	13.5	310	2.4	.34	.19	3.1
Liver Sausage	16.7	260	5.4	.20	1.30	5.7
Pork Sausage Links	10.8	450	1.6	.40	.15	2.3
Salami	23.9	430	3.6	.25	.21	2.9
Country-Style Sausage	16.2	310	1.6	.22	.19	3.1
Summer Sausage	23.5	410	2.8	.46	.36	4.1
Thuringer	17.7	290	2.8	.12	.23	4.2

SOURCE: Facts About Sausage. (1974). National Live Stock and Meat Board, Chicago.

SAUSAGE, TYPES

TABLE 2.S.9

CHARACTERISTICS AND STORAGE CONDITIONS FOR SAUSAGES

Type	Characteristics	Examples	Storage
Fresh sausages	Made of chopped, uncured meat. Usually not smoked. They are sold uncooked and must be cooked thoroughly before eating.	Fresh pork sausage Country-style sausage Bratwurst Fresh thuringer Bockwurst	Refrigerate and use within a day or two for finest flavor. Freezing is not generally recommended because product will lose some of its delicate flavor.
Uncooked smoked sausages	Similar to fresh sausage but contain a mild cure and are smoked. Must be cooked before eating.	Country-style sausage Mettwurst Italian and Polish sausage	Same as above. Use within a week.
Cooked smoked sausages	Include a large variety of table-ready meat thought of broadly as "baloney." Usually made from smoked meat. Completely cooked; can be eaten cold. Require heating only to enhance flavor.	Frankfurters Bologna Cooked thuringer Vienna sausage	Wrap well and refrigerate. Use within a week. Freeze only if necessary to prevent waste of product, and freeze for the shortest time possible. Freezing adversely affects flavor and texture.
Dry sausages	Processed by long continuous air drying. During this time the products undergo a bacterial fermentation which gives characteristic "tanginess." Some are smoked. They are ready-to-serve.	Dry salami Pepperoni Farmer cervelat Cappicola Mortodella	Wrap loosely and refrigerate. Will keep several weeks. Freezing is not recommended.
Semidry sausages	Similar to dry sausages. Usually cooked and then dried a relatively short time. Contain more moisture than fully dry sausages. They are ready-to-eat.	Cooked salami Lebanon bologna Kosher salami Cervelat	Same as above.
Cooked specialities	Made from fresh or cured meat; may be smoked. Cooked or baked and are ready-to-serve.	Luncheon meat Liver loaf Jellied corned beef Tongue loaf Head cheese or souse	Wrap well and refrigerate. Use within a week. Freezing is not recommended because the flavor of salted and spiced meat is adversely affected by freezing.

SOURCE: FRANKS, E. B. When you Buy Sausage. Ohio State Univ. Coop. Ext. Serv. Leaflet *45*.

SCOOP SIZE

TABLE 2.S.10

MEASURES AND WEIGHTS OF SCOOP SIZES

Scoop Number	Measure	Equivalent Weight (Oz)
6	$\frac{2}{3}$ cup (10 Tbsp+)	6
8	$\frac{1}{2}$ cup (8 Tbsp)	4–5
10	$\frac{2}{5}$ cup (6 Tbsp)	3–4
12	$\frac{1}{3}$ cup (5 Tbsp +)	$2\frac{1}{2}$–3
16	$\frac{1}{4}$ cup (4 Tbsp)	2–$2\frac{1}{4}$
20	$3\frac{1}{5}$ Tbsp	$1\frac{3}{4}$–2
24	$2\frac{2}{3}$ Tbsp	$1\frac{1}{2}$–$1\frac{3}{4}$
30	$2\frac{1}{5}$ Tbsp	1–$1\frac{1}{2}$
40	$1\frac{3}{5}$ Tbsp	$\frac{3}{4}$–1

SOURCE: VAN EGMOND, DOROTHY (EDITOR). 1974. Cost Management. *In* School Food Service. Avi Publishing Co., Westport, Conn.

SEED COMPOSITION

TABLE 2.S.11

CHEMICAL COMPOSITION OF SEEDS

Kind of Seed	Water (%)	Ash (%)	Crude Protein (%)	Crude Fiber (%)	N-free Extract (%)	Lipids (%)
Barley	10.6	2.8	12.7	5.4	66.6	1.9
Corn, dent No. 1	13.0	1.2	8.8	2.1	70.9	4.0
Cottonseed	9.4	4.6	19.5	22.6	24.9	19.0
Flaxseed	6.2	3.6	24.0	6.3	24.0	35.9
Oats	9.8	4.0	12.0	11.0	58.8	4.6
Peanut kernels	5.4	2.3	30.4	2.5	11.7	47.7
Soybeans	10.0	4.6	37.9	5.0	24.5	18.0
Wheat	10.5	1.9	13.2	2.6	69.9	1.9

SOURCE: MALLETTE, M. F., ALTHOUSE, P. M., and CLAGETT, C. O. Biochemistry of Plants and Animals. John Wiley & Sons, New York.

SEED, CHEMICAL COMPOSITION

TABLE 2.S.12

SEEDS: CHEMICAL COMPOSITION
Values, except as otherwise indicated, are g or mg per 100g seeds.

Species	Gross Composition					Amino Acids											Fatty Acids					Vitamins			
	Water	Protein	Fat	Carbohydrate	Ash	Arginine	Histidine	Isoleucine	Leucine	Lysine	Methionine	Phenylalanine	Threonine	Tryptophan	Tyrosine	Valine	Palmitic	Stearic	Oleic	Linoleic	Linolenic	Niacin	Pantothenic Acid	Riboflavin	Thiamin
	g/100g																g/100g fat[1]					mg/100g			
Barley (Hordeum vulgare)	11.1	8.2	1.0	78.8	0.9	0.61	0.26	0.51	0.84	0.42	0.19	0.62	0.48	0.19		0.61	9	3	33	54		3.1	0.66	0.08	0.12
Bean, lima (Phaseolus vulgaris mac.)	12.6	20.7	1.3	61.6	3.8																	2.0	0.84	0.18	0.48
Bean, mung (P. aureus)	9.8	23.3	1.0	62.0	3.9	0.30	0.21	0.12	3.2	0.74	0.25	1.2	0.60	0.17	0.66	1.9	28	8	18	40	3	2.0		0.21	0.68
Chick-pea (Cicer arietinum)	10.6	20.8	4.7	60.9	3.0																	1.6		0.18	0.49
Corn (Zea mays)	13.0	8.8	4.0	73.0	1.2	0.45	0.24	0.36	1.1	0.29	0.21	0.46	0.34	0.08		0.50	10.2	3.0	50	34		2.8	0.64	0.10	0.49
Cotton (Gossypium hirsutum)[2]	7.3	23.1	22.9	43.2	3.5	3.0	1.1	1.8	2.2	1.5	0.5	2.2	1.1	0.4	0.6	1.8	← 27 →		19	54		4.4		0.31	
Cowpea (Vigna sinensis)	10.6	22.9	1.4	61.6	3.5																	2.2		0.16	0.92
Flax (Linum usitatissimum)[2]	6.2	24.0	35.9	30.3	3.6	3.6	0.65	1.8	2.3	1.4	0.35	2.2	1.3	0.63		2.2									
Gingko (Gingko biloba)	7.3	7.2	1.6	41.2	1.7																				
Hemp (Cannabis sativa)	7.0	28	37														← 10.1 →		16	46	28				
Lentil (Lens culinaris)	11.2	25.0	1.0	59.5	3.3																	2.2		0.24	0.56
Lotus (Nelumbium nelumbo)	9.6	16.5	2.3	63.9	3.6																				
Oat (Avena sativa)	9.8	12.0	4.6	69.6	4.0	0.99	0.23	0.80	0.87	0.51	0.23	0.72	0.54	0.20	0.50	0.99	10		59	31		1.0	0.63	0.13	0.92
Pea (Pisum sativum)	11.6	23.8	1.4	60.2	3.0	2.6	0.4	1.2	1.9	1.5	0.1	1.4	1.2	0.2		1.2						3.1	1.01	0.28	0.77
Peanut (Arachis hypogaea)[2]	4.0	26.2	42.8	24.3	2.7	6.9	1.3	2.6	4.1	1.9	0.6	3.1	1.6	0.8		2.8	6.3	4.9	61	21.8		15.6	3.50	0.13	1.09
Pigeon-pea (Cajanus cajan)	13.1	21.9	1.6	59.9	3.5																	2.0		0.18	0.47
Popcorn (Zea mays praecox)	9.8	11.9	4.7	72.1	1.5																	2.1		0.11	0.39
Pumpkin (Cucurbita pepo)	2.4	22.9	31.9	13.2	3.6																	1.5		0.10	0.18
Rape (Brassica napus)	9.5	20.4	43.6	22.3	4.2												1		32	15					
Rice (Oryza sativa)	12.0	7.5	1.7	77.7	1.1	0.54	0.14	0.28	0.51	0.28	0.14	0.31	0.22	0.10		0.40	13.2	1.9	44	39		4.6	1.01	0.05	0.32
Rye (Secale cereale)	11.0	12.1	1.7	73.4	1.8	0.59	0.25	0.44	0.67	0.45	0.18	0.47	0.37	0.14		0.56	← 21 →		18	61		1.6	0.92	0.22	0.43
Safflower (Carthamus tinctorius)	6.0	12.7	30.8		3.0												← 5.8 →		16	78					
Sesame (Sesamum indicum)	5.8	19.3	51.1	18.1	5.7																	4.5		0.22	0.93
Sorghum (Sorghum vulgare)	10.0	11.2	3.5	73.8	1.5												8.5					4.5	1.04	0.13	
Soybean (Glycine soja)[2]	7.5	34.9	18.1	34.8	4.7	4.1	1.3	2.6	4.3	3.1	0.5	3.1	2.3	0.7		2.7	← 15 →		27	52	6	2.3	1.56	0.31	1.07
Sunflower (Helianthus annuus)[2]	5.0	18.5	27.8		3.3	5.46	1.43	2.78	3.71	1.45	1.61	2.39	1.64	1.14		2.70	← 11.3 →		30	60					
Wheat (Triticum esculentum)	12.5	12.3	1.8	71.7	1.7	0.63	0.31	0.58	0.91	0.35	0.22	0.70	0.38	0.19		0.64	13.8	1.0	30	49	6	4.3	1.39	0.12	0.52

[1] Component fatty acids are expressed as percent by weight of the total fatty acids of the seed.
[2] Values for amino acids are applicable to meal or flour.

SOURCE: SPECTOR (EDITOR). Handbook of Biological Data. Federation of American Societies for Experimental Biology. Bethesda, Maryland.

SEED, GERMINATION

TABLE 2.S.13

AVERAGE QUALITY, AMOUNT NEEDED FOR A TEST, AND DAYS FOR GERMINATION

Kind	*Pure seed (percent)*	*Germination (percent)*	*Weed seed (percent)*	*Size sample*	*Days for germination*
Alfalfa	99	90	0.50	⅓ cup	7
Bahiagrass	72	70	.50	1 cup	21–28
Barley	99	90	.50	1 qt.	7
Bean	99	90	.00	3 cups	7–10
Beet, field	97	75	.00	1½ qts.	14
Bentgrass	95	90	.50	¼ cup	21–28
Bermudagrass	97	85	1.00	½ cup	21
Bluegrass:					
Kentucky	85	80	1.00	½ cup	21–28
Rough	85	80	1.00	½ cup	21–28
Brome:					
Smooth	92	85	1.00	1 cup	14
Broomcorn	98	85	.50	3 cups	10
Buckwheat	97	85	1.00	3 cups	6
Canarygrass, Reed	96	80	.50	¼ cup	21
Carpetgrass	92	90	.50	½ cup	21
Chickpea	99	90	.00	1 qt.	7
Clovers:					
Alsike	97	90	1.00	¼ cup	7
Alyce	98	90	1.00	⅓ cup	21
Berseem	98	90	.50	⅓ cup	7
Bur (in bur)	90	90	.50	1½ qts.	14
Bur (out of bur)	98	90	.50	⅓ cup	14
Cluster	95	85	1.00	¼ cup	10
Crimson	98	85	.80	⅓ cup	7
Ladino and white	95	90	1.00	¼ cup	7
Persian	95	85	1.00	¼ cup	7
Red	98	90	.50	⅓ cup	7
Sour	98	90	.50	⅓ cup	14
Strawberry	97	90	1.00	⅓ cup	7
Subterranean	99	90	.50	1 cup	14
Sweet	95	90	1.00	¼ cup	7
Corn	99	90	.00	3 cups	7
Cotton	99	85	.00	1¼ qts.	12
Cowpea	98	85	.00	3 cups	8
Crotalaria: Slender leaf	99	80	.50	⅓ cup	10
Dallisgrass	70	70	1.00	1 cup	21
Fescue:					
Meadow	97	90	2.00	1 cup	14
Red, Chewings	97	80	.50	¾ cup	21–28
Tall	97	90	2.00	1 cup	14
Flax	97	85	.50	¾ cup	7
Johnsongrass	98	85	.50	½ cup	35
Kudzu	99	70	.50	1 cup	14
Lespedeza:					
Sericea or Chinese	98	90	1.00	⅔ cup	28
Common and Kobe	96	90	1.00	⅔ cup	14
Korean	97	90	1.00	⅔ cup	14
Lupine	99	90	.00	3 cups	10
Meadow foxtail	90	80	.50	½ cup	14
Medic, Black	98	90	.50	⅓ cup	7
Millet:					
Browntop	96	70	.50	⅔ cup	14
Foxtail, German, Hungarian, or Golden.	98	90	.50	⅔ cup	10
Japanese	97	90	.50	⅔ cup	10
Pearl	98	85	.50	1 cup	7
Proso	98	85	.50	1 cup	7
Oats	98	90	.10	1¼ qts.	10
Oatgrass, Tall	85	80	1.00	1 cup	14
Orchardgrass	85	85	1.50	1 cup	21

TABLE 2.S.13 (*Continued*)

Kind	*Pure seed (percent)*	*Germination (percent)*	*Weed seed (percent)*	*Size sample*	*Days for germination*
Peanuts	99	80	.00	1¼ qts.	10
Peas, Field	99	90	.00	3 cups	8
Rape, Dwarf Essex, Winter	99	90	.50	½ cup	7–10
Redtop	92	90	1.00	½ cup	10
Rescuegrass	95	85	1.00	¾ cup	28
Rhodesgrass	60	60	1.00	½ cup	14
Rice	99	90	.50	1 qt.	14
Rough pea	98	90	.00	3 cups	14
Rye	97	85	.10	3 cups	7
Ryegrass	98	90	.50	⅔ cup	14
Sainfoin	98	70	.50	2 cups	14
Sesbania	99	90	.25	¾ cup	7
Sorghum	98	85	.50	⅔ cup	10
Soybean	98	85	.00	3 cups	8
Sudangrass	98	80	.50	1¼ cups	10
Sunflower (Cult)	99	90	.00	1¾ qts.	7
Timothy	99	90	.50	⅛ cup	10
Trefoil, Big	98	80	1.00	¼ cup	10
Trefoil, Birdsfoot	96	90	1.00	¼ cup	10
Velvetgrass	95	85	.50	½ cup	14
Vetch	97	90	.50	3 cups	10–14
Wheat	99	90	.10	3 cups	7–10
Wheatgrass:					
Crested	95	85	.50	⅔ cup	14
Slender	95	85	.50	⅔ cup	14
Western	80	80	2.00	⅔ cup	28

SOURCE: ANON. Seeds: The Yearbook of Agriculture, U.S. Dep. Agric.

SHEEP BREEDS

TABLE 2.S.14

BREEDS OF SHEEP AND THEIR CHARACTERISTICS

Breed	Place of Origin	Color; Face, Ears, and Legs	Head Characteristics	Other Distinguishing Characteristics	Disqualifications
(Classified by type of wool produced)[1]					
Fine-Wool Breeds:					
American Merino	Spain	White. Reddish-brown spots may occasionally appear on lips, ears, and pasterns.	Most rams have horns, but there are some polled strains.	Distinguished from the Delaine Merinos by more skin wrinkles; the more wrinkled American Merinos being the "A" and "B" types. Strong flocking instinct. Ewes will breed out of season.	
Debouillet	On the Amos Dee Jones ranches of Roswell and Tatum, New Mexico. Ass'n organized in 1954.	White	Rams may have horns, but there are also polled strains; open face.	Comparatively smooth body; long staple.	Failure to pass inspection.

(Continued)

TABLE 2.S.14 (*Continued*)

Breed	Place of Origin	Color; Face, Ears, and Legs	Head Characteristics	Other Distinguishing Characteristics	Disqualifications
Delaine Merino	Spain	White. Reddish-brown spots may occasionally appear on lips, ears, and pasterns.	Most rams have horns, but there are some polled strains.	Comparatively smooth bodied; of the "C" type. Strong flocking instinct. Ewes will breed out of season.	
Rambouillet	France	White, brownish, or black spots are sometimes present, but discriminated against.	Most rams have horns, but there are some polled strains. Ewes are hornless.	The largest fine wool breed. Strong flocking instinct. Ewes will breed out of season.	Less than 2 normal sized testicles descended in the scrotum, short or long jaws, rolled eyelids, inverted teats, black spots or black fibers in the fleece, excess pigmentation in the hooves, broken-down pasterns, any serious bone deformity, or any other defect which will limit the animal's usefulness.
Medium-Wool Breeds:					
Cheviot	Scotland; in the Cheviot Hills between Scotland and England.	White face with a black nose. Often black spots are on the ears.	Both sexes are polled.	Stylish, alert, and active. Head and legs free from wool.	Black spots other than ears. Overshot or undershot jaw.
Dorset	England; especially in the southern countries of Dorset and Sumerset.	White and practically free from wool.	There are horned and polled strains, both of which are registered by The Continental Dorset Club. Except for the presence or absence of horns, the two strains are identical.	Ewes will breed out of season.	Black spots on body, legs, and face.
Hampshire	England; in the south-central county of Hampshire.	Rich deep brown, approaching black.	Both sexes are hornless, although rams sometimes have scurs.	Large size; early maturity.	Horns; short or long jaw; abnormal testicles; inverted eyelids.
Montadale (Columbia X Cheviot)	U.S.; by E.H. Mattingly, St. Louis, Missouri.	White	Both sexes are polled.	Face and legs free from wool.	Horns. Brown hair or spots on face, ears or legs. Black spots in the wool.
North Country Cheviot	In Scotland, from the old Long Hill sheep, but with infusion of Merino, Ryeland, and Southdown blood in formative period.	White	Nose straight to slightly Roman. Rams are sometimes horned.	Wool grades 50's to 56's mature rams weigh up to 300 pounds and mature ewes up to 200 pounds.	
Oxford	England; in the south-central county of Oxford.	Variable, from gray to brown.	Both sexes are polled. Topknot of wool.	Largest of the Down breeds.	Black fiber; stub horns.
Shropshire	England; in the central western counties of Shropshire and Stafford.	Dark face, but a gray nose is not objectionable.	Both sexes are polled, although rams frequently have scurs.	Covering of dense wool well over the poll.	Such lack of type as to render the identity of the breed doubtful; horns or stubs (not scurs); overshot or undershot jaws.
Southdown	England; in the south-eastern county of Sussex.	Light or mouse brown color preferred.	Both sexes are polled, although rams sometimes have scurs.	Superior conformation and quality of carcass.	Horns; dark poll; speckled markings on face, ears, and legs; one testicle only; black or brown fleece.

TABLE 2.S.14 (*Continued*)

Breed	Place of Origin	Color; Face, Ears, and Legs	Head Characteristics	Other Distinguishing Characteristics	Disqualifications
Suffolk	England; in the southeastern counties of Suffolk, Essex, and Norfolk.	Very black head, ears, and legs.	Both sexes are polled, although rams frequently have scurs.	The head and ears are entirely free from wool.	
Tunis (or American Tunis)	Asia; in Tunis.	Reddish brown to bright tan.	Both sexes are polled; long, drooping ears; head free from wool.	Originally, it was a fat-tailed sheep, which means that the tail was distinctly broad and fat. However, breeders have selected away from this trait. Pendulous ears. Will mate almost any season of the year.	Horns; red or black wool; one testicle; undershot or overshot jaw.
Long-Wool Breeds:					
Cotswold	England; in the Cotswold hills of Gloucestershire.	White, although grayish specks and bluish tinge are common.	Both sexes are polled, although rams frequently have scurs.	The natural wavy ringlets or curls in which the fleece hangs all over the body. The tuft of wool on the forehead. Second only to the Lincoln in size.	
Leicester	England; in the central county of Leicester.	White, but may have a bluish tinge or black spots.	Both sexes are polled.		
Lincoln	England; along the eastern coast of England and bordering the North Sea, in Lincolnshire.	White. Black spots may be present but are discriminated against.	Both sexes are polled.	The largest of all breeds of sheep. Produces the heaviest fleece of any mutton breed.	
Romney	England; in the Romney Marsh region of the County of Kent.	White	Both sexes are polled.	In comparison with other long-wool breeds; the Romney is shorter legged, more rugged, and its fleece is shorter, finer, and less open.	
Crossbred Wool Breeds[1]					
Columbia (**Lincoln rams, Rambouillet ewes**)	United States; in Wyoming and Idaho.	White	Both sexes are polled.	Open-faced, with no tendency to wool blindness.	Horns or scurs; wool blindness; uneven or light fleece; overshot or undershot jaw; colored wool; excessive folds.
Corriedale (Lincoln and Leicester rams, Merino ewes)	New Zealand	White, although black spots are sometimes present.	Both sexes are polled.		Black or brown spots. Wool blindness. Malformed mouth. Horns.

(Continued)

TABLE 2.S.14 (*Continued*)

Breed	Place of Origin	Color; Face, Ears, and Legs	Head Characteristics	Other Distinguishing Characteristics	Disqualifications
Panama (Rambouillet rams, Lincoln ewes)	United States; by Laidlaw and Brockie of Muldoon, Idaho.	White	Both sexes are polled.		Horns, scurs, or knobs; overshot or undershot mouth; excessive folds or wrinkles; colored wool; colored spots larger than 3/4 in. in diameter on clear areas; any unsound hereditary factor.
Tailless (or No Tail)	South Dak. Agric. Expt. Sta.	White	Both sexes are polled.	Usually produce tailless offspring.	
Targhee (Rambouillet rams, Lincoln-Rambouillet-Corriedale ewes)	United States; by the USDA at Dubois, Idaho.	White	Both sexes are polled.	Open-faced.	Marked scurs or horns. Noticeable coarseness of wool on the britch or tail. Noticeable defects.
Carpet-Wool Breed:					
Black-faced Highland (or Scottish Black face)	Scotland; in the highland country.	Black or mottled.	Both sexes have horns.	Striking stylish appearance. Fleece consists of long coarse outer-coat and a finer inner-coat.	
Fur-Sheep Breed:					
Karakul	Asia; in the county of Bokhara (US SR).	Black or brown.	Rams have horns, but ewes are hornless.	Drooping ears. A fat-tailed sheep. Lamb pelts suitable for fur production.	

[1]The listing of the crosses which produced each of the "crossbred-wool breeds" is given for breed history purposes only, and does not imply any lack of purity of the respective breeds. Nor does it indicate that all of them are new breeds: for example, the Corriedale, which is an old breed, was originated in New Zealand about 1880.

SOURCE: ENSMINGER, M. E. 1969. Animal Science, Interstate Printers and Publishers, Danville, Illinois. Reproduced with permission of publisher.

SHEEP MARKET CLASSES AND GRADES

TABLE 2.S.15

MARKET CLASSES AND GRADES OF SHEEP

Use Selection		Sex Classes	Age	Wt Division	(Pounds)	(Kilograms)	Commonly Used Grades
Sheep	Slaughter sheep	Ewes	Yearling	Light	90 down	40.9 down	Prime, Choice, Good, Utility, Cull[1]
				Medium	90 to 100	40.9–45.4	
				Heavy	100 up	45.4-up	
			Mature (2-year-old or older)	Light	120 down	54.5 down	Choice, Good, Utility, Cull[1]
				Medium	120–140	54.5–63.6	
				Heavy	140 up	63.6 up	
		Wethers	Yearling	Light	100 down	45.5 down	Prime, Choice, Good, Utility, Cull[1]
				Medium	100–110	45.4–49.9	
				Heavy	110 up	49.9 up	
			Mature (2-year-old or older)	Light	115 down	52.2 down	Choice, Good, Utility, Cull[1]
				Medium	115–130	52.2–59.0	
				Heavy	130 up	59.0 up	
		Rams	Yearling	All weights			Prime, Choice, Good, Utility, Cull[1]
			Mature (2-year-old or older)	All weights			Choice, Good, Utility, Cull[1]
	Feeder sheep	Ewes and wethers	Yearlings	All weights			Fancy, Choice, Good, Medium, Cull
		Ewes	Mature (2-year-old or older)	All weights			Choice, Good, Medium, Cull
	Breeding sheep	Ewes (rams occasionally purchased as breeders, but not listed in market reports)	Yearlings, 2-, 3-, or 4-yr.-olds and older	All weights			Fancy, Choice, Good, Medium, Cull
Lambs	Slaughter lambs	Ewes, wethers, and rams	Hothouse lambs	60 down			Prime, Choice, Good, Utility, Cull[1]
		Ewes, wethers, and rams	Spring lambs	Light	70 down	31.8 down	Prime, Choice, Good, Utility, Cull[1]
				Medium	70–90	31.8–40.9	
				Heavy	90 up	40.9 up	
		Ewes, wethers, and rams	Lambs	Light	75 down	34.0 down	Prime, Choice, Good, Utility, Cull[1]
				Medium	75–95	34.0–43.1	
				Heavy	95 up	43.1 up	
	Feeder lambs	Ewes and wethers	All ages	All weights			Fancy, Choice, Good, Medium, Cull
	Shearer lambs	Ewes and wethers	All ages	All weights			Choice, Good, Medium

[1] In addition to the above quality grades the following yield grades became effective March 1, 1969: Yield Grade 1, Yield Grade 2, Yield Grade 3, Yield Grade 4, and Yield Grade 5. Thus, slaughter sheep and lambs may be graded for (1) quality alone, (2) yield grade alone, or (3) both quality and yield grades.

SOURCE: ENSMINGER, M. E. 1969. Animal Science. Interstate Printers & Publishers, Danville, Illinois.

SHRIMP

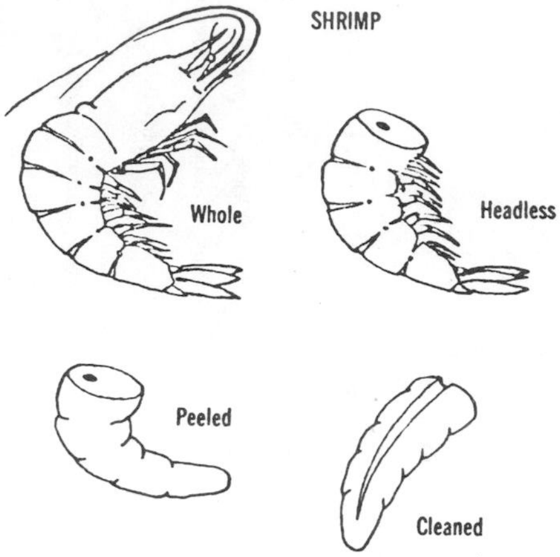

FIG. 2.S.3. FORMS IN WHICH SHRIMP ARE MARKETED

SOURCE: Food For Us All. Yearbook of Agriculture, 1969. USDA.

SIMMERING MEAT

TABLE 2.S.16

TIME-TABLE FOR SIMMERING (COOKING IN WATER) FOR LARGE CUTS AND STEWS

Cut	Average Size or Average Weight	Approximate Cooking Time	
		minutes per pound	*total hours*
Fresh beef	4 to 8 pounds	40 to 50	3 to 4
Corned beef	6 to 8 pounds	40 to 50	4 to 6
Fresh pork	Weight desired	30	
Smoked whole ham	12 to 16 pounds	18 to 20	4 to 5
Smoked half ham	6 to 8 pounds	25	2½ to 3½
Smoked picnic	4 to 8 pounds	35 to 45	3 to 4½
Stew, lamb or veal	1 to 2 inch cubes		1½ to 2*
Stew, beef	1 to 2 inch cubes		2 to 3*

* If cooking in pressure pans, follow time-table of manufacturer.

SOURCE: Cooking Meat in Quantity. National Live Stock and Meat Board, Chicago.

SODIUM HYDROXIDE SOLUTION

TABLE 2.S.17

AMOUNT OF SODIUM HYDROXIDE NEEDED FOR STRENGTH DESIRED

Sodium hydroxide solns: Specification requires 95% NaOH in sticks or pellets of caustic soda. Dissolve and dil. to 1 L.

NaOH Strength Desired Grams per Liter	Sodium Hydroxide Required Grams	
12.5	13.16	For crude fiber
30	31.58	
40	42.11	1*N* soln
50	52.63	
75	78.95	
100	105.26	
150	157.89	
200	210.53	
250	263.16	
300	315.79	

SOURCE: AOAC EDITORIAL BOARD. 1975. Official Methods of Analysis of the Association of Official Analytical Chemists, 12th Edition. Assoc. Offic. Anal. Chemists.

SODIUM-RESTRICTED DIET

TABLE 2.S.18

FOOD LISTS FOR SODIUM-RESTRICTED DIETS

List 1—Milk Products

	List 1	*List 1A*
For Mild Na Restriction	1,800 or Unrestricted Calorie Diet Each unit contains approx: carbohydrate 12, protein 8, fat 10 g; cal 170; Na 120 mg 1 unit = 1 cup Whole milk 1 cup Whole milk buttermilk 1 cup Evaporated whole milk (reconstituted) 2 Fat units plus 1 cup Nonfat buttermilk 2 Fat units plus 3 tbsp Nonfat dry milk (powder) (or amt specified on package for making 1 cup) 2 Fat units plus 1 cup Nonfat dry milk (reconstituted) 2 Fat units plus 1 cup Skim milk *N.B.:* 2 units from the meat list may be substituted for not >1 milk unit/day. AVOID: Any commercial foods made of milk—ice cream, sherbet, milk shakes, chocolate milk, malted milk, milk mixes, condensed milk, etc.	1,200-Calorie Diet Each unit contains approx: carbohydrate 12, protein 8 g, fat negligible; cal 85; Na 120 mg 1 unit = 1 cup Skim milk 1 cup Evaporated skin milk (reconstituted) 1 cup Nonfat buttermilk 3 tbsp Nonfat dry milk (powder) (or amt specified on package for making 1 cup) 1 cup Nonfat dry milk (reconstituted) *N.B.:* 1 unit from the meat list may be substituted for not >1 milk unit/day. AVOID: Whole milk or any commercial foods made of milk—ice cream, sherbet, milk shakes, chocolate milk, malted milk, milk mixes, condensed milk, etc.

(Continued)

TABLE 2.S.18 (*Continued*)

For Moderate & Strict Na Restriction	As above except that buttermilk must be unsalted. Where <500 mg of Na is necessary, use special low-Na milk products.	As above except that buttermilk must be unsalted. Where <500 mg of Na is necessary, use special low-Na dry milk products; avoid buttermilk products.

List 2—Vegetables

	Group A	*Group B*	*Group C*
For Mild Na Restriction	Each unit contains: carbohydrate, protein, fat, and cal negligible; Na varies 1 unit = ½ cup Artichoke Asparagus Beet greens Broccoli Brussels sprouts Cabbage Cauliflower Celery Chard, Swiss Chicory Cucumber Dandelion greens Eggplant Endive Escarole Green beans Kale Lettuce Mushrooms Mustard greens Okra Peppers, green or red Radishes Spinach Squash, summer (yellow, zucchini, etc.) Tomato juice Tomatoes Turnip greens Wax beans	Each unit contains approx: carbohydrate 7, protein 2, fat 0 g; cal 35; Na 9 mg 1 unit = ½ cup Beets Carrots Onions Peas Pumpkin Rutabaga (yellow turnip) Squash, winter (acorn, Hubbard, etc.) Turnip, white *N.B.:* 2 units from Group A may be substituted for 1 unit from Group B.	Each unit contains approx: carbohydrate 15, protein 2, fat 0 g; cal 70; Na 5 mg 1 unit = ¼ cup Beans, baked (no pork) ½ cup cooked Beans, Lima or navy (fresh or dried) ⅓ cup or ½ small ear Corn ½ cup Hominy ½ cup cooked Lentils (dried) ⅔ cup Parsnips ½ cup cooked Peas, split green or yellow, cowpeas, etc. (dried) 1 small Potato, white ½ cup Potatoes, mashed ¼ cup or ½ small Sweet potato *N.B.:* 1 unit from the bread list may be substituted for 1 unit from Group C.
For Moderate & Strict Na Restriction	All of the above, except artichokes, beet greens, celery, chard, dandelion greens, kale, mustard greens, spinach.	All of the above, except beets, carrots, turnips.	All of the above, except hominy.

Canned vegetables and tomato juice should be of low-Na dietetic type. Frozen vegetables must be processed without salt. (Check labels.)

TABLE 2.S.18 (*Continued*)

	List 3—Fruit Products
For all Na-Restricted Diets	Includes fresh, frozen, canned, or dried fruit Each unit contains approx: carbohydrate 10 g; protein and fat negligible; cal 40; Na 2 mg 1 unit = 1 cup Blackberries, raspberries, strawberries, watermelon ⅔ cup Blueberries ⅓ cup Apple juice or cider, cranberry juice (sweetened), pineapple juice ½ cup Applesauce, fruit cup or mixed fruits, diced pineapple; orange, tangerine, or grapefruit juice ¼ cup Apricot nectar, grape juice, prune juice 1 Apple, fig, pear, tangerine, orange, peach 2 Apricots (fresh or dried), dates, plums, prunes ½ Banana, grapefruit, mango 10 Cherries 12 Grapes ⅓ Papaya ¼ Cantaloupe ⅛ Honeydew melon 1 tbsp Cranberries (sweetened) 2 tbsp Raisins, rhubarb (sweetened) Fresh lemons and limes, unsweetened cranberries, cranberry juice, and rhubarb: Use as desired; do not count as a unit. On 1,200- and 1,800-cal diets, do not use glazed or sweetened fruits or those packed in sugar syrup.
	List 4—Bread and Cereal Products
For Mild Na Restriction	Each unit contains approx: carbohydrate 15, protein 2 g; fat negligible; cal 70; Na 5 mg 1 unit = *N.B.:* 1 unit from the vegetable list, group C, may be substituted for 1 bread unit. 1 slice — Bread 4 pieces (3½ × 1½ × ⅛ in.) — Melba toast 1 medium — Roll, biscuit, or muffin 1 cube (1½ in.) — Cornbread 2 (3 in.) — Griddle cakes ½ cup cooked — Farina, grits, oatmeal, rolled wheat, wheat meal (lightly salted) ⅔ biscuit — Shredded wheat ¾ cup — Other dry cereal 1½ tbsp — Uncooked barley 2 tbsp — Cornmeal 5 (2 in. sq) — Crackers (low-Na dietetic) 2½ tbsp — Flour or cornstarch 2 — Graham crackers ½ cup cooked — Macaroni, rice (brown or white), noodles, or spaghetti 1 (5 in. sq) — Matzo (plain, unsalted) 1½ cup — Popcorn 2 tbsp uncooked — Tapioca 1 (3 in. sq section) — Waffle, yeast

(Continued)

TABLE 2.S.18 (*Continued*)

For Moderate & Strict Na Restriction	As above except that yeast bread and rolls, quick breads, and cooked cereals must be made without salt or monosodium glutamate; all breads must be made with Na-free baking powder or low-Na dietetic mix, and the dry cereal used must have not >6 mg of Na/100 g of cereal (check the label). Avoid self-rising cornmeal; graham crackers; salted popcorn, potato chips, pretzels, and crackers.

List 5—Meat or Meat Substitutes

For Mild Na Restriction

Each unit contains approx:
carbohydrate negligible; protein 7, fat 5 g; cal 75; Na 25 mg

1 unit =

1 oz, cooked

Beef	Lamb	Rabbit
Brain	Liver (beef, calf, chicken, pork)	Tongue
Chicken		Turkey
Duck	Pork	Veal
Kidney	Quail	
Bass	Eels	Salmon
Bluefish	Flounder	Scallops
Catfish	Halibut	Shrimp
Clams	Lobster	Sole
Cod	Oyster	Trout
Crab	Rockfish	Tuna

1 oz	American cheddar or Swiss cheese
¼ cup	Cottage cheese (lightly salted)
1	Egg
2 tbsp	Low-Na dietetic peanut butter

AVOID: Salty or smoked meats or fish (e.g., bacon, luncheon meats, chipped or corned beef, ham, frankfurters, salt pork, smoked tongue, sausage; anchovies, caviar, salted and dried cod, herring, sardines, etc.), processed cheese, cheese spreads, Roquefort, Camembert, Gorgonzola.

For Moderate & Strict Na Restriction

As above except that (1) brain, kidney, and shellfish are to be avoided. (2) Canned meat, poultry, and fish are to be of low-Na dietetic type. (3) Cottage cheese should be unsalted; other cheeses are to be of low-Na dietetic type. (4) Fish, except as noted under (2), to be fresh only. (5) Eggs are limited to 1/day.

List 6—Fats

For Mild Na Restriction

Each unit contains approx:
fat 5 g; cal 45; Na negligible

1 unit =

⅛ (4 in. diam)	Avocado
1 tsp (1 pat)	Butter or margarine
1 tbsp	Cream, heavy (sweet or sour)
2 tbsp	Cream, light (sweet or sour)
1 tsp	Fat or oil, cooking
1 tbsp	French dressing
1 tsp	Mayonnaise
6 small	Nuts, unsalted

AVOID: Salted nuts, bacon and bacon fat, olives, salt pork.

TABLE 2.S.18 *(Continued)*

For Moderate & Strict Na Restriction	As above except that salted butter and margarine are to be avoided; commercial salads and dressings are to be of low-Na dietetic type.	
	List 7—Free Choice	
For Mild Na Restriction	1 unit from	List 4—Breads
	75 cal	Candy (made without salted nuts)
	2 units from	List 6—Fats
	2 units from	List 3—Fruits
	4 tsp	Sugar (white or brown)
	4 tsp	Syrup, honey, jelly, jam, or marmalade
	1 unit from	List 2—Vegetables, group C
	Flavorings and seasonings may be used as desired except that barbecue sauce, bouillon, catsup, celery salt, chili sauce, garlic salt, prepared horseradish, meat extracts or tenderizers, monosodium glutamate, prepared mustard, olives, onion salt, pickles, relishes, soy sauce, Worcestershire sauce, and cooking wines are to be avoided.	
For Moderate & Strict Na Restriction	As above except that candy is to be home-made, salt-free, or low-Na dietetic.	

SOURCE: HOLVEY, D. N. 1972. The Merck Manual, 12th Edition. Merck & Co., Rahway, N.J.

SOIL CLASSES

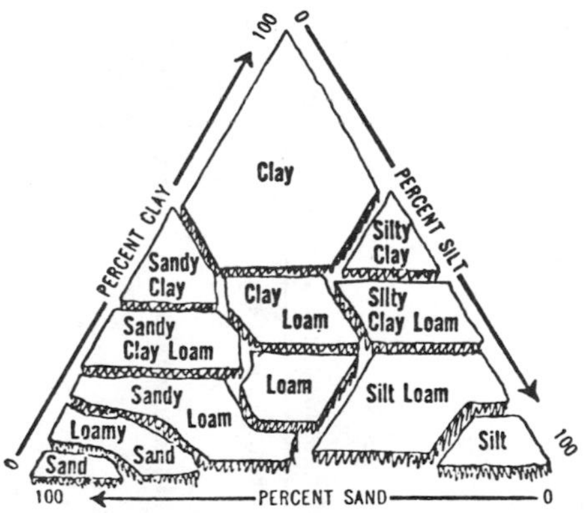

FIG. 2.S.4. THE TEXTURE TRIANGLE SHOWS THE PERCENTAGE OF SAND, SILT, AND CLAY IN EACH OF THE TEXTURAL CLASSES

SOURCE: Soil, The 1957 Yearbook of Agriculture. USDA.

SOUPS, COMPOSITION

TABLE 2.S.19

COMPOSITION OF SOUPS

Food, Approximate Measure, and Weight (in Grams)		Water (%)	Food Energy (Cal)	Protein (g)	Fat (Total Lipid) (g)	Fatty Acids: Saturated (Total) (g)	Fatty Acids: Unsaturated: Oleic (g)	Fatty Acids: Unsaturated: Lin-oleic (g)	Carbohy-drate (g)	Calcium (mg)	Iron (mg)	Vitamin A Value (I.U)	Thiamin (mg)	Riboflavin (mg)	Niacin (mg)	Ascorbic Acid (mg)
Soups, canned; ready-to-serve:																
Bean	1 cup (250 g)	82	190	8	5	2	2	Tr	30	95	2.8		0.10	0.10	0.8	
Beef	1 cup (250 g)	92	100	6	4	2	2	Tr	11	15	.5					
Bouillon, broth, consomme	1 cup (240 g)	95	10	2					0	2	1.0	0	0	0.05	0.6	0
Chicken	1 cup (250 g)	94	75	4	2	1	1	Tr	10	20	0.5		0.02	0.12	1.5	
Clam chowder	1 cup (255 g)	91	85	5	2	Tr	Tr	1	12	36	3.6					
Cream soup (asparagus, celery, mushroom)	1 cup (255 g)	85	200	7	12	7	4	Tr	18	217	0.5	200	0.05	0.20	0.1	0
Noodle, rice, barley	1 cup (250 g)	90	115	6	4	1	2	1	13	82	0.2	30	0.02	0.05	0.7	0
Pea	1 cup (245 g)	86	140	6	2	1	1	Tr	25	32	1.5	440	0.17	0.07	1.2	5
Tomato	1 cup (245 g)	91	90	2	2	1	Tr	1	18	24	1.0	1,230	0.02	0.10	0.7	10
Vegetable	1 cup (250 g)	92	80	4	2	1	1	Tr	14	32	0.8		0.05	0.08	1.0	8

SOURCE: INSTITUTE OF HOME ECONOMICS. Nutritive Value of Foods. USDA Home and Garden Bull. 72.

SOUR CREAM DRESSING

Ingredients

1 cup cream
2 tbsp vinegar & 1 tbsp lemon juice or
3 tbsp vinegar
1 tbsp sugar
1 tsp salt

Procedure

Mix the dry ingredients and add the acid. Add the cream. Stir thoroughly. Store in the refrigerator.

SOURCE: KINTNER, T. C., and MANGEL, M. Vinegars and salad dressings. Missouri Agric. Exp. Sta. Univ. Bull. *631.*

SOYBEAN COMPOSITION

TABLE 2.S.20

PROXIMATE ANALYSES OF COMMERCIAL SOYBEAN FLOURS AND GRITS.[a]

Product	Moisture %	Protein (N×6.25) %	Fat %	Crude fiber %	Ash %
Full-fat flour	5.0	41.5	21.0	2.1	5.2
Low-fat flour	5.5	46.0	6.5	3.0	5.5
Defatted flour[b]	5.0	53.0	0.9	2.9	6.0
Lecithinated flour[c]	5.5	45.2	16.4	2.4	5.3

[a]These analyses are not product standards, but are values typical for product.
[b]Available in a variety of moist-heat treatments.
[c]Available with lower lecithin contents.

SOURCE: MEYER, E. W. 1971. Soybean Flours and Grits. Proc. 3rd Intern. Congr. Food Science Technol.

SPECIFIC GRAVITIES, FATS AND OILS

TABLE 2.S.21

SPECIFIC GRAVITIES OF SOME FATS AND OILS

Fat or Oil	Specific Gravity 99°/15°C	15°/15°C	25°/25°C
Babassu			0.916-0.918
Castor		0.958-0.968	
Coconut	0.869-0.874		
Corn		0.922-0.926	0.915-0.920
Cottonseed		0.921-0.924	0.916-0.918
Kapok		0.920-0.923	
Linseed		0.931-0.938	0.924-0.931
Olive		0.914-0.919	0.909-0.915
Palm	0.849-0.856	0.921-0.925	0.914-0.918
Palm kernel	0.863-0.872		
Peanut		0.917-0.921	0.910-0.915
Safflower		0.925-0.928	
Sesame		0.920-0.926	
Soybean		0.924-0.928	
Sunflower		0.922-0.926	
Lard	0.858-0.864	0.934-0.938	0.908-0.913
Tallow (beef)	0.860-0.870	0.943-0.952	0.903-0.907
Tallow (mutton)	0.857-0.860	0.937-0.952	
Neatsfoot	0.860-0.865		
Horse		0.916-0.921	

SOURCE: MAHLENBACHER, C. V. The Analysis of Fats and Oils. Garrard Press, Champaign, Illinois.

SPECIFIC HEAT, MEAT

TABLE 2.S.22

AVERAGE SPECIFIC HEAT OF MEATS AND POULTRY

	Fresh	Frozen
Beef (lean)	0.77	0.40
Beef (fat)	0.60	0.35
Pork (ave)	0.55	0.32
Mutton (ave)	0.65	0.36
Poultry (ave)	0.80	0.48

SOURCE: GEARY, D., and GERRARD, F. 1968. Meat and Refrigeration. Meat Trades J., London, England.

SPICES, MICROBIAL CONTENT

TABLE 2.S.23

MICROBIAL CONTENT OF UNTREATED SPICES

Kind of Spice or Herb	Untreated Spice Suspensions Incubated at: 37°C (98.6°F) — Total Micro-organisms per Gram — Bacteria	Room Temp — Molds
Whole allspice	1,000,000	70,000
Ground allspice	64,000	50,000
Sweet basil	525,000	50
Whole cloves	4,400	100
Whole Zanzibar cloves	190	0
Ground China cinnamon	36,000	60,000
Crushed cinnamon	8,000	600
Ground ginger	60,000	2,000
Bay leaves	15,000	350
Ground Bandamace	2,800	400
Ground mustard	1,800	0
Ground East Indian nutmeg	1,200	700
Ground paprika	680,000	5,000
Ground red pepper	2,190,000	1,220,000
Ground white pepper	42,000	9,000
Decorticated pepper	1,780,000	70,000
Ground black pepper	10,400,000	1,300,000
Savory	4,000	450
Ground sage	270,000	20,000
Whole thyme	2,700,000	12,000
Ground thyme	35,000	30,000
Miscellaneous:		
Celery seed	1,150,000	10,000
Onion powder	6,000	0
Garlic cloves	200	20,000
Onion juice	30,000,000	100
Ground garlic powder	90,000	200
Liquid garlic	10,000	10,000
Emulsified spice oil	10	10

SOURCE: WEISER, H. H., MOUNTNEY, G. J. and GOULD, W. A. (EDITORS). 1971. Microbiology of Spices. *In* Practical Food Microbiology and Technology. Avi Publishing Co., Westport, Conn.

SPOILAGE, CARBOHYDRATE FOODS

TABLE 2.S.24

TYPES OF FOOD SPOILAGE ASSOCIATED WITH THE FERMENTATION AND METABOLISM OF CARBOHYDRATES IN FOODS

Type of Food	Spoilage	Organism
Fruit juices	Souring, CO_2	*Lactobacillus* spp.
Fruit juice concentrates	Acetification	*Acetobacter* spp.
	Slime formation, ropy and viscous	*Leuconostoc* spp.
Canned fruit	Souring, CO_2	*Lactobacillus* spp.
Bottled fruit	Alcohol, butyric acid	Osmophilic yeasts, *Clostridia* spp.
Chocolate creams	Alcoholic, CO_2	Osmophilic yeasts, *Escherichia coli*
Wines	Acetification	*Acetobacter* spp., *Acetomonas* spp.
	Slimes and off-flavors	*Leuconostoc* spp., *Lactobacillus* spp.
Beers	Off-flavors	*Saccharomyces* spp.
	Gassing and slimes	*S. lactis*
		S. fragilis
Fruits	Souring, soft rots, and bitter flavors	*Streptococcus faecalis*, *Byssochlamys fulva*, *Penicillium italicum*, *P. citrinum*, *P. digitatum*
Cucumber	Souring	*Bacillus polymyxa*
	Soft rots	*Erwinia carotovora*
Carrots and vegetables	Off-flavors	*Sclerotinia sclerotiorum*
Milk	Souring	*Lactobacillus* spp.
	Acidity and gassing	*Streptococcus* spp.
Bread	Sour flavor	*Bacillus mesentericus*
	Ropy	*Rhizopus oryzae*
Cereals	Discoloration	*R. nigricans*
	Moldy flavor	*Penicillium glacum*, *Serratia marcescens*
Vinegar	Loss of acidity	*Acetobacter*
	Slimes	*Monilia acetobutans*
Sauerkraut	Slimes	*Lactobacillus plantarum*

SOURCE: ESKIN, N. A. M., HENDERSON, H. M., and TOWNSEND, R. J. 1971. Biochemistry of Foods. Academic Press, New York.

SPOILAGE, FAT IN FOOD

TABLE 2.S.25

TYPES OF FOOD SPOILAGE ASSOCIATED WITH THE MICROBIAL DEGRADATION OF FATS IN FOODS

Type of food	Spoilage	Spoilage organism
Milk	Souring	*Streptococcus lactis*
Cream	Rancidity, free fatty acid	*S. cremoris, Oidium lactis*
Butter	Free fatty acid	*Cladosporium suaveolens*
Margarine	Rancidity, methyl ketones	*C. butyri, Candida lipolytica*
Lard	Free fatty acid	*Paecilomyces aureocinnamoneum*
Palm oil	Rancidity	
Coconut oil	Methyl ketones	*Margarinomyces bubaki*
Groundnut oil		*Staphylococcus aureus*
Cottonseed oil	Rancidity	*Lactosaprophiticus*
Corn oil	Free fatty acid	*Aspergillus tamarii*
Rapeseed oil	Lipoxidation	*A. niger*
Olive oil	Rancidity	*A. repens*
Oats	Bitterness	*A. restrictus*
Wheat	Soapiness	*Paecilomyces variotii*
Barley		*Monilia acremonium*
Biscuits		*Serratia marcescens, Pseudomonas hydrophila*

SOURCE: ESKIN, N. A. M., HENDERSON, H. M., and TOWNSEND, R. J. 1971. Biochemistry of Foods. Academic Press, New York.

SPOILAGE, PROTEIN FOODS

TABLE 2.S.26

TYPES OF FOOD SPOILAGE ASSOCIATED WITH THE MICROBIAL DEGRADATION OF PROTEINS IN FOODS

Type of food	Spoilage	Spoilage organism
Milk	Coagulation of caseins, off-flavors, rancidity, putrefaction, cadaverine	*Bacillus subtilis*, *B. cereus* *Pseudomonas putrefaciens*, *P. ichthyosmia* *Proteus vulgaris*, *Streptococcus liquefaciens*, *S. lactis*
Meats and meat products	Surface slimes, liquefaction, collagen degradation, elastin degradation, keratin degradation, putrefaction, cadaverine, putrescine, indole, amines, NH_3, H_2S, and bone taint	*Clostridium perfringens*, *Cl. welchii*, *Cl. histolyticum*, *Cl. sporogenes*, *Flavobacterium elastolyticum*, *Aeromonas* spp., *Achromobacter* spp., *Proteus* spp., *Pseudomonas* spp.
Fish, fish sausage, and fish cakes	Fishy odors, trimethylamine, dimethylamine, indole, cadaverine, putrescine, H_2S, surface slimes	*Achromobacter* spp., *Pseudomonas* spp., *Flavobacterium* spp., *Micrococcus* spp., *Sarcina* spp., *Proteus* spp., *Bacillus* spp.
Hams	Greening	*Lactobacillus viridescens*
Bacon	Putrefaction	*Clostridium sporogenes*
Chicken and turkey	Liquefaction, bone taint, rancidity	*Cl. aerofoetidum* *Cl. bifermentans* *Cl. histolyticum* *Cl. putrefaciens* *Cl. perfringens* *Pseudomonas fluorescens* *Vibrio costicolus* *Micrococcus candidus* *M. luteus*
Eggs	White rot, black rot, mixed rot, and fungal infections	*Clostridium sporogenes* *Cl. putrificum* *Cladosporium herbarum* *Penicillium glaucum*
Cheese	Moldy	*P. glaucum* *P. expansum* *Monilia sitophila*

SOURCE: ESKIN, N. A. M., HENDERSON, H. M., and TOWNSEND, R. J. 1971. Biochemistry in Foods. Academic Press, New York.

STABILIZERS, THICKENERS

TABLE 2.S.27

FUNCTIONS AND USES OF STABILIZERS AND THICKENERS

Additive	*Function*	*Type of Food*
Agar agar	Thickener	Frozen candied sweet potatoes, ice cream, frozen custard, sherbet
Sodium alginate (algins)	Water retainers	Condiments, salad dressing, cake icing, chocolate milk, dessert toppings
Carrageenan	Stabilizer	Chocolate milk, syrups for frozen products, evaporated milk, pressure-dispersed whipped cream, cottage cheese
Sodium carboxymethyl cellulose	Stabilizer, bodying agent	Ice cream, icing for baked goods, cheese spreads, dietetic canned fruit products, fruited ham glaze
Dextrin	Stabilizer	Beer, baked goods, gelatin desserts
Gelatin	Thickener	Fruit gelatins and puddings, cream cheese, cheese spreads, cheese foods
Cellulose gums	Thickener, suspender, bodying agent	Dessert mixes, cake mixes, salad dressing
Gum acacia (gum arabic)	Thickener, stabilizer	Beer, soft drinks, ice cream, imitation fruit juice drinks
Locust bean gum	Thickener, stabilizer	Cream cheese, fruit sherbert, salad dressing
Guar gum	Thickener, stabilizer, binder	Cheese spreads, baked goods, meat products
Gum tragacanth	Thickener	Pickle relish, icings, fruit juices, salad dressings

SOURCE: BERARDE, M. A. 1971. The Chemicals We Eat. McGraw-Hill Book Company, New York.

STAINLESS STEEL

TABLE 2.S.28

COMPOSITION AND PROPERTIES OF SOME TYPES OF STAINLESS STEEL[1]

Part I—Composition of Some Stainless Steels

Composition	Type 302	Type 304	Type 316	Type 430	Type 440C	Type 502
Carbon	0.08–0.20	0.08	0.10	0.12	0.95	0.10
Manganese	2.00	2.00	2.00	1.00	1.00	1.00
Phosphorus	0.04	0.04	0.04	0.04	0.04	0.04
Sulfur	0.03	0.03	0.03	0.03	0.03	0.03
Silicon	1.00	1.00	1.00	1.00	1.00	1.00
Nickel	8.00–10.00	8.00–10.00	10.00–14.00	0.00	0.00	0.00
Chromium	17.00–19.00	18.00–20.00	16.00–18.00	14.00–18.00	16.00–18.00	4.00–6.00
Molybdenum	0.00	0.00	2.00–3.00	0.00	0.75	0.00

Part II—Properties of Some Types of Stainless Steel

	Types 302 and 304		Type 316		Type 430		Type 440C		Type 502
Mechanical Properties	An-nealed	Cold Drawn	An-nealed	Cold Drawn	An-nealed	Ann. and Cold Drawn	An-nealed	Ann. and Cold Drawn	Annealed Bars
Tensile strength	75,000	100,000	80,000	90,000	75,000	85,000	110,000	125,000	65,000
Yield strength	35,000	60,000	30,000	60,000	45,000	70,000	65,000	100,000	25,000
Brinnel hardness	150	212	149	190	155	185	230	260	150
Rockwell hardness		C-33	78				B.97	C.24	B.75
Scaling temp., °F	1,650	1,650	1,650	1,650	1,550	1,550			1,150
Annealing temp., °F	1,900–2,000 and quench		1,900–2,050 and quench		Air cool from		Cool slowly		Furnace Cool
	1,650	1,650	1,650	1,650	1,500–1,400°F		1,550–1,650		1,600–1,525
Hardenable	No	No					Yes	Yes	Yes
Magnetic							Yes	Yes	Yes

[1] Percent iron not shown.

SOURCE: HALL, C. W., FARRALL, A. W. and RIPPEN, A. L. (EDITORS). 1971. Stainless Steel. *In* Encyclopedia of Food Engineering. Avi Publishing Co., Westport, Conn.

STANDARDS, PROCESSED FRUIT AND VEGETABLE PRODUCTS

TABLE 2.S.29

RELATIVE IMPORTANCE OF FACTORS INVOLVED IN USDA STANDARDS FOR PROCESSED FRUIT AND VEGETABLE PRODUCTS

Product	Absence of Defects	Color	Flavor	Character	Consistency	Uniformity	Texture	Tenderness and Maturity	Clearness of Liquor
Apples	20	20	..	40	..	20 siz.	..	..	..
Apple Butter	20	20	20	20 fin.	20	..	..	..	..
Apple Juice	20	20	60	..	..	..	..	..	..
Apple Sauce	20	20	20	20 fin.	20	..	..	..	..
Apricots	30	20	..	30	..	20 siz.	..	..	..
Asparagus	30	20	..	..	..	..	..	40	10
Green & Wax Beans	35	15	..	..	..	..	..	40	10
Dried Beans	40	..	..	40	20	..	..	..	..
Lima Beans	25	35	..	30	..	..	..	..	10
Beets	30	25	..	..	..	15	30	..	..
Berries	30	20	..	30	..	20	..	..	..
Blueberries	40	20	..	40	..	..	..	..	..
Carrots	30	25	..	..	shape	15 siz.	30	..	..
Cherries, Sweet	30	30	..	20	..	20 siz.	..	..	..
Cherries, Sour	30	20	..	30	..	20 pits	..	..	..
Corn, Cream	20	10	20	..	20	..	..	30	..
Corn, Whole	20	10	20	..	..	..	..	40	10
Cranberry Sauce	20	20	20	..	40	..	..	..	..
Figs, Kadota	30	20	..	35	..	15 siz.	..	..	..
Frozen Apples	20	20	..	40	..	20	..	..	..
Fruit Cocktail	20	20	..	20	..	20	..	..	20
Fruit Jelly	..	20	40	..	40	..	..	..	..
Fruit Preserv. (Jam)	20	20	40	..	20	..	..	..	..
Fruit Salad	30	20	..	30	..	20 siz.	..	..	..
Grapefruit	20	20	..	20	(Wholeness 20)			(Drained Wt. 20)	
Grapefruit Juice	40	20	40	..	..	..	..	..	..
Grape Juice	20	40	40	..	..	..	..	..	..
Lemon Juice	35	35	30	..	..	..	..	..	..
Mushroom	30	30	..	20	..	20 siz.	..	..	..
Olives, Green	30	30	..	20	..	20 siz.	..	..	..
Olives, Ripe	10	15	30	25	..	20	..	..	..
Orange Juice	20	40	40	..	..	..	..	..	..
Orange Juice con.	20	40	40	..	..	..	..	..	..
Orange Marm.	20	20	40	..	20	..	..	..	..
Okra	20	15	15	..	..	10	..	35	5
Peaches	30	20	..	30	..	20 siz.	..	..	..
Peanut Butter	30	20	30	..	20	..	..	..	..
Pears	30	20	..	30	..	20 siz.	..	..	..
Peas	30	10	..	..	..	..	..	50	10
Peas, Field	40	20	..	40	..	..	..	..	..
Cucumber Pick.	30	20	..	..	..	20	30	..	..
Pimientos	40	30	..	10	..	20 siz.	..	..	..
Pineapples	30	20	..	30	..	20	..	..	..
Pineapple Juice	40	20	40	..	..	..	..	..	..
Plums	30	20	..	30	..	20 siz.	..	..	..
Potatoes, peeled	40	20	..	..	..	20	20	..	..
Prunes, dr.	30	20	..	35	..	15	..	..	..
Pumpkins & Squash	30	20	..	20 fin.	30	..	..	..	..
Raspberries	20	25	..	35	..	20 siz.	..	..	..
Sauerkraut	10	15	45	15 crisp		..	..	..	15
Sauerkraut, bulk	10	15	45	15 crisp		..	..	..	15
Spinach	40	30	..	30	..	..	..	..	..
Sw. Potatoes	40	20	..	20	..	20 siz.	..	..	..
Tomatoes	30	30	..	..	(Wholeness 20)			(Drained Wt. 20)	
Tomato Juice	15	30	40	..	15	..	..	..	..
Tomato Paste	40	60	..	..	..	..	..	..	..
Tomato Pulp—pure	50	50	..	..	..	..	..	..	..
Tom. Sauce-Catsup	25	25	25	..	25	..	..	..	..
Chili Sauce	20	20	20	20	20	..	..	..	..

SOURCE: KRAMER, A. and TWIGG, B. A. (EDITORS). 1970. *In* Quality Control for the Food Industry, Vol. 1, 3rd Edition. Avi Publishing Co., Westport, Conn.

STARCH

TABLE 2.S.30

TYPES OF STARCHES USED IN SUGAR CONFECTIONERY

Type	Use and Characteristics
Unmodified maize starch	Filler for cheap cream paste, toffee cigarettes, licorice paste. Dusting powder. Can be mixed with fat for release agents; with icing sugar for Turkish Delight dusting.
Acid modified thin boiling starches	
Fluidity Nos. 30, 40	Used in gums and jellies. Generally used for open pan cooking; can also be used for continuous processes where acid is present during cooking process.
Nos. 50, 60, 70, 85	Enable high solids production, good depositing capability, can be used in combination with other gelling agents. Produce gels of high rigidity, clarity and short texture and are capable of producing a wide range of textures (soft to hard); good shelf life.
Oxidized modified thin boiling starches	Similar range of fluidity available. Produce gels of increased clarity but lack the rigidity of acid-modified starches. Produces soft eating products; can be used in combination with other starches and gelling agents.
Molding starches	
Oil bound molding starch (contains 0.12%-0.2% mineral oil)	Provides good molding characteristics at low moisture percentages. Reduces explosion hazard by suppressing dust. Oil used is not susceptible to rancidity.
Oil bound 0.75%	Can be mixed with oil-free starch in mogul plant to improve molding. Increase total oil content to suitable range 0.2%.
Oil-free molding starches	Can be mixed with heavy molding starch to rejuvenate after extended use. Excellent water absorption properties. (Molding starches based on di-glycerides as binders are also available.)
Amylopectin thin boiling (range of fluidities)	Produces gels of excellent clarity with no setback. Can be used at high concentration to produce hard texture; with other gelling agents, to provide a variety of textures. Also for continuous licorice paste production.
Modified waxy maize starches	Similar viscosity to gum arabic at same concentration. Excellent clarity, very soluble, low gelatinization temperature.
Soluble dextrin starches (range of fluidities; manufactured from maize or tapioca starches.)	For adhesive coatings and glazes. Used in panning operation as a seal. In some cases can replace natural gums. Good sheen and clarity.
Pregelatinized maize starch	Cold-water soluble; used as a tablet binder.
Physical modified oxidized starch	Cold-water soluble, easily dispersible, smooth texture, good film former, bland flavor. Used as tablet binder. Replaces gums and gelling agents in lozenge pastes, etc. Good seal for nuts, etc., in panning.

TABLE 2.S.30 (*Continued*)

Type	Use and Characteristics
Modified waxy maize starches cross bonded	For use in caramel and caramel coating, gives body with a soft eating texture, good clarity and flavor, acid-stable and resistant to long storage. Also used as a gelling agent in deposited and extruded marshmallow. Acid, heat, and shear stable.
Pregelatinized cross bonded acetylated waxy maize starches	Used where moisture is a restriction, dissolves readily in cold water even in high concentrations to form a clear smooth short texture. Gel resistant to freezing and thawing.
High amylose starches	Very high gelatinization temperature with strong set back used for quick-setting starch jellies. (High amylose can be blended with thin boiling maize starches to produce different amylopectin/amylose ratio.)

SOURCE: LEES, R., and JACKSON, E. B. 1973. Sugar Confectionery and Chocolate Manufacture. Leonard Hill Books, International Textbook Co., London, England.

STARCH, MICROAPPEARANCE

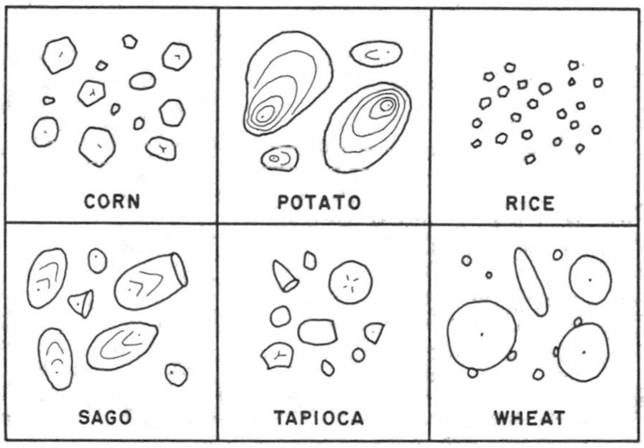

FIG. 2.S.5. MICROAPPEARANCE OF VARIOUS GRANULAR STARCHES

SOURCE: SCHOCH, THOMAS J. 1969. Starches in Foods. *In* Carbohydrates and Their Roles, Symposium on Foods. H. W. Schultz, R. F. Cain and R. W. Wrolstad (Editors). Avi Publishing Co., Westport, Conn.

STARCH, MODIFIED

TABLE 2.S.31

PROPERTIES OF MODIFIED STARCHES

Type of Modified Starch	Texture	Clarity	To Retrogradation	Terminal Viscosity	Stability: Shear	Stability: Acid	Stability: Heat	Stability: Freeze Thaw	Gelatinization Temp in Water
Roll dried maize	Short Granular	Avg	High set back	Instant cold water soluble; thick	Good	Fair	Fair	Poor	Cold water soluble
Acid modified maize	Short Smooth	Avg	High set back	Thick	Fair	Fair	Fair	Poor	63°–73°C in Water
Oxidized maize	Short Smooth	Above Avg	Soft set back	Thin	Poor	Fair	Fair	Poor	54°–64°C in Water
Moderately cross bonded waxy maize	Short Smooth	Avg	No set back at room temp; some at low temp	Thick	Good	Good	Good	Mod.	67°–77°C
Medium cross bonded waxy maize	Short Smooth	Avg	No set back at room temp; some at low temp	Thick	V. good	V. good	V. good	Fair	69°–79°C
High cross bonded waxy maize	Short Smooth	Avg	No set back at room temp; set back at low temp	Thick	Exc.	Exc.	Exc.	Poor	73°–83°C
Cross bonded acetylated waxy maize	Short Smooth	V. good	No set back	Thick	Exc.	Exc.	Exc.	Exc.	60°–72°C
Roll dried cross bonded acetylated waxy maize	Short Smooth	Above Avg	No set back	Instant cold water soluble	Exc.	Exc.	Exc.	Exc.	Cold water soluble

SOURCE: LEES, R., and JACKSON, E. B. 1973. Sugar Confectionery & Chocolate Manufacture. Leonard Hill Books, International Textbook Co., London, England.

STARCHY ROOTS COMPOSITION

TABLE 2.S.32

COMPOSITION OF THE EDIBLE PORTION (EP) AND REFUSE IN THE MATERIAL AS PURCHASED (AP)

Commodity and Description	Water	Protein	Fat	Carbohydrate Total (By Dif)	Carbohydrate Fiber	Ash	Calories (No./100 g)	Notes	Refuse in AP (%)
	(*Percent of Edible Portion*)								
Potatoes									
Potato (*Solanum tuberosum*)	78	2.0	0.1	18.9	0.4	1.0	82		15
Potato flour	7	8.5	0.4	80.0	1.7	4.1	349		0
Sweet potatoes (*Ipomoea batatas*)	70	1.3	0.4	27.3	0.8	1.0	117		17
Cassava									
Fresh (*Manihot* spp.)	62.5	1.2	0.3	34.7	1.3	1.3	146	Manioc, yuca	25
Meal and flour	14	1.5	0.6	81.5		2.4	338		0
Yautia (*Xanthosoma* spp.)[1]	65	2.1	0.4	31.5	0.8	1.0	136	Also called tanier, malanga	20
Taro (*Colocasia* spp.)[1]	72.5	1.9	0.2	24.2	0.9	1.2	104		18
Yam (*Dioscorea* spp.)[1]	72.4	2.4	0.2	24.1	0.9	0.9	105		14
Arracacha (*Arracacia xanthorrhiza*)[2]	72	1.7	0.3	24.9	0.6	1.1	108		30
Starches, pure dry	12	0.5	0.3	86.9	0.2	0.3	362	Arrowroot, corn-starch, sago, tapioca, etc.	0

[1] More information needed.
[2] More information needed, especially on refuse.

SOURCE: CHATFIELD, C. Food Composition Tables for International Use. FAO, United Nations, Rome.

STEAM, PROPERTIES

TABLE 2.S.33

PROPERTIES OF SATURATED STEAM, 0 TO 200 PSI GAGE

Psig	Temp, °F	Specific Volume, Cu Ft per Lb	Heat of the Liquid	Latent Heat, Btu/ Lb	Total Heat of Steam, Btu/Lb
0	212.0	26.79	180.0	970.4	1,150.3
1	215.3	25.23	183.4	967.2	1,151.6
2	218.5	23.80	186.6	966.3	1,152.8
3	221.5	22.53	189.6	964.3	1,153.9
4	224.4	21.40	192.5	962.4	1,154.9
5	227.2	20.38	195.3	960.4	1,155.9
6	229.8	19.45	198.0	958.8	1,156.8
7	232.4	18.61	200.6	957.2	1,157.8
8	234.8	17.85	203.1	955.5	1,158.6
9	237.1	17.14	205.4	954.0	1,159.4
10	239.4	16.49	207.7	952.5	1,160.2
11	241.6	15.89	209.9	951.1	1,161.0
12	243.7	15.34	212.1	949.6	1,161.7
13	245.8	14.82	214.2	948.2	1,162.4
14	247.8	14.33	216.2	946.8	1,163.0
15	249.7	13.88	218.2	945.5	1,163.7
16	251.6	13.45	220.1	944.2	1,164.3
17	253.5	13.05	222.0	942.9	1,164.9
18	255.3	12.68	223.9	941.6	1,165.5
19	257.1	12.33	225.7	940.4	1.166.1
20	258.8	11.99	227.4	939.3	1,166.7
21	260.5	11.67	229.1	938.1	1,167.2
22	262.1	11.38	230.8	936.9	1,167.7
23	263.7	11.09	232.4	935.8	1,168.2
24	265.3	10.82	234.0	934.8	1,168.8
25	266.9	10.67	235.6	933.7	1,169.3
26	268.3	10.32	237.2	932.5	1.169.7
27	269.8	10.00	238.7	931.5	1.170.2
28	271.3	9.86	240.1	930.5	1,170.6
29	272.7	9.65	241.6	929.5	1,171.1
30	274.1	9.45	243.0	928.5	1,171.5
32	276.8	9.07	245.7	926.6	1,172.3
34	279.4	8.72	248.4	924.7	1,173.1
36	281.9	8.40	251.0	922.9	1,173.9
38	284.3	8.10	253.5	921.1	1,174.6
40	286.7	7.82	255.9	919.4	1,175.3
42	289.0	7.56	258.3	917.6	1,175.9
44	291.3	7.32	260.6	916.0	1,176.6
46	293.5	7.09	262.9	914.3	1,177.2
48	295.6	6.88	265.1	912.7	1,177.8
50	297.7	6.68	267.2	911.2	1,178.4
52	299.7	6.50	269.3	909.6	1,178.9
54	301.7	6.32	271.3	908.2	1,179.5
56	303.6	6.14	273.3	906.7	1,180.0
58	305.5	5.98	275.2	905.3	1,180.5
60	307.3	5.83	277.1	903.9	1,181.0
62	309.1	5.69	279.0	902.5	1,181.5
64	310.9	5.56	280.8	901.2	1,182.0
66	312.6	5.43	282.6	999.8	1,182.4
68	314.4	5.30	284.4	998.5	1,182.9
70	316.0	5.18	286.1	897.2	1,183.3
72	317.7	5.07	287.8	895.9	1,183.7
74	319.3	4.97	289.5	894.6	1,184.1
76	320.9	4.86	291.1	893.4	1,184.5
78	322.4	4.76	292.7	892.2	1,184.9
80	323.9	4.67	294.3	891.0	1,185.3
82	325.4	4.57	295.9	889.5	1,185.7
84	326.9	4.48	297.4	888.7	1,186.1
86	328.4	4.400	298.9	887.5	1,186.4
88	329.8	4.319	300.4	886.4	1,186.8
90	331.2	4.241	301.8	885.3	1,187.1
92	332.5	4.166	303.2	884.3	1,187.5
94	333.9	4.093	304.6	883.2	1,187.8
96	335.2	4.023	306.0	882.4	1,188.1
98	336.0	3.955	307.4	881.1	1,188.5
100	337.0	3.890	308.8	880.0	1,188.8
102	339.2	3.826	310.1	879.0	1,189.1
104	340.4	3.765	311.4	878.0	1,189.4
106	341.7	3.706	313.5	876.2	1,189.7
108	343.0	3.648	314.1	875.8	1,189.9
110	344.2	3.591	315.3	874.9	1,190.2
112	345.4	3.538	316.6	873.9	1,190.5
114	346.6	3.486	317.8	873.0	1,190.8
116	347.8	3.435	319.1	872.0	1,191.1
118	348.9	3.385	320.3	871.0	1,191.3
120	350.1	3.338	321.5	870.5	1,191.6
122	351.2	3.292	322.7	869.1	1,191.8
124	352.4	3.248	323.8	868.8	1,192.1
126	353.5	3.204	325.0	867.3	1,192.3
128	354.6	3.160	326.2	866.4	1,192.6
130	355.7	3.118	327.3	865.5	1,192.8
132	356.7	3.078	328.4	864.6	1,193.0
134	357.8	3.039	329.5	863.8	1,193.3
136	358.9	2.999	330.6	862.8	1,193.5
138	359.9	2.961	331.8	861.9	1,193.7
140	360.9	2.925	332.8	861.1	1,193.9
142	362.0	2.890	333.9	860.3	1,194.2
144	363.0	3.856	335.0	859.4	1,194.4
146	364.0	2.823	336.0	858.6	1,194.6
148	365.0	2.790	337.1	857.7	1,194.8
150	365.9	2.758	338.1	856.9	1,195.0
152	366.9	2.726	339.1	856.1	1,195.2
154	367.9	2.695	340.1	855.3	1,195.4
156	368.8	2.665	341.1	854.4	1,195.5
158	369.8	2.635	342.1	853.6	1,195.7
160	370.7	2.606	343.1	852.8	1,195.9
162	371.6	2.578	344.1	852.0	1,196.1
164	372.6	2.551	345.1	851.2	1,196.3
166	373.5	2.524	346.0	850.5	1,196.5
168	374.4	2.498	347.0	849.7	1,196.7
170	375.3	2.472	347.9	848.9	1,196.8
172	376.2	2.447	348.9	848.1	1,197.0
174	377.1	2.422	349.8	847.4	1,197.2
176	377.9	2.397	350.7	846.6	1,197.3
178	378.8	2.373	351.6	845.9	1,197.5

SOURCE: HALL, C. W., FARRALL, A. W., and RIPPEN, A. L. (EDITORS). 1971. Steam. *In* Encyclopedia of Food Engineering. Avi Publishing Co., Westport, Conn.

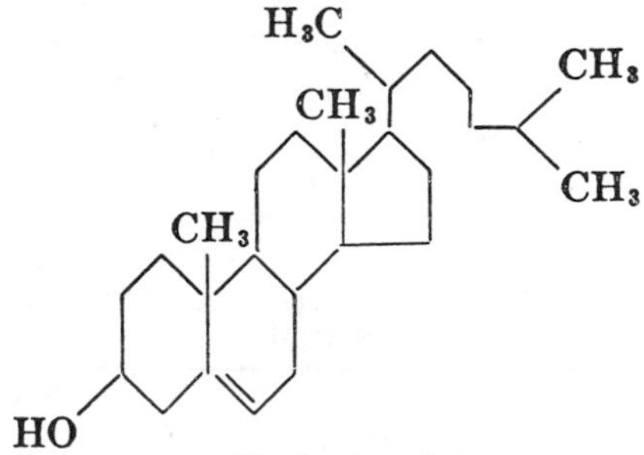

Cholesterol

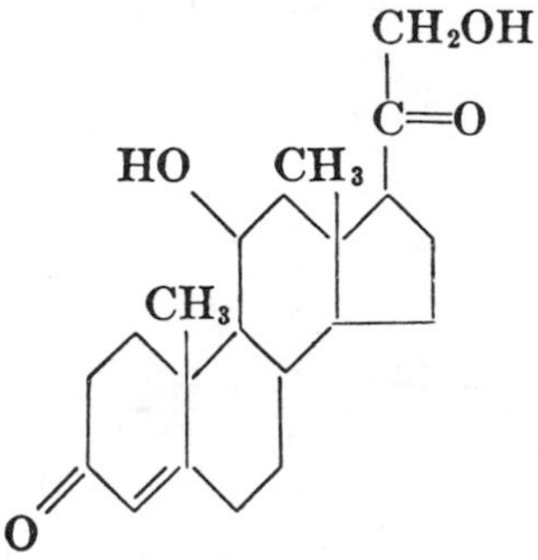

Corticosterone

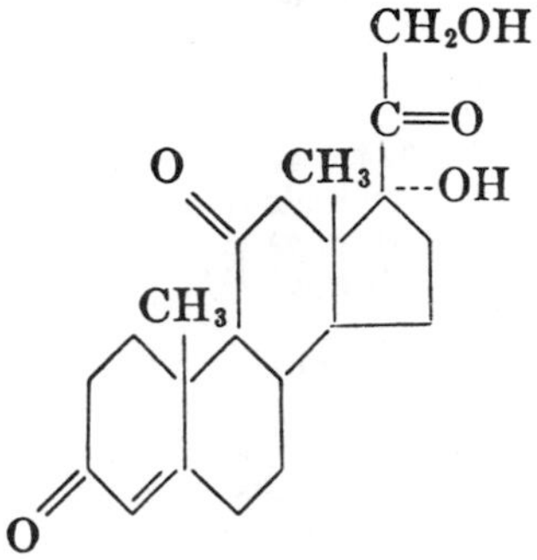

Cortisone

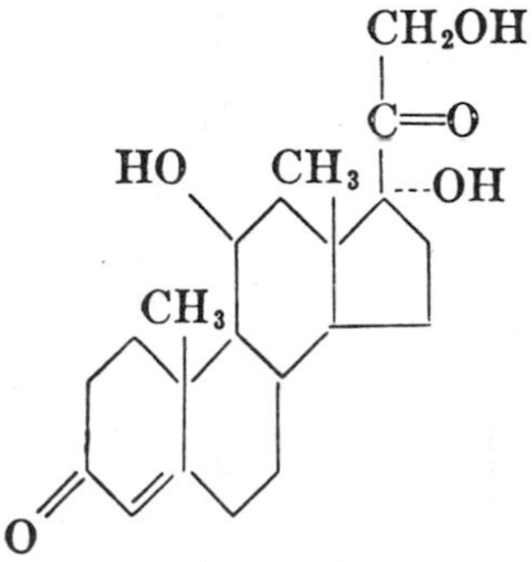

Cortisol

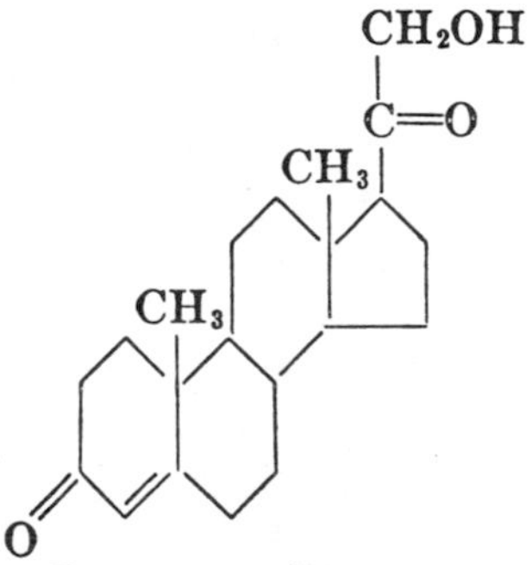

Desoxycorticosterone

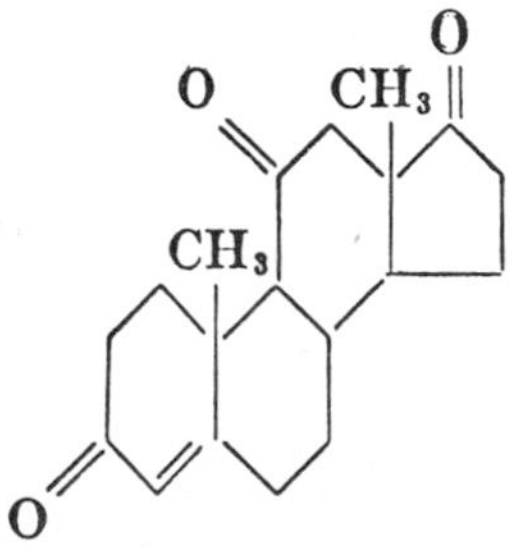

Adrenosterone

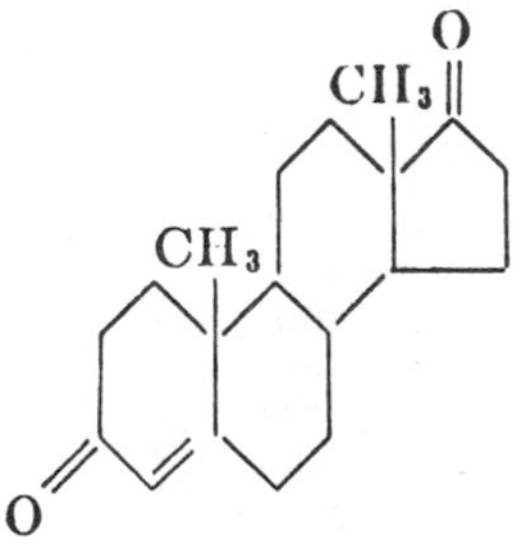

Δ^4-Androstenedione

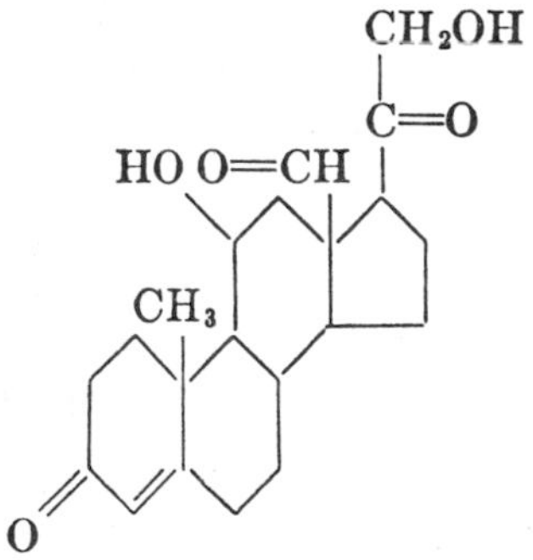

Aldosterone

FIG. 2.S.6. DIAGRAM OF THE CHOLESTEROL MOLECULE SHOWING CLOSE FAMILY RESEMBLANCE OF STEROID DERIVATIVES

SOURCE: SHIDEMAN, F. E. 1967. Take as Directed—Our Modern Medicines. Chemical Rubber Co., Cleveland. Reproduced with permission of CRC Press.

TABLE 2.S.34

STORAGE PROPERTIES OF FOODS

Commodity	Temp (°F)	Relative Humidity (%)	Approx Length of Storage Period	Avg. Freezing Point (°F)
Apples	30-32	85-88	—	28.4
Apricots	31-32	80-85	1-2 wks.	28.1
Asparagus	32	85-90	3-4 wks.	29.8
Avocados	—	85-90	—	27.2
Bananas	56-60	90-95	7-10 days	—
Beans				
Green, or snap	32-40	85-90	2-4 wks.	29.7
Lima				
Unshelled	32	85-90	2-4 wks.	30.1
	40	85-90	10 days	
Shelled	32	85-90	15 days	
	40	85-90	4 days	
Beets				
Topped	32	95-98	1-3 mos.	26.9
Bunch	32	85-90	10-14 days	26.9
Blackberries	31-32	80-85	7-10 days	28.9
Broccoli (Italian or sprouting)	32-35	90-95	7-10 days	29.2
Brussels sprouts	32-35	90-95	3-4 wks.	—
Cabbage	32	90-95	3-4 mos.	31.2
Carrots				
Topped	32	95-98	4-5 mos.	29.6
Bunch	32	85-90	10-14 days	29.6
Cauliflower	32	85-90	2-3 wks.	30.1
Celeriac	32	95-98	3-4 mos.	—
Celery	31-32	90-95	2-4 mos.	29.7
Cherries	31-32	80-85	10-14 days	—
Coconuts	32-35	80-85	1-2 mos.	25.5
Corn (green)	31-32	85-90	4-8 days	28.9
Cranberries	36-40	85-90	1-3 mos.	27.3
Cucumbers	45-50	85-95	10-14 days	30.5
Dates, Deglet Noor, cured	0-24	—	1 yr.	-4.1
Dewberries	31-32	80-85	7-10 days	—
Eggplants	45-50	85-90	10 days	30.4
Endive	32	90-95	2-3 wks.	30.9
Figs (fresh)	31-32	85-90	10 days	—
Garlic (dry)	32	70-75	6-8 mos.	25.4
Grapefruit		85-90	6-8 wks.	28.4
Grapes				
Vinifera	30-31	85-90	3-6 mos.	24.9
American	31-32	80-85	3-8 wks.	27.5
Horseradish	32	95-98	10-12 mos.	26.4
Jerusalem artichokes	31-32	90-95	2-5 mos.	27.5
Kohlrabi	32	95-98	2-4 wks.	30.0
Leeks (green)	32	85-90	1-3 mos.	29.2
Lemons	55-58	85-90	1-4 mos.	28.1
Lettuce	32	90-95	2-3 wks.	31.2
Limes	45-48	85-90	6-8 wks.	29.3
Logan blackberries	31-32	80-85	7-10 days	29.5
Melons				
Watermelon	36-40	75-85	2-3 wks.	29.2 flesh 28.8 rind
Muskmelon (cantaloupe)	32-34	75-78	7-10 days	29.0 flesh 28.4 rind
Honeydew and honey ball	36-38	75-85	2-4 wks.	29.0 flesh 28.8 rind
Cassaba and Persian	36-40	75-85	4-6 wks.	

TABLE 2.S.34 (*Continued*)

Commodity	Temp (°F)	Relative Humidity (%)	Approx Length of Storage Period	Avg. Freezing Point (°F)
Mushrooms (cultivated)	32-35	80-85	2-3 days	30.2
Okra	50	85-95	2 wks.	30.1
Olives (fresh)	45-50	85-90	4-6 wks.	28.5
Onions	32	70-75	6-8 mos.	30.1
Onion sets	32	70-75	5-8 mos.	29.5
Oranges		85-90	8-10 wks.	{28.0 flesh 27.4 peel
Parsnips	32	90-95	2-4 mos.	28.9
Peaches	31-32	80-85	2-4 wks.	29.4
Pears				
Bartlett	29-31	85-90		28.5
Fall and winter varieties	29-31	85-90	—	—
Peas (green)	32	85-90	1-2 wks.	30.0
Peppers				
Chili (dry)	—	70-75	6-9 mos.	—
Sweet	32	85-90	4-6 wks.	30.1
Pineapples				
Mature green	50-60	85-90	3-4 wks.	29.1
Ripe	40-45	85-90	2-4 wks.	29.9
Plums (including prunes)	31-32	80-85	3-8 wks.	28.0
Potatoes				
Early		85-90		—
Late	38-50	85-90	—	28.9
Pumpkins	50-55	70-75	2-6 mos.	30.1
Quinces	31-32	80-85	2-3 mos.	28.1
Radishes (winter)	32	95-98	2-4 mos.	—
Raspberries	31-32	80-85	7-10 days	29.9
Rhubarb	32	90-95	2-3 wks.	28.4
Rutabagas	32	95-98	2-4 mos.	29.5
Salsify	32	95-98	2-4 mos.	28.4
Spinach	32	90-95	10-14 days	30.3
Squashes				
Summer	40-50	85-95	2-3 wks.	—
Winter	50-55	70-75	4-6 mos.	29.3
Strawberries	31-32	80-85	7-10 days	29.9
Sweet potatoes	50-55	80-85	4-6 mos.	28.5
Tomatoes				
Ripe	40-50	80-85	7-10 days	30.4
Mature green	55-70	80-85	3-5 wks.	30.4
Turnips	32	95-98	4-5 mos.	30.5
Dried fruits		—	9-12 mos.	—
Nuts	32-45	65-75	8-12 mos.	—

SOURCE: ROSE, D. H., WRIGHT, R. C., and WHITMAN, T. M. U.S. Dep. Agric. Circ. *278*.

STORAGE, DRY

The following are recommended dry storage times for various foods:

6-12 Months

Canned Fruits and Vegetables
Honey and Peanut Butter

3-6 Months

Dry Milk Solids
Macaroni
Dry Beans and Peas
Cereals (corn meal)

3-6 Months (*Cont.*)

Flour
Sugar
Spices
Rice

3 Months

Dried Fruit

7-30 Days

Potatoes
Root Vegetables
Onions

7-10 Days

Oranges
Apples
Pears

SOURCE: Food Storage. Ohio Department of Health, Columbus.

STORAGE TIMES (°F)

TABLE 2.S.35

RECOMMENDED TEMPERATURE AND STORAGE LIFE OF VARIOUS FOODS

Food	Suggested Maximum Temperature of	Recommended Maximum Storage Life	Remarks
Candy (chocolate)	70	3 months	Wrapped or in original carton - may be frozen
Canned Goods	70	12 months	In original containers
Cereals	70	6 months	In original package
Beans, flour, rice	70	6 months	In original container or covered galvanized can
Cream filled pastries Cream pies, custards, Cream puffs, etc.	36	serve day prepared	Spoil readily; must be served the day prepared
Dairy products			
Milk - Fluid	40	5 days	In original container, tightly covered
Milk - Dried	70	3 months	In original package - If open, 38° in tight can
Milk - Evaporated	70	12 months	In cans - invert every 30 days
Butter	40	2 weeks	In waxed cartons
Cheese (hard)	40	6 months	Tightly wrapped
Cheese (soft)	40	7 days	In tightly covered container
Ice cream and ices	10	3 months	In original container, covered
Eggs	45	7 days	Unwashed - never in cardboard carton
Eggs (dried)	70	6 months	In original carton - if open, 45° in tight can
Egg whites	45	2 days	In tight container
Egg yolks	45	2 days	In tight container - cover with water
Fish (fresh)	36	5 days	Wrap loosely
Shellfish	36	5 days	In covered container

Fruits			
Peaches, Plums, Berries	45	7 days	Unwashed
Apples, pears, citrus	70	2 weeks	In original containers
Dried	70	3 months	In original containers
Gravies, sauces	36	2 days	In covered containers
Left-overs.	36	2 days	In covered containers
Meat			
Ground.	38	2 days	Loosely wrapped
Fresh meat cuts	38	5 days	Loosely wrapped
Liver & variety meats	38	2 days	Loosely wrapped
Cold cuts (sliced).	38	5 days	Wrap in semi-moistureproof (waxed paper)
Cured bacon (sliced).	38	1 to 2 weeks	May wrap tightly
Ham (tender cured).	38	1 to 2 weeks	May wrap tightly
Ham (canned).	38	6 weeks	In original container, unopened
Tongue (smoked)	38	7 weeks	May wrap tightly
Dried beef.	38	6 weeks	May wrap tightly
Poultry	36	3 days	Wrap loosely
Processed foods . . . . made with eggs, meat, milk, fish or poultry	36	serve day prepared	In covered container. Spoils rapidly Must serve day prepared
Sugar - Spices.	70	3 to 6 months	In original package - or covered galvanized can
Vegetables			
Leafy	45	5 days	Unwashed
Potatoes, onions and root vegetables.	70	7 to 30 days	Dry in ventilated container or bags

SOURCE: Food Storage, Ohio Department of Health, Columbus.

SUGAR BEET YIELD

TABLE 2.S.36

CHANGES IN THE VALUE OF THE CROP FROM INCREASES IN NITROGEN FERTILIZER APPLICATION IN GREAT BRITAIN

N dressing	*Root yield*	*Sugar*	*Payment*		*Total sugar*	*Juice purity*	*Extractable white sugar*
(cwt/acre)	(ton/acre)	(%)	(£/ton roots)	(£/acre)	(cwt/ acre)	(%)	(cwt/acre)
0·0	12·34	17·30	8·45	104·27	42·7	93·1	33·5
0 to 0·6	+3·40	−0·10	−0·05	+27·95	+11·4	−0·5	+8·8
0·6 to 1·2	+1·24	−0·45	−0·20	+7·02	+2·7	−0·4	+0·9
1·2 to 1·8	+0·06	−0·63	−0·35	−5·48	−1·9	+0·6	−2·8
(kg/ha)	(t/ha)	(%)	(£/t roots)	(£/ha)	(t/ha)	(%)	(t/ha)
0	30·99	17·30	8·59	257·44	5·36	93·1	4·20
0 to 75	+8·54	−0·10	−0·05	+69·01	+1·43	−0·5	+1·10
75 to 150	+3·11	−0·45	−0·20	+17·33	+0·34	−0·4	+0·11
150 to 225	+0·15	−0·63	−0·36	−13·53	−0·24	−0·6	−0·35

SOURCE: DRAYCOTT, A. P. (1972). Sugar-Beet Nutrition. Applied Science Publishers, Essex, England.

SUGAR CANE COMPOSITION

TABLE 2.S.37

VEGETATIVE COMPOSITION OF CANE PLANT BASED ON AVERAGE TONS OF MILLABLE CANE REAPED ANNUALLY IN NATAL FOR 12 YEARS, 1940–41 TO 1951–52, COMPARED WITH HAWAIIAN DATA

Portion of Plant	Green Weight			Dry Material			Hawaii
	Tons per Acre	Percent Millable Cane	Percent Total Plant	Percent of Green Weight	Tons Acre	Percent Total Dry Weight	Percent Total Dry Weight
Millable cane	33.35	100	57.80	32	10.72	49.02	45.23
Tops	8.38	25	14.44	26	2.18	9.95	14.60
Trash	5.04	15	8.68	85	4.28	19.53	20.59
Stubble	8.38	25	14.44	35	2.93	13.37	11.65
Roots	2.69	8	4.64	66	1.78	8.13	7.30
Young shoots	—	—	—	—	—	—	0.63
Total plant	58.04	173	100	37.75	21.91	100.00	100.00
Plant residues	24.49	73	42.2	45.6	11.17	50.98	54.77

SOURCE: BARNES, A. C. 1974. The Sugar Cane. Leonard Hill Books, London, England.

SUGAR, D-ALDEHYDO

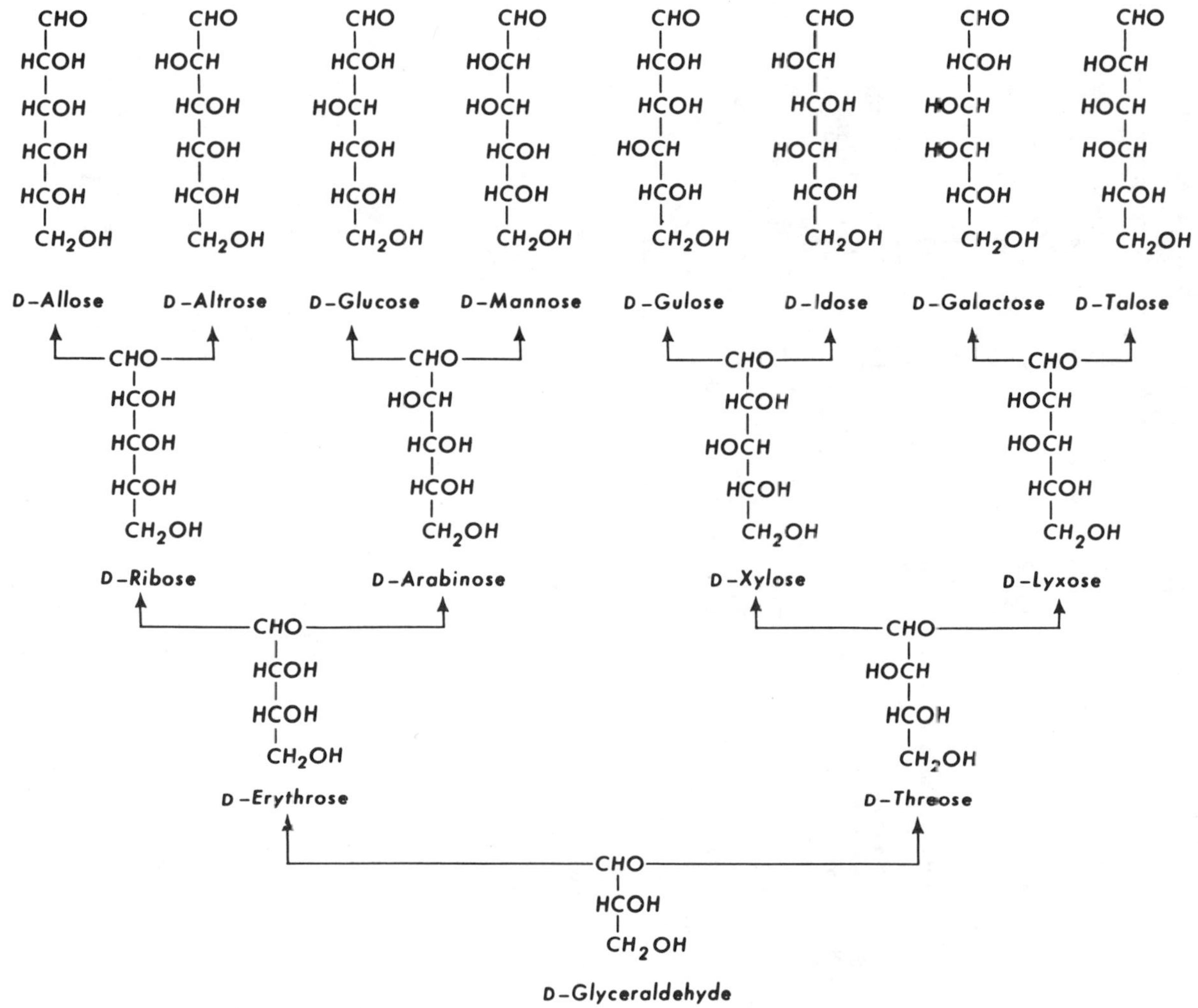

FIG. 2.S.7. FAMILY TREE OF D-ALDEHYDO SUGARS

SOURCE: SHALLENBERGER, R. S. and BIRCH, G. G. (EDITORS). 1975. Structure of Monosaccharides. *In* Sugar Chemistry. Avi Publishing Co., Westport, Conn.

SUGAR, FRUIT

TABLE 2.S.38

FREE SUGARS IN FRUIT AS PERCENTAGE FRESH BASIS

Fruit	Total Solids %	Glucose %	Fructose %	Sucrose %	Maltose %
Apple, *Pyrus Malus*	15.96	1.17	6.04	3.78	Trace
Apricot, *Prunus Armeniaca*	14.44	1.73	1.28	5.84	
Blackberry, *Rubus*	15.28	2.48	2.15	0.59	0.66
Blueberry, *Vaccinium corymbosum*	15.89	3.76	3.82	0.19	0.08
Currant, *Ribes sativum*	17.68	3.33	3.68	0.95	0.64
Gooseberry, *Ribes grossularia*	14.81	3.29	3.90	1.21	
Grape, *Vitis Labruscana*	19.13[1]	6.86	7.84	2.25	1.58
Grape, *Vitis vinifera*	17.97[1]	5.35	5.33	1.32	2.19
Peach, *Prunus Persica*	12.79	0.91	1.18	6.92	0.12
Pear, *Pyrus communis*	13.58	0.95	6.77	1.61	0.31
Plum, *Prunus domestica*	17.97	3.49	1.53	4.94	0.15
Raspberry (red), *Rubus idaeus*	20.67	2.40	1.58	3.68	
Raspberry (black), *Rubus occidentalis*	28.22	4.56	4.84	1.90	
Cherry (sour), *Prunus cerasus*	15.05	4.30	3.28	0.40	
Cherry (sweet), *Prunus avium*	22.39	6.49	7.38	0.22	
Strawberry, *Fragaria chiloensis*	9.45	2.09	2.40	1.03	0.07

[1] Soluble solids.

SOURCE: SHALLENBERGER, R. S. and BIRCH, G. G. (EDITORS). 1975. Occurrence and Properties of Sugars. *In* Sugar Chemistry. Avi Publishing Co., Westport, Conn.

SUGAR, LEGUMES

TABLE 2.S.39

FREE SUGARS IN LEGUMES

Legume	Total Solids	Glucose	Fructose	Sucrose	Raffinose	Stachyose
Fava bean,[1] *Vicia faba*	16.61		0.18	3.36	0.66	
Lima bean,[1] *Phaseolus lunatus*	26.74	0.04	0.08	2.59	0.20	0.59
Pole Lima bean[1], *Phaseolus lunatus*	24.58	0.18		2.26	0.32	0.60
Pole snap bean,[1] *Phaseolus lunatus*	10.21	0.48	1.30	0.28	0.26	
Snap bean,[1] *Phaseolus vulgaris*	7.79	1.08	1.20	0.25	0.11	0.19
Pea (Alaska)[1] *Pisum sativum*	25.54		0.08	3.00	0.06	0.06.
(Wrinkled)[1] *Pisum sativum*	22.77	0.32	0.23	5.27	0.58	0.49
Cow Pea,[1] *Vigna sinensis*	39.30	0.08	0.06	1.86	0.10	1.66
Dry bean,[2] *Phaseolus vulgaris*				2.40	0.80	3.40
Mung bean,[2] *Phaseolus aureus*				1.19	0.40	1.75
Pea bean,[2] *Phaseolus vulgaris*				2.55	0.65	3.06
Pea seed,[2] *Pisum sativum*		0.24		4.11	1.75	7.96
Soybean,[2] *Glycine Max*				4.53	0.73	2.73

[1] Sugars as % fresh basis.
[2] Sugars as % total bean weight.

SOURCE: SHALLENBERGER, R. S. and BIRCH, G. G. (EDITORS). 1975. Occurrence and Properties of Sugars. *In* Sugar Chemistry. Avi Publishing Co., Westport, Conn.

SUGAR SOLUTIONS I

TABLE 2.S.40

DEGREES BRIX, DEGREES BAUMÉ, REFRACTIVE INDEX, AND SPECIFIC GRAVITY OF SUGAR (SUCROSE) SOLUTIONS

Degrees Brix[1]	Refractive Index at 20°C	Degrees Baumé[2]	Specific Gravity 20°/20°C[3]	Degrees Brix[1]	Refractive Index at 20°C	Degrees Baumé[2]	Specific Gravity 20°/20°C[3]
0.0	1.3330	0.00	1.0000	8.2	1.3451	4.58	1.0326
0.2	1.3333	0.11	1.0008	8.4	1.3454	4.69	1.0334
0.4	1.3336	0.22	1.0016	8.6	1.3457	4.80	1.0343
0.6	1.3339	0.34	1.0023	8.8	1.3460	4.91	1.0351
0.8	1.3341	0.45	1.0031	9.0	1.3463	5.02	1.0359
1.0	1.3344	0.56	1.0039	9.2	1.3466	5.13	1.0367
1.2	1.3347	0.67	1.0047	9.4	1.3469	5.24	1.0376
1.4	1.3350	0.79	1.0055	9.6	1.3472	5.35	1.0384
1.6	1.3353	0.90	1.0062	9.8	1.3475	5.46	1.0392
1.8	1.3356	1.01	1.0070	10.0	1.3478	5.57	1.0400
2.0	1.3359	1.12	1.0078	10.2	1.3481	5.68	1.0408
2.2	1.3362	1.23	1.0086	10.4	1.3485	5.80	1.0416
2.4	1.3365	1.34	1.0094	10.6	1.3488	5.91	1.0425
2.6	1.3368	1.46	1.0102	10.8	1.3491	6.02	1.0433
2.8	1.3370	1.57	1.0109	11.0	1.3494	6.13	1.0441
3.0	1.3373	1.68	1.0117	11.2	1.3497	6.24	1.0450
3.2	1.3376	1.79	1.0125	11.4	1.3500	6.35	1.0458
3.4	1.3379	1.90	1.0133	11.6	1.3503	6.46	1.0466
3.6	1.3382	2.02	1.0141	11.8	1.3506	6.57	1.0475
3.8	1.3385	2.13	1.0149	12.0	1.3509	6.68	1.0483
4.0	1.3388	2.24	1.0157	12.2	1.3512	6.79	1.0492
4.2	1.3391	2.35	1.0165	12.4	1.3516	6.90	1.0500
4.4	1.3394	2.46	1.0173	12.6	1.3519	7.02	1.0508
4.6	1.3397	2.57	1.0181	12.8	1.3522	7.13	1.0517
4.8	1.3400	2.68	1.0189	13.0	1.3525	7.24	1.0525
5.0	1.3403	2.79	1.0197	13.2	1.3528	7.35	1.0534
5.2	1.3406	2.91	1.0205	13.4	1.3531	7.46	1.0542
5.4	1.3409	3.02	1.0213	13.6	1.3534	7.57	1.0551
5.6	1.3412	3.13	1.0221	13.8	1.3538	7.68	1.0559
5.8	1.3415	3.24	1.0229	14.0	1.3541	7.79	1.0568
6.0	1.3418	3.35	1.0237	14.2	1.3544	7.90	1.0576
6.2	1.3421	3.46	1.0245	14.4	1.3547	8.01	1.0585
6.4	1.3424	3.57	1.0253	14.6	1.3550	8.12	1.0593
6.6	1.3427	3.69	1.0261	14.8	1.3554	8.23	1.0602
6.8	1.3430	3.80	1.0269	15.0	1.3557	8.34	1.0610
7.0	1.3433	3.91	1.0277	15.2	1.3560	8.45	1.0619
7.2	1.3436	4.02	1.0285	15.4	1.3563	8.56	1.0628
7.4	1.3439	4.13	1.0294	15.6	1.3566	8.67	1.0636
7.6	1.3442	4.24	1.0302	15.8	1.3570	8.78	1.0645
7.8	1.3445	4.35	1.0310	16.0	1.3573	8.89	1.0653
8.0	1.3448	4.46	1.0318	16.2	1.3576	9.00	1.0662

(Continued)

TABLE 2.S.40 (*Continued*)

Degrees Brix[1]	Refractive Index at 20°C	Degrees Baumé[2]	Specific Gravity 20°/20°C[3]	Degrees Brix[1]	Refractive Index at 20°C	Degrees Baumé[2]	Specific Gravity 20°/20°C[3]
16.4	1.3579	9.11	1.0671	25.2	1.3726	13.95	1.1064
16.6	1.3582	9.22	1.0679	25.4	1.3730	14.06	1.1074
16.8	1.3586	9.33	1.0688	25.6	1.3733	14.17	1.1083
17.0	1.3589	9.45	1.0697	25.8	1.3737	14.28	1.1092
17.2	1.3592	9.56	1.0706	26.0	1.3740	14.39	1.1101
17.4	1.3596	9.67	1.0714	26.2	1.3744	14.49	1.1111
17.6	1.3599	9.78	1.0723	26.4	1.3747	14.60	1.1120
17.8	1.3602	9.89	1.0732	26.6	1.3751	14.71	1.1129
18.0	1.3605	10.00	1.0740	26.8	1.3754	14.82	1.1139
18.2	1.3609	10.11	1.0749	27.0	1.3758	14.93	1.1148
18.4	1.3612	10.22	1.0758	27.2	1.3761	15.04	1.1157
18.6	1.3615	10.33	1.0767	27.4	1.3765	15.15	1.1167
18.8	1.3618	10.44	1.0776	27.6	1.3768	15.26	1.1176
19.0	1.3622	10.55	1.0784	27.8	1.3772	15.37	1.1186
19.2	1.3625	10.66	1.0793	28.0	1.3775	15.48	1.1195
19.4	1.3628	10.77	1.0802	28.2	1.3779	15.59	1.1204
19.6	1.3632	10.88	1.0811	28.4	1.3782	15.69	1.1214
19.8	1.3635	10.99	1.0820	28.6	1.3786	15.80	1.1223
20.0	1.3638	11.10	1.0829	28.8	1.3789	15.91	1.1233
20.2	1.3642	11.21	1.0838	29.0	1.3793	16.02	1.1242
20.4	1.3645	11.32	1.0847	29.2	1.3797	16.13	1.1252
20.6	1.3648	11.43	1.0855	29.4	1.3800	16.24	1.1261
20.8	1.3652	11.54	1.0864	29.6	1.3804	16.35	1.1271
21.0	1.3655	11.65	1.0873	29.8	1.3807	16.46	1.1280
21.2	1.3658	11.76	1.0882	30.0	1.3811	16.57	1.1290
21.4	1.3662	11.87	1.0891	30.2	1.3815	16.67	1.1299
21.6	1.3665	11.98	1.0903	30.4	1.3818	16.78	1.1309
21.8	1.3668	12.09	1.0909	30.6	1.3822	16.89	1.1319
22.0	1.3672	12.20	1.0918	30.8	1.3825	17.00	1.1328
22.2	1.3675	12.31	1.0927	31.0	1.3829	17.11	1.1338
22.4	1.3679	12.42	1.0936	31.2	1.3833	17.22	1.1347
22.6	1.3682	12.52	1.0945	31.4	1.3836	17.33	1.1357
22.8	1.3685	12.63	1.0955	31.6	1.3840	17.43	1.1367
23.0	1.3689	12.74	1.0964	31.8	1.3843	17.54	1.1376
23.2	1.3692	12.85	1.0973	32.0	1.3847	17.65	1.1386
23.4	1.3696	12.96	1.0982	32.2	1.3851	17.76	1.1396
23.6	1.3699	13.07	1.0991	32.4	1.3854	17.87	1.1406
23.8	1.3703	13.18	1.1000	32.6	1.3858	17.98	1.1415
24.0	1.3706	13.29	1.1009	32.8	1.3861	18.08	1.1425
24.2	1.3709	13.40	1.1018	33.0	1.3865	18.19	1.1435
24.4	1.3713	13.51	1.1028	33.2	1.3869	18.30	1.1445
24.6	1.3716	13.62	1.1037	33.4	1.3872	18.41	1.1454
24.8	1.3720	13.73	1.1046	33.6	1.3876	18.52	1.1464
25.0	1.3723	13.84	1.1055	33.8	1.3879	18.63	1.1474

TABLE 2.S.40 (*Continued*)

Degrees Brix[1]	Refractive Index at 20°C	Degrees Baumé[2]	Specific Gravity 20°/20°C[3]	Degrees Brix[1]	Refractive Index at 20°C	Degrees Baumé[2]	Specific Gravity 20°/20°C[3]
34.0	1.3883	18.73	1.1484	43.2	1.4060	23.68	1.1952
34.2	1.3887	18.84	1.1494	43.4	1.4064	23.78	1.1962
34.4	1.3891	18.95	1.1503	43.6	1.4068	23.89	1.1973
34.6	1.3894	19.06	1.1513	43.8	1.4072	24.00	1.1983
34.8	1.3898	19.17	1.1523	44.0	1.4076	24.10	1.1994
35.0	1.3902	19.28	1.1533	44.2	1.4080	24.21	1.2004
35.2	1.3906	19.38	1.1543	44.4	1.4084	24.32	1.2015
35.4	1.3909	19.49	1.1553	44.6	1.4088	24.42	1.2025
35.6	1.3913	19.60	1.1563	44.8	1.4092	24.53	1.2036
35.8	1.3916	19.71	1.1573	45.0	1.4096	24.63	1.2047
36.0	1.3920	19.81	1.1583	45.2	1.4100	24.74	1.2057
36.2	1.3924	19.92	1.1593	45.4	1.4104	24.85	1.2068
36.4	1.3928	20.03	1.1603	45.6	1.4109	24.95	1.2079
36.6	1.3931	20.14	1.1613	45.8	1.4113	25.06	1.2089
36.8	1.3935	20.25	1.1623	46.0	1.4117	25.17	1.2100
37.0	1.3939	20.35	1.1633	46.2	1.4121	25.27	1.2111
37.2	1.3943	20.46	1.1643	46.4	1.4125	25.38	1.2122
37.4	1.3947	20.57	1.1653	46.6	1.4129	25.48	1.2132
37.6	1.3950	20.68	1.1663	46.8	1.4133	25.59	1.2143
37.8	1.3954	20.78	1.1673	47.0	1.4137	25.70	1.2154
38.0	1.3958	20.89	1.1683	47.2	1.4141	25.80	1.2165
38.2	1.3962	21.00	1.1693	47.4	1.4145	25.91	1.2176
38.4	1.3966	21.11	1.1704	47.6	1.4150	26.01	1.2186
38.6	1.3970	21.21	1.1714	47.8	1.4154	26.12	1.2197
38.8	1.3974	21.32	1.1724	48.0	1.4158	26.23	1.2208
39.0	1.3978	21.43	1.1734	48.2	1.4162	26.33	1.2219
39.2	1.3982	21.54	1.1744	48.4	1.4166	26.44	1.2230
39.4	1.3986	21.64	1.1755	48.6	1.4171	26.54	1.2241
39.6	1.3989	21.75	1.1765	48.8	1.4175	26.65	1.2252
39.8	1.3993	21.86	1.1775	49.0	1.4179	26.75	1.2263
40.0	1.3997	21.97	1.1785	49.2	1.4183	26.86	1.2274
40.2	1.4001	22.07	1.1796	49.4	1.4187	26.96	1.2284
40.4	1.4005	22.18	1.1806	49.6	1.4192	27.07	1.2295
40.6	1.4008	22.29	1.1816	49.8	1.4196	27.18	1.2306
40.8	1.4012	22.39	1.1827	50.0	1.4200	27.28	1.2317
41.0	1.4016	22.50	1.1837	50.2	1.4204	27.39	1.2328
41.2	1.4020	22.61	1.1847	50.4	1.4208	27.49	1.2340
41.4	1.4024	22.72	1.1858	50.6	1.4213	27.60	1.2351
41.6	1.4028	22.82	1.1868	50.8	1.4217	27.70	1.2362
41.8	1.4032	22.93	1.1878	51.0	1.4221	27.81	1.2373
42.0	1.4036	23.04	1.1889	51.2	1.4225	27.91	1.2384
42.2	1.4040	23.14	1.1899	51.4	1.4229	28.02	1.2395
42.4	1.4044	23.25	1.1910	51.6	1.4234	28.12	1.2406
42.6	1.4048	23.36	1.1920	51.8	1.4238	28.23	1.2417
42.8	1.4052	23.46	1.1931	52.0	1.4242	28.33	1.2428
43.0	1.4056	23.57	1.1941	52.2	1.4246	28.44	1.2440

(Continued)

TABLE 2.S.40 (*Continued*)

Degrees Brix[1]	Refractive Index at 20°C	Degrees Baumé[2]	Specific Gravity 20°/20°C[3]	Degrees Brix[1]	Refractive Index at 20°C	Degrees Baumé[2]	Specific Gravity 20°/20°C[3]
52.4	1.4251	28.54	1.2451	61.6	1.4455	33.31	1.2982
52.6	1.4255	28.65	1.2462	61.8	1.4459	33.41	1.2994
52.8	1.4260	28.75	1.2473	62.0	1.4464	33.51	1.3006
53.0	1.4264	28.86	1.2484	62.2	1.4468	33.61	1.3018
53.2	1.4268	28.96	1.2496	62.4	1.4473	33.72	1.3030
53.4	1.4272	29.06	1.2507	62.6	1.4477	33.82	1.3042
53.6	1.4277	29.17	1.2518	62.8	1.4482	33.92	1.3054
53.8	1.4281	29.27	1.2530	63.0	1.4486	34.02	1.3066
54.0	1.4285	29.38	1.2541	63.2	1.4491	34.12	1.3078
54.2	1.4289	29.48	1.2552	63.4	1.4495	34.23	1.3090
54.4	1.4294	29.59	1.2564	63.6	1.4500	34.33	1.3102
54.6	1.4298	29.69	1.2575	63.8	1.4504	34.43	1.3114
54.8	1.4303	29.80	1.2586	64.0	1.4509	34.53	1.3126
55.0	1.4307	29.90	1.2598	64.2	1.4514	34.63	1.3138
55.2	1.4311	30.00	1.2609	64.4	1.4518	34.74	1.3150
55.4	1.4316	30.11	1.2620	64.6	1.4523	34.84	1.3162
55.6	1.4320	30.21	1.2632	64.8	1.4527	34.94	1.3175
55.8	1.4325	30.32	1.2643	65.0	1.4532	35.04	1.3187
56.0	1.4329	30.42	1.2655	65.2	1.4537	35.14	1.3199
56.2	1.4333	30.52	1.2666	65.4	1.4541	35.24	1.3211
56.4	1.4338	30.63	1.2678	65.6	1.4546	35.34	1.3223
56.6	1.4342	30.73	1.2689	65.8	1.4550	35.45	1.3235
56.8	1.4347	30.83	1.2701	66.0	1.4555	35.55	1.3248
57.0	1.4351	30.94	1.2712	66.2	1.4560	35.65	1.3260
57.2	1.4355	31.04	1.2724	66.4	1.4565	35.75	1.3272
57.4	1.4360	31.15	1.2736	66.6	1.4569	35.85	1.3284
57.6	1.4364	31.25	1.2747	66.8	1.4574	35.95	1.3297
57.8	1.4369	31.35	1.2759	67.0	1.4579	36.05	1.3309
58.0	1.4373	31.46	1.2770	67.2	1.4584	36.15	1.3321
58.2	1.4378	31.56	1.2782	67.4	1.4589	36.25	1.3334
58.4	1.4382	31.66	1.2794	67.6	1.4593	36.35	1.3346
58.6	1.4387	31.76	1.2805	67.8	1.4598	36.45	1.3358
58.8	1.4391	31.87	1.2817	68.0	1.4603	36.55	1.3371
59.0	1.4396	31.97	1.2829	68.2	1.4607	36.66	1.3383
59.2	1.4400	32.07	1.2840	68.4	1.4612	36.76	1.3396
59.4	1.4405	32.18	1.2852	68.6	1.4617	36.86	1.3408
59.6	1.4409	32.28	1.2864	68.8	1.4622	36.96	1.3421
59.8	1.4414	32.38	1.2876	69.0	1.4627	37.06	1.3433
60.0	1.4418	32.49	1.2887	69.2	1.4631	37.16	1.3446
60.2	1.4423	32.59	1.2899	69.4	1.4636	37.26	1.3458
60.4	1.4427	32.69	1.2911	69.6	1.4641	37.36	1.3471
60.6	1.4432	32.79	1.2923	69.8	1.4646	37.46	1.3483
60.8	1.4436	32.90	1.2935	70.0	1.4651	37.56	1.3496
61.0	1.4441	33.00	1.2946	70.2	1.4656	37.66	1.3508
61.2	1.4446	33.10	1.2958	70.4	1.4661	37.76	1.3521
61.4	1.4450	33.20	1.2970	70.6	1.4666	37.86	1.3533

TABLE 2.S.40 (*Continued*)

Degrees Brix[1]	Refractive Index at 20°C	Degrees Baumé[2]	Specific Gravity 20°/20°C[3]	Degrees Brix[1]	Refractive Index at 20°C	Degrees Baumé[2]	Specific Gravity 20°/20°C[3]
70.8	1.4671	37.96	1.3546	78.0	1.4850	41.50	1.4010
71.0	1.4676	38.06	1.3559	78.2	1.4855	41.60	1.4023
71.2	1.4681	38.16	1.3571	78.4	1.4860	41.70	1.4036
71.4	1.4685	38.26	1.3584	78.6	1.4865	41.79	1.4049
71.6	1.4690	38.35	1.3596	78.8	1.4871	41.89	1.4063
71.8	1.4695	38.45	1.3609	79.0	1.4876	41.99	1.4076
72.0	1.4700	38.55	1.3622	79.2	1.4881	42.08	1.4089
72.2	1.4705	38.65	1.3635	79.4	1.4886	42.18	1.4102
72.4	1.4710	38.75	1.3647	79.6	1.4891	42.28	1.4116
72.6	1.4715	38.85	1.3660	79.8	1.4896	42.37	1.4129
72.8	1.4720	38.95	1.3673	80.0	1.4901	42.47	1.4142
73.0	1.4725	39.05	1.3686	80.2	1.4906	42.57	1.4155
73.2	1.4730	39.15	1.3698	80.4	1.4912	42.66	1.4169
73.4	1.4735	39.25	1.3711	80.6	1.4917	42.76	1.4182
73.6	1.4740	39.35	1.3724	80.8	1.4922	42.85	1.4196
73.8	1.4744	39.44	1.3737	81.0	1.4927	42.95	1.4209
74.0	1.4749	39.54	1.3750	81.2	1.4933	43.05	1.4222
74.2	1.4754	39.64	1.3763	81.4	1.4938	43.14	1.4236
74.4	1.4759	39.74	1.3775	81.6	1.4943	43.24	1.4249
74.6	1.4764	39.84	1.3789	81.8	1.4949	43.33	1.4263
74.8	1.4769	39.94	1.3801	82.0	1.4954	43.43	1.4276
75.0	1.4774	40.03	1.3814	82.2	1.4959	43.53	1.4289
75.2	1.4779	40.13	1.3827	82.4	1.4964	43.62	1.4303
75.4	1.4784	40.23	1.3840	82.6	1.4970	43.72	1.4316
75.6	1.4789	40.33	1.3853	82.8	1.4975	43.81	1.4330
75.8	1.4794	40.43	1.3866	83.0	1.4980	43.91	1.4343
76.0	1.4799	40.53	1.3879	83.2	1.4985	44.00	1.4357
76.2	1.4804	40.62	1.3892	83.4	1.4991	44.10	1.4371
76.4	1.4810	40.72	1.3905	83.6	1.4996	44.19	1.4384
76.6	1.4815	40.82	1.3918	83.8	1.5001	44.29	1.4398
76.8	1.4820	40.92	1.3931	84.0	1.5007	44.38	1.4411
77.0	1.4825	41.01	1.3944	84.2	1.5012	44.48	1.4425
77.2	1.4830	41.11	1.3957	84.4	1.5017	44.57	1.4439
77.4	1.4835	41.21	1.3970	84.6	1.5022	44.67	1.4452
77.6	1.4840	41.31	1.3984	84.8	1.5028	44.76	1.4466
77.8	1.4845	41.40	1.3997	85.0	1.5033	44.86	1.4479

Source: National Canners Assoc. (1968).

[1] Degrees Brix (or Balling) = the percent of sugar (sucrose) by weight at the temperature indicated on the instrument.

[2] Degrees Baumé $= 145 - \frac{145}{\text{Sp gr}}$ (for materials heavier than water).

$= \frac{140}{\text{Sp gr}} - 130$ (for materials lighter than water).

[3] Accepted by International Commission for Uniform Methods of Sugar Analysis.

SOURCE: KRAMER, A. and TWIGG, B. A. (EDITORS). 1973. *In* Quality Control For The Food Industry. Vol. 2, 3rd Edition. Avi Publishing Co., Westport, Conn.

TABLE 2.S.41

DEGREES BRIX, SPECIFIC GRAVITY, AND DEGREES BAUMÉ OF SUGAR SOLUTIONS

Degrees Brix or percentage of sucrose by weight	Specific gravity at 20°/4° C	Specific gravity at 20°/20° C	Degrees Baumé (modulus 145)	Degrees Brix or percentage of sucrose by weight	Specific gravity at 20°/4° C	Specific gravity at 20°/20° C	Degrees Baumé (modulus 145)
0.0	0.99823	1.00000	0.00	5.0	1.01785	1.01965	2.79
.1	.99862	1.00039	.06	5.1	1.01825	1.02005	2.85
.2	.99901	1.00078	.11	5.2	1.01865	1.02045	2.91
.3	.99940	1.00117	.17	5.3	1.01905	1.02085	2.96
.4	.99979	1.00155	.22	5.4	1.01945	1.02125	3.02
.5	1.00017	1.00194	.28	5.5	1.01985	1.02165	3.07
.6	1.00056	1.00233	.34	5.6	1.02025	1.02206	3.13
.7	1.00095	1.00272	.39	5.7	1.02065	1.02246	3.18
.8	1.00134	1.00311	.45	5.8	1.02105	1.02286	3.24
.9	1.00173	1.00350	.51	5.9	1.02145	1.02321	3.30
1.0	1.00212	1.00389	.56	6.0	1.02186	1.02366	3.35
1.1	1.00251	1.00428	.62	6.1	1.02226	1.02407	3.41
1.2	1.00290	1.00467	.67	6.2	1.02266	1.02447	3.46
1.3	1.00329	1.00506	.73	6.3	1.02306	1.02487	3.52
1.4	1.00368	1.00545	.79	6.4	1.02346	1.02527	3.57
1.5	1.00406	1.00584	.84	6.5	1.02387	1.02568	3.63
1.6	1.00445	1.00623	.90	6.6	1.02427	1.02608	3.69
1.7	1.00484	1.00662	.95	6.7	1.02467	1.02648	3.74
1.8	1.00523	1.00701	1.01	6.8	1.02508	1.02689	3.80
1.9	1.00562	1.00740	1.07	6.9	1.02548	1.02729	3.85
2.0	1.00602	1.00779	1.12	7.0	1.02588	1.02770	3.91
2.1	1.00641	1.00818	1.18	7.1	1.02629	1.02810	3.96
2.2	1.00680	1.00858	1.23	7.2	1.02669	1.02851	4.02
2.3	1.00719	1.00897	1.29	7.3	1.02710	1.02892	4.08
2.4	1.00758	1.00936	1.34	7.4	1.02750	1.02932	4.13
2.5	1.00797	1.00976	1.40	7.5	1.02791	1.02973	4.19
2.6	1.00836	1.01015	1.46	7.6	1.02832	1.03013	4.24
2.7	1.00876	1.01054	1.51	7.7	1.02872	1.03054	4.30
2.8	1.00915	1.01093	1.57	7.8	1.02913	1.03095	4.35
2.9	1.00954	1.01133	1.62	7.9	1.02954	1.03136	4.41
3.0	1.00993	1.01172	1.68	8.0	1.02994	1.03176	4.46
3.1	1.01033	1.01211	1.74	8.1	1.03035	1.03217	4.52
3.2	1.01072	1.01251	1.79	8.2	1.03076	1.03258	4.58
3.3	1.01112	1.01290	1.85	8.3	1.03116	1.03299	4.63
3.4	1.01151	1.01330	1.90	8.4	1.03157	1.03340	4.69
3.5	1.01190	1.01369	1.96	8.5	1.03198	1.03381	4.74
3.6	1.01230	1.01409	2.02	8.6	1.03239	1.03422	4.80
3.7	1.01269	1.01448	2.07	8.7	1.03280	1.03463	4.85
3.8	1.01309	1.01488	2.13	8.8	1.03321	1.03504	4.91
3.9	1.01348	1.01528	2.18	8.9	1.03362	1.03545	4.96
4.0	1.01388	1.01567	2.24	9.0	1.03403	1.03586	5.02
4.1	1.01428	1.01607	2.29	9.1	1.03444	1.03627	5.07
4.2	1.01467	1.01647	2.35	9.2	1.03485	1.03668	5.13
4.3	1.01507	1.01687	2.40	9.3	1.03526	1.03709	5.19
4.4	1.01547	1.01726	2.46	9.4	1.03567	1.03750	5.24
4.5	1.01586	1.01766	2.52	9.5	1.03608	1.03792	5.30
4.6	1.01626	1.01806	2.57	9.6	1.03649	1.03833	5.35
4.7	1.01666	1.01846	2.63	9.7	1.03691	1.03874	5.41
4.8	1.01706	1.01886	2.68	9.8	1.03732	1.03915	5.46
4.9	1.01746	1.01926	2.74	9.9	1.03773	1.03957	5.52

TABLE 2.S.41 (*Continued*)

Degrees Brix or percentage of sucrose by weight	Specific gravity at 20°/4° C	Specific gravity at 20°/20° C	Degrees Baumé (modulus 145)	Degrees Brix or percentage of sucrose by weight	Specific gravity at 20°/4° C	Specific gravity at 20°/20° C	Degrees Baumé (modulus 145)
10. 0	1. 03814	1. 03998	5. 57	15. 0	1. 05916	1. 06104	8. 34
10. 1	1. 03856	1. 04039	5. 63	15. 1	1. 05959	1. 06147	8. 40
10. 2	1. 03897	1. 04081	5. 68	15. 2	1. 06002	1. 06190	8. 45
10. 3	1. 03938	1. 04122	5. 74	15. 3	1. 06045	1. 06233	8. 51
10. 4	1. 03980	1. 04164	5. 80	15. 4	1. 06088	1. 06276	8. 56
10. 5	1. 04021	1. 04205	5. 85	15. 5	1. 06131	1. 06319	8. 62
10. 6	1. 04063	1. 04247	5. 91	15. 6	1. 06174	1. 06362	8. 67
10. 7	1. 04104	1. 04288	5. 96	15. 7	1. 06217	1. 06405	8. 73
10. 8	1. 04146	1. 04330	6. 02	15. 8	1. 06260	1. 06448	8. 78
10. 9	1. 04187	1. 04371	6. 07	15. 9	1. 06303	1. 06491	8. 84
11. 0	1. 04229	1. 04413	6. 13	16. 0	1. 06346	1. 06534	8. 89
11. 1	1. 04270	1. 04455	6. 18	16. 1	1. 06389	1. 06577	8. 95
11. 2	1. 04312	1. 04497	6. 24	16. 2	1. 06432	1. 06621	9. 00
11. 3	1. 04354	1. 04538	6. 30	16. 3	1. 06476	1. 06664	9. 06
11. 4	1. 04395	1. 04580	6. 35	16. 4	1. 06519	1. 06707	9. 11
11. 5	1. 04437	1. 04622	6. 41	16. 5	1. 06562	1. 06751	9. 17
11. 6	1. 04479	1. 04664	6. 46	16. 6	1. 06605	1. 06794	9. 22
11. 7	1. 04521	1. 04706	6. 52	16. 7	1. 06649	1. 06837	9. 28
11. 8	1. 04562	1. 04747	6. 57	16. 8	1. 06692	1. 06881	9. 33
11. 9	1. 04604	1. 04789	6. 63	16. 9	1. 06736	1. 06924	9. 39
12. 0	1. 04646	1. 04831	6. 68	17. 0	1. 06779	1. 06968	9. 45
12. 1	1. 04688	1. 04873	6. 74	17. 1	1. 06822	1. 07011	9. 50
12. 2	1. 04730	1. 04915	6. 79	17. 2	1. 06866	1. 07055	9. 56
12. 3	1. 04772	1. 04957	6. 85	17. 3	1. 06909	1. 07098	9. 61
12. 4	1. 04814	1. 04999	6. 90	17. 4	1. 06953	1. 07142	9. 67
12. 5	1. 04856	1. 05041	6. 96	17. 5	1. 06996	1. 07186	9. 72
12. 6	1. 04898	1. 05084	7. 02	17. 6	1. 07040	1. 07229	9. 78
12. 7	1. 04940	1. 05126	7. 07	17. 7	1. 07084	1. 07273	9. 83
12. 8	1. 04982	1. 05168	7. 13	17. 8	1. 07127	1. 07317	9. 89
12. 9	1. 05024	1. 05210	7. 18	17. 9	1. 07171	1. 07361	9. 94
13. 0	1. 05066	1. 05252	7. 24	18. 0	1. 07215	1. 07404	10. 00
13. 1	1. 05109	1. 05295	7. 29	18. 1	1. 07258	1. 07448	10. 05
13. 2	1. 05151	1. 05337	7. 35	18. 2	1. 07302	1. 07492	10. 11
13. 3	1. 05193	1. 05379	7. 40	18. 3	1. 07346	1. 07536	10. 16
13. 4	1. 05236	1. 05422	7. 46	18. 4	1. 07390	1. 07580	10. 22
13. 5	1. 05278	1. 05464	7. 51	18. 5	1. 07434	1. 07624	10. 27
13. 6	1. 05320	1. 05506	7. 57	18. 6	1. 07478	1. 07668	10. 33
13. 7	1. 05363	1. 05549	7. 62	18. 7	1. 07522	1. 07712	10. 38
13. 8	1. 05405	1. 05591	7. 68	18. 8	1. 07566	1. 07756	10. 44
13. 9	1. 05448	1. 05634	7. 73	18. 9	1. 07610	1. 07800	10. 49
14. 0	1. 05490	1. 05677	7. 79	19. 0	1. 07654	1. 07844	10. 55
14. 1	1. 05532	1. 05719	7. 84	19. 1	1. 07698	1. 07888	10. 60
14. 2	1. 05575	1. 05762	7. 90	19. 2	1. 07742	1. 07932	10. 66
14. 3	1. 05618	1. 05804	7. 96	19. 3	1. 07786	1. 07977	10. 71
14. 4	1. 05660	1. 05847	8. 01	19. 4	1. 07830	1. 08021	10. 77
14. 5	1. 05703	1. 05890	8. 07	19. 5	1. 07874	1. 08065	10. 82
14. 6	1. 05746	1. 05933	8. 12	19. 6	1. 07919	1. 08110	10. 88
14. 7	1. 05788	1. 05975	8. 18	19. 7	1. 07963	1. 08154	10. 93
14. 8	1. 05831	1. 06018	8. 23	19. 8	1. 08007	1. 08198	10. 99
14. 9	1. 05874	1. 06061	8. 29	19. 9	1. 08052	1. 08243	11. 04

(Continued)

TABLE 2.S.41 (*Continued*)

Degrees Brix or percentage of sucrose by weight	Specific gravity at 20°/4° C	Specific gravity at 20°/20° C	Degrees Baumé (modulus 145)	Degrees Brix or percentage of sucrose by weight	Specific gravity at 20°/4° C	Specific gravity at 20°/20° C	Degrees Baumé (modulus 145)
20. 0	1. 08096	1. 08287	11. 10	25. 0	1. 10356	1. 10551	13. 84
20. 1	1. 08140	1. 08332	11. 15	25. 1	1. 10402	1. 10597	13. 89
20. 2	1. 08185	1. 08376	11. 21	25. 2	1. 10448	1. 10643	13. 95
20. 3	1. 08229	1. 08421	11. 26	25. 3	1. 10494	1. 10689	14. 00
20. 4	1. 08274	1. 08465	11. 32	25. 4	1. 10540	1. 10736	14. 06
20. 5	1. 08318	1. 08510	11. 37	25. 5	1. 10586	1. 10782	14. 11
20. 6	1. 08363	1. 08554	11. 43	25. 6	1. 10632	1. 10828	14. 17
20. 7	1. 08407	1. 08599	11. 48	25. 7	1. 10679	1. 10874	14. 22
20. 8	1. 08452	1. 08644	11. 54	25. 8	1. 10725	1. 10921	14. 28
20. 9	1. 08497	1. 08689	11. 59	25. 9	1. 10771	1. 10967	14. 33
21. 0	1. 08541	1. 08733	11. 65	26. 0	1. 10818	1. 11014	14. 39
21. 1	1. 08586	1. 08778	11. 70	26. 1	1. 10864	1. 11060	14. 44
21. 2	1. 08631	1. 08823	11. 76	26. 2	1. 10910	1. 11106	14. 49
21. 3	1. 08676	1. 08868	11. 81	26. 3	1. 10957	1. 11153	14. 55
21. 4	1. 08720	1. 08913	11. 87	26. 4	1. 11003	1. 11200	14. 60
21. 5	1. 08765	1. 08958	11. 92	26. 5	1. 11050	1. 11246	14. 66
21. 6	1. 08810	1. 09003	11. 98	26. 6	1. 11096	1. 11293	14. 71
21. 7	1. 08855	1. 09048	12. 03	26. 7	1. 11143	1. 11339	14. 77
21. 8	1. 08900	1. 09093	12. 09	26. 8	1. 11190	1. 11386	14. 82
21. 9	1. 08945	1. 09138	12. 14	26. 9	1. 11236	1. 11433	14. 88
22. 0	1. 08990	1. 09183	12. 20	27. 0	1. 11283	1. 11480	14. 93
22. 1	1. 09035	1. 09228	12. 25	27. 1	1. 11330	1. 11526	14. 99
22. 2	1. 09080	1. 09273	12. 31	27. 2	1. 11376	1. 11573	15. 04
22. 3	1. 09125	1. 09318	12. 36	27. 3	1. 11423	1. 11620	15. 09
22. 4	1. 09170	1. 09364	12. 42	27. 4	1. 11470	1. 11667	15. 15
22. 5	1. 09216	1. 09409	12. 47	27. 5	1. 11517	1. 11714	15. 20
22. 6	1. 09261	1. 09454	12. 52	27. 6	1. 11564	1. 11761	15. 26
22. 7	1. 09306	1. 09499	12. 58	27. 7	1. 11610	1. 11808	15. 31
22. 8	1. 09351	1. 09545	12. 63	27. 8	1. 11657	1. 11855	15. 37
22. 9	1. 09397	1. 09590	12. 69	27. 9	1. 11704	1. 11902	15. 42
23. 0	1. 09442	1. 09636	12. 74	28. 0	1. 11751	1. 11949	15. 48
23. 1	1. 09487	1. 09681	12. 80	28. 1	1. 11798	1. 11996	15. 53
23. 2	1, 09533	1. 09727	12. 85	28. 2	1. 11845	1. 12043	15. 59
23. 3	1. 09578	1. 09772	12. 91	28. 3	1. 11892	1. 12090	15. 64
23. 4	1. 09624	1. 09818	12. 96	28. 4	1. 11940	1. 12138	15. 69
23. 5	1. 09669	1. 09863	13. 02	28. 5	1. 11987	1. 12185	15. 75
23. 6	1. 09715	1. 09909	13. 07	28. 6	1. 12034	1. 12232	15. 80
23. 7	1. 09760	1. 09954	13. 13	28. 7	1. 12081	1. 12280	15. 86
23. 8	1. 09806	1. 10000	13. 18	28. 8	1. 12128	1. 12327	15. 91
23. 9	1. 09851	1. 10046	13. 24	28. 9	1. 12176	1. 12374	15. 97
24. 0	1. 09897	1. 10092	13. 29	29. 0	1. 12223	1. 12422	16. 02
24. 1	1. 09943	1. 10137	13. 35	29. 1	1. 12270	1. 12469	16. 08
24. 2	1. 09989	1. 10183	13. 40	29. 2	1. 12318	1. 12517	16. 13
24. 3	1. 10034	1. 10229	13. 46	29. 3	1. 12365	1. 12564	16. 18
24. 4	1. 10080	1. 10275	13. 51	29. 4	1. 12413	1. 12612	16. 24
24. 5	1. 10126	1. 10321	13. 57	29. 5	1. 12460	1. 12659	16. 29
24. 6	1. 10172	1. 10367	13. 62	29. 6	1. 12508	1. 12707	16. 35
24. 7	1. 10218	1. 10413	13. 67	29. 7	1. 12556	1. 12755	16. 40
24. 8	1. 10264	1. 10459	13. 73	29. 8	1. 12603	1. 12802	16. 46
24. 9	1. 10310	1. 10505	13. 78	29. 9	1. 12651	1. 12850	16. 51

TABLE 2.S.41 (*Continued*)

Degrees Brix or percentage of sucrose by weight	Specific gravity at 20°/4° C	Specific gravity at 20°/20° C	Degrees Baumé (modulus 145)	Degrees Brix or percentage of sucrose by weight	Specific gravity at 20°/4° C	Specific gravity at 20°/20° C	Degrees Baumé (modulus 145)
30. 0	1. 12698	1. 12898	16. 57	35. 0	1. 15128	1. 15331	19. 28
30. 1	1. 12746	1. 12946	16. 62	35. 1	1. 15177	1. 15381	19. 33
30. 2	1. 12794	1. 12993	16. 67	35. 2	1. 15226	1. 15430	19. 38
30. 3	1. 12842	1. 13041	16. 73	35. 3	1. 15276	1. 15480	19. 44
30. 4	1. 12890	1. 13089	16. 78	35. 4	1. 15326	1. 15530	19. 49
30. 5	1. 12937	1. 13137	16. 84	35. 5	1. 15375	1. 15579	19. 55
30. 6	1. 12985	1. 13185	16. 89	35. 6	1. 15425	1. 15629	19. 60
30. 7	1. 13033	1. 13233	16. 95	35. 7	1. 15475	1. 15679	19. 65
30. 8	1. 13081	1. 13281	17. 00	35. 8	1. 15524	1. 15729	19. 71
30. 9	1. 13129	1. 13329	17. 05	35. 9	1. 15574	1. 15778	19. 76
31. 0	1. 13177	1. 13378	17. 11	36. 0	1. 15624	1. 15828	19. 81
31. 1	1. 13225	1. 13426	17. 16	36. 1	1. 15674	1. 15878	19. 87
31. 2	1. 13274	1. 13474	17. 22	36. 2	1. 15724	1. 15928	19. 92
31. 3	1. 13322	1. 13522	17. 27	36. 3	1. 15773	1. 15978	19. 98
31. 4	1. 13370	1. 13570	17. 33	36. 4	1. 15823	1. 16028	20. 03
31. 5	1. 13418	1. 13619	17. 38	36. 5	1. 15873	1. 16078	20. 08
31. 6	1. 13466	1. 13667	17. 43	36. 6	1. 15923	1. 16128	20. 14
31. 7	1. 13515	1. 13715	17. 49	36. 7	1. 15973	1. 16178	20. 19
31. 8	1. 13563	1. 13764	17. 54	36. 8	1. 16023	1. 16228	20. 25
31. 9	1. 13611	1. 13812	17. 60	36. 9	1. 16073	1. 16279	20. 30
32. 0	1. 13660	1. 13861	17. 65	37. 0	1. 16124	1. 16329	20. 35
32. 1	1. 13708	1. 13909	17. 70	37. 1	1. 16174	1. 16379	20. 41
32. 2	1. 13756	1. 13958	17. 76	37. 2	1. 16224	1. 16430	20. 46
32. 3	1. 13805	1. 14006	17. 81	37. 3	1. 16274	1. 16480	20. 52
32. 4	1. 13853	1. 14055	17. 87	37. 4	1. 16324	1. 16530	20. 57
32. 5	1. 13902	1. 14103	17. 92	37. 5	1. 16375	1. 16581	20. 62
32. 6	1. 13951	1. 14152	17. 98	37. 6	1. 16425	1. 16631	20. 68
32. 7	1. 13999	1. 14201	18. 03	37. 7	1. 16476	1. 16682	20. 73
32. 8	1. 14048	1. 14250	18. 08	37. 8	1. 16526	1. 16732	20. 78
32. 9	1. 14097	1. 14298	18. 14	37. 9	1. 16576	1. 16783	20. 84
33. 0	1. 14145	1. 14347	18. 19	38. 0	1. 16627	1. 16833	20. 89
33. 1	1. 14194	1. 14396	18. 25	38. 1	1. 16678	1. 16884	20. 94
33. 2	1. 14243	1. 14445	18. 30	38. 2	1. 16728	1. 16934	21. 00
33. 3	1. 14292	1. 14494	18. 36	38. 3	1. 16779	1. 16985	21. 05
33. 4	1. 14340	1. 14543	18. 41	38. 4	1. 16829	1. 17036	21. 11
33. 5	1. 14389	1. 14592	18. 46	38. 5	1. 16880	1. 17087	21. 16
33. 6	1. 14438	1. 14641	18. 52	38. 6	1. 16931	1. 17138	21. 21
33. 7	1. 14487	1. 14690	18. 57	38. 7	1. 16982	1. 17188	21. 27
33. 8	1. 14536	1. 14739	18. 63	38. 8	1. 17032	1. 17239	21. 32
33. 9	1. 14585	1. 14788	18. 68	38. 9	1. 17083	1. 17290	21. 38
34. 0	1. 14634	1. 14837	18. 73	39. 0	1. 17134	1. 17341	21. 43
34. 1	1. 14684	1. 14886	18. 79	39. 1	1. 17185	1. 17392	21. 48
34. 2	1. 14733	1. 14936	18. 84	39. 2	1. 17236	1. 17443	21. 54
34. 3	1. 14782	1. 14985	18. 90	39. 3	1. 17287	1. 17494	21. 59
34. 4	1. 14831	1. 15034	18. 95	39. 4	1. 17338	1. 17545	21. 64
34. 5	1. 14880	1. 15084	19. 00	39. 5	1. 17389	1. 17596	21. 70
34. 6	1. 14930	1. 15133	19. 06	39. 6	1. 17440	1. 17648	21. 75
34. 7	1. 14979	1. 15183	19. 11	39. 7	1. 17491	1. 17699	21. 80
34. 8	1. 15029	1. 15232	19. 17	39. 8	1. 17542	1. 17750	21. 86
34. 9	1. 15078	1. 15282	19. 22	39. 9	1. 17594	1. 17802	21. 91

(Continued)

TABLE 2.S.41 (*Continued*)

Degrees Brix or percentage of sucrose by weight	Specific gravity at 20°/4° C	Specific gravity at 20°/20° C	Degrees Baumé (modulus 145)	Degrees Brix or percentage of sucrose by weight	Specific gravity at 20°/4° C	Specific gravity at 20°/20° C	Degrees Baumé (modulus 145)
40.0	1.17645	1.17853	21.97	45.0	1.20254	1.20467	24.63
40.1	1.17696	1.17904	22.02	45.1	1.20307	1.20520	24.69
40.2	1.17747	1.17956	22.07	45.2	1.20360	1.20573	24.74
40.3	1.17799	1.18007	22.13	45.3	1.20414	1.20627	24.79
40.4	1.17850	1.18058	22.18	45.4	1.20467	1.20680	24.85
40.5	1.17901	1.18110	22.23	45.5	1.20520	1.20733	24.90
40.6	1.17953	1.18162	22.29	45.6	1.20573	1.20787	24.95
40.7	1.18004	1.18213	22.34	45.7	1.20627	1.20840	25.01
40.8	1.18056	1.18265	22.39	45.8	1.20680	1.20894	25.06
40.9	1.18108	1.18316	22.45	45.9	1.20734	1.20947	25.11
41.0	1.18159	1.18368	22.50	46.0	1.20787	1.21001	25.17
41.1	1.18211	1.18420	22.55	46.1	1.20840	1.21054	25.22
41.2	1.18262	1.18472	22.61	46.2	1.20894	1.21108	25.27
41.3	1.18314	1.18524	22.66	46.3	1.20948	1.21162	25.32
41.4	1.18366	1.18575	22.72	46.4	1.21001	1.21215	25.38
41.5	1.18418	1.18627	22.77	46.5	1.21055	1.21269	25.43
41.6	1.18470	1.18679	22.82	46.6	1.21109	1.21323	25.48
41.7	1.18522	1.18731	22.88	46.7	1.21162	1.21377	25.54
41.8	1.18573	1.18783	22.93	46.8	1.21216	1.21431	25.59
41.9	1.18625	1.18835	22.98	46.9	1.21270	1.21484	25.64
42.0	1.18677	1.18887	23.04	47.0	1.21324	1.21538	25.70
42.1	1.18729	1.18939	23.09	47.1	1.21378	1.21592	25.75
42.2	1.18781	1.18992	23.14	47.2	1.21432	1.21646	25.80
42.3	1.18834	1.19044	23.20	47.3	1.21486	1.21700	25.86
42.4	1.18886	1.19096	23.25	47.4	1.21540	1.21755	25.91
42.5	1.18938	1.19148	23.30	47.5	1.21594	1.21809	25.96
42.6	1.18990	1.19201	23.36	47.6	1.21648	1.21863	26.01
42.7	1.19042	1.19253	23.41	47.7	1.21702	1.21917	26.07
42.8	1.19095	1.19305	23.46	47.8	1.21756	1.21971	26.12
42.9	1.19147	1.19358	23.52	47.9	1.21810	1.22026	26.17
43.0	1.19199	1.19410	23.57	48.0	1.21864	1.22080	26.23
43.1	1.19252	1.19463	23.62	48.1	1.21918	1.22134	26.28
43.2	1.19304	1.19515	23.68	48.2	1.21973	1.22189	26.33
43.3	1.19356	1.19568	23.73	48.3	1.22027	1.22243	26.38
43.4	1.19409	1.19620	23.78	48.4	1.22082	1.22298	26.44
43.5	1.19462	1.19673	23.84	48.5	1.22136	1.22352	26.49
43.6	1.19514	1.19726	23.89	48.6	1.22190	1.22406	26.54
43.7	1.19567	1.19778	23.94	48.7	1.22245	1.22461	26.59
43.8	1.19619	1.19831	24.00	48.8	1.22300	1.22516	26.65
43.9	1.19672	1.19884	24.05	48.9	1.22354	1.22570	26.70
44.0	1.19725	1.19936	24.10	49.0	1.22409	1.22625	26.75
44.1	1.19778	1.19989	24.16	49.1	1.22463	1.22680	26.81
44.2	1.19830	1.20042	24.21	49.2	1.22518	1.22735	26.86
44.3	1.19883	1.20095	24.26	49.3	1.22573	1.22789	26.91
44.4	1.19936	1.20148	24.32	49.4	1.22627	1.22844	26.96
44.5	1.19989	1.20201	24.37	49.5	1.22682	1.22899	27.02
44.6	1.20042	1.20254	24.42	49.6	1.22737	1.22954	27.07
44.7	1.20095	1.20307	24.48	49.7	1.22792	1.23009	27.12
44.8	1.20148	1.20360	24.53	49.8	1.22847	1.23064	27.18
44.9	1.20201	1.20414	24.58	49.9	1.22902	1.23119	27.23

TABLE 2.S.41 (*Continued*)

Degrees Brix or per-cent-age of sucrose by weight	Specific gravity at 20°/4° C	Specific gravity at 20°/20° C	Degrees Baumé (modu-lus 145)	Degrees Brix or per-cent-age of sucrose by weight	Specific gravity at 20°/4° C	Specific gravity at 20°/20° C	Degrees Baumé (modu-lus 145)
50. 0	1. 22957	1. 23174	27. 28	55. 0	1. 25754	1. 25976	29. 90
50. 1	1. 23012	1. 23229	27. 33	55. 1	1. 25810	1. 26033	29. 95
50. 2	1. 23067	1. 23284	27. 39	55. 2	1. 25867	1. 26090	30. 00
50. 3	1. 23122	1. 23340	27. 44	55. 3	1. 25924	1. 26147	30. 06
50. 4	1. 23177	1. 23395	27. 49	55. 4	1. 25982	1. 26204	30. 11
50. 5	1. 23232	1. 23450	27. 54	55. 5	1. 26039	1. 26261	30. 16
50. 6	1. 23287	1. 23506	27. 60	55. 6	1. 26096	1. 26319	30. 21
50. 7	1. 23343	1. 23561	27. 65	55. 7	1. 26153	1. 26376	30. 26
50. 8	1. 23398	1. 23616	27. 70	55. 8	1. 26210	1. 26433	30. 32
50. 9	1. 23453	1. 23672	27. 75	55. 9	1. 26267	1. 26490	30. 37
51. 0	1. 23508	1. 23727	27. 81	56. 0	1. 26324	1. 26548	30. 42
51. 1	1. 23564	1. 23782	27. 86	56. 1	1. 26382	1. 26605	30. 47
51. 2	1. 23619	1. 23838	27. 91	56. 2	1. 26439	1. 26663	30. 52
51. 3	1. 23675	1. 23894	27. 96	56. 3	1. 26496	1. 26720	30. 57
51. 4	1. 23730	1. 23949	28. 02	56. 4	1. 26554	1. 26778	30. 63
51. 5	1. 23786	1. 24005	28. 07	56. 5	1. 26611	1. 26835	30. 68
51. 6	1. 23841	1. 24060	28. 12	56. 6	1. 26669	1. 26893	30. 73
51. 7	1. 23897	1. 24116	28. 17	56. 7	1. 26726	1. 26950	30. 78
51. 8	1. 23953	1, 24172	28. 23	56. 8	1. 26784	1. 27008	30. 83
51. 9	1. 24008	1. 24228	28. 28	56. 9	1. 26841	1. 27066	30. 89
52. 0	1. 24064	1. 24284	28. 33	57. 0	1. 26899	1. 27123	30. 94
52. 1	1. 24120	1. 24339	28. 38	57. 1	1. 26956	1. 27181	30. 99
52. 2	1. 24176	1. 24395	28. 44	57. 2	1. 27014	1. 27239	31. 04
52. 3	1. 24232	1. 24451	28. 49	57. 3	1. 27072	1. 27297	31. 09
52. 4	1. 24287	1. 34507	28. 54	57. 4	1. 27130	1. 27355	31. 15
52. 5	1. 24343	1. 24563	28. 59	57. 5	1. 27188	1. 27413	31. 20
52. 6	1. 24399	1. 24619	28. 65	57. 6	1. 27246	1. 27471	31. 25
52. 7	1. 24455	1. 24675	28. 70	57. 7	1. 27304	1. 27529	31. 30
52. 8	1. 24511	1. 24731	28. 75	57. 8	1. 27361	1. 27587	31. 35
52. 9	1. 24567	1. 24788	28. 80	57. 9	1. 27419	1. 27645	31. 40
53. 0	1. 24623	1. 24844	28. 86	58. 0	1. 27477	1. 27703	31. 46
53. 1	1. 24680	1. 24900	28. 91	58. 1	1. 27535	1. 27761	31. 51
53. 2	1. 24736	1. 24956	28. 96	58. 2	1. 27594	1. 27819	31. 56
53. 3	1. 24792	1. 25013	29. 01	58. 3	1. 27652	1. 27878	31. 61
53. 4	1. 24848	1. 25069	29. 06	58. 4	1. 27710	1. 27936	31. 66
53. 5	1. 24905	1. 25126	29. 12	58. 5	1. 27768	1. 27994	31. 71
53. 6	1. 24961	1. 25182	29. 17	58. 6	1. 27826	1. 28052	31. 76
53. 7	1. 25017	1. 25238	29. 22	58. 7	1. 27884	1. 28111	31. 82
53. 8	1. 25074	1. 25295	29. 27	58. 8	1. 27943	1. 28169	31. 87
53. 9	1. 25130	1. 25351	29. 32	58. 9	1. 28001	1. 28228	31. 92
54. 0	1. 25187	1. 25408	29. 38	59. 0	1. 28060	1. 28286	31. 97
54. 1	1. 25243	1. 25465	29. 43	59. 1	1. 28118	1. 28345	32. 02
54. 2	1. 25300	1. 25521	29. 48	59. 2	1. 28176	1. 28404	32. 07
54. 3	1. 25356	1. 25578	29. 53	59. 3	1. 28235	1. 28462	32. 13
54. 4	1. 25413	1. 25635	29. 59	59. 4	1. 28294	1. 28520	32. 18
54. 5	1. 25470	1. 25692	29. 64	59. 5	1. 28352	1. 28579	32. 23
54. 6	1. 25526	1. 25748	29. 69	59. 6	1. 28411	1. 28638	32. 28
54. 7	1. 25583	1. 25805	29. 74	59. 7	1. 28469	1. 28697	32. 33
54. 8	1. 25640	1. 25862	29. 80	59. 8	1. 28528	1. 28755	32. 38
54. 9	1. 25697	1. 25919	29. 85	59. 9	1. 28587	1. 28814	32. 43

(Continued)

TABLE 2.S.41 (*Continued*)

Degrees Brix or percentage of sucrose by weight	Specific gravity at 20°/4° C	Specific gravity at 20°/20° C	Degrees Baumé (modulus 145)	Degrees Brix or percentage of sucrose by weight	Specific gravity at 20°/4° C	Specific gravity at 20°/20° C	Degrees Baumé (modulus 145)
60. 0	1. 28646	1. 28873	32. 49	65. 0	1. 31633	1. 31866	35. 04
60. 1	1. 28704	1. 28932	32. 54	65. 1	1. 31694	1. 31927	35. 09
60. 2	1. 28763	1. 28991	32. 59	65. 2	1. 31755	1. 31988	35. 14
60. 3	1. 28822	1. 29050	32. 64	65. 3	1. 31816	1. 32049	35. 19
60. 4	1. 28881	1. 29109	32. 69	65. 4	1. 31877	1. 32110	35. 24
60. 5	1. 28940	1. 29168	32. 74	65. 5	1. 31937	1. 32171	35. 29
60. 6	1. 28999	1. 29227	32. 79	65. 6	1. 31998	1. 32232	35. 34
60. 7	1. 29058	1. 29286	32. 85	65. 7	1. 32059	1. 32293	35. 39
60. 8	1. 29117	1. 29346	32. 90	65. 8	1. 32120	1. 32354	35. 45
60. 9	1. 29176	1. 29405	32. 95	65. 9	1. 32181	1. 32415	35. 50
61. 0	1. 29235	1. 29464	33. 00	66. 0	1. 32242	1. 32476	35. 55
61. 1	1. 29295	1. 29523	33. 05	66. 1	1. 32304	1. 32538	35. 60
61. 2	1. 29354	1. 29583	33. 10	66. 2	1. 32365	1. 32599	35. 65
61. 3	1. 29413	1. 29642	33. 15	66. 3	1. 32426	1. 32660	35. 70
61. 4	1. 29472	1. 29701	33. 20	66. 4	1. 32487	1. 32722	35. 75
61. 5	1. 29532	1. 29761	33. 26	66. 5	1. 32548	1. 32783	35. 80
61. 6	1. 29591	1. 29820	33. 31	66. 6	1. 32610	1. 32844	35. 85
61. 7	1. 29651	1. 29880	33. 36	66. 7	1. 32671	1. 32906	35. 90
61. 8	1. 29710	1. 29940	33. 41	66. 8	1. 32732	1. 32967	35. 95
61. 9	1. 29770	1. 29999	33. 46	66. 9	1. 32794	1. 33029	36. 00
62. 0	1. 29829	1. 30059	33. 51	67. 0	1. 32855	1. 33090	36. 05
62. 1	1. 29889	1. 30118	33. 56	67. 1	1. 32917	1. 33152	36. 10
62. 2	1. 29948	1. 30178	33. 61	67. 2	1. 32978	1. 33214	36. 15
62. 3	1. 30008	1. 30238	33. 67	67. 3	1. 33040	1. 33275	36. 20
62. 4	1. 30068	1, 30298	33. 72	67. 4	1. 33102	1. 33337	36. 25
62. 5	1. 30127	1. 30358	33. 77	67. 5	1. 33163	1. 33399	36. 30
62. 6	1. 30187	1. 30418	33. 82	67. 6	1. 33225	1. 33460	36. 35
62. 7	1. 30247	1. 30477	33. 87	67. 7	1. 33287	1. 33523	36. 40
62. 8	1. 30307	1. 30537	33. 92	67. 8	1. 33348	1. 33584	36. 45
62. 9	1. 30367	1. 30597	33. 97	67. 9	1. 33410	1. 33646	36. 50
63. 0	1. 30427	1. 30657	34. 02	68. 0	1. 33472	1. 33708	36. 55
63. 1	1. 30487	1. 30718	34. 07	68. 1	1. 33534	1. 33770	36. 61
63. 2	1. 30547	1. 30778	34. 12	68. 2	1. 33596	1. 33832	36. 66
63. 3	1. 30607	1. 30838	34. 18	68. 3	1. 33658	1. 33894	36. 71
63. 4	1. 30667	1. 30898	34. 23	68. 4	1. 33720	1. 33957	36. 76
63. 5	1. 30727	1. 30958	34. 28	68. 5	1. 33782	1. 34019	36. 81
63. 6	1. 30787	1. 31019	34. 33	68. 6	1. 33844	1. 34081	36. 86
63. 7	1. 30848	1. 31079	34. 38	68. 7	1. 33906	1. 34143	36. 91
63. 8	1. 30908	1. 31139	34. 43	68. 8	1. 33968	1. 34205	36. 96
63. 9	1. 30968	1. 31200	34. 48	68. 9	1. 34031	1. 34268	37. 01
64. 0	1. 31028	1. 31260	34. 53	69. 0	1. 34093	1. 34330	37. 06
64. 1	1. 31088	1. 31320	34. 58	69. 1	1. 34155	1. 34392	37. 11
64. 2	1. 31149	1. 31381	34. 63	69. 2	1. 34217	1. 34455	37. 16
64. 3	1, 31209	1. 31441	34. 68	69. 3	1. 34280	1. 34517	37. 21
64. 4	1. 31270	1. 31502	34. 74	69. 4	1. 34342	1. 34580	37. 26
64. 5	1. 31330	1. 31563	34. 79	69. 5	1. 34405	1. 34642	37. 31
64. 6	1. 31391	1. 31623	34. 84	69. 6	1. 34467	1. 34705	37. 36
64. 7	1. 31452	1. 31684	34. 89	69. 7	1. 34530	1. 34768	37. 41
64. 8	1. 31512	1. 31745	34. 94	69. 8	1. 34592	1. 34830	37. 46
64. 9	1. 31573	1. 31806	34. 99	69. 9	1. 34655	1. 34893	37. 51

TABLE 2.S.41 (*Continued*)

Degrees Brix or percentage of sucrose by weight	Specific gravity at 20°/4° C	Specific gravity at 20°/20° C	Degrees Baumé (modulus 145)	Degrees Brix or percentage of sucrose by weight	Specific gravity at 20°/4° C	Specific gravity at 20°/20° C	Degrees Baumé (modulus 145)
70. 0	1. 34717	1. 34956	37. 56	75. 0	1. 37897	1. 38141	40. 03
70. 1	1. 34780	1. 35019	37. 61	75. 1	1. 37962	1. 38206	40. 08
70. 2	1. 34843	1. 35081	37. 66	75. 2	1. 38026	1. 38270	40. 13
70. 3	1. 34906	1. 35144	37. 71	75. 3	1. 38091	1. 38335	40. 18
70. 4	1. 34968	1. 35207	37. 76	75. 4	1. 38156	1. 38400	40. 23
70. 5	1. 35031	1. 35270	37. 81	75. 5	1. 38220	1. 38465	40. 28
70. 6	1. 35094	1. 35333	37. 86	75. 6	1. 38285	1. 38530	40. 33
70. 7	1. 35157	1. 35396	37. 91	75. 7	1. 38350	1. 38595	40. 38
70. 8	1. 35220	1. 35459	37. 96	75. 8	1. 38415	1. 38660	40. 43
70. 9	1. 35283	1. 35522	38. 01	75. 9	1. 38480	1. 38725	40. 48
71. 0	1. 35346	1. 35585	38. 06	76. 0	1. 38545	1. 38790	40. 53
71. 1	1. 35409	1. 35648	38. 11	76. 1	1. 38610	1. 38855	40. 57
71. 2	1. 35472	1. 35711	38. 16	76. 2	1. 38675	1. 38920	40. 62
71. 3	1. 35535	1. 35775	38. 21	76. 3	1. 38740	1. 38985	40. 67
71. 4	1. 35598	1. 35838	38. 26	76. 4	1. 38805	1. 39050	40. 72
71. 5	1. 35661	1. 35901	38. 30	76. 5	1. 38870	1. 39115	40. 77
71. 6	1. 35724	1. 35964	38. 35	76. 6	1. 38935	1. 39180	40. 82
71. 7	1. 35788	1. 36028	38. 40	76. 7	1. 39000	1. 39246	40. 87
71. 8	1. 35851	1. 36091	38. 45	76. 8	1. 39065	1. 39311	40. 92
71. 9	1. 35914	1. 36155	38. 50	76. 9	1. 39130	1. 39376	40. 97
72. 0	1. 35978	1. 36218	38. 55	77. 0	1. 39196	1. 39442	41. 01
72. 1	1. 36041	1. 36282	38. 60	77. 1	1. 39261	1. 39507	41. 06
72. 2	1. 36105	1. 36346	38. 65	77. 2	1. 39326	1. 39573	41. 11
72. 3	1. 36168	1. 36409	38. 70	77. 3	1. 39392	1. 39638	41. 16
72. 4	1. 36232	1. 36473	38. 75	77. 4	1. 39457	1. 39704	41. 21
72. 5	1. 36295	1. 36536	38. 80	77. 5	1. 39523	1. 39769	41. 26
72. 6	1. 36359	1. 36600	38. 85	77. 6	1. 39588	1. 39835	41. 31
72. 7	1. 36423	1. 36664	38. 90	77. 7	1. 39654	1. 39901	41. 36
72. 8	1. 36486	1. 36728	38. 95	77. 8	1. 39719	1. 39966	41. 40
72. 9	1. 36550	1. 36792	39. 00	77. 9	1. 39785	1. 40032	41. 45
73. 0	1. 36614	1. 36856	39. 05	78. 0	1. 39850	1. 40098	41. 50
73. 1	1. 36678	1. 36919	39. 10	78. 1	1. 39916	1. 40164	41. 55
73. 2	1. 36742	1. 36983	39. 15	78. 2	1. 39982	1. 40230	41. 60
73. 3	1. 36805	1. 37047	39. 20	78. 3	1. 40048	1. 40295	41. 65
73. 4	1. 36869	1. 37111	39. 25	78. 4	1. 40113	1. 40361	41. 70
73. 5	1. 36933	1. 37176	39. 30	78. 5	1. 40179	1. 40427	41. 74
73. 6	1. 36997	1. 37240	39. 35	78. 6	1. 40245	1. 40493	41. 79
73. 7	1. 37061	1. 37304	39. 39	78. 7	1. 40311	1. 40559	41. 84
73. 8	1. 37125	1. 37368	39. 44	78. 8	1. 40377	1. 40625	41. 89
73. 9	1. 37189	1. 37432	39. 49	78. 9	1. 40443	1. 40691	41. 94
74. 0	1. 37254	1. 37496	39. 54	79. 0	1. 40509	1. 40758	41. 99
74. 1	1. 37318	1. 37561	39. 59	79. 1	1. 40575	1. 40824	42. 03
74. 2	1. 37382	1. 37625	39. 64	79. 2	1. 40641	1. 40890	42. 08
74. 3	1. 37446	1. 37689	39. 69	79. 3	1. 40707	1. 40956	42. 13
74. 4	1. 37510	1. 37754	39. 74	79. 4	1. 40774	1. 41023	42. 18
74. 5	1. 37575	1. 37818	39. 79	79. 5	1. 40840	1. 41089	42. 23
74. 6	1. 37639	1. 37883	39. 84	79. 6	1. 40906	1. 41155	42. 28
74. 7	1. 37704	1. 37947	39. 89	79. 7	1. 40972	1. 41222	42. 32
74. 8	1. 37768	1. 38012	39. 94	79. 8	1. 41039	1. 41288	42. 37
74. 9	1. 37833	1. 38076	39. 99	79. 9	1. 41105	1. 41355	42. 42

(Continued)

TABLE 2.S.41 (*Continued*)

Degrees Brix or percentage of sucrose by weight	Specific gravity at 20°/4° C	Specific gravity at 20°/20° C	Degrees Baumé (modulus 145)	Degrees Brix or percentage of sucrose by weight	Specific gravity at 20°/4° C	Specific gravity at 20°/20° C	Degrees Baumé (modulus 145)
80. 0	1. 41172	1. 41421	42. 47	85. 0	1. 44539	1. 44794	44. 86
80. 1	1. 41238	1. 41488	42. 52	85. 1	1. 44607	1. 44863	44. 91
80. 2	1. 41304	1. 41554	42. 57	85. 2	1. 44675	1. 44931	44. 95
80. 3	1. 41371	1. 41621	42. 61	85. 3	1. 44744	1. 45000	45. 00
80. 4	1. 41437	1. 41688	42. 66	85. 4	1. 44812	1. 45068	45. 05
80. 5	1. 41504	1. 41754	42. 71	85. 5	1. 44881	1. 45137	45. 09
80. 6	1. 41571	1. 41821	42. 76	85. 6	1. 44949	1. 45205	45. 14
80. 7	1. 41637	1. 41888	42. 81	85. 7	1. 45018	1. 45274	45. 19
80. 8	1. 41704	1. 41955	42. 85	85. 8	1. 45086	1. 45343	45. 24
80. 9	1. 41771	1. 42022	42. 90	85. 9	1. 45154	1. 45411	45. 28
81. 0	1. 41837	1. 42088	42. 95	86. 0	1. 45223	1. 45480	45. 33
81. 1	4. 41904	1. 42155	43. 00	86. 1	1. 45292	1. 45549	45. 38
81. 2	1. 41971	1. 42222	43. 05	86. 2	1. 45360	1. 45618	45. 42
81. 3	1. 42038	1. 42289	43. 10	86. 3	1. 45429	1. 45686	45. 47
81. 4	1. 42105	1. 42356	43. 14	86. 4	1. 45498	1. 45755	45. 52
81. 5	1. 42172	1. 42423	43. 19	86. 5	1. 45567	1. 45824	45. 57
81. 6	1. 42239	1. 42490	43. 24	86. 6	1. 45636	1. 45893	45. 61
81. 7	1. 42306	1. 42558	43. 29	86. 7	1. 45704	1. 45962	45. 66
81. 8	1. 42373	1. 42625	43. 33	86. 8	1. 45773	1. 46031	45. 71
81. 9	1. 42440	1. 42692	43. 38	86. 9	1. 45842	1. 46100	45. 75
82. 0	1. 42507	1. 42759	43. 43	87. 0	1. 45911	1. 46170	45. 80
82. 1	1. 42574	1. 42827	43. 48	87. 1	1. 45980	1. 46239	45. 85
82. 2	1. 42642	1. 42894	43. 53	87. 2	1. 46050	1. 46308	45. 89
82. 3	1. 42709	1. 42961	43. 57	87. 3	1. 46119	1. 46377	45. 94
82. 4	1. 42776	1. 43029	43. 62	87. 4	1. 46188	1. 46446	45. 99
82. 5	1. 42844	1. 43096	43. 67	87. 5	1. 46257	1. 46516	46. 03
82. 6	1. 42911	1. 43164	43. 72	87. 6	1. 46326	1. 46585	46. 08
82. 7	1. 42978	1. 43231	43. 77	87. 7	1. 46395	1. 46654	46. 13
82. 8	1. 43046	1. 43298	43. 81	87. 8	1. 46464	1. 46724	46. 17
82. 9	1. 43113	1. 43366	43. 86	87. 9	1. 46534	1. 46793	46. 22
83. 0	1. 43181	1. 43434	43. 91	88. 0	1. 46603	1. 46862	46. 27
83. 1	1. 43248	1. 43502	43. 96	88. 1	1. 46673	1. 46932	46. 31
83. 2	1. 43316	1. 43569	44. 00	88. 2	1. 46742	1. 47002	46. 36
83. 3	1. 43384	1. 43637	44. 05	88. 3	1. 46812	1. 47071	46. 41
83. 4	1. 43451	1. 43705	44. 10	88. 4	1. 46881	1. 47141	46. 45
83. 5	1. 43519	1. 43773	44. 15	88. 5	1. 46950	1. 47210	46. 50
83. 6	1. 43587	1. 43841	44. 19	88. 6	1. 47020	1. 47280	46. 55
83. 7	1. 43654	1. 43908	44. 24	88. 7	1. 47090	1. 47350	46. 59
83. 8	1. 43722	1. 43976	44. 29	88. 8	1. 47159	1. 47420	46. 64
83. 9	1. 43790	1. 44044	44. 34	88. 9	1. 47229	1. 47489	46. 69
84. 0	1. 43858	1. 44112	44. 38	89. 0	1. 47299	1. 47559	46. 73
84. 1	1. 43926	1. 44180	44. 43	89. 1	1. 47368	1. 47629	46. 78
84. 2	1. 43994	1. 44249	44. 48	89. 2	1. 47438	1. 47699	46. 83
84. 3	1. 44062	1. 44317	44. 53	89. 3	1. 47508	1. 47769	46. 87
84. 4	1. 44130	1. 44385	44. 57	89. 4	1. 47578	1. 47839	46. 92
84. 5	1. 44198	1. 44453	44. 62	89. 5	1. 47648	1. 47909	46. 97
84. 6	1. 44266	1. 44521	44. 67	89. 6	1. 47718	1. 47979	47. 01
84. 7	1. 44334	1. 44590	44. 72	89. 7	1. 47788	1. 48049	47. 06
84. 8	1. 44402	1. 44658	44. 76	89. 8	1. 47858	1. 48119	47. 11
84. 9	1. 44470	1. 44726	44. 81	89. 9	1. 47928	1. 48189	47. 15

TABLE 2.S.41 (*Continued*)

Degrees Brix or percentage of sucrose by weight	Specific gravity at 20°/4° C	Specific gravity at 20°/20° C	Degrees Baumé (modulus 145)	Degrees Brix or percentage of sucrose by weight	Specific gravity at 20°/4° C	Specific gravity at 20°/20° C	Degrees Baumé (modulus 145)
90. 0	1. 47998	1. 48259	47. 20	95. 0	1. 51546	1. 51814	49. 49
90. 1	1. 48068	1. 48330	47. 24	95. 1	1. 51617	1. 51886	49. 53
90. 2	1. 48138	1. 48400	47. 29	95. 2	1. 51689	1. 51958	49. 58
90. 3	1. 48208	1. 48470	47. 34	95. 3	1. 51761	1. 52030	49. 62
90. 4	1. 48278	1. 48540	47. 38	95. 4	1. 51833	1. 52102	49. 67
90. 5	1. 48348	1. 48611	47. 43	95. 5	1. 51905	1. 52174	49. 71
90. 6	1. 48419	1. 48681	47. 48	95. 6	1. 51977	1. 52246	49. 76
90. 7	1. 48489	1. 48752	47. 52	95. 7	1. 52049	1. 52318	49. 80
90. 8	1. 48559	1. 48822	47. 57	95. 8	1. 52121	1. 52390	49. 85
90. 9	1. 48630	1. 48893	47. 61	95. 9	1. 52193	1. 52463	49. 90
91. 0	1. 48700	1. 48963	47. 66	96. 0	1. 52266	1. 52535	49. 94
91. 1	1. 48771	1. 49034	47. 71	96. 1	1. 52338	1. 52607	49. 98
91. 2	1. 48841	1. 49104	47. 75	96. 2	1. 52410	1. 52680	50. 03
91. 3	1. 48912	1. 49175	47. 80	96. 3	1. 52482	1. 52752	50. 08
91. 4	1. 48982	1. 49246	47. 84	96. 4	1. 52555	1. 52824	50. 12
91. 5	1. 49053	1. 49316	47. 89	96. 5	1. 52627	1. 52897	50. 16
91. 6	1. 49123	1. 49387	47. 94	96. 6	1. 52699	1. 52969	50. 21
91. 7	1. 49194	1. 49458	47. 98	96. 7	1. 52772	1. 53042	50. 25
91. 8	1. 49265	1. 49529	48. 03	96. 8	1. 52844	1. 53114	50. 30
91. 9	1. 49336	1. 49600	48. 08	96. 9	1. 52917	1. 53187	50. 34
92. 0	1. 49406	1. 49671	48. 12	97. 0	1. 52989	1. 53260	50. 39
92. 1	1. 49477	1. 49741	48. 17	97. 1	1. 53062	1. 53332	50. 43
92. 2	1. 49548	1. 49812	48. 21	97. 2	1. 53134	1. 53405	50. 48
92. 3	1. 49619	1. 49883	48. 26	97. 3	1. 53207	1. 53478	50. 52
92. 4	1. 49690	1. 49954	48. 30	97. 4	1. 53279	1. 53551	50. 57
92. 5	1. 49761	1. 50026	48. 35	97. 5	1. 53352	1. 53623	50. 61
92. 6	1. 49832	1. 50097	48. 40	97. 6	1. 53425	1. 53696	50. 66
92. 7	1. 49903	1. 50168	48. 44	97. 7	1. 53498	1. 53769	50. 70
92. 8	1. 49974	1. 50239	48. 49	97. 8	1. 53570	1. 53842	50. 75
92. 9	1. 50045	1. 50310	48. 53	97. 9	1. 53643	1. 53915	50. 79
93. 0	1. 50116	1. 50381	48. 58	98. 0	1. 53716	1. 53988	50. 84
93. 1	1. 50187	1. 50453	48. 62	98. 1	1. 53789	1. 54061	50. 88
93. 2	1. 50258	1. 50524	48. 67	98. 2	1. 53862	1. 54134	50. 93
93. 3	1. 50329	1. 50595	48. 72	98. 3	1. 53935	1. 54207	50. 97
93. 4	1. 50401	1. 50667	48. 76	98. 4	1. 54008	1. 54280	51. 02
93. 5	1. 50472	1. 50738	48. 81	98. 5	1. 54081	1. 54353	51. 06
93. 6	1. 50543	1. 50810	48. 85	98. 6	1. 54154	1. 54426	51. 10
93. 7	1. 50615	1. 50881	48. 90	98. 7	1. 54227	1. 54499	51. 15
93. 8	1. 50686	1. 50952	48. 94	98. 8	1. 54300	1. 54573	51. 19
93. 9	1. 50757	1. 51024	48. 99	98. 9	1. 54373	1. 54646	51. 24
94. 0	1. 50829	1. 51096	49. 03	99. 0	1. 54446	1. 54719	51. 28
94. 1	1. 50900	1. 51167	49. 08	99. 1	1. 54519	1. 54793	51. 33
94. 2	1. 50972	1. 51239	49. 12	99. 2	1. 54593	1. 54866	51. 37
94. 3	1. 51044	1. 51311	49. 17	99. 3	1. 54666	1. 54939	51. 42
94. 4	1. 51115	1. 51382	49. 22	99. 4	1. 54739	1. 55013	51. 46
94. 5	1. 51187	1. 51454	49. 26	99. 5	1. 54813	1. 55087	51. 50
94. 6	1. 51258	1. 51526	49. 31	99. 6	1. 54886	1. 55160	51. 55
94. 7	1. 51330	1. 51598	49. 35	99. 7	1. 54960	1. 55234	51. 59
94. 8	1. 51402	1. 51670	49. 40	99. 8	1. 55033	1. 55307	51. 64
94. 9	1. 51474	1. 51742	49. 44	99. 9	1. 55106	1. 55381	51. 68
				100. 0	1. 55180	1. 55454	51. 73

SOURCE: BATES, F. J. *et al*. Polarimetry, saccharimetry, and the sugars. Circ. *C440*, U.S. Dept. Comm.

SUGAR, VEGETABLES

TABLE 2.S.42

FREE SUGARS IN VEGETABLES AS PERCENTAGE FRESH BASIS

Vegetable	Total Solids %	Glucose %	Fructose %	Sucrose %
Asparagus, *Asparagus officinalis*	9.15	0.92	1.30	0.28
Beet,[1] *Beta vulgarus*	11.19	0.18	0.16	6.11
Broccoli, *Brassica oleraceae* (*botrytis*)	11.84	0.73	0.67	0.42
Brussels sprout,[1] *Brassica oleracea* (*gemmifera*)	11.45	0.66	0.75	0.41
Cabbage, *Brassica oleracea* (*capitata*)	6.67	1.58	1.20	0.15
Cabbage, *Brassica oleracea* (*capitata*), red	9.06	2.06	1.74	0.50
Carrot, *Daucus carota*	12.00	0.85	0.85	4.24
Cauliflower,[1] *Brassica oleracea* (*botrytis*)	8.05	0.83	0.74	0.67
Celery, *Apium graveolens*	8.29	0.49	0.43	0.31
Cucumber, *Cucumis sativus*	3.46	0.86	0.86	0.06
Eggplant, *Solanum melongena* (*esculentum*)	8.49	1.51	1.53	0.25
Endive, *Cichorum endivia*	5.60	0.07	0.16	0.07
Escarole, *Cichorum endivia*	6.15	0.16	0.32	0.10
Kale, *Brassica oleracea* (*acephala*)	9.74	0.27	0.21	
Kohlrabi, *Brassica oleracea* (*gongylodes*)	7.55	1.34	1.24	0.58
Leek,[1] *Allium porrum*	11.95	0.98	1.47	1.06
Lettuce, *Lactuca sativa*	4.97	0.25	0.46	0.10
Melon, Honeydew, *Cucumis melo*	12.74	2.56	2.62	5.86
Melon, Musk, *Cucumis melo* (*reticulatus*)	10.84	1.72	2.03	3.56
Melon, Water, *Citrullus vulgarus*	9.57	1.81	3.54	2.35
Okra, *Hibiscus esculentus*	10.70	1.03	1.06	0.75
Onion,[2] *Allium cepa*	11.56	2.07	1.09	0.89
Onion, green,[1] *Allium cepa*	9.59	0.56	0.76	0.86
Parsley, *Petroselinum hortense*	11.28	0.10		0.20
Parsnip,[1] *Pastinaca sativa*	20.99	0.18	0.24	2.98
Pepper, *Capsicum frutescens*	6.21	0.90	0.87	0.11
Potato, new, *Solanum tuberosum*	20.08	0.15	0.09	0.14
Potato, stored at 35°F[1]		1.04	1.15	1.69
Pumpkin,[1] *Cucurbita pepo*	7.13	1.69	1.43	1.30
Radish, white, *Raphanus sativus*	4.40	0.84	0.30	
Radish, red, *Raphanus sativus*	5.46	1.34	0.74	0.22
Rhubarb, *Rheum rhaponticum*	6.20	0.42	0.39	0.09
Rutabaga, *Brassica napobrassica*	6.69	0.38	0.34	0.07
Spinach, *Spinacia oleracea*	8.04	0.09	0.04	0.06
Squash, summer, *Cucurbita pepo*	5.55	0.77	0.82	0.09
Squash, winter, *Curcurbita pepo*	13.08	0.96	1.16	1.61
Sweet corn, *Zea mays*	22.69	0.34	0.31	3.03
Swiss Chard, *Beta vulgaris* (*cicla*)	9.20	0.17	0.09	0.06
Sweet Potato, *Ipomoea batatas Poir*	22.53	0.33	0.30	3.37
Tomato, *Lycopersicon esculentum*	5.23	1.12	1.34	0.01
Turnip, *Brassica rapa*	7.40	1.50	1.18	0.42

[1] Contains traces (0.02–0.20%) raffinose, stachyose, or both.
[2] Contains 0.24% to >1.0% raffinose and stachyose.

SOURCE: SHALLENBERGER, R. S. and BIRCH, G. G. (EDITORS). 1975. Occurrence and Properties of Sugars. *In* Sugar Chemistry. Avi Publishing Co., Westport, Conn.

SUGARS AND SWEETS COMPOSITION

TABLE 2.S.43

COMPOSITION OF SUGARS AND SWEETS

Food, Approximate Measure, and Weight (in Grams)		Water (%)	Food Energy (Cal)	Protein (g)	Fat (Total Lipid) (g)	Fatty Acids: Saturated (Total) (g)	Fatty Acids: Unsaturated: Oleic (g)	Fatty Acids: Unsaturated: Lin-oleic (g)	Carbohydrate (g)	Calcium (mg)	Iron (mg)	Vitamin A Value (IU)	Thiamin (mg)	Riboflavin (mg)	Niacin (mg)	Ascorbic Acid (mg)
Candy:																
Caramels	1 oz (28 g)	7	120	1	3	2	1	Tr	22	36	0.7	50	0.01	0.04	Tr	Tr
Chocolate, sweetened, milk	1 oz (28 g)	1	145	2	9	5	3	Tr	16	61	0.3	40	0.03	0.11	0.2	0
Fudge, plain	1 oz (28 g)	5	115	Tr	3	2	1	Tr	23	14	0.1	60	Tr	0.02	Tr	Tr
Hard candy	1 oz (28 g)	1	110	0	0				28	0	0	0	0	0	0	0
Marshmallow	1 oz (28 g)	15	90	1	0				23	0	0	0	0	0	0	0
Chocolate syrup	1 tbsp (20 g)	39	40	Tr	Tr				11	3	0.3					
Honey, strained or extracted	1 tbsp (21 g)	20	60	Tr	0				17	1	0.2	0	Tr	.01	Tr	1
Jams, marmalades, preserves	1 tbsp (20 g)	28	55	Tr	Tr				14	2	0.1	Tr	Tr	Tr	Tr	1
Jellies	1 tbsp (20 g)	34	50	0	0				13	2	0.1	Tr	Tr	Tr	Tr	1
Molasses, cane																
Light (first extraction)	1 tbsp (20 g)	24	50						13	33	0.9		0.01	0.01	Tr	
Blackstrap (third extraction)	1 tbsp (20 g)	24	45						11	116	2.3		0.02	0.04	0.3	
Syrup, table blends	1 tbsp (20 g)	25	55	0	0				15	9	0.8	0	0	Tr	Tr	0
Sugar:																
Granulated, cane or beet	1 cup (200 g)	Tr	770	0	0				199			0	0	0	0	0
	1 tbsp (12 g)	Tr	50	0	0				12			0	0	0	0	0
Lump, 1⅛ by ⅝ by ⅛ in.	1 lump (7 g)	Tr	25	0	0				7			0	0	0	0	0
Powdered, stirred before measuring.	1 cup (128 g)	Tr	495	0	0				127			0	0	0	0	0
	1 tbsp (8 g)	Tr	30	0	0				8			0	0	0	0	0
Brown, firm-packed	1 cup (220 g)	3	815	0	0				210	[1] 167	5.7	0	0	0	0	0
	1 tbsp (14 g)	3	50	0	0				13	[1] 10	0.4	0	0	0	0	0

[1] Calcium value is based on dark brown sugar; value is lower for light brown sugar.

SOURCE: INSTITUTE OF HOME ECONOMICS. Nutritive Value of Foods. USDA Home and Garden Bull. 72.

SUGARS AND SYRUPS COMPOSITION

TABLE 2.S.44

COMPOSITION OF THE EDIBLE PORTION (EP) AND REFUSE IN THE MATERIAL AS PURCHASED (AP)

Commodity and Description	Water	Protein	Fat	Carbohydrate Total (By Dif)	Carbohydrate Fiber	Ash	Calories (No./100 g)	Notes	Refuse in AP (%)
				(Percent of Edible Portion)					
Sugars and Syrups									
Sugars									
Sugar, refined				100			387	Cane or beet	0
Crude sugars from cane, palm, coconut, maple	7	1		90		2	351	Jaggery, ghur, panela, marena, piloncillo	0
Syrups									
Molasses (by-product of cane sugar)	24			(60)		4.5	232		0
Sorghum syrup (concentrated juice)	23			(67)		2.5	259	From sweet sorghum (*Sorghum saccharatum*)	0
Cane syrup (concentrated cane juice)	27			(67)		1.5	259		0
Maple syrup	34			(64)		0.7	248		0
Syrups, miscellaneous, incl. corn syrup	20			(80)		0.5	310		0
Honey	21			(75)		0.2	290		0

SOURCE: CHATFIELD, C. Food Composition Tables for International Use. FAO, United Nations, Rome.

SULFURIC ACID SOLUTION

TABLE 2.S.45

VARIOUS STRENGTHS OF SULFURIC ACID SOLUTIONS
Sulfuric Acid Solutions: Specification requires not <94% H_2SO_4 by wt.
Sp gr = 1.835 at 15°. Pour acid into excess of H_2O and dil to 1 liter.

H_2SO_4 Strength Desired	H_2SO_4 Required		
Grams per Liter	Grams	Ml	
5	5.32	3.0	
12.5	13.29	7.2	For crude fiber
20	21.28	11.6	
30	31.91	17.4	
40	42.55	23.2	
49	52.13	28.4	1*N* soln
100	106.38	58.0	
150	159.57	87.0	
250	265.96	144.9	
300	319.15	173.9	
400	425.53	231.9	

SOURCE: EDITORIAL BOARD, AOAC. 1975. Official Methods of Analysis of the Association of Official Analytical Chemists, 12th Edition. Association of Official Analytical Chemists, Washington, D.C.

SWEET POTATO AND IRISH POTATO

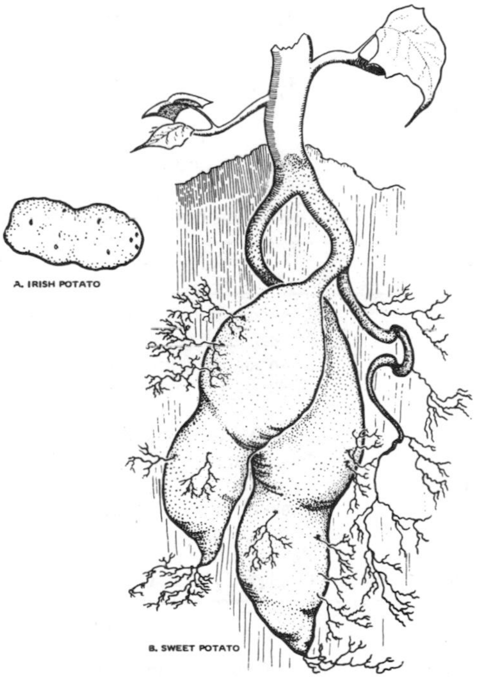

FIG. 2.S.8. ILLUSTRATING DIFFERENCE BETWEEN A FOOD STORAGE TUBER (A) AND A FOOD STORAGE ROOT (B)

SOURCE: MITTLEIDER, J. R., and NELSON, A. N. 1970. Food for Everyone. Extension Division, Loma Linda University, Cal.

SWEETENING AGENTS

TABLE 2.S.46

COMPOSITION OF CONFECTIONERY SWEETENING AGENTS

Sugar Product	Total Sugar (%)	Sucrose (%)	Dextrose (%)	Levulose (%)	Invert sugar (%)	Maltose (%)	Dextrin (%)	Ash (%)	Water (%)	Sweetening Power Sucrose = 100[1]
Sucrose	100	100								100
Corn syrup	47.63		21.19			26.44	34.68		17.65	30[2]
Corn sugar (Cerelose)	91		87.5			3.5	0.5	0.04	9.1	66
Invert sugar (Nulomoline)	80	6			74				20	98
Golden syrup	68.5	31			37.5			3.9	22.5	77
Molasses	70.36	53.6	8.76	8				4.0	20	74
Honey	76.8	1.9	34.48	40.50				0.18	17.7	97
Maple syrup	64.07	62.6			1.47				35	64
Sorghum syrup	63	36			27			2.5	23	69
Saccharin[3]										30,000-50,000
Sucrol[3]										20,000

[1] Based on the composition of the sugar products and the relative sweetness values for the different sugars as determined by Biester.
[2] The sweetening power of corn syrup varies according to the grade of the syrup, *i.e.*, degree of hydrolysis: high purity syrup = 40–45; low purity syrup = 26–29; Sweetose = 56–64.
[3] See recent FDA rulings on use.

SOURCE: JACOBS, M. B. (EDITOR). The Chemistry and Technology of Food and Food Products, 2nd Edition, Vol. *2* Interscience Publishers, New York.

SWEETENING COMPOUNDS

TABLE 2.S.47

SWEETENING COMPOUNDS USED IN MEAT PROCESSING

Sugar	Common Name	Type	Sweetening Value
Sucrose	Sugar	Disaccharide of glucose and fructose	100
Glucose	Dextrose	Monosaccharide	74-90
Fructose	Fruit sugar	Monosaccharide	173
Invert sugar		Mixture of monosaccharides; 50% glucose and 50% fructose	123-130
	Honey	65-80% invert sugar	125-173
Maltose		Disaccharide of glucose and glucose	33
	Corn syrup solids	Primarily maltose	30
Lactose	Milk sugar	Disaccharide of glucose and galactose	16
Glycogen	Animal starch	Polysaccharide	Little
Saccharin[1]	Nonnutritive sweeteners	$C_6H_4SO_2NHCO$	30,000-50,000

[1] See recent FDA rulings on use.

SOURCE: OCKERMAN, H. W. 1975. Chemistry of muscle and major organs. *In* Meat Hygiene. J. A. Libby (Editor). Lea & Febiger, Philadelphia.

SWEETNESS OF SWEETENERS

TABLE 2.S.48

DEGREE OF SWEETNESS OF VARIOUS SWEETENERS

Sugar	Degree of Sweetness
Sucrose	100
Fructose	173.3
Glucose	74.3
Corn syrup	30
Molasses	74
Honey	97
Sorghum syrup	69
Saccharin[1]	30,000-50,000
Dulcin (sucrol)	20,000

[1]See recent FDA rulings on use.

SOURCE: BRAVERMAN, J. B. S. Introduction to the Biochemistry of Foods. ASP Biological and Medical Press (Elsevier Division), New York.

SWINE BREEDS

TABLE 2.S.49

BREEDS OF SWINE AND THEIR CHARACTERISTICS

Breed	Place of Origin	Color	Distinctive Head Characteristics	Other Distinguishing Characteristics	Disqualifications
American Landrace	Denmark	White, although small black skin spots are common.	Medium lop ears, straight snout, and trim jowl.	Very long side.	Black in the hair coat. Fewer than six teats on either side. Erect ears, with no forward break.
Beltsville No. 1 (75% Landrace & 25% Poland China)	United States; by the USDA at Beltsville, Maryland, beginning in 1934.	Black with white spots.	Fairly long, narrow head with trim, light jowl and moderately large, drooping ears.		
Berkshire	England; chiefly in the south central counties of Berkshire and Wiltshire.	Black with 6 white points, 4 white feet, some white on the face, and a white switch on the tail. Any or all white points may be missing.	Medium short nose, medium dished face, and erect ears.	Striking style and carriage.	A swirl on upper half of body. More than 10% white.
Chester White	United States; chiefly in Chester and Delaware counties of Pennsylvania.	White. Small bluish spots are sometimes found on the skin, but are discriminated against.			Not two-thirds big enough for age, upright ears, off colored hair, spots on hide larger than a silver dollar, cryptorchidism in males, hernia in males or females, or swirls on body above flanks.
CPF No. 1 (Developed from San Pierre X Beltsville No. 1)	Conner Prairie Farm, Noblesville, Ind.; beginning in 1956, accepted for registry in 1964.	Black and white.	Fairly long snout; trim jowl; moderate size, drooping ears.	Moderately long and well muscled.	
CPF No. 2 (25% Yorkshire, 25% Beltsville No. 1, 50% Maryland No. 1)	Conner Prairie Farm, Noblesville, Ind.; beginning in 1959, accepted for registry in 1964.	Black and white.	Fairly short snout, small ears that jut forward.	Fairly long body and length of leg, trim middle.	

(Continued)

TABLE 2.S.49 (*Continued*)

Breed	Place of Origin	Color	Distinctive Head Characteristics	Other Distinguishing Characteristics	Disqualifications
Duroc	United States; chiefly in New York and New Jersey.	Red, varying from light to dark.	Medium size ear, tipping forward.		White feet or white spots on any part of body, any white on end of nose, black spots larger than 2 in. in diameter, swirls on upper half of the body or neck, ridgeling (one testicle) boars, or less than 6 udder sections on either side.
Hampshire	United States; in Boone County, Kentucky.	Black, with a white belt around the shoulders and body, including the front legs.	Longer and straighter in the face than most breeds; ears carried erect.		Any white on head other than front of snout, white on hind legs higher than bottom of ham, more than 2/3 of body white, solid black, white from belt running back on underline to meet white on hind quarters, an incomplete belt, one or both front legs black, a swirl, boar with one testicle, more than 2/3 undersize, or evidence of tampering to conceal faulty conformation or color markings.
Hereford	United States; by R. U. Webber of La Plata, Missouri.	Red body color, with white face, legs, and switch similar to Hereford cattle.			A white belt extending over shoulders, back, or rump; more than 2/3 white markings; no white markings on face; fewer than 2 white feet; a swirl; no marks or identification; boar with one testicle; or permanent deformities of any kind.
Kentucky Red Berkshire	United States; in Kentucky.	Red	Short upturned nose, dished face, and erect ears.		
Lacombe (55% Landrace, 23% Berkshire, and 22% Chester White)	Canada; at the Experimental Farm Lacombe, Alberta, beginning in 1947.	White	Medium-sized flop ears and a medium length, slightly dished face.	Of the 3 parent breeds, it resembles the Landrace most closely.	
Maryland No. 1 (62% Landrace X 38% Berkshire)	United States; by the USDA and the U. of Maryland, beginning in 1941.	Black and white spotted.	The ears are erect or slightly drooping and intermediate in size.		
Minnesota No. 1 (48% Landrace X 52% Tamworth)	United States; by the USDA and the U. of Minnesota, beginning in 1936.	Red with occasional small black spots.	Long face, trim jowls, and fairly erect ears.	Long-bodied, short-legged, light shoulders, and a relatively straight back.	
Minnesota No. 2 (40% Yorkshire and 60% Poland China)	United States; by the U. of Minnesota, beginning in 1941.	Black and white.	Ears of medium size, with erect carriage. Snout is shorter than Minnesota No. 1.		
Minnesota No. 3 (From following 8 lines or breeds: Gloucester Old Spot, Welsh, Large White, C-Line Poland, Beltsville No. 2, Minnesota No. 1, Minnesota No. 2, and San Pierre)	Rosemount Experiment Station, Rosemount, Minn.; breeding stock first released in 1957.	Black and red spotted; or black and white.	Moderately dished face, trim jowl, ears tilted forward and slightly erect.	Noted for rapid growth and ruggedness.	

TABLE 2.S.49 (*Continued*)

Breed	Place of Origin	Color	Distinctive Head Characteristics	Other Distinguishing Characteristics	Disqualifications
Montana No. 1 (55% Landrace X 45% Hampshire)	United States; in Montana, by the USDA and Montana State University, beginning in 1936.	Black	Drooping ears.		
OIC (Ohio Improved Chester)	United States; in Ohio, by L. B. Silver of Salem, Ohio.	White	Wide, short head and smooth dished face. Ears droop slightly.		Swirls on upper half of body, hernia, cryptorchidism, spots on skin with other than white hair, or inverted nipples.
Palouse (65% Landrace and 35% Chester White)	United States; by Washington State University, beginning in 1945.	White	Head is moderate in length; the ears are somewhat erect but inclined forward.		
Poland China	United States; in Ohio, in the Miami Valley of Warren and Butler Counties.	Black or black with white spots, with 6 white points—the feet, face, and tip of the tail.	Drooping ears		Fewer than 6 teats on a side, a swirl on upper half of body, hernia, or cryptorchidism.
Spotted	United States, chiefly in Indiana.	Spotted black and white, 50% each.		Must have at least six prominent teats on each side to be eligible for show or sale.	Brown or sandy spots; less than 20% or more than 80% white on body; boar with a swirl; small upright ears; not over half normal size; cramped or deformed feet; seriously diseased, barren or blind; or if scoring fewer than 60 points.
Tamworth	England; in the central counties of Stafford, Leicester, Warwick, and Northampton.	Red, varying from light to dark. Black spots may occur, but are objectionable.	Wide between the ears, snout moderately long and straight, neat jowl, and medium size, erect ears.		Swirls.
Wessex Saddleback	Hampshire, England.	Black, with a white belt around the shoulders and body including the front legs.	Fairly long snout, medium sized ears with forward pitch, trim jowl.		
Yorkshire (known as the Large White in England)	England	White, although black "freckles" appear.	Slightly dished face, and erect ears.		Swirls on upper third of body, hernia, hair color other than white, cryptorchidism, hermaphrodite, blind or inverted teats, total blindness, or fewer than 6 teats on each side.

SOURCE: ENSMINGER, M. E. 1969. Animal Science. Interstate Printers and Publishers, Danville, Illinois. Reproduced with permission of the publisher.

SWINE MARKET CLASSES AND GRADES

TABLE 2.S.50

MARKET CLASSES AND GRADES OF HOGS

Hogs or Pigs	Use Selection	Sex Class	Weight Divisions (lbs.)	Weight Divisions (kg)	Commonly Used Grades
Hogs	Slaughter hogs	Barrows and Gilts (often called butcher hogs)	120-140 140-160 160-180 180-200 200-220 220-240 240-270 270-300 300-330 330-360 360-400 400 lbs. up	55-64 64-73 73-82 82-91 91-100 100-109 109-123 123-136 136-150 150-163 163-182 182 up	U.S. No. 1, U.S. No. 2, U.S. No. 3, U.S. No. 4, U.S. Utility.
		Sows (or packing sows)	270-300 300-330 330-360 360-400 400-450 450-500 500-600 600 lbs. up	123-136 136-150 150-163 163-182 182-204 204-227 227-272 272 up	U.S. No. 1, U.S. No. 2, U.S. No. 3, U.S. No. 4, U.S. Utility.
		Stags	All weights		Ungraded
		Boars	All weights		Ungraded
	Feeder hogs	Barrows and Gilts	120-140 140-160 160-180	55-64 64-73 73-82	U.S. No. 1, U.S. No. 2, U.S. No. 3, U.S. No. 4, U.S. Utility, Cull.
Pigs	Slaughter pigs	Barrows, Gilts, and Boars	Under 30 30-60	13.6 13.6-27.2	Ungraded
		Barrows and Gilts	60-80 80-100 100-120	27.2-36.3 36.3-45.4 45.4-54.5	Ungraded
	Feeder pigs	Barrows and Gilts	80-100 100-120	36.3-45.4 45.4-54.5	U.S. No. 1, U.S. No. 2, U.S. No. 3, U.S. No. 4, U.S. Utility, Cull.

SOURCE: ENSMINGER, M. E. 1969. Animal Science. Interstate Printers and Publishers, Danville, Illinois. Reproduced with permission of the publisher.

T

TALLOW, BEEF, TRIGLYCERIDE MOLE PERCENT COMPOSITION

0 *Double Bonds*	
PMP	0.5
PMSt	1.0
StMSt	0.5
MPM	0.4
MPP	0.5
MPSt	0.5
PPP	1.7
PPSt	3.6
StPSt	1.8
MStM	0.3
MStP	0.4
MStSt	0.5
PStP	1.6
PStSt	3.2
StStSt	1.6
Remaining ones	0.3
1 *trans Double Bond*	
PEP[1]	0.3
PESt	0.5
PME	0.4
StME	0.4
PPE	0.8
StPE	0.7
PStE	0.6
StStE	0.6
Remaining ones	0.8
1 *cis Double Bond*	
MOP	0.5
MOSt	0.5
POP	5.8
POSt	10.5
StOSt	4.8
PMO	1.5
StMO	1.4
PPO	3.9
StPO	3.6
PStO	1.6
StStO	1.5
Transglycerides	4.5
Remaining ones	0.2
2 *cis Double Bonds*	
MOO	0.6
POO	12.1
StOO	5.9
OMO	0.5
OPO	2.1
OStO	0.5
PPL	0.3
StPL	0.2
PLP	0.5
PLSt	0.4
Transglycerides	2.3
Remaining ones	0.4
3 *cis Double Bonds*	
OOO	4.9
POL	0.8
StOL	0.4
PLO	0.7
StLO	0.3
OPL	0.6
OStL	0.2
PPLe	0.1
StPLe	0.1
PStLe	0.3
Transglycerides	1.6
Remaining ones	0.4

[1] E = Elaidic acid.

SOURCE: BOEKENOOGEN, H. A. (EDITOR). 1968. Oil, Fats and Fat Products, Vol. 2. John Wiley & Sons, New York.

TANGERINE OIL COMPOSITION

TABLE 2.T.1

CHEMICAL COMPOSITION OF TANGERINE OIL

TERPENES:

$\triangle_3$-carene
$\triangle^3$-carene
α,β-phellandrene
α-pinene
β-pinene
β-myrcene
d-limonene
α-terpinene
p-cymene
α-terpinolene
α-thujene
camphene
△-elemene
copaene
pentadecane
?
β-elemene
caryophllene
α-elemene
α,β-humulene
$C_{15}H_{24}$
$C_{15}H_{24}$
△-cadinene
sabinene
β-ocimene

ALDEHYDES:

octanal
decanal
undecanal
dodecanal
perilla
citral {neral, geranial}

ALCOHOLS:

citronellol
heptanol
octanol
nonanol
decanol
dodecanol
α,β-sabinol
linalool
citronellol
nerol
benzyl
trimethyl-benzyl
geraniol
terpinen-4-ol
α-terpineol
cis, trans-carveol
cis, trans-2,8-p-menthadiene-1-ol
1,8-p-menthadiene-9-ol
elemol
thymol
8-p-menthene-1,2-diol
1-p-menthene-9-ol

ESTERS:

decyl acetate
geranyl acetate
linalyl acetate
terpinyl acetate
methyl N-methylanthranilate

KETONES:

carvone

PHENOLS:

1,8-cineol
thymol
o-phenylphenol

ACIDS:

heptoic
caprylic
pelargonic
citronellic
capric
undecanoic
lauric

FLAVONE:

tangeretin

SOURCE: KESTERSON, J. W., HENDRICKSON, R., and BRADDOCK, R. J. 1971. Florida Citrus Oils. Florida Agric. Expt. Sta. Tech. Bull. *749*.

TANGERINE OIL PROPERTIES

TABLE 2.T.2

MAXIMUM AND MINIMUM VALUES FOR THE PHYSICOCHEMICAL PROPERTIES OF TANGERINE OILS

Type oil	Coldpressed						De-oiler
	Screw Press		FMC rotary		FMC in-line		
	Max.	Min.	Max.	Min.	Max.	Min.	
Number samples	4		3		20		1
Sp. grav. 25°C/25°C	0.8447	0.8445	0.8474	0.8454	0.8473	0.8449	0.8407
Ref. ind. η_D^{20}	1.4739	1.4738	1.4744	1.4734	1.4752	1.4736	1.4720
Ref. ind. 10% dist. η_D^{20}	1.4721	1.4720	1.4726	1.4711	1.4722	1.4713	—
Difference	0.0018	0.0018	0.0026	0.0018	0.0034	0.0015	—
Opt. rot. α_D^{25}	+93.31	+90.11	+91.18	+90.09	+93.75	+90.64	+93.67
Opt. rot. 10% dist. α_D^{25}	+94.86	+94.42	+94.21	+92.68	+96.26	+92.54	—
Difference	+4.75	+1.11	+4.12	+1.50	+4.00	+1.55	—
Aldehyde, %	1.02	0.96	1.08	0.95	1.23	1.09	1.24
Ester content, %	—	—	1.44	0.34	—	—	0.25
Evap. res., %	2.75	2.46	4.83	4.04	4.75	2.75	0.20
U.V. spectrum mμ log $E_{100\ ml}^{0.25\ g}$							
CD 1.	0.530	0.425	—	—	1.576	0.410	—
2.	0.350	0.250	—	—	0.450	0.100	—
Peak 1.	1.130	0.920	—	—	3.580	0.810	—
2.	1.430	1.310	—	—	3.080	1.099	—
mμ 1.	325	324	—	—	328.8	322.0	—
2.	270	268	—	—	272.8	266.0	—

SOURCE: KESTERSON, J. W., HENDRICKSON, R., and BRADDOCK, R. J. 1971. Florida Citrus Oils. Florida Agric. Expt. Sta. Tech. Bull. *749*.

TASTE PANEL, DIFFERENCE TESTS

TABLE 2.T.3

TYPES OF DIFFERENCE TESTS

Name	Method of presentation	Standard	Response	Probability
Single stimulus (A not A)	"A" or "B" A | ? ? ? ? . . .	One present and designated at onset of test and can be reintroduced	"A" or "not A"; "like A" or "not like A"	1/2
Paired comparison	A B or A A or B B or B A ? ? ? ? ? ? ? ?	Subjective	"Different" or "Not different"	1/2
Paired comparison	A B ? ?	Subjective	Which is saltier?, Which is tougher, etc.	1/2
Duo-trio	A | A B | ? ?	One present and designated	Which is the different sample? or Which is the same as A?	1/2
Triangle	A A B or A B B ? ? ? ? ? ?	None designated; criterion is within test	Which is the odd sample?	1/3
Triangle	A A B or A B B ? ? ? ? ? ?	None designated; criterion is within test	Which is sweeter? More acid? etc.	1/6
Dual standard	A B | A B | ? ?	Two present and designated	Which is A and which is B?	1/2
Multiple standard[a]	B ? A A A ? ? ?	None designated; criterion is within test	Which is *most* different?	1/4 (or less)
Multiple pairs	A B A B ? ? ? ? B A B A ? ? ? ?	None designated; criterion is within test	Which are A and which are B?	1/35[b]

[a] Used where standard is nonhomogeneous; all samples presented simultaneously.
[b] As shown for all correct; various higher probabilities for partially correct responses.
Adapted from Peryam (1958).

SOURCE: AMERINE, M. A., PANGBORN, R. M., and ROESSLER, E. B. Principles of Sensory Evaluation of Food. Academic Press, New York.

TEETH ERUPTION

TABLE 2.T.4

ERUPTION OF THE TEETH OF ANIMALS

	Horse	Ox	Sheep, Goat	Swine	Dog	Cat
Di 1	Birth to 1 week	Before birth	Birth to 1 week	2-4 weeks	4-5 weeks	2-3 weeks
Di 2	4-6 weeks	Before birth	1-2 weeks	6-12 weeks	4-5 weeks	3-4 weeks
Di 3	6-9 months	Birth to 1 week	2-3 weeks	Before birth	5-6 weeks	3-4 weeks
I 1	2½ years	1½-2 years	1-1½ years	1 year	2-5 months	3½-4 months
I 2	3½ years	2-2½ years	1½-2 years	16-20 months	2-5 months	3½-4 months
I 3	4½ years	3 years	2½-3 years	8-10 months	4-5 months	4-4½ months
Dc	Does not erupt	Birth to 2 weeks[1]	3-4 weeks[1]	Before birth	3-4 weeks	3-4 weeks
C	4½-5 years	3½-4 years[1]	3-4 years[1]	6-10 months	5-6 months	5 months
Dp 2	Birth to 2 weeks	Birth to 3 weeks	Birth to 4 weeks	5-7 weeks	4-6 weeks	Upper: 2 months Lower: none
Dp 3	Birth to 2 weeks	Birth to 3 weeks	Birth to 4 weeks	1-4 weeks	4-6 weeks	4-5 weeks
Dp 4	Birth to 2 weeks	Birth to 3 weeks	Birth to 4 weeks	1-4 weeks	6-8 weeks	4-6 weeks
P 1	5-6 months (wolf tooth)	None	None	5 months	4-5 months	None
P 2	2½ years	2-2½ years	1½-2 years	12-15 months	5-6 months	Upper: 4½-5 mo. Lower: none
P 3	3 years	1½-2½ years	1½-2 years	12-15 months	5-6 months	5-6 months
P 4	4 years	2½-3 years	1½-2 years	12-15 months	4-5 months	5-6 months
M 1	9-12 months	5-6 months	3-5 months	4-6 months	5-6 months	4-5 months
M 2	2 years	1-1½ years	9-12 months	8-12 months	6-7 months	None
M 3	3½-4 years	2-2½ years	1½-2 years	18-20 months	6-7 months	None

[1] The canine tooth of domestic ruminants has commonly been accounted a fourth incisor.

SOURCE: The Merck Veterinary Manual, 4th Edition. Merck & Co., Rahway, N.J., 1973.

TEMPERATURE

TABLE 2.T.5

CENTIGRADE AND FAHRENHEIT CONVERSION TABLE

INTERPOLATION FACTORS

$$C = \frac{5}{9}(F - 32)$$

$$F = \frac{9}{5}C + 32$$

Kelvin (Absolute)

$$°K = °C + 273.15$$

C°	↓	F°	C°	↓	F°	C°	↓	F°
0.56	1	1.8	2.22	4	7.2	3.89	7	12.6
1.11	2	3.6	2.78	5	9.0	4.44	8	14.4
1.67	3	5.4	3.33	6	10.8	5.00	9	16.2

Enter table at arrow with the temperature you have; Equivalent Fahrenheit is found 1 column to right and equivalent Centigrade temperature 1 column to the left.

C°	↓	F°	C°	↓	F°	C°	↓	F°
-156.7	-250	-418.0	-112.2	-170	-274.0	-72.8	-99	-146.2
-151.1	-240	-400.0	-106.7	-160	-256.0	-72.2	-98	-144.4
-145.6	-230	-382.0	-101.1	-150	-238.0	-71.7	-97	-142.6
-140.0	-220	-364.0	-95.6	-140	-220.0	-71.1	-96	-140.8
-134.4	-210	-346.0	-90.0	-130	-202.0	-70.6	-95	-139.0
-128.9	-200	-328.0	-84.4	-120	-184.0	-70.0	-94	-137.2
-123.3	-190	-310.0	-78.9	-110	-166.0	-69.4	-93	-135.4
-117.8	-180	-292.0	-73.3	-100	-148.0	-68.9	-92	-133.6

(Continued)

TABLE 2.T.5 (*Continued*)

C°	↓	F°	C°	↓	F°	C°	↓	F°
-68.3	-91	-131.8	-34.4	-30	-22.0	-0.56	31	87.8
-67.8	-90	-130.0	-33.9	-29	-20.2	0.00	32	89.6
-67.2	-89	-128.2	-33.3	-28	-18.4	0.56	33	91.4
-66.7	-88	-126.4	-32.8	-27	-16.6	1.11	34	93.2
-66.1	-87	-124.6	-32.2	-26	-14.8	1.67	35	95.0
-65.6	-86	-122.8	-31.7	-25	-13.0	2.22	36	96.8
-65.0	-85	-121.0	-31.1	-24	-11.2	2.78	37	98.6
-64.4	-84	-119.2	-30.6	-23	-9.4	3.33	38	100.4
-63.9	-83	-117.4	-30.0	-22	-7.6	3.89	39	102.2
-63.3	-82	-115.6	-29.4	-21	-5.8	4.44	40	104.0
-62.8	-81	-113.8	-28.9	-20	-4.0	5.00	41	105.8
-62.2	-80	-112.0	-28.3	-19	-2.2	5.56	42	107.6
-61.7	-79	-110.2	-27.8	-18	-0.4	6.11	43	109.4
-61.1	-78	-108.4	-27.2	-17	1.4	6.67	44	111.2
-60.6	-77	-106.6	-26.7	-16	3.2	7.22	45	113.0
-60.0	-76	-104.8	-26.1	-15	5.0	7.78	46	114.8
-59.4	-75	-103.0	-25.6	-14	6.8	8.33	47	116.6
-58.9	-74	-101.2	-25.0	-13	8.6	8.89	48	118.4
-58.3	-73	-99.4	-24.4	-12	10.4	9.44	49	120.2
-57.8	-72	-97.6	-23.9	-11	12.2	10.00	50	122.0
-57.2	-71	-95.8	-23.3	-10	14.0	10.56	51	123.8
-56.7	-70	-94.0	-22.8	-9	15.8	11.11	52	125.6
-56.1	-69	-92.2	-22.2	-8	17.6	11.67	53	127.4
-55.6	-68	-90.4	-21.7	-7	19.4	12.22	54	129.2
-55.0	-67	-88.6	-21.1	-6	21.2	12.78	55	131.0
-54.4	-66	-86.8	-20.6	-5	23.0	13.33	56	132.8
-53.9	-65	-85.0	-20.0	-4	24.8	13.89	57	134.6
-53.3	-64	-83.2	-19.4	-3	26.6	14.44	58	136.4
-52.8	-63	-81.4	-18.9	-2	28.4	15.00	59	138.2
-52.2	-62	-79.6	-18.3	-1	30.2	15.56	60	140.0
-51.7	-61	-77.8	-17.78	0	32.0	16.11	61	141.8
-51.1	-60	-76.0	-17.22	1	33.8	16.67	62	143.6
-50.6	-59	-74.2	-16.67	2	35.6	17.22	63	145.4
-50.0	-58	-72.4	-16.11	3	37.4	17.78	64	147.2
-49.4	-57	-70.6	-15.56	4	39.2	18.33	65	149.0
-48.9	-56	-68.8	-15.00	5	41.0	18.89	66	150.8
-48.3	-55	-67.0	-14.44	6	42.8	19.44	67	152.6
-47.8	-54	-65.2	-13.89	7	44.6	20.00	68	154.4
-47.2	-53	-63.4	-13.33	8	46.4	20.56	69	156.2
-46.7	-52	-61.6	-12.78	9	48.2	21.11	70	158.0
-46.1	-51	-59.8	-12.22	10	50.0	21.67	71	159.8
-45.6	-50	-58.0	-11.67	11	51.8	22.22	72	161.6
-45.0	-49	-56.2	-11.11	12	53.6	22.78	73	163.4
-44.4	-48	-54.4	-10.56	13	55.4	23.33	74	165.2
-43.9	-47	-52.6	-10.00	14	57.2	23.89	75	167.0
-43.3	-46	-50.8	-9.44	15	59.0	24.44	76	168.8
-42.8	-45	-49.0	-8.89	16	60.8	25.00	77	170.6
-42.2	-44	-47.2	-8.33	17	62.6	25.56	78	172.4
-41.7	-43	-45.4	-7.78	18	64.4	26.11	79	174.2
-41.1	-42	-43.6	-7.22	19	66.2	26.67	80	176.0
-40.6	-41	-41.8	-6.67	20	68.0	27.22	81	177.8
-40.0	-40	-40.0	-6.11	21	69.8	27.78	82	179.6
-39.4	-39	-38.2	-5.56	22	71.6	28.33	83	181.4
-38.9	-38	-36.4	-5.00	23	73.4	28.89	84	183.2
-38.3	-37	-34.6	-4.44	24	75.2	29.44	85	185.0
-37.8	-36	-32.8	-3.89	25	77.0	30.00	86	186.8
-37.2	-35	-31.0	-3.33	26	78.8	30.56	87	188.6
-36.7	-34	-29.2	-2.78	27	80.6	31.11	88	190.4
-36.1	-33	-27.4	-2.22	28	82.4	31.67	89	192.2
-35.6	-32	-25.6	-1.67	29	84.2	32.22	90	194.0
-35.0	-31	-23.8	-1.11	30	86.0	32.78	91	195.8

TABLE 2.T.5 (*Continued*)

C°	↓	F°	C°	↓	F°	C°	↓	F°
33.33	92	197.6	67.22	153	307.4	101.11	214	417.2
33.89	93	199.4	67.78	154	309.2	101.67	215	419.0
34.44	94	201.2	68.33	155	311.0	102.22	216	420.8
35.00	95	203.0	68.89	156	312.8	102.78	217	422.6
35.56	96	204.8	69.44	157	314.6	103.33	218	424.4
36.11	97	206.6	70.00	158	316.4	103.89	219	426.2
36.67	98	208.4	70.56	159	318.2	104.44	220	428.0
37.22	99	210.2	71.11	160	320.0	105.00	221	429.8
37.78	100	212.0	71.67	161	321.8	105.56	222	431.6
38.33	101	213.8	72.22	162	323.6	106.11	223	433.4
38.89	102	215.6	72.78	163	325.4	106.67	224	435.2
39.44	103	217.4	73.33	164	327.2	107.22	225	437.0
40.00	104	219.2	73.89	165	329.0	107.78	226	438.8
40.56	105	221.0	74.44	166	330.8	108.33	227	440.6
41.11	106	222.8	75.00	167	332.6	108.89	228	442.4
41.67	107	224.6	75.56	168	334.4	109.44	229	444.2
42.22	108	226.4	76.11	169	336.2	110.00	230	446.0
42.78	109	228.2	76.67	170	338.0	110.56	231	447.8
43.33	110	230.0	77.22	171	339.8	111.11	232	449.6
43.89	111	231.8	77.78	172	341.6	111.67	233	451.4
44.44	112	233.6	78.33	173	343.4	112.22	234	453.2
45.00	113	235.4	78.89	174	345.2	112.78	235	455.0
45.56	114	237.2	79.44	175	347.0	113.33	236	456.8
46.11	115	239.0	80.00	176	348.8	113.89	237	458.6
46.67	116	240.8	80.56	177	350.6	114.44	238	460.4
47.22	117	242.6	81.11	178	352.4	115.00	239	462.2
47.78	118	244.4	81.67	179	354.2	115.56	240	464.0
48.33	119	246.2	82.22	180	356.0	116.11	241	465.8
48.89	120	248.0	82.78	181	357.8	116.67	242	467.6
49.44	121	249.8	83.33	182	359.6	117.22	243	469.4
50.00	122	251.6	83.89	183	361.4	117.78	244	471.2
50.56	123	253.4	84.44	184	363.2	118.33	245	473.0
51.11	124	255.2	85.00	185	365.0	118.89	246	474.8
51.67	125	257.0	85.56	186	366.8	119.44	247	476.6
52.22	126	258.8	86.11	187	368.6	120.00	248	478.4
52.78	127	260.6	86.67	188	370.4	120.56	249	480.2
53.33	128	262.4	87.22	189	372.2	121.11	250	482.0
53.89	129	264.2	87.78	190	374.0	121.67	251	483.8
54.44	130	266.0	88.33	191	375.8	122.22	252	485.6
55.00	131	267.8	88.89	192	377.6	122.78	253	487.4
55.56	132	269.6	89.44	193	379.4	123.33	254	489.2
56.11	133	271.4	90.00	194	381.2	123.89	255	491.0
56.67	134	273.2	90.56	195	383.0	124.44	256	492.8
57.22	135	275.0	91.11	196	384.8	125.00	257	494.6
57.78	136	276.8	91.67	197	386.6	125.56	258	496.4
58.33	137	278.6	92.22	198	388.4	126.11	259	498.2
58.89	138	280.4	92.78	199	390.2	126.67	260	500.0
59.44	139	282.2	93.33	200	392.0	127.22	261	501.8
60.00	140	284.0	93.89	201	393.8	127.78	262	503.6
60.56	141	285.8	94.44	202	395.6	128.33	263	505.4
61.11	142	287.6	95.00	203	397.4	128.89	264	507.2
61.67	143	289.4	95.56	204	399.2	129.44	265	509.0
62.22	144	291.2	96.11	205	401.0	130.00	266	510.8
62.78	145	293.0	96.67	206	402.8	130.56	267	512.6
63.33	146	294.8	97.22	207	404.6	131.11	268	514.4
63.89	147	296.6	97.78	208	406.4	131.67	269	516.2
64.44	148	298.4	98.33	209	408.2	132.22	270	518.0
65.00	149	300.2	98.89	210	410.0	132.78	271	519.8
65.56	150	302.0	99.44	211	411.8	133.33	272	521.6
66.11	151	303.8	100.00	212	413.6	133.89	273	523.4
66.67	152	305.6	100.56	213	415.4	134.44	274	525.2

(Continued)

TABLE 2.T.5 (*Continued*)

C°	↓	F°	C°	↓	F°	C°	↓	F°
135.00	275	527.0	170.56	339	642.2	206.11	403	757.4
135.56	276	528.8	171.11	340	644.0	206.67	404	759.2
136.11	277	530.6	171.67	341	645.8	207.22	405	761.0
136.67	278	532.4	172.22	342	647.6	207.78	406	762.8
137.22	279	534.2	172.78	343	649.4	208.33	407	764.6
137.78	280	536.0	173.33	344	651.2	208.89	408	766.4
138.33	281	537.8	173.89	345	653.0	209.44	409	768.2
138.89	282	539.6	174.44	346	654.8	210.00	410	770.0
139.44	283	541.4	175.00	347	656.6	210.56	411	771.8
140.00	284	543.2	175.56	348	658.4	211.11	412	773.6
140.56	285	545.0	176.11	349	660.2	211.67	413	775.4
141.11	286	546.8	176.67	350	662.0	212.22	414	777.2
141.67	287	548.6	177.22	351	663.8	212.78	415	779.0
142.22	288	550.4	177.78	352	665.6	213.33	416	780.8
142.78	289	552.2	178.33	353	667.4	213.89	417	782.6
143.33	290	554.0	178.89	354	669.2	214.44	418	784.4
143.89	291	555.8	179.44	355	671.0	215.00	419	786.2
144.44	292	557.6	180.00	356	672.8	215.56	420	788.0
145.00	293	559.4	180.56	357	674.6	216.11	421	789.8
145.56	294	561.2	181.11	358	676.4	216.67	422	791.6
146.11	295	563.0	181.67	359	678.2	217.22	423	793.4
146.67	296	564.8	182.22	360	680.0	217.78	424	795.2
147.22	297	566.6	182.78	361	681.8	218.33	425	797.0
147.78	298	568.4	183.33	362	683.6	218.89	426	798.8
148.33	299	570.2	183.89	363	685.4	219.44	427	800.6
148.89	300	572.0	184.44	364	687.2	220.00	428	802.4
149.44	301	573.8	185.00	365	689.0	220.56	429	804.2
150.00	302	575.6	185.56	366	690.8	221.11	430	806.0
150.56	303	577.4	186.11	367	692.6	221.67	431	807.8
151.11	304	579.2	186.67	368	694.4	222.22	432	809.6
151.67	305	581.0	187.22	369	696.2	222.78	433	811.4
152.22	306	582.8	187.78	370	698.0	223.33	434	813.2
152.78	307	584.6	188.33	371	699.8	223.89	435	815.0
153.33	308	586.4	188.89	372	701.6	224.44	436	816.8
153.89	309	588.2	189.44	373	703.4	225.00	437	818.6
154.44	310	590.0	190.00	374	705.2	225.56	438	820.4
155.00	311	591.8	190.56	375	707.0	226.11	439	822.2
155.56	312	593.6	191.11	376	708.8	226.67	440	824.0
156.11	313	595.4	191.67	377	710.6	227.22	441	825.8
156.67	314	597.2	192.22	378	712.4	227.78	442	827.6
157.22	315	599.0	192.78	379	714.2	228.33	443	829.4
157.78	316	600.8	193.33	380	716.0	228.89	444	831.2
158.33	317	602.6	193.89	381	717.8	229.44	445	833.0
158.89	318	604.4	194.44	382	719.6	230.00	446	834.8
159.44	319	606.2	195.00	383	721.4	230.56	447	836.6
160.00	320	608.0	195.56	384	723.2	231.11	448	838.4
160.56	321	609.8	196.11	385	725.0	231.67	449	840.2
161.11	322	611.6	196.67	386	726.8	232.22	450	842.0
161.67	323	613.4	197.22	387	728.6	232.78	451	843.8
162.22	324	615.2	197.78	388	730.4	233.33	452	845.6
162.78	325	617.0	198.33	389	732.2	233.89	453	847.4
163.33	326	618.8	198.89	390	734.0	234.44	454	849.2
163.89	327	620.6	199.44	391	735.8	235.00	455	851.0
164.44	328	622.4	200.00	392	737.6	235.56	456	852.8
165.00	329	624.2	200.56	393	739.4	236.11	457	854.6
165.56	330	626.0	201.11	394	741.2	236.67	458	856.4
166.11	331	627.8	201.67	395	743.0	237.22	459	858.2
166.67	332	629.6	202.22	396	744.8	237.78	460	860.0
167.22	333	631.4	202.78	397	746.6	238.33	461	861.8
167.78	334	633.2	203.33	398	748.4	238.89	462	863.6
168.33	335	635.0	203.89	399	750.2	239.44	463	865.4
168.89	336	636.8	204.44	400	752.0	240.00	464	867.2
169.44	337	638.6	205.00	401	753.8	240.56	465	869.0
170.00	338	640.4	205.56	402	755.6	241.11	466	870.8

TABLE 2.T.5 (*Continued*)

C°	↓	F°	C°	↓	F°	C°	↓	F°
241.67	467	872.6	421.11	790	1454	765.56	1410	2570
242.22	468	874.4	426.67	800	1472	771.11	1420	2588
242.78	469	876.2	432.22	810	1490	776.67	1430	2606
243.33	470	878.0	437.78	820	1508	782.22	1440	2624
243.89	471	879.8	443.33	830	1526	787.78	1450	2642
244.44	472	881.6	448.89	840	1544	793.33	1460	2660
245.00	473	883.4	454.44	850	1562	798.89	1470	2678
245.56	474	885.2	460.00	860	1580	804.44	1480	2696
246.11	475	887.0	465.56	870	1598	810.00	1490	2714
246.67	476	888.8	471.11	880	1616	815.56	1500	2732
247.22	477	890.6	476.67	890	1634	821.11	1510	2750
247.78	478	892.4	482.22	900	1652	826.67	1520	2768
248.33	479	894.2	487.78	910	1670	832.22	1530	2786
248.89	480	896.0	493.33	920	1688	837.78	1540	2804
249.44	481	897.8	498.89	930	1706	843.33	1550	2822
250.00	482	899.6	504.44	940	1724	848.89	1560	2840
250.56	483	901.4	510.00	950	1742	854.44	1570	2858
251.11	484	903.2	515.56	960	1760	860.00	1580	2876
251.67	485	905.0	521.11	970	1778	865.55	1590	2894
252.22	486	906.8	526.67	980	1796	871.11	1600	2912
252.78	487	908.6	532.22	990	1814	876.67	1610	2930
253.33	488	910.4	537.78	1000	1832	882.22	1620	2948
253.89	489	912.2	543.33	1010	1850	887.78	1630	2966
254.44	490	914.0	548.89	1020	1868	893.33	1640	2984
255.00	491	915.8	554.44	1030	1886	898.89	1650	3002
255.56	492	917.6	560.00	1040	1904	904.44	1660	3020
256.11	493	919.4	565.56	1050	1922	910.00	1670	3038
256.67	494	921.2	571.11	1060	1940	915.56	1680	3056
257.22	495	923.0	576.67	1070	1958	921.11	1690	3074
257.78	496	924.8	582.22	1080	1976	926.67	1700	3092
258.33	497	926.6	587.78	1090	1994	932.22	1710	3110
258.89	498	928.4	593.33	1100	2012	937.78	1720	3128
259.44	499	930.2	598.89	1110	2030	943.33	1730	3146
260.00	500	932	604.44	1120	2048	948.89	1740	3164
265.56	510	950	610.00	1130	2066	954.44	1750	3182
271.11	520	968	615.56	1140	2084	960.00	1760	3200
276.67	530	986	621.11	1150	2102	965.56	1770	3218
282.22	540	1004	626.67	1160	2120	971.11	1780	3236
287.78	550	1022	632.22	1170	2138	976.67	1790	3254
293.33	560	1040	637.78	1180	2156	982.22	1800	3272
298.89	570	1058	643.33	1190	2174	987.78	1810	3290
304.44	580	1076	648.89	1200	2192	993.33	1820	3308
310.00	590	1094	654.44	1210	2210	998.89	1830	3326
315.56	600	1112	660.00	1220	2228	1004.44	1840	3344
321.11	610	1130	665.56	1230	2246	1010.00	1850	3362
326.67	620	1148	671.11	1240	2264	1015.56	1860	3380
332.22	630	1166	676.67	1250	2282	1021.11	1870	3398
337.78	640	1184	682.22	1260	2300	1026.67	1880	3416
343.33	650	1202	687.78	1270	2318	1032.22	1890	3434
348.89	660	1220	693.33	1280	2336	1037.78	1900	3452
354.44	670	1238	698.89	1290	2354	1043.33	1910	3470
360.00	680	1256	704.44	1300	2372	1048.89	1920	3488
365.56	690	1274	710.00	1310	2390	1054.44	1930	3506
371.11	700	1292	715.56	1320	2408	1060.00	1940	3524
376.67	710	1310	721.11	1330	2426	1065.56	1950	3542
382.22	720	1328	726.67	1340	2444	1071.11	1960	3560
387.78	730	1346	732.22	1350	2462	1076.67	1970	3578
393.33	740	1364	737.78	1360	2480	1082.22	1980	3596
398.89	750	1382	743.33	1370	2498	1087.78	1990	3614
404.44	760	1400	748.89	1380	2516	1093.33	2000	3632
410.00	770	1418	754.44	1390	2534	1648.89	3000	5432
415.56	780	1436	760.00	1400	2552	2760.00	5000	9632

SOURCE: OCKERMAN, H. W. 1974. Quality Control of Post-Mortem Muscle Tissue, 9th Edition. Ohio State University, Columbus.

TEMPERATURE OF VAPORIZATION, LATENT HEAT OF VAPORIZATION, BOILING POINT

TABLE 2.T.6

RELATION BETWEEN TEMPERATURE OF VAPORIZATION, LATENT HEAT OF VAPORIZATION AND THE BOILING POINT OF WATER

Temperature °F.	Inches of Vacuum (Hg)	Latent Heat B.t.u.
32	29.82	1073.4
50	29.64	1063.3
75	29.13	1049.4
100	28.07	1035.6
125	26.04	1021.6
150	22.42	1007.4
175	16.22	992.8
200	6.47	977.9
212	0.00	970.4

SOURCE: DESROSIER, N. W. (EDITOR). 1970. *In* The Technology of Food Preservation, 3rd Edition. Avi Publishing Co., Westport, Conn.

TEMPERATURES CORRESPONDING TO GAUGE PRESSURE AT VARIOUS ALTITUDES

TABLE 2.T.7

QUIDE TO PRESSURES ABOVE SEA LEVEL

Temp.	Sea	Feet above sea level							Temp.
Deg. F.	Level	500	1000	2000	3000	4000	5000	6000	*Deg. C.*
200	....	....	....	....	....	....	....	....	93.3
205	....	....	....	....	....	....	0.5	0.9	96.1
210	....	....	....	0.4	0.9	1.4	1.8	2.3	98.9
212	0.0	0.2	0.5	1.0	1.5	2.0	2.4	2.9	100.0
215	0.9	1.1	1.4	1.9	2.4	2.9	3.3	3.8	101.7
220	2.5	2.7	3.0	3.4	3.9	4.4	4.9	5.3	104.4
225	4.2	4.5	4.7	5.2	5.7	6.2	6.6	7.1	107.2
230	6.1	6.3	6.6	7.1	7.6	8.0	8.5	9.0	110.0
235	8.1	8.3	8.6	9.1	9.6	10.0	10.5	11.0	112.8
240	10.3	10.5	10.8	11.3	11.7	12.2	12.7	13.1	115.6
242	11.2	11.4	11.7	12.2	12.7	13.1	13.6	14.1	116.7
245	12.6	12.9	13.1	13.6	14.1	14.6	15.0	15.5	118.3
248	14.1	14.3	14.6	15.1	15.6	16.0	16.5	17.0	120.0
250	15.1	15.4	15.6	16.1	16.6	17.1	17.5	18.0	121.1
252	16.2	16.4	16.7	17.2	17.7	18.1	18.6	19.1	122.2
255	17.8	18.1	18.3	18.8	19.3	19.8	20.2	20.7	123.9
260	20.7	21.0	21.2	21.7	22.2	22.7	23.1	23.6	126.7

SOURCE: Processes for Low-Acid Canned Foods in Metal Containers, 10th Edition. National Canners Association Research Laboratory, Bull. *26L*.

TENDERNESS OF POULTRY

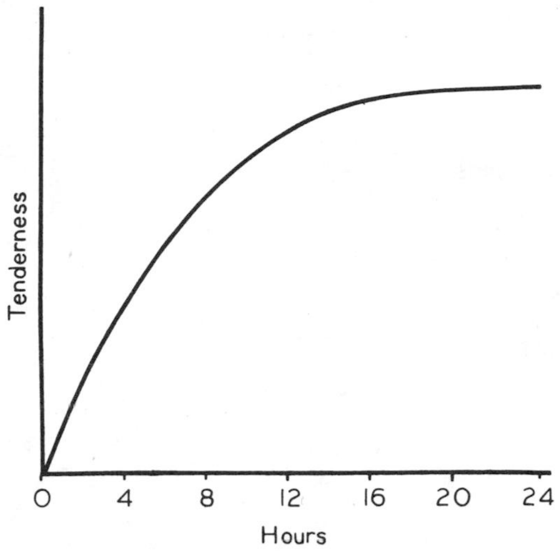

FIG. 2.T.1. EFFECT OF HOLDING TIME ON TENDERNESS OF POULTRY

The curve varies somewhat with size and kind of fowl and may vary with birds of the same lot and treatment. Maximum tenderness is reached usually at from 12 to 24 hr.

SOURCE: SNYDER, E. S., and ORR, H. L. Poultry meat. Dep. Agric. Publ. *9*, Can. Dep. Agric., Ottawa.

THERMAL-ARREST TIME

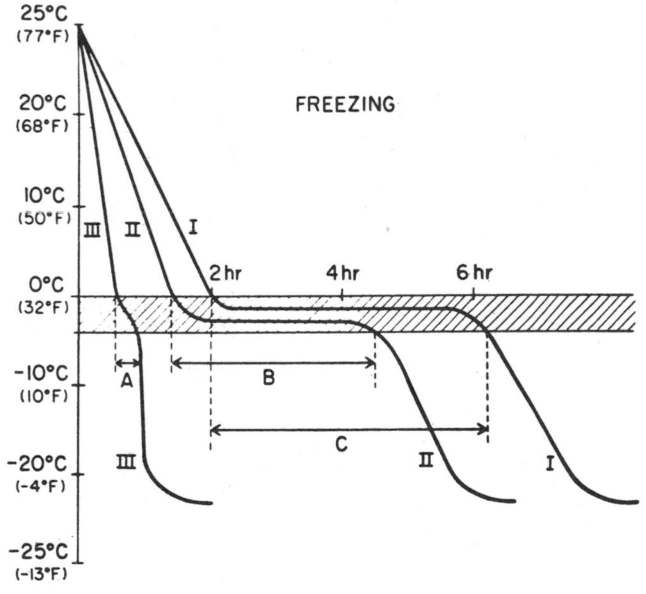

FIG. 2.T.2. THERMAL-ARREST TIME INDICATED BY A (15 MIN), B (155 MIN), AND C (250 MIN) IN THE DIAGRAM

SOURCE: BORGSTROM, G. 1968. Principles of Food Science, Vol. *1*. Macmillan Publishing Co., New York.

THERMAL-DEATH-TIME CURVE

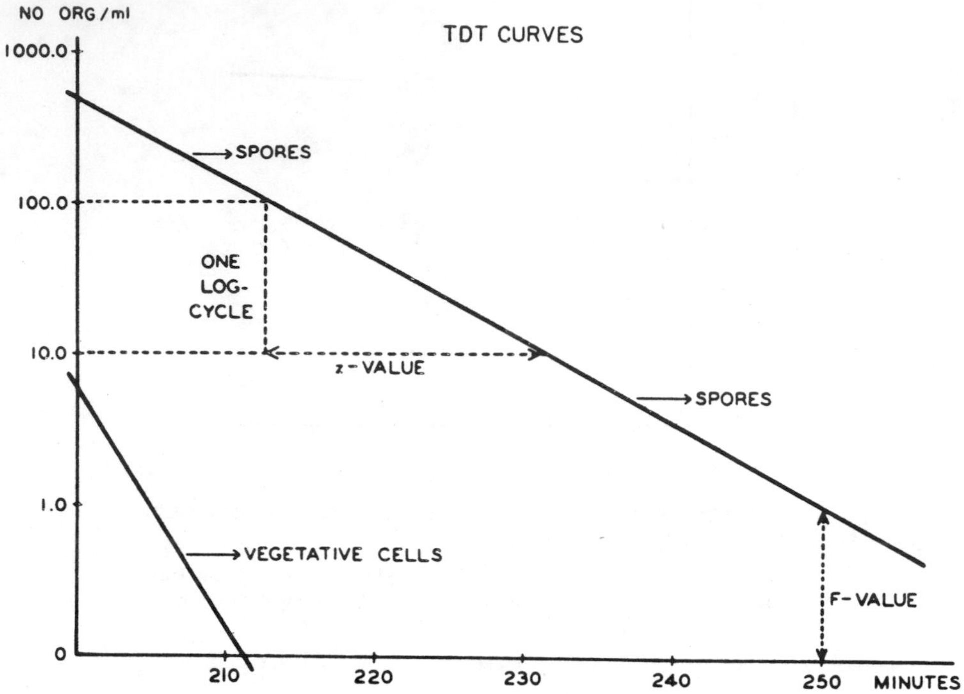

FIG. 2.T.3. THERMAL-DEATH-TIME CURVES FOR SPORES AND VEGETATIVE CELLS SHOWING z AND F VALUES

SOURCE: BORGSTROM, G. 1968. Principles of Food Science, Vol. *1*. Macmillan Publishing, Co., New York.

THERMOPHILES

TABLE 2.T.8

THERMOPHILES OF IMPORTANCE TO THE FOOD INDUSTRIES

Name	Economic Importance	Heat-Resistant Spores	Growth Temperatures Optimum Degrees F.	Growth Temperatures Range Degrees F.	Oxygen Require-ments
Streptococcus thermophilus	Grow during pasteurization of milk. Ripening agent in Swiss cheese.	None	120	77 –140	Facultative
Lactobacillus bulgaricus	Bulgaricus milk. Lactic acid manufacture.	None	120	77 –140	Facultative
Lactobacillus thermophilus	Grow during pasteurization of milk.	None	131	86 –150	Facultative
Lactobacillus delbruckii	Acidification of brewery mash. Lactic acid manufacture.	None	113	70 –140	Facultative
Bacillus calidolactis	Coagulates milk held at high temperatures.	Yes	131–149	113–167	Facultative
Bacillus thermoacidurans	Flat sour spoilage of tomato juice.	Yes	113	80 –140	Facultative
Bacillus stearothermophilus	Flat sour spoilage of canned foods.	Yes	122	113–169	Facultative
Clostridium thermo-saccharolyticum	Hard swells of canned foods.	Yes	131–143	110–160	Anaerobic
Clostridium nigrificans	Sulfide-stinkers of canned foods	Yes	131	80 –158	Anaerobic

SOURCE: DESROSIER, N. W. (EDITOR). 1970. Principles of Food Preservation by Canning. *In* The Technology of Food Preservation, 3rd Edition. Avi Publishing Co., Westport, Conn.

THIAMIN

TABLE 2.T.9

THIAMIN CONTENT OF FOODS

	Mg/100 g		Mg/100 g
Peas	0.35	Broccoli	0.10
Lima beans	0.24	Brussels sprouts	0.10
Asparagus	0.18	Oranges	0.09
Corn	0.15	Tomatoes	0.06
Cauliflower	0.11	Lettuce	0.06
Potatoes	0.10	Bananas	0.05
Watermelon	0.10	Grapefruit	0.04
Sweet potatoes	0.10	Apples	0.03
Spinach	0.10		

SOURCE: WHITE, P. L. and SELVEY, N. (EDITORS). 1974. Nutritional Qualities of Fresh Fruits and Vegetables. Futura Publishing Co., Mt. Kisco, N.Y.

THIAMIN, DAILY RECOMMENDATIONS

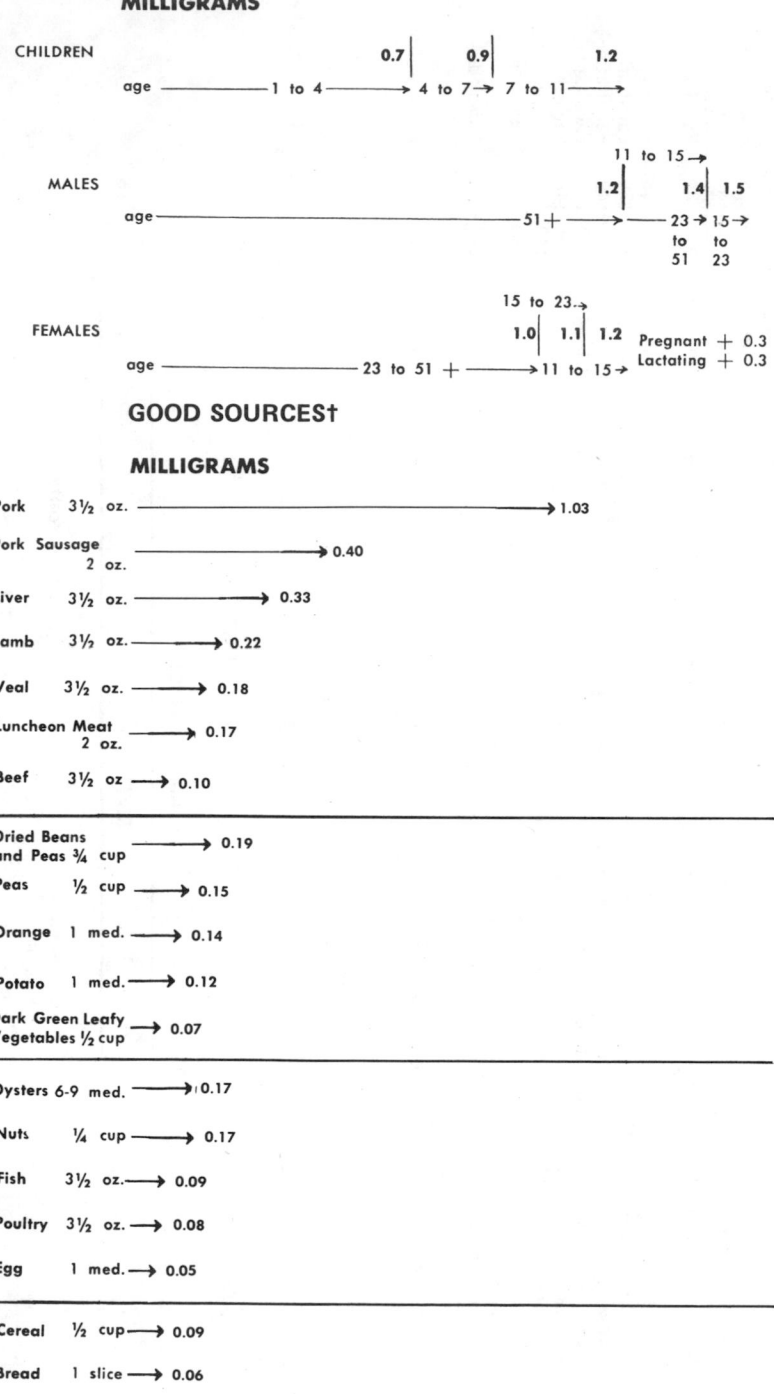

MILLIGRAMS

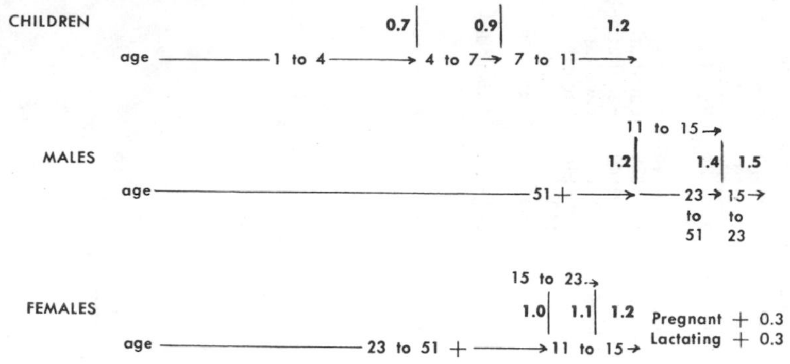

GOOD SOURCES†

MILLIGRAMS

Pork	3½ oz.	1.03
Pork Sausage	2 oz.	0.40
Liver	3½ oz.	0.33
Lamb	3½ oz.	0.22
Veal	3½ oz.	0.18
Luncheon Meat	2 oz.	0.17
Beef	3½ oz	0.10
Dried Beans and Peas	¾ cup	0.19
Peas	½ cup	0.15
Orange	1 med.	0.14
Potato	1 med.	0.12
Dark Green Leafy Vegetables	½ cup	0.07
Oysters	6-9 med.	0.17
Nuts	¼ cup	0.17
Fish	3½ oz.	0.09
Poultry	3½ oz.	0.08
Egg	1 med.	0.05
Cereal	½ cup	0.09
Bread	1 slice	0.06
Milk	1 cup	0.08

†Average nutrient content as food is served. (*Note: 3½ oz equals approximately 100 g.*)

SOURCE: Lessons on Meat. (1974). National Live Stock and Meat Board, Chicago.

THIAMIN, FOOD

TABLE 2.T.10

THIAMIN CONTENT OF FOODS, AS PURCHASED (MG PER 100 G)

Cereal Products		Fruits	0.01-0.05
Biscuits	0.035-0.060	Meat	
Bread, white	0.18	Bacon	0.40
Bread, wholemeal	0.20	Beef	0.08
Cakes	0.085-0.160	Heart	0.60
Flour, white	0.40	Kidney	0.30
Flour, wholemeal	0.28	Liver	0.30
Macaroni	0.14	Mutton	0.15
Oatmeal	0.50	Pork	1.0
Rice (highly milled)	0.08	Sausages (pork)	0.17
Semolina	0.12	Veal	0.10
Dairy Products		Nuts	0.1-1.0
Cheese	0.03	Vegetables	
Milk	0.04	Peas (green)	0.32
Eggs	0.10	Potatoes	0.10
Fish, white	0.02-0.08	Vegetables (other)	0.02-0.10
Herring	0.03	Yeast Extracts	2.4-3.0
Cod roe	1.5		

SOURCE: SINCLAIR, H. M. and HOLLINGSWORTH, D. F. 1969. Hutchison's Food and the Principles of Nutrition. Edward Arnold (Publishers), London, England.

TITER, FATS AND OILS

TABLE 2.T.11

TITER POINTS OF SOME COMMON FATS AND OILS

Fat or Oil	Titer Point °C	Fat or Oil	Titer Point °C
Babassu	22-23	Safflower	15-18
Borneo tallow	51-53	Sesame	20-25
Cacao butter	45-50	Soybean	21-23
Coconut	20-24	Sunflower	16-20
Corn	14-20	Teaseed	13-18
Cottonseed	30-37	Tung	36-37
Hempseed	14-17	Walnut	14-16
Kapok	27-32	Butterfat	33-38
Linseed	19-21	Lard	32-43
Mustard (white)	8-10	Tallow-beef	40-47
Mustard (black)	6-8	Tallow mutton	43-48
Olive	17-26	Horse fat	34-38
Palm kernel	20-28	Cod liver	18-24
Palm	40-47	Sardine	27-28
Peanut	26-32	Whale	22-24
Rape	11-15	Sperm	8-14
Rice bran	26-28	Wool fat	38-40

SOURCE: MAHLENBACHER, C. V. The Analysis of Fats and Oils. Garrard Press, Champaign, Illinois.

TOCOPHEROLS

TABLE 2.T.12

TOCOPHEROLS IN FOOD (MG/100 GM)

Food	No. of Values Averaged	α-T	α-T-3	β-T	β-T-3	γ-T	γ-T-3	δ-T	δ-T-3
Nuts and grains									
Almond	2	27.4	0.5[1]	0.3[1]	—	0.9[1]	—	—	—
Barley	5	0.4	1.3	0.3	0.7[5]	0.05[4]	0.2[3]	0.01[1]	—
Corn	11	0.6	0.2[6]	—	0.4[1]	3.8	0.5[6]	tr	—
Millet	1	0.05	—	tr	—	1.3	—	0.4	—
Oats	6	0.7	0.7	0.2[4]	0.1[4]	0.3[4]	—	—	—
Peanuts	1	9.7	—	—	—	6.6	—	—	—
Peas	3	0.5	—	—	—	6.4[3]	—	0.6[1]	—
Pecans	1	1.2	—	—	—	19.1	—	—	—
Poppy seed	1	1.8	—	—	—	9.2	—	—	—
Rice	5	0.3	tr	—	—	0.3[4]	0.5[3]	0.04[5]	—
Rye	4	0.8	1.3[4]	0.4[4]	0.9	0.6[1]	—	—	—
Walnut, English	1	0.4	—	—	—	15.8	—	1.3	—
Wheat	9	1.0	0.4[8]	0.9	2.5[7]	—	—	0.08[1]	—
Vegetable oils									
Coconut	1	0.5	0.5	—	0.1	—	1.9	0.6	—
Corn	8	11.2	—	5.0[1]	—	60.2	—	1.8[3]	—
Cottonseed	9	38.9	—	—	—	38.7	—	—	—
Neem	1	—	—	—	—	58.0	—	59.0	—
Olive	4	5.1	—	—	—	—	—	—	—
Palm	4	25.6	14.3[1]	—	3.2[1]	31.6[2]	28.6[1]	7.0[1]	6.9[1]
Peanut	11	13.0	—	—	—	21.4	—	2.1[3]	—
Rapeseed	5	18.4	—	—	—	38.0	—	1.2[1]	—
Safflower	3	38.7	—	—	—	17.4	—	24.0[1]	—
Sesame	2	13.6	—	—	—	29.0	—	—	—
Soybean	14	10.1	—	—	—	59.3	—	26.4[9]	—
Sunflower	10	48.7	—	—	—	5.1	—	0.8[3]	—
Walnut	1	56.3	—	—	—	59.5	—	45.0	—
Wheat germ	3	133.0	2.6[1]	71.0	18.1[3]	26.0[1]	—	27.1[1]	—
Mustard seed	1	8.6	—	—	—	17.6	—	5.8	—
Asparagus (fresh weight)	—	1.8	—	0.05	—	0.07	—	—	—
Carrots (fresh weight)	—	0.51	0.04	0.01	0.08	—	—	—	—
Cucumber	—	8.4	—	—	—	—	—	—	—
Mango, flesh, green	—	0.26	—	—	—	—	—	0.27	—
Mango, flesh, ripe	—	0.98	—	—	—	—	—	—	—
Muskmelon	—	10.1	—	—	—	—	—	—	—
Tomato	—	18.2	—	—	—	—	—	—	—

[1] One value reported.
[2] Slover, unpublished data.
[3] Average of two values.
[4] Average of three values.
[5] Average of four values.
[6] Average of six values.
[7] Average of seven values.
[8] Average of eight values.
[9] Average of twelve values.

SOURCE: BAUERNFEIND, J. C. 1975. Tocopherols. *In* Encyclopedia of Food Technology. A. H. Johnson and M. S. Peterson (Editors). Avi Publishing Co., Westport, Conn.

TOMATO AND TOMATO PRODUCTS, COMPOSITION

TABLE 2.T.13

COMPOSITION OF TOMATO AND TOMATO PRODUCTS, 100 GRAMS

	Tomato		Tomato Juice				Tomato			
	Fresh	Canned	Regular	Concentrated	Dehydrated	Cocktail	Purée (pulp)	Catsup	Chili Sauce	Tomato Paste
Water (%)	93.5	93.7	93.6	75.0	1.0	93.0	87.0	68.6	68.0	75.0
Food energy (calories)	22	21	19	76	303	21	39	106	104	82
Protein, gm	1.1	1.0	0.9	3.4	11.6	0.7	1.7	2.0	2.5	3.4
Fat, gm	0.2	0.2	0.1	0.4	2.2	0.1	0.2	0.4	0.3	0.4
Carbohydrate:										
total, gm	4.7	4.3	4.3	17.1	68.2	5.0	8.9	25.4	24.8	18.6
fiber, gm	0.5	0.4	0.2	0.9	3.1	0.2	0.4	0.5	0.7	0.9
Ash, gm	0.5	0.8	1.1	4.1	17.0	1.2	2.2	3.6	4.4	2.6
Calcium, mg	13	6	7	27	85	10	13	22	20	27
Phosphorus, mg	27	19	18	70	279	18	34	50	52	70
Iron, mg	0.5	0.5	0.9	3.5	7.8	0.9	1.7	0.8	0.8	3.5
Sodium, mg	3	130	200	790	3934	200	399	1042	1338	38
Potassium, mg	244	217	227	888	3518	221	426	363	370	888
Vitamin A (I.U.)	900	900	800	3300	13100	800	1600	1400	1400	3300
Thiamine, mg	0.06	0.05	0.05	0.20	0.52	0.05	0.09	0.09	0.09	0.20
Riboflavin, mg	0.04	0.03	0.03	0.12	0.40	0.02	0.05	0.07	0.07	0.12
Niacin, mg.	0.7	0.7	0.8	3.1	13.5	0.06	1.4	1.6	1.6	3.1
Ascorbic acid, mg	23	17	16	49	239	16	33	15	16	49

SOURCE: GOULD, W. A. (EDITOR). 1974. Composition of Tomatoes. *In* Tomato Production, Processing and Quality Evaluation. Avi Publishing Co., Westport, Conn.

TOMATO GRADES

TABLE 2.T.14

U.S. STANDARDS FOR GRADES OF TOMATOES FOR PROCESSING (3-1-73)

Factor	Category A	Category B	Category C	Culls
Firmness	Firm	Fairly firm	Fairly firm	Water soaked, soft, shriveled, or puffy over 20% waste
Any worm attached	Free from	Free from	Free from	Affected Tomatoes Classed as Culls
Freezing	Free from	Free from	Free from	
Worm injury	Free from	Free from	Free from	
Anthracnose	Free from	Free from	Not more than 2	

SOURCE: GOULD, W. A. (EDITOR). 1974. Tomato Grading Practices. *In* Tomato Production, Processing and Quality Evaluation. Avi Publishing Co., Westport, Conn.

TRAGACANTH SPECIES

TABLE 2.T.15

GEOGRAPHICAL DISTRIBUTION OF TRAGACANTH SPECIES

Species	Geographical Distribution
A. gummifer	Northern Kurdistan, Armenia, Asia Minor and Syria
A. kurdicus	Southern Kurdistan to Asia Minor and Syria
A. brachycalyx	Iranian Kurdistan and Luristan
A. eriostylus	Luristan
A. pycnocladus	Kermanshab (Shahu and Avroman Mts.)
A. verus	Western Iran
A. leiocladus	Western and Central Iran
A. adscendens	South Western and Southern Iran
A. strobiliferus	Eastern Iran
A. heratensis	Khorasan to Afghanistan

SOURCE: HOWES, F. N. Vegetable Gums and Resins. Ronald Press Company, New York.

TRANSIT TEMPERATURE

TABLE 2.T.16

DESIRABLE TRANSIT TEMPERATURES FOR FRUITS AND VEGETABLES

Product	Temperature (°F)	Product	Temperature (°F)
Apples	32–40	Asparagus	32–36
Avocados			
Most varieties	45	Beans (snap)	45
West Indian varieties	55	Cantaloupe	35–40
Bananas (green)	56–60	Celery	32
Cherries (sweet)	32	Cucumbers	45–50
Cranberries	36–40	Honeydew melon	45–50
Dates	40–50	Lettuce	32
Grapefruit	50–60	Onions (dry)	32–40
Limes	48–50	Peppers (sweet)	45–50
Oranges		Potatoes	
Arizona & California	40–44	Early crop	50–60
Florida & Texas	32–40	Late crop	40–50

SOURCE: WHITE, P. L. and SELVEY, N. (EDITORS). 1974. Nutritional Qualities of Fresh Fruits and Vegetables. Futura Publishing Co., Mt. Kisco, N.Y.

TRIANGULAR TASTE TEST + PREFERENCE

TABLE 2.T.17

SIGNIFICANCE IN TRIANGULAR TASTE TESTS (p = 1/6)

No. of Tasters or Tastings	Minimum Agreeing Judgments Necessary to Establish Significant Differentiation (Two-tail Test)			Minimum Correct Answers Necessary to Establish Significant Differentiation (One-tail Test)		
	Probability Level			Probability Level		
	.05	.01	.001	.05	.01	.001
5	4	4	5	3	4	5
6	4	5	6	4	4	5
7	4	5	6	4	5	6
8	5	5	6	4	5	6
9	5	6	7	4	5	7
10	5	6	7	5	6	7
11	5	6	8	5	6	7
12	6	7	8	5	6	8
13	6	7	8	5	7	8
14	6	7	9	6	7	8
15	7	8	9	6	7	9
16	7	8	9	6	7	9
17	7	8	10	7	8	9
18	7	9	10	7	8	10
19	8	9	10	7	8	10
20	8	9	11	7	9	10
21	8	9	11	7	9	10
22	8	10	11	8	9	11
23	9	10	12	8	9	11
24	9	10	12	8	10	11
25	9	10	12	8	10	12
26	9	11	12	9	10	12
27	10	11	13	9	10	12
28	10	11	13	9	11	12
29	10	12	13	9	11	13
30	10	12	14	10	11	13
31	11	12	14	10	11	13
32	11	12	14	10	12	13
33	11	13	14	10	12	14
34	11	13	15	10	12	14
35	11	13	15	11	12	14
36	11	13	15	11	13	15
37	12	14	16	11	13	15
38	12	14	16	11	13	15
39	12	14	16	12	13	15
40	13	14	16	12	14	16
41	13	15	17	12	14	16
42	13	15	17	12	14	16
43	13	15	17	12	14	17
44	13	15	17	13	15	17
45	14	15	18	13	15	17
46	14	16	18	13	15	17
47	14	16	18	13	15	18
48	14	16	18	14	15	18
49	15	16	19	14	16	18
50	15	16	19	14	16	18
60	17	19	21	16	18	21
70	19	21	24	18	21	23
80	21	24	26	20	23	26
90	23	26	29	22	25	28
100	26	28	31	24	27	30

SOURCE: ROESSLER, E. B., BAKER, G. A., and AMERINE, M. A. One-Tailed and Two-Tailed Tests in Organoleptic Comparisons. Food Res. *21*, 117.

TRIANGULAR TASTE TEST PROBABILITY

TABLE 2.T.18

PROBABILITY IN TRIANGULAR TASTE TESTS

No. of Tasters or Tastings	No. of Correct Answers Necessary to Establish Significant Differentiation			No. of Tasters or Tastings	No. of Correct Answers Necessary to Establish Significant Differentiation		
	P = 0.05	P = 0.01	P = 0.001		P = 0.05	P = 0.01	P = 0.001
7	5	6	7	57	27	29	31
8	6	7	8	58	27	29	32
9	6	7	8	59	27	30	32
10	7	8	9	60	28	30	33
11	7	8	9	61	28	30	33
12	8	9	10	62	28	31	33
13	8	9	10	63	29	31	34
14	9	10	11	64	29	32	34
15	9	10	12	65	30	32	35
16	10	11	12	66	30	32	35
17	10	11	13	67	30	33	36
18	10	12	13	68	31	33	36
19	11	12	14	69	31	34	36
20	11	13	14	70	32	34	37
21	12	13	15	71	32	34	37
22	12	14	15	72	32	35	38
23	13	14	16	73	33	35	38
24	13	14	16	74	33	36	39
25	13	15	17	75	34	36	39
26	14	15	17	76	34	36	39
27	14	16	18	77	34	37	40
28	15	16	18	78	35	37	40
29	15	17	19	79	35	38	41
30	16	17	19	80	35	38	41
31	16	18	19	81	36	38	41
32	16	18	20	82	36	39	42
33	17	19	20	83	37	39	42
34	17	19	21	84	37	40	43
35	18	19	21	85	37	40	43
36	18	20	22	86	38	40	44
37	18	20	22	87	38	41	44
38	19	21	23	88	39	41	44
39	19	21	23	89	39	42	45
40	20	22	24	90	39	42	45
41	20	22	24	91	40	42	46
42	21	22	25	92	40	43	46
43	21	23	25	93	40	43	46
44	21	23	25	94	41	44	47
45	22	24	26	95	41	44	47
46	22	24	26	96	42	44	48
47	23	25	27	97	42	45	48
48	23	25	27	98	42	45	49
49	23	25	28	99	43	46	49
50	24	26	28	100	43	46	49
51	24	26	29	200	80	84	89
52	25	27	29	300	117	122	127
53	25	27	29	400	152	158	165
54	25	27	30	500	188	194	202
55	26	28	30	1,000	363	372	383
56	26	28	31	2,000	709	722	737

SOURCE: ROESSLER, E. B., WARREN, J., and GUYMON, J. F. Significance in Triangular Taste Tests. Food Res. *13*, 503.

TRICHINOSIS

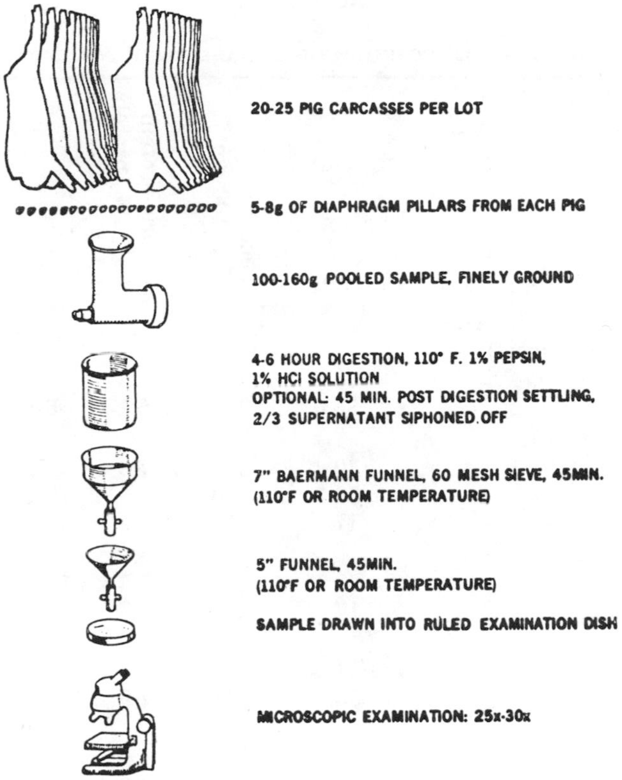
20-25 PIG CARCASSES PER LOT
5-8g OF DIAPHRAGM PILLARS FROM EACH PIG
100-160g POOLED SAMPLE, FINELY GROUND
4-6 HOUR DIGESTION, 110° F. 1% PEPSIN, 1% HCl SOLUTION
OPTIONAL: 45 MIN. POST DIGESTION SETTLING, 2/3 SUPERNATANT SIPHONED OFF
7" BAERMANN FUNNEL, 60 MESH SIEVE, 45MIN. (110°F OR ROOM TEMPERATURE)
5" FUNNEL, 45MIN. (110°F OR ROOM TEMPERATURE)
SAMPLE DRAWN INTO RULED EXAMINATION DISH
MICROSCOPIC EXAMINATION: 25x-30x

FIG. 2.T.4. SCHEMATIC OUTLINE OF MODIFIED POOLED-SAMPLE TRICHINOSIS DIAGNOSTIC TECHNIQUE

SOURCE: ZIMMERMAN, W. F. 1975. Trichinosis. *In* Meat Hygiene. J. A. Libby (Editor). Lea & Febiger, Philadelphia.

TURKEY COMPOSITION

TABLE 2.T.19

NUTRIENT COMPOSITION OF COOKED TURKEY MEATS

	Protein %	Food Energy Cal./100 gm.	Calorie-protein Cal./1% protein	Fat %	Moisture %	Ash %
Turkey, roasted and boned						
Breast (white meat)						
male	33.5	194	5.8	6.7	59	1.1
female	35.0	215	6.1	8.3	56	1.1
Leg (dark meat)						
male	30.8	224	7.3	11.2	57	1.0
female	30.3	230	7.6	12.1	56	1.0
Skin	17.7	375	21.2	33.8	45	1.0
Edible Viscera						
male	23.5	200	8.5	14.0	61	1.6
female	17.8	254	14.3	20.3	61	1.2
Smoked Turkey, bones						
Breast	31.0	207	6.7	9.2	57	2.8
Leg	30.2	221	7.3	11.1	56	2.8
Chicken, roasted and boned						
Breast	31.5	138	4.4	1.3	66	1.0
Leg	25.4	168	6.6	7.3	67	0.9

SOURCE: SNYDER, E. S., and ORR, H. L. Poultry Meat. Dep. Agric. Publ. 9, Can. Dep. Agric., Ottawa.

TURKEY VARIETIES

TABLE 2.T.20

VARIETIES OF TURKEYS AND THEIR CHARACTERISTICS

Variety	Standard Weights Adult tom (lb)	Standard Weights Adult hen (lb)	Plumage	Beak	Color of Throat Wattle	Beard	Shanks & Toes	Comments
Bronze	36	20	Black; with an iridescent sheen of red, green, bronze.	Light horn at tip, dark at base.	Red, changeable to bluish white.	Black	Dull black in young; smoky pink in mature birds.	The Broad-breasted Bronze is a sub-variety. Of all meat animals, the Broad-breasted Bronze most uniformly produces a well-fleshed carcass.
White Holland	33	18	Pure white.	Light pinkish horn.	Red, changeable to pinkish white.	Deep black	Pinkish white.	Very similar to Bronze; only white, and slightly higher in fertility.
Beltsville Small, white	23	13	Pure white.	Light pinkish horn.	Red, changeable to pinkish white.	Black	Pinkish white.	Developed by the USDA. These small turkeys are good egg producers of high hatchability.

SOURCE: ENSMINGER, M. E. 1969. Animal Science. The Interstate Printers & Publishers, Inc., Danville, Illinois.

U

UNSAPONIFIABLE MATTER

TABLE 2.U.1

UNSAPONIFIABLE CONTENT OF SOME FATS AND OILS

Oil or Fat	Unsaponifiable Matter %	Oil or Fat	Unsaponifiable Matter %
Babassu	0.2-0.8	Peanut	0.2-0.8
Cacao butter	0.2-1.0	Perilla	0.6-1.3
Castor	<1.0	Rapeseed	0.7-1.3
Chinese vegetable		Rice bran	3.0-5.0
tallow	0.5-1.5	Safflower	0.3-1.3
Coconut	<0.5	Sesame	0.9-2.3
Corn	0.8-2.0	Soybean	0.5-1.6
Cottonseed	<1.5	Sunflower	0.3-1.3
Hempseed	<1.5	Teaseed	<1.5
Kapok	0.5-1.0	Tung	<1.0
Linseed	<1.7	Lard	<0.8
Mustard seed		Neatsfoot	<0.8
(white)	0.7-1.5	Tallow (beef)	<1.0
(black)	0.7-1.5	Tallow (mutton)	<1.0
Olive	0.7-1.1	Whale	1.6-1.9
Palm	0.3-1.0	Cod	3.3-4.7
Palm kernel	0.2-0.8	Shark liver	13.0-20.0

SOURCE: MAHLENBACHER, C. V. The Analysis of Fats and Oils. Garrard Press, Champaign, Illinois.

UNSATURATED FATTY ACIDS

TABLE 2.U.2

NAME, FORMULA, AND SOURCE OF UNSATURATED FATTY ACIDS

Common Name	Systematic Name	Formula	Source
	Monoethenoid Fatty Acids		
Caproleic	9-Decenoic	$C_{10}H_{18}O_2$	Butter fat, milk fat of human, goat; sperm head oil.
Lauroleic	5-Dodecenoic	$C_{12}H_{22}O_2$	Herring oil, sperm blubber and head oil.
	9-Dodecenoic	$C_{12}H_{22}O_2$	Cochineal wax (*Coccus cacti*), cow's milk fat.
	5-Tetradecenoic	$C_{14}H_{26}O_2$	Sperm and dolphin oils, whale head oil, sardine.
Myristoleic	9-Tetradecenoic	$C_{14}H_{26}O_2$	Whale oil, shark liver oil, eel oil, turtle oil, human milk fat, depot fats.
Palmitoleic ("Physetoleic")	9-Hexadecenoic	$C_{16}H_{30}O_2$	Sperm head oil (*Physeter macrocephalus* Shaw), milk fat, seed oils, marine oils.
Petroselinic	6-Octadecenoic	$C_{18}H_{34}O_2$	Parsley seed oil, coriander, *Umbelliferae*.
Oleic	9-Octadecenoic	$C_{18}H_{34}O_2$	Olive oil, pork fat, most fats and oils.
Vaccenic	11-Octadecenoic	$C_{18}H_{34}O_2$	Butter, beef fat, mutton fat, lard.
Gadoleic	9-Eicosenoic	$C_{20}H_{38}O_2$	Cod-liver oil, many fish and marine oils.
	11-Eicosenoic	$C_{20}H_{38}O_2$	Jojoba oil.
Cetoleic	11-Docosenoic	$C_{22}H_{42}O_2$	Marine oil, shark liver, herring, sardine and other marine oils.
Erucic	13-Docosenoic	$C_{22}H_{42}O_2$	Mustard and rapeseed oils.
	Diethenoid and Polyethenoid Fatty Acids		
Linoleic	9,12-Octadecadienoic	$C_{18}H_{32}O_2$	Linseed oil, most seed fats.
Hiragonic	6,10,14-Hexadecatrienoic	$C_{16}H_{26}O_2$	Sardine oil.
Linolenic	9,12,15-Octadecatrienoic	$C_{18}H_{30}O_2$	Hempseed oil, linseed oil, walnut oil, soybean oil, seed oils.
Eleostearic	9,11,13-Octadecatrienoic	$C_{18}H_{30}O_2$	Tung oil, bagilumbang nut, essang-seed oil.
Arachidonic	5,8,11,14-Eicosatetraenoic	$C_{20}H_{32}O_2$	Liver lipid, brain, egg lecithin, glandular organs.
	4,8,12,16-Eicosatetraenoic	$C_{20}H_{32}O_2$	Sardine oil, whale oil.
Clupanodonic	4,8,12,15,19—Docosapentaenoic	$C_{22}H_{34}O_2$	Sardine oil, sturgeon oil, white fish oil, pilchard oil, cod-liver oil, other fish oils.

SOURCE: MAHLENBACHER, C. V. The Analysis of Fats and Oils. Garrard Publishing Co., Champaign, Illinois. Reproduced with the permission of the publisher.

V

VARIETY MEAT, COOKING

TABLE 2.V.1

TIMETABLE FOR COOKING VARIETY MEATS

Kind	Broiled	Braised	Cooked in Liquid
LIVER			
Beef			
3- to 4-pound piece		2 to 2½ hours	
Sliced		20 to 25 minutes	
Veal (Calf), sliced	8 to 10 minutes		
Pork			
Whole (3 to 3½ pounds)		1½ to 2 hours	
Sliced		20 to 25 minutes	
Lamb, sliced	8 to 10 minutes		
KIDNEY			
Beef		1½ to 2 hours	1 to 1½ hours
Veal (Calf)	10 to 12 minutes	1 to 1½ hours	¾ to 1 hour
Pork	10 to 12 minutes	1 to 1½ hours	¾ to 1 hour
Lamb	10 to 12 minutes	¾ to 1 hour	¾ to 1 hour
HEART			
Beef			
Whole		3 to 4 hours	3 to 4 hours
Sliced		1½ to 2 hours	
Veal (Calf)			
Whole		2½ to 3 hours	2½ to 3 hours
Pork		2½ to 3 hours	2½ to 3 hours
Lamb		2½ to 3 hours	2½ to 3 hours
TONGUE			
Beef			3 to 4 hours
Veal (Calf)			2 to 3 hours
Pork } usually sold			
Lamb } ready-to-serve			
TRIPE			
Beef	10 to 15 minutes[2]		1 to 1½ hours
SWEETBREADS	10 to 15 minutes[2]	20 to 25 minutes	15 to 20 minutes
BRAINS	10 to 15 minutes[2]	20 to 25 minutes	15 to 20 minutes

[1] On top of range or in a 300°F. to 325°F. oven.

[2] Time required after precooking in water.

SOURCE: Lessons on Meat. (1974). National Live Stock and Meat Board, Chicago.

VARIETY MEAT PERCENTAGE OF DAILY RECOMMENDED ALLOWANCES

TABLE 2.V.2

PERCENTAGE OF THE DAILY RECOMMENDED DIETARY ALLOWANCES (1973) SUPPLIED BY A 3½-OZ SERVING OF VARIETY MEAT[1]
(Man—22 Years of Age)

Food Constituent	Liver	Kidney	Heart	Brains	Sweetbreads	Tongue	Tripe
Protein	55	50	55	22	53	40	33
Calories	8	8	7	4	6	8	3
Calcium	2	2	1	16	26	2	16
Iron	176	130	51	21	31	18	16
Phosphorus	66	31	21	41	52	14	17
Magnesium	7		7				tr
Vitamin A	876	23	2	0	0	0	0
Ascorbic acid	68	27	tr	42	46	6	
Thiamin	22	34	16	7	4	4	tr
Riboflavin	248	268	75	12	9	16	8
Niacin	111	59	40	17	16	19	6
Vitamin B-6[2]	38	22	16	8	10	10	
Vitamin B-12[2]	2300	1070	224	133	307		

[1]Percentages are averages of representative values for beef, pork, lamb and veal.
[2]All values are for the cooked variety meats except vitamins B-6 and B-12 which are values for the raw product.

SOURCE: Recipes for Variety Meats. (1974). National Live Stock and Meat Board, Chicago.

VARIETY MEAT PREPARATION

TABLE 2.V.3

A GUIDE FOR BUYING AND PREPARING VARIETY MEATS

Kind	Characteristics	Buying Guide		Preparation
		Avg Wt	Servings	
Liver (Beef, veal, pork, lamb)	Veal, lamb, pork livers more tender than beef. Veal and lamb livers milder in flavor than pork and beef.	1 beef—10 lb 1 veal—2½ lb 1 pork—3 lb 1 lamb—1 lb	¾-1 lb for four	Braise, fry, broil, grind for loaves or patties.
Kidney (Beef, veal, pork, lamb)	Veal, lamb and pork kidneys more tender than beef. Also milder in flavor. Veal and lamb kidney sometimes cut with chops.	1 beef—1 lb 1 veal—¾ lb 1 pork—¼ lb 1 lamb—⅛ lb	4-6 3-4 1-2 ½-1	Braise, broil, cook in liquid, grind for loaves or patties.
Heart (Beef, veal, pork, lamb)	Beef heart is least tender but all hearts must be made tender by proper cooking.	1 beef—4 lb 1 veal—½ lb 1 pork—½ lb 1 lamb—¼ lb	10-12 2-3 2-3 1	Braise, cook in liquid, grind for loaves or patties.
Tongue (Beef, veal, pork, lamb)	May be purchased fresh, pickled, corned or smoked. Must be made tender by proper cooking. Pork and lamb usually purchased ready-to-serve.	1 beef—3¾ lb 1 veal—1½ lb 1 pork—¾ lb 1 lamb—½ lb	12-16 3-6 2-4 2-3	Cook in liquid until tender. Remove skin, serve as desired.
Tripe (Beef)	Plain and honeycomb, latter preferred. Purchased fresh, pickled or canned. Often purchased precooked, requires further cooking.	Plain—7 lb Honey comb—1½ lb	¾-1 lb for four	Precook (unless purchased cooked) in water to make tender. Then braise, fry or broil.
Sweetbreads (Beef, veal, lamb)	Divided into two parts: heart and throat sweet breads. Tender and delicate in flavor.	⅛ lb	¾-1 lb for four	Precook in water to help keep and make firm. Broil, fry, braise or cream.
Brains (Beef, veal, pork, lamb)	Very tender and delicate to flavor.	⅜ lb	¾-1 lb for four	Precook in water to help keep and make firm. Broil, scramble, fry or cream.

SOURCE: Recipes for Variety Meats. (1974). National Live Stock and Meat Board, Chicago.

VEAL CHART

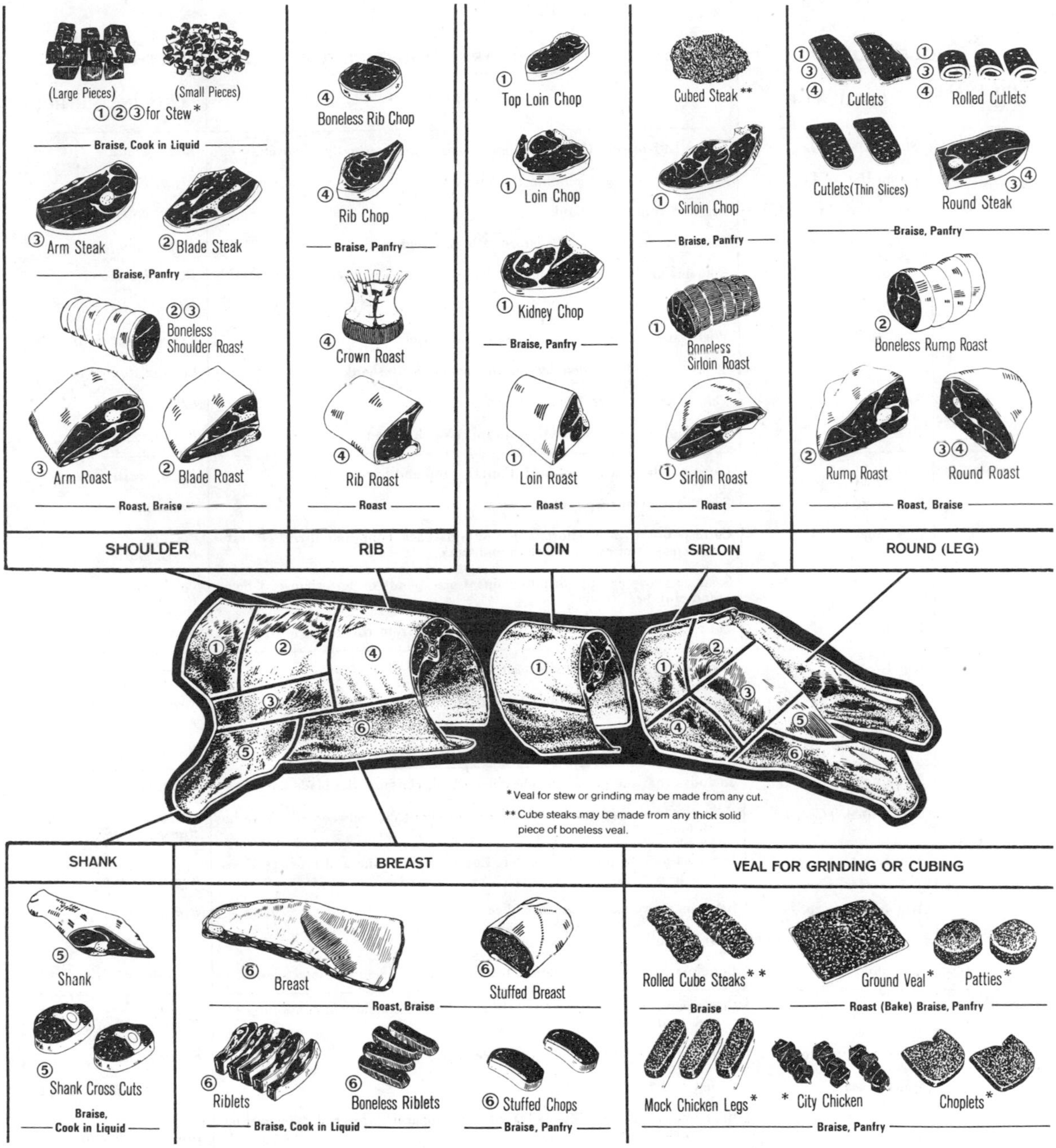

FIG. 2.V.1. RETAIL CUTS OF VEAL, WHERE THEY COME FROM AND HOW TO COOK THEM

SOURCE: Be a Smarter Shopper . . . a Better Cook. (1973). National Live Stock and Meat Board, Chicago.

VEAL CUTS

TABLE 2.V.4

WHOLESALE CUTS, RETAIL CUTS AND THEIR CHARACTERISTICS AND COOKING METHODS

WHOLESALE CUTS	RETAIL CUTS	CHARACTERISTICS	COOKING METHODS
Leg (Round)	Shank Half of Leg	Lower half of leg. Hock and part of shank bone usually removed.	*Roast; braise*
	Rump Half of Leg	Upper half of leg, including the rump.	*Roast; braise*
	Center Cut of Leg (*Round*)	Leg with rump and shank off.	*Roast; braise*
	Round Steak (*Cutlet*)	Same muscle and bone structure as beef round steaks.	*Braise; panfry*
	Standing Rump Roast	Contains aitch or rump bone, tail bone, and usually a part of leg bone.	*Roast; braise*
	Rolled Rump Roast	Boneless roll.	*Roast; braise*
	Heel of Round	Wedge-shaped boneless piece—same as in beef.	*Braise; cook in liquid*
	Hind Shank	Shank bone surrounded by varying amounts of shank meat.	*Cook in liquid; braise*
	Scallops	Thin boneless slices from any part of carcass.	*Braise; panfry*
	Rosettes	Solid boneless pieces or slices wrapped with bacon	*Braise; panfry*
Loin	Sirloin Roast	Corresponds to sirloin of beef. Contains hip and back bones.	*Roast; braise*
	Sirloin Steak	Same as above except cut into steaks.	*Braise; panfry*
	Loin Roast	Corresponds to beef short loin. Contains back bone and three separate muscles—loin eye, tenderloin and flank.	*Roast; braise*
	Loin Chop	Same as above except cut into chops. Corresponds to porterhouse, T-bone and club beef steaks.	*Braise; panfry*
	Kidney Chop	Cut to contain cross section of kidney. Made from rib end of loin.	*Braise; panfry*
Rib	Rib Roast	Similar to standing beef rib roast.	*Roast*
	Crown Roast	Rib sections "frenched" and formed into shape of crown.	*Roast*
	Rib Chop	Contains rib bone and rib eye, except chops cut between ribs have no rib bone.	*Braise; panfry*
Shoulder	Blade Roast	Includes that section of the shoulder which contains the blade bone.	*Roast; braise*
	Blade Steak (*Chop*)	Contains blade bone and rib bone except chops cut between ribs have no rib bone.	*Braise; panfry*
	Arm Roast	Includes arm section of shoulder. Contains arm bone and cross sections of 3 to 5 ribs.	*Roast; braise*
	Arm Steak (*Chop*)	Same as above except cut into slices.	*Braise; panfry*
	Rolled Shoulder Roast	Boneless roll.	*Roast; braise*
	City Chicken	Boneless cubes of veal fastened together on a wooden or metal skewer.	*Braise*
Breast	Breast	Corresponds to short plate and brisket of beef. Thin, flat cut containing rib ends and breast bone.	*Braise; cook in liquid*
	Breast with pocket	Same as above with pocket cut between ribs and lean.	*Roast; braise*
	Rolled Breast	Boned and rolled breast.	*Roast; braise*
	Riblets	Breast bone is removed (usually). Breast is separated into riblets by cutting between ribs.	*Braise; cook in liquid*
	Stew Meat	Small bone-in or boneless pieces of meat. Also made from the shoulder, shank and leg.	*Braise; cook in liquid*
Fore Shank	Fore Shank	Contains considerable bone and connective tissue. Varying amounts of lean. Rich in gelatin-forming substance.	*Braise; cook in liquid*
Ground Veal	Loaf and Patties	Usually made from flank, breast, shank and neck.	*Roast; braise; panfry*
	Mock Chicken Legs	Ground veal molded into shape of chicken legs with wooden skewer to represent leg bone.	*Braise; panfry*

TABLE 2.V.4 (*Continued*)

WHOLESALE CUTS	RETAIL CUTS	CHARACTERISTICS	COOKING METHODS
Round (and Rump)	Round Steak (*full cut*)	Round or oval in shape with small round bone. One large muscle, three smaller ones.	*Braise*
	Top Round Steak or Pot-Roast	Most tender portion of round. Is one large muscle.	*Braise; roast; panfry*
	Bottom Round Steak or Pot-Roast	Not so tender as top round. Distinguished from top round by having two muscles.	*Braise*
	Tip Roast or Steak	Triangular cut; roast may contain kneecap. Steaks are boneless.	*Braise; roast; broil; panbroil; panfry*
	Standing Rump	Triangular in shape; contains portions of aitch (rump) bone and tail bone. Knuckle end of leg (round) bone usually removed.	*Braise; roast (high quality)*
	Rolled Rump	Boneless roll.	*Braise, roast (high quality)*
	Heel of Round	Boneless wedge-shaped cut from lower part of round. Weighs 4 to 8 pounds. Has very little fat and is least tender cut of round.	*Braise; cook in liquid*
	Hind Shank	Bony, considerable connective tissue, rich in extractives.	*Cook in liquid (soup)*
Sirloin	Sirloin Steak	Contains portions of back bone and hip bone. Wide variation in bone and muscle structure of the various steaks.	*Broil; panbroil; panfry*
	Pinbone Sirloin Steak	Lies next to the porterhouse. Contains pin bone which is the forward end of hip bone.	*Broil; panbroil; panfry*
	Boneless Sirloin Steak	Any boneless steak from the sirloin.	*Broil; panbroil; panfry*
Short Loin	Porterhouse Steak	Largest steak in short loin. Loin strip and tenderloin muscles. T-shaped bone. Tenderloin larger in porterhouse than in other short loin steaks.	*Broil; panbroil; panfry*
	T-Bone Steak	Same as porterhouse except tenderloin is smaller (porterhouse and T-bone used more or less interchangeably).	*Broil; panbroil; panfry*
	Club (Delmonico) Steak	Triangular-shaped; smallest steak in short loin. Tenderloin has practically disappeared.	*Broil; panbroil; panfry*
	Tenderloin Roast or Steak	Boneless tapering muscle. Most tender cut beef.	*Roast; broil; panbroil; panfry*
Flank	Flank Steak	Oval-shaped boneless steak weighing ¾ to 1½ pounds. Muscles run lengthwise; usually scored to shorten muscle fibers. Less tender cut.	*Braise*
	Flank Steak Fillets	Sections of flank steak rolled and fastened with skewers.	*Braise*
	Flank Meat	Boneless. Coarse fibers. May be rolled, cut into stew or ground.	*Braise; cook in liquid*
Rib	Standing Rib Roast (Short Cut)	Contains two or more ribs from which short ribs and chine bone have been removed. Comparable to rib roast served in restaurants.	*Roast*
	Rolled Rib Roast	Boneless roll. Outer cover of roll consists largely of thin plate meat wrapped around rib eye.	*Roast*
	Rib Steak	Contains rib eye and may contain rib bone.	*Broil; panbroil; panfry*
	Short Ribs	Cut from ends of ribs; layers of lean and fat.	*Braise; cook in liquid*
Short Plate	Plate "Boiling" Beef	Cut across plate parallel with ribs.	*Braise; cook in liquid*
	Rolled Plate	When rolled the absence of the rib eye distinguishes this cut from the rolled rib.	*Braise; cook in liquid*
	Short Ribs	Cut from ends of ribs; layers of lean and fat.	*Braise; cook in liquid*
Square-Cut Chuck	Arm Pot-roast or Steak	Has a round bone and cross sections of 3–5 ribs. A small round muscle near the round bone is surrounded by connective tissue.	*Braise*
	Blade Pot-roast or Steak	Pot-roast contains portions of rib and blade bones. Steaks cut between ribs will not contain rib bone.	*Braise*
	Boneless Chuck	Any part of the square-cut chuck (except the neck) from which the bones have been removed.	*Braise*
	Boneless Neck	Any part of the neck without the neck bone.	*Braise; cook in liquid*
	English (Boston) Cut	A rectangular piece cut across 2 or 3 chuck ribs.	*Braise*
Brisket	Brisket	Layers of lean and fat. Presence of breast bone sure indication that cut is from the brisket.	*Braise; cook in liquid*
	Boneless Brisket	Same as above with ribs and breast bone removed.	*Braise; cook in liquid*
Fore Shank	Shank Knuckle	Knuckle or upper end of fore shank.	*Cook in liquid, braise*
	Shank Cross-Cuts	Small pieces cut across shank bone.	*Braise; cook in liquid*
Ground Beef	Loaf and Patties	Usually made from flank, shank, plate and chuck.	*Roast (bake); broil; panbroil; panfry; braise*

SOURCE: Meat Manual, 6th Edition. National Live Stock and Meat Board, Chicago.

VEAL CUTS AND USES

TABLE 2.V.5

VEAL CUTS AND HOW TO USE THEM

CUT	DESCRIPTION OF CUT	RETAIL CUTS	VEAL SPECIALTIES
LEG	Solid meat, small percentage of bone, little waste	Roasts, cutlets veal birds	Brains— Cream, scramble, fry
RUMP	Excellent quality; corresponds to rump of beef	Roast	Heart— Braise, cook in water
LOIN	Excellent quality, more bone than leg	Chops, roasts, kidney chops	Kidney— Broil, meat pie, fry, cook in water
RIB	Excellent quality	Chops, Frenched chops, roasts	Liver— Fry, broil, braise, roast whole or as loaf
BREAST	Narrow, thin strip of meat with breast bone and lower portion of ribs	Stuffed roast, stews, jellied veal	Tongue (Corned, smoked, fresh)— Cook in water
SHOULDER	Tender, juicy, and well flavored	Roast, boned and rolled roast, chops, pot-roasts	Sweetbreads— Cream, braise, broil, fry
SHANK	Little meat, fine flavor	Pressed veal, stock, stews,	
FLANK	Good flavor, no waste	Stews, pressed veal	

SOURCE: Meat Buying Manual. National Live Stock and Meat Board, Chicago.

VEAL ROASTING

TABLE 2.V.6

TIME-TABLE FOR ROASTING VEAL

Cut	Approx. Wt. of Single Roast	No. of Roasts in Oven	Approx. Total Wt. of Roasts in Oven	Oven Temperature	Interior Temperature of Roast When Removed from Oven	Minutes per Pound Based on One Roast	Minutes per Pound Based on Total Wt. of Roasts in Oven	Approximate Total Time
	pounds		*pounds*					
Leg	7 to 8	1		300° F.	170° F.	25		3 to 3½ hours
Leg	16	1		300° F.	170° F.	22		6 hours
Leg	23	1		300° F	170° F.	18 to 20		7 to 7½ hours
Loin	4½ to 5	1		300° F.	170° F.	30 to 35		2½ to 3 hours
Rack (4 to 6 ribs)	2½ to 3	1		300° F.	170° F.	30 to 35		1½ hours
Shoulder	7	1		300° F.	170° F.	25		3 hours
Shoulder	12 to 13	1		300° F.	170° F.	25		5 to 5½ hours
Cushion shoulder (with stuffing)	9 to 10	1		300° F.	170° F.	30 to 35		5 to 5½ hours
Cushion shoulder (with stuffing)		3	24	300° F.	170° F.		10 to 12	4 to 5 hours
Rolled shoulder	5	1		300° F.	170° F.	40 to 45		3½ to 4 hours
Rolled shoulder		3	20	300° F.	170° F.		14	5 hours
Rolled shoulder	9 to 10	1		300° F.	170° F.	35 to 40		6 to 7 hours
Round (rump and shank off)	20	1		300° F.	170° F.	20		6½ hours

SOURCE: Cooking Meat in Quantity. National Live Stock and Meat Board, Chicago.

VEAL WHOLESALE CUTS

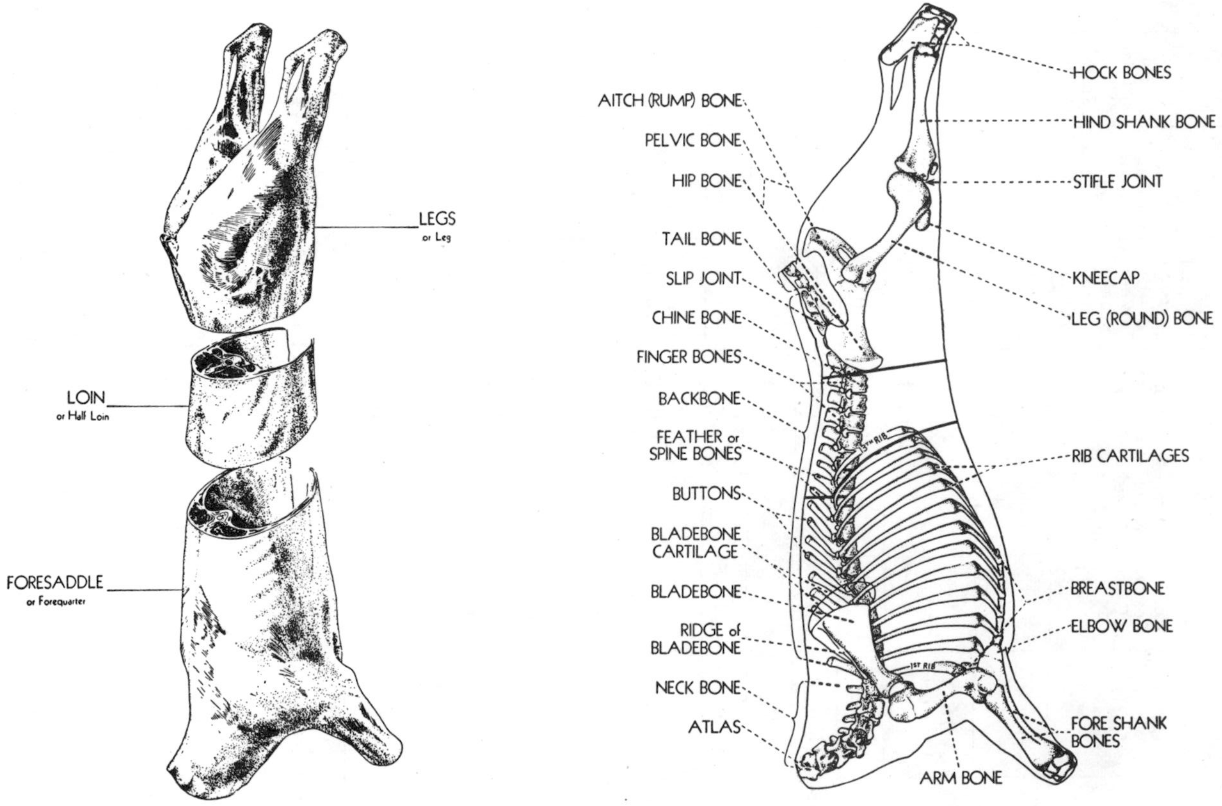

FIG. 2.V.2. VEAL WHOLESALE CUTS (LEFT); LOCATION, STRUCTURE, AND NAMES OF CARCASS BONES (RIGHT)

SOURCE: Cooking Meat in Quantity. National Live Stock and Meat Board, Chicago.

VEGETABLE BOILING

TABLE 2.V.7

BOILING GUIDE FOR FRESH VEGETABLES

Vegetable	Cooking time after water returns to boil	Approximate amount as purchased for six servings) (about ½ cup each)
	Minutes	*Pounds*
Asparagus	10 to 13 (whole)	2½
Beans, lima	25 to 27	2¾ in pods
Beans, snap (green or wax)	13 to 15 (1-inch pieces)	1
Beets	38 to 41 (whole)	2½ with tops or 1½ without tops
Broccoli	9 to 12 (heavy stalk, split)	2
Brussels sprouts	15 to 17	1½
Cabbage	6 to 8 (shredded)	1¼
	10 to 13 (wedges)	1½
Carrots	20 to 22 (whole)	1½ without tops
	18 to 20 (sliced or diced)	
Cauliflower	8 to 12 (separated)	2
	20 to 24 (whole)	
Celery	15 to 19 (cut-up)	1¼
Collards	15 to 20	1½ untrimmed
Corn	5 to 7 (on cob)	3 in husks
	6 to 8 (whole kernel)	
Kale	15 to 20	1¼ untrimmed
Okra	12 to 14	1¼
Onions, mature	11 to 15 (whole)	1¾
	10 to 14 (quartered)	
Parsnips	20 to 40 (whole)	1½
	8 to 15 (quartered)	
Peas	10 to 14	3 in pods
Potatoes	25 to 29 (whole, medium)	1½
	15 to 17 (quartered)	
Spinach	8 to 12	1½ prepackaged
Squash, acorn	18 to 20 (quartered)	2½
Squash, butternut	16 to 18 (cubed)	
Squash, yellow crookneck	11 to 13 (sliced)	1½
Squash, zucchini	13 to 15 (sliced)	
Sweetpotatoes	28 to 35 (whole)	2
Tomatoes	7 to 15 (cut-up)	1¼
Turnips	30 to 38 (whole)	1¾ without tops
	10 to 12 (cut-up)	

SOURCE: Vegetables in Family Meals, USDA Home and Garden Bull. *105*, 1975.

VEGETABLE COMPOSITION, PART I

TABLE 2.V.8

NUTRITIVE VALUES OF THE EDIBLE PART OF VEGETABLES AND VEGETABLE PRODUCTS

[Dashes in the columns for nutrients show that no suitable value could be found although there is reason to believe that a measurable amount of the nutrient may be present]

Food, Approximate Measure, and Weight (in Grams)		(g)	Water (%)	Food Energy (Cal)	Protein (g)	Fat (g)	Fatty Acids: Saturated (Total) (g)	Fatty Acids: Unsaturated: Oleic (g)	Fatty Acids: Unsaturated: Linoleic (g)	Carbohydrate (g)	Calcium (mg)	Iron (mg)	Vitamin A Value (IU)	Thiamin (mg)	Riboflavin (mg)	Niacin (mg)	Ascorbic Acid (mg)
Asparagus, green:																	
Cooked, drained:																	
Spears, ½-in. diam at base	4 spears	60	94	10	1	Tr	—	—	—	2	13	0.4	540	0.10	0.11	0.8	16
Pieces, 1½ to 2-in. lengths	1 cup	145	94	30	3	Tr	—	—	—	5	30	0.9	1,310	0.23	0.26	2.0	38
Canned, solids and liquid	1 cup	244	94	45	5	1	—	—	—	7	44	4.1	1,240	0.15	0.22	2.0	37
Beans:																	
Lima, immature seeds, cooked, drained	1 cup	170	71	190	13	1	—	—	—	34	80	4.3	480	0.31	0.17	2.2	29
Snap:																	
Green:																	
Cooked, drained	1 cup	125	92	30	2	Tr	—	—	—	7	63	0.8	680	0.09	0.11	0.6	15
Canned, solids and liquid	1 cup	239	94	45	2	Tr	—	—	—	10	81	2.9	690	0.07	0.10	0.7	10
Yellow or wax:																	
Cooked, drained	1 cup	125	93	30	2	Tr	—	—	—	6	63	0.8	290	0.09	0.11	0.6	16
Canned, solids and liquid	1 cup	239	94	45	2	1	—	—	—	10	81	2.9	140	0.07	0.10	0.7	12
Sprouted mung beans, cooked, drained	1 cup	125	91	35	4	Tr	—	—	—	7	21	1.1	30	0.11	0.13	0.9	8

Beets:																
Cooked, drained, peeled:																
Whole beets, 2-in. diam	2 beets	100	91	30	1	Tr	—	—	—	7	14	0.5	20	0.03	0.04	0.3	6
Diced or sliced	1 cup	170	91	55	2	Tr	—	—	—	12	24	0.9	30	0.05	0.07	0.5	10
Canned, solids and liquid	1 cup	246	90	85	2	Tr	—	—	—	19	34	1.5	20	0.02	0.05	0.2	7
Beet greens, leaves and stems, cooked, drained	1 cup	145	94	25	3	Tr	—	—	—	5	144	2.8	7,400	0.10	0.22	0.4	22
Blackeye peas (*See* Cowpeas)																
Broccoli, cooked, drained:																
Whole stalks, medium size	1 stalk	180	91	45	6	1	—	—	—	8	158	1.4	4,500	0.16	0.36	1.4	162
Stalks cut into ½-in. pieces	1 cup	155	91	40	5	1	—	—	—	7	136	1.2	3,880	0.14	0.31	1.2	140
Chopped, yield from 10-oz frozen pkg	1⅜ cups	250	92	65	7	1	—	—	—	12	135	1.8	6,500	0.15	0.30	1.3	143
Brussels sprouts, 7–8 sprouts (1¼ to 1½ in. diam) per cup, cooked	1 cup	155	88	55	7	1	—	—	—	10	50	1.7	810	0.12	0.22	1.2	135
Cabbage:																
Common varieties:																
Raw:																
Coarsely shredded or sliced	1 cup	70	92	15	1	Tr	—	—	—	4	34	0.3	90	0.04	0.04	0.2	33
Finely shredded or chopped	1 cup	90	92	20	1	Tr	—	—	—	5	44	0.4	120	0.05	0.05	0.3	42
Cooked	1 cup	145	94	30	2	Tr	—	—	—	6	64	0.4	190	0.06	0.06	0.4	48
Red, raw, coarsely shredded	1 cup	70	90	20	1	Tr	—	—	—	5	29	0.6	30	0.06	0.04	0.3	43
Savoy, raw, coarsely shredded	1 cup	70	92	15	2	Tr	—	—	—	3	47	0.6	140	0.04	0.06	0.2	39
Cabbage, celery or Chinese, raw, cut in 1-in. pieces	1 cup	75	95	10	1	Tr	—	—	—	2	32	0.5	110	0.04	0.03	0.5	19
Cabbage, spoon (or pakchoy), cooked	1 cup	170	95	25	2	Tr	—	—	—	4	252	1.0	5,270	0.07	0.14	1.2	26
Carrots:																
Raw:																
Whole, 5½ × 1 in., (25 thin strips)	1 carrot	50	88	20	1	Tr	—	—	—	5	18	0.4	5,500	0.03	0.03	0.3	4
Grated	1 cup	110	88	45	1	Tr	—	—	—	11	41	0.8	12,100	0.06	0.06	0.7	9

(Continued)

TABLE 2.V.8 (*Continued*)

Food, Approximate Measure, and Weight (in Grams)		(g)	Water (%)	Food Energy (Cal)	Protein (g)	Fat (g)	Fatty Acids: Saturated (Total) (g)	Fatty Acids: Unsaturated: Oleic (g)	Fatty Acids: Unsaturated: Linoleic (g)	Carbohydrate (g)	Calcium (mg)	Iron (mg)	Vitamin A Value (IU)	Thiamin (mg)	Riboflavin (mg)	Niacin (mg)	Ascorbic Acid (mg)
Carrots (*Cont.*)																	
Cooked, diced	1 cup	145	91	45	1	Tr	—	—	—	10	48	0.9	15,220	0.08	0.07	0.7	9
Canned, strained or chopped (baby food)	1 oz	28	92	10	Tr	Tr	—	—	—	2	7	0.1	3,690	0.01	0.01	0.1	1
Cauliflower, cooked, flowerbuds	1 cup	120	93	25	3	Tr	—	—	—	5	25	0.8	70	0.11	0.10	0.7	66
Celery, raw:																	
Stalk, large outer, 8 by about 1½ in. at root end	1 stalk	40	94	5	Tr	Tr	—	—	—	2	16	0.1	100	0.01	0.01	0.1	4
Pieces, diced	1 cup	100	94	15	1	Tr	—	—	—	4	39	0.3	240	0.03	0.03	0.3	9
Collards, cooked	1 cup	190	91	55	5	1	—	—	—	9	289	1.1	10,260	0.27	0.37	2.4	87
Corn, sweet:																	
Cooked, ear 5 × 1¾ in.[1]	1 ear	140	74	70	3	1	—	—	—	16	2	0.5	310[2]	0.09	0.08	1.0	7
Canned, solids and liquid	1 cup	256	81	170	5	2	—	—	—	40	10	1.0	690[2]	0.07	0.12	2.3	13
Cowpeas, cooked, immature seeds	1 cup	160	72	175	13	1	—	—	—	29	38	3.4	560	0.49	0.18	2.3	28
Cucumbers, 10-oz; 7½ by about 2 in.:																	
Raw, pared	1 cucumber	207	96	30	1	Tr	—	—	—	7	35	0.6	Tr	0.07	0.09	0.4	23
Raw, pared, center slice ⅛-in. thick	6 slices	50	96	5	Tr	Tr	—	—	—	2	8	0.2	Tr	0.02	0.02	0.1	6
Dandelion greens, cooked	1 cup	180	90	60	4	1	—	—	—	12	252	3.2	21,060	0.24	0.29	—	32
Endive, curly (including escarole)	2 ounces	57	93	10	1	Tr	—	—	—	2	46	1.0	1,870	0.04	0.08	0.3	6
Kale, leaves including stems, cooked	1 cup	110	91	30	4	1	—	—	—	4	147	1.3	8,140	—	—	—	68

Lettuce, raw:																	
Butterhead, as Boston types; head, 4-in. diam	1 head	220	95	30	3	Tr	—	—	—	6	77	4.4	2,130	0.14	0.13	0.6	18
Crisphead, as Iceberg; head, 4¾-in. diam	1 head	454	96	60	4	Tr	—	—	—	13	91	2.3	1,500	0.29	0.27	1.3	29
Looseleaf, or bunching varieties, leaves	2 large	50	94	10	1	Tr	—	—	—	2	34	0.7	950	0.03	0.04	0.2	9
Mushrooms, canned, solids and liquid	1 cup	244	93	40	5	Tr	—	—	—	6	15	1.2	Tr	0.04	0.60	4.8	4
Mustard greens, cooked	1 cup	140	93	35	3	1	—	—	—	6	193	2.5	8,120	0.11	0.19	0.9	68
Okra, cooked, pod 3 × ⅝ in.	8 pods	85	91	25	2	Tr	—	—	—	5	78	0.4	420	0.11	0.15	0.8	17
Onions:																	
Mature:																	
Raw, onion 2½-in. diam	1 onion	110	89	40	2	Tr	—	—	—	10	30	0.6	40	0.04	0.04	0.2	11
Cooked	1 cup	210	92	60	3	Tr	—	—	—	14	50	0.8	80	0.06	0.06	0.4	14
Young green, small, without tops	6 onions	50	88	20	1	Tr	—	—	—	5	20	0.3	Tr	0.02	0.02	0.2	12
Parsley, raw, chopped	1 tablespoon	4	85	Tr	Tr	Tr	—	—	—	Tr	8	0.2	340	Tr	0.01	Tr	7
Parsnips, cooked	1 cup	155	82	100	2	1	—	—	—	23	70	0.9	50	0.11	0.12	0.2	16
Peas, green:																	
Cooked	1 cup	160	82	115	9	1	—	—	—	19	37	2.9	860	0.44	0.17	3.7	33
Canned, solids and liquid	1 cup	249	83	165	9	1	—	—	—	31	50	4.2	1,120	0.23	0.13	2.2	22
Canned, strained (baby food)	1 oz	28	86	15	1	Tr	—	—	—	3	3	0.4	140	0.02	0.02	0.4	3
Peppers, hot, red, without seeds, dried (ground chili powder, added seasonings)	1 tbsp	15	8	50	2	2	—	—	—	8	40	2.3	9,750	0.03	0.17	1.3	2
Peppers, sweet:																	
Raw, about 5 per lb:																	
Green pod without stem and seeds	1 pod	74	93	15	1	Tr	—	—	—	4	7	0.5	310	0.06	0.06	0.4	94
Cooked, boiled, drained	1 pod	73	95	15	1	Tr	—	—	—	3	7	0.4	310	0.05	0.05	0.4	70
Potatoes, medium (about 3 per lb raw):																	
Baked, peeled after baking	1 potato	99	75	90	3	Tr	—	—	—	21	9	0.7	Tr	0.10	0.04	1.7	20
Boiled:																	
Peeled after boiling	1 potato	136	80	105	3	Tr	—	—	—	23	10	0.8	Tr	0.13	0.05	2.0	22
Peeled before boiling	1 potato	122	83	80	2	Tr	—	—	—	18	7	0.6	Tr	0.11	0.04	1.4	20

(Continued)

TABLE 2.V.8 (*Continued*)

Food, Approximate Measure, and Weight (in Grams)		(g)	Water (%)	Food Energy (Cal)	Protein (g)	Fat (g)	Fatty Acids: Saturated (Total) (g)	Fatty Acids: Unsaturated: Oleic (g)	Fatty Acids: Unsaturated: Linoleic (g)	Carbohydrate (g)	Calcium (mg)	Iron (mg)	Vitamin A Value (IU)	Thiamin (mg)	Riboflavin (mg)	Niacin (mg)	Ascorbic Acid (mg)
Potatoes (*Cont.*)																	
French-fried, piece 2 × ½ × ½ in.:																	
Cooked in deep fat	10 pieces	57	45	155	2	7	2	2	4	20	9	0.7	Tr	0.07	0.04	1.8	12
Frozen, heated	10 pieces	57	53	125	2	5	1	1	2	19	5	1.0	Tr	0.08	0.01	1.5	12
Mashed:																	
Milk added	1 cup	195	83	125	4	1	—	—	—	25	47	0.8	50	0.16	0.10	2.0	19
Milk and butter added	1 cup	195	80	185	4	8	4	3	Tr	24	47	0.8	330	0.16	0.10	1.9	18
Potato chips, medium, 2-in. diameter	10 chips	20	2	115	1	8	2	2	4	10	8	0.4	Tr	0.04	0.01	1.0	3
Pumpkin, canned	1 cup	228	90	75	2	1	—	—	—	18	57	0.9	14,590	0.07	0.12	1.3	12
Radishes, raw, small, without tops	4 radishes	40	94	5	Tr	Tr	—	—	—	1	12	0.4	Tr	0.01	0.01	0.1	10
Sauerkraut, canned, solids and liquid	1 cup	235	93	45	2	Tr	—	—	—	9	85	1.2	120	0.07	0.09	0.4	33
Spinach:																	
Cooked	1 cup	180	92	40	5	1	—	—	—	6	167	4.0	14,580	0.13	0.25	1.0	50
Canned, drained solids	1 cup	180	91	45	5	1	—	—	—	6	212	4.7	14,400	0.03	0.21	0.6	24
Squash:																	
Cooked:																	
Summer, diced	1 cup	210	96	30	2	Tr	—	—	—	7	52	0.8	820	0.10	0.16	1.6	21
Winter, baked, mashed	1 cup	205	81	130	4	1	—	—	—	32	57	1.6	8,610	0.10	0.27	1.4	27
Sweetpotatoes:																	
Cooked, medium, 5 × 2 in., weight raw about 6 oz:																	
Baked, peeled after baking	1 sweetpotato	110	64	155	2	1	—	—	—	36	44	1.0	8,910	0.10	0.07	0.7	24
Boiled, peeled after boiling	1 sweetpotato	147	71	170	2	1	—	—	—	39	47	1.0	11,610	0.13	0.09	0.9	25

Candied, 3½ × 2¼ in.	1 sweetpotato	175	60	295	2	6	2	3	1	60	65	1.6	11,030	0.10	0.08	0.8	17
Canned, vacuum or solid pack	1 cup	218	72	235	4	Tr	—	—	—	54	54	1.7	17,000	0.10	0.10	1.4	30
Tomatoes:																	
Raw, approx 3-in. diam 2⅛ in. high; wt, 7 oz	1 tomato	200	94	40	2	Tr	—	—	—	9	24	0.9	1,640	0.11	0.07	1.3	[3]42
Canned, solids and liquid	1 cup	241	94	50	2	1	—	—	—	10	14	1.2	2,170	0.12	0.07	1.7	41
Tomato catsup:																	
Cup	1 cup	273	69	290	6	1	—	—	—	69	60	2.2	3,820	0.25	0.19	4.4	41
Tablespoon	1 tbsp	15	69	15	Tr	Tr	—	—	—	4	3	0.1	210	0.01	0.01	0.2	2
Tomato juice, canned:																	
Cup	1 cup	243	94	45	2	Tr	—	—	—	10	17	2.2	1,940	0.12	0.07	1.9	39
Glass (6 fl oz)	1 glass	182	94	35	2	Tr	—	—	—	8	13	1.6	1,460	0.09	0.05	1.5	29
Turnips, cooked, diced	1 cup	155	94	35	1	Tr	—	—	—	8	54	0.6	Trace	0.06	0.08	0.5	34
Turnip greens, cooked	1 cup	145	94	30	3	Tr	—	—	—	5	252	1.5	8,270	0.15	0.33	0.7	68

[1] Measure and weight apply to entire vegetable including parts not usually eaten.
[2] Based on yellow varieties; white varieties contain only a trace of cryptoxanthin and carotenes, the pigments in corn that have biological activity.
[3] Year-round average. Samples marketed from November through May, average 20 mg per 200-g tomato; from June through October, around 52 mg.

SOURCE: Nutritive Value of Foods. USDA Inst. Home Econ., Home Garden Bull. 72.

VEGETABLE COMPOSITION, PART II

TABLE 2.V.9

COMPOSITION OF THE EDIBLE PORTION (E.P.) AND REFUSE IN FRESH VEGETABLES AS PURCHASED (A.P.)

Commodity and Description	Water	Protein	Fat	Carbohydrate Total (by dif.)	Carbohydrate Fiber	Ash	Calories (per 100 g)	Notes	Refuse in A.P. (%)
	(Percent of edible portion)								
Tomatoes (*Lycopersicon esculentum*)	93.8	1.1	0.3	4.2	0.6	0.6	20		3
Roots, bulbs, and tubers									
Beets, common red (*Beta vulgaris*)	87.6	1.8	0.1	9.5	1.0	1.0	42	Refuse: A.P. without tops[1]	26
Jerusalem artichokes (*Helianthus tuberosus*)	80	2.2	0.1	16.5	0.8	1.2	70		30
Leeks and green onions (*Allium porrum*, *A. odorum*, *A. cepa*)	87.8	1.8	0.2	9.4	1.2	0.8	43		53
Oca (*Oxalis tuberosa*)	83.4	2.1	0.8	12.7	—	1.0	61		10
Onions, mature (*Allium cepa*)	88.8	1.4	0.2	9.0	0.8	0.6	40		7
Parsnips (*Pastinaca sativa*)	79.4	1.6	0.4	17.6	1.7	1.0	75		35
Radishes, common, small (*Raphanus sativus*)	93.7	1.1	0.1	4.2	0.7	0.9	20	Refuse: A.P. with tops	44
Radishes, large rooted (daikon) (*R. sativus*)	93.7	1.1	0.1	4.2	0.7	0.9	20	Refuse: A.P. without tops	5
Salsify and black salsify (*Tragopogon porrifolius*, *Scorzonera hispanica*)	79.0	3.2	0.6	16.4	1.8	0.8	77		23
Turnips and rutabagas or swedes (*Brassica rapa*, *B. campestris*)	91.3	1.1	0.1	6.8	1.1	0.7	80	Refuse: A.P. without tops[2]	5
Green and yellow vegetables									
Asparagus (*Asparagus officinalis*)	92.9	2.1	0.2	4.1	0.8	0.7	21		33
Beans, broad or fava (*Vicia faba*)	77.3	7.1	0.4	14.0	2.7	1.2	71		68
Beans, lima (*Phaseolus lunatus macrocarpus*)	66.3	7.5	0.9	23.6	1.4	1.7	110		61
Beans, snap or string, young in pods (haricots) (*P. vulgaris*)	89.1	2.4	0.2	7.6	1.5	0.7	35		9
Beet greens (*Beta vulgaris*)	89.8	2.1	0.5	6.5	1.5	2.1	29		(20)
Broccoli (*Brassica oleracea botrytis*)	85.7	4.3	0.3	8.7	1.3	1.0	44		42
Brussels sprouts (*B. oleracea gemmifera*)	84.8	4.7	0.5	8.7	1.2	1.3	47		24
Cabbage, Chinese (*B. chinensis* and *B. pekinensis*)	95	1.4	0.1	2.6	0.6	0.9	14		21
Cabbage, common, headed (*B. oleracea capitata*)	91.8	1.6	0.1	5.7	1.0	0.8	25		31

Carrots (*Daucus carota*)	88.6	1.1	0.2	9.1	1.0	1.0	40	Refuse: A.P. without tops[3]	8
Chard, silver beet (*Beta vulgaris*)	91.4	1.9	0.3	4.3	0.7	2.1	22		(20)
Chicory and endive (*Cichorium intybus, C. endivia*)	93.1	1.7	0.2	4.1	0.9	0.9	20		38
Dandelion greens (*Leontodon taraxacum*)	85.7	2.7	0.7	8.9	1.8	2.0	44		(10)
Ipomoea greens (*Ipomoea* spp.)	89.5	2.7	0.3	6.1	2.2	1.4	31		10
Kale (*Brassica oleracea acephala*)	85.9	3.9	0.6	7.8	1.3	1.8	42		37
Lettuce (*Lactuca sativa*)	94.8	1.3	0.2	2.8	0.6	0.9	15		31
Mustard greens (*Brassica juncea, B. lepidum*)	92.2	2.2	0.3	4.1	0.8	1.2	23		17
Peas, fresh (*Pisum sativum*)	75.0	6.7	0.4	17.0	0.2	0.9	80		56
Peas, edible-podded (*P. sativum*)	84.9	3.4	0.2	10.6	1.2	0.9	48		(9)
Peppers (*Capsicum annuum*), green	92.8	1.2	0.2	5.3	1.4	0.5	24	Includes chilies	18
Peppers, red	89.5	1.5	0.3	8.0	1.5	0.7	36	Includes chilies	18
Peppers, unspecified	91.2	1.4	0.3	6.5	1.4	0.6	29	Includes chilies	18
Spinach (*Spinacia oleracea*)	92.1	2.2	0.3	3.9	0.7	1.5	22		19
Turnip and rutabaga tops (*Brassica rapa, B. campestris*)	89.3	3.1	0.4	5.4	1.2	1.8	30		25
Other vegetables									
Artichokes, French or globe (*Cynara scolymus*)	83.7	3	0.2	11.8	1.9	1.3	51		53
Cauliflower (*Brassica oleracea botrytis*)	91.5	2.4	0.2	5.0	1.0	0.9	25		47
Celery (*Celeri graveolens*)	93.3	1.1	0.2	4.3	0.9	1.1	20		38
Cucumbers (*Cucumis sativus*)	95.6	0.8	0.1	3.0	0.6	0.5	13		28
Eggplant (*Solanum melongena*)	92.7	1.2	0.2	5.4	0.9	0.5	24		18
Kohlrabi (*Brassica oleracea gongylodes*)	90.5	2.1	0.2	6.2	1.1	1.0	29		48
Maize (corn), green (*Zea mays*)	73.9	3.4	1.2	20.7	1.0	0.7	92		62
Punpkins, squashes and gourds, mature (*Cucurbitaceae*, mainly *Cucurbita* spp.)	89.9	1.3	0.3	7.7	1.2	0.8	33	Winter types, squash, pumpkin	32
Pumpkins, squashes and gourds, immature (*Cucurbitaceae*, mainly *Cucurbita* spp.)	95	0.8	0.1	3.5	0.6	0.6	15	Summer squashes, vegetable marrow, zucchini, etc.	17
Unspecified fresh vegetables	91.3	1.8	0.2	5.8	1.0	0.9	27	Weighted average[4]	21

[1] Refuse, as purchased with tops is 48%.
[2] Refuse as purchased with tops is 35%.
[3] Refuse, as purchased with tops is 31%.
[4] Average of the kinds important in consumption; these figures are to be applied only when no information is available on each kind. In developing the averages for these values, the weights assigned to the groups were approximately as follows, in terms of the edible portion: tomatoes, 10%; roots, bulbs, and tubers, 16%; green and yellow, 56%; other vegetables, 18%.

SOURCE: CHATFIELD, C. Food Composition Tables for International Use. FAO, United Nations, Rome.

VEGETABLE COOKING, FROZEN

TABLE 2.V.10

FROZEN VEGETABLE COOKING TIME CHART[1]

Vegetable	In Open Kettle After Water Returns to Boiling Point	Vegetable	In Open Kettle After Water Returns to Boiling Point
	Min		Min
Asparagus, cuts and tips	5–8	Kale	20–25
Asparagus, spears	8–10	Kohlrabi	8–10
Beans, green, cut	12–15	Mixed vegetables	15–20
Beans, green, Frenched	8–10	Mushrooms (sauté—do not cook in water)	10–15
Beans, lima, Fordhook	12–16	Mustard greens	12–15
Beans, lima, bush	16–20	Okra	10–20
Beans, wax, cut	12–15	Peas	6–8
Beets, whole	18–20	Peas and carrots	5–10
Beets, cubed or sliced	Heat to serve	Rhubarb	10–12
Beet greens	10–12	Spinach, chopped	3–4
Broccoli, chopped	4–6	Spinach	4–6
Broccoli	5–7	Succotash	8–10
Brussels sprouts	5–7	Squash, summer	10–12
Carrots	5–10	Squash, winter	Heat to serve
Cauliflower	5–8	Swiss chard	8–10
Corn, kernel	3–4	Turnips	8–10
Corn on the cob (defrost completely)	3–4	Turnip greens	15–20

[1]This information is based on retail size cartons and the approximate cooking times may vary with the maturity, size, and quality of the product.

SOURCE: TRESSLER, D. K. and EVERS, C. F. The Freezing Preservation of Foods, 3rd Edition, Vol. *1*. Avi Publishing Co., Westport, Conn.

VEGETABLE FROZEN YIELD

TABLE 2.V.11

APPROXIMATE YIELD OF FROZEN VEGETABLES FROM FRESH

VEGETABLE	FRESH, AS PURCHASED OR PICKED	FROZEN
Asparagus	1 crate (12 2-lb. bunches)	15 to 22 pt.
	1 to 1½ lb.	1 pt.
Beans, lima (in pods)	1 bu. (32 lb.)	12 to 16 pt.
	2 to 2½ lb.	1 pt.
Beans, snap, green, and wax	1 bu. (30 lb.)	30 to 45 pt.
	⅔ to 1 lb.	1 pt.
Beet greens	15 lb.	10 to 15 pt.
	1 to 1½ lb.	1 pt.
Beets (without tops)	1 bu. (52 lb.)	35 to 42 pt.
	1¼ to 1½ lb.	1 pt.
Broccoli	1 crate (25 lb.)	24 pt.
	1 lb.	1 pt.
Brussels sprouts	4 quart boxes	6 pt.
	1 lb.	1 pt.
Carrots (without tops)	1 bu. (50 lb.)	32 to 40 pt.
	1¼ to 1½ lb.	1 pt.
Cauliflower	2 medium heads	3 pt.
	1⅓ lb.	1 pt.
Chard	1 bu. (12 lb.)	8 to 12 pt.
	1 to 1½ lb.	1 pt.
Collards	1 bu. (12 lb.)	8 to 12 pt.
	1 to 1½ lb.	1 pt.
Corn, sweet (in husks)	1 bu. (35 lb.)	14 to 17 pt.
	2 to 2½ lb.	1 pt.
Kale	1 bu. (18 lb.)	12 to 18 pt.
	1 to 1½ lb.	1 pt.
Mustard greens	1 bu. (12 lb.)	8 to 12 pt.
	1 to 1½ lb.	1 pt.
Peas	1 bu. (30 lb.)	12 to 15 pt.
	2 to 2½ lb.	1 pt.
Peppers, sweet	⅔ lb. (3 peppers)	1 pt.
Pumpkin	3 lb.	2 pt.
Spinach	1 bu. (18 lb.)	12 to 18 pt.
	1 to 1½ lb.	1 pt.
Squash, summer	1 bu. (40 lb.)	32 to 40 pt.
	1 to 1¼ lb.	1 pt.
Squash, winter	3 lb.	2 pt.
Sweetpotatoes	⅔ lb.	1 pt.

SOURCE: Home Freezing of Fruits and Vegetables. (1971). USDA Home And Garden Bull. *10*.

VEGETABLE PLANTS

TABLE 2.V.12

HABITS AND CHARACTERISTICS OF VEGETABLE PLANTS

Common and Latin names	Plant habit[1]	Approximate seeds per ounce	Germination: Time	Germination: At temperature	Notable characteristic or requirement
		Number	*Days*	*Degrees F.*	
Artichoke—*Cynara scolymus*	P	700	7–21	68–86	Tolerates cool soil.
Asparagus—*Asparagus officinalis*	P	700	7–21	68–86	Do.
Asparagusbean—*Vigna sesquipedalis*	A	225	5–8	68–86	Requires warm soil.
Beans:					
Garden—*Phaseolus vulgaris*	A	100–125	5–8	68–86	Do.
Dry edible—*Phaseolus vulgaris*	A	100–125	5–8	68–86	Do.
Lima—*Phaseolus lunatus*	A	25–75	5–9	68–86	Do.
Runner—*Phaseolus coccineus*	A	25–30	5–9	68–86	Do.
Beet—*Beta vulgaris*	B	1, 600	3–14	68–86	Tolerates cool soil.
Broadbean—*Vicia faba*	A	20–50	4–14	68–86	Do.
Broccoli—*Brassica oleracea* var. *botrytis*.	A–B	9, 000	3–10	68–86	Do.
Brussels sprouts—*Brassica oleracea* var. *gemmifera*.	B	9, 000	3–10	68–86	Do.
Cabbage—*Brassica oleracea* var. *capitata*.	B	9, 000	3–10	68–86	Do.
Cabbage, Chinese—*Brassica pekinensis*.	A–B	18, 000	3–7	68–86	Do.
Cardoon—*Cynara cardunculus*	P	700	7–21	68–86	Do.
Carrot—*Daucus carota*	B	23, 000	6–21	68–86	Do.
Cauliflower—*Brassica oleracea* var. *botrytis*.	A–B	9, 000	3–10	68–86	Do.
Celeriac—*Apium graveolens* var. *rapaceum*.	B	72, 000	10–21	50–68	Requires cool soil.
Celery—*Apium graveolens* var. *dulce*	B	72, 000	10–21	50–68	Requires cool soil.
Chard, Swiss—*Beta vulgaris* var. *cicla*.	B	1, 600	3–14	68–86	Tolerates cool soil.
Chicory—*Cichorium intybus*	P	27, 000	5–14	68–86	Do.
Citron—*Citrullus vulgaris*	A	300	7–14	68–86	Requires warm soil.
Collards—*Brassica oleracea* var. *acephala*.	B	9, 000	3–10	68–86	Tolerates cool soil.
Corn, sweet—*Zea mays*	A	120–180	4–7	68–86	Requires warm soil.
Cornsalad (fetticus)—*Valerianella locusta* var. *olitoria*.	A–B	....	7–28	68	Tolerates cool soil.
Cowpea (southern pea)—*Vigna sinensis*.	A	225	5–8	68–86	Requires warm soil.
Cress:					
Garden—*Lepidium sativum*	A	12, 000	4–10	68	Light sensitive.
Water—*Rorippa nasturtium-aquaticum*.	P	150, 000	4–14	68–86	Tolerates cool soil.
Cucumber—*Cucumis sativus*	A	1, 100	3–7	68–86	Requires warm soil.
Dandelion—*Taraxacum officinale*	B–P	35, 000	7–21	68–86	Tolerates cool soil.
Eggplant—*Solanum melongena* var. *esculentum*.	A	6, 500	7–14	68–86	Requires warm soil.
Endive—*Cichorium endivia*	A–B	27, 000	5–14	68–86	Tolerates cool soil.
Kale—*Brassica oleracea* var. *acephala*.	B	9, 000	3–10	68–86	Do.
Kale, Chinese—*Brassica oleracea* var. *alboglabra*.	B	9, 000	3–10	68–86	Do.
Kohlrabi—*Brassica oleracea* var. *gongylodes*.	B	9, 000	3–10	68–86	Do.
Leek—*Allium porrum*	B	11, 000	6–14	68	Requires cool soil.

TABLE 2.V.12 (*Continued*)

Common and Latin names	Plant habit[1]	Approximate seeds per ounce	Germination: Time	Germination: At temperature	Notable characteristic or requirement
		Number	*Days*	*Degrees F.*	
Lettuce—*Lactuca sativa*	A	25,000	7	68	Requires cool soil. Some varieties light sensitive.
Muskmelon (including cantaloup)—*Cucumis melo.*	A	1,300	4–10	68–86	Requires warm soil.
Mustard—*Brassica juncea*	A	18,000	3–7	68–86	Tolerates cool soil.
Mustard, spinach—*Brassica perviridis.*	A	15,000	3–7	68–86	Do.
Okra—*Hibiscus esculentus*	A	500	4–14	68–86	Requires warm soil.
Onion—*Allium cepa*	B	9,500	6–10	68	Requires cool soil.
Onion, Welsh—*Allium fistulosum*	B	....	6–12	68	Do.
Pak-choi—*Brassica chinensis*	A–B	18,000	3–7	68–86	Tolerates cool soil.
Parsley—*Petroselinum hortense* (*P. crispum*).	B	18,500	11–28	68–86	Do.
Parsnip—*Pastinaca sativa*	B	12,000	6–28	68–86	Do.
Pea—*Pisum sativum*	A	90–175	5–8	68	Requires cool soil.
Pepper—*Capsicum* spp	A	4,500	6–14	68–86	Requires warm soil.
Potato—*Solanum tuberosum*	P	....	.....	68	Tolerates cool soil.
Pumpkin—*Cucurbita pepo*	A	100–300	4–7	68–86	Requires warm soil.
Radish—*Raphanus sativus*	A	2–4,000	4–6	68	Requires cool soil.
Rhubarb—*Rheum rhaponticum*	P	1,700	7–21	68–86	Tolerates cool soil.
Rutabaga—*Brassica napus* var. *napobrassica.*	B	12,000	3–14	68–86	Do.
Salsify—*Tragopogon porrifolius*	B	1,900	5–10	68	Requires cool soil.
Sorrel—*Rumex acetosa*	P	30,000	3–14	68–86	Tolerates cool soil.
Soybean—*Glycine max*	A	175–350	5–8	68–86	Requires warm soil.
Spinach—*Spinacea oleracea*	A	2,800	7–21	59	Requires cool soil.
Spinach, New Zealand—*Tetragonia expansa.*	A	350	5–28	50–86	Germinates irregularly.
Sweetpotato—*Ipomoea batatas*	P	....	.....	77	Break or remove seedcoat.
Squash—*Cucurbita moschata* and *C. maxima.*	A	200–400	4–7	68–86	Requires warm soil.
Tomato—*Lycopersicon esculentum*	A	11,500	5–14	68–86	Do.
Tomato, husk—*Physalis pubescens*	A	35,000	7–28	68–86	Do.
Turnip—*Brassica rapa*	B	15,000	3–7	68–86	Tolerates cool soil.
Watermelon—*Citrullus vulgaris*	A	200–300	4–14	68–86	Requires warm soil.

[1] This column shows the nature of the parent plant—whether it is an annual, a biennial, or a perennial species: A—annual, B—biennial, P—perennial. Plants shown as A-B or B-P may exhibit either of two kinds of behavior, depending on cultural conditions and management.

SOURCE: Seeds: The Yearbook of Agriculture. U.S. Department of Agriculture.

VEGETABLE SERVINGS

TABLE 2.V.13

APPROXIMATE SERVINGS PER CAN, POUND, AND PACKAGE

FRESH VEGETABLES	*Servings per lb*[1]
Asparagus	3 or 4
Beans, lima [2]	2
Beans, snap	5 or 6
Beets, diced [3]	3 or 4
Broccoli	3 or 4
Brussels sprouts	4 or 5
Cabbage:	
Raw, shredded	9 or 10
Cooked	4 or 5
Carrots:	
Raw, diced or shredded [3]	5 or 6
Cooked [3]	4
Cauliflower	3
Celery:	
Raw, chopped or diced	5 or 6
Cooked	4
Kale [4]	5 or 6
Okra	4 or 5
Onions, cooked	3 or 4
Parsnips [3]	4
Peas [2]	2
Potatoes	4
Spinach [5]	4
Squash, summer	3 or 4
Squash, winter	2 or 3
Sweetpotatoes	3 or 4
Tomatoes, raw, diced or sliced	4

[1] As purchased.
[2] Bought in pod.
[3] Bought without tops.
[4] Bought untrimmed.
[5] Bought prepackaged.

FROZEN VEGETABLES	*Servings per Package (9 or 10 oz)*
Asparagus	2 or 3
Beans, lima	3 or 4
Beans, snap	3 or 4
Broccoli	3
Brussels sprouts	3
Cauliflower	3
Corn, whole kernel	3
Kale	2 or 3
Peas	3
Spinach	2 or 3

CANNED VEGETABLES	*Servings per can (1 lb)*
Most vegetables	3 or 4
Greens, such as kale or spinach	2 or 3

DRY VEGETABLES	*Servings per lb*
Dry beans	11
Dry peas, lentils	10 or 11

SOURCE: Nutrition, Food at Work for You. (1968) USDA Home and Garden Bull. *1*.

VEGETABLE STORAGE I

Store in cool room, away from bright light:

Onions, mature	Rutabagas	Sweetpotatoes
Potatoes	Squash, winter	

Refrigerate, covered:

Asparagus	Cauliflower	Parsnips
Beans, snap or wax	Celery	Peas, shelled
Beets	Corn, husked	Peppers, green
Broccoli	Cucumbers	Radishes
Cabbage	Greens	Squash, summer
Carrots	Onions, green	Turnips

Refrigerate, uncovered:

Beans, lima, in pods	Peas, in pods	Watermelons
Corn, in husks	Pineapples	

SOURCE: Nutrition, Food at Work for You. (1968). USDA Home and Garden Bull. *1*.

VEGETABLE STORAGE II

TABLE 2.V.14

RECOMMENDED COLD STORAGE CONDITIONS, HEAT OF RESPIRATION AND LOSS IN WEIGHT OF VEGETABLES GROWN IN THE TROPICS

Vegetables	Temp. °F	Relative Humidity %	Storage Life Wk	Heat Evolution[a] BTU/ton-day	Weight Loss[b] %
Ampalaya	42–45	85–90	3		12.0
Asparagus	32	95	3–4	18,600	
Beans					
Bush sitao	42	88–92	4	6,881	14.0
Lima in pods	40–45	90–95	1.5–2	16,400	12.0
Lima, shelled	40	95	2	14,080	
Dolichos lablab, in pods	32–35	90	3	13,260–14,200	20.3
Snap	38–42	88	2–3	5,600	15.0
Winged	50	90	4	7,116	18.0
Beet, bunched	32	90	1.5	1,170	
Beet, topped	32–35	90–95	8–14	1,000	33.0
Betel leaves	42–45	85–90	1	13,200	2.8
Bitter Gourd	33–35	85–90	4		
Brinjal	47–50	85–90	4	4,400–6,600	17.7
Brussels Sprout	32–35	90–95	4–6		
Cabbage, wet season	32–35	92–95	4–6	3,600	
Cabbage, dry season	32–35	92–95	12	2,000–2,400	10.0
Carrot, bunched	32	90–95	4		25.0
Carrot, topped	32	95	20–24	810	20.0–35.0
Cauliflower, 'Snowball'	32–35	85–95	7	5,200–6,400	30.4
Celery	31–32	92–95	8	700	15.2
Chayote	45	85–90	4–6	1,271	4.9
Colocasia	52–55	85–90	21		
Condol	45	85	8		
Coriander leaves	32–35	90	5		
Corn, sweet	33–35	90–95	1	11,000–16,500	3.2
Corn, green	32	90–95	1.5		
Chow-Chow	52–55	90	3	5,500–6,600	10.0
Cucumber	50–53	92	2	3,960–5,500	7.2

(Continued)

TABLE 2.V.14 *(Continued)*

Vegetables	Temp. °F	Relative Humidity %	Storage Life Wk	Heat Evolution[a] BTU/ton-day	Weight Loss[b] %
Eggplant	50–55	92	2–3	9,251–13,609	9.6
Garlic (bulbs), dry	32	65	28–36	800	12.6
Ginger	45–50	75	16–24		18.9
Gourd, bottle	45	85–90	4–6		3.2
Gourd, Snake	65–70	85–90	2		
Leek	32	90–95	4–12	2,500	
Lettuce, head	32	90–95	3	640	14.0
Lettuce, leaf	32	95	1		
Mushroom	32	95	1.5	10,800	7.8
Muskmelon, cantaloupe	35–38	85–90	1.5	3,960–4,640	7.2
Muskmelon, Honeydew	45	85	4–5		
Okra	48	90	2	10,670	6.8
Onion, white	34	70–75	16–20	1,000	14.2
Onion, red	32	70–75	20–24	660	16.3
Onion, green (immature)	32	90–95	2		
Patola (Trichosanthes)	42–45	85–90	3		11.3
Pea, green	32	88–92	2–3	5,000	8.0
Pepper, sweet (green)	45	85–90	3–5	5,200	7.1
Pepper, sweet (ripe)	42–45	90–95	2	2,200	
Petsai, Brassica	32	95	1.5–2.5	2,300	15.0
Potato, Irish (8 varieties)	38–40	85	34	800–2,200	4.9
Pumpkin	35–60	70–75	24–36		3.7
Radish, topped	32	88–92	3–5	4,200	8.0
Squash	55–60	70–75	8–24		4.0–15.0
Sweet potato	50–55	80–90	13–20	1,320–6,600	8.5
Tapioca root	32–35	85	23		
Tomato					
'VC-lines', mature green	48–50	85–90	4–5	3,216–4,156	5.2
'VC-lines', ripe	45	90	1	2,860	
'Oxheart', 'Hybrid-6', 'Marathi', all green	35–38	85–90	6	3,300–4,400	4.8
'Ponderosa', yellow	42–45	85–90	3		
'Sioux', red	32–35	85–90	2	1,441–1,600	
Turnip	32	90–95	8–16	1,300	
Watermelon	45–60	80–90	2	2,400	2.0
Yam	80	60–70	3–5		

Source: Authors' unpublished data.
[a]Represents steady state heat production during storage at indicated temperatures.
[b]Loss in weight upon removal from storage at indicated storage periods. This may include trimming losses for leafy vegetables. Weight loss values are averages of several trials, some in commercial storage plants but mostly in experimental cold rooms.

SOURCE: PANTASTICO, ER. B., CHATTOPADHYAY, T. K. and SUBRAMANYAM, H. 1975. Storage and Commercial Storage Operations. *In* Postharvest Physiology, Handling and Utilization of Tropical and Subtropical Fruits and Vegetables. Er. B. Pantastico (Editor). Avi Publishing Co., Westport, Conn.

VEGETABLE YIELD

TABLE 2.V.15

AMOUNT OF FROZEN PRODUCT OBTAINABLE FROM 100-FOOT ROW

	Yield from 100-ft Row, (Avg)	Pounds of Frozen Product from 100-ft Row
Carrots	1 bu	40
Beets	1½ bu	60
Snap beans	1½ bu	20
Lima beans	12 qt shelled	18
Broccoli	75 lb	50
Spinach	40 lb	25
Peas	10 qt shelled	15
Sweet corn	60 ears	12
Cauliflower	25 heads	15
Asparagus	30 lb	20
Rhubarb	200 lb	175
Squash or pumpkin	150 lb	75

SOURCE: STOUT, G. J. The Home Freezer Handbook. Van Nostrand Reinhold Co., New York.

VEGETABLE YIELD, CANNED AND FROZEN

TABLE 2.V.16

YIELD OF VEGETABLES PROCESSED IN CANS OR FROZEN

	Approximate Amount of Cooked Vegetable Obtained From:			
	Canned (Drained)		Frozen Packages	
Vegetable	Size of Container (oz)	Cups	Size of Container (oz)	Cups
Asparagus, cut	14	1⅓	10	1¼
Beans, green or wax, cut	15½	1¾	9	1⅔
Beans, lima	16	1¾	10	1⅔
Beets, sliced, diced or whole	16	1¾	—	—
Broccoli, cut	—	—	10	1½
Carrots, diced or sliced	16	1¾	10	1⅔
Cauliflower	—	—	10	1½
Corn, whole kernel	16	1⅔	10	1½
Kale	15	1⅓	10	1⅛
Okra	15½	1¾	10	1¼
Peas	16	1¾	10	1⅔
Potatoes, French fried	—	—	9	1⅔
Spinach	15	1⅓	10	1¼
Summer squash, sliced	—	—	10	1⅓
Tomatoes, undrained	16	1⅞	—	—

SOURCE: ANON. 1969. How to Buy Canned and Frozen Vegetables. USDA Home and Garden Bulletin *167*.

VEGETABLE YIELD, FROZEN, CANNED AND FRESH

TABLE 2.V.17

APPROXIMATE AMOUNT OF COOKED VEGETABLE OBTAINED FROM FROZEN, CANNED, AND FRESH

Vegetable and style	Frozen vegetables		Canned vegetables (drained)		1 lb. of fresh vegetable as purchased—
	Size of container (ounces)	Cooked, Cups	Size of container (ounces)	Heated, Cups	Cups
Asparagus, cut	10	1¼	14	1⅓	1¾
Beans, green or wax, cut	9	1⅔	15½	1¾	2¾
Beans, lima	10	1⅔	16	1¾	1⅛
Beets, sliced, diced or whole	...	...	16	1¾	1⅞
Broccoli, cut	10	1⅓	...	...	1½
Brussels sprouts	10	1½	...	...	2¼
Cabbage, shredded	...	...	...	...	2⅓
Carrots, diced, or sliced	10	1⅔	16	1¾	2⅛
Cauliflower	10	1½	...	...	1½
Corn, whole kernel	10	1½	[1] 16	1⅔	...
Kale	10	1⅛	15	1⅓	2⅔
Okra	10	1¼	15½	1¾	2¼
Peas	10	1⅔	16	1¾	1
Potatoes	9	[2] 1⅔	...	...	[3] 1¾
Spinach	10	1¼	15	1⅓	2
Summer squash, sliced	10	1⅓	...	...	2
Tomatoes	...	...	[4] 16	1⅞	...

[1] Whole kernels with liquid; a 12 oz. can of whole kernels, vacuum pack, provides 1¾ cups.
[2] French fries.
[3] Mashed.
[4] Undrained.

SOURCE: Food For Us All. Yearbook of Agriculture, 1969. USDA.

VEGETABLES, BOILING TIME, FROZEN

TABLE 2.V.18

BOILING GUIDE FOR HOME FROZEN VEGETABLES

Vegetable	Cooking time after water returns to boil	Approximate amount of frozen vegetable for six servings (½ cup each)
	Minutes	*Ounces*
Asparagus, whole	8 to 10	24
Beans, lima	12 to 14	18
Beans, snap (green or wax), cut	7 to 9	16
Broccoli spears	6 to 8	22
Brussels sprouts	10 to 12	20
Carrots:		
Slices	6 to 8	18
Strips	7 to 9	18
Cauliflower	2 to 6	20
Corn:		
Whole kernel	7 to 9	20
On cob	4 to 8	32
Kale	8 to 10	25
Okra, whole	6 to 8	16
Peas	8 to 10	18
Spinach	2 to 6	25
Squash, summer, sliced	6 to 8	22

SOURCE: Vegetables in Family Meals. (1975) USDA Home and Garden Bull. *105*.

VEGETABLES, CANNED GRADES

U.S. Grade A or Fancy	Grade A vegetables are carefully selected for color, tenderness, and freedom from blemishes. They are the most tender, succulent, and flavorful vegetables produced.
U.S. Grade B or Extra Standard	Grade B vegetables are of excellent quality but not quite so well selected for color and tenderness as Grade A. They are usually slightly more mature and therefore have a slightly different taste than the more succulent vegetables in Grade A.
U.S. Grade C or Standard	Grade C vegetables are not so uniform in color and flavor as vegetables in the higher grades and they are usually more mature. They are a thrifty buy when appearance is not too important—for instance, if you're using the vegetables as an ingredient in soup or souffle.
Packed under continuous inspection of the U.S. Department of Agriculture	This statement may be given along with the grade name or it may be shown by itself. It provides assurance of a wholesome product of at least minimum quality.

The grade names and the statement, "Packed under continuous inspection of the U.S. Department of Agriculture," may also appear within shields.

SOURCE: How to Buy Canned and Frozen Vegetables. (1969) USDA Home and Garden Bull. *167*.

VEGETABLES, CANNING DATES

TABLE 2.V.19

OPENING AND CLOSING CANNING DATES

STATES AND TERRITORIES	Arti-chokes	Aspara-gus	BEANS Lima	Snap	Beets	Corn	Carrots	Kraut	Okra	Peas
ALABAMA				May 1-July 10 Oct. 1-Oct. 30					May 1 Sept. 1	
ARKANSAS			July 1 Nov. 15	May 5-July 5 Oct. 1-Nov. 15		July 1 July 31			June 1 Sept. 1	
CALIFORNIA	Feb. 1 Apr. 30	Apr. 1 June 30	Sept. 1 Oct. 31	Aug. 1 Oct. 15	May 5 Dec. 20					Apr. 10 June 30
COLORADO				July 15 Oct. 1	Aug. 1 Oct. 15			All Year		June 15 Aug. 1
DELAWARE		Apr. 25 June 30	Aug. 5 Sept. 30	June 20-July 20 Sept. 5-Sept. 30		July 25 Sept. 15				May 25 June 20
FLORIDA				Jan. 1-May 15 Nov. 1-Dec. 15						
GEORGIA				May 1-June 15 Aug. 20-Sept. 15					May 15 Sept. 1	
IDAHO						Aug. 1 Sept. 15				June 1 July 20
ILLINOIS		Apr. 20 June 25	Aug. 15 Sept. 30	July 5 Sept. 30		Aug. 1 Sept. 25				June 3 July 30
INDIANA				July 1 Oct. 15		Aug. 1 Sept. 30		All Year		June 1 July 30
IOWA		Apr. 25 June 25				Aug. 1 Oct. 1				June 10 July 15
KENTUCKY				June 1-July 15 Sept. 15-Oct. 15				All Year		
LOUISIANA						June 1 July 15			May 1 Sept. 1	
MAINE				Aug. 1-Sept. 15		Aug. 20 Oct. 15				July 1 Aug. 30
MARYLAND		Apr. 20 June 30	Aug. 5 Oct. 10	June 15 July 31	June 1 July 15	July 20 Sept. 15		All Year		May 20 July 15
MICHIGAN		May 10 July 1	Sept. 1 Sept. 30	July 10 Sept. 15	Aug. 1 Nov. 20	Aug. 10 Sept. 20	Oct. 1 Nov. 25	All Year		June 15 Aug. 15
MINNESOTA		May 1 July 1	Aug. 15 Sept. 30	July 20 Sept. 20	July 20 Nov. 30	Aug. 5 Sept. 1				June 15 Aug. 1
MISSISSIPPI				May 1-July 31 Oct. 1-Nov. 1					May 1 Sept. 1	
MISSOURI				June 15 Oct. 15						
NEBRASKA				July 10-Oct. 1		Aug. 10 Oct. 1				
NEW JERSEY		Apr. 20 July 1	Aug. 1 Oct. 1	July 1 Oct. 1					Aug. 20 Oct. 1	May 20 July 10
NEW YORK		May 10 July 15		July 5 Sept. 25	Aug. 1 Dec. 31	Aug. 10 Sept. 20	Sept. 15 Dec. 31	All Year		June 20 Aug. 1
NORTH CAROLINA				June 1-July 10					June 1 Sept. 15	
OHIO		May 5 July 25		July 25 Sept. 5	July 20 Nov. 30	Aug. 1 Sept. 25		Year	All	May 28 Aug. 1
OKLAHOMA				May 15-July 10 Oct. 1-Nov. 15						
OREGON		Apr. 15 July 1		Aug. 1 Sept. 5	July 1 Oct. 15	Aug. 15 Sept. 30	Aug. 20 Oct. 15	All Year		June 10 Aug. 20
PENNSYLVANIA			July 1 Oct. 1	July 15 Sept. 20	July 25 Oct. 1	Aug. 5 Sept. 20		All Year		June 1 July 25
SOUTH CAROLINA				May 20-Aug. 10 Sept. 15-Oct. 30					June 1 Sept. 15	Aug. 5 Sept. 30
TENNESSEE			Aug. 1 Sept. 20	July 15 Sept.20	July 10 Aug. 15	July 25 Aug. 30		All Year		May 15 June 15
TEXAS				Apr. 1-June 20 Nov. 1-Dec. 15	Nov. 15 May 15		Nov. 15 May 15			
UTAH			Aug. 5 Oct. 1	July 10 Oct. 15	June 1 Oct. 15	Aug. 15 Sept. 25	Aug. 15 Oct. 15	All Year		June 10 Aug. 10
VIRGINIA			Aug. 1 Oct. 10	June 10-July 15						May 15 June 5
WASHINGTON		May 1 July 1		Aug. 1 Sept. 5	July 1 Oct. 15	Aug. 15 Sept. 30	Aug. 20 Oct. 15	All Year		June 10 Aug. 20
WISCONSIN			Aug. 20 Sept. 20	July 10 Oct. 1	July 20 Nov. 30	Aug. 1 Oct. 1	July 25 Nov. 30	All Year		June 10 Aug. 20
ONTARIO, CANADA		May 5 June 30		July 15 Sept. 25	Aug. 1 Mar. 1	Aug. 10 Oct. 10	Oct. 1 Jan. 15	All Year		June 25 Aug. 1
QUEBEC, CANADA				June 25 Sept. 25	Oct. 1 Dec. 1	Aug. 25 Oct. 10	Oct. 1 Dec. 1			July 1 Aug. 5
VANCOUVER, B. C.		May 15 June 15		Aug. 1 Sept. 30		Sept. 1 Oct. 15				June 20 Aug. 1

TABLE 2.V.19 (*Continued*)

STATES AND TERRITORIES	Pickles	Pimientos	Pumpkin	Rhubarb	Spinach	Sprouts	Squash	Succotash	Sweet Potato	Tomatoes
ALABAMA		Aug. 1 Nov. 15			Feb. 20-May 30 Oct. 15-Dec. 31				Aug. 1 Feb. 1	Aug. 1-Sept. 15
ARKANSAS					Feb. 20-May 30 Oct. 15-Dec. 31					Aug. 1-Oct. 20
CALIF.	All Year	Sept. 15 Dec. 15	Oct. 1 Nov. 15		Feb. 20-Apr. 20 Oct. 1-Dec. 15				Sept. 1 Dec. 31	July 10 Nov. 10
COLO.			Oct. 1 Nov. 15				Oct. 5 Nov. 15			Aug. 15 Oct. 15
DEL.					Nov. 10 Mar. 1		Oct. 1 Nov. 5		Sept. 15 Dec. 1	July 15 Oct. 1
FLORIDA									Aug. 1 Feb. 1	Mar. 1 May 15
GEORGIA		Aug. 1 Nov. 15								Aug. 1-Feb. 1
IDAHO										
ILLINOIS			Sept. 10 Oct. 30							Aug. 1 Oct. 1
INDIANA			Sept. 15 Nov. 15					Aug. 20 Sept. 15		Aug. 1 Oct. 15
IOWA										Aug. 10 Oct. 15
KY.								Aug. 10 Aug. 30		Aug. 1 Oct. 15
LOUISIANA		Oct. 1 Dec. 1							July 20 Mar. 1	
MD.			Oct. 1 Nov. 10		Apr. 1-May 15 Nov. 1-Nov. 30		Oct. 1 Nov. 10	Aug. 18 Oct. 1	Sept. 15 Dec. 1	July 15 Oct. 15
MICHIGAN	All Year		Sept. 10 Oct. 30	May 20 June 30	June 10-July 1 Sept. 20-Oct. 20		Sept. 5 Sept. 30			Aug. 1 Sept. 30
MINN.	All Year		Sept. 10 Oct. 30							
MISSOURI					May 1 June 15				Aug. 15 Feb. 1	Aug. 10 Oct. 20
NEBR.			Oct. 1 Dec. 1							Aug. 10 Oct. 1
N. J.			Oct. 1 Nov. 1		Apr. 1-May 31 Oct. 20-Nov. 30		Oct. 1 Nov. 15		Sept. 15 Nov. 15	July 15 Oct. 15
NEW YORK			Sept. 20 Nov. 15	May 20 June 30	June 5-June 20 Sept. 25-Oct. 10		Sept. 15 Nov. 1	Sept. 1 Oct. 1		Aug. 5 Oct. 5
NORTH CAROLINA	All Year	Aug. 10 Sept. 30							Sept. 1 Dec. 31	July 10 Sept. 1
OHIO			Sept. 10 Nov. 20							Aug. 1 Oct. 1
OKLA.					Feb. 20-May 30 Oct. 15-Dec. 31					Aug. 1-Oct. 20
OREGON	All Year		Oct. 1 Nov. 30	May 1 June 10			Oct. 10 Nov. 10			Aug. 15 Oct. 1
PA.								Aug. 20 Sept. 15		Aug. 5 Oct. 5
SOUTH CAROLINA										June 30 Aug. 15
TENN.		Aug. 15 Nov. 15	Sept. 15 Nov. 15		Mar. 1-June 1 Sept. 15-Oct. 10			Aug. 10 Sept. 10	Sept. 1 Dec. 1	Apr. 25-June 1 Sept. 15-Oct. 10
TEXAS					Nov. 10 Mar. 20				Oct. 1 Feb. 1	May 15-June 20 Dec. 1-Jan. 15
UTAH			Oct. 1 Nov. 15				Oct. 1 Nov. 15			Aug. 15 Oct. 15
VIRGINIA					Apr. 1-May 25 Oct. 25-Nov. 30				Sept. 1 Dec. 15	July 15 Sept. 15
WASH.	All Year		Oct. 1 Nov. 30	May 1 June 10	Sept. 1 Oct. 15		Oct. 10 Nov. 10			Aug. 15 Oct. 1
WEST VIRGINIA										Aug. 1 Sept. 30
WISC.	All Year		Sept. 10 Nov. 20	May 10 May 30	June 1-June 20		Sept. 10 Nov. 20			Aug. 10 Oct. 10
ONTARIO, CANADA			Oct. 1 Nov. 15	May 25 June 30	May 25-June 20 Sept .20-Oct. 18					Aug. 10 Oct. 15
QUEBEC, CANADA			Oct. 1 Oct. 15							Aug. 15 Oct. 10
VANCR., B. C.			Oct. 1 Nov. 30	June 1 July 30						Aug. 1 Oct. 15

SOURCE: The Almanac of the Canning, Freezing, Preserving Industries, 58th Edition. (1976) E. E. Judge & Son, Baltimore, Maryland.

VEGETABLES, CLASSIFICATION

TABLE 2.V.20

VEGETABLE CLASSIFICATION

Family	Fruit/ Vegetable	Scientific Name	Type	Description
		Fruit Vegetables		
Cucurbitaceae	Chayote	*Sechium edule* (Jacq.) Sw.	Pepo	Outer wall is receptacle.
	Cucumber	*Cucumis sativus* L.	Pepo	Flesh of the fruit is mesocarp and endocarp. Derived from inferior ovary.
	Squash	*Cucurbita maxima* Duch.	Pepo	–Ditto–
Malvaceae	Okra	*Hibiscus esculentus* L.	Berry	Fibrous pericarp.
Leguminosae	Cowpea	*Vigna sinensis* (Stickm.) Savi ex Hassk	Legume	Derived from monocarpellary ovary; it splits along both sutures.
	Beans	*Phaseolus* sp. L.	Legume	–Ditto–
	Pea	*Pisum sativum* L.	Legume	–Ditto–
Solanaceae	Eggplant	*Solanum melongena* L. var. *esculentum*	Berry	Thin exocarp; mesocarp and exocarp fused.
	Sweet pepper	*Capsicum frutescens* L. var. *grossum*	Berry	Large internal cavity.
	Tomato	*Lycopersicon esculentum* Mill. var. *commune*	Berry	Seeds embedded in juicy flesh.
		Subterranean Vegetables		
Liliaceae	Garlic	*Allium sativum* L.	Modified skin	Compound bulb made of cloves; 3 kinds of scales.
	Leek	*Allium porum* L.	Leaves	Swollen, blanched bases but not a distinct bulb.
	Onion	*Allium cepa* L.	Bulb	Short stem with overlapping leaf bases, fleshy leaves.
Chenopodiaceae	Beet	*Beta vulgaris* L.	Storage root	Pigmented tissue.

Cruciferae	Radish	*Raphanus sativus* L.	Storage root	Fleshy root, porous when aged.
	Turnip	*Brassica rapa* L. var. *rapifera* Metz.	Modified root	Top-like organ.
Convolvulaceae	Sweet Potato	*Ipomoea batatas* (L.) Poir.	Root	Texture more rough than Irish potato.
Umbelliferae	Carrot	*Daucus carota* L. var. *sativa*	Modified root	Pigmented flesh.
Zingiberaceae	Ginger	*Zingiber officinale*	Rhizome	Bulky, underground, horizontal stem.
Solanaceae	Irish Potato	*Solanum tuberosum* L.	Tuber	Bulky, short terminal portion of stem.
Leafy Vegetables (Including flower and stem)				
Liliaceae	Asparagus	*Asparagus officinalis* L. var. *altilis*	Stem	Fleshy shoot with spirally arranged scales.
Umbelliferae	Celery	*Apium graveolens* L. var. *dulce*	Leaf	Ridged petioles and compound leaves with 3 to 7 leaflets.
	Parsley	*Petroselinum crispum* (Mill.) Nym.	Stem and leaf	Lobed and curled leaves, pinnately compound.
Compositae	Lettuce	*Lactuca sativa* L.	Leaf	Curly tips.
Cruciferae	Brussels sprouts	*Brassica oleracea* var. *gemmifera*	Buds	Adventitious side shoots.
	Cabbage	*Brassica oleracea* var. *capitata*	Staminal bulb	Forms a head.
	Cauliflower	*Brassica oleracea* var. *botrytis* DC	Curd	Consists of short internodes, branched apices and bracts.
	Kohlrabi	*Brassica caulorapa*	Stem	Globular stem, thin rind.
	Mustard	*Brassica juncea* Coss.	Leaf	Leaves with notched margin and crepe-like surface.
	Petsai	*Brassica pekinensis*	Leaf	Spatulate leaves with broad midrib.

SOURCE: PANTASTICO, ER. B. (EDITOR). 1975. Structure of Fruits and Vegetables. *In* Postharvest Physiology, Handling and Utilization of Tropical and Subtropical Fruits and Vegetables. Avi Publishing Co., Westport, Conn.

VEGETABLES, COOKING FROZEN

TABLE 2.V.21

TIMETABLE FOR COOKING FROZEN VEGETABLES IN A SMALL AMOUNT OF WATER[1]

VEGETABLE	Time to allow after water returns to boil [2]	VEGETABLE	Time to allow after water returns to boil [2]
	Minutes		*Minutes*
Asparagus	5–10	Chard	8–10
Beans, lima:		Corn:	
Large type	6–10	Whole-kernel	3–5
Baby type	15–20	On-the-cob	3–4
Beans, snap, green, or wax:		Kale	8–12
1-inch pieces	12–18	Kohlrabi	8–10
Julienne	5–10	Mustard greens	8–15
Beans, soybeans, green	10–20	Peas, green	5–10
Beet greens	6–12	Spinach	4–6
Broccoli	5–8	Squash, summer	10–12
Brussels sprouts	4–9	Turnip greens	15–20
Carrots	5–10	Turnips	8–12
Cauliflower	5–8		

[1] Use ½ cup of lightly salted water for each pint of vegetable with these exceptions: Lima beans, 1 cup; corn-on-the-cob, water to cover.

[2] Time required at sea level; slightly longer time is required at higher altitudes.

SOURCE: Home Freezing of Fruits and Vegetables. (1971) USDA Home and Garden Bull. *10*.

VEGETABLES, PANNED

TABLE 2.V.22

GUIDE FOR COOKING PANNED VEGETABLES (6 SERVINGS, ½ CUP EACH)

Vegetable	Amount of—				Cooking time
	Vegetable	Fat	Salt	Water	
	Quarts	*Table-spoons*	*Tea-spoons*		*Minutes*
Beans, snap (green or wax), sliced in 1-inch pieces	1	1½	½	⅝ cup	20 to 25.
Cabbage, finely shredded	1½	1½	¾	3 tablespoons	6 to 8.
Carrots, thinly sliced	1	2	½	3 tablespoons	10.
Corn, cut	1	1½	½	⅓ cup	15 to 18.
Spinach, finely shredded	3	2	½	-------------	6 to 8.
Summer squash, thinly sliced	1	1½	½	3 tablespoons	12 to 15.

SOURCE: Vegetables in Family Meals. (1975) USDA Home and Garden Bull. *105*.

VINEGAR, SPICED

Ingredients	%
24's Vinegar	86.0
Chillies	3.4
Pimientos	2.4
Coriander seed	2.4
Cloves (whole)	1.7
Black pepper (whole)	1.7
Mustard seed	1.2
Root ginger	1.2
	100.0

SOURCE: BINSTED, R., DEVEY, J. D., and DAKIN, J. C. 1971. Pickle & Sauce Making, 3rd Edition. Food Trade Press, London, England.

VITAMIN A

TABLE 2.V.23

VITAMIN A IN SOME FOODS

	IU/100 g		IU/100 g
Carrots	11500	Cherries	1000
Sweet potatoes	8800	Tomatoes	900
Spinach	8100	Asparagus	900
Cantaloupe	3400	Peppers	420
Apricots	2700	Corn	400
Broccoli	2500	Lettuce	330
Peaches	1330	Oranges	200

SOURCE: WHITE, P. L. and SELVEY, N. (EDITORS). 1974. Nutritional Qualities of Fresh Fruits and Vegetables. Futura Publishing Co., Mt. Kisco, N.Y.

VITAMIN A, DAILY RECOMMENDATIONS

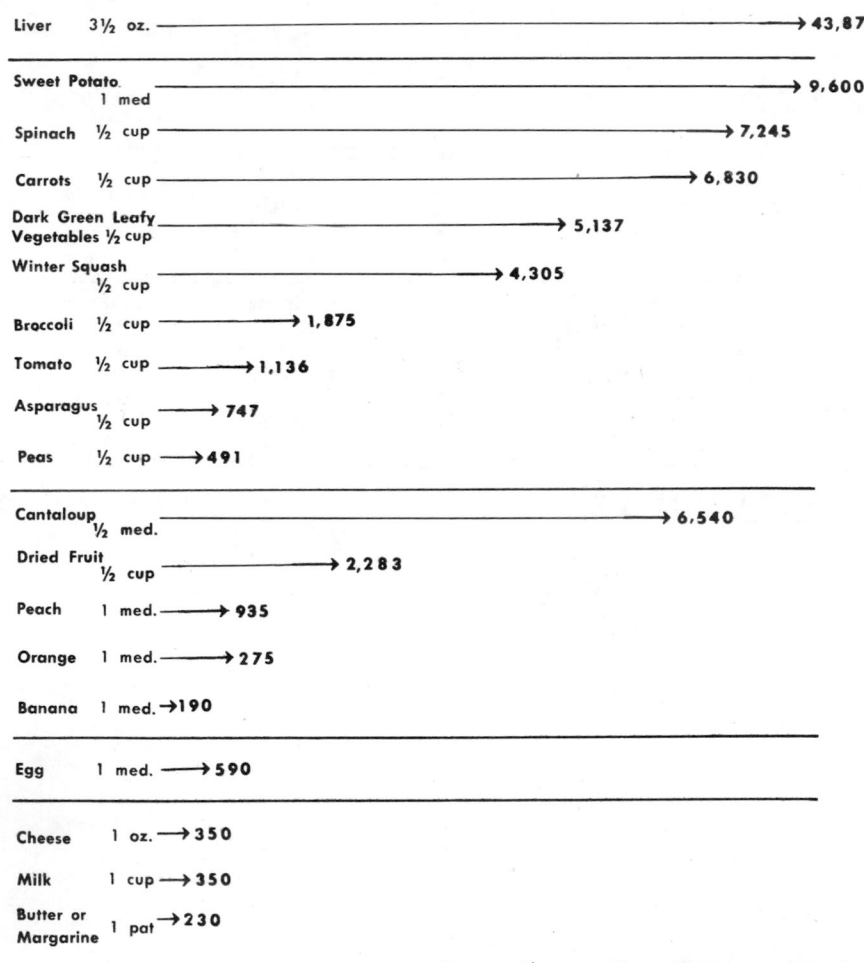

INTERNATIONAL UNITS

	Age	International Units
CHILDREN	1 to 4	2,000
	4 to 7	2,500
	7 to 11	3,300
MALES	11 to 51 +	5,000
FEMALES	11 to 51 +	4,000
	Pregnant	5,000
	Lactating	6,000

GOOD SOURCES†

INTERNATIONAL UNITS

		International Units
Liver	3½ oz.	43,875
Sweet Potato	1 med	9,600
Spinach	½ cup	7,245
Carrots	½ cup	6,830
Dark Green Leafy Vegetables	½ cup	5,137
Winter Squash	½ cup	4,305
Broccoli	½ cup	1,875
Tomato	½ cup	1,136
Asparagus	½ cup	747
Peas	½ cup	491
Cantaloup	½ med.	6,540
Dried Fruit	½ cup	2,283
Peach	1 med.	935
Orange	1 med.	275
Banana	1 med.	190
Egg	1 med.	590
Cheese	1 oz.	350
Milk	1 cup	350
Butter or Margarine	1 pat	230

†Average nutrient content as food is served. (*Note: 3½ oz equals approximately 100 g.*)

SOURCE: Lessons on Meat. (1974) National Live Stock and Meat Board, Chicago.

TABLE 2.V.24

VITAMIN A CONTENT OF OILS FROM FISHERY SOURCES HAVING COMMERCIAL IMPORTANCE IN THE UNITED STATES & ALASKA[1]

Common Name	Area in Which Fish Are Caught	Source of Oil	Per Cent of Round Weight[2]	Oil Content, %	Vitamin A Content in U.S.P. Units Per Gram of Oil	
					Range	Average
Soupfin shark	Pacific (male)	Liver	10	55–68	45,000–200,000	120,000
" "	" (female)	"	10	65–72	15,000—40,000	32,000
Grayfish (dogfish)	" -Alaska	"	10	67–72	2,000–20,000	5,000
" "	" -Hecate Strait	"	10	65–70	7,000–15,000	10,000
" "	" -Wash.-Ore.	"	10	50–70	8,000–25,000	14,000
" "	" -N. Calif.	"	10	62–68	12,000–20,000	15,000
Halibut	Pacific-area 3[3]	Liver	1.5–3	8–21	40,000–160,000	87,000
"	" - " 2[4]	"	1–1.75	17–27	20,000–65,000	40,000
"	"	Viscera[5]	2.5–5	2–5	70,000–700,000	200,000
Sablefish	Pacific	Liver	2–2.5	10–26	50,000–190,000	90,000
"	"	Viscera	3–4	5–12	90,000–250,000	125,000
Lingcod	Pacific	Liver	1–1.5	8–20	40,000–550,000	175,000
"	"	Viscera	1.8–3	4–15	10,000–175,000	40,000
Sleeper shark	Pacific	Liver	10–15	40–55	5,000–15,000	7,000
Mud shark	"	"	10–15	60–65	5,000–7,000	5,500
Great blue shark	"	"	[6]	30–45	7,000–27,000	20,000
Hammerhead shark	" -Atlantic	"	"	30–40	30,000–120,000	50,000
" "	"	"	"	55–75	20,000–150,000	60,000
" "	Atlantic	"	"	[6]	5,000–140,000	40,000
" "	Florida	"	"	[6]	10,000–125,000	50,000
Little black tip	Florida	"	"	40–60	5,000–25,000	5,000
Tiger shark	"	"	"	45–60	2,000–5,000	3,000
Sand-bar shark	"	"	"	[6]	3,000–15,000	8,000
Nurse shark	"	"	"	[6]	1,000–10,000	3,000
Dusky shark	"	"	"	[6]	5,000–60,000	25,000
Leopard shark	Pacific	"	"	40–50	1,000–5,000	3,000
Bay shark	"	"	"	60–75	2,000–20,000	10,000
Thresher shark	"	"	"	45–55	1,000–5,000	3,000
Mexican shark	"	"	"	40–50	20,000–80,000	40,000
Gray smooth hound	"	"	"	50–60	10,000–25,000	20,000
Cazon shark	Argentina-Brazil	"	7–10	30–45	10,000–200,000	50,000
Albacore tuna	Pacific	"	1.5–2	7–20	10,000–60,000	25,000
Bluefin tuna	"	"	[6]	4–6	25,000–100,000	75,000
Yellowfin tuna	"	"	"	3–5	35,000–90,000	50,000
Skipjack tuna	"	"	"	4–6	30,000–60,000	40,000
Bonito	"	"	"	4–12	15,000–60,000	35,000
Swordfish	Pacific-Atlantic	"	1.4–2.6	8–35	20,000–400,000	250,000
"	" "	Viscera	3–6	6–12	2,000–30,000	10,000

(Continued)

TABLE 2.V.24 (*Continued*)

Common Name	Area in Which Fish Are Caught	Source of Oil	Per Cent of Round Weight[2]	Oil Content, %	Vitamin A Content in U.S.P. Units Per Gram of Oil	
					Range	Average
Black sea bass	Pacific	Liver	[6]	13–20	100,000–1,000,000	300,000
Totuava	Pacific	Liver	[6]	15–25	40,000–400,000	[6]
Cod	Atlantic	"	3–5	20–60	1,000–6,000	2,000
Rosefish	"	Waste[7]	[6]	2–4	3,000–5,000	[6]
Halibut	"	Liver	1.5–2.5	15–25	40,000	"
Rockfish	Pacific	"	1–1.5	5–25	14,000–300,000	"
"	"	Viscera	1.5–2.5	2–15	15,000–125,000	"
Petrale sole	Pacific	Liver	1–1.5	6–25	4,000–175,000	"
Herring	"	Body	[6]	5–25	50–300	90
Pilchard	"	"	[6]	5–25	50–800	100
Menhaden	Atlantic	"	[6]	5–20	500	[6]

[1] These data compiled from reports of research at the laboratories of the Fish and Wildlife Service and of the Fisheries Research Board of Canada, and from articles published by representatives of commercial processors of fish livers and viscera. For the most part, the data are based on large lots of material or on samples taken over the normal season for the species.

[2] Per cent of round weight means the proportion of liver weight to the weight of the entire fish (undressed) expressed as per cent.

[3] Area 3 is defined by the International Halibut Commission regulations as follows: "Area 3 shall include all the convention waters off the coast of Alaska that are between Area 2 and a straight line running south from the southwestern extremity of Cape Sagak on Umnak Island, at a point approximately latitude 52°49′30″ N., longitude 169°07′00″ W., according to Chart 8802, published January, 1942, by the United States Coast and Geodetic Survey, and that are south of the Alaska Peninsula and of the Aleutian Islands and shall also include the intervening straits or passes of the Aleutian Islands."

[4] Area 2 includes: "all convention waters off the coasts of the United States of America and of Alaska and of the Dominion of Canada between Area 1B and a line running through the most westerly point of Glacier Bay, Alaska, to Cape Spenser Light as shown on Chart 8304, published in June, 1940, by the United States Coast and Geodetic Survey, which light is approximately latitude 58°11′57″ N., longitude 136°38′18″ W., thence south one-quarter east and is exclusive of the areas closed to all halibut fishing in Section 9 of these regulations."

[5] Viscera, unless otherwise designated, means the contents of the body cavity minus the liver, stomach, and gonads.

[6] The source from which information listed here was obtained did not supply data under this heading.

[7] Waste is the entire body of the rosefish minus the fillet or edible portion. It includes head, backbone, skin, and viscera.

SOURCE: BRODY, J. (EDITOR). Non-Fat Components of Fish Oils. *In* Fishery By-Products Technology. Avi Publishing Co., Westport, Conn.

VITAMIN A, FOOD

TABLE 2.V.25

VITAMIN A POTENCY (IU) OF FOODS PER 100 G (ABOUT 3½ OZ)

Cereals		Fruits	
Yellow maize (as carotene)	330–900	Apricots and peaches	750 (as carotene)
Flour, bread, cornflour, oatmeal, pearl barley, rice, rye, sago, etc.	none	Tomatoes	3,000 (as carotene)
		Meats	
		Beef, veal, mutton, lamb	50
		Pork and pork products	none
Dairy foods		Variety meats	
Butter	3500	Heart	200
Cheddar cheese		Kidney	1,000
Winter milk	550	Liver	
Summer milk	1400	Pig	10,000
Eggs	1000	Cow	15,000
Milk		Rabbit	25,000
Winter	100	Sheep	60,000
Summer	150	Sperm whale	440,000
		Seal	1,300,000
Fish		Vegetables	
Herring		Beans, green	600–950
Fresh	150	Cabbage	900 (as carotene)
Canned	30	Carrots	9,000
Liver oil		Peas (green)	500 (as carotene)
Cod	10,000–400,000	Potatoes	none
Halibut	3–36 million	Sprouts	300 (as carotene)

SOURCE: SINCLAIR, H. M. and HOLLINGSWORTH, D. F. 1969. Hutchison's Food and the Principles of Nutrition. Edward Arnold (Publishers), London, England.

VITAMIN A, MILK AND MILK PRODUCTS

TABLE 2.V.26

VITAMIN A CONTENT OF MILK AND MILK PRODUCTS[1]

Milk or Milk Product	Avg	Range (IU/100 g)[2]	Cheese Variety	Avg	Range (IU/100 g)
Whole milk:			Very hard:		
Fluid	156	119-176	Parmesan	1410	— (1)[3]
Condensed	276	141-352 (4)[3]	Hard:		
Evaporated	369	342-464 (4)	Cantal	1333	— (1)
Dried	1100	600-1600 (6)	Cheddar	1169[4]	750-1985 (10)
Skimmilk:			Cheshire	970	— (1)
Fluid	9	4-18 (4)	Edam	1203	733-1788 (4)
Dried	143	40-250 (3)	Gouda	1050	— (1)
Malted milk:			Gruyère	822	267-1333 (3)
Dried	1020	— (1)	Swiss	1592	954-2680 (3)
Buttermilk:			Semisoft:		
Fluid	12	4-20 (2)	Blue[5]	1935	1000-3502 (6)
Yoghurt	69	— (1)	Brick	1626	853-2400 (2)
Cream:			Chantelle	1910	— (1)
Half and half	480	— (1)	Liederkranz	3437	— (1)
Light table	880	— (1)	Limburger	1280	— (1)
Medium whipping	1336	— (1)	Port Salut[5]	1333	— (1)
Heavy whipping	1598	— (1)	Roquefort[6]	1971	900-4012 (3)
Butter	3108	2374-3836	Stilton	1235	— (1)
Ice cream	523	425-600 (4)	Tilsiter	1045	— (1)
Whey:			Trappist[5]	742	— (1)
Fluid	11	10-12 (2)	Soft:		
Dried	50	— (1)	Ripened:		
			Brie	667	— (1)
			Brinza[5]	483	(1)
			Camembert	2140	667-3612 (2)
			Unripened:		
			Cottage:		
			Creamed	291	185-397 (2)
			Uncreamed	42	9-60 (3)
			Cream	2194	1552-2819 (3)
			Neufchâtel	1495	— (1)
			Pimento Cream	3204	— (1)
			Processed:		
			Brick	1407	— (1)
			Cheddar	1705	1250-2160 (2)
			Limburger	1460	— (1)
			Swiss	1680	1390-1970 (2)

[1] Mean and range of average values obtained from various publications.
[2] IU per 100 ml for products designated fluid.
[3] Figures in parentheses indicate the number of references consulted.
[4] One high value (5,500 IU/100 g) omitted.
[5] May be made from milk of species other than the cow.
[6] Made from ewe's milk.

SOURCE: HARTMAN, A. M., and DRYDEN, L. P. Vitamins in milk and milk products. J. Dairy Sci., American Dairy Science Association.

VITAMIN C

TABLE 2.V.27

VITAMIN C IN SOME FOODS

	mg/100 g		mg/100 g
Peppers	128	Grapefruit	38
Broccoli	113	Cantaloupe	33
Brussels sprouts	102	Asparagus	33
Cauliflower	78	Tomatoes	23
Strawberries	59	Potatoes	20
Spinach	51	Corn	12
Oranges	50	Bananas	10
Cabbage	47	Apples	7

SOURCE: WHITE, P. L. and SELVEY, N. (EDITORS). 1974. Nutritional Qualities of Fresh Fruits and Vegetables. Futura Publishing Co., Mt. Kisco, N.Y.

VITAMIN D, FISH

TABLE 2.V.28

VITAMIN D CONTENT OF OILS FROM FISHERY SOURCES

Common Name	Area in Which Fish are Caught	Source of Oil	Vitamin D Content in International Units Per Gram of Oil
Albacore tuna	Pacific	Liver	25,000–250,000
Bluefin "	"	"	20,000–70,000
Yellowfin "	"	"	10,000–45,000
Skipjack "	"	"	25,000–250,000
Bonito	"	"	50,000
Swordfish	" -Atlantic	"	2,000–25,000
Mackerel, Pacific	Pacific	"	1,400
Albacore tuna	"	Waste[2]	67
Halibut	"	Liver	1,000–5,000
"	"	Viscera[3]	100–500
Sablefish	"	Liver	600–1,000
"	"	Viscera	100
Lingcod	"	Liver	1,000–6,000
"	"	Viscera	100–200
Rockfish	"	Liver	300–5,000
Cod	"	"	85–500
Ishinagi	"	"	3,800
Barracuda	"	"	2,000
Black sea bass	"	"	5,000
Beluga whale	"	"	50–100
Grayfish (dogfish)	"	"	5–25
" "	"	Body[4]	29
Ratfish	"	Liver	2–5
Soupfin shark	"	"	5–25
Herring	"	Body[5]	25–160
"	"	Liver	250
Pilchard	"	Body[5]	20–100
King salmon	"	Liver	100–500
" "	"	Offal[6]	50–150
Sockeye "	"	Liver	200–600
" "	"	Offal	100–300
Silver "	"	Liver	100–500
" "	"	Offal	100–200

(Continued)

TABLE 2.V.28 (*Continued*)

Common Name	Area in Which Fish are Caught	Source of Oil	Vitamin D Content in International Units Per Gram of Oil
Pink "	"	Liver	100–600
" "	"	Offal	100–300
Chum "	"	Liver	100–500
" "	"	Offal	50–100
Starry flounder	"	Liver	1,000
Rex sole	"	"	150
Skate	"	"	25
Mud shark	"	"	20
Snoek	South Africa	"	500–6,000
"	" "	Viscera	85
Stonebass	" "	Liver	700–1,300
Stockfish	" "	"	50–380
"	" "	Viscera	3
Kingklip	" "	Liver	85–600
Halibut	" "	"	1,000–2,000
Cod	" "	"	100
Ling	New Zealand	"	500
Yellowtail	Australia	"	9,000–17,000
Halibut	Atlantic	"	2,000
Mackerel, common	"	"	750
Rosefish	"	Waste[7]	50
Dogfish	"	Liver	3

Table Courtesy of U. S. Fish and Wildlife Service.

[1] Data on vitamin A content of most of these fish are to be found in Tables 1 and 2.

[2] Waste indicates offal from the cannery fish cleaning tables. The raw eviscerated fish is pre-cooked prior to this cleaning operation, hence some of the tuna body oil has been lost from this waste before it is made into meal and oil.

[3] Viscera indicates the contents of the body cavity minus the liver, stomach, and gonads.

[4] Body indicates the entire body of the fish minus the liver.

[5] Body indicates the entire body of the fish including the liver and viscera.

[6] Offal indicates the cannery trimmings, including heads, livers, and viscera but not eggs.

[7] Waste indicates the entire body of the rosefish minus the fillet or edible portion. It includes head, backbone, skin, and viscera.

SOURCE: BRODY, J. (EDITOR). Non-Fat Components of Fish-Oils. *In* Fishery By-Products Technology. Avi Publishing Co., Westport, Conn.

VITAMIN D, FOOD

TABLE 2.V.29

VITAMIN D CONTENT OF FOODS

	IU per 100 g		IU per 100 g
Dairy foods		**Fish**	
Butter, Empire imported	**60**	**Herrings**	
Cheese	**15**	**Fresh and cured**	**850**
Dripping	**30**	**Canned**	**170**
Egg		**Mackerel**	**700**
Whole, fresh	**60**	**Salmon, canned**	**600**
Dried	**240**	**Sardines, canned**	**1000**
Margarine	**200**	**Fish liver oils[1]**	
		Cod	**20,000**

[1] Halibut liver oils, not included in this table, run from 20,000 to 400,000.

SOURCE: SINCLAIR, H. M. and HOLLINGSWORTH, D. F. 1969. Hutchison's Food and the Principles of Nutrition. Edward Arnold (Publishers), London, England.

VITAMIN RETENTION, MEAT

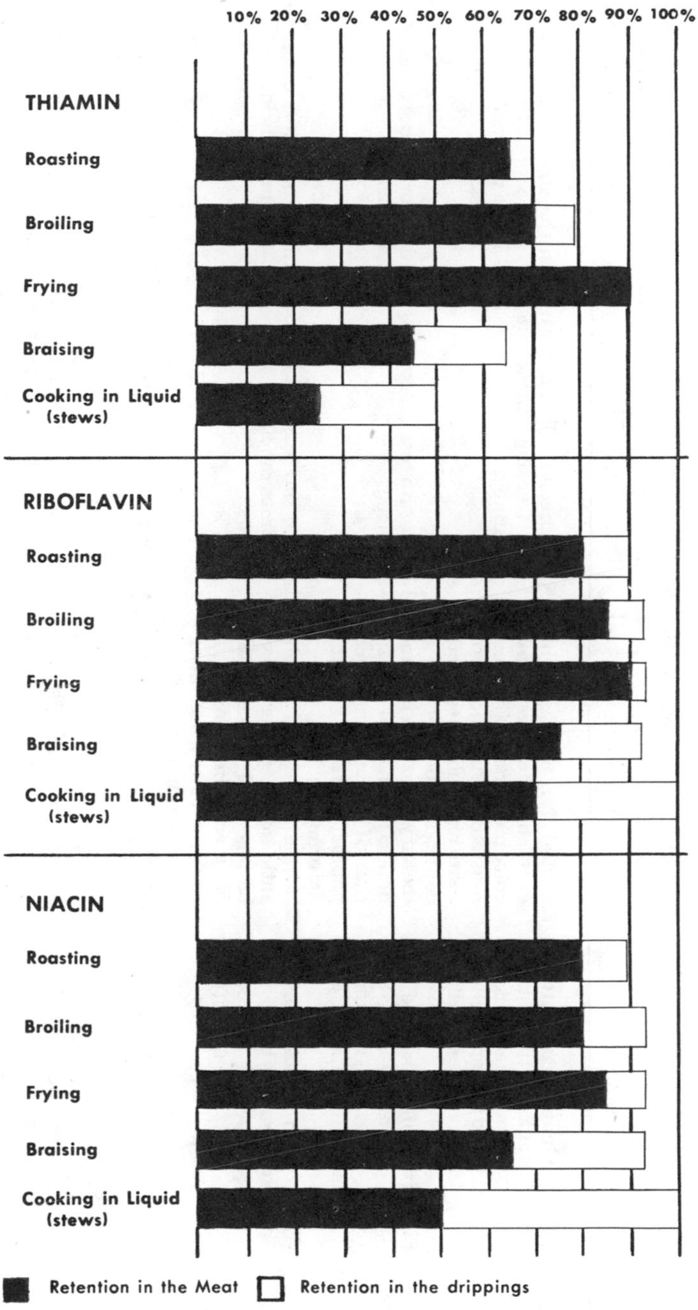

SOURCE: Lessons on Meat. (1974) National Live Stock and Meat Board, Chicago.

VITAMIN SOURCES, FUNCTIONS, AND STABILITY

TABLE 2.V.30

VITAMIN SOURCES, FUNCTIONS, AND STABILITY

	Food Sources	Functions	Effects of Processing[1]	Effects of Storage[2]
Fat-soluble vitamins				
Vitamin A and carotene	Liver, kidney, eggs, butter, whole milk, fortified skim milk, cream, cheese, dark green and deep yellow vegetables and deep yellow fruit.	Essential for healthy skin, eyes and hair; keeps mucous membranes firm and resistant to infection; prevents night blindness, and controls bone growth.	No appreciable loss by heating, freezing, preserving, or canning.	In the absence of air, stable. High storage temperatures in the presence of air result in loss.
Vitamin D (the sunshine vitamin)	Fish liver oils, sunshine on skin, vitamin D milk, egg yolk, margarine, mackerel, sardines, salmon, tuna, cod liver oil.	Necessary for teeth and bones, and normal utilization of calcium and phosphorus; prevents bone deformities.	Little or no loss unless oxidized.	Little or no loss unless oxidized.
Vitamin E	Whole grain cereal, pulses, wheat germ, soybean, cottonseed, peanut and corn oils, eggs, liver, butter, margarine.	Essential for normal muscle; antioxidant, preserving vitamins and unsaturated fatty acids in foods or the body; required for integrity of red blood cells.	Little or no loss unless food becomes rancid.	Little or no loss unless food becomes rancid.
Vitamin K	Cabbage, cauliflower, pork liver, soybean, spinach, wheat bran.	Essential for normal blood clotting.	Destroyed by irradiation.	No appreciable loss.
Water-soluble vitamins				
Vitamin B_1 (thiamin)	Liver, pork, poultry, fish, eggs, beans and peas, whole grain cereal, enriched bread, lean meat, potatoes, broccoli, collards, yeast.	Necessary for growth, fertility and lactation; promotes normal appetite; aids metabolic processes, releasing energy from food; keeps nervous system healthy and prevents irritability.	The higher and longer the heating period, the greater the loss. Loss is decreased in presence of acid and small amounts of water.	Refrigeration lessens destruction.
Vitamin B_2 (riboflavin)	Milk, cheese, ice cream, liver, meat, fish, poultry, eggs, yeast.	Assists in conversion of tryptophan to nicotinic acid; necessary for healthy skin; essential for build-	Stable to heat but may be dissolved and discarded in cooking water. Open vessels (or light) and use of	Relatively stable.

		ing and maintaining body tissues and the use of oxygen by cells.	sodium bicarbonate in cooking water will destroy riboflavin.	
Niacin	Liver, lean meats, eggs, peas, beans, nuts, peanut butter, enriched bread, whole grain cereal, yeast.	Prevents pellagra; necessary for growth and health of tissues; promotes appetite and good utilization of food in the body.	No loss during ordinary cooking processes, but may lose some in cooking water.	Relatively stable.
Pyridoxine hydrochloride	Barley, meat, cabbage, carrots, corn, cottonseed meal, milk, peanuts, peas, rice, wheat, brewers' yeast, lima beans.	Coenzyme, necessary for protein, tryptophan and fat metabolism; promotes normal red blood cell formation.	Loss occurs due to leaching of vitamin in cooking water (30%). Destroyed by high temperature, high irradiation dose, and exposure to light.	Loss increases with temperature and time of storage.
Pantothenic acid	Wheat, eggs, milk, meat, fish, yeast, molasses, oatmeal, broccoli, cabbage, cucumbers, corn, tomatoes, potatoes, peas, liver, nuts.	Essential for metabolism of carbohydrates and fats.	Fairly stable in moist heat, particularly in neutral solution; readily destroyed by prolonged dry heat in alkaline environment. Can be leached by water.	Relatively stable.
Biotin	Yeast, liver, peanuts, beans, eggs, kidney.	Important to intermediary metabolism-energy release mechanisms.	Stable to heat, but can be dissolved in cooking water.	Relatively stable.
Folic acid	Liver, dark green leafy vegetables; cauliflower, kidney, beef, veal, wheat breakfast foods, bran, black-eyed peas.	Prevents certain anemias; with vitamin C aids tyrosine metabolism in energy conversion cycles; aids in red blood cell formation.	High temperature processing is detrimental to folic acid stability.	Low temperatures of storage are preferred to room temperature to enhance stability.
Vitamin B_{12}	Liver, beef extract, dry milk, oysters, lean meat.	Prevents certain anemias and promotes good general nutrition by contributing to health of nervous system.	Very stable in neutral solutions, but loses potency in either acid or alkaline solutions. Cooking losses range from 24–90%.	More stable to storage than to processing; affected by presence of thiamin and nicotinamide in aqueous pharmaceutical preparations.
Ascorbic acid	Fresh fruits and vegetables, particularly citrus fruits and leafy vegetables.	Essential for healthy bones and strong teeth; helps to maintain body's resistance to infection; prevents capillary fragility; essential for growth and wound healing.	Most easily destroyed of all vitamins and should be processed in stainless steel or glass as a protective measure.	Foods can lose as much as 50% and more depending upon storage time and temperature. Storage at 0°F (−18°C) or below recommended for good retention.

[1] Loss of water-soluble vitamins may be large or small depending upon the processing and cooking techniques and methods that are employed.
[2] Vitamin losses in storage may be large or small depending on storage time and conditions, the product involved, and the vitamin in question.

SOURCE: THOMAS, M. H. 1975. Vitamins. *In* Encyclopedia of Food Technology. A. H. Johnson and M. S. Peterson (Editors). Avi Publishing Co., Westport, Conn.

VITAMINS

TABLE 2.V.31

DATA COVERING THE PRINCIPAL VITAMINS

Vitamin	*Principal Sources*	*Properties*	*Functions*	*Deficiency Symptoms in Man*	*Daily Allowances*	*Usual Therapeutic Dosage*
Vitamin A (Retinol)	Fish liver oils, liver, egg yolk, butter, cream, vitamin A-fortified margarine, green leafy or yellow vegetables	Oil-soluble; large doses cause toxicity	Photoreceptor mechanism of retina, integrity of epithelia, lysosome stability	Night blindness; xerophthalmia; keratomalacia	*Adults:* 1.5 mg retinal (equals 5000 U.S.P. u. or 9 mg β-carotene)[b, c]	25,000–50,000 U.S.P. u./day[c] (*see* text for higher dosage)
Vitamin D Ergocalciferol (D_2) Cholecalciferol (D_3)	Fish liver oils, butter, egg yolk, liver, ultraviolet irradiation	Oil-soluble; large doses may cause hypercalcemia	Bone formation, increases calcium & phosphorus absorption	Rickets (tetany sometimes associated); osteomalacia	*Adults & children:* 400 U.S.P. u.[c]	400–1,600 U.S.P. u./day[c] (*see* text for higher dosage)
Vitamin E Group (α, β, γ, δ tocopherol)	Vegetable oil, wheat germ, leafy vegetables, egg yolk, margarine, legumes	Oil-soluble	Intracellular antioxidant, stability of biological membranes	RBC hemolysis; creatinuria; ceroid deposition in muscle	*Adults:* 30 I.U. (equals 30 mg synthetic *dl-α*-tocopherol acetate)	50–300 I.U./day
Vitamin K (activity)	Leafy vegetables, pork liver, vegetable oils, intestinal flora after 4th day of life		Prothrombin formation; normal blood coagulation	Hemorrhage from deficient prothrombin	Not yet established; thought to be about 0.03 mg/kg	In situations conducive to neonatal hemorrhage, 2–5 mg during labor or daily for 1 wk prior; or 1–2 mg to newborn (*see* text for details)
Menadione		Oil-soluble; unstable to light; toxic in large doses				
Menadione sodium bisulfite		Water-soluble; toxic in large doses				
Phytonadione (Vitamin K_1)		Oil-soluble; unstable to heat & light				10–50 mg to counteract excessive anticoagulant (*see* text for details)
Thiamine (Vitamin B_1)	Dried yeast, whole grains; meat (especially pork, liver); enriched cereal products, nuts, legumes, potatoes	Water-soluble; I.V. may cause anaphylactoid shock	Carbohydrate metabolism; central & peripheral nerve cell function; myocardial function	Beriberi, infantile & adult (peripheral neuropathy; cardiac; acute cerebral symptoms)	*Adults:* 1.0–1.5 mg	5–30 mg/day
Riboflavin (Vitamin B_2)	Milk, cheese, liver, meat, eggs, enriched cereal products	Slightly water-soluble	Many aspects energy & protein metabolism; integrity of mucous membranes	Cheilosis, angular stomatitis, corneal vascularization, amblyopia, sebaceous dermatosis	*Adults:* 1.0–1.7 mg	10–30 mg/day
Niacin (Nicotinic acid) Niacinamide (Nicotinamide)	Dried yeast, liver, meat, fish, legumes, whole-grain enriched cereal products	Water-soluble; intolerance produces flushing, burning, itching (rare with niacinamide)	Oxidation-reduction reactions; carbohydrate & tryptophan metabolism	Pellagra (dermatosis, glossitis, GI & CNS dysfunction)	*Adults:* 15–20 mg equivalents[d]	Niacinamide 100–1000 mg/day

TABLE 2.V.31 (*Continued*)

Vitamin	*Principal Sources*	*Properties*	*Functions*	*Deficiency Symptoms in Man*	*Daily Allowances*	*Usual Therapeutic Dosage*
Vitamin B_6 Group (Pyridoxine, Pyridoxal, Pyridoxamine)	Dried yeast, liver, organ meats, whole-grain cereals, fish, legumes	Water-soluble	Essential for cellular function & for metabolism of certain amino & fatty acids	Convulsions in infancy, anemias, neuropathy, seborrhea-like skin lesions. Dependency states (*see text*)	*Adults:* 2 mg	25–100 mg/day
Pantothenic acid (Calcium pantothenate)	Dried yeast, liver, eggs, organ meats, legumes	Water-soluble	Involved in fat, protein, & carbohydrate metabolism by its relation to acetylation processes	Experimental deficiency in man characterized by fatigue, malaise, headache, sleep disturbances, nausea, abdominal & muscle cramps, vomiting, paresthesias, & impaired coordination	Not yet established; thought to be about 10 mg/day	Not known; not < 50 mg/day should be used for therapeutic trial
Folic acid (Folacin, Pteroylglutamic acid)	Fresh green leafy vegetables & fruit, organ meats, liver, dried yeast	Poorly water-soluble	Maturation of RBCs; synthesis of purines & pyrimidines	Pancytopenia, megaloblastosis (especially pregnancy, infancy, malabsorption)	*Adults:* 400 μg based on *L. casei* method or 100 μg synthetic folic acid	100 μg/day
Vitamin B_{12} (Cyanocobalamin)	Liver, meats, (especially beef, pork, organ meats); eggs, milk & milk products	Water-soluble	Maturation of RBCs; neural function; DNA synthesis, related to folate coenzymes; methionine & acetate synthesis	Pernicious anemia; fish tapeworm & vegan anemias, some psychiatric syndromes, nutritional amblyopia	*Adults:* 5 μg; based on absorption of 30% or less	1–2 μg/day I.M. to maintain remission in pernicious anemia
Vitamin C (Ascorbic acid)	Citrus fruits, tomatoes, potatoes, cabbage, green pepper	Water-soluble	Essential to osteoid tissue, collagen formation, vascular function, tissue respiration, & wound healing	Scurvy (hemorrhages, loose teeth, gingivitis)	*Adults:* 60 mg *Children:* 40 mg	100–1000 mg/day

[b] One U.S.P. u. equals 0.3 μg of retinol. 1 μg of β-carotene is equivalent to 0.167 μg of retinol.
[c] One U.S.P. u. equals 1 I.U.
[d] 60 mg. of tryptophan is equivalent to 1 mg. of niacin.

SOURCE: HOLVEY, D. N. 1972. The Merck Manual, 12th Edition. Merck & Co., Rahway, New Jersey.

VOLUME

TABLE 2.V.32

LIQUID VOLUME CONVERSION TABLE: GALLONS, QUARTS, PINTS, CUPS, AND OUNCES TO MILLILITERS

U.S. Gallons	Milliliters
1	3785.3
2	7570.6
3	11355.9
4	15141.2
5	18926.5
6	22711.8
7	26497.1
8	30282.4
9	34067.8
10	37853.1
11	41638.4
12	45423.7
13	49209.0
14	52994.3
15	56779.6
16	60564.9
17	64350.2
18	68135.5
19	71920.8
20	75706.1
21	79491.4
22	83276.7
23	87062.0
24	90847.3
25	94632.7
26	98417.0
27	102203.3
28	105988.6
29	109773.9
30	113559.2
31	117344.5
32	121129.8
33	124915.1
34	128700.4
35	132485.7
36	136271.0
37	140056.3
38	143841.6
39	147626.9
40	151412.2
41	155197.5
42	158982.9
43	162768.2
44	166553.5
45	170338.8
46	174124.1
47	177909.4
48	181694.7
49	185480.0
50	189265.3

U.S. Quarts	Milliliters
1	946.33
2	1892.65
3	2838.98
4 (gal.)	3785.31

U.S. Pints	Milliliters
½	236.58
1	473.16
2 (1 qt)	946.33
3	1419.49
4 (2 qt)	1892.65
5	2365.82
6 (3 qt)	2838.98
7	3312.14
8 (gal.)	3785.31

Cups ½ pt; 8 oz	Milliliters
¼	59.15
⅓	78.86
½	118.29
⅔	157.72
¾	177.44
1	236.58

Tablespoons (tbsp) (3 tsp; 1/16 cup)	Milliliters
½	7.40
1	14.79

Teaspoons (tsp) (⅓ tbsp)	Milliliters
¼	1.23
⅓	1.64
½	2.46
⅔	3.29
¾	3.70
1	4.93

TABLE 2.V.32 (*Continued*)

U.S. Ounces	Milliliters	U.S. Ounces	Milliliters	U.S. Ounces	Milliliters
1	29.57	44	1301.20	87	2572.82
2 (¼ cup)	59.15	45	1330.77	88	2602.40
3	88.72	46	1360.34	89	2631.97
4 (½ cup)	118.29	47	1389.92	90	2661.54
5	147.86	48	1419.49	91	2691.12
6 (¾ cup)	177.44	49	1449.06	92	2720.69
7	207.01	50	1478.64	93	2750.26
8 (cup)	236.58	51	1508.21	94	2779.83
9	266.15	52	1537.78	95	2809.41
10	295.73	53	1567.35	96 (3 qt)	2838.98
11	325.30	54	1596.93	97	2868.55
12	354.87	55	1626.50	98	2898.12
13	384.44	56	1656.07	99	2927.70
14	414.02	57	1685.64	100	2957.27
15	443.59	58	1715.22	101	2986.84
16 (pt)	473.16	59	1744.79	102	3016.42
17	502.74	60	1774.36	103	3045.99
18	532.31	61	1803.93	104	3075.56
19	561.88	62	1833.51	105	3105.13
20	591.45	63	1863.08	106	3134.71
21	621.03	64 (2 qt)	1892.65	107	3164.28
22	650.60	65	1922.23	108	3193.85
23	680.17	66	1951.80	109	3223.42
24	709.74	67	1981.37	110	3253.00
25	739.32	68	2010.94	111	3282.57
26	768.89	69	2040.52	112	3312.14
27	798.46	70	2070.09	113	3341.72
28	828.04	71	2099.66	114	3371.29
29	857.61	72	2129.23	115	3400.86
30	887.18	73	2158.81	116	3430.43
31	916.75	74	2188.38	117	3460.01
32 (qt)	946.33	75	2217.95	118	3489.58
33	975.90	76	2247.53	119	3519.15
34	1005.47	77	2277.10	120	3548.72
35	1035.04	78	2306.67	121	3578.30
36	1064.62	79	2336.24	122	3607.87
37	1094.19	80	2365.82	123	3637.44
38	1123.76	81	2395.39	124	3667.02
39	1153.34	82	2424.96	125	3696.59
40	1182.91	83	2454.53	126	3726.16
41	1212.48	84	2484.11	127	3755.73
42	1242.05	85	2513.68	128 (1 gal.)	3785.31
43	1271.63	86	2543.25		

Example: 3 qt and 13 oz = 2838.98 ml + 384.44 ml = 3223.42 ml

SOURCE: OCKERMAN, H. W. 1974. Quality Control of Post-Mortem Muscle Tissue, 9th Edition. Ohio State University, Columbus.

VOLUMETRIC SOLUTIONS, TEMPERATURE CORRECTIONS

The table below gives the correction to various observed volumes of water, measured at the designated temperatures to give the volume at the standard temperature, 20°C. Conversely, by subtracting the corrections from the volume desired at 20°C, the volume that must be measured out at the designated temperatures in order to give the desired volume at 20°C, will be obtained. It is assumed that the volumes are measured in glass apparatus having a coefficient of cubical expansion of 0.000025 per degree centigrade. The table is applicable to dilute aqueous solutions having the same coefficient of expansion as water.

TABLE 2.V.33

TEMPERATURE CORRECTION FOR VOLUMETRIC SOLUTIONS

Temperature of Measurement, °C	Capacity of Apparatus in Milliliters at 20°C						
	2,000	1,000	500	400	300	250	150
	Correction in Milliliters to give volume of water at 20°C						
15	+1.54	+0.77	+0.38	+0.31	+0.23	+0.19	+0.12
16	+1.28	+0.64	+0.32	+0.26	+0.19	+0.16	+0.10
17	+0.99	+0.50	+0.25	+0.20	+0.15	+0.12	+0.07
18	+0.68	+0.34	+0.17	+0.14	+0.10	+0.08	+0.05
19	+0.35	+0.18	+0.09	+0.07	+0.05	+0.04	+0.03
21	-0.37	-0.18	-0.09	-0.07	-0.06	-0.05	-0.03
22	-0.77	-0.38	-0.19	-0.15	-0.12	-0.10	-0.06
23	-1.18	-0.59	-0.30	-0.24	-0.18	-0.15	-0.09
24	-1.61	-0.81	-0.40	-0.32	-0.24	-0.20	-0.12
25	-2.07	-1.03	-0.52	-0.41	-0.31	-0.26	-0.15
26	-2.54	-1.27	-0.64	-0.51	-0.38	-0.32	-0.19
27	-3.03	-1.52	-0.76	-0.61	-0.46	-0.38	-0.23
28	-3.55	-1.77	-0.89	-0.71	-0.53	-0.44	-0.27
29	-4.08	-2.04	-1.02	-0.82	-0.61	-0.51	-0.31
30	-4.62	-2.31	-1.16	-0.92	-0.69	-0.58	-0.35

SOURCE: WEAST, R. C. (EDITOR). 1974–1975. Handbook of Chemistry and Physics, 55th Edition. CRC Press, Cleveland. Reproduced with permission of CRC Press.

W

WASTES, AGRICULTURAL AND INDUSTRIAL

TABLE 2.W.1

COMPOSITION OF VARIOUS INDUSTRIAL AND AGRICULTURAL ORGANIC WASTES

Material	Moisture %	Ash %	N %	P_2O_5 %	K_2O %	N Availability[1]
		Industrial				
Antibiotic wastes						
Penicillin	75.3	29.5	3.85	4.13	1.08	0.4
Streptomycin	62.6	71.9	2.20	0.52	0.06	0.7
Botanical drug wastes						
Cascara bark	75.8	9.7	0.54	0.03	0.01	0.0
Licorice roots	—	—	2.20	0.11	1.12	0.1
Pryethrum flowers	25.0	12.1	1.07	0.58	2.58	0.0
Scammony roots	36.4	13.9	1.12	0.47	2.22	0.0
Cannery wastes						
Asparagus	93.8	12.5	3.96	0.91	3.54	0.6
Beet (red)	94.2	7.0	2.57	0.52	1.92	0.5
Spinach	85.7	58.4	3.21	1.14	1.07	0.9
Sweet potatoes	90.0	10.2	1.84	0.46	0.72	0.2
Spent spice mare						
Carolina chili	16.2	8.3	3.41	1.03	3.84	0.5
Ginger	11.8	5.5	1.74	0.35	1.80	0.1
Nutmeg	37.3	4.3	1.25	0.40	1.26	0.1
Patchouli leaves	11.0	19.5	3.34	0.60	3.96	0.7
Coffee wastes						
Chaff	3.0	5.5	2.58	0.19	2.10	0.0
Grounds, fresh	62.9	0.5	1.84	0.03	0.12	0.0
Grounds, composted	58.0	—	1.65	0.22	3.00	0.2
Snuff wastes						
Stem sand	7.5	38.8	2.81	0.77	4.54	0.2
Leaf sand	3.5	74.4	0.94	0.21	1.62	0.0
Sweepings	16.9	25.1	2.91	0.49	6.90	0.4
Cocoa shells	—	—	2.71	1.17	3.06	0.2
Seaweed	—	—	3.17	—	—	0.8
Spent hops	79.1	4.4	2.13	0.66	0.42	0.3
Tea leaves	86.0	3.2	4.41	0.29	0.24	0.2
		Agricultural				
Apple pomace	—	—	1.70	—	—	0.0
Cow manure	—	—	2.50	0.50	1.40	0.8
Duck manure	—	—	3.55	—	—	0.9
Horse manure	—	—	2.85	—	—	0.5
Poultry manure plus bedding	22.6	25.6	3.58	3.02	1.62	0.8
Sawdust						
Oak	45.6	2.1	0.12	0.002	0.12	0.0
Popular	43.3	2.5	0.13	0.001	0.15	0.0
Soybeans mash	84.0	15.1	4.81	1.49	0.78	0.8
Tobacco stems	20.0	21.5	1.96	0.63	10.80	0.4
Garbage	49.3	28.5	1.07	1.16	0.12	0.0
Garbage compost	10.0	55.0	1.00	2.7	0.69	0.0
Sewage sludge	38.0	15.0	2.00	1.7	0.10	0.0

[1]Based on $(NH_4)_2SO_4$ nitrification value of 1.0

SOURCE: TOTH, S. J. 1973. Composting Agricultural and Industrial Organic Wastes. *In* Symposium: Processing Agricultural and Municipal Wastes. G. E. Inglett (Editor). Avi Publishing Co., Westport, Conn.

WATER ACTIVITY, ORGANISMS AND FOOD

TABLE 2.W.2

INFLUENCE OF a_w-VALUES ON THE MICROBIAL SPOILAGE OF FOODS

a_w–*range*	*Organisms inhibited by the lower value*	*Examples of foods having this lower* a_w–*value*
1.00-0.95	Gram-negative rods; Spores of *Bacillaceae*	Foods containing *c.* 40 wt.% sucrose or *c.* 7 wt.% NaCl
		Bread crumb
		Some types of cooked sausage
0.95-0.91	Most cocci, lactobacilli and vegetative cells of *Bacillaceae*	Foods containing *c.* 55 wt.% sucrose or *c.* 12 wt.% NaCl
		Raw ham
0.91-0.88	Most yeasts	Foods containing *c.*65 wt.% sucrose or 15 wt.% NaCl
		Salami
		Fishmeal with *c.* 10% moisture
0.88-0.80	Most moulds; *Staph. aureus*	Flour, rice, pulses, etc. with *c.* 17% moisture
		Fruit cake
		Dry sausage
0.80-0.75	Most halophilic bacteria	Foods containing *c.* 26 wt.% NaCl
		Most jams and fondant creams
0.75-0.65	Xerophilic moulds	Marzipan, marshmallow
		Fishmeal with *c.* 5% moisture
0.65-0.60	Osmophilic yeasts	Liquorice, gums
		Medium salted cod with *c.* 12% moisture
<0.60	All micro-organisms	Toffees, boiled sweets
		Raisins

SOURCE: MOSSEL, D. A. A. 1970. Microbial Spoilage of Proteinaceous Foods. *In* Proteins as Human Food. R. A. Lawrie (Editor). Avi Publishing Co., Westport, Conn.

WATER DRINKING STANDARDS

TABLE 2.W.3

COMPARISON OF STANDARDS FOR DRINKING WATER

Test	WHO Max Acceptable Concentration[1]	WHO Max Allowable Concentration[1]	U.S.PHS
Color (Hazen or platinum-cobalt scale units)	5	50	Not exceeding 15
Turbidity units	5	25	Not exceeding 3
Odor	Unobjectionable	—	Not exceeding threshold Odor number of 3 units
Taste	Unobjectionable	—	—
Iron (Fe)	0.3 mg/l	1.0 mg/l	Not exceeding 0.3 mg/l
Manganese (Mn)	0.1 mg/l	0.5 mg/l	Not exceeding 0.05 mg/l
Copper (Cu)	1.0 mg/l	1.5 mg/l	Not exceeding 1.0 mg/l
Zinc (Zn)	5.0 mg/l	15 mg/l	Not exceeding 5.0 mg/l
Calcium (Ca)	75 mg/l	200 mg/l	—
Magnesium (Mg)	50 mg/l	150 mg/l	—
Sulphate (SO_4)	200 mg/l	400 mg/l	Not exceeding 250 mg/l
Chloride (Cl)	200 mg/l	600 mg/l	Not exceeding 250 mg/l
Phenols	0.001 mg/l	0.002 mg/l	Not exceeding 0.001 mg/l
pH range	7.0-8.5	Less than 6.5 or greater than 9.2	—
Alkyl benzene sulphonates	0.5 mg/l	1.0 mg/l	Not exceeding 0.5 mg/l
Carbon chloroform extract	0.2 mg/l	0.5 mg/l	Not exceeding 0.2 mg/l
Nitrate (NO_3)	—	45 mg/l[2]	Not exceeding 45 mg/l
Fluoride (F)	1 mg/l	1.5 mg/l	1.7 mg/l (at average max daily air temp of 50-54°F) down to 0.8 mg/l (at temp of 79.3-90.5)
Toxic Substances			
Arsenic (As)		0.05 mg/l	0.05 mg/l[3]
Barium (Ba)		1.0 mg/l	1.0 mg/l
Cadmiun (Cd)		0.01 mg/l	0.01 mg/l
Chromium (Cr^{6+})		0.05 mg/l	0.05 mg/l
Cyanide (CN)		0.2 mg/l	0.01 mg/l
Lead (Pb)		0.05 mg/l	0.05 mg/l
Selenium (Se)		0.01 mg/l	0.01 mg/l
Silver (Ag)		—	0.05 mg/l

[1] "Maximum acceptable concentration" applies to a water generally acceptable by consumers. "Maximum allowable concentration": values greater than those listed would markedly impair the potability of the water.

[2] "May give rise to infantile methaemoglobinaemia."

[3] Arsenic should not be present in a water supply in excess of 0.01 mg/l where other more suitable supplies are or can be made available.

SOURCE: HERSCHDOERFER, S. M. (EDITOR). 1968. Quality Control In the Food Industry, Vol. 2. Academic Press, New York and London, England.

WATER, HARDNESS

TABLE 2.W.4

U.S. GEOLOGICAL WATER SURVEY
HARDNESS CLASSIFICATION

Class	Ppm	Gr/Gal.[1]
Soft	0–60	0–35
Moderately hard	60–120	3.5–7.0
Hard	120–180	7.0–10.5
Very hard	Over 180	Over 10.5

[1] 17 ppm = 1 gr/gal.

SOURCE: HARPER, W. J. 1972. Sanitation in Dairy Food Plants. *In* Food Sanitation. R. K. Guthrie (Editor). Avi Publishing Co., Westport, Conn.

WATER, WEIGHT AND VOLUME

TABLE 2.W.5

U.S. WATER WEIGHT AND MEASURE AT 20°C OR 68°F

One Gallon	
Weighs	8.322 lb
Weighs	3774.6 gm
Contains	3785 ml
Contains	128 fl oz
One Pint	
Weighs	1.0403 lb
Weighs	471.825 gm
Contains	16 fl oz
Contains	0.473 liters
One Liter	
Weighs	2.1987 lb
Contains	1.0569 qt
Contains	1000.00 ml

SOURCE: WOODROOF, JASPER GUY and PHILLIPS, G. FRANK (EDITORS). 1974. *In* Beverages: Carbonated and Noncarbonated. Avi Publishing Co., Westport, Conn.

WAVES, ENERGY-PRODUCING

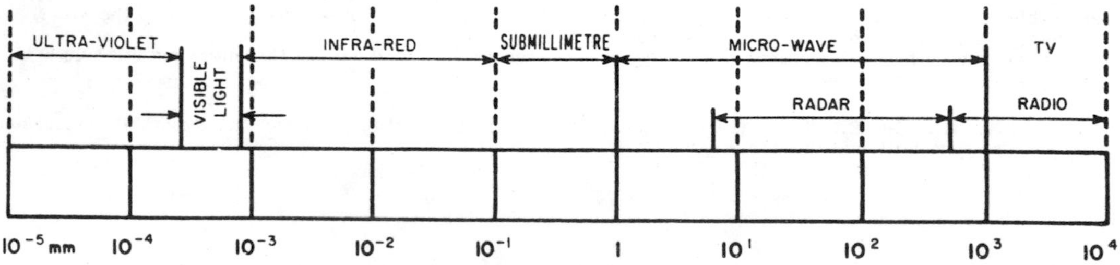

FIG. 2.W.1. WAVELENGTH SPECTRUM OF ENERGY-PRODUCING WAVES

SOURCE: BORGSTROM, G. 1968. Principles of Food Science, Vol. *1*. Macmillan Publishing Co., New York.

WAX

TABLE 2.W.6

TYPES AND COMPOSITION OF WAXES

Source	Examples	Composition
Mineral waxes	Paraffin	Straight-chain hydrocarbons, 26–30 C atoms/molecule
	Microcrystalline	Branched-chain hydrocarbons, 41-50 C atoms/molecule
	Oxidized microcrystalline	Hydrocarbons, esters, fatty acids
	Montan	Wax acids, alcohols, esters, ketones
	Hoechst waxes	Acids, esters (obtained by oxidizing montan)
	Ozokerite	Saturated and unsaturated high-mol-wt hydrocarbons
Vegetable waxes	Carnauba	Complex alcohols, hydrocarbons, resins
	Esparto	Mainly hydrocarbons
	Flax	Fatty-acid esters, hydrocarbons
	Sugarcane wax	Hydrocarbons, long straight-chain aldehydes, alcohols
	Candelilla	Hydrocarbons, acids, esters, alcohols, stearols, resins
Animal waxes	Beeswax	Hydrocarbons, acids, esters alcohols, lactones
Synthetic waxes	Fischer-Tropsch	Saturated and unsaturated hydrocarbons, oxygen compounds
	Polyethylene	Hydrocarbon

SOURCE: GRANT, J. (EDITOR). 1969. Hackh's Chemical Dictionary, 4th Edition. McGraw-Hill Book Co., New York.

WEIGHT

TABLE 2.W.7

WEIGHT CONVERSION TABLE: POUNDS AND OUNCES TO GRAMS

Pound	Grams	Pound	Grams
1	453.59	26	11,793.40
2	907.18	27	12,246.99
3	1,360.78	28	12,700.59
4	1,814.37	29	13,154.18
5	2,267.96	30	13,607.77
6	2,721.55	31	14,061.36
7	3,175.15	32	14,514.96
8	3,628.74	33	14,968.55
9	4,082.33	34	15,422.14
10	4,535.92	35	15,875.73
11	4,989.52	36	16,329.33
12	5,443.11	37	16,782.92
13	5,896.70	38	17,236.51
14	6,350.29	39	17,690.10
15	6,803.89	40	18,143.70
16	7,257.48	41	18,597.29
17	7,711.07	42	19,050.88
18	8,164.66	43	19,504.47
19	8,618.26	44	19,958.07
20	9,071.85	45	20,411.66
21	9,525.44	46	20,865.25
22	9,979.03	47	21,318.84
23	10,432.63	48	21,772.44
24	10,886.22	49	22,226.03
25	11,339.81	50	22,679.62

(Continued)

TABLE 2.W.7 (*Continued*)

Whole Ounces	Grams	Whole Ounces	Grams
1	28.35	9	255.15
2	56.70	10	283.50
3	85.05	11	311.84
4	113.40	12	340.19
5	141.75	13	368.54
6	170.10	14	396.89
7	198.45	15	425.24
8	226.80	16	453.59
Fractional Ounces	**Grams**	**Fractional Ounces**	**Grams**
1/64	0.44	17/64	7.53
1/32	0.89	9/32	7.97
3/64	1.33	19/64	8.42
1/16	1.77	5/16	8.86
5/64	2.21	21/64	9.30
3/32	2.66	11/32	9.75
7/64	3.10	23/64	10.19
1/8	3.54	3/8	10.63
9/64	3.99	25/64	11.07
5/32	4.43	13/32	11.52
11/64	4.87	27/64	11.96
3/16	5.32	7/16	12.40
13/64	5.76	29/64	12.85
7/32	6.20	15/32	13.29
15/64	6.64	31/64	13.73
1/4	7.09	1/2	14.17
Fractional Ounces	**Grams**	**Fractional Ounces**	**Grams**
33/64	14.62	49/64	21.71
17/32	15.06	25/32	22.15
35/64	15.50	51/64	22.59
9/16	15.95	13/16	23.03
37/64	16.39	53/64	23.48
19/32	16.83	27/32	23.92
39/64	17.28	55/64	24.36
5/8	17.72	7/8	24.81
41/64	18.16	57/64	25.25
21/32	18.60	29/32	25.69
43/64	19.05	59/64	26.13
11/16	19.49	15/16	26.58
45/64	19.93	61/64	27.02
23/32	20.38	31/32	27.46
47/64	20.82	63/64	27.91
3/4	21.26	1	28.35

Example: 6 lb and 14 3/4 oz = 2,721.55 + 396.89 + 21.26 = 3,139.70 g.

SOURCE: OCKERMAN, H. W. 1974. Quality Control of Post-Mortem Muscle Tissue, 9th Edition. Ohio State University, Columbus.

WEIGHT, HUMAN

TABLE 2.W.8

WEIGHTS OF PERSONS 20 TO 30 YEARS OLD

Height (Without Shoes) (ft)	(in.)	Weight (Without Clothing) Low (lb)	Average (lb)	High (lb)	Height (Without Shoes) (ft)	(in.)	Weight (Without Clothing) Low (lb)	Average (lb)	High (lb)
Men					Women				
5	3	118	129	141	5		100	109	118
5	4	122	133	145	5	1	104	112	121
5	5	126	137	149	5	2	107	115	125
5	6	130	142	155	5	3	110	118	128
5	7	134	147	161	5	4	113	122	132
5	8	139	151	166	5	5	116	125	135
5	9	143	155	170	5	6	120	129	139
5	10	147	159	174	5	7	123	132	142
5	11	150	163	178	5	8	126	136	146
6		154	167	183	5	9	130	140	151
6	1	158	171	188	5	10	133	144	156
6	2	162	175	192	5	11	137	148	161
6	3	165	178	195	6		141	152	166

SOURCE: Food For Us All. Yearbook of Agriculture, 1969. USDA.

WHEAT, AMINO ACIDS

TABLE 2.W.9

AMINO ACIDS OF WHEAT, FLOUR, AND BREAD
(g per 16 g nitrogen)

	Wheat	Flour	Bread
Alanine	3.25	2.78	2.93
Arginine	4.69	3.80	3.56
Aspartic acid	5.09	4.14	4.60
Cystine	1.97	2.11	1.88
Glutamic acid	28.5	34.5	31.7
Glycine	3.88	3.22	3.21
Histidine	1.92	1.88	1.89
Isoleucine	3.90	4.26	4.32
Leucine	6.48	6.98	7.11
Lysine	2.74	2.08	2.48
Methionine	1.76	1.73	1.90
Phenylalanine	4.42	4.92	4.80
Proline	9.85	11.7	11.1
Serine	5.06	5.44	5.45
Threonine	3.02	2.82	3.01
Tryptophan	1.09	1.02	0.97
Tyrosine	3.10	3.25	3.32
Valine	4.50	4.54	4.68

SOURCE: POMERANZ, Y. (EDITOR). 1971. Wheat Chemistry and Technology, 2nd Edition. American Association of Cereal Chemists, St. Paul.

WHEAT AND FLOUR COMPOSITION

TABLE 2.W.10

PROXIMATE CHEMICAL COMPOSITION OF A COMMERCIAL MILL MIX OF HARD RED SPRING WHEAT AND ITS PRINCIPAL MILL PRODUCTS[1]; CHEMICAL COMPOSITION (13.5% M.B.)

Product	Proportion of Wheat (%)	Protein[2] (%)	Fat (%)	Ash (%)	Starch (%)	Pentosans (%)	Total Sugars[3] (%)	Undetermined (%)
Wheat	100.0	15.3	1.9	1.85	53.0	5.2	2.6	6.8
Patent flour	65.3	14.2	0.9	0.42	66.7	1.6	1.2	1.4
1st Clear flour	5.2	15.2	1.4	0.65	63.1	2.0	1.4	2.8
2nd Clear flour	3.2	18.1	2.4	1.41	56.3	2.6	2.1	3.6
Red dog flour	1.3	18.5	3.8	2.71	41.4	4.5	4.6	11.0
Shorts	8.4	18.5	5.2	5.00	19.3	13.8	6.7	18.0
Bran	16.4	16.7	4.6	6.50	11.7	18.1	5.5	23.5
Germ	0.2	30.9	12.6	4.30	10.0	3.7	16.6	8.4

[1] Compiled from USDA mimeographed publication ACE-189 (1942).
[2] Nitrogen X 5.7.
[3] Expressed as glucose.

SOURCE: POMERANZ, Y. (EDITOR). 1971. Wheat Chemistry and Technology, 2nd Edition. American Association of Cereal Chemists, St. Paul.

WHEAT, CARBOHYDRATE COMPOSITION

TABLE 2.W.11

PROXIMATE CARBOHYDRATE COMPOSITION OF A FRENCH WHEAT AND ITS PRINCIPAL MILL PRODUCTS (% DRY MATTER)

Product	Proportion of Wheat %	Ash	Starch	Crude Fiber	Pentosans	Sugars
Wheat	100.0	1.8	68.3	2.4	8.5	4.4
Flour	77.0	0.55	81.8	0.3	1.8	2.6
Red dog flour	2.4	2.4	54.8	1.1	7.9	7.75
Shorts	3.2	4.1	24.6	6.0	24.7	10.80
Bran fine	9.1	6.1	19.3	10.4	32.4	8.35
Bran coarse	7.7	7.5	14.7	12.3	34.7	7.15
Germ 1	0.4	4.7	20.8	4.5	13.5	16.90
Germ 2	0.2	4.6	20.8	3.3	8.2	20.55

SOURCE: CERNING, J. and GUILBOT, A. 1974. Carbohydrate Composition of Wheat. *In* Wheat: Production and Utilization. G. E. Inglett (Editor). Avi Publishing Co., Westport, Conn.

WHEAT, FATTY ACIDS

TABLE 2.W.12

FATTY ACID COMPOSITION OF THE TOTAL LIPID AND TRIGLYCERIDES FROM WHEAT, BRAN, GERM, AND ENDOSPERM

	Total Lipid				Triglycerides			
Fatty Acid Methyl Esters	From Whole Wheat (%)	From Bran (%)	From Germ (%)	From Endo-sperm (%)	From Whole Wheat (%)	From Bran (%)	From Germ (%)	From Endo-sperm (%)
Myristate (C-14:0)	0.1	tr	tr	tr	tr	tr	tr	tr
Palmitate (C-16:0)	24.5	18.3	18.5	18.0	16.7	17.9	19.4	12.9
Palmitoleate (C-16:1)	0.8	0.9	0.7	1.0	0.7	0.7	0.8	1.1
Stearate (C-18:0)	1.0	1.1	0.4	1.2	0.3	0.8	0.5	0.7
Oleate (C-18:1)	11.5	20.9	17.3	19.4	16.5	20.3	19.6	15.1
Linoleate (C-18:2)	56.3	57.7	57.0	56.2	59.0	56.2	52.5	65.1
Linolenate (C-18:3)	3.7	1.3	5.2	3.1	4.3	2.9	4.5	3.5
Arachidate (C-20:0)	0.8	tr	tr	tr	1.9	0.7	0.5	0.0
Other	1.1	tr	0.8	1.1	0.7	0.8	2.4	1.5

SOURCE: POMERANZ, Y. (EDITOR). 1971. Wheat Chemistry and Technology, 2nd Edition. American Association of Cereal Chemists, St. Paul.

WHEAT GRAIN

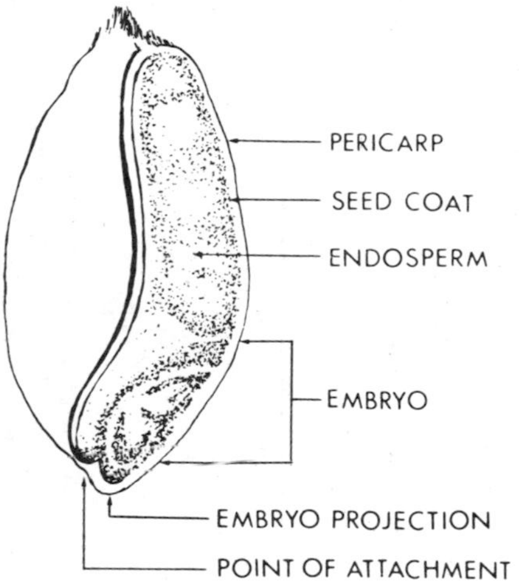

FIG. 2.W.2. SEMIDIAGRAMMATIC OF LONGITUDINAL SECTION OF A WHEAT SEED

SOURCE: WALLACE, H. A. H. 1973. Fungi and Other Organisms Associated with Stored Grain. *In* Grain Storage: Part of a System. R. N. Sinha and W. E. Muir (Editors). Avi Publishing Co., Westport, Conn.

WHEAT GRADES

TABLE 2.W.13

GRADES AND GRADE REQUIREMENTS FOR ALL CLASSES OF WHEAT EXCEPT MIXED WHEAT

Grade	Minimum test weight per bushel		Maximum limits of—						
			Defects					Wheat of other classes[1]	
	Hard Red Spring Wheat Or White Club	All other classes and sub-classes	Heat-damaged kernels	Dam-aged kernels (total)	Foreign material	Shrunken and broken kernels	Defects (total)	Con-trasting classes	Wheat of other classes (total)
	Pounds	*Pounds*	*Percent*	*Percent*	*Percent*	*Percent*	*Percent*	*Percent*	*Percent*
U.S. No. 1	58.0	60.0	0.1	2.0	0.5	3.0	3.0	1.0	3.0
U.S. No. 2	57.0	58.0	0.2	4.0	1.0	5.0	5.0	2.0	5.0
U.S. No. 3	55.0	56.0	0.5	7.0	2.0	8.0	8.0	3.0	10.0
U.S. No. 4	53.0	54.0	1.0	10.0	3.0	12.0	12.0	10.0	10.0
U.S. No. 5	50.0	51.0	3.0	15.0	5.0	20.0	20.0	10.0	10.0
U.S. Sample grade ...	U.S. Sample grade shall be wheat which does not meet the requirements for any of the grades from U.S. No. 1 to U.S. No. 5, inclusive; or which contains more than two crotalaria seeds (*Crotalaria spp.*) in 1,000 grams of grain, or contains castor beans (*Ricinus communis*), stones, broken glass, animal filth, an unknown foreign substance(s), or a commonly recognized harmful or toxic substance(s); or which is musty, sour, or heating; or which has any commercially objectionable foreign odor except of smut or garlic; or which contains a quantity of smut so great that any one or more of the grade requirements cannot be applied accurately; or which is otherwise of distinctly low quality.								

[1] Red Durum Wheat of any grade may contain not more than 10.0 percent of wheat of other classes.

SOURCE: INGLETT, G. E. (EDITOR). 1974. *In* Wheat: Production and Utilization. Avi Publishing Co., Westport, Conn.

WHEAT KERNEL

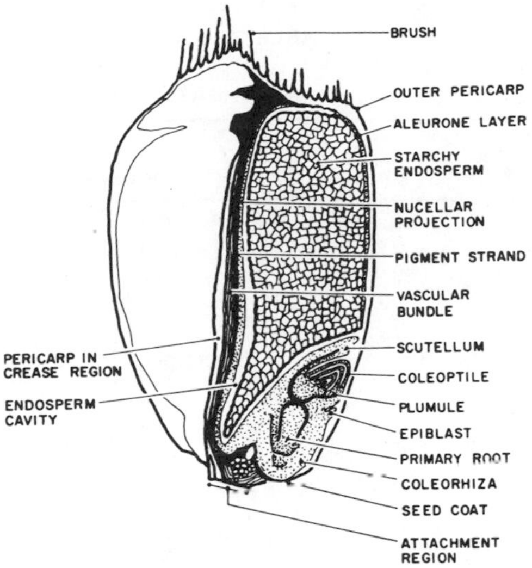

FIG. 2.W.3. CROSS SECTION OF A WHEAT KERNEL

SOURCE: BROOKER, DONALD B., BAKKER-ARKEMA, FRED W. and HALL, CARL W. (EDITORS). 1974. Principles of Grain Drying. *In* Drying Cereal Grains. Avi Publishing Co., Westport, Conn.

WHEAT KERNEL PARTS

Wheat kernel (caryopsis)

- Pericarp (fruit coat) — Bran
  - Outer
    1. Epidermis (epicarp)
    2. Hypodermis
    3. Remnants of thin-walled cells
  - Inner
    4. Intermediate cells
    5. Cross cells
    6. Tube cells
- Seed
  - Seed coat (testa, spermoderm, tegmen) and pigment strand — Bran
  - Nucellar epidermis (hyaline layer, perisperm) and nucellar projection — Bran
  - Endosperm
    1. Aleurone layer — Bran
    2. Starchy endosperm
  - Germ (embryo)
    - Scutellum (cotyledon)
      1. Epithelium
      2. Parenchyma
      3. Provascular tissues
    - Embryonic axis
      - Plumule, including coleoptile
      - Primary root, covered by coleorhiza
      - Secondary lateral rootlets
    - Epiblast

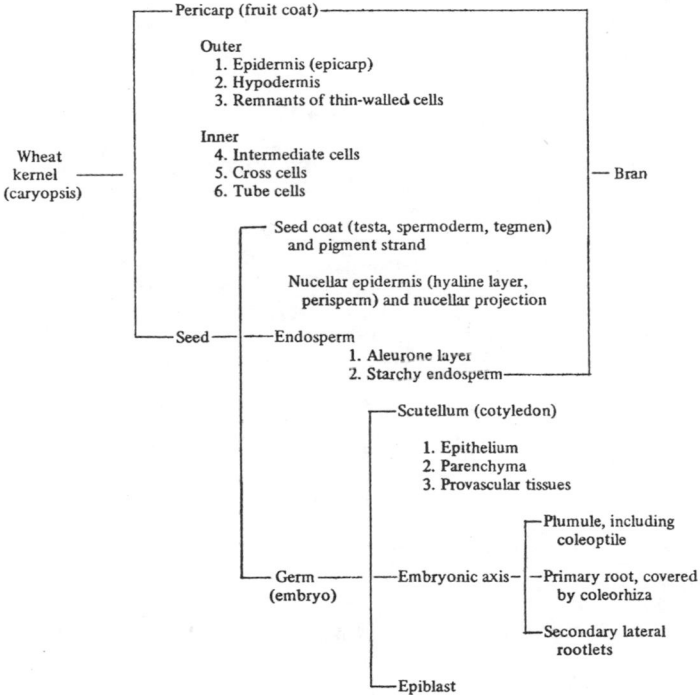

FIG. 2.W.4. PARTS OF THE WHEAT KERNEL AND THEIR RELATION TO EACH OTHER

SOURCE: POMERANZ, Y. (EDITOR). 1971. Wheat Chemistry and Technology, 2nd Edition. American Association of Cereal Chemists, St. Paul, Minn.

WHEAT, MINERALS

TABLE 2.W.14

MINERAL COMPOSITION OF WHEAT, FLOUR, AND BREAD

	Wheat	Flour (% dry basis)	Bread
Potassium	0.454	0.105	0.191
Phosphorus	0.433	0.126	0.183
Magnesium	0.183	0.028	0.034
Calcium	0.045	0.018	0.127
		(Parts per Million)	
Sodium	45	9.8	0.858%
Zinc	35	7.8	9.7
Iron	43	10.5	27.3
Manganese	46	6.5	5.9
Copper	5.3	1.7	2.3
Molybdenum	0.48	0.25	0.32
Cobalt	0.026	0.003	0.022

SOURCE: POMERANZ, Y. (EDITOR). 1971. Wheat Chemistry and Technology, 2nd Edition. American Association of Cereal Chemists, St. Paul.

WHEAT, PARTS OF GRAIN

TABLE 2.W.15

CONSTITUENTS AND CALORIE YIELDS[1] OF DIFFERENT PARTS OF THE WHEAT GRAIN[2]

Part of Grain	Starch (g)	Reducing Sugars (g)	Pentosans and Similar Carbohydrates (g)	Cellulose (g)	Crude Protein (g)	Fatty Material (g)	Ash (g)	Calories (g)
Entire kernel	58.5	2.0	6.6	2.3	12.0	1.8	1.8	310
Pericarp	0.0	0.0	34.5	38.0	7.5	0.0	5.0	175
Testa and hyaline layer	0.0	0.0	50.5	11.0	15.5	0.0	8.0	175
Aleurone layer	0.0	0.0	38.5	3.5	24.0	8.0	11.0	244
Outer endosperm	62.7	1.6	1.4	0.3	16.0	2.2	0.8	345
Inner endosperm	71.7	1.6	1.4	0.3	7.9	1.6	0.5	344
Embryo and scutellum	0.0	26.0	6.5	2.0	26.0	10.0	4.5	350

[1] Per 100 g.
[2] Moisture content: 15%.

SOURCE: AYKROYD, W. R. and DOUGHTY, J. 1970. Wheat in Human Nutrition. FAO, United Nations, Rome.

WHEAT, PARTS OF GRAIN, VITAMINS

TABLE 2.W.16

CONTENT OF CERTAIN VITAMINS[1] IN DIFFERENT PARTS OF THE WHEAT GRAIN

Part of Grain	Thiamin (mg)	Nicotinic Acid (mg)		Pyridoxine Hydro-chloride (mg)	Pantothenic Acid (mg)	Riboflavin (mg)
		Kind of Wheat				
		Soft English	Manitoba			
Pericarp, testa and hyaline layer	0.06	2.00	2.57	0.60	0.78	0.10
Aleurone layer	1.65	61.30	74.10	3.60	4.51	1.00
Outer endosperm	0.03	1.50	2.70	0.06	0.39	0.07
Inner endosperm	0.01	0.47	0.55	0.03		
Embryo	0.84	5.20	3.85	2.11	1.71	1.38
Scutellum	15.6	3.80	3.82	2.32	1.41	1.27

[1] Per 100 g; moisture content: 13%.

SOURCE: AYKROYD, W. R. and DOUGHTY, J. 1970. Wheat in Human Nutrition. FAO, United Nations, Rome.

WHEAT PRODUCTS, AMINO ACID COMPOSITIONS

TABLE 2.W.17

AMINO ACID COMPOSITIONS OF WHEAT, FLOUR AND FLOUR PROTEIN FRACTIONS
(g per 16 g N)

	Wheat	Flour	Albumin	Globulin	Gliadin	Glutenin	Residue Protein
Tryptophan	1.5	1.5	1.1	1.1	0.7	2.2	2.3
Lysine	2.3	1.9	3.2	5.9	0.5	1.5	2.4
Histidine	2.0	1.9	2.0	2.6	1.6	1.7	1.8
Ammonia	3.5	3.9	2.5	1.9	4.7	3.8	3.5
Arginine	4.0	3.1	5.1	8.3	1.9	3.0	3.2
Aspartic acid	4.7	3.7	5.8	7.0	1.9	2.7	4.2
Threonine	2.4	2.4	3.1	3.3	1.5	2.4	2.7
Serine	4.2	4.4	4.5	4.8	3.8	4.7	4.8
Glutamic acid	30.3	34.7	22.6	15.5	41.1	34.2	31.4
Proline	10.1	11.8	8.9	5.0	14.3	10.7	9.3
Glycine	3.8	3.4	3.6	4.9	1.5	4.2	5.0
Alanine	3.1	2.6	4.3	4.9	1.5	2.3	3.0
Cystine (half)	2.8	2.8	6.2	5.4	2.7	2.2	2.1
Valine	3.6	3.4	4.7	4.6	2.7	3.2	3.6
Methionine	1.2	1.3	1.8	1.7	1.0	1.3	1.3
Isoleucine	3.0	3.1	3.0	3.2	3.2	2.7	2.8
Leucine	6.3	6.6	6.8	6.8	6.1	6.2	6.8
Tyrosine	2.7	2.8	3.4	2.9	2.2	3.4	2.8
Phenylalanine	4.6	4.8	4.0	3.5	6.0	4.1	3.8

SOURCE: BUSHUK, W. and WRIGLEY, C. W. 1974. Proteins: Composition, Structure and Function. *In* Wheat: Production and Utilization. G. E. Inglett (Editor). Avi Publishing Co., Westport, Conn.

WHEAT PRODUCTS COMPOSITION

TABLE 2.W.18

TYPICAL ANALYTICAL DATA FOR U.S. WHEAT PRODUCTS

	Range of Analytical Values[1] in Typical U.S. Millfeeds			
	Bran	Shorts	Red Dog	Wheat Germ
Chemical constituent (%)				
Protein ($N \times 6.25$)	13.3-16.9	15.2-18.2	13.9-16.7	23.9-27.0
Starch	4.6-7.2	15.9-21.7	36.2-47.8	14.0-23.9
Ash	4.7-7.1	3.1-4.3	1.5-2.7	3.5-4.3
Crude fat	3.0-4.2	3.7-6.3	2.3-4.7	6.3-10.6
Crude fiber	9.2-11.6	5.6-7.2	1.2-3.2	2.7-4.0
Essential amino acids (%)				
Lysine	0.56-0.61	0.68-0.86	0.45-0.65	1.30-1.77
Methionine	0.20-0.26	0.23-0.30	0.22-0.27	0.39-0.58
Threonine	0.36-0.53	0.54-0.63	0.42-0.56	0.89-1.09
Minerals				
Phosphorus (%)	0.9-1.5	0.54-0.92	0.36-0.62	0.77-0.96
Potassium (%)	1.2-1.6	0.82-1.1	0.34-0.64	0.86-1.3
Magnesium (%)	0.39-0.64	0.20-0.29	0.08-0.20	0.20-0.25
Zinc (ppm)	56-141	62-149	19-100	100-144
Iron (ppm)	74-103	38-79	28-57	41-58
Manganese (ppm)	72-138	91-142	32-71	95-147
Selenium (ppm)	0.10-0.75	0.03-0.75	0.13-0.60	0.01-0.77
Vitamins (μg/g)				
Niacin	249-359	84-120	22-62	64-85
Pantothenic acid	29-41	17-27	9-17	18-27
Folic acid	0.8-1.4	1.2-2.0	0.4-1.2	1.4-3.0
Thiamin	5.1-7.0	16-22	14-30	19-24
Riboflavin	4.3-5.8	4.0-5.2	1.7-3.1	5.5-6.4
Pyridoxine	7.0-10.7	4.7-9.8	2.1-8.6	6.6-19.8
Alpha-tocopherol	20-28	49-82	26-37	31-200
Betaine	3,000-7,000	3,000-6,000	2,350-4,500	3,000-6,000
Choline	1,800-2,700	1,800-2,300	1,400-2,000	2,600-3,300
Lipids (%)				
Total	3.9-6.1	5.3-7.9	3.5-7.0	9.2-13.5
Nonsaponifiable	0.6-0.7	0.5-0.6	0.3-0.4	0.7-1.4
Saponifiable	2.5-4.0	3.6-5.8	2.3-4.7	6.2-9.9
Stearate	0.7-1.4	0.6-1.2	0.6-1.0	0.5-0.8
Oleate	16-22	15-20	14-20	12-17
Linoleate	59-61	55-60	57-61	56-60
Linolenate	3.7-5.4	4.8-6.4	4.2-5.8	7.3-9.7

[1] All values reported on 14% moisture basis.

SOURCE: MILNER, M. (EDITOR). 1969. Protein-Enriched Cereal Foods for World Needs. American Association of Cereal Chemists, St. Paul, Minn.

WHEAT, VITAMINS

TABLE 2.W.19

VITAMINS OF WHEAT, FLOUR, AND BREAD

	Wheat	Flour (Mg/100 g Dry Weight)	Bread
Thiamin	0.40	0.104	0.46
Riboflavin	0.16	0.035	0.29
Niacin	6.95	1.38	4.39
Biotin	0.016	0.0021	0.0029
Choline	216.0	208.0	202.0
Pantothenic acid	1.37	0.59	0.69
Folic acid	0.049	0.011	0.040
Inositol	370.0	47.0	53.0
p-Aminobenzoic acid	0.51	0.050	0.092

SOURCE: POMERANZ, Y. (EDITOR). 1971. Wheat Chemistry and Technology, 2nd Edition. American Association of Cereal Chemists, St. Paul.

WHITE SAUCE

TABLE 2.W.20

INGREDIENTS FOR 1 CUP OF WHITE SAUCE

Ingredients	Measure			
	Thin sauce		Medium sauce	
	Standard	Low-fat	Standard	Low-fat
Butter or other fat	1 tablespoon	2 teaspoons	2 tablespoons	1 tablespoon.
All-purpose flour	1 tablespoon	1 tablespoon	2 tablespoons	2 tablespoons.
Salt	¼ teaspoon	¼ teaspoon	¼ teaspoon	¼ teaspoon.
Milk	1 cup[1]	1 cup[1 2]	1 cup[1]	1 cup.[1 2]
Calories in 1 cup white sauce	290	180	420	245.

[1] Vegetable liquid may be used in place of part of milk.

[2] Use skim milk or reconstituted nonfat dry milk for milk in low-fat white sauce.

SOURCE: Vegetables in Family Meals. (1975) USDA Home and Garden Bull. *105*.

NOTE: There are no entries for the letter X in this section.

Y

YIELD GRADE MEAT

TABLE 2.Y.1

RETAIL YIELD OF CARCASS ACCORDING TO YIELD OF MEAT GRADE

Yield Grade 1: means the carcass will yield 79.8% or more in retail cuts.
Yield Grade 2: 75.2–79.7%.
Yield Grade 3: 70.6–75.1%.
Yield Grade 4: 66–70.5%.
Yield Grade 5: 65.9% or less.

SOURCE: How to Buy Meat for Your Freezer. (1969) USDA Home and Garden Bull. *166*.

NOTE: There are no entries for the letter Z in this section.